Praise for On Moral Business

"Awesome! The diversity and scope of sources and topics in this volume are incredible. This book is an essential resource for students and faculty of business and economics. It will also be highly appreciated by businesspersons who draw upon biblical, philosophical, and ethical wisdom to guide their business decisions."

— JOHN W. EBY
Coauthor of *Business through the Eyes of Faith*

"In this one volume we have all the voices of our current debates on ethical issues in economics and business life. It represents a veritable communion of saints of ethical conversation. . . . This volume will be an indispensable addition to every course exploring Christian ethics and economics. Teachers outside the theological world can find no better way to expand the horizons of their students than to use this foundational reader."

— WILLIAM JOHNSON EVERETT
Andover Newton
Theological School

"A ground-breaking event that meets an urgent need of our time. This volume will contribute significantly to the exploration of the empirical nature of ecumenical theology."

— KOSUKE KOYAMA
Union Theological Seminary,
New York

"This book is the most comprehensive attempt to date to examine business ethics from a theological perspective. It is long overdue."

— THOMAS DONALDSON
Georgetown University

"There is no other volume in business ethics that even begins to rival this one in terms of comprehensive scope, timely relevance, and judicious selection of material. It advances an integrated vision of business, morality, and religion in a way needed both by those who insulate business practices from religious ethics and by those who engage in ethical analysis apart from the realities of business life."

— DOUGLAS J. SCHUURMAN
St. Olaf College

"An exemplary collection of readings edited by a group of America's most distinguished Christian ethicists. I recommend it without reservation."

— EDMUND LEITES
Queens College, The City University of New York

"The most comprehensive set of materials on business ethics ever assembled. . . . A gold mine of riches for both scholars and business practitioners."

— DAVID A. KRUEGER
Baldwin Wallace College

"An amazing collection of texts dealing with almost every conceivable ethical and theological question related to business, markets, and corporate life on a global scale. The fact that this volume has been put together by Christians who are serious about both business and the Bible, about both human vocations and divine callings, is a tribute to the earthly vitality and spiritual strength of Christianity in this day of cynicism and confusion on so many fronts."

— JAMES W. SKILLEN
Executive Director, The Center for Public Justice

ON MORAL

BUSINESS

Classical and Contemporary Resources for Ethics in Economic Life

Edited by

Max L. Stackhouse, Dennis P. McCann, and Shirley J. Roels

with

Preston Williams

WILLIAM B. EERDMANS PUBLISHING COMPANY
GRAND RAPIDS, MICHIGAN

Collection © 1995 Wm. B. Eerdmans Publishing Co.
255 Jefferson Ave. S.E., Grand Rapids, Michigan 49503

Printed in the United States of America

02 01 00 99 98 97   9 8 7 6 5 4 3 2

Library of Congress Cataloging-in-Publication Data

On moral business: classical and contemporary resources for
  ethics in economic life / edited by Max L. Stackhouse . . . [et al.].
      p.   cm.
    Includes bibliographical references.
    ISBN 0-8028-0626-0 (pbk.)
    1. Business ethics. 2. Christian ethics. 3. Economics —
  Religious aspects — Christianity. 4. Business — Biblical teaching.
  I. Stackhouse, Max L.
  HF5387.O53   1995
  174′.4 — dc20   94-21941
                                          CIP

Scripture quotations designated NRSV are from the New Revised Version of the
Bible, copyright © 1989 by the Division of Christian Education of the National
Council of the Churches of Christ in the U.S.A., and used by permission.

Scripture quotations designated RSV are from the Revised Standard Version of the
Bible, copyrighted 1946, 1952 © 1971, 1973 by the Division of Christian
Education of the National Council of the Churches of Christ in the U.S.A., and
used by permission.

Scripture quotations designated NIV are from The Holy Bible, New International
Version, copyright © 1978 by the New York International Bible Society.

The editors and publisher gratefully acknowledge permission to reprint materials
granted by the individuals and institutions listed on pp. 962-968.

Contents

PART A: CLASSICAL RESOURCES

PART B: MODERN DEBATES

PART C: CONTEMPORARY DEVELOPMENTS

A Word to the Reader

Dennis P. McCann

My fellow editors and our publisher asked me to address a few words of encouragement to you the reader to show how one can use this anthology creatively in a variety of settings both inside and outside the classroom. The volume is large but need not be daunting if the reader understands the various and flexible ways it can be used. We have offered a collection of this size and scope because we want to provide readers with a broad array of material from which to choose selections for study and because we hope to advance the study of business ethics and economics on several fronts at once. We wanted to put together an anthology that (1) could serve simultaneously as the basis for courses in M.B.A. programs and in seminaries and divinity schools; that (2) is both a standard reference work in the history of Christian economic ethics and a timely introduction to contemporary discussions of the moral and religious significance of the modern business corporation; and that (3) faithfully surveys the range of contemporary Christian attitudes toward commerce and capitalism, while also clearing a space for interreligious dialogue about the role of multinational corporations in the global economy of the twenty-first century. We thought that such an anthology was worth presenting in a single volume because it might stimulate some mutual learning that otherwise might not occur for lack of a common ground.

Who's This Book For?

Our hope is to invite at least five different audiences to interactive conversation on this common ground. Three of these emerge from the editors' teaching experiences with diverse groups of students: (1) the ecumenical world of the modern seminary or divinity school, where most students seek professional training in Christian ministry; (2) the increasingly secular world of the business schools — even those in universities claiming religious sponsorship — where students concentrate on technical training in various aspects of business management; and (3) the mostly undergraduate Christian colleges, where business students, like all other students, are encouraged to integrate their career expectations within an explicitly theological perspective on Christian vocation. You may find yourself already participating in any one of these three groups or, perhaps, thinking of joining one of them. We realize that each group has different needs, though we also hope that at some point your studies and your professional interests will converge.

Let me illustrate one way to respect the diversity of our audiences from what I've learned while test-teaching this anthology in the classrooms of DePaul University. Though the book is divided into fifteen chapters (plus preliminaries and an epilogue) and therefore could conceivably be read at the rate of a chapter a week for a single semester's course, I cannot teach it that way. For one thing, DePaul is on the quarter system, and so classes meet usually for only ten weeks in any given quarter. In my graduate course on "Ethics and Economics," for example, I once used the material in this anthology to construct a syllabus concentrating on Part C, and prefaced this with selections from the chapter in Part B on "Recent Church Documents." For that group of mostly M.B.A. students, I wanted to emphasize how business ethics is discussed in the business community as it seeks to respond to external stakeholders, including the churches. But on another occasion, when the class was mostly M.A.L.S. students seeking a historical perspective on Christian ethical concern, I concentrated the class discussion on readings from Parts A and B, with independent research projects based on the materials in Part C. (The collection is designed to provide the student with ample material for independent study and thus may be the only book necessary for a given course.) Given the comparative nature of DePaul's program in religious studies, students have in both cases used the chapters on "Economics around the World" and "The Global Economy" to explore the university's broadly institutional commitments to multiculturalism and internationalization.

It is impossible, of course, for us to address the students' needs without our first becoming conversation partners with their teachers. This anthology, therefore, is meant to stimulate fresh inquiry among persons in a fourth group, namely, our professional peers, those of you who labor with us in the academic fields of business ethics, practical theology, and Christian social ethics generally. You will determine whether what we think we have learned with our students is also relevant for rethinking the curricula that your own students follow. What we hope to have offered you — beyond assistance in curriculum planning — is a rich and versatile benchmark text that may stimulate your own research projects in these fields. If you, like us, have been frustrated by the ignorance of Christian ethics all too often advertised as an intellectual virtue among moral philosophers currently studying business ethics and economics, here is an alternative map of the Western intellectual tradition that will allow you to place contemporary discussions of business ethics on an entirely different footing.

We also anticipate interactive conversation with a fifth audience, made up of both business professionals, on the one hand, and practicing clergy, on the other, who have discovered their own need for continuing education. Some of you may encounter this text first in an academic setting, as returning students about to complete a postponed degree program or to enter upon a new one. But many, we hope, will simply chance upon it while browsing in a bookstore, or will have it recommended to them by a friend, say, at a clergy conference or a business roundtable group. We have designed the introductory materials to the various sections of each chapter to facilitate an unguided reading of the texts, set at your own pace, with your own interests in mind. Especially in Part C, we have included a number of essays written by people like you, giving expression to their own adult moral concerns, unencumbered by professional training in ethics. You are our heroes, and we mean to support your efforts in any way we can. We also hope the anthology will stimulate the efforts of various organizations, both inside and outside the churches, to form communities of moral discourse in which all of you,

lay business professionals but perhaps clergy as well, can cultivate mutual understanding and assist one another in your common struggle to balance moral leadership and institutional responsibility.

What Made Us Do a Book Like This?

One-dimensional thinking — that's the demon we are seeking to exorcise from the study of business ethics. The editors, each in his or her own way, had often been frustrated trying to help themselves as well as their students overcome compartmentalized thinking about business, ethics, and economics. When we began this project more than five years ago, the reigning academic orthodoxies were still largely governed by the spurious ideal of value neutrality. The distortions inherent in this pose had for a time threatened further progress in the reigning paradigms of neoclassical economics, applied moral philosophy, and the various disciplines of management. Fortunately, revisionist trends are now working in each of these fields to dispel the myth of value neutrality, and these are likely to succeed without much encouragement from us. Our task, however, is to chart the theological implications of these paradigm shifts in order to recover the significance of Christian faith for business, ethics, and economics.

The fragmentation of public discourse about economics and business has, of course, many symptoms. But our own frustrations were provoked by the stunning silence about the religious values operative in various models of economics and business management. Though Max Weber's celebrated thesis on the Protestant ethic and the development of modern capitalism had already suggested — for us, as for many others — an alternative path of integrated religious and ethical reflection, we knew from experience that Weber's work had virtually no impact on how neoclassical economics analysed the actual workings of the capitalist system, how the various disciplines of management understood business corporations, or how business ethics defined the moral challenges involved in working for these corporations. We felt that our students — be they aspiring M.B.A.'s or candidates for some form of Christian ministry — were singularly unprepared to deal with the challenges of the global economy unless they were better informed about these values.

This is especially true for students preparing for careers with an international focus. If you plan to work for a multinational corporation, for example, you are likely to encounter a multiculturalism that raises theological issues heretofore reserved only for high-level interreligious dialogue. The religious terrain upon which multinational corporations operate is no longer the Protestant franchise that Weber described, nor even the American ecumenical establishment that Will Herberg celebrated in *Protestant, Catholic, Jew* (1960). The increasingly prominent multinationals based in East Asia are based on neo-Confucian values, and working in these corporations may often involve participating in Buddhist meditation practices and Shinto rituals. How can Americans evaluate the corporate culture in such firms without understanding the religious values operative in them? Conversely, how can American firms compete with them without understanding their own, still largely unacknowledged, religious assumptions?

The same point could be made about careers in Christian ministry. The pastoral care of laypersons whose working lives are played out in a multinational setting can no longer be understood as a form of prophetic witness against an essentially secular world. What philosopher Richard T. DeGeorge called "the myth of amoral business" has been unmasked as a peculiar artifact of the fleeting U.S. hegemony in international business. In the global economy, personal integrity increasingly will depend not on coping with secularism but on establishing continuity between one's own faith journey and the pluralism of religious and moral values likely to be embedded in the corporate culture. Pastors will not be in a position to assist the laity if they do not understand the spiritual environment in which the laity routinely operate.

While I could go on to suggest a similar lesson for those preparing to serve in the churches' increasingly global ministries, I am concerned here only to explain why *On Moral Business* turned out the way it did, and what's in it for you. It turned out the way it did because it is animated by a vision of the challenges of the global economy. We believe that in order to meet those challenges those concerned with business must have (1) a strong grounding in the history of Christian ethical reflection on economic questions, (2) at least a passing familiarity with the way these same questions are formulated in the world's other major religious traditions, and (3) some appreciation of how the various answers to these questions continue to have significant impact on the ways in which professionals — Christian ethicists, public policy analysts, and business practitioners — understand the morality of business and economics. The organization of this anthology reflects these concerns, more or less in that order.

What's the Book About?

If one purpose of this anthology is to educate both clergy and lay professionals to the religious and moral significance of business and economics, another purpose is to establish an agenda for research and constructive theological reflection. Though these converging purposes, for the reasons just given, require an extended anthology, we also recognize that general readers and instructors will want to make their own selections. In order to facilitate your own choices, we have divided the anthology into three parts: Part A, "Classical Resources"; Part B, "Modern Debates"; and Part C, "Contemporary Developments." Parts A and B, roughly the first half of the anthology, survey the history of Christian ethics focused on the general question of economic justice; Part C places the discussion of specifically business ethics in the context of an emerging global economy. Each part, as I suggested earlier, could be made the central focus for a course, supplemented with selections from the other two, depending on the needs and interests of the instructor and students. Though an M.B.A. course, for example, might be organized from Part C, and an M.Div. course from Parts A and B, we believe that the most effective use of this anthology would offer selections from all three parts in an effort to stretch both instructors and students beyond their previous attitudes toward business, ethics, and economics.

As its title suggests, Part A, "Classical Resources," explores biblical attitudes toward wealth and poverty, work, stewardship, and money, along with the reflections of Hellenistic philosophers, medieval Catholic theologians, and key figures in shaping the traditions of the Reformation. The organization of Part A testifies to our view that Christian moral wisdom, though rooted in the Bible, is hardly exhausted by it. Prior to the advent of modernity, Christian understandings of economics were significantly shaped by both biblical and Hellenistic values and then rethought in light of the new patterns of urban development that emerged in the high Middle Ages. How the entire premodern period, roughly coextensive with the history of Christendom, is to be interpreted will depend upon the reader's prior orientation to the Hebrew Scriptures and the Christian New Testament. Unlike subsequent chapters, which feature primary sources, the first two chapters in Part A exhibit a diverse range of contemporary biblical scholarship. We deliberately chose to model a pluralism of interpretation at the beginning of this anthology so that readers may feel free to develop their own insights into the relative significance of the historical materials. Though we believe that Christian ethics inevitably develops along the lines of a quadrilateral bounded by Scripture, tradition, reason, and experience, we do not mean to pre-empt your own effort to define an appropriate hermeneutic circle.

Part B continues, for the most part, the historical sequence established in Part A. Now, however, the focus shifts to the challenge of modernity, a challenge that eventually resulted in the dissolution of Christendom. The Christian tradition of social ethics emerges in this period as one participant among others in "Modern Debates" about morality and the marketplace. Thus we begin with Christendom's stepchild, the secular Enlightenment, here represented by some of "the Worldly Philosophers" — as Robert Heilbroner aptly named them — whose theories helped to differentiate economics from the matrix of social institutions in which it had been embedded and to make it central to our understanding of society. As the chapter on the Enlightenment unfolds, readers are invited to reconstruct the moral logic of an autonomous marketplace. The next chapter explores the processes of modernization in a variety of institutions, particularly those that are essential for supporting the marketplace's own emergent sense of morality. This is followed by a chapter on "Socialism, Capitalism, and Christianity," which charts the ways in which the Christian communities of faith tried to influence the outcome of the twentieth century's great economic debate, in order to make the economy once more amenable to religious and moral values.

Now that the emergence of a global economy seems to have eclipsed the debate over the relative merits of socialism versus capitalism, the comparative study of world religions has become an indispensable resource in the search for a new paradigm. The next chapter, "Economics around the World," offers a brief introduction to the interplay between tradition and modernity with reference to business and economic development in cultures beyond the historic influence of Christendom. We believe that the study of how other religions have regarded business and economics will tend to confirm the universality of many of the ethical concerns that surfaced in the history of Christian tradition. Christians are not alone, for example, in discerning the presence of the sacred in the ongoing struggle for economic justice.

The final chapter to Part B, "Recent Church Documents," features selections from the many official pronouncements on ethics and economics authorized by various Christian denominations over the past decade. Here, too, despite the historic diversity of various denominational traditions in Christian ethics, the theological perspectives and ethical priorities tend to converge in a variety of ways. We feel that these statements make a fitting conclusion to our survey of the history of Christian thought on economics and business, for, though very recent in origin, they cite as authoritative many of the points first made by texts presented in the previous chapters. Each statement thus provides a framework of interpretation, a perspectival reading of the quadrilateral of Scripture, tradition, reason, and experience that may be tested against both the preceding texts and the new challenges outlined in the next section of the anthology.

"Contemporary Developments," as Part C is labeled, is distinguished from Parts A and B by its intensive focus on the internal dynamics of the business corporation considered as a field of operations in which growing numbers of lay Christians exercise their vocations. But we also mean it to convey our sense that the emergence of the global economy is an epoch-making historical event whose moral challenges and opportunities may be without parallel in the previous history of Christian ethics. As Peter F. Drucker recently pointed out, the global economy is just as aptly characterized as "Post-Capitalist" as it is "Post-Communist." This should convince us, as we hope to convince our readers, that the dramatic end to the Cold War should not become a pretext for celebrating the triumph of a capitalism that no longer exists. Instead, we need to focus not only upon the public policy implications of the global marketplace but also upon the ways in which new forms of economic competition are transforming the cultures of business corporations, both here and abroad. Try to understand the nature of these changes first, if you mean to exercise your vocation by institutionalizing moral business practices within the global economy.

We believe that the ethical challenge cannot be reduced to the simplicities of making a decision either for or against socialism or capitalism as such; nor should it be regarded as simply an extension of Christianity's historic ambivalence toward modernity. Instead, Christians find themselves involved in economic struggles that cannot be resolved simply within the conventional categories of public policy analysis. Part C, "Contemporary Developments," thus is meant to chart possible new approaches, based on the realization that the perennial concerns of Christian social ethics must now be addressed in a context whose development has outrun the capacities of any existing political system for controlling it. If basic Christian commitments to the common good, and to social justice for all, are to have a role in shaping the global economy, Christians will have to rediscover that, beyond the external threat of political coercion, corporate accountability, in business as in any other institutional setting, is based on the internalization of moral vision and values.

We begin Part C, therefore, with a chapter outlining the moral significance of "The Changing Corporation." As in the chapters to follow, this one is meant to provide a mix of interpretations, so that the actualities of moral discourse within business organizations can be compared with similar efforts within religious institutions. The focus of this chapter is upon the possibilities for structural transformation. It means to illustrate recent trends in business management that have strengthened the structures for enhanced ethical accountability. It also shows how the efforts of Christian social activists in, for example, the movement for corporate social responsibility actually do play a role in developing these structures. And finally, it invites us to ponder the significance of recent discussions of economic democracy among Christian ethicists and business practitioners: Should economic democracy be seen as an alternative model for business organization or as itself indicative of the possibilities already operative in contemporary business practice?

The next chapter, "Ethics in Specializations of Business," seeks to demonstrate how Christian ethicists can contribute to the development of moral discourse in specialized business disciplines — in, for example, marketing, finance, accounting, and human resource management. In each of the subsections of the chapter, we've emphasized theological reflection wherever possible, not from any apologetic need to argue the superiority of Christian ethics, but in order to establish a common ground of shared moral concern and promising convergences in the articulation of ethical priorities and principles. Moral consensus, however extensive, does not make religious perspectives redundant in business ethics. On the contrary, such religious perspectives are often closer to the actual concerns of managers, stakeholders, and business theorists, because as a matter of fact these perspectives are more alert to the moral significance of institutional settings than the perspectives of applied moral philosophy generally have proven to be. Nevertheless, since for most of this century Christian social ethics has tended to focus, as we've seen in Part B, on the politics of economic justice at the national and international levels, this comparative advantage has yet to be fully developed. The Christian ethicists featured in this chapter must truly be regarded as pioneers.

The next chapter in Part C, "Moral Business Leadership: Origins and Outcomes," shifts the focus from corporate structure and social practice to character formation and the exercise of a Christian vocation in business. The chapter begins with a sample of religious narratives in which business people give an account of their vocations; it then moves on to discuss the positive role that corporate culture can have in helping to nurture a sense of vocation. We conclude the chapter with two different examples of how vocations may be tested in business: first, by facing the dreaded possibility of having to "blow the whistle" on business practices that are morally wrong; second, on a more positive note, by responding to the various demands that society makes upon business to exercise moral leadership, especially in the area of corporate philanthropy.

"The Global Economy," our penultimate chapter, is meant to suggest the diversity of religious resources for conceptualizing the economic challenge that multinational corporations and their managers are likely to face. The opening section, "Challenges in Emerging Global Markets," surveys a number of regional perspectives on corporate culture and economics. The impact of the world's religious traditions is evident here, as economic development seems to have been stimulated globally by a variety of religious perspectives. While multinational managers thus cannot afford to remain monocultural on the subject of business ethics, we also need to acknowledge the ways in which Christian ethicists have debated the moral significance of multinational corporations, Third-World development, and the ecological environment. A separate section is devoted to each of these in order to reflect the richness of the ongoing debates among Christian ethicists in these areas.

The anthology's final chapter, "The Ongoing Discussion," seeks to integrate the twin purposes animating this anthology by showing how Christian activists in both ministry and management are changing the churches' thinking about mission in the marketplace. The first section, "Challenges for the Church Community," features proposals for new forms of ministry within the economy. While the pastoral strategies shown here have clearly shifted from confrontation to collaboration, the second section, "Challenges for the Business Community," tries to steer the discussion to the actual experience of lay professionals in business. Breaking the inherited taboos forbidding direct expressions of moral concern in business helps to set the agenda for new forms of theological reflection. The final section, "The Call for New Christian Paradigms," while more theoretical in orientation, features some of the perspectives that are emerging from the new economic activism. We have given ourselves the last word among these by

reprinting "A Postcommunist Manifesto," which Max Stackhouse and I published a few years ago in *The Christian Century*. In retrospect, the manifesto was a promissory note: now, however, the promissory note has come due. This anthology provides an inventory of resources necessary for making good, among other things, on the claims we made for a public theology after the collapse of socialism.

The anthology was designed to meet the needs emerging in a variety of personal and institutional settings. When the editors started working together on this project some five years ago, Eerdmans suggested that their recently published anthology *On Moral Medicine: Theological Perspectives in Medical Ethics* (1987), edited by Stephen E. Lammers and Allen Verhey, might be a suitable model for our efforts. But one look at *On Moral Medicine* convinced us that Christian ethicists had been far more active for many more years in the field of biomedical ethics than they had been in the field of business ethics and economics. We convinced Eerdmans to risk publication even at this early stage in the hope that this anthology might play a creative role in stimulating further research in Christian business ethics. We make no claim that any of our chapters or subsections are definitive on any given topic; but they represent, we hope, some of the best of what's currently out there and thus will help to stimulate further inquiry.

How We Came to Work on It Together

We did not start out with a common project in mind. Though Max Stackhouse and I had known each other professionally for several years and had each become aware of Shirley Roels's growing reputation among Christian teachers in the field of business ethics, it was Jon Pott, editor-in-chief at Eerdmans, who saw in our diverse backgrounds the potential for fruitful collaboration. Max's book *Public Theology and Political Economy*, which Eerdmans had published in 1987, served as the basis for our working together, for both Shirley and I had read it and used it in our own teaching and research. I was attracted to Max's perspective because it tries to define an open and yet constructively critical stance toward capitalism, avoiding, on the one hand, the abstract and ill-informed denunciations of capitalism and business enterprise so prevalent among self-consciously radical Christians, and, on the other hand, the glib assurances of neoconservatives who, in denouncing "really existing socialism," seemed incapable of advancing the discussion of business ethics in the institutions of really existing capitalism. All three of us wanted to avoid the ideological polarizations that had dominated the 1980s, and we had all grown weary of generalized polemics on one side or another of the great economic debate.

Max's career has been dedicated to serving those who seek professional training in the Christian ministry in those denominations representing mainline Protestantism. Recently appointed to the faculty at Princeton Theological Seminary after many years at Andover Newton, Max brought to the project his deep awareness that a massive new effort in Christian education will be necessary if Christian leadership, both clergy and laity, is to maintain an effectively pastoral stance toward business and the modern professions. He wanted to dispel the clergy's virtually invincible ignorance of business practice and economic theory and the laity's resulting inability to overcome an unnecessary and ultimately self-destructive separation of religious faith from their worldly occupations. Shirley and I share Max's sense of mission, but we have tended to focus more on the training of lay professionals, who need, just as much as the clergy, an appropriate education in Christian ethics.

Shirley has carried out this mission through some fifteen years of undergraduate teaching in a variety of business subjects at Calvin College. As she once said to Max and me, "You name it, I've taught it"; her list includes marketing management, managerial accounting, human resource management, business policy and strategy, as well as management of not-for-profit organizations. Shirley has also directed Calvin College's student internship program and helped to shape Calvin's program on women in the workplace. More than either Max or myself, she is expert in the disciplines of business management and has exercised a key role in the Christian College Coalition's attempt to develop a constructive approach to business ethics. Having already collaborated with Richard C. Chewning and John W. Eby in the Coalition's seminal text *Business Through the Eyes of Faith* (1990), Shirley helped the team maintain an appropriately ecumenical balance so that *On Moral Business* remains as open to the insights of evangelical Christians as it is to those who represent liberal perspectives in Christian social ethics.

My own experience teaching business ethics at DePaul University is, I hope, complementary to that of Max and Shirley. Largely out of respect for its Roman Catholic identity, DePaul's curriculum — a joint venture between commerce and the College of Liberal Arts and Sciences — has been somewhat distinctive in its programmatic commitment to studying the religious dimensions of business ethics. Having helped to establish the goals of this interdisciplinary program at its inception in 1981, I have spent most of my time since trying to respond to the intellectual, as well as pedagogical, challenges they entail. These challenges converge in the never-ending search for suitable instructional materials. When I started out, *Full Value: Cases in Christian Business Ethics* (1978), the first fruits of an ongoing collaboration at the University of Notre Dame between Oliver F. Williams and John W. Houck, was very useful, not least because of its accessibility to undergraduates. When the U.S. Catholic bishops' pastoral letter *Economic Justice for All: Catholic Social Teaching and the U.S. Economy* (1986) became available, I used selections from it to similar effect. But no matter how pertinent the supplements chosen, students nevertheless got the impression that Christian perspectives were at best peripheral to the central concerns of business ethics.

My own search for an alternative was stimulated by prolonged conversation with a few business executives in Chicago, who wanted to explore the relationship between Christian faith and business practice. Those who know the sociological data on American business corporations will not be surprised by this development, inasmuch as executives are unusually active in their local churches, with participation rates far higher than the strikingly robust statistics reported for the American population as a whole. Indeed, most U.S. executives who express a personal interest in business ethics are usually motivated by religious faith. One such person is M. L. "Bud" Brownsberger, whose story is included in this anthology. Bud collaborated with me in writing two papers that were presented at the annual meetings of the

Society of Christian Ethics in 1988 and 1990. These papers outlined certain key features of a theocentric approach to business management. Like Max and Shirley, we hoped to show why and how religious and theological questions were central to any adequate understanding of the moral responsibilities of management.

Let me conclude these preliminary remarks by acknowledging the indispensable contribution of yet another member of our editorial team, Preston N. Williams. Preston's various responsibilities at the Harvard Divinity School did not permit him to participate in the project at the same level as Max, Shirley, and I did. Nevertheless, Preston was generous in reading and criticizing various versions of the anthology and in suggesting specific selections that tended to make the collection more inclusive of the concerns of Christian women and minorities. As one of the invited critics of the "Postcommunist Manifesto," Preston at that time declared not only his continued commitment to socialist ideals but also his pragmatism about economic progress, especially for the poor and the marginalized. We believe that, thanks to his advice and encouragement, we now have an opportunity to move Christian ethical thinking on business and economics toward a more constructive posture, without thereby confirming the suspicion that we are merely out to let business off the hook. We emphatically share with Preston the commitment to economic and social justice that is an indelible mark upon the soul of Christian social ethics, but we also are convinced — more so now than when we began this project — that such a commitment can find an authentic expression within business as it faces the unprecedented challenges of the global economy.

Whom We Must Thank

A project on this scale obviously would not have been possible without the encouragement and support of numerous colleagues in the various institutions where the editors normally work and our many friends scattered elsewhere who have helped us, if only by listening sympathetically, as we struggled to overcome one obstacle or another that stood in the way of its completion. We received significant secretarial and research support from Ms. Sheila Lloyd at Andover Newton, Mr. Lake Lambert III at Princeton Theological Seminary, Ms. Jen Candler at Calvin College, and Ms. Mary R. Garrison at DePaul University's Center for the Study of Values. Our colleagues, the members of various faculties at Princeton Theological Seminary, the Department of Religion and Society at Andover Newton Theological School, DePaul University's Department of Religious Studies, and Calvin College's Department of Economics and Business, provided indispensable feedback on our initial attempts to conceptualize the project as a whole and timely response to inquiries regarding the merits of various selections and the overall design of the various chapters. Members of the Society of Christian Ethics, notably Prof. Jon Gunnemann at the Candler School of Theology and Prof. Bill Everett, formerly of Candler and now a member of the faculty at Andover Newton, volunteered to test all or some parts of the anthology in a classroom setting. Their help was inestimable in persuading us to keep the length of this project down to what we hope are manageable proportions.

Max and I were able to discuss the anthology as a work in progress before a gathering of scholars held at the Institute for the Study of Economic Culture at Boston University in May 1991. We are especially grateful for the opportunity the Institute's director, Prof. Peter Berger, gave us to show where the project was headed in light of the "Postcommunist Manifesto." The response we received from the scholars assembled by the Institute encouraged us to continue at a crucially formative stage in the project. Last year Max was able to make a similar presentation at a much more advanced stage in the project to the faculty of the joint colloquium of the Harvard Divinity School and the Harvard Business School. We hope that our anthology will help to stimulate a proliferation of such interdisciplinary conversations at academic institutions throughout the country.

I personally wish to thank my collaborators in the business ethics program at DePaul University, starting with the former Dean of the College of Commerce, Bro. Leo V. Ryan, C.S.V., who organized the program that led to my coming to DePaul in 1981. My own Dean, Dr. Richard J. Meister, now Executive Vice-President for Academic Affairs, consistently supported this program as an essential component of the university's claim to an urban, Catholic, Vincentian identity and developed an internal program of summer research grants and academic research leave that, among other things, allowed me to begin my work on the project and to make the initial survey of selections for Part C of this anthology. The College of Commerce's Executive-in-Residence, Mr. Ron Nahser, the Chairman and Chief Executive Officer of Frank C. Nahser Advertising, Inc., encouraged me to explore the spiritual dimensions of business ethics. Our countless conversations over the years about his business, my theology, and our common struggle with Catholic tradition were as constructive an introduction to the actual practice of business ethics as I can imagine. My debt to Ron is enormous, as it is to Bud Brownsberger, a former business executive who, during the course of our collaboration, accepted the call to ministry within the United Church of Christ. It was Bud who first had the idea of developing an anthology like this one and who worked with me on a number of preliminary sketches of it.

Max, Shirley, Preston, and I wish to thank all our colleagues who have given us permission to reprint their essays in this collection. They have accepted, usually without complaint, our editorial revisions and have helped us to understand what we were up to better than we would have had we been left to our own devices. Finally, we must thank our publishers, the team at Eerdmans. In addition to Jon Pott, without whom none of this would have come to pass, we have benefited significantly from the hospitality and the suggestions made by Reinder Van Til, Ina Vondiziano, Anne Salsich, Charles Van Hof, Jennifer Hoffman, and Klaas Wolterstorff. They kept faith with this imposing project over its many months of preparation.

Introduction: Foundations and Purposes

Max L. Stackhouse

The Challenge of Business Today

The fall of Rome, the demise of feudalism, the onset of the French Revolution, the defeat of fascism, and the overthrow of colonialism do not surpass in importance what has happened in the last decades of this century. Both traditional and socialist economies have collapsed. They have proven incapable of meeting basic human needs and of sustaining a humane society for the future. Neither primal communitarianism nor scientific socialism will provide the models for tomorrow.

It is not clear, however, exactly what has triumphed. Our present economy, variously called "capitalism," a "mixed economy," or "free-market society," is changing also. No one familiar with it thinks it is perfect. Furthermore, no description of a situation can tell us how we ought to live or whether we ought to embrace or resist what is happening. The purpose of *On Moral Business* is to seek ethical guidelines for the emerging forms of economic life beyond traditionalism and socialism by studying the most profound resources we can find from the past, from around the world, and from current practices that bear on the future.

Some things are clear. The corporation, a social artifact with a long but fragile history, has become one of the strongest institutions of our day. Families split, but companies endure; governments fall, but firms expand. To be sure, businesses fail, companies fold, and corporations are bought out, but the society is preoccupied with plans for their growth. The steeples of the churches are dwarfed by the towers of industry. People say they learn more at work than they did at school. The corporation reaches across cultures; it transcends the boundaries of the nations; it serves as the predominant form of organization for nearly all social institutions; it is the primary center of production and applied technology; and it binds together people of diverse backgrounds in new global networks of interdependence and exchange. And it is changing its internal form to adapt to new global conditions. Instead of a dense, centrally controlled, hierarchical monolith serving a single country, it is becoming a network of ever-changing subunits, operating in many societies and cultures.[1]

Modern corporations are guided by teams of coordinators — managers, planners, engineers, financial experts, lawyers, personnel specialists, and market researchers — who work with employees, suppliers, customers, owners, and host communities to see that some product or service desired by some segment of the population is produced and distributed peacefully, voluntarily, and cooperatively. All who participate gain from it, and more gain when more participate, although not all gain equally; there is some evidence that the inequalities are growing, and many do not participate.

With the triumph and changing structure of the corporation, the influence and institutional bases of the great alternatives have declined. The economic futures of the so-called Second World and Third World hold little promise except insofar as they adopt one or another version of modern business. The elders of these societies and those alienated from the institutions and values of the industrialized countries may resent the fact, but it is true nevertheless.[2] Fewer and fewer people want to live in traditional systems, even if ideals from and hopes for them are treasured.

It is now doubtful that either households (families, clans, villages, or manorial estates), which dominated traditional economies, or governments (feudal, royal, military, or "people's democratic"), which dominated mercantilist and socialist national economies, can manage a modern complex economy. Of course, family firms continue to have a place in the whole economy, and families (which are themselves undergoing

1. See Robert B. Reich, *The Work of Nations: Preparing Ourselves for 21st Century Capitalism* (New York: Alfred A. Knopf, 1991).

2. See Peter L. Berger, *The Capitalist Revolution* (New York: Basic Books, 1986).

change) seek to form persons who are able to live responsibly in complex political economies. Governments also will continue to try to establish the conditions under which business can flourish: coining money, supporting education, preventing exploitation, protecting the environment, developing infrastructure, etc. In fact, family traditions will, in part, be evaluated according to their capacity to form people who are able to make their way in the world and contribute to the well-being of the commonwealth, while governments will be assessed according to their capacity to preserve a degree of law and order and to sustain a context in which business can flourish. But neither the traditional household nor the political program will be the center of the economic life of tomorrow — although new forms of Asian capital suggest new adaptations of both national and familistic corporate functioning.

But these are not all that have been removed from their positions of social centrality; the kind of capitalism that relied on unfettered laws of supply and demand to provide the world with all it needs has also been displaced. It turned out that it both led to depressions and fostered dehumanizing practices. It brought about an economic egocentricity with little place for generosity, compassion, or social justice; and, for that matter, it obscured the human capacity to betray interests for utterly irrational reasons. It is not accurate to say that "capitalism" has defeated the traditional, agricultural household economy and the industrial collectivism of socialism, if one has in mind the individualist capitalism made famous by Adam Smith. He wrote:

> Every individual is continually exerting himself to find out the most advantageous employment of whatever capital he can command. It is his own advantage, indeed, and not that of society which he has in view. But the study of his own advantage naturally, or rather necessarily, leads him to prefer that employment which is most advantageous to the society. . . . Every individual necessarily labours to render the annual revenue of the society as great as he can. . . . [But he] neither intends to promote the public interest, nor knows how much he is promoting it. . . . He intends only his own security; and by directing that industry in such a manner as its produce may be of the greatest value, he intends only his own gain, and he is in this, as in many other cases, led by an invisible hand to promote an end which was not part of his intention. . . . By pursuing his own interest he frequently promotes that of the society more effectually than when he really intends to promote it.[3]

It is surely the case that many will try to live with the convenient confidence that the well-being of the whole comes automatically from one's own self-interest. And those who are self-employed or form sole-proprietary corporations may well contribute to society. But they do so in institutions that ideas of radical individualism cannot sustain. People do not interact as isolated entities. They live in networks. We are related to others in a thousand ways, even if we are alone. We get our information from the mass media and are paid in currency whose value depends on national institutions and international exchange rates. We are a part of "living units" — cohorts, classes, cultural identity groups, political parties, clubs, friendship enclaves, and religious groups. People work in corporations or firms, large or small, and these interact with a constantly changing worldwide society that is both less atomistic than Smith thought and less collectivistic than his most ardent disciple and opponent, Karl Marx, thought. Something other than individualism has displaced traditionalism and solidarity. People, it turns out, are connected by new forms of chosen association as well as isolated by the demise of old communal solidarities.

Besides, if individual ownership of the means of production, individual initiative in business, and individual participation in a free market according to individual, rational calculations of cost and benefit are what is most natural to human beings, why are these not the case everywhere and always? In fact, the decisive kinds of individual personalities that are characteristic of modern economies and able to flourish in complex and dynamic systems arise only where certain ethical and social patterns of human interaction are present.

Those who are to manage the economies of tomorrow cannot rely on a few tired and doubtful

3. Adam Smith, *An Inquiry into the Nature and Causes of the Wealth of Nations* (New York: Modern Library, 1985).

slogans about these matters. They will have to develop a deeper sense of history and a larger regard for morality. They will have to gain a comprehension of the big picture, of major trends, of how parts relate to wholes, of how particular ends are influenced by multiple purposes. They will have to develop a view of higher principles, long-range purposes, and the character of modern changes, which alter what some thought was "nature." They will have to ask whether present systems can sustain a civilization on which individuals, family life, governments, and corporations — as well as hospitals, schools, symphony orchestras, sports teams, and much more — depend. If present systems will not sustain them, they will have to learn how to change them. To do all this they will have to attend to the deepest, broadest, and most enduring source and norm of values that can be imagined. As we will see, they will have to become theological, and they will have to relate theology to business in the context of an understanding of how cultures work.

We are at a turning point in the history of civilizations; changes in the economic order are an indicator of this. Behind the divisions between "liberals" and "conservatives," and deeper than the struggles against slavery and the "robber barons" in the nineteenth century or even against fascism and communism in the twentieth, is a transformation of even greater proportions. We face a number of structural changes that make society more directly dependent on the modern business corporation and its management.

(1) Population growth around the world demands that modern business must provide more jobs, goods, and services than ever before. As agribusiness takes over food and fiber production, the youth of the world flood to the cities, which swallow suburbs and exurbs and form links with other cosmopolitan centers around the globe. If business does not meet the needs of these vast new populations, we could face urban devastation and starvation that no social security system could contain. New forms of barbarism could again threaten civilization.

(2) New technologies make it possible for humans to cut more deeply into the fabric of the bio-physical universe than ever before. The most advanced forms of technology, outside of certain areas within specialized needs of the medical and military fields, are in the control of business — and even the medical and military technologies are developed by corporations. All this makes business, in new ways, similar to the medical and the military fields in that life and death depend on it. This places squarely on business the responsibility to exercise stewardship in regard to natural resources. And if they do not assume that responsibility in research and development, and for ecology, it will and should revert to others.

(3) The emergence of a global market makes interdependence necessary, competition unavoidable, and direct regulation of all aspects of domestic economies impossible. Both the leadership and the workforce of major corporations are increasingly pluralistic culturally. Without a capacity to think in multicultural terms, businesses will be limited to marginal operations.

(4) The emerging, and increasingly common, political culture around the world will demand of both governmental organizations and social and economic institutions one or another form of constitutional democracy, with a defense of human rights and an increasingly common legal structure. Closer agreement is necessary on, for example, patent, copyright, liability, and health and safety provisions, since we are already woven into an utterly interdependent world order. The basic principles on which these laws are based and the particular ways in which they are interpreted and applied will be fateful for business.

(5) The global reach of tomorrow's economy, and of all these related conditions, will entail increased encounters among the world's high religions. These are likely not only to bring clashes surpassing those of recent centuries when Christian traditions met simpler or secular cultures but also to demand an awareness of how religious orientations often determine cultural views of work, city life, technology, cosmopolitan values, law, and political culture.

In other words, business leaders are increasingly the stewards of civilization. Such challenges require "moral business" with a larger sense of institutional systems and a deeper sense of "professional responsibility" in the midst of a wider new global situation than most business leaders have yet confronted. Those who aspire to leadership, and those who are called to give intellectual, moral, and spiritual guidance to the economic leaders of the future, will have to think of business in new ways. The burden of leadership in the next century is likely to fall on business management in a way that has never before been the case in human history.

Business as a "Calling"?

Many people are skeptical about the morality of modern business, and there are reasons for this doubt. One reason is that business leaders have sometimes exploited workers, deceived customers, damaged the environment, and tried to manipulate family life, political power, and religion for gain. Everyone knows that these things are wrong; but they are frequent enough that business is often seen as an empirical confirmation of the reality of "original sin" in the form of greed, although it is not at all clear that business leaders are more greedy than, say, tribesmen, peasants, emperors, actresses, or sundry high priests. Another reason is that modern business is disruptive. It breaks down old ways of doing things, and, as already noted, it displaces familial and political patterns. A money economy, for example, undercuts relations built on barter or traditional status. It demands changes in prevailing cultural understandings. Skills or habits that are necessary and honored in one generation become obsolete and dispensable in the next. Modern business rewards achievement, but the achievements it rewards do not long endure.

Business has never been a "profession" in the technical sense. People seldom speak of "moral business" in the same way that they speak of just law, sound medicine, quality education, or profound religion. People who work in operations management, finance, marketing, or accounting may have as much specialized training as do other respected occupations, and they may be as amply rewarded for their work; but they are seldom seen as "true" professionals, as lawyers, doctors, professors, and clergy are.

Very ancient and very profound views of why one does what one does stand behind these distinctions. For most of human history, people were hunters, gatherers, or farmers, living by subsistence. Roles were established by sex, age, and status (as, e.g., the chief's relative). Where more complex societies were established, the crafts were honored — the mason, the potter, or the midwife, etc. But in some cultures, the idea developed that persons with exceptional abilities were given those talents because they were called by God to special responsibilities necessary to the well-being of the whole society — to religious or political leadership, especially. Among the ancient Hebrews, with parallels in Greece, India, China, Egypt, and elsewhere, roles that required both special ability and specialized training and that were indispensable to the life of the civilization were treated as "callings" or "vocations." Persons with a "calling" developed a disciplined life-style governed by a worldview and a value system that comprehended the whole and guided a practical expertise, so that they could best serve God and the people in a humane context.

The idea of a "calling" requires several things to become operative in a whole society. One of them is the vision of a complex, open, cosmopolitan civilization. It is only in such societies that great numbers of people can find the opportunities to find and carry out their vocations. The personal quest to find out what one is called to do with one's life, in other words, is intimately connected to the kind of society in which one lives. In a recent lecture, V. S. Naipaul, an Indian born and raised in Trinidad and now one of the world's premier writers, speaks of his own inner urgency and of the objective conditions necessary to fulfill it:

> I was given the ambition to write books, and specifically to write novels. . . . But books are not created just in the mind. Books are physical objects. To write them you need a certain kind of sensibility; you need a language, a certain gift of language; . . . [but to] get your name on the spine of the created physical object, you need a vast apparatus outside yourself. You need publishers, editors, designers, printers, binders; booksellers, critics, newspapers, and magazines and television where the critics can say what they think of the book; and of course, buyers and readers.
>
> I want to stress this mundane side of things, because it is easy to take it for granted; it is easy to think of writing only in its personal . . . aspect. . . . [B]ut the published book, when it starts to live, speaks of the cooperation of a par-

ticular kind of society. The society has a certain degree of commercial organization.[4]

The vision of a cosmopolitan civilization where all people with many divergent callings flourish is not natural. For most of human history, people did with their lives what their grandparents did. Whether we believe that the vision of a global community of communities wherein each person finds a way to contribute to the whole by following his or her calling is a revelation or a poetic invention of speculative philosophers, it had to be created as a moral possibility in the human imagination. In fact, it has to be constantly re-created, for the human tendency is to settle for the ordinary, to fear the extraordinary, and to avoid thinking of the whole.

The idea of "calling" implies not only a "callee" in an open, complex society; it also implies a "Caller" who wants life to be just and loving. In the biblical tradition, Abrahamic, Mosaic, and Christian, that is God. God has a purpose for a people. They are to be something more than what they are naturally. They are called, in humility but also in confidence, to be a "light to the nations" on the basis of a disclosure of the eternal truth of a godly justice.

In the New Testament, that idea is both personalized and universalized. God has a purpose for each person, and God calls that person into communities that are explicitly not tribal or political but are linked to visions of a universalistic "New Jerusalem" in a renewed cosmos, a "new heaven and a new earth." By examining their gifts, talents, and abilities in relationship to the needs of the world, people find out how God wants them to contribute to world civilization and thus why God brought them into being. The life and associations one is called to are more important than the life and community one comes from.

The response to that calling is to "express forth in a vow" or "profess" to live morally and to use those talents to fulfill the duties of that calling so far as possible. Of course, this means that one is not simply to work for oneself or one's family or nation. Egoism, group selfishness, and preferences for "one's own kind," which are everywhere present among humans, are brought under constraint by conscious commitment to principles and pur-

poses that overarch all humanity. The "professing" person is one who is dedicated to excellence in the "calling" God intends and is also willing to take upon himself or herself the responsibility of helping to spread the possibilities for all peoples by shaping a genuinely cosmopolitan civilization. Here is the root of the idea of "profession" — one which was gradually extended over the centuries from the prophet, the sage, and the priest to the statesman, the law-giver, and the healer, and to others in roles the ancient world did not know.

This idea of many kinds of persons having a vocation and developing professions in an open, complex, pluralistic society was also influenced by the vision of a cosmopolitan civilization that one can find among the Stoic philosophers at the time of the Roman Empire. But these early and fragile beginnings were not fully developed in antiquity. Only gradually did such ideas come to constitute a chief characteristic of a civilization.

The connections between the biblical and philosophical ancient world and the modern one are many, although the routes from then to now involve twists and turns that are subtle and often surprising. Again and again in history, it is by returning to these ancient sources and seeing them through fresh eyes that societies have renewed themselves. It is, indeed, partly by becoming aware of the roots and decisive developments behind present situations that one becomes a professional. *On Moral Business* will focus on influences that have brought us to the twenty-first century.

For now, let us anticipate one example of this history. The development of the idea of "calling" has gone through several changes between biblical times and the present: the formation of the monastic ideal in Catholic Christianity saw "vocation" as a personal call to holy life; the development of mysticism among the laity, and later Protestantism, carried this sense of godly work into secular life; and subsequently, the university developed specialized training for each field and gave further impetus to modern understandings of professionalism. These shifts have both refined what is implied in the earlier records and given a specific shape to modernity.[5]

---

4. V. S. Naipaul, "Our Universal Civilization," *New York Review of Books,* 31 Jan. 1991, p. 22.

5. See Karl Holl, "Die Geschichte des Worts Beruf," *Aufsaetze zur Kirchengeschichte,* vol. 3 (Tübingen, 1928); and Chapters 4 and 5, below.

David Smith recently reviewed these developments and pointed out that Calvinism stressed the idea "that the professional is called not to accept but to reform or change the world according to the ideals of his or her calling. . . . [T]he professional is called to a special responsibility for society as a whole. S/he is a public official with leadership responsibilities — physicians should work for public health, lawyers for civil rights, etc."[6] What is the proper correlative responsibility for business?

Of Careers and Professions

The historic meaning of calling and profession has largely eroded. Many think of "vocation" in the context of "vocational training" — that form of manual education given to those who do not plan to go to college. That usage, however, was a further extension of what is outlined above. It developed in the late nineteenth century in an attempt to give the ordinary worker a sense of dignity before God and society. Unfortunately, that usage now obscures some of the classical connections between vocation and profession.

Similarly, when people use the word "professional" they often mean someone who is an expert and who works full-time in their field. Thus, traditional crafts and modern trades — carpentry, plumbing, hairdressing, tennis playing, word processing — are now spoken of as "professions." Clearly, the dedication to excellence, the commitment to trustworthy standards, and the sense of serving others retain aspects of the ancient meaning of "profession." "Doing a first-rate job" is a matter of great importance to persons and for civilization as a whole. But nothing in that necessarily involves taking moral responsibility for the cosmopolitan shape of things.

Today people speak more frequently of "careers" — a term rooted historically in the image of a competitive "race course" — than of "callings." A career is a sequence of jobs with increased levels of skill, responsibility, and reward as charted out by an organization. Such "ladders" of occupational progress are both necessary to complex economic institutions and sources of great opportunity for those who find their way onto the lower rungs. Those without access to such ladders are relegated to the permanent underclass of modern societies. Yet career patterns may be designed or pursued with no sense of wider vision for either souls or civilization; it may even come to mean a scramble to the top of a prescribed pyramid as governed by the cynical slogan, "Whoever has the most toys when they die, wins."

The "classical professions," the clergy, the doctor, the lawyer, the educator, the statesman, the poet, and the architect, are not immune to careerism, but the residual meanings of vocation and profession continue to influence their self-image, their training, and their characteristic institutions in ways that are rare among business leaders.

In part, this is an accident of history. The medicine man, the judge, and the philosopher required special training and established schools in the ancient empires to cultivate their disciplines. Their character was stamped by theological views of life predominant among those monastics, mystics, and reformers who saw in them elements of the wisdom of God necessary for the preservation of civilization after the empires of the ancient world collapsed. Those professions developed further in the medieval universities and later set the tone for the "new professions," which emerged more directly from the needs of the modern nation state. Architecture, engineering, and public administration were developed in their modern forms by priestly advisors to political powers and have also come to share in an implicit ethical legitimacy, while journalism with its struggle for freedom of the press and social work with its commitments to those neglected by society were deeply influenced by clergy who saw advocacy among the people as the manifestation of the prophetic tradition under modern conditions.

In spite of some outstanding exceptions,[7] most of the overt references to anything theological in these fields is now gone, although ethical considerations remain relevant. People who go into these

6. David H. Smith, "Called to Profess: Religious and Secular Theories of Vocation," Annual Meeting of the Society of Christian Ethics, 1988.

7. See Karen Lebacqz, *Professional Ethics: Power and Paradox* (Nashville: Abingdon, 1985); and especially Eric Mount, Jr., *Professional Ethics in Context* (Louisville: Westminster, 1990).

fields are not only expected to be competent and to lead basically decent personal lives; they are to make their public decisions on morally justifiable grounds, to protect the interests of those they serve, to contribute to both the theory and the practice of what they do and show the relationship of one to the other, and to use their specialized skills in ways that enhance the quality of life in society. Both the activities that are undertaken by these professionals and the institutions in which they work — courts, hospitals, schools, churches, etc. — are seen as having inherent ethical qualities needful of protection, clarification, defense, and loyalty.

It is true, of course, that shyster lawyers, quack doctors, mad scientists, unscrupulous clergy, and all the fraudulent representatives of the other professions both are subject to legal sanction and are the butts of innumerable jokes. But these professionals are objects of sometimes well-deserved ridicule precisely because people expect them not simply to live for themselves and off their institutions but to live for others, in accord with the values built into the institutions they serve, under the ethical codes of their profession, and with the recognition that they perform an indispensable role in the civilization.

Today we face a tendency among all the professions to deny responsibility for the general shape of things. Many tend to "let politics take care of that," while they seek to become more specialized and refined in their skills. The distinguished ethicist James Luther Adams spoke of this problem when he wrote that the

emphasis on specificity of function, to be sure, represents a definitely legitimate professional responsibility. . . . But in many quarters [it also leads to an incapacity to see] the specialist responsibilities within the context of the total fabric of life. In this process, the specialist [becomes] only a segment of a person. One is reminded of the epitaph [found] in Scotland:

Here lies John MacDonald
Born a man
Died a grocer.[8]

8. James Luther Adams, "The Social Import of the Professions," in *Voluntary Associations,* ed. J. Ronald Engel (Chicago: Exploration Press, 1986), pp. 270-71.

Business has recently become so pervasive, international, and equipped with modern technology that it has become indispensable to the well-being of the common life. In the past, merchants were most often independent and isolated. It may have been morally reprehensible, but it was not disruptive of the whole civilization if they were guided by narrow interest only. When nearly all were limited in knowledge of the world and relatively poor, only the vain and foolish wanted "foreign" goods to enhance the image of grandeur, and when traders were basically fugitives from responsible living, commerce was viewed as a temptation and a snare. To be sure, some who were successful in business were noted for fairness and generosity from time to time; and no small number of people have been willing to bow before wealth in every age and on every continent. Still, business has often been viewed with suspicion by other professionals in church, government, court, hospital, and university. Images of the shady merchant, the slick dealer, the fast-talking salesman, and the unscrupulous captain of industry abound. Even a good number of people in business are haunted by the suspicion that what they do is, somehow, a morally less honorable activity than what their professional neighbors do.

A common critique of various fields today is that "it is simply becoming a business." Contemporary leaders of law, medicine, education, journalism, and sometimes religion complain that their fields are being "reduced" to "business" decisions. It is not that they are opposed to good management or being solvent, but they do not want life and thought in their fields to be governed by what they understand to be "merely" business criteria or to act in their professions as if material gain were the only goal. And they believe that "good business" means nothing else than greed, a congenital blindness to the needs of others and to justice, health, wisdom, honesty, and the common good. People often view business with suspicion, in other words, because it is thought to be constitutionally unethical in some regard or another. The "good" of "good business" is not thought to be a moral good.

Of course, people in business may be quite moral personally. People put enormous confidence in those with whom they do business, and no economic system survives without deep reservoirs of trust. People who are in business may be as moral (or no more immoral) in a great number of areas of life as people in any other field are. And many seek to develop a sense of integrity and service at the grass roots of business. Rotary International, for example, has tried to set exemplary standards for business persons. They have established a "four-way test for things we think, say, and do: Is it the truth? Is it fair to all concerned? Will it build good will and better friendships? Will it be beneficial to all concerned?" The question, however, is whether business as a practice in the future must include a new depth of professional awareness because of the new responsibilities to which business leaders are being called in our new global situation.

Economics, Law, and Culture

Three areas that always deeply influence business could, in unexpected ways, also obscure part of business's responsibility today. Influential views of economics, jurisprudence, and cultural development may deflect attention away from business ethics. The discipline of economics, for example, has developed the capacity to give us a more accurate reading of how business systems work — how, in the aggregate, societies, corporations, and communities respond to economic pressures and trends of one kind or another — than has ever been available in human history before. This is an enormous advance — as important for human understanding as were the discoveries of Galileo, Newton, and Einstein in physics or of Darwin, Mendel, Crick, and Watson in biology.

Science of all kinds tells us how things work, but it does not tell us how things ought to work or what we ought to do with the knowledge science makes possible. Economics, like physics and biology, has often been so fascinated with its capacity to describe that it has forgotten how to address the issue of what humans should prescribe. Economics developed out of moral philosophy and theology nearly two centuries ago, and it has not regained an integrated relationship to normative issues, with which it nevertheless deals. Theology, meanwhile, either abandoned economics or adopted romantic or socialist ideas until quite recently. Economics as a science thus knows little of vocation or profession, though it knows much about the division of labor and the costs and benefits of career patterns.

In consequence, people in business who take their cues primarily from economics are deprived of a language system for discussing values, ethical norms, and spiritual principles that relate to what they do. In spite of imaginative and highly visible work on values in management by Peter Drucker and Thomas Peters over the last few decades and new efforts by religiously interested and philosophically disposed economists,[9] modern business is largely without a nuanced vocabulary to deal with its own moral potentialities and limitations. The explosion of journals and books dedicated to business ethics by philosophical and theological authors in the last few decades indicates a new, though still inchoate, attempt to develop a language of morality for the modern manager and the modern corporation.

People sometimes say, "This is right in theory but it doesn't work in practice." They ought to say, "This is wrong in theory and consequently it is wrong in practice." There is no true theory which could be wrong in practice. This contrast between theory and practice is contrived by people who want to escape hard and thorough thinking. They like to abide in the shallowness of accustomed practices, on the surface of a so-called "experience." They will accept nothing but a repeated confirmation of something they already know or believe. Only those questions for truth which have challenged and disturbed centuries of practice have brought about a fundamental transformation of practice. This is true of the history of science, morals and religion.

— Paul Tillich, *The Shaking of the Foundations*
(New York: Charles Scribner and Sons, 1948), p. 115

---

9. See, for example, Amitai Etzioni, *The Moral Dimension: Toward a New Economics* (New York: The Free Press, 1988); and Severyn T. Bruyn, *A Future for the American Economy* (Stanford: University of California Press, 1991).

Much of business practice in the West is controlled by a quite sophisticated set of legal constraints that serve, for many, as the key guides to business morality. Modern business presupposes a stable fabric of law. Law, of course, means limits; there are some things that businesses cannot do and remain legitimately in business. It is one of the ironies of modern economic life that constraints are necessary in order for there to be a "free market." Lands that have not developed legal systems that simultaneously control corruption and encourage business remain underdeveloped, as one can see when one compares Eastern and Western Europe, North and South Korea, Malaysia and Singapore, or the Philippines and Japan. Another irony is that where legal systems are strong, moral debates tend to defer to them, and concern for distinctive ethical issues is underdeveloped, even though strong legal systems rest on a fabric of shared moral convictions.

Indeed, much of morality is beyond the law — both in the sense that morality is what makes some laws just and others unjust, and in the sense that much of morality has to do with how we ought to organize authority, establish policy, and arrange human relationships within the law. Some perfectly legal business transactions are morally scandalous, and some business leaders who will never be indicted are scoundrels. These may even be quite successful economically; and it is doubtful whether all moral behavior could or should be controlled legally. Law is best when it provides general guidelines for organization and action, yet preserves maximum freedom, protects persons and groups from danger or exploitation, and constrains those who subvert the capacity to live responsibly. The point is this: economics and law cannot generate business morality alone. Something in addition to them must guide business.

Business is also deeply influenced by culture; some national, ethnic, or regional cultures tend to inhibit business activity while others encourage it, as we shall see. For example, a culture influences how parents relate to children and what values are honored in school, community, and society. Such influences determine in substantial measure the preparedness of youth for the world of business, the work habits, the sense of responsibility and rights, and the forms of cultural literacy they bring to it. Those without these influences are at a great disadvantage.

Further, business has its own subcultural values that reach between groups: business leaders from China, Canada, Brazil, and Ghana can chatter away on first meeting in the same way that nurses, philosophers, and musicians can. Still further, certain larger enterprises generate their own corporate culture — working for Ford, or Apple, or Toyota, or Air India, or Amway induces distinctive styles of human relations, cooperation or conflict, even distinctive senses of humor. People who interview for jobs in any of these firms are assessed as to whether they would "fit in" as well as whether they are competent in a narrow sense, and they have to decide whether they will be happy working in that particular corporate subculture.

But culture, like law and economics, is finally unable to supply the norms for moral business. Cultures and subcultures do not themselves answer the question, for example, of how inclusive or exclusive these cultures or their workforce or the communities they serve *ought* to be. Nor do they tell us what to do when cultures or subcultures become blind to their own injustice. Since the twentieth-century struggles against Hitler, segregation, and apartheid, for example, many are aware of the fact that racism can become built into cultures and that only principles that transcend the values of a given society can change them.

Of course, business uses economics, just as technology uses physics and medicine uses biology, and all these fields depend on the civil law for some things and on culture for others; but economics, law, and culture cannot prescribe how their own principles ought to be used any more than physics or biology can. Much of what is contained in these chapters will be oriented in modern economics, law, and culture in the sense that whatever ethical vision we propose must be socially viable. But basic models — for example, of supply and demand — will not be our focus. Instead, the focus will be on those principles that *ought* to be employed so that "good business" means not only realistic economics but also "moral business" — professional practices within responsible institutions operating under just laws in vibrant cultural settings.

In brief, nothing is likely to be so useful as helping business leaders and practitioners recognize, cultivate, define, and refine their potential as professionals. It is time for business, the belated profession, to come into its own. It is the purpose of this volume to retrieve from the past those great motifs and themes that will be important also to the future, to explore resources in other cultures that can aid in our global situation, and to offer analyses of the actual practices of modern business to see what values in them need to be developed, extended, or altered. This requires, of course, the professionalization of modern business precisely in the sense that it develops among business leaders the moral and spiritual capacity to guide their increasing expertise and emerging institutions with clarity about and commitment to the well-being of the commonwealth of nations.

What Is Ethics?

The explosion of articles, books, journals, courses, and programs in "business ethics" in the last generation indicates a felt need for moral reflection among business leaders. What follows in this section is an overview of major presuppositions about the nature of ethics. This will be followed with a summary of our assumptions about the relationship of ethics to the various functions in business life and then the relationship of ethics to religion and theology. These are the themes that will be accented throughout this volume.

Ethics is about how we *ought* to live. Ethics studies the various patterns of morality that exist in the habits of persons, the fabric of communities, or the teachings of the wise and analyzes which ones ought to be followed and how we know. We need not use only the word "ought" to describe ethics; we could use the word "just" or the phrase "with integrity," or half a dozen other terms. Each term has its own emphasis, but all are about living trustworthy and honorable lives, and not living as cheats, liars, exploiters, or oppressors. Or, we could say that ethics is about how to live responsibly in general, and that professional responsibility is about how we ought to live when we are doing business. Above all, as we will see, ethics is about how God wants us to live.

The "ought" that is necessarily involved in ethics is a complex term, not a simple one. It has several parts that are often confused. Thus we must make several distinctions. One of them is this: personal ethics is not the same as social ethics, even if they are related. Note that ethics is about how *we* ought to live; it applies to us as an aggregate of persons. But in the modern world the "we" is not always clear. Each person is a member of many communities, and each has to decide which of those communities to support with enthusiasm and which to ignore or oppose. Moreover, individuals make decisions and seek to be more or less honorable with regard to their various relationships. Thus, one part of ethics treats the virtues, the development of character, and helps us decide the kind of people we ought to be. It is because of this difference between personal and social ethics that we can find saints in bad situations and scoundrels in good ones.

Institutions also have common standards and moral qualities. And it is here, as much as in personal areas, that ethics makes a difference in business. It always has a public, social dimension as well. Organizations, through complex processes, also make decisions and determine patterns of living. When Control Data decided to build plants on Indian reservations to help unemployment problems, when Johnson & Johnson decided to recall Tylenol capsules, and when General Dynamics decided to reorganize in the early 1980s, the consequences were extensive. Ethics in this social dimension is concerned with how we form polities and policies — structures and programs that channel and limit both personal inclinations and collective tendencies. Negatively, that means that unjust structures can corrupt persons or put them in perpetually compromising positions; positively, it means that moral institutions and intentional policies can at least limit the capacity of immoral persons or cultural trends from damaging the common life and perhaps even redeem damage already done.

Ethical influence, in other words, need not only flow from individual to group; it can also work the other way around. A just society or a moral organization can constrain mean people from being vicious and help decent but fragile people live life with greater integrity, while a disintegrative structure can evoke the worst from everyone. In any case, in sorting out an ethical situation we have to be clear whether the central problem is a personal one, one present in a particular institution or sector of society, or a systemic one applying to the whole of the society. The range of ethical vision will differ, even if basic principles are constant.

A second major distinction in ethics is also important: the difference between descriptive (or interpretive) analysis and prescriptive (or normative) analysis. That is, we have to learn the difference between what is and what ought to be. How we live may or may not be how we ought to live. It is also sometimes the case that how we think we ought to live is not in fact how we ought to live. Slavery as a primary instrument of production, for example, was thought to be proper for centuries. (It still is in some cultures.) Differentiated economic roles for males and females continues to be defended in many cultures today.

The modern social sciences — psychology, political science, economics, anthropology, sociology, and the like — have developed refined techniques to help us describe the moral situation. They can tell us what moral opinions prevail on just about any issue. They tell us that people with particular psychological, economic, and social backgrounds are likely to believe that the national policy on taxation *ought* to be more "progressive," while other people with other psychological, economic, and social profiles believe that the policy *ought* to be based on flat rates. As the newspapers are full of opinion polls, the textbooks of the social sciences help us understand how the moral attitudes of people are shaped by their personal, social, and cultural experience.

But these sciences, with all their vast capacity to describe how things are, intentionally do not try to tell us how they ought to be. There may be considerable overlap, of course, between what the social scientific analysis describes and what the ethical analysis prescribes; sometimes what happens is not far from what ought to happen, and sometimes our view of what ought to happen is shaped by what does happen. More frequently, the discovery of dysfunctional problems indicates the need to invoke moral imperatives. But the fact that some things are the way they are does not prove that they ought to be as they are.

This distinction between the empirical "is" and the normative "ought" also implies something very important for ethics — freedom. We humans are not altogether determined by "what is." The genetic,

economic, psychological, social, and cultural backgrounds from which we come may influence us deeply; but we do not have to remain passive before everything that has shaped us. It is possible to discover, grasp, or imagine an ideal of "what ought to be." That is an experience of moral freedom. We can then see that some pattern of life in which we were raised is limited, and we can choose to live more in accord with the ideal. Freedom may not be the highest value in life, but it is a necessary foundation of our humanity and morality.

As to what we ought to do with our freedom, we must note a threefold set of distinctions. (1) Some "ideal" things that we ought to do, ought to be done because they are right. We ought to do what is right and not do what is wrong, and everyone knows it. (2) Still other things ought to be done because they are good to do. Not to do them would be evil, or would lead to evil. (3) And still other things ought to be done because they are appropriate to the particular time, place, and situation that is at hand. Just as one does not act at a funeral the way one does at a wedding, a business leader is not a politician or a professor or a social worker or a doctor. Certain moral demands are involved in each one of these functions that are not involved in any of the others, and it is only by grasping the particular contexts in which each of these works that one can understand what the fitting thing to do might be.

These three concepts, the right, the good, and the fitting (or negatively, the wrong, the evil, and the unfitting) are decisive for ethics. In ordinary conversation these terms seem interchangeable. To say "That's right!" does not differ greatly from saying "That's good!" or "That fits!" To say that something is "inappropriate" or "sick" or "gross" is often a slang way of saying that it is "bad" (= not conducive to the good, even if not positively evil) or contrary to what is right (= wrong). But a professional level of clarity about business ethics requires greater precision than this. Each term implies something distinctive about how we ought to live and about how we can know how we ought to live. The problem is that they do not imply the same thing, and sometimes they imply contrary things. In any case, there is no end of confusion when they are mixed up.

H. Richard Niebuhr argued that these accents grow out of the different kinds of questions one asks when faced with doubt about what we should do or how we ought to live. Some people want to know, above all, "What is the law and what is the first law of my (or our) life?" These are people who understand their own humanity as "citizens," as members of a larger body that is and has to be regulated by common laws or principles. Other people want to know, instead, "What is my (or our) goal or purpose?" These people understand their humanity as "makers" or "builders." They view life as a task to be accomplished, an objective to be attained. And still others want to know, first of all, "What is going on?" These are the responders. They want to interpret a particular situation, to be equipped to respond to it, and to be accountable for their response.[10]

All through the following pages, these three themes will appear in various vocabularies, and it is important to be able to recognize some of the key ways of thinking about these three dimensions of the moral life, for they lead to different ways of deciding matters in business. In fact, each of them has a subdiscipline within ethics — deontology, teleology, and ethology.

Deontology (based on the Greek deon = binding, duty)

An ethic based on concepts of right (and wrong) attempts to answer the question "What is the law?" It seeks to state in a rational and clear fashion — usually in the form of rules or principles — what kinds of behavior are required, forbidden, or permitted. In its more complete forms, it also attempts to give the reasons for stating things this way. It tends to be based on the idea that, for all humanity, certain kinds of things are morally binding no matter what the circumstances or consequences. It is right to tell the truth, to keep promises, to honor legitimate authority, to be fair to all, and to respect the human rights of everyone. It is wrong to murder, rape, torture, exploit, or oppress people. Even if, in some extreme circumstances, we have to violate one of these principles (such as by going to war to control a tyrant or breaking a promise to save another person's life), we may morally do so only to establish the kind of right order in society where the moral laws and principles can be better observed.

This kind of thinking about ethics is very ancient. One finds it in the Hebrew Scriptures, where God's laws are given as the Commandments, in passages that deal specifically with business issues, and in teachings of Jesus that emphasize the unchanging character of this dimension of ethics:

> You shall be holy: for I the LORD your God am holy. . . .
>
> You shall not steal; you shall not deal falsely; and you shall not lie to one another . . . : I am the LORD.
>
> You shall not defraud your neighbor; . . . and you shall not keep for yourself the wages of a laborer until morning . . . : I am the LORD.
>
> You shall not render an unjust judgment; you shall not be partial to the poor or defer to the great: with justice you shall judge your neighbor . . . , but you shall love your neighbor as yourself: I am the LORD. (Lev. 19:2, 11-15, 18, NRSV)

"Do not think that I have come to abolish the law or the prophets; I have come not to abolish but to fulfill. For truly I tell you, until heaven and earth pass away, not one letter, not one stroke of a letter, will pass from the law until all is accomplished. Therefore, whoever breaks one of the least of these commandments, and teaches others to do so, will be called least in the kingdom of heaven." (Matt. 5:17-19, NRSV)

Although in a quite contrasting style, the idea that there are universal absolutes also appears in the doctrine of "eternal forms" or "archetypes" taught by the famous Greek philosopher Plato (see Chapter 3). For centuries, theologians and philosophers in these traditions have held that humans have a profound awareness of right and wrong that derives from a rather vague but still real memory of their divine origins. Some call it "common grace," while others think of it as an inherent "moral sense," but all think that general principles of justice can be known in some measure, and that this knowledge is a divine gift.

The founding fathers of the United States held one version of this view when, in the Declaration of Independence, they wrote: "We hold these

---

10. H. Richard Niebuhr, *The Responsible Self* (New York: Harper & Row, 1963), pp. 60-61 et passim.

truths to be self-evident; that all men are created equal; that they are endowed by their creator with certain unalienable rights." Another, more recent version is part of the United Nations "Universal Declaration of Human Rights." Article 1 states: "All human beings are born free and equal in dignity and rights. They are endowed with reason and conscience." The following articles then outline the rights that people have and the wrongs that may not be done.

The attempt to state universal principles is shared by all the world's religions and all the major philosophies, and the consensus is remarkable. Christian theology has a technical term for this — "*justitia originalis*" — and this "primal sense of right," what Thomas Aquinas called *synteresis,* is basic for doctrines about "natural law," "general revelation," and most theories of "conscience." Moral philosophers and theologians study these things, trying to figure out what would be the most reliable way of clarifying the first principles of right and wrong in the moral life and the basis on which they stand.

In modern theory, this way of thinking ethically has been especially accented by the followers of the influential German philosopher Immanuel Kant, a leader of the Enlightenment. In one writing that is very important for modern thought, he takes up the issue of "maxims," that is, self-evident moral principles, and the motivations for doing what is right according to them, that is, "duty."

> Now, as an act from duty wholly excludes the influence of inclination, . . . nothing remains which can determine the will objectively except the law, and nothing subjectively except pure respect for this practical law. . . . Thus, the moral worth of an action does not lie in the effect which is expected from it or in any principle of action which has to borrow its motive from this expected effect. . . .
>
> But what kind of a law can that be, the conception of which must determine the will without reference to the expected result? . . . [N]othing remains to serve as moral . . . except universal conformity of . . . [an] action to law as such. That is, I should never act in such a way that I could not also will that my maxim should be a universal law.[11]

11. Immanuel Kant, *Foundations of the Metaphysics*

Not everyone follows Kant's argument, just as not everyone follows Leviticus or Plato or Jesus or the United Nations. In fact, criticism of all these positions has increased recently, primarily because they rest on the idea that there is a divine order of things that is, at least in part, knowable by humans. Contemporary thinkers are very unsure about how to argue for that view, although they know that large percentages of the population believe that it is true, and their own suspicions about it depend on the absolute belief that telling the truth is right, and not telling it is wrong.

Whether or not the next generation of thinkers will find these kinds of arguments persuasive, these examples do show us that moral rules are part of the historic, serious thinking about ethical behavior, righteous living, and the human condition generally. Deontological thinkers believe that "universal," "absolute" principles are not arbitrary impositions or demands that apply only to those who hold certain beliefs on blind faith. Authentic, just laws and moral principles are reasonable and for everyone all the time — like the logic behind grammars that makes it possible to translate languages, the root patterns of rhythm and harmonics that make many musics possible, or the maths that make many sciences possible, all of which have also been viewed as gifts of God. Deontology, in other words, aspires to identify the skeleton of ethics, even if it cannot supply everything an ethic needs to take on flesh or spirit.

Attention to deontology reveals one dimension of doing what we ought to do as business leaders in a business-influenced, global society. Responsible professionals will have to become as clear as possible about the first principles that are to govern our personal lives and the social-economic contexts in which we wish to do business.

Teleology (based on the Greek telos = end or purpose)

Teleology attempts to address the question: "What is the goal or purpose?" Besides dealing with basic issues of right and wrong in regard to "ought," every complete ethic must also face the question

of Morals, trans. L. W. Beck (Indianapolis: Bobbs-Merrill, 1959), pp. 24-25.

of good and evil. This dimension of ethics is distinct from deontology and focuses on the identification of ends or objectives that ought to be sought. While basic principles of right and wrong are timeless — rape, theft, deception, murder, exploitation, and torture were as wrong among ancient tribes as they will be when and if Mars is colonized — our understanding of what is good and what is evil is tied to time in a particular way. We humans set goals for ourselves for the future, and we act toward those goals in ways that depart from the past and change the present. If deontology seeks for the constant and reliable, teleology seeks the novel and the dynamic.

Humans are not only different from animals because we live under higher moral principles; we also live for objectives beyond our instincts. We have purposes that invite us to action. We want to accomplish something that is not yet fully actual. When we act toward those ends, we are plunged into the future. We have to imagine a state of affairs that is not yet the case, and we have to assemble the knowledge, resources, and skills to make it come to pass. Our purposes constantly expand and contract.

The normative question for teleology is this: What goals *ought* we to seek? Some goals may be good, others may be better, and still another may be the best. The opposite may also be the case: some goals may be bad (defective), or worse than others, or even evil (destructive of good). Moreover, in human affairs the real choices at hand are often not between good and evil or even between good and best, but between evils. We have to seek the lesser evil, to prevent the worst evil from happening. Further, people sometimes intend good but do things in the pursuit of good that turn out to be quite terrible in actual result.

People have to study teleology not only because of these variations but also because of an ambiguity that is built into the question of teleology, "What goals ought we to seek?" There is both an objective and a subjective element in human purposes. One has to do with the target that is established, the goal itself. We have to figure out which goal is worth all the effort and how it fits into other goals that we might want to pursue. We must get our priorities straight — and that means deciding which goals are the most valid.

The other has to do with what we intend. This dimension of teleology touches on inclinations, dispositions, motivations, and desires that we find within ourselves. We know that most motives for what we do in life are mixed. We want to do some good in the world, and we want to get recognition and gain for ourselves. The mixtures of egoism and altruism, of self-love and neighbor-love, of dedication to excellence and willingness to cut corners, of confidence in our potential and insecurity that prompts us to constantly attempt to prove ourselves — these are deep in the human condition. Further, everyone has multiple mixed motives that bump into the mixed motives of others in every human relationship.

What is true for individuals is also true for institutions. The objectives of the school are not those of the hospital, of the law court, of the family, of the political party, or of the symphony orchestra. And all of these differ from the goals of the business corporation. Each area of human social experience has distinctive objectives, and the people in them will have different potentials and motives. The fact that people live in multiple institutions means that people often have conflicting senses of purpose. Even within one general area, such as business, different industries, companies, divisions, or functions (engineering, design, marketing, accounting, etc.) will have different goals, and each of these are populated by people who have different personal agendas and are driven by mixed motives.

Sorting out just these kinds of problems and seeing them within a larger vision of what is good is what the teleological dimension of ethics is all about. Of course, to do that one has to have a notion what the good really ought to be and what potentialities humans have to strive for it. The question "What goals ought we to seek?" turns out to be more than a matter of personal or even corporate policy; it touches one of the deepest questions of philosophy and theology: What, in the final analysis, is worth living, working, and sacrificing for?

Modern society, for the most part, has given this question a utilitarian answer: the increase of pleasure and the decrease of pain. What increases comfort and reduces suffering is approved. More than two centuries ago, the British author Jeremy Bentham was the great advocate for this point of view:

Nature has placed mankind under the governance of two sovereign masters, *pain* and *pleasure*. It is for them alone to point out what we ought to do, as well as to determine what we shall do. On the one hand the standard of right and wrong, on the other the chain of causes and effects, are fastened to their throne. . . . The *principle of utility* recognizes this subjection, and assumes it for the foundation of that system. . . . Systems which attempt to question it deal in sounds instead of sense, in caprice instead of reason, in darkness instead of light. . . .

By utility is meant that property in any object, whereby it tends to produce benefit, advantage, pleasure, good or happiness (all this in the present case comes to the same thing) or (what comes again to the same thing) to prevent the happening of mischief, pain, evil or unhappiness.[12]

Two generations later, his greatest disciple, John Stuart Mill, refined his view and tried to link it to deontological views.

The creed which accepts as the foundation of morals, Utility . . . , holds that actions are right in proportion as they tend to promote happiness, wrong as they tend to produce the reverse of happiness. By happiness is intended pleasure, and the absence of pain; by unhappiness, pain, and the privation of pleasure. . . .

Now, such a theory of life excites in many minds . . . inveterate dislike. To suppose that life has (as they express it) no higher end than pleasure . . . they designate as . . . a doctrine worthy only of swine. . . .

[However,] human beings have faculties more elevated than the animal appetites, and when once made conscious of them do not regard anything as happiness which does not include their gratification. . . . [I refer to] the pleasure of the intellect, of the feelings and imagination and of the moral sentiments. . . . It is quite compatible with the principle of utility to recognize the fact that some *kinds* of pleasure are more desirable and more valuable than others. . . .

[Further,] the happiness which forms the util-itarian standard of what is right in conduct, is not the agent's own happiness, but that of all concerned. . . .

. . . [O]ne of the strongest obstacles to the reception of the doctrine that Utility . . . is the criterion of right and wrong, has been drawn from the idea of Justice. . . . Justice implies something which it is not only right to do, and wrong not to do, but which some individual can claim from us as his moral right. . . . When we call anything a person's right, we mean that he has a valid claim on society to protect him in the possession of it, either by the force of law, or by that of education and opinion. . . .

To have a right, then, is, I conceive, to have something which society ought to defend me in the possession of. If the objector goes on to ask why it ought, I can give him no other reason than general utility.[13]

The utilitarian way of understanding the good, however, has never been without critics. The ancient Greek philosopher Aristotle was perhaps the greatest teleologist of all times, and was chief among the critics, for he knew that moral people would endure rather substantive quantities of pain and would forego a wide variety of pleasures for deeper and broader purposes.

Seeking pleasure and avoiding pain had a governing purpose:

Since . . . all knowledge and every pursuit aims at some good, [we inquire as to] the highest of all realizable goods. As to name, I suppose nearly all men are agreed: for the masses and the men of culture alike declare that it is happiness, and hold that to "live well" and "do well" is the same as to be "happy." But they differ as to what this happiness is. . . .

. . . [T]he masses, who are the least refined, hold it to be pleasure, and so accept the life of enjoyment as their ideal. . . .

Refined men with a practical turn prefer honour; for I suppose we may say that honour is the aim of the statesman's life. But this seems too superficial to be the good we are seeking . . . , [for] they wish to be honored by men of sense . . .

12. From Jeremy Bentham, *An Introduction to the Principles of Morals and Legislation* (Oxford, England, 1789), chapter 1.

13. From John Stuart Mill, *Utilitarianism* (London, 1863), chapters 2, 5.

on the ground of their virtue or excellence. It is plain, then, that in their view, virtue or excellence is better than honor. . . .

But virtue or excellence also appears too incomplete to be what we want; for it seems that a man might have virtue and . . . be inactive all his life [or] meet with the greatest disasters and misfortunes; and no one would maintain that . . . [he] is happy. . . .

The third kind of life is the life of contemplation: we will treat of it further on.

As for the money-making life, it is something quite contrary to nature, and wealth evidently is not the good of which we are in search, for it is merely useful as a means to something else.

So we might rather take pleasure and virtue or excellence to be ends rather than wealth; for they are chosen on their own account. But it seems that not even they are the end, though much breath has been wasted in attempts to show that they are.[14]

Aristotle proceeds to discuss the nature and character of happiness in a way that influenced not only the whole history of Western philosophy, and a good number of current attempts to correct the superficialities of a consumer culture, but also theology — he was known by Buddhists and used in medieval Islamic traditions, Roman Catholicism, and contemporary neoconservative movements who protest mere utilitarianism. He argued that every human potential and every activity had a natural end built into it. Thus there is a direct connection between the subjective intentions and the objective goals. The former could be stabilized by good habits that would lead more surely to the goal. Life was only truly happy when these, together, were ordered toward the highest good, and only this highest good could order the "common good" of the city.

This way of thinking was adopted and adapted by theology. The fact that theology adopted it shows that it is a very helpful way of thinking; the fact that theology adapted it shows that the world religions were not entirely satisfied with it. They did not leave it intact; they subordinated it to another vision of a still higher end. For the most

part, the religious thinkers who encountered these arguments agree that Aristotelian teleology is superior to utilitarian teleology; but they believe that both of these are too "humanistic" — the one too sensual and calculative, the other too intellectualist and political. Their validity applies, if at all, only in the short-term. They miss the long-range vision of transcendent ends entirely. The happiness of the philosopher is not the end of the eastern religions, and the biblical religions believe that God has ends in mind for humanity that these views simply do not contemplate. Happiness is better than pleasure; but the joys of heaven are better yet. The greater good for the greater number is not evil, and neither is the quest for the common good; and the contemplation of the highest good the human mind can imagine may be better; but they pale in comparison with the hope given in the vision of the New Jerusalem.

To a remarkable degree, the world religions agree about right and wrong. They do not all agree about good and evil in the ultimate sense, and people have to make a faith commitment about what ultimate ends will govern their lives. The Asian religions, for example, speak of *samsara* (release from the eternal striving toward the better) or the bliss of *nirvana* (the ultimate state of "nothingness," in which life is no longer attached to "things"); Muslims may speak of Paradise, a return to the primal state of nature as God created it; and Jews speak of the final "messianic age," when righteousness, peace, and mercy are actualized, when the knowledge of God is immediate, when the justice and fear (awe) of God is realized.

Christians, of course, believe that this ultimate end has already broken into time in the life, death, and resurrection of Jesus Christ. It is a present possibility as well as a future hope; but it is one that anticipates a cosmopolitan civilization yet to come. In the very last book of the New Testament, we read of a vision of a holy city:

> It has the glory of God and a radiance like a very rare jewel, like jasper, clear as crystal. It has a great, high wall with twelve gates . . . , and on the gates are inscribed the names of the twelve tribes of the Israelites. . . . And the wall of the city has twelve foundations, and on them are the twelve names of the twelve apostles of the Lamb.

14. Aristotle, *The Nicomachean Ethics*, trans. F. H. Peters (London: Kegan Paul, Trench, Truebner & Co., 1891).

. . . [A]nd the street of the city is pure gold, transparent as glass.

I saw no temple in the city, for its temple is the Lord God the Almighty and the Lamb. And the city has no need of sun or moon to shine on it, for the glory of God is its light, and its lamp is the Lamb. The nations will walk by its light. . . . Its gates will never be shut by day — and there will be no night there. People will bring into it the glory and the honor of the nations. . . .

. . . [T]he river of the water of life, bright as crystal, [will flow] from the throne of God and of the Lamb through the middle of the street of the city. On either side of the river is the tree of life with its twelve kinds of fruit, producing its fruit each month; and the leaves of the tree are for the healing of the nations. (Rev. 21:11–22:2, NRSV)

All of the religious visions of the ultimate end, of course, can only be stated in highly symbolic terms, and there is much variety in their interpretation. This is true in part because the ultimate ends remain in the future, and the data of that future is never available beforehand, even if glimpses of its possibilities are divinely disclosed. Thus there are a number of differences not only between but within the great traditions.

These differences are one of the key elements that divide the religions of the world, however much other things unite them. And these distinctive visions have enormous implications for how the so-called "natural ends" of teleology — utilitarian or Aristotelian or, for that matter, those of other great philosophical traditions such as the Confucian — are understood. But they all recognize that the "natural ends" have to be governed and guided — even transformed — by "divine ends" to make full sense. After all, if we pursue only the natural end of life, we find death. The meaning of all our purposes and goals and efforts come to emptiness, inevitably and finally, unless there is something beyond them. And it is only those who have a sense of a divine purpose that does not die who can put the wisdom of "natural" teleologies into a larger perspective.

The implications of a religiously inspired understanding of the purpose of life for practical business life are powerful but indirect and not widely acknowledged by modern secular thought. How can we measure the impact of fundamental orientations toward life's ultimate end, such as can be found in, say, Dante's *Divine Comedy,* Milton's *Paradise Lost,* Bunyan's *Pilgrim's Progress,* Goethe's *Faust,* or the comparable dramas of other religions — the *Mahabharata* and *Ramayana* of the Hindu tradition, for example — on the way in which people live their economic lives?

The proximate purpose of business everywhere is to increase wealth, and whenever business does not do that it fails. But what is viewed as wealth, who is to have access to and control of it, how capital is used, what criteria are used to decide how it ought to be used, and what goods and services are most treasured vary from culture to culture. That variation is guided by the value systems by which people define the purpose of their lives; and that is influenced more by religion than any recent business text admits. Even present-day "consumerism" or "materialism" is less a forsaking of all religion than the triumph in popular culture of resurgent pagan religious motifs, rather crudely mixed with aspects of culture influenced by Jewish and Christian values, as Professor Campbell has demonstrated.[15]

In the future, especially facing the global pluralism of the world's religions, professional business leaders will have to be aware of such factors. This is true in part because changes in the value system will change markets. But it is true in a larger sense because the failure to ask the deeper questions behind these changes (and to participate in the offering of normative answers to the deeper questions) will mean that business will only be of concern to cramped souls with limited horizons.

That is why we have heard so much emphasis on "social responsibility" in regard to business in the last generation. Protestant, Catholic, and Jewish leaders have been telling business that its purpose is too narrow, that its managers must become more responsive to larger human purposes, and that its corporations must operate on an explicit ethic of service to humanity and stewardship of the biophysical cosmos. Typical of these exhortations is this portion of a Roman Catholic encyclical:

15. See Colin Campbell, *The Romantic Ethic and the Spirit of Modern Consumerism* (Oxford: Basil Blackwell, 1987).

In the design of God, every man is called upon to develop and fulfill himself, for every life is a vocation . . .

But each man is a member of society. He is part of the whole of mankind. It is not just certain individuals, but all men, who are called to this fullness of development. . . . This personal and communal development would be threatened if the true scale of values were undermined. The desire for necessities is legitimate, and work undertaken to obtain them is a duty. But the acquiring of temporal goods can lead . . . to the insatiable desire for more, and can make increased power a tempting objective. Individuals, families and nations can be overcome by avarice, be they rich or poor, and all can fall victim to a stifling materialism. . . .

The Bible, from the first page on, teaches us that the whole of creation is for man, that it is his responsibility to develop it by intelligent effort and by means of his labor to perfect it, so to speak, for his use. If the world is made to furnish each individual with the means of livelihood and the instruments for his growth and progress, each man has therefore the right to find in the world what is necessary for himself. All other rights whatsoever, including those of property and of free commerce, are to be subordinated to this principle. . . .

. . . [N]ew opinions have arisen in human society — we do not know how — that considered profit as the most important incentive to encourage economic progress, free competition as the supreme form of economics, and private ownership of the means of production as an absolute right which would not accept limits or a corresponding social obligation. One cannot condemn such abuses too strongly by solemnly recalling once again that the economy is at the service of man.[16]

Such views and the way they have been spelled out by the churches and adopted by some business leaders have been resisted by several notable contemporary theorists, especially those who show no interest in connecting the purposes of business with any larger ethical or religious vision. Milton Friedman is one of the vigorous opponents of any attempt on the part of business leaders to embrace such views:

[Some] businessmen believe that . . . business is not concerned "merely" with profit but also with promoting desirable "social" ends; that business has a "social conscience" and takes seriously its responsibilities for providing employment, eliminating discrimination, avoiding pollution and whatever else may be the catch-words of the contemporary crop of reformers. . . . Businessmen who talk this way are unwitting puppets of the intellectual forces that have been undermining the basis of a free society. . . .

What does it mean to say that "business" has responsibilities? Only people can have responsibilities. A corporation is an artificial person and in this sense may have artificial responsibilities, but "business" as a whole cannot be said to have responsibilities. . . .

Presumably, the individuals who are to be responsible are business men, which means individual proprietors or corporate executives. Most of the discussion of social responsibility is directed at corporations, so in what follows I shall mostly neglect the individual proprietor and speak of corporate executives.

In a free-enterprise, private-property system a corporate executive is an employee of the owners of the business. He has direct responsibility to his employers. That responsibility is to conduct the business in accordance with their desires, which generally will be to make as much money as possible while conforming to the basic rules of the society, both those embodied in law and those embodied in ethical custom.[17]

Friedman may well be correct in thinking that business leaders have no special authority to use resources entrusted to their care to save civilization or to transform human nature according to their personal social convictions, and they do have a fiduciary relationship to those who pay them to manage other people's resources; but "profit" is surely too limited a vision of management's ends. Profit is, in fact, only an indicator of whether or

---

16. Pope Paul VI, *The Development of Peoples* (March 1967).

17. Milton Friedman, "The Social Responsibility of Business Is to Increase Its Profits," *New York Times Magazine,* 13 Sept. 1970, pp. 32-33.

not the company is doing well in the short term. And every culture and every religion approves of profit *if it does not in itself become the chief end of life, displacing all other ends, and if it contributes to the well-being of the commonwealth.* The larger task of business depends on its long-term ability to create the kinds and qualities of wealth that serve humanity and honor all that is holy. Profit is only one step and one strategy, although a necessary one over time, on the road to capitalization. In any case, the purpose is essentially productive and qualitative, not only acquisitive and quantitative. How the ultimate purposes of life can and ought to shape economic production and the sense of quality today is an urgent issue.

Friedman's remarks have another fault. He looks at economic behavior as it operates within "the basic rules of society, both those embodied in law and those embodied in ethical custom." It is precisely these nods to two other constraints on economic activity that cannot be neglected. What is and what ought to be embodied in law? That is a deontological question that controls also the boundaries of his teleology. In addition, what is the actual character of the "ethical custom" to which he bows?

Amatai Etzioni is suspicious of a good number of currently accepted practices. In his book *The Moral Dimension* he points out a number of areas in which social practice and accepted custom distort both the common life and economic theory. To cite one example, he says:

> The economic literature is replete with references to distortions the government causes in the market. Comparable attention should be paid to manipulations of the government by participants in the markets, and the effects of these manipulations on the internal structures of markets. A major way these manipulations are carried out is for corporations, banks, farmers, and labor unions to use their political power to significantly and systematically affect the outcomes of market transactions.[18]

Such considerations lead us to the third of the three basic modes of moral discourse as discussed

by Niebuhr. This one has to do with the question "What is going on?"

Ethology (based on the Greek ethos = *the values embodied in custom and common practice)*

Those who especially accent issues of right and wrong and those who debate issues of good and evil recognize that not all ethical qualities are present in a moral law that stands over us, nor in intended ends that draw us forward to great purpose. Many of the values by which we live are found in that subtle web of meanings, expectations, manners, and legitimations which hold every human organization and relationship together. A mechanic may feel as morally strange in a hospital as a nurse does in a car repair shop; a lawyer may feel as morally lost in the pit of an opera house as a musician does in a court room. But all are more or less aware of how people ought to act in their own context.

Humans and institutions depend on higher principles and a vision of ends; but they are not mere social machines that, if properly programmed by principles and ends, simply churn out a plentiful and joyous life. In fact, social institutions are rather fragile, just as individuals far too frequently turn out to be unreliable — for themselves and for others. Schools and hospitals are always on the brink of insolvency; political parties often come apart at the seams; governments fail; bands and teams break up; churches die. The threat of non-being hangs heavy over every business, corporation, and industry as well as over every life.

Just as "it takes a heap of living to make a house a home," and just as it takes character to turn an individual into a reliable person, so it takes sustained moral human interactions to make any institution viable. Roles have to be defined, habits have to be practiced, stories have to be told, friendships have to be formed, promises have to be made and kept, senses of excellence and quality have to be cultivated. These interactions are moral in the sense that a density of responsibility, accountability, and trust has to be embodied in specific contexts or things fall apart.

The cumulative effect of these interactions generates a distinct social identity. An institutional

---

18. Amatai Etzioni, *The Moral Dimension: Toward a New Economics* (New York: The Free Press, 1988), p. 217.

esprit de corps energizes human cooperation and evokes human creativity. It stamps the personality of all who work in its environment. We see this in teams of all sorts, in colleges, unions, nations, and churches, and it is also true of business institutions. No organization without such an ethos can long endure. Cooperation, responsibility, and creativity can only be bought for a while; and if they are coerced, they will soon be sabotaged. Sooner or later, people have to want to give them. And they will do so only if the ethos itself relates them significantly to others and evokes the kind of loyalty and mutual responsiveness appropriate to the kind of relationship that is involved.

Ethology is the general name given to the study of this moral fabric, although some call it "moral ecology."[19] It studies the warp and woof of operational morality as practiced in a social setting, and thus it is very close to the social sciences in the way it is understood. And this study, like economics, can be undertaken at a number of levels. We can study it in direct, interpersonal relations — such as producer/consumer, employer/employee, co-worker/associate, or buyer/seller. What are the values, the appropriate forms of "quality," the "proper" expectations and roles that shape the various relationships and functions? We may not have a very profound or prolonged relationship with a check-out clerk in a supermarket; but we are disturbed by "unseemly" comments or actions. Interactions are based on a fabric of trust, manners, and customary adaptations whereby the concerns of all are served. This is what is "fitting" to a situation; it is what is recognized as "prudent" and "appropriate" among those who are responsive to how things work and why they work that way.

It is also possible to study the ethos at a more complex level — the level of a plant, office, or corporation. Here, one can study relations to suppliers and customers, the interactions of management and labor, and the relation of the unit to competitors and the market. The time span for this kind of study would be longer, and it would be compared to previous experience. The levels of interaction and accountability would be much more complex, and the sense of what is "fitting" would depend on more explicitly established patterns in the business environment, perhaps including the analysis of practices conventional in an industry plus those written down in contracts or codes.

In either of the above cases, we would have to analyze psychological, anthropological, political, and cultural dimensions of these "economic" relationships; and we would find that many non-business but clearly ethical issues would be involved — including, for example, matters that are gender-, race-, or class-related. To grasp any of them, we would have to identify the value patterns that are built into the way people have built up senses of what is the "proper" way to do things and what is not. In other words, the "sociological" interpretation and analysis of the actual conditions under which people work together requires what cultural anthropologist Clifford Geertz has called "thick descriptions."[20]

We could also investigate, within a still larger scope, the general ethos of modern economic order, comparing it, for example, to the traditionalism of the past or the anticipated socialism of the future. This is what many, from Karl Marx, Friedrich Engels, and Vladimir Lenin to Michael Harrington, have done. They focused on the social implications of the means of production; the formation of the classes, especially the bourgeois and the proletariat; the use of force and ideology in class conflict; and the mobilization of political will to transform the socioeconomic order. Or we could take up the post-Marxist traditions from Max Weber, Talcott Parsons, Clifford Geertz, Robert Bellah, and Peter Berger, who have studied economic action crossculturally and in relation to political, ethnic, familial, technological, legal, and religious institutions and meanings. They tend to see conflict within larger patterns of institutional pluralism and degrees of moral consensus. There are other schools of economic thought, of course; but these are the ones that have dominated ethological thinking for most of the past century.

Neither of these great schools of social analysis (or their parallels in other areas of the social sci-

---

19. See Robert Bellah et al., *Habits of the Heart: Individualism and Commitment in American Life* (Berkeley: University of California Press, 1985).

20. See Clifford Geertz, *The Interpretation of Cultures* (New York: Basic Books, 1973).

ences) is basically concerned about deontological first principles or teleological ultimate ends. They are first of all concerned with the structures and dynamics and functions of why things are the way they are in society. They have competing assessments of what values reign, why they do, and how we ought to respond if we wish to sustain the common life.

If business leaders and those who advise them are to adjudicate their disputes or to make practical decisions based on the best available interpretation of social reality, it is not only necessary to grasp the factual data; it is also necessary to probe very deep presuppositions about the essence of human nature, the true nature of community, the relationship of humans to the biophysical universe, and the ultimate relationship of materiality and spirituality, morality and identity. Such matters are inevitably religious; they grind the glasses through which we interpret the factual data. This was already recognized by St. Augustine, centuries ago, when he offered an interpretation of the "city" of God — that is, the governing structure of the divine economy — in relationship to the civilizations of history:

> [T]wo cities have been formed by two loves: the earthly by the love of self, even to the contempt of God; the heavenly by the love of God, even to the contempt of self. The former in a word glories in itself, the latter in the Lord. For the one seeks glory from men, but the greatest glory of the other is God, the witness of conscience. The one lifts up its head in its own glory; the other says to its God, "Thou art my glory, and the lifter up of mine head." In the one, the princes and the nations it subdues are ruled by the love of ruling; in the other, the princes and the subjects serve one another in love.[21]

Augustine here recognizes that the deepest analysis of ethos demands the recognition of living in the whole context of God's creation of and providential care for the world and all of history, and that our relationship to the cosmos, to history, and to the Creator of it all rests in substantive measure in the quality of love by which we live out our roles in each context.

21. Augustine, *The City of God,* bk. XIV, chap. 28.

We do not understand what drives our own ethos, or anyone else's, if we do not understand what is at stake in these deep presuppositions. Nor will it be possible to change our own patterns of life, should they prove to be wrong or evil on deeper investigation and longer experience, if we do not recognize whence they came and the foundations on which they rest. Many modern efforts at social analysis, political change, and economic development have foundered on the shoals of thinking that "morals" can be accounted for by social and cultural or ideological analysis, with no awareness of this deeper level.

Such voices point to the largest context of all, the one that is decisive for all understandings of every ethos, one that focuses on the reality of sin and the necessity of grace. We humans, by grace, have been given a wonderful world and the capacity to use hearts, hands, and heads to live in it abundantly and joyously; but humans, as free creatures, are also able to distort every instruction that is right, every vision of the good, and every context that is fitting. Thus, we are in constant need of the grace that forgives and renews.

In short, the deepest and broadest ethos of all includes the mundane and the ideal, the historical and the visionary, the cosmic *and the divine*. The most profound grasp of ethos always penetrates to questions of religion. That is essential to being responsible.

Religion is high voltage; it can electrocute as well as energize, shock, or empower. More often than not it is the inner guidance system of civilizations, even when people in those civilizations are not consciously pious. We must turn to it with care, and not only because we might offend someone else's faith. Politeness counts in any ethos; but the more important reason is that only some religious traditions provide the resources to discern the moral qualities that stand at the foundations of life. That is because only some religions stress the presence of the love of God in the midst of existence — indeed, precisely in the midst of material, temporal life. Some religions only obscure or obliterate the patterns of ethos whereby love and spirituality become concrete in the context of work, exchange, production, distribution, and consumption; others merely reflect and legitimate the immoral patterns that are always also present in a sinful world.

Covenant: An Ethical Tri-unity

The right, the good, and the fitting. Deontology, teleology, and ethology. These three dimensions of morality in society, and hence of moral business, do not always coincide. More often than not, they pull in contrary directions. Ethics is not a recipe by which one can add one part rightness, one part goodness, and one part fittingness and make a moral (and profitable) cake. Rather, the mix will sometimes make an explosion or a stink. That is why the making of decisions is always necessary in practice, why clarity about modes of moral logic is vitally important, and why some integrating transcendent reference is always necessary.

What holds these three things together? Christians believe that love, God's love, is the only thing that sustains life. It alone brings all right and good and responsible things into existence and sustains them in their relationships. But what does this mean? The clue is found in the biblical idea of "covenant." That is what holds ethics together in concrete, historical experience. Covenant implies a bonded fidelity to responsive associations when they are formed under first principles of right and wrong and designed to serve those purposes that contribute to the ultimate and common good. In a flawed world, we seek relative approximations to their perfect integration, and these become the patterns of justice established in our common life. Covenantal justice is the worldly form of godly love. That demands, of course, the formation of those qualities in persons that make them willing and able to stick to principles, to sacrifice for the common good, and to engage the neighbor compassionately.

It is not clear that this can be achieved only by human will. The biblical traditions suggest that even the proximate realizations of covenant in the midst of the distortions and conflicts of human life require not only great energy, wisdom, and dedication but also gifts of grace — as we know when we see a marvelous marriage, a great school, a just law, a peaceful political order, or a religious community that heals, inspires, and guides all who come to know it toward the holiness of love. In each of these cases, a profound ethical position will recognize that the only ultimate integrating point is God. It is in the divine life alone that

covenant is perfectly actualized. Thus, if the modern corporation is to embody justice, if contemporary business is to become moral in the covenantal sense, theology will of necessity become the intimate companion to business ethics.

The Need for Theology

The word "theology" will be confusing to some who have never encountered it in relation to business, economics, or even ethics. The word may induce resentment among any who have only been exposed to infantile or oppressive religions and have left their childishness and pompous self-righteousness behind. It will frustrate the heirs of a spiritual tradition who see engagement with social and material questions as the betrayal of faith and the root of wickedness. Nevertheless, we use it, for we are persuaded that business professionals need a more profound set of resources for business ethics than most contemporary resources supply. But some definitions are necessary here.

When we use the word "theology" we do not mean the doctrines or dogmas of any particular denomination, sect, or church. There are special words for that — "creeds" and "confessions." Nor do we mean the beliefs and ritual practices of a community that has developed a standard way of coping with ultimate questions and frequent dilemmas. We have words for that, also — a "religious tradition" or a "cultic practice." Theology is nearly always related to these, but, in a deeper and broader sense, it is what assesses the relative validity of these according to the highest standards of truth and justice that are known and debated in reasonable discourse. It is the position of the editors of this volume that Christian theology is in accord with those standards — although we would acknowledge that on many points Christian theology has something to learn from others, just as others do from Christianity.

An analogy may help. If the views of different churches represent different moral and spiritual recipes, and if the views of different religions represent different moral and spiritual cuisines, theology represents a crossculturally valid and constantly self-critical quest for the ultimate principles by which humans could identify basic elements and assess the relative nutritional value of the feasts cooked up by various cooks with different recipes and cuisines.

Ethics, to be sure, is an important discipline, but it finally cannot stand alone. Ethics needs theological help, in part because it needs an ultimate center of integration, as mentioned above. But it also needs help at the attitudinal level. A generation or two may coast on the morality inherited from parents or grandparents; but the zeal, the motivation, and the commitment run dry over the generations if no theological ground sustains it. The ultimate issues about what is right, what is good, and what is fitting demand a foundation in a living reality that transcends ordinary human capabilities.

Theology has shared the task of clarifying this foundation with philosophy over the centuries, and much that goes on in all discussions of ethics is philosophical in nature. Historically, philosophy and theology were sister fields, considering much the same areas. But in the final analysis, philosophy itself proved to need a more reliable and ultimate grounding than what humans can construct out of their own reason and experience. In fact, what modern philosophy has disclosed more than any other matter is that its own foundations are groundless without God. Besides, much modern philosophy has lost interest in thinking about the ultimate questions that must, by definition, preoccupy theology and ethics. If religion moves the minds and souls of many but is unreliable unless examined by theology, philosophy moves the minds and souls of very few people, and it has little promise of shaping the future of the ethos in general or business in particular. Still, philosophy demands of all who engage in it a requirement to be reasonable and to supply arguments for what one claims. For that reason, it remains fair to say that the only serious theology will be a philosophical theology.

Nor should any who are convinced that the only serious theology is, say, a biblical theology be fretful about this. A true revelation will have nothing to fear, for it would be not only persuasive to the mind but also compelling to morality. If it is true and just, it will contribute to a deeper and broader theology and ethic; if it cannot so contribute, it is probably neither true nor just.

Minds and souls persuaded by a serious theology, however, would want to do something about it. They would grasp a sense of the higher law, they would catch a vision of the ultimate goal, and they would be able to discern something of the deepest tissues of the ethos. But they would not be satisfied with intellectual understanding alone. They would want to implement it. They would want to make that holistic understanding of life under God as real in the world as possible. In fact, life would take on the meaning of making these things real.

All who catch the theological vision are, in other words, driven into active participation in religious community and into associations for the common good.[22] Even more, the model of new community formation would have to take place also in the world of work. And here we must face the key question of what specific practices and what kinds of economic organizations can best respond to the laws of God, the purposes of God, and the mercies of God under the tough, demanding conditions of modern, globally competitive, high-technological, pluralistic life.

Such concerns have shaped every chapter of this volume. Our premise can be summarized thus: material culture with all its quite earthy ways of dealing with life are in fact more driven by the power of the Spirit than spirituality is driven by materiality. We can see this as clearly in the arena of economics with its drive toward wealth as in other areas — perhaps even more than in politics with its drive toward power, psychology with its preoccupation with sexuality, science with its curiosity about how things are, and law, education, and the arts as they express ideas of order, culture, and beauty. Something more than materiality channels the way people meet material needs, guides how people deal with one another, sets the contexts within which quite mundane interests conflict and are resolved. Of course, bad spirituality can, like bad money, drive out good; and a false morality can bend the constraints on our beastly impulses; but the only way we can know that and the only way we can attempt to overcome the damage is by the repair of "the moral and spiritual values," as people call them today, by which the theological vision of truth and justice and compassion becomes actuated in life.

22. See, for example, Robert Wuthnow and Virginia A. Hodgkinson et al., *Faith and Philanthropy in America: Exploring the Role of Religion in America's Voluntary Sector* (San Francisco: Jossey-Bass Publishers, 1990).

This volume thus presumes the indispensability of theological ethics. Only God can save humanity from our perennial tendency to self-destruct and mutually exploit, and nothing within the range of human discourse points as carefully and as completely toward God as does theology. Over the centuries it has been the God-intoxicated people and Spirit-inspired movements that have formed the channels of soul and sociality in which the wheels of civilization turn. Where malformed or ill informed, to be sure, great damage has been done. But where well formed — that is, where religion is guided by the disciplines of theology — it has a chance of generating a vibrant, creative, and sustaining ethic for both persons and the common life.

One of the things the world has learned from the collapse of Marxism-Leninism in Eastern Europe and among the recovering liberationists of the Third World is that a merely secular, practical, and material approach to civilization and to economics leads to a moral and spiritual vacuum. People do not believe it; it cannot inspire; it offers, finally, no hope. It becomes an instrument of greater imperialism and exploitation than it opposes. As the editors of this volume have discovered in our travels and study in intentionally secularized lands, a failure of theological-ethical vision destroys the fabric of society as well as the hearts and minds of persons, and thereby creative economic potentialities as well. That threat is now worldwide, as great a peril in "capitalist" as in formerly "socialist" regions.

Of course, we are not proposing that there be daily worship in factory or firm. The corporation is not a chapel, the market is not high mass, and neither the board room nor the union hall is a seminary. In fact, the imposition of a dogma or cult in the midst of business dealings can tend toward idolatry. It may well be that everyone should conduct business in a prayerful attitude — acknowledging that we live and work under a grace and a power that are not of our making, and that we are but temporary stewards of all that has been given to us. But the practice of piety in the world of work, trying to make the shop or the office into a substitute church, is not only undesirable in a day of religious pluralism; it leads us to the brink of temptations that are both spiritually seductive and morally insidious. It is spiritually seductive to us for it tends to turn religion into a form of magic —

the attempt to manipulate divine forces to accomplish human ends. It is morally insidious for it tends to identify holiness with the particular interests of the people in charge.

At the same time, to ignore theological ethics in the area of business life is to allow materialism — with its temptations to self-interest, greed, possessiveness, and opportunism — to stand as the "god" we worship. In this case, theological and ethically refined religion becomes entirely secondary or unnecessary to our "real" economic lives. This is what the Bible warns about when it preaches against Mammon, the raising of business, acquisition, or profit into the idol of our lives. All profound religion, after all, has at its depths a celebration of giving and not getting, of sharing and not possessing, of sacrificing and not only accumulating. Theological ethics thus stands in a constant tension with Mammon's temptation to make success in a purely material sense the goal of life and the rule of behavior. It cannot save humanity, even if it pretends to by drowning souls and civilizations in commodities and services. Indeed, this is the greatest threat to modern business life and contemporary business professionals.

But some religions, and Christianity is chief among them, hold that we are not to separate our faith entirely from material reality. Religious and ethical spirituality may be in tension with materiality, but it is not only opposed to it. Indeed, spirituality joins materiality, enters into it, alters it, redeems it, and ultimately transforms it so that it, too, can participate in the praise and honoring of God. Until the end of time, the tension will never be entirely resolved. That makes change always necessary; but a degree of complementarity between spirituality and materiality makes development possible. What the deepest theology and the most profound moral covenants are about is therefore directly pertinent to the area of business life — including its practical, mundane, and material dimensions — insofar as it is shaped by an ethic that preserves and transforms the world to the glory of God.

This view, which is a governing conviction of this entire volume, implies one additional, simple, but decisive presupposition that ought to be made explicit. We live in the Christian era. The Bible, the insights that arose from the formation of theology out of the encounter of biblical views with philosophy, the heritage of Hebraic, Catholic, and Protestant reflection — these are as directly pertinent to our world as is the thinking of modernity. We do not live in a post-Christian — or only a post-Enlightenment, postmodern — world, but in a world rooted in the reality we know in Christ. This reality is both constant and ever renewing — even as it now encounters present challenges, meets the world religions, and shapes a wider global context. The foundational old is not left behind; rather, it serves as the decisive resource for the future.

PART A

CLASSICAL RESOURCES

Chapter One

The Hebrew Scriptures

Modern economics has tended to separate religious or ethical theory from the science of how economic laws function and how economic relationships work (see Chapters 6 and 7). Thus many attempts to begin the study of business ethics by adopting the presumptions of the present are flawed. They unwittingly reinforce the conviction that, in reality, economics has a logic of its own that is no more influenced by the convictions of persons or human communities than is meteorology. Yet they try to induce ethical responses to economic matters. Their disjointed attempts do not settle the question of whether God is lord over both the religious convictions of people and the actual ways the world works, and thus the question how theological and economic matters are to be related in ways that are deeper than modern presumptions allow remains unresolved.

Clearly, many workers, managers, business leaders, and consumers have very strong views about religion and ethics that come from biblical traditions. They try to live their lives, at work as well as in church, by biblical principles. Further, the channels of thought by which people think about both "sacred" and "secular" matters have been deeply imprinted by Jewish and, especially, Christian ideas. Biblical themes have shaped, if not fully determined, modern industrial culture and thereby business activity around the world — even where other religious traditions are dominant or where people consciously resist modernity or Christianity (see Chapter 5).

Our first selection of texts focuses on the Bible. That is because anyone concerned with modern economic life who has not wrestled with the biblical materials that have shaped our society is not yet fully professional. The manager, union organizer, trustee, lawyer, engineer, professor of economics, or member of the clergy who attempts to speak of business matters does not know whence certain of the deepest patterns in modern business derive unless that person knows something about Scripture.

In this chapter, we will present, first, an overview of some of the important themes found in the Bible, as summarized by Professor George N. Monsma, Jr. One can find in his essay not only a compendium of the most cited Hebrew texts on economic matters, but also the fundamental dependence on familial and political structures that dominated the ancient world's thinking about economics. In his analysis, he also identifies root attitudes toward stewardship, wealth, and poverty that transcend that ancient context and have influenced Western civilization. Then we will turn to more detailed interpretations of selected biblical passages not treated extensively by Monsma. Of special importance will be a series of themes from the Hebrew Scriptures, what Christians call the Old Testament: creation and fall, exodus and covenant, and prophecy and wisdom. Throughout, we also see the interplay of deontology (the laws of God), teleology (the promises of God), and ethology (the mercies and providence of God).

Christians believe that many of these sources point to the New Testament, which gives them new twists. The continuity is stated by Stephen Mott in Chapter 2; but discontinuities have also been noted. These continuities and discontinuities have led to intense debates about the biblical understanding of wealth, poverty, money, and the role of government intervention and taxation according to biblical thought. The essays here, by Jews, Catholics, and Protestants, represent that debate.

Biblical Principles Important for Economic Theory and Practice

George N. Monsma, Jr.

A. Revelation

[Christians believe that God is revealed] to us most perfectly by becoming incarnate in the person of Jesus Christ, but God is . . . revealed, and teaches us about ourselves and the world in other ways as well. The Bible (special revelation), inspired by God, testifies to the incarnation, as well as to other actions of God in this world, and gives us guidance for our lives: "All scripture is inspired by God and profitable for teaching, for reproof, for correction, and for training in righteousness, that everyone who belongs to God may be complete, equipped for every good work" (2 Tim. 3:16-17). God has also revealed himself through the world he has created and which he upholds (general revelation):

> For what can be known about God is plain to them, because God has shown it to them. Ever since the creation of the world his invisible nature, namely, his eternal power and deity, has been clearly perceived in the things that have been made. (Romans 1:19-20)

Since these are revelations of a God who does not lie, they are consistent with each other. Special and general revelation should be used under the guidance of the Holy Spirit to illumine each other,

---

From *Through the Eye of a Needle: Readings on Stewardship and Justice*, ed. Department of Economics and Business, 3rd ed. (Grand Rapids: Calvin College, 1989).

and used together to guide our lives. Since neither is limited to some particular sphere of life, but deal with the totality of our relations with God, our fellow human beings, and the rest of God's creation, both are relevant to economics, and should be used when constructing economic theories or determining economic actions.

B. Stewardship

> The earth is the Lord's and the fullness thereof,
>   the world and those who dwell therein.
>   (Ps. 24:1)

Since God as creator is the owner of all things (including us), we are not owners of anything. We are only stewards of things that God has entrusted to us. In addition, God has given all authority to Christ, the Redeemer; as he said: "All authority in heaven and on earth has been given to me" (Matt. 28:18). In view of this all persons are called to use the economic resources they have control over (including their own labor) as God commands; we are not autonomous beings entitled to use things as we please. . . .

Regarding the purposes for which we are to use resources, the Bible consistently calls us to use them to provide justice (or equity). On the other hand I see no call in the Bible to use resources in order to continually increase the overall level of production, or to meet the desires of those with economic or political power, whatever those desires may be (these, of course, are two commonly stressed uses in our day).

God reveals himself as one who executes justice:

> For the Lord your God is God of gods and Lord of lords, the great, the mighty, and the terrible God, who is not partial and takes no bribe. He executes justice for the fatherless and the widow, and loves the sojourner, giving him food and clothing. (Deut. 10:17-18)

. . . . And God also calls his people to act justly, in the economic sphere of life as well as in other spheres. This call goes out to all people:

> A righteous man knows the rights
>   of the poor;

a wicked man does not understand
    such knowledge.   (Prov. 29:7)

. . . . But it goes out in a special way to those with governmental power, as . . . the Lord said to the king of Judah through Jeremiah:

"Thus says the LORD: Do justice and righteousness, and deliver from the hand of the oppressor him who has been robbed. And do no wrong or violence to the alien, the fatherless, and the widow, nor shed innocent blood in this place."

"Do you think you are a king
    because you compete in cedar?
Did not your father eat and drink
    and do justice and righteousness?
    Then it was well with him.
He judged the cause of the poor and needy;
    then it was well.
Is not this to know me?
    says the LORD."   (Jeremiah 22:3, 15-16)

God gives us much evidence in the Bible concerning standards for economic justice. The Mosaic economic laws are one fruitful source for guidance here. Although I do not believe that these laws, which were given for an agrarian society in a very different economic situation than our country is in today, are binding on us in their particular form, by examining them and the results they would give if followed we can learn much about what is required if an economic structure and actions within it are to be just. This is especially true when there is support for what we deduce from the Mosaic laws in other parts of Scripture.

The Mosaic laws limited the property rights of the human stewards of God's resources in such a way as to assure both short- and long-run provision of necessary material goods to all families (and individuals). They provided all people with access to food at all times through limitations on the rights of farmers to completely harvest their own crops, with the right to what remained given to the poor:

"When you reap the harvest of your land, you shall not reap your field to its very border, neither shall you gather the gleanings after your harvest.

And you shall not strip your vineyard bare, neither shall you gather the fallen grapes of your vineyard; you shall leave them for the poor and for the sojourner: I am the Lord your God" (Lev. 19:9-10),

through tithes that were partly for the poor (Deut. 14:28-29), through the right given to the poor to whatever the land produced in the sabbatical year (Exod. 23:10-11), and through the right to eat in a neighbor's field or vineyard (Deut. 23:24-25).

The poor were also given access to necessities in the short-run by means of interest-free loans which were to be canceled every seventh year:

"If there is among you a poor man, one of your brethren, in any of your towns within your land which the Lord your God gives you, you shall not harden your heart or shut your hand against your poor brother, but you shall open your hand to him, and lend him sufficient for his need, whatever it may be. Take heed lest there be a base thought in your heart, and you say, 'The seventh year, the year of release is near,' and your eye be hostile to your poor brother, and you give him nothing, and he cry to the Lord against you, and it be sin in you. You shall give to him freely, and your heart shall not be grudging when you give to him; because for this the Lord your God will bless you in all your work and in all that you undertake." (Deut. 15:7-10)

There were also restrictions against keeping a cloak or a mill (or by implication any necessity) as security for such a loan, and provisions to safeguard the dignity of the borrower (Exod. 22:25-27; Deut. 24:6, 12-13). These laws regarding food and loans gave each family access to the necessities of life at all times.

But the Lord did not stop with laws giving all persons access to basic consumption goods. He also gave laws regarding the distribution of "ownership" (stewardship) and control of the basic resources of production in the society. Israelites were not to be sold into perpetual slavery:

"If your brother, a Hebrew man, or a Hebrew woman, is sold to you, he shall serve you six years, and in the seventh year you shall let him go free from you. And when you let him go free from you, you shall not let him go empty-handed; you shall furnish him liberally out of your flock, out of your threshing floor, and out of your wine press; as the Lord your God has blessed you, you shall give to him." (Deut. 15:12-14)

If they became poor and had to temporarily serve another they were to be treated as hired servants or sojourners rather than as slaves. In addition, the land could not be sold in perpetuity; rather it was to stay with the family to whom it had been entrusted by God when the land was settled. If a family became so poor that it had to sell its land, the land was to be returned to it in the year of jubilee. The family also had the right to redeem the land at any time it was able to do so, at a price determined by the number of years until the year of jubilee (Lev. 25:8-17, 23-34). These laws, if followed, assured each family in the long-run control over the resources necessary for them to be active, decision-making, producers. . . . In the long-run none would be forced to live from the charity of others, or even to earn a living by working under the orders of others. Rather each family was given an opportunity to respond to God's call to be a steward over the world's resources by being given control over their own labor and a share of the land and working-capital needed to produce a living in an agrarian society. Note that these laws severely limited the degree to which "ownership" and control over wealth could become concentrated into a few hands. Indeed, if each family is to have the opportunity for productive, stewardly use of resources in a way that it can meet its own needs, there must be limits on the concentration of wealth, income, and economic power.

Along with these laws, the Lord gave a promise:

"But there will be no poor among you (for the Lord will bless you in the land which the Lord your God gives you for an inheritance to possess), if only you will obey the voice of the Lord your God, being careful to do all this commandment which I command you this day." (Deut. 15:4-5)

The promise and the laws were not arbitrarily linked. If the laws were obeyed there would be no families who were continually poor in the sense of not being able to provide for themselves or not

having a share in the stewardship responsibilities of the society, and those who were temporarily poor by these standards would at least be provided with access to the goods necessary for life in their society as a matter of right, as long as the weather was good enough to provide adequate harvests (and this would be part of the Lord's blessing on them if they kept his commandments). Thus we can conclude from the Mosaic laws that a society, in order to be economically just, must provide all with access to the basic necessities for life in that society, and must provide all with opportunities for producing for their own needs in a context which gives them control over their own labor and a portion of the other resources of society.

Such a judgment is reinforced by the testimony of the prophets, who conveyed the Lord's condemnation upon Israel and Judah when they failed to exercise proper stewardship of their economic resources. After the moving parable of the vineyard in Isaiah 5:1-7, the Lord condemns those who build up concentrations of wealth (houses and land) to the extent that others cannot support themselves:

Woe to those who join house to house,
  who add field to field,
until there is no more room,
    and you are made to dwell alone
    in the midst of the land.
The LORD of hosts has sworn in my hearing:
"Surely many houses shall be desolate,
  large and beautiful houses,
    without inhabitant."   (Isa. 5:8-9)

And in Jeremiah 34:8-22 the Lord condemns those who rob others of control over their own labor by re-enslaving them after they had been set free following their prescribed terms of service. The Lord also condemns the nations and their rulers for failing to uphold the rights of the poor (Isa. 10:1-4) and condemns those who live in luxury in the face of this poverty (Isa. 3:16–4:1; Amos 6:4-7). The Lord punished the people for their injustice with famine but even this did not bring them to justice, so the Lord sent them into exile (Amos 4, 5, and 6). But always there is the call to repent and turn from these evil ways; the call to establish governmental justice (see, e.g., the passage from Jeremiah 22 quoted above), and to use justly the resources God has entrusted to each of them. . . .

The New Testament speaks less about the justice or injustice of particular legal economic structures (perhaps because the people to whom it was primarily addressed had no control or influence over these). But it does continue the strong emphasis of the Old Testament on caring for the poor and being of service to those in need. . . . Christ calls all people to follow his example by giving their lives in service to others who are in need. It is clear from the teaching of Christ and the apostles that being of service to those with economic needs is an important part of the Christian life for those who have the resources which enable them to be of such service. . . This is taught in Christ's account of the last judgment contained in Matt. 25:31-46, where the things that distinguished the sheep from the goats were whether they had fed the hungry, gave drink to the thirsty, welcomed the stranger, clothed the naked, and visited those in prison. Paul calls upon the Corinthian Christians to use their abundance to supply the needs of other Christians (2 Cor. 8:8-15), and in 1 Timothy 6:18 he charges the rich "to do good, to be rich in good deeds, liberal and generous." James stresses the concern that should be shown toward the poor and calls the rich oppressors (James 1:27–2:7; 5:1-6), and he uses aid for the poor to show that a living faith will be demonstrated through works. And John, in a very moving passage, tells us the source of our ability to serve others economically, and the example we are to follow:

> By this we know love, that he laid down his life for us; and we ought to lay down our lives for the brethren. But if any one has the world's goods and sees his brother in need, yet closes his heart against him, how does God's love abide in him? Little children, let us not love in word or speech but in deed and in truth. (1 John 3:16-18)

In the New Testament as in the Old the Lord calls people to work, using their labor to provide for their families and those who are in need. For example we read in Ephesians 4:28: "Let the thief no longer steal, but rather let him labor, doing honest work with his hands, so that he may be able to give to those in need." Since all are called to work to support themselves and their families a just society must provide opportunities for this,

at least over a period of time, as was done by the Mosaic Laws. . . .

In sum then, the Biblical evidence regarding proper stewardship of God's resources indicates that:

a. those who have been entrusted with resources have only a limited right to the personal use of them or the goods they can produce.

b. Those who have been entrusted with resources have a duty to use them productively in order to meet their own family's needs and to meet the needs of others who do not have enough to meet their own needs.

c. Societies have a duty to provide just structures (including systems of property rights). For structures to be just they must at least:

  i. Assure all families access to the basic necessities of life at all times;

  ii. Provide all families with the opportunity to develop and use their God-given talents and other resources in such a way that they can provide for their own needs, at least in the long-run;

  iii. Provide all families with the economic freedom necessary to enable them to exercise responsible economic stewardship of their resources, at least in the long-run (this includes having decision-making opportunities in the use of their resources in production as well as in consumption); and

  iv. Place limits on the concentrations of wealth, income, and economic power in the society (for this is necessary in order to achieve the first three).

d. Individuals and societies must care for their natural environment, and do not exhaust its resources to such an extent that future generations lack the possibility of providing all with the things listed in *c* above.

C. Wealth

Wealth is sometimes a gift from God:

> And Isaac sowed in that land, and reaped in the same year a hundredfold. The Lord blessed him, and the man became rich, and gained more and more until he became very wealthy. He had pos-

sessions of flocks and herds, and a great household, so that the Philistines envied him. (Gen. 26:12-14)

But wealth is also sometimes the result of evil actions of men:

"For wicked men are found among my people;
    they lurk like fowlers lying in wait.
They set a trap;
    they catch men.
Like a basket full of birds,
    their houses are full of treachery;
therefore they have become great and rich,
    they have grown fat and sleek.
They know no bounds in deeds of wickedness;
    they judge not with justice
the cause of the fatherless, to make it prosper,
    and they do not defend the rights
        of the needy."   (Jer. 5:26-28)

And:

Come now, you rich, weep and howl for the miseries that are coming upon you. Your riches have rotted and your garments are moth-eaten. Your gold and silver have rusted, and their rust will be evidence against you and will eat your flesh like fire. You have laid up treasure for the last days. Behold, the wages of the laborers who mowed your fields, which you kept back by fraud, cry out; and the cries of the harvesters have reached the ears of the Lord of hosts. You have lived on the earth in luxury and in pleasure; you have fattened your hearts in a day of slaughter. You have condemned, you have killed the righteous man; he does not resist you. (James 5:1-6)

But regardless of how it has been obtained, the Bible teaches several things concerning it:

wealth:

1

It is not the most important thing in life:

Better is a little with the fear of the LORD
    than great treasure and trouble with it.
Better is a dinner of herbs where love is
    than a fatted ox and hatred with it.
                            (Prov. 15:16-17)

2

We should not put our trust in it:

He who trusts in his riches will wither,
    but the righteous will flourish like a green leaf.
                            (Prov. 11:28)

"As for the rich in this world, charge them not to be haughty, nor to set their hopes on uncertain riches but on God who richly furnishes us with everything to enjoy." (1 Tim. 6:17)

3

We should not orient our lives toward the seeking of wealth:

But those who desire to be rich fall into temptation, into a snare, into many senseless and hurtful desires that plunge men into ruin and destruction. For the love of money is the root of all evils; it is through this craving that some have wandered away from the faith and pierced their hearts with many pangs. (1 Tim. 6:9-10)

Rather we should be content with what is necessary for our lives (1 Tim. 6:6-8; Heb. 13:5-6).

4

More wealth is not always better than less wealth; we can have too much wealth for our own good as well as too little wealth. As Agur prays in Proverbs 30:8 and 9:

give me neither poverty nor riches;
    feed me with the food that is needful for me,
lest I be full, and deny thee,
    and say, "Who is the Lord?"
or lest I be poor, and steal,
    and profane the name of my God.

5

Wealth always belongs to God; we are only stewards of it, not owners of it. Thus we must use it as God commands to establish justice; to live in luxury in a world where poverty exists is a sin.

42

D. Sin

"All have sinned and fall short of the glory of God" (Romans 3:23). This sinfulness affects all aspects of our lives, including the economic aspect. Both individual and collective economic actions are affected by sin.

1

Sin causes individuals and societies to be unfaithful stewards of the resources God has entrusted to them. God condemns those who are unjust stewards, who cause and allow poverty to exist when there is enough for all. This condemnation is given both to individuals: "He who gives to the poor will not want, but he who hides his eyes will get many a curse" (Prov. 28:27), and to societies or nations. Sodom was destroyed at least in part because she was affluent "but did not aid the poor and needy" (Ezek. 16:49-50), and Israel and Judah were sent into exile at least in part because of the economic injustice in their societies (Amos 5 and 6; Zech. 7:8-14).

It is clear from the Scriptures that formal acts of "worship" and profession of faith cannot take the place of proper stewardship. The Lord says through Amos

"I hate, I despise your feasts,
    and I take no delight in your
        solemn assemblies.
Even though you offer me your burnt offerings
    and cereal offerings,
    I will not accept them,
and the peace offerings of your fatted beasts
    I will not look upon.
Take away from me the noise of your songs;
    to the melody of your harps I will not listen.
But let justice roll down like waters,
    and righteousness like an everflowing stream."
                                            (Amos 5:21-24)

and through James

What does it profit, my brethren, if a man says he has faith but has not works? Can his faith save him? If a brother or sister is ill-clad and in lack of daily food, and one of you says to them, "Go in peace, be warmed and filled," without giving them the things needed for the body, what does it profit? So faith by itself, if it has no works, is dead. But some one will say, "You have faith and I have works." Show me your faith apart from your works, and I by my works will show you my faith. (James 2:14-18)

The Lord calls for repentance, that is, for a turning from the unjust acts to just ones, and promises blessings on those who do so. As he says through Isaiah:

"Wash yourselves; make yourselves clean;
    remove the evil of your doings
    from before my eyes;
cease to do evil,
    learn to do good;
seek justice,
    correct oppression;
defend the fatherless,
    plead for the widow.
Come now, let us reason together,
    says the Lord:
though your sins are like scarlet,
    they shall be as white as snow;
though they are red like crimson,
    they shall become like wool.
If you are willing and obedient,
    you shall eat the good of the land."
                                            (Isa. 1:16-19)

2

Sin distorts both our knowledge and our wills, and both of these distortions lead to sinful economic actions, as well as sinful actions in other areas of life. Regarding their ignorance, the Lord tells the church at Laodicea through John: "For you say, I am rich, I have prospered, and I need nothing; not knowing that you are wretched, pitiable, poor, blind, and naked" (Rev. 3:17). Regarding those whose wills are turned against the Lord, he says through Isaiah:

And now, go write it before them on a tablet,
    and inscribe it in a book,
that it may be for the time to come
    as a witness for ever.
For they are a rebellious people,
    lying sons,

sons who will not hear
    the instruction of the Lord;
who say to the seers, "See not";
    and to the prophets, "Prophesy not to us
        what is right;
speak to us smooth things,
    prophesy illusions,
leave the way, turn aside from the path,
    let us hear no more of the Holy One of Israel."
Therefore thus says the Holy One of Israel,
"Because you despise this word,
    and trust in oppression and perverseness,
    and rely on them;
therefore this iniquity shall be to you
    like a break in a high wall, bulging out,
        and about to collapse,
    whose crash comes suddenly, in an instant;
and its breaking is like that of a potter's vessel
    which is smashed so ruthlessly
that among its fragments not a sherd is found
    with which to take fire from the hearth,
    or to dip up water out of the cistern."

(Isa. 30:8-14)

3

Sin keeps people enslaved to false gods (idols), which in the end bring them to ruin. Two such idolatries which are particularly involved with economics today, as well as in Biblical times, are individualism and materialism.

Individualism is the sin of putting oneself and one's own desires in the place of God and his commands. Economically it involves believing that what one has is the result of one's own actions alone, rather than a gift, in trust, from God, and putting one's own desires for the use of goods in place of God's commands regarding the use of them. Surely the warning God gave to Israel through Moses before they entered the promised land is relevant to us today as well:

"Take heed lest you forget the Lord your God, by not keeping his commandments and his ordinances and his statutes, which I command you this day: lest, when you have eaten and are full, and have built goodly houses and live in them, and when your herds and flocks multiply, and your silver and gold is multiplied, and all that you have is multiplied, then your heart be lifted up, and you forget the Lord your God, who brought you out of the land of Egypt, out of the house of bondage, who led you through the great and terrible wilderness, with its fiery serpents and scorpions and thirsty ground where there was no water, who brought you water out of the flinty rock, who fed you in the wilderness with manna which your fathers did not know, that he might humble you and test you, to do you good in the end. Beware lest you say in your heart, 'My power and the might of my hand have gotten me this wealth.' You shall remember the Lord your God, for it is he who gives you power to get wealth; that he may confirm his covenant which he swore to your fathers, as at this day. And if you forget the Lord your God and go after other gods and serve them and worships them, I solemnly warn you this day that you shall surely perish. Like the nations that the Lord makes to perish before you, so shall you perish, because you would not obey the voice of the Lord your God." (Deut. 8:11-20)

Materialism involves making goods one's god, trusting in them as one's source of security, believing that more goods are always better than fewer goods. This is contrary to the teaching of scripture in Proverbs 11:4: "Riches do not profit in the day of wrath, but righteousness delivers from death" and Hebrews 13:5: "Keep your life free from love of money, and be content with what you have; for he has said, 'I will never fail you nor forsake you.'"

E. Redemption

Christ, through his perfect life and his sacrifice on the cross, has freed those who believe on him from bondage to idolatries (including individualism and materialism). As we read in 1 Peter 1:18 and 19: "You know that you were ransomed from the futile ways inherited from your fathers, not with perishable things such as silver or gold, but with the precious blood of Christ, like that of a lamb without blemish or spot." This freedom enables those who trust in Christ to show his love for the world through a life of service to others, including economic service. This love and service was evidenced in the early church: "There was not a needy person among them, for as many as were possessors of lands or houses sold them, and brought the proceeds of what was sold and laid it at the apostles' feet; and distribution was made to each as any had need" (Acts 4:34-35). And although Christians are set free from bondage to idolatries, we must also confess with Paul that in this life "I do not the good I want, but the evil I do not want is what I do" since sin still dwells within us (Romans 7:19). No one leads a perfect life, in the economic sphere, or in any other sphere.

F. Faith influences all of life

As should be clear from the above, one's faith influences all of ones' life. We are called to show love for God and our neighbors in all of life; there can be no religiously neutral area of life. Thus all economic theories and actions are influenced by the faith of the person devising or engaging in them. And this is true both of actions with respect to "private" property and of actions with respect to governments or other social institutions.

G. Individuals cannot exist alone

People are never isolated individuals; they are *social* beings. They cannot escape their relationship to God. As the Lord said through Jeremiah: "Can a man hide himself in secret places so that I cannot see him? says the Lord. Do I not fill heaven and earth? says the Lord" (Jeremiah 23:24). It is a central teaching of scripture that our meaning in life comes from our relationships with God and with our neighbors, and not from ourselves as solitary individuals. This is clear from the fact that our basic calling in life is to love God with all our heart, soul, strength, and mind and to love our neighbor as ourself (Luke 10:25-28). Therefore at their essence economic actions, as all actions, involve relations with other beings (God and our neighbors), and thus they are social actions.

Creation and Fall

In the first book of the Bible, Genesis, we find a highly symbolic account of the creation of the world and the beginnings of human history. In fact, there are so many layers of meaning in the apparently simple story that this account has intrigued and puzzled people for centuries. The early chapters tell us that the material world and various forms of life are a good gift of God, but that material and social reality has to be seen in the context of limits and responsibilities that pervade all the decisive arenas of human activity. The first chapter says that humans are made in God's image and thus are to have dominion over all other creatures. Indeed, humans are to subdue the earth; but we are to do so under God's law, for godly ends, and in the context of care for what has been given to us.

Much debate has taken place about the meanings of the terms "dominion" and "subdue." These words do not imply rapacious exploitation; they mean "stewardship." Humans are, under God, responsible for nature. We live in it, we are to work and care for it, and we are to see that it flourishes. But we are not to be ruled by nature, for it has no power to be by itself. This means that Jewish and Christian (and, for that matter, Islamic) peoples and cultures have been resistant to views that take nature as the ultimate authority for life and thought. Instead we are to view nature as creation and see that it follows the laws and purposes of the Creator. Those who accept the biblical traditions seldom doubt that if humans have the capacity to correct clear distortions of nature — birth defects or famine by natural disaster, for example — we have the obligation to do so. At the same time, we are not to trespass basic boundaries and think that we can rule nature according to our own sovereign will. Humans are the middle term between creation and Creator. Nature is humanity's to use responsibly, creatively, and caringly, as humanity is God's to command, guide, and love.

God commissions humanity to work and to exercise freedom to do what God intends, but humanity uses freedom and labor to violate God's intentions and gifts. Humanity is not always responsible or creative or caring. The second chapter of Genesis begins a poetic narrative of how, from the start, humans distort God's guidance. Genesis 2, 3, and 4 chart implications that have great bearing on all subsequent social life — e.g., sexual, technological, cultural, and political as well as religious, for serious religion influences all of these, and they all influence economics. Several important implications for business are treated in Barry Gordon's commentary on these chapters, which is based on current scholarly study of the historical background of these passages, written or edited by the Yahwist writer, the unknown ancient writer whose preferred name for God was *JHWH* (Jehovah), translated today as "Lord God."

Genesis 1:1–4:1 (NRSV)

In the beginning when God created the heavens and the earth, the earth was a formless void and darkness covered the face of the deep, while a wind from God swept over the face of the waters. Then God said, "Let there be light"; and there was light. And God saw that the light was good; and God separated the light from the darkness. God called the light Day, and the darkness he called Night. And there was evening and there was morning, the first day.

And God said, "Let there be a dome in the midst of the waters, and let it separate the waters from the waters." So God made the dome and separated the waters that were under the dome from the waters that were above the dome. And it was so. God called the dome Sky. And there was evening and there was morning, the second day.

And God said, "Let the waters under the sky be gathered together into one place, and let the dry land appear." And it was so. God called the dry land Earth, and the waters that were gathered together he called Seas. And God saw that it was good. Then God said, "Let the earth put forth vegetation: plants yielding seed, and fruit trees of every kind on earth that bear fruit with the seed in it." And it was so. The earth brought forth vegetation: plants yielding seed of every kind, and trees of every kind bearing fruit with the seed in it. And God saw that it was good. And there was evening and there was morning, the third day.

And God said, "Let there be lights in the dome of the sky to separate the day from the night; and let them be for signs and for seasons and for days and years, and let them be lights in the dome of the sky to give light upon the earth." And it was so. God made the two great lights — the greater light to rule the day and the lesser light to rule the night — and the stars. God set them in the dome of the sky to give light upon the earth, to rule over the day and over the night, and to separate the light from the darkness. And God saw that it was good. And there was evening and there was morning, the fourth day.

And God said, "Let the waters bring forth swarms of living creatures, and let birds fly above the earth across the dome of the sky." So God created the great sea monsters and every living creature that moves, of every kind, with which the waters swarm, and every winged bird of every kind. And God saw that it was good. God blessed them, saying, "Be fruitful and multiply and fill the waters in the seas, and let birds multiply on the earth." And there was evening and there was morning, the fifth day.

And God said, "Let the earth bring forth living creatures of every kind: cattle and creeping things and wild animals of the earth of every kind." And it was so. God made the wild animals of the earth of every kind, and the cattle of every kind, and everything that creeps upon the ground of every kind. And God saw that it was good.

Then God said, "Let us make humankind in our image, according to our likeness; and let them have dominion over the fish of the sea, and over the birds of the air, and over the cattle, and over all the wild animals of the earth, and over every creeping thing that creeps upon the earth."

So God created humankind in his image,
in the image of God he created them;
male and female he created them.

God blessed them, and God said to them, "Be fruitful and multiply, and fill the earth and subdue it; and have dominion over the fish of the sea and over the birds of the air and over every living thing that moves upon the earth." God said, "See, I have given you every plant yielding seed that is upon the face of all the earth, and every tree with seed in its fruit; you shall have them for food. And to every beast of the earth, and to every bird of the air, and to everything that creeps on the earth, everything that has the breath of life, I have given every green plant for food." And it was so. God saw everything that he had made, and indeed, it was very good. And there was evening and there was morning, the sixth day.

Thus the heavens and the earth were finished, and all their multitude. And on the seventh day God finished the work that he had done, and he rested on the seventh day from all the work that he had done. So God blessed the seventh day and hallowed it, because on it God rested from all the work that he had done in creation.

These are the generations of the heavens and the earth when they were created.

In the day that the LORD God made the earth and the heavens, when no plant of the field was yet in the earth and no herb of the field had yet sprung up — for the LORD God had not caused it to rain upon the earth, and there was no one to till the ground; but a stream would rise from the earth, and water the whole face of the ground — then the LORD God formed man from the dust of the ground, and breathed into his nostrils the breath of life; and the man became a living being. And the LORD God planted a garden in Eden, in the east; and there he put the man whom he had formed. Out of the ground the LORD God made to grow every tree that is pleasant to the sight and good for food, the tree of life also in the midst of the garden, and the tree of the knowledge of good and evil.

A river flows out of Eden to water the garden, and from there it divides and becomes four branches. The name of the first is Pishon; it is the one that flows around the whole land of Havilah, where there is gold; and the gold of that land is good; bdellium and onyx stone are there. The name of the second river is Gihon; it is the one that flows around the whole land of Cush. The name of the third river is Tigris, which flows east of Assyria. And the fourth river is the Euphrates.

The LORD God took the man and put him in the garden of Eden to till it and keep it. And the LORD God commanded the man, "You may freely eat of every tree of the garden; but of the tree of the knowledge of good and evil you shall not eat, for in the day that you eat of it you shall die."

Then the LORD God said, "It is not good that the man should be alone; I will make him a helper as his partner." So out of the ground the LORD God formed every animal of the field and every bird of the air, and brought them to the man to see what he would call them; and whatever the man called every living creature, that was its name. The man gave names to all cattle, and to the birds of the air, and to every animal of the field; but for the man there was not found a helper as his partner. So the LORD God caused a deep sleep to fall upon the man, and he slept; then he took one of his ribs and closed up its place with flesh. And the rib that the LORD God had taken from the man he made into a woman and brought her to the man. Then the man said,

"This at last is bone of my bones
and flesh of my flesh;
this one shall be called Woman,
for out of Man this one was taken."

Therefore a man leaves his father and his mother and clings to his wife, and they become one flesh. And the man and his wife were both naked, and were not ashamed.

Now the serpent was more crafty than any other wild animal that the LORD God had made. He said to the woman, "Did God say, 'You shall not eat from any tree in the garden'?" The woman said to the serpent, "We may eat of the fruit of the trees in the garden; but God said, 'You shall not eat of the fruit of the tree that is in the middle of the garden, nor shall you touch it, or you shall die.'" But the serpent said to the woman, "You will not die; for God knows that when you eat of it your eyes will be opened, and you will be like God, knowing good and evil." So when the woman saw that the tree was good for food, and that it was a delight to the eyes, and that the tree was to be desired to make one wise, she took of its fruit and ate; and she also gave some to her husband, who was with her, and he ate. Then the eyes of both were opened, and they knew that they were naked; and they sewed fig leaves together and made loincloths for themselves.

They heard the sound of the LORD God walking in the garden at the time of the evening breeze, and the man and his wife hid themselves from the presence of the LORD God among the trees of the garden. But the LORD God called to the man, and said to him, "Where are you?" He said, "I heard the sound of you in the garden, and I was afraid, because I was naked; and I hid myself." He said, "Who told you that you were naked? Have you eaten from the tree of which I commanded you not to eat?" The man said, "The woman whom you gave to be with me, she gave me fruit from the tree, and I ate." Then the LORD God said to the woman, "What is this that you have done?" The woman said, "The serpent tricked me, and I ate." The LORD God said to the serpent,

"Because you have done this,

cursed are you among all animals
and among all wild creatures;
upon your belly you shall go,
and dust you shall eat
all the days of your life.
I will put enmity between you
and the woman,
and between your offspring and hers;
he will strike your head,
and you will strike his heel."
To the woman he said,
"I will greatly increase your pangs
in childbearing;
in pain you shall bring forth children,
yet your desire shall be for your husband,
and he shall rule over you."
And to the man he said,
"Because you have listened to the voice
of your wife,
and have eaten of the tree
about which I commanded you,
'You shall not eat of it,'
cursed is the ground because of you;
in toil you shall eat of it all the days
of your life;
thorns and thistles it shall bring forth
for you;
and you shall eat the plants of the field.
By the sweat of your face
you shall eat bread
until you return to the ground,
for out of it you were taken;
you are dust,
and to dust you shall return."

The man named his wife Eve, because she was the mother of all living. And the LORD God made garments of skins for the man and for his wife, and clothed them.

Then the LORD God said, "See, the man has become like one of us, knowing good and evil; and now, he might reach out his hand and take also from the tree of life, and eat, and live forever" — therefore the LORD God sent him forth from the garden of Eden, to till the ground from which he was taken. He drove out the man; and at the east of the garden of Eden he placed the cherubim, and a sword flaming and turning to guard the way to the tree of life.

Now the man knew his wife Eve, and she conceived and bore Cain, saying, "I have produced a man with the help of the LORD."

Scarcity, Faith, and Wisdom

Barry Gordon

In Genesis, there is no doubt that the problem of scarcity is an ever-present burden for the bulk of mankind. Nature is not especially beneficent, and the acquisition of the means of life is a task involving continual struggle and personal cost. Such sentiments are not uncommon in surviving examples of other early ancient writings, and they may be compared, for example, with those of the Greek poet, Hesiod (c. 700 B.C.). However, the Yahwist's treatment of scarcity has a distinctive character in that it involves the idea that humanity was not designed originally to be subject to the pressures involved. Further, the treatment denies that work is a feature of the human condition which is exclusively engendered by the pressures of scarcity. This latter is in marked contrast with the Greek tradition on the question. The origins of the economic problem, according to the Yahwist, are located in the Fall of Man. Originally, the Creator ordained that the means of life should be freely available:

> "Yahweh God caused to spring up from the soil every kind of tree, enticing to look at and good to eat . . . Then Yahweh God gave man this admonition, 'You may eat indeed of all the trees in the garden. Nevertheless of the tree of the knowledge of good and evil you are not to eat for on the day you eat it you shall most surely die.'" (Gen. 2:9, 16)

From Barry Gordon, *The Economic Problem in Biblical and Patristic Thought* (Leiden: E. J. Brill, 1989), pp. 1-8.

This situation alters radically when mankind chooses to try to capitalize on the most distinctive attribute with which it has been endowed, i.e., the gift of the ability to disobey its Creator. Instead of remaining satisfied with the beneficence of Yahweh, humans decide to take control of the entire range of their choices as consumers of the fruits of creation. In Yahwistic terms, Adam and Eve eat the forbidden fruit (Gen. 3:1-6).

Since men and women have decided to care for their own welfare as far as consumption is concerned, there is no way in which Yahweh can honor that choice except by freeing them from their former state of dependence as consumers. They must leave Eden if they are to live as they have chosen. They have taken upon themselves the problem of scarcity, a problem which it was not intended they should be obliged to face.

Given that mankind is not designed to cope with its chosen independence, it might be expected that this form of creation would quickly disappear from the face of the earth outside Eden. However, this is not the case. The reason is that these creatures were designed to be workers and were invested with the ability to innovate. They were not intended for an existence of idle enjoyment of the Creator's largesse in Paradise. Rather, they were made in the image of the God who works. Humans were settled in the Garden, "to cultivate and take care of it" (Gen. 2:15; see also 2:5).

Work precedes the Fall and the onset of scarcity. For the Yahwist, its basic rationale is not the satisfaction of the worker's needs as a consumer. Instead, its chief significance is in its fulfilling an ordinance of God which relates to man's very being. This point has been observed by a variety of modern commentators among whom is Alan Richardson. He finds that the Yahwistic texts,

> "Do not represent work as coming into being as a result of sin but as part of the very intention of God in making the world and man . . . Apart altogether from sin and the Fall, man has work to do; he has a function to perform within the created order."

There is no doubt that in Eden, although its economic viability is not in question, mankind has responsibilities. Humanity has a job to do. The Yahwist uses terms such as "to cultivate" and "to take care of," and these are, "technical terms used frequently for the service of God and observance of the commandments. They express responsibility, the burden of man faced with the divine initiative." Mankind is "burdened" in paradise. It is confronted with the phenomenon of "cost."

Man the Worker is designed to cope with the burden of opportunity cost, i.e., a foregoing of the benefits of the outcomes of the possibilities discarded in the series of choices which a work process may entail. His position is analogous to that of the Creator when he set about his work. The character of man's burden is illustrated graphically by the Yahwist through the episode of the naming of the beasts:

> "So from the soil Yahweh God fashioned all the wild beasts and all the birds of heaven. These he brought to man to see what he would call them; each one was to bear the name the man would give it. The man gave names to all the cattle, all the birds of heaven, and all the wild beasts." (Gen. 2:19-20)

This, it is obvious, is not a mean task. In fact, so the Yahwist suggests, this challenge to work like God is so severe that man alone (Adam) is granted a "helpmate." With this equally endowed co-worker, the formerly singular image of God forms "one body" (Gen. 2:20-24).

After the Fall, mankind is not denied its role of sharing in God's work. Hence, it continues to incur opportunity cost. However, because of the choice to become independent as consumers, men and women subject themselves to a second type of cost. This is "real cost," in the sense of toil, physical pain, and sweat (Gen. 3:17-19). By embracing scarcity, humanity burdens itself beyond the intention of the Creator.

Innovation and Mercy

By the end of the third chapter of Genesis, the Yahwist has presented his readership with a very bleak assessment of the human condition and of what they can expect in their lives. Nevertheless, even within that chapter there are some glimmers of hope. In the first instance, Adam and Eve do not die on the day they eat the forbidden fruit.

Further, it would seem that Yahweh is not prepared to leave them entirely to their own devices in their self-elected contest with scarcity. Discovering the need for a new type of consumption item, clothing, the first pair's somewhat meagre innovation is the loin-cloth of fig leaves (Gen. 3:7). This is a weak response to independent assessment of need, so Yahweh provides a superior substitute, clothes made out of skins (Gen. 3:21).

Immediately after the departure from Eden there is another sign of hope. The "soil" may be "accursed" because of Adam (Gen. 3:17), but this does not preclude population growth (Gen. 4:1-2). Again, in the tale of Cain and Abel the Yahwist endeavors to demonstrate at length how the merciful intervention of God is available to give rise to benefits despite, and even through, the disasters evoked by the fledgling innovations of mankind. The fundamental innovation, in this case, is the division of labor: "Abel became a shepherd and kept flocks, while Cain tilled the soil" (Gen. 4:2). This arrangement leads to competition and then to fratricide. Abel loses his life, and the murderer Cain is rendered incapable of productive activity. Yahweh tells Cain:

> "Now be accursed and driven from the ground that has opened its mouth to receive your brother's blood at your hands. When you till the ground it shall no longer yield you any of its produce. You shall be a fugitive and a wanderer over the earth." (Gen. 4:11-12)

The full weight of this sentence is tempered by God's mercy. Cain is given a special mark to prevent his being murdered in his wanderings, and the upshot is a series of striking innovations. The descendants of Cain cannot cope with scarcity by means of tilling the soil, but this handicap gives rise to a wide range of new productive pursuits:

> "Cain had intercourse with his wife, and she conceived and gave birth to Enoch. He became the builder of a town . . . Adah gave birth to Jabal: he was the ancestor of the tent-dwellers and owners of livestock. His brother's name was Jubal: he was the ancestor of all who play the lyre and the flute. As for Zilla, she gave birth to Tubal-cain; he was the ancestor of all metalworkers, in bronze or iron." (Gen. 4:17-22)

Here, out of a crime associated with a simple division of labor has come a much more complex division which would not have eventuated without Yahweh's forebearance. It can be remarked also that the process of economic development implied by the narrative is observed to be grounded in the denial of traditional pursuits to "Cain's descendants." Development, it is suggested, is born of adversity.

The next narrative in the Yahwistic sequence is that of the Flood and Noah. This offers yet further affirmations that contemporary humanity does not experience the full economic implications of the Fall. Immediately after the Fall the soil became accursed (Gen. 3:17), but after the Flood, in the Covenant with Noah that marks the beginning of a new world order, Yahweh declares:

> "Never again will I curse the earth because of man . . . As long as earth lasts, sowing and reaping, cold and heat, summer and winter, day and night shall cease no more." (Gen. 8:21-22)

If the Yahwist can be interpreted in 3:17 as contending that mankind's struggle with scarcity is due in part to a fall of Nature together with Man, then 8:21-22 suggests that he also wished his audience to appreciate that this situation pertained only before the Flood. In any event, it is clear that the readership is to understand that the element of conflict between man and soil is greatly reduced after the Covenant with Noah. Perhaps, it is a token of the reduction that Noah is associated with a distinctive innovation. He is "the first to plant the vine" (Gen. 9:20).

They may be part of a new world order, but the Yahwist does not want his contemporaries to gain the impression that they can innovate with impunity. Hence, as a final cautionary tale from primeval history he introduces the episode of the Tower of Babel. This is another occasion for the merciful intervention of God to save mankind from the adverse consequences of misdirected use of its powers. Just what the adverse consequences may be is by no means clear on this occasion.

In the Babel story, humanity (or, part of it united in Babylonia) comes together for a major co-operative enterprise. Yahweh, however, subverts the project by upsetting the ability of the workers to communicate. He decides to "confuse their language" (Gen. 11:7), and the builders are scattered over the face of the earth. God is portrayed as foreseeing that this particular enterprise is a prelude to an upsurge of further innovation: "This is but the start of their undertakings. There will be nothing too hard for them to do" (Gen. 11:6). In some unspecified manner, it is this circumstance which threatens adversity.

The Solution by Faith: Abraham

Up to this point in the analysis, man has not dealt very well with his self-imposed task of combating the pressures of scarcity. Despite man's capacity for innovation, the direct intervention of Yahweh has been necessary to promote the degree of development which has been achieved since Adam and Eve confronted the soil outside the Garden. Such a reflection on primeval history prepares the way for the Yahwist to show how his readership can cope successfully. The Solution comes . . . when Abraham is called and elected.

The Yahwist's Solution is the Solution by Faith. It involves the precise reversal of the process which evoked scarcity in the first place. Adam and Eve opted for independence. In its beginning, mankind disobeyed a command which did not appear to make sense. Noah, it is true, anticipates Abraham in that he was willing to involve himself in the seeming absurdity of constructing a queer kind of ship in the midst of dry land. This proved decisive for the future of mankind. Abraham's decision is to prove crucial for the Jewish people, at least, and he is the more significant model for them.

God tells Abraham to leave one of the main, regional centers of civilization and economic activity (Haran, or perhaps, Ur) for an unspecified destination, and Abraham accepts the command (Gen. 12:1-4). This is extraordinary since "to leave home and to break ancestral bonds was to expect of ancient men almost the impossible." In the new life that his act of faith has opened up, Abraham and his dependents prosper. He is portrayed as traveling around the Middle East. Early on in his new career, after an eventful trip to Egypt, he is said to become "a very rich man, with livestock, silver and gold" (Gen. 13:2).

This affluence, however, is not attained without cost, and a substantial cost is incurred in his initial act of faith. The act required his taking up sojourning. It required a positive response to "the radical demand of God that the way of faith requires leaving a land and accepting landlessness as a posture of faith." An even more radical demand (in the eyes of the Yahwist's audience) is made by God at a later date. Abraham is commanded to deny himself posterity as well as the ownership of land. He is to kill his only son Isaac (Gen. 22:2). The man of faith begins to commit himself to this ultimate in irrationality, but his hand is stayed by God's messenger and he is promised a well-nigh limitless posterity. In addition, the economic success continues unabated. Near the end of Abraham's life, his chief-steward can declare: "Yahweh has overwhelmed my master with blessings, and Abraham is now very rich. He has given him flocks and herds, silver and gold, men slaves and women slaves, camels and donkeys" (Gen. 24:35). There is circulating capital in abundance here. Still, the prize of land is unattained. There is only the promise (Gen. 13:17, 15:18).

The Solution by Wisdom: Jacob and Joseph

The abundance of Abraham continues with his son, Isaac (see Gen. 26:13). The same comes to apply to Isaac's second son, Jacob, who eventually, "grew extremely rich, and became the owner of large flocks, with men and women slaves, camels and donkeys" (Gen. 30:43). Nevertheless, with Jacob, a new element enters into the strategy for overcoming the threat of scarcity. That element is Wisdom.

Jacob, in his youth, is depicted as a reflective person who is by no means a man of action to rival Esau, his twin, who was first-born. Yet, through judgment of persons and circumstances, and with the aid of his mother, he secures both the birthright and blessings that custom required should be bestowed on Esau. These machinations make it prudent for him to exile himself with his mother's relatives. There, in exile, he becomes rich through exercising extraordinary managerial skill as a herdsman and breeder (Gen. 30:32-43). Subsequently, he skillfully negotiates a treaty with his irate father-in-law, Laban, and placates his brother Esau in another display of adroit diplomacy.

In the sphere of wisdom, however, the wily Jacob comes to be far outshone by "the son of his old age," Joseph. Whereas the figure of Jacob anticipates the ideal of the era of Solomon, the figure of Joseph embodies it. With Joseph we are given, "a good example of the goal toward which all training and education in Israel during the royal period directed a young man of good standing."

The boy sold into slavery rises to become grand vizier of Egypt, and in the court story which details his agrarian policy he emerges as the consultant administrator without peer (Gen. 47:13-26). Joseph manipulates the tools of macroeconomic policy to deal with the onset of scarcity on a grand scale. He combats the problem with success, while also serving the interests of his ruler. As a *political* economist, his skill is such that at the end, Pharaoh has come to own almost the entire country, but the populace gladly acclaim the administrator: "You have saved our lives. If we may enjoy my lord's favor, we will be Pharaoh's serfs" (Gen. 47:25).

There is nothing else in the Old Testament to match this story, and both its character and setting raises the question of whether something approaching economic analysis was taught in the wisdom schools of Egypt long before the Greeks took their first steps along such a path with the Sophists. There is even a possibility that the practice could have applied for a time in Jerusalem. In Solomon's day, an Egyptian-trained and perhaps Egyptian-staffed bureaucracy (1 Kings 4:1ff.) kept the books and provided the matrix for the kingdom's intellectual class.

Exodus and Covenant

One of the greatest and most famous stories of the Bible is the escape of the Hebrew people from slavery under the Pharaohs. Although most of the ancient Middle Eastern population lived in rather simple agrarian or pastoral settings much of the time, the economic situation of the region changed radically with the rise of the great empires. In a time of distress, the Hebrews had to submit to one of the most powerful of these ancient regimes, Egypt — as we already saw in the previous reading. Eventually they were reduced to slavery there by subsequent rulers who "knew nothing of Joseph."

Later, under the inspired leadership of Moses, who became one of the world's most famous leaders after an anonymous, violent, and inarticulate beginning, the slaves escaped. They crossed a sea in which their pursuers were destroyed. For a generation they wandered in the wilderness, not quite knowing what they should do. After facing many hardships, they came to Mount Sinai, where they were given the covenant with its several dimensions — the laws and statutes that formed them into a nation, a sense of purpose that charged them to become witnesses to these principles before all the world, and a new awareness of their distinctive identity as a community. And they were promised a land.

These events are recounted in the Book of Exodus, with major events summarized in the sixth, fifteenth, nineteenth, and twentieth chapters (up to verse 17). The last passage is often taken as a kind of "summary constitution" for just communities among the people of God in the biblical traditions. Over the centuries, however, major disputes have arisen within, and especially beyond, the Hebraic community as to which event in this story is the decisive one — exodus, with its mes-sage of liberation; covenant, which presumes freedom but focuses on the forms of civilization; or conquest, the seizing of land by force, implications of which still plague that region today.

Paul D. Hanson of Harvard University, one of the outstanding biblical scholars of our time, offers a historical commentary on these events, while Max L. Stackhouse points specifically to the economic significance of the Ten Commandments, the deontological part of the covenant, and to one of the most important ways in which these must be recovered by subsequent generations who wish to renew covenantal relationships.

Exodus 6:2-9 (NRSV)

Exodus 15:19-21 (NRSV)

God also spoke to Moses and said to him: "I am the LORD. I appeared to Abraham, Isaac, and Jacob as God Almighty, but by my name 'The LORD' I did not make myself known to them. I also established my covenant with them, to give them the land of Canaan, the land in which they resided as aliens. I have also heard the groaning of the Israelites whom the Egyptians are holding as slaves, and I have remembered my covenant. Say therefore to the Israelites, 'I am the LORD, and I will free you from the burdens of the Egyptians and deliver you from slavery to them. I will redeem you with an outstretched arm and with mighty acts of judgment. I will take you as my people, and I will be your God. You shall know that I am the LORD your God, who has freed you from the burdens of the Egyptians. I will bring you into the land that I swore to give to Abraham, Isaac, and Jacob; I will give it to you for a possession. I am the LORD.'" Moses told this to the Israelites; but they would not listen to Moses, because of their broken spirit and their cruel slavery.

When the horses of Pharaoh with his chariots and his chariot drivers went into the sea, the LORD brought back the waters of the sea upon them; but the Israelites walked through the sea on dry ground.

Then the prophet Miriam, Aaron's sister, took a tambourine in her hand; and all the women went out after her with tambourines and with dancing. And Miriam sang to them:

"Sing to the LORD, for he has
        triumphed gloriously;
horse and rider he has thrown into the sea."

The Birth of the Covenant

Paul D. Hanson

The shape of the development of Israel's earliest oral and literary traditions was determined through and through by the confession of the God Yahweh who delivered Hebrews from Egyptian bondage. The laws and social structures of earliest Israel were imbued so thoroughly by this same confession as to set them apart — in spite of many formal and thematic similarities — from the laws and social structures of contemporaneous neighboring cultures. As we trace these traditions back through their many stages of development, we find ourselves coming to the twelfth century as their point of origin, which is to say, within a century of the time regarded by most scholars as the time of the exodus (that is, the reign of Ramesses II in the thirteenth century B.C.E.). It seems to me to be an instance of excessive skepticism to doubt that the exodus confession arose out of a very powerful experience of some of Israel's ancestors. Within the cult, they subsequently preserved a vivid memory of their extraordinary birth as a people during the period we would now designate as transitional from the Late Bronze Age to the Iron Age, a memory recalling the escape from Egypt of a group of slaves under the leadership of a leader named Moses, an escape in which the activity of the God Yahweh was recognized.

This particular event made such a profound impact on those involved as to forge earlier impressions of divine providence and folk traditions concerning theophanies and divine promises to ancient patriarchs and matriarchs into a thematic focus capable of generating a whole new under-

standing of the nature of God and the quality of the community drawn into fellowship with God. For this reason, we are on a historically solid foundation when we draw on critically interpreted biblical sources to describe the birth of a new notion of community in the exodus; that is, in the deliverance from Egyptian slavery in which the early Hebrews recognized the redemptive activity of Yahweh.

A. Ancestral Background

The new community born of the exodus must first be seen against the background of the old order from which it emerged. In Egypt the people who were to emerge as the Hebrews of the exodus narrative belonged to a larger class of Semitic slaves who, in the course of migrations occasioned by economic necessity, had been absorbed into a society notoriously conservative in its attitudes toward religion and culture. Tensions and even open conflicts did arise within the history of relationships between pharaohs and priests in Egypt, but both were united in commitment to a social system that buttressed their own personal power and wealth, and that was accordingly deaf to the concerns of those at the bottom of the social pyramid. Although we must be cautious in describing one ancient culture for purposes of comparing with another, it is clear that the nineteenth dynasty in Egypt was a kingdom that supported the ambitious building programs of its kings and the luxury of its upper echelons through the exploitation of its human resources in a workforce living close to the subsistence level. The latter had little hope of upward mobility, and lived with the constant danger of decline into slavery through indebtedness.

The burden of such a social system weighed heaviest, of course, on the corvées of foreign slaves. Without any human rights to which they could lay claim, they were at the mercy of their overlords. Although the description of slavery in Egypt found in the opening chapters of the Book of Exodus has been shaped by theological concerns, the depictions of foreign slaves found on the reliefs of the Ramesside period leave no doubt that the experiences of Moses's kinsfolk in Egypt would have been typical of slave experience

From Paul D. Hanson, *The People Called* (New York: Harper & Row, 1986), pp. 12-15, 18-24.

throughout the ancient world. It would have been marked by an inhumane workload aimed at pressing every bit of work out of persons whose only purpose in life was deemed to be that of delivering services to their owners. The episode of the Egyptian beating the Hebrew slave in Exodus 2:11, coupled with the motif of the increased burden placed on the brickmakers, fits the usual pattern followed by masters, namely, that of maintaining a level of productivity just short of the breaking point as a means of keeping slaves in a servile state of mind, deprived of the will and physical strength necessary for resistance or rebellion.

The Egyptian system under which the Hebrews labored was a carefully structured one, the result of centuries of refinement. Perhaps its major strength was the stability it maintained in the land through the cultivation and central distribution of all available resources. Within this system, every individual was aware of his or her assigned role, and the expectations associated with that role, a fact true for slaves as well as for all other social castes. While we recognize in Moses's rebellious followers' demanding a return to the "fleshpots of Egypt" a narrative motif serving a particular theological point, it also depicts a basic social reality: even for slaves the rigidly stratified system of Egypt ordered life in a predictable manner. As the experience of some slaves in the period after the American Civil War indicates, freedom can come as a dreadful threat for those accustomed to such order, even to the point of making re-enslavement preferable to the agony of self-determination.

We still see, however, that the slaves escaping from Egypt, together with whatever other groups joined them on the basis of identifying with their experience, forged within the liminal period between bondage and self-determination a sense of personhood that viewed freedom and spiritual development as essential qualities distinguishing the human world from the realm of the beasts. They accordingly considered the static structures that had maintained their bondage as an intolerable price to pay for security. Our contrast is not intended to deny the often remarkable accomplishments of ancient Egyptian civilization, as a visit to Luxor, Gizeh, or the British Museums readily illustrates. It simply points to a difference in value systems. In the case of the Egyptian system, life was graded on a scale beginning with the "divine" Pharaoh and descending all the way down to the slave. It was only natural that from the vantage point of the upper Egyptian classes the slave was of no intrinsic value or interest, but like a beast of burden functioned as a cog in the smooth functioning of an eternal kingdom. . . .

Aided by a reconstruction of the sociopolitical background of the Genesis ancestors and their descendants, we can begin to understand the social matrix underlying the legends gathered by tradition to describe the birth and childhood of Moses. The following hints are important: The reference to the Hebrew midwives who would not collaborate with the Pharaoh because "they feared God, and did not do as the king of Egypt commanded them but let the male children live" (Exod. 1:17); the detail that Moses, while raised in the Pharaoh's palace, had his own Hebrew mother as a nurse (Exod. 2:10); the episode describing Moses's violent reaction to the situation in which "he saw an Egyptian beating a Hebrew, one of his people" (Exod. 2:11-15). These legends all bear witness to a common folk memory: these slaves were conscious of being distinct from the others by virtue of a religious tradition that had been kept alive among them, a tradition of a God who had related to their ancestors in the intimacy of a covenant of promise. This memory was the source of the conviction that their present slave status was not the inevitable result of divine decree, but an evil their God would one day redress. Interesting in this connection is the motif associated with Moses and his mother: only an upper echelon of the Hebrew slave people — to which the Egyptian system had assigned a less oppressive role — could keep alive this faith in the God who had not forgotten them. This motif reflects a social phenomenon recognized by revolutionary theorists down to our time, namely, that the masses of an oppressed people often are too drained of energy and broken of spirit to effect their own means of escape. A human catalyst, somehow spared from the depths of oppression, is required. Thus Moses, having benefited from a privileged upbringing, and yet having been nurtured within the ethnoreligious traditions of his kinsfolk by his nurse-mother, became the representative who stood firmly against both the grumbling skepticism of his broken people and the Pharaoh's hard heart. . . .

contra handout reading

B. Out of the House of Bondage: The Exodus

While the exodus event broadly construed was multifaceted and complex, it did have a nucleus that brought into sharp focus the theological meaning of the whole. We are brought close to that nucleus by the remarkable hymn found in Exodus 15, whose oral form was the product of a vivid recollection of the event of deliverance. Once again, it does not represent history reporting in the narrow sense, but should be interpreted as a response to an experience in which the encounter with historical realities led to a discernment of a deeper underlying significance. The genre used was that of the hymn. The community, newly delivered from the oppressor and recipient of God's promise of blessing and land and progeny, responded in the manner it found most fitting — through an expression of praise and gratitude to a gracious and mighty God. It seems clear that the historical episode underlying the hymn involved the escape of a band of Hebrews from the armies of the Pharaoh. In this episode, the exact details of which are beyond our ken, the majesty and compassion of Yahweh were displayed in a manner so vivid that it gave rise to an image that seemed to reveal the heart of Israel's God. Through this glorious triumph, Yahweh became Israel's "strength" and "victory" even as God had earlier been the protector of Israel's ancestors. The hymn goes on to describe that triumph: Yahweh defeated the armies of the Pharaoh, and thwarted their efforts to recapture the people of Israel. Yahweh was incomparable among the gods! The redeemer God was experienced as Israel's sustainer as well, leading the people in steadfast love, protecting them from hostile peoples, and establishing them in a place that was Yahweh's own sanctuary. Although the metaphor of God as warrior understandably creates serious problems for many modern interpreters, its importance for the system of belief of a people born of deliverance from slavery must not be overlooked.

The exodus event was a broad one and a deep one, encompassing ancestral promises, Egyptian social and religious structures, tribal customs, and many other specific happenings and concrete details not preserved by tradition. Yet its nucleus was captured by the hymn in Exodus 15. In a unique way, after a rich gestation period, the moment of Israel's birth as a community occurred in the experience of Yahweh's majesty placed at the service of an oppressed and threatened people, the experience of deliverance from the hosts of the Pharaoh at the Sea. . . . [This] became the nucleus around which developed an entire exodus pageant. This celebration echoes through the Bible as its most persistent theme. And it continues today to find annual expression in the Jewish celebration of the Passover.

C. The Yahwistic Notion of Community

. . . . What were the implications of the encounter with the God of the exodus for the development of social structures and patterns of community? First, it must be recognized that emergent Israel was a people living within a world in which slavery and the exploitation of aliens were unquestioned parts of the economic system. And as we shall see, the young community, recognizing the need for communal norms and social structures as a matter of survival within a threatening world, naturally borrowed from laws and practices existing among its neighbors. This reality, together with the obvious fact that the members of the early Yahwistic community were vulnerable to the same human passions that foster oppression and inequality in every society, serves sufficient warning against temptations to view early Israel in romantically idealistic terms. Once this grounded view is clear, however, we can go on to recognize the long-range significance of the exodus experience: for its life as a free people, this community was indebted to the God who chose to take the side of slaves against the "divine" Pharaoh. So long as this primal experience was preserved in memory, it would have a decisive impact on the development of communal values and social structures. The exodus experience cannot be understood if its social implications are not recognized clearly: in this act of deliverance, the God Yahweh annulled religious and social systems predicated on assumptions of special privilege, and abolished the caste system as a fundamental structure of human society. Again, we dare not overlook the sad fact that this understanding of the exodus experience was more often neglected than preserved in ancient Israel, because of forgetfulness and the seduction of alternate ideologies. But the simple fact of the exodus event and the God encountered in that event implanted into the consciousness of the people a reality that refused to be silenced. As godly leaders in all ages of Israelite history pointed out, that reality continued to be present with this people, true to the same saving purpose that underlay the exodus. . . .

However much denied by actual practices, there was accordingly an organic connection between the exodus event and the communal structures that were true to Israel's origins in God's gracious act of deliverance. That connection could not be preserved solely by abstract formulations of belief, but demanded a quality of life relating inextricably to systems of justice, land distribution, use of capital, treatment of vulnerable classes within the society, and the like. These institutions are not formal accidents, but essential structures already implicit in the nature of the God revealed in the exodus. Because of their ultimate source in God's nature, Israel's understanding of these structures would be deepened and refined over the entire history of its relating to the living God of the Covenant.

Thus God's deliverance of a slave people inaugurated a new order of life for Israel and, concretely, a new notion of community. Israel began to draw out some of the cardinal qualities of that new order as the Israelites lived in the wake of this memorable foundational event. Beyond these early beginnings, the act of deliverance in the exodus set in motion a dynamic process among those people who owed their freedom to that event, a process of defining themselves as the people of God. That process moved powerfully and creatively through the entire unfolding of Scripture, in spite of diverse forms of opposition from outside and from within.

The Ten Commandments: Economic Implications

Max L. Stackhouse

One of the most interesting versions of the Ten Commandments appears in Deuteronomy 5. Long before that passage was written, Moses had led the people out of slavery. Yet many did not know how to deal with their liberation. Some danced around the golden calf; some wanted to return to the security of imperial power. And in the midst of this murmuring, God offered the people a covenant — an ethic marked by the first principles of social justice.

But over the generations people forgot it. Other peoples with different backgrounds became a part of the community, and the new pluralism gave the comforting excuse to ignore old principles. Even the heirs of that grand tradition had become settled in life. Religion became routine. Some confused God's covenant with the love of freedom. Others with the pursuit of gain. Still others with the claim of special privilege due to God's favor. Some placed their confidence in the redemptive power of sexual potency, others in political or military glory, others in material plenty. The consequence was the dulling viciousness of licentious living, the blurring of principle by luxury, and the unfeeling neglect of the poor. The society began to decay from within; it became a target of foreign domination. Against this forgetting and betrayal the prophets later railed. They spoke God's truth, but they did not fully bring the people of the society to renewal.

The people had to come together again and

Adapted from a keynote address to the Convocation of the National Council of the Churches of Christ, USA, held in Cleveland, 1982.

again (see Nehemiah 8) to articulate and renew their covenant — to reaffirm in common their loyalty to the God of justice as known by ancient convictions. It is in this moment of covenant renewal that we find these words: "Not with our fathers did the Lord make this covenant but with all of us here alive this day" (Deut. 5:3).

A truly universal covenant is not only with "our fathers." Mothers, aunts, cousins, and those once foreign to us also shape our reception of the covenant. Today we properly remember *all* our forebears. Yet the truth which was with those who went before is in need of recovery and recasting in the present, for it is not restricted to the past. It becomes a present and future reality when it is remembered, for its principles are eternal. These are what structures a community, orders its freedom, and contains its impulses to conquest.

1. "You shall have no other God before me." There are many gods — even today, in the so-called secular world of economics and business. People place their ultimate confidence in all sorts of things. Wealth is one. National pride is another. So are race and sex. And progress, or financial security, or productivity, or profit, or "our lifestyle," or even freedom. Have we built, can we ever build a whole and fulfilling life on the basis of these? None of these is necessarily evil. All are potentially good. But if we acknowledge nothing beyond them to keep them in proportion, they tempt us to put our final and whole truth in passing and partial values. Then we find them commanding our loyalties, deciding our ethics, and controlling our society. Then they displace God. Then they must be criticized according to the only true "Living Standard," beyond all of these.

2. "You shall not make for yourself a graven image." Although we submit to God, we are not to be merely passive. We make things; we participate in God's creativity. But we are wrong if we presume that humans have control over everything and can raise up divine truth out of our imagination, knowledge, and craft. That presumes to assert control of heaven because we control earth or other people, or ideas. This commandment reinforces and links 1 & 3. We are today besieged by graven images. They flit across the tube, they clutter our magazines, they become idols of our minds. We pay image makers to create realities that refer to nothing and reveal less, so long as they evoke response and make themselves famous. To do this, we stereotype male and female, white and black, rich and poor, Oriental and Muslim. The idols insidiously invite us to bow down and serve them by giving our time, energy, money, or loyalties to them. But faithful people will not live by empty icons or stereotyped images.

3. "You shall not take the Lord's name in vain." How flippant we are with God's gift of communication. We swear easily. We use friendly chatter to hide crass interests. We tolerate the use of sacred language for commercial purposes. We make it hard to talk seriously about the most important things. We cheapen the currency of moral discourse. And we confront preachers on one side who attach holy words to tedium, and preachers on the other side who attach their pious rhetoric to ungodly and inhumane programs. The "Lord will not hold guiltless," says the text, "those who do these things." We must speak of all things in ways that clarify and honor all that is holy.

4. "Observe the sabbath. Six days shalt thou labor but the seventh shalt thou rest." All should work. Each has a vocation from God. But all, also, need a time for holiness, for "re-creation." This commandment cuts several ways. The work ethic is commended in the context of godly responsibility. On its own the work ethic can become an instrument of greed and compulsive pride. Sloth is a sin and all who can should work, yet we are not to be workaholics. If the world of work and the drive for success undercuts the vision of larger things, if it prevents prayer, worship, and family responsibilities by father and mother, something is wrong.

And we dare not use this commandment to accuse society's victims. A society which prevents willing people from working, or a public policy which limits access to opportunities to work or find training for work, or a pattern of business activity which condemns the needy to unrelieved, unceasing struggle merely to survive is wrong. It forces people to violate God's laws. It must be altered.

5. "Honor your father and your mother." Of course we should respect our parents. But the meaning is more. In our life-styles, in our sexuality, in our attitudes to families, to children, to the elderly, in our personal and public policies, we should so conduct ourselves that dignity is brought to those who give, sustain, and nurture

life. As we were cared for by our parents so that we have some modicum of health, of hope, and of compassion, so we must extend these to all God's people. That honors our parents.

6. "Thou shalt not kill." Few kill directly. But modern society has murderous aspects. The death penalty is a scandal before God. The world's nuclear and chemical arsenals need extensive reductions. Some abortions are murderous in intent or consequence; some trade policies and marketing structures leave people starving; and some atomic and industrial wastes threaten generations yet unborn. These holocausts by slow degrees, diffused through populations and not clearly intended by any one person in particular, are no less lethal. All who try to live under God's covenant must resist these forces of death.

7. "Neither shall you commit adultery." The family is in trouble today. The long-range economic costs are incalculable; the human cost is greater. To encourage by word or example that kind of promiscuity which breaks fidelity; to drift with the tides of indulgent self-gratification; to praise models of economy and marriage which lead to the exploitation of women and the impoverishment of children; to expect constant and increasing success from every male; to fail to reconstruct a vision of the Christian family at a time when older versions have been shown to be inadequate is simply to abandon our ethical anchors. In faith we cannot do this.

8. "You shall not steal." Pilfering, "borrowing," "liberating," or simply "using" what is the neighbor's, or a store's, or the company's, or the public's, without authority, prevents rightful owners from exercising stewardly responsibility. Property is an extension of accountable personhood as it exists in economic community; mistreating it violates not only the property, but the persons and the community. People begin to live locked up lives. Further, using resources in the present that should be preserved for the future steals from generations yet unborn; refusing to pay a fair share of the public costs of maintaining the society steals from the common good. Stolen resources — by deception, exploitation, force, embezzlement, plagiarizing, distribution of illicit goods, swindle, lack of stewardship for the future, or resistance to just taxes — are not truly property. They may be reclaimed by public authority.

9. "You shall not bear false witness." Lying, cheating, twisting information and evidence, creating false impressions, making what is bad look good, keeping silent when truth needs a voice, and failing to be direct are among the ways that we attempt to gain advantage or smooth human relations for our benefit. Though bargaining, sharp dealing, advertising, public relations, packaging, and selling "as is" have been a part of economic life since the first horse trade, misrepresentation, deception, and obscurity by legalese infect open interaction and destroy the trust necessary for commerce. They lead to litigation in all things and even to the corruption of judicial systems. We are to tell the truth in all things, so far as we can know it.

10. "You shall not covet." Here, the commandment cuts to the heart. Most commandments speak of behavior. Even if they imply internal integrity, they draw limits on public action. Since most people draw their ethical principles from the common life, that is proper. Further, most of the commandments are in the negative; they draw a boundary, telling us what is *not* morally possible, what is *beyond* the limits. That too is proper since only a negative limit allows maximum freedom and recognizes the necessity of conscience and judgment.

Most commandments deal with limits to allowed behavior: This boundary you shall not trespass. But this last commandment cuts below behavior and negative limit to touch inner motivations. These too are to be commanded. The incentives for life, including the economic parts of it, are not to be rooted in cravings or desires or lust for that which is not ours to have. All such motivations reveal an insecurity that neither things nor conquests can remove. And if we cater to them, they become obsessive. The drive to do well, to live decently, to make useful lives with the partners and talents we have been given, to have reliability and excellence acknowledged, to get a fair wage or make a fair profit or increase the capital of the commonwealth, to accomplish something worth doing and get paid for it — all of this is quite respectable. But life is not to be lived in resentment or envy, or in the incessant drive to possess more and more. That corrupts the soul and makes us distort the intent of all the commandments.

These commandments are not only for children to whom we properly teach them, nor are they only for hardened criminals who are convicted by law for violation of these principles. They are also for advertisers, for managers, for engineers, for accountants, for union members, for secretaries, and for multinational corporations. Exploitative greed ever marches at the boundaries of morality and appears in petty ways. It tempts each to appropriate for some what should be shared by all. It evokes perceived needs about things we don't need. At many levels these practices must be challenged.

The need for a renewal of covenant is ever old, ever new. It confers moral identity to a conglomeration of many tribes. It calls each to personal responsibility. It gives public integrity to the common life. Abraham Heschel states the link between godly morality for the people of God and the renewed personal identity when he writes of such moments, "I am commanded, therefore I am." Jesus knew this tradition. He lived in it. He loved in it. Indeed, he extended and deepened it by the power of sacrificial love. When he went up to the mountain, as had Moses, he was so empowered by God's love that he took the people with him to renew their covenant. He brought the people up to the mountain. He began his Sermon on the Mount with the Beatitudes, which turned misunderstandings of this ancient heritage inside out and upside down. Yet he also insisted that the ancient heritage was not to be voided. "Think not that I have come to abolish the law and the prophets, I come not to abolish but to fulfill." Not only with our fathers did the Lord make this covenant but with all of us here alive this day.

Prophecy and Wisdom

The revitalization of the covenant led in several directions. One was the fuller specification of the implications of the "holy law" or *Torah*. A great number of refinements were made, and many of the details regarding how these were to be faithfully lived were elaborated. Psalm 19, for example, not only celebrates the covenantal order built into the very structure of creation but also sings the praises of God's law — decrees, precepts, commandments, and ordinances, which are to be "more desired than gold." On the basis of this refined sense of the godly ordering of life by deontological principles, rich jurisprudential traditions developed in Jewish life and gave rise to a new genre of intellectual life, the commentaries. These commentaries became a model for applying sacred texts from the past to changing conditions.

A second tradition that arose was the prophetic tradition. Sometimes from among the cultivated and "progressive" priests, and sometimes from among the rustic and "conservative" populists, courageous and inspired leaders tried to bring the first principles of moral life back into the vision of the society. Whenever the people, especially those in advantaged positions, began to exploit others, to ignore the plight of the weak and the dispossessed, and to luxuriate in their own privilege, these prophets "spoke forth" for God's purposes. Seeing all from that vantage point, they published analyses of the evils of the current situation, warnings of doom, condemnations of those responsible, and a call for moral and social change that would drive toward the moral goal or *telos* of *shalom* — a just and loving peace.

Still a third tradition was the wisdom tradition. Scholars not only recorded, refined, and collated the aphorisms, sayings, and insights that help people cultivate character and perspective on the common contexts of life; they also translated and adapted insightful materials from surrounding cultures. Elements from Hellenic, Assyrian, Egyptian, and Babylonian cultures, for example, are easily documented by biblical scholars. This is, of course, of great significance, for it indicates that the authors of the Bible recognized that inspired truth could be found in many sources among the peoples of the world and not only from within one culture.

While all of these traditions have been of great importance for subsequent Judaic, Christian, Islamic, and modern secular thinkers, ethical reflection on business has been especially influenced by the prophetic and wisdom traditions. These inspired writers were addressing a social context and an ethos in which social position was defined by familial status or political power, for economic organizations distinct from these scarcely existed. In his essay "Property and Riches in the Old Testament and Judaism," Martin Hengel accents some of the key themes. Selections about commerce, generosity, riches, and the trades and crafts from the representative "intertestamental" book Sirach, sometimes called Ecclesiasticus, are also included in this section.

Deuteronomy 15:1-23
(NRSV)

Every seventh year you shall grant a remission of debts. And this is the manner of the remission: every creditor shall remit the claim that is held against a neighbor, not exacting it of a neighbor who is a member of the community, because the Lord's remission has been proclaimed. Of a foreigner you may exact it, but you must remit your claim on whatever any member of your community owes you. There will, however, be no one in need among you, because the Lord is sure to bless you in the land that the Lord your God is giving you as a possession to occupy, if only you will obey the Lord your God by diligently observing this entire commandment that I command you today. When the Lord your God has blessed you, as he promised you, you will lend to many nations, but you will not borrow; you will rule over many nations, but they will not rule over you.

If there is among you anyone in need, a member of your community in any of your towns within the land that the Lord your God is giving you, do not be hard-hearted or tight-fisted toward your needy neighbor. You should rather open your hand, willingly lending enough to meet the need, whatever it may be. Be careful that you do not entertain a mean thought, thinking, "The seventh year, the year of remission, is near," and therefore view your needy neighbor with hostility and give nothing; your neighbor might cry to the Lord against you, and you would incur guilt. Give liberally and be ungrudging when you do so, for on this account the Lord your God will bless you in all your work and in all that you undertake. Since there will never cease to be some in need on the earth, I therefore command you, "Open your hand to the poor and needy neighbor in your land."

If a member of your community, whether a Hebrew man or a Hebrew woman, is sold to you and works for you six years, in the seventh year you shall set that person free. And when you send a male slave out from you a free person, you shall not send him out empty-handed. Provide liberally out of your flock, your threshing floor, and your wine press, thus giving to him some of the bounty with which the Lord your God has blessed you. Remember that you were a slave in the land of Egypt, and the Lord your God redeemed you; for this reason I lay this command upon you today. But if he says to you, "I will not go out from you," because he loves you and your household, since he is well off with you, then you shall take an awl and thrust it through his earlobe into the door, and he shall be your slave forever.

You shall do the same with regard to your female slave.

Do not consider it a hardship when you send them out from you free persons, because for six years they have given you services worth the wages of hired laborers; and the Lord your God will bless you in all that you do.

Every firstling male born of your herd and flock you shall consecrate to the Lord your God; you shall not do work with your firstling ox nor shear the firstling of your flock. You shall eat it, you together with your household, in the presence of the Lord your God year by year at the place that the Lord will choose. But if it has any defect — any serious defect, such as lameness or blindness — you shall not sacrifice it to the Lord your God; within your towns you may eat it, the unclean and the clean alike, as you would a gazelle or deer. Its blood, however, you must not eat; you shall pour it out on the ground like water.

Sirach

Sirach 26:29–27:4

A merchant can hardly keep from wrongdoing,
  nor is a tradesman innocent of sin.
Many have committed sin for gain,
  and those who seek to get rich
    will avert their eyes.
As a stake is driven firmly into a fissure
    between stones,
  so sin is wedged in between selling and buying.
If a person is not steadfast in the fear
    of the Lord,
  his house will be quickly overthrown.
When a sieve is shaken, the refuse appears;
  so do a person's faults when he speaks.

Sirach 29:8-17

Nevertheless, be patient with someone
    in humble circumstances,
  and do not keep him waiting for your alms.
Help the poor for the commandment's sake,

From *The New Oxford Annotated Bible with the Apocrypha, NRSV*, ed. B. Metzger and R. Murphy (New York: Oxford University Press, 1989). Sirach is sometimes known as Ecclesiasticus, or the Wisdom of Ben Sira, and was included in earlier Bibles. This book was used among some Jews and many early Christians, but it was not viewed by later Jewish scholars or Protestants as equal to other writings of law, prophecy, wisdom, or gospel. Nevertheless, it treats economic matters in a significant way, and we conclude the survey of ancient biblical materials and economic matters with this example of a form of religio-economic practical wisdom developed in a transitional period.

and in their need do not send them away
    empty-handed.
Lose your silver for the sake of a brother
    or a friend,
  and do not let it rust under a stone
    and be lost.
Lay up your treasure according to
    the commandments of the Most High,
  and it will profit you more than gold.
Store up almsgiving in your treasury,
  and it will rescue you from every disaster;
better than a stout shield and a sturdy spear,
  it will fight for you against the enemy.

A good person will be surety for his neighbor,
  but the one who has lost all sense of shame
    will fail him.
Do not forget the kindness of your guarantor,
  for he has given his life for you.
A sinner wastes the property of his guarantor,
  and the ungrateful person abandons
    his rescuer.

Sirach 31:1-11

Wakefulness over wealth wastes away one's flesh,
  and anxiety about it drives away sleep.
Wakeful anxiety prevents slumber,
  and a severe illness carries off sleep.
The rich person toils to amass a fortune,
  and when he rests he fills himself
    with his dainties.
The poor person toils to make a meager living,
  and if ever he rests he becomes needy.

One who loves gold will not be justified;
  one who pursues money will be led astray
    by it.
Many have come to ruin because of gold,
  and their destruction has met them
    face to face.
It is a stumbling block to those who are avid
    for it,
  and every fool will be taken captive by it.
Blessed is the rich person who is
    found blameless,
  and who does not go after gold.
Who is he, that we may praise him?
  For he has done wonders among his people.

Who has been tested by it and been
found perfect?
Let it be for him a ground for boasting.
Who has had the power to transgress
and did not transgress,
and to do evil and did not do it?
His prosperity will be established,
and the assembly will proclaim his acts
of charity.

Sirach 38:24-34

The wisdom of the scribe depends
on the opportunity of leisure;
only the one who has little business
can become wise.
How can one become wise who handles
the plow,
and who glories in the shaft of a goad,
who drives oxen and is occupied
with their work,
and whose talk is about bulls?
He sets his heart on plowing furrows,
and he is careful about fodder for the heifers.
So too is every artisan and master artisan
who labors by night as well as by day;
those who cut the signets of seals,
each is diligent in making a great variety;
they set their heart on painting a lifelike image,
and they are careful to finish their work.
So too is the smith, sitting by the anvil,
intent on his iron-work;
the breath of the fire melts his flesh,
and he struggles with the heat of the furnace;
the sound of the hammer deafens his ears,
and his eyes are on the pattern of the object.
He sets his heart on finishing his handiwork,
and he is careful to complete its decoration.
So too is the potter sitting at his work
and turning the wheel with his feet;
he is always deeply concerned over his products,
and he produces them in quantity.
He molds the clay with his arm
and makes it pliable with his feet;
he sets his heart to finish the glazing,
and he takes care in firing the kiln.
All these rely on their hands,
and all are skillful in their own work.
Without them no city can be inhabited,

and wherever they live, they will not
go hungry.
Yet they are not sought out for the council
of the people,
nor do they attain eminence
in the public assembly.
They do not sit in the judge's seat,
nor do they understand the decisions
of the courts;
they cannot expound discipline or judgment,
and they are not found among the rulers.
But they maintain the fabric of the world,
and their concern is for the exercise
of their trade.

Property and Riches in the Old Testament and Judaism

Martin Hengel

I. The Prophetic Criticism of Riches and its Expression in the Torah

Before we consider the attitude of Jesus and early Christianity to property and riches, we must take a look at the Old Testament and Jewish tradition out of which early Christianity grew. Here the message of the prophets and the social legislation of the Torah had long stimulated criticism of property. The right to property was in principle subordinated to the obligation to care for the weaker members of society. Even the testimony of the first writing prophet, Amos, in the eighth century B.C. leaves nothing to be desired by way of clarity. With unsurpassable sharpness he attacks the subjection and exploitation of the poor by the rich landowners and royal officials in the northern kingdom:

> They hate him who reproves in the gate,
> and they abhor him who speaks the truth.
> Therefore because you trample the poor
> and take from him exactions of wheat,
> you have built houses of hewn stone,
> but you shall not dwell in them.
> You have planted pleasant vineyards,
> but you shall not drink their wine.
> For I know how many are your transgressions,
> and how great are your sins —
> you who afflict the righteous, who take a bribe,

Martin Hengel, "Property and Riches in the Old Testament and Judaism," *Property and Riches* (Philadelphia: Fortress Press, 1973), pp. 12-22.

> and turn aside the needy in the gate.
> (Amos 5:10-12)

> Hear this, you who trample upon the needy,
> and bring the poor of the land to an end,
> saying, 'When will the new moon be over,
> that we may sell grain?
> And the sabbath,
> that we may offer wheat for sale,
> that we may make the ephah small
> and the shekel great,
> and deal deceitfully with false balances,
> that we may buy the poor for silver
> and the needy for a pair of sandals,
> and sell the refuse of the wheat?'
> The LORD has sworn by the pride of Jacob:
> 'Surely I will never forget any of their deeds.
> Shall not the land tremble on this account,
> and every one mourn who dwells in it?'
> (Amos 8:4-8)

Amos' threats against society are continued a little later by Isaiah, in the southern kingdom. He, too, roughly attacks the dispossession practiced by the great landowners, the corruption among the judges and the mercilessness and partiality of officials:

> Woe to those who join house to house,
> who add field to field,
> until there is no more room,
> and you are made to dwell alone
> in the midst of the land.
> The LORD of hosts has sworn in my hearing:
> 'Surely many houses shall be desolate,
> large and beautiful houses,
> without inhabitant.
> For ten acres of vineyard shall yield
> but one bath,
> and a homer of seed shall yield
> but an ephah. . . .

> Woe to those who decree iniquitous decrees,
> and the writers who keep writing oppression,
> to turn aside the needy from justice
> and to rob the poor of my people
> of their right,
> that widows may be their spoil
> and that they may make the fatherless
> their prey.

What will you do on the day of punishment,
    in the storm which will come from afar?
To whom will you flee for help,
    and where will you leave your wealth?

                            (Isa. 5:8-10; 10:1-3)

. . . . At least part of the social message of the prophets was given expression in the Torah . . . which played a decisive role in King Josiah's reform and in the spiritual renewal of Israel during the exile. Examples of this are the numerous regulations contained in the Torah which protect the weak and underprivileged members of society. In Deut. 15:1ff., 12ff., the ordinance of the year of release which takes place every seven years enjoined a universal release of debts and the freeing of all who had been enslaved for debt. The prophet Jeremiah was already protesting against the breach of this practice (34:8ff.). In the fiftieth year, after seven years of release or sabbath years, the "year of jubilee" was celebrated. In this year all land that had been sold in the meantime was to be returned to its original owner or his heirs (Lev. 25:8ff.). The reason given for this "redistribution" of land was that Yahweh was the real owner of the holy land: "For the land is mine; for you are strangers and sojourners with me" (Lev. 25:23). "Each of you shall return to his property" (25:13). "What is called a sale is not really a sale; it is merely a provisional exchange of possessions; for Yahweh alone is the owner of the land. The Israelites are merely hereditary tenants on his property, who have no more ultimate right to dispose of the land which had been assigned to them than the strangers and sojourners whom they have accepted in their midst." We find the three demands for the remission of debt, the freeing of slaves and the redistribution of land in numerous attempts at social reform in the ancient world: the Jewish law attempted to institutionalize these ever-recurring basic demands of "ancient social reform," though of course it remains an open question how far the demands were ever realized. Significantly enough, the "year of jubilee" was later reinterpreted as a symbol of the eschatological liberation of Israel.

On the other side was appropriate and legitimate possession under the protection of the ten commandments, which prohibited envious covetousness of a neighbor's property. . . . The picture of the king's peace in the time of Solomon, when "Judah and Israel dwelt in safety, every man under his vine and under his fig tree" (1 Kings 4:25), became a symbol of the prophetic vision of the time of salvation (Micah 4:4; Zech. 3:10; cf. also 2 Kings 18:31).

2. Social Tensions in Early Judaism

The contrast between the great landowners and the small peasant farmers or landless tenants had already led to considerable social tensions in the late monarchy (1 Kings 21; Isa. 5:8ff.; Micah 2:2) and then again in the Persian period under Nehemiah (5:1ff.). The situation became considerably more acute in the Hellenistic period after Alexander, as the Graeco-Macedonian colonizers with their own particular approach to the world went over from the extensive exploitation hitherto usual in the East to an intensive exploitation of their subject territories. The Romans and the rulers appointed by them, like Herod and his successors, continued this form of extreme exploitation of the land. Great estates forced back the free peasant farmers, and the number of landless tenants increased, particularly after the time of Herod. We have a lively picture of the social scene in Palestine from the parables of Jesus with their landowners, tenants, day laborers and slaves; with faithful and unfaithful administrators; with remission of debts and slavery for debts. The social scene has the firm imprint of feudalism upon it. We can understand why the Jewish struggles for freedom — first of all that of the Maccabees against the Macedonian Seleucids and then later that of the "Zealots" against the Romans — were always also social struggles. When the Jewish rebels plundered Jerusalem in A.D. 66 from their base in the temple, the first thing that they burnt was the city archive with the land-registers and the accounts of debts (Josephus, *Bell,* 2, 427).

Chapter Two

The New Testament

As we turn to the New Testament, we should note that the first great distortion of Christianity, the first official "heresy," was one that claimed that Christianity was opposed to the Hebrew Scriptures. This view was proclaimed false because the God present in Christ does not differ from the God present in creation, exodus, covenant, prophecy, and wisdom. If there are differences, they are these: the truth, justice, and mercy of the one biblical God becomes in the New Testament less centered on "a people" and both more universal and more personal; a church is created that is distinct from both familial and political authority; and the ultimate purpose of God becomes actual in Jesus.

The Marcionite heretics, however, believed otherwise. They held that the God of the Jews was legalistic, wrathful, imperfect, and focused on creation; while the God of Jesus Christ was good, loving, perfect, and focused on redemption. This view, which feeds anti-Semitism and hyper-spirituality, was repudiated by the church. But it has recurred in Western culture, giving religious and ideological support to any who want to separate ethical problems of society — such as business and economics — from anything having to do with what is "truly" holy or sacred. Here, in other words, is a great split that can lead either to an anti-business attitude that claims to represent the "real" truth of the Bible while it leaves the world to its own devices, or to a pro-business attitude that finds nothing pertinent for business in biblical or theological insight.

It is true that the New Testament does not contain extended passages that focus particularly on business or economics — or, for that matter, any other area of social or political life. However, it remains an open debate as to why this is so. It may be that the decisive ethical assumptions regarding these areas are already present in the Old Testament, the Scripture of the early Christians. It could also be that the New Testament, like the Old, presents basic foundations, and that these always have to be brought into relationship with what we can learn from nonbiblical sources — philosophy, the arts and sciences, and practical experience. It could also be, however, that the Bible simply does not have anything to do with these areas — as the ancient Marcionites argued. Even if they were badly mistaken in some ways, perhaps they had this right.

Over the centuries, nearly every phrase in the New Testament has been used to advance one or another of these possibilities. In the following essay, Professor Stephen Mott of Gordon-Conwell Theological Seminary examines some of the modern debates about the pertinence of the New Testament to social, political, and economic issues. Each of the scholars he mentions is worth studying, even if Mott judges some of them as mistaken, for each represents a major alternative perspective on the use of the New Testament in regard to questions of economic issues.

The Use of the New Testament in Social Ethics

Stephen Charles Mott

Objections to using the New Testament for contemporary social ethics come from both ends of the theological spectrum. They have been raised by both biblical scholars and Christian ethicists. Denial of the legitimacy of this use of the New Testament takes three forms: 1. Denial of the social content of the New Testament; 2. denial that the New Testament is concerned with ethics; 3. denial that New Testament social thought is either available to us or practical for us today.

On the other hand, great numbers of Christians who have been involved in social change and social service consider the New Testament to be foundational to their activity. Great Christian social movements have drawn upon it. Have they been deceived about what has guided their behavior and, in the process, misused the biblical documents? When the breadth and diversity of its ethical thought is understood, the New Testament makes valid, significant, and essential contributions to Christian social ethics.

A. The Relationship between the Old and New Testaments

One of the first comments to be made regarding the contribution of the New Testament to social ethics is that without the Old Testament, it is incomplete. Christopher Wright [has] pointed out that Jesus is presented in the New Testament as

Stephen C. Mott, "The Use of the New Testament in Social Ethics," *Transformation* 1, no. 2 (April/June 1984): 21-26.

servant, he is understood as the embodiment of Israel, the people of God. He has inherited and is passing on to the new messianic community the social role and intention of Old Testament Israel. The Old Testament was the Scripture of Jesus and the early church. The statement of the later Pauline church that this Scripture was "useful . . . for instruction in righteousness" (or "education in justice," 2 Tim. 3:16) was only articulating the assumption the church made from the beginning. Old Testament ethical principles accepted by these communities were not necessarily restated; they did not need to be, for they already were in Scripture. As a result New Testament ethical topics, raised to meet ad hoc problems, do not form the entire content of the New Testament church's ethical belief. In exegesis, one must be continually alert to the "continuity of content" of which the Decalogue is only the most obvious example. Behind the New Testament lies an authoritative text which demonstrates deep concern for the social order, for justice, for the economic and social relationships of the powerful and the weak.

New Testament writers have interpreted new life in Christ in continuity with the Old Testament's social hopes and concerns. Luke 1 and 2 are an essential introduction to the whole Gospel. Jesus came to and was received by humble people of the land who were looking for the manifestation of divine power to reverse the roles of possessors and the dispossessed by bringing in social and economic justice. These chapters, which are everywhere impregnated . . . with the notion of fulfillment, reflect the fact that Christians interpreted their experiences in light of their reading of the Old Testament, including its message of justice. The writer, by the way he constructs his Gospel, reveals his agreement with their perspective. The positioning of the famous Nazareth sermon expresses a similar interpretation. Luke 4:18-21 provides the first presentation of Jesus' preaching. The passage serves as His inaugural sermon. The Old Testament text which is read identifies Jesus' mission as a comprehensive liberation understood in a Hebrew way. Likewise the Sermon on the Mount in Matthew is the first presentation of Jesus' teaching. It too is an inaugural address. The Beatitudes which begin the Sermon deal with similar groups of afflicted people (the standard recipients of justice in the Old Testament). They connect Jesus to the Old Testament concern for justice for the weak. Finally, all the Gospels introduce Jesus' public ministry with that of John the Baptist. John the Baptist, who in Q [a source quoted by Gospel writers, but whose writings do not survive] is the greatest of the prophets, is presented in each of the Synoptic Gospels as a preacher of repentance in accordance with the Old Testament prophecy of social righteousness (Mark 12:3-4 par.). In Luke, John is related to the believing remnant of chapters 1 and 2. All the Gospel writers make John a prominent link between Jesus and the Old Testament social tradition.

In addition to these important ways of structuring their Gospels, the authors reveal in other ways that they assume the Old Testament teaching on justice. In Matthew 23:23 and Luke 11:42, Jesus demands justice of his hearers. Matthew identifies this justice as belonging to the more important part of the Law. In the story of Lazarus and Dives in Luke 16, Dives wants to send Lazarus back from the dead to warn his brothers that in a social reversal of fortunes those who keep their wealth from the poor are sent into torment. He is told that they have Moses and the prophets, who are sufficient (Luke 16:29-31). This story follows the statement: "Heaven and earth can pass away more easily than one 'dot' from the Law" (v. 17). The Old Testament is both normative and adequate in its teachings about property relations. The Parable of the Wicked Husbandmen (Matt. 21:33-46; Mark 12:1-12; Luke 20:9-19) further connects Jesus to the prophetic tradition. Jesus, the son, has the same mission as the prophets of the Old Testament who are the slaves of the owner of the vineyard. All have the task of calling the leaders of the people, the farmers, to account for failing to produce the fruits of the vineyard. Matthew (21:43) states that the failure is one of not "bearing the fruits" of the Reign of God. In Q John the Baptist uses this same phrase in his demand for repentance (Matt. 3:8; Luke 3:8). Luke in 3:10-14 identifies the ethical actions required for bearing fruit ("do" [poiein] in v. 10 links with "bear" [poiein] in v. 8); the fruits are sharing economic necessities and ending oppressive activity. In the background text to the parable (Isaiah 5) the fruits are social justice (Isa. 5:7). Jesus is linked to the Old Testament social tradition in which the leaders of Israel are called to

account for their violation of God's covenant through acts of injustice. . . .

What does recognition of continuity with the Old Testament do for the study of New Testament ethics and particularly the ethics of Jesus? . . . When we only know about an individual of the past from a few written documents, . . . it is not methodologically sound to argue from silence that that person lacks specific ideas. Anyone's thought should be interpreted in terms of that person's normative culture. For Jesus the Old Testament was an important component of his culture and supplied an anthropology and social perception said to be lacking. For example, groups in the Old Testament who are to be the recipients of justice, such as the sick, the poor, the stranger, and the widow, are identified by the particular form of their need. Members of these groups frequently appear in the Gospels. From this background one perceives that Jesus intentionally responded not merely to individuals but also to groups. His response reflected both his recognition of specific human needs and the corresponding claims they pose upon the community. . . .

The Old Testament is also needed to understand [God] more fully. . . . As in anthropology, so theology, one would have only a sketch of the full biblical revelation of God if the canon contained nothing more than the Gospel writings about Jesus, or the New Testament. The Old Testament establishes what is often missed in interpretations which begin and end with the New Testament: God the Redeemer is recognized also as Creator; God's saving concerns include the whole creation, and God is concerned with the morality of the social order and not merely with the salvation of individuals or small groups of individuals. It is this perspective which is lacking in attempts to interpret the words of the sermon in Nazareth or the Beatitudes as metaphors for ideas about salvation and existence interpreted only in terms of individuals. . . .

One of the most significant consequences of interpreting New Testament ethics in continuity with the Old Testament is the impact it makes upon the concept of the Reign of God. God's Reign is a theme which sums up the hope of the Old Testament. It speaks of God's intervention in history to produce a new age in which there would be not only a new relationship of faith and obedience to God but a new social order. The coming of this new rule of God is that salvation in which God's creation is renewed in such a way that creation and redemption become merged.

In the New Testament the Reign of God formed a major part of Jesus' teaching. In Pauline thought it is linked with Christ's conquest of the cosmic powers (1 Cor. 15:24). Beyond the actual use of the term *(basileia),* recovery of God's sovereign rule over all things in the liberation of creation in Romans 8 and in the reconciliation of all things in Colossians and Ephesians is present.

Walter Rauschenbusch's statement that "the kingdom of God as a righteous social order is the message of Scripture" goes too far since no one theme can recapitulate the fullness of biblical thought, but it does draw attention to its importance. The Reign provides a context for God's universal ethical concerns. It also furnishes a concept of history into which other New Testament themes can be placed. We understand that Jesus in his ethics was proclaiming a new social order breaking into history. . . .

This understanding of the Reign of God in the Gospels is not universally accepted. It is denied by many who question the New Testament's relevance to social ethics. A logical progression can be traced from a neglect of the Old Testament context for New Testament ethics to a denial of the social aspects of the Reign of God to a dismissal of the social ethics of the New Testament. . . . [Some deny] . . . that ethical norms are connected to the Kingdom of God because Jesus is the Kingdom in person. The difficulty with this commonly held position — beyond its ambiguity — is that the Synoptic Gospels present Jesus as one who proclaims and is an agent of the Reign but who directs little attention to his own being. From the perspective of the whole of the New Testament, we understand that Jesus as the incarnation of God inaugurates and empowers God's new Reign through his life, death, and resurrection. But he is not that Reign. The Reign is the sphere where he conquers those powers which are destructive of the creation. When their defeat is accomplished at his coming again, he hands the Reign over to God. [In short] . . . the concept of a just rule and an ideal order is part of the New Testament's portrayal of Reign. The best description occurs in the Lord's Prayer: "Your Kingdom come, your will be done on earth as it is in heaven."

B. The Place of Status in Society and in the Message of the New Testament

The second crucial factor in identifying the social content of the New Testament is the importance of status in its pages. In Old Testament social ethics economic deprivation is the central concern; in the New Testament status is the key to social ethics. Even when scholars have interpreted correctly the many passages which deal with status, they have frequently failed to identify adequately the sociological characteristics of status present or to realize the importance that status has for the social system. In general the Old Testament is concerned with class while the New Testament is concerned with status. There are, however, important overlaps.

The contrast between class and status is important and helpful for our purposes, although it is a simplification because there are many forms of each. Class deals with the economic opportunities that an individual can expect in life by virtue of the group to which he or she belongs. It is related to property relations and economic power. It is objective. Status is subjective. It is based on the value the culture places on various groups of people. On account of certain characteristics, prestige and respect (or its lack) are granted by custom or law. Material rewards and opportunities may be included with status or they may be its consequence. What matters in receiving esteem or dishonor is not so much what you are as what people think you are. Both class (economic position) and status (social position) are power resources. Jesus' teaching of universal love for those who belonged to the various groupings of his social world relates to status and forms a major segment of the New Testament ethic. Another major part of this ethic, which also involves status, is the concern in the Epistles over how the new Christian communities are to be formed and who is to be included.

The story of Zacchaeus (Luke 19:1-10) is a good basis for showing the importance of the question about status in Jesus' teaching. Verse 7 stands out because structurally it is in the centre of the meeting between Zacchaeus and Jesus (vv. 5-10). It also stands in sharp contrast to Zacchaeus' joy and response to Jesus' action in seeking, receiving, and affirming him: "Everyone grumbled, saying, 'He has gone to lodge with a man who is a sinner.'" The text states that "everyone" joined in this evaluation of Zacchaeus. The whole community agreed that Zacchaeus was a "sinner." That was his status in society.

The term *sinner (hamartolos)* was not a moral description but a technical term. It was a title used to refer to a group of people who could be both identified and segregated. In the Gospels the "sinners" are the tax collectors, prostitutes, and drunkards. They are characterized by an observable lifestyle or economic activity which has been ethically condemned. In the Hellenistic world a "sinner" was the opposite of those who are right and proper ("our kind of people"). For Jewish writers it was a derogatory term of abuse. Their lifestyle had cut them off from the community. No matter what other attributes Zacchaeus had, as a tax collector he was a "sinner" and therefore cut off and despised.

Jesus was accused frequently of this intimate association with "sinners" (in the Orient table fellowship signifies sharing an intimate community of life). Why was he accused? Why was it a matter of such concern? Jesus, like Paul later, was crossing socially important boundaries. Status depends on separation and the avoidance of communications that imply acceptance and equality. Jesus by intentionally and habitually crossing those boundaries, showed how he defined status. Jesus' deliberate action is shown in his response to the accusation (verse 10) "The Son of Man has come to seek and to save the lost." (Note that in verse 9 Jesus uses the third person rather than the second: "He is a son of Abraham." Jesus is now talking about Zacchaeus rather than to him). As elsewhere (Mark 2:17 par.), Jesus defends his conduct (crossing status boundaries) by stating the purpose of his mission. His behavior is consistent with his intention.

Jesus names as "the lost" those whom his objectors call "sinners" (cf. also Luke 15:6-7). The redefinition is significant. They are not sinners to be hated and driven away. They are lost, needing to be found and rejoiced over. "Lost" implies a different status; there is something to be recovered. "He is a son of Abraham" (v. 9). He is

neither a devil; nor less than human. He is a lost child of Abraham, the very criterion for membership in the community. (In the Pauline mission the equivalent criterion is replaced by the universal "one for whom Christ died.") Jesus' mission is to locate and find these lost persons and bring them back into the community of God's people.

In Luke 15 the lost son is such a sinner. Sunken in debauchery (v. 15) he is the kind of person with whom Jesus was accused of associating at the beginning of the chapter. A strange term is used to describe the restoration of the son. He has been received back "safe and sound." The term *(hygiainein)* literally means "restored to health," but the story does not indicate that he had been sick. The point is that he had been restored to his former condition; he was "sound" socially. The purpose of justice in biblical terms is to restore to community. Jesus' way of dealing with the inequalities of status and his activity in bringing people back into community would constitute a ministry of justice. . . .

Space does not permit discussion of other groups to which Jesus extended his mission who also were hurt by their social relationships: the sick, women, children, Samaritans. But the same factors of status are present.

The status boundaries that Jesus crossed are crucial to the stability of a society. That is why he provoked hostility. Status is one of the most basic elements of a social system. It is a way of controlling people. Because of it some are weak and some powerful. This inequality is socially useful. The existence of roles is inherent in being social. They are patterns of behavior prescribed by custom or law. Roles are the way society performs its functions. They indicate how people are to behave in a situation and how they can expect others to behave. But the roles are highly differentiated in their meaning, importance, and esteem. Status is a way of matching people to roles. The chaos of constantly determining anew what to expect from others is thus avoided.

When Jesus by his actions and words challenged the existing status system, he defied a major requirement for operating a social system. To those who claim that Jesus's ministry was merely personal, we reply that he could not have done anything more basic to challenge institutions and social structures. The leadership, with vested interests in maintaining society as it was structured, were threatened by his actions. They responded with enmity against him. Threats to status bring persecution. Persons responsible for the threat "come to be defined as dangerous public enemies requiring severe repressive action."

That persecution is a topic treated by most of the New Testament writings reflects in part the challenge that the Christian message and presence presented to the societies of that day. A priority for the early church was to determine if the relationships among its members would be characterized by the status distinction of the surrounding culture. The answer was far reaching. In the new reality made present by Jesus Christ, the major status distinctions of the culture — slavery, nationality, and sex — were considered null and void (Gal. 3:28). When Paul argues in Romans that the Gentiles (who according to Ephesians had no rights in the commonwealth of Israel) have been made participants in God's community through his righteousness (or "justice," *dikaiosyne*) not by means of "works" — a category of status — but by faith, he draws upon the biblical sense of justice which involves bringing people back into community.

Although social conduct in the Christian community is directly derived from the new statement about status (Col. 3:9-16), the new ideal relates to the religious basis of status (by faith in Christ). Some have argued, as a result, that the early church did not touch the secular status systems. What is missed, however, in this criticism is the central importance of religion for status in traditional societies. Any system of stratification requires a system of belief to explain, justify, and propagate the inequalities and persuade people to accept as legitimate the fact of their inequality. In a traditional society religion provides the ideological basis for status in the system. When this base is removed, the whole system is shaken.

Matthew's Sermon on the Mount

"Without doubt," said Gandhi many years ago, "the Sermon on the Mount is the most sublime treatment of ethics the world has ever known." Few dispute it: modern non-Christians as well as Christians have found great meaning in the three chapters of St. Matthew's Gospel where, in an echo of Moses' delivery of God's commandments from the mountain and the Deuteronomist's recasting of them, Jesus delivers a message that both renews the ancient covenant and announces a new vision of the future. In the Sermon on the Mount, Jesus tells us how ultimately God wants things to turn out and how we ought to live in anticipation of what God is bringing about.

This passage of Scripture is troubling to those with a purely economic outlook, for it challenges many of the presuppositions on which modern business, at least as secular interpreters speak of it, is based. One seldom finds treatments in business ethics about the blessedness that is among the poor, the meek, the merciful, and the persecuted. Nor are business leaders told not to be anxious about what to eat, wear, or reap. They may know that they are not to be greedy or totally preoccupied with their own well-being, and they do not respect people who are. Yet they find their way in life by seeing that they and others are provided with food, clothing, shelter, and the increase of wealth generally.

The central point is this: business and economic activity and attentiveness to vocation are a part of life, and all of life is to be carried out in a larger and deeper and longer context than any particular product, contract, quarterly report, or industry or business cycle represents. In recognizing this, one finds a certain serenity in coming to clarity about what the most important dimensions of life ultimately are.

The question of how those ultimate dimensions are to relate to the proximate ones of practical life has been a central preoccupation of biblical ethics for centuries. At times, they were thought to be entirely incompatible with secular life, so that if one felt inclined to follow the ethical life-style implied by this sermon one had either to join a monastery or to become engaged in a church that stood deliberately as a counterculture to the dominant patterns of civilization.

While not prescribing these views, Lisa Cahill, one of the outstanding Roman Catholic ethicists writing today, offers a summary of one current way of drawing connections between biblical scholarship and contemporary social ethics. Of central importance is the question of whether religious matters such as those treated in the Sermon are to have direct and public implications, or whether they are essentially for the private life, or whether they are for faithful believers when they are separate from the general operations of society.

Matthew 5:1–7:29 (NRSV)

When Jesus saw the crowds, he went up the mountain; and after he sat down, his disciples came to him. Then he began to speak, and taught them, saying:

"Blessed are the poor in spirit, for theirs is the kingdom of heaven.

"Blessed are those who mourn, for they will be comforted.

"Blessed are the meek, for they will inherit the earth.

"Blessed are those who hunger and thirst for righteousness, for they will be filled.

"Blessed are the merciful, for they will receive mercy.

"Blessed are the pure in heart, for they will see God.

"Blessed are the peacemakers, for they will be called children of God.

"Blessed are those who are persecuted for righteousness' sake, for theirs is the kingdom of heaven.

"Blessed are you when people revile you and persecute you and utter all kinds of evil against you falsely on my account. Rejoice and be glad, for your reward is great in heaven, for in the same way they persecuted the prophets who were before you.

"You are the salt of the earth; but if salt has lost its taste, how can its saltiness be restored? It is no longer good for anything, but is thrown out and trampled under foot.

"You are the light of the world. A city built on a hill cannot be hid. No one after lighting a lamp puts it under the bushel basket, but on the lampstand, and it gives light to all in the house. In the same way, let your light shine before others, so that they may see your good works and give glory to your Father in heaven.

"Do not think that I have come to abolish the law or the prophets; I have come not to abolish but to fulfill. For truly I tell you, until heaven and earth pass away, not one letter, not one stroke of a letter, will pass from the law until all is accomplished. Therefore, whoever breaks one of the least of these commandments, and teaches others to do the same, will be called least in the kingdom of heaven; but whoever does them and teaches them will be called great in the kingdom of heaven. For I tell you, unless your righteousness exceeds that of the scribes and Pharisees, you will never enter the kingdom of heaven.

"You have heard that it was said to those of ancient times, 'You shall not murder'; and 'whoever murders shall be liable to judgment.' But I say to you that if you are angry with a brother or sister, you will be liable to judgment; and if you insult a brother or sister, you will be liable to the council; and if you say, 'You fool,' you will be liable to the hell of fire. So when you are offering your gift at the altar, if you remember that your brother or sister has something against you, leave your gift there before the altar and go; first be reconciled to your brother or sister, and then come and offer your gift. Come to terms quickly with your accuser while you are on the way to court with him, or your accuser may hand you over to the judge, and the judge to the guard, and you will be thrown into prison. Truly I tell you, you will never get out until you have paid the last penny.

"You have heard that it was said, 'You shall not commit adultery.' But I say to you that everyone who looks at a woman with lust has already committed adultery with her in his heart. If your right eye causes you to sin, tear it out and throw it away; it is better for you to lose one of your members than for your whole body to be thrown into hell. And if your right hand causes you to sin, cut it off and throw it away; it is better for you to lose one of your members than for your whole body to go into hell.

"It was also said, 'Whoever divorces his wife, let him give her a certificate of divorce.' But I say to you that anyone who divorces his wife, except on the ground of unchastity, causes her to commit adultery; and whoever marries a divorced woman commits adultery.

"Again, you have heard that it was said to those of ancient times, 'You shall not swear falsely, but

76

carry out the vows you have made to the LORD.' But I say to you, Do not swear at all, either by heaven, for it is the throne of God, or by the earth, for it is his footstool, or by Jerusalem, for it is the city of the great King. And do not swear by your head, for you cannot make one hair white or black. Let your word be 'Yes, Yes' or 'No, No'; anything more than this comes from the evil one.

"You have heard that it was said, 'An eye for an eye and a tooth for a tooth.' But I say to you, Do not resist an evildoer. But if anyone strikes you on the right cheek, turn the other also; and if anyone wants to sue you and take your coat, give your cloak as well; and if anyone forces you to go one mile, go also the second mile. Give to everyone who begs from you, and do not refuse anyone who wants to borrow from you.

"You have heard that it was said, 'You shall love your neighbor and hate your enemy.' But I say to you, Love your enemies and pray for those who persecute you, so that you may be children of your Father in heaven; for he makes his sun rise on the evil and on the good, and sends rain on the righteous and on the unrighteous. For if you love those who love you, what reward do you have? Do not even the tax collectors do the same? And if you greet only your brothers and sisters, what more are you doing than others? Do not even the Gentiles do the same? Be perfect, therefore, as your heavenly Father is perfect.

"Beware of practicing your piety before others in order to be seen by them; for then you have no reward from your Father in heaven.

"So whenever you give alms, do not sound a trumpet before you, as the hypocrites do in the synagogues and in the streets, so that they may be praised by others. Truly I tell you, they have received their reward. But when you give alms, do not let your left hand know what your right hand is doing, so that your alms may be done in secret; and your Father who sees in secret will reward you.

"And whenever you pray, do not be like the hypocrites; for they love to stand and pray in the synagogues and at the street corners, so that they may be seen by others. Truly I tell you, they have received their reward. But whenever you pray, go into your room and shut the door and pray to your Father who is in secret; and your Father who sees in secret will reward you.

"When you are praying, do not heap up empty phrases as the Gentiles do; for they think that they will be heard because of their many words. Do not be like them, for your Father knows what you need before you ask him.

"Pray then in this way:
Our Father in heaven,
   hallowed be your name.
Your kingdom come.
Your will be done,
   on earth as it is in heaven.
Give us this day our daily bread.
And forgive us our debts,
   as we also have forgiven our debtors.
And do not bring us to the time of trial,
   but rescue us from the evil one.

For if you forgive others their trespasses, your heavenly Father will also forgive you; but if you do not forgive others, neither will your Father forgive your trespasses.

"And whenever you fast, do not look dismal, like the hypocrites, for they disfigure their faces so as to show others that they are fasting. Truly I tell you, they have received their reward. But when you fast, put oil on your head and wash your face, so that your fasting may be seen not by others but by your Father who is in secret; and your Father who sees in secret will reward you.

"Do not store up for yourselves treasures on earth, where moth and rust consume and where thieves break in and steal; but store up for yourselves treasures in heaven, where neither moth nor rust consumes and where thieves do not break in and steal. For where your treasure is, there your heart will be also.

"The eye is the lamp of the body. So, if your eye is healthy, your whole body will be full of light; but if your eye is unhealthy, your whole body will be full of darkness. If then the light in you is darkness, how great is the darkness!

"No one can serve two masters; for a slave will either hate the one and love the other, or be devoted to the one and despise the other. You cannot serve God and wealth.

"Therefore I tell you, do not worry about your life, what you will eat or what you will drink, or about your body, what you will wear. Is not life more than food, and the body more than clothing? Look at the birds of the air; they neither sow nor reap nor gather into barns, and yet your heavenly Father feeds them. Are you not of more value than they? And can any of you by worrying add a single hour to your span of life? And why do you worry about clothing? Consider the lilies of the field, how they grow; they neither toil nor spin, yet I tell you, even Solomon in all his glory was not clothed like one of these. But if God so clothes the grass of the field, which is alive today and tomorrow is thrown into the oven, will he not much more clothe you — you of little faith? Therefore do not worry, saying, 'What will we eat?' or 'What will we drink?' or 'What will we wear?' For it is the Gentiles who strive for all these things; and indeed your heavenly Father knows that you need all these things. But strive first for the kingdom of God and his righteousness, and all these things will be given to you as well.

"So do not worry about tomorrow, for tomorrow will bring worries of its own. Today's trouble is enough for today.

"Do not judge, so that you may not be judged. For with the judgment you make you will be judged, and the measure you give will be the measure you get. Why do you see the speck in your neighbor's eye, but do not notice the log in your own eye? Or how can you say to your neighbor, 'Let me take the speck out of your eye,' while the log is in your own eye? You hypocrite, first take the log out of your own eye, and then you will see clearly to take the speck out of your neighbor's eye.

"Do not give what is holy to dogs; and do not throw your pearls before swine, or they will trample them under foot and turn and maul you.

"Ask, and it will be given you; search, and you will find; knock, and the door will be opened for you. For everyone who asks receives, and everyone who searches finds, and for everyone who knocks, the door will be opened. Is there anyone among you who, if your child asks for bread, will give a stone? Or if the child asks for a fish, will give a snake? If you then, who are evil, know how to give good gifts to your children, how much more will your Father in heaven give good things to those who ask him!

"In everything do to others as you would have them do to you; for this is the law and the prophets.

"Enter through the narrow gate; for the gate is wide and the road is easy that leads to destruction, and there are many who take it. For the gate is narrow and the road is hard that leads to life, and there are few who find it.

"Beware of false prophets, who come to you in sheep's clothing but inwardly are ravenous wolves. You will know them by their fruits. Are grapes gathered from thorns, or figs from thistles? In the same way, every good tree bears good fruit, but the bad tree bears bad fruit. A good tree cannot bear bad fruit, nor can a bad tree bear good fruit. Every tree that does not bear good fruit is cut down and thrown into the fire. Thus you will know them by their fruits.

"Not everyone who says to me, 'LORD, LORD,' will enter the kingdom of heaven, but only the one who does the will of my Father in heaven. On that day many will say to me, 'LORD, LORD, did we not prophesy in your name, and cast out demons in your name, and do many deeds of power in your name?' Then I will declare to them, 'I never knew you; go away from me, you evildoers.'

"Everyone then who hears these words of mine and acts on them will be like a wise man who built his house on rock. The rain fell, the floods came, and the winds blew and beat on that house, but it did not fall, because it had been founded on rock. And everyone who hears these words of mine and does not act on them will be like a foolish man who built his house on sand. The rain fell, and the floods came, and the winds blew and beat against that house, and it fell — and great was its fall!"

Now when Jesus had finished saying these things, the crowds were astounded at his teaching, for he taught them as one having authority, and not as their scribes.

Ethical Implications of the Sermon on the Mount

Lisa Sowle Cahill

Nowhere in New Testament interpretation are exegesis, theology, and ethics bound more closely together than in approaches to Matthew's Sermon on the Mount (Matt. 5–7). When ethical concerns are foremost, the so-called "hard sayings" (Matt. 5:38-48) command attention. . . . Jesus seems both to hold the faithful to impossible standards of concrete action and to break up the foundations of justice on which social cooperation is built. . . .

Undoubtedly the greatest impact of the historical-critical method on ethical interpretations of the Sermon on the Mount has been made by the discovery that the early church expected the imminent return of Jesus, Risen Lord and Judge, to complete the reign of God begun in his lifetime. The questions of the eschatology behind the Sermon and its relevance to the Sermon's continuing meaning have been most prominent in recent discussions of the Sermon's ethics, especially those well-informed by biblical scholarship. Standard typologies of historically and theologically important readings have highlighted the importance of this emergent modern interest. The model proposed by Joachim Jeremias is simple, representative, and of continuing influence. According to this model, the Sermon usually is seen in one of three ways: (1) a perfectionist code, fully in line with the legalism of rabbinic Judaism; (2) an impossible ideal, meant to drive the believer first to desperation, and then to trust in God's mercy; or (3) an "interim ethic" meant for what was ex-

pected to be a brief period of waiting in the end-time, and which is now obsolete. Jeremias adds his own fourth thesis: The Sermon is an indicative depiction of incipient life in the Kingdom of God, which presupposes as its condition of possibility the experience of conversion. . . .

Kingdom Ethics as Relationship and Action

In recent hermeneutics of the Sermon there is a trend to avoid the extremes of Jeremias' first three types, and to appropriate the insights of his fourth by recognizing coherence among several interdependent factors: Matthew's view of Jesus as the Messiah who fulfills Jewish expectations, Jesus' depiction of discipleship in concrete and action-oriented but extreme terms, the Sermon's eschatological "kingdom" language, and traditional Christian views of ethics, both personal and social. These factors often are tied together in some understanding of *converted relationship*. The Sermon on the Mount portrays a new relationship to God . . . , which is epitomized in and somehow made possible for others by Jesus, which individuals actually and presently experience in their own lives and communities, which transforms their relationships so that, like God, they can look even on enemies selflessly, which makes them doers of concrete actions concerned foremost with grasping the situation and meeting the needs of others they affect, and which would be so radical in its fulfillment that fullness never has been experienced. . . .

A key theme of the Sermon's depiction of the kingdom is imitation of God; to act as God does, with forgiveness and mercy, is to live in the kingdom. The Lord's Prayer, an appeal for the fullness of the kingdom, closely associates it with doing on earth the will of the Father (6:10). It is one's forgiveness of neighbor on which one's own forgiveness by God explicitly depends (6:15); the disciple prays to be forgiven as one who also forgives (6:12, 14-15). The purpose of loving even the enemy is to "be sons of your father who is in heaven" (5:45a); if one is to go beyond merely self-gratifying relationships, then one must aim to be as "perfect" in the ways of mercy and forbearance "as your heavenly Father is perfect" (5:48). The command not to judge others' failings (7:1-5) bears

Lisa Sowle Cahill, "The Ethical Implications of the Sermon on the Mount," *Interpretation* 41, no. 1 (April 1987): 144-56.

out the forgiveness theme of the prayer for the kingdom; it is our attitude toward others which will determine God's attitude of judgment or forgiveness toward us. Righteousness in God's eyes is not purity and law-abidingness, but mercifulness effective in compassionate action. Matthew's inclusion of the "Golden Rule" (7:12) urges the disciple to identify with the other, to perceive the other's concrete need as though it were the disciple's, to act toward the other as though the other were oneself. The morally right act is simply but radically the act which demonstrates the forgiving attentiveness to the needs of others disclosed by Jesus as the will of God. Love is defined in Matthew's Sermon as a way of acting, not as an emotion. However, inferable from the deeds done is an attitude toward others which might be characterized as empathy, kindness, generosity, or compassion. With this, the "dilemmas" which an ethic of love is sometimes said to pose, such as the conflict between love and justice or the impasse of a choice between two neighbors, are set aside if not answered. The mandate is not to settle such conflicts in the most prudent or effective way but to enter into them by identifying the needs of those concerned as one's own.

This theme of love as attentive forgiveness fleshes out the concrete meaning of the "hard sayings," including the baffling instruction not to resist the evil one (5:39). Although the precise original meanings of nonresistance and "one who is evil" remain unclear, it can be concluded minimally that the disciple does not approach the enemy or evildoer in hard, resistant, alienating, and self-righteous judgment but in a compassionate desire to meet the needs of wrongdoers and victims as well as possible in the circumstances. The Beatitudes are confirmatory: Those blessed with the kingdom are "poor in spirit" (5:3), "meek" (5:5), "merciful" (5:7), "pure in heart" (5:8), "peacemakers" (5:9), those who "hunger and thirst" for the "righteousness" understood throughout the Sermon as forgiveness, and those who are ready to be persecuted by those who judge by power and status, or even by the law of the scribes and Pharisees (5:10-11, 20). The phrases of the Beatitudes may well have reference to minority social position as well as to discipleship attitudes, and thus fit well with the many sayings of Jesus (in the Sermon, 6:19-21) about

the dangers that wealth and power present to the greater righteousness expected of the disciple. The more position and prestige one has to protect, the less likely one is to enter with compassionate action a situation in which one's assets are required for the well-being of others. Surrounding the Lord's Prayer are admonitions (6:1-8, 16-24) not to pray or do good works for worldly motives, especially in order to increase one's own importance, but rather out of a desire to imitate God's generosity. The often cited and seemingly naïve "lilies of the field" passage can be understood in context as an exhortation not to be caught up anxiously in one's own daily needs but to seek first of all God's kingdom and his righteousness. Action which is righteous the way God's forgiveness and attentive care are righteous is the most basic condition of the goodness experienced in the life of the disciple.

Eschatological Judgment

An obvious next question is what will sustain a compelling connection between relation to God and acts toward others. . . . When the radical, conversion-based injunctions are placed in the context of the three chapters of the Sermon and, more broadly, in that of the Gospel, they derive much of their forcefulness from accompanying warnings of the consequences for those who fall short of the law's fulfillment and of the greater righteousness enjoined by Jesus (5:17, 20). Those who fail "will never enter the kingdom of heaven" (5:20), "shall be liable to judgment" (5:22a), "will be liable to the hell of fire" (5:22), or "thrown into hell" (5:29; cf. 30b).

The insistent pairing of the twin themes of righteous action and judgment is central to Matthew 7; these themes are amplified by those of efficacious prayer and mission. As we have seen, action is an important component of spreading the gospel. It is the life of "good works" which gives "glory to your Father who is in heaven," and by which the disciples will be "salt" and "light" to the world (5:13-16). Doing the good works commended is not a distant ideal but necessary now. "Not every one who says to me 'Lord, Lord,' shall enter the kingdom of heaven, but he who does the will of my Father who is in heaven" (7:21). Although doing what is heard is hard, Jesus assures that "good things" shall be given to those who earnestly ask (7:11). The Sermon's exhortation to pray counteracts exaggerated "gift" interpretations of the kingdom, since the petitioner has a role in securing the blessings from which action springs. The warning not to be taken in by false prophets in sheep's clothing (7:15), or by trees that do not bear good fruit (7:16-20), or by those who perform showy works in Jesus' name (7:22-23), or to build one's house on "sand" by not actually living up to Jesus' words (7:24-27) suggest choice, responsibility, difficulty, and the possibility of delusion in the life of would-be discipleship. The allusions to the "narrow gate" (7:13-14) and the Lord's repudiation of "evildoers" on the "last day" (7:22-23) are explicit references to judgment. . . .

The Sermon on the Mount does not suggest a "social ethics" in any direct or usual sense. It depicts active, personal outflow of a total conversion by virtue of which ordinary religious and moral expectations are shaken to their roots and one is transfixed by Jesus' transparence to the reign of God. Sayings and imperatives with ethical content and even prima facie socio-political implications function most obviously and effectively within the parameters of the Sermon as engaging illustrations of the immediate sphere of committed discipleship. Indeed, the energy of the practical moral life must spring up here: in individual commitment within a supportive community. Martin Hengel argues historically that a fundamental difference between Jesus and the Zealot revolutionaries is that Jesus saw the primary source of evil in the world as the evil in the individual's heart rather than Roman political domination, the priestly aristocracy, or large landowners. Thus the reign of God is not brought about in the first instance by socio-political transformation but by the "transformed heart" which alone "is capable of new human community, of doing good."

Yet, even if the Sermon does not plainly dictate social objectives, it may imply them. It is particularly appropriate to draw out such implications if the realization of the kingdom is understood biblically to span races, cultures, nations, and now also generations. Inasmuch as the twentieth-century disciple has increased capacity to affect whole groups of socially and economically disadvantaged, even oppressed, persons, the broader social duties of discipleship hardly can be ignored. . . . One hardly can forgive another, show mercy in the face of his or her need, and treat the other as oneself would want to be treated, if the other is perceived as alien and approached in terms of gender, race, national, religious, or class stereotypes. To be perfect in one's compassion is to presuppose that such divisions have ceased to exist, along with the institutions which support and feed on them. . . .

Public Language

All social justice interpretations of the Sermon suggest translation into language viable in the larger social order. The Thomistic "natural law" tradition of Roman Catholics, for instance, claims that radical gospel demands support reasonable cooperation toward social justice. This is true both of those who discuss the Sermon at length, such as Hendrick and Jan Lambrecht, and of those more concerned with social problems, such as Pope John XXIII and the U. S. Bishops in their recent pastoral letter, *The Challenge of Peace*. Even without arguing that the Sermon expresses common ideals, its special insights can challenge secular society. A recent volume of the *Bangalore Theological Forum* from India addresses the power of the Sermon's message for non-Christian and even non-Western cultures.

Certainly the Sermon's integral presupposition of discipleship makes moot, from its internal viewpoint, the question whether Christian ethics can be universalized. Even though discipleship may affect the social order, it is still true that the New Testament never presents ethics autonomously. The primary question the sermon poses is not, How can the Christian speak to or affect natural moral values or social justice? nor, In what way does the Christian live differently from others? but rather, What is the fullness of discipleship like when imitation of the Father known in Jesus pervades one's existence? It is a question directed very much from inside an experience of radical commitment, of life in and with the risen Lord. The answer is that discipleship is lived only in the action which identifies the agent with the needs of the other, neighbor or enemy. . . .

Matthew's Parables

Matthew is the Gospel writer who also brings us the parables of the wise and foolish virgins and of the talents. A "parable" is a poetic narrative or saying that explains one thing by stating parallels and similarities to something else. These particular stories told by Jesus show how servants of the Lord are to employ the resources that God gives to them. Such teachings prevent one from thinking that the Sermon on the Mount and similar motifs in the Bible lead to carelessness about practical things or to a retreat from social responsibility for the sake of either "the simple joys of life" or some alleged "purity."

These stories also contain a series of presumptions. They are like an archeological discovery that an anthropologist can study in order to learn about the fabric of an entire civilization. These particular parables, for example, presume that the private ownership of property, the allocation of differing amounts of resources to people of different abilities to manage them, trade in the market, and due reward for good work are proper social metaphors for how God relates to humanity.

Further, justice is not, in these stories, equality; rather, one receives what one deserves according to how one uses responsibly the gifts one has been given for the sake of the Lord. Such points have been questioned by Christians (and others) from time to time, especially by those who focus more exclusively on certain motifs from the Sermon on the Mount and who think that the "love ethic" of the New Testament excludes judgment, accountability, and the possibility of punishment, or only means forgiveness and acceptance.

Every generation that takes such passages of Scripture and such ultimate human dilemmas seriously has to decide how to deal with the perennial questions anew: Are some levels of these parabolic moral issues deontological (and thus right for all times and places), some teleological (and thus to be assessed according to the religious vision of God's final purposes for humanity), and some primarily ethological (and thus variant according to the specific historical and cultural context in which it developed)? If so, how are they to be integrated, so far as they can be, in a particular decision in present understandings?

Leland Ryken, the widely respected evangelical teacher of business ethics, offers an insightful commentary on key assumptions and implications of the "talents" parable in an analysis of the biblical understanding of work, its responsibilities and duties under God.

Matthew 25:1-46 (NRSV)

"Then the kingdom of heaven will be like this. Ten bridesmaids took their lamps and went to meet the bridegroom. Five of them were foolish, and five were wise. When the foolish took their lamps, they took no oil with them; but the wise took flasks of oil with their lamps. As the bridegroom was delayed, all of them became drowsy and slept. But at midnight there was a shout, 'Look! Here is the bridegroom! Come out to meet him.' Then all those bridesmaids got up and trimmed their lamps. The foolish said to the wise, 'Give us some of your oil, for our lamps are going out.' But the wise replied, 'No! there will not be enough for you and for us; you had better go to the dealers and buy some for yourselves.' And while they went to buy it, the bridegroom came, and those who were ready went with him into the wedding banquet; and the door was shut. Later the other bridesmaids came also, saying, 'Lord, lord, open to us.' But he replied, 'Truly I tell you, I do not know you.' Keep awake therefore, for you know neither the day nor the hour.

"For it is as if a man, going on a journey, summoned his slaves and entrusted his property to them; to one he gave five talents, to another two, to another one, to each according to his ability. Then he went away. The one who had received the five talents went off at once and traded with them, and made five more talents. In the same way, the one who had the two talents made two more talents. But the one who had received the one talent went off and dug a hole in the ground and hid his master's money. After a long time the master of those slaves came and settled accounts with them. Then the one who had received the five talents came forward, bringing five more talents, saying, 'Master, you handed over to me five talents; see, I have made five more talents.' His master said to him, 'Well done, good and trustworthy slave; you have been trustworthy in a few things, I will put you in charge of many things; enter into the joy of your master.' And the one with the two talents also came forward, saying, 'Master, you handed over to me two talents; see, I have made two more talents.' His master said to him, 'Well done, good and trustworthy slave; you have been trustworthy in a few things, I will put you in charge of many things; enter into the joy of your master.' Then the one who had received the one talent also came forward, saying, 'Master, I knew that you were a harsh man, reaping where you did not sow, and gathering where you did not scatter seed; so I was afraid, and I went and hid your talent in the ground. Here you have what is yours.' But his master replied, 'You wicked and lazy slave! You knew, did you, that I reap where I did not sow, and gather where I did not scatter? Then you ought to have invested my money with the bankers, and on my return I would have received what was my own with interest. So take the talent from him, and give it to the one with the ten talents. For to all those who have, more will be given, and they will have an abundance; but from those who have nothing, even what they have will be taken away. As for this worthless slave, throw him into the outer darkness, where there will be weeping and gnashing of teeth.'

"When the Son of Man comes in his glory, and all the angels with him, then he will sit on the throne of his glory. All the nations will be gathered before him, and he will separate people one from another as a shepherd separates the sheep from the goats, and he will put the sheep at his right hand and the goats at the left. Then the king will say to those at his right hand, 'Come, you that are blessed by my Father, inherit the kingdom prepared for you from the foundation of the world; for I was hungry and you gave me food, I was thirsty and you gave me something to drink, I was a stranger and you welcomed me, I was naked and you gave me clothing, I was sick and you took care of me, I was in prison and you visited me.' Then the righteous will answer him, 'Lord, when was it that we saw you hungry and gave you food, or thirsty and gave you something to drink? And when was it that we saw you a stranger and welcomed you, or naked and gave you clothing? And when was it that we saw you sick or in prison and visited you?' And the king will answer them, 'Truly I tell you, just as you did it to one of the least of these who are members of my family, you did it to me.' Then he will say to those at his left hand, 'You that are accursed, depart from me into the eternal fire prepared for the devil and his angels; for I was hungry and you gave me no food, I was thirsty and you gave me nothing to drink, I was a stranger and you did not welcome me, naked and you did not give me clothing, sick and in prison and you did not visit me.' Then they also will answer, 'Lord, when was it that we saw you hungry or thirsty or a stranger or naked or sick or in prison, and did not take care of you?' Then he will answer them, 'Truly I tell you, just as you did not do it to one of the least of these, you did not do it to me.' And these will go away into eternal punishment, but the righteous into eternal life."

Work as Stewardship

Leland Ryken

The Christian doctrines that all of life is God's and that God calls people to their work are two mighty assaults against the curse of work. A third Christian doctrine follows naturally from the previous two. It is that the worker is a steward who serves God.

A steward is a person who is entrusted with a master's property. Applied to work, it means that the work we perform in the world is given to us by God. To accomplish our work is to serve God.

The key biblical text is Jesus' parable of the talents (Matt. 25:14-30). The story revolves around a master who entrusted his talents (weights of money) to three stewards before going on a long journey. Two of the stewards invested the money wisely and doubled its amount during their master's absence. The third servant, called "the wicked and slothful servant," hid his entrusted money in the ground. Upon the master's return, the industrious servants were rewarded, while the slothful servant was cast into outer darkness.

This is obviously a metaphor or allegorical story about stewardship in general. What it says about work cannot be overemphasized. At least five principles emerge.

To begin, the parable underscores the doctrine of vocation. God is the sovereign provider of all opportunities, abilities, and time for work. He provides the very materials for work. Having provided the things that make work possible, he calls people to work for him. The implication is clear: everything that makes up the activity we call work

From Leland Ryken, *Work and Leisure in Christian Perspective* (Portland: Multnomah Press, 1987), pp. 221-24.

is a gift from God. Work is owned by God and lent to his creatures.

Second, the expectations of God are clear — he expects service. The worker is a servant, actively working to produce something for his or her master. Work is thus a duty imposed by God on his creatures. Laziness and inactivity are harshly judged. We might say that the goal is work at full capacity.

Third, work becomes the arena of creaturely choice. Once the stewards have been entrusted with their master's wealth, it is up to their choice and initiative to do something with it. Moral responsibility is a necessary part of work, once we grant the premise that the worker is a steward.

Furthermore, God judges his creatures on the basis of their service. Good servants are rewarded, though not with conventional standards of reward. By contrast, the unprofitable servant is banished from God's sight and the joyful community. What matters most is obviously what the master thinks about the service and the work of his servants. The world's assessment of the servants' work is not even mentioned.

Finally, the parable of the talents reverses the customary view of the rewards of work. In the parable, the reward of the faithful stewards is the approval of their master. Financial rewards do not even enter the picture. Instead the master promises that because the workers "have been faithful over a little, I will set you over much" and he invites them to "enter into the joy of your master." This is obviously a picture of heavenly reward for those who have served God by their stewardship.

Some Practical Results of Viewing Work as a Stewardship

Several important ideas emerge from the principle that work is essentially a form of stewardship in which the worker serves God with the work that God provides. One is that work is a gift. God gives the materials for the worker and the very ability of the worker to perform the work. Gratitude for work is the natural response. To complain about a gift we have received has always been near the top of the list of ignominious behavior. Complaining about the gift of work is no exception.

The perspective of stewardship also affects our attitude toward the "ownership" of work. When work began to be viewed in primarily economic terms with the arrival of the industrial revolution, it became customary to look upon work as something the worker owns and sells to the highest bidder. As alternatives to that view, capitalism often operates on the premise that the employer owns the work of people (since work is a means of production), while socialism operates on the premise that society owns work. But the Christian view of the worker as steward suggests something truly revolutionary: God is the rightful owner of human work. There is a sense in which workers offer their work back to God.

The idea that work is a service to God also revolutionizes conventional attitudes about the goal or reward of work. Our whole cultural situation encourages us to think of our work as something we do for ourselves, our employer, or the public we serve. While we ask, "What's in it for me?" modern notions of accountability and job performance have also made us obsessed with pleasing the boss or the public. But where do we hear about pleasing God as the primary aim of work?

When we turn to the New Testament, we find an emphasis that sounds strange to modern ears:

> Whatever your task, work heartily, as serving the Lord and not men, knowing that from the Lord you will receive the inheritance as your reward; you are serving the Lord Christ. (Col. 3:23-24)

> Be obedient to those who are your earthly masters . . . as to Christ; not in the way of eyeservice, as men-pleasers, but as servants of Christ, doing the will of God from the heart, rendering service with a good will as to the Lord and not to men. (Eph. 6:5-7)

Our secular culture lacks the antennae by which to understand such a view of work, and I fear that Christians today find it just as foreign to their thinking.

It did not seem foreign to the original Protestants. Luther said that "the life of all Christians is intended for the eyes of God alone. . . . It is enough that our action is intended to satisfy and to glorify the One who sees it." The same view is expressed in a poem a young Puritan wrote on the occasion of his twenty-third birthday. John Milton's seventh sonnet opens with self-rebuke at his lack of achievement to date. But the consolation expressed in the famous ending of the poem is based on the idea of work as stewardship to God:

All is, if I have grace to use it so,
As ever in my great task-master's eye.

The most plausible interpretation of the lines is this: "All that matters is that I have the grace to use my time in such a way that I am always conscious of living in my great taskmaster's presence." The evocative epithet "my great task-master" sums up the Puritan consciousness of working for God. The identity of the worker, in this view, comes from one's relationship to God, not from the prestige or financial rating of the joy or task.

This fits in well with the distinctive contribution of Calvin to the history of work: he made the glory of God the goal of work. In the words of a modern historian,

Calvin's contention was that a person's body . . . is not his own but is God's. Thus any talents he has in the performing of his work came not from himself but from God and should therefore be used for God's enhancement and not his own. All should be done to the glory of God. Work, then, should be discharged in this spirit of glorification, of duty, and of service to Him through service to fellow men.

Here, in fact, is one of the antidotes to the syndrome of overwork that characterizes the contemporary work scene. It is hard to imagine God being glorified by the type of strain some people bring upon themselves as they pursue the advancement of their career or a lifestyle that requires overwork.

Toward a Christian Theology of Work

The first Christian doctrine that underlies a Christian theology of work is creation. Made in the image of a God who himself works, people were created to work. As originally given by God to the human race, work was a blessing. It gave purpose to life, even in paradise.

When the human race fell, work became a curse. God himself imposed this quality on work as a punishment for human sin. As a result, we do not have to apologize for finding many of our tasks unpleasant or burdensome. Christianity takes a realistic approach to work.

But work can be redeemed from many of the effects of the fall. The key elements in that redemption are a realization that common work in the world bears God's approval, the belief that God calls us to our work, and an awareness that we are stewards who serve God with the work he has entrusted to us.

Luke's Poor

The New Testament begins with several different accounts of the same story. They share much, but a pluralism is built into Christianity from the start. Matthew is concerned to show the continuities, and thereby to highlight the discontinuities, between the covenant of Moses and its radical renewal in Jesus Christ. Mark emphasizes the relation of the "non-pious" to God and hints that the "insiders" do not always get the main point.

Luke, the author of both the third Gospel and the Acts of the Apostles, refers often to matters of wealth and poverty and accents the fact that Jesus places special obligations on well-educated and well-to-do people. He emphasizes those parts of Jesus' teachings that warn against preoccupation with gain to the neglect of obedience and the ethical life. He is very critical of people who have plenty, who put their basic trust in material things or fail to share what they have with the needy.

More than the other Gospels, Luke's account has evoked intense debates over the centuries in regard to Christianity's understanding of wealth and poverty. Texts from Luke were used to argue for the necessity of communities where private property was abolished. They also inspired many to give to charity. In the nineteenth century, they prompted American Christians to develop the "Social Gospel" movement, which had great influence on the "Progressive Era" and, later, the "New Deal."

More recently, these texts have been used with Marxist modes of social analysis to interpret economic conditions in developing countries and the relations between the richer and the poorer lands. After all, Marx got his famous principle "from each according to his ability and to each according to his need" from Luke, and he wove it into his theory of the inevitable struggle of the social classes. Post-Marxist social analysis has recognized the reality of conflict but has doubted the reading of either the Bible's treatment of "rich" and "poor" or contemporary social conditions through Marxist glasses. These post-Marxist views accent the dependence of economic well-being on the quality of familial, educational, legal, cultural, technological, and political structures, and not on class structures alone. To illuminate these debates, we turn to one of the most influential contemporary scholars who treats these matters, Bruce Malina.

Wealth and Poverty in the New Testament World

Bruce J. Malina

Many Christians seek to take their moral cues for daily living from the Bible. The words and examples presented in New Testament books are seen to offer direct religious sustenance for twentieth-century people intent upon pleasing God. Such twentieth-century people find themselves in a world often assessed in terms of Gross National Product, where quantity orientation, judging one's own success in terms of numbers, is a normal occurrence. Human worth often hangs in the balance with countable money: the cost of a quality education, of necessary hospital surgery, of a house and clothing that match one's status, job searches in terms of income rather than satisfaction. When persons from this sort of background come to read the Bible, the rescue they often seek from God is in terms of the right amount of money at the right time for their own purposes. After all, the Lord exalts those of low degree, fills the hungry with good things, and sends the rich away empty (Luke 1:51-52). On the other hand, there are very well-to-do people who consider themselves "good Christians," yet would have their fellows believe they are serving God, not mammon, and who would scarcely give a thought to selling all they have and giving it to the poor. The question of the rich and poor is often settled in the minds of pious Christians of the rich persuasion by the insight that the poor are poor because they are lazy, or unfortunate, or both; and the poor know the rich are rich because they have had the

B. J. Malina, "Wealth and Poverty in the New Testament and Its World," *Interpretation* 41, no. 4 (Oct. 1987): 354-66.

breaks. Yet fortunately, most Americans still belong to a rather dwindling middle class, and the Bible has no word to the middle class. Why?

The purpose of this article is to suggest that in the eastern Mediterranean in New Testament times, "rich" or "wealthy" as a rule meant "avaricious, greedy," while "poor" referred to persons scarcely able to maintain their honor or dignity. Thus the words are not opposites and really refer to two qualitatively different spheres. Secondarily, in non-moral contexts, the "wealthy" were contrasted with the "needy" in terms of access and control of the necessities of life which were available to everyone. However, the moral problem was the essential wickedness of the wealthy who chose to serve Greed rather than God. . . .

I. Linguistic Collocation

A first step in interpreting the meaning of "poor" and "rich" or "wealthy" would be to consider the lexical company that the words keep. This is called their linguistic collocation. The words in question are used alone or in the company of other words that may clarify their ranges of meanings. For example, from passages in which the word "poor" is used without further description, we simply cannot get any idea of what the authors are referring to except by reading our own ideas into their words (e.g., Matt. 19:21; 26:9, 11; Mark 10:21; 14:5, 7; Luke 18:22; John 12:5-8; 13:29; Rom. 15:26; 2 Cor. 6:10; 8:9; 9:9; Gal. 2:10). Of course the same holds for the word "rich" (e.g., Luke 14:12; 16:1; Eph. 2:4; Rev. 2:9; 13:16).

On the other hand, there is also a series of passages in which the word "poor" is used in the company of other words that describe the condition of the person who is labeled "poor." Thus, Luke 4:18 has a quotation from Isaiah in which the poor are those imprisoned, blind, debt-ridden. Matthew 5:3-5, along with Luke 6:20-21, have the poor ranked with those who hunger, thirst, and mourn. Matthew 11:4-5 lists the blind, lame, lepers, deaf, and the dead with the poor, while Luke 14:13-21 has the maimed, lame, and the blind. Further, Mark 12:42-43 and Luke 21:2-3 speak of a poor widow, and Luke 16:20-22 tells of the poor Lazarus who was hungry and full of sores, hence ill, leprous. Finally James 2:3-6 points out the shabbily dressed poor man as truly powerless, while Revelation 3:17 considers the poor to be wretched, pitiable, blind, naked — categories similar to the list in Matthew 25:34-36, where we find the hungry, thirsty, stranger, naked, and imprisoned (but not poor!). These adjacent descriptions of the poor point to the "poor" person as one who has undergone some unfortunate personal history or circumstance.

Within these collocations, the "poor" rank among those who cannot maintain their inherited status due to circumstances that befall them and their family, such as debt, being in a foreign land, sickness, death (widow), or some personal physical accident. Consequently, from the viewpoint of the vast majority of people, the poor would not be a permanent social class but a sort of revolving class of people who unfortunately cannot maintain their inherited status. Day laborers, landless peasants, and beggars born into such situations, on the other hand, are not poor for economic reasons. Anyone who worked for a daily wage was considered "in need" and "poor" by minority, wealthy elites (e.g., Philo, *The Special Laws* IV, 195-96; LCL VIII, 128-29), mainly because of the precariousness of such a person's social position.

As for the wealthy, there is likewise a series of passages in which the word "rich" or equivalents are used with other words, giving indication of the quality of the rich condition. Thus in Mark 12:41-44 and Luke 21:1-4: Rich people control an abundance of resources from which they can give large sums and are contrasted with a poor widow. The rich are presumed by non-elites to have ready access to God (Mark 10:23-24, Matt. 19:23-24, and Luke 18:23-25) since they do in fact have ready access to the human powers that be, for example, Joseph of Arimathea (Matt. 27:57). In Luke 1:53 "rich" is the opposite of "hungry" and parallel with "mighty, proud"; similarly Luke 6:24-25: The rich are already consoled; they are among those who are full now. Luke 12:16 speaks of a rich man in a context of covetousness, that is, greed: "Take heed, and beware of all covetousness; for a man's life does not consist in the abundance of his possessions" (v. 15); this person "is not rich toward God," but lays up treasure for himself, that is, is greedy (v. 21). Thus Luke accuses the Pharisees of greed ("lovers of money," 16:14) in a context about serving God or Greed. Further, in Luke

16:19-31, a rich, well, satisfied man with a large family of brothers is contrasted with the poor, suffering, ill, and family-less Lazarus. Finally, Luke 19:1-10 tells of the rich Zachaeus who as chief tax collector takes from the poor and defrauds.

In addition 1 Timothy 6:10 points to the truism of greed as the root of all social evils. The author notes that the rich in this world are haughty, set their hopes on uncertain riches; instead these should be like God in being benevolent, liberal, and generous (1 Tim. 6:17; 2 Tim. 3:1-4 ranks avarice second after selfishness). James 1:10-11 would have the rich man face the fact that he will die while in pursuit of riches, hence act accordingly, "humbly." God's chosen, the poor, rich in faith and heirs of the kingdom, are overlooked in favor of the rich who oppress, hail to court, publicly shame the name "invoked over you" (James 2:6-7). Perhaps the fullest description of the moral quality of being rich is in James 5:1-7: The rich trust in their perishable possessions — in garments, gold, silver, fields, amassed goods; they keep back wages of laborers who work for them and harvest their fields, defraud them, condemn the righteous, kill the righteous. In Revelation 3:17-18, the rich are those who prosper, while needing nothing; they are opposed to the wretched, pitiable, poor, blind, and naked. They rank with the kings of the earth, great men, generals, and the strong (Rev. 6:15). Those presently growing rich are the merchants *(emporoi)*, those with ships at sea (Rev. 18:3, 15, 19).

Now if we take all these adjacent descriptions of the rich and group them in terms of what they have in common, it would seem that they became rich as the result of their own covetousness, or greed, or that of their ancestors. For typical of the rich is the amassing of surplus, of having more than enough and more than others. Significantly, one was presumed to have become rich by depriving others, defrauding and eliminating others, prospering by having others become wretched, pitiable, ill, blind, and naked. Thus the rich rank with persons who wield power for their own aggrandizement, such as kings and generals, or with the haughty and others who overstep their proper social rank, such as merchants.

On a morally neutral level, as frequently in the Wisdom books, the rich and poor simply mark the extremes of the social body in terms of elite and non-elite status. But in a moral context, rich meant powerful due to greed, avarice, and exploitation, while poor meant weak due to inability to maintain one's inherited social station. Consequently, the opposite of rich would not necessarily be the economically poor. In the perception of people in peasant society, the majority of people are neither rich nor poor; rather all are equal in that each has a status to maintain in some honorable way. "The Lord makes poor and makes rich" (1 Sam. 2:7). Personal value is not economic, but a matter of lineage. In this context rich and poor characterize two poles of society, two minority poles — the one based on the ability to maintain elite status, the other based on the inability to maintain one's inherited status of any rank. Why this range of meanings?

To begin with, words are rooted in social systems; they realize meanings from social systems. . . . It is the meanings of first-century Mediterranean social systems that are realized by means of words in texts from that time and place. It is thus the social system that requires us to look at the greedy and the weak rather than the economically rich and poor, for ancient Mediterranean ways of perceiving and judging differ markedly from our own. A comparative look at social structures as well as a consideration of some first-century stereotypes will illustrate the point.

II. Comparing Social Systems

It is common to distinguish four basic social institutions or structures. Social institutions or social structures are the ways or means humans use to realize basic human values. The basic social institutions are generally called kinship, economics, politics, and religion. Briefly, kinship is about naturing and nurturing people; it forms the structure of human belonging. Economics is about provisioning a group of people; it forms a society's structure for adapting to a given environment. Politics looks to effective collective action and forms the vertical organizational structure of a society. Finally religion deals with the overarching order of existence, that is, with ultimate meaning; it provides reasons for what exists and the ways of understanding that develop those reasons. Since religion forms the meaning system of a society, it

will feed back and forward into the kinship, economic, and political systems, unifying the whole by means of some explicit or implicit ideology.

Biblical literature developed exclusively within the contexts of kinship and politics. It comes from a world where there was domestic religion and political religion, as well as domestic economy and political economy. Thus biblical authors never spoke of economics purely and simply; their language was never used to express systems of meaning deriving from technology (or the means of production). The problem was not with their language, since speakers of modern Hebrew and Greek do quite well in articulating economic and religious theory. The point is that during the period from which the biblical writings date, the existing social systems simply did not have free-standing and formal religion and economics. The vocabulary and system of distinctions in the theology of the Bible, for example, worked in kinship and politics. The language of covenant and law was and is derivative of politics, just as the language of worship was and is derivative of kinship and political forms of behavior. There is no developed biblical terminology descriptive of market economies or economic theories and those abstract meanings rooted in them. Hence, biblical literature reveals a vocabulary and syntax employed to realize a range of meanings expressing belonging and power. Belonging is the social dimension rooted in kinship, while power is the social dimension rooted in politics. On the other hand, biblical literature reveals almost nothing of abstract reasoning, the social dimension typical of formal religious institutions, and of course nothing for formal economic theory. Rather, religion and its meanings are made to work through belonging and power rather than on their own terms since these terms are nearly always inflated in the form of wild assertions and exaggerations: Witness the varied stories about the intervention of God or the gods. Moreover, economic dimensions of society have to be converted through and into belonging (e.g., wealth is meaningless unless convertible into honor, and thus has no focus in and of itself). This embedded economic focus is replicated in the prohibition of interest for loans within the social body (e.g., Deut. 23:19-20). Similarly, in the Hellenistic and Roman periods, this lack of focus reveals itself in disdain for the status and role of merchant.

If all this appears somewhat abstract, consider the concrete case of the poor and the wealthy in Mediterranean village society. There wealthy, "sonless" women whose husbands have died are referred to as "poor widows." In what sense are they poor? Surely not in any economic sense. Similarly, in antiquity, the label "poor" was applied, in particular, to the vast majority of the people in any city-state who, having no claim to the income of a large estate, lacked that degree of leisure and independence regarded as essential to the life of a gentleman. . . . "[T]he poor" as recipients of a wealthy man's benevolence would primarily be unfortunate members of his own class . . . "some ought to be poor" (Aristotle) and . . . "deserve misfortune" (Cicero). If the word "poor" presently refers mainly to economics, that simply reflects our contemporary social arrangement, and says nothing about any other society. To find out what noneconomic "poor" might refer to, we will have to examine the basic social structures people use to realize and express their values. Such an exercise should enable us to see that the designation "poor" takes on a different meaning, a meaning determined by the social structure considered primary in the culture in question.

As a general rule, in both past and present societal arrangements, one or another of the basic four institutions described above maintains primacy over the others. Thus, for example:

(1) In . . . applied Marxism of the [former] Soviet Union and the Peoples' Republic of China, kinship, religion, and economics are determined by the political institutions: Politicians of one sort or another govern.

(2) In the United States and to a far lesser extent in Western Europe, kinship, religion, and politics are dominated by economics, that is, the norms of kinship, religion, and politics are (more clearly influenced by wealth). . . .

(3) In Latin America and most Mediterranean countries, religion, politics, and economics are subservient to kinship, that is, the norms of religion, politics, and economics are determined by the kinship institution. Here well-born persons rooted in the "best" families control society in their role of patrons. Latin American Liberation Theology, for example, is [largely] rooted in the

practical attempt to dislodge economics from kinship and embed it in politics.

(4) Finally, in contemporary Islamic republics in the present and in medieval Christendom, kinship, economics, and politics are governed by religion, that is, the norms of kinship, economics, and politics are determined by [religious law]. . . .

In each instance, the societal arrangement determines the meaning of specific concepts. The overriding desire for more and more goods changes its meaning in a society with the political institution in the ascendance (avarice), or with the economic institution as central (profit), or with a focal kinship institution (covetousness), or with the religious institution as paramount (blessing). Note how the meaning of the word "poor" changes when used of the oppressed (the politically unable: e.g., in the Exodus the empowerment of the poor; during the Israelite monarchy, the consolation of the poor) the indigent (the economically unable), the sick and outcast (the kinship unable: those who cannot maintain their honor by themselves), and the unbelieving — and therefore ignorant (the religiously unable: note that in Islam, unbelief is ignorance). Metaphorically speaking, all such "poor" people are marginal, at the margins of their social group. The problem for understanding specific concepts is the margin in question: Which is these margins are considered socially significant?

III. Who Were "The Rich"?

Given the model of four basic social institutions (kinship, economics, politics, and religion), economics in Mediterranean antiquity was embedded in kinship or in polity and was not a freestanding adaptive institution. Rather crudely put, the Roman Empire was structurally much like applied Soviet Marxism, while the rest of the area was structurally much like Latin American rural realities of large landed tracts owned by paternal families and served by client villagers. These are embedded economies. An embedded economy means that economic goals, roles, production, hiring, firing, planning, and the like, are determined by kinship or political considerations, either alone or primarily and not purely or primarily on the basis of "economic" considerations. . . .

[In the ancient view] wealth is meant to meet the needs of human living. It is to be used with contentment and satisfaction. Consequently, wealth is meant simply as another means for acquiring and maintaining honor. When the acquisition of wealth is an end, not a means, then the person dedicated to wealth acquisition is inherently demented, vicious, evil. Not a few of the ancients remark on this aspect of human experience. Pseudo-Pelagius (presumably ca. 400) remarked: "For persons to cease to be greedy, they must cease to be wealthy" (*On Wealth* II, PLSupp I, 1381), or again: "It is scarcely possible for a rich person to keep from committing crimes" (XX, 4; PLSupp I, 1417).

In other words, the rich might be presumed to be wicked on the basis of a series of commonly held, stereotypical assessments. Gallagher marshals a range of the cultural cues that controlled perception among second-century Mediterraneans, and thus facilitated anti-introspective judgments: that genealogy can be deduced from one's subsequent behavior and character (and behavior/character offer solid indication of one's genealogy); that social standing necessarily determines one's abilities or lack of them (and ability or inability is clear proof of one's social standing); that a person who does something for all mankind [is of divine birth (and divine birth points to benefits for all mankind)]; that kings necessarily perform valuable actions of benefit to many (hence actions that benefit many point to some royal agent). Further, magic is effective only among the ignorant and immoral; the ignorant and immoral are addicted to magic; magicians are fearsome, threatening, and suspicious persons; hence fearsome, threatening, and suspicious persons are almost certainly magicians. Good and honest persons are preoccupied with continuity and antiquity — they respect the past; hence those who advocate a break with the past, who advocate something brand new are rebellious, outsiders and deviants. In our case in point, if a person is wealthy, he or she is wicked or the heir of wicked people.

Plutarch, certainly a well-situated person by any economic standards, did not consider himself "wealthy." Rather he mocked "the wealthy" and dissociated himself and his coterie from that group because of their need for ostentation ("they consider wealth as non-wealth and a blind alley and a dead end unless it has witnesses and spectators as a tragedy. But the rest of us . . ." (*Table Talk V 5*, 679, A-C; LCL VIII, 408-11). In the treatise *On Love of Wealth* (LCL VII) he comments at length on the wealthy, noting the following stereotypical characteristics of that category of people:

(1) They put everything away under lock and seal or lay it out with money lenders and agents; thus wealthy persons go on amassing and pursuing new wealth, wrangling with their servants, farmers, and debtors (525A; 17).

(2) The wealthy are either avaricious or prodigal. The greedy miser feels compelled to acquire more and more, yet is forbidden to enjoy the acquisitions; he is miserly, unsocial, selfish, heedless of friends, indifferent to civic demands. The avaricious in general suffer hardships, lose sleep, engage in trade, chase after legacies, and truckle to others (525C; 19). Thus the greedy rich kill and destroy people without using what they destroy, and they take from others what they cannot use themselves. What they pass on to their heirs is their avarice and meanness, a warped character and no formation in basic humanity (526 B.C.; 25).

(3) The heirs of the greedy rich "catch the taint of avarice directly from their fathers," they assimilate their father's life, steal before their father is dead, then upon death become transformed persons; "There is instead interrogation of servants, inspection of ledgers, the casting up of accounts with steward and debtors, and occupation and worry that deny him his luncheon and drive him to the bath at night" (526EF; 27-29). Thus, avaricious, wealthy fathers take away leisure and freedom from their heirs, offering overwhelming and overpowering wealth.

(4) The prodigal or profligate rich persons, on the other hand, are legal blackmailers, and pursuers of legacies. They cheat and carry on intrigues and schemes, they keep track of living friends but put their wealth to no use. Yet prodigals call a truce to their acquisitiveness once they are affluent and well-provided for (525F; 23). While they too kill and destroy people as they accumulate wealth, unlike the greedy they use what they destroy (and so are better than the miserly).

(5) In between the greedy and the profligate rich are those politically well-situated, who accumulate vast amounts of wealth for political utility:

"Let kings and royal stewards and those who would be foremost in their cities and hold office engage in money-getting." These are motivated by ambition (love of honor), pretension, and vain glory and need the wealth to give banquets, bestow favors, pay court, send presents, support armies, buy gladiators (525D; 21).

What characterizes all the wealthy is their lack of contentment, of satisfaction — and this at the expense of others. Even apart from New Testament voices, such evaluations of the rich are not rare in the time and area notably from people labeled Stoics and Cynics. Such generalizations can help modern interpreters see what their first-century counterparts may have seen because of how they stereotypically saw, and one of the things they saw was the necessary wickedness of the wealthy. For this reason, it is not adequate to say that the biblical texts witness a recognition of the dangers of wealth, as modern theology often has it. Rather those texts reveal a pervasive conviction of the wickedness of the wealthy (e.g., further mirrored in the Council of Carthage in 401: "All the emperors must be requested, because of the affliction of the poor (*pauperes*) with whose suffering the church is enervated without intermission, that they delegate for them defenders against the power of the wealthy (*diuites*) with the supervision of the bishops" (CCL, CCLIX, 202).

IV. The Purpose of Wealth

True wealth, that deriving ultimately from the domestic economy as Aristotle noted, was meant to maintain human beings in a sufficiently contented way of life. People were to be satisfied with having their needs met, even in noble style. This was *autarkeia* (see 2 Cor. 9:8; Phil. 4:11; 1 Tim. 6:6; the independence of 1 Thess. 4:12). As a rule, anyone could meet this goal, as Jesus presumes in the parable of Matthew 6:25-32 and as Stoics and Cynics alike insisted. Here wealth was simply another means for acquiring and maintaining honor. Yet due to the hoarding and avarice of the wealthy, the poor were deprived of the honor due them. This is an especially acute problem for Jesus and his preaching of the restoration of Israel. As Philo noted, jubilee meant restoring "the prosperity of the past" to the present (*De Spec. Leg.* II, 122;

LCL VII, 378-79). Given the perception of limited good and an embedded economy, Jesus' injunction to give one's goods to the poor is not about self-impoverishment but about redistribution of wealth; and motives for giving to the poor are not rooted in self-satisfying charity but in God-ordained, socially required restitution.

With the rise of the first urban Christians outside of Palestine, the problem is no longer restitution and redistribution but the "conversion" of the wicked wealthy. Here the wealthy are to share their goods with their fellow Christians. This easily fit into Hellenistic common sense. As Plutarch remarked, the felicity of wealth is to parade one's possessions as in a theater, before spectators and witnesses: "With no one to see or look on, wealth becomes lackluster indeed and bereft of radiance" (*One's Love of Wealth*, 528A; LCL VII, 37). But greed was out. Even for the Hellenist, that other wealth deriving from trading, interest taking, and any other form rooted in acquiring money for the use of money was essentially suspicious, if not downright perverted. Such wealth is an end, not a means to the good life (see Aristotle, *Politics*, III, 12-20, 1257a-58a; LCL 40-49). The pursuit, acquisition, and maintenance of such wealth is inherently demented, vicious, and evil — witness the wealthy.

In sum, adequate reflection on New Testament scenarios peopled by the wealthy and the poor would require attention to the social system of the time and place. That social system had its focus on kinship and politics; it urged the perception of limited good and contentment with readily available necessities of life. Cultural criteria of the day had the word "poor" pointing to the socially impotent, while the label "rich" or "wealthy" attached to the greedy and avaricious.

Paul and the Letters

The debate over what is meant in the New Testament by "the rich" and "the poor" leads us to the letters of Paul and other early New Testament writers, for many of them lived in the world assumed by Acts. The question of the "communism" of the church portrayed in Acts has been especially debated. All serious observers agree that it was some kind of a communitarianism of distribution, and not one of planned common production. Beyond the fact that they saw the necessity of developing some sort of cooperative alliance and bonded mutuality beyond the family and outside of political control, it is not clear exactly what kind of an economic association was involved.

Obviously, complex economic organizations independent of the local or the royal household (such as corporations, stock exchanges, etc.) had not yet been invented, although certain partnerships were legal and a number of religious groups and cults were in existence that had distinctive forms of membership and ways of practicing economic discipline or giving. These, however, were almost always limited by class and status. In contrast, many early church members were people of means, some were quite poor, while most (for whom we have records) seem to have been drawn from the emerging urban classes in the crafts and trades; but that does not seem to be a central factor in membership or policy. No New Testament writer expected these factors to change by political strategy. The church was not an interest group, a political party, a commune, or a soup kitchen. It was a new, sociologically inclusive, morally and spiritually demanding, mutually supportive movement with, as yet, indistinct forms of organization.

We know that Paul collected funds from the various churches outside old Palestine to help the poor Christians in Jerusalem. He also claimed certain economic rights for himself and for others. Paul's letters to the new churches mention these things; but they do not focus on economic matters even in the ways we have seen in the Gospels, and there is no single economic perspective present in them. Still, they reveal much about how people who knew God through Jesus Christ thought God wanted people to relate to one another. Inevitably, these relations have economic implications.

In the following essay, the church historian Justo Gonzalez argues that we can best understand the events described in Acts if we see them in relation to the efforts of Paul and the authors of other early letters to form congregations faithful to the "new covenant."

From the Jesus Movement to the Urban Christians

Justo Gonzalez

. . . . Did the early Christians practice the sort of commonality described here, or is it a fictional reconstruction of the life of the early church on the part of the author? Some scholars have held the latter, arguing that what is described here is too close to the ideal community of certain Hellenistic traditions — the Pythagorean in particular — and that it is therefore no more than an attempt to depict the early Christian church as an ideal community. . . .

Another common interpretation of these passages in Acts must be mentioned. According to this interpretation, the early church did indeed have all things in common at the beginning, but this practice was soon abandoned. Usually, this interpretation includes the notion — with no basis in the texts themselves — that at least one of the reasons the Christian community in Jerusalem was poor and Paul spent so much effort on its relief was precisely the improvidence implied in this failed communistic experiment. This view is succinctly expressed in one of the biblical commentaries most commonly used today by preachers in the United States: "Whatever may have been the extent of this 'communistic' experiment at Jerusalem, it appears very soon to have broken down, first, perhaps on account of the dissension between 'Hellenists' and 'Hebrews' (6:1), and second, because the administrators who had been appointed as a result of the dispute had been driven

from the city by the Jews. Probably also the eager expectation of the Parousia led to improvidence for the future, so that the Jerusalem community was always poor."

In order to respond both to the "idyllic fiction" view and to the "economic disaster" interpretation, we have to begin by clarifying the commonality of goods to which Acts refers. First of all, the notion that people simply went out and sold all they had in order to share it with the rest is built on an incorrect interpretation of the Greek grammar. The Greek language has two forms of the past tense. One, the imperfect, indicates a continuing past action. The other, the aorist, refers to an action completed once and for all. In the texts under discussion, all verbs appear in the imperfect. Therefore, what the text says is not exactly that "they sold their possessions and goods and distributed them to all, as any had need" (Acts 2:45), but rather that they continued doing this or, as the New American Standard Bible says, "They began selling their property and possessions, and were sharing them with all, as any might have need."

The use of the imperfect tense also points to a major difference between the community described in these texts and the Hellenistic and other communes, including that of Qumran, with which it has been compared. Here the community of goods is not the guiding principle. No matter how much Luke's Gospel has made of renunciation, what is described in Acts is a community where people relinquish their possessions, not for the sake of renunciation, but for the sake of those in need. In both passages under discussion the need of the recipients plays an important role. The goal is not an abstract or dogmatic notion of unity nor a principle of purity and renunciation but meeting the needs of others.

It is inevitable in such a community that those who are most generous, such as Barnabas, will arouse the jealousy of others such as Ananias and Sapphira. Yet the very fact that the book of Acts tells the story of both Barnabas's generosity and the deception of Ananias and Sapphira immediately after describing the community of goods indicates that this is neither an attempt to paint the early community in idyllic tones, nor to describe a dogmatically communistic commune. Peter clearly tells Ananias (Acts 5:4) that he was under no obligation to sell his property, and that having

Justo L. Gonzalez, "The New Testament Koinonia," *Faith and Wealth: A History of Early Christian Ideas on the Origin, Significance, and Use of Money* (New York: Harper & Row, 1990), pp. 80-88.

sold it he did not have to bring the proceeds to the community. Thus Acts describes an imperfect community with its share of liars and jealousy. In chapter 6 the conflict between the Hellenists and the Aramaic speakers over the distribution of relief to the widows of each group will be further proof of the imperfect nature of this community. The self-understanding of this group, however, is such that "no one said that the things which he possessed was his own." Yet, the actual working out of the sharing that this implied depended both on the needs of those who had no possessions and on the free will to share on the part of the more fortunate.

As we look further at the description of this community in Acts we must pay close attention to the word *koinonía,* by which this community is described in Acts 2:42. The Revised Standard Version and the New American Standard Bible translate it as "fellowship," and the Jerusalem Bible as "brotherhood." This is the common understanding of this word, which is usually taken to refer to the inner disposition of goodwill — "fellowship" — toward other members of the group. Thus taken, what Acts 2:42 says is simply that there were good relationships within the community.

Yet *koinonía* means much more that that. It also means partnership, as in a common business venture. In this way Luke uses the related term *koinonós,* member of a *koinonía,* for in Luke 5:10 we are told that the sons of Zebedee were *koinionoí* with Peter, meaning that they were business partners. The same usage appears outside the New Testament, sometimes in very similar contexts. *Koinonía* means first of all, not fellowship in the sense of good feelings toward each other, but sharing. It is used in that sense throughout the New Testament, both in connection with material goods and in other contexts. In Philippians 3:10, what the Revised Standard Version translates as "share his sufferings" actually says "know the *koinonía* of his sufferings." In 1 Corinthians 10:16, Paul says, "The cup of blessing which we bless, is it not a participation in the blood of Christ?" The term that the Revised Standard Version translates here as "participation," with a footnote explaining that it could also be translated as "communion," is *koinonía.* Paul's letter to the Philippians, which acknowledges receipt of a gift, begins with words in which Paul is thanking the Philippians for their partnership and sharing with him. In 1:5, he says that he is thankful for the Philippians' *koinonía,* and two verses later he declares that they are "joint *koinonoí*" of grace with him, that is, common owners or sharers. At the end of the epistle, he says that they have shared in his trouble (4:14), and the term he uses could be translated as "co-koinonized." All of this leads to the unique partnership "in giving and receiving" that he has enjoyed with the church of the Philippians (4:15), and once again the word he uses literally means "koinonized." In short, *koinonía* is much more than a feeling of fellowship; it involves sharing goods as well as feelings.

Returning to Acts 2:42, it is clear that *koinonía* there is much more than fellowship: "They devoted themselves to the apostles' teaching and *koinonía,* to the breaking of bread and prayers." The four things listed here, the apostles' teaching, *koinonía,* the breaking of bread, and prayers, are taken up in almost the same order in verses 43 to 47, where we are told (1) that fear came upon every soul, and wonders and signs were done through the apostles; (2) that all who believed had all things in common; (3) that they attended the temple and praised God; and (4) that they broke bread in their homes and partook of food with glad and generous hearts. The *koinonía* is not simply a spiritual sharing. It is a total sharing that includes the material as well as the spiritual.

Having clarified the connection of the commonality of goods in Acts 2 and 4 with the idea of *koinonía,* we can now return to the question posed earlier: are there indications that such sharing of goods continued — if it ever existed — after the time that those early chapters of Acts claim to describe? Again, the question is not whether all Christians went out and sold everything at once and put it into a common treasury. As we have seen, that is not the situation that Acts describes. The question is whether we can find indications that, at other times and places in the life of the church described in the New Testament, the Christian community was a partnership that included material as well as spiritual sharing, that this sharing was to be governed by the need of the less fortunate, and that, though voluntary, this sharing and the vision behind it challenged the traditional — particularly the Roman — understanding of private property.

When the question is posed in these terms, the obvious answer is found in the collection for the poor in Jerusalem that plays such an important role in the epistles of Paul. This collection is not a responsibility added to Paul's apostleship; rather it is part and parcel of it. Indeed, as Paul himself describes his authentication by the leaders in Jerusalem, the collection for the poor was an important part of his commission (Gal. 2:10). As we look at that collection and the manner in which Paul describes it in his letters, it is clear that it continues the practice of *koinonía* described in Acts 2 and 4.

Of all the churches among which Paul worked in collecting the offering for Jerusalem, the best known is that in Corinth. Paul's Corinthian correspondence provides much information both about the economic life of Christians in that city and about how Paul understood and interpreted the collection in which he was engaged. The social structure of the Corinthian church has been amply studied. Probably the best conclusion is that of biblical scholar Wayne Meeks, that the prominent members of the Pauline churches, including Corinth, were people of "high status inconsistency." While not all the members of a church such as that in Corinth were poor, those who had greater financial resources were people whose status was limited by other factors. In any case, it is clear that marked economic differences existed among members of the Corinthian church and that these differences created difficulties, for Paul says that when they gather for the common meal some are hungry while others are drunk (1 Cor. 11:21).

Paul is clear about the deep contradiction between such behavior, which humiliates the poor, and the very nature of the church. Those who have much to eat while others do not have enough are not only humiliating the poor but also despising the church (1 Cor. 11:22). And a case could be made that Paul is referring to them when he declares that "any one who eats and drinks without discerning the body (that is, without realizing that this community is the body of Christ) eats and drinks judgment upon himself" (1 Cor. 11:29).

In any case, as Paul speaks of the collection in Corinth, he instructs his readers to set aside a certain amount on the first day every week, so that special contributions will not have to be made upon his arrival (1 Cor. 16:1-4). The phrase that the Revised Standard Version translates "as he may prosper" is difficult to translate. It certainly does not mean that they should contribute only if they prospered. More likely it means that they should set aside as much as they could. These instructions, which Paul says that he has given also to the churches of Galatia, seem to apply to a community most of whose members are neither destitute nor rich. At the same time, Paul expects the total amount he is raising to be liberal, abundant, or even lavish (2 Cor. 8:20).

Paul's theological understanding of the offering for Jerusalem is best seen in 2 Corinthians, chapters 8 and 9. Paul begins by giving the Corinthians news of the collection in Macedonia, where the response was such that "their abundance of joy and their extreme poverty have overflowed in a wealth of liberality on their part." Paul makes clear throughout his argument that the gifts he is requesting should be made voluntarily. The Macedonians have given "of their own free will" (8:3). Paul stresses that his asking the Corinthians for an offering is not a command (8:8). Their offering should be "ready not as an exaction but as a willing gift" (9:5). And "each one must do as he has made up his mind, not reluctantly or under compulsion, for God loves a cheerful giver" (9:7). Thus, just as in Acts the giving was voluntary, and Peter told Ananias that he had been under no obligation to give, so here Paul makes it clear that giving must be from the heart and not out of an exterior compulsion or a dogmatic understanding of the community of goods.

The voluntary nature of the gift does not mean, however, that no goals or guidelines apply. In this text, the goal is equality: "I do not mean that others should be eased and you burdened, but that as a matter of equality your abundance at the present time should supply their want, so that their abundance may supply your want, that there may be equality. As it is written, 'He who gathered much had nothing over, and he who gathered little had no lack'" (2 Cor. 8:13-15).

The text is unclear as to how the abundance of the recipients will supply the want of the givers. Possibly it means that the Christians in Jerusalem, though materially poor, are spiritually rich, and that from this abundance the Corinthians will profit. The idea is fairly common in later patristic thought, that the prayers of the poor have greater efficacy, and that when the rich give to the poor the latter repay their benefactors by praying for them. This may be what Paul means here. Another option, however, would be to take a clue from the phrase "at the present time" and to interpret the text as meaning that when, at some future date, the Corinthians are in need, those in Jerusalem will come to their aid.

Whatever the case may be, Paul clearly says that the purpose of the offering is to promote equality. At present, the Corinthians enjoy relative abundance, at least of material wealth. It is clear from 1 Corinthians 1:26 that the church in Corinth did not include the aristocracy of that city. Still, in comparison with those in Jerusalem they lived in abundance. It is the contrast between the need in Jerusalem and the abundance in Corinth that must be overcome by the offering. The Corinthians are to give because those in Jerusalem are in need. Thus, as in the case of the original commonality of goods in Acts 2 and 4, what controls the giving is the need of the poor.

In this context, and to strengthen his argument, Paul cites the miracle of the redistribution of manna. In Exodus 16:16-18, when God provided manna the Israelites were ordered to go and collect a certain measure of it (an omer) for each member of the household. As so often happens in human societies, "some gathered much and some little." Yet, when they measured what they had gathered, they found that it had been redistributed, so that each household had the amount that God had ordered. This is the miracle of equality, which shows the will of God and which Paul is exhorting the Corinthian Christians to imitate.

The Corinthian discussion displays a remarkable similarity to what the book of Acts describes as having taken place in the early church. True, the text does not say, "They had all things in common." But the spirit and practice are certainly similar to that found in Acts, especially if we read, not only the brief account of the commonality of goods, but also the examples of how this actually worked — or did not work — in the cases of Barnabas and of Ananias and Sapphira.

Luke/Acts was written after the epistles of Paul, in a circle with strong Pauline influence. Actually, the vast majority of the book of Acts is devoted to Paul's ministry. Therefore, rather than suggesting

that the description of the commonality of goods in Acts is due to Hellenistic influences and to the idealizing of the early community, it seems possible to take the opposite view: even though some of the phrases used in Acts 2 and 4 may have parallels in earlier Greek literature, what Luke was describing here was the understanding of the Christian *koinonía* that had been at the very heart of Paul's ministry. If so, Acts is not speaking about a brief idyllic moment in the early life of the church or of something limited to the Jerusalem community but of something that, fully practiced or not, was still part of the self-understanding of the church — at least of the Pauline churches — everywhere. . . . [T]his continued to be the case for several generations.

The Later Books of the New Testament

In the later books of the New Testament we find both the continuation of themes already present in the early Christian movement and the first adumbrations of themes and situations that will become clearer in later times.

The theme of *koinonía* continues in the Johanine Epistles. Indeed, 1 John begins by declaring that the Epistle itself is written "so that you may have fellowship *(koinonía)* with us; and our fellowship *(koinonía)* is with the Father and with his Son Jesus Christ" (1 John 1:3). The writer then goes on to say that it is impossible to have *koinonía* with God unless we have it among ourselves (1:6-7). The entire Epistle leads to the conclusion that "if any one has the world's goods and sees his brother in need, yet closes his heart against him, how does God's love abide in him? Little children, let us not love in word or speech but in deed and in truth" (3:17-18).

The existence of wandering preachers and the need to support them are reflected in 1 John 5-8. In the Deutero-Pauline literature (Titus 1:7-11) a problem appears . . . , namely, preachers who are upsetting and exploiting the community "by teaching for base gain."

Also in the Deutero-Pauline Epistles appear a number of references to the temptation involved in riches. The evil of the "last days" includes people who will be "lovers of self, lovers of money, proud, arrogant, abusive . . ." (2 Tim. 3:1-2). And the following passage clearly reflects a church in which some have, or at least are seeking, more than they need:

> There is great gain in godliness with contentment; for we brought nothing into the world, and we cannot take anything out of the world; but if we have food and clothing, with these we shall be content. But those who desire to be rich fall into temptation, into a snare, into many senseless and hurtful desires that plunge men into ruin and destruction. For the love of money is the root of all evils; it is through this craving that some have wandered away from the faith and pierced their hearts with many pangs. (1 Tim. 6:6-10).

Along the same lines, Hebrews 10:34 praises believers who "joyfully accepted the plundering of your property, since you knew that you yourselves had a better possession and an abiding one." They are also told that Moses "considered abuse suffered for the Christ greater wealth than the treasure of Egypt, for he looked to the reward" (Heb. 11:26). And they are exhorted: "Keep your life free from love of money, and be content with what you have" (Heb. 13:5).

The theme of a reward for those who do not cling to their wealth but employ it for good deeds, sounds most clearly in 1 Timothy 6:17-19: "As for the rich in this world, charge them not to be haughty, nor to set their hopes on uncertain riches but on God who richly furnishes us with everything to enjoy. They are to do good, to be rich in good deeds, liberal and generous, thus laying up for themselves a good foundation for the future, so that they may take hold of the life which is life indeed."

Here we find, not only the notion that by making good use of treasures on earth one can acquire treasures in heaven, but also the contrast between two kinds of riches. Some are "rich in this world"; others are "rich in good deeds." While the two are not mutually exclusive, they are quite distinct. . . . [A] fairly common theme in early Christian literature is that those who apparently are rich are in truth poor and vice versa. This theme appears already in the book of Revelation, where the words to the church in Smyrna, "I know your tribulation and your poverty (but you are rich)" (Rev. 2:9), contrast with the message to the church in Laodicea: "For you say, I am rich, I have prospered, and I need nothing; not knowing that you are wretched, pitiable, poor, blind, and naked. Therefore I counsel you to buy from me gold refined by fire, that you may be rich" (Rev. 3:17-18).

The Study of the New Testament Household

Economic matters are always related to family life, and thus to the relationships between male and female, parent and child, and (in most cultures around the world) householders and servants — serfs, peasants, or slaves. This is especially so in societies where the family is the primary institution of production as well as consumption, as was true in biblical times. Further, the household, and thus the economy, was politically regulated by status and the distinctive roles and rights of all. Householding male rulers made these laws, and it surprises no one that many of these laws have been patriarchal throughout most of history and in most cultures. The male rulers may well have thought that they were simply requiring for society what nature had built into life and what was demanded by the gods, so that civilization would not fall apart, but it would have been very unusual if a desire to protect their positions or power had no influence on their views.

Modern feminist scholars have confirmed what a number of dissident, protesting, and reforming groups have suggested over the centuries: many of those laws and customs were not the order of the universe but merely the conventions of an age, and they are not the divine design but the distorted inventions of privilege. Further, they are not even central to early Christian beliefs, although Christian teachings, even as represented in Scripture, reflect some accommodations to such customs and laws.

People today may have all sorts of images of, and views about, "feminism," but it is difficult to deny the importance of the evidence offered here by Elisabeth Schüssler Fiorenza for business and economic ethics. For one thing, she clarifies the process of differentiation that took place in early Christianity under the impact of the message of Jesus Christ between the religious organization and the household on the one hand and the political institution on the other. The formation of the church as an institution outside of both familial and governmental control was the most formidable challenge to patriarchy. The early baptismal formulas shatter the authority of the "head of the family" and the "rulers of the world" by relocating the primary identity of the person in a non-hereditary, non-coercive community of faith governed not by patriarchy but by a fundamental equality. That is the meaning of Galatians 3:28, "There is no longer Jew or Greek, there is no longer slave or free, there is no longer male and female; for all of you are one in Christ Jesus."

Even if parts of the church gradually reasserted patriarchal practices, such a development had several consequences for the practice of moral business. First of all, it began a series of debates about the divine character of hierarchy based on ethnicity, slavery, and gender. While many religions support such things, Christianity began a challenge to all three. The battles lasted for centuries and only recently issued in the legal abolition of slavery and the establishment of legal protections irrespective of "race, religion, national origin, or sex." Antidiscrimination may not be realized in modern societies generally or in the world of business specifically; but insofar as people believe that it should be, they are direct or indirect heirs of this tradition. Their ideals have no other origin than this.

Second, this distinction between household and faith community established a "social space," an "associational zone" that gradually won acceptance in society. This is the soil out of which charitable institutions, guilds, opposition political parties, and (of great significance for modern business life) eventually both unions and corporations grew.

And, most important for modern feminist Christians, there is a model, with both positive and negative examples, of the struggles faithful believers experience when they develop a fundamental commitment to equality between the sexes and yet a desire to live in society in spite of its powerful traces of patriarchal influence. The fact that we all have to live in a fallen world implies an inevitable tension between the ideal and the real and thus an inner pressure to reform every institution — church, family, government, and corporation — from within.

Christian Mission, Patriarchal Order, and the Household

Elisabeth Schüssler Fiorenza

The early Christian vision of the discipleship of equals practiced in the house church attracted especially slaves and women to Christianity but also caused tensions and conflicts with the dominant cultural ethos of the patriarchal household. True, women as well as men, slaves as well as free, Asians as well as Greeks and Romans, participated fully in the cult of the Great Goddess (that was popular at the time); and in such a religious context the baptismal confession of Gal. 3:28 was not utopian. However, in contrast to the public cult of the goddess, in the Christian context, the public religious sphere of the church and the private sphere of the patriarchal house were not clearly separated. Insofar as Christians understood themselves as the new family and expressed this self-understanding institutionally in the house church, the public-religious and private patriarchal spheres were no longer distinguished. In fact, it was the religious ethos — of equality — that was transferred to and came in conflict with the patriarchal ethos of the household. The Christian missionary movement thus provided an alternative vision and praxis to that of the dominant society and religion.

Colossians and the Household Code

Colossians, written by a disciple of Paul, quotes Gal. 3:28 but changes it considerably. Moreover,

From Elisabeth Schüssler Fiorenza, *In Memory of Her* (New York: Crossroads, 1983), chap. 7, pp. 251-79.

he balances it out with a household code of patriarchal submission. The relationship of Jews and gentiles was no longer a great problem and concern for the author. The separation between the Jewish and Christian communities probably had already taken place at the time of his writing. In quoting the baptismal formula Colossians mentions Greeks first and elaborates the second member of the pair circumcision and uncircumcision with "barbarian and Scythian," in order to stress that national and cultural differences and inequalities are overcome in the new humanity of Christ. Since Scythians were the proverbial boors of antiquity, it is obvious that the author of Colossians is especially interested in the opposite pair, Greek and barbarian. While the third pair of Gal. 3:28 — male and female — is not mentioned at all, Col. 3:11 also dissolves the slave-free polarization that defines the social-political stratifications of institutional slavery. Col. 3:11 no longer juxtaposes slave-free as opposite alternatives but adds them to the enumeration and elaboration of those who are uncircumcised: barbarian, Scythian, slave, freeborn.

Although the letter to the Colossians still refers to the baptismal liturgy and theology of the Asian churches, it celebrates not so much the restoration of human equality in the new community but rather "a cosmic event, in which the opposing elements of the universe were reconciled to each other." The so-called enthusiastic theology ascribed to Paul's opponents in Corinth is fully expressed here. Baptism means resurrection and enthronement with Christ in heaven, "stripping away the body of flesh" (2:11), and life in heaven rather than on earth (2:1-4; cf. 2:12, 20). The baptized are delivered from "the dominion of darkness" and transferred into "the kingdom of his beloved son" (1:13). They are "dead to the cosmos," have received a secret mystery (1:26f.; 2:2-3), and have the assurance of an inheritance among the "holy ones" in the realm of light. The writer of Colossians agrees with his audience on this theology of exaltation but disagrees with some of the Colossians on how this baptismal "symbolic universe" and drama should be remembered and made effective. While some in the community of Colossae believed that the "removal of the fleshly body" and the "new humanity" in baptism must be realized in ascetic practices and elaborate ritual

observances, the author insists on the finality of Christ's reconciliation and unification. The new "angelic religion" and the life in heaven are not to be realized by ascetic and ritual practice but in ethical behavior and communal life. Since they have been raised with Christ, they are to "seek the things that are above," and to set their "minds on the things that are above." They do so "by putting away" anger, wrath, malice, slander, and foul talk and by "putting on" compassion, kindness, lowliness, meekness, and patience, forebearing one another and forgiving each other. Above all, they should "put on love, which binds everything together in perfect harmony" (3:5-17). They should behave wisely to outsiders and be able to answer everyone (4:5f.).

This is the context of the household code (3:18–4:1), the first and most precise form of the domestic code in the New Testament. The basic form of this code consists of three pairs of reciprocal exhortations addressing the relationship between wife and husband, children and father, and slaves and masters. In each case, the socially subordinate first member of the pair is exhorted to obedience to the superordinate second. The formal structure of such a household code, then, consists of address (wives), exhortation (submit to your husbands), and motivation (as is fitting in the Lord). The only Christian element in the Colossian code is the addition "in the Lord." However, the author of Colossians quotes the code here, not because he is concerned about the behavior of wives, but that of slaves.

The expansion of the code's third pair, slave-master, indicates that the obedience and acceptance of servitude by Christian slaves are of utmost concern. Colossians asks slaves to fulfill their task with single-mindedness of heart and dedication "as serving the Lord and not men" (3:23). He not only promises eschatological reward for such behavior but also threatens eschatological judgment and punishment for misbehavior (3:24f.). The injunction to masters, in turn, is very short and has no Christian component except the reminder that they, too, have a master in heaven. Slave behavior is likened here to the Christian service of the Lord, while the "masters" are likened here to the "Master" in heaven. It is obvious that the good behavior of slaves, according to the author, is the concrete realization of Gal. 3:28, insofar as both slaves and freeborn have one Lord in heaven, Christ, and belong to the new humanity, now "hid with Christ in God" (3:3). There is no question that E. A. Judge is right when he asserts that what we hear in these injunctions is "the voice of the propertied class." We have no way of determining whether "those who are your earthly masters" are only pagan or also Christian masters. The injunction to the masters presupposes that they still have slaves who might or might not have been Christian.

In taking over the Greco-Roman ethic of the patriarchal household code, Colossians not only "spiritualizes" and moralizes the baptismal community understanding expressed in Gal. 3:28 but also makes this Greco-Roman household ethic a part of "Christian" social ethic. However, it is important to keep in mind that such a reinterpretation of the Christian baptismal vision is late — it did not happen before the last third of the first century. Moreover, it is found only in one segment of early Christianity, the post-Pauline tradition, and had no impact on the Jesus traditions. The insistence on equality and mutuality within the Christian community that seems to have been expressed by slaves as well as by women is not due to later "enthusiastic excesses" or to illegitimate agitation for emancipation. The opposite is true. Colossians shows how a so-called "enthusiastic" realized eschatological perspective can produce an insistence on patriarchal behavior as well as an acceptance of the established political-social status quo of inequality and exploitation in the name of Jesus Christ.

In discussing the *Sitz im Leben* of the household code form, exegetes have arrived at different interpretations. While a few scholars think that the demands for the obedience and submission of wives, children, and slaves are genuinely Christian, the majority sees the domestic code as a later Christian adaptation of a Greco-Roman or Jewish-Hellenistic philosophical-theological code . . . .

Aristotle, who has decisively influenced Western political philosophy . . . argues against Plato that one must begin the discussion of politics with thoughts about marriage, defined by him as a union of "natural ruler and natural subject." When slaves are added to the family, it can be called a "house." Several households constitute a village and several villages a city-state, or *politeia:*

The investigation of everything should begin with its smallest parts, and the smallest and primary parts of the household are master and slaves, husband and wife, father and children. We ought therefore to examine the proper constitution and character of each of the three relationships, I mean that of mastership, that of marriage and thirdly the progenitive relationship. [*Politics* I.1253b]

It is part of the household science to rule over wife and children as freeborn. However, this is not done with the same form of government. Whereas the father rules over his children as a monarch rules, the husband exercises republican government over the wife:

for the male is by nature better fitted to command than the female . . . and the older and fully developed person than the younger and immature. It is true that in most cases of republican government the ruler and ruled interchange in turn . . . but the male stands in his relationship to the female continuously. The ruler of the father over the children on the other hand is that of a king. [*Politics* I.1259b]

Against those who argue that slavery is contrary to nature, Aristole points to the rule of the soul over the body.

It is manifest that it is natural and expedient for the body to be governed by the soul and for the emotional part to be governed by the intellect, the part possessing reason, whereas for the two parties to be on equal [*ison*] footing or in the contrary positions is harmful in all cases. . . . Also as between the sexes, the male is by nature superior and the female inferior, the male ruler and the female subject. And the same must also necessarily apply in the case of humankind generally; therefore all human beings that differ as widely as the soul does from the body . . . these are by nature slaves for whom to be governed by this kind of authority is advantageous. [*Politics* I.1254b]

These "natural" differences justify the relationships of domination in household and state. . . .

Although the negative influence of Aristotle on Christian anthropology is widely acknowledged today, it is not sufficiently recognized that such an anthropology was rooted in Aristotle's understanding of political rule and domination. Just as he defined the "nature" of slaves with respect to their status as property and to their economic function, so Aristotle defined the "nature" of woman as that of someone who does not have "full authority" to rule, although he is well aware that such rule was an actual historical possibility and reality. The definition of "woman's nature" and "woman's proper sphere" is thus rooted in a certain relation of domination and subordination between man and woman having a concrete political background and purpose. Western misogynism has its root in the rules for the household as the model of the state. A feminist theology therefore must not only analyze the anthropological dualism generated by Western culture and theology, but also uncover its political roots in the patriarchal household of antiquity. . . .

1 Peter and the Household Code

The household code in 1 Pet. 2:11–3:12 no longer consists of three pairs of reciprocal injunctions, for it only mentions slaves, wives as well as husbands, but no children and parents. Moreover, it stresses primarily the duties of the subordinate members of the household. Its context, however, is the Greco-Roman discussion on the *politeia* with its three sections: the discussion of the duties concerning the state, those concerning the household, and those concerning marriage. This threefold division is clearly followed in pseudo-Peter's discussion of the Christian life. This discussion begins with a demand for submission even to hard and unjust masters (2:18-25), and asks Christian wives to submit themselves to their husbands, even when the latter are pagans and actively engaged against the Christian community by being disobedient to the word (3:1-6). While the passage does not contain an exhortation to masters, the admonitions to the wife are followed by a short exhortation to the husband (3:7).

Although the context of this household-code type of instruction is not that of cosmic reconciliation and heavenly enthronement as in Colossians, it is clearly connected with baptismal remembrance and instruction. The Christians are "born anew" by the incorruptible living word (1:23-25), they are elect and holy, they are the beloved who are called to an incorruptible living hope. As newborn babes they should "put off" all malice and vice (2:1), and live as "children of obedience" (1:4), so that they may "grow up to salvation" for they "have tasted the kindness of the Lord" (2:2f.). As the spiritual temple, the priestly people of God, "they should be holy" just as God is holy who called them (1:14-16). They should cast all their anxieties on God, because it is God who cares for them (5:7).

As the royal priesthood they are a holy *politeuma*, a new people who have been "liberated from the futile ways inherited from your fathers" (1:18) through the death of Christ. Here the point of conflict between the Christian community and the surrounding society is named: they have left the ancestral customs and gods of their pagan households and turned to the "living stone," Jesus Christ. However, "as God's own people," they are now "exiles in the dispersion," strangers and immigrants. As such they are deeply alienated from their own society. They have to suffer various trials, are slandered, treated as criminals, and reviled. They are therefore exhorted not to give in to their fear, not to be afraid of those who may injure (3:13) or slander them (3:16). Nonetheless, knowing that they are called to "God's eternal glory," they can have courage, for they have to suffer only for a "little while" (1:6f., 5:10f.) in order that their genuineness may be tested by fire.

It is obvious that these Christian communities of Asia Minor were a small and alienated minority group. They represent an illegal religion that had disrupted the ancestral customs and religion of their patriarchal households. Since no "masters" are addressed we can assume that the majority of their members were slaves of pagan masters and wives of pagan husbands. Because of their distinctive lifestyle and their heightened consciousness of election they were being persecuted. The writer of 1 Peter, seeking to encourage them in their trials, insists that their unjust sufferings because of Christ and their lifestyle "as God's own people" are necessary, and will last only for a "little while." At the same time he offers them a "strategy" for survival in the midst of trials and persecutions. This strategy consists in "doing good" and proving themselves faithful "law-abiding" citizens; it presupposes that "what is good" is agreed upon by Christians as well as pagans and that Christian suffering is rooted in a pagan "misunderstanding," but not in a different societal-religious ethos. The distinctiveness of Christian faith and religion is maintained only insofar as slaves and wives must be prepared to suffer for being Christians. However, for the sake of the Christian mission, they should seek to reduce suffering and tensions as much as possible by a lifestyle that is totally conformed to the customs and ethos of their pagan household and state.

The interpretational key to the household-code instructions is given in 2:12, which introduces the whole section:

Beloved, I beseech you as aliens and exiles. . . . Maintain good conduct among the Gentiles so that in case they speak against you as wrongdoers [better, lawbreakers] they may see your good deeds [your law-abiding behavior as good citizens] and glorify God on the day of visitation. [2:11a, 12] . . .

The patriarchal pattern of submission, therefore, does not so much seek to put wives back into their proper patriarchal roles and places, but seeks to lessen the tension between the Christian community and the pagan patriarchal household. Especially the conversion of wives and slaves provoked such political tensions between the Christian movement and its pagan society. This conflict was a conflict of values and allegiances between the Christian community and the patriarchal family. . . . The accusation of second-century pagan writers that Christianity destroys the household by attracting especially women, slaves, and young people can thus not just be pushed aside as unfounded slander but must be taken seriously. . . .

I have argued that the pagan perception of Christians interfering with the patriarchal order of the house was not unfounded. Insofar as Christians accepted slaves and women from pagan households as converts and members, they clearly broke the ancestral laws. Their self-understanding as the new eschatological community, the new creation, the new humanity, in which the social-political stratifications of religion, class, slavery, and patriarchal marriage are abolished, and all are equal in Christ, was an alternative vision that clearly undermined the Greco-Roman patriarchal order. The Christian message was so attractive and convincing for women and slaves, precisely because it promised them liberation from the patriarchal order and gave them a new freedom in the community of equals. . . .

Ephesians and the Household Code

Ephesians presents the "hope to which Christians are called" (1:18) as the gospel of peace (6:15). Such universal peace was accomplished by Christ's victory over the powers of darkness, a victory which did away with the gulf between Jews and non-Jews. Forgiveness of sin means liberation from the spiritually evil heavenly powers and unification of the two into one "new third race" or into the one family of God. The divine mediator has healed the breach between the world above and the world below, Christ has reconciled Jews and gentiles to a new universal harmony and peace.

The author writes to gentile Christians and reminds them, using Old Testament-Jewish and early Christian traditional materials, that they have received access to the one true God of Israel in Jesus Christ. They who have been sojourners and strangers have become fellow-citizens with the saints and angels. The dividing wall of the Temple, which is here projected into the whole cosmos and into the structure of the universe, is broken down, and a new unified humanity has come into existence in the church. Ephesians reinterprets the cosmic stress of Colossians in terms of ecclesiology. Christ is the head and source of peace for the church. His work as universal peacemaker is now to be carried out by the church, which is his *plērōma*, the sphere of his influence and the force-field of his peacemaking power. The church "embodies" the peace of Christ. Those who are baptized are a new creation (2:10), have put on the new human (4:24; cf. 4:13, the "perfect man"). They have risen with Christ and are seated with him above (2:6). By "grace they have been saved" (2:5c) and have been "sealed" with the promised Holy Spirit, the "guarantor" of their "inheritance" (1:13). They are children of God (5:1, 8).

The universal peace of Christ must be manifest in the community of Jew and gentile Christians. They are admonished to "lead a life worthy of your calling to which you have been called" (4:1). They must be eager to preserve

> the unity of the spirit in the bond of peace. There is one body and one Spirit, ... one Lord, one faith, one baptism, one God and Father of us all. [4:4ff.]

The baptismal remembrance of 2:11-22 clearly refers to the pre-Pauline baptismal formula with its opposites, uncircumcision/circumcision. The author expresses in various ways the unification of Jews and gentiles through the death of Christ and their equality in the new community of those baptized into Christ's death and resurrection. . . .

While the Colossian code clearly was interested in the patriarchally appropriate behavior of slaves, the Ephesian code elaborates upon the relationship of wife and husband in patriarchal marriage. In so doing, the author combines the traditional household code form with the church-body theology and Pauline bride-bridegroom notion found for the first time in 2 Cor 11:3. The relationship between Christ and the church, expressed in the metaphors of head and body as well as of bridegroom and bride, becomes the paradigm for Christian marriage and vice versa. This theological paradigm reinforces the cultural-patriarchal pattern of subordination, insofar as the relationship between Christ and the church clearly is not a relationship between equals, since the church-bride is totally dependent and subject to her head or bridegroom. Therefore, the general injunction for all members of the Christian community, "Be subject to one another in the fear of Christ," is clearly spelled out for the Christian wife as requiring submission and inequality.

As the church is subordinated to Christ, so the wife has to subject herself to her husband in everything. The phrase "in everything," which in the Colossian code was associated with the obedience of children and slaves, here underlines the subordinate position of the wife (v. 24). 5:22 insists that the submission of the wife to her husband is on a par with her religious submission to Christ, the Lord. The instruction to the wives thus clearly reinforces the patriarchal marriage pattern and justifies it christologically. The instructions to the wife are therefore summed up in the injunction to fear or to respect her husband (v. 33).

However, the patriarchal-societal code is theologically modifed in the exhortation to the husband. The negative demand of Colossians that men are not to be harsh with their wives is not repeated here. Instead, the husbands are three times commanded to love their wives (5:25, 28, 33). Jesus' commandment, "to love your neighbor as yourself" (cf. Lev. 19:18) is applied to the marriage relationships of the husband. Moreover, the relationship of Christ to the church becomes the example for the husband. Christ's self-giving love for the church is to be the model for the love relationship of the husband with his wife. Patriarchal domination is thus radically questioned with reference to the paradigmatic love relationship of Christ to the church.

Nevertheless, it must be recognized that this christological modification of the husband's patriarchal position and duties does not have the power, theologically, to transform the patriarchal pattern of the household code, even though this might have been the intention of the author. Instead, Ephesians christologically cements the inferior position of the wife in the marriage relationship. One could say that the exhortations to the husbands spell out what it means to live a marriage relationship as a Christian, while those to the wives insist on the proper social behavior of women. The reason for this theological shortcoming might be the author's interest in clarifying the relationship between Christ and the church, whose unity is his primary concern in the rest of the letter. His interpretation of Gen. 2:24 shows that this is the case. Although early Christian theology used this Old Testament text for understanding the marriage relationship, the author applies it primarily to the relationship of Christ and the church.

Eph. 5:21-33 thus participates in the trajectory of the patriarchal household-code tradition insofar as it takes over the household-code pattern and reasserts the submission of the wife to the husband as a religious Christian duty. At the same time, it modifes the patriarchal code by replacing patriarchal superordination and domination with the Christian command of love to be lived according to the example of Christ. On the whole, however, the author was not able to "Christianize" the code. The "gospel of peace" has transformed the relationship of gentiles and Jews, but not the social roles of wives and slaves within the household of God. On the contrary, the cultural-social structures of domination are theologized and thereby reinforced. However, it must not be overlooked that the code and its theological legitimation are not descriptive of the actual situation of women and slaves in the communities of Asia Minor. It is exhortative or prescriptive and seeks to establish a Christian behavior that is not yet realized in the life of the Christians in Asia Minor.

Toward a Summary of Implications

The roots of the Western ethics in regard to social life, and thus to business, are in the Bible. But they are not only there, and much has happened between the New Testament and contemporary life, including the encounters of biblical perspectives with nonbiblical cultures, social changes, and rather vigorous rejections of biblical thought. After all, every age has to discern, as did the early Christians, which parts of the sacred past are essentially ethological in the sense that they are expressions of passing sociocultural contexts, which parts are deontological in the sense that they state principles that are true for all times, and which parts are teleological in the sense that they point toward ultimate goals and ends for which we strive or hope, that they may become actual in the future.

The question of how we can with intellectual honesty and should with spiritual fidelity draw on classic Scriptures such as those we have reviewed in the last two chapters haunts modern life, for some aspects of modernity are the result of scriptural patterns and promises while other aspects are blatant repudiations of them. Thus, to conclude these two chapters, we pose again the question once put to John the Baptist, who represents the connection between the covenantal and prophetic tradition of Moses and that of Jesus: "What then shall we do?"

It is difficult to overestimate in this connection the social and ethical importance of the church as an organizational reality, for the church is the embodied form that answers to this question took when faithful people had to face these issues. For all its moral and spiritual weakness, the deepest roots of pluralist society are to be found in the formation of this distinctive association. All societies have religions, but they are nearly always identified with familial or political authority. The church claimed that it had a divine right to exist and that any true convert could join without the approval of the head of any household or of the government — both of whom also controlled the wealth.

The organizational implications of this development are not discussed much in Scripture, but the struggle to establish a self-governing group that could morally deal with sex, power, wealth, and ethnic pluralism is clear in almost every text. The formation of independent groups was against the law; the legal basis for the persecution of the early church was that it was an illegal organization. Nevertheless, wherever it took root, the formation of the church altered familial and political patterns, and thus economic possibilities. It established a new view of social order and civilization as well as of religion.

The church over the centuries has had to do what we have to do today: identify what from our most godly, most universalistic sense of the eternally true and just, and what from our best vision of the most ultimate future, can be related to our deepest understanding of the present, to guide our lives together.

What Then Shall We Do? On Using Scripture in Economic Ethics

Max L. Stackhouse

What we cannot do. It is no more possible to derive a contemporary, normative economics exclusively from the pages of Scripture than it is to derive a biology from Genesis, a platform for democratic politics from Amos, a welfare-policy from Luke, or a university curriculum from the letters of Paul. Several of the best contemporary efforts to relate biblical materials to issues of modern social ethics all recognize the necessity of a certain indirection of connection.

This is not to suggest that biblical resources are irrelevant to these subjects. Indeed, the whole point of Chapters 1 and 2 is to show that the biblical message is pertinent to modern economic issues. We are to care for the poor and the oppressed, to labor diligently in our vocations as well as for the establishment of just social institutions, and to exercise stewardly responsibility for God's creation. That is no small agreement. . . .

Yet the Christian consensus on these matters quickly becomes contentious. All modern commentators, for example, approve of "charity," which for centuries has been a key mark of Christian economic responsibility; but they also believe that charity is not enough. They turn to models of social-welfare democracy, democratic socialism, and democratic capitalism to interpret both the meaning of the texts and the structure of our context. None of these models of political

economy are imagined in the Bible, yet they become the glasses through which people read both texts and contexts. . . .

This is not to say that the Bible is a sociological Rorschach into which each social group may read its own ideological sensibilities. It is to suggest, however, that in using scriptural warrants for social and ethical prescription, we have no choice but to be self-conscious and self-critical about the ways in which our social presuppositions influence what we see in, what we get out of, and how we apply what we learn from Scripture.

What has been done. From the beginning, Christians encountered philosophies, sciences, and civilizations not based on the experience of thought of biblical peoples. Christians did not utterly repudiate these worlds but developed ways of encountering, honoring, and selectively adopting and adapting what could be usefully learned from "non-biblical" thought, experience, and civilization. This was held to be possible for two reasons: First, the one true God whom they knew in Jesus Christ was not merely their God, but the God of all — over all societies, peoples, and contexts. Second, in the life, teachings, death, and resurrection of Jesus Christ, the basic principles by which Christians could discern God's truth from pretentious untruth, God's justice from idolatrous injustice, and God's love from human passions had been made clear. Thus, the resources were at hand to make the necessary, if necessarily indirect, connections between what could be known about God, as witnessed by Scripture, and what could be known about truth, justice, and the care of the neighbor, as found in non-scriptural ways of life. Often, postbiblical syntheses became the guides to life, and the Scriptures themselves were probed to see how they pointed toward general themes and principles which could be contextualized in new settings. Regarding how we ought to believe, the result is called "Theology"; regarding how we ought to act, it is called "Ethics." Both entail the ongoing task of drawing selective connections between major themes of a biblically rooted faith and the intellectual-social fabric of society. Yet even this thematizing approach has become more difficult.

Of special importance in regard to economic matters is a fundamental transformation that has taken place in the modern understanding of the

Max L. Stackhouse, "What Then Shall We Do? On Using Scripture in Economic Ethics," *Interpretation* 41, no. 4 (Oct. 1987): 382-97.

relationships between religion, ethics, and economics. Adam Smith in the eighteenth century in one way and Karl Marx in the nineteenth century in another way believed both that economic developments were independent of extrinsic religious and moral influences and that, indeed, "natural" economic forces (which each claimed to have scientifically discovered) were decisive for the shape of society in general. To be sure, much divided Smith and Marx; not the least was the fact that they were asking opposite questions. Smith wanted to know why it was that some people were wealthy, since most of the world, most of the time, is poor. Marx wanted to know how it was that some people are poor, since he presumed that the natural state of affairs entailed the sharing of plenty. Nevertheless, they both believed that economics and its laws could be disembedded from the ethical and religious traditions which, for most of human history, were thought to shape economic attitudes and behaviors. Once these laws were isolated, we could know the "basic" causes of wealth and poverty. Smith accented the relationships of supply, demand, market, and division of labor; Marx accented the relationships of classes, the ownership of the means of production, and political power. Both saw material interests as the clue to human motivation and social history.

The human task in these "economistic" theories was to grasp the "scientific laws of economic life" and then to employ these laws in the service of human interests — unfettered from moralistic or religious teachings. The results, argued Smith, would insure the "wealth of nations" or, as Marx envisaged, the "classless society." Both wings of this debate were governed by a rejection of "metaphysical idealism" in favor of a "natural materialism." "Real" material needs, structures, and dynamics were phenomenal; the rest was epiphenomenal. . . .

What we might do. Modern believers have no choice but to attempt to show that at least some theological claims, ethical principles, or social themes found in Scripture may well be of more than contextual import. In one sense, that is what every missionary since Paul, every preacher since Peter, and every theologian since, perhaps, Appollos has believed. Anyone who has ever tried to understand the pertinence of the message of the text in relationship to another context where it is exposited has done the same. Pastors have always presumed that the text had trans-contextual content which only needed to be teased out and re-contextualized in a way that could become indigenized in a secondary context, transforming it in the process. Today we call this "contextualization," a process that stands in contrast to current forms of "contextualism," although the two are frequently confused.

The classical theological way of speaking about the trans-contextual character of the message in the text is to refer to the text, or at least themes in it, as revealed or inspired. That is, while every text is obviously written at a particular time and place and in a particular language (so that each text is in some sense idiosyncratic), and while a text may well point to what God has done or is doing in social-historical life (so that the text points beyond itself to convey its meanings), and while we recognize that what we have in the New Testament is the gospel *according to* Matthew, Mark, Luke, John, Paul, and others (so that the perception and application of the gospel is necessarily pluralistic), the various sources and versions point to a message which, in the final analysis, is not so divided against itself and so pluriform in its manifestations that it has no unity or coherence.

Further, even if it becomes possible to identify defensible trans-contextual normative meanings from the careful study of texts (in and beyond their own contexts), it would also be necessary to show how such trans-contextual meanings might relate to contemporary global economic realities. This requires an understanding of social contexts which is at least as complex as the hermeneutics of texts — in part because modern social contexts have already been influenced by the ways in which biblical motifs have been wedded to philosophical themes, social institutions, and economic interests over the course of two thousand years.

To cite but one example, let us briefly note the changing reputation of poverty. The texts commending "evangelical simplicity" have been interpreted to imply the sacralization of poverty. At times this issued in the identification of the oppressed with the true community of faith while elsewhere also in the necessity of monastic asceticism for those truly devoted to the religious life. The formation of cooperative, disciplined communities of production in the monasteries, as we shall see, resulted in very wealthy orders. The subsequent reassertion of the ideals of poverty on the basis of the gospel, in turn, brought vast systems of institutionalized begging. The Reformation, on the basis of a new reading of the texts, and an analysis of their context, reacted against both fat orders and thin mendicants. Luther and Calvin desacralized poverty, banned beggars, and dissolved monastic orders. Preoccupation with wealth is indeed a spiritual and social peril; but poverty is not a mark of holiness. It is to be overcome by hard work, by organized benevolence for those unable to work, and by removing artificial obstacles to new forms of economic behavior which limited productivity. This had several consequences: It led some to see wealth as proof of God's favor, and it led others to construct modern, industrial systems of production, with social welfare provisions, as a religious duty.

Today, in reaction against modern industrial societies based on these foundations (even if the members of these societies do not know whence their foundations derive), we find a repudiation of all these traditions. We see among some of the most sensitive young people a resacralization of poverty linked to presumptive guilt of affluence — namely, anyone not in poverty must be responsible for or beneficiaries of the fact that others are in poverty.

If such sensibilities are to be assessed, what is required more than anything else in our present situation is a double hermeneutic. That is, on the one hand, a hermeneutic of texts, one alert to the contexts in which they were composed, and to the contexts into which they are transposed, but seeking above all else for those thematic possibilities in the texts which are trans-contextual in importance and able to evaluate, effect, and transform contexts. Only these can be transported to new contexts, recontextualized, and make a difference in how economic life is lived. On the other hand, a hermeneutic of contexts is required, one which does not methodologically deny the fact that religiously and ethically grounded meanings can and do influence the fabric of social life. Any interpretive model of social and economic life which sees the social structure and the direction of civilizational development determined by economistic factors (or political, or sexual, or racial, or tech-

nological ones) has no place for theological or ethical conviction as effective social forces and will be doubted. If the two sides of this double hermeneutic are joined, it would mean, indeed, that we are forever caught up in a process of giving articulation to refined norms for economic life in each and every particular context. . . .

What takes place between the two levels of this double hermeneutic is less a dialectic than a quest for those possibilities which have what Max Weber called an "elective affinity." In some ways, to be sure, there will always be unresolvable tensions. Some of the deepest dimensions of faith have to do with sacrifice and are forever in conflict with every concern for material well-being. The demands of being responsible in many areas of institutional life — familial, political, and economic — are eternally distinct from the most sublime mysteries of religious truth. This is the wisdom which the saints and mystics have always known, and this is the source of a certain anti-institutionalism in many forms of religious piety. Yet the mystics and saints have seldom attempted to make their insight into a social program, which may be the contemporary temptation of some even though every effort to turn the entirely transmundane dimensions of the gospel into a political project ends in fanaticism or a triuimphalist sectarianism. Similarly, efforts to baptize "successful" economic necessities with unreserved blessing may produce a marketable piety, but at the cost of an easy conscience and cheap grace.

Yet some biblical themes do press in other directions: those of living not *by* the world but living *in* this sinful world with a sense of abundant life. The analysis of text demands the sorting out not only of the merely contextual but also the transmundane from those trans-contextual themes that can make sense in the broader conduct of life. Transcontextual norms which can shape and guide public discourse and public behavior become decisive. Further, the deeper understanding of context demands not only the tough-minded analysis of power, of economic necessity and need, but recognition of the fact that every social institution has to have a mix of stability and dynamism legitimated by one or another "metaphysical-moral vision" which renders it "meaningful" to those who engage in it. Thus, some religious orientations — those that are entirely contextual or transmundane — cannot supply moral guidelines to economic systems of global reach. Any economic system which is not simultaneously relatively stable and relatively dynamic and which is not grounded on principles accepted among the people brings only chaos, violence, and starvation. This kind of social analysis points beyond itself: It recognizes that no social hermeneutic is complete if it does not penetrate to the deepest levels of those metaphysical-moral presuppositions which are at the core of every social system — including modern, industrialized, "secular" ones. Such an analysis can tell us how specific religious and ethical visions tend to influence the structures of wealth and poverty in a civilization, and how these "ideal interests" connect with "material interests" and the necessities of production, exchange, and distribution among specific social constituencies. If we know that, we are required to be accountable for the probable consequences of any theological-ethical principles we advance as they are likely to function in relation to real economic prospects.

When we work in these ways, it quickly becomes clear how many variables have to be taken into account if we are to demonstrate that motifs from Scripture can be, and should be, taken as normative for modern economic judgments about wealth and poverty. To be sure, there is no small supply of preachers, activists, libertarians, and liberationists who will continue to quote Scripture and make preemptive judgments about what we ought to do; but the harder problem is to identify the double hermeneutical principles by which we could show that what they tell us to do is, or is not, warranted, since they do not agree.

What we must do. The current rise of confessionalist postures which abdicate the attempt to wrestle with fundamental questions of truth and justice in relationship to complex systems in favor of a "perspectival pluralism," and, indeed, the turn to contextualism, leaves us incapable of addressing economic issues on a warranted basis. . . .

But we must tell the deeper questions: Is it possible to identify any fundamental patterns of truth and justice behind the pluralism of the texts and contexts which can guide modern economic systems? Is it possible to identify how these can provide guidance to the common life in a global civilization to which we are moving? Is it possible

to argue convincingly that concerns of justice are a matter of universal truth which no one has the right to deny and which must become prudently built into modern economic systems?

The great biblical traditions have identified or presupposed some of the key theological-ethical principles which we must continue to honor and attempt to contextualize in economic life, especially where they are not contextually present. Do not lie, cheat, steal, or covet; deal as equitably with the foreigner and the stranger as with the family member and the beloved neighbor; if authority is given to someone, it must not be used to extort or gain advantage; all bounty is to be treated as a trusted and trustworthy steward treats that which is the Lord's. Honor is not to go to the rich and the powerful because they are rich and powerful but accordingly as they love mercy, do justice, and walk humbly with God. Further, the greedy accumulation of wealth which removes some from accountability to all others is contrary to God's justice and damaging to the community — it creates resentments which leave the dispossessed not only hungry but vicious. Forced poverty is equally contrary to God's justice and destructive of viable economic development. Thus, efforts to call the greedy to account, to relieve the needs of the distressed, and to convert both to a disciplined life, are always necessary.

There is a social realism in the biblical sources. Human efforts to establish equality are only temporarily successful, and we should not make idols of them. In every human situation, some people will be improvident, lazy, or dependent, while others, both rich and poor, will exploit others and put their ultimate truth in material security. Thus, no social program — by almsgiving, jubilee entitlement, or revolution — can permanently solve problems of inequity, although they may be periodically required because they can relieve some people from the threat of permanent entrapment in involuntary poverty and judge those who betray fiduciary responsibilities. The particular principles to be invoked at any given time would have to be assessed accordingly as they prompt voluntary sharing, move a society toward a stable and dynamic social system which also protects other basic values such as the freedom of worship, human rights, the reduction of violence as a means of social control, and the cultivation of convenantal senses of vocational responsibility and corporate responsibility among the people.

These principles seem, in some ways, so unremarkable that we sometimes fail to accent them. Indeed they are less than remarkable if they are taken as but another list of legalistic prescriptions. Yet if they are understood to be the ethical refractions of a foundational relationship to God, and therefore to the neighbor, society, and the cosmos, they become marks of a valid and viable economic ethic, all the more remarkable precisely because they are not present in many experiences of life, and yet are ethically universal. We fail to note their importance because they have, in fact, become woven into the fabric of common expectation, although less often in common practice, in every society influenced by Christianity. Exposure to cultures not shaped by these principles reveals how remarkable, and how necessary to viable and dynamic social economics, they are.

Closely related is the even more remarkable fact that the New Testament presses the faithful to form a new kind of community. In most societies, community is formed by familial-tribal connections or by national-military ones. Most frequently in world history, both religious and economic community — and status, class, and opportunity — is determined by these two communities. The New Testament invites to a community independent of these to form a solidarity which is not to be determined by either. The implication of ecclesial formation is, socially and historically, one of the most important, if indirect, contributions of the Jesus movement to economic life in the history of the world. In the early church, new patterns of mutual responsibility, accountability, and structured authority with voluntary participation had to be worked out. At the time, the economic focus was primarily on the obligations of distribution and the denial of the authority of cultural, sexual, racial, national, and military power to determine community patterns. But more, it meant the establishment of an institution distinct from *oikos* and *polis*. The church, in other words, became the first "trans-ethnic" and "transnational" corporation able to establish, potentially for all civilizations, the model of a social space for a new kind of human community.

For centuries after the New Testament, to be sure, the established church had a monopoly over this social space, and economically productive institutions remained essentially confined to *oikos* or *polis,* as is still the case in most traditional societies. Yet when under the impact of the rise of the cities (with which Christianity has always had an affinity, in part because here too the power of traditional familial, tribal, national, and military power is challenged), believers turned again to biblical models of the independent community and applied them to the formation of communities of production. Both individualist-capitalist analysis and collectivist-socialist analysis miss this point and thus fail to grasp much of the nature of modern economic institutions. The point is simply this: When the trans-contextual principles from the biblical sources become adopted by and incarnated in a new kind of social institution, the foundations of modern, pluralist, interdependent, and cosmopolitan, productive society are laid. . . .

What then ought we do? In the final analysis, the church has nothing to offer the world of economic life but words and example — words about how things ought to be, and how they are, examples of how to live together. It does not live by wealth and might, although some words have tremendous indirect power when they both touch on what is universally just and become incarnated in living patterns of disciplined social existence. So far as we are able, we must represent the truth and justice of God, and the best understanding of social life available, constantly clarifying their indirect connections. The words will not always join to our social experience; but if our words do not stretch toward trans-contextual principles and do not evoke communities that attempt to contextualize them in viable social systems, they will neither be believed nor have any chance to form, or transform, economic life. Mammon will win; the poor will suffer; the rich will not be brought to conviction; civilizations will wither.

113

Chapter Three

Ancient Philosophers

Philosophy can be found in the Bible, especially in those parts called "wisdom literature." However, it is not as fully developed there as it was in ancient Greek and Roman thought and among some popular teachers. Jews and Christians found much that was valid in philosophy, even if they challenged some of its premises on the basis of their religious convictions. Later, Islam's response was similar.

Philosophies are as varied as religions. But for all the differences within each, philosophy and religion are similar in that they both attempt to provide a basic understanding of the nature and character of ultimate reality and valid principles to guide thought and action. Both want to know what is true and what is just, and how we can reliably know such things.

They differ essentially in this: philosophy understands itself to be based on the innate capacities of human reason and imagination to understand reality, while religion is rooted in the conviction that humans best understand their own innate capacities when they acknowledge, by faith, a dependence on a moral or spiritual reality that is neither fully grasped by human reason nor constructed by human imagination. This does not mean, of course, that philosophies are entirely rational or independent of believed presumptions, or that religions are basically unimaginative or irrational; some philosophies celebrate the irrational, and some religions argue that faith is more reasonable than philosophy's rationality. It does mean that philosophy and religion are sometimes in tension because one focuses on human wisdom while the other focuses on divine reality.

Two great and integrative ways of thinking developed when the traditions from biblical religion interacted with philosophy and ethics as they developed in the Greco-Roman world. One of these is philosophical theology, the arrangement, analysis, and critical assessment of claims about the nature of the creation and its Creator; the other is theological ethics, the analysis of which patterns of human relations, decision making, and action are right, good, and fitting when seen in relation to God. Theology wants to know what is ultimately true; ethics wants to know what is ultimately just. Both want to know how ultimate issues relate to practical life. Such questions influenced every aspect of Western civilization — at least until certain forms of modern secular thought tried to sever these relationships, as we shall see.

The implications for economics are many, for it is the philosophical element in theology and ethics that has cut the channels of mind and thought by which many Westerners understand themselves, their world, and the divine source and destiny of both — often against business. In the following excerpts from Plato, Aristotle, Plotinus, and Cicero, we find probing questions about the relationship of social ethics to human nature and economic interests, and the relationship of business to politics and the passions. We also find influential theories about the relationship of economic behavior to the quest for human happiness, and the relationship of material goods to spirituality. If we believe that economics must be controlled by politics and that politics must be controlled by philosophy, we are heirs of the classics.

Plato

Socrates, the "gad-fly" of ancient Athens, thought he had a God-given mission to raise all sorts of biting questions about life in that fragile, proto-democratic city-state. He also gave theoretical answers to various questions posed to him by others. A number of young leaders gathered around Socrates and adopted his critical way of thinking, to the chagrin of the elders. When he was tried and executed for being "impious" of the town gods, his student, Plato, founded a school to teach his approach to life. Plato wrote a number of "dialogues" to reflect his engaged method of inquiry and debate. One key question concerned human nature; is it basically good or evil? To what degree can we trust ourselves and our neighbors?

It is sometimes suggested that only the biblical traditions teach the idea of "original sin" — the notion that the primal goodness in humanity has been so distorted that we humans always tend toward untruth and injustice. Thus we find people around us, and ourselves when we are honest about it, seeking selfish ends and taking unfair advantage of our neighbors and of the social and natural environment.

The idea of original sin, however, is not only biblical. A similar view was present in the ancient authoritative poets, such as Homer and Hesiod. It was also present in philosophy, at least since a friend of Socrates named Glaucon asked his opinion on the "parable of the rings," a dialogue that is contained in one of Plato's most famous books, *The Republic*. If the point of the parable is correct, the implications are momentous for business. Is human nature such that people would stop doing honest work and would seduce the innocent and exploit their neighbor for personal gain if they were not controlled by the fear of getting caught? If so, what principles ought to be put in place by political

authority to constrain people's tendencies to evil? As Socrates constructs a model of the economic base of the city, he imagines how it can become "fevered," driven by gluttony. And this, he suggests, leads to war. Economics may be the base of civilization, but it is also the source of violence and imperialism. Economics must be controlled by government, but what is to guide politics?

Plato's response, the remainder of the book, spells out what is suggested in this excerpt: the cure for injustice requires a sense of how the whole is constituted. It is notable that the analysis of what constitutes the whole begins by describing the various kinds of persons and activities that are necessary for society to exist. These, Socrates says, have to be politically controlled to make sure they serve the common good. This in turn requires wise philosophers who are able both to guide the rulers and to teach what is true and just to the citizens. To find that wisdom, he seeks principles that humans already know in the depths of their souls but that become obscured by the clutter of life.

Plato's arguments contain such insights that later thinkers made up the legend that Plato learned from biblical writings. Although that is unlikely, many themes from Plato were adopted as the natural ally of Jewish and Christian convictions. In any case, his view of the relationship of intellectual and moral leadership to the well-being of the common life has been much debated over the centuries, as has the capacity of natural reflection to discover what is universally true, just, and fitting to the cosmopolitan life.

116

On the Myth of the Ring and the Economics of the City

Plato

Glaucon said to me: Socrates, do you wish really to persuade us, or only to seem to have persuaded us, that to be just is always better than to be unjust?

I should wish really to persuade you, I replied, if I could.

Then you certainly have not succeeded. Let me ask you now: — How would you arrange goods — are there not some which we welcome for their own sakes, and independently of their consequences, as, for example, harmless pleasures and enjoyments, which delight us at the time, although nothing follows from them?

I agree in thinking that there is such a class, I replied.

Is there not also a second class of goods, such as knowledge, sight, health, which are desirable not only in themselves, but also for their results?

Certainly, I said.

And would you not recognize a third class, such as gymnastic, and the care of the sick, and the physician's art; also the various ways of money-making — these do us good but we regard them as disagreeable; and no one would choose them for their own sakes, but only for the sake of some reward or result which flows from them?

There is, I said, this third class also. But why do you ask?

Because I want to know in which of the three classes you would place justice?

In the highest class, I replied, — among those

goods which he who would be happy desires both for their own sake and for the sake of their results.

Then the many are of another mind; they think that justice is to be reckoned in the troublesome class, among goods which are to be pursued for the sake of rewards and of reputation, but in themselves are disagreeable and rather to be avoided.

I know, I said, that this is their manner of thinking. . . .

I wish, he said, that you would hear me . . . and then I shall see whether you and I agree. . . . To my mind the nature of justice and injustice have not yet been made clear. Setting aside their rewards and results, I want to know what they are in themselves, and how they inwardly work in the soul. . . . I will speak (first) of the nature and origin of justice according to the common view of them. Secondly, I will show that all men who practice justice do so against their will, of necessity, but not as a good. And thirdly, I will argue that there is reason in this view, for the life of the unjust is after all better far than the life of the just. . . .

Now that those who practice justice do so involuntarily and because they have not the power to be unjust will best appear if we imagine something of this kind: having given both to the just and the unjust power to do what they will, let us watch and see whither desire will lead them; then we shall discover in the very act the just and unjust man to be proceeding along the same road, following their interest, which all natures deem to be their good, and are only diverted into the path of justice by the force of law. The liberty which we are supposing may be most completely given to them in the form of such a power as is said to have been possessed by Gyges. . . . According to the tradition, Gyges was a shepherd in the service of the king of Lydia; there was a great storm, and an earthquake made an opening in the earth at the place where he was feeding his flock. Amazed at the sight, he descended into the opening, where, among other marvels, he beheld a hollow brazen horse, having doors, at which he stooping and looking in saw a dead body of stature . . . , more than human, and having nothing on but a gold ring; this he took from the finger of the dead and reascended. Now the shepherds met together, according to custom, that they might send their

From Plato, *The Republic* (Chicago: Henry Regnery, 1942), chap. 2.

monthly report about the flocks to the king; into their assembly he came having the ring on his finger, and as he was sitting among them he chanced to turn the collet of the ring inside his hand, when instantly he became invisible to the rest of the company and they began to speak of him as if he were no longer present. He was astonished at this, and again touching the ring he turned the collet outwards and reappeared; he made several trials of the ring, and always with the same result — when he turned the collet inwards he became invisible, when outwards he reappeared. Whereupon he contrived to be chosen one of the messengers who were sent to the court; where as soon as he arrived he seduced the queen, and with her help conspired against the king and slew him, and took the kingdom. Suppose now that there were two such magic rings, and the just put on one of them and the unjust the other; no man can be imagined to be of such an iron nature that he would stand fast in justice. No man would keep his hands off what was not his own when he could safely take what he liked out of the market, or go into houses and lie with any one at his pleasure, or kill or release from prison whom he would, and in all respects be like a god among men. Then the actions of the just would be as actions of the unjust; they would both come at last to the same point. And this we may truly affirm to be a great proof that a man is just, not willingly or because he thinks that justice is any good to him individually, but of necessity, for wherever any one thinks that he can safely be unjust, there he is unjust. For all men believe in their hearts that injustice is far more profitable to the individual than justice, and he who argues as I have been supposing, will say that they are right. If you could imagine any one obtaining this power of becoming invisible, and never doing any wrong or touching what was another's he would be thought by the lookers-on to be a most wretched idiot, although they would praise him to one another's faces, and keep up appearances with one another from a fear that they too might suffer injustice. . . .

Heavens! my dear Glaucon, I said, how energetically you polish them up for the decision, first one and then the other, as if they were two statues.

I do my best, he said. And now that we know what they are like there is no difficulty in tracing out the sort of life which awaits either of them. This I will proceed to describe; but. . . let me put them into the mouths of the eulogists of injustice: They will tell you that the just man who is thought unjust will be scourged, racked, bound — will have his eyes burnt out; and, at last, after suffering every kind of evil, he will be impaled: Then he will understand that he ought to seem only, and not to be, just; the words of Aeschylus may be more truly spoken of the unjust than of the just. For the unjust is pursuing a reality; he does not live with a view to appearances — he wants to be really unjust and not to seem only: —

His mind has a soil deep and fertile,
Out of which spring his prudent counsels.

In the first place, he is thought just, and therefore bears rule in the city; he can marry whom he will,. . . . also he can trade and deal where he likes, and always to his own advantage, because he has no misgivings about injustice; and at every contest, whether in public or private, he gets the better of his antagonists, and gains at their expense, and is rich, and out of his gains he can benefit his friends, and harm his enemies; moreover, he can offer sacrifices, and dedicate gifts to the gods abundantly and magnificently, and can honor the gods or any man whom he wants to honor in a far better style than the just, and therefore he is likely to be dearer than they are to the gods. And thus, Socrates, gods and men are said to unite in making the life of the unjust better than the life of the just. . . .

He proceeded: And now when the young hear all this said about virtue and vice, and the way in which gods and men regard them, how are their minds likely to be affected, my dear Socrates, — those of them, I mean, who are quick-witted, and, like bees on the wing, light on every flower, and from all that they hear are prone to draw conclusions as to what manner of persons they should be and in what way they should walk if they would make the best of life? . . .

Glaucon and the rest entreated me . . . to proceed in the investigation. They wanted to arrive at the truth, first, about the nature of justice and injustice, and secondly, about their relative advantages. I told them, what I really thought, that the inquiry would be of a serious nature, and would require very good eyes. Seeing then, I said, that we are no great wits, I think that we had better adopt a method which I may illustrate thus; suppose that a short-sighted person had been asked by some one to read small letters from a distance; and it occurred to some one else that they might be found in another place which was larger and in which the letters were larger — if they were the same and he could read the larger letters first, and then proceed to the lesser — this would have been thought a rare piece of good fortune.

Very true, said Adeimantus; but how does the illustration apply to our inquiry?

I will tell you, I replied: justice, which is the subject of our inquiry, is, as you know, sometimes spoken of as the virtue of an individual, and sometimes as the virtue of a State.

True, he replied.

And is not a State larger than an individual?

It is.

Then in the larger the quantity of justice is likely to be larger and more easily discernible. I propose therefore that we inquire into the nature of justice and injustice, first as they appear in the State, and secondly in the individual, proceeding from the greater to the lesser and comparing them.

That, he said, is an excellent proposal.

And if we imagine the State in process of creation, we shall see the justice and injustice of the State in process of creation also. . . .

A State, I said, arises, as I conceive, out of the needs of mankind; no one is self-sufficing, but all of us have many wants. Can any other origin of a State be imagined?

There can be no other.

Then, as we have many wants, and many persons are needed to supply them, one takes a helper for one purpose and another for another; and when these partners and helpers are gathered together in one habitation the body of inhabitants is termed a State.

True, he said.

And they exchange with one another, and one gives, and another receives, under the idea that the exchange will be for their good.

Very true.

Then, I said, let us begin and create in idea a State; and yet the true creator is necessity, who is the mother of our invention.

Of course, he replied.

Now the first and greatest of necessities is food, which is the condition of life and existence.

Certainly.

The second is a dwelling, and the third clothing and the like.

True.

And now let us see how our city will be able to supply this great demand: We may suppose that one man is a husbandman, another a builder, some one else a weaver — shall we add to them a shoemaker, or perhaps some other purveyor to our bodily wants?

Quite right.

The barest notion of a State must include four or five men.

Clearly.

And how will they proceed? Will each bring the result of his labors into a common stock? — the individual husbandman, for example, producing for four, and laboring four times as long and as much as he need in the provision of food with which he supplies others as well as himself; or will he have nothing to do with others and not be at the trouble of producing for them, but provide for himself alone a fourth of the food in a fourth of the time, and in the remaining three-fourths of his time be employed in making a house or a coat or a pair of shoes, having no partnership with others, but supply himself all his own wants?

Adeimantus thought that he should aim at producing food only and not at producing everything.

Probably, I replied, that would be the better way; and when I hear you say this, I am myself reminded that we are not all alike; there are diversities of natures among us which are adapted to different occupations.

Very true.

And will you have a work better done when the workman has many occupations, or when he has only one?

When he has only one.

Further, there can be no doubt that a work is spoilt when not done at the right time?

No doubt.

For business is not disposed to wait until the doer of the business is at leisure; but the doer must follow up what he is doing, and make the business his first object.

He must.

And if so, we must infer that all things are produced more plentiful and easily and of a better quality when one man does one thing which is natural to him and does it at the right time, and leaves other things.

Undoubtedly.

Then more than four citizens will be required; for the husbandman will not make his own plough or mattock, or other implements of agriculture, if they are to be good for anything. Neither will the builder make his tools — and he too needs many; and in like manner the weaver and shoemaker.

True.

Then carpenters and smiths, and many other artisans, will be sharers in our little State, which is already beginning to grow?

True.

Yet even if we add neatherds, shepherds, and other herdsmen, in order that our husbandmen may have oxen to plough with, and builders as well as husbandmen may have draught cattle, and curriers and weavers fleeces and hides, — still our State will not be very large.

That is true; yet neither will it be a very small State which contains all these.

Then, again, there is the situation of the city — to find a place where nothing need be imported is wellnigh impossible.

Then there must be another class of citizens who will bring the required supply from another city?

There must.

But if the trader goes empty-handed, having nothing which they require who would supply his need, he will come back empty-handed.

That is certain.

And therefore what they produce at home must be not only enough for themselves, but such both in quantity and quality as to accommodate those from whom their wants are supplied.

Very true.

Then more husbandmen and more artisans will be required?

They will.

Not to mention the importers and exporters, who are called merchants?

Yes.

Then we shall want merchants?

We shall.

And if merchandise is to be carried over the sea, skilful sailors will also be needed, and in considerable numbers?

Yes, in considerable numbers.

Then, again, within the city, how will they exchange their productions? To secure such an exchange was, as you will remember, one of our principal objects when we formed them into a society and constituted a State.

Clearly they will buy and sell.

Then they will need a market-place, and a money-token for purposes of exchange.

Certainly.

Suppose now that a husbandman, or an artisan, brings some production to market, and he comes at a time when there is no one to exchange with him, — is he to leave his calling and sit idle in the market-place?

Not at all; he will find people there who, seeing the want, undertake the office of salesmen. In well-ordered States they are commonly those who are the weakest in bodily strength, and therefore of little use for any other purposes; their duty is to be in the market, and to give money in exchange for goods to those who desire to sell and to take money from those who desire to buy.

This want, then, creates a class of retail-traders in our State. Is not 'retailer' the term which is applied to those who sit in the market-place engaged in buying and selling, while those who wander from one city to another are called merchants?

Yes, he said.

And there is another class of servants, who are intellectually hardly on the level of companionship; still they have plenty of bodily strength for labor, which accordingly they sell, and are called, if I do not mistake, hirelings, hire being the name which is given to the price of their labor.

True.

Then hirelings will help to make up our population?

Yes.

And now, Adeimantus, is our State matured and perfected?

I think so.

Where, then, is justice and where is injustice, and in what part of the State did they spring up?

Probably in the dealings of these citizens with one another. I cannot imagine that they are more likely to be found anywhere else.

I dare say that you are right in your suggestion, I said, we had better think the matter out, and not shrink from the inquiry. . . .

Let us then consider, first of all, what will be their way of life, now that we have thus established them. Will they not produce corn, and wine, and clothes, and shoes, and build houses for themselves? And when they are housed, they will work, in summer, commonly, stripped and barefoot, but in winter substantially clothed and shod. They will feed on barley-meal and flour of wheat, baking and kneading them, making noble cakes and loaves; these they will serve up on a mat of reeds or on clean leaves, themselves reclining the while upon beds strewn with yew or myrtle. And they and their children will feast, drinking of the wine which they have made, wearing garlands on their heads, and hymning the praises of the gods, in happy converse with one another. And they will take care that their families do not exceed their means; having an eye to poverty or war.

But, said Glaucon, interposing, you have not given them a relish to their meal.

True, I replied, I had forgotten; of course they must have a relish — salt, and olives, and cheese, and they will boil roots and herbs such as country people prepare; for a dessert we shall give them figs, and peas, and beans; and they will roast myrtle-berries and acorns at the fire, drinking in moderation. And with such a diet they may be expected to live in peace and health to a good old age, and bequeath a similar life to their children after them.

Yes, Socrates, he said, and if you were providing for a city of pigs, how else would you feed the beasts?

But what would you have, Glaucon? I replied.

Why, he said, you should give them the ordinary conveniences of life. People who are to be comfortable are accustomed to life on sofas, and dine off tables, and they should have sauces and sweets in the modern style.

Yes, I said, now I understand: the question which you would have me consider is, not only how a State, but how a luxurious State is created; and possibly there is no harm in this, for in such a State we shall be more likely to see how justice and injustice originate. In my opinion the true and healthy constitution of the State is the one which I have described. But if you wish also to see a State at fever-heat, I have no objection. For I suspect that many will not be satisfied with the simpler way of life. They will be for adding sofas, and tables, and other furniture; also dainties, and perfumes, and incense, and courtesans, and cakes, all these not of one sort only, but in every variety; we must go beyond the necessaries of which I was at first speaking, such as houses, and clothes, and shoes: the arts of the painter and the embroiderer will have to be set in motion, and gold and ivory and all sorts of materials must be procured.

True, he said.

Then we must enlarge our borders; for the original healthy State is no longer sufficient. Now will the city have to fill and swell with a multitude of callings which are not required by any natural want; such as the whole tribe of hunters and actors, of whom one large class have to do with forms and colours; another will be the votaries of music — poets and their attedant train of rhapsodists, players, dancers, contractors; also makers of divers kinds of articles, including women's dresses. And we shall want more servants. Will not tutors be also in request, and nurses wet and dry, tirewomen and barbers, as well as confectioners and cooks; and swineherds, too, who were not needed and therefore had no place in the former edition of our State, but are needed now? They must not be forgotten: and there will be animals of many other kinds, if people eat them.

Certainly.

And living in this way we shall have much greater need of physicians than before?

Much greater.

And the country which was enough to support the original inhabitants will be too small now, and not enough?

Quite true.

Then a slice of our neighbours' land will be wanted by us for pasture and tillage, and they will want a slice of ours, if, like ourselves, they exceed the limit of necessity; and give themselves up to the unlimited accumulation of wealth?

That, Socrates, will be inevitable.

And so we shall go to war, Glaucon, shall we not?

Most certainly, he replied.

Then, without determining as yet whether war does good or harm, thus much we may affirm, that now we have discovered war to be derived from causes which are also the causes of almost all the evils in States, private as well as public. (In any case, all this would have to be managed by a ruler or guardian. . . .)

He who is to be a really good and noble guardian of the State will require to unite in himself philosophy and spirit and swiftness and strength?

Undoubtedly.

Then we have found the desired natures; and now that we have found them, how are they to be reared and educated? Is not this an inquiry which may be expected to throw light on the greater inquiry which is our final end — How do justice and injustice grow up in States? for we do not want either to omit what is to the point or to draw out the argument to an inconvenient length.

Adeimantus thought that the inquiry would be of great service to us.

Then, I said, my dear friend, the task must not be given up, even if somewhat long.

Certainly not.

Come then, and let us pass a leisure hour in story-telling, and our story shall be the education of our heroes.

By all means.

And what shall be their education? Can we find a better than the traditional sort? — and this has two divisions, gymnastic [physical skills] for the body, and music [skills in musing or reflecting] for the soul.

True.

Shall we begin education with music, and go on to gymnastic afterwards?

By all means.

And when you speak of music, do you include literature or not?

I do.

And literature may be either true or false?

Yes.

And the young should be trained in both kinds, and we begin with the false?

I do not understand your meaning, he said.

You know, I said, that we begin by telling children stories which, though not wholly destitute of truth, are in the main fictitious; and these stories are told them when they are not of an age to learn gymnastics.

Very true.

That was my meaning when I said that we must teach music before gymnastics.

Quite right, he said.

You know also that the beginning is the most important part of any work, especially in the case of a young and tender thing; for that is the time at which the character is being formed and the desired impression is more readily taken.

Quite true.

And shall we just carelessly allow children to hear any casual tales which may be devised by casual persons, and to receive into their minds ideas for the most part the very opposite of those which we should wish them to have when they are grown up?

We cannot.

Then the first thing will be to establish a censorship of the writers of fiction, and let the censors receive any tale of fiction which is good, and reject the bad; and we will desire mothers and nurses to tell their children the authorized ones only. Let them fashion the mind with such tales, even more fondly than they mould the body with their hands; but most of those which are now in use must be discarded.

Of what tales are you speaking? he said.

You may find a model of the lesser in the greater, I said; for they are necessarily of the same type, and there is the same spirit in both of them.

Very likely, — he replied; but I do not as yet know what you would term the greater.

Those, I said, which are narrated by Homer and Hesiod, and the rest of the poets, who have ever been the great story-tellers of mankind.

But which stories do you mean, he said; and what fault do you find with them?

A fault which is most serious, I said; the fault of telling a lie, and, what is more, a bad lie.

But when is this fault committed?

Whenever an erroneous representation is made of the nature of gods and heroes, — as when a painter paints a portrait not having the shadow of a likeness to the original.

For a young person cannot judge what is allegorical and what is literal; anything that he receives into his mind at that age is likely to become indelible and unalterable; and therefore it is most important that the tales which the young first hear should be models of virtuous thoughts.

There you are right, he replied; but if any one asks where are such models to be found and of what tales are you speaking — how shall we answer him?

I said to him, you and I, Adeimantus, at this

Excerpts from Hesiod's *Works and Days*

From working, men grow rich in flocks
    and gold
And dearer to the deathless gods. In work
There is no shame; shame is in idleness.
And if you work, the lazy man will soon
Envy your wealth: a rich man can become
Famous and good. . . . The humble are
The poor men, while the rich are self-assured.
Money should not be seized; that gold
    which is
God's gift is better. If a man gets wealth
By force of hands or through his lying tongue,
As often happens, when greed clouds his mind
And shame is pushed aside by shamelessness,
Then the gods blot him out and blast
    his house
And soon his wealth deserts him. Also he
Who harms a guest or suppliant, or acts
Unseemly, sleeping with his brother's wife,
Or in his folly, hurts an orphan child,
Or he who picks rough quarrels and attacks
His father at the threshold of old age,
He angers Zeus himself, and in the end
He pays harsh penalties for all his sins. . . .
Shun evil profit, for dishonest gain
Is just the same as failure. Love your friends;
Approach the men who come to you, and give
To him who gives, but not, if he does not. . . .

Add to your stores, and Famine, burning-eyed,
Will stay away. Even if your supply
Is small, and if you add a little bit,
And do it often, soon it will be big.
Less worry comes from having wealth
    at home;
Business abroad is always insecure. . . .
Let wages promised to a friend be fixed
Beforehand; even with your brother, smile
And have a witness, for too much mistrust
And too much trust can both be ruinous. . . .
When the Pleiads, Atlas' daughters, start to rise
Begin your harvest; plough when they
    go down.
For forty days and nights they
    hide themselves,
And as the year rolls round, appear again
When you begin to sharpen sickle-blades;
This law holds on the plains and by the sea,
And in the mountain valleys. . . . To sow
    your seed
Go naked; strip to plough and strip to reap,
If you would harvest all Demeter's yield . . .
And later, you will not be found in need
And forced to beg from other men, and get
No help. See now, you come to me like that,
And I will neither give nor lend to you.
You foolish Perses, go to work! The gods
    have given work to men. . . .

— Hesiod, "Works and Days," in *Hesiod and
Theognis,* trans. Dorothea Wender
(Baltimore: Penguin, 1973), pp. 68-71

moment are not poets, but founders of a State: now the founders of a State ought to know the general forms in which poets should cast their tales, and the limits which must be observed by them, but to make the tales is not their business.

Very true, he said; but what are these forms of theology which you mean?

Something of this kind, I replied: — God is always to be represented as he truly is, whatever be the sort of poetry, epic, lyric or tragic, in which the representation is given.

Right.

And is he not truly good? And must he not be represented as such?

Certainly.

And no good thing is hurtful?

No, indeed.

And that which is not hurtful hurts not?

Certainly not.

And that which hurts not does no evil?

No.

And can that which does no evil be a cause of evil?

Impossible.

And the good is advantageous?

Yes.

And therefore the cause of well-being?

Yes.

It follows therefore that the good is not the cause of all things, but of the good only?

Assuredly.

Then God, if he be good, is not the author of all things, as the many assert, but he is the cause of a few things only, and not of most things that occur to men. For few are the goods of human life, and many are the evils, and the good is to be attributed to God alone; of the evils the causes are to be sought elsewhere, and not in him.

That appears to me to be most true, he said.

Well, but can you imagine that God will be willing to lie, whether in word or deed, or to put forth a phantom of himself?

I cannot say, he replied.

Do you not know, I said, that the true life, if such an expression may be allowed, is hated of gods and men?

What do you mean? he said.

I mean that no one is willingly deceived in that which is the truest and highest part of himself, or about the truest and highest matters; there, above all, he is most afraid of a lie having possession of him.

Still, he said, I do not comprehend you.

The reason is, I replied, that you attribute some profound meaning to my words; but I am only saying that deception, or being deceived or uninformed about the highest realities in the highest part of themselves, which is the soul, and in that part of them to have and to hold the lie, is what mankind least like; — that, I say, is what they utterly detest.

There is nothing more hateful to them.

And, as I was just now remarking, this ignorance in the soul of him who is deceived may be called the true lie; for the lie in words is only a kind of imitation and shadowy image of a previous affection of the soul, not pure unadulterated falsehood. Am I not right?

Perfectly right.

The true lie is hated not only by the gods, but also by men?

Yes.

Whereas the lie in words is in certain cases useful and not hateful; in dealing with enemies — that would be an instance; or again, when those whom we call our friends in a fit of madness or illusion are going to do some harm, then it is useful and is a sort of medicine or preventive; also in the tales of mythology, of which we were just now speaking — because we do not know the truth about ancient times, we make falsehood as much like truth as we can, and so turn it to account.

Very true, he said.

But can any of these reasons apply to God? Can we suppose that he is ignorant of antiquity, and therefore has recourse to invention?

That would be ridiculous, he said.

Then the lying poet has no place in our idea of God?

I should say not.

Or perhaps he may tell a lie because he is afraid of enemies?

That is inconceivable.

But he may have friends who are senseless or mad?

But no mad or senseless person can be a friend of God.

Then no motive can be imagined why God should lie?

None whatever.

Then the superhuman and divine is absolutely incapable of falsehood?

Yes.

Then is God perfectly simple and true both in word and deed; he changes not; he deceives not, either by sign or word, by dream or waking vision.

Your thoughts, he said, are the reflection of my own.

You agree with me then, I said, that this is the second type or form in which we should write and speak about divine things. . . . [This, then, is the basis for ordering justice in the State, and in the souls of citizens.]

Aristotle

Aristotle was Plato's most brilliant student. But he broke with his teacher on several key issues and established his own school. His lectures and writings formed the second great body of philosophical literature in Western intellectual history. Indeed, Alfred North Whitehead, the great twentieth-century thinker, only exaggerated somewhat when he said that "all of philosophy is but a footnote to Plato and Aristotle." Certainly many Jews, Christians, Muslims, and humanist thinkers have found as close an ally in Aristotle as they did in Plato.

Three disagreements between Plato and Aristotle are most important for the study of ethics and business. First, Aristotle does not think that we can figure things out by grasping a sense of the whole, or by discovering universal principles in the depths of the human soul, or by trying to imagine how God must be. He was convinced that we had to begin with particulars and proceed toward more general truths. He believed that we must first discover what makes particular persons virtuous, and then we will know what makes for wise leadership and prudent social practice. Both his *Ethics* and his *Politics* reflect this conviction.

Second, Aristotle had a more optimistic view of human nature. While Plato writes of the human propensity to evil — and then proposes ways to constrain it by means of political authority, education, and a philosophy based on universal principles, Aristotle begins with the assumption that everyone, indeed, everything, has a tendency to the good. If clearly understood and made actual by proper habits and measured experience, all would lead naturally to the common good and the happiness of wisdom — the goal of life. Thus, Aristotle links the analysis of the ethos directly to teleology, while Plato tends to connect it to deontological forms.

And third, Aristotle was much more fascinated by the natural sciences, such as biology, than Plato was, and he applied the methods and findings of his empirical study of the natural world to social, psychological, political, and economic matters. Of particular importance is the general theory of causation that he used in all these areas. Given the limits of his resources, it is fair to say that his powers of observation and categorization were among the greatest of any scholar in human history; and it is not accidental that his views on a range of particular questions — the nature of money, the purposes of economic activity, the relationship of commerce to virtue and justice, etc. — were held as both moral and empirical absolutes for centuries. When someone invokes Aristotle, however, it is necessary to inquire whether it is his (seldom irrelevant) demand to face the facts or his (often surpassed) interpretation of them that is in question.

These accents can be found in his writings on economics, management, and business, which occur in his treatment of the household in his *Politics*. In his view, the household is the proper locus for production and distribution, rooted in the natural relationships of master and slave, husband and wife, and parents and children, and in living close to the earth, the source of material creativity. He contrasts these relations to the artificiality of commerce, trade, and finance, which he thinks are not "fecund," that is, not really productive.

On the Management of the Household and the Perils of Trade

Aristotle

I

All associations have ends: the political association has the highest; but the principle of association expresses itself in different forms, and through different modes of government.

Observation shows us, first, that every polis or state is a species of association, and, secondly, that all associations are instituted for the purpose of attaining some good — for all men do all their acts with a view to achieving something which is, in their view, a good. We may therefore hold on the basis of what we actually observe that all associations aim at some good; and we may also hold that the particular association which is the most sovereign of all, and includes all the rest, will pursue this aim most, and will thus be directed to the most sovereign of all goods. . . .

VIII

The art of household management is distinct from that of acquisition. It has to provide a stock of requisites for the household; and the different methods by which this is

---

Aristotle, "The Theory of the Household," in *The Politics of Aristotle*, bk. 1, chaps. 1, 8-10, trans. and ed. Ernest Barker (New York: Oxford University Press, 1946).

done produce different ways of life. . . . Nature intends and provides the requisites for household use; and the acquisition of such requisites is a natural mode of acquisition. Property in them is limited to the amount required by household needs; and it is the nature of all true wealth to be so limited.

We may now study generally all forms of property and the art of acquiring it, following our normal method, the analytical and genetic method, which proceeds from the parts to the whole and from the first beginnings to the developed result. . . . The first problem which may be raised is whether the art of acquiring property is identical with that of household management, or is a part of it, or is ancillary to it; and whether, if it be ancillary, it is so in the sense in which the art of making shuttles is ancillary to the art of weaving, or in the sense in which the art of casting bronze is ancillary to the art of sculpture. . . . Either of these ancillary arts serves its master-art in a different way; the one provides it with an instrument, and the other with material.

By "material" we mean the substance from which a product is made: wool, for instance, serves the weaver as the substance from which he produces cloth; and bronze serves the sculptor in the same way. . . . That the art of household management is not identical with the art of acquiring property is obvious. It is the function of the latter simply to *provide* either instruments or materials, as the case may be, but it is the function of the former to *use* what has been provided; for what art can there be, other than that of household management, which will deal with the use of the resources of the household? But the question whether the art of acquisition is a part of it, or a separate art altogether, is one which admits of a divergence of views.

If a man who is engaged in acquisition has to consider from what different sources he can get goods and property, and if property and wealth include many different parts drawn from many different sources, we shall first have to consider these parts before we can consider acquisition as a whole. For instance, we shall have to ask whether farming is a part of the art of acquisition, or a separate art: indeed we shall have to ask that question generally, in regard to *all* modes of occupation and gain which are concerned with the provision of subsistence.

This leads to a further observation. There are a number of different modes of subsistence; and the result is a number of different ways of life, both in the animal world and the human. It is impossible to live without means of subsistence; and in the animal world we may notice that differences in the means of subsistence have produced consequent differences in ways of life.

Some animals live in herds, and others are scattered in isolation, according as they find it convenient for the purpose of getting subsistence — some of them being carnivorous, some herbivorous, and some, again, omnivorous. Nature has thus distinguished their ways of life, with a view to their greater comfort and their better attainment of what they need: indeed, as the same sort of food is not naturally agreeable to all the members of a class, and as different sorts suit different species, we also find different ways of life even inside the class of carnivorous animals — and equally in that of the herbivorous — distinguishing species from species.

What is true of animals is also true of men. Their ways of life also differ considerably. The most indolent are the pastoral nomads. . . . There are others who live by hunting. . . . Some live by fishing; etc. . . . Most men, however, derive their livelihood from the soil, and from cultivated plants.

The different ways of life, at any rate if we take into account only those who follow an occupation dependent on their own labors, and do not provide themselves with subsistence at the expense of others by exchange and petty trade, may be roughly classified. . . . But there are some who live comfortably by means of a combination of different methods, and who eke out the shortcomings of one way of life, when it tends to fall short of being sufficient in itself, by adding some other way. For example, some combine the pastoral way of life with the freebooting: others combine farming with the life of the chase; and similar combinations may similarly be made of other ways of life, as needs and tastes impel men to shape their lives.

Property of this order, that is to say, for the purpose of subsistence, is evidently given by nature to all living beings, from the instant of their first birth to the days when their growth is finished.

There are animals which, when their offspring is born, bring forth along with it food enough to support it until it can provide for itself: this is the case with insects which reproduce themselves by grubs, and with animals which do so by eggs. Animals which are viviparous have food for their offspring in themselves, for a certain time, of the nature of what is called milk.

. . . We must believe that similar provision is also made for adults. Plants exist to give subsistence to animals, and animals to give it to men. Animals, when they are domesticated, serve for use as well as for food; wild animals, too, in most cases if not in all, serve to furnish man not only with food, but also with other comforts, such as the provision of clothing and similar aids to life.

Accordingly, as nature makes nothing purposeless or in vain, all animals must have been made by nature for the sake of men. It also follows that the art of war is in some sense, that is to say, so far as it is directed to gaining the means of subsistence from animals, a natural mode of acquisition. Hunting is a part of that art; and hunting ought to be practiced — not only against wild animals, but also against human beings who are intended by nature to be ruled by others and refuse to obey that intention — because war of this order is naturally just.

It follows that one form of acquisition, i.e. what may be called the "hunting" form, is naturally a part of the art of household management. It is a form of acquisition which the manager of a household must either find ready to hand, or himself provide and arrange, because it ensures a supply of objects, necessary for life and useful to the association of the polis or the household, which are capable of being stored.

These are the objects which may be regarded as constituting true wealth. True wealth has a limit of size, determined by the purpose of the association it serves; and the amount of household property which suffices for a good life is not unlimited, nor of the nature described by Solon in the verse,

"There is no bound to wealth [that] stands fixed for men."

There *is* a bound fixed for the property needed by the art of household management, as is also the case in the means required by the other arts. All the instruments needed by all the arts are limited, both in number and size, by the requirements of the art they serve; and wealth may be defined as a number of instruments used in a household or state and needed for their respective "arts."

It is thus clear that there is a natural art of acquisition which is to be practiced by managers of households and statesmen; and the reason for its existence is also clear the reason being that it is natural for man to acquire what is naturally provided for his use. . . .

IX

The "art of acquisition" is a way of acquiring property distinct from the natural way of the household. It originates in exchange, when exchange is conducted through the medium of currency and for profit. The view thus arises that the art of acquisition is specially concerned with accumulating a fund of currency. But there is a contrary view that currency is a mere convention, and not the true object of the art of acquisition. This contrary view has its truth. There is a natural form of the art of acquisition, which is not distinct from, but a part of, the art of household management. This natural form of acquisition aims at the accumulation not of currency, but of true wealth — and therefore not at the infinite, but at the finite.

But there is a second form of the general art of getting property, which is particularly called, and which it is just to call, "the art of acquisition." It is the characteristics of this second form which lead to the opinion that there is no limit to wealth and property. There are many who hold this second form of the art of getting property to be identical with the other form previously mentioned, because it has affinities with it. In fact it is not identical, and yet is is not far removed. The other form previously mentioned is natural: this second form is not natural, but is rather the product of a certain sort of experience and skill.

We may start our discussion of this form from the following point of view. All articles of property have two possible uses. Both of these uses belong to the article as such, but they do not belong to it in the same manner, or to the same extent. The one is proper and peculiar to the article concerned; the other is not. We may take a shoe as an example. It can be used both for wearing and for exchange. Both of these uses are uses of the shoe as such.

Even the man who exchanges a shoe, in return for money or food, with a person who needs the article, is using the shoe as a shoe; but since the shoe has not been made for the purpose of being exchanged, the use which he is making of it is not its proper and peculiar use. The same is true of all other articles of property.

Exchange is possible in regard to them all: it arises from the natural facts of the case, and is due to some men having more, and others less, than suffices for their needs. We can thus see that retail trade which buys from others to sell at a profit is not naturally a part of the art of acquisition. If that were the case, it would only be necessary to practice exchange to the extent that sufficed for the needs of both parties and not to the extent of the making of profit by one of the parties at the expense of the other.

In the first form of association, which is the household, it is obvious that there is no purpose to be served by the art of exchange. Such a purpose only emerged when the scope of association had already been extended until it issued in the village. The members of the household had shared all things in common: the members of the village, separated from one another in a number of different households, had at their disposal a number of different things, which they had to exchange with one another, as need arose, by way of barter — much as many uncivilized tribes still to to this day.

On this basis things which are useful are exchanged themselves, and directly, for similar useful things, but the transaction does not go any further that is to say, no money is involved; wine, for instance, is given, or taken, in return for wheat, and other similar commodities are similarly bartered for one another. When used in this way, the art of exchange is not contrary to nature, nor in any way a form of the art of acquisition in the second sense of that term defined at the beginning of this chapter. Exchange simply served in its first beginnings to satisfy the natural requirements of sufficiency.

None the less it was from exchange, as thus practiced, that the art of acquisition in its second sense developed, in the sort of way we might reasonably expect. Distant transactions were the cause. The supply of men's needs came to depend on more foreign sources, as men began to import for themselves what they lacked, and to export what they had in superabundance; and in this way the use of a money currency was inevitably instituted.

The reason for this institution of a currency was that all the naturally necessary commodities were not easily portable; and men therefore agreed, for the purpose of their exchanges, to give and receive some commodity i.e. some form of more or less precious metal which itself belonged to the category of useful things and possessed the advantage of being easily handled for the purpose of getting the necessities of life. Such commodities were iron, silver, and other similar metals. At first their value was simply determined by their size and weight; but finally a stamp was imposed on the metal which, serving as a definite indication of the quantity, would save men the trouble of determining the value of each occasion.

When, in this way, a currency had once been instituted, there next arose, from the necessary process of exchange, i.e. exchange between commodities, with money serving merely as a measure, the other form of the art of acquisition, which consists in retail trade conducted for profit. At first, we may allow, it was perhaps practiced in a simple way, that is to say, money was still regarded as a measure, and not treated as a source of profit; but in process of time, and as the result of experience, it was practiced with a more studied technique, which sought to discover the sources from which, and the methods by which, the greatest profit could be made.

The result has been the emergence of the view that the art of acquisition is specially concerned with currency, and that its function consists in an ability to discover the sources from which a fund of *money* can be derived. In support of this view it is urged that the art is one which produces wealth and money; indeed those who hold the view often assume that wealth is simply a fund of currency, on the ground that the art of acquisition (in the form of retail trade for profit) is concerned with currency.

In opposition to this view there is another which is sometimes held. On this view currency is regarded as a sham, and entirely a convention. Naturally and inherently, the supporters of the view argue, a currency is a nonentity; for if those who use a currency give it up in favor of another, that currency is worthless, and useless for any of the necessary purposes of life. A man rich in currency, they proceed to urge, will often be at a loss to procure the necessities of subsistence; and surely it is absurd that a thing should be counted as wealth which a man may possess in abundance, and yet none the less die of starvation — like Midas in the fable, when everything set before him was turned at once into gold through the granting of his own avaricious prayer.

Basing themselves on these arguments, those who hold this latter view try to find a different conception of wealth from that which identifies it with a fund of currency and a different conception of the art of acquisition from that which makes it specially concerned with currency. They are right in making the attempt. The natural art of acquisition, and natural wealth, *are* different. The natural form of the art of acquisition is connected with the management of the household which in turn is connected with the *general* acquisition of *all* the resource needed for its life; but the other form is a matter only of retail trade, and it is concerned only with getting a fund of money, and that only by the method of conducting the exchange of commodities. This latter form may be held to turn on the power of currency; for currency is the starting-point, as it is also the goal, of exchange.

It is a further point of difference that the wealth produced by this latter form of the art of acquisition is unlimited. In this respect the art of acquisition, in its retail form, is analogous to other professional arts. The art of medicine recognizes no limit in respect of the production of health, and the arts generally admit no limit in respect of the production of their ends each seeking to produce its end to the greatest possible extent — though medicine, and the arts generally, recognize and practice a limit to the means they use to attain their ends, since the end itself constitutes a limit. The same is true of the retail form of the art of acquisition. There is no limit to the end it seeks; and the end it seeks is wealth of the sort we have mentioned i.e. wealth in the form of currency and the mere acquisition of money.

But the acquisition of wealth by the art of household management as contrasted with the art of acquisition in its retail form *has* a limit; and the object of that art is not an unlimited amount of wealth. It would thus appear, if we look at the matter in this light, that all wealth must have a limit. In actual experience, however, we see the opposite happening; and all who are engaged in acquisition increase their fund of currency without any limit or pause.

The cause of this contradiction lies in the close connection between the two different modes of acquisition that of the householder, and that of the retail trader. They overlap because they are both handling the same objects and acting in the same field of acquisition; but they move along different lines — the object of the one being simply accumulation, and that of the other something quite different. This overlap of the two modes explains why some men believe that mere accumulation is the object of household management; and in the strength of that belief they stick to the idea that they must keep their wealth in currency untouched, or increase it indefinitely.

But the fundamental cause of this state of mind is men's anxiety about livelihood, rather than about well-being; and since their desire for that is unlimited, their desire for the things that produce it is equally unlimited. Even those who do aim at well-being seek the means of obtaining physical enjoyments; and, as what they seek appears to depend on the activity of acquisition, they are thus led to occupy themselves wholly in the making of money. This is the real reason why the other and lower form of the art of acquisition has come into vogue.

Because enjoyment depends on the possession of a superfluity, men address themselves to the art which produces the superfluity necessary to enjoyment; and if they cannot get what they want by the use of that art — i.e. the art of acquisition — they attempt to do so by other means, using each and every capacity in a way not consonant with its nature. The proper function of courage, for example, is not to produce money but to give confidence. The same is true of military and medical ability: neither has the function of producing money: the one has the function of producing victory, and the other that of producing health.

But those of whom we are speaking turn all such capacities into forms of the art of acquisition, as though to make money were the one aim and everything else must contribute to that aim.

We have thus discussed the unnecessary form of the art of acquisition: we have described its nature, and we have explained why men need or think that they need its services. We have also discussed the necessary form: we have shown that it is different from the other, and is naturally a branch of the art of household management, concerned with the provision of a due amount of subsistence, and *not*, therefore, unlimited in its scope, as the other form is, but subject to definite bounds.

X

Household management is concerned with the use, and not (except in the way of general supervision) with the acquisition, of property; generally the householder should be able to count on nature supplying the means he needs. Acquisition for acquisition's sake shows its worst side in usury, which makes barren metal breed.

The argument of the last chapter provides a clear solution to the problem which we originally raised: "Does the art of acquisition belong to the province of the manager of the household and the statesman and is it thus a part of, or otherwise connected with, their art? Or is it outside that province, and should property be regarded as something on which they can simply count, and with the acquisition of which they need not concern themselves?" It may be urged, in favor of the second alternative, that just as the art of the statesman does not produce human stock, but counts on its being supplied by nature and proceeds to use her supply, so nature must also provide the physical means of subsistence — the land, or sea, or whatever it be. Then, and upon that basis, it is the province of the householder to manage properly the means which are ready to his hand. . . .

On a general view, as we have already noticed, a supply of property should be ready to hand as a provision of nature. It is the business of nature to furnish subsistence for each being brought into the world; and this is shown by the fact that the offspring of animals always gets nourishment from the residum of the matter that gives it its birth.

The natural form, therefore, of the art of acquisition is always, and in all cases, acquisition from fruits and animals. That art, as we have said, has two forms: one which is connected with retail trade, and another which is connected with the management of the household. Of these two forms, the latter is necessary and laudable; the former is a method of exchange which is justly censured, because the gain in which it results is not naturally made from plants and animals, but is made at the expense of other men.

The trade of the petty usurer, the extreme example of that form of the art of acquisition which is connected with retail trade, is hated most, and with most reason: it makes a profit from currency itself, instead of making it from the process, i.e. of exchange which currency was meant to serve.

Currency came into existence merely as a means of exchange; usury tries to make it increase as though it were an end in itself. This is the reason why usury is called by the word we commonly use, *tokos*, which (in Greek) also means "breed" or "offspring"; for as the offspring resembles its parent, so the interest bred by money is like the principal which breeds it, and as a son is styled by his father's name, so it may be called "currency the son of currency." Hence we can understand why, of all modes of acquisition, usury is the most unnatural.

Cicero

Aristotelian thought in antiquity tended toward naturalism. It was later developed by the Muslims and still later became adapted to major developments in Christian thinking, especially by St. Thomas Aquinas; but in the ancient world, it temporarily lost influence. Generally, Athens declined when Rome conquered Greece and established its empire. New forms of internationalism developed in politics, ethics, and religion as trade brought people into contact with one another. People had to begin to think in more cosmopolitan terms than the theories of city-state and household allowed.

The most impressive ethical teachings came from a group of philosophers called the "Stoics." Heraclitus, Zeno, and others gave lectures on a famous porch (or *stoa* in Greek) some three hundred years before Christ. They emphasized the idea of "natural law" as a moral concept, less as an empirical "law of nature" than as a general human ability to tell right from wrong. Because of this, it made little difference to Stoics whether one was Jewish or pagan, Roman or Greek, African or European, rich or poor, male or female. The human moral capacity was the same for all — if, that is, it was exercised with discipline and equanimity, for otherwise it became corrupted by local customs and foolish passions.

Stoics thus accented a sense of duty, a cosmopolitan sense of the human community, a moral approach to religious issues, and a studied control of the passions. Such a combination generated reliable administrators, managers, jurists, and teachers. Their honesty, incorruptibility, and impartial performance of duty brought them much respect. It is said that through these Stoics, Greece reconquered Rome from the inside. Certainly, the moral and legal fabric of the Roman Empire, perhaps the most just regime of its sort the world had ever seen, became the embodiment of "Greco-Roman" philosophy.

Cicero represents a "romanized" phase of Stoic thought. In his *Laws,* he modifies the Greek notion of justice by developing an idea of "humanity" as a chief source of authority. He emphasizes equality before a universal moral law, and thus the notion that the state must live in accord with justice and not simply impose arbitrary laws, in the same way that an individual must live in accord with ethical principles and not simply choose personal values.

One can see certain similarities between early Christianity and the Stoics, and elements of Stoic thought can be found in the New Testament and early church writings, partly because they were pervasive at that time, and partly because there were striking parallels between early church teachings and Stoic thought. Stoic ideas later were utilized by reformers among medieval, reformation, and American colonial thinkers — especially those who tried to develop a theological view of law, politics, and economics. Ideas of modern democracy, human rights, and mass markets might not have developed without the Stoics' moral challenges to the ancient tribal societies, the state-dominated political philosophy of Plato, or the household-dominated political philosophy of Aristotle, however much the Hebrews and the Greeks contributed to human understanding.

On Justice, Law, and Nature

Cicero

With respect to the true principle of justice, many learned men have maintained that it springs from Law. I hardly know if their opinion be not correct, at least, according to their own definition: for "Law (say they) is the highest reason, implanted in nature, which prescribes those things which ought to be done, and forbids the contrary." This, they think, is apparent from the converse of the proposition; because this same reason, when it is confirmed and established in men's minds, is the law of all their actions.

They therefore conceive that the voice of conscience is a law, that moral prudence is a law, whose operation is to urge us to good actions, and restrain us from evil ones. They think, too, that the Greek name for law (νομος), which is derived from νέμω, to distribute, implies the very nature of the thing, that is, to give every man his due. For my part, I imagine that the moral essence of law is better expressed by its Latin name, *(lex)*, which conveys the idea of selection or discrimination. According to the Greeks, therefore, the name of law implies an equitable distribution of goods: according to the Romans, an equitable discrimination between good and evil.

The true definition of law should, however, include both these characteristics. And this being granted as an almost self-evident proposition, the origin of justice is to be sought in the divine law of eternal and immutable morality. This indeed is

Markus Tullius Cicero, *The Laws,* trans. Francis Barham (1841), in *Introduction to Contemporary Civilization in the West,* 3rd ed. (New York: Columbia University Press, 1960), vol. 1, pp. 61-73.

the true energy of nature, the very soul and essence of wisdom, the test of virtue and vice. But since every discussion must relate to some subject, whose terms are of frequent occurrence in the popular language of the citizens, we shall be sometimes obliged to use the same terms as the vulgar, and to conform to that common idiom which signifies by the word law, all the arbitrary regulations which are found in our statute books, either commanding or forbidding certain actions.

We should seek for justice in its native source, which being discovered, we shall afterwards be able to speak with more authority and precision respecting our civil laws, that come home to the affairs of our citizens.

I shall endeavor to describe a system of Laws adapted to that Commonwealth, which Scipio declares to be most desirable in those Six Books which I have written under that title. All our laws, therefore, are to be accommodated to that mixed kind of political government there recommended. We shall also treat of the general principles of morals and manners, which appear most appropriate to such a constitution of society, but without descending to particular details.

Grant me that the entire universe is overruled by the power of God, that by his nature, reason, energy, mind, divinity, or some other word of clearer signification, all things are governed and directed. . . . Since you grant me the existence of God, and the superintendence of Providence, I maintain that he has been especially beneficent to man. This human animal — prescient, sagacious, complex, acute, full of memory, reason and counsel, which we call man, — is generated by the supreme God in a more transcendent condition than most of his fellow-creatures. For he is the only creature among the earthly races of animated beings endued with superior reason and thought, in which the rest are deficient. And what is there, I do not say in man alone, but in all heaven and earth, more divine than reason, which, when it becomes ripe and perfect, is justly termed wisdom?

There exists, therefore, since nothing is better than reason, and since this is the common property of God and man, a certain aboriginal rational intercourse between divine and human natures. This reason, which is common to both, therefore, can be none other than right reason; and since this *right reason* is what we call *Law*, God and men are said by Law to be consociated. Between whom, since there is a communion of law, there must be also a communication of Justice.

Law and Justice being thus the common rule of immortals and mortals, it follows that they are both the fellow-citizens of one city and commonwealth. And if they are obedient to the same rule, the same authority and denomination, they may with still closer propriety be termed fellow-citizens, since one celestial regency, one divine mind, one omnipotent Deity then regulates all their thoughts and actions.

This universe, therefore, forms one immeasurable Commonwealth and city, common alike to gods and mortals. And as in earthly states, certain particular laws, which we shall hereafter describe, govern the particular relationships of kindred tribes; so in the nature of things doth an universal law, far more magnificent and resplendent, regulate the affairs of that universal city where gods and men compose one vast association.

When we thus reason on universal nature, we are accustomed to reason after this method. We believe that in the long course of ages and the uninterrupted succession of celestial revolutions, the seed of the human race was sown on our planet, and being scattered over the earth, was animated by the divine gift of souls. Thus men retained from their terrestrial origin, their perishable and mortal bodies, while their immortal spirits were ingenerated by Deity. From which consideration we are bold to say that we possess a certain consanguinity and kindred fellowship with the celestials. And so far as we know, among all the varieties of animals, man alone retains the idea of the Divinity. And among men there is no nation so savage and ferocious as to deny the necessity of worshipping God, however ignorant it may be respecting the nature of his attributes. From whence we conclude that every man must recognize a Deity, who considers the origin of his nature and the progress of his life.

Now the law of virtue is the same in God and man, and cannot possibly be diverse. This virtue is nothing else than a nature perfect in itself, and developed in all its excellence. There exists therefore a similitude between God and man; nor can any knowledge be more appropriate and sterling than what relates to this divine similitude.

Nature, attentive to our wants, offers us her treasures with the most graceful profusion. And it is easy to perceive that the benefits which flow from her are true and veritable gifts, which Providence has provided on purpose for human enjoyment, and not the fortuitous productions of her exuberant fecundity. Her liberality appears, not only in the fruits and vegetables which gush from the bosom of the earth, but likewise in cattle and the beasts of the field. It is clear that some of these are intended from the advantage of mankind, a part for propagation, and a part for food. Innumerable arts have likewise been discovered by the teaching of nature; for her doth reason imitate, and skillfully discover all things necessary to the happiness of life. . . .

As the Deity, therefore, was pleased to create man as the chief and president of all terrestrial creatures, so it is evident, without further argument, that human nature has made the greatest advances by its intrinsic energy; that nature, which without any other instruction than her own, has developed the first rude principles of the understanding, and strengthened and perfected reason to all the appliances of science and art.

You may well describe these topics as grand, which we are now briefly discussing. For of all the questions on which our philosophers argue, there is none which it is more important thoroughly to understand than this, *that man is born for justice, and that law and equity are not a mere establishment of opinion, but an institution of nature.* This truth will become still more apparent if we investigate the nature of human association and society.

There is no one thing more like to another, more homogeneous and analogous, than man is to man. And if the corruption of customs, and the variation of opinions, had not induced an imbecility of minds, and turned them aside from the course of nature, no one would more nearly resemble himself than all men would resemble all men. Therefore whatever definition we give of man, it must include the whole human race. And this is a good argument, that no portion of mankind can be heterogeneous or dissimilar from the rest; because, if this were the case, one definition could not include all men.

In fact, reason, which alone gives us so many advantages over beasts, by means of which we conjecture, argue, refute, discourse, and accomplish and conclude our designs, is assuredly common to all men; for the faculty of acquiring knowledge is similar in all human minds, though the knowledge itself may be endlessly diversified. By the same senses we all perceive the same objects, and that which strikes the sensibilities of the few, cannot be indifferent to those of the many. Those first rude elements of intelligence which, as I before observed, are the earliest developments of thought, are similarly exhibited by all men; and that faculty of speech which is the soul's interpreter, agrees in the ideas it conveys, though it may differ in the syllables that express them. And therefore there exists not a man in any nation, who, adopting his true nation for his true guide, may not improve in virtue.

Nor is this resemblance which all men bear to each other remarkable in those things only which accord to right reason. For it is scarcely less conspicuous in those corrupt practices by which right reason is most cruelly violated. For all men alike are captivated by voluptuousness, which is in reality no better than disgraceful vice, though it may seem to bear some natural relations to goodness; for by its delicious delicacy and luxury it insinuates error into the mind, and leads us to cultivate it as something salutary, forgetful of its poisonous qualities. . . .

It follows, then, in the line of our argument, *that nature made us just that we might participate our goods with each other, and supply each other's wants.* You observe in this discussion whenever I speak of nature, I mean *nature in its genuine purity,* and not in the corrupt state which is displayed by the depravity of evil custom, which is so great, that the natural and innate flame of virtue is often almost extinguished and stifled by the antagonist vices, which are accumulated around it.

But if our true nature would assert her rights, and teach men the noble lesson of the poet, who says, "I am a man, therefore no human interest can be indifferent to me," — then would justice be administered equally by all and to all. For nature hath not merely given us reason, but right reason, and consequently that law, which is nothing else than right reason enjoining what is good, and forbidding what is evil. . . .

There can be but one essential justice, which cements society, and one law which establishes this justice. This law is right reason, which is the true rule of all commandments and prohibitions. Whoever neglects this law, whether written or unwritten, is necessarily unjust and wicked.

But if justice consists in submission to written laws and national customs, and if, as the Epicureans persist in affirming, everything must be measured by utility alone, he who wishes to find an occasion of breaking such laws and customs, will be sure to discover it. So that real justice remains powerless if not supported by nature, and this pretended justice is overturned by that very utility which they call its foundation.

But this is not all. If nature does not ratify law, all the virtues lose their sway. What becomes of generosity, patriotism, or friendship? Where should we find the desire of benefiting our neighbors, or the gratitude that acknowledges kindness? For all these virtues proceed from our natural inclination to love and cherish our associates. This is the true basis of justice, and without this, not only the mutual charities of men, but the religious services of the gods, would become obsolete; for these are preserved, as I imagine, rather by the natural sympathy which subsists between divine and human beings, than by mere fear and timidity.

If the will of the people, the decrees of the senate, the adjudications of magistrates, were sufficient to establish justice, the only question would be how to gain suffrages, and to win over the votes of the majority, in order that corruption and spoliation, and the falsification of wills, should become lawful. But if the opinions and suffrages of foolish men had sufficient weight to outbalance the nature of things, might they not determine among them, that what is essentially bad and pernicious should henceforth pass for good and beneficial? Or why should not a law able to enforce injustice, take the place of equity? Would not this same law be able to change evil into good, and good into evil?

As far as we are concerned, we have no other rule capable of distinguishing between a good or a bad law, than our natural conscience and reason. These, however, enable us to separate justice from injustice, and to discriminate between the honest and the scandalous. For common sense has impressed in our minds the first principles of things, and has given us a general acquaintance with them, by which we connect with Virtue every honorable and excellent quality, and with Vice all that is abominable and disgraceful. . . .

Besides this, if we weigh virtue by the mere utility and profit that attend it, and not by its own merit, the virtue which results will be in fact a species of vice. For the more a man's views are self-interested, the further he recedes from probity. It therefore necessarily happens, that those who measure virtue by profit, acknowledge no other virtue than this usurious vice. For who could be called benevolent, if none endeavored to do good for the love of others? Where could we find the grateful person, if those who are disposed to gratitude could meet no benefactor disinterested enough to deserve it? What would become of sacred friendship, if we were not to love our friends for their own sake with all our heart and soul? In pursuance of this pseudo-benevolence, we must desert our friend, as soon as we can derive no further assistance from him. What can be more inhuman! But if friendship ought rather to be cultivated on its own account, for the same reason are society, equality, and justice, desirable for themselves. If this were not so, there could be no justice at all, since nothing is more opposite to the very essence of virtue than selfish interest.

Plotinus

Many were not satisfied with either Aristotle's "naturalism" or Stoic "ethical rationality." They did not think them utterly false, but they were more attracted to certain themes from Plato — especially his emphasis on intuitive knowledge at the depth of the soul, his notion of an intelligible God (he was the first to coin the word "theology"), and his treatment of the desire of the deepest self for direct knowledge of the source and structures of meaning. Such themes anticipate much of Western mysticism as well as the depth psychology and psychiatry of today.

The result was "Neo-Platonism," and its greatest representative was Plotinus. In his *Enneads,* he used the image of a ladder of being, a great hierarchy of qualitative existence, to organize his thought about the world. At the higher levels are those realities that are known by spiritual wisdom, similar to the more "mystical" side of Plato. At the lower levels are the human and social realities, and below that, the material realities that are known by the material sciences, much as could be found in Aristotle's work. All levels are "real," but the higher levels are more enduring, while the lower ones are more temporal. Comparative scholars tell us that Plotinus's theories are, in major respects, similar to certain classical philosophies of non-Western civilizations, such as India and China.

Plotinus became the single most influential philosopher between the ancient world and the later periods when Aristotle was reintroduced to the West by Muslim scholars in the Middle Ages and Stoic theories were recovered by jurists and political theorists in the Renaissance and Reformation. Plotinus was, for example, the most important philosophical influence on St. Augustine, and through him on much of Western Christianity.

A central claim in Plotinus's view has many implications for economy and society. This is the claim that a tension stands between activities that are sensible (material, earthly, open to empirical investigation) and those activities which are spiritual (divine, heavenly, and open to intelligible investigation). One is clearly "higher" than the other, and thus no one could expect bodily (or material or economic) matters to be spiritual. Unless they are guided and controlled by what is "higher," they are devoid of intellectual and spiritual principle, as every "Sage" (anyone who is a truly wise philosopher) knows. Yet he argued against those who think that material, bodily, and economic realities are evil. All that exists is good; but higher mind is better than lower body. Thus Plotinus is the intellectual forebear of modern, wholistic theories of ecology and intelligence. Still, here is a classic statement of the view that spirituality and materialism are the great opposites within a single monistic system and that the increase of one brings the decrease of the other, a view that often made religion and business strangers if not enemies.

Such a view easily fit into the developing practices of monasticism. It also gave philosophical justifications for the attempts to preserve spiritual and intellectual life during the later decline and fall of the Roman Empire and the plunge into the "Dark Ages." Various accents in Plotinus's thought have found echoes among modern thinkers, from transcendentalist Henry David Thoreau to evolutionist Teilhard de Chardin to process philosopher Alfred North Whitehead. In any case, its greatest strength is in these questions: What holds the whole together, and what finally can we rely on when the things of the world fall apart?

On True Happiness

Plotinus

Are we to make True Happiness one and the same thing with Welfare or Prosperity and therefore within the reach of other living beings as well as ourselves?

There is certainly no reason to deny well-being to any of them as long as their lot allows them to flourish unhindered after their kind.

Whether we make Welfare consist in pleasant conditions of life, or in the accomplishment of some appropriate task, by either account it may fall to them as to us. For certainly they may at once be pleasantly placed and engaged about some function that lies in their nature: take for an instance such living beings as have the gift of music; finding themselves well-off in other ways, they sing, too, as their nature is, and so their day is pleasant to them. . . .

It may be a distasteful notion, this bringing-down of happiness so low as to the animal world — making it over, as then we must, even to the vilest of them and not withholding it even from the plants. . . .

But, to begin with, it is surely unsound to deny that good of life to animals only because they do not appear to man to be of great account. And as for plants, we need not necessarily allow them what we accord to the other forms of life, since they have no feeling. It is true people might be found to declare property possible to the very plants: they have life, and life may bring good or evil; the plants may thrive or wither, bear or be barren.

No: if Pleasure be the Term, if here be the good

of life, it is impossible to deny the good of life to any order of living things; if the Term be inner-peace, equally impossible; impossible, too, if the good of life be to live in accordance with the purpose of nature. . . .

What then is happiness? Let us try basing it upon Life.

Now if we draw no distinction as to kinds of life, everything that lives will be capable of happiness, and those will be effectively happy who possess that one common gift of which every living thing is by nature receptive. We could not deny it to the irrational whilst allowing it to the rational. If happiness were inherent in the bare being-alive, the common ground in which the cause of happiness could always take root would be simply life. . . .

Now in common use this word "Life" embraces many forms which shade down from primal to secondary and so on, all massed under the common term — life of plant and life of animal — each phase brighter or dimmer than its next: and so it evidently must be with the Good-of-Life. And if thing is ever the image of thing, so every Good must always be the image of a higher Good.

If mere Being is insufficient, if happiness demands fullness of life, and exists, therefore, where nothing is lacking of all that belongs to the idea of life, then happiness can exist only in a being that lives fully.

And such a one will possess not merely the good, but the Supreme Good if, that is to say, in the realm of existents the Supreme Good can be no other than the authentically living, no other than Life in its greatest plentitude, life in which the good is present as something essential not as something brought in from without, a life needing no foreign substance called in from a foreign realm, to establish it in good. . . .

It has been said more than once that the perfect life and the true life, the essential life, is in the Intellectual Nature beyond this sphere, and that all other forms of life are incomplete, are phantoms of life, imperfect, not pure, not more truly life than they are is contrary: here let it be said succinctly that since all living things proceed from the one principle but possess life in different degrees, this principle must be the first life and the most complete.

If, then, the perfect life is within human reach,

Plotinus, "Tractate Four," in *The Six Enneads,* trans. S. MacKenna and B. S. Page (Chicago: University of Chicago Press, 1952), pp. 12-21.

the man attaining it attains happiness: if not, happiness must be made over to the gods, for the perfect life is for them alone.

But since we hold that happiness is for human beings too, we must consider what this perfect life is. The matter may be stated thus: . . . there exists no single human being that does not either potentially or effectively posses this thing which we hold to constitute happiness.

But are we to think of man as including this form of life, the perfect, after the manner of a partial constituent of his entire nature?

We say, rather, that while in some men it is present as a mere portion of their total being — in those, namely, that have it potentially — there is, too, the man, already in possession of true felicity, who is this perfection realized, who has passed over into actual identification with it. All else is now mere clothing about the man, not to be called part of him since it lies about him unsought, not his because not appropriated to himself by any act of the will. . . .

The sign that this state has been achieved is that the man seeks nothing else.

What indeed could he be seeking? Certainly none of the less worthy things; and the Best he carries always within him.

He that has such a life as this has all he needs in life.

Once the man is a Sage, the means of happiness, the way to good, are within, for nothing is good that lies outside him. Anything he desires further than this he seeks as a necessity, and not for himself but for a subordinate, for the body bound to him, to which since it has life he must minister the needs of life, not needs, however, to the true man of this degree. He knows himself to stand above all such things, and what he gives to the lower he so gives as to leave his true life undiminished.

Adverse fortune does not shake his felicity: the life so founded is stable ever. . . .

The pleasure demanded for the Sage's life cannot be in the enjoyments of the licentious or in any gratifications of the body — there is no place for these, and they stifle happiness — nor in any violent emotions — what could so move the Sage? — it can be only such pleasure as there must be where Good is, pleasure that does not rise from movement and is not a thing of process, for all

that is good is immediately present to the Sage and the Sage is present to himself: his pleasure, his contentment, stands immovable.

Thus he is ever cheerful, the order of his life ever untroubled: his state is fixedly happy and nothing whatever of all that is known as evil can set it awry — given only that he is and remains a Sage.

If anyone seeks for some other kind of pleasure in the life of the Sage, it is not the life of the Sage he is looking for. . . .

A powerful frame, a healthy constitution, even a happy balance of temperament, these surely do not make felicity; in the excess of these advantages there is, even, the danger that the man be crushed down and forced more and more within their power. There must be a sort of counter-pressure in the other direction, towards the noblest: the body must be lessened, reduced, that the veritable man may show forth, the man behind the appearances.

Let the earth-bound man be handsome and powerful and rich, and so apt to this world that he may rule the entire human race: still there can be no envying him, the fool of such lures. Perhaps such splendors could not, from the beginning even, have gathered to the Sage; but if it should happen so, he of his own action will lower his state, if he has any care for his true life; the tyranny of the body he will work down or wear away by inattention to its claims; the rulership he will lay aside. . . .

This does not make the Sage unfriendly or harsh: it is to himself and in his own great concern that he is the Sage: giving freely to his intimates of all he has to give, he will be the best of friends by his very union with the Intellectual-Principle.

Those that refuse to place the Sage aloft in the Intellectual Realm but drag him down to the accidental, dreading accident for him, have substituted for the Sage we have in mind another person altogether; they offer us a tolerable sort of man and they assign to him a life of mingled good and ill, a case, after all, not easy to conceive. But admitting the possibility of such a mixed state, it could not be deserved to be called a life of happiness; it misses the Great, both in the dignity of Wisdom and in the integrity of Good.

Chapter Four

The Catholic Theological Traditions

Believers took Christ as their model for life. They learned about him through the Scriptures and through traditions handed down in the church. As the faith began to spread throughout the Mediterranean world — Greece, Rome, Spain, North Africa — and eventually into Northern Europe, the Slavic lands, and the Americas, believers encountered subtle philosophies based on profound forms of reason and reflecting the experience of high cultures.

Believers lived and worked at the intersection of the church and a civilization that was formed by these philosophies and the pagan cultures they expressed. They faced many practical issues of what to think and do, of how to live their lives and order the common life. They sought an integrated vision that would bring together Scripture, tradition, reason, and experience so that they could live "in but not of the world" — as many today are trying to do in the newer churches of Asia and Africa, and now again in the West in the face of neo-paganism.

The great teachers and preachers of theological ethics, as it developed between the ancient world and the modern one, were not of one mind about economic matters. As in science, medicine, and the arts, a good number of faltering steps were taken, but only some opened up wider and deeper possibilities for an economic life that was increasingly cosmopolitan while providing spiritual and moral guidance to persons, local communities, and whole societies.

Theological ethicists focused on one or another of the dimensions of ethics as they are found in Scripture, tradition, reason, and experience. Some accented the deontological dimensions, while others emphasized the teleological or ethological dimensions. Some showed acute understandings of personal ethics, but very little understanding of how production and distribution work. Some presumed that production would always be plentiful because God endowed nature with plenty, and thus they emphasized an ethic of sharing, equitable distribution, or compassion for the poor. And just as in philosophy, political theory, or judicial practice, some great teachers were conservative and cautious, while others were liberal and willing to take risks in life and thought. In the economy of God, and in the formation of business ethics, all of these made contributions, though they did not all agree.

In the richness of these variations, it is important to see the major theological and ethical teachings that lay behind root attitudes toward economic life. These teachings made new opportunities possible in addition to purely traditional practices, and they constrained destructive practices and attitudes that could have ripped souls and civilizations to shreds.

In this chapter, we find a series of brief, representative readings from the early and medieval periods of the church's teachings. These readings reveal an attempt to integrate biblical and philosophical motifs; they represent major alternative attitudes toward wealth, poverty, and work; and they express a variety of understandings of the social context of economic life. Although some of the styles will seem strange at first to readers not familiar with normative theological discourse, these readings deal with major issues that have been debated over the centuries and that are still alive today.

Clement of Alexandria

Some early Christian teachers feared the temptation of wealth as they saw it among the elites of the ancient cities. After all, many of the very wealthy people of this period were much given to ostentatious displays of wealth and massive banquets, which not infrequently led to open debauchery, on the holidays of the pagan gods. Every person of means had to decide whether or not to become a part of this social swirl.

Many found other styles of life through learning and faith, but the inclination to condemn all aspects of culture was pronounced. Some saw corruption everywhere in civilization and felt compelled to seek God and to fight the battles against temptation in the still isolation of the desert. Early forms of Christian asceticism, the disciplined control of material and bodily existence for the sake of spiritual and moral well-being, can be found here. We shall see later in this chapter how that impulse made a significant if unintended contribution to economic history.

Most believers neither went to banquets nor retreated to the desert. Most felt that God wanted them to live righteously, but in the midst of culture. The question was how? For all the benefits of civilization, family and sexuality, politics and power, culture and art, and especially wealth and goods could easily become all-consuming; they could become idols in which one put one's ultimate trust. This, then, was a theological matter. Further, they could blind one to the harshness in one's own soul or group or to the distress of the needy and lonely. Thus, this was also a moral matter. The debates over how Christians should live and participate in society were intense, and they deeply influenced subsequent basic attitudes toward material possessions.

Clement, a Greek by origin who became a leader among Egyptian Christians in Alexandria, wrote several treatises on the issue in the century after the Gospels were written. As the head of a school, he linked his understanding of the Bible with motifs from Stoic ethics to form a major wing of Christian opinion in that time. He made a distinction between the ownership and the use of property: ownership was God's; use was ours. Further, against those who took Paul's warning to Timothy that "the love of money is the root of all evil" as a demand to repudiate all wealth, Clement argued that it is theologically and ethically valid to hold the goods of the earth, *provided that* the use of those goods is for the well-being of the community, and *provided that* one becomes neither gluttonous nor idolatrous about material things. In fact, Clement believed that poverty prevents the soul from seeking God, for the body constantly demands its attention.

In the passage that follows, Clement treats one of the most difficult and widely quoted biblical texts on these questions, the story of the rich young ruler, a story told in the New Testament, with slight variations, by Matthew, Mark, and Luke.

142

Who Is the Rich Man That Shall be Saved?

Clement of Alexandria

Our Lord and Saviour was asked pleasantly a question most appropriate for Him, as the Life respecting life, the Saviour respecting salvation, the Teacher respecting the chief doctrines taught, the Truth respecting the true immortality. . . .

And having been called "good," and taking the starting note from this first expression, He commences His teaching with this, turning the pupil to God, the good, and first and only dispenser of eternal life, which the Son, who received it of Him, gives to us. . . .

But, nevertheless, this man being such, is perfectly persuaded that nothing is wanting to him as far as respects righteousness, but that he is entirely destitute of life. Wherefore he asks it from Him who alone is able to give it. And with reference to the law, he carries confidence; but the Son of God he addresses in supplication. He is transferred from faith to faith. As perilously tossing and occupying a dangerous anchorage in the law, he makes for the Saviour to find a haven.

Jesus, accordingly, does not charge him with not having fulfilled all things out of the law, but loves him, and fondly welcomes his obedience in what he had learned; but says that he is not perfect as respects eternal life, inasmuch as he had not fulfilled what is perfect, and that he is a doer indeed of the law, but idle at the true life. Those things, indeed, are good. Who denies it? For "the commandment is holy," as far as a sort of training with fear and preparatory discipline goes, leading

Clement of Alexandria, "Who Is the Rich Man That Shall Be Saved?" in *The Ante-Nicene Fathers,* vol. 2 (Grand Rapids: Eerdmans, 1951), pp. 593-99.

as it did to the culmination of legislation and to grace. But Christ is the fulfillment "of the law for righteousness to every one that believeth"; and not as a slave making slaves, but sons, and brethren, and fellow-heirs, who perform the Father's will. . . .

But he departed displeased, vexed at the commandment of the life, on account of which he supplicated. For he did not truly wish life, as he averred, but aimed at the mere reputation of the good choice. And he was capable of busying himself about many things; but the one thing, the work of life, he was powerless, and disinclined, and unable to accomplish. . . .

What then was it which persuaded him to flight, and made him depart from the Master, from the entreaty, the hope, the life, previously pursued with ardour? — "Sell thy possessions." And what is this? He does not, as some conceive off-hand, bid him throw away the substance he possessed, and abandon his property; but bids him banish from his soul his notions about wealth, his excitement and morbid feeling about it, the anxieties, which are the thorns of existence, which choke the seed of life. For it is no great thing or desirable to be destitute of wealth. . . . For thus those who have nothing at all, but are destitute, and beggars for their daily bread, the poor dispersed on the streets, who know not God and God's righteousness, simply on account of their extreme want and destitution of subsistence, and lack even of the smallest things, were most blessed and most dear to God, and sole possessors of everlasting life.

Nor was the renunciation of wealth and the bestowment of it on the poor or needy a new thing; for many did so before the Saviour's advent, — some because of the leisure (thereby obtained) for learning, and on account of a dead wisdom; and others for empty fame and vain-glory. . . .

Why then command as new, as divine, as alone life-giving, what did not save those of former days? And what peculiar thing is it that the new creature the Son of God intimates and teaches? It is not the outward act which others have done, but something else indicated by it, greater, more godlike, more perfect, the stripping off of the passions from the soul itself and from the disposition, and the cutting up by the roots and casting out of what is alien to the mind. For this is the lesson peculiar to the believer, and the instruction worthy of the

Saviour. For those who formerly despised external things relinquished and squandered their property, but the passions of the soul, I believe, they intensified. For they indulged in arrogance, pretension, and vainglory, and in contempt of the rest of mankind, as if they had done something superhuman. How then would the Saviour have enjoined on those destined to live for ever what was injurious and hurtful with reference to the life which He promised? For although such is the case, one, after ridding himself of the burden of wealth, may none the less have still the lust and desire for money innate and living; and may have abandoned the use of it, but being at once destitute of and desiring what he spent, may doubly grieve both on account of the absence of attendance, and the presence of regret. For it is impossible and inconceivable that those in want of the necessaries of life should not be harassed in mind, and hindered from better things in the endeavor to provide them somehow, and from some source.

And how much more beneficial the opposite case, for a man, through possession a competency, both not himself to be in straits about money, and also to give assistance to those to whom it is requisite so to do! For if no one had anything, what room would be left among men for giving? and how can this dogma fail to be found plainly opposed to and conflicting with many other excellent teachings of the Lord? "Make to yourselves friends of the mammon of unrighteousness, that when ye fail, they may receive you into the everlasting habitations." "Acquire treasures in heaven, where neither moth nor rust destroys, nor thieves break through." How could one give food to the hungry, and drink to the thirsty, clothe the naked, and shelter the houseless, for not doing which He threatens with fire and the outer darkness, if each man first divested himself of all these things? Nay, He bids Zaccheus and Matthew, the rich taxgathers, entertain Him hospitably. And He does not bid them part with their property, but, applying the just and removing the unjust judgment, He subjoins, "To-day salvation has come to this house, forasmuch as he also is a son of Abraham." He so praises the use of property as to enjoin, along with this addition, the giving a share of it, to give drink to the thirsty, bread to the hungry, to take the houseless in, and clothe the naked. But if it is not possible to supply those needs without

substance, and He bids people abandon their substance, what else would the Lord be doing than exhorting to give and not to give the same things, to feed and not to feed, to take in and to shut out, to share and not to share? which were the most irrational of all things.

Riches, then, which benefit also our neighbors, are not to be thrown away. For they are possessions, inasmuch as they are possessed, and goods, inasmuch as they are useful and provided by God for the use of men; and they lie to our hand, and are put under our power, as material and instruments which are for good use to those who know the instrument. If you use it skillfully, it is skillful; if you are deficient in skill, it is affected by your want of skill, being itself destitute of blame. Such an instrument is wealth. Are you able to make a right use of it? It is subservient to righteousness. Does one make a wrong use of it? It is, on the other hand, a minister of wrong. For its nature is to be subservient, not to rule. That then which of itself has neither good nor evil, being blameless, ought not to be blamed; but that which the power of using it well and ill, by reason of its possessing voluntary choice. And this is the mind and judgment of man, which has freedom in itself and self-determination in the treatment of what is assigned to it. So let no man destroy wealth, rather than the passions of the soul, which are incompatible with the better use of wealth. So that, becoming virtuous and good, he may be able to make a good use of these riches. The renunciation, then, and selling of all possessions, is to be understood as spoken of the passions of the soul.

I would then say this. Since some things are within and some without the soul, and if the soul make a good use of them, they also are reputed good, but if a bad, bad; — whether does He who commands us to alienate our possessions repudiate those things, after the removal of which the passions still remain, or those rather, on the removal of which wealth even becomes beneficial? If therefore he who casts away worldly wealth can still be rich in the passions, even though the material [for their gratification] is absent, — for the disposition produces its own effects, and strangles the reason, and presses it down and inflames it with its inbred lusts, — it is then of no advantage to him to be poor in purse while he is rich in passions. For it is not what ought to be cast away that he has cast away, but what is indifferent; and he has deprived himself of what is serviceable, but set on fire the innate fuel of evil through want of the external means [of gratification]. We must therefore renounce those possessions that are injurious, not those that are capable of being serviceable, if one knows the right use of them. And what is managed with wisdom, and sobriety, and piety, is profitable; and what is hurtful must be cast away. But things external hurt not. So then the Lord introduces the use of external things, bidding us put away not the means of subsistence, but what uses them badly. And these are the infirmities and passions of the soul.

The presence of wealth in these is deadly to all, the loss of it salutary. Of which, making the soul pure, — that is, poor and bare, — we must hear the Saviour speaking thus, "Come, follow Me." For to the pure in heart He now becomes the way. But into the impure soul the grace of God finds no entrance. And that (soul) is unclean which is rich in lusts, and is in the throes of many worldly affections. For he who holds possessions, and gold, and silver, and houses, as the gifts of God; and ministers from them to the God who gives them for the salvation of men; and knows that he possesses them more for the sake of the brethren that his own; and is superior to the possession of them, not the slave of the things he possesses; and does not carry them about in his soul, not bind and circumscribe his life within them, but is ever laboring at some good and divine work, even should he be necessarily some time or other deprived of them, is able with cheerful mind to bear their removal equally with their abundance. This is he who is blessed by the Lord, and called poor in spirit, a meet heir of the kingdom of heaven, not one who could not live rich.

But he who carries his riches in his soul, and instead of God's Spirit bears in his heart gold or land, and is always acquiring possessions without end, and is perpetually on the outlook for more, bending downwards and fettered in the toils of the world, being earth and destined to depart to earth, — whence can he be able to desire and to mind the kingdom of heaven, — a man who carries not a heart, but land or metal, who must perforce be found in the midst of the objects he has chosen? For where the mind of man is, there is also his treasure. The Lord acknowledges a twofold treasure, — the good: "For the good man, out of the good treasure of his heart, bringeth forth good"; and the evil: for "the evil man, out of the evil treasure, bringeth forth evil: for out of the abundance of the heart the mouth speaketh." As then treasure is not one with Him, as also it is with us, that which gives the unexpected great gain in the finding, but also a second, which is profitless and undesirable, an evil acquisition, hurtful; so also there is a richness in good things, and a richness in bad things, since we know that riches and treasure are not by nature separated from each other. And the one sort of riches is to be possessed and acquired, and the other not to be possessed, but to be cast away. . . .

He then is truly and rightly rich who is rich in virtue, and is capable of making a holy and faithful use of any fortune; while he is spuriously rich who is rich, according to the flesh, and turns life into outward possession, which is transitory and perishing, and now belongs to one, now to another, and in the end to nobody at all. . . .

The wealthy and legally correct man, not understanding these things figuratively, nor how the same man can be both poor and rich, and have wealth and not have it, and use the world and not use it, went away sad and downcast, leaving the state of life, which he was able merely to desire but not to attain, making for himself the difficult impossible. For it was difficult for the soul not to be seduced and ruined by the luxuries and flowery enchantments that beset remarkable wealth; but it was not impossible, even surrounded with it, for one to lay hold of salvation, provided he withdrew himself from material wealth, — to that which is grasped by the mind and taught by God, and learned to use things indifferent rightly and properly, and so as to strive after eternal life. And the disciples even themselves were at first alarmed and amazed. Why were they so on hearing this? Was it that they themselves possessed much wealth? Nay, they had long ago left their very nets, and hooks, and rowing boats, which were their sole possessions. Why then do they say in consternation, "Who can be saved?" They had heard well and like disciples what was spoken in parable and obscurely by the Lord, and perceived the depth of the words. For they were sanguine of salvation on the ground of their want of wealth. But when they became conscious of not having yet wholly renounced the passions (for they were neophytes and recently selected by the Saviour), they were excessively astonished, and despaired of themselves no less than that rich man who clung so terribly to the wealth which he preferred to eternal life.

"And Jesus answering said, Verily I say unto you, Whosoever shall leave what is his own, parents, and children, and wealth, for My sake and the Gospel's, shall receive an hundredfold." . . .

But I think that our proposition has been demonstrated, . . . that the Saviour by no means has excluded the rich on account of wealth itself, and the possession of property, nor fenced off salvation against them; if they are able and willing to submit their life to God's commandments, and prefer them to transitory objects, and if they would look to the Lord with steady eye. . . . For if, in consequence of his involuntary birth in wealth, a man is banished from life, rather is he wronged by God, who created him, in having vouchsafed to him temporary enjoyment, and in being deprived of eternal life. And why should wealth have ever sprung from the earth at all, if it is the author and patron of death?

But if one is able in the midst to turn from its power, and to entertain moderate sentiments, and to exercise self-command, and to seek God alone, and to breathe God and walk with God, such a poor man submits to the commandments, being free, unsubdued, free of disease, unwounded by wealth. But if not, "sooner shall a camel enter through a needle's eye, than such a rich man reach the kingdom of God. . . .

Cyprian

In all of the world religions, giving is seen as better than getting; sacrifice is honored, while acquisitiveness is suspect; liberality is praised, while possessiveness is condemned. Gifts, donations, and charity are intrinsic to the religious spirit. The motivations for giving may vary from religion to religion — some may give to affirm detachment from material things, some to make the "divine forces" benevolent, some to fulfill required commands, and some to display the magnanimity of the donor; but the approval of generosity as opposed to greed is universal.

In Christian thought the urge to give is understood to be rooted less in terms of the duty of the believer or the winning of spiritual merit or the display of altruism than in a response of gratitude for the gifts that God has given to humanity. This core motivation is related to a double need: the need for the self to express the love of God, which purifies the soul, and the need of a neighbor, whom we are to love.

Few of the early Christians accented these motifs as clearly as Cyprian. He was a church leader in Carthage, a thriving city in North Africa, who was driven from his post during a political persecution of Christians. During his exile, he kept the church together by means of smuggled letters and booklets of instruction, in which he used reason to argue from Scripture.

When he finally was allowed to return to his position as bishop, he proved to be one of the most effective leaders of the generation after Clement. He developed a number of guidelines for the conduct of worship and the organization of the church; but we remember him primarily as one who established decisive principles of sharing, stewardship, and charity. These themes have become a part of what is expected of the responsible person in modern societies. He took up these questions in the reading that follows by discussing "alms," an early practice of relief, aid, and religious offering.

In addition to a number of concerns which he shares with Clement about the effects of giving on the heart (or "bowels," which ancient peoples thought was the seat of the soul) of the giver, Cyprian is more clearly concerned about the effects that giving has on the recipients. He wanted to see the practical alleviation of distress among the needy. Implicit in this accent is the notion that living in want is not how God intends life to be, that social and political orders in which people have great need are contrary to God's will, and that the responsible person will undertake direct and personal concrete "works" to overcome that distortion — even though the capacity of the citizenry to influence public policy was severely limited at that time, and the Christians were a persecuted minority in any case.

147

On Works and Alms

Cyprian

. . . . The Holy Spirit speaks in the sacred Scriptures, and says, "By almsgiving and faith sins are purged." . . . Moreover, He says again, "As water extinguisheth fire, so almsgiving quencheth sin." Here also it is shown and proved that . . . by almsgiving and works of righteousness the flame of sins is subdued. And because in baptism remission of sins is granted once for all, constant and ceaseless labor, following the likeness of baptism, once again bestows the mercy of God. The Lord teaches this also in the Gospel. For when the disciples were pointed out, as eating and not first washing their hands, He replied and said, "He that made that which is within, made also that which is without. But give alms, and behold all things are clean unto you"; teaching hereby and showing that not the hands are to be washed, but the heart, and that the foulness from inside is to be done away rather than that from outside: but that he who shall have cleansed what is within has cleansed also that which is without; and that if the mind is cleansed what is within has cleansed also that which is without; and that if the mind is cleansed, a man has begun to be clean also in skin and body. Further, admonishing, and showing whence we may be clean and purged, He added that alms must be given. He who is pitiful teaches and warns us that pity must be shown; and because He seeks to save those whom at a great cost He has redeemed. He teaches that those who, after the grace of baptism, have become foul, may once more be cleansed. . . .

Therefore in the Gospel, the Lord, the Teacher of our life and Master of eternal salvation, quickening the assembly of believers, . . . commands and prescribes nothing more frequently than that we should devote ourselves to almsgiving, and not depend on earthly possessions, but rather lay up heavenly treasures. "Sell," says He, "your goods, and give alms." And again: "Lay not up for yourselves treasures upon the earth, where moth and rust do corrupt, and where thieves break through and steal. But lay up for yourselves treasures in heaven, where neither moth nor rust doth corrupt, and where thieves do not break through nor steal. For where thy treasure is, there will thy heart be also." And when He wished to set forth a man perfect and complete by the observation of the law, He said, "If thou wilt be perfect, go and sell what thou hast, and give to the poor, and thou shalt have treasure in heaven; and come and follow me." Moreover, in another place He says that a merchant of the heavenly grace, and a gainer of eternal salvation, ought to purchase the precious pearl — that is, eternal life — at the price of the blood of Christ, from the amount of his patrimony, parting with all his wealth for it. He says: "The kingdom of heaven is like unto a merchant-man seeking goodly pearls. And when he found a precious pearl, he went away and sold all that he had, and bought it."

In fine, He calls those the children of Abraham whom He sees to be laborious in aiding and nourishing the poor. For when Zacchaeus said, "Behold, the half of my goods I give to the poor; and if I have done any wrong to any man, I restore fourfold," Jesus answered and said, "That salvation has this day come to this house, for that he also is a son of Abraham." For if Abraham believed in God, and it was counted unto him for righteousness, certainly he who gives alms according to God's precept believes in God, and he who has the truth of faith maintains the fear of God; moreover, he who maintains the fear of God considers God in showing mercy to the poor. For he labors thus because he believes — because he knows that what is foretold by God's word is true, and that the Holy Scripture cannot lie — that unfruitful trees, that is, unproductive men, are cut off and cast into the fire, but that the merciful are called into the kingdom. He also, in another place, calls laborious and fruitful men faithful; but He denies faith to unfruitful and barren ones, saying, "If ye have not

Cyprian, "On Works and Alms," in *The Ante-Nicene Fathers*, vol. 5 (Grand Rapids: Eerdmans, 1951), pp. 476-82.

Charitable giving and volunteerism are on the rise in this country, thanks largely to the generous character of religious people, according to a new Independent Sector/Gallup survey.

"The caring spirit is alive and very much growing, even [among] the so-called me generation of baby boomers," said Brian O'Connell, president of Independent Sector, a coalition of 650 corporate, foundation, and voluntary organizations.

The report, released at a Washington, D.C., press conference last month, found that 75 percent of American households are contributing an average of $734 annually to charitable causes. That dollar figure represents a 20 percent increase (after inflation) from two years ago. Similarly, the number of Americans volunteering their time and talents to charitable endeavors is at 98 million, up 23 percent from 1987.

One of the most significant findings in the survey was that religious belief is a major factor in contributions of time and money. Over half of the respondents surveyed reported having made contributions to religious organizations. Moreover, 80 percent of those affiliated with a religious institution reported household contributions to charity, and nearly 60 percent volunteered.

Those who attended religious services weekly "were clearly the most generous givers of both time and money, compared with all other groups," said the report. It continued, "People who attended church regularly were far more likely to give a higher percentage of their household income to charitable causes."

In addition, survey respondents specifically identified religion as a major motivating factor. Fifty-three percent of all givers said their motive was feeling they should "help those who had less," and 43 percent said "such behavior met their religious beliefs or commitment." Those listing such motives were also significantly above the national giving averages.

"Religious organizations have been a major, if not the greatest, influence in developing the tradition of giving and volunteering to both spiritual and secular causes," the report said.

— "Religious Faith: Firm Foundation for Charity,"
Christianity Today 34, no. 17 (19 Nov. 1990): 63

---

been faithful in the unrighteous mammon, who will commit to you that which is true? And if ye have not been faithful in that which is another man's, who shall give you that which is your own?"

If you dread and fear, lest, if you begin to act thus abundantly, your patrimony being exhausted with your liberal dealing, you may perchance be reduced to poverty; be of good courage in this respect, be free from care: that cannot be exhausted whence the service of Christ is supplied, whence the heavenly work is celebrated. Neither do I vouch for this on my own authority; but I promise it on the faith of the Holy Scriptures, and on the authority of the divine promise. The Holy Spirit speaks by Solomon, and says, "He that giveth unto the poor shall never lack, but he that turneth away his eye shall be in great poverty"; showing that the merciful and those who do good works cannot want, but rather that the sparing and barren hereafter come to want. Moreover, the blessed Apostle Paul, full of the grace of the Lord's inspiration, says: "He that ministereth seed to the sower, shall both minister bread for your food, and shall multiply your seed sown, and shall increase the growth of the fruits of your righteousness, that in all things ye may be enriched." And again: "The administration of this service shall not only supply the wants of the saints, but shall be abundant also by many thanksgivings unto God"; because, while thanks are directed to God for our almsgivings and labors, by the prayer of the poor, the wealth of the doer is increased by the retribution of God. And the Lord in the Gospel, already considering the hearts of men of this kind, and with prescient voice denouncing faithless and unbelieving men, bears witness, and says: "Take no thought, saying,

What shall we eat? or, What shall we drink? or, Wherewithal shall we be clothed? For for these things the Gentiles seek. And your Father knoweth that ye have need of all these things. Seek first the kingdom of God, and His righteousness; and all these things shall be added unto you." He says that all these things shall be added and given to them who seek the kingdom and rigtheousness of God. For the Lord says, that when the day of judgment shall come, those who have labored in His Church are admitted to receive the kingdom.

You are afraid lest perchance your estate should fail, if you begin to act liberally from it; and you do not know, miserable man that you are, that while you are fearing lest your family property should fail you, life itself, and salvation, are failing; and whilst you are anxious lest any of your wealth should be diminished, you do not see that you yourself are being diminished, in that you are a lover of mammon more than of your own soul; and while you fear, lest for the sake of yourself, you should lose your patrimony, you yourself are perishing for the sake of your patrimony. And therefore the apostle well exclaims, and says: "We brought nothing into this world, neither indeed can we carry anything out. Therefore, having food and clothing, let us therewith be content. For they who will be rich fall into temptation and a snare, and into many and hurtful desires, which drown a man in perdition and in destruction. For covetousness is a root of all evils, which some desiring, have made shipwreck from the faith, and pierced themselves through with many sorrows. . . ."

Wherefore do you applaud yourself in those vain and silly conceits, as if you were withheld from good works by fear and solicitude for the future? Why do you lay out before you certain shadows and omens of a vain excuse? Yea, confess what is the truth: and since you cannot deceive those who know, utter forth the secret and hidden things of your mind. The gloom of barrenness has besieged your mind; and while the light of truth has departed thence, and deep and profound darkness of avarice has blinded your carnal heart. You are the captive and slave of your money; you are bound with the chains and bonds of covetousness; and you whom Christ had once loosed, are once more in chains. You keep your money, which, when kept, does not keep you? You heap up a patrimony which burdens you with its weight; and

you do not remember what God answered to the rich man, who boasted with a foolish exultation of the abundance of his exuberant harvest: "Thou fool," said He, "this night thy soul is required of thee: then whose shall those things be which thou hast provided?" Why do you watch in loneliness over your riches? Why for your punishment do you heap up the burden of your patrimony, that, in proportion as you are rich in this world, you may become poor to God? Divide your returns with the Lord your God; share your gains with Christ; make Christ a partner with you in your earthly possessions, that He also may make you a fellow-heir with Him in His heavenly kingdom.

Augustine

No single intellectual or spiritual leader of the first ten centuries after the New Testament was written has had as much influence on the West as the North African thinker and pastor, Augustine. Historians of ideas trace root notions behind modern psychology to him; he wedded classical political philosophy to a biblical understanding of history to form basic paradigms of the West's social and legal theory; he established a monastic movement; he was considered the best theological authority by the greatest Roman Catholic thinkers; and Protestant thought is dependent on his work. Today, a number of critics of Christianity and Western culture believe that the West will not be reformed in its basic directions until the ideas of Augustine are refuted or rejected.

He wrote relatively little specifically on economics and business, although one can find many passages that echo Clement or Cyprian, plus fragments where business is seen as redemptive. For example, he wrote this in a sermon on "The Love of Neighbor":

> Man . . . is a rational soul with a mortal and earthly body in its service. Therefore he who loves his neighbor does good partly to the man's body, and partly to his soul. What benefits the body is called medicine; what benefits the soul, discipline. Medicine here includes everything that either preserves or restores bodily health. It includes, therefore, not only what belongs to the art of medical men, properly so called, but also food and drink, clothing and shelter, and every means of covering and protection to guard our bodies against injuries and mishaps. For hunger and thirst, and cold and heat . . . produce loss of that health which is the point to be considered. Hence those who . . . wisely supply all the things required

for warding off these evils and distresses are called compassionate. . . .

Augustine's importance for ethics and economics, however, comes more from the fact that he develops a basic attitude toward God based on an understanding of the will guided by inner grace and by civilization as an exterior form of grace. Within this general framework, he shows the pertinence of biblical and theological concepts to every human activity. He drew on the Greeks, the Stoics, and especially Plotinus, but he subordinated their philosophies to a theology of love. From the standpoint of ordinary experience, life is ordered by love: what one loves determines one's purposes in life. But ultimately, the love of God is the only reliable love, for it alone accords with the ultimate purposes, laws, and grace of existence beyond the reality of sin.

The following selections are drawn from his famous work, *The City of God,* which he composed during the first quarter of the fifth century. In them, he treats the fundamental issues of good and evil and how they are to be understood in the heart, in the world, and in religion.

On Good and Evil

Augustine

"Whether Positive Evil Exists"

The explanation of the goodness of creation is the goodness of God. It is a reasonable and sufficient explanation whether considered in the light of philosophy or of faith. It puts an end to all controversies concerning the origin of the world. . . .

Thus does Divine Providence teach us not to be foolish in finding fault with things but, rather, to be diligent in finding out their usefulness or, if our mind and will should fail us in the search, then to believe that there is some hidden use still to be discovered, as in so many other cases, only with great difficulty. This effort needed to discover hidden usefulness either helps our humility or hits our pride, since absolutely no natural reality is evil and the only meaning of the word "evil" is the privation of good. . . .

"The Source of Ethical Failings"

This I know, that the nature of God can never and nowhere be deficient in anything, while things made out of nothing can be deficient. In regard to these latter, the more they have of being and the more good things they do or make — for then they are doing or making something positive — the more their causes are efficient; but in so far as they fail or are defective and, in that sense, "do evil" — if a "defect" can be "done" — then their causes are "deficient." I know, further, that when

Augustine, *The City of God*, trans. D. B. Zema and G. G. Walsh, in *Fathers of the Church*, vol. 8 (New York: Catholic University Press, 1950), selections from bks. 11, 12, 14, and 19.

a will "is made" evil, what happens would not have happened if the will had not wanted it to happen. That is why the punishment which follows is just, since the defection was not necessary but voluntary. The will does not fall "into sin"; it falls "sinfully." Defects are not mere relations to natures that are evil; they are evil in themselves because, contrary to the order of natures, there is a defection from Being that is supreme to some lesser being.

Thus, greed is not a defect in the gold that is desired but in the man who loves it perversely by falling from justice which he ought to esteem as incomparably superior to gold; nor is lust a defect in bodies which are beautiful and pleasing: it is a sin in the soul of the one who loves corporeal pleasures perversely, that is, by abandoning that temperance which joins us in spiritual and unblemishable union with realities far more beautiful and pleasing; nor is boastfulness a blemish in words of praise: it is a failing in the soul of one who is so perversely in love with other peoples' applause that he despises the voice of his own conscience; nor is pride a vice in the one who delegates power, still less a flaw in the power itself: it is a passion in the soul of the one who loves his own power so perversely as to condemn the authority of one who is still more powerful.

In a word, anyone who loves perversely the good of any nature whatsoever and even, perhaps, acquires this good makes himself bad by gaining something good and sad by losing something better. . . .

"Human Responsibility in Decision Making"

However, our main point is that, from the fact that to God the order of all causes is certain, there is no logical deduction that there is no power in the choice of our will. The fact is that our choices fall within the order of the causes which is known for certain to God and is contained in His foreknowledge — for, human choices are the causes of human acts. It follows that He who foreknew the causes of all things could not be unaware that our choices were among those causes which were foreknown as the causes of our acts.

In this matter it is easy enough to refute Cicero

by his own admission, namely, that nothing happens without a preceding efficient cause. It does not help him to admit that nothing happens without a cause and then to argue that not every cause is fated, since some causes are either fortuitous or natural or voluntary. He admits that nothing happens without a preceding cause; that is enough to refute him.

Thus, God is the Cause of all things — a cause that makes but is not made. Other causes make, but they are themselves made — for example, all created spirits and, especially, rational spirits. Material causes which are rather passive than active are not to be included among efficient causes, for their power is limited to what the wills of spirits work through them.

It does not follow, therefore, that the order of causes, known for certain thought it is in the foreknowing mind of God, brings it about that there is no power in our will, since our choices themselves have an important place in the order of causes.

Our conclusion is that our wills have power to do all what God wanted them to do and foresaw they could do. Their power such as it is, is a real power. What they are to do they themselves will most certainly do, because God foresaw both that they could do it and that they would do it and His knowledge cannot be mistaken. . . .

"On Evil"

Should anyone say that the cause of vices and evil habits lies in the flesh because it is only when the soul is influenced by the flesh that it lives then in such a manner, he cannot have sufficiently considered the entire nature of man. . . .

It is an error to suppose that all the evils of the soul proceed from the body. . . . On the contrary, the first bad will, which was present in man before any of his bad deeds, was rather a falling away from the work of God into man's own works than a positive work itself; in fact, a fall into bad works, since they were "according to man" and not "according to God." Thus, this bad will or, what is the same, man in so far as his will is bad is like a bad tree which brings forth these bad works like bad fruit.

A bad will, however, contrary as it is to nature and not according to nature, since it is a defect in nature, still belongs to the nature of which it is a defect, since it has no existence apart from this nature. This nature, of course, is one that God has created out of nothing, and not out of Himself, as was the case when He begot the Word through whom all things have been made. Though God has fashioned man from the dust of the earth, that same dust, like all earthly matter, has been made out of nothing. And it was a soul made out of nothing which God united to the body when man was created.

In the long run, however, the good triumphs over the evil. It is true, of course, that the Creator permits evil, to prove to what good purpose His providence and justice can use even evil. Nevertheless, while good can exist without any defect, as in the true and supreme God Himself, and even in the whole of that visible and invisible creation, high in the heavens above this gloomy atmosphere, evil cannot exist without good, since the natures to which the defects belong, in as much as they are natures, are good. Moreover, we cannot remove evil by the destruction of the nature or any part of it, to which the damage has been done. We can only cure a disease or repair the damage by restoring the nature to health or wholeness. . . .

"On Power and Authority"

Our first parents only fell openly into the sin of disobedience because, secretly, they had begun to be guilty. Actually, their bad deed could not have been done had not bad will preceded it; what is more, the root of their bad will was nothing else than pride. For, "pride is the beginning of all sin." And what is pride but an appetite for inordinate exaltation? Now, exaltation is inordinate when the soul cuts itself off from the very Source to which it should keep close and somehow makes itself and becomes an end to itself. This takes place when the soul becomes inordinately pleased with itself, and such self-pleasing occurs when the soul falls away from the unchangeable Good which ought to please the soul far more than the soul can please itself. Now, this falling away is the soul's own doing, for, if the will had merely remained firm in the love of that higher immutable Good which lighted its mind into knowledge and warmed its will into love, it would not have turned away in search of satisfaction in itself and, by so doing, have lost that light and warmth. And thus Eve would not have believed that the serpent's lie was true, nor would Adam have preferred the will of his wife to the will of God nor have supposed that his transgression of God's command was venial when he refused to abandon the partner of his life even in a partnership of sin.

Our first parents, then, must already have fallen before they could do the evil deed, before they could commit the sin of eating the forbidden fruit. For such "bad fruit" could come only from a "bad tree." That the tree became bad was contrary to its nature, because such a condition could come about only by a defection of the will, which is contrary to nature. Notice, however, that such worsening by reason of a defect is possible only in a nature that has been created out of nothing. In a word, a nature is a nature because it is something made by God, but a nature falls away from That which Is because the nature was made out of nothing.

Yet, man did not so fall away from Being as to be absolutely nothing, but, in so far as he turned himself toward himself, he became less than he was when he was adhering to Him who is supreme Being. Thus, no longer to be in God but to be in oneself in the sense of to please oneself is not to be wholly nothing but to be approaching nothingness. For this reason, Holy Scripture gives another name to the proud. They are called "rash" and "self-willed." Certainly, it is good for the heart to be lifted up, not to oneself, for this is the mark of pride, but to God, for this is a sign of obedience which is precisely the virtue of the humble.

There is, then, a kind of lowliness which in some wonderful way causes the heart to be lifted up, and there is a kind of loftiness which makes the heart sink lower. This seems to be a sort of paradox, that loftiness should make something up. The reason for this is that holy lowliness makes us bow to what is above us and, since there is nothing above God, the kind of lowliness that makes us close to God exalts us. On the other hand, the kind of loftiness which is a defection by this very defection refuses this subjection to God and so falls down from Him who is supreme, and by falling comes to be lower. Thus it comes to pass, as Scripture says, that "when they were lifting themselves up thou hast cast them down." Here, the Psalmist does not say: "When they had been lifted up," as though they first lifted themselves up and afterwards were cast down, but "when they are lifting themselves up, at that moment they were cast down," which means that their very lifting themselves up was itself a fall.

Hence it is that just because humility is the virtue especially esteemed in the City of God and so recommended to its citizens in their present pilgrimage on earth and because it is one that was particularly outstanding in Christ, its King, so it is that pride, the vice contrary to this virtue, is, as Holy Scripture tells us, especially dominant in Christ's adversary, the Devil. In fact, this is the main difference which distinguishes the two cities of which we are speaking. The humble City is the society of holy men and good angels; the proud city is the society of wicked men and evil angels. The one City began with the love of God; the other had its beginnings in the love of self.

Benedict

The suspicion of Mammon in some parts of the Bible was reinforced over time by the teachings of some philosophers and by various forms of spirituality that had a contempt for material and historical reality. These emphases encouraged a tradition of hermits, those who abandoned civilization, with all its necessary compromises, for a life of spiritual struggle for holiness and against destructive forces within and without. Some ascetics had disciples or devoted admirers; many lived alone in the desert; but their witness to a kind of meaning other than that found in secular society had a great impact on Christian believers, just as the sadhus of India, the forest monks of Thailand, the Taoist sages of China, and the Sufis of the Middle East have had elsewhere.

But the reclusive impulse was not the only impulse within Christianity. Its intense focus on the individual soul is matched by a drive toward fellowship. And for all Christianity's accent on a world-transcending spirituality, this faith places an equally strong emphasis on a world-affirming sense of incarnation. The spiritual realm is made present to humans in and through the earthly and temporal world.

Such motifs have combined in numerous ways in Christian history. One of the most significant for economic life is the formation of distinctive communities of committed people who separate themselves from the institutions of ordinary life. The first such stable community was formed by Pachomious in North Africa in the early 300s. A century later Augustine himself founded an order. But it was another hundred years before Benedict wrote his "Rule" for the monastic community. Benedict's Rule not only summarized much that went before but also gave monasticism in the West a distinctive stamp. He connected spirituality with the shared, planned, and disciplined modes of production as demands of the gospel, so that work became a form of prayer and technology (the tools of the day) became instruments of sacramental importance.

Some scholars have argued that without the monastic movement the church and its faith could easily have been swallowed into the feudal family or the imperial culture, depending on whoever supported it financially. But the monastic movement gave the church a base independent of family life (which was the basis of most economic production) and of politics (which was the basis of most power and prestige). In this context, the vows of "poverty, chastity, and obedience" (obedience to the abbot, and hence not to either the head of the family or the head of the regime) represented not only a particular view of Scripture and the demands of faith but also the formation of a disciplined, cooperative, productive community outside traditional structures of authority. This movement became the progenitor of numerous church reforms. Its influence can also be traced to later forms of Christian socialism, various countercultural communes, several radical and independent sects, and the independent corporation. It was a quiet but very consequential revolution brought about by communal spiritual discipline — a revolution whose effects were felt in many directions.

The Rule of Saint Benedict

Benedict

Listen carefully, my son, to the master's instructions, and attend to them with the ear of your heart. This is advice from a father who loves you; welcome it, and faithfully put it into practice. The labor of obedience will bring you back to him from whom you had drifted through the sloth of disobedience. This message of mine is for you, then, if you are ready to give up your own will, once and for all, and armed with the strong and noble weapons of obedience to do battle for the true King, Christ the Lord. . . .

Seeking his workman in a multitude of people, the Lord calls out to him and lifts his voice again: *Is there anyone here who yearns for life and desires to see good days?* (Ps 33[34]:13). If you hear this and your answer is "I do," God then directs these words to you: If you desire true and eternal life, *keep your tongue free from vicious talk and your lips from all deceit; turn away from evil and do good; let peace be your quest and aim* (Ps 33[34]:14-15). Once you have done this, my *eyes will be upon you and my ears will listen for your prayers; and even before you ask me, I will say* to you: *Here I am* (Isa 58:9). What, dear brothers, is more delightful than this voice of the Lord calling to us? See how the Lord in his love shows us the way of life. Clothed then with faith and the performance of good works, let us set out on this way, with the Gospel for our guide, that we may deserve to see *him who has called* us *to his kingdom* (1 Thess 2:12). If we wish to dwell in the tent of this kingdom, we will

never arrive unless we run there by doing good deeds. . . .

Therefore we intend to establish a school for the Lord's service. In drawing up its regulations, we hope to set down nothing harsh, nothing burdensome. The good of all concerned, however, may prompt us to a little strictness in order to amend faults and to safeguard love. Do not be daunted immediately by fear and run away from the road that leads to salvation. It is bound to be narrow at the outset. But as we progress in this way of life and in faith, we shall run on the path of God's commandments, our hearts overflowing with the inexpressible delight of love. . . .

[Chapters Regarding the Economic Life]

[T]here should be chosen from the community someone who is wise, mature in conduct, temperate, not an excessive eater, not proud, excitable, offensive, dilatory or wasteful, but God-fearing, and like a father to the whole community. He will take care of everything, but will do nothing without an order from the abbot. Let him keep to his orders.

He should not annoy the brothers. If any brother happens to make an unreasonable demand of him, he should not reject him with disdain and cause him distress, but reasonably and humbly deny the improper request. Let him keep watch over his own soul, ever mindful of that saying of the Apostle: *He who serves well secures a good standing for himself* (1 Tim 3:13). He must show every care and concern for the sick, children, guests and the poor, knowing for certain that he will be held accountable for all of them on the day of judgment. He will regard all utensils and goods of the monastery as sacred vessels of the altar, aware that nothing is to be neglected. He should not be prone to greed, nor be wasteful and extravagant with the goods of the monastery, but should do everything with moderation and according to the abbot's orders.

Above all, let him be humble. If goods are not available to meet a request, he will offer a kind word in reply, for it is written: A kind *word is better than the best gift* (Sir 18:17). He should take care of all that the abbot entrusts to him, and not presume to do what the abbot has forbidden. He will

---

From *The Rule of St. Benedict*, abridged ed. in English and Latin, with notes and commentary by T. Fry, O.S.B. (Collegeville, MN: Liturgical Press, 1981), pp. 5, 9, 13, 75, 77, 79.

provide the brothers their allotted amount of food without any pride or delay, lest they be led astray. For he must remember what the Scripture says that person deserves *who leads one of the little ones astray* (Matt 18:6).

If the community is rather large, he should be given helpers, that with their assistance he may calmly perform the duties of his office. Necessary items are to be requested and given at the proper times, so that no one may be disquieted or distressed in the house of God.

Chapter 32. The Tools and Goods of the Monastery

The goods of the monastery, that is, its tools, clothing or anything else, should be entrusted to brothers whom the abbot appoints and in whose manner of life he has confidence. He will, as he sees fit, issue to them the various articles to be cared for and collected after use. The abbot will maintain a list of these, so that when the brothers succeed one another in their assigned tasks, he may be aware of what he hands out and what he receives back.

Whoever fails to keep the things belonging to the monastery clean or treats them carelessly should be reproved. If he does not amend, let him be subjected to the discipline of the rule.

Chapter 33. Monks and Private Ownership

Above all, this evil practice must be uprooted and removed from the monastery. We mean that without an order from the abbot, no one may presume to give, receive or retain anything as his own, nothing at all — not a book, writing tablets or stylus — in short, not a single item, especially since monks may not have the free disposal even of their own bodies and wills. For their needs, they are to look to the father of the monastery, and are not allowed anything which the abbot has not given or permitted. *All things should be the common possession of all,* as it is written, *so that no one presumes to call anything his own* (Acts 4:32).

But if anyone is caught indulging in this most evil practice, he should be warned a first and a

second time. If he does not amend, let him be subjected to punishment.

Chapter 34. Distribution of Goods According to Need

It is written: *Distribution was made to each one as he had need* (Acts 4:35). By this we do not imply that there should be favoritism — God forbid — but rather consideration for weaknesses. Whoever needs less should thank God and not be distressed, but whoever needs more should feel humble because of his weakness, not self-important because of the kindness shown him. In this way all the members will be at peace. . . .

Thomas Aquinas

To call the next period of Western history the "Dark Ages" is to interpret it from only one side. It is true that the old Roman Empire fell and that forms of agrarian feudalism came to dominate life. Also, Islam, the greatest post-Christian religion, arose in Arabia and quickly expanded north into Russia, south into Africa, east into Asia, and west into Europe. It created an empire surpassing anything in the West, and it wove together new patterns of thought by combining elements from the Greek classics with the wisdom of the Qu'ran. Indeed, it was Islamic scholars who kept the thought of Aristotle alive, and eventually mediated it to the West.

However, one of the ironies of history is that the Islamic expansion and the Christian crusades of the eleventh and twelfth centuries not only threw bloody armies against each other (and in some cases against Jews from both sides) in terrible destruction; they also opened new trade routes between Asia and Europe, stimulated science, allowed scholars to discover new ideas, and began a new epoch in the development of cosmopolitan thinking. Thus this period is better called the "High Middle Ages."

The ideas of Augustine, with their many echoes from Plato and Plotinus, had been kept alive in the monasteries, and they had dominated both biblical understandings and the interpretation of social and ethical issues for half a dozen centuries. As trade, city life, and cultural vitality began to grow again, Aristotle's more naturalistic and empirical methods challenged the consensus. In this context, Thomas Aquinas rendered a new synthesis of biblical and philosophical thought, one that integrated natural, rational themes from Aristotle (whom he calls "the Philosopher") and biblical, theological themes from Augustine, as well as drawing on many others.

Thomas methodically takes up a vast array of issues, poses possible objections, interrogates a series of witnesses from over the ages, and renders a judgment about what is right (lawful). He is convinced that moral issues are not a matter of opinion but rather a matter of correct argument, seen from an integrated and comprehensive point of view that finds its final focus in the ultimate vision of God. Many consider his work to be an intellectual achievement that remains unsurpassed — even by such feats as the integrated theory of physics and cosmology developed in our own time.

Roman Catholic Christians, especially, revere the "angelic doctor" more than others and have found it unnecessary to introduce many innovations in his teachings about economic ethics or the relation of moral philosophy to business until quite recently. In fact, his arguments were used to oppose Protestants in some cases, and as we will see in several subsequent readings, aspects of Thomistic thought are still very much alive. Today many Protestants and non-Christian philosophers also find his arguments among the most cogent of any in human history.

Here we focus on two selections from his greatest work, *Summa Theologica*. One sets forth his distinction between distributive and commutative justice; the other applies the concept of business.

Of Justice, and Of Cheating

Thomas Aquinas

Of Justice, Commutative and Distributative

Here there are four points of inquiry: (1) whether there are two kinds of justice, commutative and distributive; (2) whether each strikes the virtuous mean in the same manner; (3) whether their subject-matter is uniform or manifold; (4) whether in each the just is identified with reciprocal give-and-take.

First Article: Are the Species of Justice Well-Divided into Commutative and Distributive?

The First Point: It would seem not. For that which is harmful to the many cannot be a species of justice, which serves the common good. Now it is harmful to the common good for the goods of the community to be distributed among the many, both because it would exhaust the common resources and because it would corrupt men's morals. Cicero says that *he who receives becomes worse, and ever more ready to receive more.* So therefore distribution is no part of any kind of justice.

2. Besides, we have agreed that the act of justice is to render to each what is his. But in distributing he does not receive what was his, instead there is

From *Summa Theologica* 2, II, q. 61, art. 1, trans. T. Gilby, O.P., Blackfriars ed., vol. 37 (New York: McGraw-Hill, 1975), pp. 87-101.

newly appropriated to him something which belonged to the community. This is not a work of justice.

3. Again, we have agreed that justice is in subjects as well as in rulers. Yet distribution is the office always of a ruler. Therefore to be distributive is not part of justice.

4. Also, according to the *Ethics,* distributive justice is of community goods. These, however, are the concern of general or legal justice. Consequently distributive justice is a species of that, not of particular justice.

5. Further, being engaged with one or many does not make for a difference of kind in a virtue. Now commutative justice lies in rendering one person his due, distributive in giving something to the many. Therefore they are not different kinds of species of justice.

On the Other Hand, Aristotle assigns two parts to justice, and says that one governs distributions and the other exchanges.

Reply: As we have seen, particular justice is directed towards the private person, who may be compared to the community as a part to a whole. Now with a part we may note a twofold relationship. First, that of one part to another, and this corresponds to the ordering of private persons among themselves. This is governed by commutative justice, which is engaged with their mutual dealings one with another. Second, that of the whole to a part, which goes with the bearing of the community on individual persons. This is governed by distributive justice which apportions proportionately to each his share from the common stock. And so there are two species of justice, namely commutative and distributive justice.

Hence: 1. A private person is commended for due modernation in his bountifulness, and blamed for squandering it in waste. So likewise should moderation be showed in dispensing community goods, and this is governed by distributive justice.

2. As a part and the whole are identical in a sense, so too in a sense that which is of the whole is also of a part. Accordingly when something is given to each from the goods of the community each in a way receives what is his own.

3. The act of distributing common goods is the office of him who is their guardian. Nevertheless distributive justice is also in subjects in that they

are content with the fair sharing out. Yet note that distributive justice may be from the common goods of the family, not the State, and this dispensing can be done by the authority of a private person.

4. A movement gets its character from the term it arrives at. Accordingly general or legal justice aims to conduct the dealings of private persons to the good of the community, whereas the reverse holds when that is brought to private persons, such distribution is a function of particular justice.

5. It is not merely the one and the many that gives rise to the distinction between commutative and distributive justice, it is also the difference between types or kinds of what is due, for somebody is entitled in one manner to what is his own, but in another to what is the community's.

Second Article: Do Commutative and Distributive Justice Strike the Just Mean in the Same Fashion?

The Second Point: 1. So it would seem. For we have agreed that both are contained under particular justice. Now all the specific parts of the moral virtues of fortitude and temperance take the virtuous mean in the same manner. So then also the commutative and distributive parts of justice.

2. Again, the shaping principle or form of a moral virtue consists in observing a mean determined by reason. Since, then, there is one and the same form in one virtue, it would seem that the virtuous mean is struck in the same manner by commutative and distributive justice alike.

3. Further, in distributive justice the mean is struck when attention is paid to differences of personal rank. But this is attended to in commutative justice, for instance, in imposing penalties, for a heavier sentence is incurred for offering violence to a ruler than to a private person. Both kinds of justice, then, are alike in taking the virtuous mean.

On the Other Hand, Aristotle holds that the mean is taken *in distributive justice according to geometrical proportion and in commutative justice according to arithmetical proportion.*

Reply: We have said that distributive justice gives something to a private person is so far as

something belonging to the community is due to a part. This is so much the more considerable in correspondence with the greater importance of the part in the whole. Consequently so much the more is given from the common stock as the recipient holds more responsibility in the community. Importance is assessed in an aristocracy by virtue, in an oligarchy by wealth, in a democracy by liberty, and in other regimes variously. So then the virtuous mean is taken in distributive justice, not according to an equality between thing and thing, but according to a proportion between things and persons, and in such a way that even as one person exceeds another so also that which is meted out to him exceeds that which is meted out to the other. Accordingly, Aristotle describes the mean here as being *according to geometric proportionality,* in which the even balance or equality lies in a comparative relation, not in a fixed quantity. Thus we reckon that 6 is to 4 as 3 is to 2; in each case the proportion is 1.5, since the greater number is the sum of the smaller plus a half. The excess is not, however, of simple quantity, since 6 exceeds 4 by 2, whereas 3 exceeds 2 by 1.

It is otherwise in exchanges between persons. There something is rendered to an individual person in return for something of his that has been received: this most evidently appears in buying and selling, from which originates the notion of an exchange. There the balance or equalization of thing with thing is called for, so that a man should repay the other as much as he gains in acquiring the thing which belonged to the other. Here the equality will be according to an arithmetical mean, which lies between an equal plus and minus of quantities. Thus 5 is the mean between 6 and 4, since it exceeds the first and is exceeded by the second by 1. If each has 5 to start with, and one receives 1 from what belongs to the other, he will have 6 and the other will be left with 4. Justice will be served when both are brought back to the mean, by 1 being taken from the one who has 6 and given to the other who has 4. Then both will have 5, which is the mean.

Hence: 1. With the other moral virtues the mean is taken according to right reason with respect to the doer, not to outside things. Justice, however, strikes this latter objective medium, and, consequently, in diverse fashions corresponds to the diversity in social reality.

2. Equality is the general shaping form of justice, and here both distributive and commutative justice agree, but in the first it is taken according to geometrical proportionality, while in the second according to arithmetical.

3. In the give-and-take of action and passion among men the quality of a person involved affects the quantity or size of the thing done; striking a ruler offers greater injury than striking a private person. Yet with distributive justice what counts is the quality or station of a person considered in itself, whereas with commutative justice it lies in a diversification arising from the objective condition of that which is owing.

Third Article: Is the Subject-matter Diverse for each kind of Justice?

The Third Point: 1. Apparently not. For a diversity of matter makes a diversity of virtue, as is clear in the case of fortitude and temperance. Were distributive justice and commutative justice to have diverse subject-matters, they would not be contained under one virture, namely justice.

2. Further, the dispensing, with which distributive justice is engaged, according to the *Ethics* is of money or honours or whatever can be apportioned to members of the community. There also are matters of exchanges between persons, and thus are the concern of commutative justice. Therefore the matters of distributive and commutative justice are not diverse.

3. Again, if the reason alleged for the difference of their subject-matters is the specific difference between distributive and commutative justice, then if there is no such specific difference the need for a difference of subject-matter will not arise. Now, though holding that commutative justice is one species of virtue, Aristotle admits that its subject-matter is manifold. It would not seem, then, that the two kinds of justice have different subject-matters.

On the Contrary, it is stated in the *Ethics* that *one kind of justice is the governing virtue in distributions and another kind in exchanges.*

Reply: We have said that justice is engaged with certain external activities concerning distributions and exchanges. These consist in the application or use of what is outside us, whether things or persons or works we do. Things, as when we take from or restore to another his property; persons, as when we strike or insult another or, alternatively, treat him with respect; works, as when we justly claim another's labour or do a job for him. Now if we take as subject-matter what each kind of justice employs, then there is no difference between them, for things of the same sort can be apportioned out of the common stock and be also exchanged between individuals, and likewise hard work can be a matter both of allotment by the community and also of repayment according to private contract. If, however, in the subject-matter of the two kinds of justice we stress the dominant for each in dealing with persons, using things, and performing works, then there is a difference on either side. For distributive justice governs the apportioning of community goods, whereas commutative governs the exchanging that may take place between two persons.

Of these exchanges some are involuntary, some voluntary. They are involuntary when somebody employs another's thing, person or work without his consent. This may be done secretly by deceit or openly by violence. In either way injury may be committed against another's property or person or against the person of one close to him. Against his property: if taken secretly it is called theft, if openly it is called robbery. Against his person, if his life and health be attacked, and also his good-name and dignity: the first may be done secretly, as when he is treacherously slain, struck, or poisoned, or openly, as when he is publicly executed, struck, maimed, or sent to prison. His dignity is injured secretly by false witness, detraction, and the like, whereby he is robbed of his good name; it is done openly by accusation in a court of law or public insult. Against the person of a connection of his, as when he is injured by adultery with his wife, which is usually secret, or by the enticement of a servant; it can also be done openly. Whatever injury may be done to the principal victim under the headings outlined above may also be done to persons connected with him. Yet adultery and enticement are injuries properly against him, and the latter, since a servant in a sense is his belonging, comes back to theft.

Exchanges are called voluntary when a person willingly transfers something he owns to another. If he simply passes it to another in such wise that the recipient incurs no strict debt, as when he makes a gift, this is an act of liberality, not of justice. A voluntary transfer comes under justice in so far as it involves the notion of something due. This can enter in several ways. First, when somebody simply transfers what is his in payment for something else, as happens in buying and selling. Second, when somebody transfers a thing he owns that another may have the use of it with the obligation of returning it later: if the use is granted without charge, then for things that bear fruit it is called usufruct, and for things that do not, such as cash, crockery, and so forth, it is called borrowing or lending. If there is a charge on the use, it is called renting or hiring. Third, when somebody hands over his property for safekeeping, not for use, and means to recover it, as with a deposit, or because of an obligation, as when he pledges a piece of property or stands surety for another.

In all dealings of this sort, whether involuntary or voluntary, the just mean is taken in the same sense according to a balance or equality in requital. Accordingly they all come under the same species of justice, namely commutative justice.

Hence: The reply to the objections is clear.

Fourth Article: Is the Just simply the same as the Reciprocal?

The fourth point: 1. So it would seem. For the divine judgment is purely and simply just, and this is the form it follows, that as a person does so shall he suffer; *With the judgment you pronounce you will be judged, and the measure you give will be the measure you get.* Therefore the just simply is the same as the reciprocal.

2. Further, in either kind of justice something is rendered to a person according to a certain equivalence. With distributive justice this regards his worth, which is weighed by his works in the service of the community; with commutative justice this regards the thing in which he has suffered loss. Both demand requital for what has been done. So then it seems that the just simply is the same as the reciprocal.

3. Besides, the chief reason why man should not get what he gives seems to lie with the difference between involuntary and voluntary action; he who does an injury involuntarily suffers the lighter penalty. But voluntary and involuntary are terms qualifying what is done on our side, and do not affect the just mean, which is a measure in reality, not merely according to our frame of mind. Consequently the just simply seems the same as the reciprocal.

On the Other Hand, there is Aristotle proving that the just does not always coincide with the reciprocal.

Reply: The term *contrapassum,* literally "counter-suffered," spells an exact concordance of a reaction with the antecedent action. Such a tit-for-tat most properly applies when injury is undergone caused by a man harming the person of his neighbour, for instance if he strike him let him be struck in return. The Old Law determines such a just requital; *If any harm follows, you shall give life for life, eye for eye, tooth for tooth,* and so forth. In the second place, because to take from another his property is a thing unjust, the notion of retaliation also applies there, so that one who inflicts loss on another should also suffer loss in his belongings. This, too, is contained in the Old Law; *If a man steals an ox or a sheep, and kills it or sells it, he shall pay five oxen for an ox, and four sheep for a sheep.* Finally, the notion is extended to voluntary exchanges, where there is something done and undergone on either side. Remember, however, that the passive character of undergoing something is lessened by its voluntariness. In all such cases the nature of commutative justice demands that equivalent recompense be made, namely that the reaction as repayment matches the action.

This would not always be the case were the doer to undergo the same in kind to that which he caused. Take the case, to begin with, of a subordinate who injures his superior; his action is more serious than a like action done on him in return. And so he who strikes a ruler is not only struck back, but also much more severely punished. Then take the case of one who unjustly takes another's property without the owner's consent; his action would exceed his undergoing the consequences were only that property to be taken away from him, for he who inflicted loss on another would suffer no loss of property in return. In consequence he is punished by a fine heavier than the simple disgorgement of his gain, for he did an injury, not only to a private person, but also to the commonwealth by breaking the security which is in its charge. So too neither in voluntary exchanges is requital always the give and return of things of the same sort, for sometimes they are unequal. Consequently in exchanges the equalization of what is done and what is undergone in return requires a certain proprotionate standard of measurement: for this purpose was money invented. It is in this sense that a *quid pro quo* is what is right and just for commutative justice.

Note, however, that in distributive justice such reciprocity has no place, for the equalization is not taken there according to the proportion of things to thing, or of doing an action to undergoing the reaction (whence the term *contrapassum*), but according to the proportionality of things to persons, as already explained.

Hence: 1. Divine judgment follows the form of commutative justice in that reward is the recompense of merit, and punishment that of sin.

2. When a man who has served the community is requited for his services, that is an act of commutative, not distributive justice. For distributive justice considers the correspondence, not between that which is spent and that which is received, but between that which is received by one and by another in accordance with their respective degrees.

3. The injury is augmented when the injurious action is voluntary, and is treated accordingly as a more important thing. Hence it calls for greater punishment in recompense. The difference is not in our thinking merely, but also in objective reality.

Of Cheating, Which is Committed in Buying and Selling

First, we shall consider cheating, which is committed in buying and selling: secondly, we shall consider usury, which occurs in loans. In connection with the other voluntary commutations no special kind of sin is to be found distinct from rapine and theft.

Under the first head there are four points of inquiry: (1) Of unjust sales as regards the price; namely, whether it is lawful to sell a thing for more than its worth? (2) Of unjust sales on the part of the thing sold. (3) Whether the seller is bound to reveal a fault in the thing sold? (4) Whether it is lawful in trading to sell a thing at a higher price than was paid for it?

First Article: Whether It Is Lawful to Sell a Thing For More Than Its Worth?

We proceed thus to the First Article.

Objection 1. It would seem that it is lawful to sell a thing for more than its worth. In the commutations of human life, civil laws determine that which is just. Now according to these laws it is just for buyer and seller to deceive one another; and this occurs by the seller selling a thing for more than its worth, and the buyer buying a thing for less than its worth. Therefore it is lawful to sell a thing for more than its worth.

Objection 2. Further, that which is common to all would seem to be natural and not sinful. Now Augustine relates that the saying of a certain jester was accepted by all, *You wish to buy for a song and to sell at a premium,* which agrees with the saying, *It is naught, it is naught, saith every buyer: and when he is gone away, then he will boast.* Therefore it is lawful to sell a thing for more than its worth.

Objection 3. Further, it does not seem unlawful if that which honesty demands be done by mutual agreement. Now, according to the Philosopher in the friendship which is based on utility, the

From *Summa Theologica*, 2, II, q. 77, art. 1, ed. D. Bigongiari (New York: Hafner Publishing Co., 1957), pp. 224-32.

amount of the recompense for a favor received should depend on the utility accruing to the receiver: and this utility sometimes is worth more than the thing given, for instance if the receiver be in great need of that thing, whether for the purpose of avoiding a danger, or of deriving some particular benefit. Therefore, in contracts of buying and selling, it is lawful to give a thing in return for more than its worth.

On the contrary, it is written *All things . . . whatsoever you would that men should do to you, do you also to them.* But no man wishes to buy a thing for more than its worth. Therefore no man should sell a thing to another man for more than its worth.

I answer that, it is altogether sinful to have recourse to deceit in order to sell a thing for more than its just price, because this is to deceive one's neighbor so as to injure him. Hence Tully [Cicero] says *Contracts should be entirely free from double-dealing; the seller must not impose upon the bidder, nor the buyer upon one that bids against him.*

But, apart from fraud, we may speak of buying and selling in two ways. First, as considered in themselves, and from this point of view, buying and selling seem to be established for the common advantage of both parties, one of whom requires that which belongs to the other, and vice versa, as the Philosopher states. Now whatever is established for the common advantage, should not be more of a burden to one party than to another, and consequently all contracts between them should observe equality of thing and thing. Again, the quality of a thing that comes into human use is measured by the price given for it, for which purpose money was invented, as stated in the *Ethics.* Therefore if either the price exceed the quantity of the thing's worth, or, conversely, the thing exceed the price, there is no longer the equality of justice: and consequently, to sell a thing for more than its worth, or to buy it for less than its worth, is in itself unjust and unlawful.

Secondly we may speak of buying and selling, considered as accidentally tending to the advantage of one party, and to the disadvantage of the other: for instance, when a man has great need of a certain thing, while another man will suffer if he be without it. In such a case the just price will depend not only on the thing sold, but on the loss which the sale brings on the seller. And thus it will

be lawful to sell a thing for more than it is worth in itself, though the price paid be not more than it is worth to the owner. Yet if the one man derive a great advantage by becoming possessed of the other man's property, and the teller be not at a loss through being without that thing, the latter ought not to raise the price, because the advantage accruing to the buyer is not due to the seller, but to a circumstance affecting the buyer. Now no man should sell what is not his, though he may charge for the loss he suffers.

On the other hand if a man find that he derives great advantage from something he has bought, he may, of his own accord, pay the seller something over and above, and this pertains to his honesty.

Reply Objection 1. Human law is given to the people among whom there are many lacking virtue, and it is not given to the virtuous alone. Hence human law was unable to forbid all that is contrary to virtue; and it suffices for it to prohibit whatever is destructive of human intercourse, while it treats other matters as though they were lawful, not by approving of them, but by not punishing them. Accordingly, if without employing deceit the seller disposes of his goods for more than their worth, or the buyer obtain them for less than their worth, the law looks upon this as licit, and provides no punishment for so doing, unless the excess be too great, because then even human law demands restitution to be made, for instance if a man be deceived in regard of more than half the amount of the just price of a thing.

On the other hand the Divine law leaves nothing unpunished that is contrary to virtue. Hence, according to the Divine law, it is reckoned unlawful if the equality of justice be not observed in buying and selling: and he who has received more than he ought must make compensation to him that has suffered loss, if the loss be considerable. I add this condition, because the just price of things is not fixed with mathematical precision, but depends on a kind of estimate, so that a slight addition or subtraction would not seem to destroy the equality of justice.

Reply Objection 2. As Augustine says *this jester, either by looking into himself or by his experience of others, thought that all men are inclined to wish to buy for a song and sell at a premium. But since in reality this is wicked, it is in every man's power to acquire that justice whereby he may resist and over-*

come this inclination. And then he gives the example of a man who gave the just price for a book to a man who through ignorance asked a low price for it. Hence it is evident that this common desire is not from nature but from vice, wherefore it is common to many who walk along the broad road of sin.

Reply Objection 3. In commutative justice we consider chiefly real equality. On the other hand, in friendship based on utility we consider equality of usefulness so that the recompense should depend on the usefulness accruing, whereas in buying it should be equal to the thing bought.

Second Article: Whether a Sale is Rendered Unlawful Through a Fault in the Thing Sold?

We proceed thus to the Second Article.

Objection 1. It would seem that a sale is not rendered unjust and unlawful through a fault in the thing sold. For less account should be taken of the other parts of a thing than of what belongs to its substance. Yet the sale of a thing does not seem to be rendered unlawful through a fault in its substance: for instance, if a man sell instead of the real metal, silver or gold produced by some chemical process, which is adapted to all the human uses for which silver and gold are necessary, for instance in the making of vessels and the like. Much less therefore will it be an unlawful sale if the thing be defective in other ways.

Objection 2. Further, any fault in the thing, affecting the quantity, would seem chiefly to be opposed to justice which consists in equality. Now quantity is known by being measured: and the measures of things that come into human use are not fixed, but in some places are greater, in others less, as the Philosopher states. Therefore just as it is impossible to avoid defects on the part of the thing sold, it seems that a sale is not rendered unlawful through the thing sold being defective.

Objection 3. Further, the thing sold is rendered defective by lacking a fitting quality. But in order to know the quality of a thing, much knowledge is required that is lacking in most buyers. Therefore a sale is not rendered unlawful by a fault (in the thing sold).

On the contrary, Ambrose says: *It is manifestly a rule of justice that a good man should not depart from the truth, nor inflict an unjust on anyone, nor have any connection with fraud.*

I answer that a threefold fault may be found pertaining to the thing which is sold. One, in respect of the thing's substance: and if the seller be aware of a fault in the thing he is selling, he is guilty of a fraudulent sale, so that the sale is rendered unlawful. Hence we find it written against certain people, *Thy silver is turned into dross, thy wine is mingled with water:* because that which is mixed is defective in its substance.

Another defect is in respect of quantity which is known by being measured: wherefore if anyone knowingly make use of a faulty measure in selling, he is guilty of fraud, and the sale is illicit. Hence it is written: *Thou shalt not have divers weights in thy bag, a greater and a less: neither shall there by in thy house a greater bushel and a less,* and further on: *For the Lord . . . abhoreth him that doth these things, and He hateth all injustice.*

A third defect in on the part of the quality, for instance, if a man sell an unhealthy animal as being a healthy one: and if anyone do this knowingly he is guilty of a fraudulent sale, and the sale, in consequence, is illicit.

In all these cases not only is the man guilty of a fraudulent sale, but he is also bound to restitution. But if any of the foregoing defects be in the thing sold, and he knows nothing about this, the seller does not sin, because he does that which is unjust materially, nor is his deed unjust. Nevertheless he is bound to compensate the buyer, when the defect comes to his knowledge. Moreover what has been said of the seller applies equally to the buyer. For sometimes it happens that the seller thinks his goods to be specifically of lower value, as when a man sells gold instead of copper, and then if the buyer be aware of this, he buys it unjustly and is bound to restitution: and the same applies to a defect in quantity as to a defect in quality.

Reply Objection 1. Gold and silver are costly not only on account of the usefulness of the vessels and other like things made from them, but also on account of the excellence and purity of their substance. Hence if the gold or silver produced by alchemists has not the true specific nature of gold and silver, the sale thereof is fraudulent and unjust, especially as real gold and silver can produce certain results by their natural action, which the counterfeit gold and silver of alchemists cannot produce. Thus the true metal has the property of making people joyful, and is helpful medicinally against certain maladies. Moreover real gold can be employed more frequently, and lasts longer in its condition of purity than counterfeit gold. If however real gold were to be produced by alchemy, it would not be unlawful to sell it for the genuine article, for nothing prevents art from employing certain natural causes for the production of natural and true effects, as Augustine says of things produced by the art of the demons.

Reply Objection 2. The measures of saleable commodities must needs be different in different places, on account of the difference of supply: because where there is greater abundance, the measures are wont to be larger. However in each place those who govern the state must determine the just measures of things saleable, with due consideration for the conditions of place and time. Hence it is not lawful to disregard such measures as are established by public authority or custom.

Reply Objection 3. As Augustine says the price of things saleable does not depend on their degree of nature, since at times a horse fetches a higher price than a slave; but it depends on their usefulness to man. Hence it is not necessary for the seller or buyer to be cognizant of the hidden qualities of the thing sold, but only of such as render the thing adapted to man's use, for instance, that the horse be strong, run well and so forth. Such qualities the seller and buyer can easily discover.

Third Article: Whether the Seller is Bound to State the Defects of the Things Sold?

We proceed thus to the Third Article.

Objection 1. It would seem that the seller is not bound to state the defects of the thing sold. Since the seller does not bind the buyer to buy, he would seem to leave it to him to judge of the goods offered for sale. Now judgment about a thing and knowledge of that thing belong to the same person. Therefore it does not seem imputable to the seller if the buyer be deceived in his judgment, and be hurried into buying a thing without carefully inquiring into its condition.

Objection 2. Further, it seems foolish for anyone to do what prevents him carrying out his work. But if a man states the defects of the goods he has for sale, he prevents their sale: wherefore Tully pictures a man as saying: *Could anything be more absurd than for a public crier, instructed by the owner, to cry: "I offer this unhealthy house for sale"?* Therefore the seller is not bound to state the defects of the thing sold.

Objection 3. Further, man needs more to know the road of virtue than to know the faults of things offered for sale. Now one is not bound to offer advice to all or to tell them the truth about matters pertaining to virtue, though one should not tell anyone what is false. Much less therefore is a seller bound to tell the faults of what he offers for sale, as though he were counselling the buyer.

Objection 4. Further, if one were bound to tell the faults of what one offers for sale, this would only be in order to lower the price. Now sometimes the price would be lowered for some other reason, without any defect in the thing sold: for instance, if the seller carry wheat to a place where wheat fetches a high price, knowing that many will come after him carrying wheat; because if the buyers knew this they would give a lower price. But apparently the seller need not give the buyer this information. Therefore, in like manner, neither, need he tell him the faults of the goods he is selling.

On the contrary, Ambrose says: In all contracts the defects of the saleable commodity must be stated; *and unless the seller make them known, although the buyer has already acquired a right to them, the contract is voided on account of the fraudulent action.*

I answer that it is always unlawful to give anyone an occasion of danger or loss, although a man need not always give another the help or counsel which would be for his advantage in any way; but only in certain fixed cases, for instance when someone is subject to him, or when he is the only one who can assist him. Now the seller who offers goods for sale, gives the buyer an occasion of loss or danger, by the very fact that he offers him defective goods, if such defect may occasion loss or danger to the buyer: loss, if, by reason of this defect, the goods are of less value, and he takes nothing off the price on that account: danger, if this defect either hinder the use of the goods or render it hurtful, for instance, if a man sells a lame for a fleet horse, a tottering house for a safe one, rotten or poisonous food for wholesome. Wherefore if suchlike defects be hidden, and the seller does not make them known, the sale will be illicit and fraudulent, and the seller will be bound to compensation for the loss incurred.

On the other hand, if the defect be manifest, for instance if a horse have but one eye, or if the goods though useless to the buyer, be useful to someone else, provided the seller take as much as he ought from the price, he is not bound to state the defect of the goods, since perhaps on account of that defect the buyer might want him to allow a greater rebate than he need. Wherefore the seller may look to his own indemnity, by withholding the defect of the goods.

Reply Objection 1. Judgment cannot be pronounced save on what is manifest: *for a man judges of what he knows.* Hence if the defects of the goods offered for sale be hidden, judgment of them is not sufficiently left with the buyer unless such defects be made known to him. The case would be different if the defects were manifest.

Reply Objection 2. There is no need to publish beforehand by the public crier the defects of the goods one is offering for sale, because if he were to begin by announcing its defects, the bidders would be frightened to buy, through ignorance of other qualities that might render the thing good and serviceable. Such defect ought to be stated to each individual that offers to buy: and then he will be able to compare the various points one with the other, the good with the bad: for nothing prevents that which is defective in one respect being useful in many others.

Reply Objection 3. Although a man is not bound strictly speaking to tell everyone the truth about matters pertaining to virtue, yet he is so bound in a case when unless he tells the truth, his conduct would endanger another man in detriment to virtue: and so it is in this case.

Reply Objection 4. The defect in a thing makes it of less value now than it seems to be: but in the case cited, the goods are expected to be of less value at a future time, on account of the arrival of other merchants, which was not foreseen by the buyers. Wherefore the seller, since he sells his goods at the price actually offered him, does not seem to act contrary to justice through not stating what is going to happen. If however he were to do so, or if he lowered his price, it would be exceedingly virtuous on his part: although he does not seem to be bound to do this as a debt of justice.

Fourth Article: Whether, in Trading, it is Lawful to Sell a Thing at a Higher Price Than What Was Paid For It?

We proceed thus to the Fourth Article.

Objection 1. It would seem that it is not lawful, in trading, to sell a thing for a higher price than we paid for it. For Chrysostom says (in his commentary) on Matth. xxi,12: *He that buys a thing in order that he may sell it, entire and unchanged, at a profit, is the trader who is cast out of God's temple.* Cassiodorus speaks in the same sense in his commentary on Ps. lxx,15, *Because I have not known learning, or trading according to another version: What is trade, says he, but buying at a cheap price with the purpose of retailing at a higher price?* and he adds: *Such were the tradesmen whom Our Lord cast out of the temple.* Now no man is cast out of the temple except for a sin. Therefore suchlike trading is sinful.

Objection 2. Further, it is contrary to justice to sell goods at a higher price than their worth, or to buy them for less than their value. Now if you sell a thing for a higher price than you paid for it, you must either have bought it for less than its value, or sell it for more than its value. Therefore this cannot be done without sin.

Objection 3. Further, Jerome says: *Shun, as you would the plague, a cleric who from being poor has become wealthy, or who, from being a nobody has become a celebrity.* Now trading would not seem to be forbidden to clerics except on account of its sinfulness. Therefore it is a sin in trading, to buy at a low price and to sell at a higher price.

On the contrary, Augustine commenting on Ps. lxx,15, Because I have known learning, says: The greedy tradesman blasphemes over his losses; he lies and perjures himself over the price of his wares. But these are vices of the man, not of the craft, which can be exercised without these vices. Therefore trading is not in itself unlawful.

I answer that a tradesman is one whose business consists in the exchange of things. According to the Philosopher exchange of things is twofold;

one, natural as it were, and necessary, whereby one commodity is exchanged for another, or money taken in exchange for a commodity, in order to satisfy the needs of life. Suchlike trading, properly speaking does not belong to tradesmen, but rather to housekeepers or civil servants who have to provide the household or the state with the necessaries of life. The other kind of exchange is either that of money for money, or of any commodity for money, not on account of the necessities of life, but for profit, and this kind of exchange, properly speaking, regards tradesman, according to the Philosopher. The former kind of exchange is commendable because it supplies a natural need: but the latter is justly deserving of blame, because, considered in itself, it satisfies the greed for gain, which knows no limit and tends to infinity. Hence trading, considered in itself, has a certain debasement attaching thereto, in so far as, by its very nature, it does not imply a virtuous or necessary end. Nevertheless gain which is the end of trading, though not implying, by its nature, anything virtuous or necessary, does not, in itself, connote anything sinful or contrary to virtue: wherefore nothing prevents gain from being directed to some necessary or even virtuous end, and thus trading becomes lawful. Thus, for instance, a man may intend the moderate gain which he seeks to acquire by trading for the upkeep of his household, or for the assistance of the needy: or again, a man may take to trade form some public advantage, for instance, lest his country lack the necessaries of life, and seek gain, not as an end, but as payment for his labor.

Reply Objection 1. The saying of Chrysostom refers to the trading which seeks gain as a last end. This is especially the case where a man sells something at a higher price without its undergoing any change. For if he sells at a higher price something that has changed for the better, he would seem to receive the reward of his labor. Nevertheless the gain itself may be lawfully intended, not as a last end, but for the sake of some other end which is necessary or virtuous, as stated above.

Reply Objection 2. Not everyone that sells at a higher price than he bought is a tradesman, but only he who buys that he may sell at a profit. If, on the contrary, he buys not for sale but for possession, and afterwards, for some reason wishes to sell, it is not a trade transaction even if he sells at a profit. For he may lawfully do this, either because he has bettered the thing, or because the value of the thing has changed with the change of place or time, or on account of the danger he incurs in transferring the thing from one place to another, or again in having it carried by another. In this sense neither buying nor selling is unjust.

Reply Objection 3. Clerics should abstain not only from things that are evil in themselves, but even from those that have an appearance of evil. This happens in trading, both because it is directed to worldly gain, which clerics should despise, and because trading is open to so many vices, since *a merchant is hardly free from sins of the lips.* There is also another reason, because trading engages the mind too much with worldly cares, and consequently withdraws it from spiritual cares; wherefore the Apostle says: *No man being a soldier to God entangleth himself with secular businesses.* Nevertheless it is lawful for clerics to engage in the first mentioned kind of exchange, which is directed to supply the necessaries of life, either by buying or by selling.

The Myth of Self-Interest

It was Reinhold Niebuhr who quipped that original sin was the one empirically verifiable Christian tenet. All one had to do, maintained Niebuhr, was observe one's neighbor. For the great Protestant theologian and his followers, original sin was the religious symbol cited to explain self-interest in politics. Within the school of "Christian realism" the Fall is used not only to explain but to justify political and economic arrangements premised on self-interest. Anything else would be open to the charge of naiveté, the worse failing of nonrealists.

Political and economic systems always embody an understanding of the human. Liberalism and capitalism, with their emphasis on self-interest, are founded ultimately upon a theological anthropology quite different from that which grounds a model of political economy which stresses community. . . .

Catholic doctrine acknowledged the tragic consequences of Adam's sin but insisted that the human being remained essentially intact after the Fall. Adam lost "the holiness and justice in which he had been constituted" and "incurred the wrath and indignation of God" and "was changed in body and soul for the worse," the Council of Trent taught. But human beings are not utterly corrupted and "free will, weakened as it was in its powers and downward bent, was by no means extinguished in them." Indeed, Trent specifically condemned the opinion that all human works done "before justification" (Hobbes's "state of nature") are sinful, that is, purely self-interested. Later in the sixteenth century, disputes about the sovereignty of grace and the status of human freedom led to the teaching that the original justice and holiness of Adam were "accidental," not intrinsic to the human person as human. This original justice and holiness were lost as a result of original sin, but since they were accidental qualities, human nature remained essentially unimpaired. As some Counter-Reformation Catholic theologians phrased the point, the human person, created in the image and likeness of God, might lose that likeness, consisting in original justice and holiness, but retained the image of God. Beneath these Counter-Reformation statements lies an important claim about the meaning of human existence.

Deeply ingrained in the Western Christian tradition is the Augustinian insight that, as creatures who exist solely to be the recipients of the divine self-gift, our hearts are restless until they rest in God. This insight was echoed in the central point of Thomas Aquinas's theological vision, that at the core of human existence is a natural desire to see God. Thus there is a connaturality between nature and grace; nature has an aptitude for grace. Extinguish this restlessness, this desire for the beatific vision, and what remains is no longer a *human* being. Original sin may have distorted this restlessness, it may have skewed the direction of this desire, but it has not undone God's creation: humanity remains *human*. The longing for *agape* is experienced in the call to be agapic, the call to give oneself away. Consequently, Catholic doctrine has insisted in opposition to the darker views of the Reformers that the human being, made in the image of God who is *agape,* remains in that image even after the Fall and so is capable, even if with great difficulty, of genuine other-directedness.

The secularized theological anthropology which underlies [the modern, liberal social ethic] is classically Protestant. If one were to develop a secularized theological anthropology of the Catholic view of original sin, what social ethic emerges? Unlike Hobbes, a Catholic-inspired model of society will acknowledge a need not only to minimize and restrain the evil of self-interest but also the challenge to maximize the good of self-giving. Because Catholics believe that the most important word we say about the human is grace, not sin, strategies for community must be given priority over concern for limiting or channeling self-interest. That is why Roman Catholic social thought has traditionally posited that humanity is social by nature. . . . Thus, a fundamental characteristic of Catholic social theory is its stress on the necessity for persons to express their social nature through the institutions they create to order their lives. Political and economic institutions premised on the primacy of self-interest can never embody the theological vision of a good society in the Catholic tradition.

— Michael J. Himes and Kenneth R. Himes, "The Myth of Self-Interest," *Commonweal,* 23 Sept. 1988, pp. 493, 495-96

Chapter Five

The Reformation Traditions

Background to the Reformers

As Christianity spread into northern Europe, domesticating the rather wild Germanic tribes and gradually transforming the basic patterns of life and thought, a church-dominated culture arose. Monasteries became centers of agricultural reform and economic development as well as centers of learning and piety, as we shall see in Chapter 7. The great cathedrals that tower over the towns of Europe and the spires of churches that overshadow the villages still stand as magnificent monuments to an achievement that took centuries — the Christianization of the West. Even the warring nobility saw themselves as heirs of the ancient Roman Empire, now blessed by the synthesis of Greco-Roman philosophy and biblical images and resting on a feudal economic base.

Not everyone was happy with the results. Humanists became disgusted with overbearing clergy who seemed to make all knowledge depend on views they could not believe and for which they could not supply proof. Too much rested on submission to authority, too little on argument and evidence. To clear their minds, humanists turned to the ancient classical sources afresh, or to the new secular discoveries emerging in the universities that were being formed outside the cathedrals and the monasteries. Today, we call these developments the Renaissance. It was paralleled by "the Reception" — the imposition of codes, concepts, and procedures from Roman legal traditions in North European contexts — and the reaction against it, which created clashes of rights and duties, property and claim. Opponents of these developments said that during this period the Catholic Church, which had heretofore more or less represented the common elements of the Christian faith in the West, became too much Roman and too little Catholic.

Further, the church itself fell into a degree of disunity and disarray, having several popes at one time and councils that deposed them all. In addition, some highly visible church leaders, who had taken vows of poverty, chastity, and obedience, seemed to live in relative luxury, with concubines, and with little discernable ecclesiastical discipline. Others became beggars (some out of conviction about the simple life), depending on handouts from working people, while still others became involved in the selling of "indulgences," offering certifications of forgiveness of sins upon payment of "donations" to the church. These developments took place as the entire economy shifted toward an urban, money, and trade economy (as we shall see also in Chapter 7), which put additional burdens on traditional authorities of all kinds.

These economic developments cannot fully explain the Reformation any more than they can account for the Renaissance or the Reception. Despite the importance of all of these influences, religious issues finally were the decisive ones. But these intellectual, social, and economic realities surely influenced the receptivity to the Reformers among the people, for in a church-dominated culture, religious and "secular" social factors are intentionally not kept distinct, and none of the Reformers wanted to segregate religion from daily life.

The Reformation, drawing on materials we now see as part of the Renaissance and the Reception, as well as on the Bible and the classic theological traditions, exploded in a number of directions. The Lutheran (or Evangelical) tradition is one, and the Calvinist (or Reformed) tradition is another; each took on national characteristics where it developed, as did Roman Catholicism of the subsequent "Counter-Reformation." A series of Anabaptist/Baptist (or Sectarian) traditions constitute a third stream. And all of these split, or combined, in new and fresh ways to create new movements that were subsequently to influence the religious world, such as Puritanism and Pietism, and later fundamentalism and liberalism. This chapter contains readings from representatives of the major streams of the Reformation that made distinctive historic contributions to modern economic life.

Martin Luther

As Christianity spread into northern Europe, many of the great themes from the figures in this volume — that a theological view of justice was decisive in economic life, that people in business had particular temptations and duties, that it was possible to identify just price and necessary to avoid the evil of usury, that responsibility to the neighbor, especially the poor, was a part of practical dealings, that wealth was not intrinsically evil and could serve the well-being of human persons, but that it bore distinctive enticements that could disrupt the well-being of the soul and of the society — passed into law and were enforced by officials who did not understand what was behind them. The church-dominated culture of the Middle Ages came under increased attack from without and from within.

Meanwhile, a number of religious leaders thought that far too many teachings and practices had become based on nothing but the speculations of human authorities. They wanted to return to the Bible and to the direct (without priests or philosophy) validity of the human experience of forgiveness by God's grace. As is well known, a key figure in this historic shift was Martin Luther. He, more than anyone else, inaugurated the Protestant Reformation in the early decades of the sixteenth century. He had a tremendous personal crisis as a monk about his calling and about the relationships of faith to thought and of ethics to ordinary life. His insights had a great impact on the development of modern individualism, the "work ethic," and the spiritual equality of secular callings to various forms of ministry in the church.

The significance of the Reformation for economics was great. Luther's first purpose was to reform the faith and purify the church; but he soon discovered that he could not keep the theological realm separate from the social, even if he wanted to, for every social question has roots in theological matters. Thus he addressed a wide range of issues, including business ones, with his characteristic vigor.

He preached from Scripture, letting opinions about daily experience become part of his argument. His aim was more to reach the hearts of people than to develop new insights — and that sometimes meant that he appealed to the prejudices of his small town and peasant audience. They could feel that great changes were underway, some of which they did not like, and they wanted government to stop them.

Luther's analysis of "Trade and Usury" is perhaps more dependent on Aristotle and Thomas (who adopted and amplified Aristotle's views) than he was aware, but it also contains much folk wisdom of the day — such as a nascent "labor theory of value" that later Marxist theorists thought decisive. While addressing issues of international trade, luxury items, pricing, and protectionism, he here takes up the vexing question of taking interest, one of the most fateful issues for modern economic life, for in it are contained all the questions of finance, money management, and credit, which are still under debate. Luther weaves all this together with his view of Scripture to produce a fresh spirituality, within a conservative structure, for economic life.

Trade and Usury

Martin Luther

The holy gospel, now that it has come to light, rebukes and reveals all the "works of darkness," as St. Paul calls them in Romans 13[:12]. For it is a brilliant light, which illumines the whole world and teaches how evil are the works of the world, and shows the true works we ought to do for God and our neighbor. As a result even some of the merchants have been awakened and become aware that in their trading many a wicked trick and hurtful financial practice is in use. It is to be feared that the words of Ecclesiasticus apply here, namely, that merchants can hardly be without sin [Ecclus. 26:29]. Indeed, I think St. Paul's saying in the last chapter of the first epistle to Timothy fits the case, "The love of money is the root of all evils" [1 Tim. 6:10], and again, "Those who desire to be rich fall into the devil's snare and into many useless and hurtful desires that plunge men into ruin and perdition" [I Tim. 6:9].

I suppose that my writing will be quite in vain, because the mischief has gone so far and has completely gotten the upper hand in all lands; and because those who understand the gospel are probably able in such easy, external things to judge for themselves what is fair and what is not, on the basis of their own consciences. Nevertheless, I have been asked and urged to touch upon these financial evils and expose some of them so that, even though the majority may not wish to do right, at least some people — however few they are — may be delivered from the gaping jaws of avarice. For it must be that among the merchants, as among other people, there are some who belong

From *Luther's Works*, ed. W. I. Brandt and H. T. Lehmann, vol. 45 (Philadelphia: Muhlenberg Press, 1962), pp. 245-72.

to Christ and would rather be poor with God than rich with the devil, as Psalm 37[:16] says, "It is better for the righteous to have a little than to have the great possessions of the wicked." For their sake, then, we must speak out.

It cannot be denied that buying and selling are necessary. They cannot be dispensed with, and can be practiced in a Christian manner, especially when the commodities serve a necessary and honorable purpose. For even the patriarchs bought and sold cattle, wool, grain, butter, milk, and other goods in this way. These are gifts of God, which he bestows out of the earth and distributes among mankind. But foreign trade, which brings from Calcutta and India and such places ware like costly silks, articles of gold, and spices — which minister only to ostentation but serve no useful purpose, and which drain away the money of land and people — would not be permitted if we had [proper] government and princes. But of this it is not my present purpose to write, for I expect that, like overdressing and overeating, it will have to stop itself when we have no more money. Until then, neither writing nor teaching will do any good. We must first feel the pinch of want and poverty.

God has cast us Germans off to such an extent that we have to fling our gold and silver into foreign lands and make the whole world rich, while we ourselves remain beggars. England would have less gold if Germany let her keep her cloth; the king of Portugal would have less if we let him keep his spices. Count up how much cash is taken out of Germany, without need or reason, from a single Frankfurt fair, and you will wonder how it happens that there is still a [penny] left in German lands. Frankfort is the gold and silver drain through which everything that springs and grows — or is minted or coined — here, flows out of Germany. If that hole were stopped up we should not now have to listen to the complaint that there are debts everywhere and no money, that all lands and cities are burdened with [contract] payments and milked dry by usury. But let that pass; it will go that way anyhow. We Germans must always be Germans; we never stop until we have to.

It is our purpose here to speak about the abuses and sins of trade, insofar as they concern the conscience. The matter of their detrimental effect on the purpose we leave to the princes and lords, that they may do their duty in this regard.

First. Among themselves the merchants have a common rule which is their chief maxim and the basis of all their sharp practices, where they say: "I may sell my goods as dear as I can." They think this is their right. Thus occasion is given for avarice, and every window and door to hell is opened. What else does it mean but this: I care nothing about my neighbor; so long as I have my profit and satisfy my greed, of what concern is it to me if it injures my neighbor in ten ways at once? There you see how shamelessly this maxim flies squarely in the face not only of Christian love but also of natural law. How can there be anything good then in trade? How can it be without sin when such injustice is the chief maxim and rule of the whole business? On such a basis trade can be nothing but robbing and stealing the property of others.

When once the rogue's eye and greedy belly of a merchant find that people must have his wares, or that the buyer is poor and needs them, he takes advantage of him and raises the price. He considers not the value of the goods, or what his own efforts and risk have deserved, but only the other man's want and need. He notes it not that he may relieve it but that he may use it to his own advantage by raising the price of his goods, which he would not have raised if it had been for his neighbor's need. Because of his avarice, therefore, the goods must be priced as much higher as the greater need of the other fellow will allow, so that the neighbor's need becomes as it were the measure of the goods' worth and value. Tell me, isn't that an un-Christian and inhuman thing to do? Isn't that equivalent to selling a poor man his own need in the same transaction? When he has to buy his wares at a higher price because of his need, that is the same as having to buy his own need; for what is sold to him is not simply the wares as they are, but the wares plus the fact that he must have them. Observe that this and like abominations are the inevitable consequence when the rule is that I may sell my goods as dear as I can.

The rule ought to be, not, "I may sell my wares as dear as I can or will," but, "I may sell my wares as dear as I ought, or as is right and fair." For your selling ought not to be an act that is entirely within your own power and discretion, without law or limit, as though you were a god and beholden to no one. Because your selling is an act performed toward your neighbor, it should rather be so governed by law and conscience that you do it without harm and injury to him, your concern being directed more toward doing him no injury than toward gaining profit for yourself. But where are there such merchants? How few merchants there would be, and how trade would decline, if they were to amend this evil rule and put things on a fair and Christian basis!

You ask, then, "How dear may I sell? How am I to arrive at what is fair and right so I do not take increase from neighbor or overcharge him?" Answer: That is something that will never be governed either by writing or speaking; nor has anyone ever undertaken to fix the value of every commodity, and to raise or lower prices accordingly. The reason is this: wares are not all alike; one is transported a greater distance than another and one involves greater outlay than another. In this respect, therefore, everything is and must remain uncertain, and no fixed determination can be made, anymore than one can designate a certain city as the place from which all wares are to be brought, or establish a definite cost price for them. It may happen that the same wares, brought from the same city by the same road, cost vastly more in one year than they did the year before because the weather may be worse, or the road, or because something else happens that increases the expense at one time above that at another time. Now it is fair and right that a merchant take as much profit on his wares as will reimburse him for their cost and compensate him for his trouble, his labor, and his risk. Even a farmhand must have food and pay for his labor. Who can serve or labor for nothing? The gospel says, "The laborer deserves his wages" [Luke 10:7].

But in order not to leave the question entirely unanswered, the best and safest way would be to have the temporal authorities appoint in this matter wise and honest men to compute the costs of all sorts of wares and accordingly set prices which would enable the merchant to get along and provide for him an adequate living, as is being done at certain places with respect to wine, fish, bread, and the like. But we Germans have too many other things to do; we are too busy drinking and dancing to provide for rules and regulations of this sort. Since this kind of ordinance therefore is not to be expected, the next best thing is to let goods be valued at the price for which they are bought and

let market dictate price

sold in the common market, or in the land generally. In this matter we can accept the proverb, "Follow the crowd and you won't get lost." Any profit made in this way I consider honest and proper, because here there is always the risk involved of having to suffer loss in wares and outlay, and excessive profits are scarcely possible.

Where the price of goods is not fixed either by law or custom, and you must fix it yourself, here one can truly give you no instructions but only lay it on your conscience to be careful not to overcharge your neighbor, and to seek a modest living, not the goals of greed. Some have wished to place a ceiling on profits, with a limit of one-half on all wares; some say one-third; others something else. None of these measures is certain and safe unless it be so decreed by the temporal authorities and common law. What they determine in these matters would be safe. Therefore, you must make up your mind to seek in your trading only an adequate living. Accordingly, you should compute and count your costs, trouble, labor, and risk, and on that basis raise or lower the prices of your wares so that you set them where you will be repaid for your trouble and labor. . . .

In determining how much profit you ought to take on your business and your labor, there is no better way to reckon it than by computing the amount of time and labor you have put into it, and comparing that with the effort of a day laborer who works at some other occupation and seeing how much he earns in a day. On that basis figure how many days you have spent in getting your wares and bringing them to your place of business, and how much labor and risk was involved; for a great amount of labor and time ought to have a correspondingly greater return. That is the most accurate, the best, and the most definite advice and direction that can be given in this matter. Let him who dislikes it, better it himself. I base my case (as I have said) on the gospel that the laborer deserves his wages [Luke 10:7]; and Paul also says in 1 Corinthians 9[:7], "He who tends the flock should get some of the milk. Who can go to war at his own expense?" If you have a better ground than that, you are welcome to it. . . .

Now, there are four Christian ways of exchanging goods . . . The first way is to let them rob or steal our property, as Christ says in Matthew 5, "If anyone takes away your cloak, let him have your

coat as well, and do not ask it of him again." This way of dealing counts for nothing among the merchants; besides, it has not been held or preached as common teaching for all Christians, but merely as a counsel or a good idea for the clergy and the perfect, though they observe it even less than do the merchants. But true Christians observe it, for they know that their Father in heaven has assuredly promised in Matthew 6[:11] to give them this day their daily bread. If men were to act accordingly, not only would countless abuses in all kinds of business be avoided, but a great many people would not become merchants, because reason and human nature flee and shun to the uttermost risks and damages of this sort.

The second way is to give freely to anyone who needs it, as Christ also teaches in the same passage [Matt. 5:42; Luke 6:30]. This too is a lofty Christian work, which is why it counts for little among the people. There would be fewer merchants and less trade if this were put into practice. For he who does this must truly hold fast to heaven and look always to the hands of God, and not to his own resources or wealth, knowing that God will support him even though every cupboard were bare, because he knows to be true what God said to Joshua, "I will not forsake you or withdraw my hand from you" [Josh. 1:5]; as the proverb has it, "God still has more than what he ever gave away." But that takes a true Christian, and he is a rare animal on earth, to whom the world and nature pay no heed.

The third way is lending. That is, I give away my property, and take it back again if it is returned to me; but I must do without it if it is not returned. Christ himself defines this kind of transaction in what he says in Luke 6[:35], "Lend, expecting nothing in return." That is, you should lend freely, and take your chances on getting it back or not. If it comes back, take it; if it does not, it is a gift. According to the gospel there is thus only one distinction between giving and lending, namely, a gift is not taken back, while a loan is taken back — if it is returned — but involves the risk that it may become a gift. He who lends expecting to get back something more or something better than he has loaned is nothing but an open and condemned usurer, since even those who in lending demand or expect to get back exactly what they lend, and take no chances on whether they get it back or not, are not acting in a Christian way. This third way too (in my opinion) is a lofty Christian work; and a rare one, judging by the way things are going in the world. If it were to be practiced generally, trade of all sorts would greatly diminish and virtually cease.

These three ways of exchanging goods, then, observe in masterful fashion [the biblical] matter of not presuming upon the future, and not trusting in any man or in oneself but clinging to God alone. Here all transactions are in cash, and are accompanied by the word which James teaches, "If God wills, so be it" [Jas. 4:15]. For here we deal with people as with those who are unreliable and might fail; we give our money freely, or take our chances on losing what we lend.

Now someone will say, "Who can then be saved? And where shall we find these Christians? Why, in this way there would be no trade left in the world; everyone would have his property taken or borrowed away, and the door would be thrown open for the wicked and idle gluttons — of whom the world is full — to take everything with their lying and cheating." Answer: I have already said that Christians are rare people on earth. This is why the world needs a strict, harsh temporal government which will compel and constrain the wicked to refrain from theft and robbery, and to return what they borrow (although a Christian ought neither to demand nor expect it). This is necessary in order that the world may not become a desert, peace vanish, and men's trade and society be utterly destroyed; all of which would happen if we were to rule the world according to the gospel, rather than driving and compelling the wicked by laws and the use of force to do and to allow what is right. For this reason we must keep the roads safe, preserve peace in the towns, enforce law in the land, and let the sword hew briskly and boldly against transgressors, as St. Paul teaches in Romans 13[:4]. For it is God's will that people who are not Christians be held in check and kept from doing wrong, at least from doing it with impunity. Let no one think that the world can be ruled without bloodshed; the temporal sword must and shall be red and bloody, for the world will and must be evil, and the sword is God's rod and vengeance upon it. But of this I have said enough in my little book on *Temporal Authority*.

Borrowing would be a fine thing if it were practiced between Christians, for every borrower

O LORD, who shall sojourn in thy tent?
   Who shall dwell on thy holy hill?
He who walks blamelessly, and does
     what is right,
   and speaks truth from his heart; . . .
who does not put out his money at interest,
   and does not take a bribe against
     the innocent.
He who does these things shall never
     be moved.

           — Psalm 15:1-2, 5 (RSV)

There are two sorts of wealth-getting. . . . [O]ne is a part of the management of a household (through agriculture), the other is retail trade: the former is necessary and honorable, while that which consists in exchange is justly censured; for it is unnatural, and a mode by which men gain from one another. The most hated sort . . . is usury, which makes a gain out of money itself. . . . Money was intended to be used in exchange, but not to increase at interest.

           — Aristotle, "On Wealth-Getting,"
from *On Politics* I.10.1258ab, ed. Ernest Barker
(New York: Oxford University Press, 1946)

would then willingly return what had been lent him, and the lender would willingly forego repayment if the borrower were unable to pay. Christians are brothers, and one does not forsake another; neither is any of them so lazy and shameless that he would not work but depend simply on another's wealth and labor, or consume in idleness another's goods. But where men are not Christians, the temporal authorities ought to compel them to repay what they have borrowed. If the temporal authorities are negligent and do not compel repayment, the Christian ought to tolerate the robbery, as Paul says in 1 Corinthians 6[:7], "Why not rather suffer wrong?" But you may exhort, insist, and do what you will to the man who is not a Christian; he pays no attention because he is not a Christian and has no regard for Christ's doctrine.

You still have a grain of comfort too in the fact that you are not obligated to make a loan except out of your surplus and what you can spare from your own needs, as Christ says of alms, "What you have left over, that give in alms, and everything is clean for you." Now if someone wishes to borrow from you an amount so large that you would be ruined if it were not repaid, and you could not spare it from your own needs, then you are not bound to make the loan. Your first and greatest obligation is to provide for the needs of your wife and children and servants; you must not divert from them what you owe them. The best rule to follow is this: If the amount asked as a loan is too great, just go ahead and give something outright, or else lend as much as you would be willing to give, and take the risk of having to lose it. John the Baptist did not say, "He who has one coat, let him give it away"; but, "He who has two coats, let him give one to him who has none; and he who has good, let him do likewise" [Luke 3:11].

The fourth way of exchanging goods is through buying and selling, but for hard cash or payment in kind. He who would use this method must make up his mind to rely not on something in the future but on God alone; also, that he will have to be dealing with men, men who will certainly fail and lie. Therefore, the best advice is this: whoever sells should not give credit or accept any security, but sell only for cash. If he wishes to lend, let him lend to Christians, or else take the risk of loss, and lend no more than he would be willing to give outright or can spare from his own needs. If the temporal government and regulations will not help him to recover his loan, let him lose it. Let him beware of becoming surety for anyone; let him much rather give what he can. Such a man would be a true Christian merchant; God would not forsake him, because he trusts properly in Him and cheerfully takes a chance in dealing with his untrustworthy neighbors. . . .

On the trading companies I ought to say a good deal, but the whole subject is such a bottomless pit of avarice and wrongdoing that there is nothing in it that can be discussed with a good conscience. Who is so stupid that he cannot see that the trading companies are nothing but pure monopolies? Even the temporal laws of the heathen forbid them as openly harmful to the whole world, to say nothing of divine right and Christian law.

They control all commodities, deal in them as they please, and practice without concealment all the tricks that have been mentioned. They raise or lower prices at their pleasure. They oppress and ruin all the small businessmen, like the pike eat the little fish in the water, just as if they were lords over God's creatures and immune from all the laws of faith and love.

So it happens that all over the world spices must be bought at whatever price they choose to set, and they vary it from time to time. This year they raise the price of ginger, next year that of saffron, or vice versa; so that in the end it all comes out the same: they do not have to suffer any loss, injury, or risk. If the ginger spoils or they have to take a loss on it, they make it up on saffron, and vice versa, so that they make sure of their profit. All this is contrary to nature, not only of merchandise, but of all temporal goods, which God wills should be subject to risk and uncertainty. But they have found a way to make safe, certain, and continual profit out of unsafe, uncertain, and perishable goods; though because of it all the world must be sucked dry and all the money sink and swim in their gullets.

How could it ever be right and according to God's will that a man in such a short time should grow so rich that he could buy out kings and emperors? They have brought things to such a pass that everybody else has to do business at the risk of loss, winning this year and losing next year, while they themselves can always win, making up their losses by increased profits. It is no wonder that they quickly appropriate the wealth of the whole world, for a pfennig that is permanent and sure is better than a gulden that is temporary and uncertain. But these companies are always dealing with permanent and sure gulden for our temporary and uncertain pfennigs. Is it any wonder that they become kings and we beggars?

Kings and princes ought to look into this matter and forbid them by strict laws. But I hear that they have a finger in it themselves, and the saying of Isaiah [1:23] is fulfilled, "Your princes have become companions of thieves." They hang thieves who have stolen a gulden or half a gulden, but do business with those who rob the whole world and steal more than all the rest, so that the proverb remains true, "Big thieves hang little thieves." As the Roman senator Cato said, "Simple thieves lie in dungeons and stocks; public thieves walk abroad in gold and silk." What will God say to this at last? He will do as he says through Ezekiel: princes and merchants, one thief with the other, he will melt together like lead and bronze [Ezek. 22:20] as when a city burns to the ground, so that there shall be neither princes nor merchants any more. That time, I fear, is already at the door. We do not think of amending our lives, no matter how great our sin and wrong. So, too, He cannot leave wrong unpunished.

This is why no one need ask how he may with a good conscience be a member of a trading company. My only advice is this: Get out; they will not change. If the trading companies are to stay, right and honesty must perish; if right and honesty are to stay, the trading companies must perish. The bed is too narrow, says Isaiah, one must fall out, the covering is too small, it will not cover both [Isa. 28:20].

Now I know full well that this book of mine will be taken amiss; perhaps they will toss it all to the winds and remain as they are. But it will not be my fault, for I have done my part to show how richly we have deserved it if God should come with his rod. If I have instructed a single soul and rescued it from the jaws of avarice, I have not labored in vain. . . .

Blasts trading companies!

179

John Calvin

When he was converted to Protestantism by reading Luther, whose works poured from the Gutenberg Press, no one would have predicted that this young French lawyer would become the single most powerful influence in the formation of modern business. Of course, any who believe that the root and chief characteristic of modern capitalism is greedy, self-interested, and profit-driven individualism resist the notion that religion generally or Calvin specifically had anything to do with it. Certainly Calvin focused on biblical, theological, and pastoral matters, and had nothing but contempt for such attitudes and behaviors. But if modern economic systems are not solely based on these characteristics, then religion, and specifically Calvin, might well have influenced it.

Calvin offered one thing above all to the rising cities: a vision of the holiness and power of God. The only God worth worshiping is just and righteous, pure and good, merciful and gracious. Whoever catches a glimpse of that perfection becomes immediately aware of how unjust, unrighteous, pretentious, and even downright wicked most of the things we humans think and do are by comparison. In comparison to the laws of God, the purposes of God, and the love of God, human practices and desires seem vacuous, if not vicious.

God's holiness is matched by God's power. That power not only involves the authority to forgive sins through Jesus Christ, but it empowers souls toward moral righteousness and engenders a vision of a rightly ordered commonwealth. Those called by God assume duty in the face of adversity, deny the desires of the heart if they lead away from that duty, and become disciplined servants of God's will. The justice of God becomes the fulcrum and the power of God becomes the lever whereby souls and civilizations are moved, for nothing in them is so holy that it does not need redemption or so powerful that it can resist.

Such convictions — inconceivable without the biblical record, Augustine, Thomas, Luther, and a series of social changes already at work — stimulated the transition from the classical traditions to modernity. In some ways, the impetus for this transformation is comparable only to the revolutions brought by the ancient Hebrew prophets, the rise of Islam in Arabia, the establishment of the Confucian ethic in China, or the earlier Christianization of the Mediterranean world by the church fathers, although each of these had its own distinctive direction. In any case, when Calvin's main point is grasped, everything changes and is subject to further change. All issues of economics, business, law, work patterns, technology, corporate formation, finance, and trade — and even Luther's views on these issues — are subject to reformation, to deconstruction and reconstruction.

For those who do not grasp, or accept, Calvin's main point, of course, all of this looks like fanaticism and a rather sour view of human potential. But whether one accepts it or not, it must be admitted that Calvinism consolidated a second great integration of biblical, traditional, intellectual, and social resources, one comparable only to those of St. Augustine and St. Thomas, and one that had enormous consequences for subsequent economic life.

The Moral Law and the Christian Life

John Calvin

The Functions of the Moral Law

Let us take a succinct view of the office and use of the Moral Law. Now, this office and use seems to me to consist of three parts. First, by exhibiting the righteousness of God, — in other words, the righteousness which alone is acceptable to God, — it admonishes every one of his own unrighteousness, certiorates, convicts, and finally condemns him. This is necessary, in order that man who is blind and intoxicated with self-love, may be brought at once to know and to confess his weakness and impurity. He who is schooled by the law, lays aside the arrogance which formerly blinded him. In like manner he must be cured of pride, the other disease under which we have said that he labors. So long as he is permitted to appeal to his own judgment, he substitutes a hypocritical for a real righteousness. But after he is forced to weigh his conduct in the balance of the Law, renouncing all dependence on this fancied righteousness, he sees that he is at an infinite distance from holiness, and, on the other hand, that he teems with innumerable vices of which he formerly seemed free. As in a mirror we discover any stains upon our face, so in the Law we behold, first, our impotence; then, in consequence of it, our iniquity; and, finally, the curse, as the consequence of both. But while the unrighteousness and condemnation of all are attested by the law it does not follow (if we make the proper use of it)

that we are immediately to give up all hope and rush headlong on despair. The Apostle testifies that the law pronounces its sentence of condemnation in order "that every mouth may be stopped, and all the world become guilty before God." In another place, however, the same Apostle declares that "God hath concluded them all in unbelief"; not that he might destroy all, or allow all to perish, but that "he might have mercy upon all"; in other words that divesting themselves of an absurd opinion of their own virtue they may perceive how they are wholly dependent on the hand of God; that feeling how naked and destitute they are, they may take refuge in his mercy, rely upon it, and cover themselves up entirely with it: renouncing all righteousness and merit, and clinging to mercy alone, as offered in Christ, to all who long and look for it in true faith.

The second office of the Law is, by means of its fearful denunciations and the consequent dread of punishment, to curb those who, unless forced, have no regard for rectitude and justice. Such persons are curbed, not because their mind is inwardly moved or affected, but because, as if a bridle were laid upon them, they refrain their hands from external acts, and internally check the depravity which would otherwise petulantly burst forth. It is true, they are not on this account either better or more righteous in the sight of God. Nevertheless, this forced and extorted righteousness is necessary for the good of society, its peace being secured by a provision but for which all things would be thrown into tumult and confusion. Nay, this tuition is not without its use, even to the children of God, who, previous to their effectual calling, being destitute of the Spirit of holiness, freely indulge the lusts of the flesh. For where the Spirit of God rules not, the lusts sometimes so burst forth, as to threaten to drown the soul subjected to them in forgetfulness and contempt of God; and so they would, did not God interpose with this remedy. All who have remained for some time in ignorance of God will confess, as a result of their own experience, that the law had the effect of keeping them in some degree in the fear and reverence of God, till, being regenerated by his Spirit, they began to love him from the heart.

The third use of the Law (being also the principal use and more closely connected with its proper

---

From *The Institutes of the Christian Religion*, trans. Henry Beveridge (London: James Clarke & Co., 1957), II.7; III.6-10, 14.

end) has respect to believers in whose hearts the Spirit of God already flourishes and reigns. For although the Law is written and engraven on their hearts by the finger of God, that is, although they are so influenced and actuated by the Spirit that they desire to obey God, there are two ways in which they still profit in the Law. For it is the best instrument for enabling them daily to learn with greater truth and certainty what that will of the Lord is which they aspire to follow, and to confirm them in this knowledge. Then, because we need not doctrine merely, but exhortation also, the servant of God will derive this further advantage from the Law: by frequently meditating upon it, he will be excited to obedience, and confirmed in it, and so drawn away from the slippery paths of sin.

The Life of a Christian

My intention in the plan of life, which I now propose to give, is not to extend it so far as to treat of each virtue specially, and expatiate in exhortation. It will be sufficient to point out the method by which a pious man may be taught how to frame his life aright, and briefly lay down some universal rule by which he may not improperly regulate his conduct. As philosophers have certain definitions of rectitude and honesty, from which they derive particular duties and the whole train of virtues; so in this respect Scripture is not without order, but presents a most beautiful arrangement, one too which is in every way much more certain than that of philosophers. The Scripture system of which we speak aims chiefly at two objects. The former is, that the love of righteousness to which we are by no means naturally inclined, may be instilled and implanted into our minds. The latter is, to prescribe a rule which will prevent us while in the pursuit of righteousness from going astray.

With what better foundation can it begin than by reminding us that we must be holy, because "God is holy"? When mention is made of our union with God, let us remember that holiness must be the bond; not that by the merit of holiness we come into communion with him (we ought rather first to cleave to him, in order that, pervaded with his holiness, we may follow whither he calls), but because it greatly concerns his glory not

to have any fellowship with wickedness and impurity. If the Lord adopts us for his sons on the condition that our life be a representation of Christ, the bond of our adoption, — then, unless we dedicate and devote ourselves to righteousness, we not only, with the utmost perfidy, revolt from our Creator, but also abjure the Savior himself. Ever since God exhibited himself to us as a Father, we must be convicted of extreme ingratitude if we do not in turn exhibit ourselves as his sons. Ever since Christ purified us by the laver of his blood, and communicated this purification by baptism, it would ill become us to be defiled with new pollution. Ever since he ingrafted us into his body, we, who are his members, should anxiously beware of contracting any stain or taint. Ever since he who is our head ascended to heaven, it is befitting in us to withdraw our affections from the earth, and with our whole soul aspire to heaven. Ever since the Holy Spirit dedicated us as temples to the Lord we should make it our endeavor to show forth the glory of God, and guard against being profaned by the defilement of sin. Ever since our soul and body were destined to heavenly incorruptibility and an unfading crown, we should earnestly strive to keep them pure against the day of the Lord. These, I say, are the surest foundations of a well-regulated life. Doctrine is not an affair of the tongue, but of the life, is not apprehended by the intellect and memory merely, like other branches of learning; but is received only when it possesses the whole soul, and finds its seat and habitation in the inmost recesses of the heart. To doctrine in which our religion is contained we have given the first place, since by it our salvation commences; but it must be transfused into the breast, and pass into the conduct, and so transform us into itself, as not to prove itself unfruitful. Of Self-denial. Although the Law of God contains a perfect rule of conduct admirably arranged, it has seemed proper to our divine Master to train his people by a more accurate method, to the rule which is enjoined in the Law; and the leading principle in the method is, that it is the duty of believers to present their "bodies a living sacrifice, holy and acceptable unto God, which is their reasonable service." The great point is, that we are consecrated and dedicated to God, and, therefore, should not henceforth think, speak, design, or act, without a view to his glory. If we are not our own, but the Lord's, it is plain both what error is to be shunned, and to what end the actions of our lives ought to be directed. We are not our own; therefore, neither is our own reason or will to rule our acts and counsels. We are not our own; therefore, let us not make it our end to seek what may be agreeable to our carnal nature. We are not our own; therefore, as far as possible, let us forget ourselves and the things that are ours. On the other hand, we are God's; let his wisdom and will preside over all our actions. We are God's; to him, then, as the only legitimate end, let every part of our life be directed. Let this, then, be the first step, to abandon ourselves, and devote the whole energy of our minds to the service of God.

When the Scripture enjoins us to lay aside private regard to ourselves, it not only divests our minds of an excessive longing for wealth, or power, or human favor, but eradicates all ambition and thirst for worldly glory, and other more secret pests. He who has learned to look to God in everything he does, is at the same time diverted from all vain thoughts. This is that self-denial which Christ so strongly enforces on his disciples from the very outset. Self-denial has respect partly to men and partly (more especially) to God. For when Scripture enjoins us, in regard to our fellow men, to prefer them in honor to ourselves, and sincerely labor to promote their advantage he gives us commands which our mind is utterly incapable of obeying until its natural feelings are suppressed. For so blindly do we all rush in the direction of self-love, that every one thinks he has a good reason for exalting himself and despising all others in comparison. If God has bestowed on us something not to be repented of, trusting to it, we immediately become elated, and not only swell, but almost burst with pride. The vices with which we abound we both carefully conceal from others, and flatteringly represent to ourselves as minute and trivial, nay, sometimes hung them as virtues. When the same qualities which we admire in ourselves are seen in others, even though they should be superior, we, in order that we may not be forced to yield to them, maliciously lower and carp at them; in like manner, in the case of vices, not contented with severe and keen animadversion, we studiously exaggerate them. Hence the insolence with which each, as if exempted from the common lot, seeks to exalt himself above his neighbor, confidently and proudly despising others, or at least looking down upon them as his inferiors. For this there is no other remedy than to pluck up by the roots those most noxious pests, self-love and love of victory. This the doctrine of Scripture does. For it teaches us to remember, that the endowments which God has bestowed upon us are not our own, but his free gifts, and that those who plume themselves upon them betray their ingratitude. Then by a diligent examination of our faults let us keep ourselves humble. Thus while nothing will remain to swell our pride, there will be much to subdue it. Again, we are enjoined, whenever we behold the gifts of God in others, so to reverence and respect the gifts, as also to honor those in whom they reside. God having been pleased to bestow honor upon them, it would ill become us to deprive them of it.

How difficult it is to perform the duty of seeking the good of our neighbor! Unless you leave off all thought of yourself, and in a manner cease to be yourself, you will never accomplish it. How can you exhibit those works of charity which Paul describes unless you renounce yourself, and become wholly devoted to others? Scripture, to conduct us to this, reminds us that whatever we obtain from the Lord is granted on the condition of our employing it for the common good of the Church, and that, therefore, the legitimate use of all our gifts is a kind and liberal communication of them with others. Whatever the pious man can do, he is bound to do for his brethren, not consulting his own interest in any other way than by striving earnestly for the common edification of the Church. Let this, then, be our method of showing good will and kindness, considering that, in regard to everything that God has bestowed upon us, and by which we can aid our neighbor, we are his stewards, and are bound to give an account of our stewardship: moreover, that the only right mode of administration is that which is regulated by love. In this way, we shall not only unite the study of our neighbor's advantage with a regard to our own, but make the latter subordinate to the former.

The Lord enjoins us to do good to all without exception, though the greater part, if estimated by their own merit, are most unworthy of it. But Scripture subjoins a most excellent reason, when it tells us that we are not to look to what men in themselves deserve, but to attend to the image of God, which exists in all, and to which we owe all honor and love. Whoever be the man that is presented to you as needing your assistance, you have no ground for declining to give it to him. Say he is a stranger. The Lord has given him a mark which ought to be familiar to you. Say he is mean and of no consideration. The Lord points him out as one whom he has distinguished by the lustre of his own image. If he not only merits no good, but has provoked you by ignorance and mischief, still this is no good reason why you should not embrace him in love, and visit him with offices of love. He has deserved very differently from me, you will say. But what has the Lord deserved? In this way only we attain to what is not to say difficult, but altogether against nature, to love those that hate us, render good for evil, and blessing for cursing, remembering that we are not to reflect on the wickedness of men, but look to the image of God in them.

Of Bearing the Cross: One Branch of Self-denial. The pious mind must ascend still higher, namely whether Christ calls his disciples, when he says, that every one of them must "take up his cross." Those whom the Lord has chosen and honored with his intercourse must prepare for a hard, laborious, troubled life, a life full of many and various kinds of evils; it being the will of our heavenly Father to exercise his people in this way while putting them to the proof. Having begun this course with Christ the first-born, he continues it towards all his children. For though that Son was dear to him above all others, yet we see that far from being treated gently or indulgently, we may say, that not only was he subjected to a perpetual cross while he dwelt on earth, but his whole life was nothing else than a kind of perpetual cross. Hence it affords us great consolation in hard and difficult circumstances, which men deem evil and adverse, to think that we are holding fellowship with the sufferings of Christ; that as he passed to celestial glory through a labyrinth of many woes, so we too are conducted thither through various tribulations.

We may add, that the only thing which made it necessary for our Lord to undertake to bear the cross, was to testify and prove his obedience to the Father; whereas there are many reasons which make it necessary for us to live constantly under the cross. Feeble as we are by nature, and prone to ascribe all perfection to our flesh, unless we receive as it were ocular demonstration of our weakness, we readily estimate our virtue above its proper worth, and doubt not that whatever happens, it will stand unimpaired and invincible against all difficulties. Hence we indulge in stupid and empty confidence in the flesh, and then trusting to it wax proud against the Lord himself; as if our own faculties were sufficient without his grace. Therefore he visits us with disgrace, or poverty, or bereavement, or disease, or other afflictions. Feeling altogether unable to support them, we forthwith, in so far as regards ourselves, give way, and thus humbled learn to invoke his strength, which alone can enable us to bear up under a weight of afflictions. Another end which the Lord has in afflicting his people is to try their patience, and train them in obedience.

There is singular consolation when we are persecuted for righteousness' sake. For our thought should then be, How high the honor which God bestows upon us in distinguishing us by the special badge of his soldiers. By suffering persecution for righteousness' sake, I mean not only striving for the defense of the Gospel, but for the defense of righteousness in any way. Whether, therefore, in maintaining the truth of God against the lies of Satan, or defending the good and innocent against the injuries of the bad, we are obliged to incur the offense and hatred of the world, so as to endanger life, fortune, or honor, let us not grieve or decline so far to spend ourselves for God; let us not think ourselves wretched in those things in which he with his own lips has pronounced us blessed.

Of Meditating on the Future Life. Whatever be the kind of tribulation with which we are afflicted, we should always consider the end of it to be, that we may be trained to despise the present, and thereby stimulated to aspire to the future life. We duly profit by the discipline of the cross, when we learn that this life, estimated in itself, is restless, troubled, in numberless ways wretched, and plainly in no respect happy; that what are estimated its blessings are uncertain, fleeting, vain, and vitiated by a great admixture of evil. From this we conclude, that all that we have to seek or hope for here is contest; that when we think of the crown we must raise our eyes to heaven. For we must hold, that our mind never rises seriously to desire and aspire after the future, until it has learned to despise the present life. Still the contempt which believers should train themselves to feel for the present life, must not be of a kind to beget hatred of it or ingratitude to God. This life, though abounding in all kinds of wretchedness, is justly classed among divine blessings which are not to be despised. Before openly exhibiting the inheritance of eternal glory, God is pleased to manifest himself to us as a Father by minor proofs, viz., the blessings which he daily bestows upon us. Therefore, while this life serves to acquaint us with the goodness of God, shall we disdain it as if it did not contain one particle of good? And there is a much higher reason when we reflect that here we are in a manner prepared for the glory of the heavenly kingdom. For the Lord hath ordained, that those who are ultimately to be crowned in heaven must maintain a previous warfare on the earth, that they may not triumph before they have overcome the difficulties of war, and obtained the victory. Another reason is that we here begin to experience in various ways a foretaste of the divine benignity, in order that our hope and desire may be whetted for its full manifestation.

When the earthly is compared with the heavenly life, it may undoubtedly be despised and trampled under foot. We ought never, indeed, to regard it with hatred, except in so far as it keeps us subject to sin; and even this hatred ought not to be directed against life itself. At all events, we must stand so affected toward it in weariness or hatred as, while longing for its termination, to be ready at the Lord's will to continue in it, keeping far from everything like murmuring or impatience. For it is as if the Lord had assigned us a post, which we must maintain till he recalls us.

How to Use the Present Life. If we are to live, we must use the necessary supports of life; nor can we even shun those things which seem more subservient to delight than to necessity. We must therefore observe a mean, that we may use them with a pure conscience, whether for necessity or for pleasure. Let this be our principle, that we err not in the use of the gifts of Providence when we refer them to the end for which their author made and destined them, since he created them for our good and not for our destruction. Now then, if we consider for what end he created food, we shall find that he consulted not only for our necessity,

but also for our enjoyment and delight. The natural qualities of things themselves demonstrate to what end, how far, they may be lawfully enjoyed. Has the Lord adorned flowers with all the beauty which spontaneously presents itself to the eye, and the sweet odor which delights the sense of smell, and shall it be unlawful for us to enjoy that beauty and this odor? Has he not given many things a value without having any necessary use? Have done, then, with that inhuman philosophy which, in allowing no use of the creatures but for necessity, not only maliciously deprives us of the lawful fruit of the divine beneficence, but cannot be realized without depriving man of all his sense, and reducing him to a block. But, on the other hand, let us with no less care guard against the lusts of the flesh, which, if not kept in order, break through all bounds. There is no surer or quicker way of accomplishing this than by despising the present life and aspiring to celestial immortality. He who makes it his rule to use this world as if he used it not, not only cuts off all gluttony in regard to meat and drink, and all effeminacy, ambition, pride and excessive show, and austerity, in regard to his table, his house, and his clothes, but removes every care and affection which might withdraw or hinder him from aspiring to the heavenly life, and cultivating the interest of his soul. Therefore, while the liberty of the Christian in external matters is not to be tied down to a strict rule, it is, however, subject to this law — he must indulge as little as possible; on the other hand, it must be his constant aim not only to curb luxury, but to cut off all show of superfluous abundance, and carefully beware of converting a help into a hindrance.

The last thing to be observed is, that the Lord enjoins every one of us, in all the actions of life, to have respect to our own calling. He knows the boiling restlessness of the human mind, the fickleness with which it is borne hither and thither, its eagerness to hold opposites at one in its grasp, its ambition. Therefore, lest all things should be thrown into confusion by our folly and rashness, he has assigned distinct duties to each in the different modes of life. And that no one may presume to overstep his proper limits, he has distinguished the different modes of life by the name of callings. Every man's mode of life, therefore, is a kind of station assigned him by the Lord, that he may not be always driven about at random. He only who directs his life to this end will have it properly framed; because free from the impulse of rashness, he will not attempt more than his calling justifies, knowing that it is unlawful to overleap the prescribed bounds. He who is obscure will not decline to cultivate a private life, that he may not desert the post at which God has placed him. The magistrate will more willingly perform his office, and

the father of a family confine himself to his proper sphere. Every one in his particular mode of life will, without repining, suffer its inconveniences, cares, uneasiness, and anxiety; persuaded that God has laid on the burden. This, too, will afford admirable consolation, that in following your proper calling, no work will be so mean and sordid as not to have a splendor and value in the eye of God.

Only Gain-Seekers?

The liberal and conservative economic schools are close enough to each other that each side recognizes the other as legitimate. Both groups assume that all people are motivated by the self-interested maximization of gain, and both assume that competition will steer self-interested behavior in the direction of the social good defined in terms of individual preferences. But where conservatives claim that minimal government is prerequisite to the achievement of that goal, the liberals would insist that extensive government intervention in the economy is necessary to the public good. . . .

The methodological objection many Christians make to both of these world views is that prediction and simplicity are made much too important in assessing these theories. Assuming that people always act in their own self-interest will give one good predictions most of the time. But is that all there is to a good theory? Can we say that these cardboard cut-out gain-seeking individuals reflect the image of God? To have a theory that believing Christians can accept in good conscience, we need an account of human motivation that is complex and rich enough to recognize human beings as moral agents with complicated motives for their actions. . . .

We all have our own vision of a good society, of what constitutes the public interest. Those visions may be self-centered, but more likely, if

we are serious about being Christian, they are based on religious or secular ethical norms. People act on the basis of their visions. The choices of a vocation, a home, and social and political affiliations are based on a person's conception of the public good. That conception also guides a person's daily policies and activities, including the decisions made by business managers and political officials. To understand how a particular society functions and how particular decisions are made, we must understand the commitments and visions of the people involved. .

This is an untidy vision. It does not always offer clear predictions, and it requires a lot of work in discovering people's motivations. It does not offer an unambiguous definition of the public interest, and it does not point to a single set of social arrangements that guarantee the achievement of the public good. But it does set an important task for the Christian community. . . . We can help people define for themselves a vision of a good society that conforms to biblical Christian principles. We can tell leaders in both business and government that their values matter and urge them to act out their Christian commitment in their professional lives. A Christian economic story can help us to make a little more real the old Reformed concept of the transformation of society to conform to the will of God.

— John Tiemstra, "Stories Economists Tell," *Reformed Journal* 38 (Feb. 1988): 15-16

Radical Reformers: Stadler and Winstanley

The traditions of the early church, represented in this volume by Clement and Cyprian, evolved into Eastern Orthodoxy. Roman Catholicism developed its basic directions by the Christian appropriation of classical philosophy and can be traced through Augustine and Thomas to modern Catholic debates (see Chapter 9); while Protestantism sparked many reforms under the influence of Luther and Calvin.

But another stream can also be found in Christian thought. It is comparable in some ways to the impulse to form a "pure" community found in Orthodox and Catholic monasticism. In Protestantism, a similar (but noncelibate) tendency appears in a different form. This is called the "Radical Reformation" or the "Anabaptist Movement" (because some believed that no one should be brought into the faith by baptism until they had attained the age of reason, as adults). It is from this tradition that many of the independent churches and sects of Christianity came — Baptists, Mennonites, Brethren, Amish, Quakers, etc. Many later flourished in America after religious freedom was established. Still others — Pentecostal, fundamentalist, and ethnic churches, etc. — have appeared only in the last century with similar impulses.

·These groups were often found among the less educated and less powerful parts of the population, and they were seldom treated well by the Orthodox, Catholics, Lutherans, or Calvinists — most of whom had close ties to political, military, economic, social, and technological leaders in society and saw such sectors of society as areas of Christian responsibility. But the "simple believers" saw in the Bible another, spiritual model of life, one that demanded opposition to the given patterns of the world. As the prophets opposed the kings and the privileged, and as Christ opposed the priests and Caesar, they wanted to establish a pure church in which only those who lived simple, saintly lives would have authority. Indeed, some wanted the saints to set the model for a new society, or even to seize power in the world to establish a holy commonwealth. Although they were very different, both Thomas Münzer and Oliver Cromwell were such "militant purifiers."

Ulrich Stadler from Moravia in the sixteenth century and Gerrard Winstanley from Britain in the seventeenth offer representative views from this stream on economic thought. One is more mystical, the other more rationalist; one calls for a communitarian enclave, the other for a public witness to change society; one advises patient suffering, the other prepares for conflict. Both have a vision of community that demands an alternative economic life. They deny private property and claim (as does a liberation slogan in the twentieth century) that "God has a preferential option for the poor." It is from these roots that many features of Christian Socialism and religious communitarian politics derive.

The True Community of the Saints

Ulrich Stadler

There is one communion of all the faithful in Christ and one community of the holy children called of God. They have one Father in heaven, one Lord Christ; all are baptized and sealed in their hearts with one Spirit. They have one mind, opinion, heart, and soul as having all drunk from the same Fountain, and alike await one and the same struggle, cross, trial, and, at length, one and the same hope in glory. But it, that is, such a community, must move about in this world, poor, miserable, small, and rejected of the world, of whom, however, the world is not worthy. Whoever strives for the lofty things [of this world] does not belong. Thus in this community everything must proceed equally, all things be one and communal, alike in the bodily gifts of their Father in heaven, which he daily gives to be used by his own according to his will. For how does it make sense that all who have here in this pilgrimage to look forward to an inheritance in the Kingdom of their Father should not be satisfied with their bodily goods and gifts? Judge, O ye saints of God, ye who are thus truly grafted into Christ, with him deadened to the world, to sin, and to yourselves, that you never hereafter live for the world or yourselves but rather for him who died for you and arose, namely, Christ. [They] have also yielded themselves and presented themselves to him intimately, patiently, of their own free will, naked and uncovered, to suffer and endure his will and, moreover, to fulfill

it and thereafter also to devote themselves in obedience and service to all the children of God. Therefore, they also live with one another where the Lord assigns a place to them, peaceably, united, lovingly, amicably, and fraternally, as children of one Father. In their pilgrimage they should be satisfied with the bodily goods and gifts of their Father, since they should also be altogether as one body and members one toward another.

Now if, then, each member withholds assistance from the other, the whole thing must go to pieces. The eyes won't see, the hands won't take hold. Where, however, each member extends assistance equally to the whole body, it is built up and grows and there is peace and unity, yea, each member takes care for the other. In brief, equal care, sadness and joy, and peace [are] at hand. It is just the same in the spiritual body of Christ. If the deacon of the community will never serve, the teacher will not teach, the young brother will not be obedient, the strong will not work for the community but for himself and each one wishes to take care of himself and if once in a while someone withdraws without profit to himself, the whole body is divided. In brief, *one, common* builds the Lord's house and is pure; but *mine, thine, his, own* divides the Lord's house and is impure. Therefore, where there is ownership and one has it, and it is his, and one does not wish to be one with Christ and his own in living and dying, he is outside of Christ and his communion and has thus no Father in heaven. If he says so, he lies. That is the life of the pilgrims of the Lord, who has purchased them in Christ, namely, the elect, the called, the holy ones in this life. These are his fighters and heralds, to whom also he will give the crown of life on the Day of his righteousness.

Secondly, such a community of the children of God has ordinances here in their pilgrimage. These should constitute the polity for the whole world. But the wickedness of men has spoiled everything. For as the sun with its shining is common to all, so also the use of all creaturely things. Whoever appropriates them for himself and encloses them is a thief and steals what is not his. For everything has been created free in common. Of such thieves the whole world is full. May God guard his own from them. To be sure, according to human law, one says: That is mine, but not according to divine law. . . .

From Ulrich Stadler, "Cherished Instructions," in *Spiritual and Anabaptist Writers,* ed. G. H. Williams and Angel M. Mergal (Philadelphia: Westminster Press, 1957), pp. 275-84.

In order to hold in common all the gifts and goods which God gives and dispenses to his own, there must be free, unhampered, patient and full hearts in Christ, yea, hearts that truly believe and trust and in Christ are utterly devoted. Whoever is thus free, unhampered, and resigned in the Lord from everything, [ready] to give over all his goods and chattels, yea, to lay it up for distribution among the children of God — it is God's grace in Christ which prepares men for it. Being willing and ready — that makes one free and unhampered. But whoever is not thus at liberty to give over and lay up in Christ the Lord, as indicated, should nevertheless not hold back, nor conceal, nor disavow anything but instead be willing and ready to give even when there is nothing at hand, yea, even to let the deacons in to collect in order that [at least] they might have free access in the Lord to them and at all times to find a willing, open heart ready to share. . . .

The children of God should group themselves and hold together here in misery after they have been driven out in the worst sort of way — if they can achieve this, for it is good and purposeful; however, if it [can be managed] without hardship they should not make big concentrations but rather, as opportunity affords, they should have many or at least a few [separated] houses. In brief, it belongs to all the children of God to live, to serve, to work, to seek not their own benefit but that of another, since we are all of the Lord. [Such] is their behavior on their pilgrimage.

Again, the brethren ought not to do business with each other, buy and sell like the heathen, each being rather in the Lord the Lord's own. Finally, everything should be arranged for the good of the saints of God in the church of the Lord according to time, place, propriety, and opportunity, for one cannot set up a specific instruction for everything. The hearts which are free, willing, unhampered, patient, [ready] to serve all the children of God, to have everything in common with them, yea, to persevere loyally and constantly in their service, shall remain always in the Lord. . . .

In conclusion, it is very good for the children of God, while they make their pilgrimage in misery, to assemble and hold themselves together, as well as can be achieved in the Lord, and not to take counsel concerning this with the flesh, for the flesh would never recommend it but rather wants to be and have only its own and not suffer it out with the pious. . . .

It is true abandon to yield and dispose oneself with goods and chattels in the service of the saints. It is also the way of love. Moreover, true friends have all things in common; indeed, they are called two bodies with but one soul. Yea, we learn it in Christ to lose oneself in the service of the saints, to be and become poor and to suffer want, if only another may be served, and further, to put aside all goods and chattels, to throw them away in order that they may be distributed to the needy and the impoverished. That is the highest part and degree of divine abandon and voluntary surrender to the Lord and to his people through the Spirit of grace.

In brief, a brother should serve, live, and work for the other, none for himself; indeed, one house for another, one community for another in some other settlement in the land, wherever the Lord grants it that we gather together, one communion, as a body of the Lord and members one to another. This we see in all the writings of the holy apostles, namely, how one brother, one congregation, serves the other, extends assistance and supplies to the other in the Lord. Such is the life of the elect, holy children of God in their pilgrimage. Amen.

The True Levellers' Standard Advanced

Gerrard Winstanley and others

In the beginning of time, the great Creator, Reason, made the earth to be a common treasury, to preserve beasts, birds, fishes, and man, the lord that was to govern this creation. For man had domination given to him over the beasts, birds, and fishes. But not one word was spoken in the beginning, that one branch of mankind should rule over another.

And the reason is this. Every single man, male and female, is a perfect creature himself. And the same Spirit that made the globe dwells in man to govern the globe; so that the flesh of man, being subject to Reason, his Maker, hath him to be his teacher and ruler within himself, therefore needs not run abroad after any teacher and ruler without him.

But since human flesh . . . began to delight himself in the objects of the creation more than in the Spirit Reason and Righteousness, who manifests himself to be the indweller in the five senses . . .; then he fell into blindness of mind and weakness of heart, and runs abroad for a teacher and ruler, and so selfish imaginations, taking possession of the five senses, and ruling as king in the room of Reason therein, and working with covetousness, did set up one man to teach and rule over another. And thereby the Spirit was killed, and man was brought into bondage and became a greater slave to such of his own kind than the beasts of the field were to him.

And hereupon the earth, which was made to

Gerrard Winstanley et al., "The True Levellers' Standard Advanced," in *Puritanism and Liberty,* ed. A. S. P. Woodhouse (London: Dent, 1938), pp. 379-85.

be a common treasury of relief for all, both beasts and men, was hedged into enclosures by the teachers and rulers, and the others were made servants and slaves. And that earth that is within this creation made a common storehouse for all, is bought and sold and kept in the hands of a few; whereby the great Creator is mightily dishonored: as if he were a respector of persons, delighting in the comfortable livelihood of some, and rejoicing in the miserable poverty and straits of others. From the beginning it was not so.

But for the present state of the old world, that is running up like parchment in the fire and wearing away we see proud imaginary flesh, which is the wise serpent, rises up in flesh and gets dominion in some to rule over others, and so forces one part of the creation, man, to be a slave to another. . . .

But when once the earth becomes a common treasury again — as it must; for all the prophecies of scriptures and reason are circled here in this community, and mankind must have the law of righteousness once more writ in his heart, and all must be made of one heart and one mind — then this enmity in all lands will cease. For none shall dare to seek a dominion over others; neither shall any dare to kill another, nor desire more of the

---

Poems of the Radical Reformation

When Adam wove
And Eve span,
Where was then
The gentleman?

The Father he is God alone;
　　nothing beside him ist.
All things are folded in that One;
　　by him all things subsist. . . .

And when the Father seeth it good,
　　and his set time is come,
He takes away the tyrant's food,
　　and gives it to the Son.

— From *The Diggers Mirth* (London, 1650)

earth than another. For he that will rule over, imprison, oppress, and kill his fellow creatures under what pretence soever, is a destroyer of the creation and an actor of the curse, and walks contrary to the rule of righteousness: Do as you would have others do you; and love your enemies, not in words, but in actions. . . .

The work we are going about is this: to dig up George's Hill and the waste ground thereabouts, and to sow corn, and to eat our bread together by the sweat of our brows.

And the first reason is this. That we may work in righteousness, and lay the foundation of making the earth a common treasury for all, both rich and poor. That every one that is born in the land may be fed by the earth, his mother that brought him forth, according to the reason that rules in the creation, not enclosing any part into any particular hand but all as one man working together, and feeding together as sons of one father, members of one family; not one lording over another, but all looking upon each other as equals in the creation. So that our Maker may be glorified in the work of his own hands, and that every one may see he is no respecter of persons, but equally loves his whole creation, and hates nothing but the serpent. Which is covetousness, branching forth into selfish imagination, pride, envy, hypocrisy, uncleanness, all seeking the ease and honor of flesh, and fighting against the Spirit Reason that made the creation. For that is the corruption, the curse, the devil, the father of lies, death and bondage — that serpent and dragon that the creation is to be delivered from.

And we are moved hereunto for that reason, and others which hath been showed us, both by vision, voice, and revelation. For it is showed us, that so long as we or any other doth own the earth to be the peculiar interest of lords and landlords, and not common to others as well as them, we own the curse that holds the creation under bondage. And so long as we or any other doth own landlords and tenants, for one to call the land his, or another to hire it of him, or for one to give hire, and for another to work for hire; this is to dishonor the work of creation — as if the righteous Creator should have respect to persons, and therefore made the earth for some, and not for all.

And that this civil propriety is the curse, is manifest thus. Those that buy and sell land and are landlords, have got it either by oppression or murder or theft; and all landlords live in the breach of the Seventh and Eighth Commandments, *Thou shalt not steal, nor kill.*

First by their oppression. They have, by their subtle, imaginary, and covetous wit, got the plain-hearted poor, or younger brethren, to work for them for small wages, and by their work have got a great increase; for the poor by their labor lifts up tyrants to rule over them. Or else by their covetous wit, they have outreached the plain-hearted in buying and selling, and thereby enriched themselves but impoverished others. Or else by their subtle wit, having been lifted up into places of trust, [they] have enforced people to pay money for a public use, but have divided much of it into their private purses, and so have got it by oppression.

Then, secondly, for murder. They have by subtle wit and power pretended to preserve a people in safety by the power of the sword. And what by large pay, much free-quarter, and other booties which they call their own, they get much moneys, and with this they buy land and become landlords. And if once landlords, then they rise to be justices, rulers, and state governors, as experience shows. But all this is but a bloody and subtle thievery, countenanced by a law that covetousness made; and is a breach of the Seventh Commandment, *Thou shalt not kill.*

And likewise, thirdly, a breach of the Eighth Commandment, *Thou shalt not steal.* But these landlords have thus stolen the earth from their fellow creatures, that have an equal share with them by the law of reason and creation, as well as they.

And such as these rise up to be rich in the objects of the earth. Then, by their plausible words of flattery to the plain-hearted people, whom they deceive, and that lies under confusion and blindness, they are lifted up to be teachers, rulers, and lawmakers over them that lifted them up; as if the earth were made peculiarly for them, and not for others' weal. . . .

[But] . . . the earth is the Lord's; that is man's, who is lord of the creation, in every branch of mankind. For as divers members of our human bodies make but one body perfect, so every particular man is but a member or branch of mankind; and mankind, living in the light and obedience to Reason, the King of Righteousness, is thereby made a fit and complete lord of the creation. And the whole earth is this Lord's man, subject to the Spirit, and not the inheritance of covetous, proud flesh that is selfish, and enmity to the Spirit.

That which does encourage us to go on in this work is this. We find the streaming out of love in our hearts toward all, to enemies as well as friends. We would have none live in beggary, poverty, or sorrow, but that every one might enjoy the benefit of his creation. We have peace in our hearts, and quiet rejoicing in our work, and [are] filled with sweet content though we have but a dish of roots and bread for our food.

And we are assured that, in the strength of this Spirit that hath manifested himself to us, we shall not be startled, neither at prison nor death, while we are about his work. And we have been made to sit down and count what it may cost us in undertaking such a work. And we know the full sum, and are resolved to give all that we have to buy this pearl which we see in the field.

For by this work, we are assured, and reason makes it appear to others, that bondage shall be removed, tears wiped away, and all poor people by their righteous labors shall be relieved and freed from poverty and straits. For in this work of restoration there will be no beggar in Israel. For surely, if there was no beggar in literal Israel, there shall be no beggar in spiritual Israel. . . .

John Wesley

The last of the great "classical" church leaders to be included here, John Wesley, was an Anglo-Catholic priest who, as the son of a "Radical Reformation" minister who later joined the established church, felt great empathy for dispossessed workers and farmers. The Industrial Revolution had begun in England, and the conditions for miners, workers, and mechanics were very difficult as they were economically driven from farming into industrial labor.

Unlike those calling for revolution, Wesley turned to evangelical preaching in open fields, at mines, and near factories, and he also formed "classes" — study groups for Bible literacy, prayer, and mutual edification, among the poor people. His movement not only grew rapidly in England; he also came to the United States. His disciples founded what is today the largest Protestant communion in the world, the United Methodist Church. He preached classical doctrines from the Bible, the church fathers, the Anglo-Catholic heritage, and Luther, and added to them the idea that each person should seek to experience the "warmed heart" that comes from knowing Christ directly. The effect among the people was radical. Some say that the Labour Party in England and the most "progressive" parts of "liberal Protestantism" in America have roots in Wesley's populism.

The name "Methodists" derived from the fact that Wesley inspired a methodical discipline among the laity in all areas of life, including economics. In terms of basic attitudes toward economic life, Wesley seemed to adopt many of the elements of Calvinism — although he disagreed vigorously with Calvinism on certain doctrinal points about freedom and grace. Nevertheless, it is fair to say that in developing a "work ethic" and a "transformative" business ethics, the Wesleyan movement did for the working masses at the time of the Industrial Revolution what the monks had earlier done for the spiritual athletes of the medieval world, and what Calvin did for urban leadership as modern complex civilizations began to develop: he brought a sense of God's holiness and God's power into the midst of life in a way that led to the constant discipline and creative reconstruction of every dimension of personal and social life.

It is difficult to discuss John Wesley without also mentioning his brother Charles. Charles remained an Anglican priest and disapproved of John's ordination of leadership outside that church, a development that finally led to John's break with Anglicanism. But Charles was also one of the world's great hymn writers — in any of the world religions. He composed more than 5,500 hymns, which today can be found in the hymnbook of every Christian denomination around the world. Themes that were part of John's sermons and were taken in by the mind became also part of Charles's songs and were taken in by the heart. In John's famous sermon "The Use of Money" we find motifs that are also present in Charles's hymn "Forth in Thy Name, O Lord, I Go."

The Use of Money

John Wesley

> I say unto you, Make to yourselves friends
> of the mammon of unrighteousness; that,
> when ye fail, they may receive you into ever-
> lasting habitations. — Luke 16:9

An excellent branch of Christian wisdom is here inculcated by our Lord on all His followers, namely, the right use of money, — a subject largely spoken of, after their manner, by men of the world; but not sufficiently considered by those whom God hath chosen out of the world. These, generally, do not consider, as the importance of the subject requires, the use of this excellent talent. Neither do they understand how to employ it to the greatest advantage; the introduction of which into the world is one admirable instance of the wise and gracious providence of God. It has, indeed, been the manner of poets, orators, and philosophers, in almost all ages and nations, to rail at this, as the grand corrupter of the world, the bane of virtue, the pest of human society.

But is not all this mere empty rant? Is there any solid reason therein? By no means. For, let the world be as corrupt as it will, is gold or silver to blame? "The love of money," we know, "is the root of all evil," but not the thing itself. The fault does not lie in the money, but in them that use it. It may be used ill: and what may not? But it may likewise be used well: it is full as applicable to the best, as to the worst uses. It is of unspeakable service to all civilized nations, in all the common

affairs of life: it is a most compendious instrument of transacting all manner of business, and (if we use it according to Christian wisdom) of doing all manner of good. It is true, were man in a state of innocence, or were all men "filled with the Holy Ghost," so that, like the infant church at Jerusalem, "no man counted anything he had his own," but "distribution was made to every one as he had need," the use of it would be superseded; as we cannot conceive there is anything of the kind among the inhabitants of heaven. But, in the present state of mankind, it is an excellent gift of God, answering the noblest ends. In the hands of His children, it is food for the hungry, drink for the thirsty, raiment for the naked: it gives to the traveller and the stranger where to lay his head. By it we may supply the place of an husband to the widow, and of a father to the fatherless. We may be a defence for the oppressed, a means of health to the sick, of ease to them that are in pain; it may be as eyes to the blind, as feet to the lame; yea, a lifter up from the gates of death.

It is, therefore, of the highest concern, that all who fear God know how to employ this valuable talent; that they be instructed how it may answer these glorious ends, and in the highest degree. And, perhaps, all the instructions which are necessary for this may be reduced to three plain rules, by the exact observance whereof we may approve ourselves faithful stewards of "the mammon of unrighteousness."

The first of these is: "Gain all you can." Here we may speak like the children of the world: we meet them on their own ground. And it is our bounden duty to do this: we ought to gain all we can gain, without buying gold too dear, without paying more for it than it is worth. But this it is certain we ought not to do; we ought not to gain money at the expense of life, nor at the expense of our health. Therefore, no gain whatsoever should induce us to enter into, or to continue in, any employ, which is of such a kind, or is attended with so hard or so long labor, as to impair our constitution. Neither should we begin or continue in any business which necessarily deprives us of proper seasons for food and sleep, in such a proportion as our nature requires. Indeed, there is a great difference here. Some employments are absolutely and totally unhealthy; as those which imply the dealing with arsenic, or other equally

From John Wesley, *Standard Sermons,* ed. E. H. Sugden, 2 vols. (London: Epworth Press, 1921), abbreviated in *Christian Ethics,* ed. Waldo Beach and H. Richard Niebuhr (New York: Alfred A. Knopf, 1973), pp. 372-79.

hurtful minerals, or the breathing an air tainted with streams of melting lead, which must at length destroy the firmest constitution. Others may not be absolutely unhealthy, but only to persons of a weak constitution. Such are those which require many hours to be spent in writing; especially if a person write sitting, and lean upon his stomach, or remain long in an uneasy posture. But whatever it is which reason or experience shows to be destructive of health or strength, that we may not submit to; seeing "the life is more" valuable "than meat, and the body than raiment": and, if we are already engaged in such an employ, we should exchange it, as soon as possible, for some which, if it lessen our gain, will, however, not lessen our health.

We are, secondly, to gain all we can without hurting our mind, any more than our body. For neither may we hurt this: we must preserve, at all events, the spirit of a healthful mind. Therefore, we may not engage or continue in any sinful trade; any that is contrary to the law of God, or of our country. Such are all that necessarily imply our robbing or defrauding the king of his lawful customs. For it is, at least, as sinful to defraud the king of his right, as to rob our fellow subjects: and the king has full as much right to his customs as we have to our houses and apparel. Other businesses there are which, however innocent in themselves, cannot be followed with innocence now; at least not in England, such, for instance, as will not afford a competent maintenance without cheating or lying, or conformity to some custom which is not consistent with a good conscience: these, likewise, are sacredly to be avoided, whatever gain they may be attended with, provided we follow the custom of the trade; for, to gain money, we must not lose our souls.

We are, thirdly, to gain all we can, without hurting our neighbor. But this we may not, cannot do, if we love our neighbor as ourselves. We cannot, if we love every one as ourselves, hurt any one in his substance. We cannot devour the increase of his lands, and perhaps the lands and houses themselves, by gaming, by overgrown bills (whether on account of physic, or law, or anything else), or by requiring or taking such interest as even the laws of our country forbid. Hereby all pawnbroking is excluded; seeing, whatever good we might do thereby, all unprejudiced men see with grief to be abundantly overbalanced by the evil. And if it were otherwise, yet we are not allowed to "do evil that good may come." We cannot, consistent with brotherly love, sell our goods below the market price; we cannot study to ruin our neighbor's trade, in order to advance our own; much less can we entice any, or receive any of his servants or workmen whom he has need of. None can gain by swallowing up his neighbor's substance, without gaining the damnation of hell!

Neither may we gain by hurting our neighbor in his body. Therefore we may not sell anything which tends to impair health. Such is, eminently, all that liquid fire, commonly called drams, or spirituous liquors. It is true, these may have a place in medicine; they may be of use in some bodily disorders, although there would rarely be occasion for them, were it not for the unskilfulness of the practitioner. Therefore, such as prepare and sell them for this end may keep their conscience clear. But all who sell them in the common way, to any that will buy, are poisoners general. They murder His Majesty's subjects by wholesale, neither does their eye pity or spare.

So is whatever is procured by hurting our neighbor in his soul; by ministering, suppose, either directly or indirectly, to his unchastity or intemperance; which certainly none can do who has nay fear of God, or any real desire of pleasing Him. It nearly concerns all those to consider this, who have anything to do with taverns, victualling-houses, opera-houses, play-houses, or any other places of public, fashionable diversion. If these profit the souls of men, you are clear; your employment is good, and your gain innocent; but if they are either sinful in themselves, or natural inlets to sin of various kinds, then, it is to be feared, you have a sad account to make.

These cautions and restrictions being observed, it is the bounden duty of all who are engaged in worldly business to observe that first and great rule of Christian wisdom, with respect to money, "Gain all you can." Gain all you can by honest industry. Use all possible diligence in your calling. Lose no time. If you understand yourself, and your relation to God and man, you know you have none to spare. If you understand your particular calling, as you ought, you will have no time that hangs upon your hands. Every business will afford some employment sufficient for every day and every hour. That where in you are placed, if you follow it in earnest, will leave you no leisure for silly, unprofitable diversions. You have always something better to do, something that will profit you, more or less. And "whatsoever thy hand findeth to do, do it with thy might." Do it as soon as possible: no delay! No putting off from day to day, or from hour to hour! Never leave anything til to-morrow, which you can do to-day. And do it as well as possible. Do not sleep or yawn over it: put your whole strength to the work. Spare no pains. Let nothing be done by halves, or in a slight and careless manner. Let nothing in your business be left undone, if it can be done by labour or patience.

Gain all you can, by common sense, by using in your business all the understanding which God has given you. It is amazing to observe how few do this; how men run on in the same dull track with their forefathers. But whatever they do who know not God, this is no rule for you. It is a shame for a Christian not to improve upon them in whatever he takes in hand. You should be continually learning, from the experience of others, or from your own experience, reading, and reflection, to do everything you have to do better to-day than you did yesterday. And see that you practice whatever you learn, that you may make the best of all that is in your hands.

 Having gained all you can, by honest wisdom, and unwearied diligence, the second rule of Christian prudence is "Save all you can." Do not throw the precious talent into the sea: leave that folly to heathen philosophers. Do not throw it away in idle expenses, which is just the same as throwing it into the sea. Expend no part of it merely to gratify the desire of the flesh, the desire of the eye, or the pride of life.

Do not waste any part of so precious a talent, merely in gratifying the desires of the flesh; in procuring the pleasures of sense, of whatever kind; particularly, in enlarging the pleasure of tasting. I do not mean, avoid gluttony and drunkenness only: an honest Heathen would condemn these. But there is a regular, reputable kind of sensuality, an elegant epicurism, which does not immediately disorder the stomach, nor (sensibly at least) impair the understanding; and yet it cannot be maintained without considerable expense. Cut off all this expense! Despise delicacy and variety, and be content with what plain nature requires.

Do not waste any part of so precious a talent, merely in gratifying the desire of the eye, by superfluous or expensive furniture; in costly pictures, painting, gilding, books; in elegant rather than useful gardens.

Lay out nothing to gratify the pride of life, to gain the admiration or praise of men. This motive of expense is frequently interwoven with one or both of the former. Men are expensive in diet, or apparel, or furniture, not barely to please their appetite, or to gratify their eye, or their imagination, but their vanity too. "So long as thou doest well unto thyself, men will speak good of thee." Rather be content with the honour that cometh from God.

But let not any man imagine that he has done anything, barely by going thus far, by "gaining and saving all he can," if he were to stop here. All this is nothing, if a man go not forward, if he does not point all this at a farther end. Nor, indeed, can a man properly be said to save anything, if he only lays it up. You may as well throw your money into the sea, as bury it in the earth. and you may as well bury it in the earth, as in your chest, or in the Bank of England. Not to use, is effectually to throw it away. If, therefore, you would indeed "make yourselves friends of the mammon of unrighteousness," add the third rule to the two preceding. Having, first, gained all you can, and, secondly, saved all you can, then "give all you can."

In order to see the ground and reason of this, consider, when the Possessor of heaven and earth brought you into being, and placed you in this world, He placed you here, not as a proprietor, but a steward: as such He entrusted you, for as season, with goods of various kinds; but the sole property of these still rests in Him, nor can ever be alienated from Him. As you yourself are not your own, but His, such is, likewise, all that you enjoy. Such is your soul and your body, not your own, but God's. and so is your substance in particular. And He has told you, in the most clear and express terms, how you are to employ it for Him, in such a manner, that it may be all an holy sacrifice, acceptable through Christ Jesus. And this light, easy service, He hath promised to reward with an eternal weight of glory.

The directions which God has given us, touching the use of our worldly substance, may be comprised in the following particulars. If you desire to be a faithful and a wise steward, out of that portion of your Lord's goods which He has for the present lodged in your hands, but with the right of resuming whenever it pleases Him, first, provide things needful for yourself; food to eat, raiment to put on, whatever nature moderately requires for preserving the body in health and strength. Secondly, provide these for your wife, your children, your servants, or any others who pertain to your household. If, when this is done, there be an overplus left, then "do good to them that are of the household of faith." If there be an overplus still, "as you have opportunity, do good unto all men." In so doing, you give all you can; nay, in a sound sense, all you have: for all that is laid out in this manner is really given to God. You "render unto God the things that are God's," not only by what you give to the poor, but also by that which you expend in providing things needful for yourself and your household.

If, then, a doubt should at any time arise in your mind concerning what you are going to expend, either on yourself or any part of your family, you have an easy way to remove it. Calmly and seriously inquire, "(1) In expending this, am I acting according to my character? Am I acting herein, not as a proprietor, but as a steward of my Lord's goods? (2) Am I doing this in obedience to His Word? In what scripture does He require me so to do? (3) Can I offer up this action, this expense, as a sacrifice to God through Jesus Christ? (4) Have I reason to believe, that for this very work I shall have a reward at the resurrection of the just?" You will seldom need anything more to remove any doubt which arises on this head; but, by this four-fold consideration, you will receive clear light as to the way wherein you should go.

Forth in Thy Name, O Lord, I Go

Charles Wesley

Forth in thy name, O Lord, I go,
My daily labor to pursue,
Thee, only thee, resolved to know
In all I think or speak or do.

The task thy wisdom hath assigned,
O let me cheerfully fulfill,
In all my works thy presence find,
And prove thy good and perfect will.

Thee may I set at my right hand,
Whose eyes my inmost substance see,
And labor on at thy command,
And offer all my works to thee.

Give me to bear thy easy yoke,
And every moment watch and pray,
And still to things eternal look
And hasten to thy glorious day.

— From the *Pilgrim Hymnal*
(Boston: Pilgrim Press, 1931), p. 406

PART B

MODERN DEBATES

Chapter Six

Enlightenment Theories

Biblical insights interacted with classical philosophies to create the theology and ethics, and thus the law and economic theories, that formed Western civilization. Christianity may have differed somewhat in Catholic, Protestant, Orthodox, and sectarian locales, but together these Christian traditions tamed the tribes of Europe, cut the channels of mind in which much of ethics still runs, and built the foundations for modernity. These foundations were sometimes mixed with violence and racism, patriarchy and colonialism. As elsewhere around the world, the strong and the wealthy often recognized that faith is powerful — it determines whether status and authority are viewed as legitimate or not. Thus many tried to manipulate religion for their own purposes; they often discredited what they appeared to invoke.

Just before the Reformation, France fought against England for domination of northern Europe. For centuries after the Reformation the emerging European nations attached themselves to one or another version of Christianity. "Our faith" battles raged between Protestant and Catholic princes on the Continent in the early seventeenth century, while Puritans were fighting Anglicans in England. Dissenters settled in America as missionaries joined explorers around the world. New lands and new trade routes reinforced new ways of reading the Bible, of doing philosophy, and of thinking about property, commerce, profits, and poverty.

All of this encouraged tendencies that had been present since the Renaissance. One was the attempt to separate religion from politics — and thus from economics, which was increasingly tied to politics. Whether attempting to protect religion from politics or politics from religion, they sought the "privatization" of religion and a "secularization" of the state. A second tendency was an attempt to assure national wealth by mercantilist policies — that is, politics based on the belief that economic development is best gained by governmental regulation. A third was to establish a "national philosophy" based on experience and reason, rather than on ancient authorities, to guide state and economic life and to adjudicate competing claims in religion, ethics, and society. The result was the Enlightenment, which established new channels of mind in the West that spread to all the world. All sought change, novelty, and improvement.

These Enlightenment philosophers often found the official religious dogmas to be unconvincing. Several opposed the idea of any "divine" order or purpose other than what is found in the facts of the world or the fabric of human consciousness. They considered imposed rule to be a source of distress. In the quest for a new relationship between freedom and order, they spoke less of faith than of reason, less of creation than of nature, less of providence than of progress — although some thought that God was behind all of these. These thinkers became the sources of modern protests against inherited beliefs of all kinds — and thus also the skeptical new dialogue partners of the great religions. These are the originators of the idea of "political economy," which is based on the effort to increase the material well-being of the people by the reform of governmental policy. It is in these terms that the dramas of modernity, with both its tyrannies and its license, have been written, as we can see in the following excerpts in which key concepts of modern, "liberal" societies — freedom, rights, reason, contract, and change by scientific and technological planning — are forged.

John Locke

A dominant idea of the Enlightenment is "contract," a notion that has three major elements. The first is liberty, which implies that the human will is fundamental to humanity and that choice, and neither force-imposed doctrine nor inherited condition, is the foundation of society. The second is right, which implies that humans can, in some measure, know the moral law and use it in freedom to establish a more just order. Thus our primal freedom is related to an equally primal morality. Third, we can know freedom and right by reason, which implies a capacity, given by God, to know what is just without revelation.

Not all theories of contract have all three elements in equal measure. Locke (and later Kant) is a premier example of those who argued for all three. In Locke's time, the idea of a moral law was usually discussed in terms of a "law of nature." Thus, when persons or groups exercise freedom in accord with the moral law, they have "natural rights" to do so, and the common life can reasonably be reformed on the basis of "rights."

Such ideas had been developing for a very long time. They have biblical roots and are present in the theological tradition. They had been expounded again in the face of religious conflict by the Reformed scholar Johannes Althusius (*Politica . . .* , 1605), the Jesuit Francisco Suarez (*Tractatus . . .* , 1611), the Calvinist dissident Hugo Grotius (*De Jure Belli . . .* , 1625), and the Lutheran Samuel Pufendorf (*De Jure Naturae . . .* , 1672). But the ideas were not yet widely adopted in policy — especially in economic thought.

Locke believed that they were indispensable for religion and for social order, for this is how God made the world. But there were perils close by. On the one hand, his predecessor Thomas Hobbes had argued that all ought to submit to the state, since there is no such thing as a moral order outside the dictates of the sovereign. On the other hand, the powerful Archbishop Laud was arguing that there is a moral order beyond the sovereign, but it is known through the authority of the church and the mysteries of dogma. Liberty in religion, politics, and morality was thus the exercise of disobedient license. In this context Locke argued for a social order based on freedom and moral law, and he did so on the basis of reasonable, "self-evident truths" to which philosopher and theologian, Protestant and Catholic could, and ought to, agree.

"Contract" ideas were applied first to politics, but they are pertinent to economics as well. For one thing, a primary reason for government was to protect property, which, Locke said, is a natural right, without which there can be no justice. Of course, many had argued for the necessity of private property; but most had argued that it was not a good thing so much as a concession to the fact that humans lived in a sinful world. Thus, contrary both to earlier traditions that viewed holding all things in common as the higher way and to more recent socialist efforts, Locke argued that private property is a positive good, reasonable to the mind, necessary to political orders that protect natural rights, *and intended by God*. He has been accused of fomenting "possessive individualism," but he has also been celebrated as the "principled liberal" who saw the implications of a work ethic and covenant for a theory of property rights and just contract.

Locke greatly influenced American developments. His ideas were adopted by the theologian Jonathan Edwards, who spurred the Great Awakening, a populist rebirth of religion; and they were also adopted by the authors of the U.S. Constitution.

Of Property

John Locke

Whether we consider natural reason, which tells us that men, being once born, have a right to their preservation, and consequently to meat and drink and such other things as Nature affords for their subsistence, or *revelation,* which gives us an account of those grants God made of the world to Adam, and to Noah and his sons, 'tis very clear that God, as King David says, *Psalm* cxv. 16, *has given the earth to the children of men,* given it to mankind in common. But, this being supposed, it seems to some a very great difficulty how any one should ever come to have a property in anything, I will not content myself to answer, that, if it be difficult to make out *property* upon a supposition that God gave the world to Adam and his posterity in common, it is impossible that any man but one universal monarch should have any *property* upon a supposition that God gave the world to Adam and his heirs in succession, exclusive of all the rest of his posterity; *but I shall endeavour to shew how men might come to have a property in several parts of that which God gave to mankind in common, and that without any express compact of all the commoners.*

God, who hath given the world to men in common, hath also given them reason to make use of it to the best advantage of life and convenience. The earth and all that is therein is given to men for the support and comfort of their being. And though all the fruits it naturally produces, and beasts it feeds, belong to mankind in common, as they are produced by the spontaneous hand of nature, and no body has originally a private dominion exclusive of the rest of mankind in any of them, as they are thus in their natural state, yet being given for the use of men, there must of necessity be a means to appropriate them some way or other before they can be of any use, or at all beneficial, to any particular man. The fruit or venison which nourishes the wild Indian, who knows no enclosure, and is still a tenant in common, must be his, and so his — *i.e.,* a part of him, that another can no longer have any right to it before it can do him any good for the support of his life.

Though the earth and all inferior creatures be common to all men, yet every man has a property *in his own* person. *This nobody has any right to but himself. The* labour *of his body and the* work *of his hands, we may say, are properly his. Whatsoever, then, he removes out of the state that nature hath provided and left it in, he hath mixed his labour with it, and joined to it something that is his own, and thereby makes it his property. It being by him removed from the common state nature placed it in, it hath by this labour something annexed to it that excludes the common right of other men.* For this labour being the unquestionable property of the labourer, no man but he can have a right to what that is once joined to, at least where there is enough, and as good left in common for others.

He that is nourished by the acorns he picked up under an oak, or the apples he gathered from the trees in the wood, has certainly appropriated them to himself. Nobody can deny but the nourishment is his. I ask, then, when did they begin to be his? when he digested? or when he ate? or when he boiled? or when he brought them home? or when he picked them up? And 'tis plain, if the first gathering made them not his, nothing else could. That labour put a distinction between them and common. That added something to them more than Nature, the common mother of all, had done, and so they became his private right. And will any one say he had no right to those acorns or apples he thus appropriated because he had not the consent of all mankind to make them his? Was it a robbery thus to assume to himself what belonged to all in common? If such a consent as that was necesary, man had starved, notwithstanding the plenty God had given him. We see in commons, which remain so by compact, that 'tis the taking

John Locke, "Of Property," *Second Treatise: An Essay Concerning the True End of Civil Government,* par. 23-38, 46-49, World Classic Series (London: Oxford University Press, 1947), pp. 23-34, 39-42.

any part of what is common, and removing it out of the state Nature leaves it in, which begins the property, without which the common is of no use. And the taking of this or that part does not depend on the express consent of all the commoners. Thus, the grass my horse has bit, the turfs my servant has cut, and the ore I have digged in any place, where I have a right to them in common with others, become my property without the assignation or consent of any body. The labour that was mine, removing them out of that common state they were in, hath fixed my property in them.

By making an explicit consent of every commoner necessary to any one's appropriating to himself any part of what is given in common, children or servants could not cut the meat which their father or master had provided for them in common without assigning to every one his peculiar part. Though the water running in the fountain be every one's, yet who can doubt but that in the pitcher is his only who drew it out? His labour hath taken it out of the hands of Nature where it was common, and belonged equally to all her children, and hath thereby appropriated it to himself.

Thus this law of reason makes the deer that Indian's who hath killed it; 'tis allowed to be his goods who hath bestowed his labour upon it, though, before, it was the common right of every one. And amongst those who are counted the civilized part of mankind, who have made and multiplied positive laws to determine property, this original law of nature for the beginning of property, in what was before common, still takes place, and by virture thereof, what fish any one catches in the ocean, that great and still remaining common of mankind; or what ambergris any one takes up here is by the labour that removes it out of that common state nature left it in, made his property who takes that pains about it. And even amongst us, the hare that any one is hunting is thought his who pursues her during the chase. For being a beast that is still looked upon as common, and no man's private possession, whoever has employed so much labour about any of that kind as to find and pursue her has thereby removed her from the state of nature wherein she was common, and hath begun a property.

It will perhaps be objected to this, that if gathering the acorns or other fruits of the earth,

etc., makes a right to them, then any one may engross as much as he will. To which I answer, Not so. The same law of nature that does by this means give us property, does also bound that property too. *God has given us all things richly,* I *Tim.* vi.17. Is the voice of reason confirmed by inspiration? *But how far has he given it us, to enjoy?* As much as any one can make use of to any advantage of life before it spoils, so much he may by his labour fix a property in. Whatever is beyond this is more than his share, and belongs to others. Nothing was made by God for man to spoil or destroy. And thus considering the plenty of natural provisions there was a long time in the world, and the few spenders, and to how small a part of that provision the industry of one man could extend itself and engross it to the prejudice of others, especially keeping within the bonds set by reason of what might serve for his use, there could be then little room for quarrels or contentions about property so established.

But the chief matter of property being now not the fruits of the earth and the beasts that subsist on it, but the earth itself, as that which takes in and carries with it all the rest, I think it is plain that property in that too is acquired as the former. As much land as a man tills, plants, improves, cultivates, and can use the product of, so much is his property. He by his labour does, as it were, enclose it from the common. Nor will it invalidate his right to say, Every body else has an equal title to it, and therefore he cannot appropriate, he cannot enclose, without the consent of all his fellow-commoners, all mankind. God, when he gave the world in common to all mankind, commanded man also to labour, and the penury of his condition required it of him. God and his reason commanded him to subdue the earth — *i.e.,* improve it for the benefit of life and therein lay out something upon it that was his own, his labour. He that, in obedience to this command of God, subdued, tilled, and sowed any part of it, thereby annexed to it something that was his property, which another had no title to, nor could without injury take from him.

Nor was this appropriation of any parcel of land, by improving it, any prejudice to any other man, since there was still enough and as good left, and more than the yet unprovided could use. So that, in effect there was never the less left for others because of his enclosure for himself. For he that leaves as much as another can make use of does as good as take nothing at all. No body could think himself injured by the drinking of another man, though he took a good draught, who had a whole river of the same water left him to quench his thirst. And the case of land and water, where there is enough of both, is perfectly the same.

God gave the world to men in common, but since he gave it them for their benefit and the greatest conveniences of life they were capable to draw from it, it cannot be supposed he meant it should always remain common and uncultivated. He gave it to the use of the industrious and rational (and labour was to be his title to it); not to the fancy or covetousness of the quarrelsome and contentious. He that had as good left for his improvement as was already taken up needed not complain, ought not to meddle with what was already improved by another's labour; if he did 'tis plain he desired the benefit of another's pains, which he had no right to, and not the ground which God had given him, in common with others, to labour on, and whereof there was as good left as that already possessed, and more than he knew what to do with, or his industry could reach to.

'Tis true, in land that is common in England or any other country, where there are plenty of people under government who have money and commerce, no one can enclose or appropriate any part without the consent of all his fellow-commoners; because this is left common by compact, *i.e.,* by the law of the land, which is not to be violated. And, though it be common in respect of some men, it is not so to all mankind, but is the joint property of this country, or this parish. Besides, the remainder, after such enclosure, would not be as good to the rest of the commoners as the whole was, when they could all make use of the whole; whereas in the beginning and first peopling of the great common of the world it was quite otherwise. The law man was under was rather for appropriating. God commanded, and his wants forced him to labour. That was his property, which could not be taken from him wherever he had fixed it. And hence subduing or cultivating the earth and having dominion, we see, are joined together. The one gave title to the other. So that God, by commanding to subdue, gave authority

so far to appropriate. And the condition of human life, which requires labour and materials to work on, necessarily introduce private possessions.

The measure of property nature has well set by the extent of men's labour and the conveniency of life. No man's labour could subdue or appropriate all, nor could his enjoyment consume more than a small part; so that it was impossible for any man, this way, to entrench upon the right of another or acquire to himself a property to the prejudice of his neighbour, who would still have room for as good and as large a possession (after the other had taken out his) as before it was appropriated. Which measure did confine every man's possession to a very moderate proportion, and such as he might appropriate to himself without injury to any body in the first ages of the world, when men were more in danger to be lost, by wandering from their company, in the then vast wilderness of the earth, than to be straitened for want of room to plant in. And the same measure may be allowed still, without prejudice to any body, as full as the world seems. For, supposing a man or family, in the state they were at first, peopling of the world by the children of Adam or Noah; let him plant in some inland vacant places of America, we shall find that the possessions he could make himself, upon the measures we have given, would not be very large, nor, even to this day, prejudice the rest of mankind or give them reason to complain or think themselves injured by this man's encroachment, though the race of men have now spread themselves to all the corners of the world, and do infinitely exceed the small number was at the beginning. Nay, the extent of ground is of so little value without labour that I have heard it affirmed that in Spain itself a man may be permitted to plough, sow, and reap, without being disturbed, upon land he has no other title to, but only his making use of it. But, on the contrary, the inhabitants think themselves beholden to him who, by his industry on neglected, and consequently waste land, has increased the stock of corn, which they wanted. But be this as it will, which I lay no stress on, this *I dare boldly affirm, that the same rule of propriety, (viz.) that every man should have as much as he could make use of, would hold still in the world, without straitening any body, since there is land enough in the world to suffice double the inhabitants, had not the invention of money, and the tacit agreement of men to put a value on it, introduced (by consent) larger possessions and a right to them; which, how it has done, I shall by and by shew more at large.*

This is certain, that in the beginning, before the desire of having more than man needed had altered the intrinsic value of things, which depends only on their usefulness to the life of man, or had agreed that a little piece of yellow metal, which would keep without wasting or decay, should be worth a great piece of flesh or a whole heap of corn, though men had a right to appropriate by their labour, each one to himself, as much of the things of nature as he could use, yet this could not be much, nor to the prejudice of others, where the same plenty was still left, to those who would use the same industry.

Before the appropriation of land, he who gathered as much of the wild fruit, killed, caught, or tamed as many of the beasts as he could — he that so employed his pains about any of the spontaneous products of nature as any way to alter them from the state nature put them in, by placing any of his labour on them, did thereby acquire a propriety in them; but if they perished in his possession without their due use — if the fruits rotted or the venison putrefied before he could spend it, he offended against the common law of nature, and was liable to be punished: he invaded his neighbour's share, for he had no right farther than his use called for any of them, and they might serve to afford him conveniencies of life.

The same measures governed the possession of land, too. Whatsoever he tilled and reaped, laid up and made use of before it spoiled, that was his peculiar right; whatsover he enclosed, and could feed and make use of, the cattle and product was also his. But if either the grass of his enclosure rotted on the ground, or the fruit of his planting perished without gathering and laying up, this part of the earth, nowithstanding his enclosure, was still to be looked on as waste, and might be the possession of any other. Thus, at the beginning, Cain might take as much ground as he could till and make it his own land, and yet leave enough to Abel's sheep to feed on: a few acres would serve for both their possessions. But as families increased and industry enlarged their stocks, their possessions enlarged with the need of them; but yet it was commonly without any fixed property

in the ground they made use of till they incorporated, settled themselves together, and built cities, and then, by consent, they came in time to set out the bounds of their distinct territories and agree on limits between them and their neighbours, and by laws within themselves settled the properties of those of the same society. For we see that in that part of the world which was first inhabited, and therefore like to be best peopled, even as low down as Abraham's time, they wandered with their flocks and their herds, which was their substance, freely up and down — and this Abraham did in a country where he was a stranger. Whence it is plain that, at least, a great part of the land lay in common, that the inhabitants valued it not, nor claimed property in any more than they made use of; but when there was not room enough in the same place for their herds to feed together, they, by consent, as Abraham and Lot did, *Gen.* xiii. 5, separated and enlarged their pasture where it best liked them. And for the same reason, Esau went from his father and his brother, and planted in Mount Seir, *Gen.* xxxvi. 6.

And thus, without supposing any private dominion and property in Adam over all the world, exclusive of all other men, which can no way be proved, nor any one's property be made out from it, but supposing the world, given as it was to the children of men in common, we see how labour could make men distinct titles to several parcels of it for their private uses, wherein there could be no doubt of right, no room for quarrel.

Now of those good things which nature hath provided in common, every one had a right (as hath been said) to as much as he could use, and had a property in all that he could effect with his labour; all that his industry could extend to, to alter from the state nature had put it in, was his. He that gathered a hundred bushels of acorns or apples had thereby a property in them, they were his goods as soon as gathered. He was only to look that he used them before they spoiled, else he took more than his share, and robbed others. And, indeed, it was a foolish thing, as well as dishonest, to hoard up more than he could make use of. If he gave away a part to any body else, so that it perished not uselessly in his possession, these he also made use of. And if he also bartered away plums that would have rotted in a week, for nuts that would last good for his eating a whole year, he did no injury; he wasted not the common stock; destroyed no part of the portion of goods that belonged to others, so long as nothing perished uselessly in his hand. *Again, if he would give his nuts for a piece of metal, pleased with its colour, or exchange his sheep for shells, or wool for a sparkling pebble or a diamond, and keep those by him all his life, he invaded not the right of others; he might heap up as much of these durable things as he pleased; the exceeding of the bounds of his just property not lying in the largeness of his possession, but the perishing of anything uselessly in it.*

And thus came in the use of money, some lasting thing that men might keep without spoiling, and that, by mutual consent, men would take in exchange for the truly useful but perishable supports of life.

And as different degrees of industry were apt to give men possessions in different proportions, so this invention of money gave them the opportunity to continue and enlarge them. For supposing an island, separate from all possible commerce with the rest of the world, wherein there were but a hundred families, but there were sheep, horses, and cows, with other useful animals, wholesome fruits, and land enough for corn for a hundred thousand times as many, but nothing in the island, either because of its commonness or perishableness, fit to supply the place of money. What reason could any one have there to enlarge his possessions beyond the use of his family, and a plentiful supply to its consumption, either in what their own industry produced, or they could barter for like perishable, useful commodities with others? Where there is not something both lasting and scarce, and so valuable to be hoarded up, there men will not be apt to enlarge their possessions of land, were it never so rich, never so free for them to take. For I ask, what would a man value ten thousand or an hundred thousand acres of excellent land, ready cultivated and well stocked, too, with cattle, in the middle of the inland parts of America, where he had no hopes of commerce with other parts of the world, to draw money to him by the sale of the product? It would not be worth the enclosing, and we should see him give up again to the wild common of Nature whatever was more than would supply the conveniencies of life, to be had there for him and his family.

Thus, in the beginning, all the world was Amer-ica, and more so than that is now; for no such thing as money was any where known. Find out something that hath the use and value of money amongst his neighbours, you shall see the same man will begin presently to enlarge his possessions.

Adam Smith

Smith is equaled only by Karl Marx and John Maynard Keynes among all the economists of the world, and they depended on him. He knew the ancient classics and the tradition of rights from Althusius to Pufendorf. He quoted Hobbes and Locke. Further, he saw the Protestant ethic as it had developed in Scotland and the cities of North Europe and America, with their post-feudal economies, increasing technology, proto-democratic pluralism, and thriving commerce. He also knew both Francis Hutcheson and David Hume, the greatest philosophers of his time; and, like them, he had written a major treatise on the "moral sentiments." As Athens had long ago given birth to the minds that formed the great classical traditions in philosophy and politics, Great Britain in this period mothered those thinkers who shaped a new classical tradition, this one regarding economic matters.

Smith wanted to understand the "laws of natural economy" for several reasons. In part he wanted to understand such things as property, price, wages, rents, currency, and the "cost of living" (treated by him in terms of "corn," the grains which supplied food, fueled work animals, and paid rural landlords). These were much under dispute — nobody had a very clear idea of how they were to be determined, yet everyone wanted more for less. In part he thought that an "invisible hand" of benevolent providence brought a certain balance to things over time and that societies violated that only to their peril. And in part he wanted to know how, after centuries in which most of the peoples of the world were poor, it might be possible to sustain the trends he saw around him — where larger segments of the population and some countries of the world were attaining new levels of relative affluence.

He did not begin by describing things as they are "naturally," nor did he seek "natural rights" as did Locke. He sought, as Newton had in cosmology and Hume had attempted in psychology, to discover the operative principles behind the facts, and then to show how these principles explained things as they are — and how they could be cultivated to produce desirable results. He thus introduced a utilitarian element that became important later on, and which tended to reduce concern for theology. The following selections from his 1776 book *The Wealth of Nations* focus on operative principles such as "the division of labor" as the key to increased productivity, more than on his analysis of the developments of his century. Here it is possible to see that social arrangements beyond the household and beyond the political order can be linked with technology to create wealth.

Smith argued against two alternative positions as well as refining the theory of labor. One of these positions was held by the French "physiocrats," who invented the phrase "laissez faire" to describe a free economy. They held, as had Aristotle, that only the earth was the natural source of wealth and that the biophysical order was the basis of the moral order. The second position Smith argued against was "mercantilism," the state support of commerce, with control of prices and wages, the granting of monopolies ("for efficiency"), and the constraint of foreign imports for the sake of national wealth. This is what much of the world has experienced as "capitalism." Smith believed that government should allow the free invention of things and social forms beyond what is "natural," abolish monopolies, encourage international trade, and support education, for the common good.

Of the Causes of Improvement . . .

Adam Smith

The greatest improvement in the productive powers of labour, and the greater part of the skill, dexterity, and judgment with which it is any where directed, or applied, seem to have been the effects of the division of labour.

The effects of the division of labour, in the general business of society, will be more easily understood, by considering in what manner it operates in some particular manufactures. It is commonly supposed to be carried furthest in some very trifling ones; not perhaps that it really is carried further in them than in others of more importance: but in those trifling manufactures which are destined to supply the small wants of but a small number of people, the whole number of workmen must necessarily be small; and those employed in every different branch of the work can often be collected into the same workhouse, and placed at once under the view of the spectator. In those great manufactures, on the contrary, which are destined to supply the great wants of the great body of the people, every different branch of the work employs so great a number of workmen, that it is impossible to collect them all into the same workhouse. We can seldom see more, at one time, than those employed in one single branch. Though in such manufactures, therefore, the work may really be divided into a much greater number of parts, than in those of a more trifling nature, the division is not near so obvious, and has accordingly been much less observed.

Excerpts from *An Inquiry into the Nature and Causes of the Wealth of Nations* (New York: Random House, 1776), bk. 1, chaps. 1-8.

To take an example, therefore, from a very trifling manufacture; but one in which the division of labour has been very often taken notice of, the trade of the pinmaker; a workman not educated to this business (which the division of labour has rendered a distinct trade), nor acquainted with the use of the machinery employed in it (to the invention of which the same division of labour has probably given occasion), could scarce, perhaps, with his utmost industry, make one pin a day, and certainly could not make twenty. But in the way in which this business is now carried on, not only the whole work is a peculiar trade, but it is divided into a number of branches, of which the greater part are likewise peculiar trades. One man draws out the wire, another straightens it, a third cuts it, a fourth points it, a fifth grinds it at the top for receiving the head; to make the head requires two or three distinct operations; to put it on, is a peculiar business, to whiten the pins is another; it is even a trade by itself to put them into the paper; and the important business of making a pin is, in this manner, divided into about eighteen distinct operations, which, in some manufactories, are all performed by distinct hands, though in others the same man will sometimes perform two or three of them. I have seen a small manufactory of this kind where ten men only were employed, and where some of them consequently performed two or three distinct operations. But though they were very poor, and therefore but indifferently accommodated with the necessary machinery, they could, when they exerted themselves, make among them about twelve pounds of pins in a day. There are in a pound upwards of four thousand pins of a middling size. Those ten persons, therefore, could make among them upwards of forty-eight thousand pins in a day. Each person, therefore, making a tenth part of forty-eight thousand pins, might be considered as making four thousand eight hundred pins in a day. But if they had all wrought separately and independently, and without any of them having been educated to this peculiar business, they certainly could not each of them have made twenty, perhaps not one pin in a day; that is, certainly, not the two hundred and fortieth, perhaps not the four thousand eight hundredth part of what they are at present capable of performing, in consequence of a proper division and combination of their different operations.

In every other art and manufacture, the effects of the division of labour are similar to what they are in this very trifling one; though, in many of them, the labour can neither be so much subdivided, nor reduced to so great a simplicity of operation. The division of labour, however, so far as it can be introduced, occasions, in every art, a proportionable increase of the productive powers of labour. The separation of different trades and employments from one another, seems to have taken place, in consequence of this advantage. This separation too is generally carried furthest in those countries which enjoy the highest degree of industry and improvement; what is the work of one man in a rude state of society, being generally that of several in an improved one. In every improved society, the farmer is generally nothing but a farmer; the manufacturer, nothing but a manufacturer. The labour too which is necessary to produce any one complete manufacture, is almost always divided among a great number of hands. How many different trades are employed in each branch of the linen and woolen manufactures, from the growers of the flax and the wool, to the bleachers and smoothers of the linen, or to the dyers and dressers of the cloth! The nature of agriculture, indeed, does not admit of so many subdivisions of labour, not of so complete a separation of one business from another, as manufactures. It is impossible to separate so entirely, the business of the grazier from that of the corn-farmer, as the trade of the carpenter is commonly separated from that of the smith. The spinner is almost always a distinct person from the weaver; but the ploughman, the harrower, the sower of the seed, and the reaper of the corn, are often the same. The occasions for those different sorts of labour returning with the different seasons of the year, it is impossible that one man should be constantly employed in any one of them. This impossibility of making so complete and entire a separation of all the different branches of labour employed in agriculture, is perhaps the reason why the improvement of the productive powers of labour in this art, does not always keep pace with their improvement in manufactures. The most opulent nations, indeed, generally excel all their neighbors in agriculture as well as in manufactures; but they are commonly more distinguished by their superiority in the latter than in the former.

Their lands are in general better cultivated, and having more labour and expense bestowed upon them, produce more in proportion to the extent and natural fertility of the ground. But this superiority of produce is seldom much more than in proportion to the superiority of labour and expense. In agriculture, the labour of the rich country is not always much more productive than that of the poor; or, at least, it is never so much more productive, as it commonly is in manufactures. The corn of the rich country, therefore, will not always, in the same degree of goodness, come cheaper to market than that of the poor. The corn of Poland, in the same degree of goodness, is as cheap as that of France, notwithstanding the superior opulence and improvement of the latter country. The corn of France is, in the corn provinces, fully as good, and in most years nearly about the same price with the corn of England, though, in opulence and improvement, France is perhaps inferior to England. The corn-lands of England, however, are better cultivated than those of France, and the cornlands of France are said to be much better cultivated than those of Poland. But though the poor country, notwithstanding the inferiority of its cultivation, can, in some measure, rival the rich in the cheapness and goodness of its corn, it can pretend to no such competition in its manufactures; at least if those manufactures suit the soil, climate, and situation of the rich country. The silks of France are better and cheaper than those of England, because the silk manufacture, at least under the present high duties upon the importation of raw silk, does not so well suit the climate of England as that of France. But the hardware and the coarse woolens of England are beyond all comparison superior to those of France, and much cheaper too in the same degree of goodness. In Poland there are said to be scarce any manufactures of any kind, a few of those coarser household manufactures excepted, without which no country can well subsist.

This great increase of the quantity of work, which, in consequence of the division of labour, the same number of people are capable of performing, is owing to three different circumstances; first, to the increase of dexterity in every particular workman; secondly, to the saving of the time which is commonly lost in passing from one species of work to another; and lastly, to the invention of a great number of machines which facilitate and abridge labour, and enable one man to do the work of many. . . .

This division of labour, from which so many advantages are derived, is not originally the effect of any human wisdom, which foresees and intends that general opulence to which it gives occasion. It is the necessary, though very slow and gradual, consequence of a certain propensity in human nature which has in view no such extensive utility; the propensity to truck, barter, and exchange one thing for another. . . .

As it is the power of exchanging that gives occasion to the division of labour, so the extent of this division must always be limited by the extent of that power, or, in other words, by the extent of the market. When the market is very small, no person can have any encouragement to dedicate himself entirely to one employment, for want of the power to exchange all that surplus part of the produce of his own labour, which is over and above his own consumption, for such parts of the produce of other men's labour as he has occasion for. . . .

When the division of labour has been once thoroughly established, it is but a very small part of a man's wants which the produce of his own labour can supply. He supplies the far greater part of them by exchanging that surplus part of the produce of his own labour, which is over and above his own consumption, for such parts of the produce of other men's labour as he has occasion for. Every man thus lives by exchanging, or becomes in some measure a merchant, and the society itself grows to be what is properly a commercial society. . . .

Money has become in all civilized nations the universal instrument of commerce, by the intervention of which goods of all kinds are bought and sold, or exchanged for one another.

What are the rules which men naturally observe in exchanging them either for money or for one another, I shall now proceed to examine. These rules determine what may be called the relative or exchangeable value of goods.

The word value, it is to be observed, has two different meanings, and sometimes expresses the utility of some particular object, and sometimes the power of purchasing other goods which the possession of that object conveys. The one may be called "value in use"; the other, "value in exchange." The things which have the greatest value in use have frequently little or no value in exchange; and on the contrary, those which have the greatest value in exchange have frequently little or no value in use. Nothing is more useful than water: but it will purchase scarce any thing; scarce any thing can be had in exchange for it. A diamond, on the contrary, has scarce any value in use; but a very great quantity of other goods may frequently be had in exchange for it. . . .

Every man is rich or poor according to the degree in which he can afford to enjoy the necessaries, conveniences, and amusements of human life. But after the division of labour has once thoroughly taken place, it is but a very small part of these with which a man's own labour can supply him. The far greater part of them he must derive from the labour of other people, and he must be rich or poor according to the quantity of that labour which he can command, or which he can afford to purchase. The value of any commodity, therefore, to the person who possesses it, and who means not to use or consume it himself, but to exchange it for other commodities, is equal to the quantity of labour which it enables him to purchase or command. Labour, therefore, is the real measure of the exchangeable value of all commoditites.

The real price of every thing, what every thing really costs to the man who wants to acquire it, is the toil and trouble of acquiring it. What every thing is really worth to the man who has acquired it, and who wants to dispose of it or exchange it for something else, is the toil and trouble which it can save to himself, and which it can impose upon other people. What is bought with money or with goods is purchased by labour, as much as what we acquire by the toil of our own body. That money or those goods indeed save us this toil. They contain the value of a certain quantity of labour which we exchange for what is supposed at the time to contain the value of an equal quantity. Labour was the first price, the original purchase-money that was paid for all things. It was not by gold or by silver, but by labour, that all the wealth of the world was originally purchased; and its value, to those who possess it, and who want to exchange it form some new productions, is precisely equal to the quantity of labour which it can enable them to purchase or command.

Wealth, as Mr. Hobbes says, is power. But the person who either acquires, or succeeds to a great fortune, does not necessarily acquire or succeed to any political power, either civil or military. His fortune may, perhaps, afford him the means of acquiring both, but the mere possession of that fortune does not necessarily convey to him either. The power which that possession immediately and indirectly conveys to him, is the power of purchasing; a certain command over all the labour, or over all the produce of labour which is then in the market. His fortune is greater or less, precisely in proportion to the extent of this power; or to the quantity either of other men's labour, or, what is the same thing, of the produce of other men's labour, which it enables him to purchase or command. The exchangeable value of every thing must always be precisely equal to the extent of this power which it conveys to its owner.

But though labour be the real measure of the exchangeable value of all commodities, it is not that by which their value is commonly estimated. It is often difficult to ascertain the proportion between two different quantities of labour. The time spent in two different sorts of work will not always alone determine this proportion. The different degrees of hardship endured, and of ingenuity exercise, must likewise be taken into account. There may be more labour in an hour's hard work than in two hours easy business; or in an hour's application to a trade which it cost ten years labour to learn, than in a month's industry at an ordinary and obvious employment. But it is not easy to find any accurate measure either of hardship or ingenuity. In exchanging indeed the different productions of different sorts of labour for one another, some allowance is commonly made for both. It is adjusted, however, not by any accurate measure, but by the higgling and bargaining of the market, according to that sort of rough equality which, though not exact, is sufficient for carrying on the business of common life.

Every commodity besides, is more frequently exchanged for, and thereby compared with, other commodities than with labour. It is more natural therefore, to estimate its exchangeable value by the quantity of some other commodity than by that of the labour which it can purchase. The greater part of people too understand better what is meant by a quantity of labour. The one is a plain palpable object; the other an abstract notion, which, though it can be made sufficiently intelligible, is not altogether so natural and obvious.

But when barter ceases, and money has become the common instrument of commerce, every particular commodity is more frequently exchanged for money than for any other commodity. The butcher seldom carries his beef or his mutton to the baker, or the brewer, in order to exchange them for bread or for beer; but he carries them to the market, where he exchanges them for money, and afterwards exchanges that money for bread and for beer. The quantity of money which he gets for them regulates too the quantity of bread and beer which he can afterwards purchase. It is more natural and obvious to him, therefore, to estimate their value by the quantity of money, the commodity for which he immediately exchanges them, than by that of bread and beer, the commodities for which he can exchange them only by the intervention of another commodity; and rather to say that his butcher's meat is worth threepence or fourpence a pound, than that it is worth three or four pounds of bread, or three or four quarts of small beer. Hence it comes to pass, that the exchangeable value of every commodity is more frequently estimated by the quantity of money, than by the quantity either of labour or of any other commodity which can be had in exchange for it. . . .

In that early and rude state of society which precedes both the accumulation of stock and the appropriation of land, the proportion between the quantities of labour necessary for acquiring different objects seems to be the only circumstance which can afford any rule for exchanging them for one another. If among a nation of hunters, for example, it usually costs twice the labour to kill a beaver which it does to kill a deer, one beaver should naturally exchange for or be worth two deer. It is natural that what is usually the produce of two days or two hours labour, should be worth double what is usually the produce of one day's or one hour's labour.

If the one species of labour should be more severe then the other, some allowance will naturally be made for this superior hardship; and the produce of one hour's labour in the one way may frequently exchange for that of two hours' labour in the other.

Or if the one species of labour requires an uncommon degree of dexterity and ingenuity, the esteem which men have for such talents, will naturally give a value to their produce, superior to what would be due to the time employed about it. Such talents can seldom be acquired but in consequence of long application, and the superior value of their produce may frequently be no more than a reasonable compensation for the time and labour which must be spent in acquiring them. In the advanced state of society, allowances of this kind, for superior hardship and superior skill, are commonly made in the wages of labour; and something of the same kind must probably have taken place in its earliest and rudest period.

In this state of things, the whole produce of labour belongs to the labourer; and the quantity of labour commonly employed in acquiring or producing any commodity, is the only circumstance which can regulate quantity of labour which it ought commonly to purchase, command, or exchange for.

As soon as stock has accumulated in the hands of particular persons, some of them will naturally employ it in setting to work industrious people, whom they will supply with materials and subsistence, in order to make a profit by the sale of their work, or by what their labour adds to the value of the materials. In exchanging the complete manufacture either for money, for labour, or for other goods, over and above what may be sufficient to pay the price of the materials, and the wages of the workmen, something must be given for the profits of the undertaker of the work who hazards his stock in this adventure. The value which the workmen add to the materials, therefore, resolves itself in this case into two parts, of which the one pays their wages, the other the profits of their employer upon the whole stock of materials and wages which he advanced. He could have no interest to employ them, unless he expected from the sale of their work something more than what was sufficient to replace his stock to him; and he could have no interest to employ a great stock rather than a small one, unless his profits were to bear some proportion to the extent of his stock.

The profits of stock, it may perhaps be thought, are only a different name for the wages of a particular sort of labour, the labour of inspection and direction. They are, however, altogether different, are regulated by quite sufficient principles, and bear no proportion to the quantity, the hardship, or the ingenuity of this supposed labour of inspection and direction. They are regulated altogether by the value of the stock employed, and are greater or smaller in proportion to the extent of this stock. . . .

In this state of things, the whole produce of labour does not always belong to the labourer. He must in most cases share it with the owner of the stock which employs him. Neither is the quantity of labour commonly employed in acquiring or producing any commodity, the only circumstance which can regulate the quantity which it ought commonly to purchase, command, or exchange for. An additional quantity, it is evident, must be due for the profits of the stock which advanced the wages and furnished the materials of that labour.

As soon as the land of any country has all become private property, the landlords, like all other men, love to reap where they never sowed, and demand a rent even for its natural produce. The wood of the forest, the grass of the field, and all the natural fruits of the earth, which, when land was in common, cost the labourer only the trouble of gathering them, come, even to him, to have an additional price fixed upon them. He must give up to the landlord a portion of what his labour either collects or produces. This portion, or, what comes to the same thing, the price of this portion, constitutes the rent of land, and in the price of the greater part of commodities makes a third component part.

The real value of all the different component parts of price, it must be observed, is measured by the quantity of labour which they can, each of them, purchase or command. Labour measures the value not only of that part of price which resolves itself into labour, but of that which resolves itself into rent, and of that which resolves itself into profit.

In every society the price of every commodity finally resolves itself into some one or other, or all of those three parts; and in every improved society, all the three enter more or less, as component parts, into the price of the far greater part of commodities. . . .

The increase in the wages of labour necessarily

increases the price of many commoditites, by increasing that part of it which resolves itself into wages, and so far tends to diminish their consumption both at home and aboard. The same cause, however, which raises the wages of labour, the increase of stock, tends to increase its productive powers, and to make a smaller quantity of labour produce a greater quantity of work. The owner of the stock which employs a great number of labourers, necessarily endeavors, for his own advantage, to make such a proper division and distribution of employment, that they may be enabled to produce the greatest quantity of work possible. For the same reason, he endeavors to supply them with the best machinery which either he or they can think of. What takes place among the labourers in a particular workhouse, takes place, for the same reason, among those of a great society. The greater their number, the more they naturally divide themselves into different classes and subdivisions of employment. More heads are occupied in inventing the most proper machinery for executing the work of each, and it is, therefore, more likely to be invented. There are many commodities, therefore, which in consequence of these improvements, come to be produced by so much less labour than before, that the increase of its price is more than compensated by the diminution of its quantity.

John Stuart Mill

One can seek forever in the writings of John Locke and Adam Smith and never find the word "capitalism." The idea, however, was developed by their disciples and their opponents. None of the figures of this period imagined the effects of the Industrial Revolution and the massive growth of the modern corporation, but their ideas fueled these developments, and some of their greatest disciples lead us to the next great ethicist of modern economic theory, J. S. Mill.

David Ricardo studied the relationships of labor and capital. He was a capitalist, but he also recognized that the situation of labor was rather grim. The "enclosure laws" in England, rooted in the new theories of property, had driven marginal farmers off the land, and now industrialization was driving them into unemployment or into the mines and factories at subsistence wages. Slums grew, and the reactions were many. On the one hand, the Rev. Thomas Malthus held that scarcity was made worse by the fact that the poor have more babies than the other classes. This problem could, he thought, only be solved by the survival of the strong or by the restraint of the birth rate (an idea that influenced modern attempts to reform the behavior of the poor). On the other hand, Thomas Carlyle believed in a natural plenty that had been distorted by greed. He vigorously attacked the rationalism, calculation, and individualism that brought the reorganization of everything for economic purposes. He called for a recovery of "eternal ideals" and community by those who substituted novelty for tradition, pleasure for happiness, and interests for the duty of station. Both got a wide hearing.

These theorists, for different reasons, wrote of an inevitable conflict of interest between landlords and factory owners on the one hand and tenant farmers and workers on the other — in other words, between those who got profits and those who got wages. Whereas previously the movements toward capitalism involved a tension between new and traditional ways of doing things, now we see an emerging tension between capitalist and socialist (or communitarian) understandings of the new. The interpretation of change by means of conflict and the presumption that economic factors are the decisive ones in civilization provide the basis of "economistic" understandings of the common life among many capitalists and socialists alike.

It is in this context that we turn to J. S. Mill, who, along with Jeremy Bentham, represents "utilitarianism" — that form of teleological ethics that defines the ends toward which we ought to act in terms of the greater good for the greater number, as determined by calculations of pleasure and pain and an informed sense of qualitative goods.

Mill presents an interpretation of capitalism as it emerged in the nineteenth century that is still held today by "liberal" thinkers around the world. In contrast to Hobbes and Locke, who believe that humanity is free and must find order, Mill thinks that the central issue is constrictive order, and that we must seek emancipation for those who benefit least from contemporary arrangements. He is as impatient with discussion of moral law or human rights or reason as he is with theology, for in his view all claims must be evaluated by the principle of utility — that is, according to the consequences as measured by pleasure or pain as known in the practical experience of the quality of life.

Mill also rejects the view that scarcity is natural; instead, he presumes that plenty is potentially available but that some keep others poor for their own benefit. Thus, while he affirms the necessity of competition and a free market, he also endorses socialist and communitarian experiments that promise "social change" or "social justice," terms invented in his day and destined to be used widely in ours.

Private Property and Its Critics

John Stuart Mill

. . . . Private property, as an institution, did not owe its origin to any of those considerations of utility, which plead for the maintenance of it when established. Enough is known of rude ages, both from history and from analogous states of society in our own time, to show that tribunals (which always precede laws) were originally established, not to determine rights, but to repress violence and terminate quarrels. With this object chiefly in view, they naturally enough gave legal effect to first occupancy, by treating as the aggressor the person who first commenced violence, by turning, or attempting to turn, another out of possession. The preservation of the peace, which was the original object of civil government, was thus attained: while by confirming, to those who already possessed it, even what was not the fruit of personal exertion, a guarantee was incidentally given to them and others that they would be protected in what was so. . . .

The assailants of the principle of individual property may be divided into two classes: those whose scheme implies absolute equality in the distribution of the physical means of life and enjoyment, and those who admit inequality, but grounded on some principle, or supposed principle, of justice or general expediency, and not, like so many of the existing social inequalities, dependent on accident alone. At the head of the first class, as the earliest of those belonging to the present generation, must be placed Mr. Owen and his followers. M. Louis Blanc and M. Cabet have

Excerpts from *Political Economy* (1848), pp. 201-20, 746-94.

more recently become conspicuous as apostles of similar doctrines (though the former advocates equality of distribution only as a transition to a still higher standard of justice, that all should work according to their capacity, and receive according to their wants). The characteristic name for this economical system is Communism, a word of continental origin, only of late introduced into this country. The word Socialism, which originated among the English Communists, and was assumed by them as a name to designate their own doctrine, is now . . . on the Continent, employed in a larger sense; not necessarily implying Communism, or the entire abolition of private property, but applied to any system which requires that the land and the instruments of production should be the property, not of individuals, but of communities or associations, or of the government. Among such systems, the two of highest intellectual pretension are those which, from the names of their real or reputed authors, have been called St. Simonism and Fourierism; the former defunct as a system, but which during the few years of its public promulgation sowed the seeds of nearly all the Socialist tendencies which have since spread so widely in France: the second, still flourishing in the number, talent, and zeal of its adherents.

Whatever may be the merits or defects of these various schemes, they cannot be truly said to be impracticable. No reasonable person can doubt that a village community, composed of a few thousand inhabitants, cultivating in joint ownership the same extent of land which at present feeds that number of people, and producing by combined labour and the most improved processes the manufactured articles which they required, could raise an amount of production sufficient to maintain them in comfort; and would find the means of obtaining, and if need be, exacting, the quantity of labour necessary for this purpose, from every member of the association who was capable of work. . . .

If, therefore, the choice were to be made between Communism with all its chances, and the present state of society with all its sufferings and injustices; if the institution of private property necessarily carried with it as a consequence, that the produce of labour should be apportioned as we now see it, almost in an inverse ratio to the labour — the largest portions to those who have never worked at all, the next largest to those whose work is almost nominal, and so in a descending scale, the remuneration dwindling as the work grows harder and more disagreeable, until the most fatiguing and exhausting bodily labour cannot count with certainty on being able to earn even the necessaries of life; if this or Communism were the alternative, all the difficulties, great or small, of Communism would be but as dust in the balance. But to make the comparison applicable, we must compare Communism at its best, with the régime of individual property, not as it is, but as it might be made. The principle of private property has never yet had a fair trial in any country; and less so, perhaps, in this country than in some others. The social arrangements of modern Europe commenced from a distribution of property which was the result, not of just partition, or acquisition by industry, but of conquest and violence: and notwithstanding what industry has been doing for many centuries to modify the work of force, the system still retains many and large traces of its origin. The laws of property have never yet conformed to the principles on which the justification of private property rests. They have made property of things which never ought to be property, and absolute property where only a qualified property ought to exist. They have not held the balance fairly between human beings, but have heaped impediments upon some, to give advantage to others; they have purposely fostered inequalities, and prevented all from starting fair in the race. That all should indeed start on perfectly equal terms is inconsistent with any law of private property: but if as much pains as has been taken to aggravate the inequality of chances arising from the natural working of the principle, had been taken to temper that inequality by every means not subversive of the principle itself; if the tendency of legislation had been to favour the diffusion, instead of the concentration of wealth — to encourage the subdivision of the large masses, instead of striving to keep them together; the principle of individual property would have been found to have no necessary connexion with the physical and social evils which almost all Socialist writers assume to be inseparable from it.

Private property, in every defence made of it, is supposed to mean the guarantee to individuals of the fruits of their own labour and abstinence. The guarantee to them of the fruits of the labour and abstinence of others, transmitted to them without any merit or exertion of their own, is not of the essence of the institution, but a mere incidental consequence which, when it reaches a certain height, does not promote, but conflicts with, the ends which render private property legitimate. To judge of the final destination of the institution of property, we must suppose everything rectified which causes the institution to work in a manner opposed to that equitable principle, of proportion between remuneration and exertion, on which in every vindication of it that will bear the light it is assumed to be grounded. We must also suppose two conditions realized, without which neither Communism nor any other laws or institutions could make the condition of the mass of mankind other than degraded and miserable. One of these conditions is universal education; the other, a due limitation of the numbers of the community. With these there could be no poverty, even under the present social institutions: and these being supposed, the question of Socialism is not, as generally stated by Socialists, a question of flying to the sole refuge against the evils which now bear down humanity; but a mere question of comparative advantages, which futurity must determine. We are too ignorant either of what individual agency in its best form, or Socialism in its best form, can accomplish, to be qualified to decide which of the two will be the ultimate form of human society.

If a conjecture may be hazarded, the decision will probably depend mainly on one consideration, viz. which of the two systems is consistent with the greatest amount of human liberty and spontaneity. After the means of subsistence are assured, the next in strength of the personal wants of human beings is liberty; and (unlike the physical wants, which as civilization advances become more moderate and more amenable to control) it increase instead of diminishing in intensity as the intelligence and the moral faculties are more developed. The perfection both of social arrangements and of practical morality would be, to secure to all persons complete independence and freedom of action, subject to no restriction but that of not doing injury to others: and the education which taught or the social institutions which required them to exchange the control of their own actions for any amount of comfort or affluence, or to renounce liberty for the sake of equality, would deprive them of one of the most elevated characteristics of human nature. It remains to be discovered how far the preservation of this characteristic would be found compatible with the Communistic organization of society. No doubt this, like all the other objections to the Socialist schemes, is vastly exaggerated. The members of the association need not be required to live together more than they do now, nor need they be controlled in the disposal of their individual share of the produce, and of the probably large amount of leisure which, if they limited their production to things really worth producing, they would possess. Individuals need not be chained to an occupation, or to a particular locality. The restraints of Communism would be freedom in comparison with the present condition of the majority of the human race. The generality of labourers in this and most other countries have as little choice of occupation or freedom of locomotion, are practically as dependent on fixed rules and on the will of others, as they could be on any system short of actual slavery; to say nothing of the entire domestic subjection of one half the species, to which it is the signal honour of Owenism and most other forms of Socialism that they assign equal rights, in all respects, with those of the hitherto dominant sex. But it is not by comparison with the present bad state of society that the claims of Communism can be estimated; nor is it sufficient that it should promise greater personal and mental freedom than is now enjoyed by those who have not enough of either to deserve the name. The question is, whether there would be any asylum left for individuality of character; whether public opinion would not be a tyrannical yoke; whether the absolute dependence of each on all, and surveillance of each by all, would not grind all down into a tame uniformity of thoughts, feelings, and actions. This is already one of the glaring evils of the existing state of society, notwithstanding a much greater diversity of education and pursuits, and a much less absolute dependence of the individual on the mass, than would exist in the Communistic régime. No society in which eccentricity is a matter of reproach can be in a wholesome state. It is yet to be ascertained whether the Communistic scheme would be consistent with that multiform development of human nature, those manifold unlikenesses, that diversity of tastes and talents, and variety of intellectual points of view, which not only form a great part of the interest of human life, but by bringing intellects into stimulating collision, and by presenting to each innumerable notions that he would not have conceived of himself, are the mainspring of mental and moral progression. . . .

The two elaborate forms of non-communistic Socialism known as St. Simonism and Fourierism are totally free from the objections usually urged against Communism; and though they are open to others of their own, yet by the great intellectual power which in many respects distinguishes them, and by their large and philosophic treatment of some of the fundamental problems of society and morality, they may justly be counted among the most remarkable productions of the past and present age. . . .

The most skillfully combined, and with the greatest foresight of objections, of all the forms of Socialism, is that commonly known as Fourierism. This system does not contemplate the abolition of private property, nor even of inheritance; on the contrary, it avowedly takes into consideration, as an element in the distribution of the produce, capital as well as labour. . . .

The institution of property, when limited to its essential elements, consists in the recognition, in each person, of a right to the exclusive disposal of what he or she have produced by their own exertions, or received either by gift of by fair agreement, without force or fraud, from those who produced it. The foundation of the whole is the right of producers to what they themselves have produced. It may be objected, therefore, to the institution as it now exists, that it recognizes rights of property in individuals over things which they have not produced. For example (it may be said) the operatives in a manufactory create, by their labour and skill, the whole produce; yet, instead of its belonging to them, the law gives them only their stipulated hire, and transfers the produce to some one who has merely supplied the funds, without perhaps contributing anything to the work itself, even in the form of superintendence. The answer to this is, that the labour of manufacture is only one of the conditions which must combine for the production of the commodity. The labour cannot be car-

ried on without materials and machinery, nor without a stock of necessaries provided in advance to maintain the labourers during the production. All these things are the fruits of previous labour. If the labourers were possessed of them, they would not need to divide the produce with any one; but while they have them not, an equivalent must be given to those who have, both for the antecedent labour, and for the abstinence by which the produce of that labour, instead of being expended on indulgences, has been reserved for this use. The capital may not have been, and in most cases was not, created by the labour and abstinence of some former person, who may indeed have been wrongfully dispossessed of it, but who, in the present age of the world, much more probably transferred his claims to the present capitalist by gift or voluntary contract: and the abstinence at least must have been continued by each successive owner, down to the present. If it be said, as it may with truth, that those who have inherited the savings of others have an advantage which they may have in no way deserved, over the industrious whose predecessors have not left them anything; I not only admit, but strenuously contend, that this unearned advantage should be curtailed, as much as is consistent with justice to those who thought fit to dispose of their savings by giving them to their descendants. But while it is true that the labourers are at a disadvantage compared with those whose predecessors have saved, it is also true that the labourers are far better off than if those predecessors had not saved. They share in the advantage, though not to an equal extent with the inheritors. The terms of cooperation between present labour and the fruits of past labour and saving, are a subject for adjustment between the two parties. Each is necessary to the other. The capitalists can do nothing without labourers, nor the labourers without capital. If the labourers compete for employment, the capitalists on their part compete for labour to the full extent of the circulating capital of the country. Competition is often spoken of as if it were necessarily a cause of misery and degradation to the labouring class; as if high wages were not precisely as much a product of competition as low wages. The remuneration of labour is as much the result of the law of competition in the United States, as it is in Ireland, and much more completely so than in England.

The right of property includes then, the freedom of acquiring by contract. The right of each to what he has produced implies a right to what has been produced by others, if obtained by their free consent; since the producers must either have given it from good will, or exchanged it for what they esteemed an equivalent, and to prevent them from doing so would be to infringe their right of property in the product of their own industry. . . .

*   *   *

It must always have been seen, more or less distinctly, by political economists, that the increase of wealth is not boundless: that at the end of what they term the progressive state lies the stationary state, that all progress in wealth is but a postponement of this, and that each step in advance is an approach to it. We have now been led to recognize that this ultimate goal is at all times near enough to be fully in view; that we are always on the verge of it, and that if we have not reached it long ago, it is because the goal itself flies before us. The richest and most prosperous countries would very soon attain the stationary state, if no further improvements were made in the productive arts, and if there were a suspension of the overflow of capital from those countries into the uncultivated or ill-cultivated regions of the earth.

This impossibility of ultimately avoiding the stationary state — this irresistible necessity that the stream of human industry should finally spread itself out into an apparently stagnant sea — must have been, to the political economists of the last two generations, an unpleasing and discouraging prospect; for the tone and tendency of their speculations goes completely to identify all that is economically desirable with the progressive state, and with that alone. . . .

The doctrine that, to however distant a time incessant struggling may put off our doom, the progress of society must "end in shallows and in miseries," far from being, as many people still believe, a wicked invention of Mr. Malthus, was either expressly or tacitly affirmed by his most distinguished predecessors, and can only be successfully combated on his principles. Before attention had been directed to the principle of population as the active force in determining the remuneration of labour, the increase of mankind was virtually treated as a constant quantity; it was,

at all events, assumed that in the natural and normal state of human affairs population must constantly increase, from which it followed that a constant increase of the means of support was essential to the physical comfort of the mass of mankind. The publication of Mr. Malthus' *Essay* is the era from which better views of this subject must be dated; and notwithstanding the acknowledged errors of his first edition, few writers have done more than himself, in the subsequent editions, to promote these juster and more hopeful anticipations.

Even in a progressive state of capital, in old countries, a conscientious or prudential restraint on population is indispensable, to prevent the increase of numbers from outstripping the increase of capital, and the condition of the classes who are at the bottom of society from being deteriorated. Where there is not, in the people, or in some very large proportion of them, a resolute resistance to this deterioration — a determination to preserve an established standard of comfort — the condition of the poorest class sinks, even in a progressive state, to the lowest point which they will consent to endure. The same determination would be equally effectual to keep up their condition in the stationary state, and would be quite as likely to exist. Indeed, even now, the countries in which the greatest prudence is manifested in the regulating of population are often those in which capital increases least rapidly. Where there is no indefinite prospect of employment for increased numbers, there is apt to appear less necessity for prudential restraint. If it were evident that a new hand could not obtain employment but by displacing, or succeeding to, one already employed, the combined influences of prudence and public opinion might in some measure be relied on for restricting the coming generation within the numbers necessary for replacing the present. . . .

Those who do not accept the present very early stage of human improvement as its ultimate type, may be excused for being comparatively indifferent to the kind of economical progress which excites the congratulations of ordinary politicians; the mere increase of production and accumulation. For the safety of national independence it is essential that a country should not fall much behind its neighbours in these things. But in themselves they are of little importance, so long as either the increase of population or anything else prevents the mass of the people from reaping any part of the benefit of them. I know not why it should be matter of congratulation that persons who are already richer than any one needs to be, should have doubled their means of consuming things which give little or no pleasure except as representative of wealth; or that numbers of individuals should pass over, every year, from the middle classes into a richer class, or from the class of the occupied rich to that of the unoccupied. It is only in the backward countries of the world that increased production is still an important object: in those most advanced, what is economically needed is a better distribution, of which one indispensable means is a stricter restraint on population. Levelling institutions, either of a just or of an unjust kind, cannot alone accomplish it; they may lower the heights of society, but they cannot, of themselves, permanently raise the depths.

On the other hand, we may suppose this better distribution of property attained, by the joint effect of the prudence and frugality of individuals, and of a system of legislation favouring equality of fortunes, so far as is consistent with the just claim of the individual to the fruits, whether great or small, of his or her own industry. We may suppose, for instance . . . , a limitation of the sum which any one person may acquire by gift or inheritance to the amount sufficient to constitute a moderate independence. Under this twofold influence society would exhibit these leading features: a well-paid and affluent body of labourers; no enormous fortunes, except what were earned and accumulated during a single lifetime; but a much larger body of persons than at present, not only exempt from the coarser toils, but with sufficient leisure, both physical and mental, from mechanical details, to cultivate freely the graces of life, and afford examples of them to the classes less favourably circumstanced for their growth. . . .

Whether the aggregate produce [of industry] increases absolutely or not, is a thing in which, after a certain amount has been obtained, neither the legislator nor the philanthropist need feel any strong interest: but, that it should increase relatively to the number of those who share in it, is of the utmost possible importance; and this (whether the wealth of mankind be stationary, or increasing at the most rapid rate ever known in an old country), must depend on the opinions and habits of the most numerous class, the class of manual labourers.

When I speak, either in this place or elsewhere, of "the labouring classes," or of labourers as a "class," I use those phrases in compliance with custom, and as descriptive of an existing, but by no means a necessary or permanent, state of social relations. I do not recognize as either just or salutary, a state of society in which there is any "class" which is not labouring; any human beings, exempt from bearing their share of the necessary labours of human life, except those unable to labour, or who have fairly earned rest by previous toil. So long, however, as the great social evil exists of a non-labouring class, labourers also constitute a class, and may be spoken of, though only provisionally, in that character.

Considered in its moral and social aspect, the state of the labouring people has latterly been a subject of much more speculation and discussion than formerly; and the opinion that it is not now what it ought to be, has become very general. The suggestions which have been promulgated, and the controversies which have been excited, on detached points rather than on the foundations of the subject, have put in evidence the existence of two conflicting theories, respecting the social position desirable for manual labourers. The one may be called the theory of dependence and protection, the other that of self-dependence.

According to the former theory, the lot of the poor, in all things which affect them collectively, should be regulated *for* them, not *by* them. They should not be required or encouraged to think for themselves, or give to their own reflection or forecast an influential voice in the determination of their destiny. It is supposed to be the duty of the higher classes to think for them, and to take the responsibility of their lot, as the commander and officers of an army take that of the soldiers composing it. This function, it is contended, the higher classes should prepare themselves to perform conscientiously, and their whole demeanor should impress the poor with a reliance on it, in order that, while yielding passive and active obedience to the rules prescribed for them, they may resign themselves in all other respects to a trustful *insouciance*, and repose under the shadow of their protectors. The relation between rich and poor, according to this theory (a theory also applied to the relation between men and women) should be only partly authoritative; it should be amiable, moral, and sentimental: affectionate tutelage on the one side, respectful and grateful deference on the other. The rich should be *in loco parentis* to the poor, guiding and restraining them like children. Of spontaneous action on their part there should be no need. They should be called on for nothing but to do their day's work, and to be moral and religious. Their morality and religion should be provided for them by their superiors, who should see them properly taught it, and should do all that is necessary to ensure their being, in return for labour and attachment, properly fed, clothed, housed, spiritually edified, and innocently amused.

This is the ideal of the future, in the minds of those who dissatisfaction with the Present assumes the form of affection and regret toward the Past. Like other ideals, it exercises an unconscious influence on the opinions and sentiments of numbers who never consciously guide themselves by any ideal. It has also this in common with other ideals, that it has never been historically realized. It makes its appeal to our imaginative sympathies in the character of a restoration of the good times of our forefathers. But no times can be pointed out in which the higher classes of this or any other country performed a part even distantly resembling the one assigned to them in this theory. It is an idealization, grounded on the conduct and character of here and there an individual. All privileged and powerful classes, as such, have used their power in the interest of their own selfishness, and have indulged their self-importance in despising, and not in lovingly caring for, those who were, in their estimation, degraded, by being under the necessity of working for their benefit. I do not affirm that what has always been must always be, or that human improvement has no tendency to correct the intensely selfish feelings engendered by power; but though the evil may be lessened, it cannot be eradicated, until the power itself is withdrawn. This, at least, seems to me undeniable, that long before the superior classes could be sufficiently improved to govern in the tutelary manner supposed, the inferior class would be too much improved to be so governed. . . .

It is on a far other basis that the well-being and well-doing of the labouring people must henceforth rest. The poor have come out of leading-strings, and cannot any longer be governed or treated like children. To their own qualities must now be commended the care of their destiny. . . .

It appears to me impossible but that the increase of intelligence, of education, and of the love of independence among the working classes, must be attended with the corresponding growth of the good sense which manifests itself in provident habits of conduct, and that population, therefore, will bear a gradually diminishing ratio to capital and employment. This most desirable result would be much accelerated by another change, which lies in the direct line of the best tendencies of the time; the opening of industrial occupations freely to both sexes. The same reasons which make it no longer necessary that the poor should depend on the rich, make it equally unnecessary that women should depend on men; and the least which justice requires is that law and custom should not enforce dependence (when the correlative protection has become superfluous) by ordaining that a woman, who does not happen to have a provision by inheritance, shall have scarcely any means open to her of gaining a livelihood, except as a wife and mother. Let women who prefer that occupation, adopt it; but that there should be no option, no other *carrière* possible for the great majority of women, except in the humbler departments of life, is a flagrant social injustice. The ideas and institutions by which the accident of sex is made the groundwork of an inequality of legal rights, and a forced dissimilarity of social functions, must ere long be recognized as the greatest hindrance to moral, social, and even intellectual improvement. On the present occasion I shall only indicate, among the probable consequences of the industrial and social independence of women, a great diminution of the evil of over-population. It is by devoting one-half of the human species to that exclusive function, by making it fill the entire life of one sex, and interweave itself with almost all the objects of the other, that the animal instinct in question is nursed into the disproportionate preponderance which it has hitherto exercised in human life. . . .

Hitherto there has been no alternative for those who lived by their labour, but that of labouring either each for himself alone, or for a master. But the civilizing and improving influences of association, and the efficiency and economy of production on a large scale, may be obtained without dividing the producers into two parties with hostile interests and feelings, the many who do the work being mere servants under the command of the one who supplies the funds, and having no interests of their own in the enterprise except to earn their wages with as little labour as possible. The speculations and discussions of the last fifty years, and the events of the last thirty, are abundantly conclusive on this point. If the improvement which even triumphant military despotism has only retarded, not stopped, shall continue its course, there can be little doubt that the *status* of hired labourers will gradually tend to confine itself to the description of work-people whose low moral qualities render them unfit for anything more independent: and that the relation of masters and work-people will be gradually superseded by partnership, in one of two forms: in some cases, association of the labourers with the capitalist; in others, and perhaps finally in all, association of labourers among themselves.

The first of these forms of association has long been practised, not indeed as a rule, but as an exception. In several departments of industry there are already cases in which every one who contributes to the work, either by labour or by pecuniary resources, has a partner's interest in it, proportional to the value of his contribution. It is already a common practice to remunerate those in whom peculiar trust is reposed, by means of a percentage on the profits: and cases exist in which the principle is, with excellent success, carried down to the class of mere manual labourers. . . .

The form of association, however, which if mankind continue to improve, must be expected in the end to predominate, is not that which can exist between a capitalist as chief, and work-people without a voice in the management, but the association of the labourers themselves on terms of equality, collectively owning the capital with which they carry on their operations, and working under managers elected and removable by themselves. So long as this idea remained in a state of theory, in the writings of Owen or of Louis Blanc, it may have appeared, to the common modes of judgment, incapable of being realized, and not likely to be tried unless by seizing on the existing capital, and confiscating it for the benefit of the labourers; which is even now imagined by many persons, and pretended by more, both in England and on the Continent, to be the meaning and purpose of Socialism. But there is a capacity of exertion and self-denial in the masses of mankind, which is never known but on the rare occasions on which it is appealed to in the name of some great idea or elevated sentiment. Such an appeal was made by the French Revolution of 1848. For the first time it then seemed to the intelligent and generous of the working classes of a great nation that they had obtained a government who sincerely desired the freedom and dignity of the many, and who did not look upon it as their natural and legitimate state to be instruments of production, worked for the benefit of the possessors of capital. Under this encouragement, the ideas sown by Socialist writers, of an emancipation of labour to be effected by means of association, throve and fructified; and many working people came to the resolution, not only that they would work for one another, instead of working for a master tradesman or manufacturer, but that they would also free themselves, at whatever cost of labour or privation, from the necessity of paying, out of the produce of their industry, a heavy tribute for the use of capital; that they would extinguish this tax, not by robbing the capitalists of what they or their predecessors had acquired by labour and preserved by economy, but by honestly acquiring capital for themselves. If only a few operatives had attempted this arduous task, or if, while many attempted it, a few only had succeeded, their success might have been deemed to furnish no argument for their system as a permanent mode of industrial organization. But, excluding all the instances of failure, there exist, or existed a short time ago, upwards of a hundred successful, and many eminently prosperous, associations of operatives in Paris alone, besides a considerable number in the departments. . . .

It is not in France alone that these associations have commenced a career of prosperity. To say nothing at present of Germany, Piedmont (N. Italy), and Switzerland (where the Konsum-Verein of Zürich is one of the most prosperous cooperative associations in Europe), England can produce cases of success rivaling even those which I have cited from France. Under the impulse commenced by Mr. Owen, and more recently propagated by the writings and personal efforts of a band of friends, chiefly clergymen and barristers, to whose noble exertions too much praise can scarcely be given, the good seed was widely sown; the necessary alterations in the English law of partnership were obtained from Parliament. . . . many industrial associations, and a still greater number of cooperative stores for retail purchases, were founded. . . .

Associations like those which we have described, by the very process of their success, are a course of education in those moral and active qualities by which alone success can be either deserved or attained. As associations multiplied, they would tend more and more to absorb all work-people, except those who have too little understanding, or too little virtue, to be capable of learning to act on any other system than that of narrow selfishness. As this change proceeded, owners of capital would gradually find it to their advantage, instead of maintaining the struggle of the old system with work-people of only the worst description, to lend their capital to the associations; to do this at a diminishing rate of interest, and at last, perhaps, even to exchange their capital for terminable annuities. In this or some such mode, the existing accumulations of capital might honestly, and by a kind of spontaneous process, become in the end the joint property of all who participate in their productive employment: a transformation which, thus effected, (and assuming of course that both sexes participate equally in the rights and in the government of the association,) would be the nearest approach to social justice, and the most beneficial ordering of industrial affairs for the universal good, which it is possible at present to foresee.

I agree, then, with the Socialist writers in their conception of the form which industrial operations tend to assume in the advance of improvement; and I entirely share their opinion that the time is ripe for commencing this transformation, and that it should by all just and effectual means be aided and encouraged. But while I agree and sympathize with Socialists in this practical portion of their aims, I utterly dissent from the most conspicuous and vehement part of their teaching, their declamations against competition. With moral conceptions in many respects far ahead of the existing arrangements of society, they have in general very confused and erroneous notions of its actual working; and one of their greatest errors, as I conceive, is to charge upon competition all the economical evils which at present exist. They forget that wherever competition is not, monopoly is; and that monopoly, in all its forms, is the taxation of the industrious for the support of indolence, if not of plunder. They forget, too, that with the exception of competition among labourers, all other competition is for the benefit of the labourers, by cheapening the articles they consume; that competition even in the labour market is a source not of low but of high wages, wherever the competition *for* labour exceeds the competition *of* labour, as in America, in the colonies, and in the skilled trades; and never could be a cause of low wages, save by the overstocking of the labour market through the too great numbers of the labourers' families; while, if the supply of labourers is excessive, not even Socialism can prevent their remuneration from being low. Besides, if association were universal, there would be no competition between labourer and labourer; and that between association and association would be for the benefit of the consumers, that is, of the associations; of the industrious classes generally.

I do not pretend that there are no inconveniences in competition, or that the moral objections urged against it by Socialist writers, as a source of jealousy and hostility among those engaged in the same occupation, are altogether groundless. But if competition has its evils, it prevents greater evils.

Immanuel Kant

The British Enlightenment philosophically shaped both the Puritan and the Industrial Revolutions. It had its deontological side (Locke), ethological side (Smith), and teleological side (Mill) — each with an interpretation of the human condition. They did not fully cohere. Yet they prompted the secularization of the state and the privatization of religion, and they reflected the growing neutralization of theological ethics in economics as well as the increased independence of business from both familial and political institutions. Life became increasingly complex. The bases of morality were less secure, but the nature and character of modern economics was illuminated and enhanced.

On the Continent, the Enlightenment took distinct forms, even as influences flooded back and forth across the channel with relative ease. There, the Enlightenment was less connected to extensions of religious toleration, constitutional government, and post-agriculture commerce than to intellectual movements in the universities, courts, and salons. In France, it captured the political *philosophes* — Voltaire, Diderot, Condorcet, and Holbach — and their anti-Christian (especially anti-Catholic) rationalism, which finally eventuated in the French Revolution.

In Germany, one of the greatest minds of modernity was shaken by reading the British and the French Enlightenment thinkers, and by the French Revolution generally. Immanuel Kant was deeply influenced by the Lutheran piety and morality of his parents; but he now viewed his convictions as merely a "dogmatic slumber." If the British and the French were correct, there was no way to know the difference between right and wrong in science or morality. Everything would become artificial; it could no longer be considered so natural or clearly revealed. Yet he was convinced that they

were, at least in part, correct. Kant admired the developments that linked freedom to equality in a consensual moral order and swept away centuries of superstition and tyranny, yet he feared that the new liberals bore within them the seeds of chaos in thought, opportunism in morality, and anarchy in politics, for they failed to clarify the basic principles of right and wrong that their reactionary opponents had already so long obscured. Kant spent his life arguing that principles can be known and do cohere with morality, equality, and freedom.

Late in life, Kant turned to economic questions by taking up the philosophy of law — specifically in regard to principles governing the laws of property, including intellectual property, and contract. He did not live in a pluralistic society, such as the Puritan and Industrial Revolutions had created in Britain, or in a society where political factions produced constant debate, as in France. Germany had no experience with democracy, few business corporations, and fewer independent associations (even much of family life was state controlled). Law was the primary means by which enlightened morality became operative in society.

Kant, like Locke, wanted to set forth the general principles of social justice. He thought that honest thinking would reveal to every sane adult certain basic laws, such as the duty to tell the truth, to keep promises, and to avoid treating other people as instruments. He thought that these were valid in all cultures, no matter what goals one pursued. He dismissed, in other words, ethological and teleological ethics in search of a deontological basis for morality — applied here to economic issues through law.

But we cannot limit Kant to the brief selection that follows, especially since a number of contemporary philosophers believe him to be the most important theorist for liberal societies. In a style more familiar to contemporary students, therefore, a brief selection from Harvard philosopher John Rawls, a follower of Kant, is included with him.

The Principles of the External Mine and Thine

Immanuel Kant

The meaning of "Mine" in Right.

Anything is *"Mine" by Right*, or is rightfully Mine, when I am so connected with it, that if any other Person should make use of it without my consent, he would do me a lesion or injury. The subjective condition of the use of anything, is *Possession* of it.

An *external* thing, however, as such could only be mine, if I may assume it to be possible that I can be wronged by the use which another might make of it *when it is not actually in my possession*. Hence it would be a contradiction to have anything External as one's own, were not the conception of Possession capable of two different meanings, as *sensible* Possession that is perceivable by the senses, and *rational* Possession that is perceivable only the by Intellect. By the former is to be understood a *physical* Possession, and by the latter, a purely *juridical* Possession of the same object.

The description of an Object as "*external* to me" may signify either that it is merely "different and distinct from me as a Subject," or that it is also "a thing placed *outside* of me, and to be found elsewhere in space or time." Taken in the first sense, the term Possession signifies "rational Possession." A rational or *intelligible* Possession, if such be possible, is Possession *viewed apart from physical holding or detention.*

* * *

From Immanuel Kant, *The Philosophy of Law*, trans. W. Hastie (1796; Edinburgh: T. & T. Clark, 1887), part 1, sections 1, 8, 10, 20, 22.

To have anything External as one's own is only possible in a Juridical or Civil State of Society under the regulation of a public legislative Power.

If, by word or deed, I declare my Will that some external thing shall be mine, I make a declaration that every other person is obliged to abstain from the use of this object of my exercise of Will; and this imposes an Obligation which no one would be under, without such a juridical act on my part. But the assumption of this Act, at the same time involves the admission that I am obliged reciprocally to observe a similar abstention towards every other in respect of what is externally theirs; for the Obligation in question arises from a universal Rule regulating the external juridical relations. Hence I am not obliged to let alone what another person declares to be externally his, unless every other person likewise secures me by a guarantee that he will act in relation to what is mine, upon the same principle. This guarantee of reciprocal and mutual abstention from what belongs to others, does not require a special juridical act for its establishment, but is already involved in the Conception of an external Obligation of Right, on account of the universality and consequently the reciprocity of the obligatoriness arising from a universal Rule. — Now a single Will, in relation to an external and consequently contingent Possession, cannot serve as a compulsory Law for all, because that would be to do violence to the Freedom which is in accordance with universal Laws. Therefore it is only a Will that binds every open, and as such a common, collective, and authoritative Will, that can furnish a guarantee of security to all. But the state of men under a universal, external, and public Legislation, conjoined with authority and power, is called the Civil state. There can therefore be an external Mine and Thine only in the Civil state of Society.

CONSEQUENCE — It follows, as a Corollary, that if it is juridically possible to have an external object as one's own, the individual Subject of possession must be allowed *to compel* or constrain every person, with whom a dispute as to the Mine or Thine of such a possession may arise, to enter along with himself into the relations of a Civil Constitution.

*   *   *

The General Principle of External Acquisition.

I acquire a thing when I act so that it becomes *mine*. — An external thing is *originally* mine, when it is mine even without the intervention of a juridical Act. An Acquisition is *original* and *primary*, when it is not derived from what another had already made his own.

There is nothing External that is as such originally mine; but anything external may be originally *acquired* when it is an object that no other person has yet made his. — A state in which the Mine and Thine are in common, cannot be conceived as having been at any time original. Such a state of things would have to be acquired by an external juridical Act, although there may be an original and common possession of an external object. Even if we think hypothetically of a state in which the Mine and Thine would be *originally* in common . . . it would still have to be distinguished from a *primeval* communion with things in common, sometimes supposed to be founded in the first period of the relations of Right among men, and which could not be regarded as based upon Principles like the former, but only upon History. Even under that condition the historic *Communio*, as a supposed primeval Community would always have to be viewed as acquired and derivative.

The Principle of external Acquisition, then, may be expressed thus: "Whatever I bring under my power according to the Law of external Freedom, of which as an object of my free activity of Will I have the capability of making use according to the Postulate of the Practical Reason, and which I will to become mine in conformity with the Idea of a possible united common Will, *is* mine." . . .

*   *   *

What Is Acquired by Contract?

But what is that, designated as "External," which I acquire by Contract? As it is only the Causality of the active Will of another, in respect of the Performance of something promised to me, I do not immediately acquire thereby an external Thing, but an Act of the Will in question, whereby a Thing is brought under my power so that I make it mine. — By the Contract, therefore, I acquire the Promise of another, as distinguished from the Thing promised; and yet something is thereby added to my Having and Possession. I have become the *richer in possession* by the Acquisition of an active Obligation that I can bring to bear upon the Freedom and Capability of another. — This my *Right*, however, is only a *personal* Right, valid only to the effect of acting upon a *particular* physical Person and specially upon the Causality of his Will, so that he shall *perform* something for me. It is not a *Real* Right upon that *Moral Person,* which is identified with the Idea of the united *Will of All* viewed *à priori,* and through which alone I can acquire a *Right valid against every Possessor of the Thing.* For, it is in this that all Right *in a Thing* consists. . . .

*   *   *

Nature of Personal Right of a Real Thing.

Personal Right of a real kind is the Right to the *possession* of an external object As a THING, and to the *use* of it As a PERSON. — The Mine and Thine embraced under this Right relate specially to the Family and Household; and the relations involved are those of free beings in reciprocal real interaction with each other. Through their relations and influence as Persons upon one another, in accordance with the principle of external Freedom as the *cause* of it, they form a Society composed as a whole of members standing in community with each other as Persons; and this constitutes the HOUSEHOLD. — The mode in which this social status is acquired by individuals, and the functions which prevail within it, proceed neither by arbitrary individual action, not by mere Contract, but by Law. And this Law as being not only a Right, but also as constituting Possession in reference to a Person, is a Right rising above all *mere* Real and Personal Right. It must, in fact, form the Right of Humanity in our own Person; and, as such, it has as its consequence a natural Permissive Law, by the favour of which such Acquisition becomes possible to us.

Two Principles of Justice

John Rawls

I shall now state in a provisional form the two principles of justice that I believe would be chosen in the original position. . . .

The first statement of the two principles reads a follows.

First: each person is to have an equal right to the most extensive basic liberty compatible with a similar liberty for others.

Second: social and economic inequalities are to be arranged so that they are both (a) reasonably expected to be to everyone's advantage, and (b) attached to positions and offices open to all. . . . [The Difference Principle]

By way of general comment, these principles primarily apply, as I have said, to the basic structure of society. They are to govern the assignment of rights and duties and to regulate the distribution of social and economic advantages. As their formulation suggests, these principles presuppose that the social structure can be divided into two more or less distinct parts, the first principle applying to the one, the second to the other. They distinguish between those aspects of the social system that define and secure the equal liberties of citizenship and those that specify and establish social and economic inequalities. The basic liberties of citizens are, roughly speaking, political liberty (the right to vote and to be eligible for public office) together with freedom of speech and assembly; liberty of conscience and freedom of thought; freedom of the person along with the right to hold (personal) property; and freedom from arbitrary income or organizational powers

From John Rawls, *A Theory of Justice* (Cambridge, MA: Harvard University Press, 1971), pp. 3-4, 18-19, 60-62, 64-65, 100-104.

on the ground that the disadvantages of those in one position are outweighed by the greater advantages of those in another. Much less can infringements of liberty be counterbalanced in this way. Applied to the basic structure, the principle of utility would have us maximize the sum of expectations of representative men (weighted by the number of persons they represent, on the classical view); and this would permit us to compensate for the losses of some by the gains of others. Instead, the two principles require that everyone benefit from economic and social inequalities. . . .

I wish to conclude this discussion of the two principles by explaining the sense in which they express an egalitarian conception of justice. Also I should like to forestall the objection to the principle of fair opportunity that it leads to a callous meritocratic society. In order to prepare the way for doing this, I note several aspects of the conception of justice that I have set out.

First we may observe that the difference principles gives some weight to the considerations singled out by the principle of redress. This is the principle that underserved inequalities call for redress; and since inequalities of birth and natural endowment are undeserved, these inequalities are to be somehow compensated for. Thus the principle holds that in order to treat all persons equally, to provide genuine equality of opportunity, society must give more attention to those with fewer native assets and to those born into the less favorable social positions. The idea is to redress the bias of contingencies in the direction of equality. In pursuit of this principle greater resources might be spent on the education of the less rather than the more intelligent, at least over a certain time of life, say the earlier years of school.

Now the principle of redress has not to my knowledge been proposed as the sole criterion of justice, as the single aim of the social order. It is plausible as most such principles are only as a prima facie principle, one that is to be weighed in the balance with others. For example, we are to weigh it against the principle to improve the average standard of life, or to advance the common good. But whatever other principles we hold, the claims of redress are to be taken into account. It is thought to represent one of the elements in our conception of justice. Now the difference principle is not of course the principle of redress. It does

not require society to try to even out handicaps as if all were expected to compete on a fair basis in the same race. But the difference principle would allocate resources in education, say, so as to improve the long-term expectation of the least favored. If this end is attained by giving more attention to the better endowed, it is permissible; otherwise not. And in making this decision, the value of education should not be assessed only in terms of economic efficiency and social welfare. Equally if not more important is the role of education in enabling a person to enjoy the culture of his society and to take part in its affairs, and in this way to provide for each individual a secure sense of his own worth.

Thus although the difference principle is not the same as that of redress, it does achieve some of the intent of the latter principle. It transforms the aims of the basic structure so that the total scheme of institutions no longer emphasizes social efficiency and technocratic values. . . .

The natural distribution is neither just nor unjust; nor is it unjust that men are born into society at some particular position. These are simply natural facts. What is just and unjust is the way that institutions deal with these facts. Aristocratic and caste societies are unjust because they make these contingencies the ascriptive basis for belonging to more or less enclosed and privileged social classes. The basic structure of these societies incorporates the arbitrariness found in nature. But there is not necessity for men to resign themselves to these contingencies. The social system is not an unchangeable order beyond human control but a pattern of human action. In justice as fairness men agree to share one another's fate. In designing institutions they undertake to avail themselves of the accidents of nature and social circumstance only when doing so is for the common benefit. The two principles are a fair way of meeting the arbitrariness of fortune; and while no doubt imperfect in other ways, the institutions which satisfy these principles are just. . . .

There is a natural inclination to object that those better situated deserve their greater advantages whether or not they are to the benefit of others. At this point it is necessary to be clear about the notion of desert. It is perfectly true that given a just system of cooperation as a scheme of public rules and the expectations set up by it, those who, with the prospect of improving their condition, have done what the system announces that it will reward are entitled to their advantages. In this sense the more fortunate have a claim to their better situation; their claims are legitimate expectations established by social institutions, and the community is obligated to meet them. But this sense of desert presupposes the existence of the cooperative scheme; it is irrelevant to the question whether in the first place the scheme is to be designed in accordance with the difference principle or some other criterion.

Perhaps some will think that the person with greater natural endowments deserves those assets and the superior character that made their development possible. Because he is more worthy in this sense, he deserves the greater advantages that he could achieve with them. This view, however, is surely incorrect. It seems to be one of the fixed points of our considered judgments that no one deserves his place in the distribution of native endowments, any more than one deserves one's initial starting place in society. The assertion that a man deserves the superior character that enables him to make the effort to cultivate his abilities is equally problematic; for his character depends in large part upon fortunate family and social circumstances for which he can claim no credit. The notion of desert seems not to apply to these cases. Thus the more advantaged representative man cannot say that he deserves and therefore has a right to a scheme of cooperation in which he is permitted to acquire benefits in ways that do not contribute to the welfare of others. There is no basis for his making this claim. From the standpoint of common sense, then, the difference principle appears to be acceptable both to the more advantaged and to the less advantaged individual.

G. W. F. Hegel

The consciousness of change, of undergoing and intentionally bringing about transformation, was present in most Enlightenment thinkers from the mid-seventeenth century on. But no one tried more self-consciously to offer a comprehensive interpretation of change than did Hegel. He later became quite conservative; but as the Holy Roman Empire crumbled in the aftermath of the French Revolution, and as British theories of economics and right were adopted in Europe, he wrestled with liberal issues, and his thought was the leaven for the "radical" thinking of Marx — who, of course, became the most important single theorist of political economic thought for a century and a half after Hegel's death in 1831.

Hegel believed that freedom involved the spontaneous flow of "Spirit" in history. "Spirit" (*Geist*, in German = Mind, Spirit, or animating principle) enters into material reality and re-creates reality in a dynamic process. Persons and civilizations become structured by a higher consciousness. Reason is what grasps the logic of this creative self-fulfillment.

Hegel used the word *Geist* to identify what is most real. He thought that his work provided a defense of Christianity against its critics, and it is likely that the Holy Spirit is what he was trying to trace. Yet, he argued that philosophy is superior to religion, and thus some have claimed that he only used religion to illustrate the dynamic "world process" whereby the Absolute and Ideal became actual and concrete. "Spirit" is a complex reality, constitutionally free, potentially infinite, and non-material; but it becomes actual by interacting with "nature" — passions, material forces, interests. In restless interaction, it constantly forms and breaks conventions, becoming concretely embodied in the lives of people and in the institutions of human civil society — families, corporations, religion, morality, and the state above all.

This process of concrete embodiment is the clue to all historical development, in Hegel's view. It is governed by a "dialectical logic," contradictions that join contraries in tension, as we can see in the relationships of man and woman, parent and child, master and slave, king and subjects. Indeed, conflict, which philosophy allows us to comprehend as deeper harmony, is the clue to dynamic development.

Hegel is important for business for two related reasons beyond his influence on Marx. First, his views express the love of all modern thinkers for progress. Creativity lives at the cutting edge of novelty, and development is the greater actualization of reason, freedom, justice, and true spirituality. Second, ethics after Hegel become more and more centered on the interpretation of historical life, on knowing, as it were, what is going on in the world and how to read its directions and inner dynamics. Ideas of an order other than the way things are, by which we judge the world and to which we ought to conform the world, are increasingly abandoned. Prescription is depth description. Morality is understood in terms of stages of developing consciousness that enhance freedom in the very fabric of a civil order. All is dynamic; nothing is fixed. Many over the centuries have understood ethics in terms of formal principles of right and wrong. But Hegel combined teleology with ethology, subordinating a biblical or covenantal view, which includes all three — deontology, teleology, and ethology — to this combination. "Real" life, in his view, and thus all serious ethics, is best understood as the encounter, conflict, and mutual transformation of opposites. This is how ideas and interests, passion and reason, spirit and matter, masters and slaves, self and society actualize the final goal of history — freedom.

Hegel wrote little about business life, but he believed that every aspect of life had to be interpreted in terms of the whole. Only the small-minded person, of no consequence to history, simply wanted to do his work well. Leaders must seek to understand the dynamics of social change, the role of personal development and group self-consciousness, and the importance of historical development for every aspect of life. Such views had an enormous impact on the modern social sciences — and on both corporate culture and radical social theories.

Introduction to the Philosophy of History

G. W. F. Hegel

The history of the world is none other than the progress of the consciousness of Freedom; a progress whose development according to the necessity of its nature, it is our business to investigate. . . .

The destiny of the spiritual World, and, — since this is the *substantial World,* while the physical remains subordinate to it, or, in the language of speculation, has no truth, as *against* the spiritual, — *the final cause of the World at large,* we allege to be the *consciousness* of its own freedom on the part of Spirit, and *ipso facto,* the *reality* of that freedom. But that this term "Freedom," without further qualification, is an indefinite, and incalculable ambiguous term; and that while that which it represents is the *ne plus ultra* of attainment, it is liable to an infinity of misunderstandings, confusions and errors, and to become the occasion for all imaginable excesses, — has never been more clearly known and felt than in modern times. Yet, for the present, we must content ourselves with the term itself without farther definition. Attention was also directed to the importance of that infinite difference between a principle in the abstract, and its realization in the concrete. In the process before us, the essential nature of freedom — which involves in its absolute necessity, — is to be displayed as coming to a consciousness of itself (for it is in its very nature, self-consciousness) and thereby realizing its existence. Itself is its own object of attainment, and the sole aim of Spirit. This result it is, at which the process of the World's History has been continu-

---

Excerpts from G. W. F. Hegel, *Philosophy of History* (1837), trans. Sibree (1857).

ally aiming; and to which the sacrifices that have ever and anon been laid on the vast altar of the earth, through the long lapse of ages, have been offered. This is the only aim that sees itself realized and fulfilled; the only pole of repose amid the ceaseless change of events and conditions, and the sole efficient principle that pervades them. This final aim is God's purpose with the world; but God is the absolutely perfect Being, and can, therefore, will nothing other than himself — his own Will. The Nature of His Will — that is, His Nature itself — is what we here call the Idea of Freedom; translating the language of Religion into that of Thought. The question, then, which we may next put, is: What means does this principle of Freedom use for its realization? . . .

The question of the *means* by which Freedom develops itself to a World, conducts us to the phenomenon of History itself. Although Freedom is, primarily, an undeveloped idea, the means it uses are external and phenomenal; presenting themselves in History to our sensuous vision. The first glance at history convinces us that the actions of men proceed from their needs, their passions, their interests, their characters, and talents; and impresses us with the belief that such needs, passions and interests are the sole springs of action — the efficient agents in this scene of activity. Among these may, perhaps, be found aims of a liberal or universal kind — benevolence it may be, or noble patriotism; but such virtues and general views are but insignificant as compared with the world and its doings. We may perhaps see the ideal of reason actualized in those who adopt such aims, and within the spheres of their influence; but they bear only a trifling proportion to the mass of the human race; and the extent of that influence is limited accordingly. Passions, private aims, and the satisfaction of selfish desires, are on the other hand, most effective springs of action. Their power lies in the fact that they respect none of the limitations which justice and morality would impose on them; and that these natural impulses have a more direct influence over man than the artificial and tedious discipline that tends to order and self-restrain, law and morality. When we look at this display of passions, and the consequences of their violence; the unreason which is associated not only with them, but even (rather we might say *especially*) with *good* designs and righteous aims;

when we see the evil, the vice, the ruin that has befallen the most flourishing kingdoms which the mind of man ever created, we can scarce avoid being filled with sorrow at this universal taint of corruption: and, since this decay is not the work of mere nature, but of the human will — a moral embitterment — a revolt of the good spirit (if it have a place within us) may well be the result of our reflections. Without rhetorical exaggeration, a simply truthful combination of the miseries that have overwhelmed the noblest of nations and polities, and the finest examples of private virtue, — forms a picture of most fearful aspect, and excites emotions of the profoundest and most hopeless sadness, counter-balanced by no consolatory result. We endure in beholding it a mental torture, allowing no defense or escape but the consideration that what has happened could not be otherwise; that it is a fatality which no intervention could alter. And at last we draw back from the intolerable disgust with which these sorrowful reflections threaten us, into the more agreeable environment of our individual life — the present formed by our private aims and interests. In short we retreat into the selfishness that stands on the quiet shore, and thence enjoy in safety the distant spectacle of "wrecks confusedly hurled." But even regarding history as the slaughter-bench at which the happiness of peoples, the wisdom of states, and the virtue of individuals have been victimized — the question involuntarily arises — to what principle, to what final aim these enormous sacrifices have been offered. From this point the investigation usually proceeds to that which we have made the general commencement of our inquiry. . . .

We assert . . . that nothing has been accomplished without interest on the part of the actors; and — if interest be called passion, inasmuch as the whole individuality, to the neglect of all other actual or possible interests and aims, is devoted to an object with every fibre of volition, concentrating all its desires and powers upon it — we may affirm absolutely that *nothing great* in *the world* has been accomplished without *passion*. Two elements, therefore, enter into the object of our investigation; the first the Idea, the second the complex of human passions; the one the warp, the other the woof of the vast tapestry of universal history. The concrete mean and union of the two is liberty, under the conditions of morality in a state. We have spoken of the idea of freedom as the nature of Spirit, and the absolute goal of history. Passion is regarded as a thing of sinister aspect, as more or less immoral. Man is required to have no passions. Passion, it is true, is not quite the suitable word for what I wish to express. I mean here nothing more than human activity as resulting from private interests — special, or if you will, self-seeking designs — with this qualification, that the whole energy of will and character is devoted to their attainment; that other interests (which would in themselves constitute attractive aims), or rather all things else, are sacrificed to them. The object in question is so bound up with the man's will, that it entirely and alone determines the "hue of resolution," and is inseparable from it. It has become the very essence of his volition. For a person is a specific existence; not man in general (a term to which no real existence corresponds), but a particular human being. The term "character" likewise expresses this idiosyncrasy of will and intelligence. But *character* comprehends all peculiarities whatever; the way in which a person conducts himself in private relations, &c., and is not limited to his idiosyncrasy in its practical and active phase. I shall, therefore, use the term "passion"; understanding thereby the particular bent of character, as far as the peculiarities of volition are not limited to private interest, but supply the impelling and actuating force for accomplishing deeds shared in by the community at large. Passion is in the first instance the *subjective,* and therefore the *formal* side of energy, will, and activity — leaving the object or aim still undetermined. And there is a similar relation of formality to reality in merely individual conviction, individual views, individual conscience. It is always a question, of essential importance, what is the purport of my conviction, individual views, individual conscience. It is always a question, of essential importance, what is the purport of my conviction, what the object of my passion, in deciding whether the one or the other is of a true and substantial nature. Conversely, if it is so, it will inevitably attain actual existence — be actualized.

From this comment on the second essential element in the historical embodiment of an aim, we infer — glancing at the institution of the state in passing — that a state is then well constituted and internally powerful, when the private interest of its citizens is one with the common interest of the state; when the one finds its gratification and realization in the other, — a proposition in itself very important. But in a state many institutions must be adopted, much political machinery invented, accompanied by appropriate political arrangements, — necessitating long struggles of the understanding before what is really appropriate can be discovered, — involving, moreover, contentions with private interest and passions, and a tedious discipline of these latter, in order to bring about the desired harmony. The epoch when a state attains this harmonious condition, marks the period of its bloom, its virtue, its vigour, and is prosperity. But the history of mankind does not begin with a *conscious* aim of any kind, as it is the case with the particular circles into which men form themselves of set purpose. The mere social instinct implies a conscious purpose of security for life and property; and when society has been constituted, this purpose becomes more comprehensive. The history of the world begins with its general aim — the realization of the idea of Spirit — only in an *implicit* form. . . . This vast congeries of volitions, interests and activities, constitute the instruments and means of the world-spirit for attaining its object; bringing it to consciousness, and realizing it. And this aim is none other than finding itself — coming to itself — and contemplating itself in concrete actuality. But that those manifestations of vitality on the part of individuals and peoples, in which they seek and satisfy their own purposes, are, at the same time, the means and instruments of a higher and broader purpose of which they know nothing, — which they realize unconsciously, — might be made a matter of question; rather has been questioned, and in every variety of form negatived, decried and contemned as mere dreaming and "philosophy." But on this point I announced my view at the very outset, and asserted our hypothesis, — which, however, will appear in the sequel, in the form of a legitimate inference, — and our belief, that Reason governs the world, and has consequently governed its history. In relation to this independently universal and substantial existence — all else is subordinate, subservient to it, and the means for its development. But moreover this Reason is immanent in historical existence and attains to its own perfection in and through that existence. The union of universal abstract existence generally with the individual, — the subjective — that this alone is truth, belongs to the department of speculation, and is treated in this general form in logic. — But in the process of the world's history itself, — as still incomplete, — the abstract final aim of history is not yet made the distinct object of desire and interest. While these limited sentiments are still unconscious of the purpose they are fulfilling, the universal principle is implicit in them, and is realizing itself through them. The question also assumes the form of the union of *freedom and necessity;* the latent abstract process of Spirit being regarded as *necessity,* while that which exhibits itself in the conscious will of men, as their interest, belongs to the domain of *freedom.* . . .

* * *

What is the material in which the ideal of Reason is wrought out? The primary answer would be, — personality itself — human desires — subjectivity generally. In human knowledge and volition, as its material element, Reason attains positive existence. We have considered subjective volition where it has an object which is the truth and essence of a reality, viz. where it constitutes a great world-historical passion. As a subjective will, occupied with limited passions, it is dependent, and can gratify its desires only within the limits of this dependence. But the subjective will has also a substantial life — a reality, — in which it moves in the region of *essential* being and has the essential itself as the object of its existence. This essential being is the union of the *subjective* with the *rational* will: it is the moral whole, the state, which is that form of actuality in which the individual has and enjoys his freedom; but on the condition of his recognizing, believing in and willing that which is common to the whole. And this must not be understood as if the subjective will of the social unit attained its gratification and enjoyment through that common Will; as if this were a means provided for its benefit; as if the individual, in his relations to other individuals, thus limited his freedom, in order that this universal limitation — the mutual constraint of all — might secure a small space of liberty for each. Rather, we affirm, are law, morality, government, and they alone, the positive fact and completion of freedom. Freedom

of a low and limited order, is mere caprice; which finds its exercise in the sphere of particular and limited desires.

* * *

The error which first meets us is the direct contradictory of our principle that the state presents the realization of freedom; the opinion, viz., that man is free by *nature,* but that in *society,* in the state — to which nevertheless he is irresistibly impelled — he must limit this natural freedom. That man is free by nature is quite correct in one sense; viz., that he is so according to the idea of humanity; but we imply thereby that he is such only in virtue of his destiny — that he has an undeveloped power to become such; for the "nature" of an object is exactly synonymous with its "Idea." But the view in question imports more than this. When man is spoke of as "free by nature," the mode of his existence as well as his destiny is implied. His merely natural and primary condition is intended. In this sense a "state of nature" is assumed in which mankind at large are in the possession of their natural rights with the unconstrained exercise and enjoyment of their freedom. This assumption is not indeed raised to the dignity of the historical fact; it would indeed be difficult, were the attempt seriously made, to point out any such condition as actually existing, or as having ever occurred. Examples of a savage state of life can be pointed out, but they are marked by brutal passions and deeds of violence; while, however rude and simple their conditions, they involve social arrangements which (to use the common phrase) *restrain* freedom. That assumption is one of those nebulous images which theory produces; an idea which it cannot avoid originating, but which it fathers upon real existence, without sufficient historical justification.

What we find such a state of nature to be in actual experience, answers exactly to the idea of a *merely* natural condition. Freedom as the *idea* of that which is original and natural, does not exist *as original and natural.* Rather must it be first sought out and won; and that by an incalculable medical discipline of the intellectual and moral powers. The state of nature is, therefore, predominantly that of injustice and violence, of untamed natural impulses, of inhuman deeds and feelings. Limitation is certainly produced by society and the state, but it is a limitation of the mere brute emotions and rude instincts; as also, in a more advanced stage of culture, of the premeditated self-will of caprice and passion. This kind of constraint is part of the instrumentality by which only the consciousness of freedom and the desire for its attainment, in its true — that is rational and ideal form — can be obtained. To the notion of freedom, law and morality are indispensibly requisite; and they are in and for themselves, universal existences, objects and aims; which are discovered only by the activity of thought, separating itself from the merely sensuous, and developing itself, in opposition thereto; and which must on the other hand, be introduced into and incorporated with the originally sensuous will, and that contrarily to its natural inclination. The perpetually recurring misapprehension of freedom consists in regarding that term only in its *formal,* subjective sense, abstracted from is essential objects and aims; thus a constraint put upon impulse, desire, passion — pertaining to the particular individual as such — a limitation of caprice and self-will is regarded as a fettering of freedom. We should on the contrary look upon such limitation as the indispensable proviso of emancipation. Society and the state are the very conditions in which freedom is realized. . . .

Karl Marx

In many ways, the culmination of the Enlightenment was Karl Marx. No one else stated quite so forcefully the view that society in all its aspects is an artifact constructed out of human interests and determined by the quest for liberation. He drew on British economic theory and saw in capitalism the force that destroyed feudalism. He was an heir of and contributor to German philosophy. But he was intrigued above all with French politics. He saw in the French Revolution of 1779 and the Paris uprising of 1830, which overthrew democracy, the model for going beyond both capitalist society and idealistic thought. He integrated English economics, German philosophy, and French politics around the Hegelian idea that the absolute becomes concrete in the struggle between master and slave. Reversing the priority from master to slave, on whom the master becomes dependent, he drew also on biblical, classical, traditional, and liberal history. Marxist "socialism" became a "secular religion," the center of loyalty and the ruling doctrine of economy, philosophy (including ethics, law, and history), and politics for at least half the world's people. Lenin said what many came to believe: "The thought of Karl Marx is omnipotent, because it is true."

The history of the twentieth century could be written in terms of the various responses to Marx. Reactionaries in the fascist traditions borrowed from him while hunting down communists and Marxist sympathizers everywhere (the word *Nazi*, we should not forget, is the German abbreviation for "National Socialism"). Conservatives repudiated Marx and opposed everything "liberal" that tended toward socialism.

Liberalism, however, split as Marxism grew. Some drew especially on Adam Smith, on utilitarianism, and on an almost Hegelian sense of the dynamic of history as it presses toward freedom, to support "free enterprise" — sometimes by advocating vast systems of government contracting to defend against Marxism. Meanwhile, social activists drew partly on Mill but fought Marxists for the control of "progressive groups" — unions, community organizations, advocacy and human rights groups — because they believed in the "self-evident" first principles accented, for instance, by Locke and Kant and denied by Marxists.

Modern theologians developed the "Social Gospel," "Christian realism," and various "liberation theologies" — especially Catholic, but also Protestant, Jewish, Islamic, Buddhist, and Hindu — in order to engage elements of liberalism or of socialism that they thought were valid but were ignored by their traditions. Liberation thought was especially important in the period after World War II when emerging nations declared independence from colonial influence, "liberal" views of development, and "Western" Enlightenment thinking — ironically by drawing their basic concepts from its representatives, particularly Marx.

No professional today can afford to remain ignorant of Marx. Although the communist systems of Eastern Europe have collapsed, every modern thinker who has developed a view of modern business has had to define a position in regard to this version of the Enlightenment. Basic Marxist ideas have become a part of how many now see reality: the presumption that the past is the history of oppression that needs to be left behind; the drive to mobilize the oppressed to transform society; the conviction that moral, spiritual, and religious ideas are a product of the social location in which they are developed; and the view that capitalist ("bourgeois") life-styles have destroyed community and are built on a foundation of exploitation that can be overcome by new historical developments if we but grasp the movements, feminism, and theories of "Third World" poverty.

On all of these issues, Marx wrote extensively. The best brief introduction to his thought on such matters is the first chapter of his famous "Manifesto," written in 1848 with his colleague and supporter, the radical industrialist Friedrich Engels.

The Manifesto of the Communist Party

Karl Marx (with Friedrich Engels)

A spectre is haunting Europe — the spectre of Communism. All the powers of old Europe have entered into a holy alliance to exorcise this spectre: Pope and Czar, Metternich and Guizot, French Radicals and German police spies.

Where is the party in opposition that has not been decried as communistic by its opponents in power? Where the opposition that has not hurled back the branding reproach of Communism against the more advanced opposition parties, as well as against its reactionary adversaries?

Two things result from this fact:

I. Communism is already acknowledged by all European powers to be itself a power.

II. It is high time that Communists should openly, in the face of the whole world, publish their views, their aims, their tendencies, and meet this nursery tale of the spectre of Communism with a manifesto of the party itself. . . .

The history of all hitherto existing society is the history of class struggles.

Freeman and slave, patrician and plebeian, lord and serf, guild-master and journeyman, in a word, oppressor and oppressed stood in constant opposition to one another, carried on an uninterrupted, now hidden, now open fight, a fight that each time ended either in a revolutionary reconstitution of society at large, or in the common ruin of the contending classes.

In the earlier epochs of history we find almost everywhere a complicated arrangement of society

Karl Marx and Friedrich Engels, *The Manifesto of the Communist Party* (1888), in *The Marx-Engels Reader* (New York: W. W. Norton, 1972), chap. 1, pp. 335-45.

into various orders, a manifold gradation of social rank. In ancient Rome we have patricians, knights, plebeians, slaves; in the Middle Ages, feudal lords, vassals, guild-masters, journeymen, apprentices, serfs; in almost all of these classes, again, subordinate gradations.

The modern bourgeois society that has sprouted from the ruins of feudal society has not done away with class antagonisms. It has but established new classes, new conditions of oppression, new forms of struggle in place of the old ones.

Our epoch, the epoch of the bourgeoisie, possesses, however, this distinctive feature: it has simplified the class antagonisms. Society as a whole is more and more splitting up into two great hostile camps, into two great classes directly facing each other — bourgeoisie and proletariat.

From the serfs of the Middle Ages sprang the chartered burghers of the earliest towns. From these burgesses the first elements of the bourgeoisie were developed.

The discovery of America, the rounding of the Cape, opened up fresh ground for the rising bourgeoisie. The East Indian and Chinese markets, the colonization of America, trade with the colonies, the increase in the means of exchange and in commodities generally, gave to commerce, to navigation, to industry, an impulse never before known, and thereby, to the revolutionary element in the tottering feudal society, a rapid development.

The feudal system of industry, in which industrial production was monopolized by closed guilds, now no longer sufficed for the growing wants of the new markets. The manufacturing system took its place. The guild-masters were pushed aside by the manufacturing middle class; division of labour between the different corporate guilds vanished in the face of division of labour in each single workshop.

Meantime the markets kept ever growing, the demand ever rising. Even manufacture no longer sufficed. Thereupon, steam and machinery revolutionized industrial production. The place of manufacture was taken by the giant, modern industry, the place of the industrial middle class, by industrial millionaires — the leaders of whole industrial armies, the modern bourgeois.

Modern industry has established the world market, for which the discovery of America paved the way. This market has given an immense development to commerce, to navigation, to communication by land. This development has, in its turn, reacted on the extension of industry; and in proportion as industry, commerce, navigation, railways extended, in the same proportion the bourgeoisie developed, increased its capital, and pushed into the background every class handed down from the Middle Ages.

We see, therefore, how the modern bourgeoisie is itself the product of a long course of development, of a series of revolutions in the modes of production and of exchange.

Each step in the development of the bourgeoisie was accompanied by a corresponding political advance of that class. An oppressed class under the sway of the feudal nobility, it became an armed and self-governing association in the mediaeval commune: here independent urban republic (as in Italy and Germany); there, taxable "third estate" of the monarchy (as in France); afterwards, in the period of manufacture proper, serving either the semi-feudal or the absolute monarchy as a counterpoise against the nobility, and, in fact, corner stone of the great monarchies in general. The bourgeoisie has at last, since the establishment of modern industry and of the world market, conquered for itself, in the modern representative state, exclusive political sway. The executive of the modern state is but a committee for managing the common affairs of the whole bourgeoisie.

The bourgeoisie has played a most revolutionary role in history.

The bourgeoisie, wherever it has got the upper hand, has put an end to all feudal, patriarchal, idyllic relations. It has pitilessly torn asunder the motley feudal ties that bound man to his "natural superiors," and has left no other bond between man and man than naked self-interest, than callous "cash payment." It has drowned the most heavenly ecstasies of religious fervour, of chivalrous enthusiasm, of philistine sentimentalism, in the icy water of egotistical calculation. It has resolved personal worth into exchange value, and in place of the numberless indefeasible chartered freedoms has set up that single, unconscionable freedom — Free Trade. In one word, for exploitation, veiled by religious and political illusions, it has substituted naked, shameless, direct, brutal exploitation.

The bourgeoisie has stripped of its halo every occupation hitherto honoured and looked up to with reverent awe. It has converted the physician, the lawyer, the priest, the poet, the man of science, into its paid wage labourers.

The bourgeoisie has torn away from the family its sentimental veil, and has reduced the family relation to a mere money relation.

The bourgeoisie has disclosed how it came to pass that the brutal display of vigour in the Middle Ages which reactionaries so much admire found its fitting complement in the most slothful indolence. It has been the first to show what man's activity can bring about. It has accomplished wonders far surpassing Egyptian pyramids, Roman aqueducts, and Gothic cathedrals; it has conducted expeditions that put in the shade all former migrations of nations and crusades.

The bourgeoisie cannot exist without constantly revolutionizing the instruments of production, and thereby the relations of production, and with them the whole relations of society. Conservation of the old modes of production in unaltered form was, on the contrary, the first condition of existence for all earlier industrial classes. Constant revolutionizing of production, uninterrupted disturbance of all social conditions, everlasting uncertainty and agitation distinguish the bourgeois epoch from all earlier ones. All fixed, fast-frozen relations with their train of ancient and venerable prejudices and opinions are swept away; all new-formed ones become antiquated before they can ossify. All that is solid melts in air, all that is holy is profaned, and man is at last compelled to face with sober sense his real conditions of life and his relations with his kind.

The need of a constantly expanding market for its products chases the bourgeoisie over the whole surface of the globe. It must nestle everywhere, settle everywhere, establish connections everywhere.

The bourgeoisie has through its exploitation of the world market given a cosmopolitan character to production and consumption in every country. To the great chagrin of reactionaries it has drawn from under the feet of industry the national ground on which it stood. All old-established national industries have been destroyed or are daily being destroyed. They are dislodged by new industries whose introduction becomes a life and death question for all civilized nations; by industries that no longer work up indigenous raw material, but raw material drawn from the remotest zones; industries whose products are consumed, not only at home, but in every quarter of the globe. In place of the old wants, satisfied by the production of the country, we find new wants, requiring for their satisfaction the products of distant lands and climes. In place of the old local and national seclusion and self-sufficiency we have intercourse in every direction, universal inter-dependence of nations. And as in material, so also in intellectual production. The intellectual creations of individual nations become common property. National one-sidedness and narrow-mindedness become more and more impossible, and from the numerous national and local literatures there arises a world literature.

The bourgeoisie, by the rapid improvement of all instruments of production, by the immensely facilitated means of communication, draws all nations, even the most barbarian, into civilization. The cheap prices of its commodities are the heavy artillery with which it batters down all Chinese walls, with which it forces the barbarians' intensely obstinate hatred of foreigners to capitulate. It compels all nations, on pain of extinction, to adopt the bourgeois mode of production; it compels them to introduce what it calls civilization into their midst, *i.e.*, to become bourgeois themselves. In a word, it creates a world after its own image.

The bourgeoisie has subjected the country to the rule of the towns. It has created enormous cities, has greatly increased the urban population as compared with the rural, and has thus rescued a considerable part of the population from the idiocy of rural life. Just as it has made the country dependent on the towns, so it has made barbarian and semi-barbarian countries dependent on the civilized ones, nations of peasants on nations of bourgeois, the East on the West.

More and more the bourgeoisie keeps doing away with the scattered state of the population, of the means of production, and of property. It has agglomerated population, centralized means of production, and has concentrated property in a few hands. The necessary consequence of this was political centralization. Independent, or but loosely connected provinces, with separate interests, laws, governments and systems of taxation, became lumped together into one nation, with one government, one code of laws, one national class interest, one frontier and one customs tariff.

The bourgeoisie during its rule of scarce one hundred years has created more massive and more colossal productive forces than have all preceding generations together. Subjection of nature's forces to man, machinery, application of chemistry to industry and agriculture, steam-navigation, railways, electric telegraphs, clearing of whole continents for cultivation, canalization of rivers, whole populations conjured out of the ground — what earlier century had even a presentiment that such productive forces slumbered in the lap of social labour?

We see, then, that the means of production and of exchange which served as the foundation for the growth of the bourgeoisie were generated in feudal society. At a certain stage in the development of these means of production and of exchange, the conditions under which feudal society produced and exchanged, the feudal organization of agriculture and manufacturing industry, in a word, the feudal relations of property became no longer compatible with the already developed productive forces; they became so many fetters. They had to be burst asunder; they were burst asunder.

Into their place stepped free competition, accompanied by a social and political constitution adapted to it, and by the economic and political sway of the bourgeois class.

A similar movement is going on before our own eyes. Modern bourgeois society with its relations of production, of exchange and of property, a society that has conjured up such gigantic means of production and of exchange, is like the sorcerer who is no longer able to control the powers of the nether world whom he has called up by his spells. For many a decade past the history of industry and commerce is but the history of the revolt of modern productive forces against modern conditions of production, against the property relations that are the conditions for the existence of the bourgeoisie and of its rule. It is enough to mention the commercial crises that by their periodical return put the existence of the entire bourgeois society on trial, each time more threateningly. In these crises a great part not only of the existing products, but also of the previously created pro-

ductive forces, are periodically destroyed. In these crises there breaks out an epidemic that, in all earlier epochs, would have seemed an absurdity — the epidemic of over-production. Society suddenly finds itself put back into a state of momentary barbarism; it appears as if a famine, a universal war of devastation had cut off the supply of every means of subsistence; industry and commerce seem to be destroyed. And why? Because there is too much civilization, too much means of subsistence, too much industry, too much commerce. The productive forces at the disposal of society no longer tend to further the development of the conditions of bourgeois property; on the contrary, they have become too powerful for these conditions, by which they are fettered, and no sooner do they overcome these fetters than they bring disorder into the whole of bourgeois society, endanger the existence of bourgeois property. The conditions of bourgeois society are too narrow to comprise the wealth created by them. And how does the bourgeoisie get over these crises? On the one hand by enforced destruction of a mass of productive forces; on the other, by the conquest of new markets and by the more thorough exploitation of the old ones. That is to say, by paving the way for more extensive and more destructive crises, and by diminishing the means whereby crises are prevented.

The weapons with which the bourgeoisie felled feudalism to the ground are now turned against the bourgeoisie itself.

But not only has the bourgeoisie forged the weapons that bring death to itself; it has also called into existence the men who are to wield those weapons s the modern working class, the proletarians.

In proportion as the bourgeoisie, i.e., capital, is developed, in the same proportion is the proletariat, the modern working class, developed — a class of labourers, who live only so long as they find work, and who find work only so long as their labour increases capital. These labourers, who must sell themselves piecemeal, are a commodity like every other article of commerce, and are consequently exposed to all the vicissitudes of competition, to all the fluctuations of the market.

Owing to the extensive use of machinery and to division of labour, the work of the proletarians has lost all individual character, and, consequently, all charm for the workman. He becomes an appendage of the machine, and it is only the most simple, most monotonous, and most easily acquired knack that is required of him. Hence, the cost of production of a workman is restricted almost entirely to the means of subsistence that he requires for his maintenance and for the propagation of his race. But the price of a commodity, and therefore also of labour, is equal to its cost of production. In proportion, therefore, as the repulsiveness of the work increases, the wage decreases. Nay more, in proportion as the use of machinery and division of labour increases, in the same proportion the burden of toil also increases, whether by prolongation of the working hours, by increase of the work exacted in a given time, or by increased speed of the machinery, etc.

Modern industry has converted the little workshop of the patriarchal master into the great factory of the industrial capitalist. Masses of labourers, crowded into the factory, are organized like soldiers. As privates of the industrial army they are placed under the command of a perfect hierarchy of officers and sergeants. Not only are they slaves of the bourgeois class and of the bourgeois state; they are daily and hourly enslaved by the machine, by the overseer, and, above all, by the individual bourgeois manufacturer himself. The more openly this despotism proclaims gain to be its end and aim, the more petty, the more hateful, and the more embittering it is.

The less the skill and exertion of strength implied in manual labour — in other words, the more modern industry develops — the more is the labour of men superseded by that of women. Differences of age and sex have no longer any distinctive social validity for the working class. All are instruments of labour, more or less expensive to use, according to their age and sex.

No sooner has the labourer received his wages in cash, for the moment escaping exploitation by the manufacturer, than he is set upon by the other portions of the bourgeoisie — the landlord, the shopkeeper, the pawnbroker, etc.

The lower strata of the middle class — the small tradespeople, shopkeepers, and retired tradesmen generally, the handicraftsmen and peasants — all these sink gradually into the proletariat, partly because their diminutive capital does not suffice for the scale on which modern industry is carried on and is swamped in the competition with the large capitalists, partly because their specialized skill is rendered worthless by new methods of production. Thus the proletariat is recruited from all classes of the population.

The proletariat goes through various stages of development. With its birth begins its struggle with the bourgeoisie. At first the contest is carried on by individual labourers, then by the workpeople of a factory, then by the operatives of one trade, in one locality, against the individual bourgeois who directly exploits them. They direct their attacks not against the bourgeois conditions of production themselves; they destroy imported wares that compete with their labour, they smash machinery to pieces, they set factories ablaze, they seek to restore by force the vanished status of the workman of the Middle Ages.

At this stage the labourers still form an incoherent mass scattered over the whole country, and broken up by their mutual competition. If anywhere they unite to form more compact bodies, this is not yet the consequence of their own active union, but of the union of the bourgeoisie, which class, in order to attain its own political ends, is compelled to set the whole proletariat in motion, and is, moreover, still able to do so for a time. At this stage, therefore, the proletarians do not fight their enemies, but the enemies of their enemies, the remnants of absolute monarchy, the landowners, the non-industrial bourgeois, the petty bourgeoisie. Thus the whole historical movement is concentrated in the hands of the bourgeoisie; every victory so obtained is a victory for the bourgeoisie.

But with the development of industry the proletariat not only increases in number; it becomes concentrated in greater masses, its strength grows, and it feels that strength more. The various interests and conditions of life within the ranks of the proletariat are more and more equalized, in proportion as machinery obliterates all distinctions of labour and nearly everywhere reduces wages to the same low level. The growing competition among the bourgeois and the resulting commercial crises make the wages of the workers ever more fluctuating. The unceasing improvement of machinery, ever more rapidly developing, makes their livelihood more and more precarious; the collisions between individual workmen and individual bourgeois take more and more the character of collisions between two classes. Thereupon the workers begin to form combinations (trade unions) against the bourgeoisie; they club together in order to keep up the rate of wages; they found permanent associations in order to make provision beforehand for these occasional revolts. Here and there the contest breaks out into riots.

Now and then the workers are victorious, but only for a time. The real fruit of their battles lies not in the immediate result but in the ever expanding union of the workers. This union if furthered by the improved means of communication which are created by modern industry, and which place the workers of different localities in contact with one another. It was just this contact that was needed to centralize the numerous local struggles, all of the same characters, into one national struggle between classes. But every class struggle is a political struggle. And that union, which the burghers of the Middle Ages, with their miserable highways, required centuries to attain, the modern proletarians, thanks to railways achieve in a few years.

This organization of the proletarians into a class, and consequently into a political party, is continually being upset again by the competition between the workers themselves. But it ever rises up again, stronger, firmer, mightier. It compels legislative recognition of particular interests of the workers by taking advantage of the divisions among the bourgeoisie itself. Thus the Ten House bill in England was carried.

Altogether, collisions between the classes of the old society further the course of development of the proletariat in many ways. The bourgeoisie finds itself involved in a constant battle — at first with the aristocracy; later on, with those portions of the bourgeoisie itself whose interests have become antagonistic to the progress of industry; at all times with the bourgeoisie of foreign countries. In all these battles it sees itself compelled to appeal to the proletariat, to ask for its help, and thus to drag it into the political arena. The bourgeoisie itself, therefore, supplies the proletariat with its own elements of political and general education; in other words, it furnishes the proletariat with weapons for fighting the bourgeoisie.

Further, as we have already seen, entire sections of the ruling classes are, by the advance of industry, precipitated into the proletariat, or are at least threatened in their conditions of existence. These also supply the proletariat with fresh elements of enlightenment and progress.

Finally, in times when the class struggle nears the decisive hour, the process of dissolution going on within the ruling class, in fact within the whole range of old society, assumes such a violent, glaring character that a small section of the ruling class cuts itself adrift and joins the revolutionary class, the class that holds the future in its hands. Just as, therefore, at an earlier period a section of the nobility went over to the bourgeoisie, so now a portion of the bourgeoisie goes over to the proletariat, and in particular, a portion of the bourgeois ideologists who have raised themselves to the level of comprehending theoretically the historical movement as a whole.

Of all the classes that stand face to face with the bourgeoisie today, the proletariat alone is a really revolutionary class. The other classes decay and finally disappear in the face of modern industry; the proletariat is its special and essential product.

The lower middle class, the small manufacturer, the shopkeeper, the artisan, the peasant — all these fight against the bourgeoisie, to save from extinction their existence as fractions of the middle class. They are, therefore, not revolutionary but conservative. Nay more, they are reactionary, for they try to roll back the wheel of history. If by chance they are revolutionary they are so only in view of their impending transfer into the proletariat; they thus defend not their present but their future interests; they desert their own standpoint to adopt that of the proletariat.

The "dangerous class," the social scum (Lumpenproletariat), that passively rotting mass thrown off by the lowest layers of old society, may here and there be swept into the movement by a proletarian revolution; its conditions of life, however, prepare it far more for the part of a bribed tool of reactionary intrigue.

The social conditions of the old society no longer exist for the proletariat. The proletarian is without property; his relation to his wife and children has no longer anything in common with bourgeois family relations; modern industrial labour, modern subjection to capital, the same in England as in France, in America as in Germany, has stripped him of every trace of national character. Law, morality, religion are to him so many bourgeois prejudices, behind which lurk in ambush just as many bourgeois interests.

All the preceding classes that got the upper hand sought to fortify their already acquired status by subjecting society at large to their conditions of appropriation. The proletarians cannot become masters of the productive forces of society except by abolishing their own previous mode of appropriation, and thereby also every other previous mode of appropriation. They have nothing of their own to secure and to fortify; their mission is to destroy all previous securities for, and insurances of, individual property.

All previous historical movements were movements of minorities, or in the interest of minorities. The proletarian movement is the self-conscious, independent movement of the immense majority, in the interest of the immense majority. The proletariat, the lowest stratum of our present society, cannot stir, cannot raise itself up, without the whole superincumbent strata of official society being sprung into the air.

Though not in substance, yet in form, the struggle of the proletariat with the bourgeoisie is at first a national struggle. The proletariat of each country must, of course, first of all settle matters with its own bourgeoisie.

In depicting the most general phases of the development of the proletariat we traced the more or less veiled civil war raging within existing society, up to the point where that war breaks out into open revolution, and where the violent overthrow of the bourgeoisie lays the foundation for the sway of the proletariat.

Hitherto, every form of society has been based, as we have already seen, on the antagonism of oppressing and oppressed classes. But in order to oppress a class certain conditions must be assured to it under which it can, at least, continue its slavish existence. The serf, in the period of serfdom, raised himself to membership in the commune, just as the petty bourgeois, under the yoke of feudal absolutism, managed to develop into a bourgeois. The modern labourer, on the contrary, instead of rising with the progress of industry, sinks deeper and deeper below the conditions of existence of his own class. He becomes a pauper, and pauperism develops more rapidly than population and wealth. And here it becomes evident that the bourgeoisie is unfit any longer to be the ruling class in society and to impose its conditions of existence upon society as an overriding law. It is unfit to rule because it is incompetent to assure an existence to its slave within his slavery, because it cannot help letting him sink into such a state that it has to feed him, instead of being fed by him. Society can no longer live under this bourgeoisie, in other words, its existence is no longer compatible with society.

The essential condition for the existence and sway of the bourgeois class is the formation and augmentation of capital; the condition for capital is wage labour. Wage labour rests exclusively on competition between the labourers. The advance of industry, whose involuntary promoter is the bourgeoisie, replaces the isolation of the labourers, due to competition, by their revolutionary combination, due to association. The development of modern industry, therefore, cuts from under its feet the very foundation on which the bourgeoisie produces and appropriates products. What the bourgeoisie, therefore, produces above all are its own grave-diggers. Its fall and the victory of the proletariat are equally inevitable.

Chapter Seven

Religion and Modernization

The Enlightenment established the basic channels of mind whereby most modern thinkers interpret economic life. The modern university is dedicated to the disciplines growing out of the Enlightenment. Modern public debates are conducted largely in these terms. Conservatives, liberals, and radicals alike draw on these resources, although they do so with different emphases and combine them in different ways. Most share the assumption that economies progress according to a logic that is present in the way things really work. What they debate is the location of that logic and how, precisely, it works. Is it in "a state of nature," in a division of labor or the market, in the people's experience of pleasure or pain, in the necessary categories of human thought, in the dialectic of spirit and material, or in the conflicting struggle of power and interests in history?

The various voices from the Enlightenment agreed that religion is neither a primary causative force in the formation of modernity nor necessary for the ethics to guide that formation. Ethics could be gleaned from studying what is natural — not what is "supernatural." To introduce religious questions into business, economic, political, or technological questions is an intrusion. These areas manifest an independence from, if not the outgrowing of, religious values, which, they say, had very little to do with material and practical issues anyway.

In the twentieth century, however, a number of social and historical investigations, using precisely the tools of research developed by the Enlightenment, have offered an alternative view of modernity and its roots and causes. Most people of the world, most of the time, have eked out a bare subsistence from soil or sea or forest. Of course, once in a while a great kingdom or dynasty or

civilization had risen for a century or two, gaining wealth for the privileged few from the sweat and toil of slaves and subservient peoples before falling again into the dust. The ruins of these great civilizations of antiquity are found on every continent. Progress is neither natural nor prolonged.

But modernity seemed to bring a new kind of civilization — one in which whole new classes were developing a degree of wealth and a level of rights, along with a capacity to control nature that was never dreamed of before. Could such a thing endure? If so, what were its organizing principles? Was it the abandonment of religious superstition in favor of "natural" laws, or was it the fulfillment of certain religious impulses? Was it the recovery of primal human potentialities against the pretenses of revelation, or was it the actualization of theological principles in the fabric of civilization?

What caused modernity? Why did modern technology, science, corporations, constitutional governments, human rights, markets with fixed prices, and specific forms of a work ethic — all things necessary to modern business — arise in the West, while they did not initially do so in other great civilizations?

These scholars, seldom believers themselves, suggest that modern economic systems are less a departure from or a denial of Christian values than an implementation and actualization of certain interpretations of them. The social historians and theorists represented in this chapter all argued that in fact Christianity was central to the development of modern economic life. In alliance with other factors, it generated the moral and spiritual foundations on which modern global systems now rest. Thus, they imply, the "secular" explanations that come out of the Enlightenment are not so much wrong as superficial insofar as they deny the foun-

245

dations on which their own assumptions rest. Their heirs now service a giant intellectual and social apparatus without moral and spiritual resources to guide it. And, of course, some who are opposed to modernity will also be inclined to reject both the Enlightenment and the moral and spiritual foundations on which it rests.

Throughout this chapter, two matters have implications beyond what is in the material. First, these selections are written from a socio-historical point of view. This has become characteristic of much thought in our century. If we want to know the meaning of something, including something religious, many turn to the social scientists and social historians instead of clergy, theologians, or philosophers. This implies that we can assess the consequences of the faith we hold empirically. This form of secondary evaluation has become, for many, a primary way of interpreting life. Second, these selections refer primarily to specific forms of Christianity; but the issues the authors address are not distinctly Christian. If they are correct that religiously shaped moral and cultural patterns were key to economic development in the West, then it could be that similar beliefs would be necessary for development elsewhere. By the same token, those who oppose our present ethos, or those who want to reform modern economies morally, may have to face more directly than they usually do the religious meanings on which it rests, at least in part.

On the Protestant Ethic

The most famous argument about the relationship of religion to economic life is found in Max Weber's *The Protestant Ethic and the Spirit of Capitalism*. Weber was not a believer; his wife referred to him as "religiously unmusical." But few tougher-minded social analysts have ever existed, and few have gained a comparable mastery of historical and crosscultural materials. Weber thinks that we cannot understand modern sciences, political and legal systems, or modern capitalism without reference to religion — especially one form of it, Protestant Christianity. This is so partly because of the nature of modern capitalism and partly because of the way religious ideas work in social life.

With regard to modern capitalism, we have to take the term "modern" very seriously. Weber does not think that capitalism has anything new or distinctive to do with "the impulse to acquisition, pursuit of gain, of money, of the greatest possible amount of money. This impulse," he wrote,

> exists and has existed among waiters, physicians . . . , artists, prostitutes, dishonest officials, soldiers . . . , gamblers and beggars. . . . It should be taught in the kindergarten of cultural history that this naive idea of capitalism just be given up once and for all. Unlimited greed for gain is not in the least identical with capitalism (in this modern sense). . . . But capitalism is identical with the pursuit of profit, and forever *renewed* profit, by means of continuous, rational, capitalistic enterprise.

What is "modern" is an ethic that says that people find meaning in their work, in a disciplined, ongoing, and voluntary system of production that is distinct from home, race, or regime, dedicated to methodical economic activity and measured by carefully calculated balances of credits over debits.

That is not how life has been lived around the world. This is an ascetic ethic that had to be invented, and it had to build a new kind of culture. How did that happen? Weber claims that it became dominant where the Protestant sense of religious discipline in a vocation interacted with other factors to shape a civilization.

Most people, he argues in a dozen writings, do what they do in life because they think that it is meaningful. If it works, they adopt and adapt one or another of the predominant senses of meaning that is presented to them. The sources of these senses of meaning are religious. Weber thinks that it is a demonstrable fact that religion cuts the deep channels of thought and emotion about what is worth living for and dying for, what is right and wrong. In fact, even if people may not be consciously religious, their sense of meaning may be traceable to religious influences that were long ago woven into the fabric of daily life. These influences may seem "natural," but they are really "second nature," that is, historical constructions.

Weber's argument is incomplete, as we shall see; but it is a key argument in the interpretation of modern business culture. It has been viewed as the most suggestive post-Marxist hypothesis, and it has invited a wide range of historical studies showing various connections between religious ethics and modern economic life. In this excerpt we see a treatment of Christian reformers, viewed less through the lens of a believer than through that of an enlightened scholar tracing the effects of other people's belief in making modern business a way of life in modernity.

Asceticism and the Spirit of Capitalism

Max Weber

In order to understand the connection between the fundamental religious ideas of ascetic Protestantism and its maxims for everyday economic conduct, it is necessary to examine with especial care such writings as have evidently been derived from ministerial practice. For in a time in which the beyond meant everything, when the social position of the Christian depended upon his admission to the communion, the clergyman, through his ministry, Church discipline, and preaching, exercised an influence (as a glance at collections of *consilia, casus conscientice,* etc., shows) which we modern men are entirely unable to picture. In such a time the religious forces which express themselves through such channels are the decisive influences in the formation of national character.

For the purposes of this chapter, though by no means for all purposes, we can treat ascetic Protestantism as a single whole. But since that side of English Puritanism which was derived from Calvinism gives the most consistent religious basis for the idea of the calling, we shall, following our previous method, place one of its representatives at the centre of the discussion. Richard Baxter stands out above many other writers on Puritan ethics, both because of his eminently practical and realistic attitude, and, at the same time, because of the universal recognition accorded to his works, which have gone through many new editions and

Max Weber, "Asceticism and the Spirit of Capitalism," chap. 5 of *The Protestant Ethic and the Spirit of Capitalism,* trans. T. Parsons (New York: Charles Scribner's Sons, 1958), pp. 155-64, 170-72, 180.

translations. He was a Presbyterian and an apologist of the Westminster Synod, but at the same time, like so many of the best spirits of his time, gradually grew away from the dogmas of pure Calvinism. At heart he opposed Cromwell's usurpation as he would any revolution. He was unfavorable to the sects and the fanatical enthusiasm of the saints, but was very broad-minded about external peculiarities and objective towards his opponents. He sold his field of labor most especially in the practical promotion of the moral life through the Church. In the pursuit of this end, as one of the most successful ministers known to history, he placed his services at the disposal of the Parliamentary Government, of Cromwell, and of the Restoration, until he retired from office under the last, before St. Bartholomew's day. His *Christian Directory* is the most complete compendium of Puritan ethics, and is continually adjusted to the practical experiences of his own ministerial activity. In comparison we shall make use of Spener's *Theologische Bedenken,* as representative of German Pietism, Barclay's *Apology* for the Quakers, and some other representatives of ascetic ethics, which, however, in the interest of space, will be limited as far as possible.

Now, in glancing at Baxter's *Saints' Everlasting Rest,* or his *Christian Directory,* or similar works of others, one is struck at first glance by the emphasis placed, in the discussion of wealth and its acquisition, on the ebionitic elements of the New Testament. Wealth as such is a great danger; its temptations never end, and is pursuit is not only senseless as compared with the dominating importance of the Kingdom of God, but it is morally suspect. Here asceticism seems to have turned much more sharply against the acquisition of earthly goods than it did in Calvin, who saw no hindrance to the effectiveness of the clergy in their wealth, but rather a thoroughly desirable enhancement of their prestige. Hence he permitted them to employ their means profitably. Examples of the condemnation of the pursuit of money and goods may be gathered without end from Puritan writings, and may be contrasted with the late medieval ethical literature, which was much more open-minded on this point.

Moreover, these doubts were meant with perfect seriousness; only it is necessary to examine them somewhat more closely in order to understand their true ethical significance and implications. The real moral objection is to relaxation in the security of possession, the enjoyment of wealth with the consequence of idleness and the temptations of the flesh, above all of distraction from the pursuit of a righteous life. In fact, it is only because possession involves this danger of relaxation that it is objectionable at all. For the saints' everlasting rest is in the next world; on earth man must, to be certain of his state of grace, "do the works of him who sent him, as long as it is yet day." Not leisure and enjoyment, but only activity serves to increase the glory of God, according to the definite manifestations of His will.

Waste of time is thus the first and in principle the deadliest of sins. The span of human life is infinitely short and precious to make sure of one's own election. Loss of time through sociability, idle talk, luxury, even more sleep than is necessary for health, six to at most eight hours, is worthy of absolute moral condemnation. It does not yet hold, [as Benjamin] Franklin [was later to say], that time is money, but the proposition is true in a certain spiritual sense. It is infinitely valuable because every hour lost is lost to labor for the glory of God. Thus inactive contemplation is also valueless, or even directly reprehensible if it is at the expense of one's daily work. For it is less pleasing to God than the active performance of His will in a calling. Besides, Sunday is provided for that, and, according to Baxter, it is always those who are not diligent in their callings who have no time for God when the occasion demands it.

Accordingly, Baxter's principal work is dominated by the continually repeated, often almost passionate preaching of hard, continuous bodily or mental labor. Labor is, on the one hand, an approved ascetic technique, as it always has been in the Western Church, in sharp contrast not only to the Orient but to almost all monastic rules the world over. It is in particular the specific defense against all those temptations which Puritanism united under the name of the unclean life, whose role for it was by no means small. The sexual asceticism of Puritanism differs only in degree, not in fundamental principle, from that of monasticism; and on account of the Puritan conception of marriage, its practical influence is more far-reaching than that of the latter. For sexual intercourse is permitted, even within marriage, only as the means willed by God for the increase of His glory according to the commandment, "Be fruitful and multiply." Along with a moderate vegetable diet and cold baths, the same prescription is given for all sexual temptations as is used against religious doubts and a sense of moral unworthiness: "Work hard in your calling." But the most important thing was that even beyond that labor came to be considered in itself the end of life, ordained as such by God. St. Paul's "He who will not work shall not eat" holds unconditionally for everyone. Unwillingness to work is symptomatic of the lack of grace.

Here the difference from the mediaeval viewpoint becomes quite evident. Thomas Aquinas also gave an interpretation of that statement of St. Paul. But for him labor is only necessary *naturali ratione* for the maintenance of individual and community. Where this end is achieved, the precept ceases to have any meaning. Moreover, it holds only for the race, not for every individual. It does not apply to anyone who can live without labor on his possessions, and of course contemplation, as a spiritual form of action in the Kingdom of God, takes precedence over the commandment in its literal sense. Moreover, for the popular theology of the time, the highest form of monastic productivity lay in the increase of the *Thesaurus ecclesice* through prayer and chant.

Not only do these exceptions to the duty to labor naturally no longer hold for Baxter, but he holds most emphatically that wealth does not exempt anyone from the unconditional command. Even the wealthy shall not eat without working, for even though they do not need to labor to support their own needs, there is God's commandment which they, like the poor, must obey. For everyone without exception God's Providence has prepared a calling, which he should profess and in which he should labor. And this calling is not . . . a fate to which he must submit and which he must make the best of, but God's commandment to the individual to work for the divine glory. This seemingly subtle difference had far-reaching psychological consequences, and became connected with a further development of the providential interpretation of the economic order which had begun in scholasticism.

The phenomenon of the division of labor and occupations in society had, among others, been interpreted by Thomas Aquinas, to whom we may most conveniently refer, as a direct consequence of the divine scheme of things. But the places assigned to each man in this cosmos follow *ex causis naturalibus* and are fortuitous (contingent in the Scholastic terminology). The differentiation of men into the classes and occupations established through historical development became for Luther, as we have seen, a direct result of the divine will. The perseverance of the individual in the place and within the limits which God had assigned to him was a religious duty. This was the more certainly the consequence since the relations of Lutheranism to the world were in general uncertain from the beginning and remained so. Ethical principles for the world could not be found in Luther's realm of ideas; in fact it never quite freed itself from Pauline indifference. Hence the world had to be accepted as it was, and this alone could be made a religious duty.

But in the Puritan view, the providential character of the play of private economic interests takes on a somewhat different emphasis. True to the Puritan tendency to pragmatic interpretations, the providential purpose of the division of labor is to be known by its fruits. On this point Baxter expresses himself in terms which more than once directly recall Adam Smith's well-known apotheosis of the division of labor. The specialization of occupations leads, since it makes the development of skill possible, to a quantitative and qualitative improvement in production, and thus serves the common good, which is identical with the good of the greatest possible number. So far, the motivation is purely utilitarian, and is closely related to the customary view-point of much of the secular literature of the time.

But the characteristic Puritan element appears when Baxter sets at the head of his discussion the statement that "outside of a well-marked calling the accomplishments of a man are only casual and irregular, and he spends more time in idleness than at work," and when he concludes it as follows: "and he [the specialized worker] will carry out his work in order while another remains in constant confusion, and his business knows neither time nor place . . . therefore is a certain calling the best for everyone." Irregular work, which the ordinary laborer is often forced to accept, is often unavoidable, but always an unwelcome state of tran-

sition. A man without a calling thus lacks the systematic, methodical character which is, as we have seen, demanded by worldly asceticism.

The Quaker ethic also holds that a man's life in his calling is an exercise in ascetic virtue, a proof of his state of grace through his conscientousness, which is expressed in the care and method with which he pursues his calling. What God demands is not labor in itself, but rational labor in a calling. In the Puritan concept of the calling the emphasis is always placed on this methodical character of worldly asceticism, not, as with Luther, on the acceptance of the lot which God has irretrievably assigned to man.

Hence the question whether anyone may combine several callings is answered in the affirmative, if it is useful for the common good or one's own, and not injurious to anyone, and if it does not lead to unfaithfulness in one of the callings. Even a change of calling is by no means regarded as objectionable, if it is not thoughtless and is made for the purpose of pursuing a calling more pleasing to God, which means, on general principles, one more useful.

It is true that the usefulness of a calling, and thus its favor in the sight of God, is measured primarily in moral terms, and thus in terms of the importance of the goods produced in it for the community. But a further, and, above all, in practice the most important, criterion is found in private profitableness. For if that God, whose hand the Puritan sees in all the occurrences of life, shows one of His elect a chance of profit, he must do it with a purpose. Hence the faithful Christian must follow the call by taking advantage of the opportunity. "If God show you a way in which you may lawfully get more than in another way (without wrong to your soul or to any other), if you refuse this, and choose the less gainful way, you cross one of the ends of your calling, and you refuse to be God's steward, and to accept His gifts and use them for Him when He requireth it: you may labor to be rich for God, though not for the flesh and sin."

Wealth is thus bad ethically only in so far as it is a temptation to idleness and sinful enjoyment of life, and its acquisition is bad only when it is with the purpose of later living merrily and without care. But as a performance of duty in a calling it is not only morally permissible, but actually enjoined. The parable of the servant who was rejected because he did not increase the talent which was entrusted to him seemed to say so directly. To wish to be poor was, it was often argued, the same as wishing to be unhealthy; it is objectionable as a glorification of works and derogatory to the glory of God. Especially begging, on the part of one able to work, is not only the sin of slothfulness, but a violation of the duty of brotherly love according to the Apostle's own word.

The emphasis on the ascetic importance of a fixed calling provided an ethical justification of the modern specialized division of labor. In a similar way the providential interpretation of profit-making justified the activities of the business man. The superior indulgence of the *seigneur* and the parvenu ostentation of the *nouveau riche* are equally detestable to asceticism. But, on the other hand, it has the highest ethical appreciation of the sober, middle-class, self-made man. "God blesseth His trade" is a stock remark about those good men who had successfully followed the divine hints. The whole power of the God of the Old Testament, who rewards His people for their obedience in this life, necessarily exercised a similar influence on the Puritan who, following Baxter's advice, compared his own state of grace with that of the heroes of the Bible, and in the process interpreted the statements of the Scriptures as the articles of a book of statutes. . . .

[To] recapitulate up to this point, [Protestant asceticism] acted powerfully against the spontaneous enjoyment of possessions; it restricted consumption, especially of luxuries. On the other hand, it had the psychological effect of freeing the acquisition of goods from the inhibitions of traditionalistic ethics. It broke the bonds of the impulse of acquisition in that it not only legalized it, but (in the sense discussed) looked upon it as directly willed by God. The campaign against the temptations of the flesh, and the dependence on external things, was, as besides the Puritans the great Quaker apologist Barclay expressly says, not a struggle against the rational acquisition, but against the irrational use of wealth.

But this irrational use was exemplified in the outward forms of luxury which their code condemned as idolatry of the flesh, however natural they had appeared to the feudal mind. On the other hand, they approved the rational and utilitarian uses of wealth which were willed by God for the needs of the individual and the community. They did not wish to impose morification on the man of wealth, but the use of his means for necessary and practical things. The idea of comfort characteristically limits the extent of ethically permissible expenditures. It is naturally no accident that the development of a manner of living consistent with that idea may be observed earliest and most clearly among the most consistent representatives of this whole attitude toward life. Over against the glitter and ostentation of feudal magnificence which, resting on an unsound economic basis, prefers a sordid elegance to a sober simplicity, they set the clear and solid comfort of the middle-class home as an ideal.

On the side of the production of private wealth, asceticism condemned both dishonesty and impulsive avarice. What was condemned as covetousness, Mammonism, etc., was the pursuit of riches for their own sake. For wealth in itself was a temptation. But here asceticism was the power "which ever seeks the good but ever creates evil"; what was evil in its sense was possession and its temptations. For, in conformity with the Old Testament and in analogy to the ethical valuation of good works, asceticism looked upon the pursuit of wealth as an end in itself as highly reprehensible; but the attainment of it as a fruit of labor in a calling was a sign of God's blessing. And even more important: the religious valuation of restless, continuous, systematic work in a worldly calling, as the highest means to asceticism, and at the same time the surest and most evident proof of rebirth and genuine faith, must have been the most powerful conceivable lever for the expansion of that attitude toward life which we have here called the spirit of capitalism. . . .

One of the fundamental elements of the spirit of modern capitalism, and not only of that but of all modern culture: rational conduct on the basis of the idea of the calling, was born — that is what this discussion has sought to demonstrate — from the spirit of Christian asceticism.

On Time

The modern sense of morality in business depends not only on a work ethic and a sense of honesty but also on a social psychology of time. Business people are busy; they constantly check their watches; idleness is shameful. Even if they do not punch in and punch out on the time clock, they get to work "on time" and know what it means to "quit early" or to "work late" (either one, done too often, induces guilt and indicates that something is wrong). The first mark of modern economic responsibility is being where one is supposed to be when one is supposed to be there. Further, modern industry, from assembly lines to production schedules to robotics, depends on precise timing.

In crosscultural encounters, those from more developed economies and those from less developed ones are frequently struck by different cultural senses of time. For some, life is ordered by this sense of punctuality, planning, and appointments that is identified with responsibility. Daily tasks (even for the young) are organized into scheduled units, each with its programmed number of minutes or hours. For others, life is measured by seasons or the moon or the rise and fall of the sun. A few days or hours or even years lost or gained here or there are not seen as enormously significant. Life, after all, in this view, is not about scurrying to meet the demands of production or efficiency or date books or calendars. Being is more important than doing. Time is the sea in which we swim, not the master of our days nor the servant of some higher meaning.

Every culture, of course, has had its own way of reckoning time. But the motivations for doing so vary. One reason for trying to calculate the movements of the stars or the changing of the seasons was so that the human community could more easily fit into the natural and cosmic rhythms. Indeed, this was the central reason for the development of quite advanced timepieces in ancient China. This motivation contrasts with the effort to divide time in such a way that humans could better control nature and transcend the cosmic forces in action for spiritual and moral reasons.

The idea that the efficient use of time is an ethical and theological matter and thus decisive in the basic pattern of the good life had to be developed, much as did the work ethic and the sense of honesty. It reflects a certain orientation toward meaning, God, and the world. Such a notion is important only where people believe that the Ultimate, the timeless and eternal, is in some basic way related to the proximate, the temporal and transient, and that we humans ought, for the sake of the Ultimate, to order the proximate by the rational ordering of time.

In a major book on this subject, Harvard historian David Landes traces the development of time-keeping devices in cultures where they were most extensively developed — China and Europe — and shows that moral and spiritual factors lay behind the particular use of time technology in the West. In this excerpt, he shows the intimate relationship of discipline to time and the technology of clocks that was born in the monastery but that matured among the lay business practitioners and workers in the towns.

Of Time: Work, Prayer, and Monks

David Landes

The clock did not create an interest in time measurement; the interest in time measurement led to the invention of the clock.

Where did this demand come from? Not from the mass of the population. Nine out of ten Europeans lived on the land. "Labor time," to quote the medievalist Jacques Le Goff, "was still the time of an economy dominated by agrarian rhythms, free of haste, careless of exactitude, unconcerned by productivity — and of a society created in the image of that economy, *sober and modest,* without enormous appetites, undemanding, and incapable of quantitative efforts." Town and city life, to be sure, was different. The city dweller has no natural sequence of tasks to rhythm his day. The very uniformity of his occupation makes him time-conscious; or if he is moving about, the irregular pattern of his contacts imparts a sense of haste and waste. But urban life developed late in the Middle Ages, from about the eleventh century on, and already before that there was an important timekeeping constituency. That was the Christian church, in particular the Roman branch.

It is worth pausing a moment to consider this temporal discipline of Christianity, especially of Western Christianity, which distinguishes it sharply from the other monotheistic religions and has not been adequately examined in the literature on time measurement. In Judaism the worshiper is obliged to pray three times a day, but at no set times: in the morning (after daybreak), afternoon

From David Landes, *Revolution in Time* (Cambridge: Harvard University Press, 1983), pp. 58-78.

(before sunset), and evening (after dark). A pious Jew will recite his prayers as soon as possible after the permissible time; but if circumstances require, he has substantial leeway in which to perform his obligation. Today some of the starting times of worship are given on calendars to the minute, thanks to astronomical calculations. In ancient and medieval times, however, nature gave the signals. The animals woke the Jew to prayer, and the first of the morning blessings thanks God for giving the rooster the wit to distinguish between day and night. The evening prayer could be recited as soon as three stars were visible; if the sky was cloudy, one waited until one could no longer distinguish between blue and black. No timepiece or alarm was needed.

Islam calls for five daily prayers: at dawn or just before sunrise, just after noon, before sunset, just after sunset, and after dark. Again, none of these requires a timepiece, with the possible exception of the noon prayer. I say "possible," because high noon is easily established in sunny climes by visual means. Besides, insofar as the local religious authorities wanted to set times for prayer and used clocks for the purpose, they could easily make do with the sundials and water clocks of the ancients. In most Islamic countries, the sun usually shines and water rarely freezes. Moreover, in Islam as in Judaism the times of prayer are bands rather than points, and local tradition determines how much the prayers may be delayed without impairment. In both religions prayer is a personal act, without clerical or congregational mediation, and worship, with some exceptions, need not be collective and simultaneous.

Christianity, especially monastic Christianity, differs from both. The early Christians had no standard liturgy; the new faith was not yet a church. Usage varied from place to place, and prayer was as much a function of opportunity as of obligation. Insofar as the Nazarenes were still Jews, they built on the practices of the older faith, with its morning and night recitations (Deut. 6:7, "when thou liest down and when thou risest up") or its triples office (Dan. 6:11, "he kneeled upon his knees three times a day"). But then they added their own devotions, in part to give expression to those praises and supplications that had no place in the Jewish service, in part to distinguish themselves from the "obdurate" Hebrews. By the early third century, Tertullian, acknowledging the impracticality of the Pauline ideal of ceaseless prayer (1 Thess. 5:17), recommended daily prayers prescribed by the Law, there would be devotions at the third, sixth, and ninth hours. These were the points that divided the daytime into quarters, and Tertullian asserts that they were recognized as temporal punctuation marks by all nations: "they serve to fix the times of business and they are announced publicly." Very convenient: that way there was no problem of knowing when to pray, since civil time signals would serve to summon the faithful.

The setting of prayer times by the clock was no small matter. It represented a first step toward a liturgy independent of the natural cycle. This tendency was much reinforced by the introduction of a night service, which apparently went back to the earliest days of Christianity, when the Jewish followers of Jesus, having celebrated the Sabbath, met again on Sunday for nocturnal devotions. The choice of hour had some precedent in scripture:

> I have remembered thy name, O LORD,
>   in the night . . .   (Psalm 119:55)

> At midnight I will rise to give thanks
>   unto thee . . .   (Psalm 119:62)

> I rose early at dawn and cried;
>   I hoped in Thy word.
> Mine eyes forestalled the night-watches,
>   That I might meditate in Thy word.
>   (Psalm 119:147-148)

Scriptural precedent, though, is more often sanction than cause. The early Christians had good prudential reasons for coming together in the night while Caesar slept; also a most potent spiritual motive, namely the hope of salvation. The Gospel speaks of the Bridegroom's coming at midnight (Matt. 25:6), which led the church in Constantinople to institute a midnight office. Yet such precision was the exception, indeed was deliberately avoided. Uncertainty was preferable, because more compelling. The Lord will come, it is written, "at an hour you do not expect" (Matt. 24:42-44). "If he comes in the second watch, or if in the third," blessed are the servants who are watching and waiting (Luke 12:37-38). Nocturnal

devotions, then, appropriately called vigils, were a spiritual watch for the second coming (the *parousia*) of the Lord. Pliny the Younger wrote of this practice to the emperor Trajan at the beginning of the second century: "They are wont to come together before the light."

For hundreds of years there were no rules, only practices. Rules came with monasticism — with the formation of a regular clergy (that is, a clergy subject to a *regula,* or rule) whose vocation it was to pray and pray often, and in so doing to save that multitude of the faithful whose worldly duties or inconstancy prevented them from devoting themselves entirely to the service of God. The innovator here was Pachomius in Upper Egypt in the early fourth century: against the prevailing eremitic individualism, his new order instituted a minute regulation of the collective praying, working, eating, and sleeping day. "It was there that for the first time we see realized the practice of an office in the strict sense, recited every day in the name of the church, *publicum officium,* at set hours." Among the services: vigils, the *officium nocturnum* that was later merged with and called matins. From Egypt the practice spread to Palestine, Syria, Mesopotamia, and Europe.

Still, rules varied — "they were still feeling their way." Temporal prescriptions, for example, may have been looser in the Eastern churches, where the natural diurnal cues continued to play an important role. It was in the West, in the Rule of Saint Benedict, that the new order of the offices found its first complete and detailed realization: six (later seven) daytime services (lauds, prime, tierce, sext, none, vespers, and compline) and one at night (vigils, later matins). As the very names indicate, most of these were designated and set in terms of clock hours. Hence the very term "canonical hour," which eventually became synonymous with the office itself: one "recited the hours."

This was around 530. In the centuries that followed, the Benedictine rule was adopted by other orders, including the great houses grouped around the Vatican and Lateran basilicas, thereby ensuring the eventual normalization of the canonical hours throughout Western Christendom. Progress in this direction was uneven owing to the physical insecurity of a violent age, in many parts of Europe, monastic life was disrupted for long periods by recurrent invasions and internecine strife. Besides, each house had its own interpretation of the Rule: we are talking here about customs *(consuetudines),* and there is nothing so idiosyncratic as custom.

Beginning in the tenth century external pressures eased, and the foundation of the Cluniac order (910), with its almost exclusive devotion to prayer, was the first sign of a general monastic revival. Cluny was followed by others, in particular the Cistercians (beginning of the twelfth century), under whom work regained the place it had held alongside prayer in the original Benedictine discipline. The very nature of these foundations, as expressed by the idea of an order, pressed them toward uniformity of practice and observance, and their reformism found expression not in the latitudinarianism often associated with the idea of reform today, but in the restoration of discipline. Discipline in turn had at its center a temporal definition and ordering of the spiritual life: *omnia horis competentibus compleantur* — all things should be taken care of at the proper time. . . .

Why was punctuality so important? One reason was that lateness — "God forbid!" — might make it necessary to abridge an office, in particular matins: "Let great care be taken that this shall not happen." Another, I think, was that simultaneity was thought to enhance the potency of prayer. That would also explain the requirement that devotions be chanted aloud: to sing along is to sing together. That indeed was the point of community: the whole was greater than the sum of the parts. . . .

This religious concern for punctuality may seem foolish to rationalists of the twentieth century, but it was no small matter to a monk of the Middle Ages. We know, for one thing, that time and the calendar were just about the only aspect of medieval science that moved ahead in this period. In every other domain, these centuries saw a drastic regression from the knowledge of the ancients, much of it lost, the rest preserved in manuscripts that no one consulted. Much of this knowledge was not recovered until reimported hundreds of years later via the Arabs and the Jews in Spain or, still later, from Byzantium. But time measurement was a subject or active inquiry even in the darkest of the so-called dark ages. One has only to compare Isidore of Seville's rudimentary

notions of time in his *De Temporibus* (615) with Bede's enormously popular textbook, the *De Temporum Ratione* (725) — written in the peripheral, tribal battleground that was Anglo-Saxon England — to realize the progress made in this field. . . .

Time mattered to such experts . . . , but it also mattered to the ordinary monk, for whom getting up in the dark of the night was perhaps the hardest aspect of monastic discipline. Indeed, the practical meaning of "reforming" a house meant first and foremost the imposition (reimposition) of this duty. The sleepyheads were prodded out of bed and urged to the office; also prodded during service lest they fail in their obligations. Where the flesh was weak, temptation lurked. Raoul Glaber (early eleventh century) tells the tale of a demon who successfully seduced a monk by holding out the lure of sweet sleep: "As for you, I wonder why you so scrupulously jump out of bed as soon as you hear the bell, when you could stay resting even unto the third bell . . . but know that every year Christ empties hell of sinners and brings them to heaven, so without worry you can give yourself to all the voluptuousness of the flesh. . . ."

These, I suggest, are what we now know as anxiety dreams. They clearly reflect the degree to which time-consciousness and discipline had become internalized. Missing matins was a serious matter, so serious that it has been immortalized for us by perhaps the best known of children's songs:

Frère Jacques, Frère Jacques,
Dormez-vous? dormez-vous?
Sonnez les matines, sonnez les matines,
Ding, ding, dong; ding, ding, dong. . . .

"Idleness," wrote Benedict, "is an enemy of the soul." The fixing of a daily schedule or prayer was only part of a larger ordering of all monachal activity, worldly as well as religious. Indeed, for monks there was no distinction between worldly and religious: *laborare est orare* — to work *was* to pray. hence, there were rules setting aside times for work, study, eating, and sleeping; rules prescribing penalties and penance for latecomers; rules providing explicitly for the maintenance of the clock and its nightly adjustment, so that it would wake the sacristan at the proper time. Note that at this stage, it was not the clock that worked the big bells. As "Frère Jacques" tells us, the clock merely rang loudly enough to get the bell ringer out of bed.

These were not necessarily clocks in our sense of the term. Many of them did not indicate the time or run continuously. Rather, they were what we now know as timers and associate with three-minute eggs or film developing. But these were timers that ran for hours. They were set to run during the night and served only to trip the alarm; to use the medieval terminology, they were *horologia nocturna* or *horologia excitatoria*. It is now generally agreed, moreover, that some of them made use of an escapement-type mechanism to produce a to-and-fro motion of the hammer(s) beating on the bell, and that this mechanism was often weight-driven. . . .

Bells, bells, bells. Big bells and small. Monasteries were beehives of varied activity, the largest productive enterprises of medieval Europe. Brothers, lay brothers, and servants were busy everywhere — in the chapel, the library, the writing room (scriptorium), in the fields, the mill, the mines, the workshops, the laundry, the kitchen. They lived and worked to bells. The big bells tolled the canonical hours and the major changes, and their peal carried far and wide, not only within the convent domain but as far as the wind could take it. And the little bells tinkled insistently throughout the offices and meals, calling the participants to attention and signaling the start of a new prayer, ceremony, or activity. All of this was part of a larger process of depersonalization, deindividuation. Monastic space was closed space — areas and corridors of collective occupancy and movement — so arranged that everyone could be seen at all times. So with time: there was "only one time, that of the group, that of the community. Time of rest, of prayer, of work, of meditation, of reading: signaled by the bell, measured and kept by the sacristan, excluding individual and autonomous time." Time, in other words, was of the essence because it belonged to the community and to God; and the bells saw to it that this precious inextensible resource was not wasted.

The bells, in short, were drivers — goads to effective, productive labor. It is this larger role, going far beyond reveille, that may account of the higher standard of punctuality enforced by the new monastic orders of the eleventh and twelfth

centuries. The Cistercians in particular were as much an economic as a spiritual enterprise (they would not have recognized a difference). Their agriculture was the most advanced in Europe; their factories and mines, the most efficient. They made extensive use of hired labor, and their concern for costs made them turn wherever possible to labor-saving devices. Their Rule enjoined them, for example, to build near rivers, so as to have access to water power; and they learned to use this in multifunctional, staged installations designed to exploit power capacity to the maximum. For such an undertaking, timekeeper and bells were an indispensable instrument of organization and control; and it may be that it was the proliferation of this order throughout Europe and the expansion of its productive activities that stimulated the interest in finding a superior timekeeper and precipitated the invention of the mechanical clock. . . .

The monastic clergy may have provided the primary market for timekeepers and the principal stimulus to technical advances in this domain, but the church alone cannot account for the popularity and development of the new device. . . .

Consider the new sources of demand. These consisted of, first, the numerous courts — royal, princely, ducal, and episcopal; and second, the rapidly growing urban centers with their active, ambitious bourgeois patriciates. At the very beginning, in the thirteenth and early fourteenth centuries, princes and courtiers may well have accounted for the greater part of secular demand for timekeepers. Typically they were the wealthiest members of society, the more given to luxury expenditure because they did not earn their income. (It is always easier to spend other people's money.) The preceding centuries, moreover, had been an era of sustained increase in wealth and power: population was growing, and with it the area under cultivation; trade also, and with it the yield of duties and taxes. These new resources nourished central authority and enabled it to enforce that condition of order that is in itself the best encouragement to productive activity. . . .

In the long run, though, the future of the infant clock industry lay with the bourgeoisie — originally and literally the residents of the *bourgs* (in colloquial American English, the *burgs*). Along with the crown, indeed in alliance with it, the town was the great beneficiary of the agricultural and commercial expansion of the high Middle Ages (eleventh to fourteenth centuries). Sleepy villages were becoming busy marketplaces; administrative centers and points of transshipment and exchange were growing into nodes of wholesale and retail trade and craft industry. The more successful residents of these new cities quickly came to constitute a new elite, an urban patriciate possessed of great wealth and a sense of power and self-esteem that rivaled that of the older landed elite. They were able, further, by shrewd cooperation with the crown and the construction of an urban military base, to win substantial autonomy for their municipalities, which were organized by collective agreement among the resident and by contractual arrangement with or concession from higher authority into self-administering communes. These had their own fiscal resources, so that when mechanical clocks appeared on the scene, the cities of western and Mediterranean Europe could afford to build them as complements to or successors to the cathedrals — a symbol of a new secular dignity and power and a contribution to the general welfare.

Why the general welfare? Because, just like the monastery, the city needed to know the time even before the mechanical clock became available. Here, too, necessity was the mother of invention.

We have already noted the contrast between the "natural" day of the peasant, marked and punctuated by the given sequence of agricultural tasks, and the man-made day of the townsman. The former is defined by the sun. The latter is bounded by artificial time signals and the technology of illumination and is devoted to the same task or to an array of tasks in no given sequence. The spatial compactness of the city, moreover, is an invitation to serial engagements: with careful planning (that is, timing), one can multiply oneself. To be sure, the medieval town long remained half-rural. Everybody who could, kept a *basse-cour* of chickens, roosters, rabbits, and other useful livestock; so that some of the natural time signals heard in the countryside were heard in the city as well. Still, it is one thing to receive or perceive the time; another thing to track and use it. The two environments differed radically in the temporal consciousness.

This difference was growing. (It was not to contract until the nineteenth century, with the coming of the railroad and the penetration of the country by the rhythms and servitudes of the city.) As commerce developed and industry expanded, the complexity of life and work required an ever larger array of time signals. These were given, as in the monasteries, by bells: the urban commune in this sense was the heir and imitator of the religious community. Bells sounded for start of work, meal breaks, end of work, closing of gates, start of market, close of market, assembly, emergencies, council meetings, end of drink service, time for street cleaning, curfew, and so on through an extraordinary variety of special peals in individual towns and cities. . . .

The introduction of equal hours and the habituation of urban populations to public time announcements had profound consequences for the European mentality. Medieval man, it has been observed, was innumerate as well as illiterate. How much reckoning could he do in a world that knew no uniformity of measurement? Units of distance were linked to physical characteristics that varied as people do (the English *foot*, for instance, and the French inch, called a *pouce*, which means thumb); while weights typically were converted to volume standards (a *bushel* of grain) that inevitably varied from place to place and mill to mill. Even the learned were not accustomed to using numbers. The calculation of the calendar, for example — a crucial aspect of liturgical discipline — was confined to specialist computists. The schools offered little if any training in arithmetic, and the very persistence of roman numerals was both symptom and cause of calculational paralysis.

All of this began to change in the twelfth and thirteenth centuries — just as one would expect. This was a period of growing trade, and he who trades must reckon. So must clerks and functionaries who count taxes and expenditures, and these were years of rapid development of royal power and government apparatus. It was no accident that arabic numerals came in at this time, or that books that had once resorted to metaphor now gave numbers, however erroneous, of armies, treasures, buildings, and the like.

It was the urban, commercial population that seems to have been quickest to learn the new language and techniques. Arithmetic was the province above all of the unlettered speakers of the vernacular (as opposed to Latin). Many of these learned arithmetic in the shop or on the road, but even before they entered trade, they learned to count by the bells of the clock. Not by the old church bells ringing the canonical hours; these did not mark equal units and hence did not lend themselves to addition and subtraction. But the new bells and the calculations they made possible (how long until? how long since?) were a school for all who listened and began to organize their lives around them. Meanwhile the church clung to the old ways and, so doing, yielded the rhythm of life and work to the lay authorities and the bourgeoisie. Equal hours announced the victory of a new cultural and economic order. Here indeed was an unintended consequence: the monks had wrought too well.

On Law

The work ethic with its "this-worldly asceticism" and the conviction that the disciplined use of time is central to responsible living developed, as we have seen in the previous readings, from religious roots. These attitudes injected a moral vitality into the ethos of the West, one which gave birth to modern economic life.

But this ethos had other elements as well. The root moral attitudes were embodied in and protected by specific social institutions that nurtured distinctive virtues, fomented particular life-styles, and engendered characteristic institutional patterns designed to bring ethical order to the whole of life. Every value orientation needs organizational support systems to become effective in the common life, and these systems have to be developed over time and must be able to take account of the hard conflicts that arise in every social context.

In the history of the West, no institution nurtured these attitudes or faced these conflicts over a longer period of time than the church. Before the Reformation, the church had three distinctive loci. Two of these were the monastery and the congregation. Through the actions of councils and popes, the church also generated a cosmopolitan system of jurisprudence that included, surpassed, and reorganized the legal heritage of the West on the basis of a fresh understanding of Scripture.

In the following selection from Harold J. Berman's masterwork on the history of law, we see how the church's law (canon law) promoted the possibilities of dynamic corporations, fostered principles that both gave permission for independent action and set limits to action, established the concept of "limited" political power, and legitimated the notions of corporation as an economic institution — distinct from persons, families, or states — that could use and dispose of property.

This development influenced all subsequent constitutional orders that have a theory of human rights and economic cooperation. It was decisive for modern economic life, for it depends heavily on laws that demand corporate accountability and constrain arbitrary power under universal principles. No modern business leader can afford to be ignorant of the law, or of the basic principles that stand behind its various provisions.

Berman shows how certain kinds of stability can be related to certain kinds of change. Some structures tend to promote, not inhibit, dynamic systems. Further, he shows how law comes to embody ethical principles by constructing a critical arena of value-laden decision making that is less than religious visions of holiness, but more than political uses of power. Throughout, Berman argues that, inevitably, theology stands at the base of law — and, in this case, ecclesiology stands at the root of the corporation.

259

Theological Sources of the Western Legal Tradition

Harold J. Berman

It is impossible to understand the revolutionary quality of the Western legal tradition without exploring its religious dimension. It has been said that the metaphors of the day before yesterday are the analogies of yesterday and the concepts of today. So the eleventh-century legal metaphors were the twelfth-century legal analogies and the thirteenth-century legal concepts. The legal metaphors that lay at the foundation of the legal analogies and concepts were chiefly of a religious nature. They were metaphors of the Last Judgment and of purgatory, of Christ's atonement for Adam's fall, of the transubstantiation of bread and wine in the sacrament of the eucharist, of the absolution of sins in the sacrament of penance, and of the power of the priesthood "to bind and to loose" — that is, to impose or remit eternal punishment. Other legal metaphors were chiefly feudal, though they had religious overtones — metaphors of honor, of satisfaction for violation of honor, of pledge of faith, of reciprocal bonds of service and protection. All of these metaphors were part of a unified structure of rituals and myths. (The word "myth" is used here not in the old sense of "fable" but rather in the opposite, now widely accepted, sense of "sacred truth.")

What such an exploration shows is that basic institutions, concepts, and values of Western legal systems have their sources in religious rituals, liturgies, and doctrines of the eleventh and twelfth

Harold J. Berman, *Law and Revolution: The Formation of the Western Legal Tradition* (Cambridge: Harvard University Press, 1983), pp. 165, 199-208, 215-21.

centuries, reflecting new attitudes toward death, sin, punishment, forgiveness, and salvation, as well as new assumptions concerning the relationship of the divine to the human and of faith to reason. Over the intervening centuries, these religious attitudes and assumptions have changed fundamentally, and today their theological sources seem to be in the process of drying up. Yet the legal institutions, concepts, and values that have derived from them still survive, often unchanged. Western legal science is a secular theology, which often makes no sense because its theological presuppositions are no longer accepted. . . .

To assert that a *system* of [church] law was created . . . for the first time in the century and a half between 1050 and 1200 is not to deny that a legal *order* had existed in the church from its early beginnings. The New Testament itself, especially in the Epistles of St. Paul and the Acts of the Apostles, gives evidence that there were within the Christian community legally constituted authorities that declared and applied rules concerning matters of doctrine, worship, mortality, discipline, and ecclesiastical structure. Also, from the earliest times, elders (bishops) had judged disputes between Christians and imposed sanctions for offenses committed by them. [Early documents] contained many ecclesiastical rules intended to regulate conduct and to serve as a basis of ecclesiastical adjudication. . . .

Over the centuries the canons issued by synods and ecumenical councils, as well as by individual bishops, multiplied, and occasionally they were brought together in unofficial collections, which also contained rules laid down in Scripture and in the writings of the church fathers as well as individual decretal letters and decisions of patriarchs, popes, and bishops. . . .

These ecclesiastical laws, both in the West and in the East, were heavily influenced by Roman law. Various concepts and rules of classical and post-classical Roman law were carried over, especially in matters of property, inheritance, and contracts. . . .

In addition, the laws of the church during the first millennium of its history bore the strong influence of the Bible, especially the Old Testament. From the Bible the church derived the authority of the Ten Commandments and of many other moral principles formulated as divine commands.

Beyond that, the Bible transmitted the pervasive belief in a universal order governed by the God who was both supreme legislator and supreme judge. As heir to the tradition of Israel, the church took seriously the numinous character of law, its pervasiveness in the divine order of creation. Moreover, many specific rules of conduct contained in the Old and New Testaments, as well as many Biblical examples and metaphors, were carried over into ecclesiastical canons.

Of course, the legal concepts and rules that prevailed in the church in the West from the fifth to the tenth centuries were influenced not only by Roman law and Biblical law but also, and especially, by the folklaw of the Germanic peoples, with its emphasis on honor, oaths, retribution, reconciliation, and group responsibility. [All this contributed to the formation of the first modern Western system.] . . .

The systematization of the laws of the church in the late eleventh and the twelfth centuries . . . rested on the premise that a body of law is not a dead corpse but a living corpus, rooted in the past but growing into the future. Contrary to what is sometimes supposed, this concept of legal evolution was not an invention of Edmund Burke, Friedrich von Savigny, and the "historical school" of the eighteenth and nineteenth centuries; it was a basic presupposition of Western jurists — and nonjurists — from the late eleventh and the twelfth centuries on, first in the ecclesiastical sphere and then in the secular.

These interrelated elements — (1) the periodization into old law and new law, (2) the summarization and integration of the two as a unified structure, and (3) the conception of the whole body of law as moving forward in time, in an ongoing process — are defining features of the Western legal tradition. . . .

Building on the Gregorian Reform, and especially on Gregory's *Dictates* of 1075, the canonists of the late twelfth and the thirteenth centuries attributed supreme governance *(imperium)* in the church to the pope. The pope was head of the church; all other Christians were its limbs, its members. He had full authority *(plenitudo auctoritatis)* and full power *(plenitudo potestatis)*. . . .

These powers did not attach to the pope because he was the Bishop of Rome, but they attached to the Bishop of Rome because he was

pope; that is, they attached to him not by virtue of his ordination *(potestate ordinis)* but by virtue of his jurisdiction *(potestate jurisdictionis)*. Indeed, the Archdeacon Hildebrand was elected Pope Gregory VII even though he had not yet been ordained a priest, let alone a bishop. . . . His power to decide doctrinal disputes derived solely from his jurisdiction as supreme officer of the church.

The sharp distinction between ordination and jurisdiction, made for the first time in the late eleventh and the twelfth centuries, was one of the fundamental constitutional principles of the Church of Rome. Ordination was a sacrament, that is, a sacred symbol of divine grace. . . . Jurisdiction, on the contrary, was a power conferred by the church as a corporate legal entity. It was the power to govern by law — to "speak law" *(jus dicere)* within the limits established by law. . . .

Thus the *imperium* and the *auctoritas* or *potestas* of the pope, though supreme and full, were identified also as his *jurisdictio,* which meant that they were legal in nature. But that, in turn, meant that there were legal limits to their exercise. . . .

The principle of jurisdictional limitations upon power and authority was a fundamental constitutional principle underlying the new system of canon law of the late eleventh and twelfth centuries. Yet an analysis of the ways in which the jurisdictional principle was applied requires a consideration not of constitutional law as such but rather of corporation law. According to the canonists, it was the church as a corporate legal entity that conferred jurisdiction upon individual ecclesiastical officers (pope, bishops, abbots), and it was the law of corporations that determined the nature and limits of the jurisdiction thus conferred.

The term "corporation" (*universitas;* also *corpus* or *collegium*) was derived from Roman law, as were many of the terms used to define it and many of the rules applicable to it. Yet there are substantial differences between the corporation law of the Romans and that of the twelfth-century western European jurists.

According to Roman law at the time of Justinian, the state as such (still called *populus Romanus*) was considered to be a corporation, but its rights and obligations were regulated administratively rather than in the courts and it was not subject to the civil law; however, the imperial treasury did have rights of ownership and other civil rights and obligations, and could sue and be sued in the ordinary courts. Also municipalities were corporations, with the right to own property and make contracts, to receive gifts and legacies, to sue and be sued, and, in general, to perform legal acts through representatives. Similarly, many private associations, including organizations for maintaining a religious cult, burial clubs, political clubs, and guilds of craftsmen or traders, were considered to be corporations, although the extent of their rights depended on privileges and liberties granted by the emperor. In 313, when Christianity became the official religion of the empire — and to a certain extent before that time — churches and monasteries were added to the list of associations that were considered to have the capacity to receive gifts and legacies as well as to have property and contract rights generally and the right to act as legal persons through representatives. In addition, the legislation of Justinian recognized charitable societies such as hospitals, asylums, orphanages, homes for the poor, and homes for the aged as having legal capacity to receive gifts and legacies for special purposes, with a general right of supervision preserved in the bishop of the diocese. (Neither in the East nor in the West was the concept of a corporation as a legal entity applied, prior to the late eleventh century, to the whole church — the Church Universal.)

The Roman jurists, with their intense hostility to definitions and theories, did not address in general terms the question of the relationship of the universities to the ensemble of its members. The Digest stated epigrammatically: "What is of the corporation is not of individuals," and again, "If something is owed to a corporation it is not owed to individuals; nor do individuals owe what the corporation owes." However, many questions — such as whether a corporation derives its existence and its powers from a grant by a public authority or from the will of its founders or from its own nature as an association, what powers are exercised by its officers and what cannot be done by them without the consent of the members, and how the officers are to be chosen and how and why they may be dismissed — were not discussed by the Roman jurists. Even the phrases "legal person" and "legal personality" were rarely used by them, and were never analyzed. Only in retrospect can one discern several implicit principles of

Roman corporation law that became explicit in Western legal thought in the twelfth century when corporation law first began to be systematized. Two of these were, first, the principle that a corporation has legal capacity to act through representatives, and second, the principle that the rights and duties of the corporation are distinct from those of its officers.

Roman rules of corporation law were carried by the church into the Germanic communities of western Europe. They had to compete, however, with Christian concepts of the corporate nature of ecclesiastical communities and also with Germanic concepts of the corporate nature of associations generally. St. Paul had called the church the body or corpus of Christ (1 Cor. 12:27), and he wrote to the Galatians: "for you are all one in Christ Jesus" (Gal. 3:28). Other Christian metaphors for the church were "wife," "spouse," "mother." All such personifications were meant to apply to the fellowship of believers, "the communion of saints," "the congregation of the faithful." Although it was accepted that all Christians everywhere formed a spiritual body, the main emphasis was on the spiritual unity of individual churches or individual dioceses. In that connection it was further emphasized that the prelate of the individual church — the parish priest or the bishop or some other shepherd of the flock — was united with his church in a spiritual marriage. As Christ was believed to be married to the Church Universal, so the bishop or priest was believed to be married to the local church. He represented it as the head represents the rest of the body. These Christian ideas were diametrically opposed to the ideas implicit in the treatment of churches as corporations under Roman law. This is not to say that under the Roman Empire or under Germanic emperors and kings the church opposed giving to individual churches the status of corporations under Roman law. On the contrary, it eagerly sought the protection of that status. Yet it was at least anomalous that under Roman law the Christians who composed an ecclesiastical corporation bore no responsibility for acts performed by prelates in the name of the corporation and for its benefit; and it was even more anomalous that the prelates themselves were considered to act only as agents and not, for example, as constituent members or partners within the association.

Germanic concepts of association bore some resemblance to Christian concepts of the church as "one person," a *corpus mysticum*. As Otto von Gierke, the great historian of Germanic law, emphasized, the Germanic household, or warrior band, or clan, or village was conceived to have a group personality which all the members shared; its property was their common property and they bore a common liability for its obligations. However, according to Gierke the *Genossenschaft* ("fellowship") derived its unity and its purpose not from a higher authority, whether divine or human, but solely from within itself, that is, solely from the voluntary coming together of the members to achieve an end set by themselves.

The twelfth-century canonists utilized earlier Roman, Germanic, and Christian concepts of corporate entities in developing a new system of corporation law applicable to the church. To some extent they harmonized the three competing sets of concepts. They did so, however, not as an abstract exercise in legal reasoning but in order to achieve practical solutions to actual legal conflicts that arose in the wake of the Papal Revolution: legal conflicts between the church and the secular polities as well as legal conflicts within the church. At the same time, they looked for the interrelationships among these legal conflicts and sought to systematize the underlying principles by which they were to be resolved.

The following questions illustrate the kinds of practical issues that arose in litigation in the twelfth century.

Is the head of a corporation (say, a bishop) required to consult its members (the chapter) before making a decision to sue or to answer a charge in court? Is he required not only to consult them but also to obtain their consent? What about a decision to alienate property, or a decision to confer privileges of various kinds?

Can a chapter repudiate a settlement with an opposing party made by a bishop without its consent?

How is the consent of a chapter to be expressed?

Who is to exercise the powers of the head of a corporation during a vacancy, that is, when the head has died or resigned or been dismissed?

If the clergy of a chapter may act on behalf of their bishop if he becomes incapable through ill-

ness or old age, may they do so also if he is neglectful?

Can a corporation commit crimes? Can it commit torts? Is it liable for the crimes or torts of its officers?

May an ecclesiastical corporation be formed without the permission of the pope?

If a corporation loses all its members, does it continue to exist? If not, may it be revived by one or more applicants who qualify for membership?

What happens to the property of a corporation that ceases to exist?

May a corporation create law for its members? May it select a magistrate to exercise lawmaking power in its name? May it select a judge to decide cases in its name?

May a corporation to which property has been given for a particular purpose lawfully decide to use that property for another purpose?

And a final question: would the answers to those questions be different if the corporation were not a bishopric or an abbey or some other local body, but the entire Church of Rome, headed by the sole vicar of Christ on earth?

Such practical legal questions arose once the church in the West declared itself to be a corporate legal entity — an *universitas* — independent of emperors, kings, and feudal lords. What is most striking about these questions is, first their legal formulation; second, the high degree of conscious interrelationship among them; and third (related to the second), the systematic character of the answers that were eventually given, that is, the resort to a conscious sytematization of corporation law in order to arrive at a set of satisfactory solutions.

On Usury

It is said that in-group/out-group relations are best seen at table, in bed, and at work — with whom one feasts, marries, and does business. Historically, these are determined largely by religiously grounded law and ethics. It may be difficult for some to imagine what it means to live in an environment in which all these relationships are defined by ethnicity and inherited social status; but many in history and much of the world still today believe that race and nation are sacred — as can be seen in Beirut, the Balkans, much of Africa, and the new rhetoric of "multiculturalism" today. Economic and political interests, but also the senses of "natural orders" and "our god" (or of "our culture"), are at issue. Change requires a transformation of worldview.

One area of such transformation that has been of enormous importance for business is in regard to "usury." The battles — religious, moral, and social — that have been fought around it are not over and, it seems, have to be fought in new terms in every generation. But in the following excerpt, Benjamin Nelson, the internationally regarded intellectual historian, traces how a particular sacred text prohibiting usury among members of "one's own kind" was applied over the centuries — until a theological shift altered the idea of communal "brotherhood," and legitimated the use of credit generally. In effect, this shift made every "other" a brother or sister in moral terms, and every brother and sister an "other" in business relationships. A banker ought to exercise fiduciary responsibility in regard to the resources of each customer and ought not to give special rates to those to whom she or he is related. Mortgages should be available equally to all reliable clients, and not only to "our kind." Nelson investigates the roots of the idea that we ought to do business this way.

His questions are closely related to two other issues, one more philosophical and one more ethical. The first is the notion that money, as a social artifact, was not "fecund," as Aristotle, Thomas, Luther, and both Islam and Judaism have taught. In its broadest implications, the issue is whether what is moral is what is natural, and whether making money from money should be viewed as "unnatural," and thus immoral. If it is "unnatural," banking and finance will be assigned to those "strangers" who are only marginal to society.

A related issue is the fact that, for much of history and in parts of the world still, no distinction was made between "interest" and "usury." Standards of "just price" and practices of "fixed price" for any goods and services, including money-lending, were not well established. High rates meant inability to pay, and debt meant perpetual servitude. Both creditors and debtors were reviled on all sides. Nelson shows how modern business practice depends on a now-forgotten religious change.

On the Taking of Interest

Benjamin N. Nelson

The Deuteronomic commandment on usury has had a fateful career. Its checkered fortunes over a twenty-five-hundred-year span in Orient and Occident disclose an unexplored episode in the tangled history of "transvaluations of values" which culminated in the spirit of capitalism. To follow its meanderings from the Jerusalem of the Prophets and Priests to mid-nineteenth century Europe is to survey the major phases of the ethical evolution of the West: first, the kinship morality of the tribal society; then the universal brotherhood of medieval Christianity; and finally the utilitarian liberalism of modern times. . . .

Prologue — Deuteronomy formed a cornerstone of the blood brotherhood morality of the Hebrew tribesmen. It assumed the solidarity of the *mishpaha* (clan) and the exclusion of the *nokri* (the foreigner, as contrasted with the *ger*, the protected sojourner, or the *toshab*, the resident stranger) from the privileges and obligations of the fraternity. It forbade the Hebrew to take *neshek* (usury, interest) from his brother *(ah)*, but permitted him to exact it from the *nokri*:

XXIII:19. Thou shalt not lend upon usury *(neshek)* to thy brother *(l'ahika)*; usury of money, usury of victuals, usury of anything that is lent upon usury:

XXIII:20. Unto a stranger *(nokri)* thou mayest lend upon usury; but unto thy brother thou shalt not lend upon usury, that the Lord thy God may bless thee in all that thou settest thine hand to in the land whither thou goest to possess it.

Moralists of the Middle Ages found the double-edged text a constant source of embarrassment, a simultaneous and unparalleled challenge to the Church's general prohibition of usury and the Christian program of universal brotherhood. Medieval Christianity, aspiring to universalism, rejected the Deuteronomic discrimination against the alien as anachronistic and obnoxious, and proposed to transcend the morality of clan by joining the "other" to the "brother."

The German Reformation marks the turning point in the fortunes of the Deuteronomic commandment. That age saw the issues of usury and brotherhood furnish the occasion for sanguinary social struggles between the conservative and radical elements of several Protestant nations. The alternatives at stake were posed in the following fashion: Were the fraternalistic institutions celebrated in the Old and New Testaments alike meant only for a day, or were they the expression of God's plan for all the ages? More precisely, were the Sabbatical and Jubilee releases, the prohibition of usury between brothers, and the love-communism of the Apostles in the early Jerusalem congregation mere expedients for special circumstances, or were they the supreme illustrations of God's eternal will? . . .

* * *

The chronicle of the changing interpretations of Deuteronomy in Western exegesis begins with a dictum by St. Jerome (340-420), and an elaborate commentary in *De Tobia* of St. Ambrose of Milan (340-397). They were the first authoritative Western theologians who strove to harmonize the irritating text with the ecclesiastical stand on usury. Jerome contended that the prohibition of usury among brothers in Deuteronomy had been universalized by the Prophets and the New Testament. There was, in short, no scriptural warrant for taking usury from anyone.

Ambrose proposed to account for the Deuteronomic discrimination against the alien by an appeal to Biblical antiquities. The true meaning and limits of Deuteronomy xxiii:20, he argued, were clear only in the light of the authorized war of the Chosen People against the tribes inhabiting the

From Benjamin N. Nelson, *The Idea of Usury: From Tribal Brotherhood to Universal Otherhood* (Princeton: Princeton University Press, 1949), pp. xv-xxi, 3-46, 73-82.

Promised Land. "The Law forbids you under any circumstances," Ambrose warned, "to exact usury from your brother." Who is he? Your brother is "your sharer in nature, co-heir in grace, every people, which, first, is in the Faith, then under the Roman Law." Who then, was the stranger? The Amalekite, the Amorite, the Canaanite: the notorious foes of God's people, who illegally withheld the lands which the Lord had promised to Israel for a habitation.

> From him, it says there, demand usury, whom you rightly desire to harm, against whom weapons are lawfully carried. Upon him usury is legally imposed. On him whom you cannot easily conquer in war, you can quickly take vengeance with the hundredth. From him exact usury whom it would not be a crime to kill. He fights without a weapon who demands usury: he who revenges himself upon an enemy, who is an interest collector from his foe, fights without a sword. Therefore, where there is the right of war, there also is the right of usury. . . .

With the beginning of the Crusades, alert churchmen were pained to discover that Ambrose's resolution opened the door to unwelcome economic and religious developments. They decided to throw off the double burden which his awkward defense of the Deuteronomic proviso had saddled upon Christianity by resorting to new exegetical strategies more in harmony with the economic interest of the Church and the universalist teachings of Christ.

All formulations of international economic policy were now seen to hinge on the adjustment of this issue. Unqualified acceptance of Ambrose's teaching authorized Christians to demand interest from Moslems — a few of the early commentators on Gratian's *Decretum (ca.* 1140) pointed out that this was a useful economic weapon in recovering their rightful heritage as Christians from the modern Canaanites — but it also gave the Jews in Europe *carte blanche* to continue to exact usury from their Christian debtors. There was the rub. In the eyes of the Popes, especially Innocent III (1198-1216), effective promotion of the crusades required the curtailment of all usurers, Jewish as well as Christian, clerical as well as secular. Aided by formal government licenses and priestly collusion, these

different but equally abhorred sorts of usurers were exploiting the opportunities for lush profits in commodity corners and loans on the security of lands which were thrown on the market by the crusade-bound nobility. The view of Ambrose allowed a loophole, also, for double-dealing Italian, South French, and Catalan merchants, who persisted, despite repeated papal fulminations, in providing the Saracen enemy with money and supplies.

Before long, these concerns were superseded by fears of a more radical challenge to the existing economic order and morality. By the end of the twelfth century, "manifest" Christian usurers were outstripping the Jews, and were well on their way to becoming an international menace. Like Judas Iscariot, contemporaries said, these parvenus stood ever ready to betray Christ and Christian brotherhood for thirty pieces of silver. There were even those who dared to cite God's word, Deuteronomy, against the Church probition of usury. Christian morality and feudal society were in the balance. Thus challenged, the Church felt called upon to check the economic revolution in the making by redefining the problem of the Brother and the Other.

The threat to the professed universalism of Christianity embodied in the Ambrosian analysis could no longer go unanswered. The double standard for the Brother and the Other appeared mysterious, paradoxical, anachronistic, and vicious to Christians, who were fascinated by the vision (or vocabulary) of a morality rooted in the Brotherhood of Man under the Fatherhood of God. It seemed altogether incompatible with Christ's summons to love our enemies. Had He not challenged Deuteronomy and pointed the new way in Luke vi:35:

> But love ye your enemies, and do good, and lend, hoping for nothing again; and your reward shall be great, and ye shall be the children of the Highest: for He is kind unto the unthankful and to the evil.

How mysterious the blood brotherhood morality of the Jews appeared to such Christians may be seen in the confession in St. Bruno of Asti's (d. 1123) *Expositio in Deuteronomium* that he could not perceive God's motives in permitting the Jews to take interest from aliens.

Without venturing to iron out the Ambrosian difficulty, the Second Lateran Council of 1139 declared the unrepentant usurer condemned by the Old and New Testaments alike and, therefore, unworthy of ecclesiastical consolations and Christian burial. . . .

Although it was never licit for the Jews to take interest, they were yielded permission to do so for the same reasons for which they were accorded the resort to the bill of divorcement, in order to avoid a greater evil and because it was difficult to bring them to perfection all at once. . . .

Alexander of Hales's (d. 1249) review of the arguments exhibits a different emphasis. It was not licit, he declared, to take usury from an alien even in ancient times; it was merely permitted the Jews . . . because of the hardness of their hearts. God feared that they would commit the greater sin of taking usury from a brother. Secondly, as others have pointed out, Ambrose was not discussing usury properly speaking, but tributes, exacted from infidels to promote their conversion to the faith. If interest is to be taken only from those whom we have a right to kill, we ought hardly to call it interest at all, because those whom we have a right to kill have no proper title to their goods, and therefore usury does not constitute a usurpation. . . .

Thomas Aquinas's (1225-1274) summary is brief and clear:

The Jews were forbidden to take usury from their brethren, i. e., from other Jews. By this we are given to understand that to take usury from any man is simply evil, because we ought to treat every man as our neighbor and brother, especially in the state of the Gospel, whereto all are called. . . . They were permitted, however, to take usury from foreigners, [not as though it were lawful,] but in order to avoid a greater evil, lest, to wit, through avarice, to which they were prone, according to Is. lvi:11, they should take usury from Jews, who were worshippers of God.

The special permission granted to the Jews in Deuteronomy, he replied to the inquiring Duchess of Brabant, has long lapsed. They may not legitimately retain what they have exacted from others by usury, and are bound to restitution, despite all government decrees to the contrary.

The same range of attitudes and scale of values are found in all the prominent theologians of the epoch. . . .

* * *

The German Reformation witnessed the outbreak of the modern revolt against the Hebraic and medieval Christian prohibitions of usury. Within less than three decades after the day when Luther stood before the boy Emperor at Worms, there occurred a fateful desertion of a principle which had claimed the allegiance of men in the Judaeo-Christian tradition for more than two millennia, the principle that the taking of interest from a co-religionist was utterly antithetical to the spirit of brotherhood. This step was far from being the result of deliberate hostility or indifference to cherished Jewish and medieval Christian ways of conceiving the Lord's design for man. On the contrary, the sixteenth-century revolt against Deuteronomy was set in motion by the fact that in the Reformation, for the first time in the history of Western Christianity, the long-obscured premises of the inherited communalisitc ethic were pressed to their ultimate conclusions.

Wherever the evangelical spirit took hold, visionary enthusiasts seized upon the fraternalistic core both of the Pentateuch and the Gospels to project a new Jerusalem, a Christian community so constituted that brothers should have no occasion to take usury from one another. In the critical hour, all of this proved anathema to the leaders of the Reformation (Luther, Melandchthon, Zwingli, Bucer) — a plot to discredit their own plans for a reform sponsored by the accredited civil magistrates. The Reformers met the challenge head on, accusing the extremists of conspiring to pervert the spiritual message of the Scriptures for the sake of their own carnal advantage. The Christian man, Luther cried, was free, under no obligation to observe dead Mosaic ordinances. As for the Gospels, they were not intended to take the place of the civil law of to supplant existing authorities. These utterances mark a milestone in the history of the idea of the Brother and the Other. In circles under the influence of these official leaders, unauthorized attempts to reorganize society in the light of the injunctions of Moses and Christ were henceforth to be dismissed as utopian and, even, anti-Christian. . . .

Throughout the first period of his campaign against usury, Luther takes an extremely exalted view of Christ's teaching with regard to economic activities. He accuses the medieval doctors of turning the Lord's commandments into mere counsels. There are, he says, three Christian ways of acting with respect to temporal goods. The first is to submit meekly to repeated acts of violence and extortion, as we are counseled to do in Matthew v:40. This is the most exacting of Christ's demands. The two less difficult charges laid on Christians are to give freely to those in need, and to extend loans without hope of return of the principal. These latter actions were so easy of accomplishment, Luther says, that they were even commanded to the Jews in the Old Testament. Here the Reformer verges upon the issue of the Brother and the Other. Without explicitly citing the twenty-third chapter of Deuteronomy — he refers, instead, to Deuteronomy xv:4, 7 and xvi:11 — he repeatedly emphasizes the fact that Luke vi obligated Christians to make no distinctions between friends, brothers, and enemies:

> If we look the word of Christ squarely in the eye, it does not teach that we are to lend without charge, for there is no need for such teaching, since there is no lending except lending without charge, and if a charge is made, it is not a loan. He wills that we lend not only to friends, the rich, and those to whom we are well disposed, who can repay us again, by returning this loan, or with another loan, or by some other benefit; but also that we lend to those who cannot or will not repay us, such as the needy and our enemies. . . . Thus, too, the doctrine falls which says that we are not bound to lay aside the *signa rancoris,* as has been said above; and even though they (the *doctores*) speak rightly concerning lending, yet they turn this commandment into a counsel and teach us that we are not bound to lend to our enemies or to the needy, unless they are in extreme want. Beware of this!

The second period in Luther's campaign against usury extends from the summer of 1523 to the close of the Peasant Revolts in the winter of 1525. The stormy developments of these two years compelled Luther to institute a crucial modification of his former emphasis. In the first phase of his mission, he had appeared as the inspired champion of national evangelical revolt against foreign domination. His program appeared eventually to promise a drastic reorganization of society in the light of the scriptural injunctions to brotherly love. By the close of 1525, he was indelibly stamped as an ally of the territorial princes and of the annuity-owning creditors in their opposition to the demands of the lower classes and their radical preacher leaders.

In the hour of decision, Luther turned his back upon the utopian visions of a New Jerusalem. The cataclysm of 1525 forced him to reveal that he stood four-square against the radical claims that both individuals and government were eternally obligated to observe the Mosaic and Gospel prohibitions of usury.

During his first years as a Reformer, Luther had expressed himself with great abandon in the matter of usury. The evangelical character of his successive pronouncements, especially of his two sermons on usury of 1519-1520, had quickened the hopes of interest-ridden debtors. Many who professed to be his followers assumed that he would make no compromise with the civil or canon laws permitting usury, but that he would insist on the literal fulfillment of the word of Scripture. Some must have felt that he was not only not averse to a drastic revision of the terms of onerous *Zins* contracts, but that he even favored a cancellation, at least in part, of outstanding *Zins* charges. Luther seemed not to care that a great number of these contracts were held in the name of religious foundations. On the contrary, he gave the impression of considering that situation an incentive rather than a deterrent to radical reform.

Luther's left-wing followers took heart from his forceful sermons. Soon they were surpassing Luther in their insistence on the immediate application to the contemporary scene of Mosaic and Gospel teachings on social issues. A brief reference by Luther in his *Longer Sermon on Usury* to Deuteronomy xv served Karlstadt (*ca.* 1480-1541) as a point of departure for a sweeping proposal to adopt the principles of the Hebraic releases of the seventh year as an aid in the elimination of slavery and mendicancy. Presently other evangelically minded preachers were to give new dimensions to the campaign against usury by pushing the

Deuteronomic precedents into the forefront of their agitation. . . .

Luther and Melanchthon flatly condemned all expressions of popular initiative in putting the Mosaic and Gospel laws into effect. If there was to be reform, Luther taught, it would have to come from the princes, and not the people. Luther, indeed, appears to have hoped, at one point, that the Emperor and princes would adopt the Old Testament principle of the proportionate tithe in the settlement of the *census* charges. He became especially active in advocating this measure in the summer of 1524, . . . when the peasant hosts were gathering. In the new conclusion of his *Longer Sermon on Usury* completed in the last week in June, he himself recommended the adoption of the principle behind the Jubilee year. Nevertheless, he simultaneously warned the people against taking matters into their own hands. Whatever Christ may have counseled, said Luther, in obvious reference to the situation at Eisenach and elsewhere, the civil authorities were right to use the sword against recalcitrant debtors. He insists repeatedly the Christians of the sixteenth century were no more bound by the "judicial laws" of Moses than they were by the ceremonial laws, such as the law of circumcision. His private correspondence of 1525, indeed, finds him groping toward the propositions which were to receive their classic expression at the hands of Calvin. The Christian man, Luther was to say, was in the truest sense of the Gospel free to lend his money as he chose. Not the Gospels, but the economic situation and the considerations of public utility, were of paramount importance in finding clues for the regulation of loans at interest. . . .

*   *   *

With John Calvin we stand on the threshold of a "transvaluation of values." In demolishing the inherited exegesis of Deuteronomy, Calvin departs even farther from the medieval morality than has been suspected. To Ashley, Calvin's attack on the Aristotelian, more correctly the patristic and scholastic, concept of the sterility of money seemed a "turning point in the history of European thought"; Weber declared that his recasting of the doctrine of "calling" and his enunciation of the program of *inner-weltliche Askese* were the foundations of the modern capitalist

spirit. . . . But no one has noticed that Calvin, self-consciously and hesitantly, charted the path to the world of Universal Otherhood, where all become "brothers" in being equally "others."

Calvin is the first religious leader to exploit the ambivalence of the Deuteronomic passage in such a fashion as to prove that it was permissible to take usury from one's brother. His exegesis spells the demise of Deuteronomy. He succeeded in legitimizing usury without seeming to impair the vitality either of the universalism or the fraternalism of the Christian ethic. Trained as a jurist, he was able to lend precision to the notion, crudely anticipated by Luther and Bucer, that the Mosaic and Gospel rules were to be translated in the light of the individual conscience, the equity of the Golden Rule, and the requirements of public utility.

Calvin on Deuteronomy became a Gospel of the modern era. Everyone from the sixteenth to the nineteenth century who advocated a more liberal usury law turned to Calvin for support. Even those who would not or could not mention his name were compelled to speak his words. If today we do not appeal to his teachings, it is because we have learned his lessons too well. Religious or even ethical vocabulary is no longer needed to justify the moral and economic postulates which he helped to establish.

The new coordinates assumed in Calvin's schema are exposed in the reply to Claude de Sachinas' inquiry on the problem of usury in the closing months of 1545, and in the sermons and commentaries on various books of the Old Testament during the following decades.

"If we wholly condemn usury," he begins, "we impose tighter fetters on the conscience than God himself." Scriptures forbid only biting usury (*ne-shek*), usury taken from the defenseless poor. Luke vi:35 has been perverted to imply that He commanded us to lend gratuitously, and without any hope of gain.

> . . . As elsewhere in speaking of the sumptuous feasts and ambitious social rivalry of the rich He commands rather that they invite in form the streets the blind, the lame and the poor, who cannot make a like return, so here, wishing to correct the vicious custom of the world in lending money, He directs us to lend chiefly to those from whom there is no hope of recovery.

As for Deuteronomy xxiii:19 — God had no other object in view "except that mutual and brotherly affection should prevail amongst the Israelites." The precept to lend without usury was plainly a part of the Jewish polity and not a universal "spiritual law." Else, God would not have allowed the Hebrews to lend at usury to Gentiles. The spiritual law does not admit such discriminations. The peculiar turn of the Deuteronomic text cannot be justified by appealing to God's promise to the Hebrews in respect to Canaan. The peoples of this area were not singled out for special mention. Rather, God spoke generally of all the nations of the world, including Egypt and Syria, and all the islands of the sea, in short, of all who traded with the Jews.

God has permitted many things *"pour la police des Juifs"* which are in themselves not good; therefore, He did not mean to legitimize the taking of usury from strangers. He merely left it unpunished. God showed this indulgence to the Jews, "since otherwise a just reciprocity would not have been preserved, without which one party must needs be injured." God had laid the Jews alone and not foreign nations under the obligation of the law against usury.

> In order, therefore, that equality be preserved, He accords the same liberty to His people which the Gentiles would assume for themselves; for this is the only intercourse that can be endured, when the condition of both parties is similar and equal.

Today, the Deuteronomic law must be applied to the profit of the Christians, rather than be allowed to justify the exploitation of Christians by Jews. On a correct interpretation, the text can hardly give comfort to Jewish usurers. (Here, indeed, Calvin undertakes to show how the Deuteronomic discrimination, rightly understood, reacts against the Jews of his own age.) Modern Jews are wrong, he explains, to assume that everything is permitted them so long as they practice no extortion among themselves.

> Indeed, they are doubly to be condemned. For they ought to be joined with us since God has opened the door to His church. But now the Jews have quit the place, they have been deprived and banished from the Kingdom of God, and, there-

fore, we [Christians] are reputed the Sons of Abraham, even though we be not descended according to the flesh of this race. Though then, the Jews anciently had the privilege to exercise usury against pagans, it does not mean that today they ought to burden and molest the children of God, even those who have been driven from His house and have been disowned in consequence of their rebellion and disobedience.

Thus, the specific content of the judicial law which was given to the ancient people is abrogated. There remains as residue only what is dictated by the rules of charity, equity, and justice, from which, in the first place, the old law springs, namely, the injunction not to show harshness to our needy brethren.

> The law of Moses (Deut. xxiii:19) is political, and does not obligate us beyond what equity and the reason of humanity suggest. Surely, it should be desirable if usuries were driven from the whole world, indeed that the word be unknown. But since that is impossible, we must make concession to the common utility.

However, Calvin admits, both Ezekiel xviii:5-9 and Psalms xv:5 seem to express universal opposition to usury, and what is more, to condemn the taking of *tarbith* as well as *neshek*. If, however, we take recourse to the infallible norm of justice, we discover that usury does not conflict with the law of God in every case. Hence, it follows that not all usury need be damned. There is a grave difference between taking usury in the course of business and setting up as a usurer. If a person takes profit on a loan on only one occasion, he is not called a usurer. This is not mere word play, Calvin insists. Men invent cavils, thinking to fool one another by the construction of "specious titles," but God does not admit such deceptions.

It must, nevertheless, be granted, that usury is not allowed indiscriminately in every case, at all times, under all forms, from everybody. For example: an excessive rate is objectionable; one who takes usury constantly has no place in the Church of God; interest taken from the poor is prohibited. In short, it is important to cling to the rule: usury is permissible if it is not injurious to one's brother.

Lastly, the crucial question: May it not be objected, Calvin asks, that usury ought to be outlawed today for the same reason that it was forbidden to Jews, "because among us there is a fraternal union?" His reply is epoch-making:

> There is a difference in the political union, for the situation in which God placed the Jews and many other circumstances permitted them to trade conveniently among themselves without usuries. Our union is entirely different. Therefore I do not feel that usuries were forbidden to us simply, except in so far as they are opposed to equity or charity.

Today, the "wall of partition which formerly separated Jew and Gentile is . . . broken down," the discrimination against the alien abrogated. Yet, since it is abundantly clear that the prohibition of usury among the ancient peoples was merely a part of their political constitution, it follows that

> usury is not now unlawful, except in so far as it contravenes equity and brotherly union. Let each one, then, place himself before God's judgment seat, and not do to his neighbor what he would not have done to himself, from whence a sure and infallible decision may be come to. To exercise the trade of usury, since heathen writers counted it amongst disgraceful and base modes of gain, is much less tolerable among the children of God; but in what cases, and how far it may be lawful to receive usury upon loans, the law of equity will better prescribe than any lengthened discussions.

It hardly seems necessary to elaborate any further on the niceties of Calvin's theory of usury. Reminiscence of his novelties will be found in virtually every writer to be discussed henceforth in the course of the present work. It does seem desirable, however, to add one remark — this by way of assessment or evaluation of the impact of his exegesis on the meaning and subsequent history of the idea of fraternity in the West. There is, of course, no warrant for imagining that Calvin renounces the traditional Christian summons to universal brotherhood and *caritas*. If anything, he feels called on to disallow the tampering with these precepts which he felt was countenanced by medieval authorities. Still, the specific gravity of the claim of brotherhood is radically altered by his support of the taking of interest and his reinter-

pretation of the Deuteronomic issue. Such a substitution impels our use of the phrase "Universal Otherhood." This is only one instance of the process of re-evaluation of the moral currency which has unnumbered illustrations in the history of morality. Calvin, it is true, appeals intensely for brotherhood; but there is a world of difference between a brotherhood in which interest is abominated and a brotherhood in which it is authorized. Neither the Hebrews nor the Christians of the Middle Ages would have been able to understand the latter kind of brotherhood.

On Technology

Another area on which modern business depends is technology. Every society has methods for adapting to the environment and getting food, clothing, and shelter from it. The ingenuity of various societies in doing so over the ages is amazing. But the methods of production in modern society are science based in ways that traditional societies did not imagine. Now the environment is adapted to society. Modern society is more interested in turning raw resources into goods efficiently so that they can be sold and used than is either "pure science" or "traditional technique." Some say that the chief indicator of economic viability in the future is technology.

Science-based technology, of course, has not always been an integral part of human society. It has to be developed, and this development had to be advanced by those who believed in it in the midst of a society that was divided in its assessment of science and technology. It is not true that this was essentially a battle between science and religion. What is true is that some kinds of religion have fostered and endorsed scientific thought and technological development while other kinds of religion have opposed and resisted them because they believed other forms of thought were more valid.

Some held that theology itself is a science that is properly in alliance with the natural and social sciences and technologies. The divine is understood in terms of *logos*, with its implications of logic and reasonable discourse. Others accented the tension between faith and reason and between religious experience and human discourse. Further, some saw the divine as quite other than the biophysical universe, which was viewed as "fallen" and thus in need of human efforts to transform it, to make it more in accord with divine purposes for humanity. Still others saw the biophysical universe as part of, or as the embodiment of, the divine, and therefore something that ought not to be disturbed by too much human prodding, probing, and rearranging. Contemporary debates about the relationship of development to ecology are the modern, secular manifestations of this historic debate.

In such issues we see a basic presupposition behind Robert Merton's famous writings about the relationship of religion, science, and technology. He shows that a decisive transformation occurred when that part of the religious heritage of the West which was favorably inclined to science and technology emerged into dominance at the hands of the Puritans and Pietists. He is aware of the great thinkers of the medieval world who had brought together Christian theology with the ancient sciences, and of the fact that there were pro-scientific tendencies even then; but, he argues, it was among the leading intellects of the century after the Reformation that the decisive transformations occurred. In fact, this transformation — along with other factors such as those traced in this chapter — is what generated the Industrial Revolution and the successive waves of technological and economic revolutions since.

Puritanism, Pietism, and Science

Robert K. Merton

. . . . It is the thesis of this study that the Puritan ethic . . . so canalized the interests of seventeenth-century Englishmen as to constitute an important *element* in the enhanced cultivation of science. The deep-rooted religious *interests* of the day demanded in their forceful implications the systematic, rational, and empirical study of Nature for the glorification of God in His works and for the control of the corrupt world. . . .

Robert Boyle was one of the scientists who attempted explicitly to link the place of science in social life with other cultural values, particularly in his *Usefulness of Experimental Natural Philosophy.* Such attempts were likewise made by John Ray, whose work in natural history was path-breaking and who was characterized by Haller as the greatest botanist in the history of man; Francis Willughby, who was perhaps as eminent in zoology as was Ray in botany; John Wilkins, one of the leading spirits in the "invisible College" which developed into the Royal Society; . . . and others. For additional evidence we can turn to the scientific body which, arising about the middle of the century, provoked and stimulated scientific advance more than any other immediate agency: the Royal Society. In this instance we are particularly fortunate in possessing a contemporary account written under the constant supervision of the members of the Society so that it might be representative of their views of the motives and aims of that association. This is Thomas Sprat's widely read *History of the Royal-Society of London,*

From Robert K. Merton, *Social Theory and Social Structure* (New York: Free Press, 1957), pp. 574-85.

published in 1667, after it had been examined by Wilkins and other representatives of the Society.

Even a cursory examination of these writings suffices to disclose one outstanding fact: certain elements of the Protestant ethic had pervaded the realm of scientific endeavor and had left their indelible stamp upon the attitudes of scientists toward their work. Discussions of the why and wherefore of science bore a point-to-point correlation with the Puritan teachings on the same subject. Such a dominant force as was religion in those days was not and perhaps could not be compartmentalized and delimited. Thus, in Boyle's highly commended apologia for science it is maintained that the study of Nature is to the greater glory of God and the Good of Man. This is the motif which recurs in constant measure. The juxtaposition of the spiritual and the material is characteristic. This culture rested securely on a substratum of utilitarian norms which constituted the measuring-rod of the desirability of various activities. The definition of action designed for the greater glory of God was tenuous and vague, but utilitarian standards could easily be applied.

To a modern, comparatively untouched by religious forces, and noting the almost complete separation, if not opposition, between science and religion today, the recurrence of these pious phrases is apt to signify merely customary usage, and nothing of deep-rooted motivating convictions. . . . But such an interpretation is possible only if one neglects to translate oneself within the framework of seventeenth-century values. Surely such a man as Boyle, who spent considerable sums to have the Bible translated into foreign tongues, was not simply rendering lip service. As G. N. Clark very properly notes in this connection:

There is . . . always a difficulty in estimating the degree to which what we call religion enters into anything which was said in the seventeenth century in religious language. It is not solved by discounting all theological terms and treating them merely as common form. On the contrary, it is more often necessary to remind ourselves that these words were then seldom used without their accompaniment of meaning, and that their use did generally imply a heightened intensity of feeling.

The second dominant tenet in the Puritan ethos designated social welfare, the good of the many, as a goal ever to be held in mind. Here again the contemporary scientists adopted an objective prescribed by the current values. Science was to be fostered and nurtured as leading to the domination of Nature by technologic invention. The Royal Society, we are told by its worthy historian, "does not intend to stop at some particular benefit, but goes to the root of all noble inventions." But those experiments which do not bring with the immediate gain are not to be condemned, for as the noble Bacon has declared, experiments of Light ultimately conduce to a whole troop of inventions useful to the life and state of man. This power of science to better the material condition of man, he continues, is, apart from its purely mundane value, a good in the light of the Evangelical Doctrine of Salvation by Jesus Christ.

And so on through the principles of Puritanism there was the same point-to-point correlation between them and the attributes, goals, and results of science. Such was the contention of the protagonists of science at that time. Puritanism simply made articulate the basic values of the period. If Puritanism demands systematic, methodic labor, constant diligence in one's calling, what, asks Sprat, more active and industrious and systematic than the Art of Experiment, which "can never be finish'd by the perpetual labors of any one man, nay, scarce by the successive force of the greatest Assembly?" Here is employment enough for the most indefatigable industry, since even those hidden treasures of Nature which are farthest from view may be uncovered by pains and patience. . . .

The exaltation of the faculty of reason in the Puritan ethos — based partly on the conception of rationality as a curbing device of the passions — inevitably led to a sympathetic attitude toward those activities which demand the constant application of rigorous reasoning. But again, in contrast to medieval rationalism, reason is deemed subservient and auxiliary to empiricism. Sprat is quick to indicate the pre-eminent adequacy of science in this respect. It is on this point probably that Puritanism and the scientific temper are in most salient agreement, for the combination of *rationalism and empiricism* which is so pronounced in the Puritan ethic forms the essence of the spirit of modern science. Puritanism was suf-

fused with the rationalism of neo-Platonism, derived largely through an appropriate modification of Augustine's teachings. But it did not stop there. Associated with the designated necessity of dealing successfully with the practical affairs of life within this world — a derivation from the peculiar twist afforded largely by the Calvinist doctrine of predestination and *certitudo salutis* through successful worldly activity — was an emphasis upon empiricism. These two currents brought to convergence through the logic of an inherently consistent system of values were so associated with the other values of the time as to prepare the way for the acceptance of a similar coalescence in natural science.

Empiricism and rationalism were canonized, beatified, so to speak. It may very well be that the Puritan ethos did not directly influence the method of science and that this was simply a parallel development in the internal history of science, but it is evident that through the psychological compulsion toward certain modes of thought and conduct this value-complex made an empirically-founded science commendable rather than, as in the medieval period, reprehensible or at best acceptable on sufferance. . . . It was in this system of values that reason and experience were first markedly considered as independent means of ascertaining even religious truths. Faith which is unquestioning and not "rationally weighted," says Baxter, is not faith, but a dream or fancy or opinion. In effect, this grants to science a power which may ultimately limit that of [dogma]. . . .

Perhaps the most directly effective element of the Protestant ethic for the sanction of natural science was that which held that the study of nature enables a fuller appreciation of His works and thus leads us to admire the Power, Wisdom, and Goodness of God manifested in His creation. . . . For a Barrow, Boyle, or Wilkins, a Ray or Grew, science found its rationale in the end and all of existence: glorification of God. Thus, from Boyle:

> . . . God loving, as He deserves, to be honour'd in all our Faculties, and consequently to be glorified and acknowledg'd by the acts of Reason, as well as by those of Faith, there must be sure a great Disparity betwixt that general, confus'd and lazy Idea we commonly have of His Power and Wisdom, and the Distinct, rational and affecting no-

tions of those Attributes which are form'd by an attentive Inspection of those Creatures in which they are most legible, and which were made chiefly for that very end.

Ray carries this conception to its logical conclusion, for if Nature is the manifestation of His power, then nothing in Nature is too mean for scientific study. The universe and the insect, the macroocosm and microcosm alike, are indications of "divine Reason, running like a Golden Vein, through the whole leaden Mine of Brutal Nature."

Up to this point we have been concerned in the main with the directly felt sanction of science through Puritan values. While this was of great influence, there was another type of relationship which, subtle and difficult of apprehension though it be, was perhaps of paramount significance. It has to do with the preparation of a set of largely implicit assumptions which made for the ready acceptance of the scientific temper characteristic of the seventeenth and subsequent centuries. . . .

It has become manifest that in each age there is a system of science which rests upon a set of assumptions, usually implicit and seldom questioned by the scientists of the time. The *basic* assumption in modern science "is a widespread, instinctive conviction in the existence of an *Order of Things,* and, in particular, of an Order of Nature." This belief, this faith, for at least since Hume it must be recognized as such, is simply "impervious to the demand for a consistent rationality." In the systems of scientific thought of Galileo, Newton, and of their successors, the testimony of experiment is the ultimate criterion of truth, but the very notion of experiment is ruled out without the prior assumption that Nature constitutes an intelligible order, so that when appropriate questions are asked, she will answer, so to speak. Hence this assumption is final and absolute. As Professor Whitehead indicated, this "faith in the possibility of science, generated antecedently to the development of modern scientific story, is an unconscious derivative from medieval theology." But this conviction, prerequisite of modern science though it be, was not sufficient to induce its development. What was needed was a constant interest in searching for this order in nature in an empirico-rational fashion, that is, an *active* interest in this

world and its occurrences plus a specific frame of mind. With Protestantism, religion provided this interest: it actually imposed obligations of intense concentration upon secular activity with an emphasis upon experience and reason as bases for action and belief. . . .

The cultural environment was permeated with this attitude toward natural phenomena which was derived from both science and religion and which enhanced the continued prevalence of conceptions characteristic of the new science.

On Differentiation

This chapter has focused on readings by major scholars who have traced some of the ways in which religion has created the modern ethos and established the social frameworks whereby modern economic life became possible. To conclude this chapter, we turn to a widely discussed essay by the leading American social theorist of the post–World War II period, Talcott Parsons. He offers a summary of the religious economic patterns now increasingly adopted around the world.

Several concepts are central to Parsons's work. One is "autonomy," which he defines as "independence of authoritarian control combined with responsibility defined in moral-religious terms." It is related to a second concept, "differentiation." Parsons believes that at certain turning points in history, theological influences channeled change toward pluralism, although they were opposed by other religious forces that resisted such changes and viewed the triumphant ones as having fallen away from true morality and religion. For example, church and state became separate from one another under pressures from religious groups who did not want political regimes determining the nature and content of faith, although some see that development as the political denigration of religion and the triumph of secularism. Similarly, economic institutions became increasingly distinct from political, social, and cultural ones that defined economic status according to "divinely appointed" ethnic, gender, or cultural roles. Some see this as a loss of communal tradition and the triumph of materialism and individualism; others see it as the triumph of ethical religion over traditional paganism.

Such shifts to institutional pluralism are paralleled by a personal differentiation. Individuals become more autonomous also. People increasingly make their own decisions about religious, political, cultural, familial, and economic matters — which implies, of course, increased areas of competency and more complex patterns of ethical reflection. Socially and personally, modernity brings increased independence of authoritarian control.

But this does not necessarily lead, as some claim it does, to rootlessness, egocentric individualism, and the breakdown of morality. Each sector of society and each individual person, now more clearly distinct from others, becomes more self-governing and thus more directly involved in the process of interpreting the general values that bind together the whole. It becomes possible for universalist "moral-religious" principles and purposes to be adopted and applied by many peoples and groups in terms of "responsibility." Modern industrial societies may well reflect a relative actualization, not the forsaking, of moral and theological insight, although that insight is criticized and opposed by other moral and religious, or antitheological, points of view. If so, the understanding and guidance of the ethos and the social context of modern business demands more theological commitment and ethical clarity than is frequently present in contemporary analysis.

Christianity and Society

Talcott Parsons

Perhaps the most important principle of the relation between religion and society which was institutionalized in the Middle Ages was that of the *autonomy* of secular society, of the "state" in the medieval sense, relative to the church, but within a Christian framework. The Christianity of secular society was guaranteed, not by the subjection of secular life to a religious law, but by the *common* commitment of ecclesiastical and temporal personnel to Christian faith. The Reformation may be seen, from one point of view, as a process of the extension of this principle of autonomy to the internal structure of religious organization itself, with profound consequences both for the structure of the churches and for their relation to secular society. It may be regarded as a further major step in the same line as the original Christian break with Judaism.

The essential point may be stated as the religious "enfranchisement" of the individual, often put as his coming to stand in a direct relation to God. The Catholic Church had emancipated the individual, as part of its own corporate entity, from the Jewish law and its special social community, and had given him a notable autonomy within the secular sphere. But within its own definition of the religious sphere it had kept him under a strict tutelage by a set of mechanisms of which the sacraments were the core. By Catholic doctrine the only access to Divine grace was through the sacraments administered by a duly ordained priest. Luther broke through this tutelage to make the individual a *religiously* autonomous entity, responsible for his own religious concerns, not only in the sense of accepting the ministrations and discipline of the church but also through making his own fundamental religious commitments.

This brought faith into an even more central position than before. It was no longer the commitment to accept the particularized obligations and sacraments administered by the Church, but to act on the more general level in accordance with God's will. Like all reciprocal relationships, this one could be "tipped" one way or the other. In the Lutheran case it was tipped far in what in certain senses may be called the "authoritarian" direction; grace was interpreted to come only from the completely "undetermined" Divine action and in no sense to be dependent on the performances of the faithful, but only on their "receptivity." In this sense Lutheranism might be felt to deprive the individual of autonomy rather than enhancing it. But this would be an incorrect interpretation. The essential point is that the individual's dependence on the *human* mediation of the church and its priesthood through the sacraments was eliminated and *as a human being* he had, under God, to rely on his own independent responsibility; he could not "buy" grace or absolution from a human agency empowered to dispense it. In this situation the very uncertainties of the individual's relation to God, an uncertainty driven to its extreme by the Calvinistic doctrine of predestination, could, through its definition of the situation for religious interest, produce a powerful impetus to the acceptance of individual responsibility. The more deeply felt his religious need, the sharper his sense of unworthiness, the more he had to realize that no human agency could relieve him of his responsibility; "mother" church was no longer available to protect and comfort him.

An immediate consequence was the elimination of the fundamental distinction in moral-religious quality between the religious life in the Catholic sense and life in secular "callings." It was the individual's direct relation to God which counted from the human side, his faith. This faith was not a function of any particular set of ritual or semi-magical practices, or indeed even of "discipline" except in the most general sense of living according to Christian principles. The core of the special meaning of the religious life had been the

From Talcott Parsons, *Sociological Theory and Modern Society* (New York: Free Press, 1967), pp. 402-12, 420-21.

sacramental conception of the earning of "merit" and this was fundamentally dependent on the Catholic conception of the power of the sacraments.

From one point of view, that of the special powers of the *church* as a social organization, this could be regarded as a crucial loss of function, and the Lutheran conception of the fundamental religious equivalence of all callings as secularization. My interpretation, however, is in accord with Max Weber's; the more important change was not the removal of religious legitimation from the special monastic life, but rather, the endowment of secular life with a new order of religious legitimation as a field of "Christian opportunity." If the ordinary man, assumed of course to be a church member, stood in direct relation to God, and could be justified by his faith, the *whole person* could be justified, including the life he led in everyday affairs. The counterpart of eliminating the sacramental mediation of the secular priesthood was eliminating also the special virtues of the religious. It was a case of further *differentiation* within the Christian framework.

Protestantism in its Lutheran phase underwent a process, analogous to that of the early church, of relative withdrawal from direct involvement in the affairs of secular society. With the overwhelming Lutheran emphasis on faith and the importance of the individual's *subjective* sense of justification, there was, as Weber pointed out, a strong tendency to interpret the concept of the calling in a passive, traditionalist, almost Pauline sense. It was the individual's relation to his God that mattered; only in a sense of nondiscrimination was his secular calling sanctified, in that it was just as good, religiously speaking, as that of the monk.

We have, however, maintained that the conception of the generalization of a Christian pattern of life was an inherent possibility in the Christian orientation from the beginning and it came early to the fore in the Reformation period in the Calvinistic, or more broadly the ascetic, branch of the movement. Here we may say that the religious status of secular callings was extended from that of a principle of basic nondiscrimination to one of their endowment with positive instrumental significance. The key conception was that of the divine ordination of the establishment of the Kingdom of God on Earth. This went beyond the negative legitimation of secular callings to the assignment of a positive *function* to them in the divine plan. . . .

For Protestants the Christian commitment was no less rigorous than it had been for Catholics; if anything it was more so. In both Lutheran and Calvinistic versions the conception was one of the most rigorous submission of the individual's life to divine will. But in defining the situation for implementing this role of "creature," the Protestant position differed from the Catholic broadly as the definition of the preschool child's role relative to his parents differs from that of the school-age child's relation to his teacher. Within the family, important as the element of discipline and expectations of learning to perform are, the primary focus is on responsibility of the parents for the welfare and security of their children; the permeation of Catholic thought with familial symbolism along these lines is striking indeed.

In the school, on the other hand, the emphasis shifts. The teacher is primarily an agent of instruction, responsible for welfare, yes, but this is not the primary function; it is rather to help to equip the child for a responsible role in society when his education has been completed. To a much higher degree the question of how far he takes advantage of his opportunities becomes his own responsibility. Thus the function of the Protestant ministry became mainly a teaching function, continually holding up the Christian doctrine as a model of life to their congregations. But they no longer held a parental type of tutelary power to confer or deny the fundamentals of personal religious security.

If the analogy may be continued, the Lutheran position encouraged a more passive orientation in this situation, a leaving of the more ultimate responsibility to God, an attitude primarily of receptivity to Grace. (This is the exception referred to above — one of relatively short-run significance.) Such an attitude would tend to be generalized to worldly superiors and authorities, including both ministers and secular teachers. Ascetic Protestantism, on the other hand, though at least equally insistent on the divine origins of norms and values for life, tended to cut off this reliance on authority and place a sharper emphasis on the individual's responsibility for positive action, not just by his faith to be receptive to God's grace, but to get out and *work* in the building of the Kingdom. This precisely excluded any special valuation of devotional exercises and put the primary moral emphasis on secular activities.

Next, this constituted a liberation in one fundamental respect from the social conservatism of the Catholic position, in that it was no longer necessary to attempt to maintain the superiority of the religious life over the secular. Hence one essential bulwark of a hierarchical ordering of society was removed. The Christian conscience rather than the doctrines and structural position of the visible Church became the focus for standards of social evaluation. This should not, however, be interpreted as the establishment of "democracy" by the Reformation. Perhaps the most important single root of modern democracy is Christian individualism. But the Reformation, in liberating the individual conscience from the tutelage of the church, took only one step toward political democracy. The Lutheran branch indeed was long particularly identified with "legitimism," and Calvinism was in its early days primarily a doctrine of a relatively rigid collective "dictatorship" of the elect in both church and state.

Third, far from weakening the elements in secular society which pointed in a direction of "modernism," the Reformation, especially in its ascetic branch, strengthened and extended them. A particularly important component was clearly law. We have emphasized the essential continuity in this respect between classical antiquity and modern Europe through the medieval church. Broadly, the revival of Roman secular law in Europe was shared between Catholic and Protestant jurisdictions; in no sense did the Reformation reverse the trend in Continental Europe to institutionalize a secular legal system. In England, however, as Pound has emphasized, Puritanism was one of the major influences on the crystallization of the common law in the most decisive period. This is very much in line with the general trends of Protestant orientation, the favoring of a system of order within which responsible individual action can function effectively. The protection of rights is only one aspect of this order, the sanctioning of responsibilities is just as important.

Perhaps most important of all is the fact that the change in the character of the church meant that, insofar as the patterns of social structure which had characterized it by contrast with the feudal elements in the medieval heritage were to be preserved, they had to become much more generalized in secular society. This is true, as noted, of a generalized and codified system of law. It is true of more bureaucratic types of organization, which developed first in the government field but later in economic enterprise. It is by no means least true in the field of intellectual culture. The Renaissance was initially an outgrowth of the predominantly Catholic culture of Italy, but the general revival and development of learning of the post-medieval period was certainly shared by Catholic and Protestant Europe. It is a significant fact that John Calvin was trained as a lawyer. And of course, particularly in science, ascetic Protestantism was a major force in cultural development.

It is particularly important to emphasize the breadth of the front over which the leverage of Protestantism extended because of the common misinterpretation of Max Weber's thesis on the special relation between ascetic Protestantism and capitalism. . . .

The essential point is that private enterprise in business was . . . a particularly strategic case in Western development, because of the very great difficulty of emancipating economic production over a truly broad front — on the one hand from the ascriptive ties which go with such institutions as peasant agriculture and guild-type handicraft, on the other hand from the irrationalities which, from an economic point of view, are inherent in political organization, because of its inherent connection with the short-run pressures of social urgency such as defense, and because of its integration with aristocratic elements in the system of stratification which were dominated by a very different type of orientation.

There is very good reason to believe that development of the industrial revolution *for the first time* could have come about only through the primary agency of free enterprise, however dependent this was in turn on prior conditions, among the most important of which was the availability of a legal framework within which a system of contractual relations could have an orderly development. Once there has been a major breakthrough on the economic front, however, the diffusion of the patterns of social organization involved need not continue to be dependent on the same conditions.

Weber's main point about the Protestant ethic and capitalism was the importance of the subordination of self-interest in the usual ideological sense of the conception of a religiously meaningful calling; only with the establishment of this component was sufficient drive mobilized to break through the many barriers which were inherent not only in the European society of the time but more generally to a more differentiated development of economic production. Basically this involves the reversal of the commonsense point of view. The latter has contended, implicitly or explicitly, that the main source of impetus to capitalistic development was the *removal* of ethical restrictions such as, for instance, the prohibition of usury. This is true within certain limits, but by far the more important point is that what is needed is a powerful motivation to innovate, to break through the barriers of traditionalism and of vested interest. It is this impetus which is the center of Weber's concern, and it is his thesis that it cannot be accounted for by any simple removal of restrictions.

However deep the ambivalence about the morality of profit-making may go, there can be little doubt that the main outcome has been a shift in social conditions more in accord with the general pattern of Christian ethics than was medieval society, provided we grant that life in this world has a positive value in itself. Not least of these is the breaking through of the population circle of high death rates and high birth rates with the attendant lengthening of the average span of life. Another crucial point is the vast extension of the sphere of order in human relationships, the lessening of the exposure of the individual to violence, to fraud and to arbitrary pressures of authority.

So-called material well-being has certainly not been trusted as an absolute value in the Christian or any other major religious tradition, but any acceptance of life in this world as of value entails acceptance of the value of the means necessary to do approved things effectively. Particularly at the lower end of the social scale, grinding poverty with its accompaniments of illness, premature death, and unnecessary suffering its certainly not to be taken as an inherently desirable state of affairs from a Christian point of view.

Another major theme of developments in this era which is in basic accord with Christian values is a certain strain to egalitarianism, associated with the conception of the dignity of the individual human being and the need to justify discriminations either for or against individuals and classes of them in terms of some general concept of merit or demerit. Certainly by contrast with the role of ascriptive discriminations in the medieval situation, modern society is not in this respect ethically inferior. . . .

In spite of the very great structural differences, the essential principles governing the process by which society has become more Christianized than before were essentially the same in the Reformation period as in the earlier one. Let us recall that the Christian church from the beginning renounced the strategy of incorporation of secular society within itself, or the direct control of secular society through a religious law. It relied on the common values which bound church and secular society together, each in its own sphere, but making the Christian aspect of secular society an autonomous responsibility of Christians in their secular roles. My basic argument has been that the same fundamental principle was carried even farther in the Reformation phase. The sphere of autonomy was greatly enlarged through release of the Christian individual from the tutelage of the church. This was essentially a process of further differentiation both within the religious sphere and between it and the secular.

In all such cases there is increased objective opportunity for disregarding the values of the religious tradition and succumbing to worldly temptations. But the other side of the coin is the enhancement of motivation to religiously valued achievement by the very fact of being given more unequivocal responsibility. This process was not mainly one of secularization but one of the institutionalization of the religious responsibility of the individual through the relinquishment of tutelary authority by a "parental" church.

For purposes of this discussion the Reformation period is the most decisive one, for here it is most frequently argued . . . that there was a decisive turn in the direction of secularization in the sense of abandonment of the values inherent in the Christian tradition in favor of concern with the "things of this world." As already noted, we feel that underlying this argument is a basic ambiguity about the relation of "the world" to religious orientations and that the Christian orientation is not, in the Oriental sense, an orientation of "rejection of the world" but rather in this respect mainly a source for the setting of ethical standards *for* life in this world. In line with this interpretation, the Reformation transition was not primarily one of "giving in" to the temptations of worldly interest, but rather one of extending the range of applicability and indeed in certain respects the rigor of the ethical standards applied to life in the world. It was expecting more rather than less of larger numbers of Christians in their worldly lives. It goes without saying that the content of the expectations also changed. But these changes indicated much more a change in the definition of the situation of life through changes in the structure of society than they did in the main underlying values. . . .

A common view would agree with the above argument that the Reformation itself was not basically a movement of secularization but that, in that it played a part in unleashing the forces of political nationalism and economic development — to say nothing of recent hedonism — it was the last genuinely Christian phase of Western development and that from the eighteenth century on in particular the trend had truly been one of religious decline in relation to the values of secular society. Certain trends in Weber's thinking with respect to the disenchantment of the world would seem to argue in this direction, as would Troeltsch's view that there have been only three authentic versions of the conception of a Christian society in Western history — the medieval Catholic, the Lutheran, and the Calvinistic.

Against this view I should like to present an argument for a basic continuity leading to a further phase which has come to maturity in the nineteenth and twentieth centuries, most conspicuously in the United States and coincident with the industrial and educational revolutions already referred to. . . . The present discussion has, by virtue of its chosen subject, been primarily interested in the problems of the institutionalization of the values originating in Christianity as a religious movement, which have been carried forward at various stages of its development. But values — i.e., moral orientations toward the problems of life

in this world — are never the whole of religion, if indeed its most central aspect. My suggestion is that the principal roots of the present religious concern do not lie in *relative* moral decline or inadequacy (relative, that is, to other periods in our society's history) but rather in problems in the other areas of religion, problems of the bases of faith and the definitions of the ultimate problems of meaning.

The very fact that the process of the integration of earlier religious values with the structure of society has gone so far as it has gone raises such problems. The element of universalism in Christian ethics inherently favors the development of a society where the different branches of Christianity cannot maintain their earlier insulation from each other. . . . But beyond this, for the first time in history something approaching a world society is in process of emerging. For the first time in history Christianity is now involved in a deep confrontation with the major religious traditions of the Orient, as well as with the modern political religion of Communism.

It seems probable that a certain basic tension in relation to the "things of this world" is inherent in Christianity generally. Hence any relative success in the institutionalization of Christian values cannot be taken as final, but rather as a point of departure for new religious stock-taking. But in addition to this broad internal consideration, the confrontation on such a new basis with the non-Christian world presents a new and special situation. We are deeply committed to our own great traditions. These have tended to emphasize the exclusive possession of the truth. Yet we have also institutionalized the values of tolerance and equality of rights for all. How can we define a meaningful orientation in such a world when, in addition, the more familiar and conventional problems of suffering and evil are, if not more prevalent than ever before, at least as brought to attention through mass communications, inescapable as facts of our world?

It is the inherent tension and dynamism of Christianity and the unprecedented character of the situation we face which, to my mind, account of the intensive searching and questioning, and indeed much of the spiritual negativism, of our time. The explanation in terms of an alleged moral collapse would be far too simple, even if there were more truth in it than the evidence seems to indicate. For this would imply that we did not need new conceptions of meaning; all we would need would be to live up more fully to the standards familiar to us all. In no period of major ferment in cultural history has such a solution been adequate.

Chapter Eight

Socialism, Capitalism, and Christianity

As can be seen in the last two chapters, Enlightenment thought from John Locke and Adam Smith through G. W. F. Hegel and Karl Marx challenged the connections that had been made between faith and economics in the ancient church, in the High Middle Ages, and in the Reformation, and was challenged in turn by social scientists who argued on Enlightenment grounds that religion was in fact a decisive cause in the formation of modernity. However, many continued to believe that historical, psychological, social, and ethical issues were not only distinct from religion but determinative of religion. Others held that religion may have been a decisive force in the historic formation of modernity but that modern humanity no longer needed it. Indeed, a religious doctrine or practice was now judged according to whether it is an ally or an enemy of the path to modernity. The question of truth or falsehood does not appear in their discussions of religion; rather, religion is seen as a variable aspect of culture that should adapt to new conditions. Faith becomes a means, not an end.

This view, however, has several difficulties. For one thing, in both North and South America, much of the Enlightenment was embraced without the rejection of religion that had characterized Europe. In this regard, the general populations of the Americas are like those of Asia and Africa (to whom we turn in the next chapter). However much they learn from the Enlightenment or from the universities, many believe that the truths of religion are more comprehensive and profound ways of guiding thought and work. Religion serves as a continuing guide as to what to accept or reject from the Enlightenment. Its rationality is a means, not an end.

Although these motifs were sometimes at war with each other, various affinities formed these societies into distinctive religious cultures — deeply Catholic, manorial (*hacienda*-focused), hierarchical, merchantilist, and nationalist in the South, and Protestant, individualist, democratic, corporate capitalist, and internationalist (critics say "imperialist") in the North. Both drew on elements of the Enlightenment, although in different ways, but they did so on post-Enlightenment, sometimes Romantic, nearly always religious grounds. These cultures, it might be said, always had something of a postmodern touch.

In any case, the path to modernity forked, and the conditions to which religion had to adapt were neither uniform nor clear. One way led through capitalism and the other through socialism. Those who were disadvantaged or morally disturbed by one sometimes turned to the other — often with a good bit of romantic idealization of its virtues. More often than not, it was religion that framed the criticism of existing conditions and prompted the extensive discussion about the relationships of Christianity, socialism, and capitalism, the varieties of each, and their possible interactions. This debate was carried out from the "Social Gospel" in the late nineteenth century, through Christian realism at mid-century, and in liberation theology from the 1960s to the 1980s. It has direct parallels to issues faced by other world religions, as we will see in Chapter 9, and it culminated in a series of official church statements in the last decade, as we shall see in Chapter 10. The readings in this chapter are selected to represent the range of the debate in the Americas.

Charles C. West

It is not possible here to present the history of socialism, or even the history of Marxism in relationship to religion. For one thing, now that the files are open to scholars, the debates about the inner workings of the Leninist and Stalinist years are newly underway among the scholars of Eastern Europe. It is, however, possible to trace some of the effect these years had on religion.

Marxist societies tried to separate religion totally from education, the media, public policy, economic activity, and political discourse. At the same time, anti-religious and atheistic propaganda was distributed by the party, advocated by the state, taught in the schools, and made mandatory for all legal organizations. To be sure, individuals were free to believe in their hearts whatever they wished (that could not fully be controlled in any case), although Marxism-Leninism was also presented as a total claim on the individual's deepest convictions and loyalties. A limited number of churches, temples, mosques, and synagogues were allowed to hold worship services; but none of this was to have public visibility, although it did anyway. In short, religion was weakened but not destroyed. It remains difficult, however, to trace the indirect influence of religion on the personal habits or economic behavior of believers during these years.

It is perhaps more important, however, to treat the intellectual and historical background of the interaction between Marxism and Christianity. Princeton scholar and churchman Charles West, who studied this relationship for decades, here shows the influences of the Judeo-Christian tradition on the formation of Marxism, takes up the interaction of Christianity and Marxist socialism before the tensions of the Lenin-Stalin years, and then treats some of the new dialogues between Christians and socialists after the death of Stalin.

These historic connections and new dialogues have had a more enduring effect on economic ethics around the world than did the harsher treatment of religion under Lenin and Stalin and parallel examples in China, Albania, and Burma.

284

Marxism and Christianity

Charles C. West

The Judeo-Christian tradition is both the spiritual ancestor of the Marxist movement and the view of reality that Marxism first repudiated in proclaiming its own message of judgment and hope. . . . Neither Karl Marx (1818-1883) nor Friedrich Engels (1820-1895) had a profound grasp of the Christian faith or the Jewish tradition. Though Marx was the grandson and the nephew of rabbis, his father turned to liberal Protestant Christianity, and Marx was confirmed in the state Church of the Old Prussian Union. Engels was educated in the Reformed piety of Prussian Westphalia but broke with it early in his life. Nevertheless, the Marxism they formulated shared in and interacted with the Judeo-Christian heritage in two fundamental ways: (1) Marxism continually confronted, and drew on, the heritage of radical Christianity, and (2) Marxism was a result of a process, rooted in the Enlightenment and developed by G. W. F. Hegel and the left-wing Hegelians, that transposed the structure of Christian faith and hope into a humanist key.

Marx and Engels were surrounded, in the revolutionary movements of their times, by socialists claiming Christian bases for their radical convictions. Claude-Henri de Rouvroy, Comte de Saint-Simon, the most influential mind of the French utopian socialist movement, expounded his conception of a society rationally organized for the benefit of all workers, especially the poor, in his book *Nouveau christianisme* (1825). Charles Fourier appealed to the Gospels in *Le nouveau monde* (1848) to support his proposal for ideal coopera-

From Charles C. West, "Marxism," in *The Encyclopedia of Religion*, ed. M. Eliade et al., vol. 9 (New York: Macmillan, 1987), pp. 240-48.

tive communities, which he called "the expression of the true Christianity of Jesus." Marx and Engels ignored this Christian dimension, which was admittedly unorthodox, and attacked these men and their followers as aristocratic planners for the poor, rather than as participants in the revolutionary action of the poor to overthrow the existing system. Yet they acknowledged the educative value of their goals for human society. More difficult to refute was Wilhelm Weitling. Founder of the League of the Just (which was the predecessor to the First International), a labor organizer, a revolutionary agitator, and also a passionately evangelical Christian, Weitling advocated a class war of the poor against the rich. He maintained that Jesus was the first socialist, whose "repudiation of power and riches, self-abasement and self-sacrifice" had been betrayed by the established church since Constantine. The worker's violent struggle for a new "socialism of love" was, in his view, also a modern renewal of original Christianity.

Marx attacked this point of view from the left and the right in the name of "scientific socialism." He scorned Weitling's faith as sentimentalism, and fought Weitling's demand for direct mass action as unplanned and premature. It was, however, precisely in this heritage of radical Christianity that Marxism found its own antecedents. Building on the critical New Testament studies of Bruno Bauer, Engels discovered a mass movement of "the laboring and the burdened," that is, of slaves, debt-laden peasants, and poor freedmen of the Roman empire, which expressed its revolt in early Christianity (*Bruno Bauer and Early Christianity*, 1852). This revolt had to be religious, given the hopeless social situation; but it was informed, he wrote in *On the History of Early Christianity* (1895), by an urgent this-worldly eschatology, the vehicle of which was the New Testament book of *Revelation*, which Engels, following Bauer, took to be the earliest Christian document. Only later, according to Engels, did this faith become a sacramental, trinitarian, escapist, and conformist religion. Christianity, in Engels's view, has therefore a dual character. On the one hand, in breaking with rituals and ceremonies designed to symbolize a particular culture's relation to the divine, it became the first genuinely universal religion, and hence a vehicle for the protest and revolt of all humanity against oppression. On the other hand, its doctrines of sin and sacrificial atonement turned people inward for salvation and undermined this protest. In *The Peasant War in Germany* (1874) and other writings, he applied this analysis to conflicts in the history of the church.

Engels's theme of duality was also used by the German Social Democrats, notably Karl Kautsky and Rosa Luxemburg. Its more sophisticated development, however, comes from Ernst Bloch, whose *Das Prinzip Hoffnung* (1959), *Atheism in Christianity* (1972), and other writings have influenced Jürgen Moltmann and other modern theologians. For Bloch the Judeo-Christian traditions is unique despite analogies in other traditions (e.g., Prometheus). The Judeo-Christian God is the spirit of the exodus from Egypt and a projection of human utopian hope that cannot be defined and known beforehand, but realized only in the struggle against existing order. The Bible is the early story of this struggle. Jesus was, with his projection of the kingdom of God, one of its prophets. Throughout the history of Christianity, there has been an underground of revolutionary, heretical theology which has carried this struggle forward. Bloch mentions Marcion, Joachim of Fiore, and Thomas Müntzer especially. The goal of this history, Bloch maintained, is the emergence of atheist humanity projecting its own utopias forward, guided by the science of Marxism, no longer needing the symbols of theology. But for Bloch, Marxism is the heir of the unique Judeo-Christian tradition, which for centuries has expressed human hope and energized human revolt by means of these symbols.

Marxism's indebtedness to the Enlightenment and to Hegel and the left-Hegelians is revealed in three principal stages. The first is the Enlightenment's confidence in the continuity between the human and the divine, between human reason and conscience and divine order, and therefore in the unbounded human capacity for progress. Educated in the Enlightenment tradition, Marx in his youth shared this confidence. The second stage is Hegel's conversion of that continuity into a divine-human dialectical struggle for self-realization in history through alienation (expressed in human oppression and suffering but supremely in the crucifixion of Christ) and reconciliation (the work of the Holy Spirit through human power to establish the supremacy and moral order of a

human society). The third stage is embodied in the view of the left-wing Hegelians, given definitive expression in Ludwig Feuerbach's *Essence of Christianity* (1841) that the divine dimension of this struggle is itself alienating, that God is essentially a projection of the ideal human essence onto the heavens, and that the whole doctrine and ceremony of the Christian church can be enjoyed as a celebration of the true quality of the human species, realizing itself in love between person and person.

Marx adopted Feuerbach's humanistic inversion of Christianity but radicalized it. Religion is, for him, the projection in fantasy of a humanity that finds no fulfillment in this world. It is "the sigh of the oppressed creature," at once a protest against oppression and an adaptation to it. It is the opium the people take to dull their pain and give them dreams. But it is not enough, he criticizes Feuerbach, to expose this fact; one must go on to analyze the contradictions in human society that produce religious illusions, and one must revolutionize them in practice. In doing this, Marx radicalized left-wing Hegelian humanism into an antitheology that cut all remaining links with spirituality. First, he redefined Feuerbach's concept of "species humanity" not in terms of human relationships, but as "free, conscious activity" of the species expressed in each individual (*Economic Philosophical Manuscripts of* 1844, first published 1927). The human being is a self-creator through labor, the agent who molds nature and history. Second, he rooted Hegel's concept of alienation in the expropriation of the fruits of a person's labor by others who employ or use him. The dehumanization that this produces amounts, in Marx's view, to total depravity. It divides humanity into classes between which there is no shared consciousness or conscience. It condemns society to ever-intensified class conflict, which no divine or human law can relativize. Third, Marx found the savior in this conflict to be the class most completely deprived and exploited, lacking all stake in existing order or power. In the utter negation of proletarian existence the image of true species humanity is formed, in solidarity free from all personal ambition, and in revolutionary determination. Fourth, what for Hegel is the cunning of the Spirit realizing its goals in history through the human struggle becomes for Marx the dialectical operation of the "material" laws of history, expressed in the forces of production overturning the relations of production, by means of the strategy and tactics of the revolutionary struggle. Fifth, communism for Marx, like the kingdom of God for Christians, is genuinely eschatological. Hope in its coming is not dimmed by its delayed arrival. It is always at hand. It will bring a transformation of human nature by new social conditions that, Marx believed, will be prepared in the struggle itself and in transitional socialist societies.

At all these points, the structural analogy — and therefore the challenge — of Marxism to Christianity is clear. The stage was set for later interaction. . . .

Before the death of Marx, the lines of conflict were drawn between the Christian church and Marxist socialism. Karl Kautsky, in *Foundations of Christianity* (1908), recognized Jesus as an early socialist, but was more severe than Engels in his condemnation of the other-worldliness of the Christian religion. Lenin made the propagation of atheism a subordinate but critically important task of the Communist party, before and after it seized power. On the Christian side, Pope Leo XIII, in the first year of his reign, condemned socialism as "a deadly plague" that undermines religion, the state, family, and private property (*Quod apostolici numeris,* 1878). Protestant church responses were no more friendly. The Marxist challenge, however, also stimulated some churches with a strong precapitalist tradition in ethics to elaborate their own social teachings. In 1891, Leo XIII recognized that in capitalist industrial development, "a small number of very rich men have been able to lay upon the masses of the poor a yoke little better than slavery itself" (*De rerum novarum*). Still rejecting socialism, he set forth the state's responsibility to intervene in the economic order to promote justice, the employers' duty to use wealth and power for the welfare of their workers and the public, and the workers' right to organize Catholic trade unions to assure their rights in the context of seeking harmony between classes. This encyclical laid the foundation of a Roman Catholic social reform movement, redefined forty years later in the *Quadragesimo anno* of Pius XI. A similar response arose among the Protestants with formation of the Anti-Revolutionary party by Dutch Calvinists, who were led by Abraham Kuyper. Kuyper and his party opposed "organic spheres of creation" to the individualism of the capitalists and the collectivism of the socialists. They held that the state is indeed the guardian of justice, defending the weak and curbing the abuse of power in the social realm, but also that its power, like that of a factory, is mechanical and therefore external. Justice is secured only when the communities of family, neighborhood, learning, and production are strengthened at their base.

This hardening of the front was, however, only part of the story. Revisionism, which for the most part held that evolutionary progress toward socialism is achieved by democratic means, and which barely mentioned religion, came more and more to dominate the policy of socialist parties. It also broke decisively with the idea of the economic determinism of human consciousness. "The materialist conception of history does not preclude an idealist interpretation of it," said the French Socialist leader Jean Jaurès (*Idealism in History,* 1905). Justice and right, whatever the philosophical or religious form they take, are driving principles in the history of human development alongside a realistic analysis of the powers of economic exploitation. In Britain, the democratic evolutionary socialism of the Fabians provided a context that absorbed outspoken Marxists (Henry Hyndman and the Social Democratic Federation) and active Christians of various kinds (Keir Hardie, the Church Socialist League) into the ideological mixture that became the Labor party. In the United States, the Socialist party was a turbulent mixture of Marxist, utopian socialist, and Christian ideas. A clergyman, George D. Herron, was, with Eugene V. Debs, a founder. After the death of Debs, it was led by a former Presbyterian minister, Norman Thomas, who described the party's philosophy as Marxist in "a very loose sense of the word" mixed with broader humanist ideals and psychological insights (*A Socialist's Faith,* 1951).

Christian socialists pursued their goals in various relationships to Marxist movements. In Germany Friedrich Naumann organized a Christian socialist group in the 1890s, which, however, had little influence and gradually moved to a left-liberal position. His countryman Christoph Blumhardt declared his conversion, on the grounds of his biblical Christian faith, to the Social

Democratic party. In Switzerland Hermann Kutter and Leonhard Ragaz, inspired in part by Blumhardt, founded a religious socialist movement. The young Karl Barth was also pastorally engaged with the labor union in his working-class parish of Safenwil and imbued the first edition of his *Epistle to the Romans* (1919) with a Christian socialist perspective. In the United States the Society of Christian Socialists was formed in 1889; its publication *The Dawn* published contributions by Marxists but basically promoted socialism as "the application to society of the way of Christ." In 1906 the Christian Socialist Fellowship supported the Socialist party, published parts of Marx's *Capital,* and advocated participation in the international socialist movement as a way of realizing what was variously called the Christian revolution, the economic expression of the religious life, or anticipation of God's redemption in the social sphere.

These movements did not engage Marxism with any depth of analysis. Walter Rauschenbusch, for example, used Marxism as a tool to expose the moral evils and injustices of capitalism: the spirit of competition, irresponsible power, exploitation, and the selfish profit motive. Rauschenbusch proposed economic equality, public ownership of the basic means of production, and industrial as well as political democracy imbued with a spirit of social fraternity in place of the capitalist system (*Christianizing the Social Order,* 1912). Kutter understood the socialist movement, despite its materialist atheism and emphasis on class war, to be the judgment of God on the capitalist system and on the church for its self-centered comfort therein, and, through its socialist program, to be the only effective force moving toward a more Christian social order (*They Must,* 1908). Ragaz found the Marxist socialist movement to be at heart an idealism demanding justice and prayed that this would prevail over the violence and dictatorship of Bolshevism (*Signs of the Kingdom,* 1984). Only in Russia were the ideological lines drawn so sharply that choices had to be made. There, a remarkable group of converts from revolutionary Marxism (three Orthodox Christians — historian Piotr Struwe, theologian Sergei Bulgakov, and philosopher Nikolai Berdiaev — and the Jewish philosopher S. L. Frank) formed a group that took basic issue with the dogmatic utopianism and the utter

submission of means to ends that characterized Russian Marxism, both Menshevik and Bolshevik. The group was dispersed in the revolution of 1917, but its influence continued. Berdiaev, who, in *The Origin of Russian Communism* (1937), wrote one of the most penetrating studies of that movement, continued throughout his life to expound a form of Christian communal philosophy in dialogue with the Marxist alternative.

The Russian Revolution and the Great Depression brought a new depth to Christian social reflection on Marxism and to Christian-Marxist relations. Jacques Maritain in his *Integral Humanism* (1936) contrasted the incarnation of Christ with the "absolute realist immanentism" of Marx. He called for a "secular Christian" pluralist society inspired, but not dominated, by the church toward a practical vision of the common good and composed of a structure of communities gathered around personal (family, neighborhood, cultural affinity) or functional (economic or social) foci, of which the state is the highest and most general. The struggle to realize this ideal by Christian groups within the various secular communities must be motivated by evangelical love and respect for human personhood. This philosophy inspired Christian Democratic alternatives to Marxist socialism not only in Europe between the world wars, but in Latin America as late as the 1970s, where it has been the principal opponent of liberation theology.

The most comprehensive Protestant effort to provide an alternative Christian vision, that of the Religious Socialists, was inspired by Paul Tillich. Tillich understood Marxism as "prophecy on the grounds of an autonomous self-contained world" (*The Socialist Decision,* 1933) and saw a structural analogy between Marx's thought and prophetic theology in its view of history, its analysis of human alienation in present society, and its unity of theory and practice in social involvement. According to Tillich, a socialism integrated with religion would enable society to understand its roots in the original powers of creation and its destiny in confrontation with the demand of the unconditioned (God) and could thus lead it from a bourgeois autonomy to a new theonomy that would be open to the grace of God, which informs and transforms human culture. The mission of religious socialists is to lead Marxist socialism into the depth of its historical being, lest it miss its *Kairos*. This means imbuing Marxism with an understanding of the human as spiritual and material, society as communal prebourgeois and class-divided, power as "realized social unity" and political force, and reality as rooted in "a harmony of religious and profane symbolism."

Tillich's conception had very little influence in Germany on either Social Democrats or Communists. It did, however, contribute to the thought of the Fellowship of Social Christians in America, whose leader was Reinhold Niebuhr. Niebuhr found in Marxism a tool of analysis that exposes liberal illusions about social power and the depth of social conflict. He saw the proletarian revolution as an instrument of God's judgment and of the hope for greater justice in society, despite its utopian illusions of a society without classes. The task of Christian socialists, in his view, was to work within both the church and the revolutionary movement (for Niebuhr, the Socialist party) so that the change to socialism would be marked by as little violence as possible, so that the conscience of the church would accept it, and so that the victorious proletarians would not in self-righteous vindictiveness turn justice into a new tyranny. German religious socialist principles went into defining the form of the socialist society for which the Fellowship of Socialist Christians hoped.

This was, however, a transitional position. From it Niebuhr and the Fellowship moved, together with British Christians, notably Stafford Cripps and William Temple, toward advocacy of a mixed economy that would curb private economic power and direct it toward the common good, but not at the price of creating political tyranny in a socialist society. In 1947, the word *socialist* was dropped and the group became the Frontier Fellowship. The definition of a "responsible society" by the British ecumenist J. H. Oldham and its adoption by the first assembly of the World Council of Churches in 1948 as a guide for Christian social ethics between the rejected extremes of communism and laissez-faire capitalism was the next movement in this trend. For two decades after World War II this moderate spirit reigned among social democrats, Marxists, and Christians. Socialist parties of Marxist background welcomed Christian members and leaders emerged in both Europe and Africa who were socialist and Christian. . . .

Marxist-Christian Dialogue

The discrediting of Stalin and the continuation of so many Stalinist policies led to profound reflection in the East and West about the whole range of Marxist theory and practice, including its relation to the claims of Christian faith and the practice of religion. Christian theologians responded with eager enthusiasm to the challenge. The result was that a vigorous Marxist-Christian dialogue erupted in Europe during the 1960s wherever political conditions permitted. . . .

The high point of this development was the only Christian-Marxist congress ever to be held in Eastern Europe, in Marianske Lazne, Czechoslovakia, in 1967. The Paulusgesellschaft, which published the proceedings as *Schöpfertum und Freiheit* (1968), brought to this meeting a history of several conferences and published reports involving Western European Catholic theologians (Karl Rahner, J. B. Metz, Giulio Girardi, et al.) and Marxist scholars from France (Roger Garaudy), Italy (Lucio Lombardo-Radice), Austria, and West Germany with Eastern European Marxists from Poland, Yugoslavia, and Hungary. It was a moment of revision and new direction for all involved, a triumph of Milan Machovec's belief (*A Marxist Looks at Jesus*, 1976) that dialogue, in which each risks deepest convictions in openness to the other, is indeed basic to the meaning of life. . . . [The Soviet Army, however, cut this blossom of the "Prague Spring."]

Meanwhile the dialogical relation was also attacked from another angle. The desideratum is "not a Christian-Marxist dialogue," writes José Miguez-Bonino, expressing a perspective common to Latin American liberation theology, "but a growing and overt common participation in a revolutionary project, the basic lines of which are undoubtedly based on a Marxist analysis" (*Christians and Marxists*, 1976). Marxism is the "language" by which the Christian understands how his obedience to God must be expressed in the inhuman conditions of society. Christians and Marxists find themselves together in a common struggle. This solidarity in "praxis" is basic in their view, not their opposing ideas of religion.

The question of the relation between Christianity and Marxism arises therefore, in this view, within the common enterprise. However, with this relation comes the beginning of an encounter on two levels, despite the failure of many liberation theologians to notice the fact. The first level is that of political power. Gustavo Gutiérrez authorized revolutionary struggle theologically by describing political liberation as "the self-creation of man" rooted in divine creation and fulfilled by re-creation in Christ (*A Theology of Liberation,* 1973). Basic Christian communities, founded alongside parishes throughout Latin America, have become schools of social activism against oppressing powers. But in violent revolutionary movements themselves and in the governments they form, Christians have tended to be junior partners to Marxist-Leninists, who are not tolerant of deviations from their military, economic, or political policies. Camillo Torres wrestled with this problem before joining the Colombian guerilla movement with which he met his death (*Revolutionary Writings,* 1969). The second level is the interpretation of Marxism itself. A few have taken it seriously. In *Marx against the Marxists* (1980), José Miranda has attempted a bold reinterpretation of Marx and Engels as humanists rather than determinists, as moralists rather than just scientists, and as at least open to the possibility of God. Miguez-Bonino recognizes that dialectical materialism devalues humanity and turns Marx's criticism of religion into absolute atheism. But he claims for Christians who are Marxists an equal right to interpret the movement and to prove by participation that biblical faith can lead to revolutionary action. This is the stuff of dialogue yet to come. . . .

Andrew Carnegie

The theories of eighteenth- and nineteenth-century capitalism from Adam Smith to Alfred Marshall were not universally taken as a repudiation of Christian values, as they often were by those who became involved in the Christian-Marxist dialogue. Instead, they were taken by some as the fulfillment of aspects of the gospel that had been neglected by a reactionary small-mindedness that preferred the tribal communitarianism or the peasant's earthy simplicity to the rich complexity of high culture — romantically forgetting, of course, the disease, the drudgery, the dullness, and the crushing brutality of those traditional societies.

Few articulated a Christian pro-capitalist point of view more clearly than Andrew Carnegie (1835-1919). He experienced the "rags to riches" life that many immigrants to America dream about. Born in Scotland, he came to the U.S. as a boy and took a job for $1.20 per week in a mill. Later he became a telegraph operator for the Pennsylvania Railroad, and as he began to rise through the ranks of that corporation he became aware of the importance of steel production for the future. He introduced the first Bessemer steel converters into this country, founded United States Steel, and became one of the world's richest men. He was frequently considered to be among the "robber barons" of the late nineteenth century, who appeared to some simply to be putting the best face possible on greed — as we see in the brief excerpt, included on page 293, from philosopher Charles Sanders Peirce. In this case, however, Carnegie became one of the greatest philanthropists of modern times. After his retirement at sixty-five, he spent nearly twenty years building public libraries, endowing educational and peace institutions, and writing his philosophy of the relationship of Christianity to problems of wealth and poverty. This selection is from his book *The Gospel of Wealth*.

The Administration of Wealth

Andrew Carnegie

The Problem of our age is the proper administration of wealth, that the ties of brotherhood may still bind together the rich and poor in harmonious relationship. The conditions of human life have not only been changed, but revolutionized, within the past few hundred years. In former days there was little difference between the dwelling, dress, food, and environment of the chief and those of his retainers. . . . The contrast between the palace of the millionaire and the cottage of the laborer with us today measures the change which has come with civilization. This change, however, is not to be deplored, but welcomed as highly beneficial. It is well, nay, essential, for the progress of the race that the houses of some should be homes for all that is highest and best in literature and the arts, and for all the refinements of civilization, rather than that none should be so. Much better this great irregularity than universal squalor. . . . The "good old times" were not good old times. Neither master nor servant was as well situated then as today. A relapse to old conditions would be disastrous to both — not the least so to him who serves — and would sweep away civilization with it. . . .

It is easy to see how the change has come. One illustration will serve for almost every phase of the cause. In the manufacture of products we have the whole story. It applies to all combinations of human industry, as stimulated and enlarged by the inventions of this scientific age. Formerly, articles were manufactured at the domestic hearth, or in small shops which formed part of the household. The master and his apprentices worked side by side, the latter living with the master, and therefore subject to the same conditions. When these apprentices rose to be masters, there was little or no change in their mode of life, and they, in turn, educated succeeding apprentices in the same routine. There was, substantially, social equality, and even political equality, for those engaged in industrial pursuits had then little or no voice in the State.

The inevitable result of such a mode of manufacture was crude articles at high prices. Today the world obtains commodities of excellent quality at prices which even the preceding generation would have deemed incredible. In the commercial world similar causes have produced similar results, and the race is benefited thereby. The poor enjoy what the rich could not before afford. What were the luxuries have become the necessities of life. The laborer has now more comforts than the farmer had a few generations ago. The farmer has more luxuries than the landlord had, and is more richly clad and better housed. The landlord has books and pictures rarer and appointments more artistic than the king could then obtain.

The price we pay for this salutary change is, no doubt, great. We assemble thousands of operatives in the factory, and in the mine, of whom the employer can know little or nothing, and to whom he is little better than a myth. All intercourse between them is at an end. Rigid castes are formed, and, as usual, mutual ignorance breeds mutual distrust. Each caste is without sympathy with the other, and ready to credit anything disparaging in regard to it. Under the law of competition, the employer, among which the rates paid to labor figure prominently, and often there is friction between the employer and the employed, between capital and labor, between rich and poor [sic]. Human society loses homogeneity.

The price which society pays for the law of competition, like the price it pays for cheap comforts and luxuries, is also great; but the advantages of this lay that we owe our wonderful material development which brings improved conditions in its train [sic]. But, whether the law be benign or not, we must say of it, as we say of the change in the conditions of men to which we have re-

Andrew Carnegie, "The Problem of the Administration of Wealth," *The Gospel of Wealth and Other Timely Essays* (New York: Century, 1900).

The nineteenth century is now fast sinking into the grave, and we all begin to review its doings. . . . It will be called, I guess, the Economical Century; for political economy has more direct relations with all the branches of its activity than has any other science. Well, political economy has its formula of redemption, too. It is this: Intelligence in the service of greed ensures the justest prices, the fairest contracts, the most enlightened conduct of all the dealings between men, and leads to the *summum bonum,* food in plenty and perfect comfort. . . .

So a miser is a beneficent power in a community, is he? [A] good angel [appears to be the one] who by a thousand wiles puts money at the service of intelligent greed, in his own person. Bernard Mandeville, in his *Fable of the Bees* [long ago maintained] that private vices of all descriptions are public benefits, and proves it, too, quite as cogently as the economist proves his point concerning the miser. He even argues, with no slight force, that but for vice civilization would never have existed. In the same spirit, it has been strongly maintained and is today widely believed that all acts of charity and benevolence, private and public, go seriously to degrade the human race.

[For us today] the *Origin of Species* of Darwin merely extends politico-economical views of progress to the entire realm of animal and vegetable life. The vast majority of our contemporary naturalists hold the opinion that the true cause of those exquisite and marvelous adaptations of nature for which, when I was a boy, men used to extol the divine wisdom, is that creatures are so crowded together that those of them that happen to have the slightest advantage force those less pushing into situations unfavorable to multiplication or even kill them before they reach the age of reproduction. Among animals, the mere mechanical individualism is vastly reinforced as a power making for good by the animal's ruthless greed. As Darwin puts it on his title-page, it is the struggle for existence; and he should have added for his motto: Every individual for himself, and the Devil take the hindmost! Jesus, in his Sermon on the Mount, expressed a different opinion.

Here, then, is the issue. The gospel of Christ says that progress comes from every individual merging his individuality in sympathy with his neighbors. On the other side, the conviction of the nineteenth century is that progress takes place by virtue of every individual's striving for himself with all his might and trampling his neighbor under foot whenever he gets a chance to do so. This may accurately be called the Gospel of Greed.

— Charles Sanders Peirce, "At First Blush,
Counter-Gospels," *The Monist*
(January 1893): 176ff.

---

ferred: It is here; we cannot evade it; no substitutes for it have been found; and while the law may be sometimes hard for the individual, it is best for the race, because it insures the survival of the fittest in every department. We accept and welcome, therefore, as conditions to which we must accommodate ourselves, great inequality of environment; the concentration of business, industrial and commercial, in the hands of a few; and the law of competition between these, as being not only beneficial, but essential to the future progress of the race. Having accepted these, it follows that there must be great scope for the exercise of special ability in the merchant and in the manufacturer who has to conduct affairs upon a great scale. That this talent for organization and management is rare among men is proved by the fact that it invariably secures enormous rewards for its possessor, no matter where or under what laws or conditions. . . .

Objections to the foundations upon which society is based are not in order, because the condition of the race is better with these than it has been with any other which has been tried. Of the effect of any new substitutes proposed we cannot be sure. The Socialist or Anarchist who seeks to overturn present conditions is to be regarded as attacking the foundation upon which civilization itself rests, for civilization took its start from the day when the capable, industrious workman said to his incompetent and lazy fellow, "If thou dost not sow, thou shalt not reap" and thus ended primitive Communism by separating the drones from the bees. One who studies this subject will soon be brought face to face with the conclusion that upon the sacredness of property civilization itself depends — the right of the laborer to his hundred dollars in the savings-bank and equally the legal right of the millionaire to his millions. Every man must be allowed "to set under his own vine and fig-tree, with none to make afraid," if human society is to advance, or even to remain so far advanced as it is. To those who propose to substitute Communism for this intense Individualism, the answer therefore is: The race has tried that. All progress from that barbarous day to the present time has resulted from its displacement. Not evil, but good, has come to the race from the accumulation of wealth by those who have had the ability and energy to produce it. But even if we admit for a moment that it might be better for the race to discard its present foundation, Individualism — that it is a nobler ideal that man should labor, not for himself alone, but in and for a brotherhood of his fellows, and share with them all in common, realizing Swedenborg's idea of heaven, where, as he says, the angels derive their happiness, not from laboring for self, but for each other — even admit all this, and a sufficient answer is: This is not evolution, but revolution. It necessitates the changing of human nature itself — work of eons, even if it were good to change it, which we cannot know. . . .

We start, then, with a condition of affairs under which the best interests of the race are promoted, but which inevitably gives wealth to the few. Thus far, accepting conditions as they exist, the situation can be surveyed and pronounced good. The question then arises — and if the foregoing be correct, it is the only question with which we have to deal — What is the proper mode of administering wealth after the laws upon which civilization is founded have thrown it into the hands of the few? And it is of this great question that I believe I offer the true solution.

There are but three modes in which surplus wealth can be disposed of. It can be left to the families of the decendents; or it can be bequeathed for public purposes; or, finally, it can be administered by its possessors during their lives. Under the first and second modes most of the wealth of the world that has reached the few has hitherto been applied. Let us in turn consider each of these modes. The first is the most injudicious. In monarchical countries, the estates and the greatest portion of the wealth are left to the first son, that the vanity of the parent may be gratified by the thought that his name and title are to descend unimpaired to succeeding generations. The condition of this class in Europe today teaches the failure of such hopes or ambitions. The successors have become impoverished through their follies, or from the fall in the value of land. Even in Great Britain the strict law of entail has been found inadequate to maintain an hereditary class. Its soil is rapidly passing into the hands of the stranger. Under republican institutions the division of property among the children is much fairer; but the question which forces itself upon thoughtful men in all lands is, Why should men leave great fortunes to their children? If this is done from affection, is it not misguided affection? Observation teaches that, generally speaking, it is not well for the children that they should be so burdened. Neither is it well for the State. Beyond providing for the wife and daughters moderate sources of income, and very moderate allowances indeed, if any, for the sons, men may well hesitate; for it is no longer questionable that great sums bequeathed often work more for the injury than for the good of the recipients. Wise men will soon conclude that, for the best interests of the members of their families, and of the State, such bequests are an improper use of their means. . . .

The growing disposition to tax more and more heavily large estates left in death is a cheering indication of the growth of a salutary change in public opinion. Of all forms of taxation this seems the wisest. Men who continue hoarding great sums all their lives, the proper use of which for public ends would work good to the community from which it chiefly came, should be made to feel that the community, in the form of the State cannot thus be deprived of its proper share. By taxing estates heavily at death the State marks its condemnation of the selfish millionaire's unworthy life. . . .

This policy would work powerfully to induce the rich man to attend to the administration of wealth during his life, which is the end that society should always have in view, as being by far the most fruitful for the people. Nor need it be feared that this policy would sap the root of enterprise and render men less anxious to accumulate, for, to the class whose ambition it is to leave great fortunes and be talked about after their death, it will attract even more attention, and, indeed, be a somewhat nobler ambition to have enormous sums paid over to the State from their fortunes.

There remains, then, only one mode of using great fortunes; but in this we have the true antidote for the temporary unequal distribution of wealth, the reconciliation of the rich and the poor — a reign of harmony, another ideal, differing, indeed, from that of the Communist in requiring only the further evolution of existing conditions, not the total overthrow of our civilization. It is founded upon the present most intense Individualism, and the race is prepared to put it in practice by degrees whenever it pleases. Under its sway we shall have an ideal State, in which the surplus wealth of the few will become in the best sense, the property of the many, because administered for the common good; and this wealth passing through the hands of the few, can be made a much more potent force for the elevation of our race than is distributed in small sums to the people themselves. Even the poorest can be made to see this, and to agree that great sums gathered by some of their fellow-citizens and spent for public purposes, from which the masses reap the principal benefit, are more valuable to them than if scattered among themselves in trifling amounts through the course of many years. . . .

This, then, is held to be the duty of the man of wealth: To set an example of modest, unostentatious living, shunning display or extravagance; to provide moderately for the legitimate wants of those dependent upon him; and, after doing so, to consider all surplus revenues which come to him simply as trust funds, which he is called upon to administer, and strictly bound as a matter of duty to administer in the manner which, in his judgment, is best calculated to produce the most beneficial results for the community — the man of wealth thus becoming the mere trustee and agent for his poorer brethren, bringing to their service his superior wisdom, experience, and ability to administer, doing for them better than they would or could do for themselves.

We are met here with the difficulty of determining what are moderate sums to leave to members of the family; what is modest, unostentatious living; what is the test of extravagance. There must be different standards for different conditions. The answer is that it is as impossible to name exact amounts or actions as it is to define good manners, good taste, or the rules of propriety; but, nevertheless, these are verities, well known although indefinable. Public sentiment is quick to know and to feel what offends these. So in the case of wealth. The rule in regard to good taste in the dress of men or women applies here. Whatever makes one conspicuous offends the canon. If any family be chiefly known for display, for extravagance in home, table, or equipage, for enormous sums ostentatiously spent in any form upon itself — if these be its chief distinctions we have no difficulty in estimating its nature or culture. So likewise in regard to the use or abuse of its surplus wealth, or to generous, free-handed cooperation in good public uses, or to unabated efforts to accumulate and hoard to the last, or whether they administer or bequeath. The verdict rests with the best and most enlightened public sentiment. The community will surely judge, and its judgments will not often be wrong. . . .

In bestowing charity, the main consideration should be to help those who will help themselves; to provide part of the means by which those who desire to improve may do so; to give those who desire to rise the aids by which they may rise; to assist, but rarely or never to do all. Neither the individual nor the race is improved by almsgiving. Those worthy of assistance, except in rare cases, seldom require assistance. The really valuable men of the race never do, except in case of accident or sudden change. Every one has, of course, cases of individuals brought to his own knowledge where temporary assistance can do genuine good, and these he will not overlook. But the amount which can be wisely given by the individual for individuals is necessarily limited by his lack of knowledge of the circumstances connected with each. He is the only true reformer who is as careful and as anxious not to aid the unworthy as he is to aid the worthy, and perhaps, even more so, for in almsgiving more injury is probably done by rewarding vice than by relieving virtue. . . .

Thus is the problem of rich and poor to be solved. The laws of accumulation will be left free, the laws of distribution free. Individualism will continue, but the millionaire will be but a trustee for the poor, entrusted for a season with a great part of the increased wealth of the community, but administering it for the community far better than it could or would have done for itself. The best minds will thus have reached a stage in the development of the race in which it is clearly seen that there is no mode of disposing of surplus wealth creditable to thoughtful and earnest men into whose hands it flows, save by using it year by year for the general good. This day already dawns. Men may die without incurring the pity of their fellows, still sharers in great business enterprises from which their capital cannot be or has not been withdrawn, and which is left chiefly at death for public uses; yet the day is not far distant when the man who dies leaving behind him millions of available wealth, which was free for him to administer during life, will pass away "unwept, unhonored, and unsung," no matter to what uses he leaves the dross which he cannot take with him. Of such as these the public verdict will then be: "The man who dies thus rich dies disgraced."

Such, in my opinion, is the true gospel concerning wealth, obedience to which is destined some day to solve the problem of the rich and the poor, and to bring "Peace on earth, among men good will." . . .

Besides this, there is room and need for all kinds of wise benefactions for the common wealth. The man who builds a university, library, or laboratory performs no more useful work than he who elects to devote himself and his surplus means to the adornment of a park, the gathering together of a collection of pictures for the public, or the building of a memorial arch. These are all true laborers in the vineyard. The only point required by the gospel of wealth is that the surplus which accrues from time to time in the hands of a man should be administered by him in his own lifetime for that purpose which is seen by him, as trustee, to be best for the good of the people. To leave at death what he cannot take away, and place upon others the burden of the work which it was his own duty to perform, is to do nothing worthy.

This requires no sacrifice, nor any sense of duty to his fellows.

Time was when the words concerning the rich man entering the kingdom of heaven were regarded as a hard saying. Today, when all questions are probed to the bottom and the standards of faith receive the most liberal interpretations, the startling verse has been relegated to the rear, to await the next kindly revision as one of those things which cannot be quite understood, but which, meanwhile, it is carefully to be noted, are not to be understood literally. But is it so very improbable that the next stage of thought is to restore the doctrine in all its pristine purity and force, as being in perfect harmony with sound ideas upon the subject of wealth and poverty, the rich and the poor, and the contrasts everywhere seen and deplored? In Christ's day, it is evident, reformers were against the wealthy. It is nonetheless evident that we are fast recurring to that position today; and there will be nothing to surprise the student of sociological development if society should soon approve the text which has caused so much anxiety: "It is easier for a camel to enter the eye of a needle than for a rich man to enter the kingdom of heaven." Even if the needle were the small casement at the gates, the words betoken serious difficulty for the rich. It will be but a step for the theologian from the doctrine that he who dies rich dies disgraced, to that which brings upon the man punishment or deprivation hereafter.

The gospel of wealth but echoes Christ's words. It calls upon the millionaire to sell all that he hath and give it in the highest and best form to the poor by administering his estate himself for the good of his fellows, before he is called upon to lie down and rest upon the bosom of Mother Earth. So doing, he will approach his end no longer the ignoble hoarder of useless millions; poor, very poor indeed, in money, but rich, very rich, twenty times a millionaire still, in the affection, gratitude, and admiration of his fellow-man, and — sweeter far — soothed and sustained by the still, small voice within, which, whispering, tells him, that, because he has lived, perhaps one small part of the great world has been bettered just a little. This much is sure: against such riches as these no bar will be found at the gates of Paradise.

John A. Ryan

In his remarkable new book on theories of justice in leading American Christian thinkers, Harlan Beckley points out that Pope Leo XIII's encyclical of 1891, *Rerum Novarum,* had an enormous impact on John A. Ryan. It addressed the conditions of workers who were leaving the church in favor of various socialist parties in the latter part of the nineteenth century. This encyclical was not widely taught or studied in the United States at the time. However, it was assigned to a class of seminarians, and it gave this future priest and scholar a way of relating classical Catholic moral theology to modern industrial problems. He became the leading exponent of a kind of natural law theory that did not stress biblical materials or theological doctrines, yet was intimately related to the church's pastoral responsibilities and to the practical problems of civilization.

Ryan is often compared to Protestant advocates of the "Social Gospel" such as Washington Gladden or Walter Rauschenbusch, or to the religiously motivated economists Henry George or Richard T. Ely, who were so influential in founding the discipline of economics and on whom he sometimes drew, or even to Christian ethicists Reinhold Niebuhr or James Luther Adams, who in the next generation accented the responsible use of political power in the support of democracy. But these comparisons are only partly accurate. Ryan may have agreed with them on many social policies, but the driving force of his thought was decidedly Roman Catholic and, as he says, "expedient" — even if some church authorities were perplexed by his progressive use of "their" moral theology and his sense of what was "prudential."

Ryan saw in *Rerum Novarum* the possibilities of reclaiming the tradition of Thomas Aquinas and of showing how it pertained to modern conditions in America. Indeed, he thought it could bring a democratic spirit to the ministries of the church as well as to the political economy, and he became the driving force behind the National Catholic Welfare Conference, surely the chief charitable and advocacy organization among Roman Catholics in this century.

In the writing included here, Ryan calls the church to recognize its own primary responsibilities and traditions and shows how they lead quite obviously to engagement in issues of social justice. He does not deal theoretically with the nature of socialism or of capitalism. Rather, he sees many of the issues from the standpoint of the worker, and he calls for governmental intervention to guide the economy so that the worker can support a family, live decently, join the labor movement, embrace democracy, and remain loyal to the church and the faith.

The Church and the Workingman

John A. Ryan

The Church is not merely nor mainly a social reform organization, nor is it her primary mission to reorganize society, or to realize the Kingdom of God upon earth. Her primary sphere is the individual soul, her primary object to save souls, that is, to fit them for the Kingdom of God in heaven. Man's true life, the life of the soul, consists in supernatural union with God, which has its beginning during the brief period of his earthly life, but which is to be completed in the eternal existence to come afterward. Compared with this immortal life, such temporary goods as wealth, liberty, education, or fame, are utterly insignificant. To make these or any other earthly considerations the supreme aim would be as foolish as to continue the activities and amusements of childhood after one had reached maturity. It would be to cling to the accidental and disregard the essential. Scoffers and skeptics may condemn this view as "otherworldly," but they cannot deny that it is the only logical and sane position for men who accept the Christian teaching on life, death, and immortality. Were the Church to treat this present life as anything more than a means to the end, which is immortal life, it would be false to its mission. It might deserve great praise as a philanthropic association, but it would have forfeited all right to the name of Christian Church.

Having thus reasserted the obvious truth that the Church's function is the regeneration and improvement of the individual soul with a view to the life beyond, let us inquire how far this includes social teaching or social activity. Since the soul cannot live righteously except through right conduct, the Church must teach and enforce the principles of right conduct. Now a very large and very important part of conduct falls under the heads of charity and justice. Hence we find that from the beginning the Church propagated these virtues both by word and by action. As regards charity, she taught the brotherhood of man, and strove to make it real through organizations and institutions. In the early centuries of the Christian era, the bishops and priests maintained a parochial system of poor relief to which they gave as much active direction and care as to any of their purely religious functions. In the Middle Ages the Church promoted and supported the monastic system with its innumerable institutions for the relief of all forms of distress. Under her direction and active support to-day, religious communities maintain hospitals for the sick, and homes for all kinds of dependents. . . . As regards justice, the Church has always taught the doctrine of individual dignity, rights, and sacredness, and proclaimed that all men are essentially equal. Through this teaching the lot of the slave was humanized, and the institution itself gradually disappeared; serfdom was made bearable, and became in time transformed into a status in which the tiller of the soil enjoyed security of tenure, protection against the exactions of the lord, and a recognized place in the social organism. Owing to her doctrine that labor was honorable and was the universal condition and law of life, the working classes gradually acquired that measure of self-respect and of power which enabled them to set up and maintain for centuries the industrial democracy that prevailed in the mediaeval towns. Her uniform teaching that the earth was given by God to all the children of men, and that the individual proprietor was only a steward of his possessions, was preached and emphasized by the Fathers in language that has brought upon them the charge of communism. The theological principle that the starving man who has no other resource may seize what is necessary from the goods of his neighbor, is merely one particular conclusion from this general doctrine. She also taught that every commodity, including labor, had a certain just or fair price from which men ought not to depart, and that the laborer, like the member of every other social class,

John A. Ryan, "The Church and the Workingman," *Catholic World* 89 (April-Sept. 1909): 776-82.

had a right to a decent living in accordance with the standards of the group to which he belonged. During the centuries preceding the rise of modern capitalism, when the money-lender was the greatest oppressor of the poor, she forbade the taking of interest. Among her *works* in the interest of social justice and social welfare, two only will be mentioned here: the achievements of her monks in promoting agriculture and settled life in the midst of the anarchic conditions that followed the downfall of the Roman Empire, and her encouragement of the Guilds, those splendid organizations which secured for their members a greater measure of welfare relatively to the possibilities of the time than any other industrial system that has ever existed. . . .

With regard to the moral aspect of existing social and industrial conditions, the Church does lay down sufficiently definite principles. They are almost all contained in the Encyclical, "On the Condition of Labor," issued by Pope Leo XIII. Passing over his declarations on society, the family, Socialism, the State, woman labor, child labor, organization, and arbitration, let us emphasize his pronouncement that the laborer has a moral claim to a wage that will support himself and his family in reasonable and frugal comfort. Beside this principle let us put the traditional Catholic teaching concerning monopolies, the just price of goods, and fair profits. If these doctrines were enforced throughout the industrial world the social problem would soon be within measurable distance of a satisfactory solution. If all workingmen received living-wages in humane conditions of employment, and if all capital obtained only moderate and reasonable profits, the serious elements of the problem remaining would soon solve themselves.

But the social principles here referred to are all very general in character. They are of very little practical use unless they are made specific and applied in detail to concrete industrial relations. Does the Church satisfactorily perform this task? Well, it is a task that falls upon the bishops and the priests rather than upon the central authority of Rome. For example, the teaching of Pope Leo about a living-wage, child labor, woman labor, oppressive hours of work, etc., can be properly applied to any region only by the local clergy, who are acquainted with the precise circumstances, and whose duty it is to convert general principles into

specific regulations. In this connection another extract from the private letter cited above may be found interesting and suggestive: "If the same fate is not to overcome us that has overtaken — and justly — the Church in Europe, the Catholic Church here will have to see that it cannot commend itself to the masses of the people by begging Dives to be more lavish of his crumbs to Lazarus, or by moral inculcations to employers to deal with their employees in a more Christian manner." There is some exaggeration in both clauses of this sentence. The defection of large numbers of the people from the Church in certain countries of Europe cannot be ascribed to any single cause. Some of its causes antedate the beginnings of the modern social question; others are not social or industrial at all; and still others would have produced a large measure of damaging results despite the most intelligent and most active efforts of the clergy. When due allowance has been made for all these factors it must still be admitted that the losses in question would have been very much smaller, possibly would have been comparatively easy to restore, had the clergy, bishops and priests, realized the significance, extent, and vitality of modern democracy, economic and political, and if they had done their best to permeate it with the Christian principles of social justice. . . .

The second clause of the quotation given above underestimates, by implication at least, the value of charity as a remedy for industrial abuses. It cannot, indeed, be too strongly nor too frequently insisted that charity is not a substitute for justice; on the other hand, any solution of the social problem based solely upon conceptions of justice, and not wrought out and continued in the spirit of charity, would be cold, lifeless, and in all probability of short duration. If men endeavor to treat each other merely as equals, ignoring their relation as brothers, they cannot long maintain pure and adequate notions of justice, nor apply the principles of justice fully and fairly to all individuals. The personal and the human element will be wanting. Were employers and employees deliberately and sincerely to attempt to base all their economic relations upon Christian charity, upon the Golden Rule, they would necessarily and automatically place these relations upon a basis of justice. For true and adequate charity includes justice, but justice does not include charity. However, the charity that the writer of the letter condemns is neither true nor adequate; it neither includes justice, nor is of any value in the present situation.

Let it be at once admitted that the clergy of America have done comparatively little to apply the social teachings of the Church, or in particular of the Encyclical "On the Condition of Labor," to our industrial relations. The bishops who have made any pronouncements in the matter could probably be counted on the fingers of one hand, while the priests who have done so are not more numerous proportionally. But there are good reasons for this condition of things. The moral aspects of modern industry are extremely difficult to evaluate correctly; its physical aspects and relations are very complicated and not at all easy of comprehension; and the social problem has only in recent times begun to become acute. Add to these circumstances the fact that the American clergy have for the most part been very busy organizing parishes, building churches and schools, and providing the material equipment of religion generally, and you have a tolerably sufficient explanation of their failure to study the social problem, and expound the social teaching of the Church.

The same conditions account for the comparative inactivity of the American clergy in the matter of social *works*. Up to the present their efforts have been confined to the maintenance of homes for defectives and dependents, and the encouragement of charitable societies. In some of the countries of Europe, particularly Germany and Belgium, and more recently France and Italy, bishops and priests have engaged more or less directly in a great variety of projects for the betterment of social conditions, such as, co-operative societies, rural banks, workingmen's gardens, etc. Obviously activities of this kind are not the primary duty of the clergy, but are undertaken merely as means to the religious and moral improvement of the people. The extent to which any priest or bishop ought to engage in them is a matter of local expediency. So far as general principles are concerned, a priest could with as much propriety assist and direct building societies, co-operative associations of all sorts, settlement houses, consumer's leagues, child labor associations, and a great variety of other social reform activities, as he now assists and directs orphan asylums, parochial schools, St. Vincent de Paul societies, or temperance societies. None of these is a purely religious institution; all of them may be made effective aids to Christian life and Christian faith. . . .

There is a very real danger that large masses of our workingmen will, before many years have gone by, have accepted unchristian views concerning social and industrial institutions, and will have come to look upon the Church as indifferent to human rights and careful only about the rights of property. Let any one who doubts this statement take the trouble to get the confidence and the opinions of a considerable number of intelligent Catholic trade unionists, and to become regular readers of one or two representative labor journals. We are now discussing things as they are, not things as we should like to see them, nor yet things as they were fifteen or twenty-five years ago. Persons who are unable to see the possibility of an estrangement, such as has occurred in Europe, between the people and the clergy in America, forget that modern democracy is two-fold, political and economic, and that the latter form has become much the more important. By economic democracy is meant the movement toward a more general and more equitable distribution of economic power and goods and opportunities. At present this economic democracy shows, even in our country, a strong tendency to become secular if not anti-Christian. Here again we are dealing with the actual facts of today. Consequently, unless the clergy shall be able and willing to understand, appreciate, and sympathetically direct the aspirations of economic democracy, it will inevitably become more and more unchristian, and pervert all too rapidly a larger and larger proportion of our Catholic population.

Reinhold Niebuhr

As the West faced the Depression, capitalism appeared to be collapsing and radical proposals seemed to be the alternatives. Theologians, too, turned away from the historic developments toward sectarian pacifism on one side or proclaimed dogma on the other. Niebuhr was an exception.

He had been a liberal Christian, very taken with pacifism and democratic socialism. He shared much with the Social Gospel, with progressive Catholics, with secular liberals such as John Dewey, and with democratic socialists. With the rise of Fascism and Stalinism as well as the Depression, however, Niebuhr underwent a kind of conversion. His earlier confidence in the goodness of humanity and in the capacity of right reason and good will to solve every problem seemed superficial, and he turned to what he called "Christian Realism." Through his many books, articles, and speaking engagements, he became a preacher to the nation. Advisors to Roosevelt studied him in the 1930s, and President Jimmy Carter quoted him in the 1970s.

Niebuhr's view was rooted in the teachings of the biblical prophets and of Jesus and elaborated by Augustine, the Reformers, and the modern existentialists who had a sense of the tragedies of life. Niebuhr's use of these resources meant that many saw him as "Neo-Orthodox," like the famous European theologian Karl Barth. But Niebuhr posed his Christian Realism against every "orthodoxy" as much as against liberal humanism. They both failed to recognize the ambiguities present in the heart, in the mind, and in the power struggles of civilizations — indeed, in every effort to do good, and even to establish relatively stable balances of power. He spoke of the necessity of a "proximate pessimism," even if an "ultimate optimism" was possible on the basis of God's grace that is given to contrite hearts. Both are necessary if we are neither to flee into idealistic illusion nor to become lost in cynicism.

Niebuhr never became an enthusiast for capitalism, but his Christian Realism drove him to the conviction that "the human capacity for good makes democracy possible, and the human capacity for evil makes democracy necessary." He thought that an economy that was regulated but not centrally controlled allowed greater prospects for democracy. A flourishing democracy could debate the wisdom of a little more or a little less regulation here or there without pretending it could save the world.

In certain writings, such as his *Moral Man and Immoral Society*, he stressed the realist side of things. In other writings, such as his famous *Nature and Destiny*, he argued that theology was necessary for an accurate analysis of human existence, and he was very critical of theologians who speak from such oracular heights that they do not see the ambiguities in the valleys. In the following reading, he assesses both socialism and dogmatics, in good Protestant fashion drawing on biblical sources to do so.

Marx, Barth, and Israel's Prophets

Reinhold Niebuhr

We hear much today about two types of dialectic thinking, dialectic materialism and dialectic theology; about the secularized religion of which Karl Marx is the author and the extreme reaction to it associated with the name of Karl Barth. Both of them are derivatives of a much older dialectic — that of the Hebrew prophets. Marxism is a secularized version of the prophetic interpretation of history, and Barthianism is a highly sophisticated version of the religious thought which insists upon the absolute transcendence of God. In the one case, the prophetic idea of God as working in history and giving it meaning is reduced to the idea of a logic in history which works toward the final establishment of an ideal society not totally dissimilar from the messianic kingdom of prophetic dreams. In the other case, it is denied that God works in history; the world of human history is a chaotic and meaningless thing until it is illumined by the incarnation; since all human actions fall short of the perfection of God it is denied that human actions can in any sense be instruments of God; the hope of a better world in prophetic eschatology is transmuted into a consistent otherworldliness which simply promises doom for man and all his works, as far as man is a creature of nature.

In both of these types of dialectic thinking, the true dialectic of Hebrew prophecy and the Gospels is destroyed. The significant fact about Hebrew thought is that it neither lifts God completely above history nor identifies Him with historical processes. . . .

The idea of God's transcendence seems to have been arrived at in Hebrew thought through ethical insights. The prophets denied that God was limited to His chosen people or that He depended upon their pride and success for his glory. Faith in a completely transcendent God was, in other words, their victory over polytheism and tribalism. Since everything in history is partial, relative, and imperfect, it follows that any God worthy of genuine adoration must transcend history. The God of the Hebrew prophets was transcendent as both the creator and the judge of the world, as both the ground of all existence and as its goal and end. Jewish prophecy thus rested upon the idea of creation (in which God is both distinguished from and related to the world) and it made religion dynamic by seeing the will of God not only as the ground of existence but as its ultimate fulfillment.

For the Hebrew prophets this transcendence of God never meant that the world of historic existence was meaningless or sinful as such, and that the realm of meaning and goodness was above the world. The transcendent God worked in history, and the prophets pointed out how He worked. Evil and injustice would be destroyed and good would be established. History was a constant revelation of both the judgment and the mercy of God. The insistence of modern ethical naturalism that history is meaningful, and the whole liberal idea of progress, is an essentially Hebrew concept revived to counteract the dualism of Christian orthodoxy.

The Religious Realism of Marx

But one significant point it failed to achieve the depths of Hebrew prophecy. Its logic of history was a simple logic and not a dialectic. It saw history as a realm of creativity, but not of judgment. In its appreciation of the fact of judgment and catastrophe in history, Marxism is undoubtedly closer to the genius of Hebrew prophecy than liberalism, either secular or religious. The idea of Marxism that unjust civilizations will destroy themselves is, in fact, a secularized version of the prophecies of doom in which the Old Testament abounds.

The Marxians pride themselves upon their

Reinhold Niebuhr, "Marx, Barth, and Israel's Prophets," *The Christian Century* 52, no. 2 (30 Jan. 1935): 138-40.

scientific realism by which they claim to have arrived at this knowledge. But such knowledge is the prophet of religious rather than scientific realism. It is only because life is moral and men feel that an unjust civilization ought not to survive that the scientific evidence can be finally adduced that it will not survive. But on the other hand, the prophets were too realistic to share the illusion of modern rationalism that men would resist from evil once they had discovered it. They know that evil must sometimes destroy itself in a terrible catastrophe before men will cease from their rebellion against God and His laws of justice. This pessimism is obvious in the words of Isaiah: "Make the heart of this people fat and their ears heavy — and I said, O Lord how long and He answered until their cities are wasted and without an inhabitant." In this pessimistic analysis of the stubbornness of human egoism and sin modern radicalism is, again, much closer to the prophets than most of our modern religion. . . .

The prophetic insistence upon the meaningfulness of human history is a natural consequence of the Jewish conception of the unity of body and soul. There is no suggestion in Hebrew thought of a good mind and an evil body, an idea which is the bane of all Greek ethics. Greek thought may begin with the naturalism of Aristotle but even in it the highest ethical attitude is the rational contemplation of pure being, which is a form of rational existence, transcending the historical world. The dualism of Plotinus and neo-Platonism is thus implicit in the naturalism of Aristotle and invariably works itself out. In this connection the difference between the love doctrines of the Stoics and of Jesus is significant. For the Stoics, the perfection of love is a rational achievement from which all emotions of pity have been subtracted. In Jesus, love is the achievement of the total psyche. There is in genuine prophetic ethics no moral distinction between emotion and reason or between body and mind. For this reason the Jews never had a doctrine of the immortality of the soul, but only a hope of resurrection.

Prophetic Rejection of Dualism

It is clear, therefore, that where modern naturalism protests against the dualism and idealism of

Greek thought and Christian orthodoxy, it is in line with prophetic thought. It seems to be equally clear that the unqualified distinction in Barthian thought between the finite and the infinite is a heresy from the standpoint of prophetic religion and that, in spite of important distinctions, it really falls into the errors of neo-Platonic dualism.

On the other hand, the strong insistence in prophetic thought on the transcendence of God distinguishes it from all forms of modern naturalism, whether liberal or radical. For it, historic reality is never self-explanatory or self-sufficient. Both the ground and the goal of historic existence lie beyond itself. The weightiest ethical consequences flow from this emphasis. It is never able to make an unqualified affirmation of the ultimate moral significance of any movement in history. It cannot, as democratic idealism did, identify the democratic movement with the Kingdom of God. Neither can it, as modern radical Christianity does, identify the Kingdom of God with Socialism. The Kingdom of God, the final ideal, is always beyond history. What is in history is always partial to specific interests and tainted by sin.

A stronger hold on prophetic essentials would have saved liberal Christianity from committing the error of identifying bourgeois democracy with the ethics of the Sermon on the Mount. Religious knowledge often anticipates the knowledge gained by painful experience. Through many disappointments and disillusionments we are now discovering to what degree the democratic movement was the instrument of the middle class interests and perspectives. A genuine prophetic religion would know that *a priori*. In the same way modern radical Christians incline to an identification of the Kingdom of God with Socialism. . . .

The Relativity of History

It is this relative and imperfect character of every historical movement and achievement which persuades the dialectic theologians to counsel Christians to abstain from politics as Christians, though of course they recognize the necessity of acting in an imperfect world. The dialectic materialist thinks it is possible to affirm the proletarian movement as an absolute in history. The dialectic theologian is unable to affirm anything in history as

Barthian thought:

really good. But the moral defeatism of his perfectionism is as foreign to prophetic religion as is the utopianism of orthodox Marxism. In prophetic religion there is a more genuine dialectic in which the movements of history are in one moment the instruments of God and in the next come under His condemnation. Thus Babylon and the king of the Medes are regarded by the prophets as the instruments of vengeance in God's hands. But that does not mean that they are better than others and that they will not be cut down in time. They pronounce doom upon Babylon as well as upon Israel. Their attitude toward Israel is perhaps the perfect illustration of this dialectic. They do not deny that Israel has a special mission from God ("You only have I chosen"). But this same Israel stands under the judgment of God and must not make pretensions. God's hands are in the destiny of the Ethiopians, the Syrians, and the Egyptians as well as in the history of Israel. John the Baptist warns his contemporaries, when he finds them complacent in their sense of destiny, that God is able to raise up children of Abraham from the stones.

This interpretation of ancient history has a very direct relevance to modern social problems. The Dutch and other Calvinists were not wrong in affirming the democratic movement as against monarchical reaction. Democracy was in its day an instrument of God. It was modern liberal Christianity which was wrong (having lost faith in the transcendent God) in making an easy moralistic identification of democracy and the Kingdom of God, without a religious reservation. Modern radical Christians are not wrong in affirming the fateful mission of the victims of injustice in our present civilization. The prophets of Jesus blessed the poor, not because they were morally superior as individuals to the privileged, but because they are by virtue of their position in society the forces of progress and creativity in it.

Change Comes from Below

The privileged classes of society form an "upper crust." This phrase is literally accurate. It is a crust they form. No matter how good privileged people may be, they will be inclined to defend their interests and with it the old society which guarantees and preserves them. The destructive and constructive force must come from below. Any religion which, in its perfectionism, wipes out this insight and destroys all criteria for the religious evaluation of political movements will become, for all of its talk of perfection, an instrument of the classes which are afraid of social change. If we live in a society which is unable to establish justice (as I think we do), it becomes a Christian duty to seek a just society and to appreciate the fateful mission of those whose hunger will create that society more than it will be created by our ideals. That is our duty, even if we know as Christians that human egoism and collective will-to-power will reduce the justice actually achieved by every new society to something less than perfect justice.

A Christian socialism in our day could find an adequate theology and an adequate political strategy by a return to the dialectic of prophetic religion. If it fails in that, the Christian religion will on the one hand become a little conventicle of dualists who find human history meaningless and historic crises irrelevant to the real meaning of human life; on the other it will capitulate to a secularized radicalism and to naturalistic substitutes for religion. . . .

It is idle to hope that, even at best, a prophetic religion could completely stem the tides of dualistic otherworldliness on the one hand, and of naturalistic utopianism on the other. But it is still possible to create and, above all, to reclaim a prophetic religion which will influence the destiny of our era and fall into neither defeatism nor into the illusions which ultimately beget despair.

James W. Skillen

In the 1960s and 1970s, Marxism got a new burst of attention at the hands of revisionist Marxist philosophers — especially Ernst Bloch, but also Antonio Gramsci, Roger Garaudy, Jürgen Habermas, Herbert Marcuse, and others. They had a great impact on younger believers in the last third of the twentieth century. "Liberalism" seemed religiously thin and morally powerless in the face of difficult social crises. Polish Catholics, Russian Orthodox, East German Lutherans, and Hungarian Calvinists in the East felt they had to try to form a new synthesis between their faith and the realities in which they lived in order to survive. In a different way, African preachers and missionaries, Asian ministers and educators, and especially Latin American priests and nuns tried to develop a new synthesis that could change things. And in the West, the new styles of theology attempted to use Marxism as a tool of social analysis. The "use" of Marxism, of course, meant that Marxist thought was not sufficient alone; but it was thought to be valid as social science and as criticism of much that was false in religious conventions, and many believed that revisionist Marxism and radical theology shared a common moral vision of freedom and social justice.

At the same time, Christian thought was undergoing revision. No longer did the "mainline" churches have a monopoly on public moral discourse in America. Both evangelical and Roman Catholic voices became more prominent — sometimes because they used the electronic media in new ways, sometimes because they joined the politically resurgent "New Right," but also because they developed carefully argued critical assessments of both "liberal" and "radical" ways of thinking about the relation of religion to politics and economics.

James W. Skillen represents one of the most subtle streams of evangelical, neo-conservative thinking about freedom and justice, drawn largely from a tradition initiated by Abraham Kuyper, a successful businessman, founder of the University of Amsterdam, prime minister of Holland, and leading Dutch theologian in the early twentieth century.

n Freedom, Social
, and Marxism:
A Biblical Response

James W. Skillen

The twentieth-century Marxist scholar, Ernst Bloch, argues that the Christian tradition, including its Bible, is at odds with itself. On the one hand, Christianity is saturated with elements that have prohibited the genuine emancipation and maturation of human beings. On the other hand, Christian faith has at times pushed and guided people to the most radical deeds of revolt and liberation in this world. The reason for this, says Bloch, is that in the Bible "there are in fact two Scriptures: a Scripture for the people and a Scripture against the people. . . ."

For most Marxists, Biblical revelation and the Christian tradition must be rejected because they come down on the side of human confinement and even oppression. Christians accept God, kings, parents, owners, and a host of other "legitimate authorities" who control people "from above." Genuine freedom and justice, according to the Marxist tradition, can come only when people liberate themselves by throwing off all authorities "above" and by dissolving the god-idea into human autonomy. If the Biblical testimony supports human liberation and justice, then we will have to demonstrate that fact convincingly in face of the radical and penetrating criticism of Christianity by Marxists.

James W. Skillen, "Human Freedom and Social Justice: A Christian Response to the Marxist Challenge," in *The Challenge of Marxist and Neo-Marxist Ideologies*, ed. John Vander Selt (Sioux Center, IA: Dordt College Press, 1982), pp. 23-25, 32-38, 41-48.

In this regard, Bloch believes that he has contributed something to the rehabilitation of Christianity. Careful examination, he says, shows that there are two competing forces in Christianity. By picking out the dynamic liberating power that is "for" people and setting it in opposition to the structures and authorities that are "against" people, one can recognize the healthy atheism that has always been present in Christianity. In other words, if it can be shown that Christianity is dualistic, then Marx's criticism is applicable only to the oppressive, authoritarian, myth-making, anti-liberation side of Christianity. And, says Bloch, if we can find in the Biblical tradition itself an opposition to that anti-human authoritarianism, then we can show a continuity from early revolutionary atheism in the Bible to the radical humanism of Marx and his followers.

For Bloch the dualism in Christianity is displayed sharply in its concepts of creation and salvation. The two concepts are incompatible with one another. The principle that "leads into this here-and-present world cannot also be the principle that leads out of it," says Bloch. Redemption takes people out of this world and is therefore at odds with creation. . . . The crux of Bloch's argument comes . . . where he is discussing the apocalyptic order of the "new heavens and a new earth" anticipated by some of the Biblical writers:

> But the six days of creation and Paradise . . . are not eventually restored; not even in the Apocalypse — not even in its utmost dreams, where all that remains good in and from the world is a heavenly Jerusalem. And where even this figment of religious fantasy is "coming down" — comes, therefore, from above; though it is also prepared for men — "as a bride adorned for her husband." (Rev. 21:2)

We will take these words of Bloch as our point of departure and will return to them frequently. His challenge poses most of the crucial questions for us: Is Christian faith caught between a fallen creation and an apocalyptic rebirth that will *not* restore . . . creation and its original paradise? Does Christianity really hang upon a hope for salvation that transcends human action, human responsibility, human history, human freedom? Is it nothing but a deceitful ideological pretense to teach that freedom and justice are possible for those who live in a world where God is "above," where the rules are "pre-set," and where the bondages and oppressions of this age will simply be discarded in the (imaginary) last days? Is there any validity to the Marxist charge that *real* injustice for humans is found in those economic, social, and political systems where self-direction and self-determination are not possible? Is the Biblical tradition less concerned with social and economic freedom than it is with an (imaginary) apocalyptic or spiritual freedom? If the slaveries and bondages of this world are fundamentally unjust, then is the only hope for genuine freedom and justice a revolution in this world which will entirely transform the present order and dissolve the myth about another world? Is Christianity a dualistic religion in face of which we must choose *either* for freedom, justice, and atheism *or* for apocalypse, God, and heaven above? . . .

Having set the stage with many questions and a few preliminary explorations, we come now to the central thesis. Biblical revelation not only disallows the foundations of Marxism, it must also challenge the whole framework of Marxist praxis. But Biblical revelation also thoroughly upsets much of Christianity. In fact, the Marxist challenge appears as serious as it does primarily because of the degenerate character of Christianity. The Marxist challenge displays its power not so much because of its own integral validity but because of its penetrating (often unintended) ability to uncover and displace the inadequate forms of Christianity dominant during the last one hundred years. The only adequate Christian response is one that recovers Biblical authenticity.

Biblical revelation shows us, from beginning to end, that the whole of reality is God's seven days of creation. The creation is not six days plus a temporary paradise followed by an apocalypse which discards the creation in favor of another world. The Bible does not speak of an earthly world followed by another world. The creation is God's covenantally constituted, historically dynamic, totally dependent unveiling of Himself in all things. It is a complex, historically differentiating unity destined for sabbatical fulfillment in which God's image (plural) should come to celebrate the complete realization of all their work in a feast of freedom and justice in the presence of God Himself — in the loving communion of Father, Son (the God-man, Christ), and the Holy Spirit.

Let there be no mistake; my intention is not to play with theological terms in order to arrive at something linguistically novel or clever. My concern is to discover why the Marxist challenge to Christianity can be so powerful and at the same time so far from touching the truth of God's revelation. What Marx saw when he described religion functioning as an opiate was very close to reality. What Bloch was observing in the world when he misread the Scriptures concerning creation, paradise, and apocalypse were highly dualistic forms of religion. I, for one, am willing to conclude that the Marxist challenge cannot be met by any form of accommodationist Christianity which fails to take this world seriously or fails to take Biblical revelation seriously. Augustine's accommodation to Stoic and neo-Platonic philosophy; Aquinas's incorporation of Aristotle; pietism's personalism and world flight; and liberal Christianity's secularism — these and countless other Christian syntheses either fail to take this world seriously on Biblical terms or they see religion and sometimes God, as something at the disposal of human beings for their life in this world.

But Biblical revelation no more allows for such accommodation than Marxism allows for the rehabilitation of religion. From the first chapters of Genesis, through the sabbatical legislation for Israel, through the Royal Psalms and the eschatological Prophets, on into the Gospels and Epistles of Christ's Kingdom-announcement, it is *God* who creates and keeps His creatures at *His* disposal. Moreover, the Creator-Judge-Redeemer is not a general abstract deity who hangs above this world; He is the covenant-making Lord of human history who is bringing a complex array of His own active and responsible creatures into the full judgment and blessing of His sabbath rest. God is the Creator who takes human responsibility so seriously that He entered into our humanity in Jesus Christ to restore that responsibility. The uncompromising starting point for understanding human freedom and social justice is the Biblical, covenantal story of the generations of Adam and Eve unfolding before the face of God — the God whose love and wrath define the ever present contours and atmosphere of human responsibility. . . .

307

There can be no doubt that the Biblical framework of meaning provides no ground for Marx's point of departure. The point of criticizing religion, Marx argued, is to disillusion man

> so that he thinks, acts, and shapes his reality like a disillusioned man who has come to his senses, so that he revolves around himself and thus around his true sun. Religion is only the illusory sun that revolves around man so long as he does not revolve about himself.

The religion that Marx was criticizing, however, was not the religion of Biblical revelation. So we cannot fight Marx simply by defending what he was rejecting. Rather, our starting point must be to look carefully at the Bible to see how it exposes both the dualistic forms of religion as well as Marxism. And in this regard, the first thing to notice about Biblical revelation is its unveiling of the sabbatical structure of creation.

The meaning of the sixth day of creation as told first in Genesis 1:24-31 (and interpreted in such passages as Exod. 20:8-11; Deut. 5:12-15; Psalms 8; and Heb. 2:5-18) is that the image and steward of God, male and female in their generations, find themselves charged with genuine responsibility under God's care, to serve God, neighbor, and all of nature toward the end of a sabbath rest with God. Nature and God exist not as signs of human alienation needing to be incorporated (or reincorporated) into human beings who produce themselves autonomously; rather, the six days of a differentiating creation exist as a wide range of human and nonhuman creativity through which God's human creatures find their true meaning as they serve the One who promises them fulfillment. . . .

As Míguez Bonino points out, the New Testament revelation of human meaning in relation to God's purpose is rooted in the *jubilee* tradition of the Old Testament — "the prophetic promise of God's ultimate peace — his *shalom* — a very rich expression which embraces the total welfare of the individual and the community; health, abundance, just relations, prosperity, harmonious family relations, personal fulfillment, faithfulness to God, a just government." After God liberated Israel from Egypt, He gave them the commandments of the liberated life, built upon the sabbatical rhythm leading to jubilee. Each seventh day was to be specially consecrated to God as fulfillment of the first six days. Israel would experience every week as a perpetual habit and reminder of the validity of human life pointing to God's ultimate liberating purpose. . . .

When Jesus came to dwell among us, He took to Himself the jubilee announcement as one would put on a familiar cloak. He went to Nazareth one sabbath day and entered the synagogue, as was His custom.

> And he stood up to read. The scroll of the prophet Isaiah was handed to him. Unrolling it, he found the place where it is written:
>
> "The Spirit of the Lord is on me,
>   because he has anointed me
>   to preach good news to the poor.
> He has sent me to proclaim freedom for the
>   prisoners
>   and recovery of sight for the blind,
>   to release the oppressed,
>   to proclaim the year of the Lord's favor."
>
> Then he rolled up the scroll, gave it back to the attendant and sat down. The eyes of everyone in the synagogue were fastened on him, and he said to them, "Today this scripture is fulfilled in your hearing." (Luke 4:16-21)

Jesus Christ came to fulfill God's sabbath promise — the Son of God and elder brother of His people came to lead them into the promised land. The promised land is not the old garden paradise of this age, and it is not an apocalyptic "other world" discontinuous with this age. Rather it is the original sabbath of God's rest now opened up to His people through Christ for their own day of fulfillment. The sabbath validates and completes the first six days of creation; it does not do away with them. In Jesus the climactic word has been spoken, even as through Him the first creative word was delivered (John 1:1-4; Heb. 1:1-3). He came for the judgment of sin, to establish justice, to set all things straight, so that the creation could be fulfilled in sabbath glory. Jesus came to give sight to the blind, hope to the poor, and release to the captives. . . .

One of the central differences between God's

sabbath and Marx's new world (or any human utopia) is that God's seventh day is the fulfillment of all the ages of humanity. The most that one can expect to find in Marx's post-revolutionary society is fulfillment of the last members of the human generations. All earlier generations are lost, having been reduced to means to the end. Marx cannot escape the linear confines of his dialectical historicism. The Bible, by contrast, reveals that God's seventh day is a day of judgment and resurrection for every creature that has ever lived. And not only does it confront every creature in an apocalyptic finale, but it does so in the very rhythms of this age — day to day, month to month, in every week, every seven years, every jubilee year, in the birth and death of every individual. . . .

The resurrection of Christ was not an isolated event in history, nor was it the beginning of an escape from history. His second coming will not be an apocalyptic discarding of history any more than it can be reduced to a mere symbol of existential meaningfulness in this age. Christ's coming will be a real event of the end of the resurrection harvest. It will display the final unveiling of God's sabbath rest in coincidence with the real end of the sixth-day responsibilities of all human generations. The eschatological fulfillment of freedom and justice will bring together the "not yet" and the "already" of Christ's Kingdom. As Paul says: "Then the end will come, when he hands over the kingdom to God the Father after he has destroyed all dominion, authority and power. For he must reign until he has put all his enemies under his feet. The last enemy to be destroyed is death" (1 Cor. 15:24-26). . . .

According to Biblical revelation the fulfillment of human history and of all social justice will come not through the proletarian revolution but through the second coming of Christ. The latter will, in fact, be a more complete fulfillment of all the generations of human life than Marx ever imagined. Every unjust dominion and oppression will be brought to judgment, crushed, and subjected to the rule of the perfect Judge. And the communalism to be unveiled will be the communion of the saints of all history in the fellowship of God's sabbath where the complete service of God will become the fulfillment of all freedom. . . .

And to speak of human responsibility today refers immediately to the heteronomous norms of the Creator-Redeemer which obligate us as His creatures *in this age* — norms of love, justice, and stewardship in all areas of life.

We must return, then, to a consideration of "freedom" and "social justice" in the light of the Biblical sabbatical revelation. . . .

Human freedom, I would argue, should be understood as the unfolding toward fulfillment of all human talents and responsibilities given by God in the very constitution of His historically dynamic creatures. This implies not only freedom *from* the kinds of obstruction and oppression that inhibit or prohibit responsible action, but freedom *for* genuine maturation, development, and differentiation of such responsibilities according to divine norms. Unlike the abstract individualism and collectivism of Locke and Marx, Biblical revelation stresses concrete differentiation of human freedom and responsibility. There is nothing like an autonomous individual or an undifferentiated autonomous society in the Bible. Marriage, the family, art, technical creativity, agriculture, production of shelter and clothing, animal husbandry, education, and countless other forms of human social life are recognized and interpreted as responses of creaturely freedom to the Creator's norms of love, stewardship, productivity, service, and justice. Part of the meaning of the Exodus from Egypt was that God set His people free and commissioned them to develop and enjoy all these creational possibilities. Freedom *from* oppression is not autonomy; it is freedom *for* responsibility, within the covenant, to fulfill divine mandates.

Marx was reacting so strongly against restrictive religion and against unjust forms of social differentiation that he never considered the Biblical testimony on its own terms. God's commandments do not lock up and confine human beings. They set people free to realize their true meaning as God's image. God stands in judgment against those human authorities who inhibit or prohibit other human beings from fulfilling their God-given talents and responsibilities. Divine norms (commandments) which hold for all the human responsibilities God has given to His image in this age are far more powerful, concrete, and direct in their exposure of oppression and restriction than Marx's counter-world hypothesis. Only by means of dialectical logic could Marx make it appear as if his future communal society of uninhibited free labor could function as a norm for evaluating the actual configurations of social life here and now. But the goal of creating a general, free community no more serves as a norm for the actual freedom of families, schools, enterprises, and commerce, than does the ideal of an autonomous individual. In place of the humanistic freedom-ideals of Locke and Marx, we must come to recognize the creationally normative identity of a free and responsible marriage, a free and responsible family, a free and responsible school, a free and responsible press, a free and responsible church, a free and responsible business enterprise. Freedom and responsibility before God go hand in hand. And the variety of responsibilities mentioned bear testimony to the creational legitimacy of a wide diversity of social communities and institutions.

Social Justice is intimately connected with responsible freedom. At the very least, social justice means that justice ought to rule the relationships that arise from the creative exercise of freedom in the unfolding of history.

Marriage partners, family members, scholars and scientists, and members of industrial enterprises must do justice to one another in the internal affairs of their associations and institutions. The very structures of those relations should be just, each in accord with its own nature. Social justice is part of the normative constitution of every social relationship and disallows, from the outset, any liberal notion of individual autonomy and sovereignty.

Beyond its reference to the internal character of these *differentiated* realms of freedom and responsibility, social justice also refers to the way in which these many patterns and structures of social life should be *integrated* together in public life. Marx was not so far from Jean-Jacques Rousseau in trying to imagine an ultimate realm of integrated public freedom that would transcend all the fracturing, parochial, and private interests of human social life. But Marx and Rousseau could envision a communal society only by discrediting the actual differentiation of social life that was occurring in their times. They both took great ahistorical leaps of faith. Rousseau wanted to go beyond the free differentiation of society and create a "rational state" (governed by the general will) that would generate, reconstitute, and/or ap-

prove all social differentiation. Marx wanted to go beyond the "rational state" and differentiated social order of his day to a mystically unified realm of free labor. Both of these were ideals that grew up out of the soil of the humanistic quest for autonomous freedom. Both were reactions that failed to take seriously the social differentiation process (which states and economic structures do not create) as well as the emergence of the state as a response to the need for public justice in differentiating societies. . . .

Marx was correct in relinquishing the Hegelian and liberal ideas of the "rational state," but he should have done so by way of reconsidering the Biblical view of justice. In opposing Marxism there is no need to accept the liberal and fascist states as legitimate expressions of public legal integration. Nor does one gain leverage for a critique of unjust societies by postulating the eventual disappearance of the state. Biblical revelation shows that the sovereign God appointed ministers for public justice not just as temporary restrainers of chaos but as promoters of social justice. In fact, our labor to establish public justice both manifests and anticipates Christ's global Lordship. . . .

Most of Marx's criticism of capitalism was oriented to show its eventual and necessary demise through its own internal contradictions. Since he viewed the state as a mere product of capitalism, he was unable to look critically at the failure of states, *as states,* to do justice in society. There are many ways in which governments have acted and should act to establishing just economic relations among people and to overcome the injustices of capitalism. Much of the structure of any economic system is determined by public laws of ownership, taxation, commerce, etc. It is far too eschatologically escapist to speak of the self-destruction of capitalism. We must be able to speak about the development of just economic institutions and relations now, and that requires a normative assessment of every differentiated institution and its integration in the larger public world. Marxism provides no normative basis for such an evaluation and constructive development.

Biblical Christianity is also more eschatological than Marxism because it sees Christ's final judgment and the completion of the resurrection as the fulfillment of social justice in Christ's sabbatical Kingdom. Marxism posits the end of economic

310

contradictions; Christians anticipate the fulfillment of this whole creation. For social justice this implies a much more concrete understanding of global justice than allowed by Marx. Marxism is against the state, but it can plan for the communist world order only by way of radicalizing state power to eliminate the state system. Whatever the version of Marxist politics, the use of political power is always a normless means to an apolitical end.

Christians, by contrast, should contend for the growth of an ever more integrated order of global public justice. We should not stand against the state, but neither should we absolutize its present historical form. The modern state system is no more sacrosanct than the feudal system or the ancient imperial or tribal orders of the past. States exist as responses (sometimes just, often unjust) to the demand for integrative public justice in society. To the extent that social, economic, and political integration is increasing on a global scale, new kinds and increasing numbers of international institutions of public justice are needed to govern human life justly. Nationalism, imperialism, commercialism, militarism, and many other patterns of international control that favor the power of some states over others and some peoples over others must be criticized as unjust and transformed for the sake of global justice. But it is precisely the normative responsibility of governments to do justice that provides the criterion for judging the success and failure of governments and international organizations. The Marxist postulate of the end of the state is not a norm of justice but a negatively projected goal. Christians must do more than develop strategies for the revolution; they must work, *while it is still today,* to overcome every form of social injustice. Along with many other kinds of action, this will require political deeds of fundamental significance, recognizing that a crucial dimension of pluriform social justice in the creation is global justice for all peoples. . . .

Peter J. Parish

Two issues have been debated with great intensity in America in relation to capitalism: slavery and the oppression of women. Are they due to capitalism, as many religious leaders suggest? This is the question addressed in the next two readings.

Slavery was both a business and a moral issue. Further, the economic issues have always been embedded in a political vision of how societies really work, and how they ought to work, while the ethical questions have always been embedded in both debates about the religious basis of ethical judgments and empirical arguments about how things really are. Thus, slavery is one of the areas in which the relationship of religious ethics to the basic categories of capitalism and socialism has been disputed. All parties to the dispute agree that slavery and racism are wrong. Further, they agree that the purpose of scholarship on topics of this sort is to seek truth. Thus, their disagreements are not about deontology or teleology, but about ethology.

Is it the case that slavery was, essentially, a form of modern capitalism, one that revealed the logic of exploitation between the oppressors and the oppressed — a manifestation of the insatiable quest for profits and an early, agrarian-industrial form of class warfare? In that context, was southern (especially black) religion an expression of "the sigh of the oppressed" and a tool of the oppressor to control the passions of resistance? Or is it the case that slavery was, basically, a form of quasi-feudal paternalism rooted in a religiously legitimated political ethic, which allowed some to make another race into forced serfs? Certainly the North, which was the center of moral and political challenges to slavery, was more capitalistic, more democratic, and more dedicated to an intentionally antihierarchical religious orthodoxy than the South. But what were the driving forces in the complex of slavery, and what modes of analysis allow us best to grasp the moral and economic realities of the situation?

Since the Civil Rights movement, a virtual explosion of research on such questions has taken place, often at the hands of scholars who, while seldom overtly socialists or capitalists, adopted research methods from Marxist and post-Marxist social scientists. The following excerpts from Peter J. Parish's summary and assessment of representative debates demand that we recognize the subtleties — and temptations to ideology — that lurk in the discussion of such issues.

312

Slavery, Capitalism, and Religion

Peter J. Parish

The performance of slavery as an economic institution was affected by all kinds of factors — social and racial, moral and personal, political and psychological. There is obviously deep feeling and bitter experience behind the confession of the economic historian Gavin Wright that "in the real world of uncertainty, the attempt to distinguish 'economic' from 'noneconomic' motives was hopeless." Slavery was a labor system and the foundation of a distinctive economic system, but it was much else besides.

The obvious yardstick for measuring the economic performance of slavery might seem to be profitability, but initial discussion of the profitability of slavery raises more questions than it answers. The first question is simply, profitable for whom? The answer must depend on whether slavery is being assessed as a business or as a system. If as a business, one must ask whether it was profitable for the individuals, groups, and interests involved in it: the slaveholders most conspicuously of all — or perhaps some slaveholders and not others — but also merchants and middlemen, and less obviously . . . the slaves themselves. On the second point — slavery as a system — one must ask whether the community or society as a whole benefited from slavery. Did the economy of the South gain or lose by it?

The next crucial distinction is between absolute and relative profitability. On one hand, the ques-

tion may simply be whether, on average, slave owners made a profit or a loss. In Kenneth Stampp's sensible formulation, did the average antebellum slaveholder over the years earn a reasonably satisfactory return from his investment? On the other hand, the question may be whether he could have made a greater profit by dispensing with slavery and using his resources differently. Similarly, for the South as a whole, there is a distinction between the question "Did the South gain or lose by slavery?" and the question "Could the South have done better without slavery?" Was the often assumed or alleged backwardness of the South a historical reality, and if so, was it the consequence of addiction to slave labor? . . .

The economic fortunes of slavery — subject to booms and slumps like almost any other business — fluctuated between one time or place, or indeed one person and another. Its profits, and the methods of making them, differed between the upper South and the lower South, or between the Atlantic seaboard and the lower Mississippi Valley, or between cotton and sugar plantations. Profits varied obviously, too, from one owner to another, according to the owner's business acumen, management skills, social aspirations, intelligence, and luck, not to mention the size of the owner's farm or plantation and the quality of the land. Profitability still depended on individual ability.

When all the appropriate qualifications have been made, there is now broad acceptance that many slave owners made reasonable — and sometimes handsome — profits in the pre–Civil War decades. Most authorities now agree that they received a return on their investment which was in line with, if not superior to that available elsewhere. Such a finding clearly undermines the old view of Ulrich B. Phillips and his followers that slavery often laid a burden of unprofitability upon the planters, which they shouldered because they supported and maintained the institution for other reasons. However, it does not follow that because slavery yielded a good return, profit was the only motive and ambition of slaveholders. The slave owner was not necessarily a capitalist pure and simple, just because he or she happened to make money.

The fundamental priorities of slavery and Southern slave society are involved in this discussion. If slavery was above all a rational economic

From "The Business of Slavery" and "The Lives of the Slaves" in Peter J. Parish, *Slavery: History and Historians* (New York: Harper & Row, 1989), pp. 43-61, 81-85.

system devoted to the pursuit of profit, those who controlled it would have retained their investment in it only as long as it continued to show greater profits than alternative forms of enterprise or labor organization. However, if slavery was even more important for other reasons — as an instrument of social adjustment or racial control, or as a status symbol — owners may have been content to maintain it for those reasons alone, as long as it did not prove crippingly unprofitable. There is abundant evidence on one hand that slaveholders were keenly aware of considerations of profit and loss, and plantation records show that many larger owners kept very detailed accounts and responded in a sophisticated way to movements in prices and market conditions. On the other hand, it seems likely that, if they could have read the refined, complicated, and somewhat esoteric arguments deployed in the modern debate over the economics of slavery, many would have found them unimpressive and even irrelevant — not to say unintelligible. At the same time, they surely saw slavery in a broader context; it was at the center of a well-established way of life to which they were both accustomed and attached, and the disruption or demise of which they feared above all else.

The presentation of the case for the slaveholder as businessperson was carried to new extremes by Fogel and Engerman, although it is worth recalling the extent to which Stampp had prefigured some of the more sober conclusions of *Time on the Cross*. Fogel and Engerman argue that the profitability of the business of slavery was derived from the efficiency of Southern slave agriculture, which they attribute to good management, a high-quality work force, and the economics of scale which slavery made possible. They were even bold or rash enough to put a precise figure on their claim for the superior efficiency of Southern agriculture; it was, they said, 35 percent more efficient than Northern agriculture based on free labor. This figure is derived from the "geometric index of total factor productivity," through which efficiency is measured by the ratio of output to the average amount of the inputs of land, labor, and capital. . . .

Gavin Wright challenges the claims made for the economics of scale which the employment of slave labor made possible. It is true that, although the median size of Northern and Southern farms was similar, the *average size* of farms in the cotton

South, was twice that in the Northwest. The Southern figure is distorted by the larger plantations, whereras there were very few farms in the North with more than five hundred acres. On the other hand, it is also true that cotton could be successfully and profitable grown on small and medium-sized farms as well as on large plantations. Wright discerns no significant evidence of economies of scale as such on the larger plantations. What is clear is that productivity rises in step with the proportion of cotton in the total output of a farm or plantation. Every 1 percent increase in the cotton share was accompanied by a 1 percent increase in the output per worker. The crucial advantage of the larger planter, with a substantial slave work force, lay, not in economies of scale but in his ability to devote a larger share of his production to cotton rather than to other crops. Wright calculates that "when output is valued at market prices, cotton comprised about one-quarter of the output of typical slaveless farms, but three-fifths or more for the largest slaveholding cotton plantations."

Why should this have been so? Why didn't all farmers maximize the proportion of cotton in their total output? First, it is important to remember that, for all the dominance of cotton and other staple crops in discussion of Southern agriculture, cotton amounted in 1850 to only one-quarter of total Southern agricultural output, and tobacco, sugar, and rice together to less than another 10 percent. In the case of cotton, where the main constraint upon production came in the picking of the crop, planters and farmers alike had spare capacity to devote to the cultivation of other crops. The largest Southern crop was not in fact cotton but corn, which was cheap to grow, and, very conveniently, could be both planted and harvested at times different from cotton. Among other things, corn provided food for livestock, notably hogs — and the South had two-thirds of the hogs in the United States in 1860. The consequence of the compatibility of cotton and corn production was to make the South virtually self-sufficient as far as food was concerned (although there were local imbalances), while it was also producing its great staple crops for export to distant markets. Corn also provided a vital element of stability and security, especially for the smaller farmer.

This is the key to an explanation of why the larger slaveholders devoted so much more of their production to cotton, and thus benefited from the greater efficiency provided by a larger cotton share of total output. The choice of priorities facing Southern farmers and planters was between pursuit of maximum profit, with the attendant risks, and the achievement of greater security by concentrating first on subsistence farming, and then in addition growing some cotton for cash. . . .

Gavin Wright has not only rebutted the argument that economies of scale explain much of the efficiency of Southern slave owners, he has also exposed the unrealistic and ultimately false comparison attempted in *Time on the Cross* between Northern and Southern agriculture. In doing so, he and others have undermined the case for the superior efficiency of Southern slave-based agriculture. Whatever the display of cliometric ingenuity, it is surely impossible to make a fair and illuminating comparison between a large-scale planter with fifty or a hundred slaves producing cotton for export, and the characteristic Northern family farm employing little if any labor outside the family and producing a variety of cereal and animal products, with the prospect of selling any surplus on the open market. The two operations are different in scale, structure, and purpose — and in their social and economic context. There was nothing in Northern agriculture comparable to the Southern cotton plantation. . . .

The safer conclusions to be drawn from this discussion of the business of slavery might be summarized as follows. First, slavery was on the whole profitable for most owners, and the prodigious expansion of both the cotton-growing area and the volume of the crop in the half century before the Civil War would surely seem to bear this out. But the precise measurement of profit is difficult because of the many factors involved, and the answers will vary according to the criterion of profitability adopted. Second, the profitability of Southern agriculture depended heavily on its ability to meet the massive world demand for cotton. Third, the efficiency claimed for slavery was essentially allocative rather than productive — that is, it depended not on higher output per worker, or economies of scale as such, but on the ability to allocate more of the work force to the cultivation of cash crops. Fourth, any attempt at precise measurement of the superior efficiency of Southern slave agriculture over Northern free agriculture is riddled with hazards and pitfalls. Fifth, maximization of profit may not always, even in purely economic terms, have been the highest or wisest priority of slave owners; there was always the need to balance short-term gain against longer-term well-being, and for smaller owners questions of security and self-sufficiency loomed large and altered the ratio of nonmarket to market activity. Finally, the business of slavery was always affected by noneconomic considerations arising from the centrality of slavery in the whole Southern way of life.

Indeed, the debate among economic historians about profitability has run parallel with another debate about the character, outlook, and motivation of the Southern slaveholding classes. In a nutshell, it is a debate over paternalism or profits, and which of the two occupied a higher priority in the minds of slaveholders. Fogel and Engerman are among the more emphatic of a large number of historians who regard slaveholders as essentially capitalists deeply imbued with the acquisitive instincts and the profit-making impulses of their kind — just a Southern variation on the nineteenth-century theme of the American businessperson and entrepreneur. The outstanding modern proponent of the alternative view of the slaveholder as paternalist is Eugene Genovese. In various writings over the last three decades, he has depicted the slave South as a precapitalist society which needed to use the apparatus of capitalism — banks and credit and merchants — to conduct its business with the outside world, but which in its internal structure and social relationships remained something different. In one of his earlier statements of this theme, Genovese emphasized that the basis of the position and power of the planters was their slave ownership:

> Theirs was an aristocratic, antibourgeois spirit with values and mores that emphasized family and status, had its code of honor, aspired to luxury, leisure and accomplishment. In the planters' community paternalism was the standard of human relationships. . . . The planter typically recoiled at the notion that profit is the goal of life; that the approach to production and exchange

should be internally rational and uncomplicated by social values; that thrift and hard work are the great virtues; and that the test of the wholesomeness of a community is the vigor with which its citizens expand the economy.

The planter was certainly no less acquisitive than the bourgeois, but an acquisitive spirit is compatible with values antithetical to capitalism. The aristocratic spirit of the planters absorbed acquisitiveness and directed it into channels that were socially desirable to a slave society: the accumulation of land and slaves and the achievement of military and political honors.

Genovese stressed that paternalism necessarily implied neither lack of acquisitiveness nor an attitude of total benevolence toward the slaves. If paternalist owners assumed a responsibility for their slaves, they also strove constantly to maintain and reinforce the utterly dependent status of those slaves.

No recent historian has more flatly contradicted Genovese's view of slaveholder paternalism than James Oakes. In *The Ruling Race: A History of American Slaveholders,* he agrees that the accumulation of land and slaves was the prime motive, perhaps even the obsession of nineteenth-century slaveholders, but he regards this as proof that they were a class of acquisitive entrepreneurs and capitalists, dominated by a materialist ethos and dedicated to free-market commercialism. He describes the intense pressures in Southern white society toward material success — and the ownership of more and more slaves was regarded as the yardstick of that success. The thrust of his argument is summarized in this description of the slaveholding entrepreneurs:

They actively embraced the capitalistic economy, arguing that sheer material interest, properly understood, would prove both economically profitable and socially stabilizing. But this intense devotion to the capitalistic spirit of accumulation had done much to diminish the influence of paternalistic ideals within the slaveholding class, and that spirit was never successfully reconciled with the conflicting devotion to stability and social harmony. This was the contradiction that rendered paternalism so anachronistic to the nineteenth-century South.

Genovese and Oakes are powerful and articulate recent protagonists in a debate which has continued for half a century or more about the nature of Southern slave society. When, after decades of controversy, historians find themselves at such directly opposite poles as Genovese and Oakes, it may be appropriate to ask whether the clash of rival schools of thought is promoting or obstructing a genuine understanding of a historical situation. Have the interpretations of historians become so schematic that they begin to look dogmatic? Have powerful arguments, based on deeply held convictions, strayed too far from the often untidy and many-sided historical reality of the Old South? It may be possible to reduce the controversy to more manageable proportions, without having to settle for some feeble and inadequate compromise.

First, it helps to be clear about which slaveholders are under discussion. This controversy has become not only a war of words but a war about words, and participants have sometimes been talking past each other. Genovese's emphasis is upon the planter class, the larger slave owners who in his view — and the view of many others — exercised a dominant influence in Southern society far beyond their actual numbers. Clearly, the paternalist ethos is more likely to have characterized this group than, for example, small farmers owning two or three slaves. With some justice, Genovese's critics have accused him of treating the words "planter" and "slaveholder" as almost interchangeable; however, Genovese has said that "the rough parvenu planters of the Southwestern frontier" did their best to follow the pattern of the older, more established areas of the South. In sharp contrast, Oakes puts the emphasis on the much more numerous slaveholders who were not "planters," who owned two or three, or five or ten, slaves and who were in his view individualistic, upwardly mobile, and ardent in their pursuit of profit, to the exclusion of paternalist values or anything else. This is no doubt a useful corrective to the concentration on the larger planters which has been a feature of so much of the historiography of slavery. Unfortunately, in his enthusiasm to make his case, Oakes often seems to neglect or ignore evidence to the contrary. He attempts simply to sweep the planters and their tradition of paternalism aside and to dismiss them as an atypical and anachronistic minority on the geographical and economic margins of Southern society.

Surely, as various historians have shown, there was a broad spectrum, or a continuum, of slave ownership, running from the small farmer through the medium-sized landowner to the great planter — and there is abundant evidence, too, of the preeminent position and influence of the planter class in Southern society and politics. The social composition of Southern slaveholders does not break down simply into two opposite extremes of struggling small farmers and great planters — and no one has made that point more effectively than Oakes. Similarly, individual slaveholder, great or small, did not commit unreservedly or exclusively to the goal of either paternalism or profit. Just as in their economic calculations, individual slaveholders struck their own balance between market and nonmarket activity, so too in their broader socioeconomic priorities they struck a varying balance between paternalism and profit seeking.

Part of the difficulty derives from the sophistication of much of the modern historical argument, which tends to ascribe an unrealistic degree of self-consciousness and self-examination to the slaveholders of the Old South. One may legitimately doubt whether the normal busy, sensible slaveholder sat down each day, or week or years and asked himself whether he was a paternalist or a capitalist — or whether there was indeed any unbearable tension or inconsistency in being both. In the abstract, of course, it may not be difficult to demonstrate such an inconsistency, but Southern slaveholders are not the only people who have lived their daily lives without finding the burden of such illogicality insupportable. Ironically, Oakes himself concedes this very point — and thus undermines much of his own neat and tidy argument — in the course of a discussion of the influence of religion on slaveholders:

As humans, masters were by definition complex beings, capable of holding to contradictory values, motivated by principles at odds with their behavior, torn by irreconcilable impulses intrinsic to their way of life. . . . Among its many rewards, slavery offered masters the luxury of ambivalence.

The "luxury of ambivalence" among slaveholders may help to clear the smoke of battle among his-

torians. After all, the ownership of slaves was a measure of both wealth and status, and there was no need to opt exclusively for one or the other.

In fact, a number of historians have now questioned the existence of the kind of dichotomy between paternalism and profit which Oakes describes. Reviewing *The Ruling Race*, Steven Hahn suggests that, even if Oakes is right about the slaveholders' acquisitiveness, "there are no necessary implications for their culture and ideology." He asks, "After all, what landed elite in modern history, no matter how reactionary, has not been acquisitive?" Genovese has made a very similar point more than once. Even Stanley Engerman, one of the authors of *Time on the Cross*, conceded the point, or rather asserted it unequivocally:

There need be no overriding conflict between paternal attitudes and the drive to make money. Indeed, the characteristics which some have associated with paternalism — good care . . . and personal involvement — seem to have been seen by planters as a way to higher profits as well. . . . The sometimes proclaimed conflict between paternalistic attitudes and a response to economic incentives is, for some issues, an artificial and unnecessary one.

In a valuable case study of one large planter, Drew Gilpin Faust has shown how James Henry Hammond was equally determined to transform his plantation into a profitable enterprise and to project himself as a beneficent master who would guide the development of those he regarded as backward people entrusted to his care by God.

The balance between paternalism and profit seeking varied from master to master, according to a whole range of factors, including size of holding and economic conditions — and also time. In his analysis of broad social changes in nineteenth-century America, Thomas Bender has argued that many social historians have greatly exaggerated the speed and comprehensiveness of the transition from a way of life based on the local community to a more complex, interdependent modern society. In particular, attitudes, values, and relationships often changed much more slowly than the rate of technological and economic development. Similarly, it seems likely that, at the very least, Oakes has exaggerated the rapidity and the completeness of the switch to commercialism and the entrepreneurial ethos in the minds of slaveholders.

Indeed, one subplot of the main debate over paternalism and profits has been concerned with the direction of change over time. Oakes claims that, between the Revolutionary era and the Civil War, whatever paternalist tradition existed in the South was overtaken and overwhelmed by the rising capitalist values of an expanding slave-owning society of men on the make. This challenges directly Genovese's argument that, having been in the eighteenth century essentially an economic system, slavery became the basis of an increasingly paternalist social order — particularly after the ending of the external slave trade in 1808. Placing the argument both within his own ideological frame of reference and the broader international context, Genovese argues that the early spread of European capitalism called forth a new system of slavery in the New World which in time proved incompatible with the consolidation of the capitalist world order. Slave owners then assumed the mantle of the landed aristocracy in Europe resisting the advance of the very capitalist system which had spawned them.

With or without Genovese's ideological assumptions it is possible to detect a change in the character of Southern slave society as it not merely took firm root but expanded and became an essential part of the established Southern order. If slaveholders enjoyed the "luxury of ambivalence," success and expansion also allowed them the luxury of escape from purely profit-related considerations — though not of course completely. In a justly famous essay, "The Domestication of Domestic Slavery," Willie Lee Rose has described the process. Eighteenth-century Virginia planters, according to Rose, were more concerned with the state of their crops than with establishing paternal relations with their slaves. But, emphasizing the evolutionary character of slavery, she suggests that in the nineteenth century the South was "domesticating" slavery, taming its earlier harshness and consolidating it as an integral part of Southern society. "The Old South was actually engaged in a process of rationalizing slavery, not only in an economic sense, but also in emotional and psychological terms," she says.

Much of the discussion of slavery as a business also applies to slavery as a system. The debate over profitability applies not only to the individual or plantation but to the Southern economy as a whole. It was perfectly possible, of course, for slavery to be a good business proposition for slaveholders but a poor economic proposition for the South in general. It would not be easy to demonstrate that it promoted the economic well-being of the non-slave-owning sections of the community — and the nonslaveholders were the large majority of the population. On one hand, it is true that slave ownership did provide a kind of escalator by which people might rise in Southern society, and Oakes has stressed the extent of upward (and presumable downward) mobility in Southern society and the frequency with which individuals moved in and out of ownership of one or two slaves. On the other hand, there were wide disparities in wealth among the Southern population, and this reflected the wide gap between the great planters and the poorer whites. Although the overall inequality in the distribution of wealth was little different among the white population of the North and the South, the Northern figures were distorted by the situation in the cities, where there was a substantial propertyless class — and of course such a comparison leaves out the 40 percent of the Southern population who were Negro slaves and owned no property at all. In much of the South, the poorer whites lived in constant dread of the day when they might have to compete with freed slaves, but in fact they were suffering all the time from wage levels depressed by competition from slave labor. Slavery was a rich man's joy but often a poor man's plight.

If the cotton boom held the key to Southern prosperity, then parts of the South felt the strain of sharing only indirectly in it, if at all. Various historians, including William Freehling, have shown that slavery was a declining institution in parts of the border states and the upper South before the Civil War. Cotton had converted slavery into the peculiar institution particularly, but not exclusively, in the Deep South and the Southwest. It has long been thought — and this view was reinforced by the pioneering cliometric work of Alfred H. Conrad and John R. Meyer — that the states of the upper South boosted their flagging fortunes by selling their surplus slaves to the Deep South and the Southwest. However, Fogel and

Engerman sought to show that the scale and importance of the domestic slave trade had been greatly exaggerated. It is an incontrovertible fact that there was a forced migration of several hundred thousand slaves across the South in the half century or so before the Civil War — perhaps as many as a quarter of a million in the peak decade of the 1850s alone. The controversy is about how they were transferred from the Old South and the upper South to Alabama, Mississippi, and Louisiana, and later to Arkansas and Texas. Fogel and Engerman claim that the great majority were not sold, but either moved with their owners or were sent by them to their new lands to the west. The point is important because sale was likely to mean sudden and permanent separation from family and the local slave community, whereas movement in a group usually mitigated such horrors. Various critics, notably Richard Sutch and Herbert Gutman, have undermined the argument presented in *Time on the Cross* and laid bare its slender basis in the evidence. Precise conclusions on this subject are difficult, but it seems clear enough that slave sales formed a significant part of the long-distance transfer of slaves to the Deep South and the Southwest, and that they were economically important to the upper South. When the large number of local sales is taken into consideration, there is no doubt that sale, or the prospect of sale, was indeed a looming threat in the lives of most slaves.

Slave trading could be a very profitable business, particularly for larger firms such as Franklin and Armfield. They bought between one thousand and twelve hundred slaves each year for transfer to the Southwest. Most of these were shipped from Virginia to New Orleans, and some were then sent upriver to Natchez and other places. But each year the company sent some slaves overland — perhaps one hundred and fifty — under the supervision of only three or four whites. The slaves walked a distance of several hundred miles and the journey took seven or eight weeks. Although the salve trade was an important cog in the machinery of the Southern slave economy, slave traders were ill-regarded in Southern society and were often treated with disdain even by the very planters who relied on their services.

There is now broad agreement among historians that, although the internal slave trade was ac-tive, the systematic breeding of slaves for market was very rare. The slave stud farm may have existed but it was exceptional. However, this was an era of large families and rapidly growing population, both slave and free; owners were well aware of the marketability of their slaves, and fecundity added to the value of a young female slave. It would be fair to say that slaveholders were ready to exploit the fertility of their slaves but seldom sought to increase it by forced mating. They enjoyed the profits of coition without coercion.

The much larger question arising from the discussion of slavery as a system concerns its relationship with what some have called the economic "backwardness" of the South. So many factors are involved, and so many different criteria might be applied, that it is virtually impossible to isolate the retarding effect, if any, of slavery alone. On one hand, there is a strong presumption that slavery imposed a certain rigidity and inflexibility upon the Southern economy, that the dead weight of the slave system prevented the South from seizing new opportunities, that low levels of literacy and skill inhibited economic growth, and that the depressed living standards of many Southerners, white and black, reduced the consumer capacity of the home market.

On the other hand, when the Civil War came, slavery and the economic system based on it were not in imminent danger of collapse through inefficiency or unprofitability.

The combined forces of cotton and slavery kept not only Southern agriculture but the whole southern economy on a straight and narrow path which led to rejection of other choices, and consequent retardation. The very success (and the profits) of plantation slavery and cotton cultivation removed any incentive to switch from agriculture to industrial and urban development. Some historians claim that slavery had proved its capacity to adapt to factory and cities but in the particular situation of peak cotton demand in the 1850s slaves were actually drawn out of the towns and onto the plantations because they could be more profitably used there. In towns they could be replaced by white immigrant workers; on the plantations they were irreplaceable. There are many other factors — political, social, and psychological, as well as economic — involved in the analysis of the limited development of urban and industrial slavery. . . .

Whatever the external pressures and the internal tensions, and whatever the calculations of profit and loss, there was little immediate sign of slavery losing or even loosening its grip. Slaveholders, and most nonslaveholders too, adhered to slavery above all because it was there, and they dreaded the consequence of its demise. "We were born under the institution and cannot now change or abolish it," said a Mississippi planter. He would have preferred to be "exterminated" rather than be forced to live in the same society as the freed slaves. Behind considerations of efficiency and profitability lay something much deeper still. Slave and master were locked together in a system which the one could not escape and the other would not abandon. . . .

For one thing, the basic element of fear on both sides of the master-slave relationship must never be forgotten. Whatever the paternalist impulses on the one side and the success in building a distinct slave community on the other, there remained an awareness on both sides that masters ultimately held sway over their slaves by force or the threat of force. It was this which set the limits within which everything else happened in slave society. For their part, masters were not unaware of the ways in which slaves were filling the spaces and cracks left open to them — and those masters often felt insecure and uneasy as a result. Fear was the binding agent of the master-slave relationship.

For another, much of that relationship and its effect on the slave community is encapsulated by J. William Harris: "In some respects, especially in religion . . . slavery was a kind of unacknowledged, negotiated agreement, under which a partly autonomous slave community emerged." Eugene Genovese places religion at the center of "the world the slaves made." He shows Christianity as a double-edged sword which could either sanction accommodation or justify resistance. In the everyday routine of plantation life, it brought spiritual comfort and relief to the individual slave and sustaining power to the slave community. An emotional brand of Christianity, spiced with elements of the African religious legacy, developed into a distinctive African-American religion. Conjurers and magicians as well as Christian preachers wielded influence within the community. Emotional fervor and active participation — for example, in the characteristic call-and-response style

— were features of slave prayer meetings, which were often held away from the eyes and ears of the whites, and which were quite separate from the "official" religious services provided by the master. The emphasis of slave religion was on faith and love, not on rigid doctrine or formal structure; the most constantly reiterated theme was deliverance and the coming of the promised land, in which the spiritual and the temporal were inextricably mixed. This was a religion of joy and solace, not of shame or guilt.

The work of Albert Raboteau and others has reinforced this view of a slave religion which inspired a powerful sense of community and offered leaders and spokespersons for that community. But it did more still. Lawrence Levine has shown how it helped to provide alternative standards and alternative possibilities, especially in the area of relations between slaves, left largely untouched by the master's authority. The entire sacred world of the slaves, he says:

> created the necessary space between the slaves and their owners and . . . the means of preventing legal slavery from becoming spiritual slavery. In addition to the world of the masters which the slaves inhabited and accommodated to, as they had to, they created a world apart which they shared with each other and which remained their own domain, free of control of those who ruled the earth.

Evidence from some recent local studies of slave communities lends support to the views of Genovese and Levine — particularly if the locality under the microscope is one where there were large plantations and heavy concentrations of slaves. (The picture was surely rather different in areas dominated by smaller farms.) In his study of the Waccamaw rice plantations in South Carolina, Charles Joyner comments on the religious fervor of a large slave community, although he acknowledges that such enthusiasm was not shared by all the slaves. On one hand, masters and white preachers made great efforts to proselytize the slaves. On the other hand, African influences, themselves very diverse, were still strong; voodoo was still widely practiced and conjurers exercised considerable influence within the slave community. What emerged from these diverse traditions and the slaves' adaptation to the American environment was a distinct syncretic African-Christianity — and this development is traced more broadly by Blassingame and other historians.

In a study of a very different South Carolina community, Orville Burton offers a rather different picture of the role of slave religion. He points to the revolutionary potential of some aspects of slave Christianity, notably in its emphasis on the theme of deliverance. But he also stresses the role of religion as an instrument of racial control in the hands of the whites. In his early efforts to assert his authority as a slaveholder, James Henry Hammond set out to break up black churches and stop black preaching, and urged his neighbors to do the same. He replaced the slaves' own meetings with regular white-controlled services, conducted by itinerant white preachers. But this was another battle where Hammond was unable to win a complete victory over his slaves; they continued to hold their own meetings; and Hammond remained fearful of the leadership and organization they provided in the slave community and of their potential challenge to his power.

The transformation in our understanding of slave religion achieved by Genovese, Raboteau, Levine, and others — like all such major reinterpretations — has aroused anxiety in those who fear that it may be pushed too far, and frustration in those who are anxious to press on still further. A leading member of the first school of thought is John Boles, an acknowledged authority on the religious history of the South, who examines slave religion in this broader context. In his view, the underground church with its worship conducted away from the masters has been "insufficiently understood and greatly exaggerated." Boles does not deny the existence of the importance of religious activity within the slave quarters and among the slaves themselves, but sees it as an extension or supplement to more public worship. According to Boles, many more slaves participated in the worship of white or mixed churches than in their own private gatherings. The emotionalism, the style of preaching, and the active participation of the congregation, typical of black services had their parallels in Southern white churches. The services in a white rural Baptist or Methodist church, says Boles, had more in common with black worship than with the dignified calm of a white Episcopalian service. With the exception of a few atypical areas with a very high percentage of blacks to whites, Boles thinks it likely that "in no other aspect of black cultural life than religion had the values and practices of whites so deeply penetrated." In a comparable observation, Blassingame estimates that "the church was the single most important institution for the 'Americanization' of the bondsman."

For much of the colonial period, slave owners had serious doubts about attempts to convert the slaves to Christianity. However, the coincidence in the eighteenth century of the rapid growth of the slave population and community and the development of the Southern evangelical churches led to a major change. In the nineteenth century, slaves became active members of Baptist and Methodist churches, sometimes representing a third or even half of the congregation. Boles claims that the churches were by far the most significant biracial institutions in the Old south, though he acknowledges that the races sat apart in church, and that whites dominated the churches in every way that really mattered.

It is clear, too, that slaves took what they wanted and needed from their Christian faith and worship in its various forms. The emotional and psychological strength which enabled slaves to withstand the dehumanizing aspects of their condition came in large measure from their faith. For most slaves, says Boles, Christianity provided "both spiritual release and spiritual victory. They could inwardly repudiate the system and thus steel themselves to survive it. This subtle and profound spiritual freedom made their Christianity the most significant aspect of slave culture and defused much of the potential for insurrection." But surely the faith of the slaves also kept alive the possibility of challenge to the system and the hope of deliverance.

In complete contrast to Boles, and even to Genovese, Sterling Stuckey assigns religion a central role in the essential and virtually exclusive "Africanity" of slave culture. He expresses reasonable doubts about the proportion of slaves who ever actually took part in Christian worship, but then commits himself to the extraordinary statement that "the great bulk of the slaves were scarcely touched by Christianity." Elsewhere, however, he takes a somewhat less rigid view and speaks of "the Africanization of Christianity," or a

"Christianity shot through with African values."
These would seem to be steps along the road to
recognition of a genuinely African-American religion in which Christian and African influences
interacted with each other or existed side by side.
Indeed, he has some intriguing suggestions to
offer about how the two traditions interrelated in
practice, although he always insists on the primacy
of the African influence. In a typical passage, he
discusses a ceremony common to Christianity and
many West African religions: water immersion or
baptism. He concludes that, as in most ostensibly
Christian ceremonies on slave plantations:

> Christianity provided a protective exterior
> beneath which more complex, less familiar (to
> outsiders) religious principles and practices were
> operative. The very features of Christianity
> peculiar to slaves were often outward manifesta-
> tions of deeper African religious concerns, prod-
> ucts of a religious outlook toward which the
> master class might otherwise be hostile. By oper-
> ating under cover of Christianity, vital aspects of
> Africanity, which were considered eccentric in
> movement, sound and symbolism, could more
> easily be practiced openly. Slaves therefore had
> readily available the prospect of practicing,
> without being scorned, essential features of Afri-
> can faith together with those of the new faith.

Clearly, not all the differences between the recent
historians of slave religion are reconcilable, but
such an analysis, and especially its last sentence,
could form the basis of a widely shared understanding of the interaction of two religious traditions, if only one could dispense with the insistence that the influence of one must always be
subordinate to the influence of the other.

Janet Thomas

The religious, political, and economic transformations that led to the abolition of slavery also gave rise to feminism. But while the ex-slaves, for the most part, became Christians, embraced democracy, and resisted socialism, feminists have tended to adopt socialist critiques of capitalism, of traditional religions, and of "bourgeois liberal" politics. Those seeking emancipation from any and all forms of domination frequently see the source of that domination in the structure of economics and in the sources of values and power that legitimate that system.

There are, however, several varieties of feminism, and they are not all in accord. At some levels, to be sure, agreement is widespread; feminism, capitalism, and socialism share with modern democracy and with those religions that derive from the biblical tradition the view that male and female are morally and spiritually of equal worth and that all should act as free moral agents able to recognize and be guided by the principles of justice and equity. Further, all agree that these ideas should be applied in society, but that no society fully embodies these ideals, and that therefore change is necessary. The disagreements with regard to patriarchy, as in issues of racism, come in the analysis of what the concrete situation is and which historical developments have made, are making, or could make things better. In short, all believe that some degree of "progress" is possible; but only some agree that the progress is related to capitalism, while others think that capitalism is the source of the problem.

In politics, academia, the professions, and religion, these ideas have been heatedly debated. Both interests and moral passions run hot. How these debates turn out will deeply influence the internal organization of business and the degree to which society regulates economic activity to overcome the effects of patriarchy. In a carefully balanced attempt to survey the arguments, Janet Thomas sorts through the evidence and identifies which generalizations are, and which are not, warranted.

Women and Capitalism: Oppression or Emancipation?

Janet Thomas

In the last few years, work in social history of women has centered on the transition to capitalism and the great bourgeois political revolutions — also variously described as industrialization, urbanization, and modernization. Throughout this work runs a steady debate about the improvement or deterioration brought about by these changes in the lives of women and working people. On the whole, sociologists of the 1960s and early 1970s and many recent historians have been optimistic about the changes in women's position, while feminist and Marxist scholars have taken a much more gloomy view. There has been little debate between the two sides, yet the same opposed arguments about the impact of capitalism on the status of women crop up not only in accounts of Britain from the seventeenth to the nineteenth century, but also in work on women in the Third World, and cry out for critical assessment.

I will first outline each argument and then evaluate the accounts of women's position before and after the great divide. Next, I will assess the explanations of precisely why capitalism is supposed to have these effects, and finally I will discuss some of the theoretical and empirical problems that this work entails.

The orthodoxy of modernization theorists . . . (such as William Goode and Talcott Parsons) has

Janet Thomas, "Women and Capitalism: Oppression or Emancipation," *Comparative Studies in Society and History* 30 (July 1988): 534-49.

been that industrialism would result in a massive improvement in the position of women. . . . A sketch of the conventional argument goes something like this: thanks to attendant democratic beliefs in the freedom and equality of all individuals (which ultimately extended to women in the form of suffrage), and legislative and educational changes, women have been able to enter the labor market as independent wage earners. This has led to their having far greater power within the family. The political authority of patriarchal heads of kin groups has dwindled with the loss of their economic power, as peasant societies disintegrated in the face of market intrusions. Their loss was the gain of the conjugal family; romantic love and free choice of marriage partner became the order of the day, and as women went out to work in increasing numbers, marriage became a partnership, with roughly equal decision-making powers held by husband and wife. Leisure, domestic work, and child-care are increasingly shared, and the family becomes "symmetrical." Advances in contraceptive technology allow women freedom from the burden of continuous childbearing and rearing and the ability to enter the labor market on almost equal terms with men. These changes are presumed to affect middle-class families first and then trickle down to the mass of the population by the principle of "stratified diffusion."

The picture offered by feminist and Marxist critics of the impact on women's position of capitalism, particularly industrial capitalism, is entirely different. In their reading, "the rise of capitalism is the root cause of the modern social and economic discrimination against women, which came to a peak in the last century." In the early 1970s, Marxist and feminist writers, adopting an inverted mirror image of the arguments of functional sociologists like Goode and Parsons, argued that the oppression of women is functionally necessary for the present operation of capitalism on several grounds:

1. that their cheap labor in the household provides capital with greater profit as their husbands' wages may be reduced because their wives' services, like cooking, laundry, cleaning, sex, and so on, do not have to be bought on the market;

2. that women, being partially supported by the

supposedly "family" wage, provide a cheap and flexible reserve army of labor;

✓ 3. that women are the main consumer targets of advertising campaigns and provide the continued individualist demand upon which capitalism depends.

This debate, which became increasingly scholastic in the course of the 70s, was subject to the familiar criticisms of functionalism. Most pertinent here is the point that to argue that women's position in the household contributes to the *persistence* of capitalism does not explain *why* women were relegated to the household in the first place. Consequently, Marxist feminists have recently turned to historical explanations of women's present situation in capitalism. . . .

Michele Barrett in *Women's Oppression Today* (1980) argues that the historical key to women's oppression in industrial capitalism is a complex that she terms the "family household system." This emerged when a partly pre-capitalist conception of women's place was elaborated by the bourgeoisie in the late-eighteenth and early-nineteenth centuries and was accepted by the organized working class from the mid-Victorian period. This ideology led to the expulsion of women from craft unions and the mid-century protective legislation on women's working conditions. As a result, women were forced into the domestic sphere, and the basis was laid for a sex-segregated market. The sexual divisions of labor within the household and labor market, once established, served to reinforce each other, as they continue to do today. . . .

A Golden Age?

Perhaps we should begin a critical analysis with the assumptions about women's status in the past that both sides hold. Optimists argue that prior to the Industrial Revolution, women's lot was very hard. There was a pronounced sex-typed division of labor in agriculture, with women being responsible for work inside and outside the home (particularly weeding and dairy and poultry products). Their day was considerably longer than men's, and their status considerably lower, which Shorter takes to be indexed by a number of folk sayings like:

A woman, a dog and a walnut tree
The more they are beaten, the better they be;

and the fact that they apparently addressed their husbands formally as "vous" not "tu," stood behind their husbands' chairs to serve them first at meal-times, and were supposed to take the passive role whenever the household's affairs touched the outside world. Public culture and religious culture are emphasized as being strictly patriarchal. These descriptions of the status of peasant women in preindustrial Europe echo the findings of many male anthropologists in the 1960s and 1970s who discovered the "male dominance" of most contemporary peasant societies. And the historian Alan McFarlane, attempting to construct an ideal type of peasant society, concludes: "the subordinate position of women in other peasant societies, for example in traditional India or China, has received much attention. It appears that it is not merely a result of a particular technology, plough cultivation, but related to a particular form of socio-economic organization. . . ."

Feminist anthropologists have recently attacked the myopia (and perhaps also the deafness) of male anthropologists on the issue of whether women have power in peasant societies. They argue that male anthropologists have listened only to male informants who naturally like to claim that they rule the roost. A very different picture is given if women are interviewed, and, moreover, if actual household decisions are investigated in depth. Feminist anthropologists argue that women can wield considerable power in peasant communities where kinship organization is important. They subvert the male order of things. . . .

Some historians find evidence of something of a pre-industrial Golden Age for women in the discovery that women enjoyed quite extensive property rights, particularly as widows. Widows' "free bench" entitled women automatically to continue in possession of between one-third and one-half of their husbands' land during their own life. Against this obvious presence of women as land holders in preindustrial England must be set the discriminatory terms of their tenure. Thus, free bench was often conditional upon no remarriage and also upon chaste living. Female property depended on their propriety.

In summary, in terms of their portrayal of the

era preceding industrial capitalism, the optimists emphasize the hard work, the long hours, the low pay, and especially the patriarchal culture, both nationally and at the village level, within which women found themselves. The pessimists emphasize the reciprocal rights and duties of men and women at the household level, the fact that home and work were not separated, the way that women were fully engaged in household production, and that women's position in customary law was considerably better than it later became.

. . . Most modern writers are very heavily dependent on the earlier work of Alice Clark and Ivy Pinchbeck. Clark argued that the great deterioration in womens' position occurred in the seventeenth century as a result of the rise of capitalism. In this she is followed by the modern feminist writer Roberta Hamilton, who argues "that the transition period from feudalism to capitalism rather than the process of industrialization was the most crucial." Hamilton, like Clark, sees the crucial factor as being the decline of the family as the economic unit of production. "It was this process — the decline of family and domestic industry — which shattered the interdependant relationship between husband and wife, which led to the identification of family life and privacy, home, consumption, domesticity — and with women." And Clark claims that the three most crucial seventeenth-century developments were the divisive effects of the substitution of an individual for a family wage, the withdrawal of wage-earners from home life, which prevented the employment of the wage-earner's wife in her husband's occupation, and family, the increase in wealth, which permitted the women of the upper classes to withdraw from all connection with business.

It could be said that Clark exaggerates the experience of women in the urban retail and craft work, research on whom she pioneered. In many respects, as historians of proto-industrialization have shown us, the seventeenth and eighteenth centuries actually *increased* the amount of work available in the home for many families and placed women's work at a premium. There is no necessity about work being separated from the home and family with capitalism or industrialism. Not only did the beginnings of capitalism batten on the self-exploitation of family members at home, the

beginnings of the factory system also saw whole families being employed in the same workplace, and today it may be that with the development of the microcomputer and with the decline of official employment, we shall see a return to work being based in the home. Pinchbeck thought that the Industrial Revolution was the crucial watershed for women, but unlike modern feminists she believed its ultimate result was beneficial for women "since it led to the assumption that men's wages should be paid in a family basis, and prepared the way for the more modern conception that in the rearing of children and in homemaking, the married woman makes an adequate economic contribution." Certainly, if the words of many modern working-class women are anything to go by, domesticity is preferable to work in the mills, or in the sweated trades. According to Elizabeth Robert's research on women's oral accounts of their working lives in three Lancashire towns before 1940, "women who worked full-time were certainly not regarded as emancipated by their contemporaries, rather as drudges. Women whose husbands earned sufficient money to clothe, feed and house the family preferred to have a reduced work load rather than extra income." And indeed, Roberts goes so far as to argue that "pre-war working class women in so far as they consciously thought about the question at all, perceived their emancipation as a movement away from outside paid employment and towards domesticity."

Pinchbeck also noted the phenomenon that Eric Richards subsequently attempts to document in some detail: the alleged disappearance of women from many jobs with industrialization. Richards emphasizes what appears to him to be a universal trend; a U-shaped curve in which "the highest activity rates for women are found in the least developed countries; during the initial phases of development the rates decline, and it is only in the long run that women regain their previous high degree of participation."

However, the great difficulty in this kind of statement, which proliferates in the work of development economists, is the tenuousness of the statistical base that it relies upon. In preindustrial Britain there was no census material upon which quantitative estimates of the kinds of work women were involved in might be based. We are forced to rely on the isolated cases of women working as carpenters, printers, butchers, and so on (mainly, it should be said, as widows of husbands working in these trades) which form such a large part of Alice Clark's evidence. This is not to say either that census material in the nineteenth century is particularly reliable, with its fluctuating categories referring to married women. It was only in 1871 that the occupational category entitled "wives" distinguished between those mainly employed in household duties and those assisting in their husbands' businesses. Preceding and subsequent censuses assumed that wives at home were not productively employed if they were not working for wages. So it is highly probable that many wives' involvement in their husbands' trades as small retailers or craftworkers was likely to be ignored in the census return.

Moreover, as the head of household (always preferentially described as a man) filled in the census, he probably thought of his wife as a housewife and mother and not as a worker. Eric Richards relies quite heavily on census data in his article when he claims that there was a substantial diminution of the economic role of women during the nineteenth century, owing largely to the steady contraction of homework from about 1820, a trend only reversed after the 1870s by the growth of new "non-domestic" work opportunities in "secondary" and "tertiary" industry. But because Richards does not distinguish between full-time and part-time or casual work, he ignores the possibility that the exclusion of women from some trades may have increased the use of women and particularly married women in casual and irregular employment, which would not easily be "condensed and classified into a census occupation." For example, Michael Anderson tells us, "Well over a third of all working wives in Preston in 1851 were employed in non-factory occupations, but were not recorded."

I would argue, then, against those, like Eric Richards, who claim that the nineteenth century saw the lowest point of women's participation in employment and their relegation to a purely domestic role. For many women a mixture of domesticity and casual work as needs arose was probably the norm. But of course, then as now, they represented a secondary labor market. But when had it been otherwise? Middleton's work on peasant women in feudal England seems to sug-

gest that if feminist historians wish to pursue the thankless task of seeking the origins of women's oppression today, they need to go back rather earlier than the nineteenth century. But while I am skeptical of some of the arguments claiming the large-scale movement of women out of the work force during the nineteenth century, I have no doubt that, in many respects, their legal status deteriorated in the long transition from feudalism to industrial capitalism, particularly that of married women.

In the medieval period there were very definite restraints on the husband's control over his wife's lands. But as land declined as a form of property, women lost out. A wife's personal property, which belonged to her on marriage, and all that she acquired after marriage were her husband's absolutely. With the development of capitalism, a great deal of personal property consisted of wages and salaries, which, if earned by the wife, belonged legally to her husband. Moreover, new forms of property that tended to go to the daughter, such as leasehold land and investments of monies in government funds and joint stock companies, passed into the absolute control of her husband during his lifetime.

Even that limited protection which the widow had enjoyed through her right of dower in her husband's lands had been gradually whittled away and was finally abolished in the early nineteenth century. However, a husband still retained his right by the "courtesy," as it was called, to a life interest in his deceased wife's land.

It is interesting that feminist writers on developing societies also point to the deleterious consequences of the spread of British legislation on land holding and inheritance practices for women's position.

Explanations of the Change in Women's Position

Basically, insofar as there are detailed explanations of precisely why capitalism or industrialism should have these alleged effects on the status of women, they fall into two categories; materialist and idealist. On the whole, the optimists have been idealists. Women prior to the modern period have been seen as restricted by traditional, religious, and legal forces, which have weakened under the impact of new religious, philosophical, and educational ideas about the appropriate relationship between individuals. Admittedly, Shorter, among the optimists, ostensibly wishes to stress the *economic impact* of capitalism on interpersonal relationships. But when it comes down to it, the prime mover turns out to be individualist ideas — "egoism that was learned in the market-place became transferred to community obligations and standards, to ties to the family and lineage — in short, to the whole domain of cultural rules that regulated familial and sexual behavior."

Until recently, the pessimists have been materialists. Their materialism has taken two forms: technological and biological. I will deal with these in turn. Eric Richards, for example, argues that "the transformations in the functions of women in the economy since 1700 have resulted primarily from general trends in the framework of occupations, rather than, for instance, the impact of government policy or feminist agitation (though neither has been negligible). It is from the quasi-autonomous changes in the structure of the economy, rather than from the politically initiated developments, that the past determinants of women's economic roles are to be sought." Richards emphasizes the way that the mid-nineteenth century expansion of primary industry was unsuitable for the female labor force. Snell argues that women agricultural laborers were pushed out of the harvest work force (and the correspondingly higher wage rates) in the East, "as a consequence of the region's expansion of grain production, bringing a more extensive use, by employers, of male harvest labor and heavier technology" (the male scythe rather than the female hand-held sickle), and he places these changes back in the late-eighteenth century, explicitly combating the assumption that it was Victorian ideas about women's position that gave them secondary status. Similarly, Boserup and Goody, in their work on third world women, stress the implication of different agricultural technologies for women's work: apparently, hoe cultures necessarily entail the extensive use of female labor, whereas, with plough cultivation, reliance on female labor disappears.

In relation to these arguments, it is not obvious that more advanced or heavier technologies nec-

essarily mean the end of a female presence in the work force. Certainly in the nineteenth century, mines and ironworks relied on females in a fair proportion of their heavy manual labor, as do a number of Southeast Asian societies today, and Marx's argument in *Capital* was precisely that with the coming of mechanization, female labor would replace male: "with the help of mechanical force, they destroy the monopoly that male labor had on the heavier work."

A second materialist variant is biological determinism, always hovering in Richard's account and recently receiving a lot of attention in Brenner and Ramas' critique of Barrett. Thus Richards argues that "the mid 19th century probably experienced the highest average size of family in British history, the tyranny of repeated pregnancy *and* continuous child-rearing was at a peak, and this may have helped to reduce the female participation rate." And Brenner and Ramas suggest that "because factory production in particular, and capitalist production in general, could not accommodate childbearing and early nurturing, married women were forced to seek more marginal, lower-paying kinds of work." As Barrett points out in her reply, "to be at the mercy of reproductive biology is, at the social rather than the individual level, a political decision rather than a biological determination." She says this because "other societies discovered that the age of marriage could be raised, that contraception could be practiced even before the pill had been invented, that a surplus of women could be housed and fed." Barrett herself explains the causes of what she sees as women's oppression in capitalism in terms of nineteenth-century ideology epitomized by the protective legislation of the 1840s. But we are left ignorant as to the origins of this remarkably powerful ideology and unclear about how to combat its still pervasive influence

Insofar as writers on third world women explain the deterioration in the position of women that they so graphically describe, they too (despite Boserup's excursion into technological determinism) argue that ideology has been responsible, in the form of Western cultural imperialism, where notions of the fitness of women for domestic tasks, disapproval of their extensive involvement in agriculture and trading in West Africa, for example, have led development planners to exclude women from the education and training that would enable them to enter the modern sector, to formulate property laws that nibble away at the customary rights of women, and to do all this in the smug belief that the problems of women in developing countries are attributable to their "status" in traditional society, a status that will inevitably improve as a result of European intervention. Thus, these writers have tended to play down any indigenous discrimination against women and have largely blamed European development planners and their (unexplained) imposition of an ideology of the domesticity of women.

Having summarized and assessed some of these positions, I would like to conclude by asking whether as a result of all this research one can come to any definite conclusions regarding the impact of capitalism on the position of women. I would argue that one probably cannot. The problem is partly empirical, mainly theoretical. As neither side, the optimists or the pessimists, agree on their criteria for an improvement or deterioration in the position of women, the debate is likely to continue endlessly. Optimists regard the spread of bourgeois freedoms to women, and particularly legislative and political reforms subsequent to industrial capitalism, as sufficient index of their improved status. Pessimists regard these as a mockery in the face of continued discrimination against women in the workplace.

And what of these women who are so well or badly affected by the impact of economic forces? Can one really generalize to all women? Oddly, in a book that attempts to document their deteriorating situation with development, Barbara Rogers argues that the concept of "status of women" conceals as much as it enlightens. "It ignores the enormous variety of situations in which individual women may find themselves: according to position in the family, their own and their relatives' occupation, their income, among other such elements; the variations through time for each individual, relating to age, position in the household, health, and perhaps number of children, the fact that they have a varying relationship with individual men and boys according to the various male structures and life cycles; and innumerable other factors."

In relation to the nineteenth century, a hasty view, for example, might be that single women in the working classes benefited, while married women lost out. Pahl points to the regional and life-cycle diversity in women's work opportunities and in the extent of domestic role-sharing in nineteenth- and twentieth-century Britain: a diversity that is masked by a blanket expression like "women's oppression."

It would be a help, too, if feminist historians were to adopt something like the anthropologist Karen Sack's simple checklist of indices of women's status that she uses for comparative purposes. She compares four African societies for their discrimination against women, breaking the concept down into two main divisions ("social" and "domestic" discrimination) and a number of subcategories within each (under "social," for example, go women's opportunities for political office, divorce, social disposal of wealth; under "domestic" go menstrual and pregnancy restrictions and the wife's inheritance of the marital estate). Such clarity could help to avoid the disagreements that are bound to arise when writers are imprecise about the particular aspects of women's status to which they refer.

And should one take women's subjective feelings into account when estimating oppression or emancipation? Barbara Rogers points out that "in this debate sweeping generalizations are made about half the people in a society based on statements either by outsiders or by the men in that society." But if the domesticity of women is taken as an index of oppression, and some women say they like it, what does one do? Call it "false consciousness," "culture lag," or attribute it to interviewer bias? The point is that not all contemporary women are necessarily dissatisfied by their domestic role, and their subjective feelings do need to be investigated dispassionately rather than assumed.

If one eschews the experiential and focuses at the quantitative level, then the problem becomes one of the noncomparability of the data base; one is comparing what must appear a wealth of statistics on women after the great divide, be it capitalism, industrialism, or whatever, with a hodgepodge medley of data and case studies for the preceding period. It is really impossible to judge whether women in general were more or less involved in the work force, in better or worse conditions, after industrial capitalism than before.

And precisely *when* does one take the period representative of before or after the watershed, whether it is taken to be capitalism, industrialism, modernization, or development? Historians have sought the origins of capitalism as far back as the thirteenth century; the Industrial Revolution is currently receding well back into the eighteenth century and perhaps even into the seventeenth.

Many writers of feminist history on the grand scale tend to lump whole centuries in together, as indicative of women's higher or lower status in the precapitalist past, so that we hear of thirteenth-century agricultural workers alongside eighteenth-century farmers' wives, sixteenth-century midwives alongside twelfth-century abbesses. And as Bridenthal and Koontz suggest, "these notions of linear improvement or decline are too simple. A highly technological capitalist society differs so fundamentally from a non-literate, communal one that relations of power, family and the economy defy simple comparisons. Yesterday's abbess is not today's woman priest; the medieval alewife is not the modern barmaid."

I suppose that the conclusion that I am coming to is that histories of women on the grand scale, whether optimistic or pessimistic, are amazingly premature when the available documentation is so sketchy (partly as a result of historians' neglect, until recently, of women as a respectable topic for academic investigation). And until they use more precise categories for comparison, and are clearer about the questions they wish to address, more heat than light will come out of the discussion.

Gustavo Gutiérrez

Roman Catholic influences have been strong in Latin America since the *Conquistadors*. Enlightenment theories have also been strong in the universities and governmental bureaucracies. These, however, were often suspect, for they looked very much like the French Revolution's rejection of traditional faith. Similarly, Protestantism, with its impulse toward democracy, its disposition to individualism, and its doubt about folk mysticism, was viewed with skepticism. Latin America turned to the combined authority of leading families, bureaucratic state, and official religion.

The family in Latin America was tied to a *hacienda* economy, in regard to both the elites who owned the land and the peasants who worked it, although tribal peoples had other patterns of family economy. The state, in which the military has played a strong role, was more often than not mercantilist in policy. It either managed parts of the economy directly or gave monopolies to business leaders, usually drawn from the leading families. The church, too, was closely tied to leading families and to the state. There are, of course, many variations on this pattern, but what is common to all of them is that they are built on a tripod of religiously legitimated and hierarchically ordered family and entrepreneurial efforts, and that free associations, including labor unions and opposition parties, have not been encouraged. Indeed, when "outside" organizations come into these cultures — multinational corporations, worker's movements, Protestant missions — they have tended to be captured or crushed by the tripod.

Recently, however, the traditional system is changing — or, some say, breaking down. Certainly, it is being challenged from below. Radical priests and nuns, overtly influenced by the Enlightenment and Romanticism, have formed movements that draw heavily on Marxism and establish "base communities" for worship, work, and advocacy among the poor. This movement sees the sources of poverty in the impact of capitalism on their lands, an influence that, it is believed, produced the present economic dependency. This movement also challenges the military-dominated, mercantilist state that favors the elites, and it seeks an alternative form for the hierarchical church. The intellectual expression of this movement is called "liberation theology."

Gustavo Gutiérrez is one of the most articulate and widely known advocates of this theology. His view of modernity and his rejection of development in the Western model is not only influential among Latin American Catholics; it has become the guiding theme of many progressive Catholics around the world and is widely accepted among ecumenical Protestants, including many black and feminist theologians. In short, this movement has challenged the traditional structures in Latin America and is prompting vigorous debates about the relationship of Christianity to socialism and capitalism everywhere.

Liberation and Development

Gustavo Gutiérrez

The world today is experiencing a profound and rapid sociocultural transformation. But the changes do not occur at a uniform pace, and the discrepancies in the change process have differentiated the various countries and regions of our planet.

Contemporary man has become clearly aware of this unequal process of transformation, of its economic causes, and of the basic relationships which combine to determine conditions and approaches. He examines his own circumstances and compares them to those of others; since he lives in a world where communication is fast and efficient, the conditions in which others live are no longer distant and unknown. But man goes beyond the limited expectations which such a comparison might create. He sees the process of transformation as a quest to satisfy the most fundamental human aspirations — liberty, dignity, the possibility of personal fulfillment for all. Or at least he would like the process to be moving toward these goals. He feels that the satisfaction of these aspirations should be the purpose of all organization and social activity. He knows also that all his plans are possible, able to be at least partially implemented.

Finally, history demonstrates that the achievements of humanity are cumulative; their effects and the collective experience of the generations open new perspectives and allow for even greater achievements in the generations yet to come.

The phenomenon of the awareness of differences among countries characterizes our era, due to the burgeoning of communications media; it is particularly acute in those countries less favored by the evolution of the world economy — the poor countries where the vast majority of people live. The inhabitants of these countries are aware of the unacceptable living conditions of most of their countrymen. They confirm the explanation that these inequalities are caused by a type of relationship which often has been imposed upon them. For these reasons, the efforts for social change in these areas are characterized both by a great urgency and by conflicts stemming from differences of expectations, degrees of pressure, and existing systems of relationships and power. It is well to clarify, on the one hand, that the current (and very recent) level of expectations of the poor countries goes far beyond a mere imitation of the rich countries and is of necessity somewhat indistinct and imprecise. On the other hand, both the internal heterogeneity and the presence of external determinants in these societies contribute to defining different needs in different groups. All of this causes a dynamics of action which is inevitably conflictual.

The poor countries are not interested in modeling themselves after the rich countries, among other reasons because they are increasingly more convinced that the status of the latter is the fruit of injustice and coercion. It is true that the poor countries are attempting to overcome material insufficiency and misery, but it is in order to achieve a more human society.

The Concept of Development

The term *development* seems tentatively to have synthesized the aspirations of people today for more human living conditions. The term itself is not new, but its current usage in the social sciences is new, for it responds to a different set of issues which has emerged only recently. Indeed, the old wealth-poverty antinomy no longer expresses all the problems and contemporary aspirations of mankind.

Origin

For some, the origin of the term *development* is, in a sense, negative. They consider it to have ap-

Gustavo Gutiérrez, "Liberation and Development," chapter 2 in *A Theology of Liberation,* 15th Anniv. ed. (Maryknoll, NY: Orbis Books, 1988), pp. 21-33.

peared in opposition to the term *underdevelopment,* which expressed the situation — and anguish — of the poor countries compared with the rich countries.

It would perhaps be helpful to recall some of the more important trends which helped clarify the concept of development.

First of all, there is the work of Joseph A. Schumpeter, the first economist after the English classics and Marx to concern himself with long-term processes. Schumpeter studied a capitalism characterized by a "circular flow," that is, a system which repeats itself from one period to the next and does not suffer appreciable structural change. The element which breaks his equilibrium and introduces a new dynamism is an *innovation.* Innovations are on the one hand technico-economic, since they are supposed to have originated in these areas; but they are simultaneously politico-social, because they imply contradicting and overcoming the prevailing system. Schumpeter calls this process *Entwicklung,* which today is translated as "development," although earlier renderings were "evolution" or "unfolding."

The work of the Australian economist Colin Clark represents another important contribution. Clark affirms that the objective of economic activity is not wealth, but well-being, a term understood to mean the satisfaction derived from the resources at one's disposal. He proposes to measure well-being by making comparisons in time and space. The differences among countries are shown by various indicators. His calculations show that the highest levels of well-being are found in the industrialized countries. Clark designated the road toward industrialization which poor countries are to follow as "progress" (not development).

The Bandung Conference of 1955 also played an important role in the evolution of the term, although on a different level. A large number of countries met there, especially Asian and African countries. They recognized their common membership in a Third World — underdeveloped and facing two developed worlds, the capitalist and the socialist. This conference marked the beginning of a policy which was supposed to lead out of this state of affairs. Although the deeds that followed did not always correspond to the expectations aroused, Bandung nevertheless signaled a deepened awareness of the fact of underdevelopment and a proclamation of its unacceptability.

Approaches

The concept of development has no clear definition; there are a variety of ways to regard it. Rather than reviewing them all at length, we will recall briefly the general areas involved.

Development can be regarded as purely economic, and in that sense it would be synonymous with *economic growth.*

The degree of development of a country could be measured, for example, by comparing its gross national product or its per capita income with those of a country regarded as highly developed. It is also possible to refine this gauge and make it more complex, but the presuppositions would still be the same: development consists above all in increased wealth or, at most, a higher level of well-being.

Historically, this is the meaning which appears first. What led to this point of view was perhaps the consideration of the process in England, the first country to develop and, understandably enough, the first to be studied by economists. This viewpoint was later reinforced by the mirage which the well-being of the rich nations produced.

Those who champion this view today, at least explicitly, are few in number. Currently its value lies in serving as a yardstick to measure more integral notions. However, this focus continues to exist in a more or less subtle form in the capitalistic view of development.

The deficiencies of the above-mentioned view have led to another more important and more frequently held one. According to it, development is a *total social process,* which includes economic, social, political, and cultural aspects. This notion stresses the interdependence of the different factors. Advances in one area imply advances in all of them and, conversely, the stagnation of one retards the growth of the rest.

A consideration of development as a total process leads one to consider also all the external and internal factors which affect the economic evolution of a nation as well as to evaluate the distribution of goods and services and the system of relationships among the agents of its economic life. This has been carefully worked out by social scientists concerned with so-called Third World countries. They have reached the conclusion that the dynamics of world economics leads simultaneously to the creation of greater wealth for the few and greater poverty for the many.

From all this flows a strategy of development which, taking into account the different factors, will allow a country to advance both totally and harmoniously and to avoid dangerous setbacks.

To view development as a total social process necessarily implies for some an ethical dimension, which presupposes a concern for human values. The step toward an elaboration of a *humanistic perspective* of development is thus taken unconsciously, and it prolongs the former point of view without contradicting it.

François Perroux worked consistently along these lines. Development for him means "the combination of mental and social changes of a people which enable them to increase, cumulatively and permanently, their total real production." Going even further, he says, "Development is achieved fully in the measure that, by reciprocity of services, it prepares the way for reciprocity of consciousness."

It would be a mistake to think that this point of view, which is concerned with human values, is the exclusive preserve of scholars of a Christian inspiration. Converging viewpoints are found in Marxist-inspired positions.

This humanistic approach attempts to place the notion of development in a wider context: a historical vision in which mankind assumes control of it own destiny. But this leads precisely to a change of perspective which — after certain additions and corrections — we would prefer to call liberation. We shall attempt to clarify this below.

The Process of Liberation

From the Critique of Developmentalism to Social Revolution

The term *development* has synthesized the aspirations of poor peoples during the last few decades. Recently, however, it has become the object of severe criticism due both to the deficiencies of the development policies proposed to the poor countries to lead them out of their underdevelopment and also to the lack of concrete achievements of the interested governments. This is the reason why *developmentalism (desarrollismo)*, a term derived from *development (desarrollo)*, is now used in a pejorative sense, especially in Latin America.

Much has been said in recent times about development. Poor countries competed for the help of the rich countries. There were even attempts to create a certain development mystique. Support for development was intense in Latin America in the '50s, producing high expectations. But since the supporters of development did not attack the roots of the evil, they failed and caused instead confusion and frustration.

One of the most important reasons for this turn of events is that development — approached from an economic and modernizing point of view — has been frequently promoted by international organizations closely linked to groups and governments which control the world economy. The changes encouraged were to be achieved within the formal structure of the existing institutions without challenging them. Great care was exercised, therefore, not to attack the interests of large international economic powers nor those of their natural allies, the ruling domestic interest groups. Furthermore, the so-called changes were often nothing more than new and underhanded ways of increasing the power of strong economic groups.

Developmentalism thus came to be synonymous with *reformism* and modernization, that is to say, synonymous with timid measures, really ineffective in the long run and counterproductive to achieving a real transformation. The poor countries are becoming ever more clearly aware that their underdevelopment is only the by-product of the development of other countries, because of the kind of relationship which exists between the rich and the poor countries. Moreover, they are realizing that their own development will come about only with a struggle to break the domination of the rich countries.

This perception sees the conflict implicit in the process. Development must attack the root causes of the problems and among them the deepest is economic, social, political and cultural dependence of some countries upon others — an expression of the domination of some social classes over others. Attempts to bring about changes within the existing order have proven futile. This analysis of the situation is at the level of scientific rationality. Only a radical break from the status quo, that is, a profound transformation of the private property system, access to power of the exploited class, and a social revolution that would break this dependence would allow for the change to a new society, a socialist society — or at least allow that such a society might be possible.

In this light, to speak about the process of *liberation* begins to appear more appropriate and richer in human content. Liberation in fact expresses the inescapable moment of radical change which is foreign to the ordinary use of the term *development*. Only in the context of such a process can a policy of development be effectively implemented, have any real meaning, and avoid misleading formulations.

Man, the Master of his Own Destiny

To characterize the situation of the poor countries as dominated and oppressed leads one to speak of economic, social, and political liberation. But we are dealing here with a much more integral and profound understanding of human existence and its historical future.

A broad and deep aspiration for liberation inflames the history of mankind in our day, liberation from all that limits or keeps man from self-fulfillment, liberation from all impediments to the exercise of his freedom. Proof of this is the awareness of new and subtle forms of oppression in the heart of advanced industrial societies, which often offer themselves as models to the underdeveloped countries. In them subversion does not appear as a protest against poverty, but rather against wealth. The context in the rich countries, however, is quite different from that of the poor countries: we must beware of all kinds of imitations as well as new forms of imperialism — revolutionary this time — of the rich countries, which consider themselves central to the history of mankind. Such mimicry would only lead the revolutionary groups of the Third World to a new deception regarding their own reality. They would be led to fight against windmills.

But, having acknowledged this danger, it is important to remember also that the poor countries would err in not following these events closely since their future depends at least partially upon what happens on the domestic scene in the dominant countries. Their own efforts at liberation cannot be indifferent to that proclaimed by growing minorities in rich nations. There are, moreover, valuable lessons to be learned by the revolutionaries of the countries on the periphery, who could in turn use them as corrective measures in the difficult task of building a new society.

What is at stake in the South as well as in the North, in the West as well as the East, on the periphery and in the center is the possibility of enjoying a truly human existence, a free life, a dynamic liberty which is related to history as a conquest. We have today an ever-clearer vision of this dynamism and this conquest, but their roots stretch into the past.

The fifteenth and sixteenth centuries are important milestones in man's understanding of himself. His relationship with nature changed substantially with the emergence of experimental science and the techniques of manipulation derived from it. Relying on these achievements, man abandoned his former image of the world and himself. Gilson expresses this idea in a well-known phrase: "It is because of its physics that metaphysics grows old." Because of science man took a step forward and began to regard himself in a different way. This process indicates why the best philosophical tradition is not merely an arm-chair product; it is rather the reflective and thematic awareness of man's experience of his relationships with nature and with other men. And these relationships are interpreted and at the same time modified by advances in technological and scientific knowledge.

Descartes is one of the great names of the new physics which altered man's relationship to nature. He laid the cornerstone of a philosophical reflection which stressed the primacy of thought and of "clear and distinct ideas," and so highlighted the creative aspects of human subjectivity. Kant's "Copernican Revolution" strengthened and systematized this point of view. For him our concept ought not to conform to the objects, but rather "the objects, or, in which is the same thing, that experience, which alone as given objects they are *cognized*, must conform to my conceptions." The reason is that "we only cognize in things *a priori* that which we ourselves place in them." Kant was aware that this leads to a "new method" of thought, to a knowledge which is critical of its foundations and thus abandons its naiveté and enters an adult stage.

Hegel followed this approach, introducing with vitality and urgency the theme of history. To a great extent his philosophy is a reflection on the French Revolution. This historical event had vast repercussions, for it proclaimed the right of every man to participate in the direction of the society to which he belongs. For Hegel man is aware of himself "only by being acknowledged or 'recognized'" by another consciousness. But this being recognized by another presupposes an initial conflict, "a life-and-death struggle," because it is "solely by risking life that freedom is obtained."

Through the lord-bondsman dialectic (resulting from this original confrontation), the historical process will then appear as the genesis of consciousness and therefore of the gradual liberation of man. Through the dialectical process man constructs himself and attains a real awareness of his own being; he liberates himself in the acquisition of genuine freedom which through work transforms the world and educates man. For Hegel "world history is the progression of the awareness of freedom." Moreover, the driving force of history is the difficult conquest of freedom, hardly perceptible in its initial stages. It is the passage from awareness of freedom to real freedom. "It is Freedom in itself that comprises within itself the infinite necessity of bringing itself to consciousness and thereby, since knowledge about itself is its very nature, to reality." Thus man gradually takes hold of the reins of his own destiny. He looks ahead and turns towards a society in which he will be free of all alienation and servitude. This focus will initiate a new dimension in philosophy: social criticism.

Marx deepened and renewed this line of thought in his unique way. But this required what has been called an "epistemological break" (a notion taken from Gaston Bachelard) with previous thought. The new attitude was expressed clearly in the famous *Theses on Feuerbach*, in which Marx presented concisely but penetratingly the essential elements of his approach. In them, especially in the First Thesis, Marx situated himself equidistant between the old materialism and idealism; more precisely, he presented his position as the dialec-

tical transcendence of both. Of the first he retained the affirmation of the objectivity of the external world; of the second he kept man's transforming capacity. For Marx, to know was something indissolubly linked to the transformation of the world through work. Basing his thought on these first intuitions, he went on to construct a scientific understanding of historical reality. He analyzed capitalistic society, in which were found concrete instances of the exploitation of man by his fellows and of one social class by another. Pointing the way towards an era in history when man can live humanly, Marx created categories which allowed for the elaboration of a science of history.

The door was opened for science to help man take one more step on the road of critical thinking. It made him more aware of the socio-economic determinants of his ideological creations and therefore freer and more lucid in relation to them. But at the same time these new insights enabled man to have greater control and rational grasp of his historical initiatives. (This interpretation is valid unless of course one holds a dogmatic and mechanistic interpretation of history). These initiatives ought to assure the change from the capitalistic mode of production to the socialistic mode, that is to say, to one oriented towards a society in which man can begin to live freely and humanly. He will have controlled nature, created the conditions for a socialized production of wealth, done away with private acquisition of excessive wealth, and established socialism.

But modern man's aspirations include not only liberation from *exterior* pressures which prevent his fulfillment as a member of a certain social class, country, or society. He seeks likewise an *interior* liberation, in an individual and intimate dimension; he seeks liberation not only on a social plane but also on a physchological. He seeks an interior freedom understood however not as an ideological evasion from social confrontation or as the internalization of a situation of dependency. Rather it must be in relation to the real world of the human psyche as understood since Freud.

A new frontier was in effect opened up when Freud highlighted the unconscious determinants of human behavior, with repression as the central element of man's psychic make-up. Repression is the result of the conflict between instinctive drives and the cultural and ethical demands of the social environment. For Freud, unconscious motivations exercise a tyrannical power and can produce aberrant behavior. This behavior is controllable only if the subject becomes aware of these motivations through an accurate reading of the new language of meanings created by the unconscious. Since Hegel we have seen *conflict* used as a germinal explanatory category and *awareness* as a step in the conquest of freedom. In Freud however they appear in a psychological process which ought also to lead to a fuller liberation of man.

The scope of liberation on the collective and historical level does not always and satisfactorily include psychological liberation. Psychological liberation includes dimensions which do not exist in or are not sufficiently integrated with collective, historical liberation. We are not speaking here, however, of facilely separating them or putting them in opposition to one another. "It seems to me," writes David Cooper, "that a cardinal failure of all past revolutions has been the dissociation of liberation on the mass social level, i.e. liberation of whole classes in economic and political terms, and liberation on the level of the individual and the concrete groups in which he is directly engaged. If we are to talk of revolution today our talk will be meaningless unless we effect some union between the macro-social and micro-social, and between 'inner reality' and 'outer reality.'" Moreover, alienation and exploitation as well as the very struggle for liberation from them have ramifications on the personal and psychological planes which it would be dangerous to overlook in the process of constructing a new society and a new man. These personal aspects — considered not as excessively privatized, but rather as encompassing all human dimensions — are also under consideration in the contemporary debate concerning greater participation of all in political activity. This is so even in a socialist society.

In this area, Marcuse's attempt, under the influence of Hegel and Marx, to use the psychoanalytical categories for social criticism is important. Basing his observations on a work which Freud himself did not hold in high regard, *Civilization and its Discontents,* Marcuse analyzes the *over-repressive* character of the affluent society and envisions the possibility of a nonrepressive society, a possibility skeptically denied by Freud. Marcuse's analyses of advanced industrial society, capitalistic or socialistic, lead him to denounce the emergence of a one-dimensional and oppressive society. In order to achieve this non-repressive society, however, it will be necessary to challenge the values espoused by the society which denies man the possibility of living freely. Marcuse labels this the Great Refusal: "the specter of a revolution which subordinates the development of the productive forces and higher standards of living to the requirements of creating solidarity for the human species, for abolishing poverty and misery beyond all national frontiers and spheres of interest, for the attainment of peace."

We are not suggesting, of course, that we should endorse without question every aspect of this development of ideas. There are ambiguities, critical observations to be made, and points to be clarified. Many ideas must be reconsidered in the light of a history that advances inexorably, simultaneously confirming and rejecting previous assertions. Ideas must be reconsidered too in light of praxis, which is the proving ground of all theory, and in light of socio-cultural realities very different from those from which the ideas emerged. But all this should not lead us to an attitude of distrustful reserve toward these ideas; rather it should suggest that the task to be undertaken is formidable. And the task is all the more urgent because these reflections are attempts to express a deeply-rooted sentiment in today's masses: the aspiration to liberation. This aspiration is still confusedly perceived, but there is an ever greater awareness of it. Furthermore, for many people in various ways this aspiration — in Vietnam or Brazil, New York or Prague — has become a norm for their behavior and a sufficient reason to lead lives of dedication. Their commitment is the backbone which validates and gives historical viability to the development of the ideas outlined above.

To conceive of history as a process of the liberation of man is to consider freedom as a historical conquest; it is to understand that the step from an abstract to a real freedom is not taken without a struggle against all the forces that oppress man, a struggle full of pitfalls, detours, and temptations to run away. The goal is not only better living conditions, a radial change of structures, a social revolution; it is much more: the continuous creation, never ending, of a new way to be a man, a *permanent cultural revolution.*

In other words, what is at stake above all is a dynamic and historical conception of man, oriented definitively and creatively toward his future, acting in the present for the sake of tomorrow. Teilhard de Chardin has remarked that man has taken hold of the reins of evolution. History, contrary to essentialist and static thinking, is not the development of potentialities preexistent in man; it is rather the conquest of new, qualitatively different ways of being a man in order to achieve an ever more total and complete fulfillment of the individual in solidarity with all mankind.

David Martin

Besides liberation theology, a second challenge to the traditional structure is exploding in Latin America. It is found in the rapidly growing new evangelical and Pentecostal churches (with similar developments in Africa, Asia, and now also in the former Soviet Union). These Christian developments, with certain sociological parallels to both the Hindu resurgence and Islamic fundamentalism elsewhere, repudiate humanist influences from the Enlightenment in theology and ethics, although they accept modern technology almost without reservation. They stress the importance of a personal "born again" religious experience, they accept a literal understanding of Scripture, and they tend to reject the "compromises" with culture that they think both the Roman Church and most Protestant churches have allowed.

Politically they are fiercely "populist," but they tend to judge candidates for office more in terms of their personal experience of faith or their sympathy to evangelical Christianity than in terms of any assessment of public policy. Many have only contempt for the "base communities," which they view as simply socialist political economics pretending to have been baptized. They encourage a strong family ethic among the poor — stressing the responsibility of the father for the moral and spiritual nurture of the family, a vigorous and individualist work ethic, the training of youth and those without skills, an absolute honesty in financial dealings, tithing to the church as a matter of stewardship, and the formation of enterprises and corporations outside the influence of the *hacienda*, state, or established churches. By several estimates, they represent at least ten percent of the population.

Many have been influenced or supported by North American television evangelists, but today it is the Central and South American leaders who are shaping the movement in their own ways. Thus far, the movement has very few writers, although it has many preachers, and those it does have are seldom translated. However, the noted British sociologist David Martin has spent several years studying this development, and he has published a careful and extensive study of this new cluster of movements. He compares it in its genesis and consequences to older developments in Protestantism and to various current movements in Catholicism, including liberation theology.

Religion and Economic Culture

David Martin

Peaceable Cultural Transformation

[Pentecostal] Protestantism [in Latin America] emerges at a certain point in the opening up of a society, particularly among people above the lowest level of indigence and with some independent resources of mind or money or skill. It enables such people to edge sideways into religious forms of participation, expression and responsibility which do not have directly to threaten the central stem of hierarchical power. Even where Catholicism adopts religious reforms and extends those into political reform, it retains a long-term historic identification with the socio-religious hierarchy and, indeed, the very sophistication and organic nature of its critical approach reflects that. Protestantism picks up sectors beginning to detach themselves through classic processes of differentiation or marginality, and is itself shaped by its history to fit in with a differentiated society. It is this which restricts its political scope and provides the push and shove for individual or group advancement rather than for political revolution.

Nevertheless, the shift to Protestantism does represent a revolution within the self: an ecstasis, a breaking beyond the static. In many cases it literally breaks down and breaks through the structured nature of social boundaries and the settled limits of ordinary received behavior. It "fills" and "fulfils" personalities deeply infected in their physical and psychic being with dis-ease and un-

ease. By exactly what linkages of mind and body we do not know, but there is sufficient evidence from the New Testament to the present time of a double release or discharge acting simultaneously on spirit and physical substance to restore harmonies long distorted and disturbed. When a Pentecostal speaks of life as delivered once again by a second birth in experiences of light and wind and fire, he or she dramatically symbolizes dissolutions of the past in catalytic and cataclysmic recoveries of wholeness. In Pentecostal language, that is an achievement of holiness. Such recoveries spread like forest fires along linked chains of kin and neighbors, re-forming families or creating communities which are themselves extended families-in-God. The importance of these networks for facilitating conversion can hardly be exaggerated. Rodney Stark, working in the different contexts of Mormon missions and early Christian missions among Jews of the Diaspora, has shown how faith spreads from relative to relative, neighbor to neighbor, but rarely from door to door.

[This] illustrates another generalization proposed by Stark which is the continuity between what missionaries and carriers of the faith have to offer and what is already in the inherited background. Though Pentecostalism maintains a rigorous rejection of Catholicism, it also activates elements which are actually latent in the Catholic faith. Kin relations are forged "in God," the *promesa* or promise is tested and realized in the gifts of healing and of the spirit, and godparenthood is extended to all the *hermanos* and the *hermanas*. Indeed, the women of Pentecostalism form something which is very close to a sisterhood. As they are brought into the circle of participation they more and more actively relate to each other and sustain each other.

At the same time, elements of the classic Protestant Ethic are realized, since discipline and sobriety are as vigorously embraced in ordinary life as ecstasy and release are achieved in the sphere of worship. Protestantism perhaps offers education, . . . or else it may motivate its followers to seek after education once there is the slightest chance such education is available. It may well be that the combination of discipline and educational aspiration is already stirring in some people and then, as they cast their eyes to new horizons, Protestantism emerges as one marker of

From David Martin, *Tongues of Fire: The Protestant Explosion in Latin America* (London: Basil Blackwell, 1990), pp. 202-11, 288-93.

a whole new way of life they propose to follow. The role of Protestantism is to reinforce and, indeed, sanctify their vision of comprehensive betterment. Clearly it provides them with a raft on to which people bound on the same journey may lash themselves.

That raft lies in a current which often slews in an American direction, at least for those in the immediate proximity of the United States. This is not to suggest, as many nationalist intellectuals would argue, that conversion to Pentecostalism is the straight path to Americanization. Its roots often lie, after all, in the oral traditions and oratory of black cultures and to that extent it does not inculcate the American concern with the written word. But it does bring people from all kinds of background into contact with North Americans, and with their expectations, and provides channels along which American ideas and ideas of America may move. The brothers and sisters communicate and pick up influences traveling from another world, mostly the joys of heaven but also the promise and power of the United States. Pentecostalism, after all, is about spiritual power and empowerment, and it would be surprising if some believers were not impressed by the United States as a fount of power. It may even be that Protestants from Puerto Rico, and elsewhere in Latin America, like Protestants in Korea, are more likely to migrate to the United States.

Whatever may be the truth about the pull of US power, it is evident that Pentecostalism (as well as other forms of evangelicalism) enables many of its followers to achieve a power in their lives which can simultaneously infuse them with the possibility of "betterment" and of new goods of every kind, spiritual and material, and also put them in touch with spiritual charges and discharges lodged deep in the indigenous culture, black, Indian or Hispanic. The long-term resources now drawn upon in people's lives run back both to the traditions of Protestant revival and to the ancient spirit worlds of Indian peasants and African slaves.

The Evidence Reviewed

There is a general, indeed notorious, supposition in sociological and anthropological studies that Protestantism is associated with economic success.

This supposition derives in a loose way from Max Weber and the endless debate about how the Protestant Ethic influenced, and was influenced by, the Spirit of Capitalism. But that debate has been mainly focused on the first wave of Calvinist Protestantism in the sixteenth, the seventeenth and (marginally) the eighteenth century. The debate has been less concerned with the second wave of Methodist Protestantism; and so far as the third and Pentecostal wave is concerned, the evidence we have is recent and rather fragmentary. When it comes to the second and third waves of Protestantism, they have been discussed more in terms of their contribution to democracy, to individualism and to the avoidance of violent revolution than in terms of their capacity to promote economic success. The *locus classicus* of debates over Methodism is not so much Weber as Halèvy. If Weber is invoked, it is on account of his essay on "The Protestant Sects and their Spirit of Capitalism" rather than "The Protestant Ethic and the Spirit of Capitalism."

That essay is a useful starting point because Weber stresses the way in which membership in a church, especially after a period of probation, provides a guarantee of moral qualification and, therefore, of credit. Doctrine he regards as comparatively unimportant so long as the moral qualifications required enshrine the Puritan virtues. Weber also notes, as did de Tocqueville earlier, the fantastic variety of associations to which Americans belong. They include, for example, masonic lodges as well as churches. These associations provide a means of contact, a source of mutual assistance and information, and a form of insurance. As a result, the USA is not a formless sandheap of individuals, but rather a buzzing complex of voluntary organizations. It is the transfer of that buzzing complex to Latin America (and South Korea) which is currently under way. Time and again in the studies here reviewed the emphasis falls on the importance of the fraternal network.

Of course, we are not, in fact, dealing just with small so-called sects, even though many of the groups concerned only have a few thousand adherents. As we have seen, the phenomenon of contemporary Pentecostalism has a wider provenance than ever Calvinism had in the past, and certainly more than Calvinism has today. The scale is "small" only in the sense that the people who become Pentecostals are small people and their "capitalism" is at the moment mostly "penny capitalism."

There have been a reasonable number of localized investigations concerned with the effect of contemporary evangelical religion, in particular Pentecostalism, on economic behavior, or at least touching on that issue as a major concern. There are, however, some problems about obtaining really firm evidence and these need to be set out. Once this is done it will become clear that we are dealing only with cumulative indications and with more or less sensitive observations about likely outcomes. We cannot expect to find more than plausible likelihoods. But, at least, it is not necessary to rehearse that part of the classic debate concerned with whether Protestantism or capitalism came first. *What we do need to probe are the complicated feedbacks whereby people perceive the possibility of change and so grasp and are grasped by religious ideas which can accelerate that change and/or help them to cope with it.*

A question which has arisen crucially in the original debate, and now arises once more, is the contingent nature of the connection between evangelical religion and economic advance. It is clear that capitalism in the past *could* occur without Protestantism and vice versa. Scholars have asked themselves complicated questions, for example, about pious Calvinist communities in certain parts of Holland and also Scotland which did not appear to bring forth the fruits of the capitalist spirit. Then, and again now, there is no necessary connection. The posited linkages and plausible likelihoods have to be couched in terms of frequent concurrence and mutual reinforcements. Evangelical religion and economic advancement do *often* go together, and when they do so appear mutually to support and *reinforce* one another.

Economic Advance by Non-evangelicals: "Strangers"; Mormons

The capacity shown by people of religious persuasions other than evangelical to advance themselves needs some further discussion. To take the example of the Lebanese (or "Syrians"), their ability to make good in the Caribbean, in Brazil, in the Ivory Coast and in North America presumably derives from a long historical experience of commerce in the Levant, and from the way many minorities — though not all — are in a position to exploit a particular corner of trade. A group of ethnic "strangers" willing to assist one another and to act cohesively can build up economic resources rather in the manner of the sects described by Max Weber. This they are well able to do even if they arrived, as most Syrians did, with only the resources of a hawker or a pedlar. The Chinese, too, are notoriously capable of forming a cohesive community of prosperous minor entrepreneurs, without the extra assistance from evangelical religion. Examples can be multiplied, for example the achievements of Asians in Kenya and after their expulsion from Kenya, again in Britain.

This phenomenon is, however, easily understood and familiar, and it need not erode any propositions we may tentatively put forward specifically about evangelicals and the improvement of material fortunes. Evangelicals are not usually migrant members of historic trading communities, though, of course, they *can* be. The Huguenots who went to England, Holland, South Africa and North America after 1685 were precisely such, though they can only broadly be classified as "evangelicals."

Less easily disposed of are instances of groups arising in a similar manner to evangelical Protestants and in similar environments whose members achieve comparable advances without being "Protestant." The main groups in question are the Witnesses, the Mormons and the Adventists. They need briefly to be considered.

With regard to the Witnesses there is a lack of material so far at least as concerns Latin America, though evidence gathered elsewhere suggests the same kind of capacity for economic and social improvement as found amongst evangelicals. James Beckford's fine study of Witnesses in England documents their capacity in a general and impressionistic way. Norman Long has provided further supporting documentation with regard to Witnesses in Zambia.

There are general grounds for supposing that Adventists also improve their positions somewhat, though the evidence directly derived from Latin America is fragmentary. Certainly material cited later from studies by Lewellen and Birdwell-Pheasant suggests that Adventism assists social mobility. In the Americas (North, Central and South), the Adventists build hospitals and provide schools, as well as encouraging certain practices with regard to health and diet. They constitute a kind of small-scale welfare system which can hardly fail to help forward their community.

The Mormons are an interesting case. In the first place, Rodney Stark has maintained that they are a *new* religion rather than a semi-Christian sect. Therefore, he argues, they make their maximum impact where modernization has advanced sufficiently to create a religious vacuum. This means, presumably, that they are expanding on the whole in environments already prosperous, for example Uruguay.

The position with regard to the Mormons is complicated further, and in a way highly relevant to our overall problem, by certain aspects of their proselytizing style. They have emphasized their US character and origin, and this has made them attractive to persons already well-disposed to the US way of life and even, maybe, seeking connections in the USA. These persons clearly form a distinctive subgroup. As Mark Grover in his study of Mormonism in Brazil puts it, "The number of cars that have recently become prominent at Mormon chapels provides extra-visual evidence of the success of members in following the American-influenced middle class dream. Mormons are urged to follow the original US model as closely as possible." A curious outcrop from the stress that Mormons place on their US character is that blacks were not a target population for conversion up to quite recently, and this has meant that many of those who belonged to the poorest sections of society did not, and could not, become Mormons. Indeed, in the early stages of Mormon activity in Brazil, the missionaries concentrated on the German community, which was unequivocally white, and moreover already equipped with the skills necessary to become better-off. . . .

Case Studies: Mexico

A study by Mary O'Connor of Mayos compares the impact of evangelical Protestantism with the impact of a nativistic millenarian movement. At the time of the study in the mid-seventies the Mayos numbered some 20,000 and were much better-off than most other Mexican Indians because they lived in an agriculturally developed area. They were also more integrated into Mexican society. Most spoke both Spanish and Mayo, and had acquired modern consumer goods and clothing. Those Mayos who became Protestant, which effectively means Pentecostal, initiated a major change of life, notably by gaining freedom from the fiesta system and from the obligation of *fiesteros* to give away huge quantities of food. To reject the obligations of the fiesta helped them get together more money for consumer goods and the education of their children. They also saved money by their rejection of all entertainment, especially drinking. Yet the rejection of waste and indulgence was not a rejection of wealth. Pastors encouraged their congregations to work hard, educate their children and improve their material conditions. It was not accounted a reproach to own a tape recorder or a car. Mary O'Connor claims: "Rationality in general is encouraged, [and] beliefs in witchcraft, ghosts, buried treasure and folk curing, common among the general population, are ridiculed."

The nativistic millenarian movement among the Mayos has some points in common with Pentecostal. The participants are an elect to be saved when God destroys the world; and they refuse drink and secular entertainment. However, the nativistic movement aims to regain economic and political control for Mayos and rejects all aspects of the mestizo world as evil. O'Connor identifies those who take part as having few opportunities for economic and social progress. The Protestants, on the other hand, see a chance of advancement for themselves and their families. Indeed, they already have an adequate economic base. They can become Protestant without losing their Mayo identity, which means that they can make the best of both the mestizo and Mayo worlds. O'Connor adds that traditional folk-Catholicism will probably remain the faith of the majority, though the fiestas will become increasingly secular. She also mentions that those who cease to be Protestant often do not revert to Catholicism. (That is an important point noted in some other studies and bears on the relationship of Protestantism to secularization.) . . .

Catholicism and Catholic Responses

What of the Catholic Church? First, something needs to be said about the Catholicism that remained in place in most Latin American countries up to the mid-century. As has been emphasized again and again, it is perfectly possible for whole cultures to remain cradled in Catholicism and for the Catholic Church itself either to be hollowed out from the inside by total government control *or* to be ruthlessly expelled from the body politic. Thus the universal Catholicism that was once so remarked upon was the observable clothing of multiple social practices and forms. Many central bastions of Catholic faith, such as priestly celibacy, remained remote and unintelligible. In some areas even the Eucharist had fallen into disuse.

Catholicism of this kind was too ramshackle to develop coherent strategies to deal with problems above the local level. Instead, local ecclesiastical functionaries, some of them more concerned with their careers than Catholic devotion, engaged in ad hoc maneuverings with adjacent political and social elites. They offered certain "services" to society as currently constituted and had to respond to its pressures. In short, Catholicism had been incorporated, it was passive and in the strict sense of the word it was "reactionary." It has taken something like a century for the Church to recollect itself as the Church and to reorganize and to plan, and to bring about some more active reference either to Roman teaching or, for that matter, to the foundation documents of Christianity. Thus, seen from a certain angle, the emergence of Pentecostalism and of evangelical Christianity generally represents a first incursion of Christianity understood as a biblically-based and personally appropriated faith, propagated by a distinct body of committed believers. Catholic observers candidly admit this when they speak of the spiritual vacuum which opens up once the external forms and localized practices collapse under the intense pressure of rapid social change.

The late Ivan Vallier described what this meant at the local level very appositely. When people came to church not only was the celestial hierarchy made manifest but the social hierarchy was also on parade. "Those who worshipped regularly in the same church building did not constitute a solidarity based congregation but a random assortment of differential social statuses juxtaposed in proximity for the duration of the mass." He goes on to point out that there was no need to create an active and enthusiastic lay body, since everyone was gently cradled in one and the same religious universe. This, of course, was precisely the situation in England up to the eighteenth century, and for Pentecostals and Catholics today one only has to substitute Methodists and the Church of England two hundred and fifty years ago. What the Pentecostalism of today offers then is a body of committed lay persons, actively brought into being rather than passively existing, and enjoying a solidarity based on social affinity.

Of course, Catholicism has responded in various ways to the challenge of social change and the centrality of the idea of movement. It has itself tried to become a movement, notably through the vast organization known as Catholic Action. To some extent the organization of Catholic Action reflected the recovery of the Church as a distinct body all too well, since it was cast in an Italian or Roman mold and represented the militancy of the Catholic ghetto and of "fortress Catholicism" more generally. Nevertheless, certain things are interesting about Catholic Action. Since it came into being as part of the broad process of differentiation of Church from social structure it could run counter to the interests of the secular elites who saw the Church just as a creature of their own concerns and style. Catholic Action divided the self-conscious Catholic from the automatic ritual conformity of established strata. So while it was hegemonic in aspiration it was sectional in organizational form. Indeed, it was proto-Protestant insofar as it was lay and depended on specific commitment. But beyond that it could develop in a radical direction and give birth to troublesome fraternities of revolutionary Catholic youth.

Liberation theology represents a continuation both of sectarian Protestant motifs and of this political and ecclesiastical radicalism. The point is that Catholicism itself was bringing into existence elements of Protestantism through Catholic Action and Liberation Theology. What was forming outside the walls of the Catholic Church was also germinating within: a parallel development. Yet what stayed within was marked by its Catholic inheritance, in particular the idea of the Church as promulgating norms for society as a whole and acting as moral mentor. It was adjusted to political reality in a characteristically Catholic manner and was, therefore, ready to provide political translations of the Bible, especially of the Old Testament, as well as to reformulate the doctrine of the just war to encompass revolutionary violence.

Liberation theology is, therefore, a major rival to Pentecostalism. In that role it probably has a modest welcome even from the more cautious members of the hierarchy, however much they are alarmed by its attitude to traditional Catholic organization and the primacy it affords to politics. Indeed, its very sectionalism is a further alarming installment of disarticulation.

Yet Liberation Theology is not so successful a competitor as might be expected and there are even those who see its existence as indirectly helping forward the expansion of evangelicalism. The reason is that however much it represents "an option for the poor" taken up by hundreds of thousands of the poor themselves, that option is most eloquently formulated by radical intellectuals. . . . However idealistic and decently concerned and shocked the leaders of "liberationism" may be, they are not usually "of the people." Liberation theology has a decided middle class and radical intellectual accent alien to the localized needs of "the poor." It claims to be Latin American but it is, in fact, at least as "foreign" as Pentecostalism, if not more so, with spokesmen — yes, spokes*men* — who are part of the international circuit of theological lecturers. This means that while the language of Pentecostalism is "odd" and many of its practices initially unattractive, the language of liberationism can easily remain remote. Beyond all that, it promises to pull poor people struggling mainly for survival into much larger and bloodier struggles of which they have often had more than enough.

There is, of course, one other response within Catholicism, which has proto-Protestant elements and which also competes with Pentecostalism, and that is the charismatic movement. The Catholic charismatic movement is not on anything like the same scale as evangelical Protestantism, involving up to (say) four or five million people, but is a significant force and derives part of its thrust from the rivalry. It offers communal warmth and solidarity, it brings the family together in strong affective bonds, and it establishes a moral density.

Catholic charismatics are often aligned with the renewals proposed by Vatican 2 and they reflect on the foundation documents of Christianity. They offer a focus of loyalty which can supplement or even supplant a fideistic reliance on the magisterium. Though they are, on occasion, influenced by liberation theology, and by liberal attitudes to moral issues, they also revive some aspects of traditional doctrine. They resemble Protestant Pentecostals in their avoidance of head-on political confrontations.

Of course, from one point of view the existence of Catholic charismatics can simply be regarded as another illustration of the inauguration of the Kingdom of the Spirit, *hic et ubique.* But from a narrower and less committed perspective it is a response from the Catholic side which has its own problems. Chief among these is the confusion it creates in the minds of traditional Catholics. They are bemused by a version of Catholicism that looks superficially just like Pentecostalism, and the result is that Catholics start to attend just those local churches which happen to suit their own predilections, and thereby disrupt further the tie to the locality. In two respects Catholic charismatics differ from their separated Pentecostal brethren. They are, first of all, ecumenical. This means that if you are walking out of the old world and shaking the dust of the system from your feet, then Catholic charismatics link you too closely and ironically with what was. In the second place, they are also (maybe) relatively middle class in their social provenance. At least that is true in the USA where they originated and whence much of their leadership derives. Evidence for Latin America is sparse. Thomas Chordas, in his short study, concludes that it "includes the middle class and the very poor" and suggests that the very poor come along in the wake of the middle class.

What has just been argued concerning the Roman Catholic Church has focused in part on competition between alternative channels of new religiosity: those within and those outside the Catholic Church. That competition, now endemic in Latin America, involves constant borrowing and inventiveness. In particular, kinds of participation and types of popular music are constantly being borrowed to increase the competitive edge. It is out of this competition that forms of religious associations are being devised that may well stand up to the corrosion of religious practice traditionally associated with the city. . . .

Clearly this startling and unanticipated development in Latin America, now spreading to the Eastern Pacific rim and Africa, is part of much wider global changes. The first of these is a worldwide growth of religious conservatism in Judaism, and in Islam, as well as in Christianity. A balance once supposed to be tipping automatically towards liberalism is now tipping the other way.

Peter L. Berger

The results of the debates about the relationship of socialism, capitalism, and Christianity are mixed. As we will see in Chapter 9, the debate about socialism and capitalism in relation to non-Christian religious traditions around the world remains quite unsettled. In Christianity, most denominations have issued new statements in recent years about religious faith and economic life that reflect these debates, as we shall see in Chapter 10. Still another striking development is the embrace of "neo-conservative" economic theory by scholars who are in many other respects "liberal" — a development that irritates both conservatives who want to repudiate all traces of liberalism and liberals who want to repudiate conservatism in all its forms.

Perhaps no contemporary theorist represents this latter group better than Peter Berger. This Boston University scholar has studied the comparative impact of cultural and economic modernization on the development of societies more extensively than perhaps any other scholar. His research in East and South-East Asia, Africa, Latin America, and Eastern Europe is matched only by his extensive analysis of developments in the modern West and by his writing on issues of social ethics from a Christian perspective. His studies have convinced him that the negative assumptions of many academic and religious leaders about the nature, character, and effects of capitalism are mistaken. At the same time, he is not convinced that there is a necessary positive relationship between democracy, human rights, Christianity, and development and the capitalism that he basically supports.

It is clear that he believes that the frequent charges against capitalism in regard to dependency, as others have argued in regard to slavery and women, are, at best, overstated, and he is convinced that socialism is basically a dead end; but he does not think that if we get the facts straight, we will know how we ought to build the future. While some presume that our values consciously or preconsciously determine which facts we perceive, and others think that the facts about our social location determine our values, Berger thinks that these are separate. We can get the facts straight (or straighter than we had them before), and we can also gain a (somewhat greater) degree of clarity about our values, which are distinct from the empirical facts. Yet it is the value orientation that often is the springboard of action, and thus the contributions of social science can only become meaningful when they are brought into relationship with valid cultural, ethical, and religious values. But the question of validity in these areas is not a question that factual answers can settle alone.

In the following article, Berger surveys the global situation with an eye to possible directions toward which the economy and faith must move in the future. The lessons are, regrettably, ambiguous and resistant to simple prescription.

Social Ethics in a Post-Socialist World

Peter L. Berger

The title of these observations contains two assumptions — that now is indeed a post-socialist era and that there is such a thing as social ethics. It may be worthwhile to examine both assumptions with at least a measure of skepticism.

Is this a post-socialist era? One might reply yes on two grounds.

First, empirically: There is precious little socialism left — "real existent socialism," in the old Marxist phrase — for anyone who may want to reply no. This is not only because of the spectacular collapse of, first, the Soviet empire in Europe, and then of the Soviet Union itself, though that collapse is surely the single most dramatic event of this moment in history. There is also the rapid conversion to capitalist policies (even if not always capitalist rhetoric) of formerly socialist regimes and movements almost everywhere in the world. Populist politicians in Latin America, African dictators, Communist Party officials in China and Vietnam, Swedish social democrats — more and more they all sound like economics graduates of the University of Chicago, at least when they talk about the economy. "Real existent socialism" survives in a few countries, every one a disaster (North Korea and Cuba are prime cases), and in enclaves where one has the feeling of being in a time-warp (among, for example, academics in India or in the English-speaking universities of South Africa, or in some church agencies in the United States).

Second, one might view this as a post-socialist

era for theoretical reasons: Given the historical record of socialism in this century, one can say with some assurance that all the claims made for it have been decisively falsified — be it in terms of economic performance, of political liberation, of social equality, or of the quality of life. Similar falsification has befallen every major proposition of Marxism as an interpretation of the modern world. As a theory, then, socialist ideology today impresses one as being akin to a stubborn assertion that, despite everything, the earth is flat.

Why, then, the skepticism? Well, for one thing, it is always dangerous to project a particular moment of history into the future. In the 1930s an observer of the world scene at that moment could well have concluded that fascism was the wave of the future and that it was futile, and possibly even wrongheaded, to resist (it is salutary to read about the sizable number of Western intellectuals, including Christian ones, who urged their contemporaries to recognize fascism as the revolution of the century and, if I may use a somewhat more recent phrase anachronistically, who urged them "to get on the right side of history"). And, of course, huge numbers of intellectuals until the day before yesterday were apodictically certain of a socialist future. Clearly, one should be extremely cautious when seized by the feeling that one is moving with the logic of history — a Hegelian indulgence that almost invariably ends with a great disillusionment.

In this particular instance it is not very difficult to imagine scenarios in the not-too-distant future in which there might occur resurgences of socialist policies and ideals: the failure of neo-capitalist regimes in developing societies and/or the formerly Communist countries in Europe to achieve economic take-off; the insight granted to sundry dictators and despots that, while socialism invariably immiserates the masses, it is a very good recipe for enriching those who claim to hold power as the vanguard of the masses; the "creeping socialism" (still an aptly descriptive term) brought on by massive government intervention in the economy in the name of some societal good, e.g., there could be an environmentalist road to socialism, or a feminist one, or one constructed (perhaps inadvertently) with some other building blocks of politically managed regulations and entitlements; or, last but not least, the actual resto-

Peter L. Berger, "Social Ethics in a Post-Socialist World," *First Things* 30 (Feb. 1993): 9-14.

ration of socialism, by coup or by voting, in a number of countries, beginning with Russia. For the last three years or so it has been fashionable to say that socialism is "finished." Let us not be so sure. Certainly, a rational mind has cause to conclude that socialism belongs on the scrapheap of history. But, alas, history is *not* the march of reason on earth.

With respect to our second question — Is there such a thing as social ethics? — the answer is obviously yes. There are, after all, programs with that label in academic curricula and on the agendas of church organizations. But it is nevertheless far from clear what this phrase is supposed to mean: Is there ethics that is *not* social? The morality of suicide and of masturbation are the only two areas that readily come to mind. Setting aside such hairsplitting, tempting though it be, one is left simply with usage. In that case, presumably, social ethics has been the intellectual activity through which Christians have tried to figure out the moral problems of contemporary society. That would in itself be a definition hard to quarrel with, were it not for the fact that in recent years it has come to be widely held that in the final purpose of "doing" social ethics is to draw up a blueprint for a just society and perhaps also a practical guide for getting there. Leaving aside the far from simple issue of the relation between faith and ethics, and hewing strictly to the line of social science, we have to say that blueprints for a just society have typically been one of two things — either a set of propositions so abstract that they could be filled with just about any concrete content or a set of propositions that could indeed be practically applied, which applications have led to some of the great human catastrophes of the modern age. Put as an empirical statement: Beware of the prophets of a just society!

Socialism has been attractive to many social ethicists precisely because it is clearly of the second type — a concrete blueprint, based on an allegedly scientific understanding of the forces of history and providing some reasonably clear guidelines for action. Marxism, in all its variants, has provided the most coherent blueprint of this type, that is, an exhaustive analysis of the present, a fairly clear vision of the future, and on top of all that (especially in its Leninist version), a practical method of getting to that future. All of it, of course, has been a gigantic delusion — the analysis was false, the vision was deeply flawed, and the experiments of realizing the vision have exacted horrendous human costs.

But even if one were to assent to the view that socialism is "finished," one should understand that the womb that gave birth to this phantom is not barren yet. Vilfredo Pareto's distinction between "residues" and "derivations" is useful here. "Residues" are the persistent impulses and motivations of human behavior, while "derivations" are the temporary, fugitive ideologies and program by which the underlying impulses express themselves at any given moment. In this instance, the "residue" is a deeply rooted impulse to create a perfect community on earth. Whether or not socialism is "finished," a crew of successor utopianisms are already standing in line. Leaving aside the theological proposal that utopianism is distorted eschatology, and idolatry to boot, we can subscribe to a perhaps more modest statement, to wit, that unless social ethics resolutely gives up any and all utopian visions, and not just the socialist one, it will again and again end up legitimating regimes and movements that perpetrate moral horrors. A Christian social ethics should begin with the premise that there can be no perfect community in this aeon, from which follows an enterprise of moral reflection that will be piecemeal, cautious, and open to revision.

It is a piece of folk wisdom, elevated to philosophical principle by Santayana, that one must understand history in order not to repeat its mistakes. The theological equivalent of this is the proposition that there can be no renewal without repentance. Generally speaking, neither the secular nor the theological version of this alleged truth is fully persuasive. Repentance is very often an exercise in self-indulgence, and sometimes the best way to move forward is to forget the past. In the case of the relation to socialism of Christian social ethics and Christian church bodies, however, it is probably true that history should be remembered and reflected upon, precisely because the impulses that moved it are not just in the past but very much present still.

And this history is not a very edifying one. Prior to the advent of "real existent socialism," that is prior to the establishment of the "first socialist society" in Russia, there was a certain innocence to the Christian infatuation with socialist ideals. One might even argue that this infatuation was defensible as long as the Soviet Union was the only empirical case of socialism — after all, one could blame its faults and failure on the peculiarities of the Russian case.

But the most intense infatuation with socialism in the churches came with the cultural earthquake of the late 1960s and early 1970s in the West. By then, there were many socialist societies scattered all over the globe, many of them with minimal or no connection with the Soviet Union. There followed a long and ever-changing list of socialist experiments, most of them in the Third World, each of which, we were told in turn, embodied some bright hope for a just and humane society — China, North Vietnam, Tanzania, Cuba, Nicaragua. The facts about these societies — facts about massive terror, repression, and economic misery, and, need it be said, about the persecution of Christians — were systematically ignored, denied, or explained away.

In consequence, Christian voices were prominent among those who served as mouthpieces and who created entire networks of political support for these regimes in the West. And although most Western sympathizers held no particular brief for Soviet-style socialism, their worldview did generally include the notion that the latter was morally equivalent to democratic capitalism. In this context the fate of the idea of "the church in socialist society" — *"Kirche im Sozialismus"* — in ecumenical discussion is most instructive (the idea, of course, was formulated in the German Democratic Republic under circumstances the unsavory character of which has not become clear with the opening of Stasi files).

Setting aside the question of how much real guilt there is in this sorry history and how much need for real repentance, the great need at this moment is an intellectual one: the need for a resolute cognitive reassessment. This reassessment should pay respect to the empirical reality, that is, on the one hand, the unmitigated disaster of socialism everywhere — economically, politically, and in a monstrous aggregate of human suffering — and, on the other hand, the relative capacity of democratic capitalism to lift large masses of people from abject poverty to decent levels of material life and to provide political regimes that establish respect for elementary human rights. This would mean giving up, once and for all, the endless rationalization of socialist fiascoes and the restless search for some allegedly different incarnation of "true socialism" in this or that obscure corner of the globe. It would mean accepting the fact that a market economy and a democratic polity, with all their demonstrable flaws, constitute the best bet, at least under modern conditions, for a modicum of moral decency in society. It would also mean an honest attempt to understand the actual workings of these two institutional arrangements — a market economy and a democratic polity — and their relation to each other.

It must be emphasized that such a reassessment would properly be a far cry from the triumphalism about democratic capitalism that (understandably perhaps) found favor in right-of center circles in the last few years: we must be careful not to substitute a right-leaning utopianism for the left-leaning one of the past. The market economy and the democratic polity are institutional mechanisms that, with some luck, are reasonably efficient in securing specific goals, respectively, the creation of wealth and the protection of certain human rights. As always with institutions, new and unforeseen problems (both technical and moral in nature) appear as their products.

And, of course, there are a host of problems that remain untouched even when these institutions are eminently successful in securing their particular goals. To mention but a few, the problems of the relation between men and women, of racial and ethnic hatred, of the impact of modern technology on the environment, not to mention the perennial problems of human finitude and mortality — all these problems are common to all societies. The notion that they can be solved either by the market or by democracy, or a combination of the two, is fully competitive with some of the more grandiose socialist delusions. Still, it is certainly possible to engage in moral reflection about these institutions without either romanticizing or anathematizing them.

If, in this thoroughly unmessianic spirit, we turn to the moral issues of contemporary capitalism, it is possible to distinguish two sets of issues, broadly definable as macro- and micro-dimensional. The macro-issues are those that involve the society or the economy as a whole; the micro-issues concern individual sectors or organizations within the economy, such questions as business ethics and corporate culture generally. The latter are naturally of great importance, and do in the aggregate affect the larger society. But our interest here will be the macro-level. Now, on this level, it would be easy right off to draw up a very long list of moral issues faced by capitalist societies today. For virtually no problems faced by and politically debated within these societies are without a moral dimension, including very technical economic problems (such as, say, the prime lending rate or rates of exchange between national currencies). A few specific examples of such issues follow.

First, there is the question of the sequencing of marketization and democratization.

For the time being at least, much of the world is moving toward a market economy and toward democracy. Among those who participate in the post-socialist mood of triumphalism, these two processes are commonly seen more or less as two sides of the same coin. Alas, they are not. There is, to be sure, a measure of validity to the identification. It is empirically correct, for instance, that a successful market economy releases democratizing pressures — the children of hungry peasants, once they have forgotten the hunger, become politically uppity. It is also empirically correct that a market economy is the necessary, though not sufficient, condition for democracy — there have been no socialist democracies, for reasons that can be explained sociologically. But it is *not* valid to say that one cannot have a market economy without democracy. The empirical evidence appears to suggest that, while a market economy tends eventually to generate democracy (put differently, dictatorships tend not to survive a successful capitalist development), a market economy need not have democracy in order to take off.

Indeed, it usually doesn't. None of the post–World War II success stories in East Asia took off under democratic regimes, except for Japan. And Japan's original take-off was almost a hundred years earlier, under the Meiji regime — and *that* was certainly not a democracy. Two recent success stories in other parts of the world, Spain and Chile, replicate the marketization-before-democratization pattern. And if one looks at the formerly socialist societies in Europe, one may well conclude that an important reason for their present difficulties is that they are attempting to undertake both transitions simultaneously. Nor does the earlier history of capitalism offer much comfort to the reverse-sides-of-the-same-coin viewpoint. England, where it all began, could hardly be described as a democracy in the eighteenth century; neither could France or Germany in the nineteenth. The United States may be the comforting exception. There are also some comforting cases in the more recent period — for example, Sri Lanka, or Pakistan in the 1960s. But on the whole, there is enough evidence at least to suggest that, if one wants to have both a market economy and democracy, it is better to have the former precede the latter — if you will, to have *perestroika* before *glasnost* (it being understood, of course, that Gorbachev had something other than full capitalism in mind with the former term, and something less than full democracy with the latter).

The reasoning behind such a hypothesis is not difficult to explain. It is safe to say that no economic takeoff can occur without pain. The pain, inevitably, will not be equitably distributed throughout the population. Initially, very likely, only a minority will benefit from economic growth. In a democracy, this minority is easily outvoted, especially if populist politicians agitate the majority that either feels the pain or, minimally, does not see any tangible benefits as yet. Mancur Olson has coined the useful term "distributional coalitions." By this he means vested interests that organize in order to get their slice of the economic pie by means of government actions. Olson argues that economic growth is slowed when these coalitions mature. In a wealthy, developed society such slowdowns are economically tolerable; in a poor, less-developed society a slowdown can abort the takeoff. Democracy, of course, gives distributional coalitions the free space to organize, to grow, and to influence government. By contrast, a dictatorship can more easily control those vested interests that seek to slow down or dismantle the government's economic policies.

The case of present-day China sharply illustrates both the empirical processes at issue and the resultant moral dilemma. It is not altogether clear whether what is now happening in China represents a deliberate policy of the Deng Xiaoping regime or whether in fact the regime has lost control over what happens. In any case, what is happening is a capitalist revolution, especially in the south, unfolding rapidly under a regime that continues to spout Marxist rhetoric and that has, so far successfully, curbed any moves toward democracy. Ironically, this situation strongly resembles the situation in Taiwan when the authoritarian Kuomintang regime launched the capitalist takeoff there. The China story, of course, has not ended and the present economic course could yet be arrested. In large parts of the country, though, such a reversal would be very difficult. Guangdong province (a territory, by the way, that has some eighty million inhabitants) is rapidly becoming an economic extension of neighboring Hong Kong, registering one of the highest growth rates in the world. The prosperity generated by this economic transformation is creeping up the coast toward Shanghai. It is not unreasonable to suppose that eventually some kind of political liberalization will follow the economic one.

The moral problem in a case of this kind concerns the interim period, the duration of which cannot be predicted. One need not necessarily be troubled by the delay in the advent of democracy per se; though it is terribly un-Wilsonian to do so, one can, and in fact ought to, remain open to the possibility of the benevolent autocrat. The trouble, once again, is empirical — the aforementioned correlation between democracy and human rights. Put simply, dictatorships, much more than democracies, are likely to violate human rights. The key question for the sort of "interim ethic" called for here (New Testament scholars will please forgive the term) is how many and what sorts of violations one is prepared to accept. It is not all that difficult to swallow the absence of elections (or the absence of *honest* elections, which amounts to the same thing) as the price for spreading prosperity soon and widespread prosperity eventually (especially as democracy is likely to appear as the latter occurs). But on the other hand, genocide is certainly not an acceptable price. The real question is, where are the limits? Using tanks against unarmed civilians? Using them once only? Regularly? What about a network of political prison camps? What about the use of torture by the security forces? Occasionally? Regularly? And so on.

The *real* moral dilemmas almost always get lost in current debates over human rights, especially if either democracy of the market or both of these are proposed as panaceas.

The second macro-level question concerns the range and the nature of political redistribution. It is clear that a market economy, once it has reached a certain level of affluence, can tolerate a considerable amount of governmentally managed redistribution. This, of course, is the basic lesson to be leaned from the coexistence of capitalism with the welfare state. It should also be clear that this tolerance is not without limits. If political redistribution reaches a certain level, it must either send the economy into a downward spin (wealth being redistributed faster than it is produced) or dismantle democracy (to prevent those whose wealth is to be redistributed — a population which, as redistribution expands, will be very much larger than the richest group — from resisting). Now, it would be very nice if economists and social scientists could tell us just where this level is — one might call it the social-democratic tolerance threshold. Right-of-center parties in Western democracies perceive a very low threshold (each piece of welfare state legislation another step on "the road to serfdom"); left-of-center parties believe in a very high threshold, and some in that camp seem to think that there is no limit at all. What evidence there is clearly does not support either the disciples of Hayek or Swedish social democrats; but neither, unfortunately, does the evidence locate the tilting-point. Once again, a sort of "interim ethic" is called for, full of uncertainties, and risks.

Paradoxically, the choices here are simpler in a poor society, where the amount of wealth available for redistribution is quite small. Perhaps a more accurate statement would be that in a poor society the choices *should* be simpler, if policies were to be decided upon rationally and with the general well-being of society as the goal. In fact, of course, all sorts of irrational motives are at work in every society, and what is bad for the whole society may be very good indeed for whatever clique of "kleptocrats" (Peter Bauer's term) is in charge of government. Still, the so-called "Uruguay effect," i.e., an expansive welfare state ruining the economy, becomes visible rather quickly in a poor society (though at that point it is very difficult to repair the damage). In a rich society the process of economic ruination is likely to take more time and to be less visible, with the consequence that the available choices may seem more free than they in fact are.

The moral problem here is, simply, to find a balance between economic prudence and the desire to meet this or that social need. Leave aside here the fact that some needs are artificially created and do not really arise out of genuine deprivation. Even when full allowance is made for this, there remain enough cases of real deprivation in any society to leave the moral problem in place. How much of a welfare state can a successful capitalist economy afford? How much of government intervention in the economy, not just for the sake of redistribution, but for any alleged societal good? Even if one is not a true disciple of Hayek, one must concede that the road to economic disaster (with all its ensuing human costs) is frequently paved with good intentions.

The moral problem becomes even more complicated. There are not only potential *economic* costs to political redistribution; there are costs in terms of democracy and in terms of the liberties of individuals, as well. The welfare state brings about an expansion of government power into ever more areas of social life, with government bureaucrats and governmentally authorized social workers peeking and poking into every nook and cranny of the lives of individuals. The purpose of all these interventions is almost always noble-sounding — to protect the public health, to assist children, the old, or the handicapped or some other underprivileged group, to safeguard entitlements, to watch over the expenditure of taxpayers' money, and so on and so forth.

The sum total of all these interventions, though, is what Bernard Levin has called "the nanny state," which reached its climax in the social democracies of northern Europe and which, of course, brought about a backlash even there, not only from irate taxpayers but from a lot of people who were fed up being interfered with at every turn by the agents of benevolent government. At what point, then, does well-meaning political intervention become tyrannical? How can specific social needs be met without aggrandizing state bureaucracy and depriving people, those with the putative needs, of more and more control over

their own lives? In poor societies the question can be put this way: How can the most pressing social needs be met without risking the "Uruguay effect"? In richer societies the question becomes: How can one maintain a reasonably effective welfare state without succumbing to the "Swedish disease"?

Third, there is the issue of the relation between economic development and cultural values.

Max Weber was wrong about many things, and he may even have been wrong about the strategic place he gave to the "Protestant ethic" in the development of modern capitalism. But he was almost certainly right in his assumption that some form of what he called "inner-worldly asceticism," that is, a collection of values that led to worldly activism and to delayed gratification, was necessary before a modern economic takeoff could occur. The Puritan entrepreneur was indeed a prototypical figure embodying such values. Contemporary evidence about the economic cultures of East Asia, of successful ethnic groups in different countries, or of the mobility of immigrants to this country all seems to point in the same direction: self-denial and discipline are virtues that are the condition *sine qua non* of early capitalist development.

Christian ethicists usually have no great difficulty in admiring and even recommending these virtues, also in cases where they do not fully or even partially endorse the theological and philosophical presuppositions of people who evince them (such as, for instance, Latin American Pentecostals, Muslim fundamentalists, or neo-Confucian businessmen). At the same time, Christian ethicists often decry the absence of the decline of these values in Western societies today and go on to suggest that, unless we return to the old virtues, we will go under economically; and in this they may very possibly be mistaken.

Contemporary Western societies, with America in the lead, are anything but self-denying and disciplined. They are governed by values of self-gratification and untrammeled individual freedom. From a Puritan viewpoint, of course, such values will be seen pejoratively — as expressing greed, selfishness, irresponsibility. From a different perspective, one may perceive them as joyful and liberating. Be that as it may, in this century there has been an ongoing progression in Western cultures away from the older asceticism. A quantum leap in this development came with the cultural revolution that began in the 1960s. The culture has become even more liberating in terms of the wants of individuals, more libidinally positive, if you will "softer," more "feminized." This cultural change has by now invaded significant sectors of the business world, of the bastions of capitalism. Thus far there is no evidence that this has a negative effect on economic productivity, at least as one reads the actual evidence.

This obviously poses a moral problem for those who remain committed to the older virtues. Hard work, postponing enjoyments, discipline, sobriety — all these components of the "Protestant ethic" may have been held to be good in themselves, but it certainly helped when one could credibly argue that adhering to these virtues not only pleased God but worked to one's economic advantage in this world, here and now. Conversely, there would be some embarrassment to many ethicists if putative vices like self-indulgence, sloth, and lechery could be happily practiced without visible ill-effects in the economic progress of individuals or of society.

But there is another moral problem if one takes the view that our "softer" culture will indeed harm us economically, both as individuals and, more importantly, as an entire society. This point of view regularly recurs in discussions of our competitiveness vis-à-vis East Asia in general and Japan in particular. We must change, it is said, or we will lose out in the international competition. Usually it is not so much our hedonism that is being chastised in this way (though that comes in for some invidious comparisons too) as our alleged "excessive individualism." By way of contrast, we are asked to contemplate the wonderful loyalty of the Japanese to their company and their fellow-employees.

Now, never mind how accurate this picture of East Asian economic culture is; let it be stipulated, for the sake of the argument, that the Japanese are all they are here assumed to be and that this does indeed give them a comparative cultural advantage over us. Do we really want to become more like them? Do we want the corporation to become an all-embracing *mater et magistra*? Do we want people to submerge their aspirations for self-realization in loyalty to an organization? Do we want

employees to put the company before family? And most basically, are we prepared to say that the whole history of Western individualism, including its expressions in the American political creed, can be looked at as a great mistake? And, if we say no to all these questions (as most of us surely would), how much of an economic price are we willing to pay for this position?

There are no definitive or unambiguous solutions to these or any other moral dilemmas of society. There is not, and cannot be, a design for a just society prior to the coming of the Kingdom of God. Moreover, when we start to act in society, the overwhelming probability is that our actions will either fail or will lead to consequences that we did not intend. Sometimes these consequences will be terrible. For this reason, the first and last principle of any Christian social ethics must be the forgiveness of sins. But that is a story for another time.

Chapter Nine

Economics around the World

The debate rages as to whether modernization is basically rooted in the secularization that is found in both the liberal, capitalist and radical, socialist wings of the Enlightenment, or in the dynamic reconstruction of the common life that derived from the world-transforming impulses of Christianity. In fact, these combined in various ways in the West to create explosive combinations at home and expansive impulses abroad. The history of the nineteenth and twentieth centuries reveals the clash of various definitions and combinations of democracy, rights, capitalism, socialism, and Christianity in the West and the expansion of these dynamic forces around the world. Imperialism and colonialism as well as the influence of peaceful trade and missions provoked, in turn, efforts at self-renewal within those religions and cultures that were shocked by the impact of the West. Every traditional view of life has been challenged. All now face a new, global encounter of the great religions and cultures.

Economically, most of the world's cultures were (and largely remain) agricultural. Trade was everywhere known, of course, but the social forms by which modern business is conducted — banks, factories, stock markets, regulatory agencies, constitutional rights, and especially legal provisions for incorporation — were lacking or resisted. Cultural views of work and time, wealth and poverty, technology and nature were often distinctive, and the ethical demand to subordinate family or ethnic loyalties and to elevate individual dignity and initiative seemed strange. Such ideas threatened various cultures, and the distinctions of "conservative," "liberal," and "radical" or "secular" and "religious" that were so important in Europe and America often appeared to be both alien and irrelevant in the East and South.

The West was also threatened by the new cultures it encountered, for liberals, Marxists, and reforming Christians (Protestant or Catholic, not to mention Western conservatives who resisted all of these) each thought that they had discovered universal principles by which the world could be understood. They met a series of quite complex civilizations based on other principles, also claiming universality, but rooted in other ways of thinking. Islam, Hinduism, Buddhism, and Confucianism showed intellectual, spiritual, and ethical subtleties that matched those found in the West, and they had already shown their capacity to guide high culture over time.

Meanwhile, business has become global and is everywhere conducted in contexts where the influences from all these sources have an impact — especially since the collapse of the Soviet form of secular socialism. One can meet Muslims and Hindus, Buddhists and Confucians, as well as African Catholic liberationists and Asian evangelical libertarians at work and in the mall as well as in international conferences on ecology, trade, labor, or management. It is indispensable in this context not only to understand the traditions from which modern business arose but also to glimpse what the world's great religions have to offer to modern views of economic life and the conduct of business.

It is obviously impossible to cover all the ethical views from these religions and cultures here; but it is possible to get some sense of the wider world. Several principles of selection have been used. Each religion or region is represented by sacred texts, a distinguished exponent of a point of view that has become typical in a significant way, and an outside interpreter. The selections also represent features, or critiques, of economic life and thought that these regions all tend to share — such as a tendency to do business through networks of extended family connections and centralized political authority and a tendency to view economic development in terms that are suspicious of ''the West'' in general and of modern business in particular.

Islam

The Qur'an (or Koran; the word means "recite" in Arabic) is believed by Muslims to be an exact record of the very thoughts of God, revealed to the Prophet Muhammad over a period of nearly two decades some 1,400 years ago. Those who follow Muhammad believe that this holy book of guidance reaffirms much of what was previously revealed by Abraham, Moses, and Jesus, but it also supercedes and makes clear, in an unmistakable way, what had been obscured, neglected, or distorted over the years. The central point is a call for submission (the Arabic word is *Islam*; those who do submit are called "Muslims") to the one and only God, Allah, and obedience to his commandments. These commandments, which cover all essential areas of life, including business, are believed to be the very essence of justice, which, however harsh they may seem to some, are ever tempered by the mercy of God.

It is proper to begin thinking about Islam by reading some selections from the Qur'an (actually, believers say that all translations of it are only paraphrases; it is only exact in Arabic). The selections in the first of our four readings on Islam have to do with the making of contracts and the treatment of thieves — both of which exemplify a profound sense of dependence on a clear, deontological moral law.

Our second reading is from Mahmud Shaltout, a respected Islamic scholar of the previous generation of Al Azhar University, Cairo, one of the centers of Islamic intellectual life in the modern world. Also known for his radio broadcasts to the Islamic community, he has written a widely used commentary on Islamic ethics, which treats economic issues. In this commentary, it is easy to note the ways in which Islam, like many of the great world religions, understands business essentially in the context of family life and government. Clearly these are the two most important, and distinctive, institutions of Islamic life, and more is said about them in the Qur'an and in the tradition than about any others. Ideas like those that developed in Christian history, separating church — and thus voluntary associations, including the corporation and unions — from membership in a family and from the state, are difficult to find in this context.

Islam, however, is not only a Middle East phenomenon. Not only did it experience an early, rapid expansion during its first three centuries, to stretch from Spain to India and from north Africa to the borders of Russia, but traders carried it farther east in the next several centuries, after its western territories were constricted by the Christian crusades of the Middle Ages. Today, the most populist Islamic country is Indonesia, which was converted less by conquest, as was much of the Middle East, South Asia, North Africa, and the West, than by the influence of more mystical strands of the tradition brought by Muslim traders. Indonesia, the largest of the Southeast Asian countries, now undergoing rapid modernization after overthrowing the Dutch colonial regime and a reputed tendency to turn Marxist under President Sukarno, is one of the key locations for understanding how Islam might adapt to the new global, market economy. Robert Hefner offers a progress report of his ongoing research on Islam and capitalism in Indonesia and Malaysia.

But Islam is also growing in parts of the West, both by immigration and by conversion. (The "Black Muslims" are one notable example in America.) As it grows, it is developing new methods based on classic Islamic principles, as we see in an article by Ken Brown.

Surahs from the Qur'an

2:267 Believers, give in alms of the wealth you have lawfully earned and of that which We have brought out of the earth for you; not worthless things which you yourselves would but reluctantly accept. Know that God is self-sufficient and glorious.

Satan threatens you with poverty and orders you to commit what is indecent. But God promises you His forgiveness and His bounty. God is munificent and all-knowing.

He gives wisdom to whom He will; and he that receives the gift of wisdom is rich indeed. Yet none except men of sense bear this in mind.

Whatever alms you give and whatever vows you make are known to God. The evil-doers shall have none to help them.

To be charitable in public is good, but to give alms to the poor in private is better and will atone for some of your sins. God has knowledge of all your actions.

2:272 It is not for you to guide them. God gives guidance to whom He will.

Whatever alms you give shall rebound to your own advantage, provided that you give them for the love of God. And whatever alms you give shall be paid back to you in full: you shall not be wronged.

As for those needy men who, being wholly preoccupied with fighting for the cause of God, cannot travel the land in quest of trading ventures; the ignorant take them for men of wealth on account of their modest behaviour. But you can recognize them by their look — they never impor-

From *The Koran*, trans. N. J. Dawood, 5th ed. (London: Penguin Classics, 1990), pp. 40-42, 60-61, 83-85.

tune men for alms. Whatever alms you give are known to God.

Those that give alms by day and by night, in private and in public, shall be rewarded by their Lord. They shall have nothing to fear or to regret.

2:275 Those that live on usury shall rise up before God like men whom Satan has demented by his touch; for they claim that trading is no different from usury. But God has permitted trading and made usury unlawful. He that has received an admonition from his Lord and mended his ways may keep his previous gains; God will be his judge. Those that turn back shall be the inmates of the Fire, wherein they shall abide for ever.

2:276 God has laid His curse on usury and blessed almsgiving with increase. God bears no love for the impious and the sinful.

Those that have faith and do good works, attend to their prayers and render the alms levy, will be rewarded by their Lord and will have nothing to fear or to regret.

Believers, have fear of God and waive what is still due to you from usury, if your faith be true; or war shall be declared against you by God and His apostle. If you repent, you may retain your principal, suffering no loss and causing loss to none.

If your debtor be in straits, grant him a delay until he can discharge his debt; but if you waive the sum as alms it will be better for you, if you but knew it.

Fear the day when you shall all return to God; when every soul shall be requited according to its deserts. None shall be wronged.

2:282 Believers, when you contract a debt for a fixed period, put it in writing. Let a scribe write it down for you with fairness; no scribe should refuse to write as God has taught him. Therefore let him write; and let the debtor dictate, fearing God his Lord and not diminishing the sum he owes. If the debtor be a feeble-minded or ignorant person, or one who cannot dictate, let his guardian dictate for him in fairness. Call in two male witnesses from among you, but if two men cannot be found, then one man and two women whom you judge fit to act as witnesses; so that if either of them commit an error, the other will remember. Witnesses must not refuse to give evidence if called upon to do so. So do not fail to put your debts in writing, be they small or big, together with the date of payment. This is more just in the sight of God; it ensures accuracy in testifying and is the best way to remove all doubt. But if the transaction in hand be a bargain concluded on the spot, it is no offense for you if you do not commit it to writing.

See that witnesses are present when you barter with one another, and let no harm be done to either scribe or witness. If you harm them you shall commit a transgression. Have fear of God, who teaches you; God has knowledge of all things.

2:283 If you are traveling the road and a scribe cannot be found, then let pledges be taken. If any one of you entrusts another with a pledge, let the trustee restore the pledge to its owner; and let him fear God, his Lord.

You shall not withhold testimony. He that withholds it is a transgressor. God has knowledge of all your actions.

To God belongs all that the heavens and the earth contain. Whether you reveal your thoughts or hide them, God will bring you to account for them. He will forgive whom He will and punish whom He pleases; God has power over all things.

4:1 Men, have fear of your Lord, who created you from a single soul. From that soul He created its mate, and through them He bestrewed the earth with countless men and women.

Fear God, in whose name you plead with one another, and honor the mothers who bore you. God is ever watching you.

Give orphans the property which belongs to them. Do not exchange their valuables for worthless things or cheat them of their possessions; for this would surely be a great sin. If you fear that you cannot treat orphans with fairness, then you may marry other women who seem good to you: two, three, or four of them. But if you fear that you cannot maintain equality among them, marry one only or any slave-girls you may own. This will make it easier for you to avoid injustice.

Give women their dowry as a free gift; but if they choose to make over to you a part of it, you may regard it as lawfully yours.

4:5 Do not give the feeble-minded the property

with which God has entrusted you for their support; but maintain and clothe them with its proceeds, and give them good advice.

4:6 Put orphans to the test until they reach a marriageable age. If you find them capable of sound judgment, hand over to them their property, and do not deprive them of it by squandering it before they come of age.

Let not the rich guardian touch the property of his orphan ward; and let him who is poor use no more than a fair portion of it for his own advantage.

When you hand over to them their property, call in some witnesses; sufficient is God's accounting of your actions.

Men shall have a share in what their parents and kinsmen leave; and women shall have a share in what their parents and kinsmen leave: whether it be little or much, they shall be legally entitled to their share.

If relatives, orphans, or needy men are present at the division of an inheritance, give them, too, a share of it, and speak to them kind words.

Let those who are solicitous about the welfare of their young children after their own death take care not to wrong orphans. Let them fear God and speak for justice.

4:10 Those that devour the property of orphans unjustly, swallow fire into their bellies; they shall burn in a mighty conflagration.

God has thus enjoined you concerning your children:

A male shall inherit twice as much as a female. If there be more than two girls, they shall have two-thirds of the inheritance; but if there be one only, she shall inherit the half. Parents shall inherit a sixth each, if the deceased have a child; but if he leave no child and his parents be his heirs, his mother shall have a third. If he have brothers, his mother shall have a sixth after payment of any legacy he may have bequeathed or any debt he may have owed.

You may wonder whether your parents or your children are more beneficial to you. But this is the law of God; God is all-knowing and wise.

4:12 You shall inherit the half of your wives' estate if they die childless. If they leave children, a quarter of their estate.

5:35 As for the man or woman who is guilty of theft, cut off their hands to punish them for their crimes. That is the punishment enjoined by God. God is mighty and wise. But whoever repents after committing evil, and mends his ways, shall be pardoned by God. God is forgiving and merciful.

5:40 Did you not know that God has sovereignty over the heavens and the earth? He punishes whom He will and forgives whom He pleases. God has power over all things. . . .

5:44 We have revealed the Torah, in which there is guidance and light. By it the prophets who surrendered themselves judged the Jews, and so did the rabbis and the divines, according to God's Book which had been committed to their keeping and to which they themselves were witnesses.

Have no fear of man; fear Me, and do not sell My revelations for a paltry end. Unbelievers are those who do not judge according to God's revelations.

We decreed for them a life for a life, an eye for an eye, a nose for a nose, an ear for an ear, a tooth for a tooth, and a wound for a wound. But if a man charitably forbears from retaliation, his remission shall atone for him. Transgressors are those that do not judge according to God's revelations.

After them We sent forth Jesus, the son of Mary, confirming the Torah already revealed, and gave him the Gospel in which there is guidance and light, corroborating what was revealed before it in the Torah, a guide and an admonition to the righteous.

5:47 Therefore let those who follow the Gospel judge according to what God has revealed therein. Evil-doers are those that do not base their judgments on God's revelations.

5:48 And to you We have revealed the Book with the truth. It confirms the Scriptures which came before it and stands as a guardian over them. Therefore give judgment among men according to God's revelations and do not yield to their fancies or swerve from the truth made known to you. . . .

Dealings

Mahmud Shaltout

In the name of Allah, the Beneficent, the Merciful. Within the Islamic code, which provides guidance for all human activities, the distinction between worship and dealings is made for convenience in the exposition of Islam. We have seen the nature of the true worship of Islam; in considering the dealings we shall be concerned with the dealings within the Muslim community — the family, monetary affairs, relations with fellow Muslims, and government — and dealings with non-Muslims both as individuals and nations. Islamic law has clearly stated the obligations of the Muslims in all areas of life and the penalties to be inflicted for offenses and irregularities.

Under the guidance of its code of laws Islam preaches the one God and, by acknowledging the principle of equality, asserts the unity of the human race and denounces discrimination based on color, racial, or regional differences. It aims at justice through the eradication of oppression and tyranny. It mistreats no stranger merely because he is a stranger in a strange land, nor the infidel because of his infidelity, nor the enemy because of his enmity; nor is a near relative given special treatment in Islamic law because of his relationship, nor is a friend shown partiality for his friendship, nor is a Muslim treated leniently because of his adherence to Islam. "Be steadfast witnesses for Allah in equity, and let not hatred of any people seduce you that ye deal not justly. Deal justly, that is nearer to your duty" (Surah V, 8).

The family. Marriage in Islam requires the full

From Mahmud Shaltout, "Islamic Beliefs and Code of Laws," in *Strait Path Islam Interpreted by Muslims,* ed. Kenneth W. Morgan (New York: Ronald Press, 1958), pp. 119-20, 123-26.

agreement of both parties without compulsion being brought to bear on either person. A marriage which takes place forcibly is considered null and void. When an agreement is reached between the two, the man pays to the woman the bride money, which is a token of admiration, not a purchase price or a form of remuneration. The actual amount of the bride money is determined by agreement and is the exclusive property of the prospective wife; the husband is not entitled to use it in any way without her consent.

The marriage contract is repeated in the presence of two or more witnesses. The bride says, "I marry you to myself," and the groom replies, "I accept your marriage to me." It is quite in order for the two accredited agents for the bride and groom to repeat the phrases of the marriage contract also. If the contract is not authenticated by two witnesses it is unlawful, and no marriage exists between the two. Properly witnessed, this verbal contract completes the marriage and the man and woman may establish their home.

In Islam, the husband, by virtue of his physical strength and ability to secure means of livelihood, is given the responsibility of guardianship of the wife and of the home, within the framework of their reciprocal legal rights and obligations. Such guardianship is not an autocratic authority which excludes the wife from expressing her views or from the right of consultation; it is merely a rank of honor and control which must respect the wife's point of view.

Thus it is seen that the marriage in Islam is a simple agreement between two parties without any participation by religious or civil authorities. Nor does it curtail the wife's freedom of action or her control of property, so long as she lives up to the responsibilities of married life and cares for the home and children. . . .

The family bears a special responsibility for the education of the children in Islam. The training begins with teaching the child to repeat lessons concerning Islamic beliefs and to perform correctly the worship rites. The family is also responsible for seeing that the child receives further training in the school and the mosque where legitimate and illegitimate actions and beliefs are expounded so that when the child attains maturity he will have been guided along the way to a true understanding of Islam.

Monetary affairs. Inheritance in Islam is based on the blood relationship of parents, brothers and sisters, and children, and on the marriage relationship of husband and wife without regard for sex or age in the right of inheritance. The parents, the children, and the consorts do not in any circumstances lose this right, though the amount of their share may be affected by the number of heirs. However, brothers and sisters are not entitled to inheritance in case the parents are living. If men and women are both heirs, the man receives twice as much as a woman except in the case of maternal half-brothers and half-sisters, who each get an equal share.

Islamic law has ruled that, since the man bears the support of the woman and the expenses of her children as well as the cost of her marriage, his share of the inheritance should be double that of the woman. Her share is allowed to stand her in good stead in case she loses the source of her livelihood. Islam has taken into consideration the fact that to allocate the inheritance among blood relatives and consorts strengthens bonds of affection and promotes among relatives a reciprocal interest in their common good. Jealousy would prevail and the family structure would be exposed ot disintegration if favoritism were allowed among heirs of equal standing. Thanks to this system, Islamic society has been guarded against the threat of financial tyranny which may result when the entire inheritance goes to a single person. It is also guarded against the danger which would come from paying the inheritance into the state treasury, for that would deprive members of the family of the results of the efforts made by parents, children, relatives, husbands, and wives, and would be damaging to society.

Islamic law also sets the standards for financial dealings through its regulations governing such things as the terms of sale and lease, things liable to sale and lease and those liable to neither, ways to employ capital, conditions regulating deposits, authentication of debts, and like matters which could become sources of controversy. All these financial dealings must be based on truthfulness, fidelity, and a willingness to discharge obligations.

Government. The necessity for some sort of government in the Muslim community is indicated by many texts in the Qur'an, such as, "Retaliation is prescribed for you in the matter of the

361

murdered" (Surah II, 178). "Lo! Allah command-eth you that ye restore deposits to their owners, and if ye judge between mankind, that ye judge justly" (Surah IV, 58). The obligations imposed upon the community by the Qur'an can only be discharged by the community deputizing a spokesman from its midst, a man possessing the mental qualifications, will power, and skills which enable him to secure unity of thought and cooperation in carrying out the tasks required for the common welfare. Such a man is known in Islam as the Caliph or Imam.

It is the duty of the Caliph or Imam, the leader in Islam, to consolidate public opinion, execute judgments, administer state machinery, encourage the faithful in the practice of their faith, such as prayers and the religious tax, and look after affairs of public interest. . . .

Thus in Islam we find no distinction in com-munity life between that which is called religious and that which is outside religion. In Islam reli-gion is concerned with faith and worship, and also with the upbringing, education, and guidance of the people, and with all economic and social deal-ings as to those which are legitimate and illegiti-mate, sound or corrupt; and religion is concerned with the government of the people and the ad-ministration of state machinery, with the opera-tion of all the functions of the community or na-tion. Religion provides the guiding principles for the individual and for the state. There can be no state which has a separate framework for the government and for religion. Those Islamic re-gions which separate the state from religion are following a mere private school of thought, con-trary to the teachings of Islam.

Islam recognizes equally the rights and re-sponsibilities of the individual and the communi-ty. It has built its legislation on the recognition that a man has a personality independent of his compatriots and his community, a personality which forms an element in the social structure. He has rights and obligations as an independent in-dividual and rights and responsibilities as a part of the nation to which he belongs. As an indepen-dent person, man is required by Islam to believe in God, worship Him, and to live in a manner which assures him a clear conscience; it is incum-bent upon him to work for a living, to control himself and his children, and to realize his inter-ests and maintain his existence without encroach-ing upon the life and welfare of other people. It is his right to own property and to enjoy the legiti-mate pleasures of life. As a member of the com-munity it is the divine duty of man to contribute to the general good, to guide and aid his fellow men, to do his full share in further in the social amenities of the community, and to take part in fighting the common enemy.

In return for the individual's fulfillment of his obligations, the community is required by Islam to protect the individual's life and property, and to safeguard the chastity of his womenfolk. Islam has legislated for this purpose, clearly defining the functions of the legitimate ruler who is represen-tative of the community, and outlining the penal-ties which the ruler must enforce.

Within the Islamic framework the individual and the community have defined for them the rights and obligations which ensure life and hap-piness through cooperation and equity in assign-ing privileges and tasks without encroaching upon the rights of the individual or the community. Should the individual deny to the community any of the rights due to it, he deserves God's denun-ciation, and it is the duty of the ruler to censure him on behalf of the nation. And if the society, as represented in the ruler, fails to ensure the rights of the individual, then the individual is entitled to insist upon his rights and the ruler deserves God's condemnation and anger. When the ruler does not protect the rights of the individual, the commu-nity is empowered to depose him and to replace him with a man who is able to live up to the functions of his high office.

Islam and the Spirit of Capitalism

Robert Hefner

We set no easy task for ourselves when we aspire to understand the culture and morality of capitalism. If, as we know, that task is already difficult in a Western context, it goes without saying that it poses an even greater challenge in Muslim society. Islam is unique among the world religions in having had over a millennium of political and spiritual competition with the West. It is important to remind ourselves of a few of the details of that history after the revelation of the Qur'an to the Prophet Muhammad and the consolidation of an Islamic government in Mecca: the Muslim conquests of Christian Syria, Palestine, and Spain in the seventh and eighth centuries; the Christian counterattack with the Crusades of the eleventh and twelfth centuries; the expulsion of Muslims from Spain in the final years of the fifteenth century; the progressive encroachment of the Ottoman empire on Europe's eastern flank from the fourteenth to the seventeenth century; and, finally, the West's unprecedented colonization of the Muslim world in the nineteenth and twentieth centuries. From a global perspective, it is hard to think of a contest of civilizations more sustained or intense than this one. This history has left its mark on the consciousness of Muslims and Westerners alike, shaping or misshaping each community's perception of the other.

There is an even more serious obstacle, however, to our understanding of Islam and the

Robert Hefner, "Islam and the Spirit of Capitalism," paper presented at a 1992 consultation on "Religion and Economics after Marxism," funded by the Lilly Endowment.

morality of capitalism than this troubled history. The historical awareness of a people or religious community survives by being regularly resurrected in speeches, sermons, literature, education, or other public media. Such historical remembering is inevitably selective, reshaping rather than simply retrieving the memory, since it is accomplished for reasons other than scholarly objectivity. Certainly the Western media's recent rediscovery of Islam, and their rather selective focus on certain violent elements in Muslim history, is one such example of an unfortunately limited rendering of a complex and rich civilization.

But the Muslim world has its selective renderings as well, especially as regards the West. Once, in a remote upland Muslim village in Java, Indonesia, I was shocked to see that the one item adorning the walls of a poor peasant's hut was a portrait of an Arab warrior, curved sword in hand, mounted on a glorious, armored steed. The picture portrayed the precise moment when, deftly and with a grisly explosion of blood, the warrior severed the head of an oncoming Christian knight. . . . The image was illustrative of a broader fact: This farmer from a remote village in East Java saw himself as part of a glorious and international civilization, one pitted in rivalry with a powerful and invasive West. Though anecdotal, this incident provides insight into the Muslim world today. In its own small way, my encounter with this Muslim peasant was a reminder of the way in which historical memories in much of the Muslim world have been affected by this centuries-long contest with the West.

In discussing Islam and the morality of capitalism, then, we must take care to remind ourselves of our own preconceptions as well as those of Muslims. In emphasizing this fact, I am not suggesting that scholars are condemned to an ever-changing house of mirrors, in which no one ever escapes from his own illusory subjectivity, as some of our deconstructionist colleagues would argue. On the contrary, by reflecting on who *we* are at the same time that we try to understand Muslim attitudes toward capitalism and morality, we only deepen our understanding of each other and increase the likelihood of our insights being true. It is, at any rate, from such a perspective that I wish to speak today.

Islam and Commercial Capitalism

Before discussing Islam and capitalism, it is important that we clarify just what we mean by the term "capitalism." This is more than the usual, tiresome preoccupation of academics with terminological clarification. There is a long history of debate on Islam and capitalism, and much of it is flawed by its failure to identify just what is meant by "capitalism." Such confusion has resulted in poorly formulated arguments and a lot of unnecessary intellectual obfuscation.

From the start, then, let me distinguish between commercial capitalism and industrial capitalism. By commercial capitalism I mean a form of economic organization characterized by the production and exchange of commodities for commercial profit. Such market- and profit-oriented exchange has existed for thousands of years and in many parts of the world and is by no means a uniquely Western achievement.

With regard to this type of capitalism, there is little doubt that Islam is not only compatible with capitalism but positively supportive of it. The scriptural tradition of Islam (the Qur'an and Sunnah or traditions of the prophet, as recorded in Hadith and other commentaries on the prophet's life) displays a decidedly positive attitude toward trade and commerce, and through most of history the most important sects of Islam have displayed much the same pro-market disposition.

From a historical or sociology of knowledge perspective, this affinity between Islam and commercial capitalism should not be surprising. An orphan raised by his uncle, Muhammad was himself a trader in his youth, as were several of his most influential companions, including Abu Bakar, a fabric trader who became the spiritual and political leader of the Muslim world after the death of Muhammad. Mecca and Medina, the two Arabian cities in which Muhammad established the faith, were essentially merchant towns located on old caravan routes, not European- or Asian-style urban centers servicing a large rural population. A significant portion of the population of Medina, we know, consisted of Jewish merchants, and these Jewish traders clearly influenced Muhammad's understanding of prophecy *and* commerce.

The word of God revealed through Muham-mad, the Qur'an, is striking for its mercantile imagery, the tone of which is quite unlike the peaceful pastoral and agrarian imagery that pervades the New Testament. Maxime Rodinson, a French sociologist, has observed that both the Qur'an and later Muslim tradition abound with "eulogistic formulations about merchants," not the least of which are the following quotes attributed to the Prophet: "The merchant who is sincere and trustworthy will (at the Judgment Day) be among the prophets, the just and the martyrs," and "Merchants are the messengers of this world and God's faithful trustees on Earth." In a similar vein, Umar, the second caliph or political and spiritual leader of Islam after Muhammad and Abu Bakar, is quoted by Rodinson: "Death can come upon me nowhere more pleasantly than where I am engaged in business in the market, buying and selling on behalf of my family."

There are nuances to mainline Islam that require us to qualify this portrait of Islam as proactive toward commercial capitalism. . . . There are "anti-capitalist" sentiments in Islam's scriptural tradition, the most famous of which is, of course, the prohibition on *riba*. *Riba* is a term from the Qur'an whose literal meaning is "increase." In fact, the actual practice to which this term referred at the time of Muhammad is not entirely clear. But over the centuries *riba* has been widely assumed by Muslim and Western scholars alike to mean usury, unfair interest, or interest on capital in any form. The last interpretation has been the most widely cited, and still today it makes things difficult in countries like Pakistan, Saudi Arabia, and Malaysia, where politicians and clerics have tried to establish Islamic banks. "Muslim" banks engage in various gymnastics to avoid charging interest, usually substituting some form of profit-sharing for interest payment.

Given the uneven accomplishment of Muslim banks, however, a not uncommon strategy for Muslim owners of capital has been to place their capital in the hands of non-Muslims able to charge interest. Though Saudi capital invested in American banks today provides one of the best examples of such a strategy, it is not a new trend. Centuries earlier, Middle Eastern potentates relied on Jewish (and, to a lesser extent, Christian) merchants to manage their finances and provide them with loans. In general, this was not regarded as illegitimate, since the interest-taking activities occurred outside the Islamic community.

Besides *riba,* another challenge to Islam's otherwise commercial ethos is posed by *zakat,* i.e., the duty to give a set portion of one's income as an alms payment, intended for the support of Muslim (and only Muslim) poor. Twentieth-century Muslim socialists, and there have been a good number, have argued that the obligation to pay *zakat* demonstrates the essentially socialistic nature of early pristine Islam. Despite mass poverty and atrocious inequalities, however, it is quite remarkable that — much less than in the Christian West — such a socialist interpretation of their religion has failed to take hold in most of the Muslim world, perhaps least of all among its teachers and jurists.

There are several reasons for this failure, three of which I might mention here, since they provide some broader insights into Islam and capitalism. The first reason is that the socialist interpretation of the *zakat* so blatantly contradicts the commercial ethos of the Qur'an and Sunnah that serious Qur'anic scholars have simply been unable to convince themselves that they should accept it. Second, the socialist interpretation of *zakat* has also run up against the widespread understanding among Muslim jurists that the *zakat* is first and foremost intended, not to equalize wealth, but to strengthen the cohesion of the Islamic community itself. A third point of resistance to socialist interpretations of *zakat*-almsgiving originates in the fact that, in practice, the great bulk of the *zakat* often goes to clerics, who use it to expand the landholdings that their schools, mosques, and staff need to survive.

Islam and Industrial Capitalism

If we turn to industrial capitalism, however, we find a different story and a more complex set of attitudes among contemporary Muslims. This form of capitalism refers to a system of production or exchange characterized by *(a)* production for profit in the marketplace, *(b)* carried on in firms (distinct from households) that become the dominant economic actors in society, and *(c)* regulated in such a non-monopolistic or "open" fashion that it creates structural incentives

for producers to seek competitive advantage through new economies, technologies, and market experimentations. One consequence of this last feature, the openness and intensity of competition with the resulting drive for efficiencies, is that modern capitalism has consistently engendered technological refinement unlike anything ever before seen in human history.

The political structure of industrial capitalism is distinctive as well, a point that needs to be stressed. If, throughout human history, the state has most commonly been parasitic to enterprise, siphoning off wealth from merchant groups when they became too prominent, modern capitalism has created a unique arrangement whereby government is enjoined to restrain its direct involvement in the corporate enterprise, seeing its primary role as a custodian of infrastructures and a guarantor of fair play.

These last points on the relationship between state and society present a marked contrast with the Muslim world. Muslim political history never facilitated such a peculiar balance of governmental and non-governmental organizations. Earnest Gellner has argued that the towns of the Middle East were vulnerable islands of merchant wealth and civility in a countryside dominated by tribal groups that regularly threatened to raid towns and destroy merchant wealth. In most of the Middle Eastern Muslim world, urban traders had little choice but to embrace the local potentate in exchange for protection from marauding tribesmen. They were thereby forced to accept a rather servile political dependency, a fact that preserved commercial capitalism but limited entrepreneurial initiative, accumulation, and, for that matter, the development of a vibrant middle class. The conditions required for the development of industrial capitalism — including a state committed to infrastructural expansion and the maintenance of a pluricentric balance of power in society itself — were thus conspicuously lacking.

Islam and the Spirit of Modernity

From the end of the Crusades until the late eighteenth and early nineteenth centuries, much of the Muslim world was independent — though, with the exception of parts of the Ottoman empire, it was largely economically stagnant. Throughout most of the world at this time Islam came in two social forms: folk Islam and official or governmental Islam, by which I refer to the Muslim scholars and jurists associated with governments or ruling elites. Folk Islam was comprised of saintly cults and sufi-mystical sects, all of which compromised Islam's strict monotheism but provided a more accessible and manipulable instrument for the practical and ethical needs of ordinary people.

The new Western challenge, at the time of colonialism in the nineteenth century, provoked a profound crisis of Muslim identity. Islam is a religion concerned not only with salvation in the afterworld but also with transformation of this world according to a God-given legal plan. The plan, outlined in the *sharia,* or Islamic law, is of course incomplete, and one of the problems faced by all devout Muslims is how to adjust the *sharia* to a world far more complex than that for which the law was originally formulated. Whatever the difficulties of this adaptation, however, Islam is not especially "politically modest," as Ernest Gellner once described Christianity. As a result, Western colonialism and, still today, Western cultural domination presented Muslims with a deep cultural challenge: they jeopardized the Muslim conviction that theirs is the true and only religion, the proof of which is reflected in its bearers' success in this world.

One reaction to such a crisis of self-legitimation, of course, is to deny the faith entirely, or at least most of its central aspects, and to look for a new source for social ideology. In the late nineteenth and early twentieth centuries, many elite Muslims did just this. The most famous such example is Kemal Ataturk, the modernizing ruler of Turkey, who in the years following World War I banned traditional dress (including the veil for women), outlawed the study of Arabic, reformed education to allow for a strong emphasis on science and no emphasis on religion, and, in short, embarked on a rather heavy-handed program of modernization. In effect, Ataturk attempted to substitute Western culture for Muslim culture in one fell swoop. In a somewhat more qualified fashion, the Shah of Iran later attempted the same thing.

Both efforts failed, of course, largely because they neglected to take seriously the moral *and*

political influence of Muslim clerics, as well as the appeal of Muslim identity among ordinary Muslims. Unlike their modernizing rulers, the great majority of Muslims had little need to repudiate their old moral identity and even less inclination to embrace a threateningly foreign culture. Such top-down efforts at Westernization only reinforced the conviction among much of the populace that Westernization threatened to rob them of their most cherished values.

Of course, most Muslim leaders did not repudiate their Islamic background but instead sought to revitalize it. But here, they too confronted a serious problem. The problem, of course, is that the Qur'an and the traditions of the Prophet make it all too clear that, in the scriptural scheme of things, central political authority (responsive, of course, to the needs of the people and sentiments in the bazaar) is to be a primary agent for the defense and dissemination of the faith. The Qur'an is quite clear on this. A good deal of its content is concerned with Muhammad's efforts to mobilize forces against his enemies, in terms that strike many Westerners as rather Machiavellian. Significant portions of the text are similarly concerned with how to organize the community of the faithful once its political preeminence is achieved.

Now it is true that the Qur'an is a complex document, and it is easy to find passages that provide justification for an alternative scheme of things, one less concerned with linking religion to government. But the fact is that, in their effort to combat medieval accretions to the faith, Muslim modernists have stressed the purity and the integrity of scripture, and in so doing they have made it difficult to deny that scripture does seem to demand the union of religion and politics. Having placed so much emphasis on this model of pristine Islam, modernists seem to have locked themselves into a political formula quite different from that which elsewhere engendered industrial capitalism and the peculiarly Western understanding of human rights and democracy through the separation of church and state.

This, then, is the central contrast between the capitalist West and the developing Muslim world. While politics, capitalism, and religion in the West all worked to slowly open up free spaces by creating a balance of social powers and facilitating a separation (but not finally a severance) of institutional religion from state (and economics), in the Muslim world the challenge of the West has done almost the opposite, creating a conviction that, rather than separating religion, state, and business, they should be all the more tightly wed. According to this view, Islam's failure to compete with the West was the result of Muslim society not being sufficiently Islamized. With more education and deeper faith, the promise made in Islam — that those who know true religion will prosper in this world as well as the hereafter — will be forcefully and definitively realized.

Concluding Comment

My own belief is that the Muslim world will gradually develop many of the values that the nineteenth and early twentieth century versions of reform Islam were inclined to overlook. I believe that this time is coming, and indeed it may have already arrived — however incompletely — in two of the most important countries in the Muslim world, Turkey and Indonesia. Often overlooked by the Western public because both are non-Arabic, these two countries are important in that both are experimenting with capitalism and cultural pluralism in a way never before undertaken in the Muslim world, and what happens in each will have far-reaching impact on the rest of the Muslim world.

Muslims will discover the values of democratic capitalism more quickly and less painfully, of course, if we Westerners engage them in dialogue and continue to show that we respect their conviction that moral and religious values can be maintained within a modern social order. Some of the more sensational moral excesses that Muslims perceive in Western society frighten them into believing that capitalism and religion are essentially incompatible. We can and should show them otherwise. That, at any rate, is my hope for a future we are destined to share.

Islamic Banking: Faith and Creativity

Ken Brown

Dr. Ala-ud-Din, a dentist in San Jose, Calif., had two choices: save for years to buy a house with cash, or take out a mortgage and violate the law of the Koran.

That was until a third choice emerged. A small Islamic financing company bought the house and leased it back to Dr. Din in a 15-year deal that made him a homeowner without violating the religious law that bans Muslims from paying or earning interest.

While still on the far edge of American finance, Islamic banking is making inroads as several groups of bankers and Muslim scholars work to create an interest-free banking system that relies on lease agreements, mutual funds and other methods. And a new emphasis by lenders on improving service to minorities, including black, Arab and Asian Muslims, may be the key to their success.

"I wouldn't say that this is a major part of American finance, but it's definitely growing," said Nicholas Kaiser, the president of the Saturna Capital Corporation of Bellingham, Wash., which manages two mutual funds that follow Islamic law.

At least six Islamic financial organization companies, in areas with large Muslim populations like Los Angeles, Detroit and New York, are offering mortgages and investment opportunities that comply with Islamic law.

Ken Brown, "Islamic Banking: Faith and Creativity," *The New York Times*, 8 April 1994.

Lease Deals Instead of Loans

Muslims are not allowed to pay or receive interest because the body of law of the Koran, called sharia, prohibits them from making a guaranteed profit on capital. Investors can get around the ban by making investments that involve risk, like stocks, or by carrying out lease deals rather than loans for homes and cars.

"Most of the Muslims who practice Islam would not buy houses with interest-based mortgages," said Dr. Din, who is from Pakistan.

The good news for the country's Muslims, who number three million to four million, is happening on several fronts. One group of Muslim experts is trying to put together a mortgage that complies with sharia. Others are refining lease agreements to bring them into compliance with Islam while making the agreements more palatable for lenders. And, coincidentally, car companies have embraced leasing, allowing Muslims to avoid the ethical problem of car loans.

But as Islamic banking becomes more common, some specialists warn that there is a risk that small investors will be duped by hustlers claiming to offer Islamic financial services. "You cannot invest money on faith alone, that's a very bad investment," said Vincent J. Cornell, a professor of religion at Duke University who studied Islamic banking in Malaysia.

Experts in Islamic finance say that what they propose varies only slightly from conventional banking. "The irony is that it doesn't take a lot of work, it takes creativity to convert a conventional home mortgage to a deferred payment sale" that complies with Islamic law, said Steven Thomas, the publisher of The American Journal of Islamic Finance.

Mr. Thomas, who works for a bank, has tried to use the newsletter to educate Muslims on the requirements of Islamic banking and show that it can be done in the United States. "Islamic finance is just another form of asset-based investment banking," he said.

In its most basic form, Islamic banking covers both saving and credit. Instead of being paid interest, depositors are considered shareholders and receive dividends when the bank turns a profit and lose money when it has a loss.

The Amana mutual funds, which Mr. Kaiser runs, work this way. Amana's income fund began in June 1986 and has between 1,200 and 1,300 shareholders and total assets of $11 million. Amana has relied on word of mouth among Muslim Americans to attract new investors. Its income fund has kept pace with the Standard & Poor's 500 stock index, Mr. Kaiser said.

But managing the income fund is not simple. The prohibition on interest prevents investing in bonds, as well as stocks in companies like banks that make money on interest. This makes the fund an equity fund by default.

No Sin Stocks

The income fund also does not invest in companies that make or sell liquor or have gambling operations, as well as some movie studios, following the Muslim laws against drinking, gambling and pornography. The fund's advisers recently decided to stop investing in preferred stocks because dividend payments were too regular, and now puts money only in common stock.

"It does probably hurt the performance a little bit," Mr. Kaiser said. "Banking stocks have been a good place to be for the last few years."

Such a fund, he adds, "may not be the world's greatest investment, but it does what it says it's going to do."

On the debt side of finance, Islamic banks concentrate mainly on leasing deals. For example, a bank buys a house and leases it for 30 years to a customer, who then takes ownership. The lease payments would total more than the bank paid for the house, but that is not considered interest.

"From the Islamic point of view, if I used your asset [for] my benefit, you could have used it for another benefit, so I owe you," Mr. Thomas said. . . .

Rent, Not Principal

MSI's home leases work like this: The buyer puts down about 20 percent and MSI covers the rest in a partnership agreement. The buyer, called the resident owner, pays rent on the value of the property that MSI owns, plus a little more to increase equity.

One important difference is that the home's value is reassessed every year. If the real estate market is hot, the resident owner may feel like he or she is walking up a down escalator, paying every month while owning less and less of the house, even though the value of the resident's equity remains the same, because the house is worth more. The risk goes both ways, of course, and the California real estate slump has hurt MSI, Mr. Joya said.

Critics of Islamic banking see two problems. First, they say the banks are far from interest-free but use "interest under a different name," said Timur Juran, an economics professor at the University of Southern California. The Muslim fundamentalist movement, he said, has helped accelerate the growth in Islamic banks, which now operate in about 50 countries.

Hinduism

Hinduism is less a single religion than a cluster of traditions. What holds them together is a complex interweaving of indigenous tribal religions with classic rituals and texts developed by sages and ascetics several thousand years before Christ. These have been supplemented by philosophies, hymns, epics, and legal codes. Together they form a constellation of religious beliefs and practices that has formed the longest-enduring complex civilization in the world. Influences from Buddhism, Zoroastrianism, Islam, and Christianity have at times appeared to sweep the subcontinent, but each has been absorbed by Hinduism or generated new religious developments.

Hinduism is characterized by a social theory that determines its economic ethic. Society is constituted by a hierarchy of hereditary "castes." At the top are the Brahmans, the priests, scholars, lawyers, guardians of ritual, and tutors of all others. Second are the political leaders, the royalty and warriors who preserve order in the land. Third are the producers and traders — the landowners, merchants, and moneylenders; they are to support the Brahmans and obey the rulers. And below these are the day-workers, artisans, and peasants, as well as slaves and other outcastes (some forty percent of the population).

According to the theory, this organization best allows each to pursue the proper ends of life — dharma, or the fulfillment of inherited duty; artha, or material well-being; kama, or the joys of sensuality; and moksha, or ultimate release from rebirth and the cares of life. Of course, in actual practice, a great number of subgroups do not fit easily into this classical theory; but a sense of group hierarchical status is pervasive, and the fact that these groups are hereditary means that family status plays a decisive role in who one is, what one does, and how one lives.

The texts relating to artha are the ones that deal most directly with business. Two brief samples are included here. The first fragment is from the Artha Shāstra ("Treatise on Material Gain") written by Kauṭilīya in North India at about the time of Alexander's invasion. The second is from the Tirukkural, written by Tiruvalluvar in classic South Indian style about 2,000 years ago. Wealth based on agriculture and trade is seen as an unambiguous good, although Hinduism has always given higher honor to the ascetic who renounces all material goods for the sake of spiritual realization. It is a sacred duty of rulers to create the conditions wherein families can produce. Here is a classic, traditional model of a politically supported, household economy, supported by a non- or anti-material spirituality.

The quest for wealth from outside by a "nontraditional" political economy brought challenges to India. British colonialism encouraged Christian missionaries, introduced Western education based on the Enlightenment, displaced the rule of Indian royalty, established corporations, and began industrial development. These presented challenges to Hinduism in both theory and practice. Mahatma Gandhi is perhaps the most famous of a generation of leaders who selectively adopted aspects of Western thought into a renewed Hindu worldview and helped to inspire Indian nationalism, which overthrew British rule.

Since Independence (1947), India has been torn as to how it should order its changing society. Traces of classic theories of political economy appear, but in nonreligious terms. Especially important have been the relative roles of political leadership, the landowning and commercial classes, and religious nationalists who want to reestablish a Hindu regime. The first wave of new leadership is represented by Jawaharlal Nehru, from whom our third reading on Hinduism is taken. Nehru was the first Prime Minister and founder of a new dynasty that lasted until his daughter and later his grandson were assassinated. For this generation, "socialism" was the model for countries seeking justice and modernization independent of the colonizing powers.

Western views of these developments have been divided, even among post-Marxist theorists who study India. A key question is the role Hinduism will play in the emerging enclaves of modern business and in the larger social ethos. In our fourth reading, Max L. Stackhouse discusses the theories of Max Weber and a major representative study of the new business subculture by Milton Singer.

Artha Śhāstra

Kauṭilīya

. . . Agriculture, cattle-breeding, trade, and commerce constitute the main topics dealt with in the science of economics; it is helpful on account of its making available grains, cattle, gold, raw material, and free labor. Through the knowledge of economics, a king brings under his control his own party and the enemy's party with the help of treasury and army.

The scepter [the symbol of government] is the means of the acquisition and the preservation of philosophy, the Veda, and economics. The science treating with the effective bearing of the scepter is the science of polity. It conduces to the acquisition of what is not acquired, the preservation of what has been acquired, the growth of what has been preserved, and the distribution among worthy people of what has grown. It is on it [the science of polity] that the proper functioning of society [lit., the world] depends. . . .

Other sciences treat of one or another field of human activity, while the science of policy is helpful in all respects and conduces to the stability of human society.

As the science of policy is the source of dharma, material gain, and pleasure, and as it is traditionally said to lead to spiritual emancipation, a king should always study it diligently.

Through the knowledge of the science of policy, kings and others become conquerors of their foes and conciliators of their own people. Kings who are skillful in working out the right policy always prevail.

Can the knowledge of words and their mean-

From *Sources of Indian Tradition*, ed. Wm. T. DeBary et al. (New York: Columbia University Press, 1958), pp. 244-45.

ings not be acquired without the study of grammar, and of material categories without the study of logic, and the science of reasoning and of ritual practices and procedures without the study of the [philosophy of ritual]? Can the limitations and destructibility of bodily existence not be realized without the study of the Vedānta texts?

Further, these sciences treat only of their own special subjects. They are, accordingly, studied only by such persons as follow their respective teachings. Their study implies mere adroitness of intellect. Of what avail are they to people interested and engaged in everyday affairs? On the other hand, the stability of any human affairs is not possible without the science of policy, in the same way as the functioning of the physical bodies of men is not possible without food.

The science of policy conduces to the fulfillment of all desires and is, therefore, respected by all people. It is quite indispensable even to a king, for he is the lord of all people.

Tirukkural

Tiruvalluvar

A kingdom is that in which . . . a complete cultivation, virtuous persons, and merchants with inexhaustible wealth, dwell together.

A kingdom is that which is desired for its immense wealth, and which grows greatly in prosperity, being free from destructive causes.

A kingdom is that which can bear any burden that may be pressed on it [from adjoining kingdoms] and [yet] pay the full tribute to its sovereign.

A kingdom is that which continues, to be free from excessive starvation, irremediable epidemics, and destructive foes.

A kingdom is that which is without various [irregular] associations, destructive internal enemies, and murderous savages who [sometimes] harass the sovereign.

The learned say that the best kingdom is that which knows no evil [from its foes], and, if injured [at all], suffers no diminution in its fruitfulness.

The constituents of a kingdom are the two waters [from above and below], well situated hills and an indestructible fort.

Freedom from epidemics, wealth, produce, happiness, and protection [to subjects]; these five, the learned say, are the ornaments of a kingdom.

The learned say that those are kingdoms whose wealth is not labored for, and those not, whose wealth is only obtained through labor.

Although in possession of all the above mentioned excellences, these are indeed of no use to a country, in the absence of harmony between the sovereign and the subjects.

From *Tirukkal in Ancient Scripts*, ed. G. Siromoney et al. (Tambaram: Madras Christian College, 1980), p. 149.

Indian Socialism

Jawaharlal Nehru

During the troubled aftermath of the Great War came revolutionary changes in Europe and Asia, and the intensification of the struggle for social freedom in Europe, and a new aggressive nationalism in the countries of Asia. There were ups and downs, and sometimes it appeared as if the revolutionary urge had exhausted itself and things were settling down. But economic and political conditions were such that there could be no settling down, the existing structure could no longer cope with these new conditions, and all its efforts to do so were vain and fruitless. Everywhere conflicts grew and a great depression overwhelmed the world and there was a progressive deterioration, everywhere except in the wide-flung Soviet territories of the U.S.S.R., where, in marked contrast with the rest of the world, astonishing progress was made in every direction. Two rival economic and political systems faced each other in the world and, though they tolerated each other for a while, there was an inherent antagonism between them, and they played for mastery on the stage of the world. One of them was the capitalist order which had inevitably developed into vast imperialisms, which, having swallowed the colonial world, were intent on eating each other up. Powerful still and fearful of war which might endanger their possessions, yet they came into inevitable conflict with each other and prepared feverishly for war. They were quite unable to solve the problems that threatened them and helplessly they submitted to slow decay. The other was the new socialist order of the U.S.S.R. which went from progress to progress, though often

at terrible cost, and where the problems of the capitalist world had ceased to exist.

Capitalism, in its difficulties, took to fascism with all its brutal suppression of what Western civilization had apparently stood for; it became, even in some of its homelands, what its imperialist counterpart had long been in the subject colonial countries. Fascism and imperialism thus stood out as the two faces of . . . decaying capitalism, and though they varied in different countries according to national characteristics and economic and political conditions, they represented the same forces of reaction and supported each other, and at the same time came into conflict with each other, for such conflict was inherent in their very nature. Socialism in the West and the rising nationalism of the eastern and other dependent countries opposed this combination of fascism and imperialism. Nationalism in the East, it must be remembered, was essentially different from the new and terribly narrow nationalism of fascist countries; the former was the historical urge to freedom, the latter the last refuge of reaction.

Thus we see the world divided up into two vast groups today — the imperialist and fascist on one side, the Socialist and nationalist on the other. There is some overlapping of the two and the line between them is difficult to draw, for there is mutual conflict between the fascist and imperialist Powers, and the nationalism of subject countries has sometimes a tendency to fascism. But the main division holds and if we keep it in mind, it will be easier for us to understand world conditions and our own place in them. . . .

I am convinced that the only key to the solution of the world's problems and of India's problems lies in socialism, and when I use this word I do so not in a vague humanitarian way but in the scientific economic sense. Socialism is, however, something even more than an economic doctrine; it is a philosophy of life and as such also it appeals to me. I see no way of ending the poverty, the vast unemployment, the degradation, and the subjection of the Indian people except through socialism. That involves vast and revolutionary changes in our political and social structure, the ending of vested interests in land and industry, as well as the feudal and autocratic Indian states system. That means the ending of private property, except in a restricted sense, and the replacement of the pres-

From Jawaharlal Nehru, "India and the World," in *Important Speeches of Jawaharlal Nehru* (New Delhi: Government of India Press, 1949), pp. 4-5, 13-14.

ent profit system by a higher ideal of co-operative service. It means ultimately a change in our instincts, habits, and desires. In short, it means a new civilization, radically different from the present capitalist order. Some glimpse we can have of this new civilization in the territories of the U.S.S.R. Much has happened there which has pained me greatly and with which I disagree, but I look upon that great and fascinating unfolding of a new order and a new civilization as the most promising feature of our dismal age. If the future is full of hope it is largely because of Soviet Russia and what it has done, and I am convinced that, if some world catastrophe does not intervene, this new civilization will spread to other lands and put an end to the wars and conflicts which capitalism feeds.

I do not know how or when this new order will come to India. I imagine that every country will fashion it after its own way and fit it in with its national genius. But the essential basis of that order must remain and be a link in the world order that will emerge out of the present chaos.

Socialism is thus for me not merely an economic doctrine which I favour, it is a vital creed which I hold with all my head and heart. I work for Indian independence because the nationalist in me cannot tolerate alien domination; I work for it even more because for me it is the inevitable step to social and economic change. I should like the Congress to become a socialist organization and to join hands with the other forces in the world who are working for the new civilization. But I realize that the majority in the Congress, as it is constituted to-day, may not be prepared to go thus far. We are a nationalist organization and we think and work on the nationalist plan. It is evident enough now that this is too narrow even for the limited objective of political independence and so we talk of the masses and their economic needs. But still most of us hesitate, because of our nationalist backgrounds, to take a step which might frighten away some vested interests. Most of those interests are already ranged against us and we can expect little from them except opposition even in the political struggle.

Much as I wish for the advancement of socialism in this country, I have no desire to force the issue in the Congress and thereby create difficulties in the way of our struggle for independence. I shall co-operate gladly and with all the strength in me with all those who work for independence even though they do not agree with the socialist solution. But I shall do so stating my position frankly and hoping in course of time to convert the Congress and the country to it, for only thus can I see it achieving independence.

The Hindu Ethic and Development: Western Views

Max L. Stackhouse

What is the relationship of religion to development? There are four possible answers: religion is decisive for development; it is irrelevant to development; it is correlative to development; religion is idiosyncratically related to development. Each answer carries with it a library of "evidence," a world view, a set of assumptions about what religion is and how it relates to society, and a sense of direction if any country or religious group wants to move or help others move toward development. . . . For India, the literature is growing, and the most quoted sources derive still from three western scholars: from Karl Marx, especially his comments on India in the 1850s, to Max Weber's writings on India just before World War I, to Milton Singer's interpretations of the Indian situation in the decades following independence. The influence of Marx, however, is declining rather rapidly in spite of several vigorous Marxist parties and the respectability accorded non-Leninist socialism from Nehru to Gunnar Myrdal's massive influence in the 1960s and 1970s.

The Focus of the Debate

One of the key figures in the discussion of this question, however, remains Max Weber. He has recently come under attack from Milton Singer,

---

From Max L. Stackhouse, "The Hindu Ethic and the Ethos of Development: Some Western Views," *Religion and Society* 20, no. 4 (1973): 5-33.

and he is an indirect, rebellious and disputatious child of Marx. Because of his importance, thus, it will be useful to focus on the work of Weber and his critic, Milton Singer.

Max Weber argued early in the century that, compared to certain other religious traditions, classical Hinduism did not provide, and indeed was constitutionally incapable of providing, an ethos that gives impetus toward modern, urban, industrial society. The various aspects of this relatively straightforward thesis need to be clarified before we proceed. The statement assumes that cross-cultural and comparative studies are useful; that while intensive, detailed investigation on any particular social and cultural setting is necessary to master the context about which one speaks, the salient features that give that context its uniqueness can best be found by drawing comparison and contrasts with other settings. For Weber, the two main centers for comparative work are the relationships of the Judaeo-Christian traditions of the West, especially radical Protestant forms of it, to the development of modern "capitalist" societies and the relationships of Confucian religiosity in China to the development of pre-revolutionary Chinese society.

By classical Hinduism, Weber means the fundamental perceptions of reality that are organized into the multi-colored fabric of Indian social and cultural life, embedded in the dominant psychological expectations and horizons of India and rationalized in a vast variety of ways by Hindu, Buddhist and Jain philosophers, saints, and reformers. Notice that there are three assumptions in this definition. One is that there is an identifiable pattern that can be called Hinduism. While few recognize more than Weber the fantastic richness, dynamic, changing variety, and, indeed, contradiction that is summarized in the word Hinduism, he felt that it was both possible and necessary to use such generalized terms. The possibility is closely related to his methodological use of "ideal types," that is, an abstracted model of general characteristics that obtain in a particular historical reality and based on empirical investigation, even though no specific concrete instance may meet all the characteristics of that model. These "ideal types" are not historical laws or morally "ideal"; they are conceptual artifacts by which one identifies the salient features of a phenomenon for comparative purposes. Another assumption in this definition is that whatever the disagreements and distinctive contributions made to India by tribal peoples, Muslims, Christians, Parsees, and others, the dominant organizing principles for social life, personal meaning, and cultural expression derive in various ways from the shared assumptions of Hindus, Buddhists, and Jains. . . .

This leads to closely related, final main assumption in this definition of what religion is. Weber does not confine it to doctrines or beliefs, rites or rituals. By religion he means what we might today call "meaning system," that is, a social, psychological and intellectual pattern that provides relative coherence to life. People may not cultically practice, may not know, or even may consciously reject, Hinduism or features of it, and yet find in the social-cultural institutions and meanings that it has formed their own sense of who to honor, how to choose, what to expect of themselves and others, what is important and what is not. In short they are dependent upon Hinduism, in some manner, for the meaning of their lives.

Weber, in all his work, contends that these "meaning systems" are pertinent to the dominant ethos and thereby to the kinds of economic structure and action that are present in any society. Thus, he rejects one possible answer to the opening question of this presentation: that religion is irrelevant to development. Religion is the prototypical meaning system. And, in the rejection he takes issue with the Marxist contention that there the laws and stages of history are economically determined and that to ask about subjective dimensions escape from reality. He thereby also rejects the basic assumptions of some so-called liberal economists and development experts, both in India and from abroad, that development is merely a function of capitalization and rationalized means of production. Modernization, they claim, is an autonomous, technical, economic process, and would of itself shatter the patterns of traditional religiosity, tied as they were to extended family and caste relations and mythical belief. . . .

Weber's argument about Hinduism is historically analytical and interpretative. He believed that there was such a thing as modern, urban, technological society, which he called "capitalism," a usage that is quite distinct from the Marxist-influenced usage of the term and a usage that has therefore led to more confusions than it is possible here to recite. India did not develop this kind of society, even though it had many of the preconditions for it. And when the British brought it, there was little in the society that responded eagerly and readily to it. Only slowly and painfully have parts of the Indian population moved toward such a society, and most of that movement seems still to be confined to urban and high governmental enclaves or to certain "guest peoples." Why? Weber thought that one critical factor was the influence of the "meaning system" of Hinduism. He thought that Hinduism in India, in certain respects like Confucianism in China, and in contrast to Protestantism in the West, and perhaps export Confucianism as it influenced Japan, Korea and oversees Chinese population, did not provide the social, psychological and intellectual "meaning system" that promoted modern, urban, technological development. At certain points his argument is stronger than that, for he suggests that Hinduism is incapable of providing this meaning system; while at other points he suggests that radical reform of certain dimensions of Hinduism (and Confucianism for that matter) might well produce a modified "meaning system" that would be significant for development. But his argument is primarily historical and interpretative, not predictive or prophetic in intent. Thus it is an open question as to whether his argument holds at a point in time one half century after he penned it, in spite of the fact that certain disciples and critics treat it in a fundamentalist, proof-texting way.

The reasons that Hinduism did not provide the impetus to development are fourfold. First, it was linked to the caste system. Every religion that is not mere ideological froth and spiritual fantasy has a characteristic mode of social organization compatible with its basic world-view. In the case of Hinduism, the relationship has been stronger than compatibility, it approaches identity. Weber's subtle and complex interpretation of caste shows that this conception of "divine community" has undergone numerous changes, has not been static, has been expansive to include new groups and the changing economic or political power relations of groups, and has had varying relationships to legal developments, doctrinal reform, and the division of labor. In view of recent research, it can be said that he both anticipated some of the more profound research and that he needs correction at certain critical points. Nevertheless, no social scientist known to this observer has denied or refuted Weber's essential contentions about caste: namely, that it is the dominant organizing principle of Indian society, that it is partially distinct from class thereby making an exclusively class analysis irrelevant to the Indian scene, that it is rooted in a sense of a particular form of extended family identity, that the triumph of caste defeated the possibility of the development of Indian forms of guilds or congregations or citizen (in the specific urban senses of the words) as decisive social units, thereby reinforcing village agrarian as opposed to urban technological patterns of life, that it is linked to specifiable although highly variegated forms of ritual, religious discipline, and metaphysical and moral belief, and that it is the pattern of social grouping which provides the most pervasive sense of personal identity, duty and authority. A modern urban industrial society was not, because it could not be, constructed where this religious pattern is the dominant organizing principle of society.

Second, Hinduism does not, as did Puritanism in the West and "export Confucianism" in the East, provide a metaphysical and moral interpretation of life that makes it meaningful in an ultimate sense for the individual to systematically and rationally engage in changing the world, consciously breaking with a past now seen as oppressive, and plunging in with focused energy and commitment to building a new society and a new humanity. In Hinduism, while people engage in economic and political activity with intensity and vigor, while they do create new things, and while they do change economic and political relations, the final meaning of their lives is not confirmed by or located in these activities. The grounding and destiny of their lives is ultimately not related to transforming historical activity. Their worldly lives are not seen as a means to accomplish an ultimate end, but as an end in itself on one hand, and as a time-space phenomenon separate from all ultimacy on the other. Weber identified this as "other-worldliness," in contrast to metaphysical-moral "this-worldly" senses of "vocation, and historicity."

And thirdly, the many reform movements that have brought philosophical richness and sharp criticism against many features of Hinduism from within Hinduism have not basically broken with the underlying assumptions of Hinduism. Indeed, even those who suffer at the bottom edges of Hindu society, and grouse at those higher up, participate enough in the fundamental perspectives of those they criticize that finally they accept their lot or attempt to move up as a group through "sanskritization" or as an individual through spiritual discipline devised at Hindu hands. Heterodox movements effecting or reflecting social change and upward mobility within the system provide a dynamic picture of change at one level of analysis, but a deeper level reflect no fundamental new departure over the long history of Hinduism. In short, the intellectuals, the prophets (primarily exemplary), and the mass movements against Hinduism have in the final analysis been reabsorbed into Hinduism, giving India a certain sameness yesterday, today and forever in spite of a turbulent history.

Finally, Weber sees a coherence between these three factors and other economic and political factors in India's history. Each of these three factors was shaped at crucial movements by factors of resources, technological development, economic interests and political domination; in this, Weber learned his lessons from Marx well. But he breaks with Marxism as held by scholars and activists of his day in that he is unwilling to say that material factors were totally determinative of the social, psychological and ideational ones. And he suspected that "radical" analysis of material factors was strongly tainted with romantic notions, more dangerous because they were unrecognized as such. Further, while social patterns have their own characteristic logics of development, as do psychological and ideational ones, no one of these is decisive for any other. Instead, every historically significant pattern is caused by a multiplicity of forces, material, historical and spiritual, which mutually influence one another at every juncture. This idea can best be understood by reference to his notion of "selective affinity." When a complex social cultural phenomenon is created and sustained over a long period of time, such as Hinduism, there is no single causative explanation of it. Instead one must recognize the variety of ideational, historical, material, personal and social factors that play into its creation. And in the process of creation certain features of these relatively autonomous forces bond better to certain features of other forces than do still other features. These bonding features mutually enforce the features that have the greatest propensity to bond, bringing them to dominance. That is why, for example, the religion of the intellectuals is often not that of the people; for the people selectively choose dimensions of the theoretical worldview that bond to the other forces in their lives, while that dimension of the religion selectively reinforces the other forces in their lives. In the creation of great historical movements, however, there is a coincidence of grand theory and other forces that have a "selective affinity." In India, the beliefs of the Hindu literati élites had an accordion-like expandability that allowed them to "bond" with a great many local insights and needs. Once a social phenomenon is created, once the bonding has begun to take place, an inner logic develops between what were previously relatively autonomous forces and influences, ideas and needs. The social researcher constructs models or "ideal types" of the inner logic of these phenomena as Marx did with classes, Durkheim and Redfield did with societies, and indeed every scholar does, often unreflectively. In short, a new coherency, with its own logic becomes itself a relatively autonomous force, having its own "spirit," selecting what is compatible with it from the environment and subordinating or rejecting the rest. In India, the factors caste, other-worldliness, and the domestication of protest engaged in a selective affinity between themselves and with powerful material forces and produced Hinduism. And that Hinduism was constitutionally resistant to modernization, in Weber's view.

It is in this context that we can see how Weber might answer the initial question of this paper. If by religion one means spiritual ideas or ritual divorced from their historical process of selective affinity with other forces, religion is idiosyncratically related to development. If by religion one means the inner logic, or inner "spirit" of a historically formed socio-cultural phenomenon, religion is decisive for development. It either selectively reinforces the latent possibilities toward it or selectively rejects them. . . .

A Critique

Milton Singer is the most articulate and knowledgeable representative critic of this perspective. Singer however, is manifestly less concerned with comparative research than was Weber. His focus is tightly on the Indian situation which gives a sense of concreteness and detail; but which makes it more difficult to find reference points when it comes to the question of "significance." Secondly, his understanding of the word "religion" as reflected in the usage of "Hindu" is much more delimited than in Weber. It is much more ideological, belief and ritual oriented that is "meaning system" which I think better reflects Weber. Weber uses "Hindu" in reference to a general character of the classical ethos; Singer uses it as active belief and ritual practice, and at certain points confines it more to "characterological" dispositions. In brief, Singer focuses much less on the more objective social-cultural side of Hinduism to which Weber wants to point. Third, Singer points out the passages where Weber gives sophisticated treatment to the dynamic and changing character of Hinduism and sees no compatibility of this with the attribution of more static features. . . . Singer comes from a tradition of scholarship that is suspicious about the relationship of the great doctrines to the actual functioning of religion in daily life. He was a party to a creative school of scholars who made quite a distinction between the "great tradition" and the "little traditions." Those who study the former engage in speculative and deductive attempts to understand societies by reference to the grand concepts of the literati, while the latter engage in empirical analysis of what the people think and do. . . .

In view of these perspectives on Weber's arguments, it is no wonder that Singer points out that when he explains Weber's views to Hindus they are astonished. When I explained Weber's view to Indian intellectuals in somewhat different terms, they were more responsive. On the basis of his reading of Weber, which I believe is partly precise and partly askew, he presents and intrinsically interesting set of results of an intensive study he made of nineteen industrialists of the Madras area for the announced purpose of arriving at "a more positive conclusion about the compatibility of traditional Indian society with modernization."

He documents that, among a number of leaders, whom he feels represent "the closest parallel to the successful Puritan capitalists who were the empirical basis for Weber's analysis of the Protestant Ethic and the Spirit of Capitalism" in the West, the joint family is not breaking down, nor does it represent a structural barrier to capitalistic development. Indeed, it has been transformed into the basis of a family large enough to issue stock so that they are no longer the owners directly. His argument is that the joint family provides "a nucleus of capital", a "well structured pattern of authority, succession and inheritance," "meets many of the requirements of industrial organization for direction, management, diversification and continuity." Further, he tries to show that caste is relatively unimportant in determining industrialization, although he admits that Brahmans and Nayudus tend to dominate at higher levels and Harijans at lower level jobs. More important is previous experience or training in finance, business or government service, and that their sons are being trained in technological and administrative skills, rather than classical learning. To be sure, it is the higher castes that have greater access to these possibilities. All of this is nevertheless tending to break traditional caste occupations but not all aspects of caste loyalties or ranking. Singer asks what this means for Hinduism — and argues that joint family and caste cannot be regarded as coextensive with Hinduism. This point is quite significant. Weber understands caste as a particular kind of extended family pattern structurally, psychologically, and intellectually related to other major aspects of Hinduism, as mentioned above. Instead, Singer understands Hinduism as a distinctive set of rituals and beliefs that can be isolated, as an independent variable from social and structural aspects of the dominant patterns of caste and family in India, and focuses on the 16 industrialists who are Hindu in the more limited confessional sense. He points out that what is taking place is a "compartmentalization" of religion, language, intimate family life and caste loyalties, on one side, with the public, secular, ritually neutral area of business on the other. Thus, the industrialists develop two models of life, one private and one professional, thereby preventing direct collision. Yet there is some interpenetration — cocktail parties are offered in the home for business purposes, astrologers are consulted regarding auspicious times for board meetings, and most give more or less pious attention to Ganesh, or Lakshmi, or Siva, or Hanuman, etc., for help in meeting problems of business. None consider themselves fully orthodox, but all are believers, and say they hold to the essential tenets of Hinduism. These, they hold, are really more ethical than religious: Be truthful, keep promises, do your job well, don't be wasteful of time, use wealth for the good of others, depend on yourself, provide opportunities to all, respect the dignity of labor, work for human rights and universal brotherhood, all this with rather heavy dependence upon Gandhian understandings of the Gita and *bhakta* and certain elements of the traditions.

This focus on the family and its relationship to profession is terribly interesting, for Weber argued that the Hindu identification of divine community with the peculiar form of extended, endogamous and hierocratic family pattern, *jati,* had been used as basic fact ordering economic life. If the latter is to be changed, the former must be modified. Also at stake is the question of relation of nurture, or the processes of shaping personal development to the processes of economic order, and relationship of meaning systems to both. Singer says, in effect, that compartmentalization has separated economic rationality and division of labor from family life specifically and the governing meaning systems generally; but that meaning system is not broken, it survives in so far as it is still basically related to family life. Simultaneously, a new theodicy has been devised, partly at least out of latent Hindu motifs, to legitimate modern industrial life.

Now, what are we to make of such an argument, and does it in fact refute Weber? It is clear, I think, that the information and insight he provides is intrinsically fascinating to anyone interested in the relations of religion and development, and that it does show that at least some people can adapt selected aspects of Hinduism and modern industrial life and weave an apparently meaningful pattern. In this, Singer has traced some serious new departures unrecognized or unknown by Weber and some Weberians. But I used the phrase *"apparently* meaningful pattern" intentionally. Most people everywhere, I believe, live with certain unresolved tensions between aspects of "compartments" of their lives. But it is a serious question whether any historical movement or constellation can come to dominate an ethos if that movement does not have sociological, psychological, and ideational means, at least in principle, of resolving those tensions. It is Weber's contention, as I understand him, that all the great religio-historical movements of consequence had that feature. And it is this "logic of integrity" that I find lacking in Singer's exposition, hardly resolved, in my judgment, by descriptively focusing on aspects of the compartmentalized tensions and showing that some people live in the midst of them. If that is so, Singer's work has less to do with Weber's argument than he assumes, although it has its own integrity as a serious piece of research. To investigate this possibility, let's look in closer detail at the arguments of Weber and Singer, point by point.

Weber assumed a cross-cultural, comparative framework for his study. There is none of that in Singer. In this cross-cultural analysis, Weber is trying to establish that meaning systems make a difference. There are all sorts of material factors that were developed in India that did not induce development. He begins his study of India by listing numerous such factors that have been advanced as causes of development. India, from ancient times, had:

- extensive trade
- credit-interest rates
- commercial stratum of population
- rationalistic enlightenment in various periods
- large political units of relative peace for long times
- rational organization of armies
- complex political rationality
- state contracting (and distribution of wealth)
- rational finance methods
- communication monopolies
- urban development (equal or superior to that of the earlier West)
- rational number system for precise calculability
- science (more advanced than in the earlier West)
- varieties of sociological types
- tolerance to religious and philosophical doctrines
- a system of law and justice that was open to modernizing commercial and industrial possibilities
- technical skills of craftsmen
- independent merchants
- occupational specialization
- acquisitiveness
- group solidarity among influential working classes

Yet it did not produce a modern industrial society: Why not? (He did not argue that it could not change in the future, but only that, in fact, it had not.) It did not because the basic orientation of the culture as visible in Hinduism did not provide a universalistic ethic for this — worldly activities that gave people the chance to find ultimate meaning for their lives in analysis of and transformation of the social-political order — and, in economics, the means of production, distribution and consumption — in comparison with those societies where an industrial society was produced. As well known, he calls this "otherworldliness." Now, Singer's study is not comparative even to the point of asking whence came the values, analytical orientation to economic condition, and worldview perspectives that these industrialists are adjusting to. And, if this is so, without developing a meaning system directly related to their public and economic activity, then we can expect no innovative action and only the eventual cynicism, corruption and disillusionment that has developed among western capitalist and socialist groups who have divorced life as lived from life as meaning. And, although he hints at several points to the differences between classical Hinduism and that held by these men, he does not systematically compare the two. If he is to refute Weber, on this point, he must either show, as some of the Marxist critics have been inclined to do, that meaning systems are non-causative reflections or projections of material conditions; or he must show that the patterns of behaviour of these industrialists are generated directly out of elements in the Hindu ethos itself. . . .

Closely related is a second point: Industrialists as leading business figures may or may not have anything to do with capitalism as Weber defines it. Weber is essentially interested in the rational organization of formally free labor, as part of the worldly activity that is of ultimate significance.

He begins his famous study of the Protestant Ethic with an analysis of the workers, he traces the advice of Franklin to clerks and farmers and shopkeepers, and he accents the traditions of the German Pietists, and Anglo-American Calvinists and Wesleyians — the overwhelming numbers of which were petty bourgeoisie and workers. Big businessmen and adventure capitalists, he points out, have appeared in every culture, and every age. There is, to him, really nothing very interesting about them, and they do not represent the transforming power of a culture. Nor does greed for and calculation of gain have anything to do with his special sense of the word capitalism. He writes: "Now in this sense capitalism and capitalistic enterprises . . . have existed in all civilized countries of the earth. . . . In China, India, Babylon, Egypt, Mediterranean antiquity and in the (western) Middle Ages." But what is distinctive is the development of a pervasive ethos among the formally free citizenry (bourgeoisie) which is, by its own sense of moral meaning, driven to adopt an integrated perspective involving both non-rational moral concerns and a rational ordering of behaviour that sees charts and statistics, balance books, and rational calculation as a loci for meaning in life, in a way that provides ever renewed striving for resources to reinvest for development. In this regard, Weber might well have included modern socialism in his definition, especially as it is based on the rational organization of a proletariat that, in his terms, is a "bourgeois" in so far as it is a formably free citizenry. He opposes socialism at another point — namely that — it, like modern massive corporations, has a tendency toward the totalization of bureaucracy. And that produces an "iron cage" for a culture. Indeed, socialism in practice is the bureaucratic corporation driven to its logical conclusion of a single national capitalizing corporation. Still, Weber approves socialism and bureaucracy for their tendencies toward equalization in so far as they are, in principle, "no respecters of persons." The problem of bureaucracy is that we can't live without them, and we can't live with them. Charismatics forget the former, socialists the latter. And Singer never defines what he means by the use of the term "socialism" in the title of this article. The entire structural problem of bureaucracy is ignored, al-though it is an enormous problem in India, inhibiting economic development.

But, in regard to the question of the dominant ethos, we do not only have the problem of the narrow base of Singer's study, and the fundamental misunderstanding of both capitalism and socialism in Weberian terms, but thirdly there is the question of innovative or transformative drive. Weber is deeply concerned with the problem of novelty and change in history and develops his theories of "charisma," "routinization" and "selective affinity" to deal with it. And all through his study of India, he is looking for forces of the ethos that are fundamentally transformative. Nearly one-third of the book is given over to potentially revolutionary events from the Jain and Buddhist movement through the "counter-reformation" of Hinduism, the development of the Veerashaivite and Bhakti traditions to the Brahmo Samaj, including the social economic forces which variously contributed to their development. Only the latter, he suggests, is promising; for in spite of the fact that social-material conditions at each of the previous reform periods were at a point of stress that could have broken into a revolutionary situation, they did not because they participated too deeply in the caste and "otherworldly" life-orienting meaning systems that prevented the mass of people from seizing the opportunities. This does not mean that there is not change, adjustment, and modification of the ethos — there obviously was. This history of India is a changing history; but there is not in Hinduism a high priority on social-economic innovation. The significance of this for such critics of Weber as Singer is that, once more, if they want their critique of Weber to be substantive, they must show one of two things: either they must show that in an unexpected place — namely, industrial leadership — there has emerged a new synthesis, or "selective affinity" of traditional Hindu and modern material techniques that is revolutionary for the whole culture in the sense that all touched by this new ethos will become conscious, intentional innovative agents in all areas of life, consciously participating in a transformative rationalizing drive, such as happened in the West at the hands of Protestants and as is happening in East Asia at the hands of expatriot Confucians. Singer does not present such evidence; but instead documents that businessmen from several castes have found ways of *adjusting* and *adapting* successfully to a commercial-industrial economy and a value orientation which together make up a new ethos for some urbanized élites in India. Or, to make their critique stand, he and other critics must show that, contrary to Weber, the Brahmo Samaj and the perspectives of the Hindu renaissance or Gandhi, the Bhakti religions of grace are in fact primarily Hindu in origin and are providing the meaning system for such men as these leaders, as the first fruits of at least a potentially transformative movement. There are several points in Singer's study that possibly could be developed in this direction.

He quotes, for example, one industrialist, as I mentioned, who felt that "something else" than qualifications, education, experience, muscle, brains and ambition, was using him as an "instrument" to succeed. There is an ultimate unifying force in the world according to him. . . . He would not attribute this to *karma*, but only to "something else." . . . This Brahman was in fact departing from the tradition, but he felt uncomfortable enough about it to discuss it with his guru (who approved it as his *dharma*); and he expressed grave concern that it might eventually change family patterns. This industrialist regularly consults an astrologer on family matters, permits no widow remarriage, and never brings business matters into his prayers for "that would tempt the gods too much." Wealth, however, is not to be treated as a possession, but as a trust. Now, in so far as this represents an element of reformed Hinduism, and a driving force to innovation that is peculiarly Indian, and not merely adjustment, Singer may have found the nucleus of a Hindu correlate to the transforming puritanisms East and West. . . .

One major implication of all this is that Singer has shown, I think that, with a modified Hinduism, carrying on a selective affinity process with non-Hindu culture and thereby producing a reformed Hinduism, Indians can adjust to the modern world. What he has not shown is that Weber is wrong, or that classical Hinduism can shape an ethos that would drive Indians under its influence, to engage in radical transformation of society, psychic expectations, or intellectual reconstruction into a new, spirited synthesis that presents a new model of meaning, society and economy to the world to compete with those of the West and Russia and China. Yet that is precisely what Indians demand from the major national parties, progressive intellectuals, and some of the workers and students who long for, and have not yet found, this new synthesis of meaning that can organize social life, psychic integration, and intellectual integrity to produce an ethos of development. Indeed, these groups are often quite contemptuous of, even cynical about, the kinds of adjustments which industrial leaders such as these have devised. It is true that in a country of scarce resources, they admire the fact that the industrialists are "making it"; but they see in them no vision of a new India and only a pale image of the grander moments of the past. Thus, without a new synthesis, it seems to me, there is a widespread sense of willingness to half-believe anything so long as it will provide a relatively secure position. But it is a heartless participation in both the religious life and the developmental or industrial efforts.

Buddhism, Asceticism, and Wealth

Ascetic renunciation for the sake of spiritual development had long been practiced in ancient India, often in the context of a robust quest for wealth among some and a daily struggle against poverty among many. More than twenty-five centuries ago, however, a prince doubted that either reliance on material goods or the practice of ascetic denial could bring relief from human misery. In fact, he thought they both increased human suffering. After a long search for a deeper understanding of reality, he announced a new insight into the basic causes of suffering and how to deal with it. His "enlightenment" marked the beginning of the second great world religion to arise in India. It involved a rejection of the domination of the Brahmans in society and a revision of ascetic theory and practice. Buddhism, indeed, has been called the "Protestantism of the East." It brought reforms to ancient Hinduism, and its converts sent out missionary monks in all directions. It came to influence much of Asia through its theories of reality, self, and society. It is central to belief and culture from Sri Lanka to Indonesia in Southeast Asia, and from the borders of Tibet to Japan in North and East Asia.

One of the key teachings of Buddhism is that suffering is caused by the desire for or the attachment to things. What causes this craving is, basically, ignorance about reality and the self. One becomes a monk or a nun essentially to find the bliss of enlightenment, which overcomes this inner craving. It is not that material things are particularly evil; in fact, they may be quite useful within their limits. It is that they are not "real." All "things" come into existence and then pass out of existence, and to rely on things is to live with the illusion of false security. If anything, wealth and the possession of things is a byproduct, an un-

sought result, of virtue, and they can be lost by vicious action. But the accumulation or loss of wealth is not the point. If wealth blocks the path toward enlightenment, it is the occasion for vice. The opposite is also true: poverty can be a great problem if it brings with it various cravings and desires that deflect one from the path.

To be sure, Buddhist literature takes great delight in portraying the abundant wealth of great Buddhist rulers and lands, and Buddhism has had an intimate relationship with royal power since the days of its birth, in part, some scholars say, because it provided ancient rulers with a deeper and broader theory of political economy than they had otherwise. Orders of monks are often viewed as jewels in the crown of the regime and sometimes as the regime's aids in ordering society — although Buddhism is found in many political contexts and has sometimes established a relative independence of political authority.

One key economic symbol of Buddhism, especially in the southern or Theravada tradition, here represented by Rajavaramuni, is the begging bowl. Monks live by begging, and *dana,* the giving of gifts to those in need, especially the monks, is greatly honored. At a personal level, it is a decisive link between laity and monk. Those who give to those in need manifest a respect toward virtue and a lack of desire for things. This gesture of non-attachment is held to be most virtuous when the donor does not think of the honor that comes from giving. Donations of land to monasteries by wealthy families has promoted a great deal of wealth and rather extensive landlordism in some places; but it is not the mere fact of possession but rather the potential for forming a dependence on or developing an attachment to such properties that raises moral issues for the monks.

Some scholars have argued that Buddhism, like the Brahmanism against which it rebelled, does not have an internal impetus toward an ethic of economic development, no matter how much it differs from its predecessor on other points. However, this a matter of scholarly dispute. Others argue that it is this lack of impetus to possess things which has preserved Buddhist peoples from capitalism and from succumbing to "Western" technological efforts to control everything. This evaluation is also under dispute, as we see in an article representing an important branch of the Mahayana tradition that is influential in Japan. Yamamoto Shichihei's contribution examines the legacy of Suzuki Shosan, a seventeenth-century Zen monk. He argues that this monk profoundly shaped Zen's influence on the Buddhist roots of Japanese economic life through an embedded cultural religiosity. Another of the most influential writers on development and ecology of the last generation, E. F. Schumacher, presents a widely held, current Western perspective and provides another vantage point for discussion.

Teachings from the *Suttas*

Vices to Be Avoided

1. The avoidance of the four vices of conduct (corresponding to the first four of the Five Precepts).

2. Doing no evil out of the four prejudices that are caused by love, hatred, delusion, and fear.

3. Not following the six ways of squandering wealth, viz., addiction to intoxicants, roaming the streets at unseemly hours, frequenting shows, indulgence in gambling, association with bad companions, and the habit of idleness.

4. Knowledge of how to distinguish among the four false friends, viz., the out-and-out robber, the man who pays lip service, the flatterer, and the leader to destruction, and the four true friends, viz., the helper, the man who is the same in weal and woe, the good counselor, and the sympathizer.

5. The amassing of wealth and the fourfold division of money into one part for living and doing duties toward others, two parts for business, and one part for time of need.

6. The covering of the six quarters of human relationships and their attendant mutual responsibilities, viz., child-parent, pupil-teacher, husband-wife, friend-friend, servants and workmen-master or employer monk-layman.

7. The four bases of social harmony, viz., giving, kindly words, life of service, and impartial treatment and participation. . . .

Cited in Phra Rajavaramuni, "Foundations of Buddhist Social Ethics," in *Ethics, Wealth, and Salvation: A Study in Buddhist Social Ethics,* ed. Russell F. Sizemore and Donald K. Swearer (Columbia: University of South Carolina Press, 1990), pp. 35-36, 39-40, 47.

The Noble Eightfold Path

	Magga
Pannā (wisdom)	1. Right view *(sammā-diṭṭhi)*
	2. Right Thought *(sammā-sankappa)*
Sīla (morality)	3. Right Speech *(sammā-vācā)*
	4. Right Action *(sammā-kammanta)*
	5. Right Livelihood *(sammā-ajīva)*
Samādhi (mental discipline)	6. Right Effort *(sammā-vāyāma)*
	7. Right Mindfulness *(sammā-sati)*
	8. Right Concentration *(sammā-samādhi)*

The Four Virtues Leading to Temporal Welfare

1. To be endowed with energy, industry, and skill in management,
2. To be endowed with attentiveness,
3. To associate with good people,
4. To have a balanced livelihood.

The Four Virtues Leading to Prosperity

1. To live in a good environment,
2. To associate with good people,
3. To aspire and direct oneself in the right way,
4. To have prepared oneself with good background.

The Four Virtues for a Good Lay Life

1. Truth and honesty,
2. Training and adjustment,
3. Tolerance and forbearance,
4. Liberality.

The Fourfold Deserved Bliss of a Layman

1. Bliss of ownership,
2. Bliss of enjoyment,
3. Bliss of debtlessness,
4. Bliss of blamelessness.

The Four Virtues Leading to Spiritual Welfare

1. To be endowed with confidence,
2. To be endowed with morality,
3. To be endowed with generosity or charity,
4. To be endowed with wisdom. . . .

Buddhist Attitudes toward Poverty and Wealth

Phra Rajavaramuni

The term *poverty* may sometimes be misleading. The familiar Buddhist concepts are rather contentment *(santutthi)* or limited desires *(appicchatā)*. Poverty *(daliddiya)* is in no place praised or encouraged in Buddhism. The Buddha says, "Poverty is a suffering in the world for a layman." He also says, "Woeful in the world is poverty and debt" (A.III.350, 352). Though monks should be contented and have few wishes, poverty is never encouraged even for the monks.

The possession of wealth by a king or even an average layman is often praised and encouraged in the Pāli canon. In other words, wealth is something to be amassed or sought after. Among the Buddha's lay disciples, the better known, the most helpful, and the often praised were mostly wealthy persons such as Anāthapiṇḍika. For the monks, though they are not expected to seek wealth, to be a frequent recipient of offerings can be regarded as a good qualification. Two monks may be equal in other qualifications and virtues, but the one who receives more offerings is praised. Even the Buddha praised a monk who was foremost in receiving offerings: "Chief among my disciples who are obtainers of offerings is Sivali" (A.I.24). However, these remarks must be qualified and further clarified.

The main theme in these texts is that it is not wealth that is praised or blamed, but the way one acquires and uses it. For the monks, as mentioned above, it is not acquisition as such that is blamed, nor poverty that is praised. The things that are blamed are greed for gain, stinginess, clinging, attachment to gain, and hoarding of wealth. Acquisition is acceptable if it is helpful in the practice of the Noble Path or if it benefits one's fellow members of the order. This does not mean that monks are encouraged to own possessions. Insofar as it is allowable by the *vinaya,* or monastic code, gain is justifiable if the possessions belong to the *sangha* or the community. But if a monk is rich in personal possessions, it is evidence of his greed and attachment and therefore he cannot be said to conform to Buddhist principles. The right practice is to own nothing except the basic requisites of life. Here the question is not one of being rich or poor, but of having few personal cares, easy mobility, the spirit of contentment, and few wishes, and as the monk's life is dependent for material sustenance on other people, of making oneself easy to support. With high mobility and almost no personal cares, monks can devote most of their time and energy to their work, whether for their individual perfection or for the social good. Thus, it is contentment and paucity of wishes accompanied by commitment to the development of good and the abandonment of evil that is praised. Even contentment and paucity of wishes are to be qualified, that is, they must be accompanied by effort and diligence, and not by passivity and idleness. In other words, for a monk it can be good to gain many possessions, but not to own or hoard them. It is good rather to gain much and to give it away.

The above conclusions have been drawn from such sayings in the Pāli canon as:

> Monks, possessed of five qualities the way of an elder monk is to the advantage of many folk, for the happiness of many folk, for the good of many folk; it is to the advantage and happiness of devas and man. Of what five?
>
> There is the elder, time-honored and long gone forth; well-known, renowned, with a great following of householders and those gone forth; a receiver of the requisites: the robe, alms, lodging, and medicaments for sickness; who is learned, has a retentive and well-stored mind, and those Dhammas, lovely . . . are by him fully understood

From Phra Rajavaramuni, "Foundations of Buddhist Social Ethics," in *Ethics, Wealth, and Salvation: A Study in Buddhist Social Ethics,* ed. Russell F. Sizemore and Donald K. Swearer (Columbia: University of South Carolina Press, 1990), pp. 40-47.

in theory; and he is a right viewer with an unperverted vision. He turns away many folk from what is not the true Dhamma and sets them in the true Dhamma. . . .(A.III.115)

Four Ariyan lineages; herein, brethren, a monk is content with whatever robes [he may have], commends contentment of this kind, and does not try to gain robes in improper, unsuitable ways. And he is not dismayed if he gain no robe, but when he has gained one, he is not greedy, nor infatuated, nor overwhelmed. Seeing the danger therein and understanding its object he makes use of it. Yet does he not exalt himself because of his contentment with any robes, nor does he disparage others. Whoso, brethren, is skilled herein, not slothful, but mindful and helpful, this monk is one who stands firm in the primeval, ancient Ariyan lineage. Then, again, the monk is content with whatever almsfood . . . with whatever lodging. . . . Lastly, brethren, the monk delights in abandoning [evil] and delights in developing [good]. . . . (D.III.224; A.II.27)

Furthermore, brethren, he is content with whatever necessaries, whether it be robes, alms, lodging, medicines, and provision against sickness. Furthermore, brethren, he is continually stirring up effort to eliminate bad qualities, making dogged and vigorous progress in good things, never throwing off the burden. (D.III.266, 290; A.V.23)

The monk is content with a robe sufficient to protect the body, with almsfood enough for his belly's need. Wherever he may go he just takes these with him. Just as, for instance, a bird upon the wing, wherever he may fly, just flies with the load of his wings. (E.g., A.II.209)

Monks, this holy life is not lived to cheat or cajole people. It is not for getting gain, profit, or notoriety. It is not concerned with a flood of gossip nor with the idea of "let folk know me as so-and-so." Nay, monks, this holy life is lived for the sake of self-restraint, of abandoning [evil], of dispassionateness, of the cessation of suffering. (A.II.24)

Monks, these four qualities are according to the true Dhamma. What four? Regard for the true Dhamma, not for wrath; regard for the true Dhamma, not for hypocrisy; regard for the true Dhamma, not for gain; regard for the true Dhamma, not for honors. (A.II.47, 84)

Harsh, monks, is gain, honor, and fame, severe and rough, being a stumbling block to the attainment of the supreme safety [of Nibbāna]. Therefore, monks, let you train yourselves: we shall let go the arisen gain, honor, and fame, and the arisen gain, honor, and fame will not stand overwhelming our minds. . . .

For one whether being honored or not whose collected mind does not waver, him the wise call a worthy man. (S.II.232)

One is the road that leads to wealth, another the road that leads to Nibbāna. If the Bhikkhu, the disciple of the Buddha, has learnt this, he will not yearn for honor, he will foster solitude. (Dh.75)

Wealth destroys the foolish, though not those who search for the Goal. (Dh. 355)

For the laity, as mentioned earlier, there is no instance in which poverty is encouraged. On the contrary, many Pāli passages exhort lay people to seek and amass wealth in a rightful way. Among the advantages or good results of good *karma*, one is to be wealthy. What is blamed as evil in connection with wealth is to earn it in a dishonest and unlawful way. Worthy of blame also is the one who, having earned wealth, becomes enslaved through clinging and attachment to it and incurs suffering because of it. No less evil and blameworthy than the unlawful earning of wealth is to accumulate riches and, out of stinginess, not to spend them for the benefit and well-being of oneself, one's dependents, and other people. Again, it is also evil if one squanders wealth foolishly or indulgently or uses it to cause suffering to other people:

And what, Ujjaya, is achievement of diligence? Herein, by whatsoever activity a clansman make his living, whether by the plough, by trading or by cattle-herding, by archery or in royal service, or by any of the crafts — he is deft and tireless; gifted with an inquiring turn of mind into ways and means, he is able to arrange and carry out his job. This is called achievement of diligence. (A.IV.285)

And what is the bliss of wealth? Herein, housefather, a clansman by means of wealth acquired by energetic striving, amassed by strength of arm, won by sweat, lawful and lawfully gotten, both enjoys his wealth and does good deeds therewith. (A.II.68)

Herein, housefather, with the wealth acquired by energetic striving . . . and lawfully gotten, the Ariyan disciple makes himself happy and cheerful, he rightly contrives happiness, and makes his mother and father, his children and wife, his servants and workmen, his friends and comrades cheerful and happy, he rightly contrives happiness. This, housefather, is the first opportunity seized by him, turned to merit and fittingly made use of. (A.II.67; cf. A.III.45)

Monks, if people knew, as I know the ripening of sharing gifts, they would not enjoy their use without sharing them, nor would the taint of stinginess stand obsessing the heart. Even if it were their last bit, their last morsel of food, they would not enjoy its use without sharing it, if there were anyone to receive it. (It.18)

> Like waters fresh lying in savage region
> Where none can drink, running to waste
> and barren,
> Such is the wealth gained by a man
> of base mind.
> On self he spends nothing, nor aught
> he gives.
> The wise, the strong-minded, who has
> won riches,
> He useth them, thereby fulfills his duties.
> His troop of kin fostering, noble-hearted,
> blameless, at death faring to
> heav'nly mansion.
>
> (S.I.90)

The misers do not go to heaven; fools do not praise liberality. (Dh.177)

Thus, good and praiseworthy wealthy people are those who seek wealth in a rightful way and use it for the good and happiness of both themselves and others. Accordingly, the Buddha's lay disciples, being wealthy, liberally devoted much or most of their wealth to the support of the *sangha* and to the alleviation of the suffering and poverty of others. For example, the millionaire Anātha-piṇḍika is said in the Commentary on the *Dhammapada* to have spent a large amount of money every day to feed hundreds of monks as well as hundreds of the poor. Of course, in an ideal society under an able and righteous ruler or under

a righteous and effective administration, there will be no poor people, as all people will be at least self-sufficient, and monks will be the only community set apart by intention to be sustained with the material surplus of the lay society.

A true Buddhist lay person not only seeks wealth lawfully and spends it for the good, but also enjoys spiritual freedom, not being attached to it, infatuated with or enslaved by that wealth. At this point the mundane and the transmundane intersect. The Buddha classifies lay people or the enjoyers of sense-pleasure into various classes according to lawful and unlawful means of seeking wealth, the spending or not spending of wealth for the good and happiness of oneself or others and for the performing of good deeds, and the attitude of greed and attachment or wisdom and spiritual freedom in dealing with wealth. The last, which the Buddha calls the best, the greatest, and the noblest, is praiseworthy in four respects. Such a person enjoys life on both the mundane and the transmundane planes as follows:

Mundane

1. Seeking wealth lawfully and unarbitrarily,
2. Making oneself happy and cheerful,
3. Sharing with others and doing meritorious deeds.

Transmundane

4. Making use of one's wealth without greed and longing, without infatuation, heedful of danger and possessed of the insight that sustains spiritual freedom.

This person is indeed an Ariyan or Noble Disciple, that is, one who has made great progress toward individual perfection. Of much significance, moreover is the compatibility between the mundane and the transmundane spheres of life which combine to form the integral whole of Buddhist ethics in which the transmundane acts as the completing part.

In spite of its great ethical utility, however, too much importance should not be given to wealth. The limitation of its utility in relation to the realization of the goal of *nibbāna*, furthermore, should also be recognized. Though on the mundane level poverty is something to be avoided, a poor person is not deprived of all means to act for the good of himself or herself and for the good of society. The ten ways of doing good or making merit begin with giving, but they also include moral conduct, the development of mental qualities and wisdom, the rendering of services, and the teaching of the *dhamma*. Because of poverty, people may be too preoccupied with the mere struggle for survival and thus cannot do anything for their own perfection. They may even cause trouble to society and difficulty for other people in their effort toward their own perfection. But when basic living needs are satisfied, if one is mentally qualified and makes the effort, nothing can hinder one from realizing one's individual perfection. Wealth as a resource for achieving the social good can help create favorable circumstances for realizing individual perfection, but ultimately it is mental maturity and wisdom, not wealth that bring about the realization of this perfection. Wealth mistreated and misused not only obstructs individual development, but can also be detrimental to the social good. A wealthy man can do much more either for the better or for the worse of the social good than a poor man. The wealth of a good man is also the wealth of the society. It is, therefore, conducive to the social good and thus becomes a resource for all the members of that society. In other words, acquiring wealth is acceptable if, at the same time, it promotes the well-being of a community or society. But if one's wealth grows at the expense of the well-being of the community, that wealth is harmful and becomes a problem to be overcome. If personal wealth is not the wealth of society and is not conducive to the social good, the society may have to seek other means of ownership and distribution of wealth to ensure the social good and the resourcefulness of wealth for both individual development and perfection of all members of the society.

In short, the Buddhist attitude toward wealth is the same as that toward power, fame, and honor. This is clearly expressed in the words of the great Buddhist king, Aśoka, in his Edict X, "King Piyadorshi, the beloved of the gods, does not consider prestige and glory as of any great meaning unless he desires prestige and glory for this purpose, that people may attend to the teaching of the *dhamma* and that they may abide by the practices of the *dhamma*."

Zen and the Economic Animal

Yamamoto Shichihei

The effect of a man's thought on later generations, especially when it is progressive or highly original, is rarely what he expects it will be. Were Jesus to visit the Vatican today and see the mammoth institution that has grown from the seeds of his teaching, he might well disavow it. If Karl Marx could inspect the "Gulag Archipelago" and if he were told that its facilities are the product of his thinking, he would not hesitate to separate himself from it entirely. The same is true of religious reformers. If John Calvin were shown America's capitalistic society and informed that it is the fruit of the Protestant ethic, he would probably be rendered speechless. A thought system functions in a variety of ways at a certain time within a given social context, but society itself does not change in exact conformity with the directions of that thought. Yet among the thinker's original ideas, one can often identify the seeds of later social change.

In this issue we will examine the thinking of the man whom I see as most directly responsible for the development of capitalism in Japan, Suzuki Shōsan (1579-1655). No doubt Shōsan also would be dumbfounded to hear himself labeled the father of Japanese capitalism. Certainly he did not foresee present-day Japanese society, or even the flourishing merchant culture of the Genroku and Kyōhō periods (1688-1735). Had someone explained to that staid Zen monk the effect his thought would have on Japanese society, surely he

Yamamoto Shichihei, "Zen and the Economic Animal," *Entrepreneurship: The Japanese Experience* 5 (March 1983): 1-7.

would have been appalled. Some of his followers today might take exception as well.

Unique Zen Philosopher

. . . A samurai from Mikawa (present-day Aichi prefecture), Shōsan was a retainer of Tokugawa Ieyasu, and he took part in the fighting that brought nearly three centuries of civil war to a close and led to the establishment of the Tokugawa shogunate. After peace was restored, Shōsan worked for a time as a shogunate official in Osaka. Then in 1620, for reasons known only to himself, he suddenly took the tonsure. He was aware that his action violated shogunate law and that the authorities might expropriate his entire assets and discontinue the family line, ordering him to commit ritual suicide. Fortunately they did not, and Shōsan lived to the ripe old age of 77 as a Zen monk, and a most extraordinary one at that.

. . . A large segment of the population had lost sight of their reason for living; . . . society in Shōsan's day had to adjust to peace after years of civil war. Certainly many people welcomed peace: even samurai, to some extent, had had enough of civil disorder, but the establishment of a peaceful social order deprived the warrior of his raison d'être. Gone were the days when a peasant might rise to the foremost position of power through his martial exploits, as Toyotomi Hideyoshi had done. After the third shogun, Iemitsu, it was clear that a coup d'état against the shogunate was out of the question. Many samurai remained thwarted, feeling useless. It may be that a sense of frustration prompted Shōsan to become a priest. How to resolve the contradiction — to find a reason for living in a new social environment — was the challenge Shōsan and others of his generation faced.

The biggest problem one encounters when dealing with a Japanese thinker is the lack of systematization of his ideas. Christianity has a systematic, organized theology, enabling one to consider the interrelation of religion and society within the theme of Christian social ethics. But in the case of Zen, there is no such systematic "theology," or body of religious thought. Organization is anathema to Zen.

Strangely enough, we find in the writings of Shōsan something like a systematic Zen "theology" as well as a corresponding Zen social ethic. Shōsan once remarked, "I would like to see the world governed by Buddhist laws." Though he took Buddhist orders, he by no means abandoned the world, but remained keenly interested in politics and society throughout his life. On this point alone we must surely call him a unique Zen thinker.

Perhaps the reason for the systematic approach in Shōsan's thinking is the fact that he was an anti-Christian ideologue, which is clear from his work *Hakirishitan* [Debunking the Christian Myth], partly a Zen rebuttal to Christian teachings. To challenge another philosophical system, there is no choice but to turn the logic in it against itself. To do that, you must arrange your own argument in contraposition to the other.

The Buddhist Trinity

In *Hakirishitan*, Shōsan defines the essence of the cosmos as the Buddha. This Buddha-nature cannot be seen or perceived, but it possesses three "virtues" that affect mankind, thus attesting to its existence. The three virtues he calls the Moon, the Heart, and the Great Healing King, by which he refers to three aspects of the Buddha, not three separate buddhas. His conceptualization clearly corresponds to Trinitarianism.

The Moon stands for the cosmos, the natural order. In the same way that a reflection of the moon's essence dwells within a drop of water, the Moon, the natural order, resides within every person's heart. This is the virtue of the Heart. Since humans are a part of the cosmos, their nature conforms to the cosmic order, and they need merely do as the heart commands. Naturally the concept of a holistic order is not Shōsan's alone; it is found in medieval Christian thought and in the doctrines of Chu-tzû. It is one of the fundamental ideas in the intellectual history of mankind.

If every man has a Buddha-nature, there ought to be no war, no crime, no injustice; all people should behave like buddhas. Why, then, did Japan suffer through nearly three hundred years of civil war? That is a question that preoccupied all Japanese thinkers of Shōsan's day. In Shōsan's opinion, the mind, like the body, fell victim to disease. All grief, he believed, was caused by three "poisons": greed, anger, and discontent. The mind's illnesses could be treated by the Great Healing King; to beg for a cure was to demonstrate one's faith. And if all people were cured and lived in accordance with the dictates of the Heart, there would be no more war and all social problems would disappear. They would live together harmoniously as living buddhas in a utopian society.

In Shōsan's view, to build a good society the heart of man first had to be protected from the three poisons. That required one to "become a buddha," by which he meant to live in accordance with the dictates of the Heart. One had to engage in ascetic exercise, that is, Buddhist practice, to live that way, but how? Unlike priests, who were free to spend their days in ascetic practice, the average person had to work hard and steadily just to earn a living. How could they be saved? Shōsan's answer: everyday labor was Buddhist practice if performed with the right intention. With this conception as a base, he formulated what must be called a Zen social ethic, a concrete guide to how man ought to live. As such, its effect reached far beyond the sphere of religion to affect the whole of secular society.

Work Equals Asceticism

Shōsan presents his social ethic in *Shimin nichiyō* [Daily Life for the Four Classes]. Like Baigan's *Tohi mondō*, it is written in question and answer form. Representatives of each class — samurai, farmer, artisan, and merchant — ask Shōsan how they ought to live, and he explains. *Shimin nichiyō* was later combined with *Sanbō Tokuyō* [The Three Precious Virtues] to form the work entitled *Banmin tokuyō* [Virtues of All], which Shōsan's disciple Keichū called his most important tract. It is possible that Shōsan became a monk so that he could spread the teachings embodied in this work. Since I believe *Shimin nichiyō* is the key to understanding Shōsan's philosophy, let us briefly examine its content.

In the section on farmers, a peasant asks, "We are taught that the next life (life after death) is important and that we should not spare ourselves

in Buddhist practice, but farm work keeps us so busy we do not have any time for practice. How unfair it seems that simply because we have to make a living through menial labor, we are destined to waste this life and suffer in the next. How can we attain Buddhahood?" Shōsan's answer is admirably clear: agricultural labor is Buddhist practice. It is a mistake, he says, to take time out from one's labor to pray for rebirth in Paradise. Agricultural labor itself is ascetic exercise.

You must toil in extremes of heat and cold, spade, hoe, and sickle in hand. Your mind and body overgrown with the thicket of desire is your enemy. Torture yourself — plow, reap — work with all your heart. . . . When one is unoccupied, the thicket of desire grows, but when he toils, subjecting his mind and body to pain, his heart is at peace. In this way he is engaged in Buddhist practice all the time. Why should a peasant long for another road to Buddhahood?

A peasant who followed Shōsan's advice was far more exalted than the most virtuous of priests, since priests did almost no work at all. It was a question of the frame of mind in which one worked, not the kind of work one did.

If a farmer treats his work as asceticism, not only will he achieve Buddhahood but society will be purified. Shōsan explains it like this:

Your birth as a farmer is Heaven's gift to the world, your mission being to nurture the world's people. Therefore, give yourself wholeheartedly to the way of Heaven with no thought for yourself. Serve Heaven through your farm labors. Celebrate the gods and buddhas by raising the five grains, and save the people. Make a solemn vow to administer even to insects. Chant *namu Amida butsu* with each stroke of your hoe. Work earnestly, and with each stroke of your sickle your fields will be purified. The five grains will then become pure food that will work as medicine to extinguish the desires of those who eat it.

In Shōsan's thinking, to work with all one's heart led to enlightenment and to freedom from all earthly constraints, making one a living buddha. Work itself was ascetic practice. This concept forms the basis of Shōsan's social ethic.

Japanese Religiosity

Next an artisan poses the following question. "I am busy every minute of the day in an effort to earn my livelihood. How can I become a buddha?" Shōsan answers:

> All occupations are Buddhist practice; through work we are able to attain Buddhahood. There is no calling that is not Buddhist. All is for the good of the world. . . . The all-encompassing Buddha-nature manifest in us all works for the world's good: without artisans, such as the blacksmith, there would be no tools; without officials there would be no order in the world; without farmers there would be no food; without merchants we would suffer inconvenience. All the other occupations as well are for the good of the world. . . . All reveal the blessing of the Buddha. Those who are ignorant of the blessing of our Buddha-nature, who do not value themselves and their innate Buddha-nature and fall into evil ways of thinking and behaving, have lost their way.

Since all human beings possess a Buddha-nature, to become buddhas,

> Above all you must believe in yourself. If you truly desire to become a buddha, just believe in yourself. Believing in yourself is believing in the Buddha, for the Buddha is in you. The Buddha has no desires, its heart contains no anger, no discontent, no life nor death . . . no right or wrong . . . no passions . . . no evil. . . .

Finally he says, "Believe with all your heart. Believe." Faith to Shōsan was faith in oneself; there is no absolute, monotheistic god in Shōsan's conception. Yet his exhortation to believe in oneself was not, of course, a defense of vanity.

An understanding of Shōsan's approach to religion gives us valuable insight into modern Japanese society. It is commonly asserted that the Japanese are not a religious people, but that is shockingly untrue. Only the nature of our faith differs from that of Christians or Moslems. In Japan it is the buddha of the Heart rather than God in whom one believes and to whom one is held accountable for his actions. A Japanese can say he has lost faith in God and society will pay little attention, but let him say he has lost faith in himself and he will find that he has lost his credentials as a member of society, just as an apostate Christian or Moslem would elsewhere. In either case society is understandably suspicious of one who believes he cannot be held accountable for his actions.

Japanese themselves are guilty of perpetuating the myth that they are not religious. From the middle of the Tokugawa period, Confucian influence strongly colored the daily vocabulary. Then in the early Meiji period there arose an anti-Buddhist movement which led the government to order all Buddhist expressions deleted from the state-controlled textbooks. For that reason Japanese no longer appreciate the religious meaning of the words they use. Expressions people use all the time, such as "I must have been out of my mind" (*Jibun ga shinjirarenai*, lit., "I cannot believe myself") or "To be honest with you" (*Honshin dewa*, lit., "In my heart of hearts"), are actually expressions of religious ideas. Because Japanese are not aware of the religious implications of the words they use, they do not see how deeply religion is still a part of their life and thought.

Pilgrim's Progress

The next section of *Shimin nichiyō* describes how merchants ought to live. In countries everywhere, merchants tend to be regarded with condescension or disfavor. In Tokugawa Japan, that tendency was especially strong, particularly among samurai. Shōsan, however, does not show the least contempt for commerce or the merchants who practice it.

In Shōsan's view, "Commerce is the function Heaven has assigned to those whose job it is to promote freedom throughout the country." Today we use the word "freedom" in a variety of ways, tending to forget that one basic freedom is the free access to goods. Without the distribution of goods through commerce our freedom would be impaired in countless ways. Far from holding merchants in contempt, Shōsan valued them for the vital function they perform. Considering the time in which he lived and his samurai origins, Shōsan's enlightened thinking was unusual indeed.

While Shōsan considers commerce, like all occupations, to be a godly activity, he does not value commerce in itself as much as the way it is performed — whether or not it is performed as Buddhist practice. A merchant asks, "I ceaselessly pursue my humble trade in hopes of realizing a profit, but to my great regret I will never be able to achieve Buddhahood. Please tell me the way." In his answer, Shōsan would by no means deny the merchant his profit, but he urges him first to cultivate through asceticism the sort of attitude that will bring about profits: an unbendable commitment to honesty.

Honesty is an essential element in Shōsan's philosophy. If as a merchant you realize that your job is to bring freedom to the nation and unfailingly "pursue your calling with honesty, just as fire burns and water flows downhill, so the blessings of Heaven will follow and your every wish will be fulfilled." Yet one must not delight in realizing a profit. Such behavior Shōsan calls "illusory goodness." To be content only after taking a profit encourages vanity and is sure to lead one into evil ways. Real goodness is nonillusory; one must engage in commerce with no illusions.

Shōsan provides the following concrete advice for merchants:

Throw yourself headlong into worldly activity. For the sake of the nation and its citizens, send the goods of your province to other provinces, and bring the products of other provinces into your own. Travel around the country to distant parts to bring people what they desire. Your activity is an ascetic exercise that will cleanse you of all impurities. Challenge your mind and body by crossing mountain ranges. Purify your heart by fording rivers. When your ship sets sail on the boundless sea, lose yourself in prayer to the Buddha. If you understand that this life is but a trip through an evanescent world, and if you cast aside all attachments and desires and work hard, Heaven will protect you, the goods will bestow their favor, and your profits will be exceptional. You will become a person of wealth and virtue and care nothing for riches. Finally you will develop an unshakable faith; you will be engaged in meditation around the clock.

To achieve Buddhahood a merchant must travel around the provinces distributing goods as if on a pilgrimage.

Zen Social Ethic

In Shōsan's conception, then, worldly labor is religious asceticism, and if one pursues a calling — any calling — with singleminded devotion one can become a buddha. This is Shōsan's cardinal principle. Agriculture is Buddhist practice: by earnestly working the land, not only does a peasant become a buddha himself, but the whole society is purified. If an artisan devotes himself to his calling, goods will be produced in limitless quantity for the benefit of the world. This, too, is the blessing of the Buddha, and the artisans possess a Buddha-nature. Merchants, by satisfying the demand for goods, bring comfort and convenience to the populace while achieving Buddhahood for themselves. In the section, "The Desire for Asceticism, the Virtue or the Three Treasures, and Everyday Life for the Samurai" he sums it up: "Since secular law is Buddhist law . . . it is reasonable that by following worldly law you can attain Buddhahood. . . . If you fail to use worldly law to attain Buddhahood then you know nothing of the will of the Buddha. It is your will that changes secular law into Buddhist law."

Shōsan's concept is truly unique, yet it is based on Zen. Among samurai of the time swordsmanship and Zen were considered one and the same. A samurai continually polished his skill with the sword, not to increase his ability to fight but because it was considered a form of Zen asceticism. Shōsan's genius was in expanding this concept to the other three classes. As such, his philosophy might be called a Zen social ethic based on systematic Zen "theology."

The times in which Shōsan lived surely played a part in the formation of his thinking. As explained above, society had moved from a time of civil disorder to one of peace and stability. Although order had been established and the people lived in peace, they were forced to abandon glorious dreams of great achievements and riches. As society gradually settled into the firm pattern of four classes, many people lost sight of their reason for living. Shōsan sought to resolve their distress by finding a spiritual meaning in everyday labor, and to that end, he expounded his ideas widely. He said that he wished to conquer the world with Buddhist law; his immediate goal was the establishment of a system based on the social ethic described above. He envisioned his social ethic becoming a basis for order, a sort of national morality by which people would achieve a spiritual, even religious satisfaction.

Shōsan's ideas are strikingly modern. Today it is easy to see how they could change attitudes toward work and provide an ethos for capitalism in Japan. Still, his philosophy has functioned in a variety of ways depending on the demands of the time. It can be interpreted as an affirmation of secular society, as was the philosophy of John Calvin, and that is exactly what happened. Shōsan argued that secular law was Buddhist law, but society interpreted his words to mean that Buddhist law was secular law.

Economic Animals or Zen Ascetics?

Today we still instinctually sense that it is wrong to seek profit, but that profits which naturally result from labor are acceptable, and this idea derives from Shōsan. For example, a department store will say in its advertisements, "Through and through, we are here to serve you." The founder/owner of a leading electronics maker is often quoted as saying that he never once worked to make a profit for his company, but that every effort he made throughout his career was to provide people with electrical and electronic products as cheaply as tapwater. Of course one might argue that if a business did nothing but serve society it would go broke in short order, and that companies are in business to make a profit: if they were not, they would not last long in the competitive business world of Japan. But that misses the point.

If one followed Shōsan's philosophy, however, he would conclude that because the department store was determined to provide the best service it could to its customers, it made a profit; were it to seek profits it would not only fail to realize them but might even go bankrupt. Because the electronics maker followed the dictates of the Heart, he was able to produce goods that benefited the world, and in the process he realized a profit. In Shōsan's words, "Those who care nothing for the people but think only of profit incur the wrath of Heaven, meet with misfortune, and are despised by all. If you do not love and respect everyone you will fail in everything you do." To apply Shōsan's

advice and make Buddhist law the law of the world is the best business practice.

The same attitude is shared by Japanese salesmen abroad. Someone once remarked that Japanese salesmen trekking through the wilds of Africa look for all the world like pilgrims. In a sense they are pilgrims. They are following Shōsan's admonition to treat commerce as an ascetic exercise, like a pilgrimage. They are like Muslims making their way to Mecca, except that unlike the latter, their pilgrimage will bring their company a profit.

Zen enjoys tremendous popularity in the West these days. When I travel abroad I often find myself deluged with questions. To foreigners, Zen is mysterious and obscure, the very essence of the exotic East. Whenever I am asked to explain Zen, I reply that to understand Zen one should study Japan's large trading houses. I then proceed to describe Shōsan's *Shimin nichiyō*, explaining that to Japanese work is not an economic activity, but Zen ascetic exercise. I say that this spirit is behind Japan's image as a land of "economic animals." My listeners are always amazed. They never dreamed that the influence of Zen is still so pervasive, any more than the average American is consciously aware of the ubiquitous presence of Puritan traditions in his own society. It is the same in every society; a people's intellectual heritage is transformed in various ways in response to conditions, but remains fundamentally unchanged.

Despite the strong religious coloring of Japanese society, we might be said to be anti-clerical. Shōsan's writings contain numerous statements critical of the priesthood as being unproductive. Indeed, if work itself is religious practice, what need has society for priests? Japanese respect one who exhibits a religious attitude toward work, yet they look askance at priests, and this attitude contributes to the mistaken impression that Japanese are an irreligious people. Since a person not engaged in productive labor is not engaged in ascetic exercise, Japanese regard him with the same suspicion as some Westerners do an atheist. For this reason Japanese dread retirement, an attitude that contrasts sharply with that of many Americans, who eagerly await retirement as a time of liberation.

Once, the Japanese penchant for work was attributed to the country's poverty. The fallacy of that theory is clear enough today, when Japan ranks among the world's most prosperous nations. If poverty made a people into hard workers, then the majority of the world's population ought to work far more diligently than Japanese. A religious attitude toward work, not poverty, is behind Japan's economic success.

When we have developed our economy sufficiently we will seek the way of the Buddha in other pursuits. No matter how we do it, we will continue to seek the way. And, as always, the inability to find it will be our source of greatest pain. It is this contradiction that gives rise to debate on the meaning of life. Shōsan's writings, too, reflect the same kind of philosophical considerations.

Shōsan's thought is an original Japanese philosophy developed during the Tokugawa period, when the people fashioned an independent social system with their own hands. Of course society did not develop along the lines that Shōsan envisioned. If he were shown Japanese society today and told that it is the result of his thinking, he might explode in anger. Nonetheless, there is no denying that his thought has lived on and has functioned in various ways. Let us summarize the basis of that thought.

The human heart and society must conform with the natural order. That requires all to follow the dictates of the Heart, that is, the cosmic order within oneself. Impediments to following the Heart are the three poisons. To protect oneself from them, one must follow the Great Healing King and observe the established law of health, which calls on everyone to believe that his occupation is Buddhist practice and engage in it wholeheartedly. Work should be undertaken with an honest attitude. If everyone works diligently with this attitude, society, the sum of its individual parts, becomes a buddha. At the same time, the products of that labor benefit society, and to distribute goods as if one were on a pilgrimage is to liberate everyone. Finally, a correspondence between the individual heart, society, and the cosmos will be achieved, people will enjoy spiritual satisfaction, and society will be free from disorder.

Buddhist Economics

E. F. Schumacher

"Right livelihood" is one of the requirements of the Buddha's Noble Eightfold Path. It is clear, therefore, that there must be such a thing as Buddhist economics.

Buddhist countries have often stated that they wish to remain faithful to their heritage. So Burma: "The New Burma sees no conflict between religious values and economic progress. Spiritual health and material well-being are not enemies: they are natural allies." Or: "We can blend successfully the religious and spiritual values of our heritage with the benefits of modern technology." Or: "We Burmans have a sacred duty to conform both our dreams and our acts to our faith. This we shall ever do."

All the same, such countries invariably assume that they can model their economic development plans in accordance with modern economics, and they call upon modern economists from so-called advanced countries to advise them, to formulate the policies to be pursued, and to construct the grand design for development, the Five-Year Plan or whatever it may be called. No one seems to think that a Buddhist way of life would call for Buddhist economics, just as the modern materialist way of life has brought forth modern economics.

Economists themselves, like most specialists, normally suffer from a kind of metaphysical blindness, assuming that theirs is a science of absolute and invariable truths, without any presuppositions. Some go as far as to claim that economic

From E. F. Schumacher, *Small Is Beautiful* (New York: Harper & Row, 1973), an excerpt adapted for *Parabola: The Magazine of Myth and Tradition* 16 (Spring 1991): 63-68.

laws are as free from "metaphysics" or "values" as the law of gravitation. We need not, however, get involved in arguments of methodology. Instead, let us take some fundamentals and see what they look like when viewed by a modern economist and a Buddhist economist.

There is universal agreement that a fundamental source of wealth is human labor. Now, the modern economist has been brought up to consider "labor" or work as little more than a necessary evil. From the point of view of the employer, it is in any case simply an item of cost to be reduced to a minimum if it cannot be eliminated altogether, say, by automation. From the point of view of the workman it is a "disutility"; to work is to make a sacrifice of one's leisure and comfort, and wages are a kind of compensation for the sacrifice. Hence the ideal from the point of view of the employer is to have output without employees, and the ideal from the point of view of the employee is to have income without employment.

The consequences of these attitudes both in theory and in practice are, of course, extremely far-reaching. If the ideal with regard to work is to get rid of it, every method that "reduces the work load" is a good thing. The most potent method, short of automation, is the so-called "division of labor" and the classical example is the pin factory eulogized in Adam Smith's *Wealth of Nations*. Here it is not a matter of ordinary specialization, which mankind has practiced from time immemorial, but of dividing up every complete process of production into minute parts, so that the final product can be produced at great speed without anyone having had to contribute more than a totally insignificant and, in most cases, unskilled movement of his limbs.

The Buddhist point of view takes the function of work to be at least threefold: to give man a chance to utilize and develop his faculties; to enable him to overcome his ego-centeredness by joining with other people in a common task; and to bring forth the goods and services needed for a becoming existence. Again, the consequences that flow from this view are endless. To organize work in such a manner that it becomes meaningless, boring, stultifying, or nerve-racking for the worker would be little short of criminal; it would indicate a greater concern with goods than with people, an evil lack of compassion and a soul-destroying degree of attachment to the most primitive side of this worldly existence. Equally, to strive for leisure as an alternative to work would be considered a complete misunderstanding of one of the basic truths of human existence, namely that work and leisure are complementary parts of the same living process and cannot be separated without destroying the joy of work and the bliss of leisure.

From the Buddhist point of view, there are therefore two types of mechanization which must be clearly distinguished: one that enhances a man's skill and power and one that turns the work of man over to a mechanical slave, leaving man in a position of having to serve the slave. How to tell the one from the other? "The craftsman himself," says Ananda Coomaraswamy, a man equally competent to talk about the modern West as the ancient East, "can always, if allowed to, draw the delicate distinction between the machine and the tool. The carpet loom is a tool, a contrivance for holding warp threads at a stretch for the pile to be woven round them by the craftmen's fingers; but the power loom is a machine, and its significance as a destroyer of culture lies in the fact that it does the essentially human part of the work." It is clear, therefore that Buddhist economics must be very different from the economics of modern materialism, since the Buddhist sees the essence of civilization not in a multiplication of wants but in the purification of human character. Character, at the same time, is formed primarily by a man's work. And work, properly conducted in conditions of human dignity and freedom, blesses those who do it and equally their products. The Indian philosopher and economist J. C. Kumarappa sums the matter up as follows:

> If the nature of the work is properly appreciated and applied, it will stand in the same relation to the higher faculties as food is to the physical body. It nourishes and enlivens the higher man and urges him to produce the best he is capable of. It directs his free will along the proper course and disciplines the animal in him into progressive channels. It furnishes an excellent background for man to display his scale of values and develop his personality.

If a man has no chance of obtaining work he is in a desperate position, not simply because he lacks an income but because he lacks this nourishing and enlivening factor of disciplined work which nothing can replace. A modern economist may engage in highly sophisticated calculations on whether full employment "pays" or whether it might be more "economic" to run an economy at less than full employment so as to ensure a greater mobility of labor, a better stability of wages, and so forth. His fundamental criterion of success is simply the total quantity of goods produced during a given period of time. "If the marginal urgency of goods is low," says Professor Galbraith in *The Affluent Society,* "then so is the urgency of employing the last man or the last million men in the labor force." And again:

> If . . . we can afford some unemployment in the interest of stability — a proposition, incidentally, of impeccably conservative antecedents — then we can afford to give those who are unemployed the goods that enable them to sustain their accustomed standard of living.

From a Buddhist point of view, this is standing the truth on its head by considering goods as more important than people and consumption as more important than creative activity. It means shifting the emphasis from the worker to the product of work, that is, from the human to the subhuman, a surrender to the forces of evil. The very start of Buddhist economic planning would be a planning for full employment, and the primary purpose of this would in fact be employment for everyone who needs an "outside" job: it would not be the maximization of employment nor the maximization of production. Women, on the whole, do not need an "outside" job, and the large-scale employment of women in offices or factories would be considered a sign of serious economic failure. In particular, to let mothers of young children work in factories while the children run wild would be as uneconomic in the eyes of a Buddhist economist as the employment of a skilled worker as a soldier in the eyes of a modern economist.

While the materialist is mainly interested in goods, the Buddhist is mainly interested in liberation. But Buddhism is "The Middle Way" and therefore in no way antagonistic to physical well-being. It is not wealth that stands in the way of liberation but the attachment to wealth; not the enjoyment of pleasurable things but the craving for them. The keynote of Buddhist economics, therefore, is simplicity and non-violence. From an economist's point of view, the marvel of the Buddhist way of life is the utter rationality of its pattern — amazingly small means leading to extraordinarily satisfactory results.

For the modern economist this is very difficult to understand. He is used to measuring the "standard of living" by the amount of annual consumption, assuming all the time that a man who consumes more is "better off" than a man who consumes less. A Buddhist economist would consider this approach excessively irrational: since consumption is merely a means to human well-being, the aim should be to obtain the maximum of well-being with the minimum of consumption. Thus, if the purpose of clothing is a certain amount of temperature comfort and an attractive appearance, the task is to attain this purpose with the smallest possible effort, that is, with the smallest annual destruction of cloth and with the help of designs that involve the smallest possible imput of toil. The less toil there is, the more time and strength is left for artistic creativity. It would be highly uneconomic, for instance, to go in for complicated tailoring, like the modern West, when a much more beautiful effect can be achieved by the skillful draping of uncut material. It would be the height of folly to make material so that it should wear out quickly and the height of barbarity to make anything ugly, shabby, or mean. What has just been said about clothing applies equally to all other human requirements. The ownership and the consumption of goods is a means to an end, and Buddhist economics is the systematic study of how to attain given ends with the minimum means.

Modern economics, on the other hand, considers consumption to be the sole end and purpose of all economic activity, taking the factors of production — land, labor and capital — as the means. The former, in short, tries to maximize human satisfactions by the optimal pattern of consumption, while the latter tries to maximize consumption by the optimal pattern of productive effort. It is easy to see that the effort needed to sustain a way of life which seeks to attain the optimal pattern of consumption is likely to be much smaller than the effort needed to sustain a drive for maximum consumption. We need not be surprised, therefore, that the pressure and strain of living is very much less in, say, Burma than it is in the United States, in spite of the fact that the amount of labor-saving machinery used in the former country is only a minute fraction of the amount used in the latter.

Simplicity and non-violence are obviously closely related. The optimal pattern of consumption, producing a high degree of human satisfaction by means of a relatively low rate of consumption, allows people to live without great pressure and strain and to fulfill the primary injunction of Buddhist teaching: "Cease to do evil; try to do good." As physical resources are everywhere limited, people satisfying their needs by means of a modest use of resources are obviously less likely to be at each other's throats than people depending upon a high rate of use. Equally, people who live in highly self-sufficient local communities are less likely to get involved in large-scale violence than people whose existence depends on worldwide systems of trade.

From the point of view of Buddhist economics, therefore, production from local resources for local needs is the most rational way of economic life, while dependence on imports from afar and the consequent need to produce for export to unknown and distant peoples is highly uneconomic and justifiable only in exceptional cases and on a small scale. Just as the modern economist would admit that a high rate of consumption of transport services between a man's home and his place of work signifies a misfortune and not a high standard of life, so the Buddhist economist would hold that to satisfy human wants from faraway sources rather than from sources nearby signifies failure rather than success. The former tends to take statistics showing an increase in the number of ton/miles per head of the population carried by a country's transport system as proof of economic progress, while to the latter — the Buddhist economist — the same statistics would indicate a highly undesirable deterioration in the *pattern* of consumption.

Another striking difference between modern economics and Buddhist economics arises over the use of natural resources. Bertrand de Jouvenel, the eminent French political philosopher, has characterized "Western man" in words which may be taken as a fair description of the modern economist:

He tends to count nothing as an expenditure, other than human effort; he does not seem to mind how much mineral matter he wastes and, far worse, how much living matter he destroys. He does not seem to realize at all that human life is a dependent part of an ecosystem of many different forms of life. As the world is ruled from towns where men are cut off from any form of life other than human, the feeling of belonging to an ecosystem is not revived. This results in a harsh and improvident treatment of things upon which we ultimately depend, such as water and trees.

The teaching of the Buddha, on the other hand, enjoins a reverent and non-violent attitude not only to all sentient beings but also, with great emphasis, to trees. Every follower of the Buddha ought to plant a tree every few years and look after it until it is safely established, and the Buddhist economist can demonstrate without difficulty that the universal observation of this rule would result in a high rate of genuine economic development independent of any foreign aid. Much of the economic decay of Southeast Asia (as of many other parts of the world) is undoubtedly due to a heedless and shameful neglect of trees.

Modern economics does not distinguish between renewable and non-renewable materials, as its very method is to equalize and quantify everything by means of a money price. Thus, taking various alternative fuels, like coal, oil, wood, or water-power: the only difference between them recognized by modern economics is relative cost per equivalent unit. The cheapest is automatically the one to be preferred, as to do otherwise would be irrational and "uneconomic." From a Buddhist point of view of course, this will not do; the essential difference between nonrenewable fuels like coal and oil on the one hand and renewable fuels like wood and water-power on the other cannot be simply overlooked. Nonrenewable goods must be used only if they are indispensable, and then only with the greatest care and the most meticulous concern for conservation. To use them heedlessly or extravagantly is an act of violence, and while complete non-violence may not be attainable on this earth, there is nonetheless an ineluctable duty on man to aim at the ideal of non-violence in all he does.

Just a modern European economist would not consider it a great economic achievement if all European art treasures were sold to America at attractive prices, so the Buddhist economist would insist that a population basing its economic life on nonrenewable fuels is living parasitically, on capital instead of income. Such a way of life could have no permanence and could therefore be justified only as a purely temporary expedient. As the world's resources of nonrenewable fuels — coal, oil and natural gas — are exceedingly unevenly distributed over the globe and undoubtedly limited in quantity, it is clear that their exploitation at an ever-increasing rate is an act of violence against nature which must almost inevitably lead to violence between men.

This fact alone might give food for thought even to those people in Buddhist countries who care nothing for the religious and spiritual values of their heritage and ardently desire to embrace the materialism of modern economics at the fastest possible speed. Before they dismiss Buddhist economics as nothing better than a nostalgic dream, they might wish to consider whether the path of economic development outlined by modern economics is likely to lead them to places where they really want to be.

The Chinese Philosophy

It is not clear that Confucianism is a religion, at least in the Western sense. Confucius speaks little of God, yet he draws much from the wisdom of ancient rulers who observed the Mandate of Heaven (which is also the order of nature and of right behavior in society) and thus governed in accord with virtue. What he draws from ancient sources and teaches his disciples, thus, is at least a profoundly humanist philosophy and an ethic. It has become a classic tradition embodied in a rich set of social rituals that, like a religion, established for China an ideal vision of personal character and a model of civilization.

Confucianism has been attacked by adversaries, both power-hungry warlords and legalists who sought to control society by formal principles. However, many found themselves imitating him if they wanted to gain respect in Asia. Confucianism has also been mixed with other great influences in Chinese history — Taoism with its mystical naturalism and theory of opposites, Mahayana Buddhism with its subtle adaptations of and to Chinese folk traditions, and, more recently, aspects of both Christianity and secular ideologies. The amalgam is known simply as "Chinese religion," and only rarely do people believe one of its parts exclusively. Still, Confucianism emerged after each attack and each mixture as the basic standard for Chinese personal and cultural ethics, and it spread to other cultures — most notably Korea, Japan, Taiwan, and Singapore — where it shaped other traditions with its distinctive teachings.

The two most characteristic teachings that bear on economic life are these: (1) the formation of character and (2) the establishment of right relationship, especially in all the decisive structures of life — parent/child, husband/wife, brother/brother, and ruler/subject. The person of character is loyal, truthful, respectful, diligent, generous, and sincere in all dealings. Superior people manifest a certain mastery of the self, which requires a continuous attention to duty as well as self-control, concern for propriety, and self-cultivation. Inferior people are spontaneous, uncivilized, lazy, unreliable, and out of control. The superior person, Confucius teaches his disciples, understands rightness; the inferior one comprehends only profit. Business activities thus also concern a way of being in the world.

The decisive relationships of life are woven into a great network of connectedness that extends from the nuclear family through an elaborate clan structure to the emperor's palace. All are to obey those above them and are to observe the proper rituals of honor, called "filial piety," for these signify both the right ordering of society and the proper state of mind. This allows the whole to function harmoniously and with decorum.

Critics say that this is authoritarian; but defenders point out that the status of a family or a clan is not hereditary, as in a caste system in India, and that it can be altered by accomplishment and moral behavior. Those moving up and those higher up must deserve the reverence they are due from those below, and their position must be rectified if they are undeserving. The behavior of rulers is assessed according to achievement, propriety, and conscientiousness in regard to society — people are to be appropriately educated, employed, and made content. Those in positions of responsibility are thus accountable both to the Mandate of Heaven and to all those over whom they have authority.

Samples of the ancient "Sayings of Confucius" and the advice of one of the key leaders of the Confucian revival in the eleventh century repre-

400

sent the classic tradition here. Opposition to Confucianism in the name of political realism and formal theory is seen here in the very modern writings by Mao Tse-Tung, who was chief leader of the revolution that established the Republic of China and appeared to destroy Confucian influence in Chinese society. His adaptation of communism to China can, however, be understood, not only as a giant historical event that changed the structure of world economics and inspired radical movements around the world, but also as an attempt at rectification, a calling of leadership to account, within the Confucian tradition.

More recently scholars are raising new questions as to whether or not the Confucian ethic, freed from its temptations to political authoritarianism either by emigration from China or by breaking with other cultural encumbrances through the revolution within China, has produced a new pattern of modernizing economic life, comparable to that of Protestantism in the West. Certainly it seems to have generated an ethic of achievement — apparently more within a clan- and politically-ordered structure than in an independent corporate structure. In any case, Weiming Tu here examines some of the debates about the role of Confucianism in East Asia's recent modernization.

Sayings of Confucius

There were four things that Confucius was determined to eradicate: a biased mind, arbitrary judgments, obstinacy, and egotism.

Confucius said; "Those who know the truth are not up to those who love it; those who love the truth are not up to those who delight in it."

Confucius said: "Having heard the Way (*Tao*) in the morning, one may die content in the evening."

Confucius said; "By nature men are pretty much alike; it is learning and practice that set them apart."

Confucius said: "In education there are no class distinctions."

Confucius said: "The young are to be respected. How do we know that the next generation will not measure up to the present one? . . .

Confucius said: "Shen! My teaching contains one principle that runs through it all." "Yes," replied Tseng Tzu. When Confucius had left the room the disciples asked: "What did he mean?" Tseng Tzu replied: "Our Master's teaching is simply this: loyalty and reciprocity."

Tzu Kung asked: "Is there any one word that can serve as a principle for the conduct of life?" Confucius said: "Perhaps the word 'reciprocity': do not do to others what you would not want others to do to you." . . .

Tzu Chang asked Confucius about humanity. Confucius said: "To be able to practice five virtues everywhere in the world constitutes humanity." Tzu Chang begged to know what these were. Con-

---

Confucius, "Selections from the Analects," in *Sources of Chinese Tradition*, vol. 1, compiled by Wm. T. DeBary et al. (New York: Columbia University Press, 1960), pp. 25-28.

fucius said: "Courtesy, magnanimity, good faith, diligence, and kindness. He who is courteous is not humiliated, he who is magnanimous wins the multitude, he who is of good faith is trusted by the people, he who is diligent attains his objective, and he who is kind can get service from the people."

Confucius said: "Without humanity a man cannot long endure adversity, nor can he long enjoy prosperity. The humane rest in humanity; the wise find it beneficial." . . .

Confucius said: "Riches and honor are what every man desires, but if they can be obtained only by transgressing the right way, they must not be held. Poverty and lowliness are what every man detests, but if they can be avoided only by transgressing the right way, they must not be evaded. If a gentleman departs from humanity, how can he bear the name? Not even for the lapse of a single meal does a gentleman ignore humanity. In moments of haste he cleaves to it: in seasons of peril he cleaves to it."

Confucius said: "The resolute scholar and the humane person will under no circumstance seek life at the expense of humanity. On occasion they will sacrifice their lives to preserve their humanity." . . .

Tzu Hsia asked about filial piety. Confucius said: "The manner is the really difficult thing. When anything has to be done the young people undertake it; when there is wine and food the elders are served — is this all there is to filial piety?"

Confucius said: "In serving his parents, a son may gently remonstrate with them. If he sees that they are not inclined to follow his suggestion, he should resume his reverential attitude but not abandon his purpose. If he is belabored, he will not complain."

The Duke of She observed to Confucius: "Among us there was an upright man called Kung who was so upright that when his father appropriated a sheep, he bore witness against him." Confucius said: "The upright men among us are not like that. A father will screen his son and a son his father — yet uprightness is to be found in that." . . .

Tzu Kung asked about the gentleman. Confucius said: "The gentleman first practices what he preaches and then preaches what he practices."

Confucius said; "The gentleman reaches upward; the inferior man reaches downward."

Confucius said: "The gentleman is always calm and at ease; the inferior man is always worried and full of distress."

Confucius said: "The gentleman understands what is right; the inferior man understands what is profitable."

Confucius said: "The gentleman cherishes virtue; the inferior man cherishes possessions. The gentleman thinks of sanctions; the inferior man thinks of personal favors."

Confucius said: "The gentleman makes demands on himself; the inferior man makes demands on others."

Confucius said: "The gentleman seeks to enable people to succeed in what is good but does not help them in what is evil. The inferior man does the contrary."

Confucius said: "The gentleman seeks to enable people to succeed in what is good but does not help them in what is evil. The inferior man does the contrary."

Confucius said: "The gentleman is broadminded and not partisan; the inferior man is partisan and not broad-minded."

Confucius said: "There are three things that a gentleman fears: he fears the will of Heaven, he fears great men, he fears the words of the sages. The inferior man does not know the will of Heaven and does not fear it, he treats great men with contempt, and he scoffs at the words of the sages." . . .

When Confucius was traveling to Wei, Jan Yu drove him. Confucius observed: "What a dense population!" Jan Yu said: "The people having grown so numerous, what next should be done for them?" "Enrich them," was the reply. "And when one has enriched them, what next should be done?" Confucius said: "Educate them."

Tzu Kung asked above government. Confucius said: "The essentials are sufficient food, sufficient troops and the confidence of the people." Tsu Kung said: "Suppose you were forced to give up one of these three, which would you let go first?" Confucius said: "The troops." Tzu Kung asked again: "If you are forced to give up one of the two remaining, which would you let go?" Confucius said: "Food. For from of old, death has been the lot of all men, but a people without faith cannot survive."

Neo-Confucian Teachings of Ch'eng Hao

Your servant considers that the laws established by the sage-kings were all based on human feelings and in keeping with the order of things. In the great reigns of the Two Emperors and Three Kings, how could these laws not but change according to the times and be embodied in systems which suited the conditions obtaining in each? However, in regard to the underlying basis of government, to the teachings by which the people may be shepherded, to the principles which remain forever unalterable in the order of things, and to that upon which the people depend for their very existence, on such points there has been no divergence but rather common agreement among the sages of all times, early or late. Only if the way of sustaining life itself should fail, could the laws of the sage-kings ever be changed. Therefore in later times those who practiced the Way [of the sage-kings] to the fullest achieved perfect order, while those who practiced only a part achieved limited success. This is the clear and manifest lesson of past ages. . . .

Heaven created men and raised up a ruler to govern and to guide them. Things had to be so regulated as to provide them with settled property as the means to a flourishing livelihood. Therefore the boundaries of the land had to be defined correctly, and the well-fields had to be equally distributed — these are the great fundamentals of government. The T'ang dynasty still maintained a

---

Ch'eng Hao, "Ten Matters Calling for Reform," in *Sources of Chinese Tradition*, vol. 1, compiled by Wm. T. DeBary et al. (New York: Columbia University Press, 1960), pp. 399-403.

system of land distribution based on the size of the family. Now nothing is left, and there is no such system. The lands of the rich extend on and on, from this prefecture to that subprefecture, and there is nothing to stop them. Day by day the poor scatter and die from starvation, and there is no one to take pity on them. Although many people are more fortunate, still there are countless persons without sufficient food and clothing. The population grows day by day, and if nothing is done to control the situation, food and clothing will become more and more scarce, and more people will scatter and die. This is the key to order and disorder. How can we not devise some way to control it? In this matter, too, there is no difference between past and present.

In ancient times, government and education began with the local villages. The system worked up from (the local units of) *pi, lü, tsu, tang, chou, hsiang, tsan,* and *sui.* Each village and town was linked to the next higher unit and governed by them in sequence. Thus the people were at peace, and friendly toward one another. They seldom violated the criminal law, and it was easy to appeal to their sense of shame. This is in accord with the natural bent of human feelings and, therefore, when practiced, it works. In this matter, too, there is no difference between past and present. . . .

In ancient times, government clerks and runners were paid by the state, and there was no distinction between soldiers and farmers. Now the arrogant display of military power has exhausted national resources to the limit. Your servant considers that if the soldiery, with the exception of the Imperial Guards, is not gradually reconverted to a peasant militia, the matter will be of great concern. The services of government clerks and runners have inflicted harm all over the empire; if this system is not changed, a great disaster is inevitable. This is also a truth which is most evident, and there is no difference between the past and the present.

In ancient times, the people had to have [a reserve of] nine years' food supply. A state was not considered a state if it did not have a reserve of at least three years' food. Your servant observes that there are few in the land who grow food and many who consume it. The productivity of the earth is not fully utilized and human labor is not fully employed. Even the rich and powerful families rarely have a surplus; how much worse off are the poor and weak! If in one locality their luck is bad and crops fail just one year, banditry becomes uncontrollable and the roads are full of the faint and starving. If, then, we should be so unfortunate as to have a disaster affecting an area of two or three thousand square *li,* or bad harvests over a number of years in succession, how is the government going to deal with it? The distress then will be beyond description. How can we say, "But it is a long, long time since anything like that has happened," and on this ground trust to luck in the future? Certainly we should gradually return to the ancient system — with the land distributed equally so as to encourage agriculture, and with steps taken by both individuals and the government to store up grain so as to provide against any contingency. In this, too, there is no difference between past and present.

In ancient times, the four classes of people each had its settled occupation, and eight or nine out of ten people were farmers. Therefore food and clothing were provided without difficulty and people were spared suffering and distress. But now in the capital region there are thousands upon thousands of men without settled occupations — idlers and beggars who cannot earn a living. Seeing that they are distressed, toilsome, lonesome, poor, and ill, or resort to guile and craftiness in order to survive and yet usually cannot make a living, what can we expect the consequence to be after this has gone on for days and years? Their poverty being so extreme, unless a sage is able to change things and solve the problem, there will be no way to avoid complete disaster. How can we say, "There is nothing that can be done about it?"? This calls for consideration of the ancient [system] in order to reform the present [system], a sharing by those who have much so as to relieve those who possess little, thus enabling them to gain the means of livelihood by which to save their lives. In this, too, there is no difference between the past and the present. . . .

The Dialectical Outlook

Mao Tse-Tung

The dialectical world outlook had already emerged in ancient times both in China and in Europe. But ancient dialectics has something spontaneous and naive about it; being based upon the social and historical conditions of those times, it was not formulated into an adequate theory, hence it could not fully explain the world, and was later supplanted by metaphysics. The famous German philosopher Hegel, who lived from the late eighteenth century to the early nineteenth, made very important contributions to dialectics, but his is idealist dialectics. It was not until Marx and Engels, the great men of action of the proletarian movement, made a synthesis of the positive achievements in the history of human knowledge and, in particular, critically absorbed the rational elements of Hegelian dialectics and created the great theory of dialectical materialism and historical materialism, that a great, unprecedented revolution took place in the history of human knowledge. Later Lenin and Stalin have further developed this great theory. Introduced into China, this theory immediately brought about tremendous changes in the world of Chinese thought.

This dialectical world outlook teaches man chiefly how to observe and analyze skillfully the movement of opposites in various things, and, on the basis of such analysis, to find out the methods of solving the contradictions. Consequently, it is of paramount importance for us to understand concretely the law of contradiction in things.

From Mao Tse-Tung, "On Contradiction," in *Sources of Chinese Tradition,* vol. 1, compiled by Wm. T. De-Bary et al. (New York: Columbia University Press, 1960), pp. 233-41.

The Universality of Contradiction

For convenience in exposition, I shall deal here first with the universality of contradiction, and then with the particularity of contradiction. Only a brief remark is needed to explain the former, because many people have accepted the universality of contradiction ever since the great creators and continuers of Marxism — Marx, Engels, Lenin, and Stalin — established the materialist-dialectical world outlook and applied materialist dialectics with very great success to many aspects of the analysis of human history and of natural history, to many aspects of changes in society and in nature (as in the Soviet Union); but there are still many comrades, especially the doctrinaires, who are not clear about the problem of the particularity of contradiction. They do not understand that the universality of contradiction resides precisely in the particularity of contradiction. Nor do they understand how very significant it is for our further guidance in revolutionary practice to study the particularity of contradiction in the concrete things confronting us. Therefore, the problem of the particularity of contradiction should be studied with special attention and explained at sufficient length. For this reason, when we analyze the law of contradiction in things, we should first analyze the universality of contradiction, then analyze with special attention the particularity of contradiction, and finally return to the universality of contradiction.

The universality or absoluteness of contradiction has a twofold meaning. One is that contradiction exists in the process of development of all things and the other is that in the process of development of each thing a movement of opposites exists from beginning to end.

Even under the social conditions of the Soviet Union a difference exists between the workers and the peasants; the difference is a contradiction, though, unlike that between labor and capital, it will not become intensified into antagonism or assume the form of class struggle: in the course of socialist construction the workers and the peasants have formed a firm alliance and will gradually solve this contradiction in the process of development from socialism to communism. This is a question of distinction in the character of contradictions, not a matter of the presence or absence of them. Contradiction is universal, absolute, existing in all process of the development of things, and running through all processes from beginning to end.

The Particularity of Contradiction

It is not only necessary to study the particular contradiction and the quality determined thereby in every great system of forms of motion of matter, but also to study the particular contradiction and the quality of every form of motion of matter at each stage of its long course of development. In all forms of motion, each process of development that is real and not imaginary is qualitatively different. In our study we must emphasize and start from this point.

Qualitatively different contradictions can only be solved by qualitatively different methods. For example: the contradiction between the proletariat and the bourgeoisie is solved by the method of socialist revolution; the contradiction between the great masses of the people and the feudal system is solved by the method of democratic revolution; the contradiction between colonies and imperialism is solved by the method of national revolutionary war; the contradiction between the working class and the peasantry in socialist society is solved by the method of collectivization and mechanization of agriculture; the contradiction within the Communist Party is solved by the method of criticism and self-criticism; the contradiction between society and nature is solved by the method of developing the productive forces. Processes change, old processes and old contradictions disappear, new processes and new contradictions emerge, and the methods of solving contradictions differ accordingly. There is a basic difference between the contradictions solved by the February Revolution and the October Revolution in Russia, as well as between the methods used to solve them. The use of different methods to solve different contradictions is a principle which Marxist-Leninists must strictly observe. The doctrinaires do not observe this principle: they do not understand the differences between the various revolutionary situations, and consequently do not understand that different methods should be used to solve different contradictions;

on the contrary, they uniformly adopt a formula which they fancy to be unalterable and inflexibly apply it everywhere, a procedure which can only bring setbacks to the revolution or make a great mess of what could have been done well.

In order to reveal the particularity of contradictions in their totality as well as their interconnection in the process of development of things, that is, to reveal the quality of the process of development of things, we must reveal the particularity of each aspect of the contradiction in the process, otherwise it is impossible to reveal the quality of the process; this is also a matter to which we must pay the utmost attention in our study.

A great thing or event contains many contradictions in the process of its development. For instance, in the process of China's bourgeois-democratic revolution there are the contradiction between the various oppressed classes in Chinese society and imperialism, the contradiction between the great masses of the people and feudalism, the contradiction between the proletariat and the bourgeoisie, the contradiction between the peasantry together with the urban petty bourgeoisie on the one hand, and the bourgeoisie on the other, the contradiction between various reactionary ruling blocs, etc.; the situation is exceedingly complex. Not only do all these contradictions each have their own particularity and cannot be treated uniformly, but the two aspects of every contradiction also have each their own characteristics and cannot be treated uniformly. Not only should we who work for the Chinese revolution understand the particularity of each of the contradictions in the light of their totality, that is, from the interconnection of those contradictions, but we can understand the totality of the contradictions only by a study of each of their aspects. To understand each of the aspects of a contradiction is to understand the definite position each aspect occupies, the concrete form in which it comes into interdependence as well as conflict with its opposite and the concrete means by which it struggles with its opposite when the two are interdependent and yet contradictory, as well as when the interdependence breaks up. The study of these problems is a matter of the utmost importance. Lenin was expressing this very idea when he said that the most essential thing in Marxism, the living soul of Marxism, is the con-

crete analysis of concrete conditions. Contrary to Lenin's teaching, our doctrinaires never use their brains to analyze anything concretely; in their writings and speeches they always strike the keynote of the "eight-legged essay" which is void of any content, and have thus brought about in our Party a very bad style in work.

From this it can be seen that in studying the specific nature of any contradiction — contradiction in various forms of motion of matter, contradiction in various forms of motion in every process of development, each aspect of the contradiction in every process of development contradiction at the various stages of every process of development and each aspect of the contradiction at the various stages of development — in studying the specific nature of all these contradictions, we should be free from any taint of subjective arbitrariness and must make a concrete analysis of them. Apart from a concrete analysis there can be no knowledge of the specific nature of any contradiction. We must all the time bear in mind Lenins' words: the concrete analysis of concrete conditions.

Marx and Engels were the first to supply us with an excellent model of such concrete analysis.

When Marx and Engels applied the law of contradiction in things to the study of the process of social history, they saw the contradiction between the productive forces and the relations of production; they saw the contradiction between the exploiting class and the exploited class, as well as the contradiction produced thereby between the economic foundation and its superstructures, such as politics and ideology; and they saw how these contradictions inevitably lead to different social revolutions in different class societies.

When Marx applied this law to the study of the economic structure of capitalist society, he saw that the basic contradiction of this society is the contradiction between the social character of production and the private character of ownership. It is manifested, in the contradiction between the organized character of production in individual enterprises and the unorganized character of production in society as a whole. The class manifestation of this contradiction is the contradiction between the bourgeoisie and the proletariat.

Because of the vastness of the scope of things and the limitlessness of their development, what in one case is universality is in another changed into particularity. On the other hand, what in one case is particularity is in another changed into universality. The contradiction contained in the capitalist system between the socialization of production and the private ownership of the means of production is something common to all countries where capitalism exists and develops; for capitalism, this constitutes the universality of contradiction. However, this contradiction in capitalism is something pertaining to a certain historical stage in the development of class society in general; as far as the contradiction between the productive forces and the relations of production in class society in general is concerned, this constitutes the particularity of contradiction. But while revealing by analysis the particularity of every contradiction in capitalist society, Marx expounded even more profoundly, more adequately and more completely the universality of the contradiction between the productive forces and the relations of production in class society in general. . . .

When Stalin explained the historical roots of Leninism in his famous work, *The Foundations of Leninism,* he analyzed the international situation in which Leninism was born, together with various contradictions in capitalism which had reached their extreme under the conditions of imperialism, and analyzed how these contradictions made the proletarian revolution a question of immediate action and how they created favorable conditions for a direct onslaught upon capitalism. Besides all these, he analyzed the reasons why Russia became the home of Leninism, how Tsarist Russia represented the focus of all the contradictions of imperialism, and why the Russian proletariat could become the vanguard of the international revolutionary proletariat. In this way, Stalin analyzed the universality of the contradiction in imperialism, showing how Leninism is Marxism of the era of imperialism and the proletarian revolution, and analyzed the particularity of the imperialism of Tsarist Russia in the contradiction of imperialism in general, showing how Russia became the birth-place of the theory and tactics of the proletarian revolution and how in such a particularity is contained the universality of contradiction. This kind of analysis made by Stalin serves us as a model in understanding the particularity and the universality of contradiction and their interconnection.

The Principal Contradiction and the Principal Aspect of a Contradiction

As regards the problem of the particularity of contradiction, there are still two sides which must be specially singled out for analysis, that is, the principal contradiction and the principal aspect of a contradiction.

In the process of development of a complex thing, many contradictions exist; among these, one is necessarily the principal contradiction whose existence and development determine or influence the existence and development of other contradictions.

So in studying any process — if it is a complicated process in which more than two contradictions exist — we must do our utmost to discover its principal contradiction. Once the principal contradiction is grasped, any problem can be readily solved. This is the method Marx taught us when he studied capitalist society. When Lenin and Stalin studied imperialism and the general crisis of capitalism, and when they studied Soviet economy, they also taught us this method.

Some people think that this is not the case with certain contradictions. For example: in the contradiction between the productive forces and the relations of production, the productive forces are the principal aspect; in the contradiction between theory and practice, practice is the principal aspect; in the contradiction between the economic foundation and its superstructure, the economic foundation is the principal aspect: and there is no change in their respective positions. This is the view of mechanistic materialism, and not of dialectical materialism. True, the productive forces, practice, and the economic foundation generally manifest themselves in the principal and decisive role; whoever denies this is not a materialist. But under certain conditions, such aspects as the relations of production, theory and the superstructure in turn manifest themselves in the principal and decisive role; this must also be admitted. When the productive forces cannot be developed unless the relations of production are changed, the change in the relations of production plays the principal and decisive role. When, as Lenin put it, "Without a revolutionary theory, there can be no revolutionary movement," the creation and advocacy of the revolutionary theory plays the principal and decisive role. When a certain job (this applies to any job) is to be done but there is as yet no directive, method, plan or policy defining how to do it, the directive, method, plan or policy is the principal and decisive factor. When the superstructure (politics, culture and so on), hinders the development of the economic foundation, political and cultural reforms become the principal and decisive factors. In saying this, are we running counter to materialism? No. The reason is that while we recognize that in the development of history as a whole it is material things that determine spiritual things and social existence that determines social consciousness, at the same time we also recognize and must recognize the reaction of spiritual things and social consciousness on social existence, and the reaction of the superstructure on the economic foundation. This is not running counter to materialism; this is precisely avoiding mechanistic materialism and firmly upholding dialectical materialism.

The Identity and Struggle of the Aspects of a Contradiction

Having understood the problem of the universality and particularity of contradiction, we must proceed to study the problem of the identity and struggle of the aspects of a contradiction.

Identity, unity, coincidence, interpermeation, interpenetration, interdependence (or interdependence for existence), interconnection or cooperation — all these different terms mean the same thing and refer to the following two conditions: first, each of the two aspects of every contradiction in the process of development of a thing finds the presupposition of its existence in the other aspect and both aspects coexist in an entity; second, each of the two contradictory aspects, according to given conditions, tends to transform itself into the other. This is what is meant by identity.

The agrarian revolution we have carried out is already and will be such a process in which the land-owning landlord class becomes a class deprived of its land, while the peasants, once deprived of their land, become small holders of land. The haves and the have-nots, gain and loss, are interconnected because of certain conditions; there is identity of the two sides. Under socialism, the system of the peasants' private ownership will in turn become the public ownership of socialist agriculture; this has already taken place in the Soviet Union and will take place throughout the world. Between private property and public property there is a bridge leading from the one to the other, which in philosophy is called identity, or transformation into each other, or interpermeation.

To consolidate the dictatorship of the proletariat or the people's dictatorship is precisely to prepare the conditions for liquidating such a dictatorship and advancing to the higher stage of abolishing all state systems. To establish and develop the Communist Party is precisely to prepare the condition for abolishing the Communist Party and all party systems. To establish the revolutionary army under the leadership of the Communist Party and to carry on the revolutionary war is precisely to prepare the condition for abolishing war for ever. These contradictory things are at the same time complementary.

The Role of Antagonism in Contradiction

"What is antagonism?" is one of the questions concerning the struggle within a contradiction. Our answer is: antagonism is a form of struggle within a contradiction, but not the universal form.

In human history, antagonism between classes exists as a particular manifestation of the struggle within a contradiction. The contradiction between the exploiting class and the exploited class: the two contradictory classes coexist for a long time in one society, be it a slave society, or a feudal or a capitalist society, and struggle with each other; but it is not until the contradiction between the two classes has developed to a certain stage that the two sides adopt the form of open antagonism which develops into a revolution. In a class society, the transformation of peace into war is also like that.

As we have pointed out above, the contradiction between correct ideology and erroneous ideologies within the Communist Party reflects in the

Party the class contradictions when classes exist. In the beginning, or with regard to certain matters, such a contradiction need not immediately manifest itself as antagonistic. But with the development of the class struggle, it can also develop and become antagonistic. The history of the Communist Party of the Soviet Union shows us that the contradiction between the correct ideology of Lenin and Stalin and the erroneous ideologies of Trotsky, Bukharin, and others, was in the beginning not yet manifested in an antagonistic form, but subsequently developed into antagonism. A similar case occurred in the history of the Chinese Communist Party.

Is Confucianism Part of the Capitalist Ethic?

Wei-ming Tu

In his 1974 Foreign Affairs article on the Sinic World, Edwin Reischauer grouped Japan and the four "mini-dragons" (Hong Kong, Korea, Singapore, Taiwan) together as integral parts of the Confucian cultural universe. The assumptive reason underlying Reischauer's perspective is widely accepted in the Sinological community: the spread of Confucian teaching was so extensive and penetrating in China and peripheral countries like Korea, Vietnam and Japan that, prior to the impact of the West in the mid-19th century, pre-modern Asia could be characterized as the Confucian age.

Specifically, since the 13th century in China, late 14th century in Korea, 15th century in Vietnam, and 17th century in Japan, the cultural elite shared the same moral education and the political leadership appealed to the same rutual system, both defined in Confucian terms. Every educated male adult was socialized in the same scriptural tradition, namely the Four Books with the collected commentaries compiled by Chu Hsi (the basic Confucianist canon), and every statesman employed the symbolic resources from the Confucian tradition for governing the state.

Despite a number of other religious influences, Confucian humanism must be recognized as a common discourse of the Sinic world. More than a century of Western domination has not totally undermined this moral fabric. Without stretching

Wei-ming Tu, "Is Confucianism Part of the Capitalist Ethic?" Excerpt from a paper presented at the International Conference on Culture and Development in Asia and the Pacific (March 1990), held in Fukuoka, Japan.

one's imagination, the Confucian discourse remains the "civil religion" of East Asia — including Mainland China, North Korea and Vietnam. By civil religion, I mean the value system that guides ordinary behaviour as well as gives ultimate meaning to life in society.

Post-Confucianism

This relevance of Confucian humanism to the Sinic world notwithstanding, Japan and the four mini-dragons are no longer Confucian. They have been so westernized — or more appropriately "Americanized" — that the presence of the Confucian heritage can no longer be taken for granted. Recognition of this has given rise to what modern-day scholars of the system have taken to calling "post-Confucianism."

The post-Confucian hypothesis is predicated on the assumptions that: culture matters; that values people cherish or unconsciously uphold provide guidance for their actions; that the motivational structure of people is not only relevant, but crucial to their economic ethics; and that the life-orientation of a society makes a difference in the economic behavior of its people. These assumptions are necessary for making the post-Confucian hypothesis intelligible as an explanatory model.

We must then examine the salient characteristics of the Confucian heritage and the possible bearings they might have on the distinctive features of the East Asian Development model.

"Habits of the Heart"

Inspired by Max Weber's thesis on the Protestant ethic, thrift and industriousness have often been singled out as major Confucian contributions to the modern East Asian work ethic. More elaborate attempts also seek to include family cohesiveness and respect for authority. Peter Berger, for example, includes "a positive attitude to the affairs of this world, a sustained lifestyle of discipline and self-cultivation, respect for authority, frugality, an overriding concern for stable family life."

Nevertheless, I believe it is misleading to approach the Confucian tradition as if its efficacy in modern East Asia could be reduced to disembodied values. . . . It is one thing to find genuinely creative reconstruction of Confucian philosophy, and quite another to detect the Confucian "habits of the heart" at work.

In what sense, then, has the Confucian tradition survived, after: (1) the total collapse of the imperial order; (2) the fundamental transformation of the agricultural economy; and (3) a profound change in the family-centered social structure?

Since the attack on Confucius at the May Fourth cultural movement in 1919, the demise of Confucianism has been announced time and time again for the last 70 years. The Confucian "habits of the heart," however, survived and continued to flourish. Recently, intellectual historians in mainland China, to their great surprise, have discovered that the New Confucian Humanism, is one of the most sophisticated, vibrant and creative currents of thought in contemporary China.

Intellectuals of all ideological persuasions in the People's Republic of China take it for granted that, for better or worse, the Chinese social ethic as well as the Chinese political culture are inseparably intertwined with the Confucian tradition. But the Chinese intelligentsia's obsession with the Confucian tradition is one-sided. Confucianism is not only historically complex but culturally diverse. It is not exclusively Chinese — for the Confucian tradition is also Korean, Japanese and Vietnamese.

The Individual: A Centre of Relationships

The Confucian insistence that learning is for the sake of the self, and that the self is a centre of relationships, is in sharp contrast to the doctrine of individualism in the modern West. The notion remains a powerful moral force in East Asia. This group orientation — or at least a non-individualistic approach to life — seriously challenges the assumption of Talcott Parsons: that "individualism" (or as he called it, "ego-orientation") is inevitably and intrinsically linked to modernity.

The rise of Japan and the four mini-dragons suggests an alternative path to modernity — a path that raises fundamental questions about the linkage between modernity, capitalism and individualism. It hints at the authentic possibility of a spirit of capitalism rooted in the Confucian ethic.

Such an ethic seems to have centred in a location that is much more dynamic than Parsons's lonely self: it is a self that is not an island, but rather an ever-expanding stream of interconnectedness. The ability of East Asian entrepreneurs to take full advantage of human capital — be it through demand to family loyalty, a disciplined work force or supporting staff — is not an accident. They are beneficiaries of the Confucian way of life.

Equally important, but less obvious, is that the East Asian conception of society itself is Confucian in character. The adversary relationship so carefully cultivated in American civil society is relegated to the background. Despite fierce competitiveness which generates a great deal of tension and conflict, East Asian societies are in essence "fiduciary communities" — which is to say they are founded on mutual trust and confidence. They take internal cohesiveness as a precondition for the long-term well-being of the people.

The ability of the leaders in these societies to mobilize resources on a large scale from different sectors testifies to the credibility of the basic Confucian precept: that the public good is not in conflict with private interests and that the enhancement of the wealth of the nation will eventually bring profit to all.

To be sure, the rhetoric of patriotism is so powerful that people are often blinded to the abusive use of power by the elite. But since the Confucians believe that political leaders ought to be moral exemplars as well, any revelation that the leadership is corrupt will lead to a major crisis in legitimacy. Public accountability, is, therefore, necessary for political survival. The relative ease with which industrial East Asian governments have transformed themselves into "development states" must be understood in the context of this pattern of interaction between the leaders and the populace, defined in Confucian terms.

Responsibility vs. Duty

The pervasiveness of the rhetoric of duty and the paucity of reference to rights in the public discourse must not lead us to the facile conclusion that respect for authority (or subjugation at the expense of personal dignity) is always one-sided. In the Confucian ethic, the sense of duty is pro-

portionate to the responsibility assumed. The heavier one's responsibility, the more enhanced one's sense of duty.

The Confucian dimension in the East Asian development model, it seems to me, could be summed up in three interrelated areas of concern: (1) the style of political leadership; (2) the pattern of social interaction; and (3) the path of human flourishing. The public demand that political leaders must also act as moral exemplar, and that members of the cultural elite must be socially responsible is characteristic of all Confucian societies. Political power and intellectual influence are thus laden with far-reaching ethical implications.

Path of Human Flourishing

Confucius never created a spiritual sanctuary — a sacred place (a church, a shrine, a synagogue) diametrically opposed to the secular world. Instead, he regarded the secular as sacred. For the Confucians, the world as we know it is the home and we are obligated to make our home a nourishing environment for humanity. The Confucians respect natural hierarchy — such as age differentiation in the family, the importance of status and authority in society, and the necessity of the division of labour in the economic sphere. Historically, however, the Confucian tradition has contributed to gerontocracy, authoritarianism, male domination, anti-commercialism and a host of other patterns of thought and behavior that are incompatible with the modernizing process.

But this does not mean that an East Asian politician, teacher or merchant under the influence of Confucian-derived values cannot function effectively in modern society. On the contrary, they may have more spiritual resources to tap into than their counterparts in Confucian societies.

The Confucian path to human flourishing, neither a spiritual journey to the other shore nor a salvation in the next life, is rooted in the improvability of this world and this life. While genetically it may not have contributed to the emergence of the spirit of capitalism, it seems in perfect accord with modern consciousness. Certainly the evocation of the Confucian dimension — if for nothing else — gives the intellectual discourse on the East Asian development model a far richer texture.

411

African Traditions and Developments

The religions of Africa are as diverse as its peoples and cultures. From the Islam of the Mediterranean rim and the desert tribes of the North, to the animism of jungle peoples in central Africa, to the vibrant forms of indigenized evangelical Christianity in decolonized coastal countries, to peculiar forms of Iberian Catholicism, Dutch Calvinism, and English Arminianism that flourish, along with Hinduism and Confucianism, in the industrialized cities of southern Africa, the continent is an anthropologist's dream and a traditionalist's nightmare. Everything blends into everything else and, like the land itself, proliferates new varieties of vitality.

It is true, of course, that some voices in the relatively recent field of African religious and social studies have suggested that behind the variety is a deep, common stratum of religious understanding that serves as a foundation on which all these varieties have built. In most traditions, the whole earth lives under a great creator god, the immediate influence of the spirits of the ancestors who must be heeded and appeased is closely felt, and oral traditions of wisdom — sayings, stories, proverbs, and myths — have had a great influence in the conduct of daily life and sustaining traditional patterns of existence. Several examples from these wisdom traditions are included here.

Socially, the household is the most common way of organizing economic life in the context of a tribal village, some by hunting and gathering, and others by herding or farming. Although varying in significant ways from time to time and place to place, this arrangement is similar to that reflected in Hebraic and Arabic scriptures. Both scriptures have been readily adopted through conversion to Christianity or Islam in a great number of regions. Only rarely did trade, manufacture, or finance play a decisive role in traditional African societies, al-

though mining and smelting was known early, and although Arabic and Indian traders plied the coasts and river systems and crossed the Sahara from very early on. Even today they tend to dominate commerce, while Western firms tend to dominate manufacture and finance. Frequently, this control of business by "outsiders" causes resentment.

Although strong evidence of elaborate civilizations from the past can be found, these civilizations did not develop into high cultures that still exist, as happened in the Middle East and in Asia. That made African (and comparable) tribal societies more vulnerable to imperial and colonial influence than other great traditions, and less prepared to face the cultural, technological, and organizational demands of modern corporate capitalism. This, too, causes resentment.

However, the two events that have been more disruptive to African life and culture than anything else are slavery and apartheid. A number of traditional African cultures had slavery for as long as can be traced (as was also the case in Greece, India, China, and elsewhere), but the African practice was compounded by both vigorous Arabic slave trading and American institutions of slavery, to which European slave traders catered.

The relationship of slavery to capitalism has been much debated in modern scholarship; and the fact that the West has abolished slavery under the influence of Christian and Enlightenment ideas of human rights has at least established the principle that there are social limits to the rights of ownership. The African suspicion of capitalism and property rights is reflected in various efforts to establish an "African socialism," represented here by Julius K. Nyerere's address to a Roman Catholic missionary order.

The struggles over South Africa's apartheid policies have been the defining debates since the mid-twentieth century. An enormous number of church efforts were made to alter the situation. In 1994, a new multiracial government was elected, and all sorts of new starts are being made. We include one striking new church development, described in an article by Bill Keller.

Wisdom from African Traditions

Hymn to the Nile

Praise to thee, O Nile, that issuest forth from the earth and comest to nourish the dwellers in Egypt. Secret of movement, a darkness in the daytime.

That waterest the meadows which Re hath created to nourish all cattle.

That givest drink to the desert places which are far from water; his dew it is that falleth from heaven.

Beloved of the Earth-God, controller of the Corn-God, that maketh every workshop of Ptah to flourish.

Lord of fish, that maketh the water fowl to go upstream, without a bird falling.

That maketh barley and createth wheat, that maketh the temples to keep festival.

If he is sluggish the nostrils are stopped up, and all men are brought low;

The offerings of the gods are diminished, and millions perish from among mankind.

When he arises earth rejoices and all men are glad; every jaw laughs and every tooth is uncovered.

Bringer of nourishment, plenteous of sustenance, creating all things good.

Taken from A. Adu Boahen et al., *The Horizon History of Africa* (New York: American Heritage, 1971). The "Hymn to the Nile" (p. 67) is dated 1600 B.C. "The Merchant's Wisdom" (p. 155) is by Ibn Khaldun from fourteenth-century Morocco. "Yoruba Proverbs" (p. 207) and "Zulu Wisdom" (p. 428) were recorded in the nineteenth century.

Lord of reverence, sweet of savor, appeasing evil.
Creating herbage for the cattle, causing sacrifice
   to be made to every god.
He is in the Underworld, in heaven, and upon
   earth.
Filling the barns and widening the granaries;
   giving to the poor.
Causing trees to grow according to the
   uttermost desire,
So that men go not in lack of them.

The Merchant's Wisdom

The merchant who knows his business will travel
only with such goods as are generally needed by
rich and poor, rulers and commoners alike.
[General need] makes for a large demand for his
goods. If he restricts his goods to those needed
only by a few [people], it may be impossible for
him to sell them, since these few may for some
reason find it difficult to buy them. Then, his business would slump, and he would make no profit.

Also, a merchant who travels with needed goods
should do so only with medium quality goods. The
best quality of any type of goods is restricted to
wealthy people and the entourage of the ruler.
They are very few in number. As is well known, the
medium quality of anything is what suits most
people. This should by all means be kept in mind
by the merchant, because it makes the difference
between selling his goods and not selling them.

Likewise, it is more advantageous and more
profitable for the merchant's enterprise, and a better guarantee [that he will be able to take advantage
of] market fluctuations, if he brings goods from a
country that is far away and where there is danger
on the road. In such a case, the goods transported
will be few and rare, because the place where they
come from is far away or because the road over
which they come is beset with perils, so that there
are few who would bring them, and they are very
rare. When goods are few and rare, their prices go
up. On the other hand, when the country is near
and the road safe for traveling, there will be many
to transport the goods. Thus, they will be found in
large quantities, and the prices will go down.

Therefore, the merchants who dare to enter the
Sudan country are the most prosperous and
wealthy of all people. The distance and the difficulty of the road they travel are great. They have
to cross a difficult desert which is made [almost]
inaccessible by fear [of danger] and beset by [the
danger of] thirst. Water is found there only in a
few well-known spots to which caravan guides
lead the way. The distance of this road is braved
only by a few people. Therefore, the goods of the
Sudan country are found only in small quantities
among us, and they are particularly expensive. The
same applies to our goods among them.

Thus, merchandise becomes more valuable
when merchants transport it from one country to
another. [Merchants who do so] quickly get rich
and wealthy. . . .

Yoruba Proverbs

When the day dawns the trader betakes himself
to his trade;
The spinner takes her distaff [or spindle], the
warrior takes his shield;
The weaver bends over his Asa, or sley [stoops
to his batten];
The farmer awakes, he and his hoehandle;
The hunter awakes with his quiver and bow.
The thread follows the needle.
There is no market in which the dove with the
prominent breast has not traded.
Peace is the father of friendship.
Wrangling is the father of fighting.
One here, two there, [so gathers] a vast multi-
tude.
The jaw is the house of laughter.
The young cannot teach tradition to the old.
I have tied the leopard skin round my waist;
you cannot sell me.

Zulu Wisdom

A man is not stabbed with one spear.
Even where there is no cock day dawns.
He who installs a king never rules with him.
The mouth is the shield to protect oneself.
There is no frog that does not peep out of its
pool.
No buffalo was ever beaten by its calf.
Days are things which want to be provided for.
One does not follow a snake into its hole.

On the Division between Rich and Poor

Julius K. Nyerere

Poverty is not the real problem of the modern world. For we have the knowledge and resources which could enable us to overcome poverty. The real problem — the thing which creates misery, wars and hatred among men — is the division of mankind into rich and poor.

We can see this division at two levels. Within nation states there are a few individuals who have great wealth and whose wealth gives them great power; but the vast majority of people suffer from varying degrees of poverty and deprivation. Even in a country like the United States, this division can be seen. In countries like India, Portugal or Brazil, the contrast between the wealth of a few privileged individuals and the dire poverty of the masses is a crying scandal. And looking at the world as a collection of nation states, we see the same pattern repeated. There are a few wealthy nations which dominate the whole world economically, and therefore politically; and a mass of smaller and poor nations whose destiny, it appears, is to be dominated.

The significance about this division between the rich and the poor is not simply that one man has more food than he can eat, more clothes than he can wear and more houses than he can live in, while others are hungry, unclad and homeless. The significant thing about the division between rich and poor nations is not simply that one has the resources to provide comfort for all its citizens, and the other cannot provide basic services. The reality and depth of the problem arises because the man who is rich has power over the lives of those who are poor, and the rich nation has power over the policies of those which are not rich. Even more important is that our social and economic system, nationally and internationally, supports these divisions and constantly increases them, so that the rich get ever richer and more powerful, while the poor get relatively ever poorer and less able to control their own future.

This continues despite all the talk of human equality, the fight against poverty, and of development. Still the rich individuals within nations, and the rich nations within the world, go on getting richer very much faster than the poor overcome their poverty. Sometimes this happens through the deliberate decision of the rich, who use their wealth and their power to that end. But often — perhaps more often — it happens "naturally" as a result of the normal workings of the social and economic systems men have constructed for themselves. Just as water from the driest regions of the earth ultimately flows into the oceans where water is already plentiful, so wealth flows from the poorest nations and the poorest individuals into the hands of those nations and those individuals who are already wealthy. A man who can afford to buy only one loaf of bread a day contributes to the profit accruing to the owner of the bakery, despite the fact that the owner already has more money than he knows how to use. And the poor nation which sells its primary commodities on the world market in order to buy machines for development finds that the prices it obtains, and the prices it has to pay, are both determined by the "forces of the free market" in which it is a pygmy competing with giants.

> For he that hath, to him shall be given; and he that hath not, that also which he hath shall be taken away from him.

Both nationally and internationally this division of mankind into the tiny minority of rich, and the great majority of poor, is rapidly becoming intolerable to the majority — as it should be. The poor nations and the poor peoples of the world are already in rebellion against it; if they do not succeed in securing change which leads towards greater justice, then that rebellion will become an explosion. Injustice and peace are in the

Julius K. Nyerere, "On the Division between Rich and Poor," address to the Ninth General Assembly of the Maryknoll Sisters (Fall 1970), Maryknoll, New York.

long run incompatible; stability in a changing world must mean ordered change towards justice, not mechanical respect for the *status quo*. It is in this context that development has been called another name for peace.

Man is the Purpose

The purpose of development is man. It is the creation of conditions, both material and spiritual, which enable man the individual, and man the species, to become his best. That is easy for Christians to understand because Christianity demands that every man should aspire towards union with God through Christ. But although the Church — as a consequence of its concentration upon man — avoids the error of identifying development with new factories, increased output, or greater national income statistics, experience shows that it all too often makes the opposite error. For the representatives of the Church, and the Church's organizations, frequently act as if man's development is a personal and "internal" matter, which can be divorced from the society and the economy in which he lives and earns his daily bread. . . .

My purpose is to suggest to you that the Church should accept the fact that the development of peoples means rebellion. At a given and decisive point in history men decide to act against those conditions which restrict their freedom as men. I am suggesting that, unless we participate actively in the rebellion against those social structures and economic organizations which condemn men to poverty, humiliation and degradation, then the Church will become irrelevant to man and the Christian religion will degenerate into a set of superstitions accepted by the fearful. . . .

For man lives in society. He becomes meaningful to himself and his fellows only as a member of that society. Therefore, to talk of the development of man, and to work for the development of man, must mean the development also of that kind of society which serves man, which enhances his well-being, and preserves his dignity. Thus, the development of peoples involves economic development, social development, and political development. And at this time in man's history, it must imply a divine discontent and a determination for change. For the present condition of men must be

unacceptable to all who think of an individual person as a unique creation . . . of a living God. We say man was created in the image of God . . . but under present conditions we are creatures, not of God, but of our fellow men. Surely there can be no dispute among Christians about that. For mankind has never been so united or so disunited; has never had such power for good nor suffered under such evident injustices. Men's capacity has never been so clear, nor so obviously and deliberately denied.

The world is one in technological terms. Men have looked down on the earth from the moon and seen its unity. In jet planes I can travel from Tanzania to New York in a matter of hours. Radio waves enable us to talk to each other — either in love or abuse — without more than a few seconds elapsing between our speech and the hearing of it. Goods are made which include materials and skills from all over the world — and are then put up for sale thousands of miles from their place of manufacture. Yet at the same time as the interdependence of man is increased through the advance of technology, the divisions between men also expand at an ever-increasing rate. . . . [It] would take a Tanzanian 40 years to earn what an American earns in one year, and we are not the poorest nation on earth. . . .

So the world is not one. Its peoples are more divided now, and also more conscious of their divisions, than they have ever been. They are divided between those who are satiated and those who are hungry. They are divided between those with power and those without power. They are divided between those who dominate and those who are dominated, between those who exploit and those who are exploited. And it is the minority which is well fed, and the minority which has secured control over the world's wealth and over their fellow men. Further, in general that minority is distinguished by the color of their skins and by their race. And the nations in which most of that minority of the world's people live have a further distinguishing characteristic — their adoption of the Christian religion. These things cannot continue, and Christians, above all others, must refuse to accept them. For the development of men, and the development of peoples, demands that the world shall become one and that social justice shall replace the present oppressions and inequalities.

Man is a Member of Society

In order to achieve this, there must be economic development and equitable distribution of wealth. The poor nations, the poor areas, and the poor peoples must be enabled to increase their output; through fair distribution they must be enabled to expand their consumption of the goods which are necessary for decency and for freedom.

For what is required is not simply an increase in the national income figures of the poor countries, nor a listing of huge increases in the production of this crop or that industry. New factories, roads, farms, and so on, are essential; but they are not enough in themselves. The economic growth must be of such a kind, and so organized, that it benefits the nations and the peoples who are now suffering from poverty. This means that social and political development must go alongside economic development — or even precede it. For unless society is so organized that the people control their own economies and their own economic activity, economic growth will result in increased inequality, both nationally and internationally. Those who control a man's livelihood control a man; his freedom is illusory and his equal humanity is denied when he depends upon others for the right to work and to eat. Equally, a nation is not independent if its economic resources are controlled by another nation; political independence is meaningless if a nation does not control the means by which its citizens can earn their living.

In other words, the development of peoples follows from economic development only if this latter is achieved on the basis of the equality and human dignity of all those involved. And human dignity cannot be given to a man by the kindness of others. Indeed, it can be destroyed by kindness which emanates from an action of charity. For human dignity involves equality and freedom, and relations of mutual respect among men. Further it depends on responsibility, and on a conscious participation in the life of the society in which a man moves and works. The whole structure of national societies and of international society is therefore relevant to the development of peoples. And there are few societies which can now be said to serve this purpose; for there are few — if any — which both accept, and are organized to serve, social justice in what has been called the Revolution of Rising Expectations.

Let us be quite clear about this. If the Church is interested in man as an individual, it must express this by its interest in the society of which those individuals are members. For men are shaped by the circumstances in which they live. If they are treated like animals, they will act like animals. If they are denied dignity, they will act without dignity. If they are treated solely as a dispensable means of production, they will become soulless "hands," to whom life is a matter of doing as little work as possible and then escaping into the illusion of happiness and pride through vice.

Therefore, in order to fulfill its own purpose of bringing men to God, the Church must seek to ensure that men can have dignity in their lives and in their work. It must itself become a force of social justice and it must work with other forces of social justice wherever they are, and whatever they are called. Further, the Church must recognize that men can only progress and can only grow in dignity by working for themselves, and working together for their common good. The Church cannot uplift a man; it can only help to provide the conditions and the opportunity for him to cooperate with his fellows to uplift himself. . . .

Within the rich countries of the world the beneficiaries of educational opportunity, of good health, and of security must be prepared to stand up and demand justice for those who have up to now been denied these things. Where the poor have already begun to demand a just society, at least some members of the privileged classes must help them and encourage them. Where they have not begun to do so, it is the responsibility of those who have had greater opportunities for development to arouse the poor out of their poverty-induced apathy. . . .

In the poor countries . . . [they have] this same role to play. It has to be consistently and actively on the side of the poor and unprivileged. It has to lead men towards Godliness by joining with them in the attack against the injustices and deprivation from which they suffer. It must cooperate with all those who are involved in this work; it must reject alliances with those who represent Mammon, and cooperate with all those who are working for Man.

A Surprising Silent Majority in South Africa

Bill Keller

Encountered at his work in the Mamelodi West Clinic, where he tends to the inhabitants of a black township east of Pretoria, Dr. Jonathan Maaga is the model of a new South African, progressive in his opinions, generous in his services to the community, a thoroughly modern man. He counsels his patients about AIDS and family planning. He spends a couple of days every week at a satellite clinic he set up in an abandoned bus in a squatter camp, Mandela Park. He has sent four children to college. On April 27, he will take a break from vaccinating homeless babies to cast the first vote of his life. Mindful of the large and petty humiliations inflicted upon him by apartheid during his 56 years and a great admirer of "the old man," as he calls Nelson Mandela, Maaga will vote for the African National Congress.

Close that window now and open another. It is Easter weekend and Maaga is driving his 10-year-old orange Mercedes north into the Transvaal, where the stark jut of the Drakensberg Mountains subsides into rocky valleys of red earth and thorn trees. He has changed his hospital whites for a proletarian khaki suit and black peaked cap. Pinned to his lapel is a small silver star, like a sheriff's badge, etched with the letters Z.C.C. and backed by swatches of green and black cloth. Three hours north of Pretoria, he slows behind an endless caravan of overloaded vehicles streaming into a scrub-covered saddle of land. The doctor parks and joins a million other pilgrims, identically dressed, carrying bedrolls and paraffin cookstoves

into the bush for a weekend of ecstatic surrender and thoughtless obedience.

The doctor, so accustomed to giving orders, becomes a part of the crowd, beyond counting, that behaves with the discipline of a regiment at war, or a herd. One marshal, passing through the crowd, need only clap his hands and a highway opens. At the signal for prayer, worshipers by the hundreds of thousands fall at once to their knees.

Throughout the weekend, circles of men leap and smash the earth with their heavy white shoes, to exorcise devils. Away from view, the ill and heartsick have silvery needles poked into their lower legs and nostrils to drain the bad humors they believe infect their blood. Or they are splashed with holy water and caressed by the healing hands of prophets.

This is the Zion Christian Church, the mysterious center of the largest and fastest-growing religious movement in southern Africa.

In Africa, there is nothing unusual about a worldly man of affairs seeking comfort in a church that practices bloodletting and exorcism and frenetic ritual dancing, or, for that matter, dropping by a witch doctor for an herbal remedy and some guidance from the ancestors. An African is no more surprised by this than, say, New Yorkers would be by the fact that their Governor believes a wafer of bread can be transformed into the body of Jesus Christ.

All the same, it is a revelation that a man of education and enlightened views would feel at home in this particular church. For the Zion Christian Church — known to all as the Zed-See-See — is no liberation church, nor an institution that puts much stock in black intellectual accomplishment. It is not the sort of pulpit from which Archbishop Desmond Tutu thunders about Christian justice. On the contrary, the Z.C.C. has declined every invitation to enlist its legions of believers — most of them poor and semiliterate — in the campaign against apartheid.

Among black intellectuals and liberation activists, the Zionists are regarded with faint scorn, as Uncle Toms, the collage of star and cloth a badge of complacency, even collusion. Whites, those who pay any mind to such things, count the church's huge membership as confirmation that many blacks are content to be subservient. White employers know that men and women adorned with

Bill Keller, "A Surprising Silent Majority in South Africa," *New York Times Magazine*, 17 April 1994.

the silver badge are quicker than most to respond to a white man's instructions with a deferential "sir" or "master." When President F. W. de Klerk talks about the "silent majority" of God-fearing, law-abiding blacks who he imagines will vote for him, the Zionists are exactly what he has in mind.

De Klerk has almost certainly misjudged the politics of the Zionists — like Maaga, they will probably support the A.N.C. — but he is onto something with his talk about a silent majority.

Western images of black South Africans are portraits of turmoil, of young men scampering before police armor, of Zulu reactionaries brandishing spears or AK-47's, of frenzied election rallies in remote townships and of the patriarchal statesmanship of Nelson Mandela. It is an easy mistake to assume, therefore, that South African blacks constitute a nation of revolutionaries.

Obscured by the revolutionary images, the great secret is that the majority of black South Africans are deeply conservative people. It's not that they are content to be governed by white men but that they are wary of sudden change, that they are devoutly religious, that they find solace in land and family and tradition, that they are intensely respectful of authority. The silent majority craves stability as much as opportunity, and more than it craves justice.

The Zionists are the foremost preachers of this cautious life, and in this year of liberation and elections, they are baptizing multitudes as never before, flourishing in the slums and the villages. Set aside the consuming question of racial oppression and it may be that the Zion Christian Church is a more accurate reflection of black South Africa than is the African National Congress. Strange as it may seem, this is probably good news for the African National Congress.

* * *

On a Sunday in black South Africa, the townships are florid with Zionists. Zionism comprises thousands of sects and autonomous congregations, and each seems to have its own sartorial scheme of robes, headdresses, staves and badges. You may find an entire parish of 20 men and women in starched white robes and blue sashes assembled under a jacaranda tree for a scriptural discourse. At intervals along the urban creeks of Soweto, you see Zionists, bright as bouquets, gathered to dunk

new members in the foul water. Zionists whirl giddily to drumbeats in the dim corners of parking garages and empty highrise warehouses in downtown Johannesburg.

Journalists were waiting outside a migrant worker hostel in Duduza township on a recent Sunday, anticipating a climactic showdown between Zulu workers and A.N.C. partisans. Suddenly, rapturously oblivious to the armored personnel carriers of police and the spear-wielding Zulu warrior impis posed for impending combat, a troupe of Zionists danced through the scene on the way to church.

The Zionist sects differ from one another mainly in their choice of prophet-healers and costumes. In their faith and shibboleths, they are one, a single powerful tributary from the river of African Christianity.

In a sense, the more educated Zionists will tell you, they began as a liberation movement. It was in the churches of the subcontinent that the issues of racial separation first came to a head. Long before the apartheid visionary Henrik F. Verwoerd dreamed up the idea of separate homelands, the Dutch Reformed Church authorized separate congregations along racial lines. At the same time, white missionaries, by educating a generation of blacks, also sowed the seeds of black struggle.

The initial break with the European churches came in the 1890's, when black preachers who had visited America returned home to form independent offshoots of the missionary churches. "Ethiopians," they called themselves, from Psalms 68:31: "Ethiopia shall soon stretch out her hand to God." The name had political resonance, too, Ethiopia being one of two black-ruled countries on the continent. The rituals and sacraments remained more or less the same as in the white Methodist or Lutheran churches, at least in the beginning, but the governance was black.

For many blacks, however, the Ethiopian movement was still a form of European colonialism. The second big schism, just after the turn of the century, produced the Zionists, the name originating from a symbol of faith's antiquity, the Mount of Zion in Jerusalem. Again, the movement took some of its inspiration from America, especially from the Christian Catholic Apostolic Church in Zion, based in Illinois.

The Zionists embraced the mysteries of Africa

and incorporated them in a way the European churches could not. Ecstatic utterances, prophesy, initiation and purification rites, taboos, exorcism of demons, all fixtures of African myth, were synthesized with the notions of the trinity, crucifixion and resurrection.

In a Zionist church, a man is welcome if he has several wives. Nobody scoffs when he speaks of "the ancestors," who in much of Africa form a powerful other-world support system.

"A guy would go to a white church and say, 'Look, I think I'm seeing witches at night flying over my house,'" says Ezra Mantini, a journalist and a member of the Z.C.C. council. "The priest would say, 'You need to see a psychologist.' The guy is insulted. He thinks, 'This priest says I'm retarded.' A black church will say: 'Let's trace the family tree. Is there anything wrong with your ancestors?' Because black churches regard the family tree as more important than just solving things on the surface. In this church, the guy feels at home."

The thing Africans missed most desperately in the Western churches was healing. African society has always accorded an important place to sangomas, the diviners and traditional healers who act as intermediaries with the ancestors, prophesying and prescribing remedies of herbs and animal parts. Mainstream churches either dismiss sangomas as a heathen superstition or, in the more liberal congregations, tolerate them as a harmless form of psychotherapy. The Zionists take them very seriously — as competition, to be supplanted. A newcomer baptized into the Z.C.C. must surrender all his sangoma medicines to be burned on the spot.

The more urbanized Zionists make compromises with Western medicine. They vaccinate their children. They visit clinics. But the healing power of the church is the heart of the faith, and every Zionist has at least one story.

For Maaga, the testimonial regards the time when his car overheated on a trip to church headquarters in the northern Transvaal. As he wrenched off the radiator cap, a geyser of searing water exploded into his face.

"My right eye went white," he told me one day over coffee in the clinic lunchroom. "My wife said, 'Let me rush you quickly to hospital.' I felt, no, if I go to the hospital and the eye goes blind, then I shall regret it for the rest of my life."

He decided, instead, to return home to Mamelodi where he had a jug of tea blessed by the church. His wife, who is not a Zionist, told him he was throwing away his eyesight.

"I said if it becomes blind, hard luck. I drove home and bathed my eye in the tea. The following day, the eye was fine. At that point in time, that was my faith. With faith healing, you have got to believe absolutely. If you have a doubt in your mind, you better try something else."

Academics working from South African census data put the number of Zionists at 5 million of South Africa's 30 million blacks. At least two million of them belong to the Zion Christian Church. (The Z.C.C. claims more than six million members throughout all of southern Africa.) In the last decade, membership of the Z.C.C. has doubled, while almost every one of the established churches has shrunk.

"They are steadily becoming the predominant movement in southern Africa," says Prof. Gerhardus Oosthuizen, a religious scholar who specializes in independent African churches.

They are also amazingly fissile. A church outgrows the house where it meets and it splits. An ambitious parishioner feels he has enough Holy Spirit in him to go it alone and he starts his own church. Professor Oosthuizen estimates that there are 4,800 Zionist churches and upwards of 100 different reasons why they split.

There are mom-and-pop Zionist churches that consist of little more than a single extended family and chain-store churches whose adherents number in the tens of thousands. And then there is the Zion Christian Church, which has built the faith of the rural poor and the working proletariat into a secretive and regimental corporate enterprise.

*　　*　　*

To an outsider, the Z.C.C. lacks the sweet intimacy and apparently spontaneous joy of the little congregations that can gather under a single tree. But it compensates by offering its believers the security of a powerful institution, which is especially comforting for the many rural blacks, like Jan Kolobe, who suddenly find themselves at sea in the teeming, politically fractious urban townships.

When Kolobe arrived four years ago in Alexandra, the densely populated black township adjoining Johannesburg, he was 33. The township

David Bosch, a leading liberal South African theologian, has said that "the South African is a religious animal." Indeed, unlike many Western nations, South Africa has not yet set aside religion as merely a Sunday ritual. South Africa in fact has a higher percentage of church members than any other nation in Africa; according to the 1980 census, almost 84 percent of the population claim church membership.

The Roman Catholic Church is the fastest growing denomination among South Africa's blacks, with a black membership that has increased from 24,000 in 1911 to 1.7 million in 1980; there are almost 400,000 white Catholics, over 260,000 coloreds and some 21,000 Asians. Only the Methodist Church has more black members. Most black Christians belong to small, independent sects that often combine Pentecostal fervor with traditional African rituals. Many of these sects resemble Protestant fundamentalist denominations in the United States.

— Richard E. Sincere, Jr., "The Churches and Investment in South Africa," *America*, 3 March 1984, pp. 146-47

---

was a confusion of tribal ways and city manners, impersonal and often violent. He found pickup work on a construction crew and rented a shack in the congested, reeking slum that sprawls like a precinct of Calcutta along the Jukskei River. Before long, he was convulsed by some kind of food poisoning. An acquaintance took him to the Zion Christian Church, where the congregants prayed over him and splashed him with blessed water. It reminded him of the witch doctors he used to visit back home. He felt better. More important, for the first time since he arrived in the township, he felt like he belonged.

This was no easy, hour-on-Sunday church. The Zionists prescribed a complete change of life. No drinking, no smoking, no pork, a pacifist approach to conflict and total commitment to the Zion Christian Church. Kolobe did not find the adjustment hard.

"That's why I say it is like a witch doctor," he says. "The things they prohibit you from doing, you now find yourself not wanting to do them."

Most evenings, Kolobe spends an hour at a prayer meeting, where congregants sing hypnotic hymns, listen to Scripture and seek healing. His Sundays are given over entirely to the church, which in Alexandra consists of a large fenced yard near the Jukskei.

At the gate, men and women line up separately in their church uniforms to be frisked and have their ID's checked. By the time the service begins several thousand are packed into the yard, perched on benches under a corrugated tin canopy and spilling in squatting regiments out onto the sun-blasted dirt. Many worshipers are sweating and serene from a morning of ritual dancing. A few have gone off in pairs with ministers to make confession.

The service is part catharsis, part commerce, with everything going on at once. Two microphone-wielding preachers — one speaking Zulu, the other Sotho — alternate scriptural exhortations, hymns and announcements in the frantic cadence of a bilingual rap duet. Another minister leads away 50 novitiates to be baptized in the oily water of the Jukskei, then brings them back for presentation to the crowd. Throughout the service, a constant procession of worshipers edges forward, bending at the waist and falling on their knees at the wooden desk that serves as a pulpit, proffering items to be blessed: jugs of water, packets of tea and coffee, jars of Vaseline, school notebooks.

The Alexandra church is simultaneously a spiritual refuge and a processing center for rural blacks new to the city. At a desk on the side, a woman collects payments for the church burial society, an insurance scheme to assure dead family members get a proper casket. Between Scriptures, the minister announces a meeting of the church chamber of commerce, where aspiring entrepreneurs can learn how to open a bank account and keep books. The church also runs a scholarship program and directs members into reading classes. Near the end of the service, a minister rises to read the names of companies that have job openings.

"The companies trust us because there is so much trouble caused by drinking and stealing, and those things don't happen in our church," Jan Kolobe says. The church found him a job as a trainee security guard at Jan Smuts Airport, and he is now earning enough to send money to his family.

As Elkana Matshidza, a primary school headmaster assigned to be my translator and minder during the service, explains, the church's claim to uplift its members does not rest entirely on faith healing.

"We sing and dance vigorously, which is good for health," he says. "We encourage our people to eat well — more vegetables, roughage and dairy products, no pork. We don't smoke. We don't drink. So naturally they get healthy. We encourage thrift, hard work and devotion to family. So naturally they get richer. We keep our members very busy, especially on the weekend, so they have very little time for mischievous things."

In addition, the church discourages sexual promiscuity, not a bad commandment in a country infested with the lethal AIDS virus. It demands that members refrain from violence, a healthy rule in communities plagued by wife-beating and political conflict. And that silver star, the object of intellectuals' derision, often invests the wearer with a life-prolonging aura of neutrality.

Kolobe says he is not planning to vote. He thinks it is "fine" that blacks are finally being allowed to choose their leaders, but the matter is not high on his agenda, not in his life plan. He tries not to think about it.

At a time of meteoric hopes, Kolobe's ambitions seem amazingly humble. He wants to keep his job, maybe eventually move from the shantytown into one of the tiny bungalows nearby. To survive. To go along. To be left alone. He is not unusual. Laying aside the question of racial equality, blacks in South Africa are as far from being bomb throwers as are South African whites.

A survey by the Markinor opinion company in January 1991, for example, found blacks expressing surprisingly high levels of respect for institutions they have every reason to despise — the legal system, the press, the Parliament in which they have never been represented, even the police. They valued hard work. ("In the long run, hard work usually brings better life," they agreed, as opposed to luck, connections or handouts.) Asked to characterize themselves, 60 percent of urban blacks said they were "traditional" or "middle of the road" on social matters. They are deeply religious, believe in free enterprise and are patriotic. ("How proud are you to be a South African?" the poll asked; 88 percent said "very" or "quite," the same as whites.) Asked about the best way to change their society, 56 percent said they preferred "gradual improvement by reforms."

For the next Government, these constituents of the black silent majority could be both a blessing and an impediment. Their deference to authority and their stoicism may help offset the feverish expectations of young militants, some of whom demand a BMW in very township garage. On the other hand, they could prove a source of resistance if the A.N.C. tries to push an aggressive social agenda — women's rights, for example, or the displacement of traditional tribal councils with more "democratic" authorities.

*　　*　　*

Engenas Lekganyane, the son of farm workers, founded the church in 1910, the year that South Africa was united. He had been trained as a Scottish Presbyterian, which may explain the incongruous presence at the Easter gathering of a marching brass band, heavy on tubas and drums, accompanied by a black man in full kilts. By the evidence of the enterprise he left behind, the founder had both charisma and business sense.

Lekganyane persuaded a white farmer to sell him a piece of land where the first converts built a small settlement, which the Bishop called Zion City. In 1925, the Zionist settlement consisted of 515 men and 411 women. Seventeen years later, the Z.C.C. had 28,000 followers at 50 churches around the country.

Over the years, the church expanded its holdings to encompass a neighboring valley, which is farmed to supply the church mill and bakery. The original Zion City has grown. It sits on a slope overlooking the valley, which makes a natural amphitheater for the million pilgrims who come on Easter weekend, the holiest occasion in the church calendar.

I loop down a dirt road and pass under an arch that announces, in Sotho, Afrikaans and English: "You Are Peacefully Welcome at Moria City."

"Have you any firearms?" a guard in Z.C.C. uniform inquires at the gate. "Cameras? Tobacco?" The Z.C.C. has long been secretive to the point of paranoia, shunning journalists, scholars and other outsiders curious about the rituals and politics of such a powerful institution. It is almost exactly one year since I requested an interview with the current Bishop, and I still have no guarantee he will speak to me. His advisers, I understand, have encouraged him to cultivate a mystique.

I sign in at the guardhouse and, with an escort in the passenger seat, drive up the road into a neat, dusty town shaded by ancient acacia trees. The town is an eerie hive of industry, as crews in their khaki uniforms prepare for the Easter throngs, building great wooden barns where vendors will feed the multitudes, sprucing up the hanger-size church with the large green neon star on top, checking the wires that run to speaker poles on the vast campground below. Knots of ministers in business suits, newly arrived for pre-Easter conferences, wait outside the general store and sip tea in the restaurant. They study me with justifiable suspicion. I am the only white person in sight, the only non-Zionist and undoubtedly the only person with the word "Orwellian" on the tip of his tongue.

The current Bishop, His Grace the Right Rev. Barnabas E. Lekganyane, 39, is the grandson of the founder, third in a dynasty. The Bishop lacks the magnetism of his grandfather, but he also lacks the ostentation of his father, Bishop Edward, whose self-indulgences included a collection of 45 imported automobiles.

The interview lasts for an hour, but the Bishop utters no more than a dozen words to me directly. He leaves the answering to his maternal uncle, Emmanuel Motolla, reputedly the protective gray cardinal of the church, and to two younger members of the church council who had vouched for me. From time to time, the Bishop leans over to whisper a suggestion to his uncle, who relays it: "On the matter of nonviolence, the Bishop is deeply rooted in the Scripture and he has just come up with one text: love thy neighbor as thyself." When I address a question directly to the young Bishop, he reacts with a deer-caught-in-the-head-lights look, but answers succinctly, then nods to his uncle to elaborate. He gives every impression that he can't wait for this unfamiliar ordeal to be over.

Whatever his personal charisma, the Bishop is an indispensable part of the Z.C.C.'s advantage over rival churches. Believers tend to trust the healing power that flows continuously from a dynasty. There are many cases of Zionist congregations swelling to huge size, only to fracture in a chorus of squabbling successors when the patriarch dies. The Bishop has three sons, one of whom will eventually be groomed to lead the dynasty into its fourth generation.

* * *

In their first decades, the Zionists got a hard time from white Christians. Their response to various indignities, in most cases, was not to rise up but to hunker down. The ministers of Zion churches were mostly unschooled men and they operated in rural areas where challenging authority was even more foolhardy than in the cities.

When I ask Jonathan Maaga, who is no apartheid patsy, about the Zionists' reputation for subservience, he says whites were simply drawing their own conclusions from a perfectly normal black survival strategy.

"The whites in South Africa have never understood the black man," the doctor says. "Suppose there is a Z.C.C. member, and he works for you. And you say to him, 'Yes, I learned that in church you worship the Bishop.' He's not going to say, 'No, we don't pray to the Bishop.' He's going to say, 'Yes,' And do you know why? That keeps you happy, and the man retains his job. Now suppose you say to your employee that you don't like Mandela, he's a bloody fool. That man is never going to say no. He's going to agree with you.

"This is what we tell our people: Supposing the man calls you a fool and you don't object. What does it take away from you? Nothing, except that that man will keep you employed and you can feed your children. So that the man never really comes to know what you think. He thinks he does, but he doesn't.

"And that has been a national strategy. It has been like that all over. And this is why the white in South Africa has never come to grips with us. Everybody knows that if you want something out of the white man, you say, 'Oh yes, my big boss!'"

The Z.C.C. shunned the anti-apartheid movement and cozied up to authority, seeking refuge in Romans 13:1: "Let every person be subject to the governing authorities. For there is no authority except from God, and those that exist have been instituted by God." The church defended tribal chiefs and leaders of the black homelands that were invented as part of grand apartheid. Many Zionists recall being mocked by school classmates as backward, simpleminded and cowardly. In 1985, four months after Archbishop Tutu was awarded the Nobel Peace Prize for standing up to the apartheid state, at a time when activism was still treason and police were shooting protesters in their backs at places like Langa township, the Zionists invited the President, P. W. Botha, to their annual Easter worship service. The white President moved among a million black worshipers confident, no doubt, that he had discovered a vast repository of black support.

Ezra Mantini, a church council member who finds the memory uncomfortable, says: "I'm sure Botha went back and boasted to his friends: 'Forget about those noisemakers like Tutu. Here are five, six million people who are prepared to die for us.' It was a tense time and the church played into his hands."

Still, Mantini adds, it did not bother the believers, who understood all too well the need to sometimes say, "Oh yes, my big boss!" In the year after Botha's visit, the church baptized a record number of new members.

Something else contributes to the smirking confidence of white politicians about the Z.C.C.: the role of a white couple who have a lock on the church business enterprises. For a share of the proceeds, Marc and Claudine de la Harpe run the multimillion-dollar burial society and the bus company that provides transport for many Zionists in the north. Marc de la Harpe has also insinuated himself into a postion as a church spokesman. Many white politicians and journalists have come away with the impression that the conservative del la Harpes hold great sway over this vast black constituency.

In the past five years, however, the church has slowly begun to change, with the rise of several younger, more worldly members into leadership positions. The de la Harpes have been marginal-ized and the church has begun to contemplate a greater secular role.

The political posture of the Z.C.C. has shifted from obeisance to neutrality. The Bishop has issued messages telling Zionists they are free to engage in politics, as long as they keep the church out of it: no political T-shirts at church, no silver stars at campaign rallies. The Bishop has met secretly with Nelson Mandela and other political leaders. On Easter Sunday this year, the Bishop invited the leaders of six political parties to come pray (but not speak) in Zion City. There was no mistaking the affections of the crowd, judging from the joyous murmur that greeted Mandela when he arrived, standing in the back of a Nissan pickup truck with seven security men.

Many church members say if the Bishop tells them to vote for one party or the other, they will eagerly do so. The Bishop declines to do so, and to prevent any hint of political leaning has instructed the 3,000 top ministers of the church to refrain from voting. After considerable internal debate, however, he used his Easter message, three weeks before the election, to tell the faithful they should vote and should even feel proud to wear their badges to the polls.

"As a Z.C.C. member, please be aware that it is your vote that will insure progress, prosperity and preservation of Christian values in the new South Africa," he intoned to the multitude spread below the church on the Zion City hillside. By Z.C.C. standards this was a breakthrough, since the church has members in the Inkatha Freedom Party and the tiny Azanian Peoples Organization, both of which are boycotting the election.

The fact that the church historically has shied away from politics did not mean its members were shills for white power, or happy with apartheid.

In fact, it is a well-kept secret outside the church that some of South Africa's best-known militants are Zionists. Peter Mokaba, an electrifying A.N.C. youth leader, and Sam Shilowa, the head of South Africa's most powerful labor federation and a member of the Central Committee of the South African Communist Party, both grew up in the Z.C.C. and still regard themselves as members in good standing, although they are not observant. For a South African, this bit of un-advertised information is comparable to discovering Jesse Jackson's name on a list of Jimmy Swaggart's contributors.

Zionists are heavily represented among the shop stewards of major unions, which are an important source of voter mobilization for the A.N.C.

"There are some people, including the whites around the Bishop, who have tried to make the Z.C.C. a conservative church," says Mokaba, who arranged the Bishop's meetings with Mandela. "But that has not worked. The members of the church are poor, and inevitably they are going to be in the struggle. The Bishop is still very much accessible to us. He knows, I think, the feeling of the broad membership of his church."

Maaga agrees: "Look, we suffered so much under the apartheid system that I don't believe many people are really going to forget that very soon. All those who remember that, I don't think are going to vote for anybody else other than the A.N.C."

*　　*　　*

The Rev. Desmond Mpilo Tutu, the Anglican Archbishop of Cape Town, sits in the study of the serene and priceless suburban estate called Bishop's Court, looking as ecclesiastical as it is possible to look in a bright blue warmup suit. We have been discussing the Zionists and I have just proposed that the Z.C.C., with its well-behaved membership and its abstemious life style and its Romans 13:1 view of authority, might be a force for stability. The Nobel laureate seems to be wrestling with his internal censor. If so, he loses.

"I almost puke," says the Archbishop, then proceeds to qualify his summary judgment. Tutu concedes that the Zionists satisfy an African yearning his own church does not. The missionary churches had blundered by treating blacks as "benighted natives" and denigrating everything African as uncivilized. Up to a point, he says, South African blacks are at home in the Christianity brought from Europe, but "deep down inside, you have something which says, 'This does not touch the wellspring of my psyche.'"

He admires the Zionists, too, for their ability to cushion the shock of township life for rural newcomers. "The independent churches are very smart," he says. "They had a kind of natural wisdom in how you dealt with people in a kind of holistic way."

This much the Archbishop will grant the Zionists, but no more. He is aggrieved that such a powerful black institution had been so silent during the years of oppression and so detached from such charitable undertakings as hospitals and schools.

But more than political complacency, what disturbs him about the Zionists is their, to his mind, pandering to the human craving for simplistic answers. Tutu grew up next door to a Zionist family and has spent much of his life pulling the opposite direction —away from fundamentalism, toward complexity, toward the exercise of the human mind on the wonderful conundrums of Christianity. After all, he says, Jesus spoke in conundrums — "He said, 'Go and do likewise.' Go and do likewise *what?*"

"People like to have a list. People like the business of not having to make decisions for themselves. They like things pre-packaged." He fumes at the folly of raising black South Africans to follow rules unthinkingly.

"I don't buy that. I'm good because I do not drink? Rubbish."

Before ushering me to the door, he concludes: "St. Augustine said, 'Love God, and do what you like.'"

Later I report this conversation to Maaga, the most thoughtful of my Z.C.C. interlocutors, a man I knew had already adjusted church precepts when they did not suit his experience.

"Maybe he is right," says the doctor, with a gentle shrug. "Except that his church does not cater to the grass roots."

*　　*　　*

If it is up to Maaga and the other more civic-minded members of the Z.C.C., the church will enlarge its social role. It already has the scholarship program and the chamber of commerce. Maaga has been pushing for an AIDS awareness program and a social-services scheme that would enlist churchwomen as intermediaries between needy illiterates and the government programs supposed to help them. Besides helping the members, these programs would give the more educated members something to do. For in the Z.C.C., advancement is based on healing powers, not on academic credentials, and Zionists with schooling are often frustrated that their learning means nothing.

The church, however, is a cautious institution that tends to chew over new ideas with an infuriating lack of urgency. There was supposed to be a voter education program this year, but it never got off the ground. One day when I was complaining of my frustration with the church hierarchy, Maaga told me he had arranged a meeting between the Bishop and some birth control specialists, hoping to enlist the church in support of family planning.

"If these girls can't control themselves, why don't they use contraception?" the Bishop asked. There was a stunned silence. "But contraception is not allowed by the church," one of the church elders said. "Where have I ever said so?" the Bishop replied. "Where has my father, or my grandfather ever said so? It's the old ladies who are against it." Then he turned to Maaga: "Your job is to convince these old ladies. On one condition: don't split the church."

Elated, Maaga went home and waited patiently for the Bishop to issue the official encyclical that would set his family planning program in motion. And waited. And waited. How long has it been, I asked. "Three years now," the doctor said. "So don't feel so bad."

It may be too much to hope, then, that the Zion church will relieve some of the demands on the new Government. But even if the new programs fail to materialize, the Zionists say, their culture of nonviolence, hard work and respect for authority is bound to be an asset to the A.N.C. as it scrambles to keep up with racing expectations.

"At the end of the day, politicians want stable societies," says Ezra Mantini. "They want peaceful societies. They want investors to come in. They want people to work. The politicians like someone who makes noise when it suits them. But as soon as they get into power, they want everyone to keep quiet. The guy who was supposed to be a stooge is suddenly a good guy for them."

Chapter Ten

Recent Church Documents

The 1980s signaled a new awareness on the part of church leaders regarding economic matters. Partly because the "Cold War" drew to a close, the widespread reading of history primarily in terms of political and military power began also to decline. At the same time, Margaret Thatcher in England, Ronald Reagan in the U.S., and Helmut Kohl in Germany, to mention only some of the more prominent world leaders, declared an end to the vague but widespread suspicion that "socialism" was the most moral path to the future. Their views were hotly debated and roundly condemned in many circles, but the focus of the discussion was altered. Crises that faced nations East and West, North and South, were recognized as both economic and ethical. While there is never any way to avoid the importance of personal morality in the conduct of business, and while government will and should play a role in regulating business to prevent exploitation and to protect the weak, the crises could not be met on the basis of the theories of Karl Marx or Adam Smith or even the attempt to synthesize them by John Maynard Keynes. For the first time in history, the ethical focus turned as much to the moral nature, structure, and responsibilities of corporations as to the morality of persons and governments.

This took place in the context of expansive new global developments. There was a resurgence of religion, most often in its more orthodox and even fundamentalist forms, and increased use of cybernetic and robotic production (which in a different but compatible sense put a premium on symbolic work and lowered the value of physical work and the less educated workers). Class mobility and the attack on discrimination based on race and sex, while not entirely victorious, reduced the sense of group solidarity — and brought a sense of the loss of community. No small amount of sympathy for socialism allied with a nostalgia for simpler societies. But by the time communism collapsed and socialist parties were voted out in country after country, nearly every major Christian denomination had issued statements on the relationship of faith to work, tax policy, welfare, income distribution, consumption patterns, homelessness, and poverty among the disadvantaged in the context of new reflections on the corporations. These documents both summarize previous convictions and point toward a still incomplete moral consensus. This chapter offers a representative sample of excerpts from current official church teachings.

Religious authorities have, of course, always taught about the ethics of marriage and the family, about law and social order, about politics and power, about the creative arts and culture, and about education and wisdom on the basis of their deepest convictions about faith and God. Such topics bring those convictions into ethical interaction with the raw issues of the world and allow the ultimate issues to shape our responses to proximate ones. Because this has always been the case, we can find in the theological heritage a profound, if too often neglected, repository of broad, deep, and wide resources for dealing with economic issues — as are collected in this volume — in both the historic tradition and modern reflections, even if many believe that the moral core of our modern, economics-driven society is eroding. Now, the churches are turning also to issues of poverty and wealth, business and economics, productivity and technology with a new vigor, seeking new ways of stating ancient truths for these times and new ways to grasp the present.

Even more, they are seeking to engender new developments. After all, it appears that religion, insofar as it is believed by people, becomes woven into the fabric of life. Taken as the basis for ethics, it can become the guiding factor in shaping both character and civilization. And the kind of religion (or ideology, or faith, or basic convictions) one has is decisive for the way the social order and the structure of personality are formed. Thus theological issues are critical for the cultivation of human communities and for human well-being, even if they are not determinative for the ultimate destiny of the soul or the fate of the universe. Those matters are in the hands of God. On earth, piety predetermines polity and policy and thus personality.

Lutheran Statement

Among the first ecclesiastical treatments of the economy in recent decades was the 1980 statement of the Lutheran Church in America. Setting a pattern that was to be followed in several denominations, the most comprehensive authoritative body of the faith community — in this case, the Biennial Convention — offered a general analysis of how the faith, as it is believed, is to be used to identify key issues in the common economic life and to guide behavior in both business life and political decisions that influence the economy. The intent was to lead church members to personal and concerted action for justice — which, as this statement says, is "distributive love." Because the churches had not often addressed economic issues in this way, quite condensed definitions of the nature of economic life, as seen from a theological and ethical vantage point, are set forth.

Almost never are long prescriptions given as to how, exactly, one is to act in economic life; but quite substantive lists of principles to be followed in making economic decisions are developed — principles such as equity, accessibility, accountability, and efficiency. Further, out of the debates about the possible relationships of Christianity to capitalism and to socialism, on which the churches had not reached wide agreement in the 1980s, the statements give a good bit of attention to the nature of work and of property, and to issues of the relative role of government in economic and business activity. The governing conclusion of the Lutheran statement is that economic activity is not to be separated from our life under God, our social context as a part of the wider human community, or our stewardly care of the material resources of the earth that are given to us by God. All of these elements can be seen in this statement from the Lutheran Church in America.

429

Economic Justice: Stewardship of Creation in Human Community

The Lutheran Church in America

Introduction

God wills humanity to exercise justice in its stewardship of creation. Holy Scripture declared that the earth is the Lord's and that persons created in God's image are divinely authorized to care for this earth and to share in its blessings. Since human community is dependent on responsible stewardship, God commands that persons deal equitably and compassionately in their use of the earth's limited resources in order to sustain and fulfill the lives of others.

It is in obedient gratitude for all the gifts of God that we in the Lutheran Church in America commit ourselves in faithful love to struggle for economic justice as an integral part of the witness and work of God's People in the world.

Economy in Society

The word, "economy," is derived from the Greek words which mean the ordering of the household. In this basic sense, economy denotes the activity of persons in the management of all the resources (natural, human, and manufactured) of this world.

An economic system is the pattern of relation-

"Economic Justice: Stewardship of Creation in Human Community," adopted by the Tenth Biennial Convention of the Lutheran Church in America, Seattle, Washington, June 24–July 2, 1980.

ships, processes, institutions, and regulations, together with the values underlying them, by which the activities of production, distribution, and consumption are carried out in and among societies and cultures.

Economic policies and institutions develop through social custom and political decision. The allocation of the resources, burdens, and benefits of the economy is variously done by traditional habits, by individual choice in the marketplace, by governmental regulation, by the action of corporations, or by all of these. Likewise the institutional constraints on economic activity are made by these means separately or in combination.

Economic activity is embedded in the total life of a society. Relations of production and distribution reflect the prevailing patterns of power as well as the values by which a society lives. The material allocations within a society are both an effect and a cause of the basic character of that society. The economic choices of the members and institutions of a society reflect what a society is and influence what it is becoming.

The fundamental questions underlying any economic system are therefore political and moral in nature. There are always technical questions that are peculiar to the operation of any given system, but the basic issues are not technical in character. For example, who may work? What should motivate our labors? By whom and how should it be decided what to produce, where to distribute, and how much to consume? Who determines, and how, the "fairness" of prices, profits, wages, benefits and strikes? How do we balance economic production and environmental protection? Do our economic practices reflect or reinforce child exploitation, sexism, ageism, racism, or anti-Semitism? The answers, never final, emerge qualified and compromised from the field of contending interests, powers, and moral claims.

The organization of economic life has undergone vast changes throughout the course of history, and no economic "system" has ever shown itself to be permanent. The appearance of new conditions, the development of new technologies, and the evolution of social values and political structures have all occasioned the alteration or replacement of economic institutions and relationships.

It is in such a world of continual change, amid

graphic evidence of both progress and exploitation, that the Holy Spirit calls the church to bear witness to God's sovereign reign in our midst. As the Lord of history God acts in society to judge and fulfill the daily efforts of all people in their economic theory and practice.

Theological Foundations

All persons are intended to respond in worship and work as one human family according to the Creator's love: to propagate, nurture and extend human life and enhance its quality; to protect and use wisely the world's resources; to participate with God in the continuing work of creation; and to share equitably the product of that work to the benefit of all people.

In a world broken by sin the Creator lovingly enables the doing of justice. Into such a world God calls the redeemed in Christ to be advocates and agents of justice for all.

The Image of God

Human life depends totally on a loving Creator. All persons are made in God's image for a life of trust, obedience, and gratitude.

Life under God is also meant to be life in community. There is no humanity but co-humanity; for one cannot be human alone. It is only together that persons can realize their creation in God's image. This image is reflected as persons respond in love and justice to one another's needs. Male and female persons are created equally in the image of God (Gen. 1:27). It is in the basic human relationships of domestic, political, and economic life that persons share in their common humanity. God's love encompasses all people, and God intends that stewardship be practiced for the benefit of the entire human family.

Created in the image of God, persons are together stewards of God's bounty. They are accountable to God for how they use, abuse, or neglect to use the manifold resources — including their own bodies and capacities — which God has placed at their disposal. Reflecting God's cosmic dominion as Creator, they are called to care for the earth and "have dominion over," but not callously dominate, every living thing (Gen. 1:28).

Work

Work, the expending of effort for productive ends, is a God-given means by which human creatures exercise dominion. Through work, persons together are enabled to perpetuate life and to enhance its quality. By work they are both privileged and obligated to reflect the Creator whose work they are.

Although sinful rebellion issues in burdens of toil and alienation, the forgiving and renewing Lord holds out the possibility of work as useful and satisfying, prompting the Psalmist's prayer, "Establish the work of our hands" (Ps. 90:17).

Work is thus meant for persons in community, not persons for work. While participation in the community of work is meant to enhance personal well-being, the identity of persons created in God's image is neither defined by the work they do nor destroyed by the absence of work. What a person *does* or *has* does not determine what one *is* as the personal creature of a loving Creator.

Christian identity is also not to be equated with the work Christians do. As new persons in Christ, Christians have been set free and empowered to exercise their vocation through many roles, occupations among them. However, Christians do not equate baptismal vocation in God's kingdom with economic occupations in the world.

Justice

Justice may be described as distributive love. It is what God's love does when many neighbors must be served with limited resources. Justice is the form of God's creating and preserving love as that love is mediated by reason and power through persons and structures in community life. Injustice dehumanizes life and prevents full participation in co-humanity. Justice is therefore viewed simply as that which people need to be human.

God mandates the doing of justice (Micah 6:8). The specific content of that justice, however, is not directly revealed but is discovered as life is lived amid claim and counterclaim. The discernment of justice involves every aspect of the human being. It is a task of reason, requiring the counting, measuring and classifying of factors that admit to such analysis. It is intuitive, involving the capacity for empathy. It is political, involving the struggle for power among competing groups. Above all, it is moral, involving the fundamental human capacity to know what enhances and what destroys the being, and dignity of the person. That capacity, conscience, grows and is nurtured in the creative interaction of persons and groups, in the recollection of and reflection on past experience, and in the confronting of new situations.

Therefore the doing of justice is the proper stewardship of the social and material resources of creation in which our co-humanity in God's image is being realized.

Social justice refers to those institutional and legal arrangements which promote justice for all the members of society.

In addition to being the way in which God's providential love is expressed socially, justice is also the way in which sinful persons are required to do for others what, in their self-centeredness, they would not otherwise do to meet their neighbors' collective needs.

Because human beings, both individually and collectively, are self-centered, self-serving, and self-justifying, their defining and doing of justice are inevitably tainted by the rationalization of special interest. This sinful rationalization often leads to such errors as the pitting of benevolence against justice and the confusion of justice with righteousness.

Social justice should not be pitted against personal benevolence (often called charity) or corporate benevolence (often called philanthropy); but neither should benevolence be substituted for justice. In its true sense, benevolence is the loving response directly to others in need; in its false sense, it is the vain attempt to purchase a good conscience and to avoid the demand for justice. Rightly understood, benevolence and justice complement each other as different forms of the Creator's providential love.

Neither personal nor corporate benevolence can accomplish what a society is required to do for its members under justice, but a society cannot remain sound if it leaves no room for benevolent acts.

Justice and righteousness, as these terms are used in this statement, are not to be confused or identified with each other. Righteousness denotes the redeeming activity of God in Christ which effects the forgiveness of sin, new life, and salvation. It frees and empowers God's faithful servants to act lovingly and justly in the world, not merely out of prudent self-regard, but also sacrificially for their neighbors' sake.

The attempt to equate human justice and divine righteousness distorts Christ's Gospel and undermines God's law. In the name of liberty, such self-righteousness enslaves; in the name of life, it kills; in the name of abundance, it lays waste. God's holy wrath is provoked when humans presume to rule society by a spurious "gospel," thereby weakening the possibility of realizing justice, peace, and civil order under God's law. . . .

Government

In a sinful world God intends the institutions of government to be the means of enforcing the claims of economic justice. Government should neither stifle economic freedom through excessive regulation, nor abdicate its responsibility by permitting economic anarchy. Legitimate governmental activity normally includes such functions as: protection of workers, producers, and households from practices which are unfair, dangerous, or degrading: protection of the public from deceptive advertising and from dangerous or defective products or processes; encouragement and regulation of public utilities, banking and finance, science and education; environmental protection: provision for the seriously ill and disabled, needy, and unemployed; and establishment of an equitable system of taxation to support these functions. Compliance with these and other legitimate governmental activities should be affirmed, even as their improvement and correction are sought through appropriate political means.

In extreme situations, when governmental institutions or holders of political power engage in the tyrannical and systematic violation of basic human rights, and when the means of legal recourse have been exhausted or are demonstrably inadequate, then non-violent direct action, civil disobedience, or, as a last resort, rebellion may become the justifiable and necessary means of establishing those conditions within which justice can again be sought and enjoyed.

Economic Justice

Economic justice is that aspect of social justice involving the material dimension of social relationships and the social activities of production, distribution, and consumption of goods and services. Economic justice denotes the fair apportioning of resources and products, of opportunities and responsibilities, of burdens and benefits among the members of a community. It includes the provision for basic human need, fair compensation for work done, and the opportunity for the full utilization of personal gifts in productive living.

Economic justice includes the elements of equity accessibility, accountability, and efficiency.

Understood as equity or fairness, economic justice does not mean economic equality. It is rather the result of a discerning of, and response to, the various needs of the members of a society, respecting differences without being partial to power or special interest. Equity implies a sense of the common good and a care for the diversity of gifts and human resources that contribute to it. At the same time it provides for those minimal necessities which, in a given social and cultural setting, are prerequisites for participation in society, and it provides for those members of the society who, because of circumstances not of their making, cannot provide for themselves.

Accessibility includes both the formal entitlements to political participation and legal redress, and such substantive entitlements (e.g., nutrition, shelter, health care, basic education, minimum income and/or employment) as are needed for entrance into the social and economic community. It also includes the provision of the means by which the members of a community may participate in decisions which affect the quality of the common life and that of future generations.

Accountability implies that economic actors must be held answerable to the community for the consequences of their behavior. Government property establishes the legal means whereby people may secure compensation for injury incurred, as a result of economic decisions which have not taken account of their likely impact on personal and community well-being.

Efficiency requires a responsible use of resources that is genuinely productive by minimizing waste. This productivity is conserving not only of material resources and time, but also of human resources and the environment. The economy should be structured to permit the calculation of efficiency so as to take account of social and ecological waste.

Persons should be permitted and encouraged to participate in fundamental as well as market decisions governing the economy. Members of a society should be co-determiners of the quality of their economic life. Such co-determination, requiring differing structures appropriate for differing situations, is the basic right of persons whom God has created in co-humanity as responsible stewards.

Stewardship requires careful forethought. Planning is vital to the stewardship of material resources at all levels of human life: personal, familial, communal, and political. Planning on economic matters is more than technical. Questions of basic human value are involved in both specifying economic goals and devising the means of achieving them.

Planning should therefore be sufficiently pluralistic in character to assure the possibility of self-correction and prevent domination by one or a few special interests. It should be done on a scale and level of social life which provide for the greatest practical degree of participation and co-determination.

God has implanted in the human creature the capacity and initiative to define the problems of material existence in community and to effect positive change. No person or community should relinquish that initiative or capacity, and social and political institutions should be designed to encourage such initiative at the local and intermediate levels of society. A society is healthier when its members are encouraged to participate responsibly in determining their own lives rather than being only the passive consumers of goods and services. . . .

Property

The concept of property is a legal means of determining responsibility for the use of resources and humanly-produced wealth. Property may be held by individuals, by business corporations, by cooperative or communal self-help organizations, or by government. In whatever manner it is held, property is held in trust and its holder is accountable ultimately to God and proximately to the community through its constituted authorities for the ways in which the resource or wealth is, or is not, used.

While the holder of wealth-producing property is entitled to a reasonable return, as determined contextually by the society, the holder of such property may not assert exclusive claim on it or its fruits. Justice requires that wealth be both productive and contributory to the general well-being through both the provision of new opportunities and the alleviation of human need.

The private ownership of property is a humanly devised legal right which can serve as a means for the exercise of that responsible stewardship which constitutes the divine image. Private property is not an absolute human right but is always conditioned by the will of God and the needs of the community. The obligation to serve justifies the right to possess. The Creator does not sanction the accumulation of economic power and possessions as ends in themselves.

Conclusion

We affirm the inseparability of the economy from the whole of human life. The criticism and reshaping of economic relations and institutions is a fundamentally moral task in which Christians should be actively involved. Economy rightly understood, is the God-given stewardship of life.

In Christ the People of God are freed and enabled individually and corporately to participate in the quest for greater economic justice and the achievement of the conditions of human well-being. As a worldwide community of brothers and sisters, the church can summon the human family to care for the earth responsibly while God yet gives us time.

The U.S. Bishops' Pastoral Letter

The Roman Catholic Bishops' Pastoral Letter of 1986 is clearly the most discussed of the contemporary church statements. Already before this letter was issued many bishops had joined Protestant and Jewish leaders in support for the civil rights movement in America and in opposing American military policies in Vietnam; already the debates about undue American influence in Latin America had been under wide discussion in religious circles; and already the bishops had issued a letter on nuclear weaponry, a letter that had brought about a major public debate about the morality of building, using, and threatening the use of these weapons of mass destruction. The capacity of religious leaders to lift the level of public moral discourse on issues of policy was widely recognized.

Equally important, the bishops decided in this case not only to hold a number of hearings around the country to gain information but also to issue several preliminary drafts of the statement and to allow the public — economists, politicians, labor leaders, and laity from many other walks of life — to offer critical responses, which were used in revisions. While the internal structure of the Roman Catholic Church, and, indeed, of most religious groups, involves structures of authority that are not fully democratic, this responsiveness to commentary and critique introduced a democratic element and brought about an enormous engagement in the issues. It prompted some Protestant groups to follow a similar procedure, and, in fact, some twenty-seven Protestant denominations eventually commended this letter to their own members for study. Nothing like that has happened since the Reformation. Similarly, the document was studied in university courses on public policy, business ethics, and political economics. It is doubtful that any church document has commanded that kind of attention since the Enlightenment.

In this document, two levels of moral discussion are set forth: authoritative teachings and considered advice. Church leaders believe that they have a responsibility to set forth as clearly as possible the first principles of ethical life, or deontology, and the broader vision, or teleology, by which all economic systems are evaluated. But the empirical assessment of economic life and the technical knowledge of economic practices, which are dealt with by ethological understanding, are matters on which laypersons with specialized knowledge in these areas can and should inform clergy and the society at large.

Economic Justice for All: Catholic Social Teaching and the U.S. Economy

National Conference of Catholic Bishops

Brothers and sisters in Christ:

. . . We write to share our teaching, to raise questions, to challenge one another to live our faith in the world. We write as heirs of the biblical prophets who summon us "to do justice, to love kindness and to walk humbly with our God" (Mi. 6:8); and we write as followers of Jesus, who told us in the Sermon on the Mount: "Blessed are the poor in spirit. . . . Blessed are the lowly. . . . Blessed are those who hunger and thirst for justice. . . . You are the salt of the earth. . . . You are the light of the world" (Matt. 5:1-6, 13-14). These words challenge us not only as believers, but also as consumers, citizens, workers and owners. In the parable of the Last Judgment, Jesus said, "I was hungry and you gave me to eat, thirsty and you gave me to drink. . . . As often as you did it for one of these the least of my brothers, you did it for me" (Matt. 25:35-40). The challenge for us is to discover in our own place and time what it means to be "poor in spirit" and "the salt of the earth" and what is means to serve "the least among us" and to "hunger and thirst for justice."

Followers of Christ must avoid a tragic separation between faith and everyday life. They can neither shirk their earthly duties nor, as the Second Vatican Council declared, "immerse ourselves in earthly activities as if these latter were utterly

---

National Council of Catholic Bishops, *Economic Justice for All* (Washington, DC: U.S. Catholic Conference, 1986), in *Origins* 16, no. 24 (27 Nov. 1986).

foreign to religion and religion were nothing more than the fulfillment of acts of worship; and the observance of a few moral obligations" (Pastoral Constitution on the Church in the Modern World, 43).

Economic life raises important social and moral questions for each of us and for society as a whole. Like family life, economic life is one of the chief areas where we live out our faith, love our neighbor, confront temptation, fulfill God's creative design and achieve our holiness. Our economic activity in factory, field, office or shop feeds our families — or feeds our anxieties. It exercises our talents — or wastes them. It raises our hopes — or crushes them. It brings us into cooperation with others — or sets us at odds. The Second Vatican Council instructs us "to preach the message of Christ in such a way that the light of the Gospel will shine on all activities of the faithful." In this case we are trying to look at economic life through the eyes of faith, applying traditional church teaching to the U.S. economy. . . .

Ethical Norms for Economic Life

Biblical and theological themes shape the overall Christian perspective on economic ethics. This perspective is also subscribed to by many who do not share Christian religious convictions. Human understanding and religious belief are complimentary, not contradictory. For human beings are created in God's image, and their dignity is manifest in the ability to reason and understand, in their freedom to shape their own lives and the life of their communities, and in the capacity for love and friendships. In proposing ethical norms, therefore, we appeal both to Christians and to all in our pluralist society to show that respect and reverence owed to the dignity of every person. Intelligent reflection on the social and economic realities of today is also indispensable in the effort to respond to economic circumstances never envisioned in biblical times. Therefore, we now want to propose an ethical framework that can guide economic life today in ways that are both faithful to the Gospel and shaped by human experience and reason.

First we outline the *duties* all people have to each other and to the whole community: love of neighbor, the basic requirements of justice and the special obligation to those who are poor or vulnerable. Corresponding to these duties are the *human rights* of every person; the obligation to protect the dignity of all demands respect for these rights. Finally these duties and rights entail several *priorities* that should guide the economic choices of individuals, communities and the nation as a whole.

The Responsibilities of Social Living

Human life is life in community. Catholic social teaching proposes several complementary perspectives that show how moral responsibilities and duties in the economic sphere are rooted in this call to community.

Love and Solidarity

The commandments to love God with all one's heart and to love one's neighbor as oneself are the heart and soul of Christian morality. Jesus offers himself as the model of this all-inclusive love: "Love one another as I have loved you" (John 15:12). These commands point out the path toward true human fulfillment and happiness. They are not arbitrary restrictions on human freedom. Only active love of God and neighbor makes the fullness of community happen. Christians look forward in hope to a true communion among all persons with each other and with God. The Spirit of Christ labors in history to build up the bonds of solidarity among all persons until that day on which their union is brought to perfection in the kingdom of God. Indeed Christian theological reflection on the very reality of God as a trinitarian unity of persons — Father, Son and Holy Spirit — shows that being a person means being united to other persons in mutual love.

What the Bible and Christian tradition teach, human wisdom confirms. Centuries before Christ the Greeks and Romans spoke of the human person as a "social animal" made for friendship, community and public life. These insights show that human beings achieve self-realization not in isolation, but in interaction with others.

The virtues of citizenship are an expression of Christian love more crucial in today's interdependent world than ever before. These virtues grow out of a lively sense of one's dependence on the commonweal and obligations to it. This civic commitment must also guide the economic institutions of society. In the absence of a vital sense of citizenship among the businesses, corporations, labor unions and other groups that shape economic life, society as a whole is endangered. Solidarity is another name for this social friendship and civic commitment that make human moral and economic life possible.

The Christian tradition recognizes, of course, that the fullness of love and community will be achieved only when God's work in Christ comes to completion in the kingdom of God. This kingdom has been inaugurated among us, but God's redeeming and transforming work is not yet complete. Within history, knowledge of how to achieve the goal of social unity is limited. Human sin continues to wound the lives of both individuals and larger social bodies and places obstacles in the path toward greater social solidarity. If efforts to protect human dignity are to be effective, they must take these limits on knowledge and love into account. Nevertheless, sober realism should not be confused with resigned or cynical pessimism. It is a challenge to develop a courageous hope that can sustain efforts that will sometimes be arduous and protracted.

Justice and Participation

Biblical justice is the goal we strive for. This rich biblical understanding portrays a just society as one marked by the fullness of love, compassion, holiness and peace. On their path through history, however, sinful human beings need more specific guidance on how to move toward the realization of this great vision of God's kingdom. This guidance is contained in the norms of basic or minimal justice. These norms state the *minimum* levels of mutual care and respect that all persons owe to each other in an imperfect world. Catholic social teaching, like much philosophical reflection, distinguishes three dimensions of basic justice: commutative justice, distributive justice and social justice.

Commutative justice calls for fundamental fairness in all agreements and exchanges between individuals or private social groups. It demands re-

spect for the equal human dignity of all persons in economic transactions, contracts or promises. For example, workers owe their employers diligent work in exchange for their wages. Employers are obligated to treat their employees as persons, paying them fair wages in exchange for the work done and establishing conditions and patterns of work that are truly human.

Distributive justice requires that the allocation of income, wealth and power in society be evaluated in light of its effects on persons whose basic material needs are unmet. The Second Vatican Council stated: "The right to have a share of earthly goods sufficient for oneself and one's family belongs to everyone. The fathers and doctors of the church held this view, teaching that we are obliged to come to the relief of the poor and to do so not merely out of our superfluous goods." Minimum material resources are an absolute necessity for human life. If persons are to be recognized as members of the human community, then the community has an obligation to help fulfill these basic needs unless an absolute scarcity of resources makes this strictly impossible. No such scarcity exists in the United States today.

Justice also has implications for the way the larger social, economic and political institutions of society are organized. *Social justice implies that persons have an obligation to be active and productive participants in the life of society and that society has a duty to enable them to participate in this way.* This form of justice can also be called "contributive," for it stresses the duty of all who are able to help create the goods, services and other nonmaterial or spiritual values necessary for the welfare of the whole community. In the words of Pius XI, "It is of the very essence of social justice to demand from each individual all that is necessary for the common good." Productivity is essential if the community is to have the resources to serve the well-being of all. Productivity, however, cannot be measured solely by its output in goods and services. Patterns of production must also be measured in light of their impact on the fulfillment of basic needs, employment levels, patterns of discrimination, environmental quality and sense of community.

The meaning of social justice also includes a duty to organize economic and social institutions so that people can contribute to society in ways that respect their freedom and the dignity of their labor. Work should enable the working person to become "more a human being," more capable of acting intelligently, freely and in ways that lead to self-realization.

Economic conditions that leave large numbers of able people unemployed, underemployed or employed in dehumanizing conditions fail to meet the converging demands of these three forms of basic justice. Work with adequate pay for all who seek it is the primary means for achieving basic justice in our society. Discrimination in job opportunities or income levels on the basis of race, sex or other arbitrary standard can never be justified. It is a scandal that such discrimination continues in the United States today. Where the effects of past discrimination persist, society has the obligation to take positive steps to overcome the legacy of injustice. Judiciously administered affirmative-action programs in education and employment can be important expressions of the drive for solidarity and participation that is at the heart of true justice. Social harm calls for social relief.

Basic justice also calls for the establishment of a floor of material well-being on which all can stand. This is a duty of the whole of society, and it creates particular obligations for those with greater resources. This duty calls into question extreme inequalities of income and consumption when so many lack basic necessities. Catholic social teaching does not maintain that a flat, arithmetical equality of income and wealth is a demand of justice, but it does challenge economic arrangements that leave large numbers of people impoverished. Further, it sees extreme inequality as a threat to the solidarity of the human community, for great disparities lead to deep social divisions and conflict.

This means that all of us must examine our way of living in light of the needs of the poor. Christian faith and the norms of justice impose distinct limits on what we consume and how we view material goods. The great wealth of the United States can easily blind us to the poverty that exists in this nation and the destitution of hundreds of millions of people in other parts of the world. Americans are challenged today as never before to develop the inner freedom to resist the temptation constantly to seek more. Only in this way will the nation avoid what Paul VI called "the most evident form of moral underdevelopment," namely greed.

These duties call not only for individual charitable giving but also for a more systematic approach by business, labor unions and the many other groups that shape economic life — as well as government. The concentration of privilege that exists today results far more from institutional relationships that distribute power and wealth inequitable than from differences in talent or lack of desire to work. These institutional patterns must be examined and revised if we are to meet the demands of basic justice. For example, a system of taxation based on assessment according to ability to pay is a prime necessity for the fulfillment of these social obligations.

Overcoming Marginalization and Powerlessness

These fundamental duties can be summarized this way: *Basic justice demands the establishment of minimum levels of participation in the life of the human community for all persons.* The ultimate injustice is for a person or group to be actively treated or passively abandoned as if they were non-members of the human race. To treat people this way is effectively to say that they simply do not count as human beings. This can take many forms, all of which can be described as varieties of marginalization or exclusion from social life. This exclusion can occur in the political sphere: restriction of free speech, concentration of power in the hands of a few or outright repression by the state. It can also take economic forms that are equally harmful. Within the United States, individuals, families and local communities fall victim to a downward cycle of poverty generated by economic forces they are powerless to influence. The poor, the disabled and the unemployed too often are simply left behind. This pattern is even more severe beyond our borders in the least-developed countries. Whole nations are prevented from fully participating in the international economic order because they lack the power to change their disadvantaged position. Many people within the less-developed countries are excluded from sharing in the meager resources available in their homelands by unjust elites and unjust governments. These patterns of exclusion are created by free human beings. In this sense they can be called forms of social sin. Acquiescence in them or failure to correct them when it is possible to do so is a sinful dereliction of Christian duty.

Recent Catholic social thought regards the task of overcoming these patterns of exclusion and powerlessness as a most basic demand of justice. Stated positively, justice demands that social institutions be ordered in a way that guarantees all persons the ability to participate actively in the economic, political and cultural life of society. The level of participation may legitimately be greater for some persons than for others, but there is a basic level of access that must be made available for all. Such participation is an essential expression of the social nature of human beings and of their communitarian vocation.

Human Rights: The Minimum Conditions for Life in Community

Catholic social teaching spells out the basic demands of justice in greater detail in the human rights of every person. These fundamental rights are prerequisites for a dignified life in community. The Bible vigorously affirms the sacredness of every person as a creature formed in the image and likeness of God. The biblical emphasis on covenant and community also shows that human dignity can only be realized and protected in solidarity with others. In Catholic social thought, therefore, respect for human rights and a strong sense of both personal and community responsibility are linked, not opposed. Vatican II described the common good as "the sum of those conditions of social life which allow social groups and their individual members relatively thorough and ready access to their own fulfillment." These conditions include the rights to fulfillment of material needs, a guarantee of fundamental freedoms and the protection of relationships that are essential to participation in the life of society. These rights are bestowed on human beings by God and grounded in the nature and dignity of human persons. They are not created by society. Indeed society has a duty to secure and protect them.

The full range of human rights has been systematically outlined by John XXIII in his encyclical "Peace on Earth." His discussion echoes the U.N. Universal Declaration on Human Rights and implies that internationally accepted human-rights standards are strongly supported by Catholic teaching. These rights include the civil and political rights of freedom of speech, worship and assembly. A number of human rights also concern human welfare and are of a specifically economic nature. First among these are the rights to life, food, clothing, shelter, rest, medical care and basic education. These are indispensable to the protection of human dignity. In order to ensure these necessities, all persons have a right to earn a living, which for most people in our economy is through remunerative employment. All persons also have a right to security in the event of sickness, unemployment and old age. Participation in the life of the community calls for the protection of this same right to employment, as well as the right to healthful working conditions, to wages and other benefits sufficient to provide individuals and their families with a standard of living in keeping with human dignity, and to the possibility of property ownership. These fundamental personal rights — civil and political as well as social and economic — state the minimum conditions for social institutions that respect human dignity, social solidarity and justice. They are all essential to human dignity and to the integral development of both individuals and society, and are thus moral issues. Any denial of these rights harms persons and wounds the human community. Their serious and sustained denial violates individuals and destroys solidarity among persons.

Social and economic rights call for a mode of implementation different from that required to secure civil and political rights. Freedom of worship and of speech imply immunity from interference on the part of both other persons and the government. The rights to education, employment and social security, for example, are empowerments that call for positive action by individuals and society at large.

However, both kinds of rights call for positive action to create social and political institutions that enable all persons to become active members of society. Civil and political rights allow persons to participate freely in the public life of the community; for example, through free speech, assembly and the vote. In democratic countries these rights have been secured through a long and vigorous history of creating the institutions of constitutional government. In seeking to secure the full range of social and economic rights today, a similar effort to shape new economic arrangements will be necessary.

The first step in such an effort is the development of a new cultural consensus that the basic economic conditions of human welfare are essential to human dignity and are due persons by right. Second, the securing of these rights will make demands on *all* members of society, on all private-sector institutions and on government. A concerted effort on all levels in our society is needed to meet these basic demands of justice and solidarity. Indeed political democracy and a commitment to secure economic rights are mutually reinforcing.

Securing economic rights for all will be an arduous task. There are a number of precedents in U.S. history, however, which show that the work has already begun. The country needs a serious dialogue about the appropriate levels of private- and public-sector involvement that are needed to move forward. There is certainly room for diversity of opinion in the church and in U.S. society on *how* to protect the human dignity and economic rights of all our brothers and sisters. In our view, however, there can be no legitimate disagreement on the basic moral objectives.

Moral Priorities for the Nation

The common good demands justice for all, the protection of the human rights of all. Making cultural and economic institutions more supportive of the freedom, power and security of individuals and families must be a central, long-range objective for the nation. Every person has a duty to contribute to building up the commonweal. All have a responsibility to develop their talents through education. Adults must contribute to society through their individual vocations and talents. Parents are called to guide their children to the maturity of Christian adulthood and responsible citizenship. Everyone has special duties toward the poor and the marginalized. Living up to these responsibilities, however, is often made difficult by the social and economic patterns of society. Schools and educational policies both public and private often serve the privileged exceedingly well, while the children of the poor are effectively abandoned as second-class citizens. Great stresses are created in family life by the way work is organized and scheduled, and by the social and cultural values communicated on television. Many in the lower middle class are barely getting by and fear becoming victims of economic forces over which they have no control.

The obligation to provide justice for all means that the poor have the single most urgent economic claim on the conscience of the nation. Poverty can take many forms, spiritual as well as material. All people face struggles of the spirit as they ask deep questions about their purpose in life. Many have serious problems in marriage and family life at some time in their lives, and all of us face the certain reality of sickness and death. The Gospel of Christ proclaims that God's love is stronger than all these forms of diminishment. Material deprivation, however, seriously compounds such sufferings of the spirit and heart. To see a loved one sick is bad enough, but to have no possibility of obtaining health care is worse. To face family problems, such as the death of a spouse or a divorce, can be devastating, but to have these lead to the loss of one's home and end with living on the streets is something no one should have to endure in a country as rich as ours. In developing countries these human problems are even more greatly intensified by extreme material deprivation. This form of human suffering can be reduced if our own country, so rich in resources, chooses to increase its assistance.

As individuals and as a nation, therefore, we are called to make a fundamental "option for the poor." The obligation to evaluate social and economic activity from the viewpoint of the poor and the powerless arises from the radical command to love one's neighbor as oneself. Those who are marginalized and whose rights are denied have privileged claims if society is to provide justice for *all*. This obligation is deeply rooted in Christian belief. As Paul VI stated: "In teaching us charity, the Gospel instructs us in the preferential respect due the poor and the special situation they have in society: The more fortunate should renounce some of their rights so as to place their goods more generously at the service of others." John Paul II

has described this special obligation to the poor as "a call to have a special openness with the small and the weak, those that suffer and weep, those that are humiliated and left on the margin of society, so as to help them win their dignity as human persons and children of God."

The prime purpose of this special commitment to the poor is to enable them to become active participants in the life of society. It is to enable *all* persons to share in and contribute to the common good. The "option for the poor," therefore, is not an adversarial slogan that pits one group or class against another. Rather it states that the deprivation and powerlessness of the poor wounds the whole community. The extent of their suffering is a measure of how far we are from being a true community of persons. These wounds will be healed only by greater solidarity with the poor and among the poor themselves.

In summary, the norms of love, basic justice and human rights imply that personal decisions, social policies and economic institutions should be governed by several key priorities. These priorities do not specify everything that must be considered in economic decision making. They do indicate the most fundamental and urgent objectives.

a. The fulfillment of the basic needs of the poor is of the highest priority. Personal decisions, policies of private and public bodies, and power relationships must all be evaluated by their effects on those who lack the minimum necessities of nutrition, housing, education and health care. In particular, this principle recognizes that meeting fundamental human needs must come before the fulfillment of desires for luxury consumer goods, for profits not conducive to the common good and for unnecessary military hardware.

b. Increasing active participation in economic life by those who are presently excluded or vulnerable is a high social priority. The human dignity of all is realized when people gain the power to work together to improve their lives, strengthen their families and contribute to society. Basic justice calls for more than providing help to the poor and other vulnerable members of society. It recognizes the priority of policies and programs that support family life and enhance economic participation through employment and widespread ownership of property. It challenges privileged economic power in favor of the well-being of all. It points to the need to improve the present situation of those unjustly discriminated against in the past. And it has very important implications for both the domestic and the international distribution of power.

c. The investment of wealth, talent and human energy should be specially directed to benefit those who are poor or economically insecure. Achieving a more just economy in the United States and the world depends in part on increasing economic resources and productivity. In addition, the ways these resources are invested and managed must be scrutinized in light of their effects on non-monetary values. Investment and management decisions have crucial moral dimensions: They create jobs or eliminate them; they can push vulnerable families over the edge into poverty or give them new hope for the future; they help or hinder the building of a more equitable society. Indeed they can have either positive or negative influence on the fairness of the global economy. Therefore, this priority presents a strong moral challenge to policies that put large amounts of talent and capital into the production of luxury consumer goods and military technology while failing to invest sufficiently in education, health, the basic infrastructure of our society and economic sectors that produce urgently needed jobs, goods and services.

d. Economic and social policies as well as the organization of the work world should be continually evaluated in light of their impact on the strength and stability of family life. The long-range future of this nation is intimately linked with the well-being of families, for the family is the most basic form of human community. Efficiency and competition in the marketplace must be moderated by greater concern for the way work schedules and compensation support or threaten the bonds between spouses and between parents and children. Health, education and social service programs should be scrutinized in light of how well they ensure both individual dignity and family integrity.

These priorities are not policies. They are norms that should guide the economic choices of all and shape economic institutions. They can help the United States move forward to fulfill the duties of justice and protect economic rights. They were strongly affirmed as implications of Catholic social teaching by Pope John Paul II during his visit to Canada in 1984: "The needs of the poor take priority over the desires of the rich; the rights of workers over the maximization of profits; the preservation of the environment over uncontrolled industrial expansion; production to meet social needs over production for military purposes." There will undoubtedly be disputes about the concrete applications of these priorities in our complex world. We do not seek to foreclose discussion about them. However, we believe that an effort to move in the direction they indicate is urgently needed.

The economic challenge of today has many parallels with the political challenge that confronted the founders of our nation. In order to create a new form of political democracy they were compelled to develop ways of thinking and political institutions that had never existed before. Their efforts were arduous and their goals imperfectly realized, but they launched an experiment in the protection of civil and political rights that has prospered through the efforts of those who came after them. *We believe the time has come for a similar experiment in securing economic rights: the creation of an order that guarantees the minimum conditions of human dignity in the economic sphere for every person.* By drawing on the resources of the Catholic moral-religious tradition, we hope to make a contribution through this letter to such a new "American experiment": a new venture to secure economic justice for all.

Working for Greater Justice: Persons and Institutions

The economy of this nation has been built by the labor of human hands and minds. Its future will be forged by the ways persons direct all this work toward greater justice. The economy is not a machine that operates according to its own inexorable laws, and persons are not mere objects tossed about by economic forces. Pope John Paul II has stated that "human work is a key, probably the essential key, to the whole social question." The pope's understanding of work includes virtually all forms of productive human activity: agriculture, entrepreneurship, industry, the care of children, the sustaining of family life, politics, medical care and scientific research. Leisure, prayer, celebration and the arts are also central to the realization of human dignity and to the development of a rich cultural life. It is in their daily work, however, that persons become the subjects and creators of the economic life of the nation. Thus it is primarily through their daily labor that people make their most important contributions to economic justice.

All work has a threefold moral significance. First, it is a principal way that people exercise the distinctive human capacity for self-expression and self-realization. Second, it is the ordinary way for human beings to fulfill their material needs. Finally, work enables people to contribute to the well-being of the larger community. Work is not only for oneself. It is for one's family, for the nation and indeed for the benefit of the entire human family.

These three moral concerns should be visible in the work of all, no matter what their role in the economy: blue-collar workers, managers, homemakers, politicians and others. They should also govern the activities of the many different, overlapping communities and institutions that make up society: families, neighborhoods, small businesses, giant corporations, trade unions, the various levels of government, international organizations and a host of other human associations including communities of faith.

Catholic social teaching calls for respect for the full richness of social life. The need for vital contributions from different human associations — ranging in size from the family to government — has been classically expressed in Catholic social teaching in the "principle of subsidiarity":

"Just as it is gravely wrong to take from individuals what they can accomplish by their own initiative and industry and give it to the community, so also it is an injustice and at the same time a grave evil and disturbance of right order to assign to a greater and higher association what lesser and subordinate organizations can do. For every social activity ought of its very nature to furnish help (*subsidium*) to the members of the body social, and never destroy and absorb them."

This principle guarantees institutional pluralism. It provides space for freedom, initiative and creativity on the part of many social agents. At the same time it insists that *all* these agents should work in ways that help build up the social body. Therefore in all their activities these groups should be working in ways that express their distinctive capacities for action, that help meet human needs and that make true contributions to the common good of the human community. The task of creating a more just U.S. economy is the vocation of all and depends on strengthening the virtues of public service and responsible citizenship in personal life and on all levels of institutional life.

Without attempting to describe the tasks of all the different groups that make up society, we want to point to the specific rights and duties of some of the persons and institutions whose work for justice will be particularly important to the future of the U.S. economy. These rights and duties are among the concrete implications of the principle of subsidiarity. . . .

Working People and Labor Unions

Though John Paul II's understanding of work is a very inclusive one, it fully applies to those customarily called "workers" or "labor" in the United States. Labor has great dignity, so great that all who are able to work are obligated to do so. The duty to work derives both from God's command and from a responsibility to one's own humanity and to the common good. The virtue of industriousness is also an expression of a person's dignity and solidarity with others. All working people are called to contribute to the common good by seeking excellence in production and service.

Because work is this important, people have a right to employment. In return for their labor, workers have a right to wages and other benefits sufficient to sustain life in dignity. As Pope Leo XIII stated, every working person has "the right of securing things to sustain life." The way power is distributed in a free-market economy frequently gives employers greater bargaining power than employees in the negotiation of labor contracts. Such unequal power may press workers into a choice between an inadequate wage and no wage at all. But justice, not charity, demands certain minimum guarantees. The provision of wages and other benefits sufficient to support a family in dignity is a basic necessity to prevent this exploitation of workers. The dignity of workers also requires adequate health care, security for old age or disability, unemployment compensation, healthful working conditions, weekly rest, periodic holidays for recreation and leisure and reasonable security against arbitrary dismissal. These provisions are all essential if workers are to be treated as persons rather than simply as a "factor of production."

The church fully supports the right of workers to form unions or other associations to secure their rights to fair wages and working conditions. This is a specific application of the more general right to associate. In the words of Pope John Paul II, "The experience of history teaches that organizations of this type are an indispensable element of social life, especially in modern industrialized societies." Unions may also legitimately resort to strikes where this is the only available means to the justice owed to workers. No one may deny the right to organize without attacking human dignity itself. Therefore we firmly oppose organized efforts, such as those regrettably now seen in this country, to break existing unions and prevent workers from organizing. Migrant agriculture workers today are particularly in need of protection, including the right to organize and bargain collectively. U.S. labor law reform is needed to meet these problems as well as to provide more timely and effective remedies for unfair labor practices.

Denial of the right to organize has been pursued ruthlessly in many countries beyond our borders. We vehemently oppose violations of the freedom to associate, wherever they occur, for they are an intolerable attack on social solidarity.

Along with the rights of workers and unions go a number of important responsibilities. Individual workers have obligations to their employers, and trade unions also have duties to society as a whole. Union management in particular carries a strong responsibility for the good name of the entire union movement. Workers must use their collective power to contribute to the well-being of the whole community and should avoid pressing demands whose fulfillment would damage the common good and the rights of more vulnerable members of society. It should be noted, however, that wages paid to workers are but one of the factors affecting the competitiveness of industries. Thus it is unfair to expect unions to make

concessions if managers and shareholders do not make at least equal sacrifices.

Many U.S. unions have exercised leadership in the struggle for justice for minorities and women. Racial and sexual discrimination, however, has blotted the record of some unions. Organized labor has a responsibility to work positively toward eliminating the injustice this discrimination has caused.

Perhaps the greatest challenge facing U.S. workers and unions today is that of developing a new vision of their role in the U.S. economy of the future. The labor movement in the United States stands at a crucial moment. The dynamism of the unions that led to their rapid growth in the middle decades of this century has been replaced by a decrease in the percentage of U.S. workers who are organized. American workers are under heavy pressures today that threaten their jobs. The restrictions on the right to organize in many countries abroad make labor costs lower there, threaten American workers and their jobs, and lead to the exploitation of workers in these countries. In these difficult circumstances, guaranteeing the rights of U.S. workers calls for imaginative vision and creative new steps, not reactive or simply defensive strategies. For example, organized labor can play a very important role in helping to provide the education and training needed to help keep workers employable. Unions can also help both their own members and workers in developing countries by increasing their international efforts. A vital labor movement will be one that looks to the future with a deepened sense of global interdependence.

There are many signs that these challenges are being discussed by creative labor leaders today. Deeper and broader discussions of this sort are needed. This does not mean that only organized labor faces these new problems. All other sectors and institutions in the U.S. economy need similar vision and imagination. Indeed new forms of cooperation among labor, management, government and other social groups are essential and will be discussed in Chapter 4 of this letter.

Owners and Managers

The economy's success in fulfilling the demands of justice will depend on how its vast resources and wealth are managed. Property owners, managers and investors of financial capital must all contribute to creating a more just society. Securing economic justice depends heavily on the leadership of men and women in business and on wise investment by private enterprises. Pope John Paul II has pointed out, "The degree of well-being which society today enjoys would be unthinkable without the dynamic figure of the business person, whose function consists of organizing human labor and the means of production so as to give rise to the goods and services necessary for the prosperity and progress of the community." The freedom of entrepreneurship, business and finance should be protected, but the accountability of this freedom to the common good and the norms of justice must be assured.

Persons in management face many hard choices each day, choices on which the well-being of many others depends. Commitment to the public good and not simply the private good of their firms is at the heart of what it means to call their work a vocation and not simply a career or a job. We believe that the norms and priorities discussed in this letter can be of help as they pursue their important tasks. The duties of individuals in the business world, however, do not exhaust the ethical dimensions of business and finance. The size of a firm or bank is in many cases an indicator of relative power. Large corporations and large financial institutions have considerable power to help shape economic institutions within the United States and throughout the world. With this power goes responsibility and the need for those who manage it to be held to moral and institutional accountability.

Business and finance have the duty to be faithful trustees of the resources at their disposal. No one can ever own capital resources absolutely or control their use without regard for others and society as a whole. This applies first of all to land and natural resources. Short-term profits reaped at the cost of depletion of natural resources or the pollution of the environment violate this trust.

Resources created by human industry are also held in trust. Owners and managers have not created this capital on their own. They have benefited from the work of many others and form the local communities that support their endeavors. They are accountable to these workers and com-

munities when making decisions. For example, reinvestment in technological innovation is often crucial for the long-term viability of a firm. The use of financial resources solely in pursuit of short-term profits can stunt the production of needed goods and services; a broader vision of managerial responsibility is needed.

The Catholic tradition has long defended the right to private ownership of productive property. This right is an important element in a just economic policy. It enlarges our capacity for creativity and initiative. Small and medium-sized farms, businesses and entrepreneurial enterprises are among the most creative and efficient sectors of our economy. They should be highly valued by the people of the United States, as are land ownership and home ownership. Widespread distribution of property can help avoid excessive concentration of economic and political power. For these reasons ownership should be made possible for a broad sector of our population.

The common good may sometimes demand that the right to own be limited by public involvement in the planning or ownership of certain sectors of the economy. Support of private ownership does not mean that anyone has the right to unlimited accumulation of wealth. "Private property does not constitute for anyone an absolute or unconditioned right. No one is justified in keeping for his exclusive use what he does not need, when others lack necessities." Pope John Paul II has referred to limits placed on ownership by the duty to serve the common good as a "social mortgage" on private property. For example, these limits are the basis of society's exercise of eminent domain over privately owned land needed for roads or other essential public goods. The church's teaching opposes collectivist and statist economic approaches. But it also rejects the notion that a free market automatically produces justice. Therefore, as Pope John Paul II has argued, "One cannot exclude the socialization, in suitable conditions, of certain means of production." The determination of when such conditions exist must be made on a case-by-case basis in light of the demands of the common good.

U.S. business and financial enterprises can also help determine the justice or injustice of the world economy. They are not all-powerful, but their real power is unquestionable. Transnational corporations and financial institutions can make positive contributions to development and global solidarity. Pope John Paul II has pointed out, however, that the desire to maximize profits and reduce the cost of natural resources and labor has often tempted these transnational enterprises to behavior that increases inequality and decreases the stability of the international order. By collaborating with those national governments that serve their citizens justly and with intergovernmental agencies, these cooperations can contribute to overcoming the desperate plight of many persons throughout the world.

Business people, managers, investors and financiers follow a vital Christian vocation when they act responsibly and seek the common good. We encourage and support a renewed sense of vocation in the business community. We also recognize that the way business people serve society is governed and limited by the incentives which flow from tax policies, the availability of credit and other public policies. These should be reshaped to encourage the goals outlined here.

Businesses have a right to an institutional framework that does not penalize enterprises that act responsibly. Governments must provide regulations and a system of taxation which encourage firms to preserve the environment, employ disadvantaged workers and create jobs in depressed areas. Managers and stockholders should not be torn between their responsibilities to their organizations and their responsibilities toward society as a whole.

Citizens and Government

In addition to rights and duties related to specific roles in the economy, everyone has obligations based simply on membership in the social community. By fulfilling these duties, we create true commonwealth. Volunteering time, talent and money to work for greater justice is a fundamental expression of Christian love and social solidarity. All who have more than they need must come to the aid of the poor. People with professional or technical skills needed to enhance the lives of others have a duty to share them. And the poor have similar obligations; to work together as individuals and families to build up their communi-

ties by acts of social solidarity and justice. These voluntary efforts to overcome injustice are part of the Christian vocation.

Every citizen also has the responsibility to work to secure justice and human rights through an organized social response. In the words of Pius XI, "Charity will never be true charity unless it takes justice into account. . . . Let no one attempt with small gifts of charity to exempt himself from the great duties imposed by justice." The guaranteeing of basic justice for all is not an optional expression of largesse but an inescapable duty for the whole of society.

The traditional distinction between society and the state in Catholic social teaching provides the basic framework for such organized public efforts. The church opposes all statist and totalitarian approaches to socio-economic questions. Social life is richer than governmental power can encompass. All groups that compose society have responsibilities to respond to the demands of justice. We have just outlined some of the duties of labor unions and business and financial enterprises. These must be supplemented by initiatives by local community groups, professional associations, educational institutions, churches and synagogues. All the groups that give life to this society have important roles to play in the pursuit of economic justice.

For this reason it is all the more significant that the teachings of the church insist that *government has a moral function: protecting human rights and securing basic justice for all members of the commonwealth.* Society as a whole and in all its diversity is responsible for building up the common good. But it is government's role to guarantee the minimum conditions that make this rich social activity possible, namely, human rights and justice. This obligation also falls on individual citizens as they choose their representatives and participate in shaping public opinion.

More specifically, it is the responsibility of all citizens, acting through their government, to assist and empower the poor, the disadvantaged, the handicapped and the unemployed. Government should assume a positive role in generating employment and establishing fair labor practices, in guaranteeing the provision and maintenance of the economy's infrastructure, such as roads, bridges, harbors, public means of communication and transport. It should regulate trade and commerce in the interest of fairness. Government may levy the taxes necessary to meet these responsibilities, and citizens have a moral obligation to pay those taxes. The way society responds to the needs of the poor through its public policies is the litmus test of its justice or injustice. The political debate about these policies is the indispensable forum for dealing with the conflicts and trade-offs that will always be present in the pursuit of a more just economy.

The primary norm for determining the scope and limits of governmental intervention is the "principle of subsidiarity" cited above. This principle states that in order to protect basic justice government should undertake only those initiatives which exceed the capacity of individuals or private groups acting independently. Government should not replace or destroy smaller communities and individual initiative. Rather it should help them to contribute more effectively to social well-being and supplement their activity when the demands of justice exceed their capacities. This does not mean, however, that the government that governs least governs best. Rather it defines good government intervention as that which truly "helps" other social groups contribute to the common good by directing, urging, restraining and regulating economic activity as "the occasion requires and necessity demands." This calls for cooperation and consensus building among the diverse agents in our economic life, including government. The precise form of government involvement in this process cannot be determined in the abstract. It will depend on an assessment of specific needs and the most effective ways to address them. . . .

A New American Experiment: Partnership for the Public Good

For over 200 years the United States has been engaged in a bold experiment in democracy. The founders of the nation set out to establish justice, promote the general welfare and secure the blessings of liberty for themselves and their posterity. Those who live in this land today are the beneficiaries of this great venture. Our review of some of the most pressing problems in economic life today shows, however, that this undertaking is not yet complete. Justice for all remains an aspiration; a fair share in the general welfare is denied to many. In addition to the particular policy recommendations made above, a long-term and more fundamental response is needed. This will call for an imaginative vision of the future that can help shape economic arrangements in creative new ways. We now want to propose some elements of such a vision and several innovations in economic structures that can contribute to making this vision a reality.

Completing the unfinished business of the American experiment will call for new forms of cooperation and partnership among those whose daily work is the source of the prosperity and justice of the nation. The United States prides itself on both its competitive sense of initiative and its spirit of teamwork. Today a greater spirit of partnership and teamwork is needed; competition alone will not do the job. It has too many negative consequences for family life, the economically vulnerable and the environment. Only a renewed commitment by all to the common good can deal creatively with the realities of international interdependence and economic dislocations in the domestic economy. The virtues of good citizenship require a lively sense of participation in the commonwealth and of having obligations as well as rights within it. The nation's economic health depends on strengthening these virtues among all its people and on the development of institutional arrangements supportive of these virtues.

The nation's founders took daring steps to create structures of participation, mutual accountability and widely distributed power to ensure the political rights and freedoms of all. We believe that similar steps are needed today to expand economic participation, broaden the sharing of economic power and make economic decisions more accountable to the common good. As noted above, the principle of subsidiarity states that the pursuit of economic justice must occur on all levels of society. It makes demands on communities as small as the family, as large as the global society and on all levels in between. There are a number of ways to enhance the cooperative participation of these many groups in the task of creating this future. Since there is no single innovation that will solve all problems, we recommend careful experimentation with several possibilities that hold considerable hope for increasing partnership and strengthening mutual responsibility for economic justice.

Cooperation Within Firms and Industries

A new experiment in bringing democratic ideals to economic life calls for serious exploration of ways to develop new patterns of partnership among those working in individual firms and industries. Every business, from the smallest to the largest, including farms and ranches, depends on many different persons and groups for its success: workers, managers, owners or shareholders, suppliers, customers, creditors, the local community and the wider society. Each makes a contribution to the enterprise, and each has a stake in its growth or decline. Present structures of accountability, however, do not acknowledge all these contributions or protect these stakes. A major challenge in today's economy is the development of new institutional mechanisms for accountability that also preserve the flexibility needed to respond quickly to a rapidly changing business environment.

New forms of partnership between workers and managers are one means for developing greater participation and accountability within firms. Recent experience has shown that both labor and management suffer when the adversarial relationship between them becomes extreme. As Pope Leo XIII stated, "Each needs the other completely: Capital cannot do without labor nor labor without capital." The organization of firms should reflect and enhance this mutual partnership. In particular, the development of work patterns for men and women that are more supportive of family life will benefit both employees and the enterprises they work for.

Workers in firms and on farms are especially in need of stronger institutional protection, for their jobs and livelihood are particularly vulnerable to the decisions of others in today's highly competitive labor market. Several arrangements are gaining increasing support in the United States: profit sharing by the workers in a firm; enabling employees to become company stockholders; granting employees greater participation in determining the conditions of work; coopera-

tive ownership of the firm by all who work within it; and programs for enabling a much larger number of Americans, regardless of their employment status, to become shareholders in successful cooperations. Initiatives of this sort can enhance productivity, increase the profitability of firms, provide greater job security and work satisfaction for employees, and reduce adversarial relations. In our 1919 Program of Social Reconstruction we observed "the full possibilities of increased production will not be realized so long as the majority of workers remain mere wage earners. The majority must somehow become owners, at least in part, of the instruments of production." We believe this judgment remains generally valid today.

None of these approaches provides a panacea and all have certain drawbacks. Nevertheless we believe that continued research and experimentation with these approaches will be of benefit. Catholic social teaching has endorsed on many occasions innovative methods for increasing worker participation within firms. The appropriateness of these methods will depend on the circumstances of the company or industry in question and on their effectiveness in actually increasing a genuinely cooperative approach to shaping decisions. The most highly publicized examples of such efforts have been in large firms facing serious financial crises. If increased participation and collaboration can help a firm avoid collapse, why should it not give added strength to healthy businesses? Cooperative ownership is particularly worthy of consideration in new entrepreneurial enterprises.

Partnerships between labor and management are possible only when both groups possess real freedom and power to influence decisions. This means that unions ought to continue to play an important role in moving toward greater economic participation within firms and industries. Workers rightly reject calls for less-adversarial relations when they are a smokescreen for demands that labor make all the concessions. For partnership to be genuine it must be a two-way street, with creative initiative and a willingness to cooperate on all sides.

When companies are considering plant closures or the movement of capital, it is patently unjust to deny workers any role in shaping the outcome of these difficult choices. In the heavy manufacturing sector today, technological change and international competition can be the occasion of painful decisions leading to the loss of jobs or wage reductions. While such decisions may sometimes be necessary, a collaborative and mutually accountable model of industrial organization would mean that workers not be expected to carry all the burdens of an economy in transition. Management and investors must also accept their share of sacrifices, especially when management is thinking of closing a plant or transferring capital to a seemingly more lucrative or competitive activity. The capital at the disposal of management is in part the product of the labor of those who have toiled in the company over the years, including currently employed workers. As a minimum, workers have a right to be informed in advance when such decisions are under consideration, a right to negotiate with management about possible alternatives and a right to fair compensation and assistance with retraining and relocation expenses should these be necessary. Since even these minimal rights are jeopardized without collective negotiation, industrial cooperation requires a strong role for labor unions in our changing economy.

Labor unions themselves are challenged by the present economic environment to seek new ways of doing business. The purpose of unions is not simply to defend the existing wages and prerogatives of the fraction of workers who belong to them, but also to enable workers to make positive and creative contributions to the firm, the community and the larger society in an organized and cooperative way. Such contributions call for experiments with new directions in the U.S. labor movement.

The parts played by managers and shareholders in U.S. corporations also need careful examination. In U.S. law, the primary responsibility of managers is to exercise prudent business judgment in the interest of a profitable return to investors. But morally this legal responsibility may be exercised only within the bounds of justice to employees, customers, suppliers and the local community. Corporate mergers and hostile takeovers may bring greater benefits to shareholders, but they often lead to decreased concern for the well-being of local communities and make towns and cities more vulnerable to decisions made from afar.

Most shareholders today exercise relatively little power in corporate governance. Although shareholders can and should vote on the selection of corporate directors and on investment questions and other policy matters, it appears that return on investment is the governing criterion in the relation between them and management. We do not believe this is an adequate rationale for shareholder decisions. The question of how to relate the rights and responsibilities of shareholders to those of the other people and communities affected by corporate decisions is complex and insufficiently understood. We therefore urge serious, long-term research and experimentation in this area. More effective ways of dealing with these questions are essential to enable firms to serve the common good.

Local and Regional Cooperation

The context within which U.S. firms do business has direct influence on their ability to contribute to the common good. Companies and indeed whole industries are not sole masters of their own fate. Increased cooperative efforts are needed to make local, regional, national and international conditions more supportive of the pursuit of economic justice.

In the principle of subsidiarity, Catholic social teaching has long stressed the importance of small- and intermediate-sized communities or institutions in exercising moral responsibility. These mediating structures link the individual to society as a whole in a way that gives people greater freedom and power to act. Such groups include families, neighborhoods, church congregations, community organizations, civic and business associations, public interest and advocacy groups, community-development corporations and many other bodies. All these groups can play a crucial role in generating creative partnerships for the pursuit of the public good on the local and regional level.

The value of partnership is illustrated by considering how new jobs are created. The development of new businesses to serve the local community is key to revitalizing areas hit hard by unemployment. The cities and regions in greatest need of these new jobs face serious obstacles in attracting enterprises that can provide them. Lack of financial resources, limited entrepreneurial skill, blighted and unsafe environments, and a deteriorating infrastructure create a vicious cycle that makes new investment in these areas more risky and therefore less likely.

Breaking out of this cycle will require a cooperative approach that draws on all the resources of the community. Community-development corporations can keep efforts focused on assisting those most in need. Existing business, labor, financial and academic institutions can provide expertise in partnership with innovative entrepreneurs. New cooperative structures of local ownership will give the community or region an added stake in businesses, and even more important, give these businesses a greater stake in the community. Government on the local, state and national levels must play a significant role, especially through tax structures that encourage investment in hard-hit areas and through funding aimed at conservation and basic infrastructure needs. Initiatives like these can contribute to a multilevel response to the needs of the community.

The church itself can work as an effective partner on the local and regional level. Firsthand knowledge of community needs and commitment to the protection of the dignity of all should put church leaders in the forefront of efforts to encourage a community-wide cooperative strategy. Because churches include members from many different parts of the community, they can often serve as mediator between groups who might otherwise regard each other with suspicion. We urge local church groups to work creatively and in partnership with other private and public groups in responding to local and regional problems. . . .

Cooperation at the International Level

If our country is to guide its international economic relationships by policies that serve human dignity and justice, we must expand our understanding of the moral responsibility of citizens to serve the common good of the entire planet. Cooperation is not limited to the local, regional or national level. Economic policy can no longer be governed by national goals alone. The fact that the "social question has become worldwide" challenges us to broaden our horizons and enhance our collaboration and sense of solidarity on the global level. The cause of democracy is closely tied to the cause of economic justice. The unfinished business of the American experiment includes the formation of new international partnerships, especially with the developing countries, based on mutual respect, cooperation and a dedication to fundamental justice.

The principle of subsidiarity calls for government to intervene in the economy when basic justice requires greater social coordination and regulation of economic actors and institutions. In global economic relations, however, no international institution provides this sort of coordination and regulation. The U.N. system, including the World Bank, the IMF and the GATT, does not possess the requisite authority. Pope John XXIII called this institutional weakness a "structural defect" in the organization of the human community. The structures of world order, including economic ones, "no longer correspond to the objective requirements of the universal common good."

Locked together in a world of limited material resources and a growing array of common problems, we help or hurt one another by the economic policies we choose. All the economic agents in our society, therefore, must consciously and deliberately attend to the good of the whole human family. We must all work to increase the effectiveness of international agencies in addressing global problems that cannot be handled through the actions of individual countries. In particular we repeat our plea made in "The Challenge of Peace" urging "that the United States adopt a stronger supportive leadership role with respect to the United Nations." In the years following World War II the United States took the lead in establishing multilateral bodies to deal with postwar economic problems. Unfortunately, in recent years this country has taken steps that have weakened rather than strengthened multilateral approaches. This is a shortsighted policy and should be reversed if the long-term interests of an interdependent globe are to be served. In devising more effective arrangements for pursuing international economic justice, the overriding problem is how to get from where we are to where we ought to be. Progress toward that goal demands positive and often difficult action by corporations, banks, labor unions, governments and other major actors on the international stage. But whatever the difficulty, the need to give priority to alleviating poverty in developing countries is undeniable; and the cost of continued inaction can be counted in human lives lost or stunted, talents wasted, opportunities foregone, misery and suffering prolonged, and injustice condoned.

Self-restraint and self-criticism by all parties are necessary first steps toward strengthening the international structures to protect the common good. Otherwise, growing interdependence will lead to conflict and increased economic threats to human dignity. This is an important long-term challenge to the economic future of this country and its place in the emerging world economic community. . . .

The Christian Vocation in the World Today

This letter has addressed many matters commonly regarded as secular, for example, employment rates, income levels and international economic relationships. Yet the affairs of the world, including economic ones, cannot be separated from the spiritual hunger of the human heart. We have presented the biblical vision of humanity and the church's moral and religious tradition as a framework for asking the deeper questions about the meaning of economic life and for actively responding to them. But words alone are not enough. The Christian perspective on the meaning of economic life must transform the lives of individuals, families, in fact, our whole culture. The Gospel confers on each Christian the vocation to love God and neighbor in ways that bear fruit in the life of society. That vocation consists above all in a change of heart: a conversion expressed in praise of God and in concrete deeds of justice and service.

My comments on the first draft of the pastoral will be somewhat critical, but they are made in a spirit of very strong appreciation. The bishops have succeeded in launching a major economics and morality debate at a time it is badly needed. . . .

The general pattern of exegetical and theological exposition is fine: creation, covenant and community as the baseline themes, embodied in Jesus and carried on by disciples. But not enough has been made of this for the church and economic life in view of the faith as a covenantal and eschatological faith. . . .

Interesting things happen when we turn to the policy section of the draft and draw out consequences that might follow if the primary biblical legacy were made more determinative for Christian approaches to economic life, for interpreting economic life in the light of the Gospel (the bishops' stated task).

Early on in the draft the bishops write: "There is no clear consensus about the nature of the problems facing the country or about the best ways to address these problems effectively. The nation wonders whether it faces fundamentally new economic challenges that call for major change in its way of doing business or whether adjustments within the framework of existing institutions will suffice."

When it says, "The nation wonders whether . . . ," it really means, "The bishops' staff wonder whether. . . ." Reflecting their unsettled judgment, the draft vacillates between two half-formed paradigms in part two.

One is, I apologize to the bishops, "Son of New Deal." The effort is to find policies of participation by the poor that, by way of critical governmental intervention, "mainstream" the poor into channels essentially left intact for the already affluent, who hold prevailing power. The market's definitions of social reality are basically accepted and the effort is to find policies that temper the morally unacceptable side of market-society reality.

The other half-formed paradigm is the call for "a new experiment in economic democracy,"

grounded in legally guaranteed socioeconomic rights and carried out with a central place for cooperative endeavors, using the subsidiarity principle. Such a paradigm, if elaborated, would address wealth, poverty and basic human needs all simultaneously in the process of structural change that alters poverty and wealth together. Such a notion does not accept the market's definitions of social reality as the controlling ones, even when it would use the market in major ways.

One economic half-paradigm — Son of New Deal — correlates roughly with the biblical legacy of God as consoler of the poor; the other, a new experiment in economic democracy, correlates roughly with God as empowerer of the poor. The weakest portion of part one is the concluding section on the church; this is because the covenantal and eschatological character of biblical faith is not simultaneously carried over into the church's own self-understanding as that affects its economic life.

What would happen to the draft if God as empowerer of the poor, and the church as the community anticipatory of the Kingdom, got better press among the bishops?

The church would be more definitely a church of the poor. In the draft it is not yet that, despite the theological call to join Jesus with the poor (54). What happens in the draft, with the long Constantinian hangover that wants everyone on board dialoguing, especially the influence-wielders, is that the potential theological radicals of part one undergo a transformation to become the prescriptive moderates of part two. (Prescriptive moderates, I hasten to add, not in contrast to the present Administration, or even majoritarian American views, but relative to the Exodus covenant and the Jesus community, where the faith of the bishops has its roots.)

— Larry Rasmussen, "Economic Policy: Creation, Covenant, and Community," *America* 152, no. 14 (4 May 1985): 365-67

A Mainline Protestant Position

In this section of this chapter, we turn to an example of recent "liberal" or "mainline" Protestant thinking on economic issues. It is drawn from a study document drafted for the United Church of Christ (UCC), the heir of the old Congregational Church of the New England Puritans as it has subsequently united with branches of the Evangelical and Reformed Churches and with a number of liberal, independent congregations formed after the Civil War. Many issues and perspectives in this statement are also found in parallel documents issued by Methodist, Presbyterian, and other church bodies connected with the National and World Councils of Churches.

The UCC document was prepared for study by delegates to the General Synod of the church and for congregational study. Pronouncements by this church do not become authoritative when they are delivered by church leaders but only when and if they are accepted by the people in the congregations. This theory of authority represents a theologically based view of radical democracy, characteristic of this church's heritage. It appears in this document in the proposal for "economic democracy." The "puritan" side of this heritage, which often (and falsely) is thought to apply especially to sexuality, aims to purify all behavior that is beyond the constraint of morally ordered community life, although within covenanted marriage, constitutional government, and regulated economies a rather robust freedom is encouraged. The claim of this document is that modern corporations have developed beyond the capacity of any community of discipline to constrain them. Thus, it is tempting for the freedom that is proper within covenanted structures of accountability to become irresponsible. This contention was challenged by other branches of the church, which issued counterstatements to this study document, as is characteristic of this tradition.

In this debate, the role of biblical reference is more frequent and direct than in most Roman Catholic documents. Further, Scripture is used not only as the central source of deontological principles and the primary locus of a teleological vision of God's ultimate purposes for humanity; Scripture is also used as a paradigmatic model for interpreting the events of the present. Contemporary developments, current trends, and characteristic experiences in the present are seen as examples of patterns and dynamics that are best illuminated by noting how they replicate decisive situations on which the ancient prophets spoke. While all may not agree on the specific analogies that are drawn between biblical texts and current experiences, it is precisely debates about these parallels that constitute one of the primary modes of moral discourse in modern Protestant traditions.

453

Christian Faith and Economic Life

United Church of Christ

As You Did It to the Least of These, So You Did It to Me

The Parable of the Great Judgment

In the parable of the great judgment (Matt. 25:31-46), Jesus describes a Divine Judge who assembles all the nations and separates them from one another. The judge places the righteous at the right and offers the blessings of the kingdom:

> for I was hungry and you gave me food, I was thirsty and you gave me drink, I was a stranger, and you welcomed me, I was naked and you clothed me, I was sick and you visited me, I was in prison and you came to see me (Matt. 25:35-36; all biblical quotations in this study paper are from the Revised Standard Version rendered into inclusive language).

When the righteous ask when they did so, the Judge answers, "Truly, I say to you, as you did it to one of the least of these my brothers and sisters, you did it to me" (Matt. 25:40).

Conversely, the Judge consigns the unjust to eternal punishment:

> for I was hungry and you gave me no food, I was thirsty and you gave me no drink, I was a stranger and you did not welcome me, naked and you did

Christian Faith and Economic Life, ed. Audrey Chapman Smock (New York: United Church Board for World Ministries, 1987).

not clothe me, sick and in prison and you did not visit me (Matt. 25:42-43).

When they ask when had they refused to minister, the Judge responds, "Truly, I say to you, as you did it not to one of the least of these, you did it not to me." (Matt. 25:45).

As the incarnation of the divine in the realm of history, the very "image of the invisible God" (Col. 1:15), Jesus of Nazareth told parables for specific purposes — not only to entertain, nor to remind his audiences of historical events, not even to communicate basic societal problems. Through parables, Jesus sought to help his hearers understand basic truths in order that they might become faithful to God. Thus this parable is more than a story about a divine judge who comes to separate the righteous from the unjust. In a variety of ways the parable discloses God's fundamental relationship with and intentions for humanity.

Like other biblical passages, the parable demonstrates God's presence within the economic and material dimensions of human life. The Divine Judge represents Christ at the second coming, evaluating the worth of the nations, both the individual members and the institutions they created, by how they fulfilled basic human requirements. Have they fed the hungry, brought drink to the thirsty, clothed the naked, provided shelter to the homeless and cared for the infirm and the prisoner? Far from offering a spiritualized concept of faith, the parable exhibits God's unbounded sensitivity to material human need. As in the parable of the unfaithful steward, Jesus here bids humanity to organize the gift of the creation so that all members of the human household will have "their portion of food at the proper time" (Luke 12:41). Whatever else it may be, Christian theology is also economic theology.

The parable of the great judgment links faithfulness to God with care of and concern for the human community. In it, God judges humanity not only through meditation, prayer, fasting, almsgiving, worship or study of Scripture. It tells us that concrete service and sharing in the life of the community provide a way to God. Thus the parable radically identifies love of God with love of neighbor.

The parable touches on several themes in Jesus' teachings: concern for the poor, the infirm, the excluded. These appear time and again, from his announcement at the opening of his ministry that he had come to preach good news to the poor (Luke 4:18), to his blessing the poor and promising them the kingdom of God in the Beatitudes (Luke 6:20), to his gathering of the outcasts and impoverished as full members of the community around him. Like the prophets, Jesus taught that the worth of a society is measured not by its power, wealth, or size, but by how it cares for its poorest and weakest members. Jesus' call for social relationships based on service also echoes his reminder to the disciples that "If anyone would be first, that person must be last of all and servant of all" (Mark 9:35). And his condemnation of those who did not share their resources and possessions resembles his rebuke of the rich as, for example, in the parable of the rich man and Lazarus (Luke 16:19-31).

The parable also conveys that Emmanuel, God with us, God immanent in the creation and in the community of believers, comes in the form of "the least of these," whoever and wherever they might be. The wretched of the earth are more than "the object of Christian love or the fulfillment of a moral duty; they are the latent presence of the coming Saviour and Judge in the world, the touchstone which determines salvation and damnation." When individuals or society fail to recognize Christ among the poor, when the powerful do not use their resources for the benefit of the suffering and needy, the parable judges that as they did it not to one of the least, they did it not to Christ.

For a century, the hope that society could provide for the basic needs of all citizens has rested on a faith in progress and a belief in the possibilities for unlimited economic growth. Industrialized economies, whether capitalist or socialist, whether controlled by the logic of the market or by state planning, have subscribed to a production ethic in which the increased output of goods and services has been a major societal goal. Imbued with the power and potential of technology, industrial cultures have worked to tame the forces of nature and to unlock the secrets of the earth. They have aspired to a standard of living and a plethora of goods inaccessible even to kings and queens in centuries gone by.

And the rise in productivity has been spectacular. Between 1950 and 1980 world output almost quadrupled in real terms, that is, after subtracting the effect of inflation, we had almost four times as many goods and services in the world in 1980 as we had in 1950. This rapid economic growth reached every continent and was unprecedented in human history. . . .

But have we managed God's creation so as to provide each member of the human family with the basic necessities of life? . . .

Current data on poverty in the world and within our own country indicate that the situation has not improved. The world continues to be divided between the one-third who are affluent and the two-thirds who are poor. The overwhelming majority of people still lack access to the basic necessities of life. Their poverty forces them to live without sufficient food, with hunger and malnutrition always lurking. The global distribution of income consigns whole groups and communities to the margins of subsistence with the lifelong possibility that any crop failure, any unexpected problem, any unanticipated expense will eliminate their thin cushion of survival. As catastrophe strikes, time and again, those particularly at risk are children under five, pregnant and lactating mothers, and the aged. Most appalling, massive starvation, malnutrition, and hunger persist in the midst of a considerable global food surplus. . . .

The current global economic crisis reflects the inadequacies of traditional economic models. Many people today sense the failure and question the appropriateness of contemporary economic approaches and the values and priorities underlying them. Many people now ask, "Why can't we create an economic system in which all people participate and all are nurtured?" It is that concern which this paper seeks to address. . . .

Biblical Mandates for Economic Life

Christian Concern for Economic Life

Christian faith summons the Christian community to show concern for the economic dimensions of life. The Old and New Testaments disclose a God whose love and compassion for the creation have no limits, a God "who executes justice for the oppressed; who gives food to the hungry" (Ps. 146:7), a God whose incarnation, Jesus Christ, came "that they may have life, and have it abundantly" (John 10:10). As the Bible attests, God's love and commitment to the world are not confined to the spiritual realm, the church, or matters relating to worship. "For the Lord is a God of Justice" (Isa. 30:18). Scripture abounds in passages dealing with such aspects of economic life as wealth, poverty, justice, hunger, access to livelihood, and distribution of goods. It does so because economic matters relate to God's covenantal care and relationship with humanity. . . .

In Genesis God is the creative power, the force who brings the universe into being and furnishes the earth with abundance so that all people can meet their needs. In contrast to religious doctrines which elevate the spiritual at the expense of the material, God pronounces the things of the creation to be good, worthwhile in and of themselves. The Genesis story presents God as planting a garden in Eden, placing Adam and Eve in the garden to till and keep it, and making available every plant that is pleasant to the sight and good for food. The garden of Eden represents the fullness of life, the sufficiency of resources with which God endowed the earth and human society so that all might have the basic means for life. But Adam and Eve, the progenitors of humanity, violate God's prescriptions. In so doing they introduce scarcity and suffering into God's good creation.

The exodus is a second major biblical tradition in which God acts as the Economist. The story of God's people begins, "Once we were slaves . . ." in the house of Pharaoh. Scripture reveals that God heard the cries of the slaves in Egypt, felt their suffering and suffered with them. In responding, God did not console the people of Israel with promises of spiritual freedom in their slavery: God led them out of bondage, out of oppression, and this is how they became God's chosen people.

After God led the people of Israel out of slavery, God made a covenant . . . in order to keep Israel from falling again into an economy of slavery. The terms of the covenant, embodied in the Torah (the first five books of the Old Testament), had many provisions for economic life, with special emphasis on the needs of the poor. The Torah provided Israel with the way to live faithfully to God and responsibility to the community. . . .

But Israel forgot and violated its covenant. During the monarchy, radical class distinctions developed with significant differences in wealth, power, and privilege. Yet another time, God spoke through the prophets and denounced this inequality, greed, and oppression. Prophet after prophet warned that an economic system based on economic exploitation and indifference to the needs of the poor was contrary to God's intentions. . . .

Jesus' ministry comprises the fourth great biblical tradition relevant to understanding God as the Economist. As recounted in the Gospels, Jesus called into the "household of Israel" all those who had been systematically excluded: the sinners, the poor, the women, the leprous, the oppressed. Through proclaiming the good news, through his parables, his signs and wonders, his fellowship with the common people of the land, Jesus depicted God as a gracious host and God's household as an economy that gives life to those excluded by the public economy.

Like the Hebrew prophets who took their stand with the poor, Jesus embodied the messianic promise to the poor and alienated. Living with and as one of the poor of his day, Jesus incarnated God's presence among and concern for the needy and alienated. In the Gospel of Luke, Jesus inaugurated his public ministry in his home town of Nazareth by announcing that:

The Spirit of the Lord is upon me
because God has anointed me
    to preach good news to the poor.
God has sent me to proclaim release
    to the captives
and recovery of sight to the blind,
    to set at liberty those who are oppressed,
    to proclaim the acceptable year of the Lord.
                    (Luke 4:18)

Jesus identified his ministry with the good news to the poor anticipated in Isaiah 61:1-2, and incarnated the radical hope of a new age. Thus Jesus concluded reading the text from Isaiah by telling those in the synagogue that "Today this scripture has been fulfilled in your hearing" (Luke 4:21). In the Beatitudes he promised that those who are poor, those who hunger, those who weep, and those who are persecuted were blessed or favored by God and thus will be cared for in the kingdom which was initiated in his ministry (Luke 6:20-22).

Faithfulness to God, according to Jesus, precluded dividing life into compartments of a religious segment for God and another segment for economic life. Thus Jesus announced that we cannot serve two masters, God and mammon (Matt. 6:24). He warned that the covetous accumulation of wealth will constitute an impediment to the service of God. . . .

Christian Principles of Economic Justice

The biblical vision of an economically just society can be stated in six interrelated principles. These provide both a standard against which to measure contemporary economic systems and a goal inspiring the faith community in its efforts to bring a more just order into being.

Fulfilling Basic Material Needs

In light of the parable of the great judgment, *a just economic system fulfills the basic material needs of all members of the human community and enhances the life opportunities of the poor, the weak, and groups at the margin of society.* As has already been stated, Scripture confers the role of stewards or economists on members of the faith community, calling us to organize God's gifts so that all persons can lead meaningful lives with their basic needs satisfied. The type of economic institutions and systems established and the policies pursued determine the level of economic productivity and the extent to which the nature of the goods and their distribution contribute to providing the means of life for all persons within the society. With the high level of interdependence within the world economy, national institutions and policies also affect the prospects and well-being of other countries.

To assure that everyone in God's household receives what it takes to live, the productivity of economic institutions is important. But it is contrary to a biblical perspective on economics to make productivity an idol. The Torah sets clear limits on economic life designed to protect the security and well-being of the poor and landless, the integrity of the community, and the needs and rights of the earth. For the prophets, fair distribution of resources and fulfillment of covenantal

relationships with all members of the community had a higher priority than economic efficiency or increases in agricultural productivity. Jesus cautioned against the single-minded accumulation of possessions, frequently criticizing the rich (Luke 6:24; 8:4-15; 16:19-31; 18:24-25) and warning, "Take heed, and beware of all covetousness, for a person's life does not consist in the abundance of possessions" (Luke 12:15). In a series teachings, Jesus admonished the rich to share their wealth (Luke 18:18-23; 12:32-34; 19:1-10), and not merely to invest it wisely on the Jerusalem stock market in order to receive better returns.

While affirming the significance of economic activity in providing for the basic needs of all members of society, Scripture underscores the need to evaluate economic systems on broader grounds in addition to, or other than, productivity or efficiency. It is not sufficient to measure the success of an economy by its gross national product, to let the mysterious and impersonal "market" decree that some people such as bankrupt farmers, the unemployed and underemployed and their children, and the dependent aged are "surplus." Aggregate measures of production like the gross national product and the per capita income tell us little regarding the usefulness of the goods produced, the extent to which all members and groups within society receive fair access to the means and benefits of production, or the extent to which the system of production conserves resources, promotes community building, benefits the poor, and allows for meaningful forms of work.

A major criterion for a faith-centered economics is whether particular institutions and policies enhance the life opportunities of the poor, the weak, and the groups at the margins of society. This mandate represents a contemporary application of Jesus' ministry of incarnating God's presence among, and bringing good news to the poor and of the prophetic mandate to protect the poor, widows, and orphans, the groups most vulnerable in biblical societies. It is also a reflection and extension of God's love for all persons. As John Bennett explains, "God's love for all persons implies a strategic concentration on the victims of society, on the weak, the exploited, the neglected persons who are a large majority of the human race." Bennett makes clear that he does not mean that God loves some people less than others, but that in loving all, God has a special concern for those whom society neglects. . . .

Economic Democracy

A just economic system is inclusive, involving all people in responsible, participatory, and economically rewarding activity. Western political democracy is rooted in the covenant tradition of the Protestant reformers. It was the rediscovery of the Old Testament covenant tradition by Calvinist thinkers that paved the way for the emergence of democratic theory. The Hebrew covenant is a life relationship between God and the chosen people established to embody righteousness within the human community. The covenant between God and humanity is a model of relationships among people, expressed in the covenant of mutual responsibility and commitment. All people are called to participate in, and to share the fruits of, creation and redemption. Those economic conditions that thwart full participation or that generate inequality and injustice therefore are as odious as despotic rulers. Just as governments finally became the property of those who are governed, so the economy belongs to the people who through it are fed and housed and inspired to produce for the needs of their neighbors and for the well-being of the whole community.

Economic democracy envisages an economic system in which all people participate and through which all are nurtured. It assumes basic economic rights and the exercise of those rights through widespread social participation. Echoing Thomas Jefferson's belief that economic dependency makes a mockery of freedom, economic democracy appropriates the best of our political tradition into the economy itself. In so doing, it contributes to the fullness of human community.

Economic democracy entails framing economic issues in ways that informed citizens can consider policy alternatives, make intentional decisions, and express their views. Economic democracy also involves facilitating and empowering the poor and other disadvantaged groups to participate on a more equal basis in the political decision-making process. Additionally, economic democracy assumes wide participation in ownership and management of economic institutions and structures. In a modern economy participation might include worker, community, or public ownership; participatory management systems representing worker and community groups; establishment of and monitoring public standards of accountability for private economic institutions; and some form of planning.

As the well-known passage from 1 Corinthians recognizes, in God's economy:

> There are varieties of gifts, but the same Spirit, and there are varieties of service, but the same Lord; and there are varieties of working, but it is the same God who inspires them all in everyone. To each is given the manifestation of the Spirit for the common good (1 Cor. 12:4-7). . . .

Human Community

A just economic system builds and enhances human communities wherein people can live with dignity and well-being. Such communities reflect and preserve the intrinsic worth and sacredness of human beings. They also facilitate expression of the love of neighbor. The community of our concern, the community to which we are responsible, is not limited to our families, our colleagues in life and work, our fellow citizens, our political allies. It extends to all humanity.

Contrary to the preoccupation with individual salvation so characteristic of American Christianity, Scripture has a very strong community and social dimension. The Bible emphasizes the intrinsic need for persons to live in community in order to achieve fulfillment and well-being and to be faithful to God's intentions. In the Old Testament the individual entered into a relationship with God through membership in the covenant community that defined mutual rights and responsibilities to God and one another. As recounted in the gospels, Jesus began calling followers almost immediately after initiating his public ministry. Once formed, this community of grace played a central role in his ministry.

Paul, so often interpreted as interested only in individual conversion, actually spent most of his ministry nurturing communities, not converting individuals. He invested his time in such efforts because he believed that the gospel bound women and men to one another as well as to God. For

Paul one cannot be a follower of Jesus apart from living within a community whose shared life reflects the gospel faith.

For Christians, all persons are included in the household of God. The Torah redefined the poor, the landless, the widow, the orphan, and the stranger as brother and sister. Jesus set tongues wagging because he entered into conversion with Syro-phoenician and Samaritan women, violating two taboos of his time. The parable of the Good Samaritan made clear that neighborliness crossed ethnic and religious barriers. In an international economy, we are enabled and called to hold a world-wide understanding of those who constitute our neighbors and to create economic institutions which provide for the basic needs of all members of the human community.

Social divisions based on doctrines of inequality and embodied in practices which disadvantage or discriminate against specific groups of persons constitute an affront to the Christian affirmation of the equality and worth of all human beings and the inclusiveness of the community. Racial class, and gender discrimination, expressions of prejudice that are often reflected in the operation of economic institutions, deny fundamental Christian beliefs. Whether expressed directly or more subtly through institutional processes, this domination and exploitation contradict the dignity of the person and love of neighbor. Equality of opportunity therefore is a requirement of Christian economic principles. . . .

Human Rights

A just economic system respects the human rights of its members and enhances the level of freedom in the society. Economy and government are made for people and not human beings for the economic and political systems. . . .

Scripture conceptualizes persons as moral and social beings created to live in communities linked by relationships of mutual caring and responsibility. Thus economic conditions and patterns of behavior which exclude or oppress any part of the community are considered to be affronts to the dignity and humanity of the individual as well as the integrity and faithfulness of the community. In the biblical view the absence of external or coercive authority has meaning only as a prelimi-

nary to facilitating individual commitment and faithfulness. Paul asks that we use our freedom as an opportunity through love to be servants of one another and to obey Christ's new covenant.

Within a biblical context then human rights and freedom consist of the ability to have material needs satisfied, to live in meaningful communities in which members respect and care for one another, to worship and be faithful to the intentions of the God of peace and justice. . . . It recognizes nine dimensions of human life in which people everywhere have basic needs. It recognizes the right of every person to:

- food and clean water;
- adequate health care;
- decent housing;
- meaningful employment;
- basic education;
- participation in community decision-making and the political process;
- protection from torture;
- protection of rights without regard to race, sex, sexual orientation, religion, national or social origin. . . .

Viable Economic System

A just and viable economic system is based on a responsible and equitable use of the earth's limited resources. Faithfulness and respect for the Creator entail reverence for the whole of creation. "The earth is the Lord's and the fulness thereof" (Ps. 24:1). The economy of God encompasses the entire created order, not just humanity. The story of the creation in Genesis states that "God saw everything that had been made, and behold it was very good" (Gen. 1:31). . . .

The environmental crisis forces choices about the quality and direction of the economy in order to assure a sustainable future for the planet. Economic justice requires systems of production whose use of finite resources recognizes needs and rights of future generations, protecting nature, the environment, and the biosphere. An ecologically sustainable system is one in which the size of the population, the pattern and use of resources, and the rate of pollution are within the capacity of the earth to support and maintain an acceptable quality of life for all people for an indefinite future.

This need for sustainability also raises serious questions about the possibilities for unlimited growth and the justification of American consumerism. . . .

[These principles need today to be applied to our new situation, some key features of which we can identify:]

Corporations

In Western market economies, the corporation has become the most successful form of social-economic organization for production of goods and provision of services. In its profit-oriented form, it has out-produced, out-employed, out-trained, and out-distributed every other way of arranging common economic activity in human history. It is the place where the various professions find a structure to work together and bring their expertise to a common focus — lawyers, economists, engineers, managers, accountants in interaction with skilled and unskilled workers. The profit-oriented corporation is also the organizational basis of the "free press" and media, publishing houses, research, and educational institutions.

It is important to note that the Western experience with the "capitalist" corporation is really quite different from the rest of the world. In parts of the world where feudalism was not displaced by the kind of social, political, and economic development which accompanied the development of the market economy, corporations were not formed by the middle class. Nor did they have the same independence. In contrast to North Europeans and Americans, most people from Central Europe, Eastern Europe and the developing countries have encountered the corporation in the form of a state corporation, a colonialist trading company, or the local subsidiary of a foreign multinational corporation. . . .

National governments of industrialized societies seek to regulate certain aspects of corporate behavior, with varying degrees of success, but state administrations, local communities, and employees often have little influence. Even the nominal owners, the shareholders, generally have little control over the managers of these vast bureaucratic hierarchies. The concentration of economic power in large corporations has given them influence over cultural values, elections and political processes, and even personal relationships, as well as threatening the fabric of pluralism that has undergirded American political, social, and economic life. . . .

The emergence of the corporation as one of the most powerful, pervasive, and effective institutions in the modern world underscores the need to address the relationship between corporations and the political and social order. The Christian principles of economic justice . . . offer the basis for beginning to reconsider corporate roles, ownership patterns, and modes of operation in relationship to the wider society. The goals of such a reformation would be to assure the preservation of pluralism and the productivity of the corporation while promoting greater responsibility and accountability to the community, broader participation in corporate decision-making, and greater justice in the impact of the corporation on the wider community. . . .

The Global Economy

In the post-World War II period the United States, as other countries, has been operating in the context of a global economy. An unprecedented surge in economic output, which made the world output almost four times as large in 1980 as in 1950, stimulated a major increase in international trade. Progressive decolonization and the initiation of major development programs in the newly independent countries added actors and markets to the international economic arena. The evolution of major corporations — American, European, Japanese, and Eastern European — into multinational empires resulted in the mobility of capital and global investment, production, and marketing strategies. . . .

Interdependence also results from the globalization of problems and issues. As the report of the Independent Commission on International Development Issues noted, "We are increasingly confronted, whether we like it or not, with more and more problems which affect mankind as a whole, so that solutions to these problems are inevitably internationalized." In the contemporary world, societies with differing political systems and economies confront similar challenges: overcoming poverty, development of renewable energy sources, depletion of resources and minerals, ecological changes, environmental pollution, redistribution of employment, employment creation, and adjustment to new technologies. . . .

Economic interdependence unfortunately has not generated the evolution of international institutions with a wide base of participation able to plan shared strategies and undertake projects and programs on behalf of the wider community. The Bretton Woods system established in 1944 by the dominant industrialized capitalist countries focused on two things, the establishment of currencies convertible into other currencies with fixed but adjustable exchange rates and the facilitation of international flows of goods and capital. To achieve these goals, three interlocking multinational institutions were created: the General Agreement on Tariffs and Trade (GATT) to promote and manage world trade, the International Monetary Fund (IMF) to maintain a system of stable exchange rates and provide short-term loans to countries with balance of payments deficits, and the International Bank for Reconstruction and Development (World Bank) to supply long-term loans to governments for development.

By 1971, however, the Bretton Woods system was no longer adequate to deal with the scale, complexity, and interdependence of the world economy. The United States' decision to cease exchanging gold for dollars at a fixed rate in that year marked its disintegration. In subsequent years the world economy has lunged from one crisis to another with no means to promote sustained and equitable development or to avert future shocks. . . . Prolonged periods of recession and the ravages of inflation have depressed growth, increased unemployment, exacerbated uneven levels and patterns of economic development, and produced a terrible toll in human suffering and poverty, particularly in the poorest and most vulnerable economies. . . .

Poverty in the U.S. Economy

. . . Any discussion of poverty in America must recognize both good news and bad news. The good news is that the United States has created a society in which the vast majority of its citizens have living standards which the medieval kings would have envied. Until this century, no country had more than one-third to one-half of its citizens living above a subsistence level of income. But the bad news must not be forgotten: poverty in the United States remains a present reality for an unacceptably large number of our citizens. In a country of affluence, tens of millions of Americans still live on the edge of economic disaster. . . .

Far from being shared equitably, the burden of poverty falls especially heavily on a few groups — blacks, Hispanics, Native Americans, women who head households, and children. Blacks and Native Americans are three times more likely than whites to live in poverty, Hispanics more than twice as likely. Compared with the 11 percent of white Americans who are poor, an appalling 34 percent of the black population and 28 percent of Hispanics live in poverty.

The incidence of poverty is particularly high among children. More than one in five of today's children live in households below the poverty line. Almost half (48 percent) of all black children live in poor households, and 39 percent of Hispanic children.

The "feminization of poverty" has been another trend in recent years. Over one third (34 percent) of female-headed households are poor. Poverty is particularly pervasive in households headed by minority women: more than half of all families headed by a single black women (52 percent) or a single Hispanic woman (53 percent) are below the poverty line. And for children in these homes the situation is especially bleak. Children living in a female-headed single parent home are four times more likely to be poor than those in two-parent homes.

Moreover, there is increasing evidence, such as the resurgence of hunger and the growing problem of homelessness, that this recent rise in poverty has brought deteriorating living conditions. The Physician Task Force on Hunger in America has compiled a deeply disturbing report. Issued in February 1985, the report states that "It is our judgment that the problem of hunger in the United States is more widespread and serious than any time in the last fifteen years." It concludes that some 20,000,000 Americans suffer from hunger. Of this number, over 15,000,000 people live below the poverty line but do not receive food stamp assistance.

These facts must be deeply disturbing to all Americans. The economic security that many of us have come to take for granted is denied to too many of our fellow citizens. Commenting on these numbers, the Catholic Bishops declare, "That so many people are poor in a nation as rich as ours is a social and moral scandal that we cannot ignore." We agree. . . .

How can we alleviate poverty in the United States? For a start there is a need to adopt a strategic option on behalf of the poor and disadvantaged in the formulation of government spending priorities. Less than three percent of the gross national product is now devoted to programs designed primarily to assist the poor, such as food stamps, welfare, and Medicaid. The recurrent debate over spending for poverty programs typically involves tiny fractions of the gross national product, with 97 percent of national resources for all practical purposes excluded from consideration. A country which spends nearly four times as much of its national resources on military expenditures as on poverty programs needs to reflect on Jesus' injunction "as you did it not to one of the least, you did it not to me" (Matt. 25:45).

Currently, there are an interlocking set of programs which provide some form of "social safety net," but which vary enormously in the extent to which they serve different groups in society. The group best protected is the elderly, who receive Social Security income (if they have contributed in earlier years) and the related Medicare benefits. They have gone from a group that is disproportionately poor in the 1960s, to a group that is disproportionately nonpoor in the 1980s. . . .

The second-largest set of welfare programs is aimed at women with children. The program we typically call "welfare" is Aid to Families with Dependent Children (AFDC), which provides minimum income guarantees to single-parent households. These households also have access to Food Stamps and to Medicaid. AFDC income levels are determined separately by each state and vary widely. In no state do AFDC payments provide income up to the poverty line, and in only a few states do AFDC and Food Stamps together put a household within 75 percent of the poverty line. . . .

There are many criticisms of this system. Among the reforms and changes that are regularly suggested are:

- Federalize AFDC and standardize support levels, so that people in all parts of the country face similar welfare options. . . .
- Provide a cash subsidy, . . . allowing low-income households to make their own budget decisions.
- Extend coverage of Medicaid, the low-income health insurance program.
- Establish a negative income tax. . . .
- Provide job training and job placement for AFDC participants who are judged able to work.
- Implement a program of national public service jobs as "jobs of last resort" for those who are unemployed and unable to find private sector jobs. . . .
- Provide better day care options for poor women. . . .

There are no easy policy solutions to the problems of unemployment and poverty in our society. But we cannot ignore these issues; there is great injustice in an affluent economy where 33 million people are poor. We must seriously pursue policies that address the needs of the groups in our society for whom the current set of educational and job opportunities has not been adequate. We must reshape our budgetary and economic priorities to assure that all of our citizens can participate fully in our society.

Poverty in the World Economy

Poverty in America is magnified many times over in the world economy. While one in seven Americans is poor, two-thirds of the global population lack adequate income, food, clothing, shelter, or medical care. In a world whose technology has made it possible to eliminate poverty, the overwhelming majority of the members of the human family still live on the margin of economic survival. The situation is particularly bleak in the 35 countries classified as low-income economies. . . .

These trends can be seen most clearly in Africa, the continent in which the poorest countries in the world are located. In contrast with countries like South Korea, Mexico, Brazil, Taiwan, and Saudi Arabia, which are approaching the threshold of self-sustaining development, the situation is worsening in much of sub-Saharan Africa. In a region already characterized by extremes of poverty, per capita incomes have been decreasing over the past decade. The World Bank predicts declining per capita income for sub-Saharan Africa through 1995, at which point it estimates that 65 to 85 percent of the population will be living below adequate subsistence levels. . . .

For over ten years Third World leaders, supported by international task forces, members of the religious community, and concerned citizens groups have argued that rather than dealing with the symptoms of current economic problems, it is necessary to address the underlying causes. They have called for major structural changes in international economic and financial institutions. The Pronouncement Affirming the United Church of Christ as a Just Peace Church adopted in 1985 supports the establishment of a more just international order in which poor nations would have a greater role in the policies and management of global economic institutions.

While differing in emphasis and detail, proposals for a more just international economic order generally include some or all of the following components:

- Greater availability of finance to Third World countries on more favorable terms, including a major restructuring of the International Monetary Fund and reduction of the debt burden of Third World countries;
- Measures to improve the terms and conditions of trade which are chronically unfavorable to Third World countries, including elimination of trade barriers, and efforts to create new markets for Third World products;
- Cooperation to achieve international food security, including adequate agricultural reforms, a greater focus on food crops, massive investments in agricultural programs and projects in Third World countries;
- Provision of greater and more assured Third World access to the technology and resources needed for development;
- Adoption of models for development which focus more on meeting key national or basic human needs and which promote more equitable income distribution within Third World countries;
- Establishment of new international institutions which are better able to address international economic problems and needs and which provide for more equitable participation by Third World countries. . . .

To be able to address the global economic crisis and promote greater international economic justice, such international economic institutions would have to facilitate new initiatives in international cooperation, direct and mobilize international development initiatives, operate on a representative and participatory basis, and undertake global management of major international resources. As envisaged here, the institutions would have responsibilities for the care of the environment, natural resource usage, international trade and finance, communications, and regulation of transnational corporations. . . .

The reluctance of the United States and other industrialized countries to accept international economic reforms consigns the overwhelming majority of God's children, those in present and future generations, to a life of poverty and deprivation. This refusal to relinquish the advantages conferred by the present international economic order may be predictable, but it is not in keeping with the Christian principles of economic justice. At this critical turning point of world history, faithfulness requires a new model of behavior, one which is inspired by the inclusiveness of the Christian community and the sacrifice of a Savior who gave up his own life in order that the world might be redeemed.

Exclusion and Discrimination in the U.S. Economy

Whose economy is it anyway? We opened the study with the affirmation that from a biblical perspective the economy belongs to God. It is part of creation. This means that all members and groups within society should have equal access to the rewards of economic participation. An economic system which excludes some individuals from full participation, or which reinforces and promotes inequality among groups, therefore, contradicts our principles of economic justice.

Few contemporary economic systems allow all people to participate fully. One major indication of this is the high and growing levels of unemployment throughout the world. In western Europe in 1985 nearly one person in five was out of work. And in the Third World, the International Labor Organization estimates that 500 million people are unemployed or underemployed. A recent sample of 21 developing countries shows that the number of unemployed doubled in a decade.

And even among those who find work, evidence of racism, sexism, ageism, and other forms of discrimination limit the access of these citizens and abridge their economic right to share in the fullness of creation. A system which promotes disparities based on race or gender fundamentally contradicts Christ's affirmation of the intrinsic worth of all individuals and the inclusiveness of the human community.

It is important to note that discrimination is not confined to overt acts of prejudice on the part of individuals. An economic system whose structures and arrangements systematically exclude people of color or women from equitable participation is also discriminatory. Institutional racism and sexism do not require intentional or willful efforts on the part of any individual to hurt some groups and to favor others. Like other forms of institutional evil, institutional racism and sexism can be embedded in the accepted "rules of the game" within the economy.

In the United States, our own economy has clearly become more inclusionary in many ways over the last several decades. The large increase in women's labor force participation, coupled with major equal employment opportunity laws, has opened up large numbers of occupations where women were once completely unwelcome. In similar ways, attempts to hire and train handicapped workers and to provide them with basic public services (as basic as toilet facilities) have been an effort to encourage greater participation in our society and to open up economic access. People of color have also seen large improvements. Since the mid-1960s, we have worked hard at lessening discrimination in access to jobs, to housing, to educational opportunities, and to more closely comparable wages.

However, we are still a long way from providing a fully inclusive society. . . . The data on wage and employment inequities indicate that rather than promoting an inclusive and equitable labor market, the operation of the market often rein-

forces and promotes inequality. To achieve equitable access to jobs, it is therefore necessary to engage in active efforts to open up employment, and to dismantle discriminatory structures. But U.S. policymakers show less and less willingness to deal with this serious problem. Attempts by the Department of Justice to dismantle affirmative action programs, and to cut funds to Equal Employment Commissions, has left many workers without any readily available form of institutional or legal protection against unfair treatment. Additionally the burden of the recent effort to cut Federal spending has fallen disproportionately on the income of peoples of color: the average black family lost three times as much in income and benefits in the budget cuts of the early 1980s as did the average white family, while the average Hispanic family lost twice as much. . . .

How is it possible to begin to deal with economic exclusion? For a start, it is necessary to acknowledge the existence of institutional racism and sexism and to seek to understand and dismantle the complex web of structures and processes which sustain these patterns of inequality. A strong commitment to assuring equal job access to people of color and to women is necessary at all levels of government — federal, state and local. The persistence of wage differentials between females and males suggests the need for attention to the relationship between classification and compensation systems for women. Many of the reforms advocated in the section on poverty would improve the life prospects of people of color and women. As actions of the General Synod recognize, justice and the empowerment of oppressed groups entail comprehensive programs involving education, employment, medical care, prison reforms, legal aid, community organizing, and political action, as well as active efforts to combat individual racism. . . .

Economic Democracy

Economic democracy describes an economic system in which all people participate and through which all are nurtured. As our second principle in Chapter Three stated, "A just economic system is inclusive, involving people in responsible, participatory and economically rewarding activity." Economic democracy is built on the assumption that all individuals have certain basic economic rights and these rights are best guaranteed through widespread participation in economic decision-making. Like constitutional democracy, economic democracy is achieved only through common ackowledgement of realistic and just rules. Recognizing the possibility of both human sin and human goodness, economic democracy calls for the establishment of institutional structures that reinforce those human characteristics that promote the common welfare. How does an economic system include all people in participatory and economically rewarding activity? . . .

The underlying assumption of economic democracy is that all individuals have inherent economic as well as political rights. To recognize this explicitly we are proposing that an Economic Bill of Rights be adopted as an amendment to the U.S. Constitution. The suggested wording follows:

> The right of the people to access to employment, food, shelter, and health care should not be abridged.

Such an amendment would mean a fundamental shift away from the view that the market, left alone, can guarantee livelihood to all.

The rationale for an economic bill of rights is simple. Guaranteeing economic rights is a profoundly biblical concept. As earlier sections of this paper and the Catholic bishops' pastoral letter have made clear, the covenant between God and Israel contained explicit instructions that Israel provide the basic necessities of life to all members of the community. It was not just incumbent on individuals to provide charity to those in need, though that was stressed. It was also intended that the polity, the government, make it possible for all members of the society to have access to those things necessary to sustain life. The New Testament broadened the community to include the whole human family. These principles are still valid today.

All people are both political *and* economic beings. While the rights accorded in the U.S. Bill of Rights — freedom of speech, freedom of religion, freedom of assembly — are central, access to employment, food, shelter, health care, and education are also essential. The Universal Declaration of Human Rights, adopted by the United Na-

tions General Assembly on December 10, 1948, incorporates a range of economic, social, and cultural rights, as well as civil and political rights. In 1964 the Council for Christian Social Action of the United Church of Christ voiced strong support for the United Nations' Human Rights conventions and specifically for the Universal Declaration of Human Rights. And as noted, both the Twelfth General Synod's Pronouncement on Human Rights and the Fifteenth General Synod's Pronouncement Affirming the United Church of Christ as a Just Peace Church recognize the right of every person to have basic economic needs met.

Hopefully people will obtain access to these basic necessities through the private sector, through jobs with privately owned firms. But this amendment would make it incumbent on government to provide access to these necessities if the private sector failed to do so. It might be implemented in a variety of ways, i.e., through the government becoming the employer of last resort, through subsidies to private firms to provide jobs, or through guaranteed annual incomes, negative income taxes or some other devices.

Some will argue that there is a crucial difference between a political and an economic bill of rights in that political rights do not cost anything. But political rights have their costs, too. Authoritarian regimes can move faster in bringing about sweeping changes in the economy. Having rights to vote, to participate, to challenge government and business slows down economic policy-making. But we, as a society, have concluded that the benefits of democratic participation far outweigh the costs.

It is clear that an economic bill of rights would bring profound changes to the U.S. economy which cannot be predicted at this time. But standing in the tradition of the prophets and Jesus, we cannot do otherwise than to issue this call. It is in our interests to live in a more decent, more humane, more just world. We need a vision, for where there is no vision, people perish.

This proposal deals only with the economic rights of people in the United States and in this sense it is only an interim step. Although it is not clear at this moment in history how it is possible to guarantee the basic economic rights of all human beings, the achievement of such universal economic rights is the goal. As worshipers of a

God "who executes justice for the oppressed; who gives food to the hungry" (Ps. 146:7), we are called to find ways to assure that all human beings, as a matter of fundamental human right, attain an existence worthy of human dignity.

The Economy and the Environment

One of the principles identified in this paper is that a just and viable economic system is based on a responsible and equitable use of the earth's limited resources. The World Council of Churches has coined the phrase: a just, participatory, and sustainable society. Christians have special reason to conserve and protect the physical environment that nurtures the whole of the created order. Faithfulness and respect for the Creator entails reverence for the whole of creation. As stewards of God's creation, we act as God's caretaker for present and future generations.

Modern economies, whether capitalist, socialist or community, whether industrialized or developing, have pursued economic growth at the expense of the environment. The resultant ecological crisis has four major components: population pressure, depletion of resources, pollution of the environment, and production and storage of hazardous wastes. . . .

Population densities and growth rates create pressures on the environment. . . . Moreover, the highest rates of population growth are in the poorest countries. In contrast with the declines registered in developed countries, many countries in Africa are experiencing increases both in fertility and in overall rates of population growth. Sub-Saharan Africa has unprecedented high rates of growth: the continent averages about three percent annual growth, and some countries, like Kenya, are approaching four percent. This means that in a region where the economy cannot generate sufficient food or employment and where governments cannot provide basic service for the current population, they will have to deal with double the number of people in about 20 years time. Of the Third World population, about 80 percent live in countries whose governments consider their fertility rates too high and would like to reduce them.

Population growth rates and densities have both exacerbated hunger and poverty and led to environmental deterioration in many areas. The effort to keep up with increased world food demand has placed major pressures on the earth's cropland. Since mid-century, little new arable land has been available to cultivate, and most increases in food output have had to come from increasing yields. The agricultural practices adopted by many farmers to improve production accelerate rates of soil erosion. Record rates of population growth in the Third Word have forced farmers onto dry, steep, and mountainous lands which are inherently susceptible to erosion once the natural cover is removed. Excessive loss of topsoil in many regions of intense agricultural production has led to a decline in the soils' fertility. As soil erosion and other ecological constraints slow increases in food production, industrial development competes for the use of the available land.

In the case of many natural resources formed over periods of millions of years, the human race has consumed more in the twentieth century, sometimes in a very few decades of the twentieth century, than in all past history. Burgeoning growth in the world's population, the insatiable demands of industrial production, careless exploitation of minerals, and erosion of arable land have placed serious constraints on the finite resources of the earth. . . .

[Further], pollution of the environment threatens both the earth and its inhabitants. A century of haphazardly producing and disposing of toxic wastes now endangers on earth's rivers, lakes, oceans, and air. Acid rain resulting from the release of sulfur dioxide and nitrogen oxides into the air during the burning of coal, oil, and other fossil fuels imperils lakes, rivers, and forests, has reduced crop yields, and comprises a health hazard in some areas. . . .

[And] in our throw-away society, industrial production generates enough solid waste each year to build a wall 75 feet wide and 200 feet high along the U.S.-Canada border. . . . In disposing of these toxic wastes, companies generally have utilized landfills, many of which leak and constitute a danger to adjacent communities. Since the overwhelming majority of these landfills are located in predominantly poor and minority communities, the resultant national toxic injustice crisis can be condemned both as a violation of stewardship, as well as a form of injustice and discrimination. . . .

The compelling need for better stewardship of

the earth and the environment involves transformation of both attitudes and practices. The three-way covenant described in Scripture linking God, humanity, and the earth requires taking seriously environmental and ecological limits to growth and considering the detrimental impact of current technologies and patterns of consumption. Just as Scripture enjoined the Israelites to allow the land to remain fallow and recuperate during the seventh, or sabbath, year, industrial economies need to factor the needs of the earth into production processes. . . .

As stewards of this earth, we must recognize the fragility of the ecosystems which sustain all of creation. This will require us to identify and enforce limits on economic growth. It should lead to the establishment of international agencies able to bring about effective cooperation between nations on environmental matters. . . .

The Economy of the Church

The parable from the Gospel of Matthew with which this study paper began tells of a great judgment in which a Divine Judge separates the righteous from the unfaithful. The Judge evaluates the worth of the nations according to how they have fulfilled basic human needs — whether they fed the hungry, brought drink to the thirsty, clothed the naked, provided shelter to the homeless, and cared for the infirm and the prisoners. The Judge informs the righteous, "Truly, I say to you, as you did it to one of the least of these my brothers and sisters, you did it to me" (Matt. 25:40).

As this paper has explored the management of the household of creation by current economic systems, it has noted that nearly two thousand years after Jesus told the parable of the great judgment the majority of the human community still does not have the basic necessities of life. Despite a spectacular rise in economic productivity, despite the technological ability to eliminate hunger and poverty, the world remains divided between the one-third to whom much is given and the two-thirds of the human family who experience overwhelming and crushing deprivation. According to the parable of that great judgment, "as you did it not to one of the least of these you did it not to me" (Matt. 25:45).

How do we begin faithfully to manage the resources of the earth and care for the global household so that all members of the human family can satisfy their basic needs? Three changes are necessary: one is our own conversion. First, this entails adopting a new understanding of economic life consistent with Christian principles of economic justice and pursuing patterns of behavior more consonant with the biblical perspective of economic activity. Second, this turning away from the idols of contemporary society to ground our lives in a sustained relationship with God involves the reconstitution and renewal of communities defined by shared religious values and commitments and bound together by a sense of mutuality. At this narrowest, such a covenantal community might consist of a house church or a single congregation and at its broadest a new covenantal relationship among God, the global household, and the entire created order. Third, discipleship calls the faithful to the design, advocacy for, and management of a more just economic system for our own country and for the global economic order. These three requirements are not sequential. They represent three interrelated dimensions of the transformation of society toward the image of economic justice and wholeness presented in Scripture.

One of the most important criteria for assessing these documents is the consistency of their analyses and recommendations with the theological and moral traditions out of which the churches speak, and secondarily with their reading of the contemporary situation. This is clearly a complex issue concerning which only summary judgments can be offered here.

Seldom do the proposals for change seem congruent with the radical character of the gospel challenge or with the disturbing descriptions of massive human suffering arising from hunger and malnutrition, and from unemployment, much less with the descriptions, sometimes bordering on the apocalyptic, of the numbers of children living in poverty. If such profound problems do not call for an alternative economic system, one would at least expect proposals for significant changes in the existing one, some plan for altering the motivating spirit of present structures, or, at the very least, an analysis suggesting that the present problems are aberrations in a system that can and should be set right. But these are not forthcoming. Thus one must wonder to what extent the structural/systemic thesis about the nature of these problems helps us to understand our situation and to take corrective action, and to what extent it leaves us helpless before a set of systems, institutions, and structures which generate and embody our problems but defy our corrective intervention. One possible explanation is that to attempt to address structural/systemic problems, without addressing some of the major constituent elements of those structures (business corporations) directly as moral and morally accountable agents is to shadowbox around the real issues.

While some of these documents do acknowledge the difficulty of privileged middle-class groups assessing the system from which they benefit, these documents must still be faulted for not putting to the churches challenges commensurate with the seriousness of the problems they portray and the potential radicalness of the biblical foundations they cite. Relatively little is said about the affluence of the few in the midst of the suffering of the many or of its symbolic if not actually causal significance. The churches' members are challenged to listen to the sufferers, to exert their influence in the public sphere on their behalf, and on occasion, to make some minor adjustments in lifestyle. But there is no facing of the larger issue of whether North American Protestants' understanding of the fullness of life and of the appropriate ways to relate to the world's needy have been shaped more by the consumer society and its conceptions of success and the good life than by the gospel with its quite different perspectives; no document asks whether the life of the churches and their members, and even these documents themselves, are more shaped by the economic and political realities to which they have become accustomed than by the biblical and theological traditions out of which they propose to speak.

Seldom if ever are Christians addressed as influential actors responsible *in their vocations* for seeing that, within their power, justice is done. They are not seriously challenged to ask questions about the human impact of their routine economic actions as workers, managers, consumers, and owners on their fellows; neither are they brought to see the connections between their economic choices and activities as individuals and as parts of those larger structures. At this point one wonders whether the structuralist, systemic approach has removed too much responsibility from individual agents, whether we have failed to see that individuals' sense of vocation connects significantly with the impact of larger structures and systems on all our lives.

Nor are the churches as communities of faith and as moral agencies sufficiently challenged out of this often disturbing litany of ills. They are not asked to reconsider on any fundamental level their generally comfortable juxtaposition of gospel and culture. They are not asked to consider what it means for the privileged few to struggle to be the church in a desperately needy world.

— Paul F. Camenisch, "Recent Mainline Protestant Statements on Economic Justice," *Annual of the Society of Christian Ethics* (1987): 71-73

Conservative and Evangelical Statements

The conservative and evangelical churches have seldom issued pronouncements on social issues. Ordinarily, they rely more heavily on the character of individual believers and have a low estimate of church hierarchy and bureaucracy. Groups of local leaders sometimes gather and issue "reports," "declarations," "affirmations," or "calls" that invite local pastors or lay leaders to respond in one way or another. Religion, in the evangelical tradition, is personal and local; and if it is not, it is viewed as possibly not authentic. At the same time, few traditions have missionary programs as active as those of the evangelical churches, and neither Roman Catholic nor mainline Protestant believers nor the adherents of any other major world faith give as high a percent of their personal budgets to support needy people and to develop programs to help people as do evangelicals. The popular slogan "Think Globally; Act Locally" is reversed among evangelicals, for local churches become learning centers from which actions become global.

In the spring of 1987, some forty conservatives who have been active in mission, relief, and development work gathered in the Swiss town of Villars to seek a renewal of focus for their work in view of the changing world situation, the fresh awareness of needs in the "Third World," and the flurry of economic teachings by fellow Christians, many of which they felt were not clearly enough rooted in biblical principles. In fact, they felt that some church statements used secular ideologies to interpret biblical texts and relied too much on public policy approaches to problems that were essentially religious, personal, and familial. Over a period of five days, they engaged in intense discussion, Bible study, debate, prayer, and private reflection, seeking to discern the "biblical mandates for relief and development" more clearly. As a result, those gathered felt that they were called upon to issue a statement reflecting their concerns.

Three years later, a larger group of evangelicals numbering some one hundred theologians and economists, development experts, ethicists, business managers, and church leaders met in Oxford, England. The groundwork for this conference had been laid in an earlier Oxford conference. In January 1987, thirty-six Christians from all continents and a broad range of professions and socio-political perspectives came together at Oxford to discuss contemporary economic issues in a way that was both faithful to the scriptures and grounded in careful economic analysis. (The papers from that conference were published in *Transformation* 4, no. 3/4 [1987].) They authorized a three-year process to attempt to draft a comprehensive statement on Christian faith and economics. In this project, groups of economists and theologians met all over the world in regional conferences, addressing issues under four headings: stewardship and creation; work and leisure; the definition of justice and freedom; government and economics. A separate paper on micro-enterprise was also undertaken. These regional discussions and studies were then drawn together to form the issues for analysis and debate at the Second Oxford Conference on January 4-9, 1990, which resulted in the Oxford Declaration included here.

Bound together by a common faith in Jesus Christ, they speak of a number of issues also addressed by other church teachings, but they also show a new evangelical awareness of cultural pluralism that faces the church in our time and of the importance of technology, which forces us to new thinking about our relationships with creation. On every issue, they emphasize "Christian distinctives," the particular insight that believers bring to these issues from their faith perspective.

The Villars Statement on Relief and Development

A World in Need

The extent of hunger and deprivation around the world is a reality haunting modern times. Confronted with disaster, disease, and chronic poverty, relief and development agencies have provided massive material assistance. Yet for all the resources expended, hunger and deprivation appear to be increasing. The sad reality is that so much effort has produced little in long-term results.

This reality calls us as Christians to reassess the work of relief and development in light of God's Holy Word. It is our conclusion that the consistent application of Biblical teaching will require a reorientation of relief and development practices, and that this may involve a change in our understanding of human need and in strategies to relieve suffering.

"Relief and development" is an expression that recognizes two Biblical principles. Relief refers to the insistence in both Testaments that the people of God must help the hungry and oppressed. Development stems from the Biblical vision of a people exercising their proper stewardship of God's gifts — of societies that are productive, healthy, and governed justly. Together relief and development envision substantial improvement in economic and human well being.

We acknowledge our own sinfulness and fallibility, and we recognize that other committed Christians may not agree with all our convictions.

"The Villars Statement on Relief and Development," *Stewardship Journal* 1, no. 1 (Winter 1991): 3-5.

Nevertheless, we are compelled by God's Word and by the reality of human suffering to share our convictions with Christians and others. We do not claim to have spoken the final word. Thus we offer the following conclusions of the Villars consultation for research, dialogue, and open debate among all who claim Christ as Lord.

Issues of Concern

With this as our goal, we raise our concerns over the following issues:

1. The failure to operate from a distinctively Biblical perspective in both methods and goals.
2. The tendency to focus on meeting material needs without sufficient emphasis on spiritual needs.
3. The attempt to synthesize Marxist categories and Christians concepts, to equate economic liberation with salvation, and to use the Marxist critique, without recognizing the basic conflict between these views and the Biblical perspective.
4. The emphasis on redistribution of wealth as the answer to poverty and deprivation without recognizing the value of incentive, opportunity, creativity, and economic and political freedom.
5. The attraction to centrally controlled economies and coercive solutions despite the failures of such economies and their consistent violation of the rights of the poor.
6. A disproportionate emphasis on changing structures without recognizing the frequency with which this only exchanges one oppressive structure for another.
7. The danger of utopian and ideological entrapment, whether from the left or the right.
8. Neglecting to denounce oppression when it comes from one end or the other of the political spectrum.
9. Focusing on external causes of poverty in exploitation and oppression without confronting those internal causes that are rooted in patterns of belief and behavior within a given culture.
10. The need to make conversion and discipleship an essential component of Christian relief and development work, and to carry this out in conjunction with the local church.
11. The need to apply the teaching of the Bible as a whole in the areas of personal life, family, and work, but equally in the shaping of the culture and social life.
12. The need to reaffirm the Biblical support for the family as the basic social and economic unit and its right to own and control property, and to stand against any ideology that would diminish the family's proper role in any of these areas.
13. The need to oppose a false understanding of poverty which makes poverty itself a virtue, or which sanctifies those who are poor on the basis of their poverty.

Biblical Perspective

In response to these issues we draw attention to the following Biblical teaching and its implication for relief and development:

1. God created mankind in His own image, endowing man with freedom, creativity, significance, and moral discernment. Moreover, prior to the Fall man lived in harmony with all of God's creation, free from pain, suffering and death.
2. The devastating reality of sin and evil (hunger, oppression, deprivation, disease, death, and separation from God) is the result of man's rebellion against God, which began at the Fall and continues through history.
3. The causes of hunger and deprivation, therefore, are spiritual as well as material and can only be dealt with adequately insofar as the spiritual dimension is taken into account.
4. Man's rebellion against God affects every aspect of human existence. The Fall resulted in God's Curse on creation and in destructive patterns of thought, culture, and relationships, which keep men and women in bondage to poverty and deprivation.
5. The work of Christian relief and development, therefore, must involve spiritual transformation, setting people free from destructive attitudes, beliefs, values, and patterns of culture. The proclamation of the gospel and the making of disciples, then is an unavoidable dimension of relief and development work — not only for

eternal salvation, but also for the transformation of culture and economic life.

6. When people were held in bondage to hunger and deprivation by unjust social structures, the Bible consistently denounced those who perpetuated such oppression and demanded obedience to God's law. The Biblical emphasis, then, is not on "sinful structures" but rather on sinful human choices that perpetuate suffering and injustice.

7. God's ultimate answer for suffering and deprivation is the gift of His only Son, Jesus Christ, who broke the power of sin and death by His own death and resurrection. The decisive victory was won on the cross in the atoning death of Christ for all who would believe Him. The final victory will be accomplished when Christ returns in power and glory to reign with His people. Until that time all who claim Jesus as their Lord are called to care for those in need as the Holy Spirit enables them and to share the only message of true hope for a broken world.

Conclusion

Therefore, in light of the issues raised and the Biblical perspective outlined here, we encourage research, dialogue and debate among all who claim Christ as Lord, so that we may serve Him more faithfully and work together more effectively.

The Oxford Declaration on Christian Faith and Economics

Preamble

This **Oxford Declaration on Christian Faith and Economics** of January, 1990 is issued jointly by over one hundred theologians and economists, ethicists and development practitioners, church leaders and business managers who come from various parts of the world. We live in diverse cultures and subcultures, are steeped in differing traditions of theological and economic thinking, and therefore have diverse notions as to how Christian faith and economic realities should intersect. We have found this diversity enriching even when we could not reach agreement. At the same time we rejoice over the extent of unanimity on the complex economics of today made possible by our common profession of faith in our Lord Jesus Christ.

We affirm that through his life, death, resurrection, and ascension to glory, Christ has made us one people (Galatians 3:28). Though living in different cultures, we acknowledge together that there is one body and one Spirit, just as we are called to the one hope, one Lord, one faith, one baptism, and one God and Father of us all (Ephesians 4:4).

We acknowledge that a Christian search for truth is both a communal and also an individual effort. As part of the one people in Christ, each of us wants to comprehend the relevance of Christ

"The Oxford Declaration," *Transformation* 7, no. 2 (April-June 1990): 7-18.

to the great issues facing humanity today together "with all the saints" (Ephesians 3:18). All our individual insights need to be corrected by the perspectives of the global Christian community as well as Christians through the centuries.

We affirm that Scripture, the word of the living and true God, is our supreme authority in all matters of faith and conduct. Hence we turn to Scripture as our reliable guide in reflection on issues concerning economic, social, and political life. As economists and theologians we desire to submit both theory and practice to the bar of Scripture.

Together we profess that God, the sovereign of life, in love made a perfect world for human beings created to live in fellowship with God. Although our greatest duty is to honour and glorify God, we rebelled against God, fell from our previous harmonious relationship with God, and brought evil upon ourselves and God's world. But God did not give up on the creation. As Creator, God continues patiently working to overcome the evil which was perverting the creation. The central act of God's redemptive new creation is the death, resurrection, and reign in glory of Jesus Christ, the Son of God, and the sending of the Holy Spirit. This restoration will only be completed at the end of human history and the reconciliation of all things. Justice is basic to Christian perspectives on economic life.

Justice is rooted in the character of God. "For the Lord is righteous, he loves justice" (Psalm 11:7). Justice expresses God's actions to restore God's provision to those who have been deprived and to punish those who have violated God's standards.

A. Creation and Stewardship

God the Creator

1. From God and through God and to God are all things (Romans 11:36). In the freedom of God's eternal love, by the word of God's omnipotent power, and through the Creator Spirit, the Triune God gave being to the world and to human beings which live in it. God pronounced the whole creation good. For its continuing existence creation is dependent on God. The same God who created it is present in it, sustaining it, and giving it bountiful life (Psalm 104:29). In Christ, "all things were created . . . and all things hold together" (Colossians 1:15-20). Though creation owes its being to God, it is itself not divine. The greatness of creation — both human and non-human — exists to glorify its Creator. The divine origin of the creation, its continued existence through God, redemption through Christ, and its purpose to glorify God are fundamental truths which must guide all Christian reflection on creation and stewardship.

Stewardship of Creation

2. God the Creator and Redeemer is the ultimate owner. "The earth is the Lord's and the fullness thereof" (Psalm 24:1). But God has entrusted the earth to human beings to be responsible for it on God's behalf. They should work as God's stewards in the creative, faithful management of the world, recognising that they are responsible to God for all they do with the world and to the world.

3. God created the world and pronounced it "very good" (Genesis 1:31). Because of the Fall and the resulting curse, creation "groans in travail" (Romans 8:22). The thoughtlessness, greed, and violence of sinful human beings have damaged God's good creation and produced a variety of ecological problems and conflicts. When we abuse and pollute creation, as we are doing in many instances, we are poor stewards and invite disaster in both local and global eco-systems.

4. Much of human aggression toward creation stems from a false understanding of the nature of creation and the human role in it. Humanity has constantly been confronted by the two challenges of selfish individualism, which neglects human community, and rigid collectivism, which stifles human freedom. Christians and others have often pointed out both dangers. But only recently have we realised that both ideologies have a view of the world with humanity at the centre which reduces material creation to a mere instrument.

5. Biblical life and world view is not centred on humanity. It is God-centred. Non-human creation was not made exclusively for human beings. We are repeatedly told in the Scripture that all things — human beings and the environment in which they live — were "for God" (Romans 11:36; 1 Corinthians 8:6; Colossians 1:16). Correspond-

473

ingly, nature is not merely the raw material for human activity. Though only human beings have been made in the image of God, non-human creation too has a dignity of its own, so much so that after the flood God established a covenant not only with Noah and his descendants, but also "with every living creature that is with you" (Genesis 9:9). Similarly, the Christian hope for the future also includes creation. "The creation itself will be set free from its bondage to decay and obtain the glorious liberty of the children of God" (Romans 8:21).

6. The dominion which God gave human beings over creation (Genesis 1:30) does not give them licence to abuse creation. First, they are responsible to God, in whose image they were made, not to ravish creation but to sustain it, as God sustains it in divine providential care. Second, since human beings are created in the image of God for community and not simply as isolated individuals (Genesis 1:28), they are to exercise dominion in a way that is responsible to the needs of the total human family, including future generations.

7. Human beings are both part of creation and also unique. Only human beings are created in the image of God. God thus grants human beings dominion over the non-human creation (Genesis 1:28-30). But dominion is not domination. According to Genesis 2:15, human dominion over creation consists in the twofold task of "tilling and taking care" of the garden. Therefore all work must have not only a productive but also a protective aspect. Economic systems must be shaped so that a healthy ecological system is maintained over time. All responsible human work done by the stewards of God the Sustainer must contain an element of cooperation with the environment.

Stewardship and Economic Production

8. Economic production results from the stewardship of the earth which God assigned to humanity. While materialism, injustice, and greed are in fundamental conflict with the teaching of the whole scripture, there is nothing in Christian faith that suggests that the production of new goods and services is undesirable. Indeed, we are explicitly told that God "richly furnishes us with everything to enjoy" (1 Timothy 6:17). Production is not only

necessary to sustain life and make it enjoyable; it also provides an opportunity for human beings to express their creativity in the service of others. In assessing economic systems from a Christian perspective, we must consider their ability both to generate and to distribute wealth and income justly.

Technology and its Limitations

9. Technology mirrors the basic paradox of the sinfulness and goodness of human nature. Many current ecological problems result from the extensive use of technology after the onset of industrialization. Though technology has liberated human beings from some debasing forms of work, it has also often dehumanised other forms of work. Powerful nations and corporations that control modern technology are regularly tempted to use it to dominate the weak for their own narrow self-interest. As we vigorously criticise the negative effects of technology, we should, however, not forget its positive effects. Human creativity is expressed in the designing of tools for celebration and work. Technology helps us meet the basic needs of the world population and to do so in ways which develop the creative potential of individuals and societies. Technology can also help us reverse environmental devastation. A radical rejection of modern technology is unrealistic. Instead we must search for ways to use appropriate technology responsibly according to every cultural context.

10. What is technologically possible is not necessarily morally permissible. We must not allow technological development to follow its own inner logic, but must direct it to serve moral ends. We acknowledge our limits in foreseeing the impact of technological change and encourage an attitude of humility with respect to technological innovation. Therefore continuing evaluation of the impact of technological change is essential. Four criteria derived from Christian faith help us to evaluate the development and use of technology. First, technology should not foster disintegration of family or community, or function as an instrument of social domination. Second, persons created in the image of God must not become mere accessories of machines. Third, as God's stewards, we must not allow technology to abuse

creation. If human work is to be done in cooperation with creation then the instruments of work
must cooperate with it too. Finally, we should not
allow technological advancements to become objects of false worship or seduce us away from dependence on God (Genesis 11:1-9). We may differ
in what weight we ascribe to individual criteria in
concrete situations and therefore our assessment
of particular technologies may differ. But we
believe that these criteria need to be taken into
consideration as we reflect theologically on technological progress.

11. We urge individuals, private institutions,
and governments everywhere to consider both the
local, immediate, and the global, long term ecological consequences of their actions. We encourage corporate action to make products which
are more "environmentally friendly." And we call
on governments to create and enforce just frameworks of incentives and penalties which will encourage both individuals and corporations to
adopt ecologically sound practices.

12. We need greater international cooperation
between individuals, private organisations, and
nations to promote environmentally responsible
action. Since political action usually serves the
self-interest of the powerful, it will be especially
important to guarantee that international environmental agreements are particularly concerned to protect the needs of the poor. We call
on Christians everywhere to place high priority on
restoring and maintaining the integrity of creation.

B. Work and Leisure

Work and Human Nature

13. Work involves all those activities done, not for
their own sake, but to satisfy human needs. Work
belongs to the very purpose for which God originally made human beings. In Genesis 1:26-28, we
read that God created human beings in his image
"in order to have dominion over . . . all the earth."
Similarly, Genesis 2:15 tells us that God created
Adam and placed him in the garden of Eden to
work in it, to "till it and keep it." As human beings
fulfil this mandate, they glorify God. Though fall-
en, as human beings "go forth to their work"

(Psalm 104:23) they fulfil an original purpose of
the Creator for human existence.

14. Because work is central to the Creator's
intention for humanity, work has intrinsic value.
Thus work is not solely a means to an end. It is
not simply a chore to be endured for the sake of
satisfying human desires or needs, especially the
consumption of goods. At the same time, we have
to guard against over-valuation of work. The essence of human beings consists in that they are
made in the image of God. Their ultimate, but not
exclusive, source of meaning and identity does not
lie in work, but in becoming children of God by
one Spirit through faith in Jesus Christ.

15. For Christians, work acquires a new dimension. God calls all Christians to employ through
work the various gifts that God has given them. God
calls people to enter the kingdom of God and to live
a life in accordance with its demands. When people
respond to the call of God, God enables them to
bear the fruit of the Spirit and endows them individually with multiple gifts of the Spirit. As those
who are gifted by the Spirit and whose actions are
guided by the demands of love, Christians should
do their work in the service of God and humanity.

The Purpose of Work

16. In the Bible and in the first centuries of the
Christian tradition, meeting one's needs and the
needs of one's community (especially its underprivileged members) was an essential purpose of
work (Psalm 128:2; 2 Thessalonians 3:8; 1 Thessalonians 4:9-12; Ephesians 4:28; Acts 20:33-35).
The first thing at issue in all fields of human work
is the need of human beings to earn their daily
bread and a little more.

17. The deepest meaning of human work is that
the almighty God established human work as a
means to accomplish God's work in the world.
Human beings remain dependent on God, for
"unless the Lord builds the house, those who build
it labour in vain" (Psalm 127:1a). As Genesis 2:5
suggests, God and human beings are co-labourers
in the task of preserving creation.

18. Human work has consequences that go beyond the preservation of creation to the anticipation of the eschatological transformation of the
world. They are, of course, not ushering in the
kingdom of God, building the "new heavens and

a new earth." Only God can do that. Yet their work makes a small and imperfect contribution to it — for example, by shaping the personalities of the citizens of the eternal kingdom which will come through God's action alone.

19. However, work is not only a means through which the glory of human beings as God's stewards shines forth. It is also a place where the misery of human beings as impeders of God's purpose becomes visible. Like the test of fire, God's judgment will bring to light the work which has ultimate significance because it was done in cooperation with God. But it will also manifest the ultimate insignificance of work done in cooperation with those evil powers which scheme to ruin God's good creation (1 Corinthians 3:12-15).

Alienation in Work

20. Sin makes work an ambiguous reality. It is both a noble expression of human creation in the image of God, and, because of the curse, a painful testimony to human estrangement from God. Whether human beings are tilling the soil in agrarian societies, or operating high-tech machinery in information societies, they work under the shadow of death, and experience struggle and frustration in work (Genesis 3:17-19).

21. Human beings are created by God as persons endowed with gifts which God calls them to exercise freely. As a fundamental dimension of human existence, work is a personal activity. People should never be treated in their work as mere means. We must resist the tendency to treat workers merely as costs or labour inputs, a tendency evident in both rural and urban societies, but especially where industrial and post-industrial methods of production are applied. We encourage efforts to establish managerial and technological conditions that enable workers to participate meaningfully in significant decision-making processes, and to create opportunities for individual development by designing positions that challenge them to develop their potential and by instituting educational programmes.

22. God gives talents to individuals for the benefit of the whole community. Human work should be a contribution to the common good (Ephesians 4:28). The modern drift from concern for community to preoccupation with self, sup-

ported by powerful structural and cultural forces, shapes the way we work. Individual self-interest can legitimately be pursued, but only in a context marked by the pursuit of the good of others. These two pursuits are complementary. In order to make the pursuit of the common good possible, Christians need to seek to change both the attitudes of workers and the structures in which they work.

23. Discrimination in work continues to oppress people, especially women and marginalised groups. Because of race and gender, people are often pushed into a narrow range of occupations which are often underpaid, offer little status or security, and provide few promotional opportunities and fringe benefits. Women and men and people of all races are equal before God and should, therefore, be recognised and treated with equal justice and dignity in social and economic life.

24. For most people work is an arduous good. Many workers suffer greatly under the burden of work. In some situations people work long hours for low pay, working conditions are appalling, contracts are non-existent, sexual harassment occurs, trade union representation is not allowed, health and safety regulations are flouted. These things occur throughout the world whatever the economic system. The word "exploitation" has a strong and immediate meaning in such situations. The God of the Bible condemns exploitation and oppression. God's liberation of the Israelites from their oppression served as a paradigm of how God's people should behave towards workers in their midst (Leviticus 25:39-55).

25. Since work is central to God's purpose for humanity, people everywhere have both the obligation and the right to work. Given the broad definition of work suggested above (cf. para 13), the right to work here should be understood as part of the freedom of the individual to contribute to the satisfaction of the needs of the community. It is a freedom right, since work in its widest sense is a form of self-expression. The right involved is the right of the worker to work unhindered. The obligation is on every human being to contribute to the community. It is in this sense that Paul says, "if a man will not work, let him not eat."

26. The right to earn a living would be a positive or sustenance right. Such a right implies the obligation of the community to provide employment opportunities. Employment cannot be

guaranteed where rights conflict and resources may be inadequate. However the fact that such a right cannot be enforced does not detract in any way from the obligation to seek the highest level of employment which is consistent with justice and the availability of resources.

Rest and Leisure

27. As the Sabbath commandment indicates, the Biblical concept of rest should not be confused with the modern concept of leisure. Leisure consists of activities that are ends in themselves and therefore intrinsically enjoyable. In many parts of the world for many people, life is "all work and no play." While masses of people are unemployed and thus have only "leisure," millions of people — including children — are often overworked simply to meet their basic survival needs. Meanwhile, especially in economically developed nations, many overwork to satisfy their desire for status.

28. The first pages of the Bible tell us that God rested after creating the universe (Genesis 2:2-3). The sequence of work and rest that we see in God's activity is a pattern for human beings. In that the Sabbath commandment interrupted work with regular periods of rest, it liberates human beings from enslavement to work. The Sabbath erects a fence around human productive activity and serves to protect both human and non-human creation. Human beings have, therefore, both a right and an obligation to rest.

29. Corresponding to the four basic relations in which all people stand (in relationship to non-human creation, to themselves, to other human beings, and to God), there are four activities which we should cultivate in leisure time. Rest consists in the enjoyment of nature as God's creation, in the free exercise and development of abilities which God has given to each person, in the cultivation of fellowship with one another, and above all, in delight in communion with God.

30. Worship is central to the Biblical concept of rest. In order to be truly who they are, human beings need periodic moments of time in which God's commands concerning their work will recede from the forefront of their consciousness as they adore the God of loving holiness and thank the God of holy love.

31. Those who cannot meet their basic needs without having to forego leisure can be encouraged by the reality of their right to rest. The right to rest implies the corresponding right to sustenance for all those who are willing to work "six days a week" (Exodus 20:9). Modern workaholics whose infatuation with status relegates leisure to insignificance must be challenged by the liberating obligation to rest. What does it profit them to "gain the whole world" if they "forfeit their life" (Mark 8:36)?

C. Poverty and Justice

God and the Poor

32. Poverty was not part of God's original creation, nor will poverty be part of God's restored creation when Christ returns. Involuntary poverty in all its forms and manifestations is a result of the fall and its consequences. Today one of every five human beings lives in poverty so extreme that their survival is daily in doubt. We believe this is offensive and heart breaking to God.

33. We understand that the God of the Bible is one who in mercy extends love to all. At the same time, we believe that when the poor are oppressed, God is the "defender of the poor" (Psalm 146:7-9). Again and again in every part of scripture, the Bible expresses God's concern for justice for the poor. Faithful obedience requires that we share God's concern and act on it. "He who oppresses a poor man insults his maker, but he who is kind to the needy honours Him" (Proverbs 14:31). Indeed it is only when we right such injustices that God promises to hear our prayers and worship (Isaiah 58:1-9).

34. Neglect of the poor often flows from greed. Furthermore, the obsessive or careless pursuit of material goods is one of the most destructive idolatries in human history (Ephesians 5:5). It distracts individuals from their duties before God, and corrupts personal and social relationships.

Causes of Poverty

35. The causes of poverty are many and complex. They include the evil that people do to each other, to themselves, and to their environment. The causes of poverty also include the cultural attitudes and actions taken by social, economic,

political and religious institutions, that either devalue or waste resources, that erect barriers to economic production, or that fail to reward work fairly. Furthermore, the forces that cause and perpetuate poverty operate at global, national, local, and personal levels. It is also true that a person may be poor because of sickness, mental or physical handicap, childhood, or old age. Poverty is also caused by natural disasters such as earthquakes, hurricanes, floods, and famines.

36. We recognise that poverty results from and is sustained by both constraints on the production of wealth and on the inequitable distribution of wealth and income. We acknowledge the tendency we have had to reduce the causes of poverty to one at the expense of the others. We affirm the need to analyse and explain the conditions that promote the creation of wealth, as well as those that determine the distribution of wealth.

37. We believe it is the responsibility of every society to provide people with the means to live at a level consistent with their standing as persons created in the image of God.

Justice and Poverty

38. Biblical justice means impartially rendering to everyone their due in conformity with the standards of God's moral law. Paul uses justice (or righteousness) in its most comprehensive sense as a metaphor to describe God's creative and powerful redemptive love. Christ, solely in grace, brought us into God's commonwealth, who were strangers to it and because of sin cut off from it (Romans 1:17-18; 3:21-26; Ephesians 2:4-22). In Biblical passages which deal with the distribution of the benefits of social life in the context of social conflict and social wrong, justice is related particularly to what is due to groups such as the poor, widows, orphans, resident aliens, wage earners and slaves. The common link among these groups is powerlessness by virtue of economic and social needs. The justice called forth is to restore these groups to the provision God intends for them. God's law expresses this justice and indicates its demands. Further, God's intention is for people to live, not in isolation, but in society. The poor are described as those who are weak with respect to the rest of the community; the responsibility of the community is stated as "to make them strong"

so that they can continue to take their place in the community (Leviticus 25:35-36). One of the dilemmas of the poor is their loss of community (Job 22:5; Psalm 107:4-9, 33-36). Indeed their various needs are those that tend to prevent people from being secure and contributing members of society. One essential characteristic of Biblical justice is the meeting of basic needs that have been denied in contradiction to the standards of scripture; but further, the Bible gives indication of how to identify which needs are basic. They are those essential, not just for life, but for life in society.

39. Justice requires special attention to the weak members of the community because of their greater vulnerability. In this sense, justice is partial. Nevertheless, the civil arrangements in rendering justice are not to go beyond what is due to the poor or to the rich (Deuteronomy 1:17; Leviticus 19:15). In this sense justice is ultimately impartial. Justice is so fundamental that it characterises the personal virtues and personal relationships of individuals as they faithfully follow God's standards. Those who violate God's standards, however, receive God's retributive justice, which often removes the offender from society or from the divine community.

40. Justice requires conditions such that each person is able to participate in society in a way compatible with human dignity. Absolute poverty, where people lack even minimal food and housing, basic education, health care, and employment, denies people the basic economic resources necessary for just participation in the community. Corrective action with and on behalf of the poor is a necessary act of justice. This entails responsibilities for individuals, families, churches, and governments.

41. Justice may also require socio-political actions that enable the poor to help themselves and be the subjects of their own development and the development of their communities. We believe that we and the institutions in which we participate are responsible to create an environment of law, economic activity, and spiritual nurture which creates these conditions.

Some Urgent Contemporary Issues

42. Inequitable international economic relations aggravate poverty in poor countries. Many of these countries suffer under a burden of debt service which could only be repaid at an unacceptable

price to the poor, unless there is a radical restructuring both of national economic policies and international economic relations. The combination of increasing interest rates and falling commodity prices in the early 1980s has increased this debt service burden. Both lenders and borrowers shared in creating this debt. The result has been increasing impoverishment of the people. Both lenders and borrowers must share responsibility for finding solutions. We urgently encourage governments and international financial institutions to redouble their efforts to find ways to reduce the international indebtedness of the Third World, and to ensure the flow of both private and public productive capital where appropriate.

43. Government barriers to the flow of goods and services often work to the disadvantage of the poor. We particularly abhor the protectionist policies of the wealthy nations which are detrimental to developing countries. Greater freedom and trade between nations is an important part of reducing poverty worldwide.

44. Justice requires that the value of money be reliably known and stable, thus inflation represents poor stewardship and defrauds the nations' citizens. It wastes resources and is particularly harmful to the poor and the powerless. The wealthier members of society find it much easier to protect themselves against inflation than do the poor. Rapid changes in prices drastically affect the ability of the poor to purchase basic goods.

45. Annual global military expenditures equal the annual income of the poorest one-half of the world's people. These vast, excessive military expenditures detract from the task of meeting basic human needs, such as food, health care, and education. We are encouraged by the possibilities represented by the changes in the USSR and Eastern Europe, and improving relations between East and West. We urge that a major part of the resulting "peace dividend" be used to provide sustainable solutions to the problems of the world's poor.

46. Drug use and trafficking destroys both rich and poor nations. Drug consumption reflects spiritual poverty among the people and societies in which drug use is apparent. Drug trafficking undermines the national economies of those who produce drugs. The economic, social, and spiritual costs of drug use are unacceptable. The two key agents involved in this problem must change: the rich markets which consume drugs and the poorer countries which produce them. Therefore both must urgently work to find solutions. The rich markets which consume drugs must end their demand. And the poorer countries which produce them must switch to other products.

47. We deplore economic systems based on policies, laws, and regulations whose effect is to favour privileged minorities and to exclude the poor from fully legitimate activities. Such systems are not only inefficient, but are immoral as well in that participating in and benefitting from the formal economy depends on conferred privilege of those who have access and influence to public and private institutions rather than on inventiveness and hard work. Actions need to be taken by public and private institutions to reduce and simplify the requirements and costs of participating in the national economy.

48. There is abundant evidence that investment in small scale enterprises run by and for the poor can have a positive impact upon income and job creation for the poor. Contrary to the myths upheld by traditional financial institutions, the poor are often good entrepreneurs and excellent credit risks. We deplore the lack of credit available to the poor in the informal sector. We strongly encourage governments, financial institutions, and Non-Governmental Organisations to redouble their efforts to significantly increase credit to the poor. We feel so strongly about this that a separate statement dedicated to credit-based income generation programmes has been issued by the conference.

D. Freedom, Governments, and Economics

The Language of Human Rights

49. With the United Nations Declaration of Human Rights, the language of human rights has become pervasive throughout the world. It expresses the urgent plight of suffering people whose humanity is daily being denied them by their oppressors. In some cases rights language has been misused by those who claim that anything they want is theirs "by right." This breadth of application has led some to reject rights as a concept, stating that if everything becomes a right then nothing will be a right, since all rights imply corre-

sponding responsibilities. Therefore it is important to have clear criteria for what defines rights.

Christian Distinctives

50. All human interaction is judged by God and is accountable to God. In seeking human rights we search for an authority or norm which transcends our situation. God is that authority; God's character constitutes that norm. Since human rights are a priori rights, they are not conferred by the society or the state. Rather, human rights are rooted in the fact that every human being is made in the image of God. The deepest ground of human dignity is that while we were yet sinners, Christ died for us (Romans 5:8).

51. In affirmation of the dignity of God's creatures, God's justice for them requires life, freedom, and sustenance. The divine requirements of justice establish corresponding rights for human beings to whom justice is due. The right to life is the most basic human right. God created human beings as free moral agents. As such, they have the right to freedom — e.g., freedom of religion, speech, and assembly. Their freedom, however, is properly used only in dependence on God. It is a requirement of justice that human beings, including refugees and stateless persons, are able to live in society with dignity. Human beings therefore have a claim on other human beings for social arrangements that ensure that they have access to the sustenance that makes life in society possible.

52. The fact that in becoming Christians we may choose to forego our rights out of love for others and in trust of God's providential care does not mean that such rights cease to exist. Christians may endure the violation of their rights with great courage but work vigorously for the identical rights of others in similar circumstances. However it may not be appropriate to do so in some circumstances. Indeed this disparity between Christian contentment and campaigning on behalf of others in adverse situations is a witness to the work and love of God.

53. All of us share the same aspirations as human beings to have our rights protected — whether the right to life, freedom, or sustenance. Yet the fact of sin and the conflict of competing human rights means that our aspirations are never completely fulfilled in this life. Through Christ,

sin and evil have been conquered. They will remain a destructive force until the consummation of all things. But that in no way reduces our horror at the widespread violation of human rights today.

Democracy

54. As a model, modern political democracy is characterised by limited government of a temporary character, by the division of power within the government, the distinction between state and society, pluralism, the rule of law, institutionalisation of freedom rights (including free and regular elections), and a significant amount of non-governmental control of property. We recognise that no political system is directly prescribed by scripture, but we believe that biblical values and historical experience call Christians to work for the adequate participation of all people in the decision-making processes on questions that affect their lives.

55. We also recognise that simply to vote periodically is not a sufficient expression of democracy. For a society to be truly democratic economic power must be shared widely and class and status distinctions must not be barriers preventing access to economic and social institutions. Democracies are also open to abuse through the very chances which make them democratic. Small, economically powerful groups sometimes dominate the political process. Democratic majorities can be swayed by materialistic, racist, or nationalistic sentiments to engage in unjust policies. The fact that all human institutions are fallen means that the people must be constantly alert to and critical of all that is wrong.

56. We recognise that no particular economic system is directly prescribed by scripture. Recent history suggests that a dispersion of ownership of the means of production is a significant component of democracy. Monopolistic ownership, either by the state, large economic institutions, or oligarchies is dangerous. Widespread ownership, either in a market economy or a mixed system, tends to decentralise power and prevent totalitarianism.

The Concentration of Economic Power

57. Economic power can be concentrated in the hands of a few people in a market economy. When

that occurs political decisions tend to be made for economic reasons and the average member of society is politically and economically marginalised. Control over economic life may thus be far removed from a large part of the population. Transnational corporations can also wield enormous influence on some economies. Despite these problems, economic power is diffused within market-oriented economies to a greater extent than in other systems.

58. In centrally planned economies, economic decisions are made for political reasons, people's economic choices are curtailed, and the economy falters. Heavy state involvement and regulation within market economies can also result in concentrations of power that effectively marginalise poorer members of the society. Corruption almost inevitably follows from concentrated economic power. Widespread corruption so undermines society that there is a virtual breakdown of legitimate order.

Capitalism and Culture

59. As non-capitalist countries increasingly turn away from central planning and towards the market, the question of capitalism's effect on culture assumes more and more importance. The market system can be an effective means of economic growth, but can, in the process, cause people to think that ultimate meaning is found in the accumulation of more goods. The overwhelming consumerism of Western societies is testimony to the fact that the material success of capitalism encourages forces and attitudes that are decidedly non-Christian. One such attitude is the treatment of workers as simply costs or productive inputs, without recognition of their humanity. There is also the danger that the model of the market, which may work well in economic transactions, will be assumed to be relevant to other areas of life, and people may consequently believe that what the market encourages is therefore best or most true.

The Role of Government

60. Government is designed to serve the purposes of God to foster community, particularly in response to our rebellious nature (Romans 13:1, 4; Psalm 72:1). As an institution administered by human beings, government can exacerbate problems of power, greed, and envy. However, it can, where properly constructed and constrained, serve to limit some of these sinful tendencies. Therefore it is the responsibility of Christians to work for governmental structures that serve justice. Such structures must respect the principle that significant decisions about local human communities are usually best made at a level of government most directly responsible to the people affected.

61. At a minimum, government must establish a rule of law that protects life, secures freedom, and provides basic security. Special care must be taken to make sure the protection of fundamental rights is extended to all members of society, especially the poor and oppressed (Proverbs 31:8-9; Daniel 4:27). Too often government institutions are captured by the economically or socially powerful. Thus, equality before the law fails to exist for those without power. Government must also have regard for economic efficiency and appropriately limit its own scope and action.

62. The provision of sustenance rights is also an appropriate function of government. Such rights must be carefully defined so that government's involvement will not encourage irresponsible behaviour and the breakdown of families and communities. In a healthy society, this fulfilment of rights will be provided through a diversity of institutions so that the government's role will be that of last resort.

Mediating Structures

63. One of the phenomena associated with the modern world is the increasing divide between private and public sectors. The need for a bridge between these two sectors has led to an emphasis on mediating institutions. The neighbourhood, the family, the church, and other voluntary associations are all such institutions. As the early church did in its context, these institutions provide citizens with many opportunities for participation and leadership. They also provide other opportunities for loyalty in addition to the state and the family. Their role in meeting the needs of members of the community decreases the need for centralised government. They also provide a channel for individuals to influence government, busi-

ness, and other large institutions. Therefore Christians should encourage governments everywhere to foster vigorous voluntary associations.

64. The future of poverty alleviation is likely to involve expanded microeconomic income generation programmes and entrepreneurial development of the so-called "informal sector" as it becomes part of the transformed formal economy. In this context, there will most likely be an even greater role for Non-Governmental Organisations. In particular, church bodies will be able to make a significant and creative contribution in partnership with the poor, acting as mediating institutions by virtue of the churches' long-standing grass-roots involvement in local communities.

Conclusion

65. As we conclude, we thank God for the opportunity God has given us to participate in this conference. Through our time together we have been challenged to express our faith in the area of economic life in practical ways. We acknowledge that all too often we have allowed society to shape our views and actions and have failed to apply scriptural teaching in this crucial area of our lives, and we repent.

We now encourage one another to uphold Christian economic values in the face of unjust and subhuman circumstances. We realise, however, that ethical demands are often ineffective because they are reinforced only by individual conscience and that the proclamation of Christian values needs to be accompanied by action to encourage institutional and structural changes which would foster these values in our communities. We will therefore endeavour to seek every opportunity to work for the implementation of the principles outlined in this **Declaration** in faithfulness to God's calling.

We urge all people, and especially Christians, to adopt stewardship and justice as the guiding principles for all aspects of economic life, particularly for the sake of those who are most vulnerable. These principles must be applied in all spheres of life. They have to do with our use of material resources and lifestyle as well as with the way people and nations relate to one another. With girded loins and burning lamps we wait for the return of our Lord Jesus Christ when justice and peace shall embrace.

A Papal Encyclical

In 1991, Pope John Paul II published his most extensive social encyclical, titled *Centesimus annus* because it was issued one hundred years after his predecessor, Leo XIII, issued *Rerum Novarum* and began the modern tradition of Catholic social teachings. It was also issued a century after the Baptist "Father of the Social Gospel," Walter Rauschenbusch, wrote his first draft of the message that was to shape mainline Protestantism in this century and force evangelical Christians to clarify their views.

No modern church document has so fully treated the emerging theological approaches to business and economic life as has this new encyclical. It not only draws on ecumenical sources but also reflects the pope's own encounter with communism in Poland and the collapse of the economies of Eastern Europe.

John Paul accepts that a reformed capitalism will be the basis of economic life in the future. At the same time, he is sharply critical of the alienation, consumerism, possessiveness, and ecological damage that threaten to dehumanize life, and he recognizes that these are among the factors that have driven many to accept the false prophecy of socialism. He acknowledges a creative place for a work ethic, profits, markets, capital, self-interest, initiative, and technical ingenuity, and he recognizes that it is the absence, not the presence, of these that brings about marginalization of some peoples. But even a "new capitalism" has not yet overcome a number of difficulties. It does not by itself overcome alienation when people are far from God, truth, and communion with others.

These economic emphases are connected to a deeper and more enthusiastic embrace of constitutional democracy and of human rights than is frequently found in Roman Catholic teaching. Further, John Paul argues that all of these are deeply informed by the social and religious realities that stand at the core of civilization. Thus, all areas of public discourse — economic, political, legal, social, and even global — must be informed by a recognition of transcendent truth. In this connection, he shows a more direct reliance on biblical principles than many who are part of the Roman tradition.

It is likely that mainline Protestants and evangelicals, as well as people of other faiths, will study this Catholic and genuinely ecumenical document.

Centesimus annus

John Paul II

The centenary of the promulgation of the encyclical which begins with the words *"rerum novarum,"* by my predecessor of venerable memory Pope Leo XIII, is an occasion of great importance for the present history of the church and for my own pontificate. It is an encyclical that has the distinction of having been commemorated by solemn papal documents from its 40th anniversary to its 90th. It may be said that its path through history has been marked by other documents which paid tribute to it and applied it to the circumstances of the day. . . .

Toward the "New Things" of Today

The commemoration of *Rerum Novarum* would be incomplete unless reference were also made to the situation of the world today. The document lends itself to such a reference because the historical picture and the prognosis which it suggests have proved to be surprisingly accurate in the light of what has happened since then.

This is especially confirmed by the events which took place near the end of 1989 and at the beginning of 1990. These events, and the radical transformations which followed, can only be explained by the preceding situations, which to a certain extent crystallized or institutionalized Leo XIII's predictions and the increasingly disturbing signs noted by his successors. Pope Leo foresaw the negative consequences — political,

From John Paul II, *Centesimus annus* (On the Hundredth Anniversary of *Rerum Novarum*), ed. Daughters of St. Paul (Boston: St. Paul Books, 1991), in *Origins* 21, no. 1 (16 May 1991): 1-17.

social and economic — of the social order proposed by "socialism," which at that time was still only a social philosophy and not yet a fully structured movement. It may seem surprising that "socialism" appeared at the beginning of the pope's critique of solutions to the "question of the working class" at a time when "socialism" was not yet in the form of a strong and powerful state, with all the resources which that implies, as was later to happen. However, he correctly judged the danger posed to the masses by the attractive presentation of this simple and radical solution to the "question of the working class" of the time — all the more so when one considers the terrible situation of injustice in which the working classes of the recently industrialized nations found themselves.

Two things must be emphasized here: first, the great clarity in perceiving, in all its harshness, the actual condition of the working class — men, women and children; second, equal clarity in recognizing the evil of a solution which, by appearing to reverse the positions of the poor and the rich, was in reality detrimental to the very people whom it was meant to help. The remedy would prove worse than the sickness. By defining the nature of the socialism of his day as the suppression of private property, Leo XIII arrived at the crux of the problem.

His words deserve to be reread attentively: "To remedy these wrongs [the unjust distribution of wealth and the poverty of the workers], the socialists encourage the poor man's envy of the rich and strive to do away with private property, contending that individual possessions should become the common property of all . . . ; but their contentions are so clearly powerless to end the controversy that, were they carried into effect, the workingman himself would be among the first to suffer. They are moreover emphatically unjust, for they would rob the lawful possessor, distort the functions of the state and create utter confusion in the community." The evils caused by the setting up of this type of socialism as a state system — what would later be called *real socialism* — could not be better expressed. . . .

In contrast, from the Christian vision of the human person there necessarily follows a correct picture of society. According to *Rerum Novarum* and the whole social doctrine of the church, the social nature of man is not completely fulfilled in the state, but is realized in various intermediary groups, beginning with the family and including economic, social, political and cultural groups which stem from human nature itself and have their own autonomy, always with a view to the common good. This is what I have called the "subjectivity" of society which, together with the subjectivity of the individual, was canceled out by "real socialism." . . .

Reading the encyclical within the context of Pope Leo's whole magisterium, we see how it points essentially to the socioeconomic consequences of an error which has even greater implications. As has been mentioned, this error consists in an understanding of human freedom which detaches it from obedience to the truth and consequently from the duty to respect the rights of others. The essence of freedom then become self-love carried to the point of contempt for God and neighbor, a self-love which leads to an unbridled affirmation of self-interest and which refuses to be limited by any demand of justice. . . .

It is on [such a] basis [that] . . . the events of recent years can be understood. Although they certainly reached their climax in 1989 in the countries of Central and Eastern Europe, they embrace a longer period of time and a wider geographical area. In the course of the '80s, certain dictatorial and oppressive regimes fell one by one in some countries of Latin America and also of Africa and Asia. In other cases there began a difficult but productive transition toward more participatory and more just political structures. An important, even decisive, contribution was made by the church's commitment to defend and promote human rights. In situations strongly influenced by ideology, in which polarization obscured the awareness of a human dignity common to all, the church affirmed clearly and forcefully that every individual — whatever his or her personal convictions — bears the image of God and therefore deserves respect. Often the vast majority of people identified themselves with this kind of affirmation, and this led to a search for forms of protest and for political solutions more respectful of the dignity of the person.

From this historical process new forms of democracy have emerged which offer a hope for change in fragile political and social structures weighed down by a painful series of injustices and resentments as well as by a heavily damaged economy and serious social conflicts. Together with the whole church, I thank God for the often heroic witness borne in such difficult circumstances by many pastors, entire Christian communities, individual members of the faithful and other people of good will; at the same time I pray that he will sustain the efforts being made by everyone to build a better future. This is, in fact, a responsibility which falls not only to the citizens of the countries in question, but to all Christians and people of good will. It is a question of showing that the complex problems faced by those peoples can be resolved through dialogue and solidarity rather than by a struggle to destroy the enemy through war.

Among the many factors involved in the fall of oppressive regimes, some deserve special mention. Certainly the decisive factor which gave rise to the changes was the violation of the rights of workers. It cannot be forgotten that the fundamental crisis of systems claiming to express the rule and indeed the dictatorship of the working class began with the great upheavals which took place in Poland in the name of solidarity. It was the throngs of working people which foreswore the ideology which presumed to speak in their name. On the basis of a hard, lived experience of work and of oppression, it was they who recovered and in a sense rediscovered the content and principles of the church's social doctrine. . . .

The second factor in the crisis was certainly the inefficiency of the economic system, which is not to be considered simply as a technical problem, but rather a consequence of the violation of the human rights to private initiative, to ownership of property and to freedom in the economic sector. To this must be added the cultural and national dimension: It is not possible to understand man on the basis of economics alone nor to define him simply on the basis of class membership. Man is understood in a more complete way when he is situated within the sphere of culture through his language, history and the position he takes toward the fundamental events of life such as birth, love, work and death. At the heart of every culture lies the attitude man takes to the greatest mystery: the mystery of God. Different cultures are basically different ways of facing the question of the meaning of personal existence. When this question is eliminated, the culture and moral life of nations are corrupted. For this reason the struggle to defend work was spontaneously linked to the struggle for culture and for national rights.

But the true cause of the new developments was the spiritual void brought about by atheism, which deprived the younger generations of a sense of direction and in many cases led them, in the irrepressible search for personal identity and for the meaning of life, to rediscover the religious roots of their national cultures and to rediscover the person of Christ himself as the existentially adequate response to the desire in every human heart for goodness, truth and life. This search was supported by the witness of those who in difficult circumstances and under persecution remained faithful to God. Marxism had promised to uproot the need for God from the human heart, but the results have shown that it is not possible to succeed in this without throwing the heart into turmoil. . . .

Moreover, man, who was created for freedom, bears within himself the wound of original sin, which constantly draws him toward evil and puts him in need of redemption. Not only is this doctrine an integral part of Christian revelation, it also has great hermeneutical value insofar as it helps one to understand human reality. Man tends toward good, but he is also capable of evil. He can transcend his immediate interest and still remain bound to it. The social order will be all the more stable, the more it takes this fact into account and does not place in opposition personal interest and the interests of society as a whole, but rather seeks ways to bring them into fruitful harmony. In fact, where self-interest is violently suppressed, it is replaced by a burdensome system of bureaucratic control which dries up the wellsprings of initiative and creativity. When people think they possess the secret of a perfect social organization which makes evil impossible, they also think that they can use any means, including violence and deceit, in order to bring that organization into being. Politics then becomes a "secular religion" which operates under the illusion of creating paradise in this world. But no political society — which possesses its own autonomy and laws — can ever be confused with the kingdom of God. The Gospel parable of the weeds among the wheat (cf. Matt. 13:24-30, 36-43)

teaches that it is for God alone to separate the subjects of the kingdom from the subjects of the Evil One and that this judgment will take place at the end of time. By presuming to anticipate judgment here and now, man puts himself in the place of God and sets himself against the patience of God.

Through Christ's sacrifice on the cross, the victory of the kingdom of God has been achieved once and for all. Nevertheless, the Christian life involves a struggle against temptation and the forces of evil. Only at the end of history will the Lord return in glory for the final judgment (cf. Matt. 25:31) with the establishment of a new heaven and a new earth (cf. 2 Pet. 3:13; Rev. 21:1); but as long as time lasts the struggle between good and evil continues even in the human heart itself.

What sacred Scripture teaches us about the prospects of the kingdom of God is not without consequences for the life of temporal societies, which, as the adjective indicates, belong to the realm of time, with all that this implied of imperfection and impermanence. The kingdom of God, being in the world without being of the world, throws light on the order of human society, while the power of grace penetrates that order and gives it life. In this way the requirements of a society worthy of man are better perceived, deviations are corrected, the courage to work for what is good is reinforced. In union with all people of good will, Christians, especially the laity, are called to this task of imbuing human realities with the Gospel. . . .

Private Property and the Universal Destination of Material Goods

In *Rerum Novarum*, Leo XIII strongly affirmed the natural character of the right to private property, using various arguments against the socialism of this time. This right, which is fundamental for the autonomy and development of the person, has always been defended by the church up to our own day. At the same time the church teaches that the possession of material goods is not an absolute right and that its limits are inscribed in its very nature as a human right.

While the pope proclaimed the right to private ownership, he affirmed with equal clarity that the "use" of goods, while marked by freedom, is subordinated to their original common destination as created goods as well as to the will of Jesus Christ as expressed in the Gospel. Pope Leo wrote: "Those whom fortune favors are admonished . . . that they should tremble at the warnings of Jesus Christ . . . and that a most strict account must be given to the Supreme Judge for the use of all they possess"; and quoting St. Thomas Aquinas, he added: "But if the question be asked how must one's possessions be used, the church replies without hesitation that man should not consider his material possessions as his own, but as common to all," because "above the laws and judgments of men stands the law, the judgment of Christ."

The successors of Leo XIII have repeated this twofold affirmation: the necessity and therefore the legitimacy of private ownership as well as the limits which are imposed on it. The Second Vatican Council likewise clearly restated the traditional doctrine in words which bear repeating: "In making use of the exterior things we lawfully possess, we ought to regard them not just as our own but also as common, in the sense that they can profit not only the owners but others too"; and a little later we read: "Private property or some ownership of external goods affords each person the scope needed for personal and family autonomy, and should be regarded as an extension of human freedom. . . . Of its nature private property also has a social function, which is based on the law of the common purpose of goods." I have returned to this same doctrine, first in my address to the third conference of the Latin American bishops at Puebla and later in the encyclicals *Laborem Exercens* and *Sollicitudo Rei Socialis*.

Rereading this teaching on the right to property and the common destination of material wealth as it applies to the present time, the question can be raised concerning the origin of the material goods which sustain human life, satisfy people's needs and are an object of their rights.

The original source of all that is good is the very act of God, who created both the earth and man, and who gave the earth to man so that he might have dominion over it by this work and enjoy its fruits (Gen. 1:28). God gave the earth to the whole human race for the sustenance of all its members, without excluding or favoring anyone.

This is the foundation of the universal destination of the earth's goods. The earth, by reason of its fruitfulness and its capacity to satisfy human needs, is Gods' first gift for the sustenance of human life. But the earth does not yield its fruits without a particular human response to God's gift, that is to say, without work. It is through work that man, using his intelligence and exercising his freedom, success in dominating the earth and making it a fitting home. In this way he makes part of the earth his own, precisely the part which he has acquired through work; this is the origin of individual property. Obviously he also has the responsibility not to hinder others from having their own part of God's gift; indeed he must cooperate with others so that together all can dominate the earth.

In history, these two factors — work and the land — are to be found at the beginning of every human society. However, they do not always stand in the same relationship to each other. At one time the natural fruitfulness of the earth appeared to be and was in fact the primary factor of wealth, while work was, as it were, the help and support for this fruitfulness. In our time, the role of human work is becoming increasingly important as the productive factor both of non-material and of material wealth. Moreover, it is becoming clearer how a person's work is naturally interrelated with the work of others. More than ever, work is work with others and work for others: It is a matter of doing something for someone else. Work becomes ever more fruitful and productive to the extent that people become more knowledgeable of the productive potentialities of the earth and more profoundly cognizant of the needs of those for whom their work is done.

In our time in particular there exists another form of ownership which is becoming no less important than land: the possession of know-how, technology and skill. The wealth of the industrialized nations is based much more on this kind of ownership than on natural resources.

Mention has just been made of the fact that people work with each other, sharing in a "community of work" which embraces ever widening circles. A person who produces something other than for his own use generally does so in order that others may use it after they have paid a just price mutually agreed upon through free bargaining. It is precisely the ability to foresee both the needs of others and the combinations of productive factors most adapted to satisfying those needs that constitutes another important source of wealth in modern society. Besides, many goods cannot be adequately produced through the work of an isolated individual; they require the cooperation of many people in working toward a common goal. Organizing such a productive effort, planning its duration in time, making sure that it corresponds in a positive way to the demands which it must satisfy and taking the necessary risks — all this too is a source of wealth in today's society. In this way the role of discipline and creative human work and, as an essential part of that work, initiative and entrepreneurial ability becomes increasing evident and decisive.

This process, which throws practical light on a truth about the person which Christianity has constantly affirmed, should be viewed carefully and favorably. Indeed, besides the earth, man's principal resources is man himself. His intelligence enables him to discover the earth's productive potential and the many different ways in which human needs can be satisfied. It is his disciplined work in close collaboration with others that makes possible that creation of ever more extensive working communities which can be relied upon to transform man's natural and human environments. Important virtues are involved in this process such as diligence, industriousness, prudence in undertaking reasonable risks, reliability and fidelity in interpersonal relationships as well as courage in carrying out decisions which are difficult and painful, but necessary both for the overall working of a business and in meeting possible setbacks.

The modern business economy has positive aspects. Its basis is human freedom exercised in the economic field, just as it is exercised in many other fields. Economic activity is indeed but one sector in a great variety of human activities, and like every other sector, it includes the right to freedom as well as the duty of making responsible use of freedom. But it is important to note that there are specific differences between the trends of modern society and those of the past, even the recent past. Whereas at one time the decisive factor of production was the land and later capital — understood as a total complex of the instruments of production — today the decisive factor is increasingly man himself, that is, his knowledge, especially his scientific knowledge, his capacity for interrelated and compact organization as well as his ability to perceive the needs of others and to satisfy them.

However, the risks and problems connected with this kind of process should be pointed out. The fact is that many people, perhaps the majority today, do not have the means which would enable them to take their place in an effective and humanly dignified way within a productive system in which work is truly central. They have no possibility of acquiring the basic knowledge which would enable them to express their creativity and develop their potential. They have no way of entering the network of knowledge and intercommunication which would enable them to see their qualities appreciated and utilized. Thus, if not actually exploited, they are to a great extent marginalized; economic development takes place over their heads, so to speak, when it does not actually reduce the already narrow scope of there old subsistence economies. They are unable to compete against the goods which are produced in ways which are now and which properly respond to needs, needs which they had previously been accustomed to meeting through traditional forms of organization. Allured by the dazzle of an opulence which is beyond their reach and at the same time driven by necessity, these people crowd the cities of the Third World where they are often without cultural roots and where they are exposed to situations of violent uncertainty without the possibility of becoming integrated. Their dignity is not acknowledged in any real way, and sometimes there are even attempts to eliminate them from history through coercive forms of demographic control which are contrary to human dignity.

Many other people, while not completely marginalized, live in situations in which the struggle for a bare minimum is uppermost. These are situations in which the rules of the earliest period of capitalism still flourish in conditions of "ruthlessness" in no way inferior to the darkest moments of the first phase of industrialization. In other cases the land is still the central element in the economic process, but those who cultivate it are excluded from ownership and are reduced to a state of quasi-servitude. In these cases it is still possible today, as in the days of *Rerum Novarum,* to speak of inhuman exploitation. In spite of the great changes which have taken place in the more advanced societies, the human inadequacies of capitalism and the resulting domination of things over people are far from disappearing. In fact, for the poor, to the lack of material goods has been added a lack of knowledge and training which prevents them from escaping their state of humiliating subjection.

Unfortunately, the great majority of people in the Third World still live in such conditions. It would be a mistake, however, to understand this "world" in purely geographic terms. In some regions and in some social sectors of that world, development programs have been set up which are centered on the use not so much of the material resources available but of the "human resources."

Even in recent years it was thought that the poorest countries would develop by isolating themselves from the world market and by depending only on their own resources. Recent experience has shown that countries which did this have suffered stagnation and recession, while the countries which experienced development were those which succeeded in taking part in the general interrelated economic activities at the international level. It seems therefore that the chief problem is that of gaining fair access to the international market, based not on the unilateral principle of the exploitation of the natural resources of these countries but on the proper use of human resources.

However, aspects typical of the Third World also appear in developed countries, where the constant transformation of the methods of production and consumption devalues certain acquired skills and professional expertise, and thus requires a continual effort of retraining and updating. Those who fail to keep up with the times can easily be marginalized as can the elderly, the young people who are incapable of finding their place in the life of society and in general those who are weakest on part of the so-called Fourth world. The situation of women too is far from easy in these conditions.

It would appear that on the level of individual nations and of international relations the free market is the most efficient instrument for utilizing resources and effectively responding to needs.

But this is true only of those needs which are "solvent" insofar as they are endowed with purchasing power and for those resources which are "marketable" insofar as they are capable of obtaining a satisfactory price. But there are many human needs which find no place on the market. It is a strict duty of justice and truth not to allow fundamental human needs to remain unsatisfied and not to allow those burdened by such needs to perish. It is also necessary to help these needy people to acquire expertise, to enter the circle of exchange and to develop their skills in order to make the best use of their capacities and resources. Even prior to the logic of a fair exchange of goods and the forms of justice appropriate to it, there exists something which is due to man because he is man, by reason of his lofty dignity. Inseparable from that required "something" is the possibility to survive and at the same time to make an active contribution to the common good of humanity.

In Third World contexts, certain objectives stated by *Rerum Novarum* remain valid and in some cases still constitute a goal yet to be reached, if man's work and his very being are not to be reduced to the level of a mere commodity. These objectives include a sufficient wage for the support of the family, social insurance of old age and unemployment, and adequate protection for the conditions of employment.

Here we find a wide range of opportunities for commitment and effort in the name of justice on the part of trade unions and other workers' organizations. These defend workers' rights and protect their interests as persons while fulfilling a vital cultural role so as to enable workers to participate more fully and honorably in the life of their nation and to assist them along the path of development.

In this sense, it is right to speak of a struggle against an economic system, if the latter is understood as a method of upholding the absolute predominance of capital, the possession of the means of production and of the land, in contrast to the free and personal nature of human work. In the struggle against such a system, what is being proposed as an alternative is not the socialist system, which in fact turns out to be state capitalism, but rather a society of free work, of enterprise and of participation. Such a society is not directed against the market, but demands that the market be appropriately controlled by the forces of society and by the state so as to guarantee that the basic needs of the whole of society are satisfied.

The church acknowledges the legitimate role of profit as an indication that a business is functioning well. When a firm makes a profit, this means that productive factors have been properly employed and corresponding human needs have been duly satisfied. But profitability is not the only indicator of a firm's condition. It is possible for the financial accounts to be in order and yet for the people — who make up the firm's most valuable asset — to be humiliated and their dignity offended. Besides being morally inadmissible, this will eventually have negative repercussions on the firm's economic efficiency. In fact, the purpose of a business firm is not simply to make a profit, but is to be found in its very existence as a community of persons who in various ways are endeavoring to satisfy their basic needs and who form a particular group at the service of the whole of society. Profit is a regulator of the life of a business, but it is not the only one; other human and moral factors must also be considered, which in the long term are at least equally important for the life of a business.

We have seen that it is unacceptable to say that the defeat of so-called "real socialism" leaves capitalism as the only model of economic organization. It is necessary to break down the barriers and monopolies which leave so many countries on the margins of development and to provide all individuals and nations with the basic conditions which will enable them to share in development. This goal calls for programmed and responsible efforts on the part of the entire international community. Stronger nations must offer weaker ones opportunities for taking their place in international life, and the latter must learn how to use these opportunities by making the necessary efforts and sacrifices and by ensuring political and economic stability, the certainty of better prospects for the future, the improvement of workers' skills and the training of competent business leaders who are conscious of their responsibilities.

At present, the positive efforts which have been made along these lines are being affected by the still largely unsolved problem of the foreign debt of the poorer countries. The principle that debts must be paid is certainly just. However, it is not right to demand or expect payment when the ef-

fect would be the imposition of political choices leading to hunger and despair for entire peoples. It cannot be expected that the debts which have been contracted should be paid at the price of unbearable sacrifices. In such cases it is necessary to find — as in fact is partly happening — ways to lighten, defer or even cancel the debt compatible with the fundamental right of peoples to subsistence and progress.

It would now be helpful to direct our attention to the specific problems and threats emerging within the more advanced economies and which are related to their particular characteristics. In earlier stages of development, man always lived under the weight of necessity. His needs were few and were determined to a degree by the objective structures of his physical makeup. Economic activity was directed toward satisfying these needs. It is clear that today the problem is not only one of supplying people with a sufficient quantity of goods, but also of responding to a demand for quality: the quality of the goods to be produced and consumed, the quality of the services to be enjoyed, the quality of the environment and of life in general.

To call for an existence which is qualitatively more satisfying is of itself legitimate, but one cannot fail to draw attention to the new responsibilities and dangers connected with this phase of history. The manner in which new needs arise and are defined is always marked by a more or less appropriate concept of man and of his true good. A given culture reveals its overall understanding of life through the choices it makes in production and consumption. It is here that the phenomenon of consumerism arises. In singling out new needs and new means to meet them, one must be guided by a comprehensive picture of man which respects all the dimensions of his being and which subordinates his material and instinctive dimensions to his interior and spiritual ones. If, on the contrary, a direct appeal is made to his instincts — while ignoring in various ways the reality of the person as intelligent and free — than consumer attitudes and lifestyles can be created which are objectively improper and often damaging to his physical and spiritual health. Of itself, an economic system does not possess criteria for correctly distinguishing new and higher forms of satisfying human needs from artificial new needs which hinder the formation of a mature personality. Thus a great deal of educational and cultural work is urgently needed, including the education of consumers in the responsible use of their power of choice, the formation of a strong sense of responsibility among producers and among people in the mass media in particular as well as the necessary intervention by public authorities.

A striking example of artificial consumption contrary to the health and dignity of the human person, and certainly not easy to control, is the use of drugs. Widespread drug use is a sign of a serious malfunction in the social system; it also implies a materialistic and in a certain sense destructive "reading" of human needs. In this way the innovative capacity of a free economy is brought to a one-sided and inadequate conclusion. Drugs, as well as pornography and other forms of consumerism which exploit the frailty of the weak, tend to fill the resulting spiritual void.

It is not wrong to want to live better; what is wrong is a style of life which is presumed to be better when it is directed toward "having" rather than "being" and which wants to have more not in order to be more, but in order to spend life in enjoyment as an end in itself. It is therefore necessary to create lifestyles in which the quest for truth, beauty, goodness and communion with others for the sake of common growth are the factors which determine consumer choices, savings and investments. In this regard, it is not a matter of the duty of charity alone, that is, the duty to give from one's "abundance" and sometimes even out of one's needs in order to provide what is essential for the life of a poor person. I am referring to the fact that even the decision to invest in one place rather than another, in one productive sector rather than another, is always a moral and cultural choice. Given the utter necessity of certain economic conditions and of political stability, the decision to invest, that is, to offer people an opportunity to make good use of their own labor, is also determined by an attitude of human sympathy and trust in providence, which reveals the human quality of the person making such decisions.

Equally worrying is the ecological question which accompanies the problem of consumerism and which is closely connected to it. In his desire to have and to enjoy rather than to be and to grow, man consumes the resources of the earth and his own life in an excessive and disordered way. At the root of the senseless destruction of the natural environment lies an anthropological error, which unfortunately is widespread in our day. Man, who discovers his capacity to transform and in a certain sense create the world through his own work, forgets that this is always based on God's prior and original gift of the things that are. Man thinks that he can make arbitrary use of the earth, subjecting it without restraint to his will as though it did not have its own requisites and a prior God-given purpose, which man can indeed develop but must not betray. Instead of carrying out his role as a cooperator with God in the work of creation, man sets himself up in place of God and thus ends up provoking a rebellion on the part of nature, which is more tyrannized than governed by him.

In all this, one notes first the poverty or narrowness of man's outlook, motivated as he is by a desire to possess things rather than to relate them to the truth and lacking that disinterested, unselfish and aesthetic attitude that is born of wonder in the presence of being and of the beauty which enables one to see in visible things the message of the invisible God who created them. In this regard, humanity today must be conscious of its duties and obligations toward future generations.

In addition to the irrational destruction of the natural environment, we must also mention the more serious destruction of the human environment, something which is by no means receiving the attention it deserves. Although people are rightly worried — though much less than they should be — about preserving the natural habitats of the various animal species threatened with extinction because they realize that each of these species makes its particular contribution to the balance of nature in general, too little effort is made to safeguard the moral conditions for an authentic "human ecology." Not only has God given the earth to man, who must use it with respect for the original good purpose for which it was given to him, but man too is God's gift to man. He must therefore respect the natural and moral structure with which he has been endowed. In this context, mention should be made of the serious problems of modern urbanization, of the need for urban planning which is concerned with how people are to live and of the attention which should be given to a "social ecology" of work.

Man receives from God his essential dignity and with it the capacity to transcend every social order so as to move toward truth and goodness. But he is also conditioned by the social structure in which he lives, by the education he has received and by his environment. These elements can either help or hinder his living in accordance with the truth. The decisions which create a human environment can give rise to specific structures of sin which impede the full realization of those who are in any way oppressed by them. To destroy such structures and replace them with more authentic forms of living in community is a task which demands courage and patience.

The first and fundamental structure for "human ecology" is the family, in which man receives his first formative ideas about truth and goodness, and learns what it means to love and to be loved, and thus what it actually means to be a person. Here we mean the family founded on marriage, in which the mutual gift of self by husband and wife creates an environment in which children can be born and develop their potentialities, become aware of their dignity and prepare to face their unique and individual destiny. But it often happens that people are discouraged from creating the proper conditions for human reproduction and are led to consider themselves and their lives as a series of sensations to be experienced rather than as a work to be accomplished. The result is a lack of freedom, which causes a person to reject a commitment to enter into a stable relationship with another person and to bring children into the world or which leads people to consider children as one of the many "things" which an individual can have or not have, according to taste, and which compete with other possibilities.

It is necessary to go back to seeing the family as the sanctuary of life. The family is indeed sacred: It is the place in which life — the gift of God — can be properly welcomed and protected against the many attacks to which it is exposed and can develop in accordance with what constitutes authentic human growth. In the face of the so-called culture of death, the family is the heart of the culture of life.

Human ingenuity seems to be directed more toward limiting, suppressing or destroying the sources of life — including recourse to abortion, which unfortunately is so widespread in the world — than toward defending and opening up the possibilities of life. The encyclical *Sollicitudo Rei Socialis* denounced systematic anti-childbearing campaigns which, on the basis of a distorted view of the demographic problem and in a climate of "absolute lack of respect for the freedom of choice of the parties involved," often subject them "to intolerable pressures . . . in order to force them to submit to this new form of oppression." These policies are extending their field of action by the use of new techniques to the point of poisoning the lives of millions of defenseless human beings as if in a form of "chemical warfare."

These criticisms are directed not so much against an economic system as against an ethical and cultural system. The economy in fact is only one aspect and one dimension of the whole of human activity. If economic life is absolutized, if the production and consumption of goods become the center of social life and society's only value, not subject to any other value, the reason is to be found not so much in the economic system itself as in the fact that the entire sociocultural system, by ignoring the ethical and religious dimension, has been weakened and ends by limiting itself to the production of goods and services alone.

All of this can be summed up by repeating once more that economic freedom is only one element of human freedom. When it becomes autonomous, when man is seen more as a producer or consumer of goods than as a subject who produces and consumes in order to live, then economic freedom loses its necessary relationship to the human person and ends up by alienating and oppressing him.

It is the task of the state to provide for the defense and preservation of common goods such as the natural and human environments, which cannot be safeguarded simply by market forces. Just as in the time of primitive capitalism the state had the duty of defending the basic rights of workers, so now, with the new capitalism, the state and all of society have the duty of defending those collective goods which, among others, constitute the essential framework for the legitimate pursuit of personal goals on the part of each individual.

Here we find a new limit on the market: There are collective and qualitative needs which cannot be satisfied by market mechanisms. There are important human needs which escape its logic. There are good which by their very nature cannot and must not be bought or sold. Certainly the mechanisms of the market offer secure advantages: They help to utilize resources better; they promote the exchange of products; above all they give central place to the person's desires and preferences, which in a contract meet the desires and preferences of another person. Nevertheless, these mechanisms carry the risk of an "idolatry" of the market, an idolatry which ignores the existence of goods which by their nature are not and cannot be mere commodities.

Marxism criticized capitalist bourgeois societies, blaming them for the commercialization and alienation of human existence. This rebuke is of course based on a mistaken and inadequate idea of alienation derived solely from the sphere of relationships of production and ownership, that is, giving them a materialistic foundation and moreover denying the legitimacy and positive value of market relationships even in their own sphere. Marxism thus ends up by affirming that only in a collective society can alienation be eliminated. However, the historical experience of socialist countries has sadly demonstrated that collectivism does not do away with alienation but rather increases it, adding to it a lack of basic necessities and economic inefficiency.

The historical experience of the West, for its part, shows that even if the Marxist analysis and its foundation of alienation are false, nevertheless alienation — and the loss of the authentic meaning of life — is a reality in Western societies too. This happens in consumerism, when people are ensnared in a web of false and superficial gratifications rather than being helped to experience their personhood in an authentic and concrete way. Alienation is found also in work when it is organized so as to ensure maximum returns and profits with no concern whether the worker, through his own labor, grows or diminishes as a person, either through increased sharing in a genuinely supportive community or through increased isolation in a maze of relationships marked by destructive competitiveness and estrangement, in which he is considered only a means and not an end.

The concept of alienation needs to be led back to the Christian vision of reality by recognizing in alienation a reversal of means and ends. When man does not recognize in himself and in others the value and grandeur of the human person, he effectively deprives himself of the possibility of benefiting from his humanity and of entering into that relationship of solidarity and communion with others for which God created him. Indeed, it is through the free gift of self that man truly finds himself. This gift is made possible by the human person's essential "capacity for transcendence." Man cannot give himself to a purely human plan for reality, to an abstract ideal or to a false utopia. As a person, he can give himself to another person or to other persons, and ultimately to God, who is the author of his being and who alone can fully accept his gift. A man is alienated if he refuses to transcend himself and to live the experience of self-giving and of the formation of an authentic human community oriented toward his final destiny, which is God. A society is alienated if its forms of social organization, production and consumption make it more difficult to offer this gift of self and to establish this solidarity between people.

Exploitation, at least in the forms analyzed and described by Karl Marx, has been overcome in Western society. Alienation, however, has not been overcome as it exists in various forms of exploitation, when people use one another and when they seek an ever more refined satisfaction of their individual and secondary needs while ignoring the principal and authentic needs which ought to regulate the manner of satisfying the other ones too. A person who is concerned sorely or primarily with possessing and enjoying, who is no longer able to control his instincts and passions or to subordinate them by obedience to the truth, cannot be free: Obedience to the truth about God and man is the first condition of freedom, making it possible for a person to order his needs and desires and to choose the means of satisfying them according to a correct scale of values, so that the ownership of things may become an occasion of growth for him. This growth can be indeed as a result of manipulation by the means of mass communication, which impose fashions and trends of opinion through carefully orchestrated repetition without it being possible to subject to critical scrutiny the premises on which these fashions and trends are based.

Returning now to the initial question: Can it perhaps be said that after the failure of communism capitalism is the victorious social system and that capitalism should be the goal of the countries now making efforts to rebuild their economy and society? Is this the model which ought to be proposed to the countries of the Third World, which are searching for the path to true economic and civil progress?

The answer is obviously complex. If by *capitalism* is meant an economic system which recognizes the fundamental and positive role of business, the market, private property and the resulting responsibility for the means of production as well as free human creativity in the economic sector, then the answer is certainly in the affirmative even though it would perhaps be more appropriate to speak of a *business economy, market economy* or simply *free economy.* But if by *capitalism* is meant a system in which freedom in the economic sector is not circumscribed within a strong juridical framework which places it at the service of human freedom in its totality and which sees it as a particular aspect of that freedom, the core of which is ethical and religious, then the reply is certainly negative.

The Marxist solution has failed, but the realities of marginalization and exploitation remain in the world, especially the Third Word, as does the reality of human alienation, especially in the more advanced countries. Against these phenomena the church strongly raises her voice. Vast multitudes are still living in conditions of great material and moral poverty. The collapse of the communist system in so many countries certainly removes an obstacle to facing these problems in an appropriate and realistic way, but it is not enough to bring about their solution. Indeed, there is a risk that a radical capitalistic ideology could spread which refuses even to consider these problems in the a priori belief that any attempt to solve them is doomed to failure, and which blindly entrusts their solution to the free development of market forces.

The church has no models to present; models that are real and truly effective can only arise within the framework of different historical situations through the efforts of all those who responsibly confront concrete problems in all their social, economic, political and cultural aspects as these interact with one another. For such a task the church offers her social teaching as an indispensable and ideal orientation, a teaching which, as already mentioned, recognizes the positive value of the market and of enterprise, but which at the same time points out that these need to be oriented toward the common good. This teaching also recognizes the legitimacy of workers' efforts to obtain full respect for their dignity and to gain broader areas of participation in the life of industrial enterprises so that, while cooperating with others and under the direction of others, they can in a certain sense "work for themselves" through the exercise of their intelligence and freedom.

The integral development of the human person through work does not impede but rather promotes the greater productivity and efficiency of work itself, even though it may weaken consolidated power structures. A business cannot be considered only as a "society of capital goods"; it is also a "society of persons" in which people participate in different ways and with specific responsibilities, whether they supply the necessary capital for the company's activities or take part in such activities through their labor. To achieve these goals there is still need for a broad associated workers' movement directed toward the liberation and promotion of the whole person.

In the light of today's "new things," we have reread the relationship between individual or private property and the universal destination of material wealth. Man fulfills himself by using his intelligence and freedom. In so doing he utilizes the things of this world as objects and instruments and makes them his own. The foundation of the right to private initiative and ownership is to be found in this activity. By means of his work man commits himself not only for his own sake, but also for others and with others. Each person collaborates in the work of others and for their good. Man works in order to provide for the needs of his family, his community, his nation and ultimately all humanity. Moreover, he collaborates in the work of his fellow employees as well as in the work of suppliers and in the customers' use of goods in a progressively expanding chain of solidarity. Ownership of the means of production, whether in industry or agriculture, is just and legitimate if its evades useful work. It becomes illegitimate, however, when it is not utilized or when it serves to impede the work of others in an effort to gain a profit which is not the result of the overall expansion of work and the wealth of society, but rather is the result of curbing them or of illicit exploitation, speculation or the breaking of solidarity among working people. Ownership of this kind has no justification and represents an abuse in the sight of God and man.

The obligation to earn one's bread by the sweat of one's brow also presumes the right to do so. A society in which this right is systematically denied, in which economic policies do not allow workers to reach satisfactory levels of employment, cannot be justified from an ethical point of view nor can that society attain social peace. Just as the person fully realizes himself in the free gift of self, so too ownership morally justifies itself in the creation, at the proper time and in the proper way, of opportunities for work and human growth for all. . . .

PART C

CONTEMPORARY DEVELOPMENTS

Chapter Eleven

The Changing Corporation

As we approach the twenty-first century, corporate forms of organization are the primary frameworks for global economic activity. While by national and international law the corporation is primarily a legal structure for engaging in collective activity, the corporate form is not static. During this century some corporations have grown into massive entities with thousands of employees. Others are more akin to extended family businesses that find legal advantages from incorporation. Now in an era of downsizing, the small entrepreneurial knowledge corporation is carving a new economic niche.

Nevertheless, as we have seen, the corporation as a mode of organized cooperation not only has its roots in the history of moral communities; it also remains, in its many forms, a source of great moral significance for the lives of customers, employees, shareholders, and communities. Adults spend more daily functional hours in the workplace than anywhere else. With loosened ties to extended families, communities of origin, and the authority of the church, the corporate workplace, whether or not it would choose to, exerts substantial influence in shaping purpose, motives, and behavior. Some highly visible corporate players in the 1980s staged ugly dramas of greed, injury, anger, and fraud. Such entities adversely affected the lives of thousands of people. Yet, if immoral corporate behavior can cause such adverse effects, why can't moral corporate behavior lead to different results?

It must be granted that the legal structure of the corporation, in and of itself, is not usually seen as moral or immoral. Yet a corporation does shape the beliefs and actions of its participants and partners by its mission, organizational structure, internal culture, systems, processes, and modes of accountability.

How should the moral significance of the corporation be understood as we approach the twenty-first century? What themes of faith and moral belief should permeate its influence? How could the corporation be reinvented to broaden societal participation and accountability? What are the responsibilities of business participants in shaping a moral future responsive to all stakeholders in the enterprise? The readings in Chapter 11 will address these issues.

Section 1 begins by providing a framework for understanding the roots of the corporation and moral/theological themes that should be woven into its future. Section 2 examines the means by which corporate accountability can be strengthened. Section 3 explores opportunities for employee participation in both profits and decision making as morally significant issues.

Section 1: Moral Significance and Corporate Organization

To envision the corporation of the future requires consideration of its past development and present state; and if we wish that future to be a moral one, we are also required to construct a more public discussion to connect corporations to their moral and spiritual underpinnings. The purpose of this section is to investigate such moral and spiritual connections as we consider purposes and roles for corporations in our global future.

Max Stackhouse examines the roots of the modern corporation and argues that they are religious. The church created the first social-institutional center independent of both household and state. Thus the church served as the model for other forms of communal effort, including the economic corporation. Yet Stackhouse is not satisfied with current embodiments of the corporation. He believes that faith and theology must inform the structures and activities of corporations to a much greater degree now than they have in the past century. Concepts such as vocation, sin, and covenant are needed to match the moral power of corporate structures with their economic power.

In arguing that business is a social practice, Dennis McCann and M. L. Brownsberger provide further exploration of corporate purposes as sources of moral influence in society. After describing Alasdair MacIntyre's concept of a social practice, they reject his neo-Aristotelian view of the corporate and managerial motive as simple acquisitiveness, thus placing business outside of social practice. Using Peter Drucker's understanding of business purposes, McCann and Brownsberger argue that business activity is a social practice with nothing intrinsically immoral in its fabric.

Stewart Herman and Don Shriver elaborate on this assertion by exploring the religious and moral values operative in business visions of the corporation. If business is indeed a social practice, then Herman's argument for covenantal models as preferable to contractual ones is thought provoking. He suggests that businesses should model themselves on covenants as described in Scripture, and he provides a substantial analysis of God's covenant with humanity as background for his argument. A distinctly different view of manager/employee relations grows from his recommendation of the covenantal framework.

Shriver raises a crucial question for understanding the manager's role in the social practice of business. He examines the frameworks that managers have adopted to serve justice. By tracing the history of the corporation in both its societal role and its organizational structure, Shriver suggests that there have been three stages of managerial development. What began as paternalism and hierarchy at the turn of the century had evolved by mid-century into a paradigm of the management team within a circle of influence. Now, however, Shriver pleads for a new paradigm of ethical standards and accountability, one less vunerable to shifting sources of influence, one in which managers assume roles as leaders becoming partners in new learning.

Implicit in these authors' reflections are the fundamental questions all corporate leaders must ask: Where are the roots of our businesses? What are our purposes? What moral vision is fundamental to business as a social practice? What frameworks for understanding the manager's role must be cultivated to accomplish these purposes?

Spirituality and the Corporation

Max L. Stackhouse

The Corporation: In Need of Theological Assessment

. . . The continued growth of the influence of the corporation in modern life seems, in the short term, to be confirmed by the fact that in recent years the democratic socialist nations in Europe have all moved steadily away from state capitalist (socialist or Fascist) tendencies. They have denationalized industry and strengthened the corporations in a process called "privatization." This pattern is being followed in Africa, where various attempts at "African socialism" have brought economic disaster. And this pattern is present in the rising stars of Asia — notably Japan and now China — countries in which it is grafted onto other religiocultural traditions. The United States and Canada now have more intercorporate trade with Asia than with Europe, a phenomenon shifting the center of commercial life from the Atlantic community to an emerging and vigorously capitalist Pacific community of nations. And despite the current vigor of liberation theology in Latin America, the larger nations of that region are also turning to a renewal of democratic patterns with increased roles for corporations, while socialist efforts elsewhere end only in the sharing of poverty.

Yet very few efforts have been made to deal with the corporation in religious or theological terms. Modern public theology has addressed economic questions in some detail — particularly in regard

From Max L. Stackhouse, *Public Theology and Political Economy* (Grand Rapids: Eerdmans, 1987), chap. 7, pp. 113-36.

to duties of equity in distribution. We know that we have a spiritual and moral obligation to care for poor people, and to act politically to see that oppressed groups are given a decent chance in economic life. But we have given very little theological attention to the decisive center of production: the corporation. Modern spiritualities have stressed the importance of identifying with the poor and reading the gospel through their eyes. But theologians have seldom thought about one of the most influential social institutions of modern economies, one now sweeping the world. . . .

Defining the Corporation

Where did the corporation come from? What are its foundations? Where is it going? How shall we assess it morally? Is there any spirituality connected with it that can be approved, or is it simply the organized unleashing of the greed that the majority report of the church's traditions always suspected to be present in nonagricultural production, trade, commerce, and finance?

We know that there are two dead-end answers to these questions. One comes from the fundamentalist emphasis on individualistic salvation, the religious parallel to laissez-faire capitalism. It is a matter of no small irony that today's most celebrated opponents of "secular humanism" are frequently the perpetrators of one of the most virulent forms of ideological secular humanism when it comes to economic life. They have uncritically accepted the utilitarian, Enlightenment understandings of individualistic economics, the modern heirs of which — Ludwig von Mises, Friedrich Hayek, and Ayn Rand, among others — would be contemptuous of fundamentalist religion, and of the idea that religion should influence economics. These fundamentalists obscure the ways in which this ideological construct in fact works out psychologically, legally, and sociologically. In their zeal to support "individual" economic and religious responsibility, they idolize the family as the locus for the accumulation and control of wealth. It is no accident that fundamentalists who baptize this form of secular humanism have a weak ecclesiology and a preference for any political regime that will protect the traditional family and capitalist values.

The other dead-end answer is offered by liberationism when it consciously or preconsciously adopts anticorporate views because of its attraction to Marxist modes of social analysis. This perspective sees the development of corporations as the result of the ascendency of an essentially alienated yet controlling class over a dispossessed class, a problem that requires solution by revolutionary action and the political control of all means of production. Such an orientation, if the revolution succeeds, turns the whole society into a single corporation managed by the revolutionary party. Those who control the guns also control the factories; those who control the army also control the food. Each "enterprise" becomes a department of state and is required to make economic decisions on the basis of the approved political ideology. Neither of these options considers it possible to accept the moral or spiritual legitimacy of the corporation, to see it as a viable social institution.

Ought we then turn to "business" to find ways of understanding the corporation? We will find that doing so is not very helpful. Many business leaders have not focused on the basic social, historical, and spiritual foundations of their own institutions and activities. Most simply presume a social, historical, and spiritual context in which corporate patterns of doing business appear to be settled, and they proceed to carry out — with as much dispatch, energy, efficiency, and profitability as they can muster — the tasks at hand. Like the physicist who takes no interest in the structure of the university or the surgeon who gives little attention to the question of what makes a hospital run, many in business are blind to the character of the structures in which they live and move and have their being. Several years ago a team of scholars at Harvard Business School inquired into the worldviews of American business leaders. The still unsurpassed result, *The American Business Creed*, demonstrated that most business leaders hold an outmoded ideological view of their sphere of expertise that does not correspond with what they do every day or with the kinds of social interactions that actually dominate their lives.

Unfortunately, it is also not possible to turn to many contemporary economists on this matter. Most seem to be so preoccupied with developing econometric models of how specific functions work that they ignore larger questions of political economy. Yet those concerned with the clarification of a public theology for political economy cannot let the matter rest. Nor should we simply reduplicate what business leaders or economists do. We want to assess the moral viability of the contexts they presume, the spiritual and moral character of the great mechanisms of productivity that they staff. Above all, we want to know whether corporations must remain the enemy of the most spiritually, ethically, and socially concerned people, as sometimes now seems to be the case.

Where then shall we turn and what questions shall we pose if we want to understand production and the social forms that govern it? I think that we will have to inquire more deeply into the social and religious history behind the modern business corporation. It is the product, empirically, of a minority tradition in the history of religion and society. This minority tradition induced a particular kind of spirituality and a particular social orientation to the world that have roots in the history of the church and that have produced a "non-natural" form of organization with its own internal logic that is today both triumphant and suspect.

The first thing to say about the business corporation is that it is a *persona ficta,* an artifact with its own internal "spirit" or "character" and with legal standing as an agent, an actor, in human affairs. Owners, managers, and workers come and go in the corporation, but the corporation lives on. It can sue and be sued, issue contracts, hold, buy or sell property, migrate from country to country, "get married" in mergers, produce offspring in the form of subsidiaries, be granted citizenship in other lands, grow and expand, or shrink and be executed by being dissolved. The corporation may be owned by individuals, families, other corporations, governments, labor unions, or church pension funds. It may be managed by males or females, blacks or whites, old or young. Hindus or Muslims, Jews or atheists. Workers may spend forty years in its employ, or there may be an employee turnover every five years. All this will make no essential difference regarding what it does or does not do. The corporation, for all its massive influence, is founded on a very narrow base. It is a community of persons designed for efficient production that must base every decision on the question of whether or not it can continue to produce. This is determined by whether or not it is likely to reap a legal profit that will perpetuate its existence. If it does not make a profit, or if it does so by illegal means, its managers will be fired, its owners will sell their interest in it, and it can be taken into receivership for either revitalization or dissolution. If it does make a profit, it is in principle immortal.

How did such a thing come about? The story is too complex to recount in full here, but clues can be found in the work of nineteenth-century legal historians, by leading social theorists early in this century, and in several newer works. The roots of the phenomenon are decidedly religious, in spite of the fact that much of traditional religion resisted — and still resists — the corporation.

The Religious Roots of the Corporation

The early church established the household of faith, an *oikoumene*, a spiritual network of persons who were one in Christ who also formed a social-institutional center independent of both the traditional *oikos* and the regime. In doing so, the church established in practice, and later in law, the notion that it was possible to form collective identities that were "non-natural" in origin and that were dedicated to the transformation of every aspect of life. At first, as we see in the Book of Acts, the church established a community only of consumption, not of production. Yet this set the precedent for disciplined use of economic resources by an organized group independent of familial or imperial control.

Throughout its early period, Christianity seems to have been most appealing precisely to those marginal groups that were not engaged in land-holding, in agricultural production, or in the service of the rulers. It seems to have been quite attractive to urban workers — not only urban slaves but artisans, traders, tent-makers, and the like. In brief, Christianity has been linked from its inception to urbanized peoples involved in producing and trading. Those tied to the land and its duties of *oikos* were called pagans; those who gave primary loyalty to regime were called idolaters. Against these, the church developed its own corporate structures and disciplines that were to be

the prototypes of later corporate structures of many kinds.

Much later, as the medieval cities developed, stimulated in part by the new methods of production introduced into northern Europe by the monastic missionaries, a series of legal provisions established the city itself as a corporation. Like the church, it was also independent of *oikos* and regime. In addition, hospitals, schools, and other charitable corporations were formed on the analogy of the church and its order.

At the hands of Protestant lawyers, during the period when protodemocratic political institutions were also being formed, this long tradition was extended by the formation of the limited-liability corporation, developed specifically for commercial purposes. This made it possible for people to invest in companies without risking personal, familial, or political capital distinct from that which was invested. Imbued with the Protestant work ethic, a dedication to "covenantal relationships," an inclination to bring all aspects of life under disciplined rational control, a drive toward the democratization of piety, politics, and social relationships of all kinds, and a radicalization of the sense of vocation, the limited-liability corporation developed the concept of "trustee" and invented a new social form for stewardship. The patterns consequently developed contributed to and grew with the Industrial Revolution as it introduced modern technologies of production and new occupational possibilities on a massive scale. The ethos of the corporation, which still bears the marks of this history in its deepest fabric, continues to imbue all those working in the corporation with values rooted in this history: common economic action demands a work ethic, a set of values separate from familial and political control, a discipline guided by rational control, at least a sense of "profession," and a stewardship of wealth that is not one's own. Workers and managers in modern corporations continue to be drawn into an ethos wherein these moral and spiritual presuppositions are seen as "natural," although the overt theological foundations have largely been replaced by utilitarian and contractual understandings of human relationships, and mammon has become, for many, the reigning deity.

Today, in the United States, where these developments are, if anything, more prevalent than anywhere else in the world, approximately thirteen percent of the population (and of the gross national product) is related to political and military matters, about seventeen percent of the work force is employed in nonprofit organizations, and only about three percent of the population is in the hands of corporations, and the profits derived make possible churches, schools, hospitals, the arts, welfare services, and various research institutes. Corporations have created more wealth than most of humankind can imagine, and they seem likely to do so in the foreseeable future. What was once rooted in *oikos* and transformed by *oikoumene* has become a corporate economy — now significantly independent not only of *oikos* and *polis* but of *oikoumene* as well.

In this context it is important to ask what "profit" is. In one sense that is what drives the corporation, and it is dedication to profit that occasions the most frequent critique of the idea that there is some viable spirituality in corporate life. Profit has a very technical and precise meaning, and organizing for it is not to be equated too quickly or too simply with either the motivation of greed or the impulse to acquisition. Max Weber already pointed that out in 1918, although theologians more than anyone else seem to have missed the point. Greed and the impulse to acquisition — indeed, the "pursuit of gain, of money, of the greatest possible amount of money" — in themselves have nothing to do with what is distinctive to the modern corporation's "profit."

> This impulse existed and has existed among waiters, physicians . . . artists, prostitutes, dishonest officials, soldiers, nobles, crusaders, gamblers, and beggars. One may say that it has been common to all sorts and conditions of men at all times and in all countries of the earth. . . . It should be taught in the kindergarten of cultural history that this naive idea of . . . capitalism must be given up once and for all.

This is so because profit involves a difference between assets and liabilities as indicated by a balance sheet figure, itself derived from the formally calculated pluses over minuses after an analytical assessment has been made on standardized principles. Profit is the estimated claim on wealth that can be used as capital for new efforts to create wealth. It is most frequently associated with the *constraint* of greed, of the impulse to acquire by chance, adventure, or expropriation and to consume. Further, profit can be understood only in the context of ongoing institutions such as corporations and exchange marts. Individuals, families, schools, hospitals, pirates, a tribe that discovers oil on its property, or a church that is the beneficiary of a will may have gains of which they want more or expenses of which they want fewer, but they do not have profits unless they are organized as corporations that produce goods and services and have rationally calculated costs and claims on income. And it is precisely such calculations that break the power of non-economic values over economic decision-making. In accounting procedures, profits serve to indicate whether previous calculations have been correct, whether economic activity has been conducted with relative efficiency and disciplined control, and whether the gain has been acquired irrespective of any special political, familial, or cultural influence that might interfere with economic calculation. This understanding of profit applies to socialist as well as capitalist economies, although in socialist economies the state calculates, collects, and deploys profits. State capitalism turns the entire nation-state into a single corporation with government as the manager of both production and markets.

Today there is another form of corporate capitalism that reigns in some regions. In the East and many developing lands, old familial networks have been incorporated into a kind of "shogunate" corporation that is highly paternalistic, patriarchal, hierarchical, and wedded by family connections to those who control government. In India, subcastes have become corporations. And in Latin America, Indonesia, and the Philippines, military elites closely tied to the government are awarded control over corporations to form a kind of "crony capitalism." In these settings, the utilitarian, contract-based corporations exported from the West have little historic connection with the theological-ethical traditions that I outlined earlier. They have no history of breaking with the power of traditional familial and political institutions: instead, they reinforce them. Further, there seldom exists a legacy of law, a societal ethos, or genuine competition to control their behavior. Corporations thus are very different in the Third World than they are in the corporate capitalist West, or under state capitalism, and they are intensely resisted for good reasons.

At present there are no institutions at the international level that can control these institutions except other corporations that do a better job of producing at a lower price. And we must acknowledge that the drive to capture markets has led all forms of modern corporate production to engage political forces in imperialistic ways. In fact, in developing countries, most of the Western-based, trans-national corporations betray the very foundations of what I have been attempting to set forth. More often than not, such corporations do not maintain the relative independence from either the leading households or the political regime that they attempt to maintain at home. They form alliances (or subsidiaries) with elite households and with military-political authorities to gain monopolistic controls, and they function as cartels to preserve the economic control of landed aristocracy over peasantry, which has been the pattern for centuries. They incline toward the fascist form of state capitalism, and they are properly opposed by both democratic capitalism and all democratic socialism as well as by every serious public theology. The obvious difficulties in which Third World countries currently find themselves are in part due to the failure of Western-based corporations to export their own fundamental assumptions and to equip the peoples to undertake corporate development, and the making of profits, on their own.

Such failures inhibit the capacity of concerned Western Christians to enhance things beyond productivity in these lands — namely, human rights and the prospects for democracy. Even in the rising economies of Asia, transnational corporate involvements have not brought about demonstrable respect for human rights or viable democracy, although they have brought about technological transformations and increased professionalization, the consequences of which are not yet clear. It could be that human rights, democracy, technology, professional development, and corporate productivity are among the things (besides Christianity) that the West has to offer the world, and that development of these things in modernizing

cultures is being inhibited by contemporary corporate policies that ally corporations too closely with political authority and indigenous feudal elites, and that do not attend to the deeper principles on which corporate activities are grounded.

Reforming the Spirituality of the Corporation

If the discussion of these matters thus far can serve as a rough outline of social and spiritual factors that we must deal with in a responsible stewardship of modern political economies, and if we are fundamentally committed to a public theology that hopes to make the Word enfleshed in this kind of world, what shall the *oikoumene* now offer to corporate life?

We will have to make some very fundamental and fateful decisions before we proceed very far. One involves answering a basic question: Which form of corporative organization do we want to champion? There are only three major choices institutionally. Shall we call for state-engineered corporative life, which is the socialist route? Shall we foster an *oikos*-based corporative model, which dominates the Third World? Or shall we endorse the model of the independent corporation, an endorsement implicit in the direction the West has taken in the past? The question could be put another way: Who do we want to have calculating and making the profits and thus controlling capitalization — governments, elite families, or stockholders? I do not think it will do for ecumenical leadership to continue to duck this issue by continuing to ignore the questions of production and concentrating only on distribution, however important it is to maintain ethical witness on that front.

I think that we had better choose the model of the independent corporation (although in some situations the state-socialist model may have to be employed temporarily to remove elite families from their present positions of economic exploitation). We should do so because, in the long run, it is the system most inclined to support and sustain the prospects for human rights, democratic participation in political life, and the reduction of feudal, patriarchal, and caste structure in family life. Of course, we must beware here, because making such a choice can easily be seen as simply a sanctification of Yankee corporate capitalism and a conscious or preconscious attempt to wrap the American way of life in the Christian flag and drape it around the world. These I do not intend, and hence any move in the direction I suggest must be coupled with simultaneous prophetic judgment against and pastoral reformation of many current corporate policies. . . .

In order to carry out prophetic judgment against and reformation of corporations, we will have to make a second decision. Do we think that corporations have any real or potential spiritual foundations? If they do not, we can have no transformative communication base with them. We would have to see them only as mechanisms, as humanly populated machines that could be constructed or deconstructed, that break down and can be repaired, but that could not in principle be reformed by any spiritual or moral transformation.

This question is not new, although it is neglected. A generation ago, F. W. Maitland and Ernest Barker, among others, researched the question of whether institutions have souls. On the whole, they argued, it cannot be held that institutions, like people, stand before the gates of heaven. Institutions can neither go to heaven nor suffer in hell. Yet that does not mean that corporations cannot have a character, even a certain esprit de corps that can be assessed on moral and spiritual grounds. It is quite possible that these *personae fictae*, which are more *ficta* than *persona*, have an inner quality that can be reformed and renewed. . . .

If this is so, what resources from our theological tradition shall we bring to bear on the reformation of the spirituality of production as it appears in the modern corporation? Let me close this chapter by listing five motifs from the governing themes of a public theology that might become the counterpoints of preaching and teaching, pastoral care, and the development of a stewardly leadership able to carry their commitments and ministries into the world of the productive corporation:

1. Vocation. From the calling of Abraham and Moses to the calling of the prophets and disciples, through the various refinements in the history of the tradition, the notion that each person was put in the world by God to serve some particular purpose and is called to serve the whole of humanity in the economy of God is a profound and penetrating insight. A vocation is not simply a job or an occupation. It comes from God and may require sacrificial suffering, discipleship, and *kenosis*. The concept has its most important application in regard to personal life, but it has social dimensions as well. Further, every institution has *its* particular vocation. Schools are to seek the truth and understanding; hospitals are devoted to healing and the care of the sick; symphonies are meant for making music. Is it possible that corporations as cooperative endeavors, as well as the people in them, have a vocation from God to do what they do? Surely this means that they must contribute to the material well-being of the human community with the particular skills and products they offer — plumbing supply, meatpacking, energy resources, or whatever — and that they must do so in a way that makes a profit.

If this is possible, common corporate vocations must be carried out under the watchful eye of the living God with no less diligence than our personal quests for vocational fulfillment. A vocation under God is proactive — not merely reactive. Not only does it minister to those harmed by bad economic policy or corporate decisions; it steels the soul for economic initiative and engenders a willingness to take moral risks. Were the sense of vocation to be reborn in modern corporations among stockholders, management, and labor, the shape of corporate economies might change.

To accent such matters is the responsibility of clergy and theologians. Who in government, in labor unions, in business schools or economic departments speaks of these matters? It is *our* task, one we will have to address again, and more fully, later on.

2. Moral Law. In some circles today it seems quaint to speak of moral law, and many are so afraid of sounding self-righteous (as those who talk about it a great deal often do) that they avoid speaking of it. And yet the reluctance to speak clearly about fundamental principles or right and wrong allows people in corporate life to be satisfied on the one hand with mere legality, and on the other hand with whatever is strategic or efficient. This has allowed many to lose sight of the basic principles of human rights that must be

met as a condition of any viable structure of economic life. Corporations, especially those in such places as South Africa and developing countries, must see to it that their activities enhance human rights. And if this is not the case, they must not be surprised if churches, workers' groups, opposition parties, and oppressed minorities form coalitions to convert them.

3. Liberation. In the West, millions of middle-class people have found their economic liberation — against the expectations of many — in the disciplined, cooperative sharing of vocations in corporations. Yet many on the underside of Western economies have not had this experience, and many more around the word are oppressed by corporations. If there is to be a remedy for this problem, it will mean that the long-range planning that every corporation now does and the intervening steps taken to carry out those plans must speak to this question: Does this project somehow contribute to the liberation of those not free in a way that draws them also into communities of economic responsibility?

4. Sin. There is something tragic in all of economic life. Every act of production involves the destruction of some resource that has been given to humanity in creation, and every pattern of distribution entails disproportionate gain for some at the expense of others, and every act of consumption involves waste. Further, every organized center of economic activity thus far developed involves the domination of some over others. Let us never think that we humans can find our salvation in economic activity and its rewards, or in the building of one specific kind of economic order, including that centered in the corporation. Many corporations engender a kind of loyalty that borders on the totemic at best, on the idolatrous at worst. The tendencies to worship mammon are with us all, and can easily demand that the corporation become mammon's temple. Especially because the corporation can provide a kind of immortality, it can require human sacrifice on its altar. These perils are already suggested in the commandment that tell us that six days shall we labor, but that we must remember the Sabbath, to keep it holy. Our necessary efforts at production are disciplined and restrained by the constant and regular repair or the One who creates what we can never produce, distributes what no human system

can apportion, and receives out of our willingness to consume less that we obviously could.

5. Covenant. In the face of our modern political economies, we must work out a convenantal structure for the corporation in ways framed by these other doctrines and in ways echoing the ecclesiological roots of the corporation. And we must attempt to structure economic influence by patterns that reflect what we have learned about political distributions of power. The future of corporate polity will surely demand the democratization of decision-making, the sharing of power, and the participation of labor in setting guidelines for corporate policy around the world. And this means the pluralization of economic authority and a political, social, and ethical openness to corporate formation in underdeveloped regions of the world, which state capitalisms of the left and the right do not presently encourage.

To this list one might easily add Creation. The modern corporation is — besides those things already discussed — the seat of modern technology that alters the structures of nature. It therefore has many implications for how we relate to the biophysical universe as a creation of God.

Management as a Social Practice: Rethinking Business Ethics after MacIntyre

Dennis P. McCann and M. L. Brownsberger

... Let us consider whether business management, contrary to MacIntyre's own view, can be regarded as a social practice. In order to pursue this line of inquiry, we must attend to MacIntyre's definition of a social practice. The term is introduced systematically in his chapter on "The Nature of the Virtues" in *After Virtue*:

> By a 'practice' I am going to mean any coherent and complex form of socially established cooperative human activity through which goods internal to that form of activity are realized in the course of trying to achieve those standards of excellence which are appropriate to, and partially definitive of, that form of activity, with the result that human powers to achieve excellence, and human conceptions of the ends and goods involved, are systematically extended [175].

In order to count as a practice, the activity in question must be socially established and cooperative; it must be governed by standards of excellence that are constitutive, at least partially, of the activity itself; and it must yield "internal goods" by meeting those standards of excellence. The definition implies an indispensable connection

Dennis P. McCann and M. L. Brownsberger, "Management as a Social Practice: Rethinking Business Ethics after MacIntyre," *Annual of the Society of Christian Ethics* (1990): 223-45.

between virtue and social practices: "A virtue is an acquired human quality the possession and exercise of which tends to enable us to achieve those goods which are internal to practices and the lack of which effectively prevents us from achieving any such goods" (178). Thus virtues are cultivated in the context of social practices: they are the habits that help us achieve the internal goods that an authentic social practice ought to produce.

Clearly, MacIntyre's is a normative theory of social practices. Not all human activities will meet his stipulations, but for different reasons. "Planting turnips is not a practice; farming is." Presumably, the difference is that planting turnips or anything else is but an element in a practice, an activity whose purpose can only be understood by placing it in the context of an integrated whole, in this case, farming. So, some activities are ruled out as practices because they are only variable elements in a larger stable pattern of behavior. On the other hand, MacIntyre insists that "practices are not to be confused with institutions":

> Chess, physics and medicine are practices; chess clubs, laboratories, universities and hospitals are institutions. Institutions are characteristically and necessarily concerned with what I have called external goods. They are involved in acquiring money, power and status as rewards. Nor could they do otherwise if they are to sustain not only themselves but also the practices of which they are the bearers. For no practices can survive for any length of time unsustained by institutions [181].

Institutions differ from the practices which they sustain in two ways: (1) Institutions characteristically generate "external goods," while genuine social practices are focused on internal goods. (2) Though institutions therefore organize the resources necessary for social practices, social practices are also thereby rendered vulnerable to the "corrupting power of institutions."

This association of corruption with institutions rests on MacIntyre's differentiation of two classes of goods, only one of which is identified with virtue, and his belief that we must often choose one at the expense of the other. Throughout the discussion in *After Virtue*, justice, courage, and truthfulness are listed as goods internal to social practices, while money, power, and status are external goods provided by institutions. Though MacIntyre is quick to affirm the desirability of such external goods, and though he readily concedes that successful performance in the various practices is often rewarded with external goods, he must insist at the same time that external goods are a threat to virtue:

> Yet notoriously the cultivation of truthfulness, justice and courage will often, the world being what it contingently is, bar us from being rich or famous or powerful. Thus although we may hope that we can not only achieve the standards or excellence and the internal goods of certain practices by possessing the virtues *and* become rich, famous and powerful, the virtues are always a potential stumbling block to this comfortable ambition. We should therefore expect that, if in a particular society the pursuit of external goods were to become dominant, the concept of the virtues might suffer attrition and then perhaps something near total effacement, although simulacra might abound [183].

This is, according to MacIntyre, exactly what happens in a liberal society whose ethos is dominated by the social characters of the manager and the therapist. Bureaucratic logic makes it all but impossible for such practitioners to recognize any good internal to their practices other than the externally measured good of effectiveness. With the "obliteration of the distinction between manipulative and nonmanipulative social relations," a confusion which MacIntyre regards as an essential feature of the character of the manager, the moral basis for understanding any human activity as a social practice disappears. . . .

How does managing a business fit into MacIntyre's normative theory of social practices? A business enterprise, like a chess club or a university, is clearly an institution. Is managing such an institution a social practice? Can management be conceived as exercising a function analogous in businesses to that represented, as in the previous paragraph, by politics? Though a full answer to these questions is not possible until we confront MacIntyre's attitude toward commerce generally, a preliminary answer can be had by comparing moral descriptions of contemporary business management with MacIntyre's notion of a social practice. Is the fit between the two sufficiently plausible to cast suspicion upon MacIntyre's own view of the character of the manager? We think that it is.

What alternative descriptions of business management are relevant here? Peter Drucker's classic statement, *The Practice of Management,* is a plausible candidate. . . .

Drucker defines management teleologically as "the dynamic, life-giving element in every business" and as the "specifically economic organ of an industrial society" whose functions are: (1) economic performance: "managing a business," (2) the transformation of human and material resources: "managing managers," and (3) organization of productive activities: "managing workers and work." Each of these three functions structures a major area of Drucker's statement as a whole.

The first function, economic performance, differentiates business enterprises from all other institutions serving society. Given the fundamental and pervasive fact of scarcity, business enterprises are specifically designed to organize as efficiently as possible the human and material resources required for the production and distribution of economic goods. The purpose of a business, however, is "to create a customer"; it is not to make a profit, though profit clearly is "the test of [the] validity" of this institution's activities (35-37). This distinction between the function and the purpose of a business is a crucial one, but one which is ordinarily overlooked. Most people, when asked to formulate the purpose of a business, will assert offhandedly that it is "to make money" rather than "to create a customer"; if they consider both, they will construe the latter as merely a means to the former. Drucker's insistence on precisely the opposite conclusion is not a convenient exercise in verbal gymnastics, but a true ordering of the actual causes of business activities, as those causes are understood by those who administer the activities, namely business managers. . . .

Drucker's way of defining the function of economic performance in terms of creating a purposive relationship between market institutions and their customers gets to the heart of MacIntyre's distinction between the goods of excellence and the goods of effectiveness. For creating a new form of association for mutual economic betterment, rather that merely for maximizing profits, suggests that managing such relationships not only might have its own characteristic form of moral excellence, but also that as such it would qualify as a social practice within institutions focused upon a society's economic development. . . . In Drucker's theory of business management, the external good of profit is made subordinate to the internal good of creating a customer. Drucker holds that recognizing this good is contingent upon a society's general attitude toward the marketplace: the purpose of a business is unintelligible apart from the market institutions that define the scope of its activities. Thus managing such activities could be regarded as a social practice if the *telos* of society, the common good, is furthered through such activity, and/or if the practice of management can succeed in this purpose only by achieving the internal good appropriate to it.

When we turn to Drucker's other two functions of business, this pattern of teleological definition is confirmed; furthermore, his specific observations on "managing managers" and "managing workers and work" suggest not only that business management could be a social practice, but that it must be such if managers are to succeed even in meeting their employers' economic goals. It is clear that Drucker's approach to human resources is not compatible with MacIntyre's description of the manager; Drucker does not describe relations that are manipulative or narrowly preoccupied with managerial "effectiveness." Drucker regards every employee as potentially a manager, and he hopes to achieve a stage of industrial organization in which "self-control" or self-management is the normal condition. Such a scheme requires "responsible workers" whose potential contributions can be actualized if their supervisors learn to motivate them through "careful placement, high standards of performance, providing the worker with the information needed to control himself, and with the opportunities for participation that will give him a managerial vision" (304). Here the policies that Drucker advocates clearly presuppose, contrary to MacIntyre's expectations, that there is in business an institutionally significant distinction between effectiveness based on manipulation and that based on informed consent. Though he

is careful to point out the limits to worker participation in managerial decision-making processes (365), he insists that the only way to increase the productivity of human resources over the long term is to manage them for mutual accountability.

Finally, Drucker insists upon the indispensable link between managerial success and personal integrity:

> One can learn certain skills in managing people, for instance, the skill to lead a conference or to conduct an interview. One can set down practices that are conducive to development — in the structure of the relationship between manager and subordinate, in a promotion system, in the rewards and incentives of an organization. But when all is said and done, developing men still requires a basic quality in the manager which cannot be created by supplying skills or by emphasizing the importance of the task. It requires integrity of character. . . .
>
> It may be argued that every occupation — the doctor, the lawyer, the grocer — requires integrity. But there is a difference. The manager lives with the people he manages, he decides what their work is to be, he directs it, he trains them for it, he appraises it and, often, he decides their future. The relationship between a merchant and a customer, professional man and client requires honorable dealings. Being a manager, though, is more like being a parent, or a teacher. And in these relationships honorable dealings are not enough; personal integrity is of the essence [348-49].

Such integrity, however, is not the result of taking courses in business ethics. Drucker argues that here is "one qualification that the manager cannot acquire but must bring with him." Rather than counting against our view that managing a business is a social practice, we understand Drucker to be saying that the *telos* that ought to govern the activities of managers lies beyond the scope of management itself. At the same time, however, Drucker insists that ultimately the task of management is educative: "The one contribution he is uniquely expected to make is to give others vision and ability to perform. It is vision and moral responsibility that, in the last analysis, define the manager" (350).

This brief outline of Drucker's interpretation

of the practice of management fails to do it justice, for it is in the details of the analysis that his vision of the moral meaning of management becomes plausible, descriptively as well as normatively. Nevertheless, what little we have presented of his thought should be a sufficient basis from which to infer Drucker's response to our question: Is management a social practice, in MacIntyre's sense of the term? "How could it not be a social practice?" might be Drucker's reply. Analytically, we might press him to specify the internal good that is achieved by the practice of management. His answer, we infer, would be "service," understood as a form of empowerment. Nevertheless, Drucker's view of the manager's internal responsibilities suggests a view of service that is not completely symmetrical with the one operative in the business's external relationship of service to its customers.

In their internal operations, managers serve their fellow employees by helping them to become participants in a cooperative endeavor whose scope would have remained beyond the capacities of any of them, considered as individuals. Clearly, Drucker's assumptions regarding this type of managerial empowerment involve normative beliefs about human nature and the common good not significantly different from those that inform MacIntyre's neo-Aristotelian perspective. . . . Where Drucker parts company with MacIntyre . . . is in his understanding of the form of empowerment operative in the ultimate purpose of business enterprise, namely, creating a customer. His questions "What is our business?" and "Who is the customer?" are answered by appealing to consumer sovereignty rather than to an overriding notion of the common good. Both questions determine the specific meaning of the service a business provides by asking what the customer actually values and whether the business is capable of fulfilling those expectations profitably (54-61). The question might have been answered in a more Aristotelian fashion by reflecting on what is intrinsically good either for the customer or for society as a whole. It is, then, Drucker's view that managers serve customers by empowering them to decide for themselves what the meaning of the good life may be, subject to the constraints imposed by law and the limits of their financial resources. Such a view of consumer

sovereignty is hardly indefensible, but it does rest upon arguments of the philosophically liberal type concerning a just market system — arguments of the type that MacIntyre disparages. As a result, any strict analogy between the activity of management and Aristotelian politics breaks down at this point. Nevertheless, despite the lack of symmetry in Drucker's understanding of the meaning of service, we believe that it does represent a genuine internal good, whose moral characteristics entitle us to qualify managing a business as a social practice. . . .

Drucker's perspective, however, forces us also to reconsider the moral meaning of commerce, as MacIntyre retrieves it from Aristotle's *Politics*. MacIntyre is right, of course; Aristotle does indeed consider trade or money-making as unnatural and therefore immoral. . . . Our focus here, however, is not an analysis of Aristotle but an analysis of MacIntyre's use of Aristotle's negative view of the place of money-making in the good life. Does *pleonexia* (understood as "simple acquisitiveness") adequately describe the basic motive for going into business, with the result that managing a business, no matter how enlightened the management, inevitably must fail to meet the moral standards implicit in MacIntyre's notion of a social practice? We think not, and here are our reasons.

First of all, we have no quarrel with MacIntyre's conviction that simple acquisitiveness — that is, "acting so as to have more as such" — is a vice and inevitably an offense against justice when it is pursued to the exclusion of all the other purposes that together constitute the good life. The question is whether such acquisitiveness can rightly be identified as the structural imperative of the successful economic performance that is the essence of a business enterprise. Can simple acquisitiveness account for the situation that MacIntyre apparently regards as typical of business management, that is, the situation of structural pathology in which a desire for external goods (or the "goods of effectiveness") completely overshadows a person's or a group's presumably natural affinity for internal goods (or the "goods of excellence")? We are skeptical about both the explanation for and the alleged frequency of this pathology among business managers.

Secondly, if MacIntyre is right to think that

pleonexia provides the sole motive for going into business, then Drucker is necessarily wrong about the limited role of profit in explaining the purpose of a business. We think that Drucker is right, though some economists who fancy themselves the defenders of "free enterprise" (such as Milton Friedman) assert that the only sufficient motive for business activity is "profit-maximization." To the extent that these views are coherent, they highlight the fact that within the discipline of neo-classical economics there are not theoretical limits to the pursuit of higher profits. However, as Drucker insists, a whole range of practical constraints are imposed upon management to the extent that the firm must remain in business (35-36). "Profit-maximization," when pushed to the limit, would entail a complete sell-off of business assets. The next balance sheet might look impressive; but it would also be the last one the firm would ever issue. Drucker's nuanced view of the role of profit relative to the purposes of a business enterprise, therefore, cannot be dismissed as an idealist's special pleading. If management is to fulfill those purposes, its practices cannot be motivated by *pleonexia*.

Thus, if profit is merely the standard by which an enterprise's success in meeting its objectives is measured, then not only is the so-called profit-motive only marginally relevant for explaining managerial behavior, but it can hardly be identified with MacIntyre's simple acquisitiveness. Nevertheless, we believe, thirdly, that the appearance of a connection between the two is so impressive that we must explain the simulacrum of vice, if you will, inherent in common perceptions of profit. What is the actual context in which profit functions as a measure of successful business performance? This measurement is unlike the rating systems used to measure the performance of athletic teams, such as the coaches' poll for the fictive "National Championship" in collegiate football. Though a school's ranking in such ratings may have a significant impact on its ability to attract a range of external goods, including unrestricted endowment funds, the standard of measurement itself is not calibrated in such goods. The profits reported in the quarterly report of a business, however, are stated as quantities of real money, which are disbursed to those investors who have title to them through some sort of share holding.

Among its customary moral obligations, management has a fiduciary responsibility to these shareholders, the ultimate owners of the enterprise, to maximize the return on their investment, consistent with the overall objectives of the business. The simulacrum of simple acquisitiveness is explained by the fact that there is, in the nature of the case, no fixed standard of profitability.

Managers are confronted, instead, with the volatility of our increasingly competitive capital markets, dominated by institutional investors whose own fiduciary responsibilities apparently commit them to short-term strategies for managing investments that are in competition with one another. As a result, business managers can never rest content with the secure knowledge that, with regard to their own firm's profitability, enough is enough. The dynamics of the capital markets in which businesses compete for investors may change virtually overnight, and a rate of return that was sufficient to attract investors in one set of circumstances may no longer be competitive. Activities that an outside observer is tempted to explain in terms of either greed or, as MacIntyre has it, "acting so as to have more as such," can just as plausibly be explained by reference to the understandable anxiety that managers must experience in trying to chart reasonable goals for the firm while coping with the basic instabilities of the capital markets.

We are not asserting that business managers are entirely innocent of simple acquisitiveness. An insightful characterization of their moral situation should be more realistic than that. Just as sin — as Reinhold Niebuhr once taught us — is an inevitable but hardly necessary outcome of the basic anxiety provoked by our experience of finitude and freedom, so something like the vice of *pleonexia* may well result from a manager's protracted struggle to still the anxiety produced by the uncertainness of securing a business's finances. In the ordinary course of business there is fertile soil where *pleonexia* may take root. We insist, however, that such irresponsible behavior is not a necessary consequence or defining feature of the work of managing a business's finances.

If this analysis of the so-called profit-motive is on target, then, as we have indicated, the challenge that it represents for the practice of management is a systemic one. Drucker, you will recall, wisely counsels managers to seek a balance among the various objectives of a business, including its performance of shareholders; this balance, he repeatedly insists, finally reflects the moral and intellectual integrity of management. He also notes that integrity can neither be taught to managers nor produced by them; it is not something a business can control. Our analysis suggests that the likelihood of achieving this balance may depend upon still another factor not entirely within management's control, namely, the firm's vulnerability to the vicissitudes of the capital markets. To the extent that the volatility of these markets directly contributes to a demoralizing instability in business management, their current mode of operations is a systemic obstacle to actualizing Drucker's vision of management as a social practice.

A significant part of the challenge represented by managing a business today involves overcoming this obstacle. Though the operations of the capital markets are properly a matter for public policy, there are a variety of strategies open to business managements seeking to enhance their own stability, including taking a company private by buying back its outstanding stock and/or initiating employee stock ownership plans in, which the firm increasingly is owned by those who work for it. Since such strategies can only succeed in particular cases, a truly systemic overhaul of the regulatory framework in which our capital markets operate may be required for the common good.

Whatever the precise solution to the problem of enhancing the stability of business management, our analysis clearly indicates the irrelevance of Aristotle's view of commerce, at least in its classical form. However comforting it may have been to MacIntyre, Aristotle's declaration that money making is to be despised as an "unnatural" way to obtain wealth is simply innocent of any true understanding of modern business economics. The interest paid to lenders, contrary to Aristotle, should be regarded as a "user fee" for capital. The accumulation of savings is socially necessary for without it there can be no investment, and without investment over the long run the level of business activity is likely to stagnate, precipitating a decline in living standards. To receive a return on one's investment is to be compensated for the opportunities foreclosed by trusting one's savings to this enterprise rather than to another. There is nothing inherently unnatural about profiting from the productivity of money, unless all the strategies designed to produce an increase of goods or economic growth are also suspect morally. In a modern society, it is difficult to see how such a verdict can be reconciled with the common good.

By ignoring what history and experience have to tell us about the actual performance characteristics of various economic systems, MacIntyre moralizes Aristotle's argument, with the result that our righteous desire to avoid the vice of *pleonexia* becomes an excuse for not investigating very carefully the moral meaning of the social practices upon which the economic welfare of the community inevitably depends. Neither Aristotle nor MacIntyre gives us sufficient reason for thinking that commerce is any less moral than any of the other organized activities that constitute our public world. The playing field, upon which the perennial struggle between vice and virtue unfolds, is just as level in business management as it is in religion, education, politics, medicine, or any other social practice we care to imagine. Business ethics after MacIntyre thus is possible if, and only if, MacIntyre's neo-Aristotelian theory of virtue cultivated within social practices can be detached from his idealizing nostalgia for the Greek polis and grafted onto the stock of opportunities for communal existence opened up by characteristically modern forms of voluntary association. Modern business enterprises are but one of those forms of association.

The Potential for Building Covenants in Business Corporations

Stewart W. Herman

What exactly is the potential for covenantal relations in modern business corporations? The question arises because during the past several years, at least five theologically minded business ethicists have proposed the idea of covenant as a normative model for explaining how large bureaucratic corporations ought to function. These prescriptions are challenging because covenantal norms hold business practitioners to a morally higher standard than the *quid pro quo* of contractual obligations. Douglas Sturm holds corporations to the norms of peace, justice, and steadfastness, while Charles McCoy and William May challenge executives to exercise moral leadership.

I am inclined to agree with these ethicists that a covenantal potential exists in corporations. Yet this potential is not obvious, for it is generally eclipsed by contract as the central term which explains how corporations operate. The contractual bond is the primary source of legal and moral leverage against malfeasance in corporations, because it is the primary description of the relationship between management and employees. Covenant-minded business ethicists therefore face the difficult task of making a covenantal basis to corporations appear as real and as firm as this contractual basis. I suspect the contractual description is too firmly established to be displaced, but it could be supplemented and modified by a covenantal description. What is

needed then is to demonstrate how the idea of covenant captures a descriptive dimension of corporations that the idea of contract misses. If Clifford Geertz is right that religious moral visions become compelling insofar as they appear "really real," the covenantal norms asserted by Sturm and others will become more persuasive as they are grounded in a description of the corporation that renders those norms obvious and compelling.

Here, I will focus on the relationship between managements and employees rather than, as is often done, the relation between corporations and society. My principal claims are that corporate settings involve managements and employees in relations which are more than contractual and that this "more than" opens the door to develop a plausible and powerful covenantal ethic for management-employee relations. This redescription and appraisal of the corporation in covenantal terms proceeds in three steps. First, I will argue that the cement that holds corporations together is not simply contracts, but a broad array of "influence strategies," which managements and employees apply to shape each other's thinking and acting. For an account of these strategies, I draw upon organization theory and organizational behavior, two closely related social-scientific fields which attempt to explain how large organizations function. This redescription renders the logic of covenanting directly relevant to explaining how corporations function, because one signal feature of covenants — in contrast to contracts — is that they are vehicles through which parties aim at forming, even transforming, the character and actions of each other. Second, I will interpret the biblical history of divine Covenant-building from an organizational perspective in order to generate a normative model for covenant-building in corporations. Managements and employees are driven to influence each other by a logic of interdependence compounded of vulnerability and contingency. This dynamic correlates with the logic of divine Covenant-building attested to in the canonical record of God's history with God's people. The important fact for organizational struggles is that the influence strategies used by God affirm the moral agency and freedom of God's people by not attempting to vanquish or manipulate the contingency that these stubborn Covenant partners pose to God. Third, I abstract

Stewart W. Herman, "The Potential for Building Covenants in Business Corporations," *Annual of the Society of Christian Ethics* (1992): 201-22.

The primary ethical question, however, is not what is predictable. Nor is it what is possible. Nor is it what will enable the human species merely to survive. It is rather what will conduce to the common good. Human life is intrinsically relational. It is lived in a set of contexts — a biosphere (the relationship between self and nature), a sociosphere (the relationship between self and other) and a psychosphere (the relationship between self and self). The common good is that texture of relationships in which the life of all is enhanced by the actions and dispositions of each one. Its common name is sympathy. Its profound meaning is love. Its ordinary, everyday demand is justice. Its grounding is ultimately ontological. That is, the common good is not an abstract principle imposed upon the reality of the world. It is a quality that derives from the structure of experience. It is the deepest impulse and profoundest need of all being. The suffering and misery that result from its violation are themselves witness to its presence.

Thus, to assess the full significance of the culture of the corporation, to interpret the meaning of the world that it manifests within itself (the meso- and microscopic views), the world that it produces through its agency (the macroscopic view), and the world that it tends to promote for the future even if it should itself disappear (the chronoscopic view), it must be measured by its conformity to the common good. The ultimate judgment of the corporation and its culture, like the ultimate judgment of all life, is whether and to what degree within the ongoing passage of history, it bodies forth some creative advance within the community of being.

In sum, the corporation, like the Sabbath, was not made for its own survival. Its legitimacy depends on whether its meaning is truly representative of the meaning of life itself.

— Douglas Sturm, "Corporate Culture and the Common Good," *Thought* 60, no. 237 (June 1985): 158

from this normative model two general guidelines: that authentic covenant-building requires that managements and employees acknowledge their vulnerability to each other, and that they be generous in their application of influence strategies to each other. . . .

A. Corporations as Constructed of Influence Strategies

The modern corporation, perhaps more than any other form of association, exemplifies the dense interplay of intentional efforts to shape human action and character — and efforts to resist such shaping. A corporation comes into being when two or more people seek to coordinate their behavior towards particular productive or economic ends. The basic units in this form of association are human action of two sorts: particular productive tasks, such as operating a drill press or processing insurance claims at a video display termi-

nal, and the actions that direct, coordinate, and motivate individuals to perform such tasks. If productive tasks are the bricks, and are performed by employees, the coordinating actions constitute the mortar of a business enterprise, and are performed by management. (The distinction is relative in that most individuals in corporations are both employees and part of management, depending on whether they look up or down the corporate hierarchy.)

In explaining how large organizations function, most organization theorists have been preoccupied with the mortar. They have asked, how does the needed coordination of human action come about? What orients and integrates human action around particular purposes? What motivates employees to perform work designed by managements? And how do employees affect managerial expectations about the content of work and other terms of the relationship? Organization theorists realized early that if the coordination and performance of productive tasks required no more than strictly mechanical behavior, corporations would need to be held together by no stronger glue than contracts. Contracting partners take the character of each other as given and seek only particular performances from each other, as Joseph Allen has noted. But the organization theorists have been no more satisfied than theological ethicists with the conventional idea that contracts suffice to explain human action in corporations. For reasons spelled out in the next section, neither managements nor employees can define themselves to explicitly defined contractual relations. They seek to shape the manner in which they are valued by each other in order to further their respective chosen ends. In so doing, they engage in forming and even transforming each other — and themselves.

B. The Influence Strategies Used in Corporate Settings

A brief catalogue will serve to illustrate the dense interweaving of influence strategies in organizational settings. A series of psychologists (beginning in the 1920s), social psychologists (1930s), sociologists (1940s), political scientists (1950s and 1960s), and economists (1970s) have brought the tools of their disciplines to bear upon organizations. They have discovered at least eight of these strategies. The concept of an influence strategy has not yet emerged as comprehensive organizing principle in the fields of organization theory or organization behavior, but it does appear to be a useful rubric for sorting through the profuse accumulation of concepts and theories in these fields. While the first two (exchange and bureaucracy) reflect a contractual understanding of the relationship, the remaining six (leadership, therapy, delegation, socialization, bargaining, and resistance) cannot be shoehorned into exacting stipulation-centered thinking.

The first influence strategy identified by theorists is that of "exchange," through which managements seek to shape employee thinking about the value of their labor. As early as 1903, Frederick Taylor, an engineer, was arguing that sufficient pay would render employees willing to accept a second form of influence: "bureaucracy." Here, "bureaucracy" refers to the procedures, rules, and commands through which managements seek to

channel the actions of employees. These first two strategies lend themselves to contractual specification and provide the basic cement, as well as the basic explanatory paradigm, of corporations. But they provided only the point of departure for those early theorists who began to appreciate that contractual descriptions hardly sufficed to explain how large organizations survived and flourished.

The early theorists aimed to improve organizational practice rather than provide value-neutral descriptions. They recommended, rather than simply reported, the use of influence strategies. Executives such as Henri Fayol, James Mooney, and Chester I. Barnard urged managers to exercise bold and visionary "leadership" in order to unite the energies of employees in pursuit of a coherent vision of organizational purpose. In a different vein, social scientists began half a century ago to prescribe a "therapeutic" strategy, in two versions. Social psychologists identified with Harvard University during the 1930s and 1940s suggested that managements could render workers more productive by making them happy — by immersing them in small workgroups which would serve to dispel the neuroses of isolated individualism. During the 1950s and 1960s, humanistic psychologists counseled managers to assist employees to "realize" their innate potentials in order to liberate their energies in the direction of achieving managerial goals. Somewhat similarly, business consultants such as Peter Drucker began to urge managements to "delegate" managerial work to employees as a means of fostering managerial work to employees as a means of fostering managerial commitment and drive in them. . . .

During the 1950s, theorists, beginning with Herbert A. Simon at Carnegie Mellon University, drew upon cognitive psychology to suggest that managements "inculcate" employees by establishing an environment of perception and purpose which shapes their thinking and acting. More recently, organization theorists influenced by cultural anthropology have observed a more comprehensive "socialization" strategy, where managements integrate employees into cohesive "corporate cultures." But in organization theory, perhaps the most prominent model of strategic influence today is "bargaining." This strategy emerged first in the 1960s, when theorists realized that influence does not work simply from top down, but in both directions. These theorists turned to interest-group theory to argue that managements and employees cultivate discrete bases of power and attempt to shape each other's expectations in order to secure their own interests.

. . . Radical organization theorists, always suspicious of managerial strategies, have contributed an eighth strategy: "resistance," or the multitude of ways in which employees strive to reduce managerial control and change managerial thinking. Resistance strategies range from mild measures to safeguard employee autonomy, such as stockpiling parts on an assembly line; through use of work-rules, planned absenteeism, and covert slowdowns to frustrate management control; to more extreme measures such as heedless waste or sabotage.

This catalogue of influence strategies suggests that descriptions of how corporations function are impoverished to the extent that they are reductively contractual. Contrary to the principal assumption of the contractual paradigm, contracts are not likely to induce either managements or employees to abandon their attempts to control or influence each other. The contractual paradigm ignores the question of what extra-contractual influence strategies managements and employees use to secure what each wants from the other, and even whether or not exchange and bureaucracy strategies are used coercively in a manner to which contract law is blind. If academic and other observers are to be believed, the coercive impact of these strategies can be powerful. Some strategies — particularly bureaucracy and socialization — have been pilloried precisely for their capacity to oppress or warp the moral character of managements and employees.

Of course, it would be foolish to assume that managements and employees are always fiendishly clever and successful in cultivating and eliciting particular tendencies for thinking and acting. But neither should the intended outcomes of willed strategies be the only focus of concern. An important sub-theme in the organizational literature is that influence strategies shape those who apply them as much as those who are targeted. Robert Merton in his classic 1940 essay explained how individuals imprint themselves with a "bureaucratic personality" by exercising bureaucratic influence. William H. Whyte, Jr., outlined how a typical 1950s manager became an "organization man" by participating in, rather than resisting

or exploiting, the human-relations conformity pressed upon him. More recently, Michael Maccoby has explained how managers enact four types of personality they bring to corporate settings. Recent best-selling success manuals advise ambitious individuals to shape their own characters in the direction of becoming expert bargainers.

It is this connection between corporate setting and character that makes "covenant" a viable term for explaining and appraising the quality of relationship between managements and employees. The signal difference between contract and covenant as associational terms is that contracts aim no higher than to secure stipulated behaviors from each contracting party, while covenanting partners seek to form, even transform, each other in the direction of a more adequate relationship. The two terms are not entirely disjunctive. Like a contract, a covenant has a prehistory of negotiation, where one or both parties seek to institute the relationship in formal terms. But this dynamic quality is reduced or eliminated in a contractual relationship once the terms of performance have been spelled out. A covenant, in contrast, remains a dynamic, interactive relationship. The consent of both parties simply formalizes and ratifies the continuing history of the efforts by both parties to render each other more adequate covenant partners. The relationship between managements and employees trespasses from contractual onto covenantal terrain when neither party is satisfied with hands-off contractual relations, and therefore seeks to shape the manner in which each values the other. In so doing, they engage in forming and even transforming the characters of themselves and each other.

I. Divine Covenant-Building from an Organizational Perspective

So far I have used "covenant" as a descriptive, operational, and not necessarily theological term. Once provided with this term for describing how character is shaped in corporate settings, covenantal theorists can proceed to ask when such influences work in the direction of fostering a theologically genuine Covenantal relationship ("Covenant") between managements and employees. To render the divine Covenant a compelling prescription, some strong correlation must be found between the logic behind the intentional strategies of influence that managements and employees apply to each other and the process by which God and God's people influence each other in the direction of Covenantal mutuality.

Theologians have proposed a variety of ways to conceptualize, in terms analogous to human intentionality, how God seeks to shape the character of God's covenant partners. Augustine and Aquinas outline a persuasion aimed at reason and beyond reason; Luther envisions a dialectic of love and wrath; Calvin, a tutelage in unchanging divine precepts; Barth, a divine command which paradoxically functions also as permission. No doubt a theologically informed Covenant between managements and employees might be conceptualized on the basis of any of these divine influence strategies, as when the National Conference of Catholic Bishops applied the Thomistic model of persuasion to unite managements and employees around the values of human dignity, justice, and the common good.

Here I will review the influence strategies God applies to God's people in the biblical narrative accounts of divine Covenant-building. But in order to draw the correlation between the biblical material and management-employee relations most closely, I will redescribe the Covenantal history through what might be termed an organizational perspective. . . .

It is risky if not foolhardy to abstract comprehensive themes from the whole biblical canon, particularly from the millennium-long series of texts which narrate the history of God's people. An organizational perspective elicits one generalization that appears defensible, however. The "historical" texts which narrate the history of Israel and of the church assume that the relationship between God and God's people evolves amid conditions of vulnerability and contingency on both sides.

The people are subject to a host of vicissitudes, collective and personal. In rough order of appearance, these include slavery, hunger and thirst, tribal warfare, economic exploitation, personal enmities, invasions, deportations, diseases, and "evil spirits." Since God, in God's sovereign freedom, intervenes at particular times and in particular ways to rescue the people from their vulnerability, God presents the people with a contingency that exceeds their control. At the same time, God is vulnerable because the people present God with contingency. They are promiscuous in their search for powerful divine aid to cope with their vulnerabilities. Their memories are short, their fears great, and their hearts often rebellious. Their pride and weaknesses lead them into harming themselves and others, sometimes in the same unspeakably cruel ways by which their enemies harm them. At the same time, the people are resilient and capable of change, even fundamental change. Sometimes they thirst for God, and their hearts can be converted to Covenantal trust and loyalty. From within their midst God lifts up heroes of exemplary righteousness. . . .

God copes with the contingent behavior of the people by applying strategies intended to elicit their faith as trust and loyalty. More than one strategy is needed because the changing situations of their lives preclude the evolution of one universal mode of influence.

1. From the time of the Patriarchs through the Exodus and Wandering, God applies a dialectic of "promising" and "testing." Abraham, Moses, and the people respond in kind by questioning, bargaining with, and testing God to determine the degree of God's commitment and power.

2. Between the Conquest and the end of the Monarchy, God seeks to "deter" abuses of kingly and priestly power through indictments announced by the Prophets, and threats of future punishment.

3. The Exile costs the people not only their political sovereignty, but more important, their confidence that God would never abandon the Covenant. God responds with various strategies of affirmation or terms of intimate sympathy to comfort the people in their extreme vulnerability.

4. During the Roman Occupation, God in Jesus assumes a readiness of the disciples to renew the Covenant. He applies "teaching" to elevate and refine their understanding of Covenantal law (Matthew) and God's partiality to the vulnerable (Luke). And he uses "recruitment" to transform the disciples into willing instruments of the Kingdom, preparing them for the "delegation" needed to sustain the fellowship (John) or carry God's Covenant-building mission to the ends of the world (Luke-Acts). . . .

Overall these strategies reflect the commitment of God to accept, rather than suppress, the contingency posed by wayward and unreliable Covenant partners.

The logic of Covenanting generates a profound irony. Covenant, as the very instrument God employs to render the people trustworthy, renders God vulnerable to their oft-repeated failure to be trustworthy Covenant partners. The long canonical history of broken Covenants and revised influence strategies suggests that nothing short of the unreserved vulnerability of God to human contingency will serve to elicit the fundamental trust and loyalty appropriate to Covenant partners. Hence, the incarnation, and of course, the cross. Of course, this logic of vulnerability and contingency in Covenanting is not universal in the canonical text; it is more evident in the Prophets than the Wisdom literature, more evident in Hosea than Amos, more evident in the Synoptic Gospels than in John. Moreover, a supercessionist argument is not being made here. From Abraham to the Resurrection there is no essential change in God's strategy to create Covenant partners from the widening circle of God's people. The vulnerability of God to the Covenantal infidelities of God's people is evident from Sinai on. There is no essential difference between the refusal of God to abandon or destroy God's unworthy people in the Pentateuch and the unqualified vulnerability of Jesus Christ in the New Testament. The long historical arc is relevant principally because it is the lengthening continuity of such vulnerability that establishes Covenantal fidelity.

II. Normative Guidelines

The major aim of a Covenant-building ethic within a corporation will be to foster the growth of a genuine, inclusive mutuality and trust between employees and managements in a manner consistent with loyalty to God's Covenant. The heuristic value of such an ethic will reside in its capacity to make two kinds of discriminations. The first is the relatively obvious distinction between Covenantal and overtly anti-Covenantal relations, as when managements openly exploit employees or employees categorically refuse to extend any trust toward well-meaning and honorable managements. The second is the less obvious distinction between inauthentic and authentic Covenantal relations, as when some participants

in a corporation bind themselves in a mutuality that excludes or devalues other parties inside or outside the corporation.

Constructing such an ethic involves more than articulating norms, which are static. In keeping with its focus upon interactive behaviors, it needs to be asked: when do the influence strategies managements and employees apply to each other serve to generate an authentic Covenantal quality of trust and trustworthiness? In formal outline, the answer appears simple: when the influence strategies they use reflect the influence strategies God applies. The biblical model suggests that such an ethic will need to make reference to both deterrent and affirmative strategies, as situationally appropriate. On the one hand, anti-Covenantal or inauthentic Covenantal relations often call for the deterrent strategies of prophetic indictment and threat. These strategies, which clearly are part of the Covenant-building process, long have been used by critics of business. . . .

C. Mutual Vulnerability

On the other hand, the sincere covenant-building efforts of managements and employees call for affirmative strategies as well. . . . First, the most genuine Covenants are built as the influence strategies managements and employees apply to each other acknowledge and reflect mutual vulnerability as well as power. . . . The fascinating, and for a Covenantal ethic encouraging, feature of business corporations is that all sides usually are vulnerable in some degree to the contingencies posed by the other. While employees are vulnerable to management for wages, safe working conditions, and some degree of meaning in their work, managements are vulnerable to employees for some degree of efficiency, honesty, and reliability. The mutuality of these vulnerabilities provides the occasion for authentic Covenantal trust-building measures. . . .

The route to Covenanting lies through the realization that neither management nor employees can fully control the other, even if the power to ruin the other's projects or interests always remains available. The parties then may find themselves in a position where they must entrust themselves to each other in some degree, and a new history of trust-building gestures may begin. . . .

D. Generous Use of Influence Strategies

A second, much different recommendation is suggested by the biblical logic of Covenant-building. Corporations will be more Covenantal to the extent that managements and employees are generous and comprehensive in their application of influence strategies to each other. This generosity and comprehensiveness is mandated by the plenitude of God, who applies a full range of influence strategies, as situationally appropriate, to shape the people of God. . . .

The eight strategies described earlier have evolved specifically in organizational contexts. Each is an appropriate vehicle of influence because each pertains to a particular slice of human motivation elicited by participation in organizations. Exchange appeals to material desires and wants; bureaucracy to a penchant for obedience; leadership to expansive vision; delegation to the drive for mastery; therapy to the urge for psychological security and self-realization; inculcation to habitualness; socialization to the desire for moral order and meaning; bargaining to the desire for autonomy; and resistance to an egalitarian impulse.

Nevertheless, any one of these strategies applied in abstraction from consideration of the others implies a devaluation of its target. For example, the fault with bureaucratic management is less the apparatus of rules and procedures itself than with the arrogant managerial assumption that rules and procedures constitute the only appropriate means of shaping the behavior of employees. . . .

One illustration will have to suffice. On the surface, bureaucracy appears a strategy which is exceedingly resistant to Covenantal use. This powerful anti-Covenantal potential cannot be extirpated from bureaucratic influence strategies, for it is rooted in impersonality, distance, and segmentation, to which bureaucracy subjects human agents. Nevertheless, participation in bureaucracy also can inculcate universalistic, fair-minded habits of normative thinking. Objective structures of rules and policies can serve as tools and resources of individuals to demonstrate their trustworthiness by protecting others from arbitrary treatment. For example, sociologist Vicki Smith recently described how branch managers used the bureaucratic apparatus of a large California bank, at some risk to themselves, to protect employees from attempts by senior management to engage in wholesale, unwarranted layoffs. These branch managers co-opted the device of training seminars to build solidarity among themselves, made constructive use of the difficult objectives imposed by senior management to organize and motivate employees for greater achievement, and in general used what margin of discretion the bureaucratic apparatus permitted in order to deflect the harsh policies of senior management.

III. Applications to Business Ethics and Beyond

The relevance of the idea of Covenant to business ethics derives from a correlation between the logic of contingency, vulnerability, and influence strategies evident in the Biblical history of Covenant-building and a similar logic in management-employee relationships. In effect, covenants of one sort or another are being made and broken daily in corporations, as managements and employees seek to shape each other's actions and expectations. Like God and God's people, managements and employees are vulnerable to the contingencies they pose to each other. This vulnerability encourages them to influence, if not seek to control, the thinking and the acting of each other. They are strongly tempted not to let their relationship be confined to the strict *quid pro quo* of contracts. . . .

This paper generates no new knowledge regarding the specific content of Covenantal norms. But it outlines a means of "operationalizing" the idea of Covenant so that managements and employees might have some idea how Covenants actually are built — or vitiated — in corporate settings. In so doing, it suggests a new direction for approaching the question of character so central to discussions in Christian ethics today. Just as the characters of God and God's people emerge from a long history of efforts to shape each other, the characters of managements and employees emerge from the influence strategies they apply to each other. One task of ethics, then, is to borrow from the organization theory and other social-scientific sources descriptions of what influence strategies operate in different forms of human association. Such data will enable ethicists to construct compelling accounts of how relationships in a variety of social contexts might be become Covenantal.

Three Images of Corporate Leadership and Their Implications for Social Justice

Donald W. Shriver, Jr.

In a speech before a luncheon club in Raleigh, North Carolina, in the nineteen-sixties, the local traffic court judge remarked: "People are always telling me what is 'just' and 'unjust.' Their certainty about justice really perplexes me. For me, justice is the search for justice."

One can detect in the remark a lawyer's focus on procedure and a judge's daily experience of clashing cries for justice. "Search" for him, however, was apparently a more substantive professional-personal commitment that he could express in terms of procedural rules or particular principles of justice. Doubtless he entertains many such rules and principles; but he wraps them about, so to speak, in a metaphor which seems to function as a boundary and a symbol of his self-image as a professional.

The image of the business manager in American society of the past hundred years embodies a seldom acknowledged notion, explicit or implicit, of the manager's role in serving justice in the business enterprise and its host society. The compounds of these images stem from historical evidence of how managers have thought of their roles and how outsiders have thought of them. My hypothesis is that, especially in the past century, the men and (the few) women who have ascended to the upper ranks of office in corporations have been heirs and architects of changing paradigms of justice in relation to their work in the corporation.

A quiet companion hypothesis is that one vital role of Christian ethicists, in their role as commentators on these changes, is to call attention to them, to give them names which highlight their reality in preparation, perhaps, for the coming of new realities. If we could accurately describe ethics as now present in the world of work, we might go a long way towards building the bridge from descriptive to normative ethics and to overcoming the insulation of the one from the other. The recent rage for business ethics to the contrary, ethics have been a "real presence" in the world of economic relations for a long time, and economic realities have shaped ethical reflection on those realities. Facts and values intermingle in human life. It is high time that those who have specialized in putting the two asunder turn their attention to properly marrying them again.

I. Justice on a Pyramid: The Ironic Legacy of the Liberal Capitalist Entrepreneur

If the Apostle Paul little imagined that he was laying the foundations of a worldwide bureaucratic church, Adam Smith as little imagined that he was preparing the way for General Motors. Determined to distangle economic transactions from the mercantilist policies of the British crown, Smith called economics back to what he believed was its primitive origin: a seller and a buyer of some thing which each deemed of value. In that transaction, free of royal regulation, lay Smith's challenge to state bureaucracy and political manipulation. Let self-interested individuals make their contracts with each other; let them curb each other's propensity for getting the best of one another; and, in the free play of countless, competing small contracts, let there arise a system, the market, which will spell the death of monopolies of wealth and power. Thus economics would theoretically be based where an emerging democratic political order was beginning to be theoretically based: on individual interests and agreements between individuals concerning mutual interests.

This vision of economic society was profoundly

Donald W. Shriver, Jr., "Three Images of Corporate Leadership and Their Implications for Social Justice," paper presented at Union Theological Seminary, New York, New York, January 7, 1991.

antagonistic to the spirit of hierarchy; and Smith's preferred world of competing tradespeople was hardly an overture to the modern world of competing mega-corporations. Composers of those corporations turned lightly aside from such a vision. A hundred and twenty-five years after the publication of *The Wealth of Nations,* John D. Rockefeller reflected on the success of his industrial empire with the observation that free price competition leads to "idiotic senseless destruction" and sheer waste in the economy; and his views were echoed by the actions, if not by the rhetoric, of Andrew Carnegie, Cornelius Vanderbilt, and Theodore Roosevelt. Roosevelt was simply reflecting on the history of late-nineteenth century business corporation when, in blunt contradiction to the spirit of Adam Smith, he accepted his party's nomination for the presidency in 1912 with the words:

> "Unrestricted competition as an economic principle has become too destructive to be permitted to exist, and the small men must be allowed to cooperate under penalty of succumbing before their big competitors."

Bigness begets bigness; "combination" and "cooperation" father inefficiency; and the large corporation is the mother of prosperity. These become the watchwords of the new capitalism. "The day of combination is here to stay. Individualism has gone never to return." Rockefeller himself said it; and even if Andrew Carnegie did continue to preach the virtues of individualism, the corporation he had created was on its way to becoming the largest industrial organization in the world, United States Steel.

Discrepancies between what they did and what they said were nothing new among American economic and political leaders. We know that the glories of rugged individualism persisted in their speeches right through the 1980's. But Rockefeller and Roosevelt were being candid about the business practices of their own era when they openly contradicted Adam Smith's vision of those who produced wealth for nations. The production of petroleum, electricity, railroads, and forty-story buildings required large organization, often generously subsidized by governments. The major actors in the world economy of the future would be such organizations, not some infinite number of little companies of tradespeople in all the little places of earth.

And what was the shape of these organizations? They were pyramids, controlled paternalistically by their founders, as hierarchical as any mercantilist government. Legitimated by the success of their individual initiative and by their legal ownership of corporate assets, these nineteenth century entrepreneurs used the freedoms of market and polity to move bottom-up into wealth and power; and the result of their efforts was a new form of economic organization, initially free of government regulation, in which they were the unchallengeable, top-down authorities, strictly analogous to military officers. As Robert E. Wood, then president of Sears, Roebuck candidly put it: "We stress the advantages of the free enterprise system, we complain about the totalitarian state, but in our individual organizations we have created more or less a totalitarian system in industry, particularly in large industry."

Such candor constitutes one of the great ironies of a century of American acclaim for the economic liberalism of Adam Smith.

As the discussion below about a second reigning image of corporate management will suggest, the history of the business corporation over the past hundred years can be read as the history of challenge to his ironic outcome of the previous century. It can also be read as the continued, vestigial survival of the corporate pyramid. Many outside observers of both types of organizations continue to believe that the pyramid of authority has been steeper in corporate and military structures than in any democratic government or any church. Henry Clay Frick's resistance to labor unions in the 1892 Homestead Strike and Henry Ford's resistance to them in the 1920's were of a piece with the philosophy; "To the founder goes the control." The judge of justice in this system was the founder. Like other architects of industrial paternalism, of course, Mr. Ford's provision for the highest average industrial wage of the time gave him understandable human reason to expect his workers to be grateful, just as the Swiss managers of Nestle, S. A., had reason, fifty years later, to expect famished mothers in poor countries to appreciate the real benefits of infant breast milk substitutes.

Whether in rhetoric or reality, by the nineteen-fifties a sea-change had overcome this style of corporate management, such that few mid-twentieth century CEOs would agree to tag these nineteenth-century business attitudes as "managerial." By 1950, from many directions the corporate pyramid was being challenged, in part by the results of its initial successes. Auto workers, once grateful for a wage of $5 a day, develop a sense that a super-profitable company owes them more than $5 a day. Unwilling to believe that "combination" is only for corporate mergers, they combine in unions. Auto engineers, educated to new technologies, discover that the boss is not always right in his technical judgments. Shop foremen, who have never met "the boss," know that he is not always right on how to manage a production line. And outside observers in the community, especially if they happen to be under the influence of a young pastor named Reinhold Niebuhr, suspect that success in selling Model-T automobiles to middle America is no guarantee of moral authority, inside or outside the Ford Motor Company. In 1927, Niebuhr had become one of Henry Ford's most vocal public critics. From the viewpoint of his twelve years as a working pastor in Detroit, for example, he commented on the cost of a recent shutdown of the Ford plants for retooling:

"I have been doing a little arithmetic and have come to the conclusion that the [new] car cost Ford workers at least fifty million in lost wages during the past year . . . Mr. Ford . . . has a way of impressing the public even with his mistakes . . . Naive gentlemen with a genius for mechanics suddenly become the arbiters over the lives of hundreds of thousands. Their moral pretensions have been credulously accepted at full value. No one bothers to ask whether an industry which can maintain a cash reserve of a quarter of a billion ought not make some provision for its unemployed. It is enough that the new car is a good one."

In an irony that Niebuhr himself would have been the first to appreciate before he questioned the analogy, the pyramid of the nineteenth century corporation had a parallel (and a rival) in the pyramid which he modeled for Christian social ethics. The model had its debts to his experience in Detroit. Whatever wisdom comes with business success, Niebuhr observed, moral obtuseness comes too. And part of the obtuseness, he discerned, consists of a failure to see that human society is an unruly combination of aims, interests, and other "organic facts of existence" which only a dictator considers utterly controllable and only an idealist considers subject to exact calculations of justice. If there is an exact calculation of justice, it exists in the mind of the Great Judge who is God; and, Christians believe, even in God perfect justice takes the form of a perfect love, which eludes even the most devout of individual Christians, not so speak of any secular social structure. Citizens of the latter are left with yearnings after a justice which even the most honest revolution realizes imperfectly. They are left empirically with a fractured, battered, often tragic upward surge of cooperation among humans for the cause of justice, which falls back perpetually into new conflicts between vital interests. "Those of us who make adjustments between the absolute ideal of our devotion and the necessities of the immediate situation lack peace, because we can never be sure that we have our adjustment at the right place." My Raleigh traffic court judge would have liked that.

In his appreciation of the fractious, untamable, many-leveled conflicts of interests in a society, Niebuhr shared some kinship with Adam Smith. His theory of justice in society was profoundly indebted to liberalism. In his sense that organizations are based on some agreements about a justice that link and transcend vital interests, he identified the ethical usefulness of various hierarchies of control; and from this pragmatic level of the Niebuhrian pyramid Henry Ford might have derived some rationale for his paternalism. But Niebuhr saw all paternalisms as both undermined from human vitality below and overruled by divine justice from above. His appreciation of the morality of industrial leaders was reserved for those who managed to infuse their use of power with a sense of limit and repentance.

Whether or not in the moral sense, a new generation of industrial leaders was about to change its mind about the shape of management required for a complex, large, world-competitive, profitable corporation. Except in a few pockets of industrial America, old-style paternalism was to give way to at least the masks of a "managerial revolution." Its leaders would prefer to see themselves, not atop a pyramid, but surrounded by a circle of influences needing to be composed by managers into policy.

II. Justice in a Circle: The Birth of Management as a Profession

Looking back on the era, one can readily conclude that the years 1940-1970 saw the climax of the nineteenth century American business corporation. Having contributed mightily to Allied victory in World War II, many of these "industrial giants" developed yet more gigantically — in number of employees, fixed assets, stock investments, access to war-devastated world markets, new technologies, science-based production techniques, organizational proliferation to national and global scales, vertical and horizontal integration, various forms of government subsidy, stock appreciation, rising wages, and contribution to Gross National Product. This staggering era of growth of the "Galbraithian" corporation will probably go down as unique in American history.

In this time of unparalleled growth and prosperity, formal leadership of many of the corporations founded in the nineteenth century passed, sometimes to third and fourth generation family members, but most often to able people recruited by them or Boards to manage companies of a size, complexity, and power which would have outrun the capacities of even the geniuses of the first generation.

James Kuhn summarizes the characteristics of the post-war corporations as: (1) the pursuit of economic growth, with stability; (2) an embracing sense of social responsibility; (3) a bureaucratic, hierarchical organizational structure; and (4) an authoritarian relationship with employees. The comparison with their nineteenth century predecessors is striking in only one respect here: an "embracing" sense of social responsibility. How did that sense get expressed, and what did it have to do with the ethics of justice in the role-definition which many corporate leaders came to adopt for themselves?

The new name of these leaders was "manager," and the name carried associations of many of the changes just catalogued. "Professional management" was a role unknown to Adam Smith (who supposed that an economy chiefly needed people who make and people who sell things) and a role lowly esteemed by the tycoons of the nineteenth century (who wanted superintendents under their own personal control). Unburdened by majority ownership of stock by the founder or his children, the twentieth century mega-corporation grew under the protection of law that made stockholders — thousands of them — the formal owners of the firm and made a Board of Directors their representatives. The latter came to see their chief power as the election of executive officers, who were expected to run the company. As an active substitute for the old personal owner-founder, neither the mass of stockholders nor the Board fell heir to the old power. The new, key actors in the new corporation was the Chief Executive Officer and the "management team" directly responsible to the CEO. Irving Olds, chairman of U.S. Steel in the "good old days" from 1940 to 1952, once remarked: "Directors are merely the parsley on the fish."

The situation of their work as corporate leaders was different enough now to spawn some new definitions of their roles as "organizational men." Reflecting a thirty-year development, one such definition came to expression in 1981 from the elite Business Roundtable:

> "Balancing the shareholder's expectations of maximum return against other priorities is one of the fundamental problems confronting corporate management. The shareholder must receive a good return but the legitimate concerns of other constituencies also must have the appropriate attention."

A business corporation, according to this new view, with its skeptical turn towards the stockholders, is a social entity with great power for good or ill in the lives of thousands of human beings. Stockholders are only one group of these constituencies, and they are not always the one whose interests should be uppermost in the minds of managers. As Andrew C. Sigler, chairman of Champion International and president of the Roundtable put it in the midst of the great debates of the nineteen-eighties about the ethics of corporate takeovers, "What right does someone who owns the stock for an hour to decide a company's fate? That's the law, and it's wrong." "Wrong" here had to mean "unjust." Sigler was implying that no single group of constituents of the corporation stood automatically at the top of the hierarchy of interests and control. Managers have an obligation to protect one constituency against the overriding power of another.

But the most elaborate, specific version of the "embracing" social responsibility charter for the work of the corporate manager was written out in 1971 by the Committee for Economic Development. No business manager, taking this job-description seriously, would be likely to think of him or herself as merely perched on the pinnacle of a pyramid; instead, the business manager sits in the center of an embracing circle of interests, pressures, needs and values:

"The modern professional manager also regards himself, not as an owner disposing of personal property as he sees fit, but as a *trustee balancing the interests of many diverse participants and constituents in the enterprise,* whose interests sometimes conflict with those of others. The chief executive of a large corporation has the problem of reconciling the demands of employees for more wages and improved benefits plans, customers for lower prices and greater values, vendors for higher prices, government for more taxes, stockholders for higher dividends and great capital appreciation — all within a framework that will be constructive and acceptable to society. This interest-balancing involves much the same kind of political skill as is required in top government posts. The chief executive of a major corporation must exercise statesmanship in developing with the rest of the management group the objectives, strategies, and policies of the corporate enterprise. In implementing these, he must also obtain the 'consent of the governed' or at least enough cooperation to make the policies work. And in the long run the principal constituencies will pass judgment on the quality of leadership he is providing to the corporate enterprise."

This statement is remarkable on many counts, some of them ethical. On the face of it, social-corporate responsibility means seeing oneself, as manager, surrounded by constituent groups to each of whom some justice is due. Management is at the center of a multi-radii circle, charged with policymaking responsibility that joins interest to interest, establishes priorities among them, and effects economic policy with potentially benign ripple effects for the entire society. Especially remarkable here is the apparently modest attention accorded to market signals and to government regulation as prime constraints on the work of corporate managers. Government and markets in 1971 were already imposing more restraints on corporate policy than might be suspected from this rhetoric. On occasion, presumably, the competent manager must judge between this whole body of pressures and take action accordingly, and this may mean defying one or another of the pressures, including markets, law, and regulatory commissions.

Two other things are missing from this array of stated pressures: (1) a posited *standard of judgment* which a manager might be obligated to invoke for the making of the complex decisions here alleged as normal, and (2) the *identification of accountability* to any one or several of the constituencies, *especially in the actual formulation of decisions.* The former standard would have inherent ethical content, for it would be a measure for distinguishing more and less important ethical claims of interest groups. The latter would admit others besides management as agents into the decision-making process.

If this statement of responsibility were not so all-embracing, one might excuse the C.E.D. for not suggesting principles for managerial preference-assignments among various constituencies. Had they included such principles, however, they might have found it difficult to maintain the circle-of-constituencies image of themselves. Robert Nozick's liberal theory, for example, suggests to managers that they are primarily fulfillers of contracts. John Rawls' Difference Principle would call them to pay heed to policies that will lessen the unequal distribution of society's resources. And, of course, classic capitalist profit-maximizing ethics simply calls them to do the efficient, profitable thing, leaving to other social agents the enactment of various alleged ethical responsibilities to society. This latter has been Milton Friedman's criticism of "the social responsibility of business" for several decades. Managers as described by the Business Roundtable and the C.E.D., in fact, fitted the image which Friedman criticized in 1962: they arrogate a public function to themselves and, therefore, "sooner or later, [they will be] chosen by public techniques of election and appointment," bringing on a society that incorporates them into a democratic or not-so-democratic socialism.

But it was Peter Drucker, and it would have been Reinhold Niebuhr, who attacked this ambitious notion of managerial responsibility as its greatest point of weakness: Its arrogation of power. Drucker compared this image of the manager to that of the enlightened despots of eighteenth century Europe: able people, armed with benevolent intentions and total authority. Neither the board of directors nor the consumer has any rightful authority to tell business managers what to do in this scheme, not to mention labor unions. Though eventually all the constituencies will indeed "pass judgment on the quality of leadership" a manager is providing — who can stop them from doing so anyway? — they have no principled and structured place in the decision-making itself.

Corporate social responsibility in this metaphor, embodied in the business manager, takes the form of a circle whose many voices should be taken into account; but nobody is there *with* management in the account-taking. There is little celebration here of that reality of American society wherein law and public interest groups are free to call business to account for certain infringements on law and interest. In this sense, the circular image of management does not take sufficient account of already-developed power-relations in the economy and the polity. Instead, what this images *does* unwittingly suggest — a vestige in spite of appearances — is the old nineteenth century hierarchical pyramid; for, sitting at the center of the managerial circle, a C.E.O. is sitting atop a round tower, so to speak, not on a flat surface. The constituents are petitioners who put in their pleas from the lower level. Nobody out there is legitimately the challenger of business policy. Business managers are hired because, given opportunity and resources, they will make good decisions. Why worry about "paternalism" if the decisions are really good?

Earlier in this century, business leaders entertained briefly Frederick W. Taylor's theory of "Scientific Management," which sought to identify objectively "the one best way" to perform a manufacturing operation. The popularity of the theory faded, not only because workers objected to it, but because it posed a threat to management's responsibility for judging the one best way. In mid-century, Elton Mayo's "Human Relations" approach to industrial peace and efficiency gained prominence, promising, with the tools of psychology and sociology, to take account of the full scope of worker's human needs. But managers themselves were in control of the accounting here, too.

"Mayo's contribution to managerial ideology lay in his emphasis upon managers as an elite — trained, rational, and possessed of a kind of industrial noblesse oblige. He saw no need for unions, government regulations, or outside pressures to guide managers in the fulfillment of their social responsibilities. . . . Cooperation [in this ideology] has almost always been defined as employees joining managers in pursuit of managerial goals. By definition managers are the source of ideas, suggestions, or production know-how."

By this definition, management is an autocratic occupation, an allegation which socialist critics of advanced capitalism have long made loudly and clearly. The justice of the allegation is suspect, in many parts of the world in the nineteen-nineties, in view of the propensity of many recent socialist systems for tolerating bureaucratic political autocracy in a society-wide framework that is more hierarchical by far than the framework in which western corporations have developed. The right to be *the* person or the elite that defines justice in any society is the right at issue here; and the issue crosscuts most of the debates between democratic capitalists and democratic socialists in this century. The economic and political organizations produced by advocates of both ideologies have shown tragic tendencies towards elitist autocracy. The one advantage of recent democratic orders has been in the fact that one autocratic elite can sometimes challenge another, a form of liberalism which has its own integrity as well as irony.

Parenthetically and with like irony, business has an economic interest in productivity which has belatedly been shown to be ill-served by autocratic modes of industrial management. The case can be made that American industrial leaders suffered the declines of the 'seventies and 'eighties because they learned too slowly the advantages of democratic mutuality for the efficiency of the productive process. Newer democracies like Japan and Germany made that discovery first, as they cut down on American-style levels of managerial hierarchy, developed close factory-floor partnerships between managers and (other!) workers, and offered their worldwide customers products whose performance exceeded those of their American competitors.

One can sharpen the irony, indeed the mystery, here by asking the questions: At a time when paternalism was on the decline in family relations, educational relations, and political relations in the culture of the United States, why has the world of American business been so slow to root out paternalism and to substitute for it a search for forms of corporate human relations distinctly compatible with a democratic ethos? What structural changes in the responsibilities of management would have to be made for democracy to become a functioning way of work inside the business corporation?

There are many answers being proposed to the latter question these days among the friends and enemies of capitalism. Some of them involve great changes in patterns of ownership, marketing, government-corporate cooperation, profit-sharing, power-sharing, and other mandated consultation between corporate leaders and their constituencies. The advocates of such structural changes, I believe, are calling for a change of the business manager's self-image more profound than the change that occurred superficially in the transition from the nineteenth century capitalist-owner to the twentieth century business executive. And, in their lack of agreement on any one set of structural changes, these critics seem to be calling for business leaders who lead as *learners*.

III. Justice on a Journey: The Business Leader as Partner in Learning

Journeys are best described in stories. This third image of corporate leadership, still taking shape in contemporary history, can best be expressed in certain stories of leaders who broke decisively in their behavior with both the pyramid and the circle-precedents of their predecessors.

The first is Louis B. Lundborg, who in 1970 was CEO of the Bank of America. In the late spring of that year, Vietnam-War-enraged demonstrators burned down the office of that bank in Isla Vista, California. A few weeks later Lundborg delivered a speech to the Rotary Club of Seattle under the title, "The Lessons of Isla Vista." The lesson to business leaders, he said, was this:

"I would suggest . . . that each of us find a college-age youth — student or not — and spend some time with him, to find out what's going on in that world that is crowding in on our heels. And if you do — remember that God gave you two ears and only one tongue — use them in that proportion."

Not many professional educators on American campuses in this period were more "responsive" to youthful collective anger than was this business executive.

Two other, more recent cases illustrate corporate relationships with constituencies hard to identify specifically. One such constituency was a majority of people in the Republic of South Africa. The other was a mass of unknowable, potential customers of a potentially dangerous drug product. In each case, corporate leaders took a step from mere listening to the voices of a diverse constituency to making *partnerships* with that constituency. In turn some doors opened on the possibility that both sides will be learning from each other in the future. Justice for them becomes a search, and the search is promising, not only for the initial partners but for others who may be added to their ranks from yet-unknown quarters.

The first corporation is the United States' largest producer of diesel engines, which until the early nineteen-eighties had done extensive business in South Africa. The respect it enjoyed from government officials there was such that they offered the company a contract, worth business of some $50 million a year, to build a plant for producing diesel engines for use in the military as well as the government-owned transportation systems of the country. Should the company accept this contract? That anyone at headquarters should even raise this question was a mark of a managerial ethos conditioned by factors new to the business world of the 'eighties. *Apartheid* was beginning to be under public attack in the world's newspapers, churches, labor unions, local governments, annual stockholder meetings, and national legislatures. Having done business in South Africa for thirty or more years, the American company's management, by questioning the proposed contract, was stepping into a new moment of its own history. And — as their decision turned out — that moment consisted in a company refusal of the contract.

Asked later why his fellow managers and he turned it down (especially in light of the subsequent fact that the contract soon went to a West German company), the C.E.O. of the American company said simply, "It would have been against the character of our company."

Companies do have "character," and standing alone the remark would be grist for those ethicists who believe that ethics is more about character than about principles, decisions, policies, and balances of power. Just as likely, however, the case and the remark should be grist for those who believe that the most powerful boundaries of ethics are historical, narrative, and dramatic in nature. Characters develop over time, and the development is likely to compose a story. In the 'seventies and 'eighties some American business leaders did a lot of listening to the enemies of *aparthied* inside and outside of South Africa — and found themselves listening more intently to the advocates of sanctions, for example, than to resisters of sanctions against that country. Similarly, leaders of the U.S. Congress in this period reported that popular American support of sanctions, rather than internal congressional concern, prompted them to pass the sanctions of 1986; and this political development illustrates how one group of people, responding to the "intrusion" of new voices, learn to direct policy into a direction it probably would not otherwise have taken. The democratic story is full of such chapters: its authors mean it to be open to just such intrusions.

Sure to go down in the history of business as a case of remarkable social responsibility on the part of a single high-placed executive, is the case of James Burke of Johnson and Johnson in the Tylenol scare of 1982. Six people in Chicago were dead of capsule-poisoning when Burke, after extensive consulting of his fellow managers, decided to remove almost $100 million of the product from shelves throughout the country. While the case illustrates extraordinary personal courage and conviction about the priority value of individual human lives, it also illustrated a style of decision-making rather unusual in the annals of American industry. Burke not only called in his management team for consultation but also opened the doors of his headquarters to news reporters, telling them all the information he had in hand and asking them for more information. As a result, Burke said later, "the company was getting some of its more accurate and up-to-date information about what was going on around the country from the reporters calling in for comment."

Burke got advice from the F.B.I., the Food and Drug Administration, and his own management associates. Virtually none of them recommended what he finally did: recall all the product. Here, surely, is an instance when the moral preferences of a C.E.O. won out over the apparent cautious prudence of associates, when the personal character of a leader was more decisive than the uncertain collective character of a large corporation, when old-style autocracy in management seemed to serve a great social good. Yet, even here, students of the narrative framework of ethics, as lived out in business history, have much data to ponder. The history of J & J had made possible certain ranges of justice which in another time and organization might have been ignored as economically unacceptable. Tylenol was manufactured by a subsidiary company wholly owned by J & J — McNeil Consumer Products. A loss of $100 million would have wiped out this subsidiary, had it been required to bear the burden for Burke's decision. Since J & J assumed the burden, Burke could later report, with some justice, "Often our society rails against bigness, but this has been an example of where size helps. If Tylenol had been a separate company, the decisions would have been much tougher. As it was, it was hard to convince the McNeil people that we didn't care what it cost to fix the problem."

But J & J did care for costs, and that was evident in its failure for three years to move out of all (tamper-vulnerable) capsule forms of its product line into (tamper-proof) caplet forms. In 1985 another death occurred from the ingestion of a capsule, and J & J moved finally to caplets. One might say that Burke and his company courageously crossed one frontier in 1982, but took three years to read the messages of old and new experience to prompt the crossing of another in 1985.

Doubtless the world's drug companies have a lot to learn in the 1990's about the good and the evil potentials of drug-marketing around the globe; and veterans of the corporate responsibility movement — one thinks of the Nestle boycott — have much reason to be on their lookout for such exploitations as the dumping of untested products in Third World countries. The general lesson in all of these developments, for corporations, their customers, and their critics, is that the world is on a journey into a future so filled with the new and the unpredictable that the people who are the least prepared for this future will be the ones who think that they are the best prepared. To put it more prosaically: the future belongs to the teachable.

In their book, *Board Games*, Fleischer, Hazard, and Klipper explore the unanticipated, unwelcome learning now occurring in the relationships of CEO's, their boards, and law courts in wake of the avalanche of takeovers in the 1980s. The impact of global competition and arbitrator manipulations has been profound on the shifts of authority upwards from managers to boards. Now language about multiple, circular responsibility is apt to apply to boards rather than managers. It is they who "have responsibilities that affect everyone's welfare. . . . Change in the economic environment . . . has expanded the nature of director responsibility." Furthermore, the majority of the directors of Fortune 500 corporations are now "outsiders," that it, persons not employed by the company, so that having "achieved supremacy in number . . . now they have achieved supremacy in power." But this language, which seems to betoken a mere shift upward from manager to board "supremacy," is misleading. The newly assertive actors in corporate policymaking include the courts who administer the corporation laws of the states. These laws are ancient in the republic, many of them made when Adam Smith's understanding of the rights of ownership held full sway, when notions of stock manipulations were little imagined,

and world corporate competition was little on the horizon.

Having newly discovered the intrusive power of old law and new court decisiveness, some boards are asserting their own version of a multiple-faceted image of their responsibilities by passing charter amendments expressly allowing "consideration of non-financial factors" in corporate policymaking. And new statutes in some states (e.g. Ohio and Pennsylvania) already legitimate such amendments. All of this impels the authors of *Board Games* to conclude their book with the ringing summary: "Above all [boards] are accountable to shareholders. It is expected. It is demanded by the free market. And it is the law." But the mood and direction of their previous account of these contemporary events in corporate affairs are not so neat and conventionally capitalistic. Stockholders are on the move, law is on the move, world markets are on the move, and boards have to be on the move, too — into perplexities and strategies they have never faced before. The most significant summation of *Board Games* comes four pages before the ringing conclusion quoted above: "Whatever the boardroom ethos may once have been it is now one of care, inquiry, and diligence." It is, in a word, an ethos for learners.

Such a claim sounds deceptively simple, for it is almost a cliche now to say that in a competitive, information-driven, global economy, those who know how to learn from new conditions will be in the best position to shape those conditions. As counsel for a shift in management style, the claim could be reduced to another form of the advice, "Pay attention to your markets." Insofar as discerning a future market is far more complex than reading a record of past sales, this is not trivial advice; for consumers of the future will be imitating those who founded the corporate responsibility movement of the 1970s: they will demand, and sometimes organize boycotts to effect their demand for, products that meet a variety of standards. Future sales of automobiles, refrigerators, and medicines worldwide will have increasingly to respond to knowledge and preferences in consumers related to ecology, health, and safety. Such demands, in the early nineteen-sixties before they learned to listen to Rachel Carson and Ralph Nader, manufacturers of these products blithely ignored. Consumers have learned a few things in the meantime, governments and organized volunteers have learned, and even the once-self-confident leaders of large bureaucracies like General Motors have learned, too. Insofar as they have learned well, they have learned the importance of *continuing* to learn and to open themselves to claims for justice from previously silent participants in the society. Among the silences that are being broken in contemporary human experience, for example, are those once ascribed to ecosystems, which once went as unheard as the cries of non-unionized coal miners.

The difference between the "all-embracing," circular responsibility of the CEO model and the new learning-model relates to structural and not merely ideological change. Structural facilitation of such learning is the economic frontier of American business organization in the nineties. How do we structure relations of production and distribution in ways that make it *difficult* for all parties affected by the transactions to *ignore* each other? Labor unions have long served this function in some corporations. Consumer or other "public" representations on corporate boards have been a step in the same direction. Various degrees of employee-ownership, mandated consumer input into product-design, and politically-enforced standards of community benefit to be considered when a company enters or leaves that community — all of these are important experiments in crossing the line from managerial autonomy (and its inclination to autocracy) to *interdependence* between the corporation and the lives of people whom it affects.

The most pervasive shift in all of these structural innovations is that from a closed, protective style of management to an openness to new partnerships across the spectrum of its internal and external human relations. H. Richard Niebuhr's paradigm of responsibility is the one best fits the requirements for a model of ethics here, along with Carol Gilligan's similar, less systematic paradigm. For both Niebuhr and Gilligan, our truly "original position" as humans is our rootedness in the particulars of some historic society. In the midst of these particulars, we are called to respond to somebody else's actions, trying as best we can to understand the meaning of those actions for us and them. Thus we are embarked on a process, a journey, in which there is much waiting, consul-

tation, argument, and changes of direction along the way. In that way we discover new things about the origins and meanings of the journey itself, only possible through a trusting, loyal solidarity with our partners. We are learning from them while they are learning from us. And there is no easy withdrawal from the learning process: complex power structures of law, government, voluntary associations, markets, employees, boards, and management itself see to that.

John Raines put the essence of this shift memorably in a recent article. His own inquiry into a "relational theory of justice" comports closely with my inquiry here. His words fit the world of business management as well as the other organization worlds in which all live:

"The process of becoming fully human is not simply that we must learn, but that we must always learn *more*, making the work more and more familiar and in so doing expanding the dimensions of our effective intentionality.

"This process is misinterpreted if viewed as expanding our power to dominate and to control. All intentionality remains co-intentionality, so that what we expand is our capacity to collaborate."

Do these signs of change in the internal and external expectations of leadership in the business corporation add up to portents of profound change in the course of business history? The future will tell us. Meantime, it is vital to add, for everyone interested in the shaping of that history through the formal education of future business managers, a note from the realm of that education. Speaking from her study of students now enrolled at the Harvard Business School, Professor Sharon Parks writes of seeing in many business school students "an elegant blend of quest and integrity." That blend is not far from the image of fidelity to partnerships of learning which I see as vital to the leadership which the next generation of Americans will need in their institutions generally. Parks describes the professional, ethical education that might help meet that need:

"It is not difficult to teach ethical systems to bright young adult minds. The difficult task is to teach moral courage . . . the capacity to act in new and life-bearing ways. This can be accomplished only as we allow the truth of interdependence to lead us into an ethic of connection. . . . When we see the *connections*, when we become connected to the truth that was 'other,' we undergo it, we suffer it, we experience compassion. . . . That passion may first take the form of rage and grief but can later give rise to energy, and to a hope grounded in a conviction of possibility . . .

"But to sustain [this] connection, conviction and courage, we need each other."

From the contractual world of Adam Smith to this world of selves in permanent, unavoidable partnership, is a long journey. One cannot read the history of American corporations without hoping that its leaders will see just this journey as the one mandated for the next chapter of business history.

Section 2: Structuring Organizations for Accountability

It is critical to call corporate structures to moral accountability. However, it is equally important to recognize the particular means by which moral accountability is exercised and moral decision making improved. There are several focal points for enhancing moral outcomes. Michael Rion focuses on the individual manager and the daily routine ways in which ethical decisions are made. He describes the recurring moral issues managers face and suggests ways in which to improve their decision making. Patrick Murphy turns attention, not to individual managers, but to structural approaches corporations might use to encourage ethical decision making. He discusses corporate credos, ethics education programs, and corporate codes.

Harold Williams shifts the focus in another direction. What is the role of the board of directors in fostering the ethical accountability of corporations? How far should corporate boards go beyond the firm's fiduciary responsibilities to its stockholders in honoring its social responsibilities to employees, consumers, and other stakeholders? How should boards of directors understand the relationship between these two dimensions of corporate responsibility? What does the law require and what does the law allow? Williams suggests that some changes in board composition for many companies could improve the range and depth of corporate accountability.

Each of these authors is aware of the moral weight corporations exercise. Each wants to call corporations to greater moral accountability. Together they contribute different pieces of the moral puzzle, focusing on different actors and different strategies. Pinpointing responsibility for moral fiduciary decisions is a continuing challenge. Each author desires moral results, but the path to that emerging picture is still being created.

Ethics and Management in the Corporate Arena

Michael R. Rion

A corporate marketing director worries whether a potential sale in a South American country might implicate her company in repressive police activities. Who can she talk to? What will they say? Another manager, in personnel, is puzzled whether a proposed compensation scheme is "fair." How does he understand what fairness means? Meanwhile, a purchasing agent for the company wonders what to do about a proposed trip to visit a vendor's plant, all expenses paid. Does corporate policy tell him how to respond? Or does he simply rely on his own judgment? And, in another part of the company, a recently graduated MBA interviews for a financial analyst position. She wonders whether this is the kind of company she wants to work in? What are its values and how do they fit with hers? Can she make a career here without compromising her integrity?

Everyday in every company decisions and questions like these arise naturally. The examples all highlight ethical dimensions of business decisions that are simply part and parcel of business life. Ethical issues and questions need not be imported into an otherwise "sterile" business environment. The challenge, rather, is to provide managers like the ones in these illustrations with support, encouragement and organizational resources to recognize the issues, to assess them ethically as well as financially, and to make sound ethical and managerial judgments.

Based on intensive experience with a corporate

Prepared for Angelo State University Symposium, 1985, by Michael Rion, Resources for Ethics and Management, West Hartford, Connecticut.

responsibility program at Cummins Engine Company, as well as teaching and consulting opportunities with managers from other major corporations, I want to offer some observations about the nature of management and how we can best think about meeting this challenge to strengthen ethical management in business firms. Following some comments about the individual manager's perspective and context, I will discuss some of the most typical ethical issues that arise in management and how we might think usefully about them. I will conclude with some thoughts about critical elements for sustaining ethical management, as well as some of the obstacles to that effort that inevitably arise in the complex affairs of these all too human enterprises.

The Manager's Perspective and Context

I begin with the individual manager's situation. Too often, we discuss ethics and management as though reality were "theory driven." That is, we know something about ethical theory and we then derive what it is that managers should know, or what rules they should follow, or what factors they should weigh as though they had all the time in the world to explore these considerations. Our theories are critically important, and we need always to be prepared to challenge the blinders of practice with a broader normative perspective. But it is just as critical to understand what goes on in the life of a manager day to day if we hope to influence what she does and how she thinks about the issues that confront her.

Lest this initial focus on individual managers mislead us into an individualistic reductionism of corporation behavior, first a word about corporations (and other organizations) as, themselves, moral agents. Certainly organizations are in no sense "persons," but through individual persons in organizational roles, organizations do act purposively and reflectively without regard to particular individuals in the roles at a given time. That is, while the individuals in the roles actually do the thinking and analysis — there is no ephemeral corporate conscience or "mind" — their analysis and reflection and decisions are shaped profoundly and not always consciously by organizational structures, policies, values and culture. And, of course, the interaction and summative impact of a variety of individual role decisions may well be different from individual intentions precisely because the sum total is shaped by organizational factors.

This organizational perspective is important to remember, but my focus here on individual managers reflects the simple fact that one critical dimension in corporate moral responsibility is the impact of the many decisions of individual managers throughout the organization every day. There is more to be said about organizational ethics than the sum total of individual actions, but these actions account for a significant dimension of corporate impact.

We can see this in both dramatic and mundane arenas. Certainly in such major issue areas as questionable payments, regulatory compliance, and product safety, the individual managers are often directly responsible for whether the corporation ends up with a reputation for integrity or a public relations and legal scandal. But there are thousands of smaller decisions that will never make the news, decisions affecting the lives and finances of many individuals and companies. Individual managers decide how best to treat a "problem" employee, how vigorously to pursue affirmative action and honest performance review, what to do for a loyal supplier when a sharp downturn hits his own business, how much disclosure to offer a customer when discussing a performance problem, and so on.

All of the elements I will discuss later for strengthening ethical management owe their effectiveness in large measure to how well they shape the decisions and behavior of individual managers. If we look carefully at the circumstances in which managers typically operate, several features affecting the manager's ability to act responsibly are evident.

The first is *complexity* and *ambiguity*. The company "stands behind its products," but does that mean that Smith should offer a settlement beyond warranty requirements in this case? What are the financial implications? Is it fair to other customers? Or, another company explicitly prohibits bribery. Does that mean that Carlson loses a major order because some goods with papers in legal order cannot get across a border without an "expediting" payment? Even with a stated company

policy, managers often face uncertainty in interpreting the policy in particular cases and weighing competing claims on their action.

This is, of course, nothing new. The purpose of management roles and of managers with good judgment is precisely to move from overall corporate objectives and policies to particular decisions and actions. Ability to work with complexity and to accept ambiguity often separates a successful, rising manager from one who "plateaus" at a particular level of responsibility. The point here is simply that this complexity and ambiguity pertains to the ethical dimensions of management decisions as well. It is perfectly appropriate for an ethicist or a senior manager to articulate a principle — such as being honest with customers — and to acknowledge that tough cases will arise. The manager who has to decide what, exactly, to tell today's customer right now lives those tough cases; she is the "practitioner" of ethics, for good or ill.

A second aspect of management is that managerial decisions typically constitute a flow of interrelated decisions rather than an ordered set of single decisions to be resolved serially. In the course of planning a production run, developing a marketing and sales strategy for a particular customer, purchasing goods and services needed to meet a production schedule, assessing the social-political climate in a foreign investment, or training, developing and deploying personnel, the elements in the manager's world simply do not hold still. Events change, opportunities become contingent upon other opportunities and actors, one decision closes off some options and opens others.

What degree of product information and counter argument regarding a competitor's product is ethically responsible, for instance, when the customer changes her own strategy during the negotiations and the competitor presents a new marketing angle? Certainly many actions are simply unethical regardless of the circumstances, and many positive responsible actions are generally applicable, but the grey areas between these two are broad and attributable, in part, to this characteristic flow in the decision process.

While managerial decisions flow in a complex and interrelated fashion, the manager is also faced with the rapidity of the decision process and the necessity to act. Individual managers typically handle this complex flow with quick decisions; there are simply too many simultaneous issues and demands on their time to allow for deliberative consideration in every case. Indeed, a critical skill for managers is precisely the ability to know when to stop the process for careful deliberation because they simply cannot stop it everytime. The manager who slows down the process too often will miss the opportunity to decide in many cases and, ultimately, fail to carry out the managerial task.

Those of us in academic and staff roles may have some difficulty imagining just how real is this rapidity. Practically, it means deciding what fair treatment to a customer or supplier means in a quick telephone discussion while another call is on hold and two people are waiting at the door with other important issues to discuss. Or, it means determining responsible foreign business conduct in the midst of a complex negotiating session in another country where delay means losing the business. And, most of all, for many managers — especially successful managers with broad areas of responsibility — it means dealing with these and other issues in the midst of a schedule and range of decisions that simply, humanly does not allow for slow deliberation for any but the exceptional issue.

Strengthening the manager's eye for the exceptional issue and helping him to shape the normal business style ethically is a central part of the challenge to business ethics.

Finally, it is my experience that individual managers experience a strong sense of accountability and responsibility for their decisions and actions. Stereotypes of bureaucratic buckpassing notwithstanding, managers typically recognize their own accountability with the system and accept responsibility for their actions. This is often not only in the sense of management authority and organizational accountability, but also in the broader sense of personal integrity and moral responsibility for personal choices in the managerial role. To be sure, there are many opportunities and temptations to "pass the buck," to make a decision and absolve oneself of responsibility on the theory that the corporate policy or circumstance allows no other choice. Managers are human and thus susceptible to these excuses and rationalizations. But because they are human

they are, typically, keenly aware of their own role and responsibility.

This awareness can lead to genuine and positive interest in ethical management; it can also lead simply to an uncomfortable conscience and a lingering anxiety beneath the daily flow of decisions. And, it may lead to a quite conscious narrowing of the sense of responsibility. Precisely because I recognize and accept that I am accountable for my actions, I may look for ways to limit that accountability (by, for instance, never acting without clear corporate policy or precedent). Any, indeed all, of these reactions characterize managers in any given company. My observation is simply that these all flow from a recognition and acceptance of one's own accountability, not a denial of it.

I have drawn for you what I think is an accurate picture of management from the perspective of most corporate managers at various levels in their organizations. Typically well paid and eager to perform, these men and women have accepted responsibility for managing a rapid flow of complex and often ambiguous decisions across a whole range of corporate activity. How do we encourage and sustain ethical sensitivities and commitments in this kind of world?

Certainly a basic requisite is simply good management itself. Good management is not sufficient for ethical management ("what's good for General Motors . . ."), but it is clearly essential. Many examples of ethical problems in management arise from a failure to plan effectively and an inflexibility unsuited to the flow of decisions I have described. Poor decisions now may eliminate options or pose unacceptable tradeoffs down the road that could have been avoided with better management in the first place. Furthermore, good management considerations will often be consistent with ethical precepts, as for instance in treating employees with respect and being a trustworthy supplier.

Management in the context I have described is best when it is anticipatory and affirmative, coordinating resources to meet changing circumstances, anticipating possible competing claims and dilemmas while there is still time for choice. Without that kind of good management, ethical management will be even more difficult than it already is.

Within this context, there are distinctive features of managerial judgment essential to making ethical decisions. Closely linked to anticipatory management is the importance of creative moral imagination, the capacity simply to recognize ethical issues, to rise above too restricted a horizon in assessing an issue and seeing the stakes involved for those affected. Managers then need appropriate conceptual "handles" to analyze ethical dimensions of an issue. Just as the manager has concepts and rules of thumb to assess return on investment, market target volumes or when to close a negotiation, so she needs help in knowing whether fairness is the right category for a particular decision, whether an alleged bribe really is a bribe, and so on. Managers need familiarity with these concepts to bring them to bear easily in their dynamic world. Furthermore, managers need to develop the capacity with ethical issues as with financial and other managerial dimensions to reach judgments, to resolve the issue or to know when to slow down the process for further analysis and reflection.

Moreover, managers increasingly need the ability to articulate their ethical reasoning in order to explain and to defend their decisions on occasion to peers and supervisors, to the public perhaps, and — most importantly — to themselves. Given their sense of accountability and responsibility, many managers are particularly open to learning about ethics in large measure to gain more confidence that they are exercising their roles responsibly. That confidence comes finally from a sense of personal integrity and the ability to convince oneself of the rightness of one's actions.

What is required, then, for the manager to enable effective and ethical business performance is dynamic anticipatory management, enriched by moral imagination and the capacity to assess and resolve ethical issues within the complex flow of daily decision making. This is what policies and structures and training programs are designed to encourage and sustain. Before I say something about those sustaining structures, let's explore further the manager's perspective in a few issues areas and how ethics comes to bear on these issues.

Although it's always presumptuous and perhaps misleading to catalogue issues, there are three issue areas that arise most frequently in the management settings I am familiar with. These are:

1. The nature and extent of role responsibility — that is, I know something may be wrong here, but is it my job to worry about it?
2. The meaning of fairness — is what I don't like unfair? is fairness equal treatment?
3. The range and limits of moral responsibility in other cultures — do I pay the bribe or not? is it a bribe? are we imposing our values on other countries?

I offer these as examples of real dilemmas that real managers worry about because they arise while they go about their regular work in the context I described earlier. While we cannot take time to analyze each of these in detail — time and other agendas press upon lecturers as well as managers — I want to offer some brief reflections on each to stimulate your thinking about ethics in the corporate arena.

Role Responsibility

Philosophers often begin reflections on business ethics with the classical distinctions between utilitarian and deontological ethics, perhaps with some interesting twists added to the familiar dichotomy. Will cost/benefit assessment lead me in one direction on this issue, while commitment to formal principles requires something else? In my experience consulting with and teaching ethics to managers, I'm convinced this is the wrong starting point. The first question the manager often asks is, "Do I have a responsibility here, or is this somebody else's problem?" For example, "I've done a lot for this troubled employee; shouldn't his family or a social service agency take over?" Or, "We make the product to quality specs, is it really any of our business how the customer uses it?" Claims are made upon the manager all the time by various stakeholders (and his or her own conscience), and a critical issue is sorting out those claims to determine which ones really belong on the manager's lap instead of somewhere else.

For this reason, I prefer to begin developing conceptual resources for ethics in management with a simple role responsibility framework. Specific principles and even the familiar utilitarian/deontology schema come in later on particular issues.

I cannot here fully outline the framework I

have found useful in management settings, but let me summarize the central concepts. We begin with a recognition of multiple stakeholders to whom the corporation has responsibilities. In the course of doing its normal business, every company affects — for good or ill — not only stockholders, but employees, suppliers, customers, public agencies, local communities, and so on. All of these have a legitimate stake in certain actions of the company, they are stakeholders. Now, not all of their claims for response from the company are legitimate, nor can most companies fully meet all the legitimate claims of its many stakeholders, for these claims sometimes conflict. But the first point is simply to recognize that business has a responsibility for its impact on all its stakeholders.

We can further understand this responsibility by considering a simple distinction between negative and affirmative responsibilities. Simply put, the responsibility not to harm others is more stringent than the responsibility positively to help others. The essential moral minimum to avoid harm is virtually universal.

Consider an encounter with a beggar on the streets of a major city. Some of us would give her money, others would not. Perhaps a few of us might even assist her to the nearest soup kitchen or even take her home to give her support. There are lots of good things we might do for the beggar, and many reasons why one of us would do one thing, and another a different response. But we would all agree, surely, that we ought not intentionally to knock the beggar down, and if, indeed, we accidentally do so, we ought to help her up.

This homely example applies to business as well as individual responsibility. Business corporations can do all sorts of good things for the world, and corporate philanthropy offers examples of what can be done in great variety of ways. And for a variety of reasons, some corporations do more than others in foundation giving and charitable contributions. But businesses are primarily designed to develop and deliver quality goods and services in the marketplace, not to become public service and welfare agencies, so these "good deeds" will always necessarily be limited, just as the individual is limited in ability to respond to the beggar.

But every business, in the course of doing its routine work, affects people all the time and, like the individual "minding his own business" walking down the street, business corporations are obliged to avoid harm to those with whom they come into contact and to compensate for harm they do cause. This sounds passive, but in fact it requires imaginative practice management in the corporate context where decisions and actions flow quickly and impacts for good or ill occur all the time. Potential for harm in the business context includes actual material injury (e.g., toxic exposures in a plant, financial loss), restriction of basic rights and freedoms (e.g., invasion of privacy, absence of due process), and violation of basic ethical principles (e.g., breaking promises, unfair treatment).

This relatively simple point about more stringent responsibility for avoiding and correcting injury offers managers a helpful framework for assessing their role responsibility. It suggests a way to sort out whether a particular problem is legitimately on the manager's desk or not. "Did I cause the problem? Am I doing all I can to conduct this operation in ways that do not injure the affected stakeholders?"

If, for instance, an employee with a history of personal problems that negatively affect work performance asks for another chance, the manager needs to assess whether the company has contributed to the person's problems, whether the manager herself has made commitments, how fairly and consistently company policies are being followed in similar cases, and so on. Or, consider the plant manager in a small community where community leaders are asking for greater leadership and financial commitment from the company in resolving a pressing community need. There may be good reasons for the company to do more, but the manager must assess carefully first the direct impact of its business activities on its many stakeholders — including its direct impact on the community — before launching into other projects that reach beyond the boundaries of the company's direct impact.

Within this framework, issues of cost/benefit calculation arise, as do the meaning of such key principles as truthtelling, promisekeeping, and fairness. But it is useful to begin with the role responsibility question as the avenue into these substantive principles, for that is how the questions typically arise for managers.

Fairness

One of these questions that frequently arises concerns fairness. I can think of no other ethical term that more quickly leaps to managers' tongues in the corporate arena, or for that matter, among people generally. We are quick to sense inequities and cry foul, to suggest that certain decisions are not fair. Certainly in corporate management, one hears of fairness across the range of business activity: a shop floor employee figures that his wages are not fair when he reads about the bonuses for senior officers, a marketing person worries whether differential treatment for two different customers is really fair, a product engineer chafes under government-directed design parameters which he thinks are unfair, a community group believes the company is unfair in its distribution criteria for philanthropic dollars.

And here is where careful moral reasoning can make contributions to management ethics. The manager may be clear about role responsibility — for instance, he knows he is responsible for fair performance review, she knows her treatment of a supplier must be fair — and even have some time to sort out the nature of that responsibility. What sometimes happens next is a kind of paralysis stemming from the power of moral language. Fairness is such a loaded term that the manager may too quickly identify a particular meaning — typically, identical treatment — with the moral force of the concept and find it difficult to move forward because that particular meaning does not work well in the case at hand. Or, different participants in the case have different views of what is fair and they accuse one another of unfairness.

Some clear thinking helps here. The essence of fair treatment is treating like things alike. On that, we typically agree but the difficulty lies in determining which categories are relevant, and which are not, for differential treatment. Disagreements about fairness are disagreements about what constitute relevant differences. In distributing votes, for instance, we say that only a few differences are relevant, such as age and legal status. But when we provide salary and promotions, we do not use the same standard; it would be unfair, we say, to pay everyone the same. Relevant differences in compensation include such job related factors as contribution and productivity. In both cases — compensation and votes — we determine what are relevant differences by looking to the nature of the good that is being distributed. In Michael Walzer's felicitous phrase, we look to the particular sphere of justice, to the particular relationships and goods that are at stake in a particular distribution.

Thus, for instance, if a compensation system provides profit-linked bonuses for higher level managers on the theory that their performance more directly effects profits than does that of lower level employees, then the same difference is relevant when profits are down and salaries have to be cut — the higher level managers ought to bear a larger burden. Better yet, perhaps the company begins to assess its assumptions and determines that all employees contribute sufficiently to profits so that there are no relevant differences apart from those reflected in basic salary scales. Then, as many companies are doing, they might turn to a profit-sharing system for all employees.

Reasonable people will disagree in tough cases about what constitute relevant differences. How much should potential be considered, apart from actual performance, in compensation rewards, for instance? Or, to take a critical controversy at the moment, are salary-based market considerations that cause women in jobs of demonstrably comparable worth to be paid less than men relevant to a particular company's compensation system or not? Clearer thinking about fairness will not magically yield agreeable solutions every time. But it will provide a better framework for sorting out specific challenges in management and contribute to more thoughtful resolution of confusions and conflicts about management responsibility.

International Involvement

Even more complicated challenges for managers emerge when American businesses go overseas. Issues of bribery, safety standards, employment policies, and host country politics raise constant questions about whether and how we can operate abroad with faithful commitment to our own ethical standards.

It is important, first, not to overestimate the differences between cultures. We are too quick to note the prevalance of bribery, for instance, as a reason for participating in it, while ignoring the fact that a visitor to this country might make the same judgment about tax obligations.

Cross-cultural research suggests that virtually every culture has certain common moral concepts — such as not harming others and keeping promises — rooted in social cooperation. But these deeply rooted common themes end up in different specific interpretations because cultures differ in fundamental orientation and in concepts that go deeper than ethical norms.

Thus, for instance, two cultures may both affirm respect for human persons, but one defines persons broadly while another limits the concept to members of a single tribe. Or, both may affirm the dignity of elderly community members, but one group understands that dignity to allow or even require abandoning the elderly in times of scarcity, while another abhors such treatment. At this level, there truly are cultural differences that affect ethical judgment, and reconciling the two "versions" of ethics may be impossible. But, this need not lead to sheer cultural relativism in management ethics, that is, to a "do as the Romans do" attitude. One reason is the common ground that does exist; another reason concerns the notion of managerial role responsibility.

Many perceived "cultural" differences in ethics are actually differences in how willing people are to tolerate divergence from a norm which is itself universally held. The actual judgments differ between cultures, but not because the cultures lack common values. Consider bribery, for example.

We typically read about cases where bribery appears to be commonly accepted in other cultures. Yet it is reasonable to conclude that nearly all countries have a prohibition against bribery. Most have laws against bribery, and public examples — e.g., the public scandal when Japanese officials accepted bribes from Lockheed — reveal that the society condemns bribery as some sort of violation of public morality.

In fact, of course, bribery occurs regularly in many of these countries. The point is that widespread systemic bribery in a given country — e.g., border guard payments — does not mean the country has different basic ethical values. Rather, the society simply tolerates greater divergence from a common ethical norm than we do in the United States because of low pay in public service, long-standing patterns of corruption, and centu-

ries old customs. For example, Mexico's President has been committed to reducing corruption (i.e., lifting up the common norm), but there is ambivalence in the culture about what can be accomplished. "It doesn't matter if they steal a bit," says a Mexican cab driver of the police, "but they shouldn't steal so much." Here we see the toleration of variation from the norm!

This tolerance of bribery does not result from irreconcilable relativism in ethics. When an American business person enters another culture, there is a common ground from which to approach the issue. If the American insists upon a more strict standard, he or she is not introducing an alien norm but rather judging differently the circumstances that justify falling short of the norm.

But then the charge arises that the American is "imposing" our values on the other culture. Here it is critical to understand role responsibilities carefully. Consider the bribery question further.

When an American company refuses to make payments that might be standard acceptable practice in the host nation, is this "cultural imperialism"? No, for the company is not "imposing" its values on the host country. Rather, it is saying, "Here is how we will do business. If that is not appropriate or sufficient, then we simply will not engage in business here." As a particular American company, it has every right to govern its conduct in this way, for it is the company that suffers any negative consequences.

What about a local company owned and operated independently by a national of the host country? Should the American company who works with this local firm condemn it for cooperating with local practices? Not necessarily, for this might indeed be an unfair imposition of our own values. National firms have fewer options than do foreign investors. Furthermore, there may be payments prohibited by the American company that are clearly tolerated even by the most reputable local firms. It may be best for the American company to expect the local firm to be as vigorous in upholding their own standards as the former is in its own standards. Different roles lead to distinctive responsibilities.

The issue of role responsibilities and cultural differences also arises in considering social-political issues in investments abroad. Is it appropriate to consider "American" social-political values in deciding on business with other countries? Can we make consistent judgments between, for example, sales and investments in South Africa, Chile, Russia, China, and so on?

Time does not permit a thorough discussion of these important issues, but I will sketch briefly the considerations I believe to be helpful in making management decisions. It begins with the "avoid harm" framework I mentioned earlier. The American business seeks to avoid harm in its business activities abroad, and this does not "impose" its values on another country. As an American firm, it puts limits on its own actions and says, "Here is how we will conduct business in your country if we are to be there at all." The host country may reply, "Then go elsewhere," and it has that right.

Some elements of this approach are relatively clear, for example, minimum standards for employee safety, compensation and opportunities; honest, fair dealing with customers and governments, and specific policy areas such as bribery. These elements are most clear where they involve direct management; actions such as employment and sales. But the concern to avoid harm extends to the wider impact of product use and operating presence in a nation.

The general principle on these broader social-political issues is that investment and doing business in a country ought to contribute positively to economic development beneficial to host countries. To that end, negotiations with host governments and nationals seek to fulfill mutually beneficial goals. Furthermore, the more a country's policies appear to frustrate equitable social and political development, the more carefully should the American firm evaluate whether it can avoid harm by involvement in repressive settings.

For certain "benign" products — e.g., medical supplies, food, clothing, certain kinds of equipment — there is a presumption in favor of involvement. Only particularly problematic political or economic circumstances could create conditions where the political-social significance of investment would counter its positive economic impact. Other products — e.g., military equipment, strategic goods — have a more direct bearing on the political climate and the presumption for investment is more readily challenged by the direct impact of the product.

The role responsibility of American companies, then, is to assess their impact in the host country. But how do they venture across the border without unreasonable demands on very different countries?

Briefly, I would argue for some minimal criterion for assessing problematic situations along these lines. What is troublesome is a society which fails to work toward providing basic material needs to its population and/or one whose political system represses the possibility for the development of culturally appropriate, indigenous forms of political expression by its citizens. Particular countries and particular business deals — sales, licensing, direct investment — may or may not be appropriate in light of this minimal criterion. Some of the considerations in particular cases would include: What are the dominant characteristics of the host country? Are there trade offs between material needs and political rights? What is the historical context and direction? Are there signs of new directions or old patterns? What is the "policy" context? What do the policies of the United States, other nations and the United Nations suggest about strategies and prospects for change?

Using this framework, I would for instance conclude that at least many companies doing business in South Africa today ought to withdraw because their products and presence provide both tangible and symbolic support to the entrenched regime. I would argue, however, that companies with appropriate opportunities in the non-military sector ought to be involved in the Peoples Republic of China. In either case, and countless others, the issue comes down to an assessment of the host country dynamics and the impact of the particular decision being considered. Sales to domestic commercial firms are different from military sales; license agreements are different from sales, and direct investment is different still. The point of my discussion is simply to illustrate the point that American companies legitimately have these issues on their agenda as they do business around the world and that they can sort out their responsibilities with some care.

My remarks for the last few minutes about role responsibility, fairness, and international involvement have simply illustrated the range of ethical issues that can arise in management and some of the perspectives from ethics that can illuminate managerial choices. On these and countless other issues, managers continue day-in and day-out to face decisions and opportunities where ethical dimensions are simply baked into the overall texture of management.

Critical Elements in Management Ethics

But how do we support managers in ways that encourage responsible actions and positive (or, at least, minimally negative) impact of corporate activity on people, institutions, the environment, and the fabric of community? What all of us with managerial responsibility or teaching and consulting roles struggle with is how best to encourage, sustain and strengthen that kind of behavior and impact. Too often, advocates of one particular strategy — for instance, codes of ethics, corporate trouble-shooting roles, ethics training, and so on — proceed as though that strategy were the lynchpin to bring ethics more effectively into the corporate environment.

My own experience with Cummins Engine Company, as well as my observations of other settings, convinces me that a whole set of elements are essential, that they are decidedly interdependent, and that, therefore, the whole effort resembles a fragile house of cards. No one element, alone, can create or sustain ethical management without all the others, and weakness in even one element can undermine the overall effort in much the way the house of cards is vulnerable without each of its supporting members.

I use the house of cards metaphor intentionally, not to suggest that business ethics is in any sense a sham, but rather to emphasize the precarious nature of ethical management in the world I described above. Ethics is not yet a standard dimension of managerial training, nor is a sophisticated and thorough approach to ethics a standard dimension of managerial practice. Given the pressures of managerial life, therefore, ethics is easily pushed off the agenda. For this reason, I argue that sustaining ethical management requires explicit and steadfast attention to all the elements described below.

There are at least five key elements although I make no pretense that this list is exhaustive:

1. A clear corporate ethos of "culture" that encourages responsible behavior
2. Top management commitment to nurture that ethos
3. Specific policy guidance on difficult issues
4. Staff support to assist line managers on an internal consulting basis
5. Development of managerial awareness and competence through ethics training.

These elements can all be incorporated into any organization in ways appropriate to its culture. I will discuss each of them with special but not exclusive reference to Cummins Engine Company.

1. Corporate Ethos

Corporate culture is one of the newest buzz words in contemporary management discussions, and like most buzz words, the concept highlights an important truth despite the excessive claims typically made for the latest theory. The truth here is that individual organizations do, indeed, have distinctive cultures; that is, they have distinctive patterns of interaction, values, symbols, and stories that shape an identity and image of the organization. And employees know that this culture shapes and limits their own patterns, sometimes consciously, sometimes despite themselves.

Consider Cummins as an example. It was founded in the early 1900's by an entrepreneurial chauffeur to the local banking family in the small southern Indiana town of Columbus. Clessie Cummins' venture into diesel engines was financed by the Irwin family at a loss for many years. Early letters and documents make clear that one of the founding interests was to provide jobs for local young people. As the company grew under the leadership of its chairman of more than 30 years, J. Irwin Miller, this initial sense of social responsibility was strengthened at every step. The company developed a clear ethos in which ethical responsibility was explicitly affirmed and expected. It was also, incidentally, an ethos that emphasized innovation, product quality and customer service. That history has continued to shape the company's identity and guide its decisions. Indeed, many managers explain their decision to join Cummins precisely because of its socially responsible and innovative ethos.

Notice how deeply rooted is this culture in the company's history. Each company has its own history, its own distinctive story, that has helped to shape its contemporary identity and ethos. This identity contributes to shaping individual role behavior into organizational action rather than simply personal decisions. Where that ethos encourages ethical management, it can be lifted up, celebrated and reinforced. Where the culture is indifferent to ethics, or even perhaps hostile, strategies for culture change must be an explicit part of any initiatives in management ethics. Indeed, the other four elements described below can serve as strategies to change culture or to reinforce it, depending upon the existing ethos.

The importance of corporate culture means that those who seek to sustain ethical management must pay explicit attention to corporate history and culture. Even in a setting with a less supportive culture, there may be resources in the company's history or in the industry's history and practice that can be appealed to in shifting values within the organization. Changing a culture indifferent or hostile to ethics is difficult, but ignoring it will doom specific efforts to failure. And ignoring a positive culture is folly, for it is the greatest resource management can rely upon in sustaining ethical management.

2. Top Management Commitment

The importance of senior management commitment to ethics is virtually a platitude, but no less important for that. Conscientious chief executive officers can not, alone, impose ethical management, but their initiative and support is essential. The CEO needs to be articulate, visible and firm in explaining corporate philosophy and policies, reinforcing commitment to those policies regularly, and upholding the philosophy and policy in tough cases. Symbolic cases where the CEO has supported ethics, even at a financial loss, become part of the lore in the organization and give support to middle level managers as they, in turn, seek to uphold ethical practices. Likewise, the CEO's actions are under special scrutiny in tough cases and even the perception that ethics have been compromised will undermine commitment to ethics lower in the organization. The CEO may not be able to impose ethics unilaterally, but if the top person is not supportive of ethics, even the most responsible organization will begin to "backslide" in its commitments.

Cummins Engine Company is an excellent example of the importance of senior management commitment. J. Irwin Miller became CEO in the early 1930s when the company was still a small start-up operation. At the helm during the company's rapid growth in the 1950's and 1960's, Miller was clear and vigorous in his insistence that business be done with high ethical standards. His personality and leadership were critical contributions to the developing ethos of the organization. The company's current chairman, Henry B. Schacht, continues this leadership role with similarly articulate and firm commitment to ethical management.

This affirmation of top management commitment, incidentally, ought not to be focused exclusively upon the CEO. In most major corporations, senior managers for various functional areas (e.g., the persons with overall responsibility for marketing, manufacturing, research and so on) play leadership roles in their divisions akin to the role of the CEO in whole corporation. Their role in supporting ethical management is nearly as critical as that of the CEO. This senior management group as a whole plays a crucial role in modeling ethical behavior as it decides central policy issues and strategic plans.

A word about so-called whistleblowing policies provides an appropriate transition here from top management commitment to policy guidance. As senior managers seek to reinforce ethical management, perhaps nothing sends so powerful a message as a serious effort to hear and act upon concerns raised by responsible lower level managers. The senior manager who doesn't want to hear quickly convinces subordinates that ethics is alright only if it does not reduce immediate profits or cause headaches for higher levels. In contrast, the executive who reinforces managers who report questionable practices and who raise ethical concerns as part of the business analysis can convince his or her subordinates to risk raising questions in ambiguous situations. Clear policy commitments that encourage such question-raising and seek to protect subordinates when they do raise questions are important here. But senior managers need to recognize that protection is not always possible, that persons may take risks of subtle reprisals if they raise certain issues. Special vigilance in encouraging the raising of ethical issues and monitoring the protection of those who risk criticizing is always essential.

3. Policy Guidance

Many companies adopt codes of ethics, and there is often a debate about whether codes will make corporations ethical. Posed in that way, the question is not very helpful. Of course, a code will not guarantee ethical management, for policies do not automatically yield compliance. Indeed, a code without compliance may do more harm than good. But codes and policy guidance are important elements in the whole process of ethical management.

General ethical principles embodied in a code or policy statement serve to remind employees of the company's commitment unambiguously. This may be a brief and simple statement (for instance, Johnson and Johnson's long-standing policy statement) or a more elaborate discussion of rationale and key principles. The importance of such statements should be appreciated but not overestimated. Without the other elements described here, a general philosophy statement neither helps people determine what to do nor encourages them effectively to act ethically. But a vigorously supportive CEO who never puts anything down on paper risks not being taken seriously and tying the ethics commitment too much to his or her own personality.

Policies or codes of ethics ought also to move beyond general philosophy into particular issues where specific policy guidance can be given to managers. Often the best intentioned manager may be puzzled about the practical implication of a broad "do good, avoid harm" philosophy statement. Cummins, for example, has not only a general policy statement but also specific policies on topics selected according to line managers' perceptions of the need for guidance. Thus, Cummins has policies on such topics as questionable payments, political participation, meals and gifts, and defense sales. Most companies, like Cummins, have some sort of policy book and policy process, and these ethics policies can fit into that framework as part of the ongoing working guidance given to managers.

Obviously, policies cannot cover every managerial decision. If they could, the problem of sustaining ethical management would be simplified immeasurably. The importance of developing some explicit ethics policies is twofold. First, the very act of being explicit and specific beyond the philosophy statement tells managers that the company is serious about its philosophy. And, where policies can be developed, managers have greater guidance in making difficult decisions and some assurance that they will be supported by senior management where a tough decision guided by a policy yields some disappointing financial results.

Indeed, one strategy for initiating greater sensitivity to ethical management, even in a company whose culture has historically been indifferent to ethics, is to canvass managers about areas where they are puzzled about their decisions and would welcome policy guidance. Developing policies in response to this canvass and working to interpret and implement them can be a significant contribution to cultural change and reinforcement of ethical management.

4. Staff Support

Cummins has long had a Corporate Responsibility Department whose function is to support ethical management throughout the organization. The department has three basic functions, each of which is important to sustaining ethical management regardless of the particular organizational structure. One function is policy development and interpretation. The department provides the staff support to management in developing particular policies, takes the initiative in making policies known to employees, and assists line managers in interpreting the policies in particular cases. Secondly, the department serves as a consulting resource to managers at every level on questions of ethics in business decisions. Managers often need an outside perspective to help them think through difficult or puzzling issues. This assistance ranges from a telephone conversation or brief meeting to long term involvement on a project team assessing a major business decision or policy question. Finally, the department works on management development through an ethics training program.

While Cummins happens to have a Corporate

Responsibility Department, other companies fulfill some or all of these functions through different staff groups. Personnel, public policy, community relations, and law departments are examples. Some organizations have an ombudsperson role to help spot problem areas and offer support to aggrieved or puzzled employees. Wherever the responsibility is lodged, staff support capable of helping managers in these three functions is an essential component of ethical management. Managers can and will act ethically without any help, but the staff support strengthens their ability to do so.

5. Education and Development

After all is said and done, ethical management still rests finally upon individual judgments throughout the organization. Therefore, the recruitment of ethically sensitive managers and support for developing their ethical judgment is a final critical element here. Recruitment judgments are always complicated, but a company can be clear about its values and the interviewers can be alert to the applicant's values in an effort to recruit managers who are committed to the same basic ethical principles as is the company. Cummins Chairman Schacht once noted that a critical characteristic of new employees ought to be the "capacity for moral outrage," that is, the willingness to raise ethical issues rather than bury them. Though difficult to "measure" or identify in the abstract, this characteristic is symbolic of the crucial dimensions of personal character and integrity needed for ethical management.

More manageable, perhaps, is the task of supporting managers once they are part of the company. I need not repeat here the descriptions of the Cummins ethics training program summarized elsewhere. Suffice to say that such training programs are an essential component in strengthening ethical management. Training enhances awareness and skills in dealing with ethical issues in management, and it exposes managers to staff resources for seeking assistance when they encounter difficult issues in the future.

We sometimes speak of institutionalizing management ethics, that is, building the process of ethical management into the systems, structures and culture of an organization. If we are successful in doing so, ethical management will be sustained without depending unduly on a particular personality in the organization or an unusual time in the company's history and interaction with the public. The five elements outlined here are vehicles for institutionalizing ethics. As such, they contribute to shaping an ethical organization whose managers fulfill their organizational roles with ethical sensitivity.

The company that attends explicitly and in depth to these five elements begins to build ethics into its culture. Each element is crucial and depends, in important ways, on all the other elements. Where top management is committed but fails to provide staff support and ethics training, the effort will fall short of the CEO's dreams. And where a staff department initiates effective training without a clear policy framework and senior level support, the result may be frustrated managers. But the more effectively a company encompasses all of these elements, the stronger the foundation of ethical management. Indeed, perhaps the house of cards can become a sturdy dwelling over time.

Obstacles to Management Ethics

All that I have said thus far speaks to the possibilities for strengthening ethical management. Lest we deceive ourselves, however, in self-congratulatory good spirits about management ethics, it is important to recognize the obstacles against which the elements I have described are working.

Many observers and critics would cite the system itself as the most profound obstacle. How can ethics be introduced into profit-making enterprises in a capitalist system, they argue, when the system itself fosters self-interest as its "motor." This question is an important one as we consider what forms and limits ought to guide our particular political economy. Meanwhile, corporate organizations continue to have substantial impact on the lives of people all around the world. My experience with Cummins and elsewhere convinces me that this impact can be shaped to minimize harm and that this is a critical task even as we assess the broader questions of social policy and economic structures. Furthermore, many of the questions of ethical management strike me as quite similar in not-for-profit and public agencies; the problems of ethical management stem less from the "profit motive" than from single-minded goal-directed activity on behalf of an organization. Therefore, it is important to look at that activity in the business context to identify the more immediate obstacles to ethical management.

Perhaps we can see these obstacles most clearly by referring again to the characteristics of the manager's world I outlined earlier. The complexity and ambiguity of many decisions simply reflects reality. A senior executive has to decide whether current and upcoming business conditions warrant a layoff. The ethical implications are profound since many people may suffer because of her business judgment, needlessly so if she is wrong. Yet that judgment is a most difficult one. The sheer size of many corporate organizations, the complexity of their products and communications systems, the uncertainties of information, and the rapidly changing world around the company all make it difficult for even the most conscientious manager to make good judgments every time. As one pundit put it, "For every human problem, there is a solution that is simple, neat, and wrong!" Training and staff support resources aim to help the manager, but the world is still complicated and we human beings are a finite lot!

We encounter our finitude again in the rapid flow of management decisions and the necessity for action. In the fast-paced goal directed activity of management, it is difficult to focus on broader questions, to discern hidden dimensions of a decision. Even conscientious managers simply miss a lot in the flow of information across their desks. For instance, the marketing director for an overseas region may be so preoccupied with 20 different orders and negotiations on a given morning that he fails to notice an order with questionable social-political or ethical implications.

The goal is to build ethical sensitivity into management so integrally that these issues emerge naturally in the same way that financial concerns arise now. But, for now, even the best and most responsible managers have to be reminded to raise their sights. Here is yet another reason for policy guidance and staff support. Often it is the different perspective from a staff group or policy process that highlights a dimension the line manager has missed.

When we turn to managerial accountability and responsibility, we encounter another dimension of human limitation. Our forebears would have called it, unashamedly, original sin; perhaps we are better understood today if we speak of fallibility. In either case, the reference is to the historically dependable tendency of human persons to overestimate our capacity to achieve the good, and to underestimate our capacity for harm. Our distinctive fallibility is not perversity or intentionally unethical behavior; it is, rather, the problem of unintended consequences of well-intentioned actions. We see it in the innovative product that turns out to have unforeseen safety problems, or the personnel decision that solves one issue only to create new ones. Despite our best efforts, we can no more escape this human limitation to business than we can in other arenas of life.

Indeed, managerial responsibility within a large organization poses a particular danger here. Excessive loyalty to narrowly conceived organizational goals can lead well-intentioned individuals to take actions in behalf of those goals that most persons would condemn from a broader perspective. A good example of how unfortunate such "loyalty blinders" can be is provided in a Wall Street Journal account of General Electric's problems with price fixing, bribery and fraud over the last several years. In each case, executives took actions that were certainly unethical and often illegal, despite firm corporate policies on legal compliance and ethical behavior. While some of the individuals may well have been intentionally unethical, it is more likely that most of them simply failed to look beyond the immediate opportunity to serve the corporation's interests as they saw it.

Awareness of these obstacles should not be read as a counsel of despair; it is, rather, a reminder that humility is one of the virtues that ought to characterize those who seek to strengthen ethical management. Individual ethical judgment in management is critical to shaping corporate impact for good rather than ill, and it can be strengthened by the elements I have described. At the same time, we must remember how far we must travel, in a given company and across industry and commerce to achieve significant improvements in ethical management, and we must recognize the obstacles to avoid discouragement or premature self-satisfac-

tion with our efforts. Each company and each individual with some responsibility or opportunity
to address these issues can start somewhere within
the set of elements I have described. There is no
excuse for failing to try.

Creating Ethical Corporate Structures

Patrick E. Murphy

What is an ethical company? This question is not
easy to answer. For the most part, ethical problems
occur because corporate managers and their subordinates are *too* devoted to the organization. In
their loyalty to the company or zest to gain recognition, people sometimes ignore or overstep ethical boundaries. For example, some sales managers
believe that the only way to meet ambitious sales
goals is to have the sales reps "buy" business with
lavish entertaining and gift giving. This over-
zealousness is the key source of ethical problems
in most business firms.

Employees are looking for guidance in dealing
with ethical problems. This guidance may come
from the CEO, upper management, or immediate
supervisors. We know that ethical business practices stem from an ethical corporate culture. Key
questions are, How can this culture be created and
sustained? What structural approaches encourage
ethical decision making? If the goal is to make the
company ethical, managers must introduce structural components that will enhance ethical sensitivity.

In this paper, I examine three promising and
workable approaches to infusing ethical principles
into businesses:

- corporate credos that define and give direction
  to corporate values;
- ethics programs where companywide efforts
  focus on ethical issues; and

Patrick E. Murphy, "Creating Ethical Corporate
Structures," *Sloan Management Review* 81 (Winter
1989): 81-87.

- ethical codes that provide specific guidance to employees in functional business areas.

Below I review the virtues and limitations of each and provide examples of companies that successfully employ these approaches.

Corporate Credos

A corporate credo delineates a company's ethical responsibility to its stakeholders; it is probably the most general approach to managing corporate ethics. The credo is a succinct statement of the values permeating the firm. The experiences of Security Pacific Corporation (a Los Angeles-based national bank that devised a credo in 1987) and of Johnson & Johnson illustrate the credo approach.

Security Pacific's central document is not an ethical code per se; rather, it is six missionlike commitments to customers, employees, communities, and stockholders. The credo's objective is "to seek a set of principles and beliefs which might provide guidance and direction to our work" (see Table 1, p. 550).

More than 70 high-level managers participated in formulating a first draft of the commitments. During this process, senior managers shared and analyzed examples of ethical dilemmas they had faced in balancing corporate and constituent obligations. An outside consultant, hired to manage the process, helped to draft the language. Ultimately more than 250 employees, from all levels of the bank, participated in the credo formulation process via a series of discussion groups.

Once the commitments were in final form, management reached a consensus on how to communicate these guiding principles to the Security Pacific organization. Credo coordinators developed and disseminated a leader's guide to be used at staff meetings introducing the credo; it contained instructions on the meeting's format and on showing a videotape that explained the credo and the process by which it was developed. At the meetings, managers invited reactions by posing these questions: What are your initial feelings about what you have just read? Are there any specific commitments you would like to discuss? How will the credo affect your daily work? Employees were thus encouraged to react to the credo and to consider its long-run implications.

Security Pacific's credo was recently cited as a model effort, and it serves internally both as a standard for judging existing programs and as a justification for new activities. For example, the "commitment to communities" formed the basis for a program specifically designed to serve low-income constituents in the area. However, this credo should not be considered the definitive approach to ethics management. First, the credo could be interpreted simply as an organizational mission statement, not as a document about ethics. Indeed, the examples supporting the credo and the videotape itself do stress what might just be called good business practice, without particular reference to ethical policies. And second, the credo has not been in place long enough for its impact to be fully assessed.

Any discussion of corporate credos would be incomplete without reference to Johnson & Johnson, whose credo is shown in Table 2 (p. 551). This document focuses on responsibilities to consumers, employees, communities, and stockholders. (The current J&J president, David Clare, explains that responsibility to the stockholder is listed last because "if we do the other jobs properly, the stockholder will always be served.") The first version of this credo, instituted in 1945, was revised in 1947. Between 1975 and 1978, chairman James Burke held a series of meetings with J&J's 1,200 top managers; they were encouraged to "challenge" the credo. What emerged from the meetings was that the document in fact functioned as it was intended to function; a slightly reworded but substantially unchanged credo was introduced in 1979.

Over the last two years, the company has begun to survey all employees about how well the company meets its responsibilities to the four principal constituencies. The survey asks employees from all fifty-three countries where J&J operates questions about every line in the credo. An office devoted to the credo survey tabulates the results, which are confidential. (Department and division managers receive only information pertaining to their units and composite numbers for the entire firm.) The interaction at meetings devoted to discussing these findings is reportedly very good.

Does J&J's credo work? Top management feels

Table 1   The Credo of Security Pacific Corporation

Commitment to Customer

The first commitment is to provide our customers with quality products and services which are innovative and technologically responsive to their current requirements, at appropriate prices. To perform these tasks with integrity requires that we maintain confidentiality and protect customer privacy, promote customer satisfaction, and serve customer needs. We strive to serve qualified customers and industries which are socially responsible according to broadly accepted community and company standards.

Commitment to Employee

The second commitment is to establish an environment for our employees which promotes professional growth, encourages each person to achieve his or her highest potential, and promotes individual creativity and responsibility. Security Pacific acknowledges our responsibility to employees, including providing for open and honest communication, stated expectation, fair and timely assessment of performance and equitable compensation which rewards employee contributions to company objectives within a framework of equal opportunity and affirmative action.

Commitment of Employee to Security Pacific

The third commitment is that of the employee to Security Pacific. As employees, we strive to understand and adhere to the Corporation's policies and objectives, act in a professional manner, and give our best effort to improve Security Pacific. We recognize the trust and confidence placed in us by our customers and community and act with integrity and honesty in all situations to preserve that trust and confidence. We act responsibly to avoid conflicts of interest and other situations which are potentially harmful to the Corporation.

Commitment of Employee to Employee

The fourth commitment is that of employees to their fellow employees. We must be committed to promote a climate of mutual respect, integrity, and professional relationships, characterized by open and honest communication within and across all levels of the organization. Such a climate will promote attainment of the Corporation's goals and objectives, while leaving room for individual initiative within a competitive environment.

Commitment to Communities

The fifth commitment is that of Security Pacific to the communities which we serve. We must constantly strive to improve the quality of life through our support of community organizations and projects, through encouraging service to the community by employees, and by promoting participation in community services. By the appropriate use of our resources, we work to support or further advance the interests of the community, particularly in times of crisis or social need. The Corporation and its employees are committed to complying fully with each community's laws and regulations.

Commitment to Stockholder

The sixth commitment of Security Pacific is to its stockholders. We will strive to provide consistent growth and a superior rate of return on their investment, to maintain a position and reputation as a leading financial institution, to protect stockholder investments, and to provide full and timely information. Achievement of these goals for Security Pacific is dependent upon the successful development of the five previous sets of relationships.

Table 2   Johnson & Johnson Credo

We believe our first responsibility is to the doctors, nurses, and patients, to mothers and all others who use our products and services. In meeting their needs everything we do must be of high quality. We must constantly strive to reduce our costs in order to maintain reasonable prices. Customers' orders must be serviced promptly and accurately. Our suppliers and distributors must have an opportunity to make a fair profit.

We are responsible to our employees, the men and women who work with us throughout the world. Everyone must be considered as an individual. We must respect their dignity and recognize their merit. They must have a sense of security in their jobs. Compensation must be fair and adequate and working conditions clean, orderly, and safe. Employees must feel free to make suggestions and complaints. There must be equal opportunity for employment, development, and advancement for those qualified. We must provide competent management, and their actions must be just and ethical.

We are responsible to the communities in which we live and work and to the world community as well. We must be good citizens — support good works and charities and bear our fair share of taxes. We must encourage civic improvements and better health and education. We must maintain in good order the property we are privileged to use, protecting the environment and natural resources.

Our final responsibility is to our stockholders. Business must make a sound profit. We must experiment with new ideas. Research must be carried on, innovative programs developed and mistakes paid for. New equipment must be purchased, new facilities provided, and new products launched. Reserves must be created to provide for adverse times. When we operate according to these principles, the stockholders should realize a fair return.

strongly that it does. The credo is often mentioned as an important contributing factor in the company's exemplary handling of the Tylenol crises several years ago. It would appear that the firm's commitment to the credo makes ethical business practice its highest priority. One might question whether the credo is adequate to deal with the multitude of ethical problems facing a multinational firm; possibly additional ethical guidelines could serve as reinforcement, especially in dealing with international business issues.

When should a company use a corporate credo to guide its ethical policies? They work best in firms with a cohesive corporate culture, where a spirit of frequent and unguarded communication exists. Generally, small, tightly knit companies find that a credo is sufficient. Among large firms, Johnson & Johnson is an exception. J&J managers consciously use the credo as an ethical guidepost; they find that the corporate culture reinforces the credo.

When is a credo insufficient? This approach does not offer enough guidance for most multinational companies facing complex ethical questions in different societies, for firms that have merged recently and are having trouble grafting disparate cultures, and for companies operating in industries with chronic ethical problems. A credo is like the Ten Commandments. Both set forth good general principles, but many people need the Bible, religious teachings, and guidelines provided by organized religion, as well. Similarly, many companies find that they need to offer more concrete guidance on ethical issues.

Ethics Programs

Ethics programs provide more specific direction for dealing with potential ethical problems than general credos do. Two companies — Chemical Bank and Dow Corning — serve as examples. Although the thrust of the two programs is different, they both illustrate the usefulness of this approach.

Chemical Bank, the nation's fourth largest bank, has an extensive ethics education program. All new employees attend an orientation session at which they read and sign off on Chemical's code of ethics. (This has been in existence for thirty years and was last revised in May 1987.) The training program features a videotaped message from the chairman emphasizing the bank's values and ethical standards. A second and more unusual aspect of the program provides in-depth training in ethical decision making for vice presidents.

The "Decision Making and Corporate Values" course is a two-day seminar that occurs away from the bank. Its purpose, according to a bank official, is "to encourage Chemical's employees to weigh the ethical or value dimensions of the decisions they make and to provide them with the analytic tools to do that." This program began in 1983; more than 250 vice presidents have completed the course thus far. Each meeting is limited to twenty to twenty-five senior vice presidents from a cross-section of departments; this size makes for a seminarlike atmosphere. The bank instituted the program in response to the pressures associated with deregulation, technology, and increasing competition.

The chairman always introduces the seminar by highlighting his personal commitment to the program. Most of the two days is spent discussing case studies. The fictitious cases were developed following interviews with various Chemical managers who described ethically charged situations. The cases are really short stories about loan approval, branch closings, foreign loans, insider trading, and other issues. They do not have "solutions" as such; instead, they pose questions for discussion, such as, Do you believe the individual violated the bank's code? Or, What should X do?

Program evaluations have yielded positive results. Participants said they later encountered dilemmas similar to the cases, and that they had developed a thinking process in the seminar that helped them work through other problems. This program, while it is exemplary, only reaches a small percentage of Chemical's 30,000 employees. Ideally, such a program would be disseminated more widely and would become more than a one-time event.

Dow Corning has a longstanding — and very different — ethics program. Its general code has been revised four times since its inception in 1976 and includes a seven-point values statement. The company started using face-to-face "ethical audits" at its plants worldwide more than a decade ago. The number of participants in these four-to-six-hour audits ranges from five to forty. Auditors meet with the manager in charge the evening before to ascertain the most pressing issues. The actual questions come from relevant sections in the corporate code and are adjusted for the audit location. At sales offices, for example, the auditors concentrate on issues such as kickbacks, unusual requests from customers, and special pricing terms; at manufacturing plants, conservation and environmental issues receive more attention. An ethical audit might include the following questions.

- Are there any examples of business that Dow Corning has lost because of our refusal to provide "gifts" or other incentives to government officials at our customers' facilities?
- Do any of our employees have ownership or financial interest in any of our distributors?
- Have our sales representatives been able to undertake business conduct discussions with distributors in a way that actually strengthens our ties with them?
- Has Dow Corning been forced to terminate any distributors because of their business conduct practices?
- Do you believe that our distributors are in regular contact with their competitors? If so, why?
- Which specific Dow Corning policies conflict with local practices?

John Swanson, manager of Corporate Internal and Management Communications, heads this effort; he believes the audit approach makes it "virtually impossible for employees to consciously make an unethical decision." According to Swanson, twenty to twenty-three meetings occur every year. The Business Conduct Committee members, who act as session leaders, then prepare a report for the Audit Committee of the board. He stresses the fact that there are no shortcuts to implementing this program — it requires time and extensive interaction with the people involved. Recently the audit was expanded; it now examines internal as well as external activities. (One audit found that some salespeople believed manufacturing personnel needed to be more honest when developing production schedules.) One might ask whether the commitment to ethics is constant over time or peaks during the audit sessions; Dow Corning may want to conduct surprise audits, or develop other monitoring mechanisms or a more detailed code.

When should a company consider developing an ethics program? Such programs are often appropriate when firms have far-flung operations that need periodic guidance, as is the case at Dow Corning. This type of program can deal specifically with international ethical issues and with peculiarities at various plant locations. Second, an ethics program is useful when managers confront similar ethical problems on a regular basis, as Chemical Bank executives do. Third, these programs are useful in organizations that use outside consultants or advertising agencies. If an independent contractor does not subscribe to a corporate credo, the firm may want to use an ethical audit or checklist to heighten the outside agency's sensitivity to ethical issues.

When do ethics programs come up lacking? If they are too issue centered, ethics programs may miss other, equally important problems. (Dow's program, for example, depends on the questions raised by the audit.) In addition, the scope of the program may limit its impact to only certain parts of the organization (e.g., Chemical Bank). Managers who want to permanently inculcate ethical considerations may be concerned that such programs are not perceived by some employees as being long term or ongoing. If the credo can be compared with the Ten Commandments, then ethics programs can be likened to weekly church services. Both can be uplifting, but once the session (service) is over, individuals may believe they can go back to business as usual.

Tailored Corporate Codes

Codes of conduct, or ethical codes, are another structural mechanism companies use to signal their commitment to ethical principles. Ninety percent of Fortune 500 firms, and almost half of all other firms, have ethical codes. According to a recent survey, this mechanism is perceived as the most effective way to encourage ethical business behavior. Codes commonly address issues such as conflict of interest, competitors, privacy, gift giving and receiving, and political contributions. However, many observers continue to believe that codes are really public relations documents, or motherhood and apple pie statements; these critics claim that codes belittle employees and fail to address practical managerial issues.

Simply developing a code is not enough. It must be tailored to the firm's functional areas (e.g., marketing, finance, personnel) or to the major line of business in which the firm operates. The rationale for tailored codes is simple. Functional area or divisions have differing cultures and needs. A consumer products division, for example, has a relatively distant relationship with customers, because it relies heavily on advertising to sell its products. A division producing industrial products, on the other hand, has fewer customers and uses a personal, sales-oriented approach. A code needs to reflect these differences. Unfortunately, very few ethics codes do so.

Several companies have exemplary codes tailored to functional or major business areas. I describe two of these below — the St. Paul Companies (specializing in commercial and personal insurance and related products) and International Business Machines (IBM).

The St. Paul Companies revised their extensive corporate code, entitled "In Good Conscience," in 1986. All new employees get introduced to the code when they join the company, and management devotes biannual meetings to discussing the code's impact on day-to-day activities. In each of the five sections, the code offers specific guidance and examples for employees to follow. The statements below illustrate the kinds of issues, and the level of specificity, contained in the code.

- Insider Information. For example, if you know that the company is about to announce a rise in quarterly profits, or anything else that would affect the price of the company's stock, you cannot buy or sell the stock until the announcement has been made and published.
- Gifts and Entertainment. An inexpensive ballpoint pen, or an appointment diary, is a common gift and generally acceptable. But liquor,

lavish entertainment, clothing, or travel should not be accepted.

- Contact with Legislators. If you are contacted by legislators on matters relating to the St. Paul, you should refer them to your governmental affairs or law department.

The "Employee Related Issues" section of the code is the most detailed; it directly addresses the company's relationship to the individual, and vice versa. This section spells out what employees can expect in terms of compensation (it should be based on job performance and administered fairly), advancement (promotion is from within, where possible), assistance (this consists of training, job experience, or counseling) and communications (there should be regular feedback; concerns can be expressed without fear of recrimination). It also articulates the St. Paul Companies' expectation of employees regarding speaking up (when you know something that could be a problem), avoiding certain actions (where the public's confidence could be weakened), and charting your career course.

The company also delineates employee privacy issues. The code outlines how work-related information needed for hiring and promotion is collected. (Only information needed to make the particular decision is gathered; it is collected from the applicant/employee where possible. Polygraphs are not used.) The St. Paul informs employees about what types of information are maintained. Finally, information in an individual's file is open to the employee's review.

The code covers other important personnel issues in depth, as well. It touches on equal opportunity by mentioning discrimination laws, but the emphasis is on the company recognition of past discrimination and its commitments to "make an affirmative effort to address this situation in all of its program and practices." Data acquired from the St. Paul supports this point. Between 1981 and 1986, hiring and promotion increased 60 percent for minorities in supervisory positions and 49 percent for women in management — even though overall employment rose only about 3 percent during this time. In addition, the code informs employees that the company will reimburse all documented business expenses. And it covers nepotism by stating that officers' and directors' relatives will not be hired; other employees' rela-

tives can be employed, so long as they are placed in different departments.

Being an ethical company requires providing clear guidelines for employees. The St. Paul Companies' extensive discussion of personnel policies does just that. Employees may strongly disapprove of certain policies, but they are fully informed. The termination policy, for example, states that employment is voluntary and that individuals are free to resign at any time; the company, too, can terminate employees "at any time, with or without cause." Some people may consider that policy unfair or punitive, but at least the rules of the game are clear. One limitation of the code is that all sections are not uniformly strong. For example, the marketing section is only one paragraph long and contains few specifics.

The second illustration is of a code tailored to the company's major line of business. IBM's "Business Conduct Guidelines" were instituted in the 1960s and revised most recently in 1983. New employees receive a copy and certify annually that they abide by the code. It has four parts; the most extensive section is entitled "Conducting IBM's Business." Since IBM is, at its core, a marketing and sales organization, this section pertains primarily to these issues.

Six subsections detail the type of activities IBM expects of its sales representatives. First, "Some General Standards" include the following directives, with commentaries: do not make misrepresentations to anyone, do not take advantage of IBM's size, treat everyone fairly (do not practice reciprocal dealing). Second, "Fairness in the Field" pertains to disparagement (sell IBM products on their merits, not by disparaging competitors' products or services). In addition, it prohibits premature disclosure of product information and of selling if a competitor already has a signed order. Third, "Relations with Other Organizations" cautions employees about firms that have multiple relationships with IBM (deal with only one relationship at a time, and do not collaborate with these firms).

The fourth and fifth sections address "Acquiring and Using Information for or about Others." The code spells out the limits to acquiring information (industrial espionage is wrong) and to using information (adverse information should not be retained). Employees must determine the confidentiality of information gathered from others. The final section outlines IBM's policy on "Bribes, Gifts, and Entertainment." The company allows customary business amenities but prohibits giving presents that are intended to "unduly influence" or "obligate" the recipient, as well as receiving gifts worth more than a nominal amount.

One might contend that it is easy for a large, profitable company like IBM to have an exemplary code. On the other hand, one could also argue that a real reason for the company's continued success is that its sales representatives do subscribe to these principles. Is this a perfect code? No. The gifts area could use more specificity and, even though the company spends millions of dollars a year on advertising, that subject is not addressed in any section of the code. Further, IBM's legal department administers the code, which may mean that problems are resolved more by legal than ethical interpretation.

When should a company use a tailored code of ethics? If a company has one dominant functional unit (like IBM), or if there is diversity among functional areas, divisions, or subsidiaries, then a tailored code might be advisable. It allows the firm to promulgate specific and appropriate standards. Tailored codes are especially useful to complex organizations because they represent permanent guidelines for managers and employees to consult.

When should they be avoided? If a firm's leaders believe specific guidelines may be too restrictive for their employees, then a tailored code is an unsatisfactory choice. Codes are not necessary in most small firms or in ones where a culture includes firmly entrenched ethical policies. If a credo is similar to the Ten Commandments, and programs are similar to religious services, then tailored credos can be considered similar to the Bible or to other formal religious teachings. They provide the most guidance, but many people do not take the time to read or reflect on them.

Conclusion

My research on ethics in management suggests several conclusions that the corporate manager may wish to keep in mind.

There Is No Single Ideal Approach to Corporate Ethics.

I would recommend that a small firm start with a credo, but that a larger firm consider a program or a tailored code. It is also possible to integrate these programs and produce a hybrid: in dealing with insider trading, for example, a firm could develop a training program, then follow it up with a strongly enforced tailored code.

Top Management Must Be Committed.

Senior managers must champion the highest ethical postures for their companies, as James Burke of J&J does. This commitment was evident in all the companies described here; it came through loud and clear in the CEOs' letters, reports, and public statements.

Developing a Structure Is Not Sufficient by Itself.

The structure will not be useful unless it is supported by institutionalized managerial processes. The credo meetings at Security Pacific and the seminars at Chemical Bank are examples of processes that support structures.

Raising the Ethical Consciousness of an Organization Is Not Easy.

All the companies mentioned here have spent countless hours — and substantial amounts of money — developing, discussing, revising, and communicating the ethical principles of the firm. And in fact there are not guarantees that it will work. McDonnell Douglas has an extensive ethics program, but some of its executives were implicated in a recent defense contractor scandal.

In conclusion, let me add that managers in firms with active ethics structures — credos, programs, and tailored codes — are genuinely enthusiastic about them. They believe that ethics pay off. Their conviction should provide others with an encouraging example.

Corporate Accountability: The Board of Directors

Harold M. Williams

The Parameters of Accountability

In considering the structure and role of the corporation, in our society, the first problem is to determine what it is that society expects the corporation to be accountable for. The consequences of any gap between the public's perceptions, business' responsibilities and the private sector's own understanding of its role are bound to be adverse, and any systematic gap almost inevitably means that the private sector responds to its critics in ways which exacerbate the problem.

Unfortunately, the corporate sector has proven disturbingly blind to the trends and changes in public attitudes. . . .

The Mechanisms of Accountability

In considering the state of corporate accountability and the balance of corporate power, it is traditional to begin — and end — with the proposition that management is accountable to the board of directors and the board of directors is in turn, elected by and accountable to, shareholders. Unfortunately, as we know, those propositions are often more in the nature of myths. The truth is that shareholder elections are almost invariably routine affirmations of management's will and that the historic and traditional shareholder is now a vanishing breed. Most stock today is pur-

Harold M. Williams, "Corporate Accountability: The Board of Directors," *Vital Speeches of the Day* 44, no. 15 (15 May 1978): 468-72.

chased by people and institutions whose sole intention is to hold for a relatively brief period and to sell at a profit. They do not perceive themselves as owners of the company, but rather as investors — or speculators — in its income stream and the stock market assessment of its securities. Perhaps one of the starkest illustrations of this fact is that securities analysts, even for major institutions, rarely involve themselves with corporate governance issues; in fact, they typically do not even make recommendations on proxy voting of securities purchased on their recommendation.

Despite efforts, such as the Commission's current inquiry, to enhance the quality of shareholder information and to revitalize shareholder democracy, I believe it is unrealistic to expect that the shareholder constituency will of itself prove an effective vehicle to keep corporate power accountable. Because of the nature of the majority of these shareholders, they are fully protected if adequate information is made available, if fraud and overreaching are prevented in securities trading, and if a fair and orderly securities market is maintained. To some extent, the decline in ownership of equities may indicate that even this function is not being well discharged. It is vital that individuals and institutions be willing to invest in a system they trust and in which they perceive they have a reasonably inviting opportunity for gain. However, many companies do not seem to appreciate that their cavalier treatment of shareholders is alienating them from what should be one of their strongest natural constituencies against government intervention.

The second traditional assumption regarding corporate accountability is also open to question. Many boards of directors, although by no means all, cannot truly be said to exercise the accountability function. The board itself is a mini-society, with all the forces of cooption and cooperation, desire for compatibility, and distaste for divisiveness, which characterize any group. Moreover, the board environment is not particularly conducive to nurturing challenge when the majority of directors are beholden — as employees, suppliers of goods or services, or due to other conflicting roles — to the chairman and chief executive. Even friendship itself often inhibits vigorous directorship, although a strong independent director, asking hard questions, in my judgment, performs an act of true friendship. Dissenting directors are, however, rare, and for some reason, they often seem to have short tenure. Thus, the board, in effect, often insulates management rather than holding it accountable.

Creating a New Environment of Accountability

With this perspective on corporate accountability and the existing mechanisms of corporate governance in mind, I will turn to the core question — whether we can improve the existing process and make it work better, or whether we should take steps to modify or replace it.

Let me dispose of the second set of alternatives first. I have not heard any proposals for structural change which I am prepared to accept today. And, perhaps because I die hard, I believe the existing system can be made substantially more effective. I believe we are dealing with a delicate mechanism — one which can and should function more effectively. Yet I am concerned with suggestions for what appear to be simple solutions — suggestions which are too often lacking in full appreciation for the consequences, including the unpredicted consequences. We need to understand what gets splashed on when we make waves. I believe that the superior economic achievement of our private enterprise system and our unequalled political and personal freedom are three closely intertwined and mutually reinforcing characteristics of our society. We need to be cautious in tampering with their balance. Direct intervention, through corporate governance legislation, into how business is run may, over time, seriously disturb that balance.

If, on the other hand, corporations are to preserve the power to control their own destiny, the larger corporations need to be able to assure the public that they are capable of self-discipline and that they will appropriately contain and channel their economic power — both real and perceived — in a fashion which is consistent with both the discipline of the marketplace and the non-economic aspects of the public interest. Mechanisms which provide that assurance must become effective structural components of the process of governance and accountability of the American

The fact of the breadth of the corporation's constituency is almost universally recognized today, but the consequences are seldom perceived. What I believe this expanded constituency necessarily means is that the large corporation has ceased to be private property — even though theoretically still owned by its shareholders — and has become, in essence, a quasi-public institution. As a society, we depend on private enterprise to serve as the instrument through which to accomplish a wide variety of goals — full employment, equal economic opportunity, environmental protection, energy independence, and others. When viewed in light of these social implications, corporations must be seen as, to a degree, more than purely private institutions, and corporate profits as not entirely an end in themselves, but also as one of the resources which corporations require in order to discharge their responsibilities. And, to the extent that business is perceived as failing to discharge those responsibilities, the argument is strengthened, not only for federal corporate governance legislation, but for federal taxation to transfer profits to the common weal.

corporation. The major part of the responsibility for the effectiveness of those structures, and for assuring the public of the corporation's responsibility and accountability rests with the leaders of the corporate sector and with the lawyers who counsel them.

The first requirement, if government involvement in the mechanisms of corporate decisionmaking is to be obviated, is that those in business understand and recognize the gap which much of the public perceives. Hopefully, discussions such as this Institute will help. The Commission's own hearings on shareholder participation in corporate governance and shareholder rights can also make an important contribution to this educative process — not solely through any rule proposals that may evolve, but also, and perhaps primarily, by focusing attention on the issue of corporate accountability. Heightened awareness of the problems and obstacles to effective accountability can stimulate self-help in reaching solutions. I believe that the very existence of the proceedings, the amount of attention focused on the issues and the number of people who appeared and covered the hearings contributes to that function. Similarly, shareholder proposals and shareholder litigation will also have a constructive effect in stimulating companies to recognize the problem of accountability.

Second, effective accountability depends on identifying certain tension-producing forces and putting them to work in the corporate environment. We need to support the creation and institutionalization of pressures which operate to balance the natural forces that otherwise exist. For example, management quite naturally is the source of pressure for a totally compatible, comfortable, and supportive board. We need to create a countervailing force that works against that tendency toward comfort. Certainly, the relationship between management and the board should not, by any means, be antagonistic, but tension is essential.

In concrete terms, how can this environment be created? The ideal board, in my opinion, would be constructed as follows: First, since the board guards two thresholds — that between ownership and management and that separating the corporation from the larger society — it must be recognized that there are some people who do not belong on boards — members of management, outside counsel, investment bankers, commercial bankers and others who might realistically be thought of as suppliers hired by management. Some of these, as individuals, can and do make excellent directors. Yet all must be excluded unless a mechanism can be designed whereby they can establish their ability to function on a basis independent of their management-related role.

Second, ideally, management should not be represented on the board by other than the chief executive. Such a board environment would not preclude other members of management, counsel, and bankers from being present to contribute their expertise to the deliberations in an uncontentious context. Yet, when it comes to the discussion and vote, the independent director would not be faced with, and discouraged or worn down over time by, what is so often a stacked majority against him.

Third, I believe that the chief executive should not be the chairman of the board. Control of the agenda process is a powerful tool, and the issues presented at board meetings should be determined by a chairman who is not a member of management. The substance and process of board deliberations, and the priority which the board assigns to the matters before it, should not be management's prerogatives. And this also means that hard decisions concerning what the board will take up when time is short and the issues are many should not be dictated by management. Finally, the intimidating power of the chair, when occupied by a chief executive in situations where the majority of the board are indebted to him for their directorship, is avoided.

The type of board I have described is an ideal. I recognize that many companies cannot immediately adopt it in all its aspects, but at the same time, there are few public corporations which cannot utilize some of these concepts. For example, it should be apparent by now that I favor a board of independent directors. In this context, committees of independent directors remain important, but primarily as a vehicle for organizing and dividing up the work of the board. Given a lesser number of independent directors, then committees composed exclusively of independent directors for audit, nomination of directors, executive compensation, public policy, and conflict of interest, become essential. But even this will not be adequate unless the board, as structured, understands and accepts its responsibility and concerns itself with the corporate environment and its compatibility with the essential corporate responsibilities.

Section 3: Democratizing the Corporation

The possibilities for radical institutional change are a compelling concern for those who understand the corporation's power for both good and ill within the framework of market capitalism. Some writers have begun to look for a way to honor both the need for individual accountability and a sense of empowered community in the workplace. They believe new leads may be found in the emerging movement for democratization.

John Cort asks whether the policy of employee ownership practiced by the Mondragon communities of Spain may offer a time-tested model of economic democracy inspired by a Christian concern for empowering the poor. Shirley Roels offers an explanation of the two main threads within the movement for economic democracy — participation in decision making and participation in ownership — and gives reasons suggesting why Christians in business should be attracted to this movement. "Theory Fastball" embodies the thinking of Max DePree, longtime leader of the Herman Miller Corporation, on how to implement communal participation in both decision making and ownership in a North American context.

Robert Massie's analysis extends the discussion of the movement for economic democracy by considering the changes that have occurred in the relationships of corporate managers and their stakeholders as a result of the churches' struggle against apartheid in South Africa and the related shareholder divestment movement. The logic of participation in that movement pushed the churches actively to exercise their rights as corporate shareholders and pushed corporations to recognize shareholders as stakeholders, with legitimate moral as well as financial claims upon the organization. Massie analyzes the resulting shifts in the ideology and the experience of corporate democracy, so that the possibilities opened up in the divestment movement will not be forgotten, now that South Africa has abandoned apartheid.

Together these writers form a convincing argument based on biblical evidence for transforming the structure and culture of the corporation while preserving its legal form. Such changes point out a path that could enhance the prospects for social justice, both inside the corporation and among its various constituencies.

Is Mondragon the Way?

John C. Cort

In St. Thomas More's *Utopia* there is an interesting conversation between More and Hythloday, the adventurer who had returned to Europe and was reporting to More and his friends the wonders of that (almost) perfect society.

"Social evils may be allayed and mitigated," Hythloday says, "but so long as private property remains, there is no hope at all that they may be healed and society restored to good health."

More disagrees: "On the contrary, it seems to me that people cannot live well where all things are in common. . . . The hope of gain will not drive them; they will rely on others and become lazy."

Hythloday responds: "I do not wonder that it appears so to you, since you have no idea of such a state. But if you had been with me in Utopia and had seen their customs and institutions as I did at first hand for the five years that I spent among them, you would frankly confess that you had never seen a people ordered so well as they were."

Of course we know that Hythloday did not spend five minutes in Utopia. There was no Hythloday and no Utopia. They were both creations of Thomas More's imagination.

Nevertheless, the question that bothered More in 1516 is, if anything, even more bothersome in 1983: to what extent is private ownership, or common ownership, or some combination of the two necessary to or consistent with a Christian society?

The careful phrasing of the question indicates that we have here not one but several questions. However, if we start with the assumption that private ownership as we know it in America, with vast wealth and well over 10,000,000 unemployed,

is not consistent with a Christian society, then we can reduce these questions to one question: is there a better way that, unlike Utopia, has stood the test of time and experience?

The answer, on the evidence, may well be, "Yes, there is such a way, and it can be found in the town of Mondragon in the Basque region of Spain."

Consider the evidence.

In 1954 Father Jose Maria Arizmendi, inspired by the social teaching of the Catholic Church, helped five of his former students to organize a workers, or producer, cooperative. Two years later they had raised enough money to build a small factory and, with 24 workers, began producing small stoves.

Today, just short of 30 years later, there are in the Mondragon Cooperative Movement, spread throughout the four Basque provinces of Spain and a smaller Basque area of France, 85 industrial cooperatives employing 20,000 worker-member owners and including the top Spanish producers of consumer durables such as refrigerators, stoves, washing machines, and dishwashers.

Of these 85 cooperatives not one has been a failure. A recent study reveals that between 80 and 90 percent of all small business start-ups in America fail within five years. These two contrasting facts make up the most convincing evidence that Mondragon is on to something important.

In addition to the 85 industrial cooperatives there are 70 other cooperatives of different kinds with perhaps another 5,000 full time worker-owners. *Of these only one, a fishermen's co-op, has been a failure.* They include:

- 43 cooperative schools with about 31,000 students and over 1,000 staff members. Membership and leadership are also drawn from the parents and students.
- One higher education cooperative including polytechnic and professional colleges and a business school, which serves over 8000 students and includes 240 teachers and professors.
- 14 housing cooperatives with over 1,200 apartments.
- Six agricultural/food cooperatives.
- One consumer/worker cooperative with 45 stores, 70,000 consumer-members and over 800 worker-members.

John C. Cort, "Is Mondragon the Way?" *New Catholic World* 226, no. 1354 (July/August 1983): 152-54.

- One technological research cooperative, with 60 research workers, which developed the first robots in Spain and has kept Mondragon abreast of the most sophisticated advances in industrial technology.
- One social security and medical cooperative covering 47,768 beneficiaries. Under Spanish law members of a cooperative are considered self-employed, do not come under the national system, and must provide their own social security and health insurance.
- One bank-credit union-managerial assistance cooperative that serves as the financial, administrative nerve center of the entire movement and binds all the cooperatives to each other by a Contract of Association. This Bank of the People's Labor (*Caja Laboral Popular* or CLP) has 120 branches throughout the Basque region, serves about 500,000 customers, has over 1000 worker-members, and is the twenty-sixth largest bank in Spain. Most of its members are employed in the banking division, but what makes the CLP unique in the world of development banking is its Empresarial (or entrepreneurial) Division. Here the business of launching new co-ops and assisting both new and old co-ops has been developed into a science whose incredible record of success cannot fail to impress the most sceptical observer.

Although this science has been refined in recent years the basic formula was the work of Father Arizmendi and the founders of the first cooperative, ULGOR. Before becoming a priest Father Arizmendi had fought in a Basque detachment of the Loyalist army against France, had been captured, and at one point was under sentence of death. Later, assigned by his bishop to work with unemployed youth in Mondragon, he concluded that what they needed was technical training. He organized a street-corner campaign to raise funds and founded the *Escuela Profesionel Politecnica,* a polytechnical college that began turning out engineers who had a knowledge of Catholic social doctrine and some commitment to that passage in Pius XI's *Quadragesimo Anno* that calls for workers to be "made sharers of some sort in the ownership, or the management, or the profits" of the firms in which they work.

When five of the graduates started ULGOR and asked him to help them, Arizmendi wrote a cooperative constitution that went all the way with *Quadragesimo Anno* and made the workers sharers in the ownership *and* the management *and* the profits. It provided that everyone who worked in the stove factory was a member of the co-op, and *only* those who worked there could be members.

Power was exercised and divided democratically, but also intelligently and practically. Each member had one vote, and only one vote, from the maintenance man to the manager, and a general assembly elected the board of directors, which in turn appointed the manager and gave him the power to manage. In addition to electing a broad to represent their interests as owners the members elected a "social council" to represent their interests as workers.

Producer cooperatives are not a new phenomenon. They have been around for about 150 years, since Parisian craftsmen formed workingmen's associations in 1834 under the leadership of the Christian socialist Philippe Buchez. The ratio of successes to failures has not been impressive, mainly because of one or more of the following factors: incompetent management, inadequate capital, weak commitment on the part of the workers, a tendency in successful cooperatives for the members to sell out to conventional buyers because shares in the co-op have been permitted to become so valuable that new members cannot afford to buy in. The operation, in short is a success but the patient dies.

In the Pacific Northwest, for example, there are a number of highly successful plywood cooperatives in which membership shares are worth as much as $50,000. Young workers cannot afford to buy in and the co-ops are forced to hire nonmembers as conventional employees, thereby reducing worker commitment and productivity. The older workers finally conclude that their only hope of cashing in their shares is to sell the entire co-op.

At Mondragon they have avoided these pitfalls and booby traps in the following ways:

1. The polytechnical college, with a strong infusion of Christian idealism, has produced competent managers and supervisors who have been willing to work in a cooperative enterprise where the maximum salary is limited to three times the minimum, which is pegged at slightly better than the prevailing wage in the area.

2. Adequate capital is provided by (a) a substantial but not prohibitive membership fee payable in installments over two years; (b) the retention of 20 percent of the profits as a reserve fund for the use of the co-op; (c) the payment of 70 percent of the profits into each member's "individual capital account," which is payable with interest on retirement or resignation but meanwhile is available as a loan to the co-op and also may be tapped to cover operating losses; (d) the capital accumulated by the CLP, the People's Labor Bank, which is available as loans to the Mondragon co-ops as needed.

Spanish law requires that 10 percent of the profits must be spent for "social purposes" to benefit the community. Most of this money has gone into the co-op schools and colleges. The resulting good will affects financial stability as it encourages people to become depositors in the bank and customers for co-op goods and services.

3. Worker commitment and high productivity is assured by (a) the confidence that every member has the same vote as a top executive; (b) the realization that 70 percent of the profits are going into his or her account; (c) the fact that every member has made a substantial cash contribution as a membership fee and therefore wants to protect that investment.

Unions have tended to be wary of cooperatives because they break down the adversary relationship between labor and management with which union leaders feel comfortable. Nevertheless, more and more labor leaders are being compelled to look at the Mondragon model as a way of saving the jobs of their members when union plants are faced with closings.

Not long ago the Trades Union Congress of Wales in Great Britain made a visit and in-depth study of Mondragon and began looking for funds to start a similar operation in Wales to create jobs for 10,000 of its unemployed members. Said George Wright, general secretary of the Welsh TUC, "Our organization is tired of being a field ambulance for capitalism."

In this country the Industrial Cooperative Association has been working with union leaders to convert companies threatened with closure into producer co-ops, as well as providing technical assistance and loans to new ventures. Last summer an ICA delegation visited Mondragon in a group that included Msgr. George Higgins of Catholic University, the well-known labor priest. ICA economist David Ellerman has written a 54-page report of this visit that, to this writer's knowledge, is the best thing available on Mondragon for the money ($6.00 from ICA, 249 Elm St., Somerville, MA 02144). Ellerman has since revealed that the Archdiocese of Boston is interested in the possibility of sponsoring a Mondragon-type venture, and a diocesan representative has joined the ICA board.

All over the world thoughtful people — especially thoughtful Christians, but also thoughtful socialists — are asking if there isn't a better way than either traditional private ownership or public ownership of the means of production. Mondragon has characteristics peculiar to itself: the Basque pride, separateness, and strong sense of fraternity. But there is something there that cries for imitation. If it can be put in one sentence it might be this: When applied with intelligence, the democratic process works as well in the field of production as it does in the field of politics. Maybe better.

In his encyclical *Laborem Exercens* Pope John Paul II wrote that in every productive enterprise there should be "a priority of labor over capital" and that the economy should be so organized that "each person is fully entitled to consider himself or herself a part-owner of the great work bench at which they are working with everyone else." He added:

A way toward that goal could be found by associating labor with the ownership of capital, as far as possible, and by producing a wide range of intermediate bodies with economic, social and cultural purposes; they would be bodies enjoying real autonomy with regard to the public powers, pursuing their specific aims in honest collaboration with each other and in subordination to the demands of the common good, and they would be living communities both in form and substance, in the sense that the members of each body would be looked upon and treated as persons and encouraged to take an active part in the life of the body.

That sounds just like Mondragon.

Evangelical Christians and Economic Democracy

Shirley J. Roels

Introduction

Recently many evangelical Christian groups seem reluctant to jump on the bandwagon of cultural change. We are skeptical about changes in social roles and cultural values. We reason that they are based on secular philosophies of life, can be fads of little lasting value, or can occur for pragmatic reasons that are never consciously evaluated.

Such reluctance has not always been the case. There is a tradition of social change that was spearheaded by evangelical Christians. In England during the late 1700s and early 1800s, William Wilberforce, a convert to Methodism and member of the British Parliament, along with other Christians, led the movement against the slave trade and after twenty years secured its abolition. They believed that the Bible called for this social reform, and they led the charge to convince the secularists of their day.

The movement for economic or workplace democracy of the 1970s and 1980s could be such an opportunity for evangelical Christians. It is more than a fleeting fancy. It involves more than pragmatic efficiency. Although it has been supported to date primarily by secular humanists, it need not rely on such a philosophical base for its support. Instead of lagging behind, evangelical Christians should be leading the charge toward economic democracy in the workplace. The bases for this change fit well with our biblical ideas of work, human nature, justice, and community.

Not previously published.

In my efforts to link evangelical theology to workplace democracy I will do the following:

1. discuss the nature of the economic democracy movement;
2. outline basic biblical principles on work that undergird the call for changes in the workplace;
3. link these perspectives with specific issues in structuring work, organizations, and ownership;
4. recognize the lingering effects of sin on our visions for the future.

Economic Democracy Defined

Calls for employee participation in the workplace are not new. Since the Industrial Revolution there has been concern about the proper relationship between employers and employees. The cooperative ownership experiments in England during the mid-1800s were one attempt to alter rigid employer/employee distinctions. Labor unions, which expanded dramatically from the 1930s through the 1950s, often bargained not only for wage increases but also for authority in the structuring of work. In the 1960s the notion of cooperatives was resurrected, though now the focus was more on consumer/supplier relationships.

What is new is the seriousness and scale of the movement for economic democracy in the late 1970s and 1980s. The campaign has a variety of labels. One hears the terms "economic democracy," "workplace democracy," "quality of work life," "participation circles," "employee stock ownership plans" (ESOPS), and "co-ops" bantered around freely. Yet each of these terms reveals an important and central change in perspectives on work. Each title envisions a change in the nature of employee participation in the lives of organizations.

One helpful way to view these changes is shown in the chart on page 564.

The key differences in the diagram revolve around two questions. To what degree are employees involved in decision making? To what degree are employees involved in ownership of the organization? While it is dangerous to caricature any category or company, the explanations below may focus our discussion.

EMPLOYEE PARTICIPATION GRID

High • Employees share a majority of profits and ownership		Wierton Steel, Inc.	Oregon Plywood Co-op Scott Bader Common- wealth Mondragon Cooper- atives
Moderate • Employees share systematically a minority of profits and ownership			Herman Miller, Inc. Steelcase, Inc. *
Low • Private or Public Stockholders • No comprehensive employee ownership • No profit sharing system	J. P. Stevens	General Motors	Ford Motor Co. Chrysler, Inc.
	Low • Employees perceived as small cogs in total operations of organization • Frequently a struggle to unionize	**Moderate** • Employers have genuine interest in adequate compensation, employee support, and good working conditions	**High** • Use of quality circles • Structured employee councils consulting with management • Japanese style consensus decision making

Levels of Ownership Participation (vertical axis label)

• Job Enrichment Programs •

Levels of Decision Participation

* Although Steelcase, Inc. is privately owned, the company has a strong profit sharing plan

---

On the left side of the decision participation continuum are organizations that allow for very limited employee involvement. Employees either accept their role as small cogs in the machinery of the organization or balk at the lack of involvement. In the latter case employees may struggle to unionize. In the moderate group are companies that are more concerned about the welfare of their employees. Often such companies exhibit a genuine interest in providing adequate wages, a solid package of indirect benefits, safe and pleasant working conditions, and a good network of employee services and support. While employer concern is laudable, this second group stops short of full employee participation. The question considered by this middle group is "What can we do for our employees?", an approach that sounds paternalistic. The question not seriously considered is "How can we involve our employees in the decision life blood of the company?"

That last approach is the one taken by groups on the right side of this continuum. They believe that supporting employees is not just a gracious favor. Rather, it is an essential part of building their internal operating culture. Many of these companies have formed small groups of employees who, together with their supervisor, regularly use paid working time to sift through company problems and suggest ways to solve them. These problem-solving groups are called quality circles, participation action circles, or other nomers that denote collective decision making. Some companies in this group have used the model of representative government. Elected employee councils control decisions ranging from job assignment to smoking policy.

Note that the job enrichment movement straddles the moderate and high participation groups. In concept the purpose of job enrichment is to expand the range of authority and responsibility a person has within his or her job. The intent is to make jobs more interesting and fulfilling for employees. Sometimes job enrichment programs are shaped predominantly by the employer, a moderate participation approach. Sometimes they are directed primarily by the employees themselves, a high participation approach.

The vertical continuum raises a different question. To what degree do employees participate, not in the decision making, but in the economic risks and rewards of the company via gain sharing plans (also commonly called profit sharing plans) and the ownership of company stock?

The very bottom of the continuum represents companies in which profits are distributed to private or public stockholders, and not in any direct way to employees. In addition, in these companies there is no systematic plan by which employees hold common stock unless they are in the upper management echelons.

In the moderate block one finds companies that have encouraged some participation in the firm's economic returns via profit sharing or stock share plans. Profit sharing bonus plans may be

Scanlon plans, Rucker plans, or some other unique formula for sharing profits with employees based on performance against a set of predetermined objectives.

ESOPS, employee stock ownership plans, are one legal U.S. form of employee ownership whereby employees can own some shares of company stock. However, many companies have been motivated primarily by the tax advantages ESOPS provide to the firm, rather than by concerns for employee ownership. Other companies have introduced variations of employee stock ownership as attractive means to recruit and retain senior managers.

Whatever the reasons, employees in this category of firms receive a minority of the profits and hold a minority of the stock. Typically ESOPS hold less than five percent of company stock, although the percentage of employee ownership may be slightly higher under some other plans.

At the top of this vertical continuum are companies in which the majority of the ownership shares are held by employees. These structures are typically called cooperatives, although an Israeli kibbutz and the Scott Bader Commonwealth of Great Britain are based on the same principles. In such entities employees hold all or a majority of the firm's ownership. Employees share in the rewards and risks according to their ownership shares.

This grid structure should be handled carefully. Firms can fall at different points on the grid. A firm in which stock is broadly distributed to employees may also have strong participation in their decisions by workers. Yet it is possible for a firm to have a stock ownership plan but still to have very limited worker participation in decisions. It is also possible to have high levels of decision participation but low participation in profits and ownership. It is even possible that a firm may not fit this two-dimensional grid. A company could have high profit sharing and high decision participation but no participation in ownership by employees.

In general, however, the push to shift from the bottom left to the top right of this participation and ownership grid is the core of the movement labelled "economic" or "workplace democracy." It involves combined changes in decision making, profit sharing, and employee ownership — in sum a change in one's philosophy of business.

Biblical Principles of Work

Why should evangelical Christians feel a need to promote this shift from the bottom left to the top right of the grid? Because promoting this shift fits so well with our Christian beliefs about the nature of work and workers. If we use the Bible as the framework for our business philosophy, it is difficult to deny that these changes should occur.

The Bible discusses human work from many different vantage points. Four vantage points that will prove helpful in our discussion are the biblical concepts of trusteeship, image-bearing, economic justice, and human community.

Trusteeship

The biblical concept of *trusteeship* begins in Genesis with creation and the role of humans within it. In Genesis 1:28, just after the creation of humankind, God charges them to

Be fruitful and multiply, and fill the earth and subdue it; and have dominion over the fish of the sea and over the birds of the air and over every living thing that moves upon the earth.

In Genesis 2:15 God puts man in the Garden of Eden "to till it and keep it."

It is clear that God gave humans *dominion* over the earth from the beginning. What did that dominion involve? It required men and women to take on responsibility with corresponding authority. Each of the two was given power over the earth and its creatures. This power was for the purposes of working the world and of taking care of it, a balance of development and conservation.

Does this dominion imply that humans own these resources? No. The Bible underscores time and again that God is both creator and owner of resources. In Psalm 50, the voice of the Lord says:

For every wild animal of the forest is mine,
    the cattle on a thousand hills.
I know all the birds of the air,
    and all that moves in the field is mine.
If I were hungry, I would not tell you,
    for the world and all that is in it is mine.
                    (Psalm 50:10-12)

The New Testament adds to this understanding of ownership by cautioning us

Do not store up for yourselves treasures on earth, where moth and rust consume and where thieves break in and steal, but store up for yourselves treasures in heaven. . . . For where your treasure is, there your heart will be also. (Matthew 6:19-21)

The parable of the ten minas in Luke 19 gives us the motif of God as the property owner who gives different talents to each servant to be used to further the master's interests. Scripture repeatedly emphasizes that God is the owner.

What then is our position as humans? We are not owners of creation in its natural, human, machine, or monetary form. Our job is one of trusteeship. We are servants for the Master who expects us to exercise the knowledge, skill, and power bestowed on us.

All of this does not require that we throw away the legal structure of private property. However, we look at private ownership differently. It becomes a mechanism that trustees can use to accomplish God's purposes. It becomes a right that has obligations to the human community attached. Private property carries trusteeship responsibility toward God, toward the people God has created, and toward creation.

Humans as Images of God

The Genesis account of creation also describes humans as images of God. In Genesis 1:26 God says:

Let us make humankind in our image, according to our likeness.

And in Genesis 1:27 the author writes,

So God created humankind in his image, in the image of God he created him; male and female he created them.

Hundreds of books and articles have been written about humans as images of God. The exact meaning of this image is a source of continuous discussion by theologians. However, some core elements of this concept are relevant for our discussion.

First, humans as images of God are creatures in relationship. God is already in relationship as Father, Son, and Holy Spirit. God is in relationship to the humans God has created. If humans are images of God, we, too, must be in relationship to God and to other humans. Without relationships both between God and humans and among humans that are cultivated and grow, we are less than fully human. We are less than true images of God.

The nature of these relationships in a perfect world was one of complete harmony. Man and woman walked and talked with God in the Garden of Eden. The first human community between the man and woman was one of total commitment, total interdependence, and a perfect intertwining of needs, resources, and responsibilities. This is the model for humans in community, humans as images of God.

Second, image-bearing humans were made as the crown of creation. Their creation position was one of great dignity. Humans were the last and most complex work of our Creator God. They were endowed with talents, skills, and knowledge far beyond those of the other creatures. They had far more authority and responsibility than the other creatures.

Humans as images of God are meant to have power. Naming the animals was no small delegation of authority. In biblical times the name given determined the creature's nature. The name giver had that power. Throughout the Old Testament God endowed power and expected performance that frequently exceeded the wildest dreams of its recipients. Joseph, Moses, Deborah, Elijah, Esther, Daniel — all were ordinary people from whom God expected great effort to further the Kingdom.

God expects performance from each of us to the utmost of our abilities to further the Kingdom in our world. God is concerned about what we do with the earthly resources entrusted to each one of us. Our Creator monitors our decisions about how resources are used, what is produced, how it is produced, and how it is marketed. Each human is charged to be the best possible trustee of each decision and resource within his or her control.

Finally, that humans are images of God implies that humans are beings who have the ability and responsibility to make decisions. That capacity was part of creation, although humans abused that decision-making capacity in eating from the tree in the garden. Yet God's design was for humans who make choices. They could choose names for animals. They could choose what food to eat. They could even choose to disobey God — the ultimate choice for each person. The capacity to make choices is a significant and natural part of us as created beings.

Economic Justice

Providing the Basics

The themes of economic justice are woven throughout both the Old and New Testaments. One theme was the obligation to care for the disadvantaged by providing access to the necessities of life. Every seventh year the crops were not to be sowed or harvested for the expressed purpose of leaving the land available for the poor (Exodus 23:11). In Leviticus 19:9-10 the law states:

> When you reap the harvest of your land, you shall not reap to the very edges of your field, or gather the gleanings of your harvest. You shall not strip your vineyard bare or gather the fallen grapes of your vineyard; you shall leave them for the poor and the alien.

This theme of concern for the disadvantaged was carried on in the New Testament as well. In James 1:27 the author writes:

> Religion that is pure and undefiled before God, the Father, is this: to care for orphans and widows in their distress. . . .

Beyond access to necessities, a second rule of economic justice concerned the ability of everyone to provide for his or her household. Not only should there be access to the necessities of life; there should also be opportunity to hold the resources required to provide for one's household. People were not to be permanently cut off from income-generating resources.

In Old Testament society the primary resources included land and flocks. Holding land was the economic opportunity to grow crops, to plant vineyards, and to raise sheep or cattle. In an agrarian society, land was a key resource that guaranteed a household's economic position.

God did not allow a household to be permanently cut off from this primary resource. In the account of rules for the Year of Jubilee God tells the children of Israel:

> The land must not be sold in perpetuity, for the land is mine; with me you are but aliens and tenants. Throughout the land that you hold, you shall provide for the redemption of the land. (Leviticus 25:23-24)

In verses 25-28 God goes on to explain how the redemption of the land should occur. Either the original owner or a relative of the original owner could buy back the land. However, if the original owner did not have the means to buy it back, then

> what was sold shall remain with the purchaser until the year of Jubilee; in the year of Jubilee it shall be released and the property shall be returned. (v. 28)

The point of this action would seem to be that economic justice requires a renewal of each household's long-term claim on a resource crucial for its economic livelihood.

The recurring thesis of these and other passages is that the disadvantaged in a society should have access to the necessities of life. This included the opportunity to be part of the economic life of the community. If the poor were willing and able to work, there was opportunity for work and for the rewards of work. In addition, the disadvantaged should not be permanently cut off from income-generating resources within the community.

Differences in Talents and Outcomes

Not only is access to necessities and resources required, but the Bible also concerns itself with the distribution of the results of work. Some Christians argue that Scripture teaches that equal standards of living should prevail for all workers. Beyond providing access to necessities and key resources, they believe that *equal* rewards should result.

However, the Scriptures do not seem clearly to support that thesis. Instead, we find in Scripture the concept of equitable relations between re-

sponsibilities, risk taking, and reward. In Matthew 25, the parable of the talents indicates that the servants were responsible to take risks commensurate with the different talents entrusted to them. Despite differences in talents, the concern was whether they did the best with what they had in their control. On that basis two of the servants were rewarded with greater responsibilities. The unrewarded servant was the one unwilling to take risks with the talent given.

Paul reinforces the respect for work performance in Ephesians 4:28 when he writes,

> Thieves must give up stealing; rather let them labor and work honestly with their own hands, so as to have something to share with the needy.

If people benefited from hard work, they were not condemned because there was an unequal distribution of rewards. However, if their motivation was money, if they behaved unethically in acquiring wealth, if they flaunted their wealth, and if they lacked concern for the disadvantaged, they were harshly condemned.

When differences in resources, talents, risk taking, and reward did occur, those with accumulated wealth had greater responsibilities for the community. Paul, in 1 Timothy 6:17-18, writes,

> As for those who in the present age are rich, command them not to be haughty, or to set their hopes on the uncertainty of riches, but rather on God who richly provides us with everything for our own enjoyment. They are to do good, to be rich in good works, generous, and ready to share.

Scripture seems to recognize that work performance among other variables will result in different outcomes. However, the rule is one of generosity and sharing, so that

> The one who had much did not have too much, and the one who had little did not have too little. (2 Corinthians 8:15)

Biblical Community

One more biblical theme has a powerful effect on work. Work and the results of work are described as cooperative efforts. The point of work was to glorify God by building up the human community. In 1 Corinthians 12, in his discussion of gifts, Paul writes,

> Now there are varieties of gifts, but the same Spirit; and there are varieties of services, but the same Lord; and there are varieties of activities, but it is the same God who activates all of them in everyone. To each is given the manifestation of the Spirit for the common good. (1 Corinthians 12:4-7)

Paul goes on to describe the work of the Christian community as the work of a human body. He argues:

> But as it is, God arranged the members in the body, each one of them, as he chose. If all were a single member, where would the body be? As it is, there are many members, yet one body. (1 Corinthians 12:18-20)

No parts of the body are to be considered disposable or inferior.

> On the contrary, the members of the body that seem to be weaker are indispensable, and those members of the body that we think less honorable we clothe with greater honor, and our less respectable members are treated with greater respect. (1 Corinthians 12:22-23)

The point of these passages is that, in our work for Christ and God's Kingdom, maintaining and enriching a sense of community is a crucial part of the process. We are mutual servants of each other. Some may argue that these passages are models for the Christian church, not for society at large. Yet if the church that Christ heads is the city on the hill, is it not logical to emulate the model? If our work in organizations is to unfold the Kingdom, then despite differences in talent and capacity for work, doing so in harmony and community is required.

In summary, these biblical themes describe God's ordained humans as powerful trustees and decision makers promoting economic justice and as people in community. Each created human being is charged with these obligations but also has these rights by nature.

Biblical Ideals Linked to Participation and Ownership

How are these scriptural ideas about humans and economics linked to issues of employee participation and ownership of organizations?

Participation in Decisions

Let's start by addressing the issue of employee participation in decision making. Why should evangelical Christians vigorously work for the greatest employee participation?

Our biblical vision of each human being was as a person who has responsibility, authority, and choice-making capacities. Each person is charged to develop his or her talents and be a trustee of resources. How can a person be a decision-making trustee before God in jobs that require no decisions and give no control over resources? Can an assembly worker whose job requires only that he or she press a button so that a machine welds four joints on each passing item sense trusteeship? The sense of decision making is very limited in this job structure.

However, you may not be able to do away with this job easily. Somehow the work must be done. Yet aren't there ways to allow for broader participation for that employee? Can't the employee's job be enlarged to include responsibilities for defects in inputs and outputs, maintenance of smoothly functioning machines, knowledge of what to do when machines break down? Could that assembly worker be included in regular decision making about quality of raw materials, ways to improve machine productivity, the frequency of routine machine maintenance, and the flow of goods in process through the plant? All such changes would increase the opportunities for that employee to become a fuller trustee, fuller decision maker, more fully human.

We cannot be utopian in our vision. Each person has different talents, skills, knowledge, wisdom, and personal circumstances. Not every person is equipped to make all decisions. The market research manager should have a different scope of decision making than the supervisor in accounts payable, simply because of differences in capability. It may not be wise for someone with heavy family or community responsibilities to push for the broadest decision authority at work at the same time.

Nor would it be a particularly effective business community if every individual was involved in every decision. The good of the whole firm and its ability to compete requires some specialization of expertise and the decisions based on them.

Yet, the biblical picture is one in which talents are matched with resources and opportunities to be trustees. Every human has gifts. Every human should have decision-making opportunities. The question we must ask is whether many jobs in our culture do an adequate job of matching talents and responsibilities. All too often the answer is no.

Bob Schuler, manager of General Motors Island Division Trim Plant, tells this story. At a 1978 GM union-management conference an older man pointed out that GM's hourly workers are effective leaders in their families and communities but "when they come back into the plant you tell them to park their brains at the door because all you want is their hands." Schuler went on to say that this was a turning point for him. He is now intent on using workers' brains as well as their hands.

What this story suggests is that we have not done a good job of matching talents with responsibilities in the past. As our industries redress that balance via quality circles, team management, and other mechanisms for decentralizing business choices, we should applaud, encourage, and enact such changes ourselves. In doing so we contribute to humans as God created them, as choice-making, responsible, talented trustees.

Participation in Profits and Losses

This first conclusion may be a fairly easy one for us to endorse. Let's now raise a second question. Does the biblical vision of humans and economic justice require *direct* participation in the profits and losses of the firm? We are not asking about an individual's job. Instead we're asking about the financial results of our collective work. Can we as Christians be completely comfortable with traditional allocations of profits?

To answer that question we must first understand how profits are distributed in business. Profits end up in many different places. They become retained earnings that provide some of the capital for future company growth. They are the source

of returns to public or private stockholders in the form of dividends and growth in stock value. They reward upper-level managers who work long hours and carry worries home. They are the basis for contributions to charitable and community needs. They are the basis on which salaries and fringe benefits can be increased. It is naive to assume that profits in most traditional companies do *not* benefit employees. They do in the form of job security, job opportunity, faithful stockholders, the possibility of wage increases, and a better quality of community life.

Yet there are unanswered questions. Are the benefits noted above too far removed to develop a sense of community and of responsibility? Is *direct* distribution of some profits via employee profit sharing plans a better way for employees to share in the firm? If so, what constitutes an equitable distribution of profits?

Let's examine first whether direct allocation of profits is a sound biblical idea. The biblical concepts of economic justice and community we explored earlier argue for an equitable relationship between risk and return and the building of social community in the process. Does direct allocation of profits reflect that scriptural viewpoint?

One characteristic of profit sharing is the accountability it instills for the effort of the whole firm community. Each firm member contributes to the performance of every other firm member. Profit sharing encourages that sense of interdependence within the community since profits are the results of communal efforts. Profit sharing and loss sharing create a community of risk takers.

Individual wage increases do not build this sense of mutual identity and contribution. Wage increases are given to reflect increased costs of living and/or meritorious individual performance. They may serve the individual, but they do not build community.

Second, profit shares can emphasize our accountability for the end results. If the company turns out quality microwaves to the right markets at the right price and in the right places, the company may flourish and rewards flow back to employees. Each person feels some measure of responsibility for the decisions that were made along the way. Each member feels accountable for results. If humans were created to be accountable and responsible for the effort of the community as a whole, then profit sharing is one mechanism that accentuates these aspects of human beings. We build a community of risk and return as well as developing individuals who take risk and are rewarded. People together enjoy the fruits of their efforts or together suffer in the pain of their mistakes.

If we accept the thesis that Christians ought to encourage firm-wide profit sharing, the second question is how those profits should be distributed. In a recent newspaper article one of the major North American automakers was criticized for its distribution of profits. The corporation decided to pass out $169 million of its $2.14 billion profit in bonuses to executives but put nothing into profit sharing for blue collar workers. Each of 5,000 high-level employees averaged $33,000 in bonuses. UAW workers received zero in bonuses. Some would argue that that's understandable. Top-level executives have more education, skill, experience, and responsibility. To some degree such gaps may reflect legitimate differences between risk, responsibility, and return.

The problem is that beyond a certain point, gaps in return become fissures that cannot be bridged. The distances become too great. Human community breaks down. Lower-level employees are alienated while upper-level employees or stockholders relish their good fortune.

If this example is indicative of an acceptable system of bonus distribution, something is quite wrong. When our method of distributing profits results in alienation within the firm community, Christians should be disturbed.

What is fair? What is equitable? A good answer to that question would be a consultant's goldmine. The answer will differ from one firm to another. It must consider the education, experience, skill, and even longevity of employees. However, some examples of rules about the range of distribution might help. In Ben and Jerry's, Homemade, Inc., a Vermont based maker of premium ice cream, the rule is that compensation for top-level employees should never exceed five times what the lowest level employees make. In the Oregon Plywood Co-ops the range is three to one. The point is that in the distribution of profit shares employers must consider the biblical call for equity between risks, responsibility, and return and then balance those with the scriptural mandate to build up the firm's human community.

There is one final problem in the equity gaps that can occur in profit sharing. Let me suggest that we see the relationship between employee risk and return far too narrowly.

Usually when we think of business risk we have mental pictures of financial risk. Buying a stock is a financial risk. Its value may go up or down. Starting your own business is an economic risk. Competitive forces could push you to bankruptcy. Or such a risk could propel you toward a standard of living about which you've only dreamed.

Yet risks are not only economic. Of course a person could lose their job. Yet, for employees the risks they take in joining any employer go beyond their financial bottom lines. For some workers, particularly in manufacturing, the risks are physical. For others, dealing with customers all day is a psychological risk. In all cases commitment to an employer is a risk of your personal, family, and community future. Ask former workers whose companies have closed plants. Many have lost a way for their families to stay in their community. They have lost future opportunities for developing their skills and knowledge. They wonder what life would have been like if they had chosen a different employer twenty years ago.

The point is that in distributing rewards perhaps we underestimate the risk employees take in joining a given firm. To decide what is an equitable distribution of profit shares we must take these risks into account.

Christian concern for economic justice and enhanced human community support the desirability of equitable direct profit sharing. However, we need to travel one further step in our analysis. How should we look at the structure of ownership?

Participation in Ownership

Our models of firm ownership are few. We think of private ownership, where an individual or small group of investors hold all company stock. We think of public ownership via stock sold on the open market to individual and institutional investors. We think of state ownership, an option we decry as socialism. Then we debate which of these forms of ownership is the most efficient and the most just. But we envision little else.

We need to look for other models based on biblical principles. To start we must go back to our concept of biblical trusteeship. The right to be a trustee is an inherent part of humans. It is part of our image as God created us. Each of us was expected to be a trustee of the material and human world. There is no question of ownership. The only question is what are the most biblical approaches to structuring our trusteeship.

How is this right to trusteeship worked out in the firm? Is trusteeship only control over the resources immediately needed to do one's job? Or does trusteeship require a sense of responsibility for the whole enterprise? In other words, does trusteeship require that employees hold the firm's capital stock? Or is trusteeship a developmental process by which we become ready to be trustees over a greater and greater pool of resources as our commitment to the organization grows?

To begin to answer these questions we must first examine the role of stock in a company. Common stock is viewed as one of several sources of financing for a company. When stock is issued, the buyers of the stock exchange their cash for title to stock shares. These people who have title to the stock have secured three rights. They have a claim on the assets of the firm. They have the right to any increase in the value of the stock shares and accompanying dividends. They have the right to vote on key decisions about the directors and managers of the company and the financial structure of the firm. While distant stockholders in very large companies may not take these rights too seriously, stock does convey a right to share in the returns on risk and to participate in key decisions of this business firm community. Are these rights which should be extended to all employees?

In the previous sections of this paper I argued that developing trusteeship requires that we cultivate a sense of the interrelationship of resources, risk, and return. We have also noted that being creatures in the image of God requires decision-making participation. We have also suggested that building community interdependence within the firm is an important Kingdom characteristic. When companies deny employees the opportunity to own stock they withhold a key avenue for building accountability, participation, and community. Furthermore, lack of participation in holding stock creates another problem. It denies access to an income-generating resource for the economic development of each household whose future is uniquely tied to the future of this firm.

Without broad employee participation in ownership, what happens? All too frequently in public companies a network of detached institutional and individual owners watches stock values, gambling that they'll go up. If they are sluggish or decline they simply sell the stock, severing ownership. There is no real community between investors and employees. Is there ever a real concern for the products, the customers, the firm's human community?

While we need not abolish all publicly held shares of stock, a different balance of ownership seems better. Majority ownership by those accountable to and for the firm's products, customers, and internal community seems to logically place the burden and joys of trusteeship where they belong.

Our models of ownership need expansion. As Christians we need to make more room for employee ownership. More employee ownership is a better route in light of the biblical calls for trusteeship, image bearing, community, and economic justice.

Principles and Remaining Problems — the Effects of Sin

If we could live in the Garden of Eden again the transition to greater participation in decision making, broader profit sharing, and wider stock holding within the firm would be easy. Yet until Christ returns we remain in a sinful world. In planning for these changes we must recognize limitations. We must structure all effort carefully around imperfectly motivated people, limits on human capacities, and an amorphous concept of equity.

Despite our created natures, sinful people don't always shine as trustees. They may reject the satisfactions of a more complex job for a boring job that leaves the responsibilities with someone else. They may be unable or unwilling to share the risks and headaches of participation. They may not even perceive the value of profit shares or ownership when comparing their lot with employees of other firms.

Human beings can make poor decisions, motivated primarily by short-term, self-serving indulgence. Without safeguards, employee ownership could lead to decisions to enjoy the profits now and shortchange future research and machinery requirements. The group decisions of non-Christian peers could make things difficult for Christian workers in some instances.

The key is to build in checks and balances to prevent misdirected or uninformed persons from destroying the firm community. Even the most participative, one-hundred percent employee owned cooperatives have unbreakable rules about profit retention for future company growth and appropriate methods of profit distribution. Every plan must be clearly and continuously explained to employees to be effective.

Every person's talent, skill, and knowledge has its own unique limitations. To ask a barely literate laborer to make complex decisions about strategies for market share growth ignores the state in which we are. As we grow in participation we must carefully match individuals with appropriate spheres of influence at appropriate times in their lives. Then we must help individuals to develop their potential for greater involvement. But it is no service to the individual or the firm community to push any person beyond their created, acquired, or circumstantial capacities.

Finally we must deal with the equity problem. We all have inherent rights to be trustees, but what counts in distributing varying shares of our trusteeship? Is it desires, ability, performance, education, or experience? How broad should differences in decision making, profit sharing, and ownership be from the bottom to the top of the organization? Commitment and faithful service over time are worthy of reward. Those with the greatest commitment may also have taken the greatest risks. Yet the needs to build community must balance the resulting inequities.

What Can Be

During the 1940s a Catholic parish priest in the Basque region of Spain taught a handful of young cathechumens about church teachings on work, wealth, and community. These young men, with their priest's guidance, formed the first Basque cooperative in Mondragon, Spain. They believed that God had created people to work together, to share the decisions, the ownership, and the rewards. Today there are over 200 Mondragon cooperatives employing over 20,000 people. They are the top producers of quality home appliances in Spain, which are exported all over Europe. They are supported by a modern research and development facility, an economic development bank, their own technical college, and a host of other services, all cooperatively owned and managed. A council of worker-owners hire the general managers and make strategic business decisions. Each worker is also an owner, sharing the risks of losses and the rewards of profit. In thirty years, a poor, destitute people have turned this region into one of the most economically powerful regions in Europe. And it started with a few Christian principles about work, wealth, and community.

For American Christians who embrace the need for greater economic democracy, the road ahead has potholes of uncertainty, ambiguity, and mistake. But I am convinced that biblical trusteeship, image bearing, justice, and community call us to lead this effort. And when we do, we may be awed at what God will do through us.

Theory Fastball

Max De Pree

The common wisdom these days seems to be that American managers have to learn to motivate employees to be more effective and more productive. Based on my 35 years of experience at Herman Miller, I'm going to take the risk of disagreeing with the common wisdom. Employees bring their *own* motivation. Managers have to start by understanding that. What people need from work is to be liberated, to be involved, to be accountable, and to reach for their potential. At Herman Miller, we believe that more and more people are winning the struggle for identity and meaning at work, and fewer are losing out to anonymity and frustration. It is our job as managers to help them *all* be winners.

Now, that may sound like a tall order for a furniture company based in the unlikely sounding town of Zeeland, Michigan, where there are no bars, no pool halls, and no theatres. But we've found that what people want, and care about, and work for is pretty much the same in Zeeland as it is in a lot of other places where we have offices, places like Atlanta and Dallas, where they *do* have bars and pool halls. The relationship of Herman Miller and its employees has developed over the years because we have had some very special people working with us, people who have made a significant contribution to Herman Miller. They were able to make their contributions because D. J. De Pree, founder of Herman Miller (and, to keep the record straight, my father), had the strength to abandon himself to the wild ideas of others. In the 1930's, when he knew the company couldn't survive by making period reproductions and im-

itating European designs much longer, he listened when the famous designer Gilbert Rhode walked in and told him that modern life was going to require a different kind of furniture — furniture that required better craftsmanship and precise manufacturing techniques. He told D. J. that Herman Miller shouldn't make furniture, it should make a new way of life.

When Rhode died, D. J. was left with a company that had a commitment to design, but no designer. How was he going to get designers to come to Zeeland, Michigan? He did it by inviting designers to come to a place where they could have a free hand — a company in which design is as important as sales or production. D. J. promised that no design would be changed without the designer's participation and approval. There would be no reliance on market research; the company would not be concerned with what was already popular. If designers and top management thought something was good, it would be put into production. D. J. and the early designers made one very important decision, one that it took a lot of courage to make, and they stuck with it: They decided that there was a market for good design.

Gilbert Rhode had introduced a number of original design concepts, such as the sectional sofa and the Executive Office Group (which had 15 components out of which 400 things could be made). The next important designer D. J. brought in was George Nelson. And Nelson brought in Charles Eames, who revolutionized furniture design. Some of Eames' more significant design innovations were:

- Molded plywood chairs
- The Eames lounge chair and ottoman
- Molded plastic chairs that are stackable
- Tandem sling seating

Eames designs were honored by the Museum of Modern Art in 1946 in the museum's first one-man show.

In 1960, The Herman Miller Research Corporation was founded, and the sculptor/artist/inventor Robert Propst was put in charge of it. He was told that he could look for new ideas, concepts, and solutions to problems without any regard for what Herman Miller could or should make.

From Max De Pree, *Leadership Is an Art* (New York: Doubleday, 1987).

Here are some of the projects he has undertaken:

- The development of a litter for burn victims.
- A mechanical, automatic bed-chair for quadriplegics.
- An office van for a quadriplegic lawyer with handicapped clients.
- A design of an environment for a new approach to business school education at Southern Methodist University.
- The Action Office System which allows workers to use multiple work surfaces and display areas to shape an office for their individual needs (the first "open office").
- The Coherent Structures, or Co/Struc, system of mobile containers, frames, carts, and rails designed to streamline the service functions of a hospital.

But commitment to research, innovation, and design has only been part of the Herman Miller story. There has also been a commitment to the community — each year Herman Miller makes a sizable donation to non-profit organizations, charities, and colleges in the communities in which its offices and factories are located. For example, when the people of Zeeland decided to turn the main street of the town into a mall, they were able to complete the project with no Federal or state funds, partly due to the leadership of Herman Miller. We contributed money, of course, but more important, we contributed people with special talents who could help get the job done.

And there is one more commitment that Herman Miller has made — in some ways the most important one. It is the commitment to all the people who work with us to turn a designer's vision into a real chair.

Let me illustrate the importance of this commitment with a story:

Theory Fastball

In the mid-60's, my wife's brother, Jim Kaat, was a major league baseball pitcher with the Minnesota Twins, and their team won the pennant. They played the Los Angeles Dodgers in the World Series, and my brother-in-law had the unique op-portunity of pitching against the famous Sandy Koufax three times in that World Series, winning one and losing two, which is not a bad record against a man of Koufax's outstanding talent.

After the World Series, I had the chance to ask my brother-in-law about Koufax's greatness. He explained that the man is unusually talented, is beautifully disciplined and trained, and was probably, in his prime, the greatest pitcher in baseball. "In fact," he said, "one of the real problems with playing against Koufax is that he is the only major league pitcher whose fastball could be heard to hum from the opposing dugout. It was a real problem because the opposing batters, instead of being noisily active in their own dugout, would sit silently and listen for that fastball to hum. They would take their turn at the plate already intimidated."

This led me to make what, at the time, was a glib comment, but what I have since come to realize was a fundamental management principle. I told my brother-in-law that I could give him the answer to the problem of Koufax's fastball. When he asked me what that was, I said, "Make me his catcher."

You see, I am such an unskilled catcher that Koufax would have to throw the ball more slowly to me, and we would thus deprive him of his greatest weapon. The point, of course, is that in the process of work many of us are outstanding pitchers, able to throw the telling fastball, but it is also true that those pitchers can only be effective if there are many of us who are outstanding catchers.

And while Herman Miller has become *famous* because of its star pitchers — our designers — we have only been *successful* because of the outstanding catchers who produced and sold their designs. In fact, we like to think we have been more than successful. When we talk about success, we are talking about being number 735 on the *Fortune* 1000 (and 49th in return on investment!). But at Herman Miller, we also talk about the difference between being successful and being exceptional. Being successful is meeting goals in a good way — being exceptional is reaching your potential.

There are two practices I want to mention here that are part of the process of building exceptional "battery mates." And then I want to share with you some of the assumptions behind the practices, some questions, a vision of what work can and should be, and finally, I propose a series of personal rights.

The Scanlon Plan

First, there's the Scanlon Plan. Using a Scanlon Plan may not be the easiest way to run a business, but we're convinced that it's the best way. It allows our people the opportunity to develop their potential as individuals. And it allows the company — the collection of those individuals — to prosper more than it could hope to otherwise.

There are four primary Scanlon principles relating to all Herman Miller people, regardless of level or location:

- Identity — They should feel they belong and that they are meaningfully involved and responsible.
- Participation — They should feel that they not only have the possibility of influencing the decision process, but the responsibility to do so.
- Equity — They should realize a fair return for their personal investments.
- Accountability — They should be responsible within their respective jobs for the overall success of the organization.

Scanlon involves everyone, from the president to the newest salesperson or production worker, in the management of the company through a network of work teams, caucuses, and councils. Also, Scanlon provides a system for communicating the corporation's performance on a monthly, quarterly, semi-annual, and annual basis. The monthly performance measurement is reflected in a bonus paid to all full-time employees in proportion to their base pay.

Employee Ownership

The other practice I want to mention is really a process that started more than 20 years ago, when stock was sold to a small group of executives who were making a career commitment to the company. This was the beginning of employee ownership at Herman Miller. Today, we are one of the few public companies in the United States that has 100% of its full-time regular employees (who have completed one year of service) as stockholders.

Employee stock ownership is, of course, synergistic with the participative management process of the Scanlon Plan. But it is important to understand that nothing is being *given*. Ownership is *earned* and *paid for*. The heart of it is profit sharing, and there is no sharing if there are no profits. There is no soft-headed paternalism at play here. Rather, there is a certain morality in connecting shared accountability with shared ownership. This lends a rightness and a permanence to the relationship of each of us to our work and to each other. Our employees have proved that they agree with the idea of shared ownership. Over 40% purchase additional stock through monthly payroll deductions.

There are some important implications of employee stock ownership. The first has to do with risk. I don't think there's a serious investor in the stock market who doesn't know that there are losses as well as gains, and that the action of external forces (in spite of good performance by Herman Miller) makes our stock price unpredictable. And while it's great to work for gains, one also has to be ready for the losses.

Second, as owners, we become more accountable for our personal performance. Owners can't walk away from business concerns. So, as owners, the accountability of all of us begins to change.

Third, we're now in a unique competitive position. I can't think of a single one of our competitors who can say to a customer, "When you place your order with us, *everyone* serving you is an owner." This is particularly important when one realizes that in the "systems furniture" business the only effective relationship between customer and supplier is a long-term relationship based primarily on quality of design and of product and of service. To me, then, employee ownership is a competitive necessity. For Herman Miller employees stock ownership is a declaration of identity. (The other day I was having lunch in the cafeteria with one of our employees from Human Resources, who said to me, "Max, I never dreamed I'd be a capitalist.")

While the employee stock ownership program seems like the end of a 20-year process, it is really the beginning of a transition to a new way of working and serving together. This new situation demands new attitudes on our part. And, as you know, changes in skills and changes in behavior are always easier to make than changes in attitude.

New Assumptions

So here are the assumptions on which these changes are based:

My first assumption is that the great majority of us in the western world who work can be properly classified as volunteers. Our mobility and flexibility, along with our "group power" (and we belong to a number of groups, many of them advocate groups), along with our loyalty to our disciplines, make us different from the previous generations of workers.

The second assumption is that while the physical environment surely counts, what *really* counts is the management environment. I believe that the management environment is an expression of the personal philosophy of the leaders of an organization.

My third assumption is that for most of us who work, there exists an exasperating discontinuity between how we see ourselves as persons and how we see ourselves as workers. This sense of discontinuity is best understood, I believe, when one thinks about a series of personal questions asked from the perspective of the one with whose productivity we're concerned:

- Does what I do count?
- Does what I do make a difference to anybody?
- Why should I come here?
- Can I be somebody here?
- Is there *for me* any rhyme or reason here?
- Can I "own" this place?
- Do I have any rights?
- Does coming here add any richness to my life?
- Is this a place where I can learn something?
- Would I show this place to my family — or am I ashamed to show it to them — or does it just not matter?
- Is there anybody here I can trust?
- Is this place open to *my* influence?

We in management are prone to search for the key to productivity in money and "perks" and in the complexity of materialism. And it is so easy to lose our way in politically-dictated "togetherness." Managers today are so afraid of change and of disruption and of tension — and yet, these are exactly what we need: constructive change, renewing disruption, and creative tension.

To eliminate that sense of discontinuity and to restore a sense of coherence in our lives, perhaps we should give poets and philosophers the opportunity to lead and manage corporations for a time. I say that because I believe that what is needed is a vision of what work can be and should be. Work is one of our greatest privileges, and I believe that work should be and can be

- productive and rewarding,
- meaningful and maturing,
- challenging and demanding,
- enriching and fulfilling,
- healing and joyful.

A Person's Rights

I would like to suggest that one way to begin implementing this vision may be to consider a short series of person's rights:

The Right to be Needed

Managers must provide workers with a genuine opportunity to use their gifts — their own individual gifts. In the long run, I'm convinced that this is the best way to meet the group's needs. If you have a great shortstop, don't ask him to play first base.

The Right to Understand

There are a lot of things wrapped up in this right — the right to understand the company mission, the right to understand personal career opportunities, the right to understand the relationship between the employee and the company (and I'm not talking about the union contract). One of the ways Herman Miller encourages understanding is tied back to the Scanlon Plan. The second Friday of every month is Scanlon Day, which is devoted to meetings designed to ensure that every employee knows what is going on in the company. At those meetings, we not only talk about the Scanlon results, we talk about customer service performance, quality performance, field problems and opportunities, production goals for the immediate future, special business programs, and much more. Employees are encouraged to ask questions about the Scanlon results and the company's performance.

The Right to be Involved

Managers need to arrange for involvement. And this is something not to be taken lightly. A manager can't invite people to contribute their ideas and then ignore the contributors. Translating the ideas into action has to be a cooperative process. All Herman Miller managers understand that it is mandatory to follow up and respond to employee suggestions — even if the response is, "We aren't going to do it."

The Right to a Covenantal Relationship

There is a difference between a covenant relationship and a contractual one. Both are commitments. A contractual relationship tends to be legal, based on reciprocity, and frequently fails under the pressures of conflict and change. A covenantal relationship, on the other hand, is one which is based on shared commitments to ideas, to issues, to values, and to goals. Covenantal relationships enable work to have meaning and to be fulfilling. They make possible relationships that can manage conflict and change. At Herman Miller, the covenant between employee and company includes an understanding that job security is directly related to performance — we all need to perform, or no one's job is secure.

The Right to Affect One's Own Destiny

Few elements in the work process are as important to personal dignity as the opportunity to influence one's own future. Managers must not evaluate, transfer, promote, or otherwise affect the life of an employee without the involvement of the person concerned.

The Right to be Accountable

To be accountable, an individual needs the opportunity to make a contribution to the group's goals, to share in the ownership of the group's problems, and to have this contribution measured according to previously understood and agreed standards of performance. Managers need to establish an adult-to-adult relationship with their employees.

The Right to Appeal

Managers must build into their organizations a nonthreatening avenue of appeal to ensure against any arbitrary leadership behavior which may threaten any of the PERSON'S RIGHTS. In fact, I'd like to suggest that the most important responsibility of leaders is to guarantee these rights to those they lead.

Those assumptions, that vision of work, and that sense of a person's rights are behind the practices of Herman Miller.

In earlier years, D. J. De Pree used to speak of the "impounded energy" in our products. He was referring to the thought, the caring, the consciousness of quality that went into our design and manufacturing processes. Now, when I think of impounded energy, I see it in terms of the whole company. There's energy there, and excitement.

Cooperative Capitalism

Yes, we live in turbulent times. Yes, interest rates are high, international competition is increasing, demographic trends are producing a changing work force. But I can't help but be optimistic.

I'm optimistic that something new and positive is starting to happen to the capitalist system in the United States.

Historically, capitalism has been fraught with adversarial relationships — labor versus management, supplier versus producer, retailer versus consumer. But it's important to remember how young the United States is, and how young the idea of capitalism is. I believe we're at the threshold of achieving all that capitalism can become.

There is much that can be done to improve our system, and at Herman Miller we are committed to doing everything we can to move the capitalist system from those historical, adversarial postures to a person-oriented posture of cooperation. I believe that, in our own way, in our own company, we have the opportunity to affect our own destiny.

I believe that what Herman Miller is doing should be part of our vision as a Nation. Herman Miller is committed to being an example of a corporation that practices a new level of capitalism —a shared and humanistic capitalism. Fortunately, there are a lot of good companies out there doing the same kind of thing. And that is where our hope lies.

Corporate Democracy and the Legacy of the South African Divestment Movement

Robert Kinloch Massie

Twenty years ago, on May 21, 1971, an event took place at the annual meeting of the General Motors Corporation in Cobo Hall in Detroit which marked the beginning of a new era in corporate governance. On that day, the Presiding Bishop of the Episcopal Church, John Hines, resplendent in his purple clerical shirt, appeared at the microphone during the time reserved for questions and asked the board of directors of the nation's largest auto company to support a shareholder resolution filed by his church which asked the firm to withdraw from South Africa.

This was not the first time that church leaders had tried to change corporate policies — there had already been considerable disagreement over civil rights and the war in Vietnam. Nor was it the first time that corporate executives had found their normal somnolent annual meetings turned into political boxing rings — this had already taken place at Eastman Kodak, Chase Manhattan Bank, and even General Motors the year before, when a movement sponsored by Ralph Nader had criticized the homogeneity and unresponsiveness of the board. What was significant was that the head of a major religious denomination, one which counted many members of the elite in its pews, had come to challenge the head of a cor-

Robert Kinloch Massie, "Corporate Democracy and the Legacy of the South African Divestment Movement," *The Christian Century*, 24 July 1991, pp. 716-20.

poration in person. Even more important was what Hines said in his letter and in his speech. Though, as one would expect, he based part of his argument for General Motors' withdrawal on the moral outrage of apartheid, he did not stop there. He argued that the Episcopal Church, which possessed 12,574 shares of General Motors stock, had the right to make such a request because the church was an *owner* of the corporation.

The assertion of ownership cut General Motors Chairman James Roche and his bevy of managers to the quick. Less than six weeks before Roche himself had rejected criticisms of General Motors' social behavior by arguing that his primary moral obligation was to the stockholders, who were the legal owners. "Management must be responsive to the wishes of the stockholders," he had told a group of executives in Chicago, "Management is obliged to inform the stockholders of the costs and benefits [of different actions and] . . . then managers must abide by the owner's decisions. Through his proxy every stockholder has the right to decide and must exercise it."

Like most American executives, Roche thought this was safe to do, because stockholders were normally invisible and mute. Nearly forty years before, Adolph Berle and Gardiner Means had demonstrated in their landmark book, *The Modern Corporation and Private Property*, that corporate shares had become so widely disbursed that ownership had effectively been separated from control. This separation had been increased by the so-called "Wall Street Rule," a tradition which dictated that persons satisfied with managerial performance held on to their stock; if they became dissatisfied, they sold it to someone else, who retained it as long as they remained content. In such a system, possession equalled approval. Managers rarely heard from shareholders because all the malcontents conveniently bailed out.

Even if a few cantankerous shareholders squawked, the executives still had little to fear because they controlled, through the annual ritual of proxy voting, the majority of all outstanding shares of the corporation. They were also protected from litigation under the so-called "Business Judgment Rule," which forbade judicial reversal of decisions taken in good faith. While a corporate executive might occasionally run into trouble with the bankers and other suppliers of

capital, a strong culture united executives in different businesses. Difficulties could be further reduced by inviting bankers, lawyers, and other business people to join the corporate board. At the time of Hines's confrontation with Roche, the board of General Motors was made up of twenty-four men. Twenty-three of them were white business stalwarts. The twenty-fourth and most recent appointee was the Rev. Leon Sullivan, the pastor of the Zion Baptist Church in Philadelphia and the founder of training programs for inner city young people. Sullivan had been picked only a few months before in response to the Nader challenge, thereby becoming the first black among the thousands of directors of top American companies. Sullivan surely caused the directors to question their decision to appoint him when, at that same tumultuous annual meeting, he stood up and supported Bishop Hines in a passionate sermon against investment in South Africa.

To understand the effect of the South African divestment question on corporate democracy, we need briefly to consider the myths and realities of corporate governance. Though it sounds bizarre, American capitalists today govern their corporations in almost exactly the same way that the Communist Party used to run the Soviet government. Like the Politburo, American corporate governance rests on an illusory theory of democracy which disguises the self-perpetuating dictatorship of an elite. Like the Politburo, the fiction is symbolized in an annual farce in which a single slate officials — selected by the man at the top — was elected unanimously by an invisible electorate. Like the Politburo, the fiction also requires a few occasional appearances in public to give the illusion of responsiveness, though the obscure venue, the tight agenda, and the blizzard of propaganda usually control the unpredictable. Only two significant differences exist. The first — of immense importance — is that the American corporation, though striving to free itself from the control of the states, is still ruled by the laws and the courts of the United States federal government. The second is that at the annual public appearance a few precious minutes are offered each year to the tiny number of intrepid shareholders who managed to locate the microphone. And it was from that microphone that the bishop launched his challenge.

The last two decades have witnessed a dramatic

surge in the use of shareholder resolutions by religious denominations to present their points of view to American managers. Not long after the confrontation in Detroit several Protestant denominations banded together to form the Interfaith Center on Corporate Responsibility, a group designed to distribute information, analyze investment portfolios, and coordinate the filing of resolutions. In its twenty year history ICCR has filed thousands of resolutions with thousands of companies on issues like Third World debt; tobacco and infant formula marketing; nuclear weapons manufacture; environmental standards; non-discriminatory employment practices in the United States, South Africa, and Northern Ireland; animal rights; and affordable housing. By 1991 ICCR's membership had risen to 55 Protestant denominations and more than 200 Roman Catholic archdioceses and orders.

The continuous filing of such shareholder resolutions has gone a long way towards implementing the vision of corporate democracy which a post-depression Congress wrote into law in the securities acts of the early 1930s. Though the churches' appeals are restricted to five hundred words and buried inside pages of pro-management prose, the simple requirement that a potentially embarrassing message must be included in a mailing to millions of disinterested shareholders has prompted managers to negotiate with the churches. Each year approximately one quarter of all resolutions are withdrawn by their religious proponents after managers have agreed in private meetings to provide the requested information or change the relevant policy.

Sometimes corporations take longer to react, but religious perseverance has usually paid off. In 1978, nearly seven years after Polaroid first reviewed their policies towards South Africa, executives of Eastman Kodak wrote to the head of the United Church of Christ Board of World Ministries and informed him that they would bar all sales of film and equipment to military and police if the church would withdraw its resolution. The Episcopal Church filed resolutions with Dresser Industries for four straight years asking them to sign the Sullivan employment principles; when the church filed a fifth time in 1984, Dresser executives announced at their annual meeting that they had decided to sign. In 1985, when the United

Church boards joined the New York City Employee Retirement System in filing a resolution asking Manufacturers Hanover not to make loans to South Africa, the bank executives committed themselves to such a policy in a private letter in exchange for the withdrawal of the measure. And in 1986, in an article in the *Wall Street Journal*, John Bryan, the chairman of Sara Lee, reported that he had finally decided to withdraw the firm from South Africa because he had been barraged by requests from major shareholders, including religious denominations, to leave. "No shareholder said 'Stay in,'" Bryan commented, "You can debate the moral question of whether it's better to stay or go, but the shareholder is the one who owns us. If he says 'Get out,' and it can be done without penalizing the company, that's what you do."

Bryan's candor was unusual. Managers, who struggle to carve out a range of discretion from the thicket of conflicting demands by customers, suppliers, employees, governments, and shareholders almost never admit that they were pressured to take any actions by anyone. When asked about shareholder resolutions or divestment, corporate executives usually point to the low percentage of total votes which most resolutions receive and argue that their influence is negligible. This, of course, neglects the resolutions which were withdrawn prior to voting. Moreover, preliminary research has shown that the true threshold for corporate response to shareholder activism is not a majority of 51% (which would be equivalent to the loss of control of the company) but around 10%. Few executives are willing to offend that many shareholders for very long, especially if the changes can be made swiftly, cheaply, and with little fanfare. As a result, hundreds of corporate reports have been written, policies altered, and changes implemented as the price of removing the irritant introduced by religious communities.

Even more important for the future of corporate democracy has been the effect of the continuous stream of shareholder resolutions on the policies of formerly dormant institutional investors. Institutional investors are organizations who control large chunks of other peoples' money, entities like universities, municipalities, foundations, religious denominations, public and private pension funds, and other endowments. When, in the early years, activists filed blunt demands for cor-

During 1985 the Trinity Center and the Resources Committee of the Trinity Church Vestry revised the Parish's policy on procedures relating to its social responsibility in investments. In Fall 1985 the Vestry approved the updated policy, which includes procedures for identifying ethical issues and for taking actions such as voting on shareholder resolutions.

In October 1985 Trinity Church held a four-part colloquy on South Africa. Twenty-five internationally-known speakers from business, foundation, government and religious communities of the United States, South Africa and England participated in discussions of the current crisis in South Africa.

Also at this time, the 68th General Convention of the Episcopal Church issued a resolution urging "the Church Pension Fund, all dioceses, parishes and affiliated institutions of the Episcopal Church to examine their portfolios with a view to identifying and divesting any holdings of companies doing business in South Africa and Namibia."

In accordance with Trinity Church's updated policy on social responsibility in investments, Dr. Robert Ray Parks, Rector of Trinity Church, named a special Ad Hoc Committee of the Vestry to study in depth the issue of Trinity's investments in companies doing business in South Africa.

In January 1986, the Ad Hoc Committee discussed a proposal for divestment submitted by the Trinity Center. The recommendation of the Ad Hoc Committee was taken up at the February 1986 meeting of the Vestry, which voted to divest the parish of all investments in companies doing business in South Africa effective immediately.

In concert with the discussion of Trinity's investments in South Africa, the Trinity Grants Board carefully reviewed its existing commitments to programs in that country. In February 1986 the Grants Board announced a program of grants to indigenous church groups in South Africa, with a commitment of $250,000 for 1986. The grants are intended to support indigenous work towards the amelioration of social and economic conditions in South Africa.

— Trinity Center for Ethics and Corporate Policy,
"Position Paper on South Africa," March 1986

---

porate withdrawal from South Africa, most of the trustees and officers of institutional investors thought the idea rash and voted instinctively with management. However, as the activists filed more reasonable requests — for information, for the improved labor practices named after Leon Sullivan, for a cessation of sales to the military or police — the institutional investors, under pressure to divest their stock in the companies completely, found the resolutions more and more appealing. Soon thousands of institutional investors across the nation had set up internal deliberative groups to evaluate the activists' claims and the corporations' responses. With each successive year the activists' claims seemed more acceptable and managers' assurances that American corporate investment would ease apartheid seemed less persuasive. By the end of the 1980s, hundreds of large investors were voting tens of millions of shares in favor of shareholder resolutions, which, only a few years before, would have seemed a radical challenge to management.

Perhaps most startling of all was the decision by some huge investors not just to *vote* for resolutions, but to begin *filing* them independently of ICCR. There is, for example, the remarkable story of Ned Regan, the Republican comptroller of the State of New York throughout the 1980s. Regan, by virtue of his office, was the sole trustee of the New York State Common Retirement Fund, a pension fund for state employees which totalled more than $30 billion during his tenure. Regan came under fierce pressure from Democrats throughout the state, including the governor and the comptroller of New York City, to divest the fund of companies doing business in South Africa. Regan refused, citing his fiduciary obligations to the plan beneficiaries. Instead, he announced, he would do something which he thought would be more effective: he would file resolutions with 104 companies in which the fund held millions of shares asking those firms to leave South Africa.

For American corporate managers who had grown accustomed to the presence of religious activists at annual meetings, the sudden appearance of the Republican comptroller of the State of New York, backed by millions of shares and demanding that the company leave South Africa, came as a nasty shock. It is worth noting that within a few months after Regan began his campaign in 1986, major corporations such as General Motors and IBM threw in the towel and sold their South African subsidiaries.

So what conclusions are we to draw? I would suggest that there are three.

1. First of all, the South African divestment movement revitalized the shareholder resolutions system and provided both the precedents and the mechanisms for the introduction of many other issues. As a result, we have witnessed in the last two decades the development of a non-governmental system by which moral issues can be introduced into managerial calculations through the capital markets. Moreover, we have seen that such activism has not been restricted to religious leaders but has now become a tool used by a wide variety of institutional investors.

2. Pension funds, which began growing at an enormously fast rate after the passage of federal legislation in 1974, now control more than half of all the commonly traded stock in the United States. This has led to several completely unexpected developments. Some of the investors have become so large that it is difficult for them to divest from major American companies because there is nowhere else for those funds to go. The result is that the managers of those large funds are taking an increasing interest in how the companies they own are being run — thus reversing the separation of ownership and control identified by Berle and Means.

These huge new vats of money have not gone unnoticed. In several epic battles between managers and corporate raiders, the targeted executives tried to use corporate pension funds to defend their positions without regard to the finan-cial consequences for the pension beneficiaries. The Department of Labor took notice and has ruled that corporate pension funds cannot simply vote with management on all shareholder proposals, as they consistently had in the past, but most show evidence that they had engaged in some rational deliberation about what was best for the pension recipients. In the public sphere, the colossal economic power of pension funds has become a hot political issue. In California, for example, Republican Governor Pete Wilson has attempted to take control of the immense state employee and teacher pension boards in order simultaneously to siphon off $1.6 billion in surplus funds to balance his budget and to rein in the board's highly visible role as a shareholder activist. Since both efforts contradict Congress' attempts to insure that pension assets are protected and that shareholders exercise their "democratic" rights in the marketplace, this is a form of boardroom piracy.

3. Corporate managers, who for more than a century have insisted that their only obligation was to the shareholder, are now being squeezed by a "scissors effect." One blade of the scissors are the social activist shareholders who want the company to pay attention to their issues. The other blade are the financially motivated investors who, having witnessed the lengths to which managers went in the merger-mania of the 1980s to extend their empires or protect their jobs with the shareholders' money, now insist that the managers pay more attention to profits. The result of this new pressure on managers from shareholders of both varieties has been the steady repudiation in management circles and business schools of the core idea of shareholders as owners. Now we hear increasing talk about the importance of the "stakeholders" and "constituencies" whose conflicting interests can only be reconciled through the benign despotism of wise (and autonomous) managers. Unfortunately, some state legislatures have been deluded by these new-found sensitivities and frightening talk of raiders and have been persuaded to pass anti-takeover mechanisms which had the effect of insulating top management from the mechanisms of shareholder accountability. Corporate executives have also petitioned the SEC to make it more difficult for religious and other activists to exert capital market pressures.

In sum, the South African divestment movement has brought about some ironic shifts in the idealogy and the reality of corporate democracy. Even as the dream of worker ownership of the means of production collapsed in communist countries around the planet, it was unexpectedly becoming a reality through the medium of the capitalist pension fund. While twenty years ago businesses used to talk about obligations to the shareholder and churches used to talk about obligations to the community, the language is now often reversed. And finally, though the great edifices of corporate law and finance theory have resided for more than a century on the premise that directors are the elected representatives of shareholders, those same directors, many of them lawyers and economists, are now endorsing proposals to reduce or eliminate the last vestiges of democratic shareholder control.

Though debates about corporate governance can be arcane, they are not idle exercises. As countries coalesce into free trade zones, as corporations burst the bonds of nations the way they once burst the bonds of states, the legitimation and use of capital market techniques by activist church groups and institutional investors will be one of the few remaining means of influencing the choices of the twenty-first century managerial elite. That elite, of course, will resist both the concept and the practice, but this should not deter those who believe that the global investment, employment, safety, and environmental decisions should reflect theological commitments to justice. American churches had the prescience and persistence to transform a moribund system of capital market accountability into a mechanism of control in this country; now, in cooperation with the international network of the faithful, they must help bring corporate democracy to the world.

Seven major American multinational companies, uncertain what will be expected of them after the South African elections this spring, are considering support for a new code of corporate conduct being developed by South African churches.

The seven — Borden, Bristol-Myers, Squibb, Colgate-Palmolive, Ingersoll-Rand, International Paper, Kimberly-Clark and Pfizer — all indicated a willingness to talk with the South Africans about how they could help put the code into practice, according to the Interfaith Council on Corporate Responsibility, a New York-based organization that coordinates stockholder activities by church groups.

In return, the Interfaith Council, which had placed shareholder resolutions concerning South Africa on the agendas of the companies' annual meetings this year, said yesterday that it was withdrawing those resolutions.

The 10-point code contains broadly worded provisions on equal opportunity and affirmative action programs, training and education, labor union rights, community relations, consumer protection, environmental practices and support for local black-owned businesses. It also assumes, but does not spell out, a system to monitor each company's adherence to the code.

"At this point, several different models are being discussed and no one has been asked to endorse a monitoring system or to pay anything to develop one," said Donna Katzin, director of the Interfaith Council's South Africa program.

Reasons for Corporate Support

One reason the companies are showing interest in the code is their belief that it will have wide backing in South Africa and may serve as an alternative to harsher legislation.

In addition, many of them believe that a code developed by South Africans would be applied to all multinational companies, creating a more level playing field than existed in the 1980's, when they were under greater pressure from advocacy groups and politicians in the United States to actively fight apartheid than were their European and Japanese competitors.

Monitoring is the major point of contention. Church groups and some other investors eager to support South Africa's move to majority rule want a system that will allow them to grade corporate behavior. The companies endorse the goals in the South African churches' code and similar codes developed by South African unions and the African National Congress, saying their own performance in recent years has exemplified what the codes call for.

But they want to be free of reporting responsibilities that they feel will add unnecessary costs to their operations and some companies have come out against the codes.

"It's another layer of costly reporting that would be superfluous," said Richard Kryzanowski, general counsel of the Crown Cork and Seal Company, which along with the United Technologies Corporation has decided to oppose shareholder resolutions calling for support of the code.

A Cost of Doing Business

Most multinational companies that stayed in South Africa have contended with performance ratings, which they considered burdensome and hoped to see disappear after the elections on April 27. The ratings began in 1977 when 12 American companies embraced a code of conduct developed by the Rev. Leon H. Sullivan, who believed that American companies could undermine the apartheid system by supporting economic and educational opportunities for blacks.

Eventually, more than 190 companies endorsed the Sullivan Principles. The endorsers submitted annual data on their treatment of ethnic and racial minorities, community investment and other matters to Arthur D. Little Inc., which was retained to rate them. Starting in 1985, those that did not submit the data and had more than 25 employees were required by a Presidential order to make similar reports to the State Department.

In 1987, Mr. Sullivan moved away from his earlier set of principles, advocating corporate divestiture to fight apartheid. An Industrial Support Unit, set up by companies determined to keep the Sullivan Principles alive, now has just 55 members and is scheduled to dissolve after April 27.

The State Department program could also be dismantled if President Clinton determines that the election was free and fair.

— Barnaby J. Feder, "Seven Companies May Back a South African Code," *New York Times*, 25 Feb. 1994

Chapter Twelve

Ethics in Specializations of Business

Few managers are involved in simply managing business as a whole. Small-scale entrepreneurs and family business managers may be; but most business managers are concerned with one part of an overall operation. These managers recognize that business is subdivided into functional areas, each of which has its own driving force and focus of concern. Often, in fact, these functions attract people of different personalities with diverse skills and knowledge.

For many business professionals it is in these specialized functions of business that moral intent must be matched with effective decision making. In these specialized areas are the moral questions over which they have specific jurisdiction. Particularly in larger companies, managers recognize that, while they have limited control over the entire business culture, they have significant influence over their unique areas of expertise. These professionals need more concrete ethical guidance beyond general discussions about business's moral mission and role in society.

To a great extent, the field of business ethics is constituted by the professionals' demand for concrete ethical guidance. Many textbooks deploy the conventional paradigms of applied moral philosophy in an effort to meet this demand. In his introductory essay to this anthology, Max Stackhouse acknowledged these paradigms: deontology and teleology. But he also went beyond the conventional to make explicit the normally neglected third paradigm, ethology, often described as the ethic of responsibility, and he showed how in all three of these paradigms ultimately religious values are operative.

This ethical triad that Stackhouse characterizes as a covenantal ethic for business is especially useful for clarifying our ethical responses to the complex demands of managerial decision making. It is presupposed in this chapter, especially, as the ethical framework in which to evaluate the moral significance of the professional specializations in business.

While some business educators would suggest more than four business specializations, they would likely agree that the four discussed in this chapter are essential ones. It is not possible to sustain an effective business without attention to marketing, finance, accounting, and human resource management.

The purpose of this chapter is to recognize the unique ethical challenges presented by specialized functions within business organizations. Weaving such strands of the firm's moral fabric is an important factor determining the integrity of a corporate culture.

Section 1: Marketing

Every professional marketer could list what textbooks call "the four P's of marketing": product, promotion, place, and price. Together Paul Camenisch, John Kavanaugh, Jon Gunneman, and William Kehoe address these four P's, calling for a deeper understanding of their meaning and conscious attempts to make marketing choices that improve the communal quality of life.

Camenisch argues that since a product or service is the heart of a business, it is also a central focus for ethical concern. At this juncture resources are transformed into life sustaining and enhancing goods and services. Thus choices about product development, design, and delivery are critical to business ethics.

Kavanaugh looks primarily at issues of promotion. He concerns himself with the "cultural tyranny of consumerism" that can occur when products and their promotion negatively affect personal identities and lifestyles, community life, and the practice of economic justice. His words are a warning to producers, marketers, and consumers, suggesting that not all products and promotional strategies enrich individuals and their communities.

Gunneman's emphasis on the ethical principle governing market exchange leads us to consider the issue of place. How does physical location, the geographical and cultural space separating the parties in an economic exchange, affect justice in market exchanges? Gunneman argues that justice and fair exchange occur in the context of shared social meanings, and he wonders whether there is any justice when the lack of shared cultural context amounts to an unequal competence in the exchanging parties. His reflections alert us to the moral hazards to be found in a world where global markets, by definition, are creating a place that transcends local and national boundaries.

Finally, Kehoe tackles the problem of ethics in pricing. At a very concrete level he identifies a multitude of real ethical thresholds operative in pricing decisions. Then, by examining price fixing, he digs deeper into the reasons why pricing behavior can become unethical and suggests several systemic ways for improving ethics in pricing.

Decisions about product, promotion, place, and price are the focus of marketing managers. By giving each of the dimensions of marketing some serious scrutiny, these authors may help us to target our ethical concerns — be they deontological, teleological, or ethological — more effectively.

586

Business Ethics: On Getting to the Heart of the Matter

Paul F. Camenisch

Many current discussions of business ethics seem in the end to locate the ethical concern some distance from the central and essential activity of business. One way this is done is to assume that the content of business ethics is no more and no less than the prevailing moral code of the society as applied to business activities. Business persons and institutions, like all other citizens, are expected to refrain from murder, from fraud, and from polluting the environment. But we cannot limit business ethics to such matters. In fact, perhaps we ought not even call this *business* ethics for the same reasons that we do not say that parental ethics prohibits my brutalizing my children. That is not parental ethics but just ethics plain and simple. This constraint arises from what it means to be a decent human being, not from what it means to be a parent. Similarly, the prohibition upon murdering to eliminate a business competitor is not part of a *business* ethic, for it does not arise from what it means to be engaged in business, nor does it apply to one simply because one is engaged in business. It too arises from what it means to be a decent, moral human being.

The second way of moving ethical issues to the edge of business's activities usually occurs under the rubric of "business's social responsibilities." The most remote of the issues raised here involve the question of whether corporations should devote any of their profits to philanthropic, educational and other sorts of humanitarian undertakings. This is a controversial issue which will not be easily resolved, but even if we concluded that this was a social responsibility of business, it would again fail to be business ethics in any specific and distinctive sense. It would simply be the application to this corporate member of a general societal expectation that members of a society existing in extensive interdependence with and benefiting from that society ought, if able, to contribute some portion of their wealth to such worthy causes. It should in passing be noted that there are persuasive grounds for rejecting this form of social responsibility for business.

Another class of social responsibilities urged upon business is somewhat closer to business activity as such since they can be fulfilled in the course of business's central activity of producing and marketing goods and services. These are the negative duties of neither creating nor aggravating social ills which might arise from business activity such as discriminatory employment, advancement and remuneration along racial, sexual or other irrelevant lines, dangerous working conditions, and avoidable unemployment or worker dislocation.

Still we have not reached the heart of business ethics for we have said nothing of the ethics which come to beat on business *as business,* on business at its very heart and essence. But what is this "heart" of the business enterprise and how and why are business ethics to be grounded in it?

Imagine a corporation which observes all the moral claims already noted — it does not commit fraud or murder, it freely contributes from its profits to various community "charities," its employment practices are above reproach, and it sells quality products at a fair and competitive price while securing for its investors a reasonable return on their investment. So far so good. Its moral record is impeccable. But imagine that the only conceivable use of its products is for human torture. Can we say that here there are no moral or ethical judgments to be made? That the kind of service or product which is at the heart of the enterprise is entirely inconsequential in any and all moral assessments of that enterprise? I do not see how morally sensitive persons or societies can set aside their moral perceptions at this point.

Paul F. Camenisch, "Business Ethics: On Getting to the Heart of the Matter," *Business and Professional Ethics Journal* 1, no. 1 (Fall 1981): 59-68.

Of course one good reason for resisting this suggestion is the great difficulty in making such assessments of goods and services. *Whose* assessments will prevail? We might get general agreement on instruments of human torture — although even here I would not expect unanimity. But what of other goods such as napalm, Saturday-night specials, pornographic materials, junk foods, tobacco, liquors, etc., and services such as prostitution, the training of military mercenaries, or even the provision of such, or the training of the armed forces of repressive regimes, offensive-oriented "survival" courses, the construction of the usually redundant fast-food outlets along suburban slurp strips? In addition to these items in which virtually everyone should be able to see some detrimental elements, there is an additional class of items which some would list here because of their use of limited, even nonrenewable, resources for no purpose beyond momentarily satisfying the whimsey of the indiscriminate wealthy, the bored, the vain, or of increasing corporate profits.

Of course we meet here not only the question of what sorts of moral criteria can properly be applied to business and its products, but also problems of the proper rights and freedoms of consumer-citizens in a free society, problems of censorship, of paternalism, etc. But if the only questions business ethics is permitted to raise concern issues finally tangential to the central activity of business, then business ethics is at best of limited value, and is at worst a hoax, for it would cover over with a veneer of moral approbation enterprises which at their very heart might well be quite irresponsible or even thoroughly reprehensible.

But how do we carry business ethics to the very heart of the business enterprise? I would argue that we can begin by asking the question of what the business sector is and claims to do, what its distinctive function is in the larger society of which it is a part. The norms, both moral and otherwise, for the conduct of an agent, whether individual or corporate, can be determined only after we have established what that agent's relations are to other agents in the moral community, what role the agent plays in relation to them, what the agent's activities in the context of that community aim at.

This approach to business ethics is parallel to the approach some, including this author, have taken to the question of professional ethics by asking what the professions are and claim to be in relation to the larger society in order to establish the starting point for professional ethics. This parallel becomes more than simply interesting or incidental when we note that increasingly many business persons want to see themselves, and to be seen by others as professionals. Before wrapping themselves too tightly in this title, however, business persons should be reminded that historically the label "professional" has had several dimensions, two of which are especially relevant here. There is of course the element of professional prestige and status which is not only known to the business community, but which most likely is a significant element in business's desire for the professional label. But there has also been a persistent moral element in that label, a claim, sometimes implicit, but often explicit, that in their professional activities professionals are oriented to their client's and the society's well-being and not primarily to the professional's own benefits, an orientation some have labeled altruistic. And one crucial question being raised currently not only by the extension of the professional label to previously non-professional groups, but also by the current practices of some of the traditional professions, is whether the prestige element can survive the demise of the moral element, or whether the latter is not a major ground for the former. But whatever the final answer to this question, in appropriating for itself the label of "profession" business will be perceived by many as making a moral commitment analogous to that of the traditional professions such as law and medicine.

It is important to remember as we seek a definition of business and its essential function that frequently, especially in the context of moral concerns, definitions represent "ought" statements as well as "is" statements, that they express what the thing defined ought to be, not just what it already is. It is my intention here to exploit this dual potential of definitions.

In looking for the essential or definitive element in business I would suggest that it is necessary and helpful to see business as one form of that activity by which humans have from the beginning sought to secure and/or produce the material means of sustaining and then of enhancing life. It is plausible to assume that in earlier times individuals and small groups did this for themselves in immediate and direct ways such as gathering, hunting and fishing, farming, producing simple tools and weapons, etc. With the passage of time developments such as co-operative efforts, barter and monetary exchange modified this simple and idyllic situation. Business, I would suggest, enters this picture as that form of such activities in which the exchanges engaged in are no longer motivated entirely by the intention of all participants to secure goods or services immediately needed to sustain and/or enhance their own lives, but by the design of at least some of the participants to make a profit, i.e., to obtain some value in excess of what they had before the exchange which is sufficiently flexible that it can be put to uses other than the immediate satisfaction of the recipient's own needs and desires. It should be noted that this last point is as much or more a matter of defining business, as it is of charting its historical emergence.

In the above statement I am suggesting that there are two essential elements in any adequate definition of business, the *provision of goods and services,* and the fact that this is done with the intention of making a *profit*. The first of these shows business's continuity with the various other human activities just noted by which life has been sustained and enhanced throughout the ages and enables us to understand business in relation to the larger society. The second is a more specific characteristic and sets business off from the other activities by revealing its distinctive internal dynamic. But this element does *not* sever business's connection with those predecessors. The crucial moral points to be made here are that moral/ethical issues arise around both of these elements and that the most important ones concern the "goods and services" element, i.e., the connection between business and the larger society of which it is a part.

This appears to put me in definite tension with Milton Friedman who attempts to ground business ethics, or at least that portion of it which he calls the social responsibility of business, in the profit element only: "In . . . [a free] economy, there is one and only one social responsibility of business — to use its resources and engage in ac-

tivities designed to increase its profits so long as it stays within the rules of the game, which is to say, engages in open and free competition, without deception or fraud."

Of course it is unfair to Friedman to say that for him the maximization of profit is business's only moral duty since he may assume that playing by the rules of the game and that even conducting oneself so as to make a profit in such a "game" would bring additional restraints to bear on business, restraints which many of us would consider to be *moral* restraints. Nevertheless, Friedman's statement does seem to put undue emphasis on business's profit-making function in answering the question of its social and/or moral responsibility.

But however one interprets Friedman's statement, we do here encounter a question fundamental to our present point. This is the question of whether, in defining business and understanding it as a moral reality, we should focus primarily on its goal of producing goods and services or of generating a profit. One can attempt to resolve this question in several ways. There is the rather common sense way of looking at the way most persons generally apply the label "business." A producer of goods and services intending to make a profit but failing to do so is still, by most accounts, engaged in business. Of course some might respond that the concept of profit is still crucial to this activity's being considered business even though here it is present in intention only. But consider the other side. What if profit is present but the provision of goods and services is entirely absent as in a bank robbery. Most, I take it, would deny that here we have just another instance of business, or even an instance of business of a rather unusual sort. Most would simply want to deny that the bank robber was engaged in business at all. Of course one might salvage the position that business is defined by profit-making and yet avoid having to consider the bank robber a businessman by arguing that profit is not just any kind of gain at all, but is a particular sort of gain or is gain realized only under certain circumstances. But even this move would tend to support my position that a single simple concept of profit is not by itself sufficient to define what we mean by business. Whether these additional defining characteristics are written into a more complex definition of profit or are seen as additional to profit is a matter of indifference in terms of the present argument.

Secondly, one could take a more reflective, analytical approach and ask what the relation between these two elements — providing goods and services and profit-making — is, to see if that relation grants a kind of priority to either of them. I would argue, consistent with the above scenario of the emergence of business, that business's primary function, like that of the activities it supplants, is the producing of goods and services to sustain and enhance human existence. Profit then, given the way business functions in the marketplace, becomes one of the necessary means by which business enables itself to continue supplying such goods and services. This would mean that the goods and services element must be given priority in our understanding of business as a social reality and in our moral/ethical response to it. For in the absence of goods and services which are really *goods* and *services,* the making of a profit is at best morally irrelevant. In the absence of the end sought, the means for achieving it are otiose.

Admittedly this understanding of the relation between the production of goods and services and the making of a profit does not reflect the perception of many persons currently engaged in business. They might argue that the relation is precisely the reverse. But is not just such a reversal of ends and means the rock which has wrecked a good many commendable human enterprises? Nor am I the first to suggest that the current outlook should be reversed. Peter Cohen writes concerning his experience at Harvard Business School:

> For two years it has been: You've got to make a better product because, with a better product, you will make a greater profit.
>
> What if they had told the story the other way around? . . .
>
> What if they had told us: You've got to make a profit because, without a profit, you will never be able to develop a better product.
>
> The profit would still be made . . .
>
> Still — you would have a whole new ball game.

Finally, in trying to settle the question of the relation between profits on the one hand and goods and services on the other, one might look at business in terms of its social function and ask why societies have generated and now support and sustain business. Surely it is not for business's own sake, nor for the sake of the few who own and manage businesses so that they can make a profit. Society has no need for profit-making as such. But rather, societies generate, encourage and sustain business because societies need the available raw material transformed into needed goods and services, and because business in its contemporary form has been conspicuously successful in doing just that. In fact, in the current setting it may be that only business has the resources and the knowhow to do that job on the needed scale.

All three of these ways of addressing the relation between these two elements would seem to confirm my position that the provision of goods and services can, perhaps must, be given priority over the profit element in our understanding of business. The major implication of this position for the resulting business ethics would be that the assessment of business as such and of specific business enterprises would begin with the question of whether the goods and services produced thereby serve to enhance or detract from the human condition, whether they contribute to or obstruct human flourishing. Implicit here is the suggestion that businesses engaged in producing goods and services which do not contribute to human flourishing are engaged in a morally questionable enterprise, and those engaged in producing goods and services inimical to human flourishing are engaged in immoral activity. And these judgments hold even if the moral records of these businesses on all the above "peripheral" matters are beyond reproach. For if business has a positive function in society, then the basic moral judgments to be made about it must focus on its performance of that function and not on its avoidance of the grosser moral failings or its performance in areas outside that central societal role. Just as Richard Nixon did not show himself to be a good President by announcing, "I am not a crook," so ITT does not show itself to be a morally commendable enterprise by maintaining that it did not help overthrow the Allende government. Being a good president requires more than not being a crook and being a good business (in the same sense of "good") requires more than abstaining from subversive activities.

Of course this suggestion concerning the heart of business ethics is rife with problems. Chief among them is the question of how we define the human flourishing which business is to serve. While we cannot resolve this question here, raising it at least serves to demonstrate that business ethics, like any serious ethics, will need to develop a philosophical or theological anthropology, a view of humanity and what its proper pursuit, its appropriate fulfillment is.

Some, of course, will argue that the only proper answers to such questions are the ones given by consumers in the marketplace as they use their purchasing power to vote for or against the various answers business implicitly offers in the form of diverse goods and services. While this may be an acceptable answer when one focuses exclusively on the relation between the individual consumer and the marketplace, it is clearly inadequate when we focus on the marketplace in relation to the total society, its present condition and needs and its future prospects. And clearly it is unrealistic, even irresponsible, to attempt to view an enterprise as large and as extensively intertwined with the total fabric of the society as is business only in its relation to individual consumers and their choices. Furthermore, the "marketplace as voting booth" answer to these questions is a costly trial and error method. And given advertising and other forms of demand formation, the significance of consumer "votes" is very unclear. Yet to have such judgments made by any agency outside the marketplace has serious implications for citizen-consumer freedom and rights in a free society.

In light of these difficult problems it might be tempting to give up the search for criteria by which to assess the performance of business at the level of its central function. And yet there are at least three important reasons for attempting this assessment in spite of the obvious problems. As we become increasingly aware of the limits of the earth and its resources within which all of humanity both present and future must live, and of the fact that in our present setting only business has the means and the know-how to transform those resources on any significant scale into the needed goods and services, it becomes increasingly clear that the total society has a crucial stake in, and should therefore have a say about what business does with this our common legacy. As Keith Davis has suggested, ". . . business now has a new social role of . . . trustee for society's resources . . ." The knowing use of non-renewable resources to make products of little or no human value and/or with short useful life solely for the sake of an immediate profit thus becomes a serious dis-service to the larger society. An ethic of the sort here proposed provides a framework within which we could raise the question of how this trusteeship can best be exercised.

Secondly, this enterprise of assessing business in terms of its contribution to human flourishing is called for and legitimated by the fact that business in its various activities is already propagating, whether consciously or not, a view of humanity and of what human flourishing consequently means, views which of course assign a major role to the consumption of the goods and services business produces. Even if this view of humanity is only implicit or perhaps especially if it is implicit, its content and potential impact call for assessment by parties outside the business sector.

Finally, the difficult task of responding to business on these central issues is worth undertaking because of the role business plays in contemporary America and similar societies. In observing the role of business and related economic matters in contemporary America one might almost suggest that we have moved from a sacralized society dominated by religious concerns, through a secularized one in which various major sectors attained considerable autonomy in their own spheres, to a commercialized or an economized culture in which the common denominators which unify and dominate all areas of activity are business related or business grounded considerations such as dollar-value, profitability, marketability, efficiency, contribution to the gross national product, etc. And as Thomas Donaldson and Patricia Werhane have written:

> There may be nothing inherently evil about the goals of economic growth, technological advance, and a higher material standard of living; but critics such as Galbraith have argued that when these become the primary goals of a nation there is a significant lowering in the quality of human life. Economic goals are able to distract attention from crucial human issues, and freedom, individuality,

and creativity are lost in a society dominated by large corporations and economic goals.

If the above is a plausible interpretation of the role of business, broadly understood, in contemporary America, and of some of its implications for human flourishing, then it should be obvious that we have need for an ethic which responds to the central activity of business, since the crucial human implications of such cultural domination by business arise from this central function and not from the less central concerns often raised in business ethics.

I would not, however, so heighten the differences between what I have called the central and the peripheral questions of business ethics as to suggest that there is no significant relation between them. It should be remembered that I suggested that the latter matters were peripheral as matters for *business* ethics, not as matters of ethics as such. As matters of ethics these central and peripheral matters have the common core which distinguishes all ethical matters and which I would again state in Peter Baelz's language by citing their relation to human flourishing. They differ primarily in their proximity to the core activity of business which, I have argued, is the transformation of available resources into life sustaining and enhancing goods and services. Thus just as a business institution, policy or practice, which fails in these central activities is morally deficient, so a business ethic which cannot or does not assess these activities is conceptually deficient.

I would also admit that I am led to stress the central matters primarily to balance the extensive attention being paid to the peripheral matters. With few exceptions we have too easily assumed that if a product or service can be marketed at a profit, its production is a legitimate, even a commendable business undertaking and that participation in those processes is a commendable activity for morally sensitive agents since it contributes to the flow of goods, services and money essential to the economic life of the society. But I am arguing that while these considerations may be adequate business criteria for assessing an undertaking, they are not adequate ethical criteria. We must also ask how such activity affects human flourishing directly through the kind of products or services it provides, and through the responsible or

irresponsible use of limited and often non-renewable resources. While these central questions must be given adequate attention, the peripheral matters are still a significant part of any complete business ethic.

But why should business submit to the scrutiny and recommendations of an ethic such as is proposed here? One answer would be because such an ethic is predicated on what business *is* — one important part of society's efforts to enable its members to flourish, specifically that part which deals with the provision of the material means for sustaining and enhancing life.

"Of course," the critic might respond, "this answer works *if* we agree on what you say business is. But if we maintain that business must be defined and understood in terms of its own internal dynamics and goals, e.g., profit-making, rather than in terms of society's needs and goals, then the answer falls apart." True enough. But given business's extensive interdependence with society — its reliance on society's educational system to provide educated workers, on society's maintenance of transportation systems, of a stable social and political setting in which to do business, of a legal system by which business can adjudicate its disputes with competitors and customers, of what E. F. Schumacher has called the "infrastructure" — it is naive to suggest that business is a self-sufficient and self-contained entity which can define its own goals and functions entirely independently of the society's goals and needs. As Robert A. Dahl has written:

> Today it is absurd to regard the corporation simply as an enterprise established for the sole purpose of allowing profit making. We the citizens give them special rights, powers, and privileges, protection, and benefits on the understanding that their activities will fulfill purposes. Corporations exist only as they continue to benefit us . . . Every corporation should be thought of as a social enterprise whose existence and decisions can be justified only insofar as they serve public or social purposes.

Furthermore, anyone who argues that business should be permitted to define its own goals and purposes and thus its own ethics independently of societal interests will have to explain why business should be granted latitude at this point that is denied to other major sectors of societal activity such as politics, education, or the traditional professions such as law and medicine. (This last of course is of special interest and relevance in light of the fact already noted that increasing numbers of business persons wish to be considered professionals.) And the questions raised here cannot be put to rest by facile references to the public vs. the private sector. First of all, much of education and certainly most of the legal and medical professions are not in the public sector. So that would not explain or justify different treatment for business at this point. But more fundamentally, such a response would miss the basic question being raised here, the question of whether in a society as complex and interdependent as ours there actually is a "private sector" in the simple, straightforward sense suggested by that response.

There are numerous varied matters which are legitimately included in any adequate definition of business ethics. In fact, in a nascent field such as this it is as yet impossible to say with any certainty what is within and what is without its borders. But it does seem clear that any business ethic that does not respond first and foremost to business's contribution to or detraction from human flourishing through its essential and definitive activity of generating life sustaining and enhancing goods and services will have failed to lay a foundation from which to address all other questions for it will not yet have gotten to the heart of the matter.

Challenging a Commodity Culture

John Kavanaugh

In the central sections of John Paul II's great christological encyclical, *Redeemer of Humankind,* he launches into an unexpected and complicated reflection upon the spirituality of economic systems. But what, one might ask, does the following of Christ have to do with being "slaves to production"? And why does the relationship between faith and economics haunt the doctrine of the pope whether he is in Brazil condemning slavery "to consumerism," in England recommending the vow of poverty as an act of resistance to the "tyranny of consumerism," or in Canada delivering a ringing indictment of the economic life and priorities of the industrialized nations of the North?

The answer lies in his dialectical view of human experience. Such a view provides a key to unlocking the complexities we face in trying to imagine an alternative way of life to the consumerist world of cultural capitalism.

Life, faith, Jesus Christ, all collide in the complex maze which makes up our cultural reality and which makes the question of "alternative living" frustratingly problematic.

John Paul is quite aware of this complexity. That is why all of his sermons, letters, and speeches are so densely dialectical. All of the "compartments" of our lives are connected. Everything is related to everything else. There is a politics, even an economics, of sex. There is a spirituality of economic and social systems. There is a sociology of grace. There is sin in political reality. All touches all.

John Kavanaugh, "Challenging a Commodity Culture," *Commonweal,* 2-16 Nov. 1984, pp. 606-12.

A living faith must be seen in such a context. If it is real and effective it will be dialectical, not something fragmented or compartmentalized. To accept Christ as way, truth, and life, consequently, is to allow him to enter every dimension, inhabit every space, penetrate every experience.

Our faith lives in and through space and time. It emerges in history only as inculturated, as embodied in concrete political, economic, social, and symbolic forms. And yet, if faith is collapsed into these cultural expressions, if it serves as little more than the legitimation of the nation or culture in which it lives, it is lost.

It is for this reason that John Paul II, whenever he advances a Christology which reveals the human person as pre-eminently valuable, created in the image of God, and transformed in Christ, insists that this liberating and saving truth may be suppressed by the force of advanced industrial society's cultural myths. Instead of freedom in Christ, we can be trapped into a subtle domination by the world of things. This domination is systemic and dialectical. It is brought about, even when we do not perceive it happening, by a formation system which is made up of the social-political system ("the whole organization of community life"), the economic order ("the production system"), and the educative blandishments of the media ("the means of social communication").

To speak of an "alternative way of life" in such a cultural formation system, consequently, is to address a whole network of inter-acting alternatives which live and thrive precisely in relationship to each other and their common connection in Christ. But, too often people of faith unwittingly choose only one area of alternative "resistance" and neglect the others. Some choose interiority, convinced that if they are able to maintain a citadel of solitude, they will be able to withstand the siege of depersonalizing forces. Yet, without community or familial support, without some expression in style of life or some commitment to social reordering, solitude alone does not provide an integrated, sustainable alternative praxis.

Others have sought community, hoping that they might be able to find some solace in the covenants of family, communion, or friendship. However, if this is the only dimension that changes in their lives, they soon discover the same cultural webs of isolation, violence, manipulation, and pretense duplicated in their patterns of relating to each other. Without the insights of social analysis, without the honesty of being known and accepted as a sinner before God, without the gentle suasion of the marginal and disenfranchised, without the expansive passion for justice, communities so easily turn in upon themselves in a Hobbesian nightmare of all against all.

Still others think that simplicity, "cutting back" and plodding toward frugality might offer some route of resistance. But the strategy fails utterly if it is unaccompanied by insight into the ways that consumerism infects far more than how we eat or what we wear or how we save and earn. The use of media as narcotic, the fear of relationship, the avoidance of commitment, the numbing of social consciousness, and the privatization of morality are all more profound cultural expressions of the tyranny of consumerism.

Social activism? Is there any more evidence or argument needed to suggest that such a maneuver, if it is uncomplemented by the truth of prayer, the praxis of community, the detachment of simplicity, and the immediacy of compassion leads to burn-out, involuted resentment, and a brooding sense of hopelessness?

Just as Christ penetrates every experience of a committed life, so also any response to Christ as a living alternative to the dominant cultural gospel must touch every dimension. Any "alternative way of life," if it is to be a true alternative, must be dialectical. It must be systemic. It must be wholehearted. And so, let us now examine five areas of our lives where the economic gospel of our culture tries to establish its hegemony in wholistic, integrated, and dialectical fashion. In each of these areas — each always in mutual relation to the others — our lives of faith will have to be engaged, and a living alternative to the cultural tyranny of consumerism will thereby be embodied.

An advertisement from the 1970's which was touting the formative power of *Playboy* purred, *"Good news for American Business: Today's young men are no longer committed to poverty. . . ."* What else is "good news for American Business"? What kinds of behavior will a culture based upon the demand for continually expanding consumption try to induce in its people?

"I Found Myself in a McCall's Catalogue." Thus, buying is transformed into our most interior ex-

perience. Our identities, pretentiously stolen from us, are now available for purchase. Our very being is collapsed into possessions and appearances. We *are* how we look, what we eat, and the way we buy. This is an economic phenomenon. It is also, critically, a spiritual phenomenon. It is not merely that we live by pretense and external appearance, not merely that we fill most of our waking moments with the media and the products that the media hustle, but that we are taught to fear the reality of who we are in solitary truth. "*Nikon: What would life be without it?*" Do advertisers really hope to imbue us with the subtle suspicion that we might go out of existence if we are not producing or somehow attached to the most real world of objects? The very condition of life is purchase, they say. We eat Life in cereal boxes. We smoke Merit and True.

In the context of a culture whose "formation system" is premised upon the interior drive of persons to produce, possess, and consume more, solitary prayer becomes an act of economic resistance, a radical alternative to the commercial imperatives of culture.

Whether one is a professional white-collar worker, a skilled or "unskilled" laborer, a family person, a single person, or a member of a religious community, the solitude of prayer is an intrinsic part of any dialectical response to consumerist culture. It may be perceived as a waste of time in terms of human productivity (it is not), it may be accosted as an insult to the logic of "self-made-men-and-women" (it is), and it may be a terror to any of us who want to avoid the fact of our utter creatureliness. But the commitment to prayer will inevitably bring us into contact with the deepest meaning of our personhood. Who am I when I cannot point to what I wear or achieve or collect? What am I when I cannot possess or control?

The fruit of solitary prayer is the simple but stunning fact that the great gift we have to offer the world, our God, and each other is the poverty of the human heart, possessing nothing other than its power to say, "I believe, I hope, I love." We may be told that we can believe in Remington, trust Woolite, or that Musk is love; but with the encounter of God in silence, the phenomenon of personal reality is revealed. And it is a truth that, while it may be "bad news" for American business,

unleashes the human being into an engagement of personhood in each of the other arenas of life.

So a run-of-the-mill *Cosmopolitan* article, "Passion for Possessions," ominously reveals our dread of relationship and flight to commercialism. As a people, in so many ways we are taught to seek out what an American Motors advertisement called "*a problem-free relationship.*" Yet, as C. S. Lewis reminded us in *The Four Loves,* if we want never to experience the problematic pain of love, we should give our hearts to no person. We should love only things, and our hearts will not be broken. They will become unbreakable, impenetrable, like the dead objects of our love.

The economic myths and demands of our culture have massive influence on our relationships, our covenants. They attempt to channel our loves, our passions, and our desires into things; and if at the same time we experience a painful absence of human convenantal intimacies in our lives, we may buy ourselves to death.

Friendship, family intimacy, and community are economic realities But they are counter-values for capitalism. "The best things in life really are free."

Our communities, so often fragmented by liturgies of media worship, and our families, so often regimented by dictates of productivity and achievement, carry within their very identities the seeds of resistance to consumerism. In relationship, as in prayer, our truth can be known. Such activities are neither easy nor without risk. The pre-eminently human enterprises of faith, hope, and love never are. Moreover, all covenants take time. It takes time to allow myself to be known and thereby loved as I really am. That is why a committed relationship in the midst of a society that lives by efficient speed and quick pretense, where "looking good is everything," is an act of economic disengagement and courageous resistance.

If we spend one half hour a day more in relationship — talking with a community friend, walking for a while with our spouse, "wasting time" with our children, speaking the truth to a brother or sister, we will find ourselves empowered to resist much of the institutionalized craving of our acculturated appetites. Such craving is, after all, little more than an attempt to fill up the stark emptiness of a life berift of covenant or intimacy.

We breathe injustice. It's everywhere. It's hopeless. What can one man, one woman do? And so, in so many rhetorical ways we ape the commodity culture that has formed us in the image and likeness of things. Things are expendable. People come and go, die, starve, burn, are aborted, are executed. And we, we the living, the conscious? Who are we — so passive, so helpless, so determined and thing-like, so susceptible to the laws of supply and demand? The received wisdom of our culture tells us that nothing can be done. And not much worry ought to be expended. To hope for otherwise is to be a pollyanna, to be hopelessly naïve, to be headed for a "guilt trip." Things feel no guilt.

"Face the facts, the real world." The reality principle here is one of human expendability — in the midst of massive waste and with the help of stunning negligence. Meanwhile we sell parakeet diapers, Calvin Klein diapers, and designer clothes for our cabbage patch adoptees. Justice is passé. *"Sip it with arrogance,"* an ad for drinks says. And, with the height of consumerist arrogance: *"For the price of a small house you could own this chair."*

The capitalist reality principle is so powerful that when the pope speaks to us of Christ's justice whereby the third world nations of the South will "rise up to judge the rich nations of the North," we say, surely he cannot mean us. Surely his talk of economic imperialism, of mountains of munitions cannot refer to us; we, so helpless and passive, cannot respond.

Thus, systematic injustice is two-edged. We can become as helpless as the things we adore. Depersonalization is intrinsically related to injustice. Underlying all violence is a human being that has been reduced to the status of an object. To kill a person is literally to "thingify" a person. Violence and injustice — in all of the subtle institutional, political, and interpersonal forms — are the cultural mirrors of the "thingified" self. Not being able to tap into the splendor of human personhood encountered in either solitude or solidarity, there is no subjective or intersubjective referent for the affirmation of the inherent worth of persons. There is no reason not to be unjust.

Consequently, when we imagine an alternative way of life in the context of our culture, we must include the heroics of social commitment — against all the wisdom that it is unrealistic, against all the cultural prudence that advises we will get nowhere, against all the socio-psychological warnings that we not appear foolish.

As men and women of faith, a faith grounded in Jesus Christ, we can see that justice is not some liberal program of social planning and one-worldism. Quite the contrary, it is the very exigency of the Gospel. For the Christian, justice is the very embodiment of faith and love: faith in the revelation of Jesus and love for the human person who is revealed by Jesus as the very face of God. The issues of hunger, imprisonment, homelessness, and economic injustice are not those of some social commissar. They are the very flesh of faith, the criteria of the Last Judgment which Jesus himself sets up as standards for following him and for encountering him on this earth.

After Jesus, everything is different. "As often as you have done this to the least" — any and all, not merely the innocent, are included in this notion — "you have done it to me." "This is my body," Jesus says in the sacrament of communion whereby all human flesh, even in its least forms — unborn, imprisoned, dirty, homeless, communist or capitalist, oppressed or oppressor, the damaged, the ugly, the unproductive — is rendered holy.

This spiritual, theological, and political insight is in absolute contradiction to the criteria of worth established by our cultural conscience where human value is a function of beauty, utility, innocence, whiteness, blackness, wealth, or masculinity.

Christ shatters all of this. Not only are we all judged capable of responding freely to the call of justice, but we are all deemed worthy of just action.

We must note, however, that the commitment to justice is not simply an insight, but an embodied reality. Each must act. Anywhere and on any level. Each must commit — not for the sake of some myopic one-sided issue, but for the sake of our Christ in faith. We will not be able to do it all, but we will be able to do something. This is to change the given order. This is to embody our commitment to an alternative way of life. Conviction must be given concrete specificity in our culture. We picket. We inform. We gather information. We protest. We undergo the threat of arrest. We look foolish. For the old, for the poor, for the unborn, for the disenfranchised, for peace, for the future now threatened by our nuclear nuptials, for the millions in misery neglected by the bullheaded excesses of capitalism.

This area of praxis will be prodded and sustained by prayer. It will be confirmed and supported by our community and covenantal exchange. It will be concretely expressed in the "style of our lives."

Buying, consuming, and possessing can become acts of violence. Such behaviors are related not only to justice in the world, but also to fairness in our covenantal lives, and self-love or self-hatred in our interior lives.

Simplicity of life is not a matter of bean sprouts and old jeans. It is not grounded in some special virtue of want or frugality. No, if simplicity has any intelligibility, it is found in the value of persons over things, the primacy of labor over capital, the worth of humanity over property. This is definitively revealed in our faith, in the saving action and teachings of Jesus. "Traveling light" is a response, not out of guilt or trendy narcissistic asceticism, but out of love for persons and personal life.

Things are for persons. This truth is behind every style-of-life-question we might ask. Can things bring us closer together or force us apart? Do things provide an escape from myself and from God in solitude, or do they enhance the possibilities of encountering the Holy in all persons? Our questions are not so much ones of "cutting back" as they are of integration and personalization.

When we live more simply, we have more time for solitude, more time to savor and appreciate the things that we actually have. We are less cluttered by assaults from the media. We have more time for each other, more time to "waste" in relationships, more time to appropriate our lives together in family or in community. When we live more simply, we are more able to respond to the problems of injustice in the world — not only by sharing of what we do not need, but also by time for greater availability in service and social action.

Thus, cutting back television-viewing — a style of life matter — will influence my time available for prayer or reflection. It will affect my morning and evening hours. It will have an impact on my own self-understanding. It will also modify my openness to relatedness. No longer will it dominate the meals I take in community, set the pattern of conversation with my family, fill up my life with the average thirty-hours-a-week of watching commercials, soap operas, sports, or shows with canned laughter.

In a similar manner, greater simplification in my patterns of consuming, entertaining, or dressing will profoundly affect my sense of driveness to possess more and newer things. It will invite me into discussion with friends of families over our so-called needs, desires, and wants as consumers. It may well enlarge my leftover income that might be put to the service of others.

Once we see the integrated way that our style-of-life decisions are related to other areas of our lives, it becomes easier to live more simply.

The final dimension of our "lived alternative" to the gospel of capitalism is that of opening ourselves to the vulnerable, those so unable to cover up their wounds that they serve us as living refutations of such dogmas as "self-made-persons" and "fulfillment in things." The marginal are unable to cram themselves into the consumerist parameters of "meaningful existence" or the categories of commercial thought. All the products of the market will not ease their existence or make the pain go away. The only reality that can encounter them, be touched by them, or help them, is personal reality.

The Teresas of Calcutta, the Jean Vaniers, the Dorothy Days, the Dom Helder Camaras — all speak to us of the empowerment we receive "from the poor." Why do they insist that "we receive so much from them"? What is it that we receive that cannot be bought? It is ourselves. It is the irreplaceability and value of our own human personhood.

If we structure into our lives an ongoing contact with the marginal people of our society, we will sustain and be sustained by them. It is so easy, even with prayer, to be deluded into a false consciousness about our true identity and purpose. It is so possible, even with community life, to hide from the marginal persons both outside and within our families and communities. It is so seductive, even while living simply, to ignore the plight of those for whom simplicity is no option — for whom it is at best a dream of wild imagination. It is so easy, even if working for justice, to forget the immediacy of compassion, of personal presence.

In each area of our lives there is a humanity that is poor and disenfranchised, that hungers and hides, that grows old and feeble and dies. This is what must be encountered — our own frightening fragility as persons. But this is also what we may most tragically evade. For in finding the precious personhood of the disposssessed, we will discover our very own personhood which we need never fear losing.

The young priest was terrified. He was in a strange country. He was with strange people. And they acted strangely. Handicapped. In this L'Arche community hidden in India. And yet the young priest had wanted to help. But at night he would shiver. Not from cold, but from shame. The thought of his fear. He was surely as frightened as the "Mongoloid" man who had arrived on the same day, who was in his thirties, too, who was separated for the first time from his hovel and his mother, who could only sit crouched on the floor and blow away the dust. The priest's fears were different. Of dirt. Of the loss of control. Of the terrible failure. Of some strange mentally-mutilated person drifting into his room at night.

It was on the third weekend, more dreaded than longed for, after dragging himself back to the community of handicapped that the priest, still fearful, was halted by a grab at his leg. The man with Downs syndrome, staring at the floor that he was cleaning with his breath-broom, stuck out his shaky hand, not looking, but refusing passage until that hand would be held and shaken.

At the gesture of friendship and sympathy, the fears of the priest finally melted away. Pretenses dissolved, the rigid controls eased.

We are all handicapped, he said to himself. It's just that some of us can pretend better than others.
— An anonymous story

Those who cannot pretend, who cannot "make it" with success and achievement, minister in marvelous ways to those who are tempted to pretend that they are something better than they are. Those who cannot pretend to be anything other than human engage the humanity of those for whom they reach. They reveal the truth that the most splendid gift we bestow upon each other is not some object, but our personhood. This is the outcome of prayer and of relationship. This is the meaning of justice and simplicity. Herein we discover that it is the human heart and hand which, no matter what the conditions of our woundedness, is most subversive and healing in a world of commodity consciousness.

The school of compassion is our final element in the "living alternative" to cultural capitalism. It is the world of irreplaceability. It is a world where we encounter the utter uniqueness of each person and the utter universality of our shared human nature. It is a world where, even if the only gesture we are able to offer is blowing the dust from the ground and offering an innocent hand of welcome, we do something mighty and majestic.

A full dialectic of personal living is the only alternative to the dialectics of domination and the idols of capitalism. Our "manner of living" will be authentically alternative when it is whole, abiding with our aloneness and with our solidarity, informing our just action and our simplicity, engaging us in our learning from the marginal and unprotected.

Capitalism and Commutative Justice

Jon P. Gunnemann

Introduction

Disputes about justice in capitalist societies typically center on distribution. Behind the distributional interest most often lies a commitment to some kind of egalitarianism or what Michael Walzer has called "simple equality." The ethical problem then is to balance this commitment with other moral claims such as liberty, efficiency, merit, creativity, and the like. There are good reasons to worry about distribution but my purpose in this paper is to argue that in a capitalist market society we ought chiefly to worry about commutative justice.

There are several reasons for considering commutative justice central to the analysis of market capitalism. The most obvious is that the distinctive human activity in a market society is exchange and commutative justice is, as Aristotle first noted and the entire Western tradition agrees, the form of justice appropriate to exchange. If we want to understand market society, we must understand exchange, and if we wish to judge the justice of a particular market society or set of market relations, we must look at the justice of exchange. The classical economists knew this (they were relatively uninterested in distributive justice, a point for which they are often criticized), as did that great critic of capitalism, Karl Marx, who often ridiculed redistributional programs and whose critique of the exchange of labor was based on a

notion, even if unstated, of commutative justice. Indeed, distributive justice is somewhat out of place in relation to the market, having its home rather in the membership of a polity: How should a given polity distribute its various benefits and burdens among its members? Exchange within a polity may affect distribution and be affected by distributional patterns, but the exchange itself must be judged by commutative justice.

Second, if market exchange is a valuable social activity, commutative justice helps preserve its value. I accept without argument here many of the standard benefits associated with market exchange: liberty, efficiency, incentive for work and for creativity, even a certain sociality and conviviality. Further, market exchange is useful in the face of numerous rationality problems connected with economic life (this is really the connection to efficiency and in part to liberty). I even give some credence to early arguments given for capitalism, as reported by Hirschman, that the pursuit of interest in exchange can lead to more peaceful social relations, within and among nations. But the basic point is that all these benefits depend on the justice of exchange.

A third reason for concern about commutative justice follows directly: to protect exchange and the market from capitalism. The point is not to do away with capitalism but to recognize that capitalism and market society are not the same, and to show how key aspects of capitalism seriously distort the market. Many virtues claimed for capitalism are in fact virtues of market exchange and part of my intention is to reclaim the market from a variety of recent champions of capitalism who tend to equate the two.

My purpose, then, is to offer a critique of capitalism using the stringent standards of the justice of the market. These standards, I suggest, can help us understand more about the kinds of limits that should be placed on capitalism than can principles of distributive justice. These standards are also old and I have very little new to say about them. But they are curiously neglected in much modern discussion.

Commutative Justice

Commutative justice is rooted in the fundamental moral prohibition against harm. In exchange,

Jon P. Gunnemann, "Capitalism and Commutative Justice," *Annual of the Society of Christian Ethics* (1985): 101-23.

harm is avoided when there is equivalence of exchange, harm is done when there is not equivalence. The problem is to determine equivalence.

In the texts of Aristotle and Thomas Aquinas, the question of equivalence devolves on the problem of the "just price." In both, a distinction is made between a given price of a commodity and its just price or true value. I agree with Schumpeter that this distinction does not involve a metaphysical notion of value or price — rather the true value or just price is represented by the normal competitive price, the common estimation of value under normal competitive conditions.

In spite of various efforts to establish a true price based on labor and other costs of production, the notion that a just price is the one obtaining under normal competitive conditions has worn well over the centuries. It represents Adam Smith's view and, as nearly as I can tell, the view of virtually all modern economists. The task that remains is to clarify what counts as normal competitive conditions.

Here again, there are no great mysteries. From Aristotle on, monopoly, the existence of only a single seller in the market, is the first distorter of the just price. But beyond this, and more important, I think, is the notion of a common estimation of value. A just exchange can take place only when those exchanging have some shared meanings about what it is that they are exchanging, and some roughly equal competence in judging the commodities, their quality, and their value. Without such shared meanings and without equal competence there is always the possibility of a gross misestimation of equivalence on the part of at least one party, and when that happens normal competitive conditions do not obtain.

When Adam Smith discusses the "natural price," he discusses the competitive conditions existing in what he calls "a society or neighborhood." It is evident here and in all the examples he gives on exchange and pricing that Smith has in mind individuals trading directly with each other, individuals who, although they may be relative strangers by the standard of traditional social bonds, clearly inhabit a world of shared meanings and mutual knowledgeability. It is because this world is relatively circumscribed, and its members mutually knowledgeable about the goods they exchange, that Smith can point to the remarkable

advantage given to a supplier who brings goods some distance to the market: if the demand and price goes up in the market, the distance permits the supplier to keep this a secret from others in his region who might compete with him in supplying and thus bring the price down again. In such a situation, the person may enjoy what Smith calls "extraordinary profits," based on an unnatural price and, therefore, on an unjust exchange. But Smith notes, revealingly, "Secrets of this kind . . . can seldom be long kept; and the extraordinary profit can last very little longer than they are kept."

I will return to this point on distances and secrets. Here I only wish to underscore that the paradigm of the just exchange for Smith (and for virtually all modern market economics) is an exchange between two individuals who inhabit a world of shared meanings (that is, shared understandings and expectations about the goods they exchange) and who are mutually knowledgeable about these meanings and goods. Such exchangers are peers. It is not an accident that contemporary theories of justice depend on virtually identical accounts of the background conditions for just human interactions. I have in mind, of course, the stipulations for John Rawls's "original position" and the characteristics of Juergen Habermas's "ideal speech situation." Especially with the latter, the conditions which make for undistorted communication replicate the conditions for just exchange. Justice is done, and the prohibition against harm respected when mutually competent persons inhabiting a world of shared meanings exchange goods or enter into contracts and agreements.

What we need to do, then, is to look closely at the criteria of shared meanings and of mutual competence in relation to modern capitalist society. I take up the question of shared meanings first, then the problem of mutual competence.

Shared Meanings and Exchange

Shopping (going to market) in another culture is so pleasurable because of the display of goods that are unavailable in our own culture and which often have mysterious meanings or embody aesthetic qualities different from our own. The results of exchange while traveling in exotic situations is the display in Western homes of artifacts from another culture in which the original meaning of the artifacts has little to do with their new context. Their original meaning, for example, may have been religious and ritualistic but they are now displayed in a consumer culture where they symbolize cosmopolitanism, affluence, liberalism. We know also of reversals of this kind of cultural displacement: the discarded objects of Western consumer culture have taken on religious meaning in the Cargo Cults of the South Pacific. And we know that the meanings of one market context can affect the meanings of another: The Japanese used wood-block prints to wrap pottery and porcelain being shipped to Europe in the nineteenth-century and when the Europeans admired and began to collect them (they influence the development of Impressionism) wood-block printing was re-estimated in Japan, moving from the status of a craft to an art. The distance between market contexts and their meanings can be historical as well as cultural as, for example, with the high price commanded now by antique peasant furniture, or with the use of the artifacts of medieval ascetic monasticism in the decor of some of Europe's most opulent hotels.

I will deal with the importance of distance between market contexts in the next section. Here I use the example of distances to demonstrate how much the exchange of goods and the price depend on cultural meanings. As Mary Douglas and Baron Isherwood, two anthropologists, have pointed out, economists tend to ignore the social meaning of goods because of their "theoretical individualism." Theoretical or methodological individualism reduces the notion of goods to subsistence and need, perhaps extended by notions of envy and social competition. But in fact, goods carry social meanings and the justice of their exchange depends on the meanings they have.

It is not possible here to develop a theory of social goods and meanings, but one aspect of such a theory illustrates one of the most critical issues for commutative justice, namely, the delimitation of goods that may be exchanged in the market at all. Although in human history virtually everything conceivable has been for sale at some time or another, no society considers all goods legitimately exchangeable in the market. Arthur Okun has suggested that in our society the notion of

rights demarcates those things which may not be sold: votes, freedom of speech, the right to trial by jury, all of those things guaranteed in the Bill of Rights plus many more hammered out in our political history such as the right to go on strike — these are "bans on exchange." Michael Walzer has taken up Okun's analysis in the phrase "blocked exchanges," and offers his own list of "the full set of blocked exchanges in the United States today." As Walzer puts it, "it is a feature of the sphere of money that it abuts every other sphere; that's why it is so important to fix its boundaries. Blocked exchanges set limits on the dominance of wealth." And, therefore, blocked exchanges limit the market and determine those things that can be exchanged, if at all, only unjustly.

The domain of rights represents at least a portion of our society's set of shared convictions about what it means to be human, about the nature of political and civic life, and the like. And, as Walzer points out, these meanings, and thus the goods that are excluded from exchange, vary historically and culturally although I doubt that what is excluded is quite as relative as he seems at times to suggest. The important point, however, is that one of the central tasks of any society, and of ethics, is the determination of what exchanges should be blocked, the erection of barriers (Walzer calls them boundaries and fences) to effect the blocking, and continued vigilance in guarding the barriers. The task here is really two-fold:

On the one side, we need constantly to clarify what may enter the market and what not. Even though there is consensus in our society on a substantial domain of rights, there are numerous areas about which there is no consensus where we have not been able to decide as a society what meaning we attach to goods. These are areas of genuine dispute where some may claim that the goods should be excluded from the market while others are eager to let the market be the chief mechanism for distributing them. We are sure, for example, about goods such as freedom of speech, religion, and voting, but not sure about education, medicare, and labor. Our uncertainty about the meaning of such goods can have more than one cause. It may stem from historical changes in the social location of the goods, from cultural and technological changes, or from a particular ideological history.

Take education, for example. Its traditional home was in the family and the church, later in the neighborhood, often still closely attached to family and church. But increasingly education is in the hands of governments, not only local governments but also state and national government. The background for the involvement of governments is that we have always considered education a right (and a duty); the state schools guarantee that even those who are poor will have a good education. Education is also deeply influenced by corporate America and the market—one has only to look at the sources of funding for higher education and at changes in curricula. The consequence of these historical changes is a displacement of the good of education from its original contexts and meanings. Whether this displacement and shift in educational goods is applauded or deplored depends on the meanings one attaches to them, but the fact that we have a flowering of new private (often so-called "Christian") schools, proposals for a market voucher system, and the like, shows how far we are from consensus on the meaning of educational goods. The idea that education should be given over to market principles without careful discussion of the moral and political meaning of education would be a disaster. Similar disagreements surround medical care because of the vast changes caused by technology, the transformation of the medical profession, and the intrusion of large corporations into medically related fields.

I will not pursue these two issues (education and medical care) any further here, but only reiterate that one of the fundamental tasks of social ethics in modern market society is to help clarify the extent to which, if at all, such disputed areas of social meanings and goods should be given over to market coordination. I am more interested in this regard in the third area of controversy I mentioned above, labor. Is labor a good to be exchanged in the market? The controversy here is not a new one coming from recent historical developments, but one that goes back to the beginnings of market society when "free labor" began to replace the traditional ties of labor. It is a controversy in which, as Charles Lindblom notes, classical liberal theory has been blind. If labor is all that one has to offer for exchange, then the termination of that exchange relationship in a bad labor

market is a drastic form of injury and the exchange itself is unjust because the goods being exchanged cannot conceivably have equivalent social meanings. Yet labor continues to be conceived in most liberal economic theory as a commodity.

Now it is evident that the growth of free labor has coincided with an increase in personal freedom. If the alternative to the free exchange of labor is the lifetime, paternalistic employment of Japanese enterprises, or the early tracking of examination systems in some socialist societies, we may be less inclined to abandon labor as a commodity. But there are ways of establishing a right of labor which can avoid these alternatives, a mix of guaranteed work with market distribution. Such solutions have costs, but the fundamental ethical question is the social meaning of labor and work. Only when that has been established can decisions about labor and the market be made.

One of the tasks of ethics, then, is the continual mapping of the limits of the market in relation to continually changing social activities; and the devising of policies consistent with this demarcation. But the second task is equally as important: the continual policing of the boundaries on the map. The problem is evident: even in those areas where there is a consensus in social meaning, goods blocked even by constitutionally sanctioned rights continue to be affected and even determined by the market. To quote Lindblom again, our "expensive legal system is open to the rich, inaccessible to the poor for civil law, and hostile to the poor in criminal law." Or one could look at problems in freedom of speech and freedom of the press in relation to the control of mass media by large corporate interests. The principled establishment of blocks to exchange does not by itself protect blocked goods from market forces.

The reason is that market relations simply tend to grow. As Walzer puts it,

One can conceive the market as a sphere without boundaries, an unzoned city—for money is insidious, and market relations are expansive. A radically *laissez-faire* economy would be like a totalitarian state, invading every other sphere, dominating every other distributive process. It would transform every social good into a commodity. This is market imperialism.

Part of the reason that money and market relations are expansive is due to human moral weakness, including greed, envy, sloth, lust, and the other classic vices. At least since Esau we have known that in moments of weakness people will sell rights and that there will always be a buyer waiting to offer a price. But money is insidious and the market expansive for other reasons as well, and some of these are subjectable to human control, even in imperfect societies of imperfect human beings. To understand these causes of market imperialism and unjust exchanges, we have to look at the exchange relation itself.

Exchange Relations and Mutual Competence

At the heart of Robert Nozick's *Anarchy, State, and Utopia* is his now famous Wilt Chamberlain story, offered as an example of how free exchange will alter any given distribution or, to use Nozick's phrase, "how liberty upsets patterns." Nozick proposes that we begin with our favorite equitable distribution and then suppose that Wilt Chamberlain, who is in great demand by basketball teams, freely makes a contract with a team in which he receives twenty-five cents for every ticket sold. In a season, a million people come to see Chamberlain play and cheerfully pay for tickets, also in a free exchange. At the end of the season, Chamberlain is $250,000 richer and the original distributional pattern has been upset. Every exchange was freely entered into, and no one is unhappy.

I like this story almost as much as everyone who reprints it in textbooks on justice, but for different reasons: it demonstrates nicely what is wrong with most contemporary moral analysis of the market. There is no question that free exchange will transform distributional patterns, and Nozick is on to something important in his criticism of theories of justice that rely on a particular distributional end-state rather than attending to the changing distributions through myriads of daily transactions in history. In this regard, the approach I am taking here, focusing on exchange itself, is closer to Nozick than to Rawls. But Nozick's understanding of exchange is superficial and abstract, as removed from actual history as Rawls's "original position."

The Wilt Chamberlain example is deeply deceptive and filled with counter-factual interpretations. Nozick portrays the exchange as one between the people and Chamberlain himself: "Each of these persons *chose* to give twenty-five cents of their money to Chamberlain." They could have spent it on other things (including *Dissent* and *Monthly Review,* Nozick notes for benefit of potential leftist critics) but "converged on giving it to Wilt Chamberlain in exchange for watching him play basketball." Are they not entitled to dispose of their money as they please, and "to give it to, or exchange it with, Wilt Chamberlain?" But not a single person who paid for a ticket exchanged anything with Wilt Chamberlain. They purchased tickets from the agents of a massive corporation which had in turn arranged something with Chamberlain and the team. None of this is mentioned in the account Nozick gives. In fact, think what else is left out of this account: Chamberlain's negotiation through an agent who has something of a monopoly in representing athletes; the fact that by far the largest portion of the ticket price went not to Chamberlain but to the capitalist enterprise for marketing and overhead as well as for profit; the fact that marketing for immensely large numbers of people and the costs of running athletics of this kind are subsidized and controlled by the mass media and the business interests they represent. Nozick portrays this as a simple exchange between parties face-to-face, such as in the paradigm example I have discussed where there are shared meanings about the goods and mutual competence. But in fact the fundamental exchanges, the ones that drive Chamberlain's price up and determine how and where the sport should be played, are exchanges between massive institutions on a variety of levels. The fans were not paying Wilt Chamberlain to play — they were buying mass entertainment, carefully marketed, packaged, and presented. It would be ludicrous to talk about exchange equivalence between Chamberlain and the people who bought tickets.

Nozick's example is all the more disingenuous because he later makes it sound as if the example would work in a socialist society as well as in a capitalist society. Imagine that Chamberlain lived in a socialist society and, having worked all day (for the state, I assume), decides to earn additional money by playing basketball at night, working overtime as it were. Nozick implies that the same redistributions would take place. But of course they would not. Chamberlain would certainly earn some extra money, some modest redistribution would take place, but, without benefit of the capital, marketing, and media of the capitalist society, we would be talking about relative chicken-feed — enough perhaps to provide incentive to play basketball in the evenings but not to the tune of hundreds of thousands of dollars.

In fact, imagining Chamberlain working as a moonlighting entrepreneur in a socialist society gives us a better idea of what face-to-face transactions in sports would look like. I think they would look much like those connected to a four-man softball team which used to tour the country when I was a boy: The King and His Court it was called. They would challenge any local team to a game and all the townspeople would pay their two or three dollars to watch the King pitch wondrous curve balls, drop balls, rise balls and combinations thereof between his legs, blind-folded, from second base — but all at the embarrassment of the local team who mostly fanned at air. Eddie Fiegner may have lived well off his earnings — perhaps he even became a millionaire, although I doubt it. But he worked long nights and long seasons, traveling in cars and buses. He was working class and he shared meanings with most of the working class men he played against. The exchange of money for play there was at least close to the kinds of exchanges that Adam Smith had in mind. In a socialist society, in the evenings, that is what Wilt Chamberlain might do. But he would not become a rich man — certainly not a celebrity. Indeed, it is likely that if he attempted to charge prices that would earn him too much, he would be run out of town for having violated the shared meanings.

This example of the capitalist and socialist Chamberlain demonstrates clearly, I think, the fundamental difference between a capitalist market society and merely a market society. A market society is characterized by a high degree of "presence," where, as I have already suggested, participants occupy a world of shared meanings, are mutually knowledgeable about the goods they exchange, and, typically, exchange directly with each other. It is this "presence" to each other that helps assure mutual competence in exchange. A capitalist society, by contrast, is characterized by

distances, and especially by distances in market contexts. I shall try to give more complexity to this notion shortly but the essential idea is expressed by the distance between the market where Chamberlain negotiates with his capitalist employers, and the market where consumers purchase entertainment. Without that distance and the capacity to bridge that distance, the profits would be modest.

The fundamental points here are two: (1) the big profits, those which Adam Smith called "extraordinary profits" and which distort the just price, are to be made in such distances; and (2) making those profits requires something to bridge the distances. That something is a form of power and it is called capital. As will become evident, I use the notion of distance both literally and figuratively: it refers to distances of both space and time between market contexts. Let me now try to clarify and illustrate these points.

Ferdnand Braudel, in his monumental *Civilization and Capitalism, 15th-18th Century,* has made the distinction between capitalism and market economy a fundamental motif running through all three volumes. I rely heavily on his account for much of the historical material I relate here. Capitalism, Braudel makes clear (he is by no means the first to do this), has its home first in trade, circulation, and marketing, not in production and industrialism. This is not at all surprising: the first distances to be covered were the physical distances between markets and this was made possible by the development of money, permitting easy transportation of capital, and by the growth of a merchant class. And as we know, these merchants were not highly regarded — because they were mobile, because they had neither king nor prince, and because of the wealth they amassed, they were not part of the shared meanings of the local markets. But these same merchants also opened up trading European markets where there had been chiefly local markets.

The making of money through trade has long been suspect. Aristotle, distinguishing retail trade from the acquisition of necessities, called the latter honorable but the gaining of wealth through exchange "justly censured," and "unnatural," linking it to usury. Aquinas followed suit. The modern world, at least in its capitalist forms, has long ceased to censure the middleman, and there is good reason not to. But it is worth looking closely at the reasons for suspicion. The fundamental reason is power in the form of capital including, for the merchant, money, ships, and special concessions from ruling authorities. This power is what Anthony Giddens calls "storage capacity," the ability to hold resources through time and over distance in order to find a market and price more favorable than the original context. Capitalist exchange is not a single exchange but a chain of exchanges mediated by capital, yielding potentially much higher profits than possible in the simple exchange of markets under normal competitive conditions. But only potentially: there are also higher risks and it is of course these risks that help to justify at least some of the higher return) because much can happen over time and space. This is why there is always an element of speculation in capitalism — true capitalism does not exist without speculation about another time, or another place.

(I might add as an aside that I learned while visiting an abbey ruin in Yorkshire, England, this past year that Benedictine monks were involved in speculative capitalism as early as the 13th century. They built the sheep industry along capitalist lines, selling the wool crop to Italian bankers long before the shearing season. The Italians had to speculate about the market months in advance. It is the earliest account of futures trading of which I have heard.)

With the growth of industrialism, capitalism shifted its home (although never entirely) from trade to production. This is the capitalism we know chiefly through the work of Marx. The "means of production," that storage capacity of factories, machinery, and labor, spanning the distance between raw materials and a growing mass market, provided the power for the generation of great wealth. Then came finance capitalism, where the storage capacity is in money and credit.

The picture is far more complicated, of course, than this simple linear development from trade to industrialism to finance. All forms of capitalism have always exited simultaneously; it is only that the speculative thrust of capitalism always takes to that form where the great profits are most easily to be made, and that means that the meaning of capital constantly shifts. To complete the picture of modern capitalism we would have to look at

storage power or capital in information, in technology and research facilities, in communications networks, and the like. Hilton Hotels learned long ago that it could give over equity ownership and even management to indigenous populations provided it could control the service contract for management and the world-wide reservations system. Third World countries have wrestled for equity and management control only to discover that real control, that is, the effective capital, lay in research and development, the storage capacity bridging the distance between the modern university or knowledge industry and actual production. Capital, as Marx understood, is infinitely flexible and will always find a new distance to span.

Now the point of all this is not that all exchange in a capitalist market society is inherently unjust, nor that capitalism must go. It may be well, in fact, to argue the other side for a moment. As I have already indicated, the risks attached to speculation have made possible remarkable advances in the development of the modern economy. I do not think that one has to approve of all of these developments in order to recognize the genuine achievements. Further, immense concentrations of capital in one form or another are essential for a host of modern undertakings, whether it be the design and building of a jet-liner or the development of mass transportation. Nor does the problem necessarily change if one shifts such undertakings to governments. Governments have perhaps as much power for storage capacity as anyone, and the ability to abuse it; they are often the largest capitalists. The storage-power is intrinsic to the large-scale organization of modern societies. but the fact that storage power is ubiquitous in both the private and public domains is only stronger argument for policing it.

Let me consider here briefly a variety of contemporary situations in which capitalism distorts or seriously threatens to distort market exchange, preventing equivalence and justice. In the example I gave earlier, Adam Smith noted that a merchant, aided by distance, might for a short time keep secret from other suppliers a change of price in the distant market. Smith anticipated that such secrets could not long be kept. But the distances now are greater and the secrets more complex. The secret is, in essence, a monopoly of information; its effect on exchange is the same as any other monopoly. Combined with distances of space and time, it creates the extraordinary profits of modern capitalism. In fact, the capitalist is drawn to the distances in part because the secrets are easier to keep. Here are some examples of various combinations and kinds of secrecy and distance, all of which prevent mutual competence in exchange.

1. Most of the first transnational corporations were extraction industries, removing natural resources from poor nations and shipping them to the industrial nations. There would be no commensurability between the price of the resource in the local market and the price in the industrial market. Copper, for example, has little use in an undeveloped economy but is of strategic importance in advanced economics. Now, competition between transnationals may help to keep prices down but even if so this ignores the sellers in the original markets if the company has a monopoly there, which in the past it usually did. The problem is that having intellectual knowledge that one's resources are worth, say, ten times more in another market is not sufficient without power. The most effective expression of power with regard to extraction industries has been nationalization but this has rarely been a long-term solution and does not work well with other forms of industry where the health of the production depends on technological knowledge, marketing knowledge, and communication networks with other industries and markets. This form of knowledge does not exist on paper but is embodied in an infrastructure of civil servants and economic advisors who can interpret information, police transactions, and make decisions. To be underdeveloped is precisely to lack such an infrastructure. Therefore, there is not mutual competence in exchange between the seller and the ultimate buyer in another market. The sophistication of modern corporations in maintaining secrets, storing knowledge, and using this for competitive advantage is extraordinary. Among the devices is transfer-pricing, exchanges between divisions of the same corporation in different countries completely removed from any market and at prices set to permit invisible capital flow from one country to another as well as to be able to report profits and losses in the most favorable tax situations.

2. The close connection between university research and modern industrial technology has spawned the Route 128's, Silicon Valley, and a host of other university science parks. Fortunes have been made with knowledge as the bridge spanning the distance between the market which originally supports a researcher (e.g., a government grant or tuition from students) and the market of advanced technology. Similar examples abound in medical science. The problem here is not simply the absence of mutual competence and equivalence at the ends of the chain of exchanges but also the potential and actual distortion of the contexts of meaning for those exchanges. Educational institutions and the education within them are changed; medical care is transformed. Capitalist exchange transforms the meanings as well as the criteria for competence in other spheres.

3. Plant closings and relocations depend as much as anything else on the remarkable mobility of capital in modern economies but it is important to point to the lack of mutuality of competence in the exchanges involved. Management is free to negotiate with other municipalities, with other states, and even with national governments about capital movement for more attractive returns. In most cases, labor is left out of such negotiations and is often kept completely ignorant, in spite of the fact that the planned new exchanges affect them directly and destructively, probably more than any other party to the exchange. The incommensurable exchange between labor and business is the root cause. If labor were afforded equal competence in that exchange, their contracts would guarantee involvement in the other exchanges.

4. The consumer market is designed as often as not to prevent equal competence in exchange. The image-laden, highly manipulative nature of most mass-media advertising virtually guarantees purchases made on grounds other than knowledge of the goods exchanged. Imagine what consumer advertising would be like if the seller were interested in making the consumer equally competent. We in fact have a model for this in trade journals where producers sell to each other, where there is trade among peers. Such advertisements are information-intensive, promising more information if needed. And such advertising should be the standard for all advertising, although I am aware of the difficulties here. It seems clear to me, however, that the criterion of mutual competence rules out advertising aimed at children and adolescents. But

the role of mass media in the consumer market, as well as its powerful effect in other spheres such as politics, suggests that the problems may lie deeper than advertising itself, that the modern development of mass media may have created a new sphere of human communication requiring the articulation of a new set of rights and prohibitions. As part of this the mass media may need to be protected from markets or from private capital as the only way to preserve fundamental political rights as well as competence in exchange.

This list could go on. Indeed, no account of the distortions of exchange and the infringement on rights to the modern world is really complete without mentioning professional monopolies such as the AMA and the ABA. But I hope that I have made my fundamental point: that it is the nature of capitalism in its most aggressive forms to distort free exchange, that speculative capitalism, which is where the great profits are, depends on asymmetry of competence in exchange, that, in short, markets need constant protection from capitalism. There is, as I confessed earlier, nothing terribly new about this, being simply an interpretation of the old criticism that capitalism tends toward monopoly. But sometimes old truths need restating.

And it follows from this that the task of ethics is not merely the demarcation of the appropriate boundaries of the market but also the interpretation and criticism of the multitude of exchanges in the modern world, displaying the distortions and the serious harms being done.

Some Concluding Suggestions

What I have said is chiefly analysis and diagnosis, not prescription. Prescription would require not merely a book but, I suspect, concerted interdisciplinary effort by many. But let me here make a few concluding comments by way of summarizing and suggesting directions.

First, it may be useful to restate why redistribution cannot by itself correct the problems I have been discussing. Redistribution may be important simply to keep people alive, and distributional justice is some measure of how a society regards its members. But aggregate statistics on income and wealth distribution tell nothing about what has entered or not entered market exchange nor do

they indicate whether there has been disruption of communities and families or corruptions of domains and rights. To know these things, we need to look at specific exchanges and measure them by commutative justice.

Second, we need to be suspicious about references to markets in general, or to exchange relations in general, and especially to the free market. These are abstractions. The exchanges in real world economies are complex and of many different kinds; they take place between very different kinds of exchangers. Without knowing specifics about the exchange — what is being exchanged by whom and under what circumstances — we cannot judge the justice of the exchange.

Third, following from the complexity and variety of exchange, there cannot be one simple solution to the problems of commutative justice. There must be different solutions for the differing forms and contexts of exchange.

Fourth, such solutions clearly require political planning and, indeed, it can be argued that "free markets" have always required the protection of governing authority. Planning of any kind is not without its problems but it needs to be remembered that in situations where non-equivalent exchanges and contracts already exist, so-called free market solutions to economic problems always favor the stronger party in the exchange while the costs of the solutions are paid by the weaker party.

Finally, the market needs to be "liberated" and secularized if you will, freed from its connections to capitalism and demystified in relation to the quasi-religious claims made about it. I have tried to do that here, first by clarifying how capitalism and the market differ, but second by avoiding much theological discussion. Too much has been claimed for markets and there has been too much bolstering with metaphysical and theological claims. Most of the discussions that argue for market economies on the basis of claims about human nature, or on the basis of theological claims about the world and history, turn out to be chiefly quasi-theological arguments about capitalism and socialism. My proposal is that we start more modestly and empirically. Markets are ubiquitous throughout human history and clearly serve a number of immensely valuable social functions. We live in a society which is, in large part, a market society. In a world of pluralism and of large and complex organizations, it is inevitable and even desirable that exchanges of immense variety and complexity take place. Given this, the central ethical task is to be sure that the exchanges are just. The appropriate standard is, virtually everyone agrees, commutative justice, rooted in the prohibition against harm. If that standard is taken seriously, I have argued, much (not all) of capitalism, which is historically a late arrival by comparison to markets, is unjust.

What we want is a society of just exchanges. To have that we must know what may or may not be exchanged in the market; and we must work to establish the conditions for mutual competence in exchange.

Ethics, Price Fixing, and the Management of Price Strategy

William J. Kehoe

Pricing is perhaps the most difficult area to examine from an ethical viewpoint of all the areas of marketing because of the complexity of the price variable. Pricing decisions are made at all levels of a distribution system. They are influenced by the profit goals of the firm and are constrained by federal and state laws. As Walton observed, "perhaps no other area of managerial activity is more difficult to depict accurately, assess fairly and prescribe realistically in terms of morality than the domain of price."

It may be because of the complexity of price along with the greater appeal of ethical issues in other marketing areas that there is limited literature on the ethics of pricing. The available literature is found in business ethics books in sections on pricing, in articles dealing with sales force and buyer/seller issues, in articles dealing with marketing management issues, in articles dealing with price fixing, in various review and theoretical articles on ethics, and in a variety of articles dealing with codes of ethics.

Concept of Price

Price is a designation (usually monetary) used to facilitate exchange of product or service at a par-

William J. Kehoe, "Ethics, Price Fixing, and the Management of Price Strategy," chap. 6 in *Marketing Ethics: Guidelines for Managers*, ed. Patrick E. Murphy and Gene R. Laczniak (Lexington, MA: Lexington Books/D.C. Heath, 1985), pp. 71-83.

ticular time and place and to particular specifications. Theoretically, price is determined in a way that maximizes profit. More realistically, pricing decisions are made on either a cost-plus basis, a target rate of return basis, a competition-oriented basis, or through analysis of the demand for the product/service.

Ethically, any price set by a firm should be either equal or proportional to the benefit received. The critical questions are, What are the benefits? How are they perceived by the consumer? For example, if a perceived benefit of a product is the status gained from the use of the product, does such a benefit justify charging a higher price for the product? If a product is defined in the larger sense as a bundle of want-satisfying qualities, the answer to the status/price question is different than if the product is more narrowly defined.

In a sense, a manager might use analysis by "proportionate reason" in considering the price/benefit question; that is, are there features of the action of charging a higher price, given some perceived benefit of the product, that justify the higher price as moral, even though the action may also have some form of wrong? For example, is it wrong to charge a price that yields extraordinary profit to the firm even if the market is willing to pay the price?

Concept of Profit

Most businesspeople would argue that business is entitled to profit so it can continue to exist in the long run. Profit is a reward to the organization for being successful in providing well-designed goods and/or services for the public, for risk taking, for efficient management, for effective marketing, and for being sensitive to the needs of its clients and other publics.

Profit is defined in economics as the excess of total revenue over total cost. Profit may also be defined as the return enjoyed by the organization on some balance sheet or income statement entry as the result of engaging in a successful exchange relationship. For example, the return on sales, the return on assets, the return on invested capital, and so on are used to describe the profit situation of a firm.

Both business and the public expect an organization to earn reasonable profit. Profit that appears too large, either in terms of its absolute magnitude or in terms of comparison with other firms, is considered by some people as unethical, especially if the profit has been preceded by prices that are perceived to be too high.

The petroleum industry is a case in point. Since about 1970, prices have increased dramatically. At the same time, petroleum companies are reporting record revenue and profit. The question becomes, is the profit reasonable or is it a windfall profit? Does the profit adequately reward the organization for risk taking and for effectiveness and efficiency in operations? When judged on the basis of return on invested capital, one might argue that there is a need for additional profit in the petroleum industry. Of course, such an argument must recognize the caveat that the industry is capital intensive.

It is not easy to judge the reasonableness of profit, and it is far more complex to decide whether the profit is ethical. A reasonable profit is one that rewards a firm for its contribution to the public good; allows a firm to reward shareholders competitively in its dividend payment; enables a firm's stock to compete in the equity market with other stocks and with bonds, certificates, and savings account; provides reinvestment for growth in the organization; and recognizes the degree of risk undertaken by a firm.

If a firm earns a reasonable profit using these criteria, is it also an ethical profit? Based on utilitarian ethical base, the argument could be advanced that a reasonable profit enables a firm to continue to produce goods and services for the benefit of society; that is, the greater good of society is being satisfied by a firm's having a reasonable profit.

Even though the greater good of society may be served by reasonable profit, one cannot conclude the profit is ethical solely on a utilitarian ethical base. Other important questions must be brought to the analysis. Was society in any way injured in making the profit? Injury could occur from actions by the firm such as deceptive advertising, pollution, price fixing, fraud, concealed product defects, and so on. Were the employees of the organization adequately and fairly paid for their work in producing the product? Were the poor and disadvantaged afforded the opportunity of the product, or were they defined as a market segment of low interest to the firm? These and other questions must be addressed when judging whether a reasonable profit is also an ethical profit.

Ethical Issues in Pricing

Identifying the Issues

There is an expansive realm of ethical issues in pricing. Issues may be raised at all levels of the distribution channel, across different market structures and competitive situations, and across industry types. Murphy and Laczniak have identified the following ethical issues in pricing:

1. determining a fair price that meets corporate objectives while not taking advantage of consumers;
2. altering the quality and/or quantity of merchandise without changing the price;
3. practicing price discrimination with smaller accounts;
4. using multiple pricing deals at the retail level;
5. excessively marking up products that are given as premiums;
6. using lower quality merchandise for end-of-month sales;
7. adding high markups to products sold by a franchisor to a franchisee;
8. engaging in price fixing.

Other ethical issues, identified by Dubinsky, Berkowitz, and Rudelius and Dubinsky and Gwin include:

9. having less competitive prices or terms of sale for those buyers who use a firm as their only supplier;
10. providing gifts, prizes or purchase volume incentive bonuses to some customers and not to others;
11. obtaining information on a competitor's price quotation in order to requote or rebid;
12. using a firm's economic power to force premium prices on a buyer;
13. using reciprocity practices.

Beyond these issues, other pricing activities of questionable ethics identified in this research include:

14. the situation of a manufacturer printing a suggested retail price (list price) on a product or its package with the knowledge the retailer does not intend to sell at the suggested retail price but intends to mark over the price to give the impression the item has been marked down — the list price should be the price at which an item is usually and customarily sold, according to the FTC in a case examining the meaning of list;
15. the practice of pricing branded products higher than generic products — Benson notes that "no ethic has been determined" regarding the pricing practices of branded versus generic products;
16. using special price codes (as in automobile dealerships with used cars) so that the consumer cannot easily compare prices;
17. failing to put the price on the product or to post it at the point of purchase, as is often done in the case of a retailer's use of UPCs;
18. bribery of purchasers to cause them to accept higher prices on items in the purchase order;
19. failure of retailers to pass on to consumers discounts to which they are entitled;
20. the practice of psychological pricing (e.g. intending that the consumer will perceive $299 as "about $200").

Choosing an Issue

A single issue, price fixing, is chosen for further analysis. This choice was made because the ethics and legality of price fixing have an extensive literature; price fixing is not only one of the oldest but also a contemporary ethical issue in pricing; and the conclusions, recommendations, and implications taken from an analysis of the ethical issue in price fixing may be generalized to other pricing situations.

Price Fixing

Price fixing is an illegal activity. It is forbidden by antitrust legislation. Antitrust law has been described by Austin as a set of laws that forms an externally imposed code of conduct and ethics that stipulate:

1. Business firms must not conspire to monopolize a market.
2. Business firms must not conspire to allocate shares of a market among themselves.
3. Business firms should not conspire to agree jointly as to the prices at which products will be sold.

The Sherman Antitrust Act of 1890, the Clayton Act of 1914, the Federal Trade Commission Act of 1914, and the Robinson-Putman Act of 1936 comprise what is commonly referred to as antitrust law.

Price fixing is any practice in which a firm conspires with other firms to set minimum or maximum prices, set production quotas, rig bids, eliminate discounts, limit price advertising, or pressure distributors to sell at suggested retail prices (so-called vertical price fixing). Lawyer explained how to conspire to fix prices but admonished that a firm may not benefit by conspiring even if it does not get caught.

The penalty for being convicted of price fixing is severe. A convicted firm can be required to pay three times the total overcharges made by all price fixers in a market. Under the proposed Antitrust Equal Enforcement Act, each company would have its liability for damages limited to the percentage of total industry sales it realized during the conspiracy. As an example, presently, a major manufacturer convicted of price fixing is liable for $700 million in damages, while under the proposed legislation, the damages would be reduced — that is, limited — to $53 million.

Examples of price fixing activities have been reported in the literature. The best known examples are from the electrical manufacturing and folding carton industries. These are presented here and their similarities are noted to suggest guidelines for operating ethically.

Electrical Manufacturers' Case

In the electrical manufacturers' case, price was decentralized. This meant that operating managers were allowed to determine price and that signifi-

cant pressure was applied on the managers to make profit goals. This, combined with the fact that collusion was perceived to be condoned by management, led to a conspiracy to fix prices in the industry.

In price fixing litigation in 1961, General Electric, Westinghouse, and other manufacturers were charged with conspiracy. The electrical manufacturing industry is an oligopoly market. In an oligopoly, there are few sellers, a substantial share of the market is controlled by a small number of the firms, and the firms are affected by each other's pricing practices, especially if the products are undifferentiated. There is an interdependence in pricing in an oligopoly because the number of firms is so few that any firm immediately notices and is affected by the pricing decisions of a competitor. An oligopoly, therefore, tends to establish price uniformity, particularly in an undifferentiated oligopoly. This is accomplished by each firm carefully monitoring the pricing actions of competitors and maintaining similar prices or by price leadership, collusion, or conspiracy.

Folding Carton Industry Case

The folding carton industry is significantly different from the electrical manufacturing industry; it is not an oligopoly. At the time of its price fixing litigation in mid-1970, the industry had over 450 companies, with the largest controlling under 10 percent of the market. Its products were undifferentiated and there was a job order nature to the business in which each job was costed and priced individually. This forced the pricing decision and authority lower in the organization and effectively decentralized the decision.

Management in the folding carton industry appraised individual performance on the basis of profit and volume. The market was crowded, there was widespread participation by employees in trade associations, and the corporate legal staffs were reactive and allowed managers to engage in questionable price practices.

Synthesis

The following company-level similarities identified by Sonnenfeld and Lawrence in these two case examples suggest company situations where there may be pressure to price in an unethical fashion:

1. undifferentiated products;
2. decentralized pricing;
3. pressure to achieve profit goals;
4. collusion perceived to be condoned by top management;
5. reactive versus anticipatory corporate legal staffs;
6. general ethical rules as opposed to specific ethical rules;
7. no ethical compliance procedures or ethical audits.

Reasons for Unethical Pricing Behavior

Price fixing is illegal. However, even in the absence of law, the expectation would be that ethics would prevent price fixing. In fact, it did not and has not.

When Sonnenfeld interviewed senior executives and divisional managers from four of the ten largest producers in the folding carton industry, he received role-biased responses to the question, why does your company have difficulty avoiding price fixing? The senior executives attributed price fixing to dispositional factors such as individual uncontrollable variations in human morals, obedience, and intelligence. They felt violators should be punished as a deterrence to others and recommended employee selection surveillance, reward tightening, and policy clarification as ways to prevent price fixing in the future. The divisional managers blamed price fixing on situational factors like declining demand and treated violators as conscientious people who happened to be caught.

A probable reason why senior executives blamed the individual for price fixing while divisional managers blamed the situation is that the divisional managers were closer to both the individual and the situation than the senior executives. Beyond these proximate reasons of individual and situation, there are other reasons for unethical behavior. A study sponsored by the Business Roundtable suggested that unethical corporate behavior is caused by at least six organizational reasons:

- Corporate objectives and review procedures that overemphasize the profit criterion. If profit goals are overemphasized, line managers may perceive that profit should be placed above ethical considerations. In both case examples discussed earlier, pressure to achieve profit goals contributed to price fixing behavior. As Clasen observed, when the choice is between profit margins and ethics at the line management level, profit margins are often chosen.
- Ethical standards without a concomitant control system. If the ethical standard is, for example, never to lower product quality without also reviewing the necessity of a price adjustment, this standard will become ineffective if it is not monitored by management, particularly if line management is profit oriented. This is because a single job objective is being emphasized.
- Allowing the law to be a surrogate for corporate ethics. This should never be permitted to occur. Rather, as stated in the Caterpillar Tractor Company's Code of Worldwide Business Conduct, "the law is a floor. Ethical business conduct should normally exist at a level well above the minimum required by law." In situations where the law is vague or permissive, the highest integrity should be expected.
- Ambiguous corporate policies. If policy is unclear as to the ethical conduct that is expected in making a pricing decision, the employee may be unsure whether the policy is to be observed. In the absence of the requirements of law in a particular pricing practice, management should determine if its policy specifically indicates the expected behavior on the part of the employee and the outcome if the behavior is not performed. For example, the policy of the IBM Corporation is clearly never to discuss price with competitors. If such a discussion ever occurs, the IBM policy is that the representative "should leave in a manner that will be noticed and remembered by others at the meeting."
- Misreading public concern about corporate ethics. The public has become increasingly concerned about business ethics. In a major ethical incident (for example, bribery by a large corporation), the public becomes sensitive about the ethical conduct of all business firms. In

such a situation, price leadership actions, for example, while legal, may be questioned on the basis of ethics.

· Amoral decision making. When profit is the criterion in the pricing decision, ethical implications of the decision and its impact on people are often overlooked. For example, the situation of establishing higher prices in a captive market, like a lower income neighborhood where people shop at the neighborhood retail outlet, is a situation of being more concerned about profit and less concerned about people, except to the extent that people affect profit projections.

These six organizational reasons, together with the proximate reasons of individual disposition and situation, give insight to reasons for questionable ethics in pricing. These reasons, in turn, are useful in formulating guideline for improving pricing ethics. . . .

Management Guidelines

Organizations should take pragmatic steps to improve ethical practice in pricing. Recommended here are steps involving four areas: the employee, the market situation, the corporation, and the consumer.

The Employee

Education of the employee in the concept of ethics is critical to improving ethical practice in pricing. The educational program, in its content and pedagogy, should seek to increase the employee's sensitivity toward the ethical dimension of the pricing decision, to imbue an understanding of ethical theory and concepts to enable the employee to analyze ethical issues in pricing decision, to develop a capacity for resolution of ethical issues, and to enable the employee to recognize when to seek professional help from management. The corporate position and its code of ethics should be promulgated and examples of likely ethical situations and dilemmas presented and discussed during the educational program. Both positive and negative outcomes should be explored. Finally, the educational program should cause ques-

tions of ethics to be routinely reported to and discussed with management. This is the obverse of a monitoring system and will enhance compliance.

The Market Situation

Guidelines for pricing ethics might be approached by analyzing pricing from two market viewpoints. At one extreme, the pricing decision is decentralized, the product is homogeneous, and the field sales representative has a wide range of pricing authority. At the other extreme, pricing is highly centralized, the product is differentiated, the price is administered by marketing management, and the field sales representative has little authority to deviate from the established price. In the former, ethics in pricing is addressed at the field sales level, while in the latter, it is addressed at the management level.

The more decentralized the pricing decision, the greater is the number of individuals who will have some degree of pricing authority. If the market is highly competitive, prices are quoted on a job basis, and the product is differentiated, it behooves management to be especially concerned that employees remain ethical and legal in pricing. In such a situation, ethics must be institutionalized in the firm, especially in the marketing area.

The Corporation

Purcell has recommended institutionalizing ethics in the corporation by placing an ethics committee on the board of directors; by establishing, promulgating, and using a corporate code of ethics; and by including ethics modules and courses in management training programs. Similarly, ethics must be institutionalized in the marketing area of the corporation. This may be accomplished by:

1. including a session on ethics at the annual sales meeting;
2. building an ethics module into the orientation program of new employees;
3. including discussion of ethics in the annual review meeting with marketing employees (the purpose here is to gain insight into individual dispositional factors that might influence pricing ethics);

4. briefly discussing ethics on a quarterly basis in employee newsletters;

5. requiring sales representatives to certify that they have not knowingly violated laws or ethical policy in securing any purchase order they submit to the firm;

6. circulating articles on ethics to the sales representatives;

7. inviting consultants and/or educators to conduct regular seminars on ethics.

The Consumer

One of the most important things a firm can do to improve ethics in pricing is to recognize that the consumer is an equal partner with the firm in the exchange relationship. The consumer brings needs and expectations to the exchange, is entitled to be fairly treated in the pricing process, and has certain rights that should be respected by the firm. What follows is a statement of consumer rights in pricing:

> A consumer is entitled to receive fair value for the money spent to purchase a product or service. He or she has the right to expect that the price was realistically and analytically arrived at by the firm and was calculated to give the firm a reasonable profit (defined earlier in this chapter). The price should be fully disclosed by being stated in advertisements for the product or service, posted at the point of sale, and placed on the product (although the use of UPCs confounds this requirement). The price on the product should be the price at which the seller is willing to enter an exchange. It should not be artificially high so it causes the buyer to believe he or she has received a bargain when the price is lowered in negotiation to its intended level. When the product is changed in quality or quantity, the customer is entitled to receive a proportional change in price. Price changes should be promptly announced and completely implemented. Questions concerning price should be honestly answered. Customers are always entitled to fair and equal pricing treatment in the marketplace.

These are several advantages to a firm in adopting the statement of consumer rights in pricing. Internally, the statement becomes a code of pricing ethics that sensitizes employees to the necessity of being ethical in pricing and in other marketing activities. Externally, the statement communicates to potential clients that the firm is oriented toward being ethical in pricing.

Conclusion

In the beginning of this chapter, Walton's observation on the difficulty in examining ethical issues in pricing was noted. That observation still stands. Price is a complex marketing variable, and it is difficult to assess ethically.

While ethics in pricing is difficult to assess, certain conclusions may be drawn that are of value to management. A firm may have difficulty with ethics in pricing when:

1. the market is at overcapacity or characterized as an oligopoly;
2. products are undifferentiated;
3. pricing is on an individual job basis;
4. profit is the primary evaluative criterion;
5. top management is perceived not to be concerned about pricing ethics;
6. employees have regular and frequent opportunities to meet with competitors;
7. ethical rules and compliance procedures are lax.

If one or several of these characteristics is present, management must be concerned with ethics in pricing. To ensure ethical practices in pricing, management should audit pricing policy and practice, institutionalize a concern for ethics in pricing, and establish a means for reviewing the pricing activity. In situations where the characteristics listed here are not present, competition should not be considered a sufficient guarantee of ethical pricing; rather, management must remain vigilant and monitor pricing decisions. These actions will ensure ethics in pricing.

Beyond ethics in pricing, management and employees should aspire to be ethical in all aspects of work. Pope John Paul II, in his Encyclical *Laborem Exercens (On Human Work)*, asks that employees be ethical in all aspects of work. The encyclical states "that man, created in the image of God, shares by his work in the activity of the Creator and that, within the limits of his own human capabilities, man in a sense continues to develop that activity, and perfects it as he advances further and further in the discovery of the resources and values contained in the whole creation." In the presence of this profound concept of work, is it too much to ask that managers be ethical in the work of pricing?

Section 2: Finance

Borrowing, lending, saving, and investing have been part of our experience in the marketplace for centuries. They have always raised moral and religious questions. Thomas Aquinas, John Calvin, Martin Luther, and many before them discussed the morality of charging interest in commercial transactions given the laws in Deuteronomy. Yet in this century financial activities have been transformed in new and complex ways. The instruments by which businesses work with money have proliferated at an astounding rate in the past two decades. Not only are businesses far more calculating about their cash flows, working capital, inventory-carrying charges, and capital budgeting; they are also involved with vast global networks of banks, capital markets, institutional investors, and governmental agencies. Both inside and outside of businesses the complexity of the financial world has exploded.

Somehow faith and finance are subtly connected. Yet of all areas of business enterprise, this is one of those least explored by religious ethicists. The last two decades should have been a wake-up call for those concerned with business ethics. The tragedies left in the wake of the savings and loan debacle, the Black Monday market crash of October 1987, insider trading, and hostile corporate takeovers are encouraging ethicists to ask anew about faith and finance.

Robert Bachelder, former banker and now a Protestant minister, suggests that the web of American religious traditions connecting the pursuit of wealth with its ethical moorings has slipped away. As a result, managing financial transactions has been transformed from a public trust into some weird kind of video game. The goal is no longer to be an economically productive fiduciary; instead the goal is winning for its own sake.

Dennis McCann reinforces Bachelder's point of view but assigns some of the blame for this moral failure to the churches' cavalier disdain for the routine activities of finance. McCann shows, for example, how the tradition of Catholic social teaching preserved certain medieval prejudices against money making. The modern papal condemnation of "the accursed internationalism" of finance, McCann argues, has retarded the development of any systematic treatment of money, banking, and financial markets. Instead, successive popes turned their attention to championing the cause of those marginalized in the global financial system. Only in the 1986 American Catholic bishops' letter does McCann begin to see a constructive basis for ethical reflection on how businesses and financial institutions handle savings and investment.

Yet the faith and finance connection is not a one-way path. Not only should faith effect finance, but finance also influences faith. As Paul Hessert observes, financial concepts continue to have considerable effects on religious thinking in everyday life. He argues that the abstract quantifications of money affect the human sense of value, identity, legitimacy, and future in important ways that we ignore to our detriment.

This is only a beginning. Complexity in the field of finance continues to grow as investment options proliferate and markets are shaped by global telecommunications. The issues of moral principle and action are complex. If any field is ripe for further discussion of moral choices, this is it.

Have Ethics Disappeared from Wall Street?

Robert S. Bachelder

Soon after the financial scandal broke last year involving Ivan Boesky, the Wall Street arbitrager, I spoke with a dean of Harvard University's Business School at a suburban Boston church. Not wanting to sound moralistic, I wondered aloud if insider trading in securities might be ethically ambiguous since some argue that it promotes market efficiency. To my surprise, this dean of one of America's educational bastions of capitalism replied sharply with a moralist's simplicity:"There's nothing ambiguous about it. It's illegal and immoral — sheer greed."

However, something troubled the dean even more than financial corruption:

> At Harvard we have lots of good and thoughtful young people. They would not commit illegal acts in their business. But business education doesn't do a very good job of teaching them how to incorporate their values in business.

To help instill values at an early age, he has been teaching Sunday school for a dozen years.

The effect in the past of the Protestant ethic, observed historian Richard Hofstadter, was to heighten generally the sense of personal responsibility and create a strong sense of civic consciousness. And Henry James, the literary expositor of this sensibility, said that "responsibility is glory." Not surprisingly, this outlook helped significantly to shape the ethos of American finance.

Robert S. Bachelder, "Have Ethics Disappeared from Wall Street?" *Christian Century*, 15-22 July 1987, pp. 628-30.

As economics writer Leonard Silk points out, the 20th-century American establishment is rooted in the 19th-century Unitarian Church in Massachusetts. The Unitarian clergy reminded the Boston merchants with some success that wealth carries responsibilities as well as privileges. In this they drew upon their Puritan antecedents. As Cotton Mather told his Boston congregation in 1701:

> God has made man a sociable creature. We expect benefits from human society, it is but equal that human society should receive benefits from us. We are beneficial to human society by the works of that special occupation in which we are to be employed, according to the order of God ["A Christian at His Calling," *The Annals of America: 1493-1973*, Vol. I (Encyclopaedia Britannica, 1976), p. 39].

Uncontrolled land speculation was an issue for the Unitarians. They disliked even *legal* land speculation since it contributed nothing to the commonwealth, and since success resulted more from luck than from diligent labor. Historian Daniel Howe observes that the Unitarian clergy fomented considerable dissent in Massachusetts against the U.S. annexation of Texas by portraying the Texans as irresponsible speculators who had entered Mexico at their own risk.

Through the 19th century, the Protestant establishment became less ecclesiastical and more secular, but it remained concerned with shaping business by the values of service and disinterestedness. Quite a few of the establishment were sons of New England ministers, and many more were educated in New England church schools and colleges. As Silk suggests, the Unitarian heritage helped form the basis for the modern social responsibility creed that David Rockefeller articulated in the 1970s as business being a "public mission" with public responsibilities. Of course, the Protestant establishment's practice always fell short of its professed moral standards: the decline of the Puritan ethic into an ethic of individualist capitalism has been well chronicled. After a visit to New York, the English novelist Anthony Trollope wrote in 1857 in *Barchester Towers* that everyone "worships" the dollar. Twelve years later, Jay Gould and James Fisk perpetrated the great gold conspiracy. And the crash of 1929 was abetted by Wall Street's financially irresponsible practices.

Whatever the moral failures or outright hypocrisy of the old establishment, however, Wall Street's current ethos is even more lamentable. Today, moral aspirations themselves are rejected as being worthy subjects for business enterprise. In the Reagan era, extreme free-enterprise ideology, which has always been popular with entrepreneurs and small business people, is staging a takeover of the more exalted bastions of American finance. This stringent creed, eschewing mention of responsibility and social obligation, maintains that the only way to run a business (or even a country) is to concentrate on maximizing profits in the near term. It has found some of its more fervent apostles among the younger investment bankers.

The more profound implications of this development, however, have been overlooked for the most part. The elder investment bankers are appalled that younger members of the fraternity who are already making $1 million a year, such as the convicted insider trader Dennis Levine of Drexel Burnham Lambert, are trying to make even more through illegal insider trading. How can they be so greedy? the elders ask. Currently, the financial periodicals are printing jeremiads about the destructiveness of greed. But greed is not the feature of financial life that should worry us most. We can survive greediness. The quintessential financier J. P. Morgan was probably as greedy as is anyone on Wall Street today. He took a lot from society, but he left even more. Within a few years he created U.S. Steel Corporation, General Electric and International Harvester, all of which produced many jobs and contributed to the commonwealth. In contrast, today's rash of takeovers has little such value.

Wall Street's recent scandals have diverted attention from an even more serious financial phenomenon: ordinary, perfectly legal corporate takeovers that pass for investment banking. To paraphrase Max Weber, the connection between the pursuit of wealth and ethical meaning has come undone. Or as novelist Gore Vidal comments, Puritan virtue is dead and there is nothing to replace it.

What is really disturbing is that so much of investment banking's acquisition and merger ac-

tivity has ceased to be economically productive. Economic activity has an inherently moral purpose to provide the material undergirding for our common life by allocating scarce capital in ways that will promote economic growth. To a late 20th-century church that speaks about "economic democracy" and "solidarity with the poor," these may seem like modest goals, morally speaking. But now even these goals are becoming remote from financial activity.

In 1986, some 3,500 companies or corporate division totaling $159 billion changed hands. In the past four years over 12,000 mergers and acquisitions valued at almost $500 billion have taken place. This activity has been spurred by the prevailing market ideology, by the concomitant deregulation of the financial markets and the growth of the financial services industry, and by the combination of a fairly sluggish economy with a hot stock market that encourages paper profiteering rather than investment in plant and product. Some of these takeovers are proper: Chrysler's 1987 acquisition of American Motors Corporation gives it much-needed production and distribution capacity at an economical price. Robert Lessin of Morgan Stanley thinks that takeovers will increasingly feature such legitimate goals and be prudently financed. That is encouraging.

However, many takeover targets are companies having no relation to the business of the firms that are raiding their stocks. Takeovers generate large fees for investment bankers, increased share prices for stockholders of the acquired companies, and great gains for the raiders, who, after running up the stocks of their acquired companies, often liquidate their assets; but these maneuvers add little if anything to the economy's productive output, and they often mean a loss of jobs through devastating restructurings. Indeed, according to Irwin Friend, emeritus professor of finance at the University of Pennsylvania's Wharton School, stockholders in the raiding companies do not even benefit appreciably from takeovers, which raises the question of whether the raiders are fulfilling their fiduciary responsibilities to their own shareholders. More important, however, is the deterioration in the combined balance sheets that may occur after a firm has been acquired in a hostile takeover or through the threat of a takeover. Felix Rohatyn of Lazard Frères, a New York City investment-banking firm, observes that the mergers of Occidental and Cities Service, of Chevron and Gulf, and of Mobil and Superior have all had this effect.

Carl Icahn, chairman of Trans World Airline, and other raiders say that takeover threats force inept, bloated management, or the "corpocracy," to shape up and become more competitive, but this is not true for the most part. Rather, as Anthony Solomon, former president of the Federal Reserve Bank of New York, observes, the targets of takeovers tend to be well-run companies that have a commitment to the long-term potential of an industry despite temporarily unfavorable circumstances that lead the market to undervalue their stocks. Even if they are not acquired, such companies often are hurt by being forced to pay "greenmail" — to buy back their own stock at inflated prices from the raider in return for dropping the threat.

Further, much of the takeover activity is financed with low-quality, high-yield bonds known as junk bonds. And takeover target companies often assume significant additional debt themselves in order to appear less attractive. This erosion of credit quality, and the high level of debt built up on corporate management, pose dangers for the future. Economist John Kenneth Galbraith fears that when corporate earnings drop, as they must at some point in the business cycle, the debt burden will become unsupportable; and then we will wonder, as we did with Penn Square Bank and with the loans to Latin America, how we could have been so foolish.

When the distinguished firm of Salomon Brothers decided to go into the junk bond takeover business, Henry Kaufman, the most respected economist on Wall Street, resigned from the firm's executive committee. He sounded the traditional theme of the Wall Street establishment at its best: "I am not sure that this whole trend makes a new contribution to society as a whole. We cannot escape the fact that we have some financial responsibility. We are not just in the business of pushing companies around" (quoted in the *New York Times,* November 16, 1986).

If much of the takeover business on Wall Street has ceased to be an economic activity, then what is it? It could be called an athletic contest. Young investment bankers speak about "putting compa-

nies into play," about getting corporate managers interested in deals that would not occur to them on their own. Max Weber noted that as the pursuit of wealth becomes devoid of religious and ethical meaning, "it tends to become associated with purely mundane passions, which often actually give it the character of sport" (*The Protestant Ethic and the Spirit of Capitalism*). This is the picture that lawyer-writer Louis Auchincloss presents in the novel *Diary of a Yuppie* (Houghton Mifflin, 1986). The lawyer and takeover specialist Robert Service describes without compunction the current moral climate:

It's all a game, but a game with very strict rules. You have to stay meticulously within the law; the least misstep, if caught, involves an instant penalty. But there is no particular moral opprobrium in incurring a penalty, any more than there is [in] being offside in football. A man who is found to have bought or sold stock on inside information, or misrepresented his assets in a loan application, or put his girl friend on the company payroll, is not "looked down on," except by sentimentalists. He's simply been caught, that's all. Even the public understands that. Watergate showed it. You break the rules, pay the penalty and go back to the game [pp. 26-27].

This is why insider trading is not the most disturbing financial phenomenon on Wall Street today. It is only the consequence of legitimate economic activity transformed into sport. And this transformation reflects in turn an even more serious development: the collapse of the Protestant ethic of responsibility that traditionally connected finance to socially desirable ends that transcend personal ambition.

A poignantly appropriate symbol for the separation of financial activity from the moral values that once informed it is the configuration of the old Protestant establishment's shrine, Harvard University. On one side of the Charles River, in Cambridge, Massachusetts, stands the college, the nursery of Puritan preachers, Unitarian moralists and their secular descendants. On the other side of the river, in Boston, stands the business school, founded only in this century, with its students eager to be catechized in the extreme free-enterprise creed. In John Marquand's novel *The Late*

George Apley (1936), the Boston Brahmin banker described the business school as a "damnable example of materialism," and he looked the other way when he motored by. But today we are getting used to the fact that traditional values and financial practice occupy separate spheres of existence.

If we are to enjoy a viable economic future, however, we need some other approach than either revulsion or complacency. The importance of responsibility and community needs to be heard in the financial district. The insider-trading scandals expose a deeper crisis in values in our financial leadership that must be confronted now by government and society before the economy suffers further damage. Legislative and regulatory reforms are needed to curb current abuses and preserve the soundness of our financial system. Investment banker Rohatyn has made several proposals in this regard that would promote responsible behavior. These include limiting the number of junk bonds that can be acquired by federal- and state-insured institutions, and specifying to company directors and officers that achieving the best short-term investment returns is not their main fiduciary responsibility. As Rohatyn acknowledges, these reforms will be opposed by powerful lobbies. It would be good to see the churches advancing such reforms through their public policy offices, along with their more traditional support for antipoverty measures.

There is in addition to this political work, as the Harvard Business School dean suggested, the task of shaping the culture's moral ethos, of reconnecting religious and ethical values to the pursuit of wealth so that it has a genuinely economic purpose. One hopes the churches will have a constructive role here. The Roman Catholic bishops' and several Protestant denominations' recent papers dealing with the relationship between Christian faith and economic life have begun this work. These proposals can help us to develop suitable understandings of economic responsibility through the end of the 20th century. . . .

Michael Thomas, a former Lehman Brothers partner, characterizes Wall Street's current mentality with a reference to Charles Dickens's *Martin Chuzzlewit*. Young Martin inquires of a man he meets on the streets of New York City, "Pray, Sir, what is the source of all virtue?" The man replies: "The source of virtue? Dollars, Sir! Dollars!"

The Protestant ethic had the power for much of U.S. history to keep America's financial establishment from taking such foolishness with perfect seriousness. It infused the financial system with a working moral capital, with the understanding, in Cotton Mather's words, that business must be "beneficial to human society" as well as profitable. Now that this capital is almost exhausted, one wonders, to borrow a favorite biblical phrase from the Puritan preachers, if the "day of trouble" may be close at hand. Will our financial temples have to fall on our heads, as Galbraith predicts, before we are brought back to our senses?

The Church and
Wall Street

Dennis P. McCann

... There exists no systematic treatment of savings and investment, money, banking and financial markets in the whole of Catholic social teaching. These topics are touched upon only in passing, in an approach to economic and social justice that has been shaped primarily by the Roman church's concern for the working poor of the industrialized nations, and more recently, the destitute majorities of the so-called third world. Catholic social teaching's perspective, however, consists for the most part in prophetic protest. The tradition typically directs its criticisms equally against both Marxist socialism and laissez-faire capitalism. Since the core of the protest concerns the godless "materialism" that is explicit in the one and allegedly implicit in the other, it is difficult to determine what the constructive alternative might be. The encyclical of Pope Pius XI, *Quadragesimo Anno* (1931), comes closest to defining it, but the modified "corporativism" that would organize society along the lines of some sort of vocational guild system seems so uncomfortably close to the aspirations of Italian Fascism that this alternative has usually been referred to ever so vaguely as "Tercerismo." The spirit animating this tradition is that of a humane aristocrat profoundly uneasy with modernity in all its forms.

What Catholic social teaching has to say on topics related to the investment industry is not very promising. The low point comes fairly early on in the tradition, with *Quadragesimo Anno*'s condemnation of the "accursed internationalism

of finance" (QA, par. 109). Yet this encyclical, written at the height of the Great Depression, at least is aware of the role of financial markets in modern industrial economics. After having defended in classical terms the right to private property, *Rerum Novarum*, an encyclical written by Pope Leo XIII in 1891, warns the "wealthy" that "the just ownership of money is distinct from the just use of money" (RN, par. 35). The point is made by way of introducing an exhortation to almsgiving:"No one, certainly, is obliged to assist others out of what is required for his own necessary use or for that of his family, or even to give to others what he himself needs to maintain his station in life becomingly and decently:'No one is obliged to live unbecomingly.' But when the demands of necessity and propriety have been sufficiently met, it is a duty to give to the poor out of that which remains. 'Give that which remains as alms'" (RN, par. 36). It is striking that this passage could still have been written in 1891. Wealth is conceived in essentially static terms as is the social order as a whole. One's station in life seems fixed for all eternity. It simply does not occur to the Pope that one might actually help the poor more by saving and investing one's surplus in some form of productive enterprise.

Quadragesimo Anno, on the other hand, does mean to take into account "the changes which the capitalist economic system has undergone since [Pope] Leo's time" (QA, par. 104). But at the core of Pope Pius XI's condemnation of "the accursed internationalism of finance" lies the conviction that an economic "dictatorship has succeeded free competition." The investment industry serves as the high command in this economic dictatorship:"In the first place, it is obvious that not only is wealth concentrated in our times but an immense power and despotic economic dictatorship is consolidated in the hands of a few, who often are not owners but only the trustees and managing directors of invested funds which they administer according to their own arbitrary will and pleasure.

"This dictatorship is being most forcibly exercised by those who, since they hold the money and completely control it, control credit also and rule the lending of money. Hence they regulate the flow, so to speak, of the lifeblood whereby the entire economic system lives, and have so firmly in their grasp the soul, as it were, of economic life

Dennis P. McCann, "The Church and Wall Street," *America* 158, no. 4 (30 Jan. 1988): 85-94.

that no one can breathe against their will" (QA, pars. 105-106).

I have quoted these passages in full because I want you to feel the sting of the papal rhetoric. Such statements later were to provide the pretext for the paranoid fantasies of the Catholic "Radio Priest," the Rev. Charles Coughlin, who enthralled and harangued American listeners during the early years of the New Deal era. Father Coughlin, in my view, merely added color and even cruder invective to a papal perspective that in the climate of the 1930's all too easily lent itself to anti-Semitic exploitation.

Nevertheless, there are subtleties in *Quadragesimo Anno*'s teaching that should not elude us, even if they did escape the like of Father Coughlin. The discerning, if not forgiving, reader can find in this encyclical the basis for a more constructive approach to savings, investment and financial markets. In a brief section devoted to "Obligations With Respect to Superfluous Income," the letter expands upon *Rerum Novarum*'s exhortation to almsgiving. Now the list of medieval virtues commended to the wealthy is expanded to include "beneficence and munificence." The latter, in particular, suggests that the reservation of savings for investment sometimes can promote the common good: "Expending larger incomes so that opportunity for gainful work may be abundant, provided, however, that this work is applied to producing really useful goods, ought to be considered" (QA, par. 50).

Further on in the encyclical, the point is restated as a general principle: "Those who are engaged in producing goods, therefore, are not forbidden to increase their fortune in a just and lawful manner; for it is only fair that he who renders service to the community and makes it richer should also, through the increased wealth of the community, be made richer himself according to his position, provided that all these things be sought with due respect for the laws of God in accordance with faith and right reason. If these principles are observed by everyone, everywhere and always, not only the production and acquisition of goods but also the use of wealth, which now is seen to be so often contrary to right order, will be brought back soon within the bounds of equity and just distribution" (QA, par. 136). Taken out of context, this principle might seem to re-

quire an endorsement of capitalism as such: but in the Pope's view, capitalism must be severely criticized precisely for failing to demonstrate "due respect for the laws of God in accordance with faith and right reason."

When we turn from these Depression-era statements to those of the 1960's and beyond, the tone of condemnation is less evident, but the lack of understanding for the positive role of money, banking and financial markets remains. The encyclical of Pope John XXIII, *Mater et Magistra* (1961), for example, echoes its predecessors' distinction between just use of property and its just ownership, but now the point is expressed as the familiar concern for the consequences of separating the ownership of "capital in very large productive enterprises . . . from the role of management" (MM, par. 104). *Mater et Magistra*'s response is not to abolish private ownership, but to distribute it more widely through "all the ranks of the citizenry" (MM, par. 113). What role financial markets might play in such a redistributive process is never clarified. Indeed, Pope John mentions the investment industry only in discussing the plight of farmers: "Wherefore, the general welfare requires that public authorities make special provision for agricultural financing, but also for establishment of banks that provide capital to farmers at reasonable rates of interest" (MM, par. 134). Presumably, financial markets cannot be relied upon to deliver capital to this sector of the economy at a fair return to investors.

So far, then, the papal perspective addresses the investment industry, if at all, mostly to protest the sufferings endured by industrial laborers and farmers, whose lives too often must bear the brunt of the dynamism — what economist Joseph Schumpeter called the "creative destruction" — generated by free-market activity. Among its other achievements, the Second Vatican Council endowed Roman Catholicism with a self-consciously global sense of mission.

Since the council, the church has become a strong advocate for the poor of the third world. *Guadium et Spes*, one of the most impressive documents to emerge from the council, made these comments on the role of financial markets in third-world development: "Investments for their part must be directed toward providing employment and sufficient income for the people both now and in the future. . . . They should also bear in mind the urgent needs of underdeveloped countries or regions. In monetary matters they should beware of hurting the welfare of their own country or of other countries. Care should also be taken lest the economically weak countries unjustly suffer any loss from a change in the value of money" (GS, par. 70).

Ever faithful to the traditional pattern of Catholic social teaching, *Gaudium et Spes* thus addresses the investment industry out of a sense of solidarity with the apparent victims of modern capitalist development. Neither here, nor anywhere else in the tradition, is there an attempt to understand money, banking and financial markets on a systematic basis.

Pope Paul VI's encyclical, *Populorum Progressio* (1967), which was published shortly after the closing of Vatican II, dramatizes the church's new concern for "underdeveloped" nations, and in this context further qualifies the church's traditional defense of the natural right to private property. This right, for example, cannot be used to justify the rapacious conduct of third-world elites:"[The Second Vatican Council] teaches not less clearly that . . . plans for excessive profit made only for one's own advantage should be prohibited. It is by no means lawful, therefore, that citizens with abundant income derived from the resources and work of their native land transfer a large part of their income to foreign countries, looking solely to their own private advantage, giving no consideration to their own country on which they inflict obvious harm by this conduct" (PP, par. 24). Although the encyclical does not make the point explicitly, the investment industry, of course, would have to be considered an accomplice in this "unlawful" activity, to the extent that it provides the means by which such transfers can be made quickly and at relatively low cost.

The papal passion for justice, however, is not matched by any clarity in economic analysis. Rather than breaking new ground in understanding the emerging global economy, *Populorum Progressio* falls back on the condemnations of *Quadragesimo Anno* and unconvincingly argues that "pernicious opinions about economics" are at the heart of the problem:"But out of these new conditions opinions have somehow crept into human society according to which profit was considered the chief incentive to foster economic development, competition the supreme law of economics, private ownership of the means of production an absolute right which recognizes neither limits nor concomitant social duty. This type of unbridled *liberalism* paved the way for a type of tyranny rightly condemned by our predecessor Pius XI as the source of the *internationalism of finance* or *international imperialism*. Such economic abuses will never be rejected as completely as they ought to be because the economy must only serve man, a point about which it is fitting once more to give a serious admonition. But if it must be admitted that so many hardships, so many injustices and fratricidal conflicts whose effects we feel even now, trace their origins to a form of *capitalism*, one would falsely attribute those evils to industrial growth which more correctly are to be blamed on the pernicious opinions about economics which accompanied that growth. On the contrary, justice demands that we admit that not only the organization of labor but also industrial progress made a necessary contribution to promote development" (PP, par. 26).

Alas, it is difficult to make coherent sense out of this papal pronouncement. The point seems to be that though capitalism is evil, industrial growth is a positive moral good. Furthermore, ideology, or avoiding "pernicious opinions" regarding the economy, seems to be a surer path to development than understanding the structural constraints — political and cultural, as well as economic — upon it. On the other hand, the statement makes what appears to be a bitter concession to realism, namely, that the abusive structures symbolized as the "internationalism of finance" will never be extirpated, so long as the economy serves only "man." What we have here is truly reactionary. Instead of making a set of recommendations that might enlist the investment industry more effectively for the task of third-world development, the Vatican is arming itself for ideological combat.

Yet one must ask: Against whom or what is the Vatican protesting? Have conditions in the third-world given new life to the obsolete ideology of laissez-faire liberalism? Or have they merely unmasked once more the essentially inhumane reality of capitalism? If so, why not say so, and get on with the business of developing an alternative? Instead, *Populorum Progressio* leads us backward once more to a Tercerismo, rendered all the more implausible for its self-righteous otherworldliness. What is an economy for, if not to serve the needs of "man"? Is it impossible that the laws of God somehow are already operative in the ambiguous workings of international finance? For any number of reasons, even after the council, the Vatican was simply unprepared to consider that possibility.

The encyclicals of the current Pope, John Paul II, indicate at least the intention of a more systematic approach to economics. His most significant letter, *Laborem Exercens* (1981), in this context provides an opening for further reflection. Between the lines one can discern this Polish intellectual locked in struggle with Marxist and neo-Marxist anthropology, even as he attempts to put Catholic social teaching on a firmer philosophical foundation. The dialogue with Marxism is at once the great strength and the great weakness of the encyclical, for it heavily colors the Pope's formulation of the encyclical's central principle, namely, "the priority of labor over capital." Rightly, the Pope wants to shift attention toward the process of production; and, in terms reminiscent of both Marx and Aquinas, he insists that "in this process labor is always a primary efficient cause, while capital, the whole collection of means of production, remains a mere instrument or instrumental cause" (LE, section 12). But inasmuch as labor includes the activities of all who participate in a production process, including its managers, the "priority of labor" principle amounts to a reassertion of the priority of person over things.

Most interesting in this context, however, is *Laborem Exercens*'s corresponding redefinition of "capital." Capital, being the "the whole collection of means of production and the technology connected with these means," is nothing other than "the historical heritage of human labor." To consider capital independently of its historic relationship to human labor is to be guilty of the error of "economism" (LE, section 13). Economism is a fundamental mistake, for the failure to grasp the necessary interdependence of labor and capital is at the root of the ideological conflict between "liberalism" and Marxism, and the "socioeconomic class conflict" which has marred the industrial era (LE, section 11).

But what is economism, if not the tendency to treat both labor and capital as commodities for sale on the open market? Consider the Pope's assertions: "Opposition between labor and capital does not spring from the structure of the production process or from the structure of the economic process. In general, the latter process demonstrates that labor and what we are accustomed to call capital are intermingled; it shows that they are inseparably linked. . . . Guided both by our intelligence and by faith that draws light from the word of God, we have no difficulty in accepting this image of the sphere and process of man's labor. It is a consistent image, one that is humanistic as well as theological. In it man is the master of the creatures placed at his disposal in the visible world. If some dependence is discovered in the work process, it is dependence on the giver of all the resources of creation and also on other human beings, those to whose work and initiative we owe the perfected and increased possibilities of our own work. All that we can say of everything in the production process which constitutes a whole collection of things, the instruments, the capital, is that it conditions man's work; we cannot assert that it constitutes as it were an impersonal subject putting man and man's work into a position of dependence" (LE, section 13).

Laborem Exercens is to be welcomed for insisting upon the religious significance of human labor, and for pointing out how utterly counterproductive and needless, both in theory and in practice, is an adversarial relationship between labor and capital. But this good news rings rather hollow so long as Catholic social teaching is unable or unwilling to spell out in equally promising terms the relationship between this kind of "capital" and the ordinary workings of finance capital.

The point is that none of the "means of production" described by the Pope would exist, had not some agent, either an individual, or a private corporation or a parastatal organization [a government-owned business] invested in them. Investment, as anyone who has ever attempted to start up a small business or purchase a home must know, comes from one of two sources, either savings or loans, or some combination of both. Investment funds, *Laborem Exercens* might say, are "capital" in the sense that they represent a surplus created in the courses of the production process; but what the encyclical appears unable to deal with is the actual liquidity of such surpluses. They exist not in the form of a "means of production," such as a factory or a machine tool, but as a certain quantity of the recognized means of exchange. Investment "capital" thus exists as money; but the encyclical leaves us guessing whether it is possible to think about money or to manipulate it in any rationally self-interested way without being guilty of the error of "economism."

Such, in my view, is the legacy of Catholic social teaching as it has developed under papal auspices. On the whole, the Vatican's position strikes me as reactionary, but unless we are simply to dismiss it from our deliberations, it can and ought to be understood sympathetically as an important protest against the social costs of modern industrial development, whether capitalist or socialist in its origins. By the time Pope Leo XIII initiated the modern tradition of Catholic social teaching, the ancient papal condemnations of usury had already been allowed to slip into oblivion; nevertheless, the overall impression created by these modern encyclicals is medieval. They continue to exhibit an inordinate fear of the mobility of capital, and the separation of capital ownership and its management, made possible by new communications technologies and the new social and legal institutions characteristic of modern industrial capitalism. As we have seen, obligations and virtues that once made sense in a relatively static and immobile society, for example, the "almsgiving, beneficence and munificence" praised in *Quadragesimo Anno*, are still preached without regard to the macroeconomic function of savings and investment in a capitalist economy. The pursuit of profit is routinely viewed with deep suspicion, as is the very liquidity of wealth.

However tempting this suspicion may be when considering specific abuses such as the flight of investment capital from the so-called third world, it must be understood in light of papal social teaching's traditional bias against international finance. . . . The point is relatively easy to make in abstract theological terms: Papal social teaching has yet to come to terms fully with modernity. But what is at stake concretely in this observation is the tradition's inability or unwillingness to transcend a bias inherent in the feudal, agrarian society of medieval Europe. This bias identifies morality with stability, fixed social classes and generalized cultural immobility.

I have often wondered about the source of this bias, for I do not find it prominently featured in the Bible. Ultimately, this bias may be inherent in the church's adoption and adaptation of the Roman pattern of diocesan administration, for this pattern reinforced and nurtured tendencies toward the centralization of resources and their administration, fixity of residence and all forms of social and economic stability. Under these circumstances the Roman Catholic Church became less a community of Eucharistic memory and more and more a community based on permanent land tenure and hierarchical forms of religious and social authority.

While it is true that under these same circumstances the medieval Christian ethic of social charity may have emerged and flourished, by the same token they also produced an ethos that could hardly be conducive to economic growth. Saving was typically confused with miserliness, and the investment function to a great extent was both condemned and relegated to a mostly tolerated pariah caste. My point is that this uncomprehending hostility to the institutions of capital formation was not an aberration, the result of a tragic failure of economic insight; rather, I see it as a systemic imperative in a Christendom most fundamentally committed to a geographically based pattern of social stability — namely, the Roman Catholic diocese.

I conclude that the hostility directed against the "accursed internationalism of finance" still evident in the modern papal social encyclicals is an important index of just how deeply ingrained this bias is. It also suggests that any attempt to discover resources for an "ethic for the investment industry" in Catholic social teaching will have to find a way to overcome this bias. The papal condemnations and warnings, in short, cannot be taken at face value. As they stand, they simply are not a reliable guide to public morality in this area.

Until most recently, the reflections of the U.S. Catholic bishops have done little but echo the biases of papal social teaching. This is particularly true of the Depression-era statements issued by the national Catholic Welfare Conference on behalf of the bishops. These go out of their way to dramatize Pope Pius XI's opinions regarding the "accursed internationalism of finance."

Nevertheless, even these statements prudently

call for further study of "the whole intricate problem of money and credit," a task that apparently was never carried out under the formal sponsorship of the bishops. The "Statement of Social Problems," issued Nov. 28, 1937, is one of their better statements: "Pius XI calls attention to the tremendous economic power exercised by those who hold and control money and are able therefore to govern credit and determine its allotment. This control, moreover, is exercised by those who are not the real owners of wealth, but merely the trustees and administrators of invested funds. Responsibility is thus divorced from ownership. Nevertheless, they hold in their hands the very soul of productions since they supply its lifeblood and no one can breathe against their will.

"The increasing ration of debt to total wealth has also had its influence on lessening the responsibility and advantage which should attach to the ownership of property. It makes for insecurity. Its relationship, moreover, to the cost of living or a reasonable price level needs careful inquiry. Further study should be given, likewise, to the whole intricate problem of money and credit so that such evils as exist in the present system may be brought to light and suitable remedies introduced" (SSP, pars. 13 and 14).

Being issued in 1937, as it was, this document's moderate tone, compared to the papal rhetoric on which it depends, suggests that perhaps the bishops were already quietly distancing themselves from the "prophetic" utterances of Father Coughlin.

But in light of the U.S. Catholic Conference's recent pastoral letter, "Economic Justice for All: Catholic Social Teaching and the U.S. Economy" (1986), all such statements must be regarded as prehistoric. . . .

Like its constituency, the letter reflects a renewed sense of engagement with the American experiment in cultural pluralism and representative government. It attempts to address both Catholics and concerned citizens in a way that is consistent with the American pattern of religious denominationalism. Its reflections on the need for "a new cultural consensus . . . in order to meet the demands of justice and solidarity" (JA, par. 83), its insistence that the "preferential option for the poor" is not just a spiritual challenge to Catholics, but the litmus test for defining "moral priorities

for the nation as a whole" (JA, pars. 85-88), and finally, its call for a "new American experiment" in democracy in order to implement these priorities (JA, pars. 95, 295-325), all suggest that the Roman Catholic community may now be willing and able to play a critical role in the continual testing of the social covenant that we all honor as Americans. Moreover, the pastoral letter embodies a process of adult moral dialogue that it open to all perspectives — including those dissenting from the mainstream of Catholic social teaching. Because it is so open-ended, the pastoral-letter process itself may be the single most important contribution that the letter may make to the discussion of ethics in the investment industry.

But if the process is that promising, it is reasonable to expect that the pastoral letter already will have yielded some fresh thinking on money, banking and financial markets. And so it does, at least as compared with papal social teaching. In a section of the letter that outlines what various sectors of the economy can contribute to the work for social justice, the bishops address the concerns of those who own and manage productive capital. Though much of what is said here echoes recent statements of Pope John Paul II, it does place them in a more realistic and appreciative estimate of the challenges facing the business community as a whole.

The bishops begin by stating an important principle: "The freedom of entrepreneurship, business and finance should be protected, but the accountability of this freedom to the common good and the norms of justice must be assured" (JA, par. 110). Recognizing the crucial contribution of "owners [investors] and managers" to economic development, the pastoral letter thus establishes the baseline of an ethic of responsibility: All work, including at least by implication work in the investment industry, must be seen in ultimately religious terms as a "vocation, and not simply a career or a job" (JA, par. 111). All those who are involved in the ownership and management of productive capital should collaborate in order to see that a proper balance of freedom and accountability is achieved.

The pastoral letter, however, tries to go beyond Pope John Paul II's call for an end to the essential adversarial relationship between labor and capital. In ways not evident in *Laborem Exercens*, the U.S.

bishops begin to grasp the unique challenges involved in the ownership and management of finance capital: "Resources created by human industry are also held in trust. Owners and managers have not created this capital on their own. They have benefited from the work of many others and from the local communities that support their endeavors. They are accountable for those workers and communities when making decisions. For example, reinvestment in technological innovation is often crucial to the long-term viability of a firm. The use of financial resources solely in pursuit of short-term profits can stunt the production of needed goods and services; a broader vision of managerial responsibility is needed" (JA, par. 113).

Yet the vision that the bishops hope to inspire within the business community is neither utopian nor reactionary. It is not simply based on a sense of moral outrage mingled with nostalgia for the preindustrial world now irretrievably lost. Consider the following observation: "Business people, managers, investors and financiers follow a vital Christian vocation when they act responsibly and seek the common good. We encourage and support a renewed sense of vocation in the business community. We also recognize the way business people serve a society is governed and limited by the incentives which flow from tax policies, the availability of credit and other public policies. These should be reshaped to encourage the goals outlined here" (JA, par. 117).

Now that strikes me as an extraordinary concession. Instead of blindly denouncing "greed," as papal social teaching typically did, the bishops here speak favorably about "incentives." This implies that financial markets, along with government macroeconomic policy, may provide significant opportunities as well as constraints upon what any business may do in serving society. Hence the exhortation that follows upon this observation: "Businesses have a right to an institutional framework that does not penalize enterprises that act responsibly. Government must provide regulations and a system of taxation which encourage firms to preserve the environment, employ disadvantaged workers and create jobs in depressed areas. Managers and stockholders should not be torn between their responsibilities to their organizations and their responsibilities to society as a whole" (JA, par. 118).

This, too, is extraordinary. In a statement already studded with claims regarding economic rights, the bishops are claiming that businesses have a right to an appropriate regulatory environment, one that will seek to insure that the organizational imperatives and social responsibilities of businesses will not be made to appear at cross purposes with one another — in short, create a regulatory framework in which both investors and managers can do well while doing good.

This more constructive approach to the situation of moral responsibility facing investors and managers should not be dismissed as a sell-out to business interests. The religious and moral vision that the bishops preach still contains a "preferential option for the poor" at its core. But the option for the poor, as I understand it, is not just another "prophetic" call for the redistribution of existing wealth. Consistent with their overall theological interpretation of the human condition, the emphasis is upon empowerment, overcoming societal "marginalization" — in short, upon enabling people, especially poor people, to make a productive contribution to society as a whole.

Among the "moral priorities for the nation" that the bishops discern in this option is the following: "*The investment of wealth, talent and human energy should be specially directed to benefit those who are poor or economically insecure.* Achieving a more just economy in the United States and the world depends in part on increasing economic resources and productivity. In addition, the ways these resources are invested and managed must be scrutinized in light of their effects on non-monetary values. Investment and management decisions have crucial moral dimensions: They create jobs or eliminate them; they can push vulnerable families over the edge of poverty or give them new hope for the future; they help or hinder the building of a more just society. Indeed they can have either positive or negative influence on the fairness of the global economy. Therefore, this priority presents a strong moral challenge to policies that put large amounts of talent and capital into the production of luxury consumer goods and military technology while failing to invest sufficiently in education, health, the basic infrastructure of our society and economic sectors that produce urgently needed jobs, goods and services" (JA, par. 92).

Not surprisingly, given their very broad focus, the bishops do not work out precisely how the investment industry should contribute to implementing this national priority. But it should be clear that just as the investment industry, like all forms of private enterprise, has a right to an adequate regulatory environment to allow it to do well while doing good, it also has inescapably social responsibilities.

What some of those social responsibilities might be can be inferred from various policy recommendations that the bishops make in Chapter Three of the pastoral letter. Particularly significant, given the fact that the letter as a whole does not pretend to offer a systemic analysis of our nation's economic problems, are the bishops' remarks on "The U.S. Economy and the Developing Nations: Complexity, Challenge and Choices." The title alone suggests the tone of the discussion: There are no villains here, only an enormously complicated set of problems that will require the good will and creativity of all concerned in order to achieve a just solution. Under the heading of "Finance," then, the pastoral letter discusses the third-world debt crisis. As one might expect, the option of the poor is invoked to plead on behalf of the debtor nations for a more flexible approach to debt management (JA, par. 274). But the bishops also try to draw some long-term lessons from the crisis so that it may not be repeated.

Here, noting the inadequacy of the Bretton Woods institutions, the pastoral letter insists that whatever reforms might be contemplated in the system of international finance, they must include a concern for the social impact of the system on all parties affected, including the poor: "The United States should promote, support and participate fully in such reforms and reviews. Such a role is not only morally right, but is in the economic interest of the United States; more than a third of this debt is owed to U.S. banks. The viability of the international banking system (and of those U.S. banks) depends in part on the ability of a debtor countries to manage those debts. Stubborn insistence on full repayment could force them to default — which would lead to economic losses in the United States. In this connection we should not overlook the impact of the U.S. budget and trade deficits on interest rates. These high rates exacerbate the already difficult debt situa-

tion. They also attract capital away from investment in economic development in third-world countries" (JA, par. 277).

In the absence of a new Bretton Woods, of course, it is impossible to demand that the investment industry alone compensate for the lack of a competent international authority capable of coordinating macroeconomic policies worldwide for equitable development. But the social responsibilities of the investment industry would at least include active collaboration with the U.S. Government and other international authorities in seeking a solution. Minimally, this would mean not blocking efforts to reconstruct an appropriate regulatory framework for international financial markets, even though such efforts might have a significant short-term impact on the profit margins of various investment banking firms.

Chapter Four of the pastoral letter, "A New American Experiment: Partnership for the Public Good" (JA, pars. 295-325), is also suggestive of a new agenda for social responsibility in the investment industry. . . . Here, among other things, the bishops encourage socially innovative forms of entrepreneurship that promise to bridge the chasm between the ownership and management of productive capital. Their theological understanding of justice as empowering people for greater social participation leads them to consider seriously the prospects for profit-sharing plans, employees' buying out the previous stockholders and managing the firm themselves, and other strategies for cooperative ownership (JA, par. 300).

Furthermore, the experiment in democracy would include some attempt to increase shareholder rights and recognize shareholder responsibilities for the overall management of the firm (JA, par. 306). Here the breadth of the pastoral letter's moral vision is evident, as well as some of its implications for the investment industry: "The parts played by managers and shareholders in U.S. corporations also need careful examination. In U.S. law, the primary responsibility of managers is to exercise prudent business judgment in the interest of a profitable return to investors. But morally this legal responsibility may be exercised only within the bounds of justice to employees, customers, suppliers and the local community. Corporate mergers and hostile takeovers may bring greater benefits to shareholders, but they often lead to decreased concern for the well-being of local communities and make towns and cities more vulnerable to decisions made from afar" (JA, par. 305).

If a business corporation is to respond to the pastoral letter's moral vision, it will have to consider redefining the manager's fiduciary responsibility in terms that include all those who have a stake in it. Here, too, as the various legal and institutional reforms necessary to enforce this broadened notion of fiduciary responsibility come under discussion, the investment industry's active collaboration would be essential.

The American contribution to Catholic social teaching thus can be summarized as a quest for a new vision of the economy that for their first time is genuinely open to the aspirations and achievement, as well as the failures, of the American experiment in capitalist democracy. This vision of a participatory society that has successfully overcome the marginalization of its social and economic minorities, and insofar as it has, has also succeeded in solving the problem of "competitiveness" or declining productivity, affords a perspective in which the ethics of the investment industry can more fruitfully be discussed than it might have been discussed solely on the basis of papal social teaching. There is more to ethics, of course, than moral vision; but without moral vision it is very difficult to establish any unifying sense of purpose that might transcend the imperatives of the immediate situation.

Theology and Money

Paul Hessert

At the west end of George Street in eighteenth-century Edinburgh stands imposing St. George's Church. At the other end of the street, complementing the classical facades of the town houses, was meant to be St. Andrew's Church — the two churches fixing the ends of the broad avenue. (This part of Edinburgh was built at the time of the joining of the kingdoms of England [St. George] and Scotland [St. Andrew] — as the official name for Great Britain indicates: "the United Kingdom.") But St. Andrew's Church was never built at that location. Instead, the spot was preempted by the British Linen Bank. Thus bank and church face each other from opposite ends of the most imposing street of the "new town." The juxtaposition may have been only fortuitous in the growth of classical Edinburgh, but it is symbolic of a closer relationship between theological and financial structures than is usually recognized.

I should like to explore certain features of the relationship between theology and finance. My focus is not the lament that money seems to be god to some people but rather the effects on religious life and thought that the monetary *structure* has. This structure trains us to think in certain ways. It is derived from the fundamental notion which first generated money and then was universalized by money, that "reality" is quantifiable, that it can be divided into identical units and so be measured, compared, and manipulated.

Paul Hessert, "Theology and Money," *Explor* 4, no. 2 (1978): 21-32.

From Quantity to Quantifiability

Greek philosophers in antiquity suggested that the plurality of our experienced world can be explained as the application of different numbers and ratios to otherwise homogeneous "stuff." Democritus taught that reality was particles in motion. Weights and measures have been used for thousands of years to bring order into agriculture, architecture, navigation, and commerce. But money models an even more universal quantification.

Lengths, areas, and volumes each had separate measures and each kingdom or even city had its own measures for them. But money provided a virtually universal approach to quantity. Even before the development of modern atomic theory, monetary conceptualization regarded the world as a vast aggregate of identical units whose significance was determined by their relative numbers.

For the merchant, money-lender, or capitalist, money is not only the vehicle of buying and selling but of reliable evaluation more generally. The king's crown, for example, may be "priceless" because of its mystical associations and traditions, but the money-lender computes its value on the basis of the gold and gems it contains, perhaps even setting a price on the skill of the artisan who made it and, today on the demands of museums and collectors. "Priceless" is not a category of modern financial life. Public auction or sealed bidding can put a price on the priceless.

What the merchant and banker gave the culture was not just a monetary system of exchange but this *idea* of universal quantification. In the sixteenth century, the function of money was thought to rest on its intrinsic preciousness: the actual gold or silver of the coin was of comparable value to that of the goods for which it was exchanged. In the seventeenth century, however, its preciousness began to be thought to depend on its exchange function: the metal merely *stood for* a value. Today, the entirely abstract monetary unit prices even gold. What supports the "worth" of money today is the industrial production and military (symbolic?) power of nation in relation to the other nations. In other words, the basic unit of modern quantification is a matter of convention: it is conceptual and abstract. Quantification extends beyond the immediate realm of finance to everything as an *idea*. "Everything that exists exists in a measurable quantity" is the creed of our culture. We doubt it at our peril.

The abstract unit dominates our relating different classes of things to each other. This contrasts with other cultures where even numbers are distinguished from each other qualitatively rather than quantitatively. For us, four is merely one more than three and one less than five. But in many cultures, three is a divine or heavenly number while four is an earthy number — four elements, four winds, four corners of the earth. In this case, four is not merely one more than three but belongs to an entirely different realm. In our totally quantified culture, on the other hand, such radically different things as human life and auto construction are put on the same continuum: the cost of relocating a dangerously vulnerable gas tank on a particular model car is balanced against the cash outlay for settlements of lawsuits lodged by accident victims or their surviving relatives. "Industry has to have an incentive," a news report reads, "and what they understand is money."

Business, built around such abstract quantification, tends to understand itself as "making money" rather than making products. The last decades have seen numerous viable businesses bought up and then shut down, not because demand for their products fell off, but because they were used as tax write-offs and the like. It was easier to make money by such manipulation than by manufacturing and selling a useful item. For many businesses today, the sale of goods is only incidental to the sale of credit, which is the real "money-maker."

The epitome of quantification in business is cost-accounting which divides an operation into the smallest possible units for which the cost of each in relation to its return is a given period of time can be computed. Unprofitable units, not otherwise essential to the operation, are eliminated, thus realizing an overall increase in profits. The manager of a shoe store, thinking of serving his customers, might stock shoes of all sizes, even though comparatively few people buy very wide or very narrow shoes. But the large chain shoe departments carry only the medium widths of shoes because the odd sizes have relatively smaller sales, "move" more slowly, and thus cost more per unit to stock. Instead of viewing the operation as a whole — a transportation system, clothing needs of a community, proper nutrition — cost accounting atomizes it so that responsibility is assumed only for those fragments which in themselves remain profitable.

The exceedingly narrow view involved in cost-accounting is particularly evident in regard to ecological concerns. For example, cost-accounting makes it economically necessary for manufacturers to use disposable containers for most products, but cost-accounting does not take into consideration the community's cost of disposing of these containers. The New York telephone company no longer recycles old telephone directories because of the cost, but the city must spend an additional million annually to dispose of them. Abstracting the telephone company from the total community conceals this cost.

Human beings, too, are translated into this type of unit thinking. Cost-accounting has been used by medical administrators to determine who will receive extended care and who will be allowed to die. Even theological schools are evaluated on the basis of their "per student cost."

Quantification and Structure

Quantifying reality entails structuring reality in a particular way. It is to this implicit *structure* that we now turn.

Increment

Since one thing is related to another by the relative number of units each contains, anything can be made larger (and better!) by increasing the number of units in it. The production of a factory can be doubled by doubling the number of machines and workers. The huge Napoleonic armies which altered the face of Europe were created by drafting the populace into them.

This idea of incremental expansion differs from the notion of organic development and critical size where a careful balance of various factors prevents giganticism by forcing a division at a particular stage of growth. A cell does not merely increase in size indefinitely but divides into two cells. Quantification tends to ignore such qualitative jumps and simply keeps on adding units, expecting more of the same as a result.

Future

Incremental expansion requires the future as its proper "space" to grow. Conversely, the future is the incremental expansion of the present. Hence, future is continuous with the present. Improving the present incrementally brings the future into being.

This means that the "improving future" is a *structural* counterpart to quantification. A quantified world *must* have a future as the possibility of its indefinite expansion. The future is thus structurally posited as the significance of present effort. The "improving future" is a cultural axiom posited along with quantification, not a phenomenon independently verified by empirical evidence.

Credit

Money is important to this improving future not only as the general model of quantification but directly as credit, the claim on the future. To have money is to be safe for the future, to be delivered from the arbitrariness of chance. Savings and salvation (both come from the same root word) go together. In this sense, money represents the future even more than wealth. In relation to pension plans, for example, wealth is less a present possession than a secure future. Often a young couple will find themselves "pension poor" because future security claims so much of their income.

Present wealth is in a sense discounted future, that is, it is future value less the improvement of intervening time. Interest-taking (as against the old concept of usury) and the monetary economy developed together. Usury exacts its price from a victim — the person in dire straits who must borrow to survive and whose borrowing calls his survival into question. Usury is therefore "blood money." Interest, on the other hand, exacts its price from the future, not from the person involved. It is based on the expectation of a "good deal," on improvement effected by time. If on the one hand, future improvement is present value plus interest, on the other hand, present value is improved future less interest — the future discounted. When a person takes out a loan, the interest will be added to the face amount of the loan and then repayment of the total amount will be worked out; or else payments on the face amount of the loan will be worked out but the borrower will receive only the face of the loan less interest.

Money gives substance to "dealing in futures" by bringing the future into the present through discounting. Cost-accounting can conceal the anticipation of an improved future by making the units of comparison so small that the larger scene is forgotten. Some businesses have managed to show a profit up to the very day they went bankrupt.

The Inner/Outer Dichotomy

Even more important to theology is the structural distinction between "inner" and "outer." What is quantifiable, and because it is quantifiable is subject to the universal mediation of money, is "real." Those things which elude this kind of quantification are "spiritual" — love, loyalty, tradition, courage, honor, family pride, and the like. There is no common unit which brings these two different realms together. Here, money fails to mediate. Inner and outer aspects of human life are separated. Indeed, the inner ceases to be the inside of the outer and becomes something entirely different and alien. There is no "one-to-one" relationship between them. For example, my father's credit was good because he was a "man of his word"; my credit today is good only in relation to my earning power.

Only through rhetoric, manifest most compellingly in advertising, are these "spiritual" values brought into juxtaposition with the quantified "real" world. Corporation policy is determined on a strict cost-accounting basis (moving factories from one state to another to obtain cheaper labor or tax advantages), but corporation advertising is full of language concerning "spiritual" values — community services, personal concern, respect for tradition, and ecological sensitivity. "We're involved," the ads claim. "We do not just provide transportation; we offer the fulfillment of life!"

No "price" can be set on the inner person. But by this fact that inner person is locked in peculiar isolation. Protected from monetary evaluation ("there are some things that money cannot buy"), this inner person cannot come to expression except in personal feelings, in those aspects of art which are thought to be expressions of inner feelings, and — tragically and increasingly — in violence. On the other hand, the outer person and world are protected from arbitrary schemes of personal feeling: "regardless of your feelings, this is a dollars-and-cents world."

Though separated, the two realms mutually depend on each other. The only way the inner person can affect the world is by entering into the external monetary scheme ("honesty pays"). In our culture, personhood itself is tied to money: one does not really exist as a public person without checking account, credit cards, and a "social security" number. This is why discriminatory credit policies have been attacked by women. But the only way the world can affect the inner person is in the call to "spiritual" values in advertising and rhetoric. As Matthew Fox, commenting on *Time* magazine's portrayal of religion, put it, advertising is the sacrament of modern culture. We might say that the images used in advertising are the icons of modern culture — the interface between two worlds which otherwise never meet. On the one hand, these images move us at our deepest inner levels; but on the other hand they are exploited quantitatively.

Religious Legitimation

Quantification, by dealing with certain aspects of life, identifies these as real and outer. By the same means, quantification isolates a realm called "inner" and "spiritual," designating it (by default) as less than real. Religion does not so much challenge this structure in order to give an independent validity to the spiritual. Rather, it supports quantification by accepting at face value its own province of the "spiritual" which quantification relegates to it. In other words, religion in our culture legitimates this quantified and secularized version of reality. One might say, the power behind modern secularization is religious!

Religion's acceptance of this basic dichotomy of inner and outer, in other words, is more important culturally than any expertise in the realm of the spiritual. And it demonstrates its acceptance of the division by shaping its own institutional life in terms of the quantified structure of reality. Church hospitals are as insistent to have a prospective patient's medical insurance card as secular institutions are. Church publishing houses are as geared to the market as the secular ones are. This does not mean that church people are worldly rather than spiritual, but only that their spirituality is defined by the structure which quantification provides. . . .

But at the same time, the church has a Scripture, tradition, and cumulated experience which speak of sin forgiven, guilt absolved, dividing walls thrown down, the future made present. Both the language of the cross (Ro 3:24, Col 2:13-14) and Christian apocalyptic (Rev 21:1-2) accept the quantified world only to destroy it in the cancellation of debt and in the inauguration of a new heaven and earth. The future they proclaim is no extension or expansion of the past. Incremental improvement does not lead to it — only death and resurrection: "I have been crucified with Christ; . . . and the life I now live in the flesh I live by faith in the Son of God . . ." (Gal 2:20).

Section 3: Accounting

If one presumes that humans act as economically rational beings with perfect data, then accounting is unrelated to ethics. In such a scenario accounting provides only disembodied numerical summaries of detail without intervening interpretation or judgment. None of the authors found in this section believes this scenario to be true. Each of them sees accounting as interpretive work and thus a matter for ethical reflection and action.

For Ian Stewart, the accountant is an agent in community with others. Thus an accountant develops meaning from data. For Stewart the creation of meaning necessarily requires a moral agent since meaning can only be created in community. Stewart argues that giving an account must serve larger human and environmental purposes and that the accountant is ultimately responsible to God whose gift of freedom makes us accountable.

Philip Piaker takes a different tack. He agrees that accounting is a profession embedded with moral meaning. However, his challenge is for the accounting firm to create the ethical environments in which accountants will thrive. Piaker observes that, since professionals desire to live by ethical standards, it is simply sensible to provide an environment responsive to their needs. While his reasoning is somewhat pragmatic, his observations about latent desires to behave morally within the accounting profession are astute.

Even if one agrees that accountants are moral agents because they deal in interpretive work, it is not enough simply to exhort accountants to be ethical. What must concretely be done to improve the ethical practices of accountants? As the American Institute of Certified Public Accountants recognized in its 1993 report, the growth of global competition, the development of more complex financial instruments, and new technologies heighten the ethical challenges already faced by accountants. Fraud in reporting must be detected and prevented; financial reports must be meaningful to those who use them; auditor independence must be insured; the legal liability system must be reformed; and self-regulation must have teeth.

If one is willing to grant that accounting creates meaning, then accountants are moral agents. If accountants are moral agents, the range of their accountability is vast. If the range is vast, then the means of insuring ethics are complex. While structural changes can help, they cannot relieve any individual accountant of the accountability that religious faith requires. Behind the network of organizational efforts to improve ethical behavior will always be the voice of Proverbs 20:10: "Differing weights and differing measures — the LORD detests them both" (NIV).

Accounting and Accountability: Double Entry, Double Nature, Double Identity

I. C. Stewart

Introduction

The basic activity of accounting is "giving an account." The primary function of the accountant is getting private or semiprivate information from the accountor (the managers) and abstracting it in a more public manner for whomever the accountees may be. The accountees are no longer the owners and creditors, but nowadays the list includes suppliers, employees, investment advisors, business connections of various types, the government, and the public in general. The problem of discerning the truth of this information flow from accountor to accountee gives rise to the auditing profession. In terms of the accountability relation, the auditor comes between the accounter and the accountees to assure the integrity and the trustworthiness of the information.

The particular concern, of course, it that the accountors might engage in bluffing. By being given an intentionally deceptive message, accountees are unable to act in ways that might act otherwise. In his report on the collapse of the Principal Group, the Edmonton-based financial empire, the Court-appointed investigator concluded that the company literature, designed to attract investors, clearly did not paint a true financial picture of the struggling empire. The investi-

gator says the chairman of the Group, Mr. Donald Cormie, that he "deliberately permitted the companies to carry on while he took steps to disguise their true financial situation." The investigator reported that the glossy 1985 annual review of the Principal Group contained a statement by the Chairman that the Group had made a profit of $607,000 in 1985, when the audited statements showed it suffered a $25.7 million loss. The $1.2 billion financial empire collapsed two years later in 1987. Meanwhile, a lot of people lost their life savings because of the misleading information put out by the Group.

This case highlights the elasticity of generally acceptable accounting principles. Although the accountant's judgment is more bounded nowadays than in the past, nevertheless, considerable discretion remains, enough for accounting practice to be described as an interpretive art. The purpose of the first section of this paper is to engage in a little accounting hermeneutics by considering the accountant as a producer of "text." The emphasis is not on the double entry structure of accounts but on the interpretive act of making an account.

The second section of the paper examines the assumptions about human nature which underlie the interpretive act of making an account. The third section takes up the notion of accountability, and following William Schweiker's analysis, suggests that accountability enacts a doubleness crucial to our moral identity. In the final section, the paper outlines some of the implications for accounting practice of this construal of accountability.

Double Entry Languages

Accounting texts use three languages: English (in British Columbia), double entry and mathematics. It is the last two which best characterize the work accountants do. Accounting practice is framed by an over-arching metaphor of numeracy. The columns of figures with their dual structure and mathematical accuracy create a presumption that the accountant's work is objective, that the accountant is representing reality "as is" through the use of members that are objective and value free. The profit and loss, for example, is not thought of as a "mere" matter of interpretation, dependent

I. C. Stewart, "Accounting and Accountability: Double Entry, Double Nature, Double Identity," *Crux* 26, no. 2 (June 1990): 13-20.

on the accountant's perspective, values or skill. The accountant is paid not merely to provide his/her point of view on the profit and loss status of the firm, but to state the objective facts of the matter.

The truth is that the adequacy of accounts is no simple matter of their calculative accuracy, which can be determined independently of the concrete circumstances of the persons who make them. Accounting, as Don Lavoie points out, should be understood as a language; that is, a process of bidirectional and interpersonal communication. Language, Lavoie states, "is not just talk, it is our way of seeing the real world." So modern accounting is a way of writing the world. Gareth Morgan notes how the numerical view highlights those aspects of organizational reality that are quantifiable and built into the accounting framework (for example, flows of costs, revenues, and other values), but ignores those aspects of organizational reality that are not quantifiable in this way. Morgan illustrates this way: "Just as we might attempt to rate the quality of last night's dinner on a scale of 1-10, and in giving it a '9' capture that it was indeed a very good meal, the accountant's numerical form of representation provides a very 'thin' and limited characterisation. It leaves much of the quality and overall experience of the meal out of account. The metaphor 'it was a 9' remains silent on so many things." So Morgan concludes by emphasizing that "accountants are always engaged in *interpreting* a complex reality, partially, and in a way that is heavily weighted in favour of what the accountant is *able* to measure and *chooses* to measure, through the particular schemes of accounting to be adopted."

An Interpretive Art

What are some of the interpretive acts accountants make in drawing up accounts? The first involves the question of what items or events qualify for recognition on the financial statements. For example, in the balance sheet, the question of which assets or liabilities to include or exclude depends on how intangible, uncertain, unenforceable, unidentifiable, or non-severable the item is that it ceases to be part of the organization. For example, some New York banks now have what are described as "financial engineers" whose task it is to come up with new financial instruments to window dress the client's balance sheet.

Once a decision has been made to recognize certain items on the financial statements, the next step is to determine how these items are to be measured. A number of attributes could be chosen such as historic cost, current cost, net realizable value and present value. Answers to these recognition and measurement questions will define the size, health, structure, and performance — in other words — the reality of the organization.

Peter Miller and Ted O'Leary have recently noted how the numerical view can also be allowed to shape the reality of the organization through the routine operation of the organization's *internal* accounting system, for example, people, students, patients, and work teams become profit centres generating revenues and expenses. Where financial considerations become a major issue, the data generated can exert a decisive influence on the accountant's reality construction.

Miller and O'Leary observe how by the use of standard costing and budgeting the accountant constructs a particular field of visibility. The accountant renders visible certain crucial aspects of the function of the enterprise. Standard costing enmeshed the factory worker within a calculus of efficiency and later moved on by means of the budget to do the same for executives. By surrounding individuals with norms and standards by which inefficiencies and wastes are rendered visible, a whole range of calculation programmes and techniques come to dominate the life of the individual, and accounting becomes part of the network of power relations that are built into the very fabric of organizational life.

So the accountant's role should not be seen as a merely technical one. The accountant is not an uncontested figure who reveals a pre-existing reality, a real of fact, a realm of measurable efficiency.

Accounting is more like a photograph — it is taken from a particular vantage point, with a particular lens, at a particular time, for a particular purpose. In a sense, accountants do reflect reality, for example, cash at bank corresponds to the number of monetary tokens held by the bank. But accounting is also constitutive, and people act on the basis of the picture which is painted.

It is important, however, to emphasize that there are often close affinities between the kinds of professional judgments which are made by accountants. Moreover, accounts are more than an expression of the subjective whims of various accountants. There are such things as generally acceptable accounting principles. The point to be emphasized in the present context is that accounts are not objectivistic in the sense of a pointer-reading science. To argue that accounting is like a barometer, or speedometer, for example, is to grossly misunderstand its nature.

It is the softness, then, of accounting numbers that is the reason why managers are so interested in them for they can manipulate them where they may be motivated to do so.

Managers' Choice of Accounting Procedures

The most widely accepted explanatory theory of managers' choice of accounting procedures is based on the economics theory of the firm. This theory borrows on the property rights literature because of its emphasis on rights established by contract. Under this view, the firm is not a separate entity; rather it is composed of individuals who have contracted with the legal entity for certain property and it is these individuals who have objectives, namely, to maximize their utility. The firm is viewed as a team of self-interested individuals who recognize that their own welfare depends on the firm's success in competition with other firms. Each of the individuals comprising the firm contributes some input to the firm's productive process (raw materials, capital, managerial skills, labour). These individuals supply in expectation of earning a rate of return on their investment. Each recognizes that the other individuals will take action to maximize their utility so that conflicts of interest are bound to arise. To reduce these conflicts, the individuals write *contracts* that will specify each individual's specific rights in the firm's outputs under various contingencies, for example, specifying how the cash flows will be distributed in the event of bankruptcy.

Accounting is an integral part of these contracts, both in the drawing up of the terms of the contract and the monitoring of them. Contracts will not reduce the costs of conflict unless the firm can determine if the contract has been breached.

Empirical research has shown that two financial contracts are particularly important in explaining managers' choice of accounting procedures. These are management compensation contracts and debt contracts.

Management compensation contracts are one means of aligning the managers' interests with the shareholders. Typically, managers are given a bonus which is a function of their net income. In this situation managers obviously have strong incentives to prefer income increasing accounting procedures. If managers controlled the calculation of net income, bonus plans would not exist for incentive purposes. To offset the managers' optimism, conservative accounting procedures are specified in the compensation contract.

Debt contracts usually contain a covenant that is designed to protect the debtholders from the managers using borrowed money for their own purposes and leaving them with a shell. Typically, the covenant specifies that the debt shall not exceed a certain proportion of total assets, or that net income shall cover interest on debt by a certain multiple. Again, managers running close to these restrictions have strong incentives to adopt income increasing accounting procedures. The reason for this is that infringement of debt covenants would entail costly renegotiation and possibly higher interest rates which would reduce net income and with it managers' bonus payments and the value of their share options.

Research has shown that there is one other key variable in managers' choice of accounting procedures and that is political costs. The theory here builds on the economic theory of the political process in which the political process is viewed as a competition for wealth transfers. To the extent that a given firm is subject to potential wealth transfers in the political process (chiefly via taxes and regulations of various sorts), its managers are hypothesized to adopt accounting procedures that reduce the size of the transfer. For example, managers of the large oil companies use accounting procedures that reduce net income in order to defuse arguments that they are profiteering.

The empirical tests to which the theory of managers' choice of accounting procedures has been put show a very high degree of support for this sort of research. It seems to be widely accepted today that managers, far from presenting a true and fair view of their corporations' operations and financial positions, choose those accounting procedures that will maximize their own self-interests. And the auditing profession, far from balancing the scales in favour of the public interest, appears to be sliding relentlessly into retailing representations in almost any way management might want. "Accountants," as John Nelson observes, "are rapidly becoming guns for hire with no code of honour to give their services adequate direction or justification."

Sociobiology and Behaviour Theory

This view from the accounting and economics literature that every agent is actuated only be self-interest is also consistent with sociobiology and behaviour theory. The modern incarnation of Darwin's evolutionary biology is known as sociobiology. The central dogma of evolutionary biology is that significant characteristics are passed from parents to offspring in the genes. Not all organisms will be successful at surviving and reproducing, and thus not all genes will be equally likely to pass from one generation to the next. The genes that do survive will be the ones that make successful organisms. As a result only genes that see to the successful pursuit of self-interest by organisms will survive. The implication of this line of thinking is that selfishness — the single-minded pursuit of genetic self-interest — is a biological fact of life, a natural necessity. What sociobiology has done is extend the concept of economic self-interest to domains of life that have been excluded by economists — domains including social relations within a group, relations between parents and offspring, and relations between mates. Human selfishness is clearly seen as a reflection of a natural law since it is of a piece with the selfishness of ants, birds, fish and other living organisms.

In behavior theory (also cast in the shadow of Darwinism), organisms engage in essentially random activity. Some of that behaviour has favourable consequences; it results in states of the environment that organisms want, that are reinforcing. The behaviour that results in reinforcing consequences and only that behaviour, continues to occur; other less successful behaviour drops out. Because of this natural selection by reinforcement of behaviour that works, the organisms that are seen have learnt to do just the right thing to produce the outcomes they want or need. So just as the maximization of reproductive success drives the evolution of the species, the maximization of reinforcement or self-interest drives the development of individuals.

This picture of organisms as pursuers of reinforcement maximization fits nicely with the model of rational economic man. As Barry Schwartz concludes, "when we add these three disciplines together, they converge on a picture of self-interested, acquisitive human nature that is truly formidable." The economist now says that people by their very natures are greedy economic men and women and can now turn in defense to sociobiology and behaviour theory. The sociobiologist contends that birds and fish do not live in an artificially created free market society and yet they pursue self-interest also. The behaviour theorist has evidence that human flexibility and diversity are themselves governed by principles of self-interest maximization.

In the sections that follow, the question of how one thinks with and yet gets beyond notions of rational agency centering on a self-realizing "I" are addressed.

Double Nature

It must be recognized at the outset that the deterministic, naturalistic approach is a necessary postulate of the scientific enquiry, and as John Macmurray has noted, serves not merely to dictate its methodology, but also to isolate the aspect of personal behaviour which is amenable to the method. This is true of all the research outlined here from the accounting, economics, sociobiology and behavioural literature. "The method is to search for patterns of behaviour which recur without change, and to formulate these in 'laws' of general application." The result is an objective knowledge of other persons, knowledge that is *impersonal*.

It was Macmurray who showed that the *personal* is constituted by personal relatedness. The unit of the personal is not the "I" but the community of the YOU and I. This community is not merely a matter of fact (upon which all scientific knowledge is based) but it is also a matter of intention. Macmurray contrasts personal and impersonal knowledge in this way: "The one assumes and implies that men are free agents, responsible for their behaviour, choosing their mode of action in the light of a distinction between right and wrong; the other that all human behaviour follows determined patterns, and that the laws which we obey are, like those which govern all natural objects, discoverable by objective scientific methods of investigation. This duality of knowledge, personal and impersonal, is the concrete statement of the antinomy of freedom and determinism."

This corresponds to the double element in man. On the one hand, man's creatureliness is emphasized in the deterministic, naturalistic view of man, and on the other hand, man's freedom is emphasized in man's agency as determinative.

As Macmurray concludes, "The question is not whether the personal conception of men as free agents or the scientific conception of man as a determined being is correct. Both are correct." Macmurray goes on to explain that this is possible because they do not refer to the same field. Science is a deliberate attempt to improve and extend generalized knowledge of man. "Its field of reference is the genus *Homo sapiens*, that is to say, the class of existents which are identifiable by observation, as possessing the factual characteristics by which objects are assigned to this class." The concept of the personal, by contrast, Macmurray argues, is not an exclusive concept. It is primarily the field in which we know one another as persons in relation. It includes the objective knowledge of one another we possess, but it does not take the scientific account as a complete account — as absolute and not relative — so that it entails the rejection of the personal conception, with the freedom it implies. It is the attempt by accountants, economist, sociobiologists and behaviourists to bring human existence under one sign only — that of nature — that must be objected to. It cannot be agreed that scientific research fixes human nature as always and only self-interested, permanently putting it outside the pale of argument. But while, on the one hand, Christians cannot accept a morality which regards sin as a given; neither, on the other hand, can they appeal to personal agency as the source of self-determination as though man's powers of rational, moral and creative thought could bring his life to fulfilment. As V. A. Demant put it, "The root of sin and non-fulfilment lies not in man's finitude, but in his disobedience to the laws of his being set by his creator."

As Demant notes, each of these poles denies one aspect of man's double nature. History seems to swing from the perversions of one to exaggerations of the other. Secularism cannot find a point of unity behind the duality. There can only be a unity between freedom and dependency as it is recognized that Christian freedom, given by the Holy Spirit, must be accompanied by respect for the moral order which exists.

If economic forces are to be rendered morally responsible, the starting point must be to emphasize Macmurray's insights of the person as agent and personal existence constituted by the relation of persons. For if there is no moral agency, then as Francis and Arrington observe, "the whole question of accountability dissipates . . . a subject who acts based on an involuntary inheritance from 'nature' cannot be accountable for those actions simply because s/he has no capacity to act otherwise." And if this is true, mankind has become slaves to its own creations and the earth is subject to unending exploitation under the aegis of efficiency.

Accountability

As Macmurray defines it, free agency is purposive action, and action is defined by intention. Alasdair MacIntyre describes it this way: "To identify an occurrence as an action is . . . to identify it under a type of description which enables us to see that occurrence as flowing intelligibly from a human agent's intentions, motives, passions and purposes. It is therefore to understand action as something for which someone is accountable, about which it is always appropriated to ask the agent for an intelligible account." In a similar vein, William Schweiker has put it this way: "giving an account is providing reasons for character and conduct, ones held to be understandable to others and thereby rendering life intelligible and meaningful."

Schweiker argues that giving an account is crucial for moral life. "The ability to engage freely in purposive actions, to undergo, interpret and evaluate actions and relations, to make judgments of praise and blame, and to account for all of these activities is constitutive of the being of an agent."

Double Identity

For it to be "appropriate to ask the agent for an intelligible account," to use MacIntyre's words, "there must be some norms, values, and beliefs that one shares in common with the agent — there must be some pre-understandings that warrant the attempt to place the agent in the position of responding to such a request." This makes giving an account intrinsically a social act. To be accountable is first, as Macmurray put it, to be persons-in-relation or an individual-in-community.

As Schweiker has pointed out, this is why "when I say something about my life I do not simply instantiate the identity of the 'I'. On the contrary, there is enacted a pre-given relation to myself as an actor and to others. Not surprisingly, when this doubleness in identity is brought to light, by whatever means, it can evoke a shock of self-recognition, understanding, a sense of pride, flat denial, shame or simple evasion about who we are and what we are doing."

Schweiker argues that this otherness found in personal identity is also present in corporations. It inheres in the fiduciary relation between a company and the accountant. It is enacted when the accountant portrays relations relative to the larger community of accounters. Schweiker admits that persons and corporations are different and radically so, but he contends that the activity of accounting enacts a doubleness crucial to moral identity. This is because it evokes some awareness of pre-given relations to others, relations subject to claims about what is good and evil.

Then secondly, Schweiker notes that because identity so engendered is deeply social, the motive of being accountable is never simple unadorned self-interest. It entails a constitutive relation to others beyond simple contractual relations. This means that the reasons why people do things are infinitely complex. Humans are accountable to God, their church communities, their families, their environment, their colleagues, and so on. Action is defined by intention, and so the purpose of accountability is to reveal the agent's intentions, passions motives, purposes, not simply to presuppose the single motive of self-interest.

Finally, Schweiker argues that this construal of accountability says something about the limits of responsibility and its scope. Schweiker suggests that agents are normally only accountable for actions they intended and/or undertook either directly or through the aid of others. However, he argues that the limits of accountability must be set within its scope. Insofar as giving an account is a rendering forth of the social and temporal structure of life, that scope is indeed considerable. It potentially opens onto an unlimited horizon of community. The structure of giving an account raises the question: accountable to whom and whose needs are to count?

What Are the Implications for Accounting?

Schweiker draws attention to two sorts of conflicts faced by accountants and offers some guidance on adjudicating between them. The first is a conflict of trusts or loyalties. Insofar as the moral identity of a corporation is enacted through giving an account, then one norm of the accounting profession is that of integrity or truthfulness founded on trust. Hence the conflicts of loyalties that accountants have between their own moral integrity and the demands made on them by clients or the companies they work for. The dilemma for the accountant is to decide which relation of trust ought to override the other. Is the accountant the loyal agent of the corporation? For example, if management were to ask the accountant to change accounting procedures to achieve an increase in income must the accountant oblige? Or, does the accountant have a fiduciary obligation to render a truthful identity of that company and her or himself?

Then giving an account not only understands moral identity around some norms but also addresses the question of what and whose goods the accountant serves. Clearly, the accountant serves the goods of the agent (the accountor) and those others to whom the agent is responsible (the accountees). In other words, the self-interest of managers is always met and tested by other needs and goods. This meeting, Schweiker argues, is "clarified through the activity of the accountant who, in the portrayal of an agent's identity, specifies that identity's interdependence with others, those to whom one is then accountable." Social responsibility, therefore, and concern for the common good must be part of the work of the accountant who takes on the burden of understanding his task as that of giving an account.

Just as there are conflicts of trusts so there are conflicts of goods. Which accountees' goods are to be pursued? For example, employees often sacrifice their health for corporations; corporations often sacrifice the common good to advance their own interests, for example, plant closures, pollution, and waste disposal. How then can the accountant adjudicate in these conflicts? If an accountable identity is constituted with others and open potentially to the whole horizon of time and community, Schweiker argues that this implies:

1. consideration of the needs of others in the determination of courses of action since those others help to constitute an accountable identity:
2. in conflict situations, there is a presumption on behalf of the priority of the common good and the needs of others. Thus private goods cannot override public goods.

Giving an account renders economic forces servants of larger human and environmental purposes without negating the singularity of their identities or motives. This is how the accounting profession can help marshall economic forces as powers for moral purposes. Yet it also means that the accountant cannot be made servile to corporate intentions and values because the accountant ultimately is the agent of a fiduciary relation through the scope of time and community. The accountant is then both an internal and external critic: *internal* because s/he is bound through a fiduciary relation to the corporation and its discourse; *external* because the accountant's perspective reaches beyond corporate intentions.

Epilogue

Schweiker's construal of accountability seems consistent with the emphasis found in biblical ethics on the need to prefer others' needs over one's own self-interests. But his notion needs to be radicalized further. Biblical ethicists would want to claim that as agents they live and act and have their being before God. Their decisions must be taken with a sense of accountability to God for the natural world and for one another, for the Christian life is a life in community. In this context, giving an account often takes the form of confession to God and to one another, as it did for Augustine who confessed his failure of trust and professed his thankfulness for God's faithfulness.

In summary, accounting is an interpretive art. Although the area for the exercise of professional judgment is somewhat more bounded than it used to be, managers and their accountants are free agents responsible for their choice of accounting procedures in writing the world. However, the scientific research agenda in accounting assumes that managers and their accountants follow a determined pattern, one dictated by their self-interests. Similar patterns of behaviour have been observed by scientists working in the fields of economics, sociobiology and behaviour theory. The challenge presented by these research programmes is that they do not have regard for the conception of man as a moral agent. As seen by the writers cited here, moral identity is constituted by the relation of persons. Insofar as the moral identity of a corporate agent is interpreted by the accountant in giving an account, accounting practice is determined by an internal ethic of truthfulness. This requires the development of character sufficient to sustain accountants in this task. Insofar as an accountable identity is constituted with others (the larger community of accountees), social responsibility and concern for the common good must also be part of the work of an accountant. But more than this, the activity of all people, wherever they live and work, must be undertaken with a sense of accountability to God for the natural world, for one another and for themselves.

Accounting and Sentiment

Philip M. Piaker

While sentiment is not generally perceived as linked to accounting, in my view it lies a the heart of accounting. Kenneth Boulding saw accounting as a twin, albeit an uncongenial one, tied to economics. Others think it is just arithmetic, passionless as calculations tend to be, devoid of refined feeling, and to the small extent that it evokes emotions, those can only be avarice, greed and meanness of spirit.

Such a view might be correct if accounting were separated from the framework of sentiment which gave birth to it two centuries before Paciolo, and within which it has fermented and thrived. It has this in common with other great institutions: When we wring sentiment out of medicine, art, literature, or music, all we have left is technique, sometimes brilliant technique, but mere technique nevertheless. But in order for the arts to transcend technique to reach greatness, the right stuff is needed, and that right stuff is "heart" or "soul" or what I call "sentiment."

Sentiment seems a particularly appropriate term to describe the proper attitude for accountants, since its Latin root — *sentire* — also gives us *sentinel*, and it is as sentinels that we serve when we assume our auditing role.

All of the great accountants I have known, either personally or through their writings, manifest a regard for virtue, a commitment to uphold the moral underpinnings of society, and a basic assumption that moral sentiment (ethics) is at the root of accounting. They know their mission is to seek truth and communicate it within the province of their particular expertise. They don't

Philip M. Piaker, "Accounting and Sentiment," *C.P.A. Journal* 54 (Nov. 1984): 6, 8-9.

need cookbook rules about how to "bake the accounting cake." Common accounting techniques when coupled with the passion for truth are in almost every case a sufficient guideline.

Ethics it seems to me derives its orientation as much from feelings and attitudes which we call values as from pure reason alone. We have all known persons of impeccable logic and strong reasoning power who nevertheless behave like scoundrels. They are hollow people because they condemn those very sentiments which I associate with the great among us in accounting, in business, in education, in every field.

William James in talking of religion spoke of "the will to believe." In respect to ethics, I speak of the feeling, the desire, the love to be righteous. Ethics, I claim, has a base in sentiment as well as in reason.

Accounting is, of course, part of the warp and woof of business, and within business, we have recently observed a flood of books and articles on ethics. I have seen more publications emerge on ethics in the last 3 years than in the last 3 decades. These include, besides ethics of business, legal ethics, ethics of medicine, of genetic engineering, and of scientific research.

How can we explain this rush of concern? Can it be that, in our social evolution, we have developed a need as pressing as the basic drives? I'll hypothesize that we have developed a requirement for ethical gratification which satisfies our sentimental sense. We need to feel that the decision we reach and the actions we take are just ones. We want the comfort that comes from knowing our behavior is supported by reason, tuned to noble goals and devoid of foreseeable ugly consequences. The pride we take in our work is commensurate with the quality of ethics and sentiment which permeates our approach to our work. Firms which provide this kind of supportive environment are ones in which managers and staff can gratify their ethical needs and bring closure to their sentimental drives.

Now, not every one believes this. Some executives resist the notion that ethics is a topic to be taken seriously in a management context. They could see the value of concepts provided by accounting, finance, production, statistics, marketing and even organizational behavior. But ethics, they think, should be reserved for preachers, religious school classes or perhaps for professors who like soft ideas because they are not comfortable with hard data.

I am suggesting that, on the contrary, the top companies and the top accounting firms of the next decade will be the ones who early on see the link between ethics on the one hand and motivation, commitment, and achievement on the other. We have gone beyond our purely economic relationships, which stem from providing a service or from financing, producing and marketing goods. We have now come to stress our moral relationships as well.

Whether it is a battlefield at Thermopylae, a science program putting men on the moon, or a production project like the IBM PC, it is ideology which develops the momentum that carries the day.

But it's not the content of ideology which supplies the drive. It is the sense of commitment and purpose which sharing a common ideology gives to its members. This gives rise to a sense of mission which gives victories. I suggest that when CPA firms deliberately insist on an ethical framework for decisions, a certain sentiment is released which energizes the kind of commitment I am talking about.

When our country was young, we had the makings of a shared ideology. People believed in hard work, savings, thrift and honesty. Our schools taught it, and we learned it at our mother's knee. Much of our literature and public utterances also gave voice to those ideas.

In recent decades, our intellectual leaders, even those in our great universities, seem to have lost faith in that vision. They question whether business and the professions are fair, whether by their very nature they can be ethical. Business is seen at best as a game where the rewards go to the money grubbers and to those who are good at bluffing and to the charlatans. Unfortunately, there are too many examples which have been provided to them to flesh out their case.

The resulting cynicism has a stifling effect on the motivation of professional leaders and business managers to make the goals of the firm congruous with the goals of just society. Some of our best young people, therefore, shun careers in business or accounting. Some are even attracted to flirt with alternative economic or social systems because they see no ethical or sentimental content in our own.

But it is no accident that the development of individual freedom and political liberty in western society largely parallels the development of accounting and industry. Nor is it coincidence that intellectual excitement and great ideas are associated in frameworks which are also hospitable to accounting.

We only tell half the story when we say the bottom line of business is profit. In an ethical business, profit is earned not only to survive but also to provide a needed product or service to society, employment to people, opportunity to them to do creative things, to develop, to be challenged, and to derive satisfaction from the work. It is a seamless web where every one of these goals depends on and contributes to the achievement of the other goals. And one of the goals is the achievement of ethical gratification and the encouragement of certain sentiments.

In an ethical environment, employee morale is high, and productivity is heightened. It may perhaps be seen as an extension of what sociologists had previously described as the need for status and prestige. What I am suggesting is that perceived integrity brings special status with it but only in a society which is itself sufficiently uncynical to prize integrity.

To Maslow's hierarchy of the needs for food, clothing, respect, and self-actualization we can add the need for that special sense of being an *ethical human being*. It is in the next step flowing from self-esteem. This sense provides a center of gravity for enhanced career satisfaction and heightened morale.

If ethical gratification is the next evolutionary step above narrow ego gratification, then the corporation and the accounting profession must be so structured as to provide for it. We must reinforce the new emphasis on ethics as an important dimension of accounting and of management.

In this sense, we can look at accounting ethics as being a kind of shorthand summary extracted from tradition, religion, social values, and past wisdom. It is necessary for group survival and for survival of the profession and of our institutions. It is demanding in that it asks the individual to sacrifice a portion of his or her self-interest for the benefit of the larger group. It takes the form of agreement guidelines for conduct and acceptance of the rules of the game in order to achieve group cohesion and harmony.

Ethics are shaped by the need for institutional survival but it goes beyond survival. Like the arts, it is both a process and an end in itself. It enhances the quality of life in the process of contributing to the survival and meaning of that life.

There appear to be five main levers which govern the ethical environment. These are family, religion, education, the sentiment of top management, and the public media.

We absorb these precious ethical attitudes early in life, or we find it hard to learn them later. Our religion, whether it comes in traditional garb or in humanism, anchors these sentiments. Education gives the intellectual reinforcement to our feelings about being ethical. The sentiments of the top partners and managers work down to the staff level. They either provide positive reinforcement to the ethical sentiment or else they drive it underground. The ethics at the top set the tone for the style of the whole firm. In the meantime, our media provide the negative reinforcement of public indignation and threatened sanctions against malefactors.

The accounting lapses which writers like Professor Briloff and Professor Hoxsey, 60 years earlier, have illuminated don't take place in a vacuum. They can only occur in an overall environment where top management suffers from the lack of integrity. But when we cure accounting lapses, we also encourage overall managerial probity. And when we demand general business ethics, we are diminishing management pressure on accountants to bend with the winds of deceptive reporting.

At the end of the last century, our profession achieved greatness because the "midwives" attending its birth in America were people of the highest moral stature who didn't shrink from identifying ethics as a center of gravity around which to construct a new profession. New times may require new leadership, new technology, and new approaches. But not all change requires discarding the wisdom of the past. To the extent that we are unabashed in preserving the ethical roots of our beginnings, our profession will preserve the best base from which to face the new challenges. Computers, statistics, and regression analyses can enhance our profession and the society which we serve only when they are harnessed to the right sentiment which drives them.

Meeting the Financial Reporting Needs of the Future: A Public Commitment from the Public Accounting Profession

The Board of Directors of the American Institute of Certified Public Accountants

The United States has the best financial reporting system in the world. It makes possible the efficient allocation of capital that fuels economic growth. Capital markets depend on reliable financial information to operate; and financial decision-makers depend upon the independent auditors for assurance that information is indeed reliable.

This is a time of exceptional challenge for the financial reporting system and, hence, for the accounting profession. The challenges come both from the economy itself and from the concerns of the public.

The globalization of the economy, the explosion of technology, the complexity of business transactions, and other forces have thrust the financial system into a new age. As the pace of economic change accelerates, so does the need of reliable and relevant information. To stay the best, our financial reporting system must be as dynamic

---

"Meeting the Financial Reporting Needs of the Future: A Public Commitment from the Public Accounting Profession," the Board of Directors of the American Institute of Certified Public Accountants, 1211 Avenue of Americas, New York, NY 10036-8775, June 1993.

as the financial markets themselves. Independent auditors must constantly strive to improve their services to add continuing value to the users of financial information.

No matter how sound the financial reporting, however, it is without value if the user does not perceive it to be sound. In the end, trust is the financial markets' only asset; without it, they cease to function. Public confidence in the financial reporting system has been shaken in recent years by highly publicized business failures. Such events have raised questions about the effectiveness of the independent audit function and the integrity, objectivity, and competence of independent auditors and the self-regulatory system that governs them. Action is needed to solidify the public trust in the financial reporting system.

In the pages that follow, we detail the steps we believe will improve the value of financial information and the public's confidence in it.

The United States has the best financial reporting system in the world — and the AICPA is determined to keep it that way.

The Challenge to Change

We are undertaking reforms in the pursuit of five principal goals:

- improving the prevention and detection of fraud;
- enhancing the utility of financial reporting to those who rely on it;
- assuring the independence and objectivity of the independent auditor;
- discouraging unwarranted litigation that inhibits innovation and undermines the profession's ability to meet evolving financial reporting needs; and
- strengthening the accounting profession's disciplinary system.

These goals cannot be fully achieved through the efforts of accountants alone. Improving financial reporting invites the collaborative participation of not only the accounting profession, but also management, boards of directors, legislators, regulators, legal advisors, and the users of financial information. We encourage all participants in the

financial reporting system to work together toward reforms that will benefit everyone.

The independent Public Oversight Board made a valuable contribution to this effort when it recently issued a special report, "In the Public Interest: Issues Confronting the Accounting Profession." The POB made twenty-five separate recommendations to improve financial reporting and the quality of independent audits for consideration by Congress, the Securities and Exchange Commission, the AICPA's SEC Practice Section (SECPS), the Financial Accounting Standards Board, the AICPA's Accounting Standards Executive Committee (AcSEC), the AICPA's Auditing Standards Board, other components of the AICPA, accounting firms, and audit committees. We applaud these recommendations.

Obviously, implementation of so many recommendations by so many parties will not be easy. We will strive to adopt those that can be implemented by the AICPA; we encourage the other parties to do the same. And, we are committed to additional reforms to achieve the five goals set forth above.

Improving the Prevention and Detection of Fraud

Fraudulent financial schemes are the stuff of headlines and spicy news reports. Fraud justifiably engenders public outrage. While few business failures involve fraud, their corrosive effect on public confidence is widespread. The public looks to the independent auditor to detect fraud, and it is the auditor's responsibility to do so.

To strengthen the audit function by providing earlier notification to the government of possible illegal activity, the AICPA has endorsed proposed Federal legislation known as the Financial Fraud Detection and Disclosure Act.

We also support the recommendations of the POB in this area. The recommendations call for new guidelines to assist auditors in assessing the possibility of management fraud, additional auditing procedures when there is a heightened likelihood of fraud, and a renewed and tough-minded emphasis on the importance of professional skepticism.

More can be done. Every participant in the

financial reporting process has a stake in preventing wrongdoing and all should be expected to share the responsibility. Management, for example, should renew its emphasis on ethical values throughout the organization. It is also critical that an open line of communication with the independent auditor be maintained. Therefore, advisers, such as attorneys, should be called upon to bring to the independent auditor's attention instance so suspected financial fraud so that the auditor can, to the extent possible, confirm or dispel those suspicions. Regulators who possess such knowledge should also be required to make that information known to the auditors.

We also can do a better job of learning from past mistakes. The accounting profession will establish a systematic process for reviewing past cases of fraud to learn how the financial statements were manipulated, how detection was initially avoided, what audit procedures did detect or might have detected the illegality, and how audits can be changed to prevent a reoccurrence. The results, which will be disseminated throughout the accounting profession, will serve as the basis for continuous improvement in auditing.

Making Financial Reports More Useful

Financial decision-makers confront change on a daily basis. The integration of financial markets, the impact of technology, the entry of new competitors, the introduction of new and more complex financial products — all of these have made investing a different business than it was just a few years ago. These innovations automatically bring with them changes in the kind of financial information needed. If the accounting profession is to fulfill its obligation to the public, it must not remain static.

The AICPA has launched an effort to ensure that financial reporting moves with the times. Our Special Committee on Financial Reporting is looking at far-reaching ways to make financial reports more relevant to the realities of today's marketplace by anticipating the financial information needs of the 21st century. This is a wide-ranging and intensive effort. We are ruling out no possibilities as we examine what changes to the existing accounting model should be made to

meet user needs in the short and long term. We expect the Special Committee to complete its work within a year.

In the interim, we are taking more immediate steps to improve the utility of financial reports. In this fast-changing economic environment, investors can't afford to look only backwards. They need to anticipate. To serve this need, the AICPA's Accounting Standards Executive Committee, consistent with a recommendation by the POB, has issued a proposal to require management to disclose risks and uncertainties that could significantly affect the company's operations or financial condition. We urge AcSEC to complete its work with all deliberate speed.

To provide further assurance to the investing public, we join the POB in calling for a statement by management, to be included in the annual report, on the effectiveness of the company's internal controls over financial reporting, accompanied by an auditor's report on management's assertions. An assessment by the independent auditor will provide greater assurance to investors as to management's statement. The internal control system is the main line of defense against fraudulent financial reporting. The investing public deserves an independent assessment of that line of defense, and management should benefit from the auditor's perspective and insights. We urge the SEC to establish this requirement.

Finally, the SEC should require audit committees to include a statement in the annual report describing their responsibilities and how these responsibilities were discharged. This will increase the attention that audit committee members give their crucial responsibilities. It will increase the attention that audit committee members give their crucial responsibilities. It will also increase the attention paid to their views by management and other directors.

Assuring Auditor Independence

The credibility of the independent audit is essential to public trust, the keystone of the financial reporting system. The accounting profession prides itself on the integrity and objectivity of its members. The future of our profession, not to mention our livelihood, rests on this reputation.

A few recent high-profile financial scandals have, however, called auditors' independence into question. Neither the accounting profession nor the financial markets can afford an erosion of public confidence. For that reason, auditors must scrupulously preserve their objectivity, in reality and appearance. We therefore call on the SEC and other regulatory bodies to prohibit public companies and other organizations with public accountability from hiring the partner responsible for their audit for one year after the partner ceases to serve that client.

Additional steps can be taken, with the support of the business community, to secure public confidence in the independent audit and the financial reporting system. SEC registrants and other publicly accountable organizations should be required to have audit committees composed entirely of independent directors whenever practicable. The audit committee members should be charged with specific responsibilities, including overseeing their financial reporting process, and recommending appointment of the entity's auditors.

Rationalizing the Liability System

The accounting profession is determined to fulfill its public mission. In that spirit, we urge reform of a debilitating and unreasonable liability system that is undermining our ability to carry out this commitment. Under the doctrine of joint and several liability, an accounting firm can be forced to pay for damages that admittedly were caused by another party. Restrictions on firms' form of organization hold every partner liable to the full extent of his or her personal assets for the action of any colleague.

For fear of unreasonable liability, auditors are reluctant to introduce innovations that the financial markets urgently need, such as assurance on forward-looking financial data. Some firms are refusing to audit smaller, high-risk companies; often, these are high-technology companies whose success is vital to the nation's economic growth and competitiveness. Moreover, accountants' liability exposure damages the profession's ability to attract and retain highly qualified people, which has an adverse impact upon the profession's ability to serve American business and the investing public.

The need for liability reform is clearly evident from the exploding cost of unwarranted litigation affecting the entire accounting profession, costs that, if not absorbed by the marketplace, could force firms into bankruptcy. The cost of litigation is now the profession's fastest-growing expense. The risk of unreasonable liability has caused some firms to cease providing audit services, an outcome that is not in the public interest.

In the words of Sophocles, things have reached "the point beyond which even justice becomes unjust." The threat of mammoth liability frequently forces firms to settle rather than fight, no matter what the merits of the case. In too many cases, the justice system has ceased to distinguish the guilty from the innocent.

Accountants should not pay for others' mistakes simply because they are the only ones left standing after a financial collapse. People should be held responsible only for the damage they cause; simple fairness and common sense demand it. The system of joint and several liability should be replaced with proportionate liability except in cases of "knowing fraud." Accounting firms should be allowed to practice in corporate form so that an accountant can go to work without worrying that his or her family could lose their home even though the accountant had no involvement in an alleged audit failure. We do not ask to be held harmless for our wrongdoing. We ask only that we not be prevented by unwarranted liability from doing our job to the best of our ability.

Finally, all litigation in federal and state courts involving the same alleged audit failure should be consolidated into one federal suit to remove incentives for the procedural gamesmanship that plagues our legal system.

Sharpening the Teeth of Self-Regulation

The effectiveness of the accounting profession in governing itself and disciplining its members is essential to public confidence in the financial reporting system. That there be no doubt in the public mind of the profession's commitment to punishing wrongdoers in its ranks, we recommend a strengthened system to discipline those guilty of substandard work or professional misconduct — individual CPAs as well as firms. There is no room in our profession for "bad apples." This system should reside in the profession with oversight by the government and should be national in scope. It should apply to auditors of SEC registered companies and other publicly accountable entities.

The profession's disciplinary system provides an effective mechanism for investigating and reprimanding accountants who fail to comply with professional standards. As it is currently structured, though, the profession's disciplining of an alleged wrongdoer within its ranks must await the conclusion of litigation involving that party. Those court proceedings can take years — up to a decade or longer. We propose a system under which investigative and disciplinary actions would take place regardless of whether legal proceedings were also under way. Accountants would know that their profession will respond swiftly to any alleged misconduct or substandard performance. The system we propose would be both timely and forceful. Punishment would extend to the imposition of fines and, under the oversight of the appropriate regulatory agencies, loss of privilege to audit publicly accountable entities.

To enable the profession's disciplinary mechanism to function on a timely basis and to preserve the effectiveness and fairness of both that mechanism and the civil liability system, the two must be insulated from one another. Information gathered and findings reached by the disciplinary structure should not be admissible in civil proceedings. Since each forum pursues its unique objectives and may involve different standards of proof and rules of evidence, one should not be allowed to bias the other.

Further to ensure a speedy and efficient disciplinary system, a way must be found to eliminate parallel, sequential or multiple investigations and proceedings. Now, a firm or individual is subject to investigations by the SEC, state board(S) of accountancy, the Quality Control Inquiry Committee of the SECPS, and the Joint Ethics Enforcement Program of the AICPA and state CPA societies. For investigations within the private sector, one proceeding before a professional body with genuine "teeth" should be acceptable to both the public and private sectors.

In addition to a forceful disciplinary mechanism, we support measures recommended by the POB to strengthen the accounting profession's self-governance. These include requiring firms to make specific investigations into alleged audit failures, and requiring that those investigations be tested in the peer review process; expanding the responsibilities of SECPS's Quality Control Inquiry Committee; and strengthening continuing professional education for auditors.

Together, these self-regulatory reforms will renew and strengthen the accounting profession's historical commitment to holding its members to the highest standard of integrity and objectivity.

Conclusion

The auditor provides assurance to participants in the marketplace that financial statements may be reasonably relied upon. That assurance assists the efficient allocation of capital which fuels economic growth. Of course, no assurance can be absolute against unpredictable economic forces, and no audit can categorically guarantee the discovery of sophisticated, collusive fraud. The AICPA is dedicated, however, to the twin goals of adding continuing value to the financial information investors need in a fast-changing world and strengthening the prevention and detection of fraud to preserve the pubic trust.

The accounting profession is proud of its history as guardian of the financial reporting system. And the AICPA is proud of its role in helping accountants to carry out their duties. The initiatives laid forth here represent one more milestone in an unending journey of self-improvement.

Section 4: Human Resources

The traditional image of the "Personnel Office" has been left behind by contemporary organizations. The scope of human resources management is no longer limited to hiring, training, and payroll. Knowledge about human motivations and incentives to work has increased for more than three decades. Government regulation of the employment process has also grown dramatically during that same period. Together, both greater knowledge and numerous laws have broadened the scope of those who facilitate the work of others; and with these broadened roles should come increased moral responsibility for people at work. The issues are numerous: fairness in recruiting and selection, equity in compensation, appropriate job analysis and design, responsible orientation and training, renewed organizational structures, and accepted employee rights. In all of these areas, ethical decisions are the responsibility of those who manage other human beings. Which perspectives can guide us as we try morally to manage structures and processes affecting the work of others? Only a few authors could be included in this section; but their viewpoints represent important points of ethical understanding for the future of relations among people at work.

Elmer Johnson, from his many years of experience at General Motors, suggests alternatives to the adversarial employer/employee relationships that have characterized most of the twentieth century. He argues that the time is ripe for more participative forms of partnership in our work, for complex organizations of "complementary, mutually supportive members," a description that sounds strikingly like 1 Corinthians 13. He argues for a radically different approach to corporate structures and hierarchies, one that facilitates responsibility, commitment, and control. Taken as a whole, his ideas would lead to significant changes in the design of jobs.

Lennie Copeland forces her readers to think beyond the legal mandates for equal employment opportunity. She argues that organizations must value workforce diversity and seize the benefits that differences in race, ethnicity, and gender can bring to the work environment. Copeland argues that multiculturalism in the workplace can be a blessing, but only if it is a managed phenomenon. She suggests that if organizations do not manage diversity, diversity will manage them.

Barbara Andolsen, a professor of Christian social ethics, examines the moral issues raised by the wholesale use of video display terminals in the workplace. She argues that our capacity for recognizing the ethical issues involved in the deployment of computerized office technology is dependent on the model of moral agency employed. In looking at clerical workers and their stress levels, she argues that a feminist ethic which is more bodily and relational can help us achieve an expanded, more social understanding of the moral person. Such a model, she claims, will alert us to our corporate responsibility for reducing occupational stress. Hers is a promising exploration of the technological implications of honoring a commitment to human dignity in the workplace.

These authors discuss only a sample of the many moral concerns that should affect those who manage people at work. Yet they do provide insight into the relationships between organizations and the individuals of which they are composed. The relationship, of course, is a two-way street. Those who can exert moral responsibility for systems of work will reap the harvest they have sown.

Shaping Our Economic Future: Dignity in the Work Place

Elmer W. Johnson

. . . . Over the last 10 or 15 years I have spent a good deal of time reading about and reflecting upon the "macro" issues of economic justice and seeking to define and articulate sound positions on these issues. Important as this quest is, I have undergone a change of thinking over the last three years. I have come to the conclusion that most of us in business can make a much bigger contribution to the cause of economic justice if we concentrate primarily on brightening the corner where we are. . . .

It is sad to consider how deeply imbued we have become by the seemingly tragic conflict between market efficiency and investor returns on the one hand, and equity to employees on the other. Many managers have long justified their authoritarian style toward employees on the ground that they, the managers, have a special trust: they must keep costs down and protect the interests of the stockholders. If they don't, no one else will. Over the years this adversary relationship has also been built into our legalistic, rule driven structure governing labor-management relations and collective bargaining in decisions by the NLRB and the courts. For decades elected union representatives maintained their power by demonstrating their confrontational skills in dealing with management, and the union leader who dared to work for a more cooperative kind of

Elmer W. Johnson, "Shaping Our Economic Future: Dignity in the Work Place," *Vital Speeches of the Day* 52, no. 11 (15 March 1986): 332-35.

relationship ran high risks of political defeat. And so, over the years, the habitual dispositions of both managers and union representatives became fixed almost beyond redemption. Almost — but not quite.

Traditional management behavior has come under siege. A new but really very ancient concept has come to the fore. The idea is very simple and yet profound. First, contrary to all our inherited learning, all of us who are employees of an enterprise are members one of another. We each have differing gifts and talents and resources. We need each other. Second, while there are necessarily different levels of authority and responsibility in the enterprise, we are all equal as human beings, and our personal and spiritual goals far transcend the commercial goals of the enterprise. Accordingly, respect for all persons is fundamental. Third, there is no basic conflict between these human values and our legitimate business purposes. They are mutually reinforcing.

I happen to accept these assumptions. I object strongly to those corporate leaders who, with great conviction, adopt credos along the following lines: "Our ability to make a profit in an ethical manner is the most important single measure of our contribution to society." Milton Friedman could not have expressed it better. And yet, there is something wrong. Surely, ethics has to do with identifying positive human goods, ends and obligations and should not be treated merely as some kind of constraint on profit-making activities.

The truth is that the large corporation is a complex organization consisting of complementary, mutually supportive members. Its fundamental social contribution is to provide products and services of superior quality and value. This is the goal that can unite all employees and give them a sense of partnership and high calling. The corporation cannot do well in this function unless it also does well in its other responsibilities: providing a work environment that is respectful of the equal and inestimable dignity and worth of all persons and that enables all employees to realize their capacities for growth in individual and team performance; providing a superior return to stockholders on their investment; and conducting its operations so as to protect legitimate social interests.

This kind of philosophy holds out the promise

that an employee can be both a productive participant in the enterprise and a responsible citizen. Management should communicate to its employees the symbiotic relationship between business and society. If top management both believes in and acts in light of this kind of vision, it will have taken one of the most fundamental steps in removing the blinders from tunnel vision managers bent only on short-term profits.

To our shame we have found by now that our continued industrial vigor as a nation really hangs, not so much on new technologies or on more brilliant financial deals, but almost entirely on whether we can forge a new kind of human partnership among managers and employees.

I recall Alfred North Whitehead, in his *Adventures in Ideas*, noting that the realization of certain long-held dreams and ideals must await the fullness of time: namely, the appropriate developments in technology and/or the gradual growth of the "requisite communal customs, adequate to sustain the load of their exemplification." He was referring to the external conditions that facilitated the abolition of slavery in the 19th century. This truth is equally apt in referring to the external conditions of our time that now facilitate and demand the formation of a new quality of human partnership among the employees at all levels of our large corporations.

Why do I sense that the time is ripe for such a historic breakthrough? First and foremost, the long-standing divorce between ethics and economics is no longer countenanced by the leadership of our churches, our universities or among the leaders of our best-run unions and companies.

Second, those managers and union representatives who are connected with heavy manufacturing have been forced by their global competitors to think much more seriously about the human aspects of the work place and about the mutually reinforcing relationship between human values, workmanship, quality and long-term return on investment. This startling revelation, that there is no long term conflict between these human values and human productivity, which strangely has come to broad daylight only in the last few years, is shaking American manufacturing know-how to its very foundations.

Yet, it is one thing to discover the new learning and quite another to put it into effect. For one thing, it calls for a major cultural change among our management and union leadership. Further, it turns out that management and organizational genius remains the *sine qua non* of competitive leadership. But this genius has been newly focused on the relationship between the manufacturing process and human factors. The new learning may be summarized, in no particular order, as follows:

1. A highly centralized, bureaucratized management scheme undermines quality and productivity because the masses of employees rightly sense that their feelings, insights and suggestions are not considered, even in respect to decisions of utmost relevance to the meaningfulness of their work lives: the design of the production system and their particular work stations. Accordingly, managers tap only a fraction of their associates' potential for quality workmanship and innovation.

2. If their full potential is to be tapped, a radical change in management philosophy and style will be required — one that solicits pertinent input from the persons most affected by decisions and that sincerely considers that input in arriving at the most quality- and cost-effective decisions on a long-term basis. Decisions must be made at the appropriate level of responsibility, capacity and control. When a group decision will affect persons beyond that group, a higher line of management must review the decision in light of that potential impact. Once the decision is made in this sensitive manner and is carefully communicated, all affected employees are obligated to support and implement that decision. This process is called participative management in the work place. It starts and ends with a great deal of mutual listening.

3. The new philosophy also calls for the team concept. Under the new production system, each plant employee is assigned to a team consisting of a half dozen or more members with a Team Leader. The success of each team is vital to the organization's overall success. Teams have the following attributes:
   a. Each member shares responsibility for the performance of the total team and actively supports other team members. When a problem occurs during production at a

team's work station, there is no longer any effort to allocate individual blame. Rather they address what went wrong *in the system* and cooperate to figure out the best remedy.

b. Each member is expected to help meet team goals and define additional goals. The performance of each team is evaluated on a regular basis, and both the process and the results are communicated back to the members.

c. Each team is an accountability center for achieving quality goals, monitoring and improving quality standards, meeting production goals and schedules, training new team members, handling its own housekeeping chores, cooperating and communicating effectively with other teams, maintaining safety standards, and continually searching for ways to make each other and the company more efficient and one's own job easier and simpler to perform.

d. With this increased participation in decision-making and this team control over each local work station on the factory floor, there follow certain individual obligations to the team. A high attendance rate among all team members is critical. Many U.S. manufacturing plants have become noncompetitive because of high absenteeism. By forging the kind of new human partnership that I have described, we can strive to break away from this pattern. High attendance becomes an important factor in determining benefits and promotions. Conversely, a failure to notify the company for three consecutive work days should be sufficient cause of termination. There are also appropriate penalties for late arrival.

e. Each team member is expected to become proficient in his or her own job and in all other assignments within each functional group of teams.

This then is the team concept.

4. Another aspect of the new partnership is the provision of individual and team awards and incentives for attendance, quality, productivity, and so forth.

5. One of management's responsibilities is to provide the team members with a work environment that is conducive to a high quality of workmanship — doing things right the first time. Traditionally the best minds in the manufacturing companies have often been allocated largely to product engineering and planning and to finance and business planning. But in the last several years, increasingly, some of the best minds are working on all aspects of the production system. Experts in materials management and in manufacturing processes are being carefully listened to by top management. When these experts cry out against tendencies toward ever more proliferation of products, parts and options, they speak with an authority they didn't have ten years ago. They are concerned over the adverse consequences of undue complexity in terms of quality and cost effectiveness, together with the workers' loss of pride of workmanship. These experts help determine the design of new products based on such considerations as enhancement of quality workmanship, durability and repairability, reduction in costs and so forth.

6. These experts in the production system have also introduced a whole new way of dealing with suppliers and receiving incoming parts. Suppliers are graded among each other based on the quality of their parts on arrival. They receive report cards. Shipments receiving poor grades are sent back in their entirety, but emissaries for the Company work closely with committed suppliers to carry out root cause analyses that lead to permanent solutions. In the case of suppliers receiving the highest grades for a sustained period, their shipments go right to the plant floor without any initial inspection. The best suppliers are rewarded with more business. The worst are terminated. Aside from this day-to-day routine, the Company interacts with its best suppliers to create new and better products. There are technical forums where team members can meet with supplier representatives to solve problems and create new efficiencies.

7. These experts in materials management and manufacturing systems listen carefully to the person on the floor. The old assembly line, where the machine was master over man, is obsolete. In its place, the workers and the production system experts have devised a system that makes man master of the machine. For

example, any team member, under this enlightened new system, can bring the entire plant to a screeching halt if he or she has a problem. No one is expected to keep the line moving if quality will suffer. At the same time no one lightly pulls the line that stops the plant. There is great visibility to the process. Signs light up to indicate the exact location of the problem. There are also whistles and chimes, etc. No one wants to be tagged as a laggard. Repeaters can be stigmatized if the problem is their own.

8. One of the logical fall outs of participative management and the team concept and the new expertise is that we can get rid of a few layers of management. They merely get in the way. Over the last 20 years, sadly, the ratio of salaried worker to hourly workers in large manufacturing companies has risen rather significantly. Thus, top management has a heavy responsibility to face up promptly to this problem if our manufacturing companies are to remain viable and competitive. Many middle managers will simply have to be retrained for other assignments.

9. This brings me to the final attribute of the new partnership. We have recently discovered that all the things I have talked about are unlikely to be realized except in a context of high employment security and mutual trust. In my own company, a major step to this end was accomplished with the 1982 and 1984 Labor Agreements. The 1984 agreement says, basically, that, subject to certain contractual obligations, the company is free to outsource and that it is free to adapt to new technologies — as it must if it is to remain competitive in the world. But, says the agreement, when dislocations occur and the affected employees cannot be immediately re-assigned, they will go into a Job Bank with full pay where they will be retrained for new jobs. We are already discovering that with this kind of protection, we can now aspire to the kind of partnership I have described. People can't participate and be creative if they are insecure.

I said earlier that there is no long term conflict between these human values and our legitimate business goals. Along with the new revelation as

to participative management and team play, we have discovered that we have been tragically misled for many years by our acceptance of a woefully inadequate definition of costs. It is only in recent years that we have learned that compilation of costs of production is not over when the product goes out the door. We now know, to our dismay, that this short-term view of costs is false. In our legal system and a moral climate, costs come to comprehend the long term consequences of failing to deliver high quality, durable, reliable, easily repairable, damage-resistant products. These costs include long-term warranty liability, government recalls, class action suits, long-term arbitration arrangements in settlement of government actions, large jury verdicts, criminal litigation and ultimately and perhaps worst of all, the permanent loss of customer goodwill.

It is in light of this recent discovery as to the nature of true costs that I have come to believe, even more firmly that I did before, that in the long term, dignity in the work place and return on investment go together like a horse and carriage or even like love and marriage. The bottom line is just that. It's the result of doing everything else right by the employee and the customer.

Learning to Manage a Multicultural Work Force

Lennie Copeland

Trend-watcher John Naisbitt says, "The big challenge of the 1980s is not the retraining of workers but the retraining of managers." The rapidly changing demographic makeup of the American work force is one reason why this is true. Now, for the first time in history, white males are the minority — only 46 percent. The U.S. Department of Labor projects that within just a few years, 75 percent of those entering the work force will be minorities and women.

The labor pool is not only changing, it is shrinking. In the 1990s, there will be four to five million fewer entry-level workers each year than in 1980. The consequences are clear. Organizations that want the most productive employees will have to put aside old definitions of "corporate fit" and employ people of different colors and cultures. They will have to compete for women, minorities and others who are different from the norm in age, appearance, physical ability and lifestyle. But that's not all. They also will have to develop and retain them.

Erroneous Assumptions

Diversity is emerging as one of the most serious issues in the workplace today, yet most employers are not prepared to deal with it. Nor are their managers. Many managers grew up having little contact with other cultures. They are actually "cul-

turally deprived," and their graduate school texts did not cover the kinds of situations that arise in today's multicultural settings.

Most traditional models of human behavior and management methods as well as many of the recommendations in recent best-sellers such as *The One-Minute Manager* and *In Search of Excellence,* are based on implicit assumptions of a homogeneous white male work force. The most widely taught theories of motivation mirror the white male's own experience and attitudes. Some of those methods can be startlingly counterproductive when applied to women or to blacks, Asians, Hispanics or American Indians.

For example:

- A manager, thrilled with a new technique developed by one of his American Indian employees, rewarded her with great fanfare and congratulations in front of her peers — just as the management books suggest. Humiliated, she didn't return to work for three weeks.
- After learning that a friendly pat on the arm or back would make workers feel good and motivated, a manager took every chance to pat his subordinates. His Asian employees, who hated being touched, avoided him like the plague. Several asked for transfers. (If he had treated female employees this way, he could have had other problems on his hands.)
- Fresh from a course on delegation, a production supervisor asked his primarily Filipino staff to alert him to any problems with some new equipment. Instead, they used masking tape and other makeshift remedies to get the machines working.
- Concerned about ethics, a manager declined a gift offered him by a new employee, an immigrant who wanted to show gratitude for her job. He explained the company's policy about gifts. She was so insulted she quit.
- In a similar situation, a new employee's wife (an Eastern European) stopped by the office with a bottle of champagne, fully expecting everyone present to stop and celebrate the new job. When people said "hello" and returned to work, she was mortified. Her husband quit within a few days.
- Trying to implement his company's policy of participatory management, a manager asked

Lennie Copeland, "Learning to Manage a Multicultural Work Force," *Training* 25 (May 1988): 48-49, 51, 55-56.

his Hispanic employees to work together to come up with solutions to some problems. Bitter ego battles ensued, as well as incidents of insubordination. Work came to a stop. This manager found he had undermined his own authority. In an ingenious "save," he appointed Hispanic women to facilitate the teams. The women were able to get input from the men by asking their "advice" and funneling their ideas to management.

Managing Diversity

Some organizations are taking aggressive steps to meet the demographic challenge of the 1990s. Digital Equipment Corp. has a "director of valuing differences." Honeywell has a "director of work-force diversity." Avon has a "director of multicultural planning and design."

Many companies, such as Bank of Boston and GTE, offer management courses dealing with race and gender. Mobil set up a special committee of executives to select high-potential women and minorities for critical line positions, moving them from staff functions to the mainstream of the oil business. Security Pacific Bank has established minority networks and support groups to encourage personal and professional growth of minority managers. The Equitable has business resource groups that meet with CEO John B. Carver to discuss issues pertaining to women, blacks and Hispanics. Carver signs off on the groups' suggestions and directs a senior manager to execute them. At the end of each quarter, he reviews progress.

"It is absolutely clear that we have to manage diversity right now and much more so in the future," says David Kearns, president and CEO of Xerox Corp. "American business will not be able to survive if we do not have a large diverse work force, because those are the demographics — no choice! The company that gets out in front of managing diversity, in my opinion, will have a competitive edge."

The current interest in multicultural diversity is embraced by equal employment opportunity specialists, who view it as the chance that EEO never had. It puts their issues in the mainstream. In a company that values diversity, says Daisy

Chin-Lor, director of multicultural planning and design at Avon, "EEO goes beyond numbers. It takes on real meaning. Valuing diversity is more than EEO-driven, it's part of the management process."

But simply throwing different people together does not create a productive work environment — or even a genuinely diverse one. People tend to cluster with people like themselves, those with whom they feel comfortable and who confirm old stereotypes. It is harder to manage a group of people who have different wants and ideas about how work is to be done. Prejudice and cultural misunderstandings cause conflict, bad decisions and poor results. Productivity may decline unless diversity is deliberately managed and managed well.

The reality today is that most organizations must deal with diversity at entry levels simply because of the demographics of the labor pool. At the same time, organizations need diversity at the top where more complex tasks need different perspectives. The upshot is that effective managing of diversity is a requirement at all levels.

Beyond Equality

Managing diversity is conceptually different from equal employment opportunity, which was primarily a battle against racism and prejudice. To *value* work-force diversity is to manage in a way designed to seize the benefits that differences bring.

In the past, experts say, we actually conspired to ignore differences. Advocates of civil rights downplayed cultural heritage because differences were regularly used as evidence of minority group inferiority. Well-meaning whites went along with the conspiracy because they were embarrassed by differences that they indeed did see as marks of inferiority. Consequently, "we are all equal" came to mean "we are all the same." Even now, many of those who say they value diversity take umbrage when actual differences are discussed. There's a fine line between recognizing cultural norms and promulgating stereotypes.

The consequence of viewing all people as the same is that the majority culture is seen as the standard. Those who don't conform are regarded as not measuring up to that standard. For example, equality for women at work came to mean that women had to become like men: aggressive, competitive, wearing dark suits, talking about sports. "The problem with measuring everyone against that white male standard," says Gerald Adolph, a management consultant and principal at Booz Allen & Hamilton, "is that you set up a sizable portion of your work force for failure."

Being blind to differences is not the aim. As Price Cobbs, a management consultant and coauthor of *Black Rage* puts it, "When people say, 'I don't even notice you are black,' what they are really saying is 'You have overcome that handicap,' or 'I don't value the difference — I see you as just like me.' It is just as bad to ignore differences as it is to emphasize them, or to treat them as deficits, or to treat everyone in a group as the same."

Santiago Roderiguez, head of affirmative action at Stanford University, says that fair treatment is more important than equal treatment. "Part of being a professional is being analytical, making choices, discerning between options and acknowledging that people are stimulated by different needs, operating with different styles. A good manager knows that individuals react differently for a variety of reasons, one of which is culture."

Still, some consider it demeaning to say that different people in the workplace have different needs. Avon's Chin-Lor counters with a wonderful analogy: "If I were planting a garden and I wanted to have a number of flowers, I would never think of giving every flower the same amount of sun, the same amount of water and the same soil. I'd be sure to cultivate each individual type of flower differently. Does that mean the rose or the orchid is less because I have to do more with them? Certainly not!"

What Every Manager Needs to Know

If managers are to be trained to value diversity, what do they actually need to learn? What barriers must they overcome to work effectively with people who are different from themselves or different from the mainstream?

Many EEO and human resources development professionals seem to agree that four major problem areas need attention:

1. stereotypes and their associated assumptions,
2. actual cultural differences,
3. the exclusivity of the "white male club" and its associated access to important information and relationships, and
4. unwritten rules and double standards for success, which are often unknown to women and minorities.

Stereotypes and assumptions

Some experts say stereotypes are not necessarily bad — it's what we do with them. I disagree. Stereotypes are bad because they are so powerfully effective in preventing differentiated thinking about people who belong to the stereotyped group. As defined by Gordon Allport in his classic book, *The Nature of Prejudice*, "A stereotype is an exaggerated belief associated with a category. Its function is to justify (rationalize) our conduct in relation to that category."

Stereotypes hurt individuals when invalid conclusions are reached about them and when those conclusions remain untested and unchanged. Take this scenario: A white male manager walks through the office, passing two black men talking at the watercooler. He is slightly irritated. Why are they standing there wasting time? A moment later he passes two women coming out of the ladies room talking. He wonders what they are gossiping about and hopes they get back to work quickly. He comes upon two white men leaning on the walls of a cubicle, also talking. He thinks nothing of it.

What are his assumptions? The women and minorities are "goofing off," but the white men are talking business. Since he hasn't really listened to the conversations, he doesn't realize that the women and the black men were talking business while the white men happened to be talking about their children. Instead, his misinterpretation of what he saw will only strengthen his bias that women and minorities don't work hard enough.

Many stereotypes have some basis in truth, but there are so many exceptions that it is a mistake to apply notions about a group to any one individual. Even when an individual seems to fit a stereotype, it's important to analyze all the assumptions that are being made. For example, take an Asian engineer who is quiet, modest and hardworking. He avoids eye contact and doesn't speak out in brainstorming sessions. When he applies for a promotion, he doesn't really sell himself. His boss' conclusion: "He is a good technician, but he lacks management skills."

It's entirely possible that the white manager fails to realize that the Asian has successfully (if indirectly) led many of his team's projects for some time. He could be coached in areas where he is lacking, as a white candidate would be. And what about the criteria the boss is using to define "management skills"? Is aggression really needed, or might intelligence, persistence and the ability to foster group collaboration be equally or more effective in getting to the same goal? Managing a diverse work force requires managers to learn new ways to recognize talent. This means laying aside some assumptions and looking beyond style at results.

Unwritten rules

Each organization has its own culture, and that culture reflects attitudes about what is important, how the organization does its work, how employees are to behave and how they are to be rewarded. In most companies, the values are male, white and based in European traditions, not because these ways are better than others but because the organization reflects the values of the people who control it. It is important for all employees to know what those values are because they define the ground rules for success.

In some organizations many of the rules are explicit, even written. In most, however, the rules are ambiguous, unwritten and may be completely inconsistent with written policy. A problem for women and minorities is that they aren't aware of many of the rules that are obvious to people in the mainstream. White men may not share the rules because it never occurs to them that everyone is not aware of them or because they don't want to seem patronizing.

Even when coaching women and minorities, managers sometimes inadvertently contribute to failure. In one company, men would train other men by putting them on the equipment and then coaching them. But they trained women by showing them how the equipment worked without giving them "hands-on" practice. In another com-

pany, men training men used correct technical terminology for the equipment, but when they trained women they referred to the "gizmo" or the "thingamajig with the little curlicue on top." They assumed that the women could not handle technical terminology and thus hindered their training.

A team is a winning team when all the players know the rules. Because so many white male managers are only subconsciously aware of the rules and double standards, they need to learn to identify their organizations' culture and rules, and how to pass on that information to women and minorities. This means providing all employees with what they need to know about career advancement, communication, leadership, management, organizational culture, power, networking, interpersonal skills and all the other unwritten rules, norms and cues for success.

But this does not mean that women and minorities should do all the changing. An employer who recognizes the value added by diversity will strive to nurture differences, not reduce everyone to white male clones. Valuing diversity may mean changing the rules to accommodate differences in style and perspective. The aim of sharing the rules is to give everyone choices, recognizing that no organization is going to change completely overnight. Employees who know the rules can proceed to take care of their careers while they (and management) work to change the system.

Membership

Relationships are central to achievement, and being a member of the "club" is as important as hard work and competence. When a white man and a woman (or minority employee) are competing for a promotion, the decision maker may be heard to say, "I just don't know Mary as well as Bob." Most of us prefer to have lunch and socialize after work with people most like ourselves. As a result, people in the mainstream fail to include those who are different and thus exclude them from important information and relationships.

Women and minorities complain that they must prove themselves while white men automatically assume membership in the club. They are kept in training too long, given just one more assignment, one more test. White men are given promotional opportunities sooner under the assumption that they will rise to the occasion. The catch-22 is that when people are not given challenging assignments, they never have the chance to learn by experience or to develop the track record that will reduce others' feelings of risk about them.

Managers impede their own people in this way. They need to learn to make deliberate efforts to include people in work-related and social events. Managing the diverse work force requires conscious team building, networking and mentoring to bring others into the mainstream.

Cultural differences

It's obvious that cultures are different. No one disputes that some people prefer sushi to tacos or wienerschnitzel. Why then do so many managers (and management gurus) assume that what works with one employee will work with others? Cultural differences affect the values people bring to the workplace. Different people feel differently about their roles in an organization, how they can make a contribution and how they want to be recognized for their efforts.

What motivates one worker might completely inhibit another — for example, rewarding people who don't like to be touched with pats on the back, or publicly recognizing people who don't like to be isolated from the group. Workers unintentionally humiliated in this manner may be less productive. Then, typically, the manager who made the mistake will fall back on stereotypes to explain an employee's disappointing behavior: "Well, what can you expect, Hispanics are like that."

In some multicultural workplaces many diverse people work side by side: Laotians, Cambodians, Vietnamese, Chinese, Korean, Salvadorean, Guatemalan, Mexican, Peruvian and so on. Managers in these mixed settings may ask, with some panic, "How can I possibly learn about all these cultures?" Experts answer, "Of course you can't learn everything there is to know about all cultures, but the more you know, the better able you will be to do your job. If you don't understand and value your employees, how can you hope to motivate and supervise them?"

It's also important to understand your own culture, whether you are Indian, Asian, Hispanic, black or white. Many whites, particularly those of European heritage, don't think of themselves as having a culture. They think "culture" is something quaint that minorities have.

Promoting Differences

Says Xerox's Kearns, "There's a lot of discussion about compromise in promoting women and minorities, and I would like to get it out of our vocabulary because it's not necessary. If you give people the right experiences, then the normal measurement system of competence and results will prove itself."

Many people expect women, minorities and others outside the mainstream to do all the adapting. But it has to be a two-way street. While women and minorities must perform, build relationships, learn the rules and work to become members of the club, managers must share the rules, invite people into the club, accommodate cultural differences, create climates that support diversity and establish systems that enable different types of employees to succeed.

Valuing diversity is an established mode of operation in some companies and unheard of in others. But even the most progressive organizations have some offices, divisions or regions of the country where more work needs to be done. Plenty of companies have given lip service to the idea of managing a diverse work force, but end up with few changes because they have failed to establish accountability.

Kearns insists that making sure you have the right balance in your work force at all levels "is something you have to measure and you have to target just like you do profits or market share." At Xerox, he went about this by identifying successful white males and studying where they had been and what they had done to get ahead. Then Kearns set targets and put in place a process to ensure that women and minorities got the same types of experiences.

Four essentials in managing a diverse work force are really a matter of changing old habits:

- Periodically stop and ask, "What's going on here? What assumptions am I making?"

- Make sure all your employees are invited into the club.
- Share the unwritten rules and change them to nurture diversity.
- Be sensitive to individual differences: appreciate diversity.

Occupational Stress Is a Moral Issue: Lessons in Front of a VDT

Barbara Hilkert Andolsen

Stress as an Occupational Health Hazard among Clerical Workers

.... Occupational stress is one of the most serious, job-related threats to the health of clerical workers who constitute one of the largest segments of the work force. "If loss of limb and back strain [were] the characteristic occupational hazards of the industrial age, then job stress is *the* characteristic hazard of the computer age." Prolonged occupational stress diminishes the quality of a worker's daily life. Occupational stress has been correlated to symptoms such as indigestion; neck, shoulder, or back pain; headache; chronic exhaustion; insomnia; anxiety and depression. Moreover, prolonged exposure to stress increases a person's risk of coronary disease, stroke, and mental illness.

Clerical workers report high levels of stress-related disease. One study by the National Institute for Occupational Safety and Health [NIOSH] concluded that the occupations of secretary and office manager ranked among the dozen occupations with the highest incidence of stress-related disorders. In the Framingham study on coronary heart disease, female clerical workers showed an increased incidence of such heart disease. Women who were clerical workers where almost twice as

Originally published under the title "The Social Self at the VDT: Exploring the Advantages and Limitations of the Relational Model of Agency," *Annual of the Society of Christian Ethics* (1988): 205-20.

likely as housewives, blue-collar, or other white-collar women to develop coronary heart disease. One NIOSH study found the clerical workers who operated video display terminals had one of the highest stress ratings ever recorded. It was higher than the rate for air traffic controllers.

There are many aspects of clerical jobs which may — alone or in interaction — lead to increased stress. These include boring, monotonous work; under-utilization of ability; close, unsupportive supervision; high production demands; machine pacing; low decision-making power; lack of career development; and/or uncertainty about continued employment. The widespread automation of office jobs may intensify occupational stress. In one San Francisco Bay study, computerized clerical work involved heavy work loads, fast machine-paced work, boring tasks, and lack of opportunities for career advancement. VDT operators were required to do work which provided little intrinsic satisfaction. Their work procedures were rigidly defined by others. VDT operators were under constant pressure to meet high production standards. The VDT system included monitoring capabilities which tallied output and errors. Thus, the workers were now confronted with the possibility of continuous monitoring of their job performance.

The level of control over their work processes which clerical workers have is a crucial health issue. Studies show that lack of control over one's work increases both physiological and psychological stress. In contrast, workers who have high job demands but who also have high decision latitude do not suffer adverse health effects. As one journalist succinctly puts it: "stress is the disease of the highly pressured and the unempowered."

Occupational stress poses a serious risk to the health of clerical workers. This threat to their bodily well-being is potentially an interesting and important issue for bioethics. However, at present, such questions of occupational health and safety are almost never raised in bioethics literature. . . .

Why is it that the problem of occupational stress experienced by clerical workers is currently invisible to bioethicists? I contend that it is, in part, because bioethicists too often presuppose an individualistic model of the self. Such a model is not suited to a discussion concerning occupational health hazards, for debate about such problems requires attention to persons *as members of a group*. . . .

In contrast to the individualistic model, both feminist and communitarian critics insist that a model of the moral agent as one embedded in relationships which have specific histories is the more appropriate and more accurate paradigm. One very important suggestion about constructing new models comes from Larry Churchill who points out that "The first sign of our sociability is our bodies . . ." Our bodies present us with vivid reminders that we are related to and dependent upon other persons, not self-creating or invulnerable. Careful attention to our bodily experience from birth to death throws elements of the liberal paradigm into serious question.

Feminist scholars who root their work in women's experience usually take bodily experience quite seriously. For both physiological and cultural reasons, many women have particularly sharp, body-based knowledge that we humans are unavoidably related to one another. Many women who have borne or nursed a baby or who have been primary caregivers for young children, the sick, the frail elderly, and the dying cannot ignore the connection between the body and sociality without falsifying their own experience.

It is with one and the same body that the self moves through a series if fragmented social roles in modern life. This bodily unity is one source of questions about the usefulness of distinctions which theorists make concerning human experiences. For example, the fragmented view of a person as a worker divorced from his or her other social roles and responsibilities obscures the destructive synergism between workplace strains and "outside" pressures, such as family obligations. As a result, the magnitude of stresses imposed upon the worker's body-self is seriously underestimated.

Loss of a sense of bodily connectedness facilitates a lack of attention to those social and historical dimensions which are intertwined in our bodily existence. The body is *a social body,* situated within a particular community and sharing in that community's specific historical patterns of location within a precise social context would lead us to recognize that health prospects are not determined entirely by some biological lottery or by personal health practices, but are also influenced in significant ways by our concrete social and historical circumstances.

The embodied self's moral choices are not fully intelligible if they are situated against the backdrop of specific social and historical settings. As a feminist ethicist, I want to particularize MacIntyre's call for "narrative history of a certain kind" as an essential genre for ethics. I insist that we need to interpret moral actions in the context of *a matrix of intersecting concrete histories.* Our moral understanding of virtually all human actions would be enriched and deepened by serious attention to historical patterns of gender and class relations. In many cases, racial or ethnic history is also of vital importance. Careful attention to the intersections of gender, race, and class would influence what we perceive as urgent issues for discussion in bioethics. For example, health hazards faced by women performing nursing, clerical, or housekeeping tasks are often ignored, because dualistic cultural traditions present these tasks as "natural" to women. The heavier health burdens borne by the poor in American society (who are disproportionately Black, Hispanic, and Native American) cry out for sustained concern. . . .

Occupational Stress as a Moral Issue

An emphasis on moral agents as radically autonomous selves tends to "lead our eye" toward moral issues which give the appearance of being decided by a single person. Insofar as communitarian and feminist critics stand a better chance to recognize the ethical questions raised by patterns of work which increase levels of stress with concomitant health risks. Let me examine three implications arising from this discussion of models of moral agency for policies addressing occupational stress as a health hazard for clerical workers.

First, the model of the self with which we work may influence in subtle ways the solutions which we can imagine for the problems which we propose and the parties whom we identify as responsible to implement those solutions. A model of the solitary self could dispose one to seek individualistic answers. In the case of health burdens related to occupational stress, there are individual solutions which would appear attractive within the classic liberal framework, but which are ulti-

mately inadequate. There are individual health practices which exacerbate or mitigate the impact of occupational stress on the body. Increased consumption of alcohol, other drugs, or cigarettes seriously compounds the harmful negative impact of stress. An individualistic model of the self might narrow our view of solutions leading us to exhort workers to improve their health habits.

While improving employee health habits is worthwhile, it is by no means a comprehensive solution. A more adequate solution would involve transforming stressful working conditions. Clerical workers need a greater control over their work processes for the sake of their bodily health. That realization turns our attention to power relationships which determine working conditions. We must concentrate on class, race, and gender dynamics in the clerical workplace and consider how workplace relationships must be restructured in order to support effective concern for clerical workers' health.

An individualistic model of the moral decision-maker also influences whom we identify as responsible parties when confronted with health-care issues. The greater emphasis on the social nature of the self raises additional questions about *the moral accountability of groups,* such as health-care providers. Among physicians, direct individual responsibility to protect the health of clerical workers threatened by occupational stress would be limited to a few occupational health researchers, members of corporate medical staffs, and public health officers. However, a greater sensitivity to social relationships would lead ethicists to examine more closely the obligations of groups of health-care professionals, such as the American Medical Association. A more social perspective in bioethics might cause ethicists to question whether the medical association should take an aggressive stance in developing policies to safeguard the health of workers in automated offices.

However, this social perspective involves more than identifying the responsibilities of groups of physicians. The obligations of clerical workers as a social group must be addressed as well. Their collective action to protect their own health is more important in the long term than the actions of a professional association without strong ties to the specific work environment. Finally, this perspective introduces changes in our understanding of the obligations of those managing diverse workplaces. . . .

The study of occupational stress makes it empirically plain that the relational context to be taken into account should not be limited to the boundaries of the "public" workplace. Rather "private" space — the home — must also be examined.

In order to accurately describe the health burdens thrust upon some clerical workers, it is essential to consider gender relations across the public/private divide. An adequate description of health-threatening stress experienced by clerical workers must include an exploration of what is called the double burden or double day. These terms refer to the combination of employment duties and domestic responsibilities assumed by many wage-earning women in industrial and post-industrial societies. This particular pattern of female obligations evolved with the development of industrialization which shifted the location of certain forms of production from the family farm or shop to the factory or office. At first, many married women — especially middle-class women — remained at home where they continued to perform household maintenance and childrearing tasks. However, throughout this century there has been a steady rise in the percentage of married women who work for wages. In the post–World War II era, a flood of White, married women entered the labor force, pushed by pressures on middle-income family budgets, drawn by a rapid increase in clerical and service jobs, and inspired by a feminist ideal of economic self-reliance. Since most men have been reluctant to increase significantly their share of domestic duties, married women (and single heads of households) have ended up carrying a double burden.

This stress which workers experience in their "personal" lives combines with job-related stress in ways which put a greater strain on their health. Women who have heavy household responsibilities and who also work in stressful occupations are at increased health risk. The Framingham study found that it was clerical workers *with children* who were more likely to develop coronary heart disease. In the Framingham study, there is some evidence that gender and class intersect to put even more strain on a woman's health. Researchers found that marriage to a man in a blue-collar job also correlated to increased risk of coronary heart disease for female office workers. A woman who had a clerical job, had children, and was married to a man in a blue-collar position was three times more likely to manifest coronary heart disease than a non-clerical mother. The Framingham data suggests that economic status and responsibility for the well-being of children combine with features of clerical work to increase the risk of heart disease.

Occupational stress may combine with family burdens to increase a woman's risk of experiencing stress-related disease. Stressful clerical duties can also combine with the strains of dealing with racism in a fashion which imperils the health of Black clerical workers. Such racism is pervasive in all aspects of social life, not neatly confined to the workplace. Unfortunately, we do not know as much as we should about whether the stresses which Black women experience in a racist society actually interact with job-related stress to threaten their lives, because there has been relatively little research on occupational stress as experienced by minority women. Nevertheless, the scattered data available gives cause for concern.

Black women clerical workers are over-represented in clerical categories, such as mail handler, telephone clerk, and key-punch operator, which lend themselves to stressful job design — low control, machine pacing, etc. In the National Survey on Women and Stress, Black women who used VDTs reported using the machines more intensively than their White counterparts. Reflecting on these results, researchers speculate that Black women are concentrated in back-office data-processing or word-processing positions which require heavy computer use, while White women predominate in the more varied, less stressful secretarial or "front office" position.

The liberal tendency to compartmentalize the self's experience — separating it into segments such as the "public" and "private" — obscures dimensions of the problem faced by workers whose job stress is compounded by the double burden and/or by racism. Too narrow a definition of the problem tends to correlate with too narrow a perspective on potential solutions. Developing a comprehensive response to occupational stress hazards requires that we imagine new patterns for distributing "private" household burdens and that we envision a broad social program to eliminate racial prejudice.

Third, this case suggests that we need to recast our understanding of the traditional liberal value of autonomy. As we have seen, stress-related diseases are one of the body's responses to a "lack of clout." Clerical workers are threatened with serious bodily harm because they lack the power to control their working conditions. It is not erroneous to say that their bodily ills result from a lack of autonomy.

Ironically, bioethicists are unable to identify and analyze occupational stress as a moral issue because this problem is distorted and harmful relationality is obscured by preoccupation with individualistic modes of thought. Once identified, however, it seems that solutions to this health threat lie in the direction of changing existing relations between clerical workers and management, allowing clerical workers more opportunity and power for self-determination of work process — a greater scope for autonomous individuality. A thorough reexamination of the concept "autonomy," one which carefully differentiates autonomy from sovereign and atomistic individualism, goes far beyond the limits of this paper. However, feminist thought suggests autonomy needs to be reconceptualized as the power of self-determination *experienced in and through rightly ordered relationships.*

Clerical workers need to be recognized as moral subjects who are entitled to make choices about their work processes. In this case, autonomy is the *freedom and power* necessary for clerical workers to participate in a meaningful way in the determination of their own working conditions. Paradoxically, bioethicists need to ponder the question: what forms of relationships among clerical workers, between workers and manager, among workers, managers and government regulators, etc., are necessary in order to create and sustain a sphere of autonomous individuality for clerical workers?

Occupational stress is a social phenomenon which cannot be addressed, or even fully identified, by ethicists relying upon a conception of agency that assumes the sovereign solitude of an agent occupied in isolated moral decisions. Only through the expanded social model of the moral self can bioethics begin to address and to evaluate the management policies, the power dynamics, the intersections of race and class, and the work conditions which contribute to the incidence of occupational stress.

Chapter 13

Moral Business Leadership: Origins and Outcomes

Chapters 11 and 12 examined the changing challenge of business accountability. Yet reinventing the corporate world in such sweeping ways requires an understanding of the origins of moral decision making and the nature of business decisions as they actually occur. Change can occur only when ethically grounded individuals intersect with morally sound corporate cultures in an ethical decision-making process. The first section of this chapter focuses on how, in fact, Christians have come to recognize the ultimately religious significance of their business careers.

Such persons are gifted with a sense of vocation that emerges from the specific circumstances of their business responsibilities. Their stories are tales that interweave personal faith, corporate culture, and ethical reflection. They suggest that personal narrative, more or less explicitly informed by the rich narrative traditions of the Bible, is still the bedrock of Christian ethical concern. Restated in the categories outlined in Max Stackhouse's introductory essay to this volume, they tend to confirm the existential priority of ethology over both deontological and teleological paradigms of moral reasoning. A covenantal ethic is still simply an attempt to weave our personal stories into the unfinished tapestry of biblical narrative before it is a mandate to resolve ethical dilemmas in a certain way. This, of course, is the basis of its irreducibly religious claim.

Section 2 seeks to extend the scope of biblical and personal religious narrative to institutions. The narratives chosen show how personal calling may intersect with corporate culture. They also illustrate by example how personal values can shape business cultures. The capacity for transformative action within the corporation is what is commonly regarded as business leadership. Here the narratives suggest that Christian faith may be just as decisive a leadership trait as the other factors cited in the burgeoning literature of leadership studies.

Even when a sound basis for ethical decision making has been constructed by the intersection of moral individuals with ethical organizational cultures, difficult decisions must still be made. They will challenge people of faith in both their individual and collective responses. Section 3 considers some of the challenges that arise as Christians must sort out the requirements of their faith. The examples chosen are both negative and positive. Negatively, we're dealing here, of course, with the problem of evil as it surfaces within a corporate setting, what business ethicists discuss under the rubric of "whistleblowing." Positively, and conversely, we are concerned with the opportunities for doing good, over and above the minimal morality of sound business practice. The essays provide orientation to the history and contemporary reality of corporate social responsibility.

Section 1: Personal Moral Vision and the Calling to Business

Demonstrated expertise and moral sensitivity to the issues raised in any one of the business specializations is hardly a sufficient basis for ethical decision making in business. The picture is incomplete without the stories of individuals who have struggled to understand the religious and moral significance of their business careers. Three contemporary autobiographies have been chosen to illuminate the relationship between Christian faith and a sense of vocation in business.

M. L. Brownsberger describes his transformation from an ordained Methodist minister to a pharmaceutical manufacturing executive. His story illustrates the search for concepts of Christian calling that fit public work in business. He wrestles with what it means to be a public Christian in the boardroom, the manufacturing plant, and the executive office.

Joseph Sullivan tells another story. He describes how Catholic social teaching is related to his work as chairman and chief executive officer of a fertilizer and chemicals company, but also how his faith propelled him into his work with international refugees. He strongly believes not only that Catholic teaching has nurtured his public life but also that his business involvement has consistently nurtured his faith.

The third contemporary autobiography, that of a female Episcopalian, Penelope Washbourn, describes her transition from theologian to banking executive. She chronicles the shifts in her own thinking about calling and then surveys the lot of women in the banking world. Her challenge to the church is the development of a theology of calling that can encompass both paid and unpaid work.

Each of these stories in its own way illustrates a person's search for religious worth and value in the business world. Each of these people has asked the questions, "What am I doing here?" and "How can I be moral?" They have arrived at a variety of answers since their stories arise from unique personal histories and intersections with different communities of faith. Yet, taken together, their stories suggest a depth dimension to the practice of management that business ethicists should not ignore in their fascination with the paradigms of applied moral philosophy.

Fred Catherwood's piece goes beyond autobiography to reflect theologically on the root reasons why Christians must regard their business lives through the eyes of faith. For him this is the significance of the familiar Protestant work ethic. He believes that the Christian calling to be God's economic trustees requires its adherents to work hard with high standards for self-motivation and competence in both one's mental and physical contributions.

John Haughey's reflections tacitly presuppose this insight and move on to an analysis of the habits of the heart — the Christian affections, as he calls them — that give rise to a vivid sense of personal vocation. He suggests that prayer and active participation in a Christian community are indispensable resources for those seeking to exercise their Christian vocation in business. Given the normally shifting allegiances of our affections, active engagement in the spiritual life of the church provides as much assurance as we can ever get that our hearts will not betray us as we confront difficult moral choices in business.

Christian Faith and Business: A Story

M. L. Brownsberger

Each of us, I suspect, is on various journeys about which we could tell many stories. One of my journeys is trying to figure out the relation between Christian faith and the 40-50 hours a week I "do business." Or in other language, trying to understand the relation of my person and my place. This became a problem for me because the longer I was in business, the wider the gap between the person I had been and thought I was and the person I was becoming in the office. I'd like to share my story with you and three notions I am finding helpful in the hope that you might hear some echoes in your stories. Joan Rivers used to ask "Can we talk?" Later, I hope you might be stimulated enough to say "yes."

The theme of this story is the relation between persons and places. On the place side of the equation, I remember my first real job working in a steel fabricating plant for a summer. My naive eagerness made my work colleagues so uncomfortable that one finally took me aside and said, "What are you trying to do, make us look bad? Relax. Slow down. They'll get the work they want." I was presented with a choice: I could either be a jerk and make problems for these people for whom this was their livelihood or I could back off and try to fit in. The point about places is that they do pre-exist us. In each place we occupy, we give and receive feedback as to what is expected, what is right and wrong, what is heroic and what isn't and the range of what will be tolerated. Part

of the process of establishing a relation to those places is learning how to accommodate ourselves to the values and expectations that are already there. Peer pressure or corporate cultures have a way of forcing square pegs to fit into round holes.

On the person side of the equation, the boss on my second summer job introduced me to my work group by indicating that I was energetic, eager to succeed, wanting to learn and was going to be a valuable asset to the team. Needless to say, we all got the message with the result that we all performed well, encouraging each other, and discovering better ways of doing things. The boss was cheering us on. He made us look good; we made him look good. We were all better off. I learned that even though I was at the bottom of the pecking order, my potential could be recognized and my best self could be confirmed. There was a kind of congruence between my person and my place and with that, a budding sense of identity was reinforced and ambition was born. In the process of making the place part of our person and our person part of the place, we become organized and focused and begin to discover meaning and purpose — we begin our journeys.

I've been involved in a number of places: in the church as an ordained minister; in the university as a dean of students; in local government as the Director of a Human Rights Commission; and now, in business as a Vice President of a pharmaceutical manufacturing firm. In my previous lives, whether in the church or university or in the institutionalized civil rights movement, what I sought was work that was congruent with an ethic. What I found was a work that was the ethic. So when I heard the calls for justice roll down like waters, or "doing for the least of these . . .", I felt a correspondence between my person and my places. I was an advocate seeking to empower people no matter the place. To me, the places supported my person; my person was congruent with my places. My person was organized around an ethic and focused. The ethic was the work; the work was the ethic. I was at home. It was a nice way to go.

Then I was fired. Or, as I prefer to think of it, I was "politicked" out of the Human Rights job. My person now had no place. Being denied a place — whether a marriage, a relationship, recognition, or a job — is to be denied an organizing relation

M. L. Brownsberger, "Christian Faith and Business: A Story," Chicago Theological Seminary *Register*, Fall 1989, pp. 56-63.

which creates meaning and value, significance and purpose. It is not unlike being homeless. For in the relation of person and place feedback is given and received and you come to know in very personal and practical ways who you are, what you're good at, what you're respected for. For me, no place meant no feedback and no feedback meant no purpose and no purpose meant no organizing identity. I was rendered powerless. The bottom fell out — not a new thought to those who have gone through it.

My wife's family made us an offer we couldn't refuse — to join their pharmaceutical manufacturing firm. We accepted with the elan of the disillusioned idealist — cynically thinking we'll take care of #1 for a while. But seventeen years of ethical congruence between person and place is not an expectation that can for long go unmet — no matter how rationalized. I again sought an ethic in the work but butted up against some sharp contrasts that "fuzzied up" things: where my "product" was personal empowerment no matter the place, I was now responsible for putting out an impersonal product (a pill) into an equally impersonal market; where I was once committed to face to face, "I-Thou" relations I was now involved in instrumental "I-It" relations based solely on performance; where I once sought to empower people I was now firing people, rendering them, in effect, as powerless as I once was; where I was educated for and committed to being a helper I now find employees rightly suspicious of such apparent paternalism — especially coming from one who judges their performance and whose name appears on their paycheck; where I used to be paid from voluntary contributions or taxes I now get a check that is the direct result of production planning and scheduling, financial recording and reporting, systems creation and maintenance, drug chemistry and technology, and regulatory compliance — all of which tends to wonderfully concentrate the mind on profits. The ethical congruence that related my person and my places had become fuzzy; there was only person and place. I could not see the ethic in the work; I could not see the work as the ethic. Some other disillusioned idealist might say that it's about time I grew up, or welcome to the real world, or idealism like a putting touch is the first thing to go with age, or they might quote Paul about giving up childish things.

Be that as it may, my person and my place got out of sync.

I looked to my theological mentors for guidance only to discover that most echoed Tillich in 1957: "(Socialism) . . . is the only possible economic system from a Christian point of view." When I looked to my pastoral mentors I heard them saying something I might have said: "If I had been interested in business I wouldn't have gone into the ministry." All seemed to be speaking in such strong "prophetic" or "therapeutic" accents, that it was and is nearly impossible for them to speak constructively to those responsible for the day to day operation and performance of the economic and other existing systems. The prophetic and the therapeutic had little to say to my place. The prophetic "accent" questioned the basic assumptions of the capitalistic system of which I was a part, saying, in effect, the nature of that system is such that the ethic can never be the work nor the work, the ethic. The therapists simply ignore the system, saying, in effect, that places, work, can never be the ethic because the ethic, as Robert Bellah critically describes it, resides in the personal privacy of the individual and tends to be, curiously, whatever makes you feel good. The prophets seemed to politicize ethics and the therapists seemed to psychologize theology, and neither were of much help. Since I am paid to perform and not reform, to act and not simply cope, I found myself ignoring both. I had work to do in the Board room, the manufacturing plant and the office — the present realities of my place.

The combination of the accents and lack of pastoral interest led me to wonder whether my place has any place in the Church. Indeed, as time went on, I, like a number of others, was forced to conclude that my person in my place does not have sufficient public significance to warrant a positive, constructive or even conversational response from academic and pastoral leadership — a theme repeated with some regularity over the past 25 years in the Christian Century and most recently by Mr. William Weiss, Chairman and CEO of Ameritech in a talk at Fourth Church. Yet, paradoxically, this same leadership wonders and worries about the growing privitization or "invisibility" of religion, to use Thomas Luckman's word, and about the "sidelining" of the mainline. I wonder if, by ignoring the relation of persons and places, of people and their work, my mentors may be encouraging that which they seek to overcome: a private Sunday that bears little relation to our public Mondays.

But the habits of 17 years of congruence persisted. I was and am still convinced that the Judeo-Christian faith is a public faith, to be lived, in Hannah Arendt's phrase, "where all can see" or in Biblical language, or the other side of the bushel. (Matt. 5:14-15) So, in finding little help, I decided I had to figure things out for myself. In this process of trying to discover some congruence between my person and my places, or, an ethic in the work, I've come across three notions I'm finding helpful: the notion of being a public person or self, the notion of responsibility and the notion of the work of God's Word and Spirit, God's two hands, being reconciliation — which might have something to do with being a responsible public person.

This past summer I had opportunity to co-teach an introductory course in business ethics. Bookstores being an addiction, I'd leave work early, park and walk down Wabash to Kroch's, people watching along the way. There were the strollers, the gawkers, the shufflers, those who can't seem to walk in a straight line, and the decisive who seem to be aiming at an invisible target in some undefined distance. One day, as one of the decisives was coming toward me, something about her seemed familiar. Recognition dawned: she was a family friend. I hardly recognized her: she walked and looked and dressed different; her mouth was set different, her eyes were targeted on some secret horizon. I knew she had a career so I assumed she was on her way to some contact. My mind being what it is, I had this image of the Bears during pre-game warm-ups: in uniform, loosely tense, determined, wearing their "task masks," focused not on the immediate but on what was to be, all of which is captured by the phrase "game face." I knew my friend from my private life of family gatherings, church and quiet evenings — those times when we were vulnerable together. Out here, in public, was my first glimpse of her "task mask." We met. At the mention of her name, her eyes left that secret horizon, focused on the intruder, registered surprise and the game face was replaced by the eyes and mouth of the person I knew in my private life. In observing this transformation, the idea of there being a difference between a person's public self and a person's private self began to take shape.

I'm convinced that the difference is real. In my private life, I am irreplaceable in my family, accepted in my church, and appreciated in my various social and political activities. In public, at work, I am accepted only if I perform, appreciated only if my results exceed my paycheck, and am replaceable if I don't perform or produce. I can be fired. In my private life, fidelity to the life my wife and I have created is perhaps the core value; in my public life, trustworthiness to the terms of both the formal and informal employment contract is that place's core value. In my private life, face to face, I-Thou relations of intimacy and depth are the norm; in my public life with employees, colleagues, customers, suppliers, the relations are, at base, instrumental, I-It relations, the comradery and occasional friendships notwithstanding. In our public places, the only reason you and I might be together in a particular work place is because someone else has decided that our combined skills and talents will produce the desired economic results. The relations of our private life are relations of our own choosing; in our public life, the relations are based on the criteria and the choosing of someone else. In short, the difference between our private and public lives is caught by the word "vulnerable." In private, we allow ourselves to be and become vulnerable — that's what home and church are for; in public, at work, we really can't risk it.

If our work is our public life, the question then is whether there is or can be an ethic in that work that can cohere person and place. For business people, this is not an easy question. Indeed, for a lot of us, business ethics is a fuzzy fad that appears to be little more than creating a rationalized barn door after the unethical horse has escaped into the public mead. But if I understand the Gospel, we are called to be the light of the world, called to be Christians on the other side of the bushel. If our work is our public life, then our work is the public place, the context in which we as public selves are recalled to be public Christians. That sounds good, but we don't need more preaching. What we do need are some specifics as to how we do this. The notion of public self then, provides the context; the notion of responsibility provides those specifics. The following is a composite of a number of stories. From it I think we can get some specifics.

As Director of Community Relations in a University community, issues current on campus usually slopped over into the town. In principle, we were one jurisdiction; in practice we were two with informal agreements between the City Manager and the University President establishing the operating arrangements. Generally, the President called the shots since he had a State-wide power base. In 1969, women and minority students were very much involved in their respective movements and were very sensitive about the discriminatory practices both on-campus and in off-campus shops and rental properties. When they approached the Human Rights Commission for redress, I tapped my network of Vice Presidents, Directors, graduate assistants, dorm counselors, campus ministers, students and friends to take the temperature, identify the hidden agendas and determine at least some of the issues and their causes. Members of the Commission did the same. I was quite impressed with the breadth and depth of our collective access to the various information networks. On the basis of our access and information and in working with the students, we all felt that approaching the City Council before taking other more direct or legal action would generate the most positive and reasonable action. We prepared an agenda item to that end.

I had tried to keep the City Manager informed along the way but his secretary had instructions that all department heads had to submit written appointment requests along with an outline of what was to be discussed and proposed actions. I did so a number of times with no response and did so again with the agenda item. I was denied access again, but this time did get a response: a rejection of the Commission's proposal. The Commission was irate that an administrator would undercut their appointive power, as was I. The next Council meeting was a shambles. Some Commission members were able to warn one or two Council people but most were ignorant of the background and were blindsided by the now demonstrating students. The Council and City Manager looked bad; I looked worse — we all lost. I was blamed for "not controlling my people"; my networks shut down; I lost whatever credibility I had; we were all rendered powerless. I had been undercut. Neither the Manager nor I were able to control the relations between our actions and their

consequences. I found out later that the President called the Manager and indicated that the issues were trivial, and that "we'll handle things from here." He couldn't and didn't with the consequence that some relatively simple issues became exceedingly complex and emotionally difficult.

Why? The Manager, in not appreciating the access the Commission and I had to various information loops, cut himself off from that access thereby denying himself needed information. And, I was cut off from his. When it came time to develop alternative actions and make choices and organize the political and legal resources to effect those choices, we were all in the dark. We had rendered ourselves irresponsible. We did not self-consciously set out to be that way; we just were. Had we had access to each other's knowledge of what was going on, our alternatives would have increased, our capacity to choose enhanced, our resources made more appropriate and all would have met the community standards of being responsive to citizen grievances.

On reflection, I wondered what we should have done if we were going to behave responsibly as an organization. I asked, if people are to be responsible, what conditions must exist? The language of the composite story sets them out: If people are to be responsible they must have access, knowledge, alternatives, choices, resources with which to implement those choices, standards against which to measure the outcomes — and one more: the commitment of others to supply all that. Both the Manager and the President failed to provide any and all. When all these conditions are in reasonable balance, however, we are in what Herbert Spiro calls a "fair situation of responsibility" — a balance that, when it exists, empowers me to act. I am enabled to exercise my power and you, yours.

To be responsible is to be enabled to exert one's power, to be enabled to act, to perform, to produce in ways consistent with and knowledgeable of what is going on and with what is expected. It is to be enabled to control the relation between our actions and their consequences. As women and minorities have discovered, to be deprived of any of the conditions is to be rendered powerless. And as women and minorities as well as myself have discovered, because we can be denied the conditions necessary for responsible action, we can not be powerful by ourselves. We make each other responsible. By providing access, knowledge and alternatives, I tried to make my boss, the Manager, responsible; had he provided access to his knowledge and resources, he would have made me, his subordinate, more responsible. Together, we could have enhanced each other's power, increased each other's capacity to act and, in the end, rendered the organization's mission more effective.

Responsibility then, is a relational notion: it is reciprocal — I create the conditions for you, you create the conditions for me and we both become better off. If we are both better off, then we can say there is a moral imperative here: Create, maintain and improve situations of responsibility for yourself and others. Perhaps there is an ethic in the work. For if the work of managing of any organization entails public decision making for which we will be held publicly accountable by bosses, Boards, stockholders, etc., and decision making depends on having access to information so that alternatives can be formulated and decisions made and resources amassed according to standards, then there is indeed an ethic in the work that is real and that is specific: the ethic of responsibility.

The third notion is theological: the reconciling work of God's two hands.

The theme of my story has been the relation between our person and our places. I have suggested that the relation organizes our talents, focuses our attention and directs our energies and interests towards the purposes the places are there to serve. The question then is what principle will we choose to govern the organizing process? Taking care of #1, the acquisition of money and power or even self-fulfillment are possibilities. No matter what we choose, we will choose out of a belief that the consequences of that choice will make us better off. And that's true! We have been organized and focused and so enabled to derive a sense of meaning and value and receive some very real and measurable rewards. But organizing principles not only organize in, they also organize out: they function as principles of selectivity or, blinders, determining to a large extent what we will see and, more importantly, what we won't see. Even recognizing these possibilities and limitations, we can still be responsible in our efforts to

take care of #1, our pursuit of power and profits. The imperative of responsibility, in my judgment, is a fairly adequate and specific description of how it's done. It is possible to be responsible without being self-consciously Christian about it.

But that's the point. We live and must be effective in many worlds. The language of any one may be non-productive in any of the others. That we compartmentalize our faith and its language is not surprising. Given the many worlds we live in, boxing things up may be a very rational and productive thing to do. However, having been involved in a number of places and fired from one, I find the organizing principles of any one place to be inadequate and self-serving and the subsequent principles of selectivity to be narrow and provincial. I've tried boxing things up and it doesn't work. Because for me, the relation between person and place is fundamentally and unavoidably ethical, an ethic for that relation must do at least two things: it must allow us to function effectively in our places while at the same time providing a broader vision of our own and others' needs and potential. For without that vision, we die. My places and my person and the persons in my places are therefore envisioned as being together in the larger place of God. We all participate in the ongoing creative work of the two hands of God: God's Word and Spirit.

By Word and by Spirit God creates, not out of nothing, but by organizing, directing, focusing the unorganized, the misdirected, the unfocused random powers of chaos into the systems, the places we call creation. The creative work of God's two hands, Word and Spirit, is organization. But prior to being organized, the powers that be must be willing to be brought together so they can be organized. Reconciliation is prior to creation. In the Biblical imagery and sequence, the Spirit of God broods over the waters of chaos, willing them to join together, to be reconciled; the Word of God organizes them: "Let there be light."

We are called to be Christians in public, to be faithful on the other side of the bushel. We are called to be agents of God's Word and Spirit though the exercise of our words and our spirit. Bible thumping in business, however, is counterproductive. But the organizing principle of being responsible agents of God's Word and Spirit through our words and spirit allows our spirit to become sensitized to the need for reconciliation, to the needs of others for empowerment: for access, knowledge, choices, resources, standards. Through the Word of God, our words organize and direct and focus the visions of others so that we are all better off. The ethic is in the work because the work is part of the work of God. The work is the ethic because through it we are reconciled, created and empowered to be responsible. In the end, we are enabled to be in control of the consequences of our actions. As a manager then, the notion of God's two hands, Word and Spirit, reconciliation and creation, are principles of organization and selection that transcends any particular place, defines the relation between my person and my places, and is that which drives me to fulfill my responsibility in God's place by pursuing the imperative of responsibility as an agent of reconciliation.

I'll stop here, even though the journey and its story will continue. I can say that the language of responsibility is most useful in the public places of my life — the Board room, the manufacturing plant and the office. I can also say as an executive managing a business, I find it most appropriate and productive to define my person as being joined hand in hand with God empowering both the powerful and the powerless though my words and spirit, as seeking justice and mercy, and as trying to make and keep human life responsible and therefore, human.

The Christian Vocation of a Business Leader

Joseph P. Sullivan

My remarks today can be summed up in two convictions about faith and work that have emerged from my 30-year experience in business and my 53-year experience in faith.

The first is that the workplace provides significant opportunities to inform and buttress one's faith. The second is that the Catholic social tradition has the potential to offer valuable insights in addressing the complex issues that a chief executive officer faces in today's turbulent economic environment. This potential, while largely unfulfilled, can be developed if laity and church professionals commit themselves to this effort.

Currently I am chairman and chief executive officer of a company that employs over 1,500 people in the manufacture and distribution of fertilizer and chemicals primarily to the agricultural segment of our economy, but also to homeowners, golf courses and institutions. Its volume is over $350 million. It was formed in the last 18 months from the divisions of two very large companies which were purchased with a relatively small amount of equity capital and a large amount of debt. Thus we, the leveraged-buyout firm which my partner, Jay Proops, and I founded, leveraged our capital with debt, from which the term "leveraged buyout" or "lbo" emanates.

Much has been written about leveraged buyouts recently. Concerns have been expressed about whether they are in the public interest. Frankly, it is hard to see in some well-publicized cases whether anybody — shareholders, employees, the public — but a select few benefit.

Joseph P. Sullivan, "The Christian Vocation of a Business Leader," *Origins* 16 (16 Oct. 1986): 325-28.

This new form of financing, however, can be used in a constructive way, and our first acquisition was a case in point. The division which we purchased would have been liquidated had not a buyer been found. In our judgment, 600 jobs were saved, most of them in agricultural areas, because we were able to employ this type of financing productively.

We operate throughout the United States, but principally in the Midwest and Southeast. And we operate in a very difficult environment, given the severe economic problems that have beset American farmers — our principal customers — in the last few years.

Our objectives in managing this company are to produce a profit and create a positive environment for the individuals who work for the company and for the long-term health and survivability of the company itself. Some of the principles and strategies we try to follow are:

1. We keep reminding ourselves that we, as a company, do not invest people with human dignity. They have it before, during and after employment with us. As managers, what we can do is to provide an environment that can enhance that dignity. A key way to do this is to demand and reward high performance.

   Demands for high performance in the '50s and '60s were often equated with being unfair or even cruel to individuals. In point of fact, the lax standards that developed in many American companies during this relatively trouble-free economic period seem to me to have been a denial, rather than an affirmation, of human dignity.

2. We will be successful only insofar as we adapt our products and services to changing needs and improve the quality of these products and services. It is not easy in the very difficult agri-business environment to spend money on product and service development and improvement in quality. We believe, however, that these tasks are even more critical in tough times and, if we perform them well, our customers will be better served and we will improve our position long term in the marketplace.

3. We delegate authority and responsibility as much as we can within the company. A corollary to this emphasis on responsibility at the field level is a very limited chain of command. At the present time, there are only three managerial levels between myself and a salesperson or retail unit manager. Remember, this is a $350 million company.

4. We place a great deal of emphasis on mutually establishing responsibilities and objectives, and rewarding achievement of objectives promptly and generously. Once again, we put a major emphasis on the outstanding performance of individuals and small teams.

5. We work hard at providing full knowledge of the company's performance to all of our people. We do more than send out occasional reports, although these are a useful tool. At least twice a year we give a report of our stewardship to all of our people. Responsibility for performance is a principle we all adhere to, not just people in the field.

6. We place a great deal of emphasis on training and development. What we are trying to do is provide an environment where every employee can develop to his or her fullest possible potential. Perhaps the most significant statistic with respect to this activity is that our top officers, including myself, spend about five weeks each year functioning as primary instructors in classroom situations where we identify business opportunities and problems and how to grow from them. We find that this is as valuable a learning experience for us as it is for our student-employees.

7. Our company is committed to growth. We grow through internal development of products and services, and also through acquisition. In these days of an unforgiving environment this is a key issue that all chief executive officers must face. I will deal with this issue more fully later on.

8. We are great believers in formal employee-assistance programs. These programs have proven highly successful in dealing with personal problems of employees, particularly alcoholism and other drug dependencies. Any employee who is not achieving a desired performance level because of a personal problem has the opportunity to seek assistance through our employee-assistance program. If the poor performance persists after such an intervention, we have no alternative but to fire that

employee. To do otherwise would be a fundamental disregard for that individual's human dignity and would also be clinically counterproductive.

9. We believe we have a special opportunity to motivate our people to become more involved in their community. Our retail units are located in farm communities. As such, they are generally one of the three or four largest businesses within the town. All of them recognize today the great problems besetting people in agricultural areas. We support our people in activities which lead to ameliorating the difficult conditions that many farmers and their families have to face. We are particularly supportive of involvement in self-help groups within the community. It is very gratifying to see the commitment that our people have made to such programs.

In sum, what we have tried to do is establish a positive environment for individual and company growth which emphasizes placing responsibility on individuals, operating in a decentralized setting dedicated to helping the customer and our company long term. Finally, we ask our people to go beyond themselves and get involved in their own communities.

The results have been excellent. We are completing a profitable year. Despite heavy overall losses in the industry, we are growing, and, most important, establishing a positive position for the future.

You will notice that my frame of reference as a businessman is growth, the survivability of a firm, market shares, and improving products and service. What does this have to do with Christian values? How does one find God in that kind of world? Our religious language fits easily into the work of the Mother Teresas of this world. But have we a religious language that fits the kind of work I do? And do we need one? I presume this is the "unchartered territory" that this consultation is intended to enter.

A logical follow-up question to be asked of one's own work experience is whether it provides a useful extension for involvement in the larger community. My judgment is that business management does provide a useful past for service to the general community and, as important, special skills to enhance the common good.

Looking back, my commitment to solving the problems of world hunger and refugees was honed by my day-to-day work in agriculture, food marketing and production. In parallel with many business people, my involvement with support of education is in no small part motivated by the recognition that the economic well-being of individuals and society are based increasingly on the technical competence and human understanding that only comes with a trained mind.

But even more important, the skills that derive from business experience — organizing people, raising funds, solving logistic problems — are crucial per se in volunteer activities and provide a sense of confidence so critical to these efforts. These talents are a special legacy that business people can bring to community service.

The best way to illustrate my point is to relate the story of the American Refugee Committee. This was a group started in 1978 by a remarkable Chicago businessman, Neal Ball. Neal brought together a group composed largely of business people to help alleviate in some way the plight of Southeast Asian refugees. Out of this sprung an organization that now runs two hospitals in Thailand and one in the Sudan which serves Ethiopian refugees.

The dedicated doctors and nurses of ARC, who serve in these remote and often dangerous settings for at least six months at minimum salary, directly minister to refugees, but have also trained over 500 barefoot doctors. These barefoot doctors work with their people and often provide the only medical service available to these isolated humans. We have many illustrious participants in this program, among them Dr. Hang Nor of *The Killing Fields* fame.

Started as a one-year project, we recently completed our eighth year of service.

The logistics, funding and medical-delivery challenges that ARC has had to solve have ranged from difficult to heart-stopping. I'm convinced that the disproportionate support that business people have given to ARC has been based heavily on a chance to test the skills they've developed in their day-to-day activities.

One memory of this experience stands out. We started a political action organization, the Emergency Task Force for Indo-Chinese Refugees, in 1979 to support legislation which ultimately became the Immigration Act of 1980.

In this effort we were supported by many business people who, on their own, went to Washington to lobby legislators. They all got great satisfaction out of this experience, not the least of which was the incredulous reaction of their congressman or senator when they realized that they were lobbying for a cause that would have no impact whatsoever on their bottom line.

To this point, we've emphasized the positive impact that the workplace can have on one's faith. This does not shield us, however, from confronting basic ethical issues that the reality of a sluggish world economy and the increasing intensity of competition place before us.

I'd like to address, all too briefly, two questions that test a chief executive officer charged with the responsibility of running a substantial business and trying at the same time to recognize his responsibility as a Christian.

First, let's look at the issue of growth. It would be very easy and, indeed, it is becoming somewhat fashionable, to concentrate on trimming businesses in the 1980s.

Growth is always fraught with risk, especially in this economy. The best justification for growth is that an organization that doesn't grow becomes static and sluggish. People in a static or sluggish organization become mean-spirited. Individuals become frustrated, with the resulting loss of commitment and ultimately the departure of talented people. This is true of any institution that becomes static. Look, if you will, at the morale level of your local school districts.

In a larger sense, the only way to solve the severe unemployment, and equally severe but far more insidious underemployment, of talented people today is for businesses to commit themselves to growth wherever feasible. Common good requires it.

Not all, but most firms in the United States and Western Europe can grow if they are creative and dedicated to this concept.

Dedication to the concept of growth rests on the moral and Christian issues that business, in the last analysis, is carried on for the sake of the common good.

The pace of growth, however, is the key to success. Simply stated, we must avoid the ego trips that seem to especially characterize the acquisition programs of many companies. All too often in these cases chief executive officers are more interested in the excitement of the hunt for companies than in building a solid growth program.

There are many ways to grow. Let me emphasize just one.

I don't think there is a firm in the United States today that can't do a better job in improving the quality of goods and services that they provide to the customer. Too little attention has been given to the thousands of little and big hurts that emanate from unsatisfactory products and services. All too often, in our quest for reducing cost to harvest quick profits, we have ignored the needs of the consumer and ultimately the long-term health of our company. Infusion of pride in products and services must start at the top. Along with that must come a commitment to new approaches of serving the customer. I would suggest that a commitment to excellence in service combines good business and good Christian responsibility.

The second key issue confronting a president trying to fulfill his responsibility as a Christian today is, How do we streamline our business for survival in a responsible, moral way? My study of business in the United States leads me to the conclusion that most companies in the United States can be better managed with far fewer organizational layers.

Faced with the need to become more streamlined, how can this be done in a moral way within a company? My approach is the following:

First, streamlining must be approached in a paced way. Typically businesses panic after one or two bad quarters and insist on a percentage cut in personnel that tends to cut across all functions and departments. This is irresponsible from both a business and moral standpoint. A studied approach to this problem avoids the often catastrophic impact that an across-the-board cut has on people and the company as a whole.

Second, the president must foster a greater understanding of the total business enterprise among all employees. All too often the president of a company does not begin to meet his basic responsibility of ensuring that the total organization understands the mission and the purpose of the business. This challenge becomes even greater as the skills required to run a major business becomes more complex. High skill levels often lead to fragmentation of objectives. The total mission of the company becomes blurred by parochial objectives. Communicating clearly on a firsthand level the goals and accomplishments of the total business is a paramount objective of the company president. It leads always to improved performance.

If, after careful analysis of both short-term and long-term needs of the business, it is necessary to reduce staff, then the president of the company must face up to the responsibility of providing help to the people who are asked to leave the organization. The first part of that responsibility is to remember we are dealing with human beings. Wherever possible at our company the person responsible talks face to face with the employee to be dismissed. Sending a computer list to the personnel department is too easy. I believe that the recognition that a manager will perform this difficult task on a one-to-one basis motivates that manager to find ways to improve performance.

Helping the dismissed employee relocate is another essential with us. Fortunately, today there are skilled professionals in out-placement functions providing this service. Combined with liberal separation policies, such programs go a long way to preserve the terminated employee's financial position and self-respect.

In summary, we must recognize that terminating employees is a burdensome moral issue. One must recognize the difficult trade-offs that are involved between preserving the health of the business and helping to enhance the dignity of the individual. The problem must be faced, however, in light of the more demanding business environment.

But what help, if any, can Catholic tradition be to the owner or manager in addressing these complex issues?

That is a very sensitive issue for me in that for most of the 30 years I've been in business, Catholic teaching seldom seemed to address the moral and ethical issues that I was faced with as a manager. On the negative side, I can recall only one homily that had anything really relevant to say concerning the issues a manager faced.

I think of business as a vocation. It serves an obvious public function: It creates employment, and it offers needed products and services to sustain and enhance life. Business has been a major source of technological advancement.

Yet rarely have I heard business described as a vocation, either by the clergy or by the laity. We as Catholics tend to apply to business the same highly individualistic rhetoric that American culture generally does. A happy exception is the bishops' pastoral on the American economy and, of course, this consultation. The challenge we face is not only to do our work responsibly; it is also to find meaning in our work. Wouldn't the Christian concept of vocation help in this regard?

Catholic publications, when they address the issues of business, invariably emphasize the structural issues of capitalism vs. socialism. Occasionally they focus on the problems or dangers of multinationals, often in a way that displays a meager understanding of the dynamics of international business and economics.

In sum, for a long period being Catholic and a manager in the marketplace was made a more solitary, often lonely, endeavor because of little enrichment from the church. Fortunately, this situation is changing — and for the better.

Individual Catholics and Catholic institutions are at the forefront of the increasing dialogue concerning corporate ethics and social responsibility. De Paul and Notre Dame are pathfinders in this effort.

Another encouraging sign is the increase in study and discussion groups of business people who reflect on ethical and moral issues affecting business. Many of these are under Catholic auspices. Courses, especially at the graduate level of business schools, are dealing with these subjects. In all of these efforts Catholic business people are prominent.

I view with optimism the process by which the bishops' pastoral letter on the economy was developed. After a shaky start, there was a real attempt to involve Catholic business people and thinkers in a wide variety of positions.

And why not? Catholic social thought contains a treasure trove of ideas that can be used in addressing these issues.

Take the issue of growth. What better way to develop the principle of subsidiarity — a concept largely kept alive through the efforts of Father Andrew Greeley — spelled out so clearly in the encyclical *Quadragesimo Anno* over 50 years ago, than through "intrapreneurship" — the establishment of small, creative, working groups in large organizations dedicated to growth, new-product development and improved services that are now increasing in popularity throughout industry.

What better extension of the principle of pluralism, once again spelled out in *Quadragesimo Anno,* than the development of quality circles wherein small groups of people at the front-line level address the challenge of improving product quality and services, thereby producing more revenue for the firm?

For the past 30 years I have devoted the professional skills and energy I have to business. Like you, I have to search for the connections between my faith and my work. It hasn't been easy. The business environment, especially today, is intensely competitive. My work as chairman and chief executive officer demands intense concentration and tends to be all-absorbing. There are few occasions when I have had the opportunity to reflect with others on the connection between business and faith.

Nevertheless, as I reflect on my business career, I've been greatly nourished by my business experience. I've learned in an intensely competitive environment that human values need not be abandoned. I've felt the spiritual uplift that comes from a group of disparate people coming together and achieving a result that far exceeds reasonable expectations. I've witnessed how a depressed community can be transformed into a hopeful one when we have succeeded in turning a company around and preventing a shutdown. And I've been enriched to see my fellow business practitioners go beyond themselves and use their skills to reach out and help both their immediate and unseen communities. Msgr. George Higgins writes eloquently in a recent issue of America on "The Social Mission of the Church in the Future" and endorses a spirituality of hope. What better foundation for such spirituality than through these experiences. Work can and does inform faith.

The real question for the future is whether Catholics — laity and clergy in partnership — recognize the promise and challenge of our economic system and what the Catholic tradition can bring to it. Will they work together and harvest the mutual benefits that the combination of business-management expertise and Catholic tradition and teaching can provide?

In order to achieve this desired end, the most important step is to build a greater understanding among church professionals concerning the world of business and particularly the issue facing business managers on a day-to-day basis. Massive changes have occurred in this world in the last 10 years — in technology, the competitive environment and organizational structure. If church professionals are to make a meaningful contribution to a ministry in the business world, if they are to help owners and managers deal with the "hard choices" spoken of in the bishops' pastoral letter, if indeed the bishops' pastoral letter is to be the real start of a process rather than an isolated event, then church professionals must make special efforts to understand this environment. Laity, on their part, should and, I believe, will work to increase this understanding.

The direction of these efforts should embrace not only better understanding of the economic system per se, but should also include opportunities for increased familiarity with the management process itself.

In sum, church professionals, with the help of the laity, must approach this task with the same enthusiasm and commitment as those who ministered to the union movement in years past. In today's world owners and managers need the kind of committed, informed ministry that the church provided to the working class 50 years ago. The quality and credibility of the clergy's role in such a ministry will be enhanced through a joint, sustained commitment to learn.

In closing, I would like to reflect not on an article from the Harvard Business Review nor on an excerpt from the increasing body of literature on the ethics and morality of business, but on the classic book for people of all ages, *The Little Prince,* by Antoine de Saint-Exupery. Saint-Exupery, the pilot, philosopher and writer killed in combat in World War II, wrote of the little prince who, on his journey from a far-off planet, visited a businessman who went through life owning, administering, counting and banking the stars. But in that poetic and powerful final chapter the little prince exhorts Saint-Exupery, the pilot in the desert, rather to listen, laugh, be comforted and refreshed by the stars.

I earnestly hope that in a milieu that often resembles that desert that those of us who are business people choose the latter course.

Women in the Workplace

Penelope Washbourn

An essay authored by an employee of the world's largest bank needs some explanation in the context of a theological journal. While it may not be academic fashion to describe the point of view of the author, in this situation and for this topic I believe it is important that readers know aspects of my personal biography. It will help to explain the background of my argument. A woman in the workplace writing about "women in the workplace" may be very close to her subject, or indeed guilty of special pleading. Our personal history fashions our intellectual habits and often causes us to value or discredit another's perspective. On the issue of women's employment it is evident that many people, men and women, feel a high degree of ambiguity about the subject.

I was raised in a middle class, professional household with the typical sex role distinction between my parents. What was perhaps atypical was that both of my parents had degrees and that my mother had worked at paid employment prior to marriage. Like many other women in the 1930s, marriage represented for her an involuntary (or voluntary) exit from the workplace. During the war years, however, she worked at cooking for a firestation and was an air raid warden. The model of women's role as married women I received as a child was standard for the post-war generation of middle class people. A married woman's role was in the home, often struggling to make ends meet, caring for children, marketing, sewing, cleaning, and supporting her husband's career. In my mother's case, her return to occasional paid employment was gradually made by turning a

hobby into a skill that could be sold on a consulting basis. My mother would not have conceived of going permanently into the workplace, even during those years when four children put a major strain on the family budget. How is it then that I, having been raised with such a role model, find myself at my place of employment from 8:15 a.m. to 4:45 p.m. fifty weeks a year?

I never thought of myself as a wage earner, a supporter of a household, even when I was getting my first job as a professor of religion. I was driven by an ideal: to study religion, and to achieve academic heights by receiving my doctoral degree. It had been evident several years previously that the option of the ministry was not open to me as an Episcopalian (at that time), nor was that option particularly appealing. The only other choice was to teach. My drive to go into teaching theology was primarily to put into use this precious credential I had achieved after so many years. I never thought of my teaching career as "employment." The wage earning aspects of my career were of secondary importance. After marriage, having two salaries was not a reflection of economic necessity, but the result of two professional careers. Like many other women raised in the middle class traditional home, I had "backed into" a career. I had no clear goal in high school for thinking of myself as potentially having a lifelong career, of being able to support myself or a family. My continued teaching during my early childbearing years was partly motivated out of a fear that if I, as a woman, took time out from my career, I would lose ground to my male colleagues and would demonstrate to them that women academics were only able to be marginal. Being a token woman had its burdens. More importantly, focusing all my energies on babies and household activities was never a choice for me. At every cost, I wanted to preserve the intellectual, social, and personal contacts that the workplace provided for me. The alternative was certain depression, anxiety, and isolation. At this point the support from members of my own family for my academic career mysteriously evaporated. They seemed to be saying "why complain about problems with day care, babysitters, bundling kids into snow suits to drop them off at preschool before work, and sick children? All these problems would be solved if you didn't work." They seemed to assume that careers

Penelope Washbourn, "Women in the Workplace," *Word and World* 4, no. 2 (1984): 159-64.

were for women who did not have the responsibility of child raising.

A major shift in my attitude to employment came when I left the full-time academic life. When we moved to San Francisco for a better lifestyle, I found I was forced to turn my teaching skills into marketable employment in the business world. There were four months after the move when I was unemployed. Never before had we experienced that one limited academic salary would be radically inadequate to support a family of four and insufficient to pay the mortgage. As I looked for employment, I experienced for the first time what men must feel all the time, as well as single parents. I thought: the security of this family depends on *my* wage earning ability; I am responsible for it. I *must* take shared fiscal responsibility. My current job may not be the complete ideal, but it enables us to maintain our standard of living. For the first time, I have a job and not a career.

This personal digression demonstrates a perception: It is very hard for those of us who work in the ministry, teaching, and counseling to comprehend the conditions of the workplace that affect men and women alike, and particularly those that affect women. These professions in the church are closer to the state of being self-employed, rather than being a wage earner, an "employee." Very often the place of work for church professionals is located in or near the home. Academics and ministers often have studies at home where they prepare sermons and lectures, do research, and conduct counseling. Most critically a large portion of the day is self-scheduled, and there is no direct supervision for professional people. For Christians the motivation to enter the professional ministry or teaching comes from a sense of vocation, or service to others, of love for God and the belief that one can contribute to the spiritual, educational, and emotional growth of others. The poor pay is justified in terms of the other values that the profession contributes to individual fulfillment.

The "workplace" is something completely different from the world of the clergy or the counseling and teaching professions. The "workplace" may be some distance from the home and involve a commute in urban areas. Since increasing numbers of people are moving into an urban environment, the pattern of rural communities where home and work have been one, or at least close to one another, is an experience shared by a decreasing percentage of America's people. The "workplace" is a reflection of the industrial revolution, when local cottage industry was centralized into efficient, standardized manufacturing operations. After this revolution, men — and some women — left the home at dawn and joined other millhands to labor intensely for 12 to 14 hours six days a week. Our modern concept of work, of having a job, for the majority of employees — men and women, blue and white collar — is based on this image of the "workplace." This separation of the domestic, private arena from the workplace of paid employment is scarcely two hundred years old. As many studies have shown, prior to the industrial revolution both men and women were engaged in activity that contributed to the economic health of the household. Men and women were equally involved in domestic tasks as were children. It is only since the enormous industrial growth in the cities and the prevailing nineteenth century ideals inherited from Europe that a sharp separation of the home and workplace has occurred. This change has dramatically affected the view of women's appropriate work during the past century. In a study entitled *Women Have Always Worked*, Alice Kessler-Harris has examined the pattern of women's work since the Colonies, both paid and unpaid. Several significant points emerge: As the meaning of "work" changed during the industrial revolution, women's labor was associated more exclusively with the domestic arena. Men's paid employment was considered "work" while women were encouraged to emulate the middle class ideal of creating a haven of domestic tranquility for the husband and family. Of course, poor women and immigrant women always worked and aspired to reach the level of economic security where they would no longer have to "work." As the result of restricting the meaning of work to "paid employment," women have continued to undervalue their economic contribution to society in their family responsibilities as well as in their contributions to the physical, emotional and spiritual health of society. Our society similarly undervalues their domestic work. It only becomes "work" when someone else is paid to do it. Many women experience guilt for employing other women to do their cleaning and support their childcare so that they can go out to the "workplace." A more usual scenario is that women will do two jobs. Studies have shown that when women take employment men do not (in this country or in the Soviet Union) significantly increase their domestic work to share the burden of the domestic responsibilities.

Our Christian views of vocation and Luther's view of the vocation of marriage were not built upon a modern industrial view of career or post-industrial marriage. By describing marriage as a vocation it may have been easy for later generations of Christians to interpret this according to societal notions of appropriate sex roles for men and women. To call marriage a vocation for men and women alike did not mean that women should stay home and that men should go to work in the workplace as the last two centuries have idealized. Luther himself demonstrated an understanding that one can have a multiplicity of roles, or "offices" and "stations," which may include one's occupation and other social relationships.

I work in an organization of 63,000 employees. Of those employees 74% are women, and their average age is 35. The statistics reveal an important fact: the enormous growth of women in the world of employment, particularly in white collar jobs, and the increase in the numbers of working mothers. In the last decade working mothers of children under 6 increased from 31 to 46 percent. A large number of these women are single heads of families; indeed the percentage of women in the workplace generally continues to rise. By 1972 the typical middle class family had two wage earners to compete with rising inflation. Only a small percent of households in this country fit the ideal of the nuclear family — a husband supporting a non-earning wife with children at home.

Most of the jobs that women do are not properly described as "careers" with opportunities for growth, but fit into the dominant women's job ghettos: the domestic, the clerical service industry, nursing, and teaching types of jobs. The gap between men's salaries and women's salaries for similar positions continues to widen each year. This is the result of continued sex segregation of women into low paying jobs. In my organization

women fill most of the "prime time" positions. They are employed for six hours a day while the bank is open to customers. The flexibility of schedule enables women to send their children off to school before coming to work and to be at home as they return. The very flexibility women prize costs them dearly in terms of benefits, long term career promotability, and opportunity for professional growth. The woman's job is used to supplement the family income and to fit in with the husband and family's schedule, but not to provide another career path for the wife during the childbearing years.

Women are still socialized to believe that the domestic arrangements are their primary responsibility. They tend to assume that the problem of coordinating family and work responsibilities is their own individual problem, and they seek private solutions for it. The stress of our current domestic and work arrangements on employed women is well described in psychological and sociological literature. Industries have not provided adequate child care facilities. Hours of work largely follow the inflexible traditional patterns. Women are trying hard to demonstrate their value to the male world of the profession by denying the need for any special favors. However, the structure of the modern home and family is based on the assumption that one domestic partner is at home to send the children to school, receive delivery of goods, services, and repairs, be available to nurse sick children, take children to the doctor and be at home for school vacations. For 15 to 20 years of life the workplace and its demands conflict with needs of the raising of the family. In its isolation the modern family struggles to juggle sick babies, school inservice days, and trips to the doctor. In the world of employment each of these activities is seen as an erosion of an employee's full value to the company. Every time a woman asks her supervisor for time off to attend to family responsibilities, her lack of commitment to her work is noted. Full commitment of time and energy to company goals is the mark of career oriented individuals. But family oriented men and women often find radical conflict in dedicating such total loyalty in order to be successful.

In spite of the ambiguity of the role and the pressures women face in juggling careers, job, and family, the workplace offers continuing appeal for economic and other reasons. The workplace has become for us the purveyor of worth or value. We ask people "what do you do?" in America; this is a quite unusual question in other societies. If we don't "do" anything we feel bad, lacking in appropriate value. This is the cause of the loss of identity for women without paid employment. What I "do" is what I am paid for. Wages are a conveyor of society's worth and self-identity for the individual.

The Christian church may resist these values and preach service for love and no money, and yet money has become a symbol for being valued in the eyes of society. Women's quest for equality in wages is part of the need for the recognition of self-worth. Likewise any profession such as the ministry that is seriously underpaid in comparison to its secular counterparts causes its members continual need for self-apology and rationalization of unequal status.

Another major reason that women stay in the workplace, in spite of its conflicts with domestic arrangements, is that there is not better mechanism for social interchange and for personal growth and development. The social interactions — the sense of belonging to an organization with complex purposes beyond oneself as an individual, and the interaction with technology — provide the possibility for growth that individual women desire. Our domestic arena — focused on home, school, church, and volunteer activities as an exclusive role — cannot match the opportunity for individual recognition and growth offered by the workplace.

The challenge for the church is major. It should not assume that woman's vocation is to make an exclusive identification with the role of mother. In each of our roles there is opportunity for sin by making it the center of our lives to the exclusion of the needs of others. A self-sacrificial role can become sinful if it reflects a fundamental lack of self-love and a desire to be seen as righteous. Similarly the exclusive identification with career to the exclusion of the needs of self or family is sin, for it puts work first. Women in the workplace may currently have too high a desire to prove themselves in the world of employment and not be sufficiently critical of its imposed values.

The church can support women and men in their quest for wholeness and a human social ar-rangement for work and domestic life. By supporting families through providing care in the communities for the children of working parents, and by enhancing parent's coping abilities, particularly during early child-bearing years, churches can help women and men build a network of support. In a time of change in employment patterns, the church needs to understand the world of work and its conditions. Industry and corporations have been driven primarily by economic considerations. The church can play a major role in the continuing need to shape the "world of work" to a more flexible and humane environment supportive of raising the next generation and caring for our aging. Unfortunately, lacking first hand understanding of the realities of the "workplace," the church's theology of work remains romantic. As women move into the workplace in greater numbers, the weakness of our present social system becomes clear. The struggle women face to play the dual roles illustrates the inherent conflict between our domestic and public institutions. Many men today find they too can no longer fit the model of the man who puts his career first, and then they suffer loss of social prestige and income when they take on more of the parenting role. The fundamental question of the church is how we can allow the many roles we have in life to co-exist — in such a way that they support each other — so that they can become the opportunity for grace for women as well as men.

The Protestant Work Ethic: Attitude and Application Give It Meaning

Fred Catherwood

In the years following the Reformation it became apparent that there was an essential difference between the developing Protestant ethic and the preceding ethic in their attitudes toward work. The latter tended to see the physical world as evil and to him the saint was one who had no part in it. To the Protestant, the evil was within. As our Lord said, "All these things come from within, and defile the man."

The Protestant position was based on the nature of man as unfolded not only by our Lord, but throughout the Bible. The natural resources of the world were created by God and were given to man for his use. "Let us make man in our image . . . and let them have dominion over the fish of the sea, and over the fowl of the air, and over the cattle, and over all the earth" (Gen. 1:26). After the fall of man, the conditions are changed, but the objective is the same. "In the sweat of thy face shalt thou eat bread" (3:19). The commission that was given to Adam was also given to Noah: "Be fruitful, and multiply, and replenish the earth" (9:1).

David set out one of God's purposes for man on earth: "Thou madest him to have dominion over the works of thy hands; thou hast put all things under his feet" (Ps. 8:6). Man is a spiritual being, but he has been put on earth to fulfill the purposes of God, and one of these primary and basic purposes is that he should control and administer the natural resources of the world. He demonstrates the nature and purpose of God to those who do not believe by obedience to this basic commandment.

If a Christian is to be true to these principles, he does not work simply to make money or to pay the bills. He works because it is part of the divine order that he should work. Even Christian slaves had to remember this: "Servants, obey in all things your masters according to the flesh; not with eye-service, as men-pleasers; but in singleness of heart, fearing God" (Col. 3:22). Clearly, whatever our work is, we must do it with enthusiasm and not grudgingly or because we are driven to it. It appears to have come more naturally to the early Christians to evangelize than to work, and the exhortation to work is a constant refrain in Paul's epistles. "And that ye study to be quiet, and to do your own business, and to work with your own hands, as we commanded you; that ye may walk honestly toward them that are without, and that ye may have lack of nothing" (1 Thess. 4:11-12). Not only must a Christian work, he must work as if for God and he must work wholeheartedly. "Whatsoever thy hand findeth to do, do it with thy might" (Eccl. 9:10). Our Lord's parable of the talents praises those who made maximum use of their resources and condemns the man who made no use of his because they were small.

It would be fair to deduce from this teaching that it is the duty of the Christian to use his abilities to the limit of his physical and mental capacity. He has a duty to train himself and develop his abilities, both academically and experimentally, to the limit that his other responsibilities allow. He should not be content to administer, but should try to improve and innovate. He should not stop until it is quite clear that he has reached his ceiling.

Values in Vocation

Ultimately we all must decide for ourselves on the limits beyond which we cannot stretch our physical and mental powers. We must decide too on the proportion of time and energy we give to family and to spiritual devotions. This is a matter in which extremes are easy and a balance difficult. God has laid down that one day in seven should

Sir Fred Catherwood, "The Protestant Work Ethic: Attitude and Application Give It Meaning," *Fundamentalist Journal*, September 1983, pp. 22-24, 48.

be devoted to Him, and we should go out of our way to see that no secular affairs spill over into that day. The family has a call on our time, and no Christian has a right to allow his work to make his wife a widow or his children orphans.

It is not possible to achieve all these objectives at once without a fair degree of method and self-discipline. These are regarded today as rather old-fashioned virtues, and the modern world seems more concerned with a reduction of stress than with an increase in standards of service. The more complex our work and the less other people can see for themselves what we are doing and why, the more important it is that we should set our own standards. "The professional must always determine himself what his work should be and what good work is. Neither what he should do, not what standards should be applied, can be set for him" (Peter Drucker, *The Practice of Management*). Christians, especially, must organize their lives and work, must set their own high standards, and must examine the quality of their work continuously and critically against those standards.

Poor personal relationships usually come from lack of self-control and are another great cause of dissipation of emotional energy. There are, of course, people who are particularly difficult, fussy, and touchy, and we all have to work with them from time to time. But the person who is determined to control his antipathies and who refuses to let people get under his skin, who rides all personal misunderstandings lightly and refuses to take umbrage, will find that he has a good deal more energy left for his job than his more sensitive colleague. Yet nothing is a greater source of strength than a sense of competence, a feeling of being on top of the situation and having the initiative. This sense of competence is not confined to Christians, but a Christian who does not feel it, and particularly a Christian who has allowed his job to "get on top of him," should examine the quality of his work to see whether he has been setting his standards and keeping to them as he ought.

Putting the Mind to Work

The sloppy thinker will waste hours of his own and others' time and energy in fruitless fussing.

He is full of second-hand ideas and will run everything "the way we used to run it." If he is in charge of others, he will keep them chasing after countless red-herrings and will refuse to see the points he does not want to see.

The man who has trained and disciplined his mind and who is able and willing to use it constructively will think a problem through. He will have the versatility required to examine and assess new evidence. His self-assurance in critical decisions and under pressure of persons and events will be based, not on ignorance or prejudice, but on knowledge. This is not something with which we are all born, but it is something most of us can acquire. Many people begin to achieve a tough mental discipline through university or professional examinations in an exact science, but this alone is not enough; it is necessary to keep the mind at full stretch for several years before the habit becomes ingrained.

To those who have not faced the problems, stresses, and strains of industrial life, these last paragraphs may seem somewhat discursive and academic. But those who have to make critical decisions affecting the material well-being of their fellows will know the misdirections of human effort that can be caused by sloppy thinking. The most common failing in industrial management today is not that people will not work the hours or the overtime, but that they will not put their minds to work. It is something that may take a long time to catch up with us and may indeed never catch up at all — except with our successors!

It is this quality of intellectual integrity that Christians, above all people, should possess. Our creed is that we are here to serve not ourselves but others; we should, therefore, be much more conscious than others of our standards of service. The standards we set for ourselves should be higher and tougher than others set for us. We should look more closely and critically at our performance than they do.

While high standards and an honest mind are essential, we should not belittle the value of sheer hard work. Long hours alone are not enough, but a Christian is called to use his talents to the full, to work with all his might, to run the race of life as if there were only one prize and he must obtain it. A race is not run, it is true, in a flat-out spurt, but it does require determination and endurance, the ability to keep going when others have stopped, and the reserves for the spurt when occasion demands it. All this sounds melodramatic, of course, to the man of the world, a little unnecessary and liable to spoil a man's health and his enjoyment of the natural pleasures of life. But those whose lives and happiness are dependent on the results do not see it that way. The men in the plant and their families depend on us [management] to find the markets to keep them in employment, and to maintain the level of technical expertise and efficiency that will keep their firm competitive. They do not grudge the manager his necessary relaxation, but they know the difference between the manager who is working and one who is cruising. The Christian should be the man who is known in the jargon as "the self-starter." He does not require pushing; he hardly needs supervision. He goes straight for the tough problem and cracks it. When a critical decision has to be made, he is the one who will have done his homework.

Today there seems to be a feeling that we are reaching the saturation point in personal wealth and that soon we ought to invest not in goods, but in leisure. Whatever others may decide for themselves, this attitude would seem to be wrong for Christians. The excessively long hours of the past were onerous and made it difficult for a man to carry out his responsibilities to his family and his church. But working hours now are not normally unreasonable, and there can be no case for sitting back when there is so much want in the world. Even in Britain and the United States, the care of the aged, medicine, and education are almost bottomless pits, and it will be a long time before their needs are satisfied. Abroad, hundreds of millions are living at no more than subsistence level, and many of these primary-producing countries are dependent on a high and rising level of activity in the industrial nations for any increase in their own low standard of living. However, our duty to work arises from clear and explicit instructions in the Bible and not indirectly through our duty to our neighbor. Many of those who first followed the Protestant ethic had long since satisfied their own small personal needs. In an age when poverty was regarded as an ineradicable evil, they went on working regardless, because the Bible told them that this was right. It is just as well for us that they did.

The Work Ethic in Decline

As the twentieth century draws to a close, the Protestant work ethic is in visible decline. All the talk is of shorter working hours and greater leisure. As the buoyant economic optimism of the fifties and sixties ran out, so workers were more inclined to lower the pace of work in order to keep their jobs. The technology of the industrialized countries is being taken up by countries that have their own kind of ethic. No one who has visited Singapore, Hong Kong, Korea, or Japan can fail to be impressed with their technical mastery and skeptical of the idea that the older industrialized countries can now ease up and work half-time. Compared with Eastern cultures, the Protestant culture rests on individual responsibility. A man and a woman answer directly to their Creator for all they do with the talents He has given them. Eastern cultures fit more easily with the collectivism of mass production. Maybe by trying to force society too far into that collectivist mold, we risk breaking the feeling of personal responsibility, which is still a very powerful force in our culture. Certainly collectivism creates impossible dilemmas for Christians as they try to reconcile group-oriented consciences with decision.

Christians are often criticized for being too individualistic, and there is a lot of talk about "structural sin," which appears to refer to the embodiment of human selfishness in the structures of society. This criticism overlooks the Christian's own group, which is the church. We believe in individual salvation, which the church cannot gain for us, and in individual responsibility before God, for which the church cannot substitute. But we also believe in the collective authority and discipline of the church, though this may not be too much in evidence today. Therefore, there is a sense in which the Christian is the real collectivist in a shattered and atomized society. . . .

The Christian doctrine of work should lead to the creation of wealth, not by the destruction of the world's natural resources, but by their proper use. Christians believe that mankind holds the natural resources of the world in trust from God and that these should not only be passed on to succeeding generations intact but, as in the parables of the talents and the pounds, improved in the passing. No generation should leave behind deserts and dustbowls, nor should they leave natural hazards. It requires great skill and ingenuity to improve standards for a rising population, to lift the poor off the poverty line, to feed the starving. It should not be done by squandering natural resources, and the weight of poverty is much too heavy to be lifted by simple redistribution. New ways have to be found of creating and distributing wealth, and this calls for immense dedication and very hard work by those who work in the countries that are the dynamo economies of this world, especially by the professionals who control these economies. It requires political skill too, because the obstacle is not technical knowledge; rather, it is our ability to organize production, to put our immense technical knowledge to work, to en-courage investment, to get men and women to work willingly in teams and not to take advantage of their position to take more than they contribute, but instead to put more in than they take out. Our theoretical knowledge is way ahead of our ability to apply it, because its application depends on trust in one another — trust by the investor in the company and mutual trust by those who work in the company.

It is the duty of each generation to re-examine its attitudes by Christian standards, and it is to be hoped that we, in our generation, may rediscover the sense of the purpose which a Christian should have in his earthly vocation and the sense of harmony which we should have with the world that God created for our use.

An acquaintance recently told me why his father, a hardworking small-business man and lifelong believer, had stopped attending church.

Faced with demands from his workers he did not feel he could afford, the entrepreneur had taken a strike. One Sunday in church this entrepreneur listened in distress as his pastor told the congregation it was "morally imperative" that none of them cross the picket line. The pastor had not taken the trouble to learn anything about the strike or about business conditions. He had simply assumed that labor is right and business wrong.

Another businessman received a note from his pastor telling him he was committing a sin by failing to yield to the demands of a striking union.

I could fill a substantial part of this magazine with similar stories. Many business people have stopped active participation in their religious communities because they are tired of the ministers' or priests' open and usually ill-informed hostility to free enterprise.

It is unfortunate that many priests, ministers and rabbis seem to believe that business people sin more than the rest of us. How? By owning, controlling or manipulating a disproportionate percentage of "society's" wealth. Is it surprising that so many business people have decided to sleep late on the Sabbath?

Religion must begin to treat entrepreneurship as a vocation. All lay people — business people included — have a special role to play in the economy of salvation. They share in the task of furthering the faith when they use their talents in a way consistent with their religion. They have their own assignment in the mission of the people of God. Everyone has talents, and God wants us to cultivate them and treat them as gifts. If the gift happens to be for business or stock trading or investment banking, its possessor should not be condemned because of his or her trade.

Much of the problem arises from economic ignorance among the clergy. Just look at seminary curricula. You will search far and wide to find a single course in the basic dynamics of how an economy works.

At the same time, certain assumptions are adopted in the courses that seminarians do take. Many graduates leave seminary with the view of the market economy as a means for dividing the economic pie and think that people who get a big piece are taking away from someone else.

That is a childish view. A market economy is about expanding the pie, providing people with jobs, services and investment opportunities.

Every clergyman should read and think about George Gilder's extraordinary book, *Wealth and Poverty,* written a decade ago. Gilder made an eloquent case for infusing moral legitimacy into entrepreneurship.

It is a mistake to associate capitalism with greed, he said. When people accept the entrepreneurial vocation, they focus on the needs of others. They must give the public what it needs and wants, and even discover needs and wants so subtle they are imperceptible to others. Business people in a market economy cannot be self-centered and be successful.

Before Gilder, an entire school of economics grew up around an insight of Joseph Schumpeter. It is entrepreneurship, Schumpeter said, more than any other economic institution, that prevents economic and technological stagnation. Entrepreneurs, as agents of change, prod the economy to adjust to population increases, resource shifts, changes in consumer needs and desires. Without entrepreneurship, we would live in a stagnant economic world, mired in economic swamps like those socialism created in Central Europe, where entrepreneurship was declared immoral and made illegal.

Many clergy have focused too much on the gains of entrepreneurs, as if wealth itself is somehow unjust, but lost sight of the risks they take. Long before entrepreneurs see a return on their ideas or their investments, they must give up their time and property. They pay out wages even before they know whether they have accurately forecast the future. They have no assurance of profit. When investments do return a profit, much of it is reinvested and some goes to charities and religious institutions. Is that immoral?

When economic risks prove to have been a mistake, are priests and ministers there with words of comfort? Unfortunately, all too often they see the economic losses that fall on capitalists as punishment for greed. But the truth is that whether entrepreneurs win or lose, they put themselves on the line, and make the future a little more secure for the rest of us.

This is not to underplay a pastor's proper function of given spiritual direction. Clergymen must remind people of the seriousness of sin and call them to virtue. They must challenge those in the business vocation when they go astray. But this spiritual direction should be based on sin as traditionally understood, and not on misguided views of economics.

Religious leaders must learn something about economics. Then they will come to understand that the entrepreneurs often are the greatest men and women of faith among us.

— Robert A. Sirico, "A Worthy Calling,"
Forbes, 22 Nov. 1993, p. 162

Affections and Business

John C. Haughey, S.J.

The general thesis I wish to develop here is that those interested in a more ethical business climate or in business ethics should examine the affections that influence business decisions. As a discipline, business ethics appears to ignore these. But it is affections that affect and guide business decisions. Some affect these decisions for the good while others generate unethical behavior. The more beneficial affections can be cultivated, and those that prompt anti-social decisions can be isolated and checked.

It is not novel to tie the study of ethics to an examination of affections. Affections were of great interest to philosophers in the eighteenth and nineteenth centuries. Adam Smith and Jonathan Edwards were among those who concentrated on their analysis. Max Scheler is one of the twentieth-century philosophers who made the affections the centerpiece of his phenomenology. This paper will not be Schelerian, Edwardian, or Smithian, however. It will be closer to an exercise in pastoral theology than an effort in philosophy or ethics. Its understanding of affections owes more to William Spohn, S.J., a moral philosopher from the Jesuit School of Theology in Berkeley, California, than from the aforementioned authors. The two of us, in turn, would have been introduced to the importance of affections in decision-making by those who formed us in the spirituality of Igatius Loyola.

A description/definition of affections as they are being viewed here is in order. Affections are

John C. Haughey, S.J., "Affections and Business," Proceedings of the Second National Consultation on Corporate Ethics, Center for Ethics and Corporate Policy, Chicago, IL, May 13-15, 1987.

dispositions of the heart that lead to actions. I say dispositions to distinguish them from feelings which I see as more fleeting and volatile than affections. I say these are of the heart since these dynamic dispositions are not rationally arrived at. Affections become habits of the soul that generate enormous moral (or immoral) energy. Affections have a kinship with virtues and vices. The former facilitate excellence in moral behavior; the latter make immoral behavior likely. To a large extent affections predetermine our choices. They flow into and direct our judgments and shape our attitudes. They also create the life-flow that leads us into circumstances that we would not experience if those affections were absent.

Affections are an inextricable part of persons' sense of themselves, their feeling selves, their whole selves. We are in many ways more explained by our affections than we are by our jobs or by self-definitions that abstract from our affections. Affections are of two kinds: positive or attractions, and negative or repugnances (disaffections).

A more essentialist view of the complex character of the human being would locate affections closer to emotions which in turn would be distinguished from the mind or the will or, for that matter, from ideas or choices. But a more existential view of the person is not comfortable with such abstractness or compartmentalization. It sees the person more concretely, in terms of his/her history and experiences.

Affections come to be because of experiences. They continue to be a force in one's life as long as there is some connection with the initial experience. If the experiences that gave them their initial life are not fed by on-going corresponding experiences they will fade in their power and influence. For example, the young, especially the young male, experiences competition in athletics and develops an affection for it. It need not cease when a person enters the adult competitive arena of business. There is simply a transfer of the affection of competition from one to the other arena.

Most affections are culturally generated or re-inforced. The generating culture can be the general one or a very particular one, a subculture if you please. Among the most effective generators of affections in our society are business and religion. (This is simply an observation; one that I can't prove.) The general culture has heroes who embody affections. Again, these heroes frequently come from either business or religious faith. Lee Iacocca, for example, "made it." He took Chrysler from the brink to being competitive and lucrative (another affection). Martin Luther King is a symbol of racial justice. Mother Theresa is a symbol of compassion for the hopeless and helpless.

Affections have an object, something which incites them. Take religion for example: In general, God is the primary object of religious affections. The ordinary religious affections incited by the presence of this "object" (if we can refer to God this way) are love or awe or trust. Worship services seek to put believers in touch with God and thus, if successful, serve to strengthen these affections. There are secondary objects of religious faith, of course, such as justice, love, peace, compassion, etc.

The particular matter we wish to focus on here is the relationship of the affections of the business executive to his or her business conduct. I contend first of all that the main influences on business conduct are affections that have been generated by the world of business itself. Growth, productivity, efficiency, the bottom line, being competitive — these are constitutive aspects of the Western business enterprise. But they also can be seen as affections. These objectives of the business enterprise frequently become affections. The movement from being an objective to being an affection depends on how much the business person has become invested in the company and its objectives. One can go from being efficient as an objective to internalizing efficiency as an affection etc. if one's job comes to mean that much to one.

Much of the literature on business ethics fails to address the situations and conduct of business because of the neglect of the affectivity of the business person. Business ethics tends to address reason and concentrate on norms. Norms are doubtless an important component in ethical conduct, especially when there is real obscurity about the right and wrong course of action to be followed. But obscurity about the right or wrong course of action in any objective sense is infrequent. Frequent, on the other hand, is wrong conduct stemming from affections that have focused on and been incited by the business atmosphere and its above-mentioned objective. Growth, efficiency, the bottom-line, competition — these are not wrong either as objectives

or as affections if they are kept in the locus proper to them. Meaning what?

Business and all the objectives that make it what it is must be kept in the relative grid of value proper to them. These objectives, and the affections that correspond to them, easily leave their place in the order of value and function as absolutes. Being competitive or beating the competition, for example, can become all-consuming, and we lose sight of the absolute value of the human person. Business was made for persons, those involved in it, and those served by its products. Persons are not to be reduced to means to business-generated ends. People are ends in themselves, even the people who have to be "beaten."

Affections have their own "rationality." They tend to make their own judgments, "judgments of affectivity." These differ from "judgments of rationality" which seek a more explicit reasoning process. Affections carry with them an immediate clarity and, simultaneously, a propulsion to take this or that action. The morality of this or that action will depend both on the object of the affections and whether the affections in question are in harmony with other extra-business affections. If an affection that has been generated within the business enterprise dominates all extra-business affections, then wrong conduct is as certain to follow as night follows day. . . .

I am specifically interested in the religious symbols that can penetrate and rearrange the affectivity of business people. Although I suppose I always knew about the connection, it came home most forcefully to me from a remark made by someone I was interviewing about what was most helpful to him in making decisions. He was an executive in one of Washington's Federal agencies. "Good Liturgy" was his reply. "How could this be," I queried? "It gets me in touch with the deeper dimensions of the issue that I otherwise deal with on their own technical and narrow terms."

His explanation was not as clear to me as was his conviction of the importance of being brought via symbols into the world of God, belief, religion, etc. At the core of the efficacy of this evocation of a deeper horizon of values are the Scriptures. They give affections a narrative and a critique. They shape the affections which can remain "brute data" if they are not brought to clearer definition. Scriptural symbols as liturgical prayer evoke affections, legitimatizing some and critiquing others.

The executive's observation led me to realize that prayer, whether personal or communal, sporadic or habitual, is an effective way of generating countervailing affections. These countervailing affections take the measure of affections for competition, efficiency, profit, growth, etc. that are generated in the business atmosphere. Intentional activity is necessary for the generation of religious affections. But prayer is this kind of activity. Belief as such, or simple assent to beliefs, will not suffice to generate countervailing affections. To counter affections that are nurtured all day long in the business culture, these extra-business affections need to be cultivated by intentional activity in order to attain a sufficient level of intensity to hold their counterparts in check. The self-activity of prayer can be personally intitiated or evoked by effective liturgy.

To be more concrete, major business decisions are nerve-racking. So much is at stake, possibly even the future of the enterprise, at least the reputation of the decision-maker(s), or even their jobs. Having to make complex weighty decisions tends to generate negative affections such as fear or insecurity or the feeling of being very much alone in the responsibility. Entry into prayer or liturgy or the Scriptures can mitigate some of this insecurity or fear or sense of being alone with the responsibility. For example, I have found a number of executives helped by internalizing some of the Scriptural metaphors of immediate providence such as "the Lord is my Shepherd" (Psalm 23). The point here is that an extra-business affection has been generated (through presumably not *ab ovo*) that speaks directly to the turmoil the person is experiencing in the business situation. Internalizing the symbol of immediate providence doesn't clarify the decision as such. But it reduces the negative affections — fear and insecurity — so that the decision can be weighed on its own merits without the weight of negative affections intruding on or paralyzing the decision-maker. A larger horizon has opened up, and the newly sensed breadth helps bring the moral agent to the freedom needed to choose the course of action that a lack of freedom made difficult. The symbol evoked a sense of the whole that enabled the partiality of the business affections and the negative affections to be seen for what they were.

Another example of a countervailing affection comes even closer to a formally ethical issue than the previous one. A CEO whose bank holding company has become one of the major banks in the country (via recent acquisitions) has found himself in the inner circle of "blue chippers." He now receives calls from those in the exclusive club describing "unbelievable deals." While he does not see these as illegal, à la insider trading, he says, "they do not feel right to me" because the privileged position of the callers makes them privy to moments in international and national finances that the public is not in on. As he explains it, his enticement is not to the money that can be made by him and his company, but rather to the allure "to belong." One really comes to belong, apparently, if one follows up on the privileged disclosures. "If you ignore these, you will be back out on the margins where you were for all the previous years of your banking career."

The affection here is the power of belonging. A countervailing affection would be one that met this need to belong to this exclusive "club of blue chippers." But the CEO has found a way of cultivating the needed countervailence; the seductiveness is reduced considerably by an on-going, warm experience of belonging to a family of worshippers. They face into a different horizon and, therefore, they embody and pursue different values. It is the affective sense of really belonging to this family that helps the CEO feels the ill-fittingness of the other community's allure with its different way of belonging.

For countervailing affections to be effective they must constrain the business affection. An unconstructed affection for growth or profit becomes the vice of avarice. The unconstrained affection for competition becomes cruelty or at least an indifference to people's needs, feelings, and rights. An unconstrained affection to calculate exclusively in terms of the bottom line leads to the instrumentalization of people. An unconstrained propensity for efficiency leads to disastrous company morale and subtle forms of sabotage that disgruntled employees devise to punish management. At the same time, it should be obvious that none of these business affections, or the objectives from which they derive, are intrinsically immoral or inevitably flawed. It is in the countering of their propensity to overreach that they remain useful and ordered to the common good.

The business firms that would be ethical should examine this matter of the affections that are given a privileged place in the operation. The firm might find means to honor in word and in deed the people, ways, and institutions that generate these extra-business affections. Active faith is not the only source of affections capable of thwarting the potentially unbridled affections generated by business. A good companion can be a source, as well as a spouse or a loving family, an avocation or a diverting hobby. There is, however, a dimensionality to religion that if fully utilized can meet every one of the business affections and keep them ordered to the common good. Judaism and Christianity can supply a rich trove of symbols. Their congregations are capable of creating the conditions that generate and celebrate those symbols.

To take just one example, let us consider competition vs. community. Both the competitive company and the person who would be competitive seek to differentiate themselves from their competition. They would lift themselves above their peers, individuating themselves, and seeking to be different from rather than similar to their competition. The religions encourage the opposite. Being one with and being for your neighbors, colleagues, peers, even enemies, is what they would engender in their adherents. Christianity goes so far as to use the bold metaphor of "member" (of a larger whole, the body) to describe the depth of association believers have and seek with one another. It seems that competition in business would be a decent thing if competitors were simultaneously experiencing the kind of interaction with people that was bonding. The humanizing effect of the latter would almost certainly deter unbridled competition or rugged individualism. I say almost certainly rather than certainly because some people seem to operate with a split consciousness that makes them capable of being both Dr. Jekyll the predator and Mr. Hyde the socially responsible citizen.

There will always be a tension between the worlds of business and religious faith, and there should be. Business will always concentrate on production, competition, and the bottom line; religious faith will be more concerned with distribution, community, and the finish line. I think there has been a neglect not only of the affections but also of the value of religion by those interested in a climate of business ethics.

Scope, in a word, is one of the important contributions religion can bring to the affections and to the business person. When a person's life becomes all business, it ceases to be human.

Section 2: When Personal Calling Meets Corporate Culture

The stories in the previous section unfolded with little explicit attention to the backdrop of particular organizations in which these people work. The focus, of course, was on the personal religious factors that motivated these people to find an ethical pathway. Yet their discoveries depended in part on the organizations with which they intersected.

Organizational cultures and their values exercise a powerful influence upon the development of individual life stories for either good or ill. William May begins our reflection on corporate culture by observing that the cultivation of the traditional business virtues, while necessary, is not sufficient. He argues that collective virtues in organizations must be born and nourished. Since corporate power is a privilege bestowed by society, according to May, corporations must necessarily cultivate a public-spirited commitment to the common good. May describes corporate covenantal responsibilities for both commutative and distributive justice. He then proceeds to discuss the virtues that good leaders must develop, seeing such leaders as both open-minded teachers and ready learners on a daily basis.

William Weiss's remarks on corporate culture are based on his experience as the chairman and chief executive officer of the Ameritech Corporation. He understands the role of corporate values and describes key values that should shape a corporate identity. Weiss is not naive, however. He acknowledges that businesses always make choices based on their *perceptions* of good and evil, perceptions that often reflect only a partial understanding of reality. He therefore cautions against easy answers, recognizing that even the best corporate intentions don't always result in the best outcomes.

The nature of corporate culture is further explicated by J. Irwin Miller, past chairman of Cummins Engine Company. Miller, too, is a realist. He recognizes that the God-given moral sense within humans is always tempered by one or another cultural context. He admits that religious commitment itself may become a tool for good or ill in business. Still, Miller is convinced that Christian faith, properly understood, allows business participants to extend themselves beyond personal self-seeking. Particularly in a time of massive corporate reengineering, care for others is critical. Miller insists that Christian commitment is a healthy foundation for the character, trust, and loyalty that will be critical to corporate success in the future.

Dennis Bakke's essay may serve as a timely counterpoint to the personal testimony of Christian executives like Weiss and Miller. He reminds business leaders that Christian faith is not simply a prime business asset. People of faith should be ethically and socially responsive, not for strategic business reasons, but because such actions are simply right and good. Bakke refuses to compromise on this point: ethical business decision making must involve more than a concern for valid outcomes; eventually, our experience in business must lead us to question the quality of our total response to God.

Each of these thinkers believes that religious values should shape corporate foundations, operating beliefs, and applied principles. They know from their own experience and observation that organizations and individuals have symbiotic relationships. Individuals bring their histories of faith, value, and experience; but present business cultures influence the futures of those individual beliefs and commitments.

The Virtues of the Business Leader

William F. May

The Subject of Virtue

. . . . While reflection on the virtues may not deserve preeminence of place, it constitutes an important part of the total terrain of ethics. Unfortunately, contemporary moralists, with some recent exceptions, have not been too interested in the clarification and cultivation of those virtues upon which the health of personal and social life depends. Reflection in this area is likely to seem rather subjective, elusive, or spongy ("I wish my physician were more personal"), as compared with the critical study of decisions and structures. From the utilitarian perspective, moreover, emphasis on the virtues appears to ignore the question of results. John Stuart Mill once argued that there is nothing independently good about sacrificial action. Its goodness depends entirely on its producing a good outcome. Our modern shorthand for Mill's concern is "the bottom line."

The novelist, Melville, argued to the contrary and in favor of the virtues. The Benthamites, he observed, would never have urged Lord Nelson to risk his life on the bridge of his ship. Nelson's heroism would not have produced the greatest net balance of good over evil; his loss would have looked bad on a cost/benefit analysis sheet. Melville's comment slyly suggests that the field of ethics does not reduce to the utilitarian concern

William F. May, "The Virtues of the Business Leader," from the Proceedings of the Second National Consultation on Corporate Ethics, 13-15 May 1987, Center for Ethics and Corporate Policy, Chicago, Illinois, ed. David A. Krueger.

for *producing* good. Ethics must deal with virtues as well as principles of action, with *being* good as well as *producing* good. This essay will explore some of the virtues central to business leadership.

Especially today attention must be paid to the question of professional virtue. The growth of large-scale organizations has increased that need. While the growth of bureaucracies has increased the opportunities for monitoring performance (and therefore would appear to lessen the need for virtue), in another respect bureaucracies make the society increasingly hostage to the virtue of the professionals who work for them. Huge organizations wield enormous power with which to cover the mistakes of their employees. Further, and more important, the opportunity for increased specialization which they provide means that few other people — whether lay or professional — know what any given expert is up to. The professional had better be virtuous. Few may be in a position to discredit him or her. The knowledge explosion is also an ignorance explosion; even the knowledgeable expert is ignorant and dependent in much. If knowledge is power, then ignorance is powerlessness. Although institutions can devise mechanisms that limit the opportunities for the abuse of specialized knowledge, ultimately one needs to cultivate virtues in those who wield that relatively esoteric and inaccessible power. One test of character and virtue is what a person does when no one else is watching. A society that rests on expertise mobilized in huge organizations needs more people who can pass that test.

The Traditional Virtues of the Marketplace: Industry, Honesty, and Integrity

Emphasis on the traditional virtues runs the danger of missing the full scope of corporate ethics. It does so, not simply because applied ethics must include the criticism of structures and the articulation of principles that will help the practitioner solve quandaries, but because middle class reflection on the virtues conventionally restricts itself to a short list of the virtues viewed as the moral presuppositions of the marketplace; namely, industry, honesty, and integrity.

The marketplace, so the argument goes, cannot function as a wholly impersonal mechanism that makes no demands upon the virtue of those who participate in it. The marketplace breaks down unless it can presuppose the virtue of industry, without which goods will not be produced; and the virtues of honesty and integrity, without which their free and fair exchange cannot take place.

Emphasis on these virtues alone, however, leaves much to be desired under the conditions of the marketplace in twentieth-century society. The personal virtues of industry, honesty, and integrity do not begin to touch the systemic issues of modern economic life. Preaching the virtue of industry hardly touches the structural issue of the employable unemployed. Commending to Midwestern farmers the personal virtues of honesty and integrity hardly spares them financial ruin. Nor do homilies on these personal virtues address the "externalities" of pollution, injurious products, hazards of the workplace, or the disrepair of our cities.

Emphasis on these particular virtues also misses the organizational issue in the twentieth-century. We live, after all, in the age of the large-scale organization. As Alisdair MacIntyre observed, the ruling theoretician of the modern world is neither Karl Marx of the East nor Adam Smith of the West, but rather the sociologist, Max Weber. Marx and Smith have supplied the ideological content for the conflicts of our times — communism vs. capitalism; but Max Weber has described the social form that has triumphed in both East and West, irrespective of content, the large-scale organization. The traditional virtues of nineteenth-century capitalism, while addressing some of the moral presuppositions of Adam Smith's marketplace, hardly deal with the moral presuppositions of the dominant institution in the marketplace, the corporation.

Corporate Virtue

The corporation requires, beyond the individual virtues of industry, honesty, and integrity, the more social virtues that dispose the members of a large, complex organization to work together. The philosopher, A. W. H. Adkins (of *Merit and Responsibility,* 1960) might have designated these the cooperative, as opposed to the competitive, virtues. Henry Cabot Lodge of Harvard Business School long ago observed that Lockian individualism had to give way in our time to the more organizational demands of teamwork.

But the virtues associated with teamwork are not enough. In his *History of Ethics,* Alisdair MacIntyre rightly called them "secondary virtues." MacIntyre's term tends to deprecate virtues associated with process rather than substance, those particular strengths of character which do not flow from shared substantive goals but rather which the large-scale organization requires in pursuing any goal whatsoever, including those that may be quite immoral. Emphasis upon the cooperative virtues alone — skills in acting in concert with others — systematically brackets the key moral question which the corporation ought to face, namely, the substantive question of the aim and goal of the enterprise.

If we are to attend in this essay to more than the virtues of process and include the virtue of substance, we will have to reckon with what, for want of a better term, I shall call "public spiritedness." The business leader must possess not simply the three traditional virtues of industry, honesty, and integrity, or the secondary cooperative virtues that make one artful in acting in concern with others, but also, substantively and preeminently, if I am right about the power and privilege of business in the modern world, public-spiritedness. I would define public-spiritedness as the art of acting in concert with others for the common good. This definition includes both a subjective and an objective element. On the subjective side, the art of acting in concert with others summarized the virtues of process. On the objective side, the definition acknowledges that the leader must open out to questions of the common good.

The Objective Element in Public Spiritedness

Why should the business leader orient to the question of the public good? After all, the leader heads what we distinctively characterize as a *private* enterprise with responsibilities traditionally restricted to private investors. Is it not, at the least, a distraction — at the worst, a corruption of the enterprise — to expect the leader, *qua* business leader, to be public-spirited? Should we not, at the most, concede the possibility of an occasional act of charity, a grace note of generosity, to ease the organization's way in the community at the level or PR, but not more?

I will argue that both the power and privilege of the corporations and the professionals who largely work for them in the setting of the modern democracies require us to rank public spiritedness among the cardinal virtues required of the business leader.

We mislead ourselves if we think of business merely as one private interest group among others in a market economy. That may have been the vision of things at the time the framers of the Constitution devised our mechanism of checks and balances — in and through which diverse interest groups might successfully limit one another. Today, however, the business community wields a power that vastly exceeds that of any other group in our society — churches, synagogues, labor organizations, service organizations, and the like. In a market economy, business leaders make decisions on major aspects of production and distribution which in other societies might be reserved to the government. Business people decide on the industrial technology, patterns of work organization, the locations of industries, market structures, resource allocation, and executive compensation and status. These decisions have momentous public impacts, for good or for ill, not only on investors, but also on workers, neighbors, consumers, suppliers, and satellite service industries, upon the air we breathe, upon the water we drink and bathe in, and upon the forests and lakes to which we would retreat of a weekend. While engaged in what we call private enterprise, business leaders are, in effect, "public officials" in a market economy. Taking the long view of Western history, Charles E. Lindblom has observed that two institutions shape the modern world just as surely as the church and the state shaped the medieval world: these preeminent institutions are business and government.

Further, the public power that business wields is not merely a power that business itself has created. Business enjoys extraordinary privileges from public largesse in a modern democratic society. To cite but a few in the U.S.A.: road improvements, railroads, airports, enclosure acts, tax offsets, tax credit for research and investments that are indulged far more than necessary, the business rental of Defense Department plants at favorable rates, urban renewal projects to help retailers, tax free perquisites, and fringe benefits.

Business also receives special treatment at the hands of the law and governmental officials. Strikingly enough, corporations can still use the services of an officer accused of crimes, but labor unions cannot. More important than this special privilege, business leaders expect government officials to take seriously their judgment on policy matters affecting the business climate. While the government can forbid some actions, it cannot directly command business to perform, hence it behooves presidents and prime ministers to confer with business leaders. Their formal and informal veto power in the society is enormous. Their capacity to create convulsive impacts on traffic patterns, school systems, parking accommodations, sewage plants, police and fire departments, and other public facilities without having to face the answering veto power of others points to an extraordinary power that can no longer be defined as wholly private. The business leader is an unelected, even though carefully selected, public functionary. His or her power, privilege, and role demand the virtue of public-spiritedness.

The heavy involvement of professionals in running corporations provides a further moral basis for accepting a responsibility to the public good. The business community largely employs, organizes, and deploys the services of professionals who work for and often lead the major corporations — lawyers, accountants, engineers, and experts with advanced degrees out of MBA programs across the land. Historically, the concept of a profession invokes the notion of public responsibility. The term "profession," and the more ancient, though less often invoked, words, "vocation" and "calling," have a public ring to them that the terms "job" and "career" do not. (A "career" reminds us of the word "car," the automobile, literally, a self-driven vehicle. A career supplies us with a kind of self-driven vehicle through life; it enters the public thoroughfares, but for its own private reasons and toward its own private destination.) It ill behooves a professional to sever his or her calling from all question of the common good and to instrumentalize it to private goals alone. Pro-

fessionals are often licensed by the state; the society invests in their education; they generate their own public standards of excellence; and they are expected to conform to these standards and to accept responsibility for their enforcement in the guild. Professionals, particularly as they increasingly work for and lead our huge corporations, have become the new rulers of the West. Our society does not transmit power today on the basis of blood. We largely wield and transmit a knowledge-based power acquired in the university from which the corporations then benefit as they attract the services of the vast majority of talented young lawyers, accountants, and engineers.

But how does one begin to specify the public responsibilities of corporations and of the leaders and professionals that largely direct them?

In my judgment, the first substantive goal of the corporate leader is economic performance at a profit. Without a profit, the institution fails of its investors and workers. It runs the risk of institutional suicide. Moreover, this goal of economic service at a profit is itself a corporation's primary public duty. We falsely interpret the institution and its basic goal if we define it wholly as a private enterprise and think of public service exclusively as something additional and marginal that follows upon it. A market economy allows for the specialization of institutions, and the marvelous economies of scale which that specialization permits. Through marketplace exchange, individuals and corporations do contribute to the well-being of the society at large. The specialized production of goods and services and their public exchange acknowledge unashamedly the fact of human interdependence and provide a specific mechanism for service a wide variety of human needs.

This basic assessment rejects two extremes. First, it would reject the insistence of the Left in the Sixties that any and all communities must be 1) self-sufficient and 2) ready to stop work before lunch on any given day to respond to the particular moral test which the Left chose for them to solve by that afternoon. I accept the good sense of a division of labor within and among institutions and the overriding single mission and public service which each performs.

But this interpretation would also reject that narrowing of public service and the community so served which Milton Friedman articulated when he declared that the corporation has a sole aim and purpose of serving investors by maximizing profits. The limitless goal of maximizing profits imposes a pressure of "ever more," "ever more," on business leaders. It makes a social good out of the vice of avarice. It forgets what the Greeks long ago knew: that temperance is a precondition of the social virtue of justice or public-spiritedness. Temperance, whether of individuals or institutions, does not demand the extinguishing of desires, but it does require their restraint. If we are to render justice to another, if we are to render to another his or her due, we must be able to keep our desires regulated, our appetites under control. That restraint translates into the goal of economic performance at a profit.

Further, the rejection of the formula, "maximizing profits," rests upon the conviction that those who are due something include more than stockholders. They include those who have been called stakeholders in the enterprise. Stockholders are important stakeholders in a company, but by no means the only ones. Workers, customers, neighbors, and the public at large have in varying way a stake in its performance, sometimes indeed a larger stake than stockholders who may dart in and out of their investments more readily than workers and neighbors can disengage themselves from a company and its fortunes.

This argument, however, rests on little more than the consonance of the two words — "stock" and "stake" — unless one can show why obligation should extend beyond stockholders in an enterprise. The ancient notion of a covenant offers some help in this effort. The concept of a covenant expands obligation beyond the limits of commercial contract (the stockholder's purchase), and takes corporate responsibility a notch deeper than token expressions of corporate philanthropy (contributions to the local community chest drive). Very briefly: a covenantal ethic concentrates on those obligations that arise in relationships between several parties that are deep-going, responsive, and reciprocal. It acknowledges a two-way process of giving and receiving that occurs in extended exchanges between parties, from which permanent obligations and agreements arise that give shape to the future. This deep and growing sense of responsibility between parties is at issue in the notion of a stakeholder. Much has happened

between two parties (between a corporation and its workers, a corporation and its neighbors) that gives them a stake in what each does. They are covenanted together.

In contrast, the ideal of philanthropy presupposes a one-way street from give to receiver. The philanthropist pretends to be pure giver alone; others relate to him as pure receiver. When the philanthropist loses interest, he moves on. That is why corporate responsibility reduced to philanthropy alone trivializes corporate ethics. As admirable as philanthropy may be, it expresses a generosity too occasional, too sentimental, too patronizing, too arbitrary to express the full depth of business responsibility in the modern world. The corporation does not give as pure benefactor alone. It has already received much from the community — not only the investment of stockholders, but also the labor of workers, the ambiance and services of the community in which it is located, the privilege of incorporation by the state, and all the protection bestowed upon persons under the due process clause of the Constitution. Its indebtedness to the society is great.

Moreover, not all this indebtedness can be toted up in commercial, contractualist terms. The corporation, to be sure, pays its workers and its taxes, but these transactions also build up a life between people and institutions that goes deeper than transient marketplace contacts. Exchanges deepen relations even while they "discharge" obligations. That is why the word covenant is to be preferred to contract in defining the moral obligations of the corporation.

Formally considered, the concepts of contract and covenant are first cousins. They both include an agreement between parties and an exchange; they look to reciprocal future action. But, in spirit, contract and covenant are quite different. Contracts involve buying and selling. Covenants include further ingredients or giving and receiving. Contracts can be filed away, but a covenant becomes a part of one's history and shapes in unexpected ways one's self-perception and perhaps even destiny. The decision-making of a corporation is massively contractual. But that decision-making rests upon a covenantal base that charters its life, grants it protection, and endows its enterprises with a public significance and responsibility.

Perhaps we are in a position now to see why the virtues of the business leader must include more than industry, honesty, and integrity. Those are the virtues of a purely commutative justice — the virtues that obtain in the fulfillment of duties based on contracts between private parties. Public spiritedness, however, suggests a more spacious obligation to distributive justice (above and beyond the mechanism of the marketplace). Professionals and business leaders wield an immense power and control fatefully the distribution of goods and burdens. The powers they wield and the goods and burdens they control are of a public magnitude and scale.

Although the government has a primary responsibility for ministering justice (the old term for distributive justice), professional and business leaders also have a "ministry" to perform. When the state alone accepts responsibility for distributive justice, a general sense of obligation for distributive justice diminishes in the citizenry and the social virtue upon which fair distributions depend loses the grounds for its renewal. Professionals and leaders particularly need to accept some responsibility for ministering justice to sustain a sense of public-spiritedness in the society at large.

The Subjective Element in Public Spiritedness: The Art of Acting in Concert with Others

We return now to the virtues of process, though properly understood, they should point in the direction of moral substance. The art of acting in concert with others entails more than a generalized disposition to cooperativeness. That disposition alone supplies us with little more than the virtues of fellowship, not leadership. The distinctive virtues of leadership consist of prudence and courage and the complex arts of persuasion, partly intellectual and partly moral, apart from which cooperativeness, at any level, often signifies little more than the presence of timidity and avarice rather than the existence of a full-strength virtue.

The special importance of the virtues of prudence and courage becomes clear if we distinguish the tasks of business leadership from those of management and administration. The word, "management," emphasizes a custodial function;

the manager, at work in any large-scale organization, handles a huge volume of work by invoking rational, impersonal routines. But the corporation, as opposed to some other bureaucracies, cannot afford to reduce itself wholly to routine. The business corporation has to deal with the market — which forces its leaders daily and relentlessly to cope with uncertainty — the uncertainty of customers, raw materials, transportation, energy costs, and changes in taste and habit. Thus some analysts would reserve the term "bureaucracy" for public institutions or nonprofit service organizations as distinct from corporations that must maintain flexibility and adaptability, if they would survive and flourish in the vagaries of the marketplace. Indeed, the corporation that would eliminate uncertainty through routine would generate its own uncertainties. The very effort to eliminate risk itself imposes risks in creating rigid, inflexible procedures. Business leaders cannot eliminate risk but must figure out the right risks to take.

For this and other reasons, top management seeks to interpret itself in the language of leadership. The term "leadership" invokes etymologically the notion of a journey. Leadership means "going." Going where? Into the unknown. Into the not-yet-fully-revealed. Into the X of the future. Invariably, seminars on leadership link leadership with the decades ahead: "Leadership in the Twenty-First Century." Leadership connects the present to the future, a future relatively opaque — partly self-determined and partly determined by forces and factors beyond one's control.

Leadership consists of what the German philosopher, Martin Heidegger, called "Vorlaufen" (literally, running ahead of oneself; or, less literally, anticipation). Anticipation in our specific context includes several ingredients: first, the selection of goals — resolving upon a destination; second, determining the route to these goals; and third, as the old English root for leadership suggests, causing others to go by showing the way. In business, top management assumes these tasks as its chief responsibilities.

Leadership requires facing the uncertainty of the future, the ultimate uncertainty of which no rational structure can ever fully eliminate or ignore. This state of affairs requires two virtues in the business leader: prudence and courage. It may seem strange to introduce these traditional, personal virtues into the discussion. In fact, the large-scale organization often seeks to institutionalize them so as not to place an extraordinary personal demand on the executive for either virtue. . . .

Prudence or Discernment Must Head the List of Virtues which the Good Leader Requires

At the heart of leadership is anticipation. The task of anticipation requires the selection of goals, the determining of the route to those goals, and the persuasion of others to move in their direction by showing the way. Casuists amongst moral theorists tend to downgrade the importance of prudence because they rely on the articulation of a set of general rules that will show the way in handling any and all cases. To that degree they tend to downgrade the importance of the concrete insight of the practitioner. Correspondingly, they trivialize prudence into a merely adroit selection of means in the pursuit of ends, a crafty packaging of polices. The virtue of prudence, to be sure, deals with fitting means to ends, but, as a virtue, it consists of much more than the "tactical cunning" of which Machiavelli speaks or the safe playing by the book to which the bureaucrat reduces the virtue. The bureaucrat, like the casuists amongst the moralists, downgrades the importance of routines, regulations, and procedures as a way of coping with any and all problems. We need, therefore, to have recourse to the classical moral tradition to retrieve some sense of the role of prudence in the moral life.

The medieval moralist gave a primary place to the cardinal virtue of prudence of the grounds that being precedes goodness. One is not equipped to respond fittingly and appropriately to the world unless one has undistorted access to the world as it is. An openness to being underlies both being good and producing the good. The marks of prudence include: *memoria* — being true to the past (rather than retouching, coloring, falsifying the past); *docilitas* — defined as openness to the present, the ability to be still, to be silent, to listen; and *solertia* — readiness for the unexpected. Prudence is the eye of the soul. In effect, the soul must be open to the past, present, and future. Practitioners in the helping professions must evince these three

dimensions of prudence. The world did not need Freud to tell us that the effective counselor must help the patient be open to his past and therefore resist the temptation to distort, retouch, color, or falsify it. Similarly, the effective counselor must be capable of docility. Docility has nothing to do with a bovine complacency. It requires sufficient discipline to listen attentively to any and all signals that the patient presents in the interview. Finally, the truly effective counselor must be sufficiently open to the future as to be ready for the unexpected. He runs the risk of missing the patient and his uniqueness if he reduces the needful intervention to past solutions to past problems.

The need for prudence in the helping professions has its analogue in the demands placed upon the business leader. He had better not retouch the past so as to obscure from himself its lessons. He requires sufficient restraint, discipline, and openness to the present to catch its nuances, its distinctiveness. And, even as he lays down his plans for the future, he is ill advised if he does not at the same time position himself to be ready for the unexpected. Mario Savio went for the jugular vein in the mid-1960s when he complained that the modern bureaucrat tends to be unacquainted with novelty. The business leader can ill afford that special obtuseness about the future.

When, however, the prudent leader has done his or her best in interpreting the past, in sifting the present, and in peering, as best as he or she can, into the contingency of the future, one must *still* shoulder uncertainty. One needs, to be sure, the wisdom to know what risks to undertake but, also, the courage to undertake them.

Courage Has a Passive and an Active Mode — Both Are Important

In its passive mode, courage takes the shape of endurance, stamina, and resilience. Most hard decisions, no matter how prudently chosen have their coefficient of adversity. St. Thomas once defined courage as firmness of soul in the face of adversity. Most tough decisions include two decisions: The first is the obvious decision — what are we going to do? The second is the less noticed decision — the decision to make good on the decision. Whatever the original decision, one needs some resoluteness of will, for, in hard cases, even the best of decisions will unravel without some staying power in the midst of adversity. And, further, if and when the decision goes wrong, one needs resilience. One needs the wisdom to recognize a mistake for what it is, but also the resilience to pick oneself off the floor in its aftermath, not to engage in personal recriminations, and to move on to the next task. Courage in its passive mode is crucial to the morale of the organization. Chester I. Barnard once wisely emphasized the importance of executive *energy*.

In its active mode, courage requires the capacity for attack, not dodging but attacking problems. We need not accept the restrictively military connotations of the term in the setting of aristocratic societies. Attack requires pressing ahead into those anticipations that cannot be fully fathomed but yet have been chosen. Basic planning and secondary, contingency planning are modes of the attack. The opposite of attack is evasion. At this point, the connection between prudence and courage becomes clear. The evasive person avoids the painful lessons of the past, turns a deaf ear to what is happening about him, and closes himself off from the contingent future. The virtues interconnect.

Finally, the full definition of leadership includes not simply running ahead of oneself into the future, but also showing the way to others. "Showing the way" can have two meanings which open up two very different notions of leadership. Ancient Sparta symbolizes one kind of leadership; ancient Athens, the other. Sparta, as a military society, depended upon leadership by command and obedience. It was an essentially taciturn society; it relied on the bark of command and the grunt of obedience. Athens, as opposed to Sparta, created a political rather than a military culture. It relied on the word *(logos)* or, more precisely the art of persuasion *(rhetor),* to function as a society. The persuasive word constitutes the essence of the art of politics, the art of acting in concert with others. Hence the importance of rhetoric in Athenian education. The truly effective citizen and leader was the man (a male chauvinist society, to be sure) who knew how to teach, how to persuade his colleagues. And what was true of politics applied also to the professions, certainly to the most revered of them, the physician. The truly scientific physician, who had access to first principles, who

knew *why* he did things and not just *how* he did them, differed from the "rough empirics," the merely trained technicians, in that he *taught* his patients. He did not merely dispense technical services or give opaque orders; he explained what he was up to in his treatment program. "Words are to a prescription what a preamble is to a constitution." It provides the explanatory background that makes sense of the regimen. Thus political life and the professional relationship depended upon something more than command and obedience. They depended upon the teaching arts that address human judgment in the choice of means and ends.

To what culture should the modern corporation spiritually belong? Sparta or Athens? In arguing here for the primacy of Athens, one need not exaggerate. No large-scale organization, public or private, can wholly substitute persuasion for command. An effective President of the U.S.A. must be a skillful teacher to the nation, but no President can afford to restrict his or her decisions to the boundaries of what can be fully explained or defended by persuasion. The board meeting of a corporation or a committee meeting of its executives hardly resembles a seminar. It must often reach a decision and adjourn before everyone has yielded to persuasion. But when one governs exclusively by command rather than persuasion, one controls behavior rather than leads people, and one fails to prepare another generation for leadership.

In the politically healthy organization, teaching takes place in three directions: from above to below; horizontally; and from below to above.

1. The top manager heretofore has tended to control his or her world by command within and by manipulation and pressuring without. But managers have greatly exaggerated the necessity of inscrutability within and secretiveness without; they overlook the cost of these two tactics. When one governs within exclusively by command rather than persuasion, one secures conforming behavior but no enlistment of the active imagination in a shared vision. Further, coping with the outside world exclusively by manipulation (some advertising) and bullying (heavy metal lobbying) generates distrust. False claims and threats produce skepticism and re-

sentment. Neither the customer nor the government listens to the merits of the case. Top management should accept a teaching responsibility both without and within if it would "show the way" by persuasion.

Upper level managers accept implicitly a further teaching responsibility of a less public nature: they must act as mentors in bringing along their junior colleagues. In some respects, Americans may not address this obligation as wisely as business leaders in other countries. In America, the boss or sponsor, more often than not, serves as mentor to subordinates. The mixture of the two roles sometimes skews and sometimes corrupts the relationship. The Japanese have spared themselves this difficulty by designating as mentors senior persons who do not exercise direct line authority over their junior colleagues. The Japanese thus avoid the dangers of parentalism with avuncularism. The French system differs from both the American and the Japanese systems. It encourages mentoring among equals. Workers do not compete against one another directly for promotion through performance. Promotion comes through external examination. The French system, whatever its other defects, reduces face-to-face competitiveness and encourages more solidarity and mutual support on the office floor among colleagues at the same level. However accomplished, mentoring contributes to building responsibility throughout the corporate culture.

2. Serving effectively on committees and writing persuasive memoranda depend heavily on skills in speaking and writing out — horizontally — to colleagues. Those skills depend partly on the command of substance partly on skills in presentation to a wider audience of intelligent peers, and partly on a sensitivity to decorum. The social vector in relationship to peers is neither up, nor down, but out. It is collegial. Nothing so poisons the relationship to peers than obsequiousness on the one hand, or condescension on the other, or even worse, the fatal stupidity of choosing to teach others what they already know.

3. Junior colleagues, especially in staff positions, accept implicitly a corresponding obligation to teach their superiors on policy issues in their role as advisers. Such teaching, of course, in a purely contractualist setting means transmitting information that the boss can use instrumentally to reach preestablished goals. A great deal of teaching in professional life does just that, and should do that. But in a more inclusive covenantal setting, the adviser needs some space to raise substantive moral questions about goals. Otherwise, the very meaning and social justification for the professional, the knowledge expert, and the business leader diminish. Presumably, the professional generates power through knowledge placed at the service of human needs. It would be odd so to restrict the scope of this advisory service in the corporate setting as to provide the middle manager with less moral power than Balaam's ass, who posed an awkward question or two about the direction in which his master rode, or with less freedom to contest, argue, and explain than the maidservants possessed in Molière's comedies. The art of acting in concert with others reduces to a nimble timidity in subordinates if it can raise no substantive questions whatsoever about the common good. Undoubtedly corporations might change their structures to encourage their staffs to offer more prudent and courageous counsel. But any such proposed reforms would take us beyond the subject of the virtues to more structural and institutional issues in applied ethics.

Minerva's Owl: Building a Corporate Value System

William L. Weiss

I'm grateful for the opportunity to take part in this seminar on corporate ethics and values.

This is not only a chance for me to benefit from your research and thoughtful consideration of important issues. It is also an opportunity for me to offer some ideas of my own.

The theories generated in academia have significant long-term influence on the business community.

But it is also important for business people to join in the academic debate so we can help define these values. Just as a business can benefit from academic concepts, academic concepts can benefit from the pragmatism born of business experience.

A useful analogy comes from an article by Irving Kristol in the July 16 *Wall Street Journal.* Kristol writes and I quote from the text:

> The trouble with most economists is that, though they may teach the virtues of markets, they don't really believe in economics — in the truths established by a chain of rigorous reasoning that begins with hypothetical models and reaches to conclusions in the real world. To criticize an economic policy by saying that "it might work in practice but not in theory," would be regarded as somewhat peculiar by most people. But not by economists, who are doing it all the time, as they blandly subordinate obvious economic realities to their sovereign economic analysis.

William L. Weiss, "Minerva's Owl: Building a Corporate Value System," presented to the Workshop on Business Ethics, DePaul University, Chicago, Illinois, 26 July 1984.

Substitute "ethics" for "economics." Our task is to discuss and crystalize issues of a corporate value system — values that have meaning and are useful in reality, as well as in the forum that created them.

In short, we should be able not just to *define* a value system — we must be able to *live* by it!

Reexamining Inherited Values

Ameritech — the corporation I head — is in an unusually favorable position to reflect on values. We are a new corporation, half a year old. We are in the process of building a corporate culture for ourselves. We want to build our value system thoughtfully — by reexamining the values we inherit from our past, and by establishing fresh values appropriate to our new circumstances.

There is a saying attributed to Hegel that "Minerva's Owl takes flight only in the gathering dusk."

Minerva, as you know, is the goddess of wisdom, and so, I presume, of culture.

In my opinion, old cultural values are becoming obsolete. A new environment will bring forth new values, on which we will build a new corporate culture.

The dusk is beginning to gather on many years of regulatory orders, court decisions, and arbitrary changes in our industry. The competitive marketplace is beginning to rule.

Let us hope that the Owl of Wisdom can now take flight. As a way to begin, I will discuss some principles that can serve as the framework for the corporate values I wish to bring into focus today.

Determining a Value System

First, there is a question — that of corporate conscience. Is there such a thing? Or is it only the individual who has a conscience?

Conscience is a practical judgment about the morality of a concrete action or decision. Ultimately this means that the corporation's leadership must determine its value system and lead the management team to behavior that conforms to it.

I am not suggesting that individuals do not have their *individual* values — the ethical guidance system for their own lives.

It is clear to me that I cannot check my own value system at the door when I arrive at the office. I should be as comfortable at work as I am at home. I translate my own behavior into being willing to look into the mirror in the morning. I suspect this is not unique to me.

Cicero said, "The best audience for the practice of virtue is the approval of one's own conscience" (Disputations, II, 26). However there does result a *corporate* culture which effectively creates a *corporate* conscience. Given sufficient time, this set of ethical standards does begin to have its own momentum.

So a corporation *can* instill within its basic policy structure and patterns of behavior a corporate culture, a corporate conscience that can prevail.

Perhaps this is not "conscience" in the strict sense. I don't mean to get into a technical discussion about terminology. Whatever you call it, I am saying that a corporation can create a moral *environment,* a distinct set of *values* and *standards,* to which it holds its people accountable. If a person's individual values are significantly different, he will soon find he is in the wrong place. It is a key responsibility of corporate leadership to set the pattern and tone of this "conscience."

Ameritech wants to build a value system — a conscience — that will provide the momentum to prevail, and to endure. We want it to be a strong value system, one that insists that falling short of its standards will not be acceptable.

Second, reality is essentially ambiguous. Dilemmas arise not just between good and evil, but, most commonly, between the good *and* the good.

Difficult Choices

We are, of course, dealing with *perceived* good and *perceived* evil. There is often good even in a perceived evil. The choice is most difficult when one must decide which is the lesser of two perceived evils and choose accordingly.

This is why a manager must sometimes make a decision — one over which he has, perhaps, agonized — a decision that appears unethical to many.

Let me cite an example. Suppose there is a trend in business — as there has been — to offer financial incentives to encourage early retirement. A chief executive does not favor such a plan, and plainly says so to his employees. On the basis of his work, many employees take early retirement — employees who might have waited for the incentive to be offered, had the chief executive not expressed his views.

A year and a half later, the course of events in the business dictates that you *must* offer such incentives. What do you do? What comes first — the corporation's financial health, or your previously expressed views — which to the employee body were accepted as your given word?

You can walk down the whole list of such pragmatic questions and ask, "What is the *reality* of this issue?" There are very few easy answers.

The ideal exists only in the mind. The world itself is concrete, and human behavior is determined not only by principle but by circumstances.

Now, I am not attempting to establish that the end justifies the means — or that changed circumstances necessarily change one's obligation to ethical consistency. Perhaps the least I can offer is that a corporate conscience at least forces one to weigh a decision — any decision — within that framework.

A *third* principle is that values are related to purpose which is the governing value.

Every decision, every action, is for a purpose. Society's purpose for business is to contribute to economic well-being by producing and distributing goods and services. Making a profit is required to stay in business.

Interdependent Objectives

The various constituencies of business have their own objectives: share owners expect a return on their investment; employees look to it for a living, customers expect quality service and products at acceptable prices.

These are not necessarily conflicting interests, nor is it appropriate to ask which takes precedence. They are all *interdependent* — it is *together* that they produce results and share the benefits of the enterprise.

My experience tells me that, in business, if you spend much time trying to deal with the issues of integrity and ethics, you realize that there is no way to define a standard that makes ethical behavior easy.

No Easy Answers

But if you raise the level of consciousness about your responsibility, there is a good probability your decisions will tend to be more ethical — made within the integrity of the situation — than they would otherwise be.

That's poor solace for those who would opt for easy answers. But it *is* the reality. The complexity of our large corporations makes it almost impossible to anticipate all the ethical implications of a particular policy decision. What seems to be perfectly ethical at one level may be totally different at another — and it will be so evaluated by the people who eventually feel its effects.

It could not have been foreseen, for example, when the internal combustion engine was invented, that it would eventually cause a major problem by polluting the atmosphere.

So the inventor was not faced with an ethical dilemma. But now that we know the true implications of this form of power, what should the response be?

The tension between the environmentalist and the industrial managers illustrates my point — there are no easy answers. But ethical progress comes as a result of this heightened awareness.

With those thoughts as background, let me now mention some of the values I would like to see develop in my own corporation's emerging culture.

I say *some* of the values. Because we are still evolving our value system, still forming our identity, still thinking carefully about what we want to be.

My list of values starts with these:

- The dignity of the individual
- Openness to people and to ideas
- Optimum standards of service
- Entrepreneurship
- Synergism
- Leadership through competence
- Behavior based on values

Let me comment briefly on each of these.

The Dignity of the Individual

It is important to treat people with dignity. This has been repeated so frequently that just the saying seems trite. But, all current literature emphasizes that the truly successful corporations are those which have this as their dominant value.

It means not just saying it — but living it.

It means leading people to self-realization and giving them the freedom to achieve it.

I need not elaborate on this one. So many of the other values stem directly from it.

Openness to People and to Ideas

I would like to depart from the cultural norm that presupposes that each of us does the job better than anyone else.

This attitude means that we can't openly accept the ideas of others which might allow us to do the job, not just well, but better.

When Japanese business people visit our country, what do they want to know? The answer is simple — anything you tell them.

They'll take an idea home and, rather than dismiss it out of hand, they'll always be willing to try it. They want to be winners, and they don't care where the idea comes from.

It is said that the ancient Greeks and the Americans are originators. The ancient Romans and the Japanese are the assimilators.

It is good to be creative. But it is also good to be able to accept a good idea from wherever it comes.

Optimum Standards of Service

Ameritech comes from a culture in which service was a supreme value. This value is even more important to us now than it was before.

Previously, people had nowhere else to go for our products and services. Today the telecommunications industry is increasingly competitive.

Service is a value from our past that we must and will keep. We are determined to offer not just *good* service, not just *excellent* service, but the *best*.

We owe this to our customers. We owe this to our share owners, too. Because without being the best we will not earn the return share owners expect from us, we will not achieve the purpose for which we are in business.

Entrepreneurship

To give top quality service, and to treat people with dignity, you must give them significant latitude to accomplish their responsibility.

Ameritech is the parent corporation of 18 companies. The word "parent" implies leading for those for whom it is responsible to a mature, constructive future.

This is why we encourage initiative, why each of our companies is a distinct profit center. This is why we have chosen a decentralized rather than a centralized organizational structure, one that permits the subsidiary companies to operate within the fabric of a broad strategic plan.

We are firmly convinced that if we give people the freedom and motivation to do things on their own, the collective effort will be greater than the sum of the parts.

Synergism

This value tells us to move away from insularity and provincialism, to recognize that the corporation is part of the environment, part of the Gestalt.

It tells us to maximize the individual's contribution for the benefit of the whole corporation.

It tells us that our corporation is part of a larger social environment. We recognize that any business exists at the pleasure of society. A successful business must, therefore, take society's expectations into account.

We further recognize that our corporation, and our industry, have a role in shaping the general environment. We are determined, therefore, actively to promote public policy which we judge necessary to keep that environment healthy and to improve it, whenever possible.

Leadership through Competence

Ameritech intends to develop managers who assert their power through competence rather than coercion.

We believe in offering the maximum freedom to our people. Institutions of higher learning

treasure academic freedom. In business, we should treasure the freedom to manage our jobs.

Ameritech operates with a lean corporate staff. It does so because we are convinced that elaborate hierarchy is restrictive and debilitating and restrains creativity and initiative.

Behavior Based on Values

If behavior contradicts our espoused values, this leads to what the psychologists call "cognitive dissonance."

When a corporation enunciates a set of standards and does not abide by them — when we talk one way but *act* another — people are torn in two directions, become cynical, and cease to take the value system seriously.

This undermines the drive to corporate identity *and* to excellence.

It is important, therefore, to encourage behavior consonant with the corporations' values — even before the realization of attitude changes, which may require more time.

A few years ago, one company was visited by representatives of the Department of Labor and found to be out of compliance with the Affirmative Action agreement to which it was committed.

Management had worked for a long time to change attitudes. Yet the company was out of compliance.

So top management decided to change *behavior* and to worry about attitudes later.

Achieving Affirmative Action targets became a factor in management appraisal. The targets were met. Later, it is good to observe, attitude changes followed the behavior. The company now behaves in a way that is appropriate to its values.

Allow me a concluding remark. Although my corporation comes from a definite heritage, it is young. We are in the process of building a new corporate culture.

Guardians of the Vision

Corporate culture is largely a matter of shared values, which are the dominant ideas of the business. These values must be communicated; they must be *shared.*

I am acutely aware that culture is shaped by a

handful of people who are the guardians of the vision, *and* the shapers of the corporate conscience.

I know it is most especially the role of the chief executive officer to define the character of the business and to establish the corporate culture.

This is a responsibility I take seriously. And I am grateful for this opportunity to think through some of my ideas and attempt to articulate them.

Ameritech's culture is still in the process formation. There is still going to be a great deal of discussion about our values, an evolution of the culture itself.

I have three personal goals for my corporation.

- I would like each person in the organization to have a sense of pride in everything he or she does. I want them all to have the feeling that what they do is important, and that they have done the best job that could possibly have been done.
- I want everyone in Ameritech to have respect for one another, respect for their co-workers and for their ideas and aspirations . . . respect for our customers and their needs and expectations. Respect for others, in my book, is an essential characteristic. Without it, you cannot have *self-respect*.
- Finally, I want us to *trust* ourselves and to trust one another, so that together we can achieve more than we ever thought possible.

It is to achieve these goals that I am working to lay the foundation of a set of corporate values.

How Religious Commitments Shape Corporate Decisions

J. Irwin Miller

The corporate world is a complex world, and human beings, individually and collectively, still baffle themselves and defeat understanding.

How then shall one tackle the subject assigned?

After many false starts, I decided to begin with observations about the "corporate world" as I have experienced it, to proceed with guesses as to how that world appears to be changing, and somewhere along the line to hazard a few thoughts as to how "religious commitments" might and might not provide a reliable guide through this still little-known land.

The Corporate World

Let us begin then with a brief discussion of the corporate world. The most important opening comment I can make is: One lone person almost never makes a complete decision all by himself or herself. Many persons are involved in even small decisions. The use of the team in decision-making is spreading.

Members of corporations and members or teams are individual humans, with different inheritances, different genes, different experiences, and different views of "religion," however we like to define that difficult word. Can a group or a team possess anything that could be called a "religious

J. Irwin Miller, "How Religious Commitments Shape Corporate Decisions," *Harvard Divinity Bulletin,* Feb.-March 1984, pp. 4-6.

commitment," something different from the commitments held individually by its members? To what extent should the "boss's" personal commitments carry through the corporation and override the commitments of subordinates? To what extent should an individual hazard the execution of an agreed-upon plan by interposing his or her own "religious commitments"?

That is one category of questions. Another category is, what kinds of corporate decisions are we talking about? Are we talking about competition for example? What is "Christian" competition or "ethical" competition? How does a manager improve market share at the expense of competitors and remain consistent with Christian teaching? How does he "lose his life," "turn the other cheek," "walk the second mile," "love his neighbor as himself" in the world of economic competition?

Then there is the "hostile takeover," so popular today. Economically it is often very much more profitable to take over another corporation against its will than to invest capital in the long process of developing, tooling, marketing and establishing a new product. Do "religious commitments" have any bearing here?

Or the whole world of people, and here let us use as example a common retirement decision. "Good old Joe" has headed a department for ten years, is vigorous, has done a better than fair job, but he dreads his sixty-fifth birthday. He passionately does not want to retire. He has no real interests other than his job, and his wife does not look forward to having him home for lunch every day. Right behind "good old Joe" is a quite able person, 20 years younger, fully capable of doing the job, and almost certain to do it better. Do "religious commitments" urge you to retire Joe on schedule, sending him to an idle frantically boring existence, perhaps to a heart attack, or to condemn the able younger person to five or more years of continued underemployment, and the department to mediocre leadership?

Advertising? What if "all the competition does it," gaining sales and market share for a quite-ordinary product by inventing hi-tech names for it and casting around it an irresistible aura of words? Do "religious commitments" permit you to do it too, or do they urge you to lose out in the marketplace, laying off people in the process?

Or bribes? If you, the boss, are willing to pay some third-world cabinet minister a considerable but affordable bribe, you will secure a long-term contract, which will increase employment and profits. If you refuse, your own standard of living may not suffer, but you will have to lay off 1,000 workers to keep the company solvent, and the West Germans will not hesitate to pay the bribe and take the contract.

More often than not, you, the boss, pay little price personally for following your "religious commitments," and you may even gain a warm feeling of self-righteousness from the praise you receive from churches and editors. Meanwhile, persons who had no part in your decision pay a very real price indeed — the laid-off workers, the man retired against his will, shareholders, suppliers, communities.

Let me suggest that you not relax too much while I wrestle with this subject. You Divinity students who are headed for the parish ministry may be plunged into the middle of such questions your first week on the job. What will you say to your parishioner, the middle-level manager, aged 55, ten years from retirement, two kids in college, at his age unemployable elsewhere, when he says to you:

Pastor, I'm responsible for our Jakarta, Indonesia, office. The corporation I work for has a written policy of *no bribes*. I agree with it in principle.

But next week a shipment of spare parts urgently needed by our customers, valued at $1,000,000, will arrive in Jakarta. Our employee there is waiting for me to tell him what to do. If he slips the customs official $100, the shipment will be promptly cleared. If he refuses to do so, we will never see those parts again — except on the black market.

As a Christian, do I tell him to pay the bribe or not?

If I call company headquarters, the answer I will probably get is 'You know the policy. If you can't manage without running to headquarters with every little problem, maybe we'd better find another man for your job.' If I tell him to pay, we violate company rules. Then, when I go by the book and tell our Jakarta employee 'no bribe,' and we lose a million-dollar parts shipment, headquarters will scream 'what kind of manager are you anyhow, losing a million dollar shipment?!'

Pastor, as a Christian, married, two kids to educate, ten years from retirement, a pension to preserve, what do I do? I've got to call Jakarta this afternoon.

Now, you will have many options. The shortest one is to say "Do right. Don't do wrong. Glad you came to see me. My door is always open." If you pick that one, you had better be braced for four-letter words, however.

Another option will be to tell him that corporate America is a cruel system indeed, that it must be changed in the interest of equity and justice not only for exploited workers, but as well for trapped middle managers like himself. You can even add that, as a convinced Christian, you are going to dedicate your own ministry to working for political, economic, and social change. That may hearten him, but what if he goes on to say, "That's great, but what do I tell our employee in Jakarta this afternoon?"

You can also say "Let's pray about it." This might or might not work. It will probably not work if your prayer is no more than conventional connected phrases of professional pulpit language. It might work if your man is comfortable with prayer, and if you are yourself confidently clear about the range of issues involved in his problem, and can so present them that he can be helped to see how to work toward an answer.

There are other options too, but as a Christian minister one of your options is not to bug out, not to say "Well, I am not a businessman. I really know nothing about international trade practices. You certainly have a tough problem all right."

All corporate decisions are tough, and they are tough because, out in the world of organized human endeavor the decision-maker almost never has the luxury of choosing between right and wrong, instead nearly always finds himself or herself forced to choose between two wrongs.

Either way he or she goes injures someone. Either way he or she can be fairly accused of having caused hurt, of acting insensitively, of being concerned only with pursuing the dollar. In addition, it is the peculiar nature of corporate decisions that usually someone else gets hurt — not the decision-maker.

Commitment in a Murky World

In this complex, baffling world, how then do religious commitments shape decisions? The correct answers is "in ways both good and bad."

Religious commitments have from the beginning of recorded history been used by decision-makers to justify what they wanted to do. *"Quantum religio potuit saudere malorum,"* says the poet Lucretius. I shouldn't have to translate that either in Harvard or in a Divinity school, but I will: "How great are the evils to which religion has been able to persuade (men)." Rulers, popes, churches, individual men and women have used religion to justify doing what they want.

We once had a customer who proclaimed "The Lord is my partner" and maintained an exhausting preaching schedule every weekend. Because the Lord was his partner, he felt he could do no wrong, and we came to know that no agreement or contract with him was worth the paper it was written on. An experienced bank examiner told me that, if a small-town banker was exceptionally pious, it was the examiner's rule to go over his books at least twice, and if, in addition, he sang in the choir, they gave his records a third look. Today we have also the Ayatollah Khomeini, who at least some of us consider to be using religion rather than being led by it.

Then there is another human response to religious commitments. One can simply wall them off from the difficult demands of business life and the real world. Sir John Bowring, who was in 1854 Superintendent of British Trade in China, could precipitate and win the second opium war with China, and over fierce Chinese resistance, force the Chinese to introduce Indian opium into their country. During the same years this man of many talents could compose and leave for us the great hymns, "God is love; His mercy brightens / All the path in which we rove," as well as "Watchman, tell us of the night, / What its signs of promise are" and "In the cross of Christ I glory, / Towering o'er the wrecks of time."

Nor is this capacity for compartmentization confined to commercial types and to great rulers. I have seen professors of theology and ethics maintain deceitful private lives. As a long-time trustee of educational institutions, I have observed fiercely liberal faculties, willing to write and demonstrate for the rights of minorities and women, but never to admit either to their own departments, claiming that they would not be party to lowering "quality" through submission to quotas. We have read of scholars who from envy put down fellow scholars, and of research fellows who entered false data in their reports.

We don't like to look at our real unvarnished behavior. It is uncomfortable to be reminded that hell is probably inhabited less by sensational criminals than by ordinary, dull people of only mildly shabby thoughts and motives.

I have a reason for this approach to our subject. I want us to remember clearly that the world of decision-making is a very murky world indeed, that the people who inhabit it are just like ourselves, neither better nor worse, and that it is in such a world that we must all exercise our religious commitments, corporate, group, or individual.

I want us not to forget that there is a sense in which religious commitments can be quite neutral. Just as a hammer can be used either to drive a nail or smash a thumb, so religious commitments can be used to make us feel very good while doing what we want to do, or they can be a reliable guide through the darkness that we create of ourselves.

I don't want to harp on this, but to me there is something unique and especially frightening about exercising religious commitments, when that exercise involves a price paid by another person. The CEO says to "good old Joe" at 65, "You've got to go. It's not fair to Bill, who has been waiting ten years for a crack at your job. I have to be fair in this thing." But the CEO himself keeps on working, sometimes past retirement age.

The President of the United States says "we" must stay in Lebanon. It is not moral to let international terrorism go unpunished. But *he* will not pay the price for being "moral." Only young marines and their families will pay.

The Morality within Us

So now we turn to "religious commitments." I have so far discussed decisions with a moral content only in terms of the price paid for living up to the "moral content." In all this I have not meant to imply that we are somehow freer in a decision-

making world from which religious commitments are excluded, or that in such a world the prices paid are less onerous, or perhaps not at all painful.

At this point, considering that we are in a Divinity school, it should not be embarrassing to quote Scripture. Consider this very familiar passage from the Ten Commandments:

> Honor your father and your mother, that your days may be long in the land which the Lord, your God gives you.

And these less familiar ones from the book of Proverbs:

> My son, do not forget my teaching but let your heart keep my commandments; For length of days and years of life and abundant welfare will they give you.

> Let not loyalty and faithfulness forsake you; bind them about your neck, write them on the tablet of your heart.

> Trust in the Lord with all your heart, and do not rely on your own insight. In all your ways acknowledge Him and He will make straight your paths.

> Be not wise in your own eyes; fear the Lord, and turn away from evil. It will be healing to your flesh and refreshment to your bones.

> Honor the Lord with your substance and with the first fruits of all your produce; Then your barns will be filled with plenty, and your vats will be bursting with wine. (Prov. 3:1-10)

And one from the New Testament:

> Do not be anxious about your life, what you shall eat, nor about your body, what you shall put on. . . . Instead seek His kingdom, and these things shall be yours as well.

Why do I give you these quotes, so familiar in our culture as to have become little more than clichés or the subject of the very dullest sermons? Well, it is only the first half of each quote that has become the cliché. No one seems to notice the second half of each. It is our custom to treat it as a throw-away line:

> That your days may be long. . . .

> He will make straight your paths. . . .

> Abundant welfare will they give you. . . .

> It will be healing to our flesh and refreshment to your bones. . . .

> All these things shall be yours as well.

If we are permitted to change the sign of this language to the negative, it is asserting that the opposite kind of behavior, the flaunting of the Judaeo-Christian ethic, as unmitigated disaster, here and now, individually and collectively.

Let's examine this.

There are two principal concepts of ethics in the Western world. One is that of Aristotle. To state it in simplistic terms, Aristotle viewed ethics as conduct which is generally recognized or which is generally accepted by society at a given time. For him ethics were evolutionary and changing in nature and could be expected to vary from culture to culture or from century to century.

The Judaeo-Christian view, as exemplified in the passages I have just quoted, asserts that there are laws of human behavior which are akin to and to which we are as subject as we are to the laws of the physical universe. It maintains that in any age or in any culture we violate the laws of human behavior at the same peril with which we violate the law of gravity, that "love your neighbor as yourself" was as valid in Sumer and Akkad as it is in Kalamazoo. This view further assumes that each of us really *knows* these laws of behavior or, as Dr. Johnson said, that "we need more often to be reminded than informed."

Two illustrations: In Victorian England the prevailing sentiment was for the sanctity of property rights. When, therefore, in 1846 at the height of the potato famine, Mrs. Gerrard in County Galway, Ireland, evicted on one day all 300 of her tenants, none of whom was in arrears, so that her holdings might be turned into a grazing farm, Lord Brougham, speaking, in the House of Lords, felt she was acting most ethically indeed. Said he,

"Property would be valueless and capital would no longer be invested in cultivation of land if it was not acknowledged that it was the landlord's undoubted, indefeasible, and most sacred right to deal with his property as he wishes." His Lordship asserted this to be a most ethical act, indeed a "sacred right," because it was in accord with the prevailing tone and sentiment of the ruling class at that time.

Illustration number 2: Huckleberry Finn has just helped Miss Watson's slave, Jim, escape. Both were on a raft in the Mississippi, but Huck left to go ashore as they floated past Cairo, Illinois. Here speaks Huck:

> Conscience says to me, "What has poor Miss Watson done to you that you could see her nigger go right off under your eyes and never say one single word?" . . . Right then along comes a skiff with two men in it with guns, and they stopped, and I stopped. One of them says: "What's that yonder?" "A piece of a raft" I says, "Do you belong to it?" "Yes, Sir." "Any men on it?" "Only one, Sir." "Well, there's five niggers run off tonight. Is your man white or black?"

> I didn't answer up prompt. I tried to, but the words wouldn't come. I tried, for a second or two, to brace up and out with it, but I warn't man enough — hadn't the spunk of a rabbit. I see I was weakening, so I just give up trying, and up and says "he's white."

Huck, unlike His Lordship, felt he was acting unethically. He had told a lie. He had violated the law, and gone against prevailing custom as well.

It is remarkable and significant that you and I, in this room, will come down unanimously in condemning the "ethical act" of Mrs. Garrett, and again unanimous in approving the morality of Huck Finn's answer. The Judaeo-Christian assertion that there are abiding laws of human behavior that hold through centuries, through changing cultures, customs, and laws is implanted deep in us. Even Aristotle, in a weak moment, understood this when he said, "In so far as we may, we should practice immortality and omit no effort to live in accordance with the best that is in us."

Fascinating phrase, "the best that is in us." The best that is in us is probably specifically what Christianity is about. It is in this sense that we are called children of God, that we are exhorted to be perfect.

An earlier Greek, Aeschylus, in the *Eumenides,* sounds like our quotes from Proverbs: "Him who pitieth suffering men Zeus pitieth, and his ways are sweet on earth." And Socrates adds to the chorus. When Glaucon in *The Republic* says that Socrates' "City of God" is too ideal and after all does not exist "anywhere on this earth." Socrates lets him have it, again reminiscent of Proverbs with its promise: "Glaucon, whether such a city exists in Heaven or ever will exist on earth, the wise man will live after the manner of that city, having nothing to do with any other, and, in so looking upon it, will set his own house in order."

What a promise!

Now I have done all this quoting in order to remind ourselves that the subject of human behavior has since very ancient times been in the thoughts of humans and that there may be more unconscious agreement than we think.

Is "human behavior" what religion is about? And is that what is meant by the subject assigned me, the effect of religious commitments on corporate decision-making?

Here I must give expression to a very personal bias. I believe that somewhere out there truth exists. Even that may not be so in our terms of definition, but I believe it. I believe also that humans are by nature consumed to discover truth, and forever tormented that they cannot find it. The Old Testament says, "He has put eternity into man's mind, yet so that he cannot find out what God has done from the beginning to the end." And Paul says, "Now we see through a glass darkly," an understatement if there ever was one.

So in the midst of uncertainty we invent certainty. Unable to sample the wine in the bottle, we become arrogant connoisseurs of bottles, labels, and tin foil, that is to say the niceties of doctrine, and proclaim others orthodox or heretical according to how they feel about the bottles, the labels, and the tin foil, not about the wine.

Wisdom in the Workplace

We do not know the origin of the word *religion.* It could mean our tie back to God. Or it could also mean those standards of conduct and belief which bind us. There is no exact word for *religion* in New Testament Greek. If we inspect our concordance, we will find only six instances (and three different words) in the whole Bible which we translate *religion* versus over 500 references to the word *love.*

So in this talk I am operating on the assumption that we are to discuss how our religious commitments should affect *our behavior toward others,* collective and individual, in the world of corporate decision-making.

Let me begin with some negative statements about the times in which we live, and in which we have to exercise our religious commitments: There is a conviction broadly held today that human relations, individually and collectively, are inescapably adversary.

The marriage relationship, for example: There is a new custom, to write a contract before marriage, specifying not commitments to each other, but retained individual rights, and the limits of the responsibilities of each partner, how many nights out!

Or in business: M.B.A.'s learn in business schools to be hesitant to commit to employer or to peers. But be certain to determine one's own career ladder, which comes before anything else.

Single-minded pursuit by the corporation of maximum profits restrained only by limits of the law, the teaching today's reigning school of economists, encourages stretching the law, exploitation of positions of power, pursuit of maximum overtime by shop workers, polluted streams and rivers, and dropping the word "bribe" in favor of "sensitive payment."

The universities: Shortages of tenured positions involve putting down the supposed competitor as much as proving one's own race worth. The flank attack on some enthusiastic adjective is often a more prized and useful strategy than thoughtful open-minded consideration of substance. Women's Lib too often leaves the poor to gain their own rights, and white males battle against what they happily call "reverse discrimination."

Single-minded pursuit of one' own self-interest, exploiting or disregarding others, is dignified today for the individual by such phrases as "self-fulfillment" and "identity crisis." For groups of individuals it seeks to gain respectability by means of phrases like "national honor," "free enterprise," and "worker solidarity." The fashionable current school of philosophy, whether it intends to do so or not, dignifies raw personal self-seeking.

To all this I must ask, "When has it ever worked?" Let me pass over the great lessons of history: Athens and her colonies, Rome and her corrupt and competing emperors, the Borgia Pope, Alexander VI, Britain and the massacre at Amritsar, or the Boer War, or our own President Wilson's landing at Vera Cruz.

Let's go straight to American business.

I have time only for assertions. Perhaps you can make me justify myself later with your questions. American business is not competing well in this world, in good part because at every level, shop floor to top management, it is substantially over-staffed. Work simplification, job descriptions, organization charts all now tend to reinforce the great American phrase, "That's not part of my job."

So we have the most exquisite division of work, not only under union contract (as management likes to suppose) but throughout the ranks of management itself. And we have highly paid men and women unhappily doing trivial work, and we are only beginning to discover that unnecessary costs mean uncompetitive costs, and loss of markets, and, of course, finally loss of jobs, with persistently high unemployment.

Back to the Old Testament: "Whatsoever thy hand findeth to do, do it with thy might." This ancient wisdom is being rediscovered in a few very exciting spots. With reasonable confidence, I think we can say that the result in several corporations is that at least a third fewer persons can perform the same operation better, faster, with fewer mistakes, higher quality, better pay, a say in how the work is done, and a rewarding feeling in the job, all with lower prices for consumers.

The promises from Proverbs!

Perhaps at this point you would like to puncture my not-so-innocent enthusiasm by asking, "Yes, but who's going to employ all these people we don't need for today's work?" That's a fair question, and there are at least three comments to be made in return. The first is that they may not be employed anyhow, if lower-cost producers drive them from the marketplace. The second is a return question: Are there today no unmet needs in the society that need filling? Are there no new prod-ucts that might be imagined to make life easier or more fun? Is there no hunger to be relieved, or poverty to be addressed? The third is an admission: change is coming so rapidly that there will be inescapable hardship. Ancient skills will disappear as did the skills of cottage industry on the coming of the Industrial Revolution. The old will suffer most and will be least amenable to retraining. Our nation has a high and most prudent responsibility to see that the hardships of the rapid change are shared equitably, top to bottom, and not borne only by those least able to bear them.

We went through such an experience once, only at a much more gradual pace. In 1800 over 85 percent of our working population was employed in agriculture. Today it is less than 2 percent, and very few persons any longer know how to sharpen a scythe. This time the speed of change is out of our control. We have only the privilege of reacting to it, extracting benefit from it if we can. The power to arrest it, or slow it down, I believe, is not ours.

How shall we react to it humanely and intelligently? How shall we avoid social chaos and personal tragedy in the face of its lightning speed? I think that here is where our religious commitments could give us a nudge, if we will permit them to do so. They might help us to bring our corporate and national behavior into line with those everlasting laws which each of us knows all too well, laws which we are too fearful to practice in so much of our corporate conduct.

To mention just a few, we can modify our concept of the job — from one which reduces each job to its very simplest, to one which utilizes the full intelligence, capacity, education, and experience of the job-holder. There is a "wisdom of the workplace," largely untapped by American industry. Utilizing it to the full will avoid costly error. It will lower costs, and improve quality, and it will produce men and women who are fully challenged and excited about what they do, because they have a say in what they do and in what happens to them, and because they are consulted. This may indeed be the new definition of "full employment": men and women who are for the first time fully employed.

Religious commitments may also urge us to find new profitable work for those displaced and to commit our own capital to such ventures.

There are some further implications of this way

of working. We are beginning already, I think, to see the disappearance of *rank*. The concept of the "supervisor" is becoming less than useful. "Rank" has usually meant, in the final analysis, "Never mind what you think. Do it. I'm the boss." Rank sets little value on the "wisdom of the workplace" and undervalues opinions of subordinates, precisely because they are subordinate. The principles of rank in the future can be very costly indeed.

The very word, "supervisor" in its etymology means looking over (someone's shoulder) to see that he does his work right. In our present work culture, the responsibility for doing accurate, quality work is not that of the person doing the work. It is the responsibility of the supervisor, who is there to check on him. The worker's responsibility is to satisfy his boss, a fundamentally humiliating, depersonalizing way to spend your life.

I think this is changing. Instead of a pyramid of rank and supervision, I believe we are moving toward a division of responsibilities. In such a world, each person becomes responsible for what he or she does.

Inspectors, technicians, those who carry multiple responsibilities are there — not to boss — but to help, to train, to bring to bear other resources, to offer judgment. We are beginning to discover the wisdom of each person's accepting full responsibility for doing well, efficiently, and on time, the task assigned, and for giving full cooperation to all others who are a part of his or her workstream.

It is only a guess on my part that this kind of change is developing in America. Old habits are hard to change, and we may not change. If we fail to change, I think it is the end of us. After all, we have already lasted longer than Athens did.

If we change too slowly, we shall become an impoverished nation, highly paid in dollars of no value. But, if we lead change, then once more all the promises can be ours.

These are no new thoughts. In 1927, fifty-seven years or two generations ago, Owen D. Young, head of General Electric, spoke these words here in Cambridge, at the opening of the Harvard Business School:

I hope the day may come when these great business organizations will truly belong to the men who are giving their lives and their efforts to them, I care not in what capacity. Then they will use capital truly as a tool and they will be all interested in working it to the highest economic advantage. Then an idle machine will mean to every man in the plant who sees it an unproductive charge against himself. Then every piece of material not in motion will mean the man who sees it an unproductive charge against himself. Then we shall have zest in labor, provided the leadership is competent and the division fair. Then we shall dispose, once and for all, of the charge that in industry organizations are autocratic and not democratic. Then we shall have all the opportunities for cultural wage which the business can provide. Then, in a word, men will be as free in co-operative undertakings and subject only to the same limitations and chances as men in individual businesses. Then we shall have no hired men. That objective may be a long way off, but it is worthy to engage the research and efforts of the Harvard School of Business.

Then, too, we must deal with this question of unemployment, which I regard as the greatest economic blot to our capitalistic system. There is no answer except that the managers of business have not yet learned how to make their system function so that men willing and able to work may do so. There is no limit to the consumption of the world. It is limited only in its individual compartments. We cannot wear more than so many clothes, and so we may have over-production in individual lines. But there are innumerable wants of men yet unserved, and as long as culture grows, these wants will outrun our capacity to produce the things to satisfy them. The world does not owe men a living, but business, if it is to fulfill its ideal, owes men an opportunity to earn a living.

How sad for the generations of workers in the intervening years, how sad for our country, that neither the Harvard Business School nor the American business community heard the words of Mr. Young! Had they listened the Golden Age might already be within our grasp.

I am unable to wind up these remarks without a comment for the benefit of the young about the criteria for employment which all this implies. In a world where more and more persons must be self-motivated, must essentially do their work unsupervised, must gain knowledge of the whole process of which they are a part, and must self-lessly work for the perfection of that process, and for the success of their neighbors, in such a world the customary criteria — college degrees, class standings, professional certificates, even experience — while still important, will nevertheless take second place to unfamiliar words like character, commitment, trust, loyalty, faithfulness.

Perhaps this is a good place to turn again to Proverbs:

> Let not loyalty and faithfulness forsake you. Bind them about your neck. Write them on the tablet of your heart. . . .

and the promise:

> It will be healing to your flesh, and refreshment to your bones.

Is this where "religious commitments" and "corporate decisions" intersect? If it is, I can tell you it will be hardest of all for the chief executive officer and the university-trained manager to understand, to accept, and to accommodate to the change required.

Demanding loyalty, faithfulness, and trust from their employees is natural and easy. Can managers in turn learn what it means, *themselves* to offer commitment and trust first, before they receive it, taking the high risk in confidence of the promise?

The affairs of men and women are today in greater disarray than at any time I can remember. That is not at all to say that once there were the good old times. Rather, we have come to a time, through our own cleverness, when the whole race is crowded together, elbow to elbow, by the airplane, the city, the telephone, TV, and now the computer. There remains little individual or national privacy.

No one did this to us. We did it to ourselves.

If we allow ourselves to yield to aggressive irritation and recrimination, we are surely done for. If, however, we are somehow able to act, individually and collectively, in reasonable accordance with that great phrase, "the best that is in us," we might even construct for ourselves a Golden Age. That is the promise, and it is the right and duty of religion in every age, not alone to cry "repent, lest you perish," but to remind us of the promises as well.

Values Don't Work in Business

Dennis Bakke

If you'd step back a number of years with me to the industrial revolution, I'd like to think about the fundamental assumptions that the industrial revolution was based on regarding people and organizations, the key fundamental assumptions that people had in mind during that time upon which they based the organizations and the treatment of people in organizations and enterprise situations. I'd love to hear your ideas on that; but I'll give you my own perspective, that people were basically considered inputs, capital, material, and labor. . . . And labor, the very word used by economists, has probably done as much harm in the understanding of who people are and of their place in enterprise and organization than any other single word used by economists.

People were considered machines, sometimes super machines, but definitely an input. That was the assumption. Some people were the thinkers and the planners, and other people were the doers. People could not be trusted, and therefore a chain of command and a control system were necessary. Finally, you wanted efficiency in organization — a wonderful concept when it deals with machinery but a terrible concept when it deals with people. The concept of efficiency — and I don't mean just business efficiency — has done irreparable harm to the way we operate our institutions, our organizations; it doesn't belong in any organizational setting.

Dennis Bakke, "Values Don't Work in Business," edited from an audiotaped extemporaneous speech given at Calvin College, Grand Rapids, Michigan, 16 April 1991.

My hypothesis today is that most of these assumptions, although prettied up and dressed up in new clothes and new techniques, fundamentally still exist in almost all of our churches, almost all of our colleges, all of our hospitals, and most of our businesses.

I'd like to switch gears a bit now and talk about AES, the company my co-founder and I started. In AES we are trying a different approach from this in terms of fundamental assumptions. Some of this will be very familiar to a lot of you who probably have gone much further than we have in some of these areas, but we have tried to make a start. I should mention that AES is not a Christian company, and it employs no more than an ordinary number of Christians. But we started the company with a very strong set of values, and I'll go through them, four of them, and they're really not unusual, as you'll see.

The first is integrity. By integrity we mean wholeness or completeness, that the organization and what it does fits together in some kind of integral totality. What we do and say in one part of the organization is related to all the other parts. The company is integrated, a unified whole.

The second value is fairness, justice in the biblical sense. I don't mean equality, but I mean fairness. We have tried very hard to figure out how to deal with both integrity and fairness in terms of objective measurement. It's very hard. The best we'd probably do in the fairness area is just to make sure that everyone always asks one question inside our company, that when every decision is made, someone says, "Is that fair? Would you feel the same way about this if you were on the other side of the table?" Whether it's with a customer, a fellow AES person, or someone outside the company in the community we need to act with integrity and fairness.

The third value is social responsibility. By social responsibility, of course, we mean the interaction of the whole company with the outside world. Through our social interaction, all of what we do is redeemed. Perhaps at this point it would be a good idea to step back and look at what we think is the purpose of all companies and all enterprise. Many people would say that the main or only purpose of business is to turn a profit. Certainly when I talked at Northwestern University last night and asked those folks what was the purpose of business, that was a predominant answer.

We don't believe that. In fact, we believe that the purpose of business, and I dare say a lot of nonprofit and government organizations as well — the purpose of enterprise in general — is to steward resources to meet a need in society. I think it's very important for AES that we start with that kind of premise, because everything else follows from that premise. The purpose of our business is to steward the resources of minds, capital, material, and creativity that we have been given in order to meet a need in society — in our particular case, a need for electricity around the world. The other values I've mentioned — integrity, fairness, and social responsibility — follow from that stewardship. What we want is for the whole company to be redeemed in the sense that all of what we do is to meet a need in society, and part of that is the extra dimension of social responsibility.

We carry these three values out in the company in a number of ways. We try to have the very safest plants. We try to have plants that are tremendously good citizens in our communities. And we've had a special emphasis on the environment, because our plants have the potential for tremendous emissions. We use coal, for example, which could be a tremendous environmental problem; but we've tried to make our plants the cleanest in the world. In every plant we've built we've tried to do some innovative thing to lessen our impact on the environment.

For example, in one plant in Texas we take the sulphur out of the fuel with a limestone scrubber, a technology that a lot of other people use. Limestone is calcium, and when we take the sulphur out we get a calcium sulphate. Then we add an extra molecule and dry it and make it into gypsum. We sell it to US Gypsum, six miles away, and US Gypsum then makes it into wallboard. Last year we made about 3 percent of the new housing starts worth of wallboard from the waste products from that plant. So we have essentially a closed-cycle power plant in terms of solid waste.

Our plant that probably has gotten the most attention is our plant in Connecticut. About three years ago, the question of global warming had not quite hit the popular press but was very evident to our own studies and concern in Washington, where our principal office is. We were concerned that we produce a huge amount of CO_2, and CO_2 looked like it was one of the gases that could cause a global warming. We looked around for some high-tech solutions and couldn't come up with anything for a long time, but finally one of our people said, "You know, trees eat CO_2, they're a great CO_2 eater. Why don't we plant trees?" So we tried to figure out how much CO_2 a 180 megawatt power plant would produce in forty years and how many trees it would take to absorb it. We found out one other interesting fact. It didn't matter where you planted the trees. It only takes about two or three weeks for the mixing of the winds and the like to equalize the benefits around the world. So we went around the world looking for a place to plant some trees, and we ended up finding a program with CARE in Guatemala where we're planting 52 million trees over the next ten years to offset the entire CO_2 emissions from this power plant in Connecticut for the next forty years.

We're going to do that with all of our plants from here on in. Not because we have to, not because anyone has suggested that — in fact, people thought it was somewhat crazy — but because we believe it's consistent with our social responsibility values.

The final value we've tried to instill in AES is fun, a somewhat inelegant term, but we couldn't think of anything else to call it. We really want to have fun, and by fun we don't mean party-type fun, but we mean creating an environment where people can use their gifts and skills in such a way that they reach out to meet needs in society. Now, we've tried some interesting things to make that happen. The first thing we had to do, though, was to think hard about what assumptions about people might help in creating an organization that might be fun. And we had to reject the ones I described to you earlier that come out of the industrial revolution. I mean really reject them as a deliberate, fundamental decision. At first it was easy, because the people who were working with us in the early stages of development of the company were MBA's coming out of Harvard. But later as we started building power plants and hiring people with different kinds of backgrounds, there was the tendency to forget or not understand the assumptions we were making about people when we set those plants up. Since we didn't know anything about operations, we went with very much the traditional ways of doing things to start with

— very successfully, by the way. But we gradually realized that the assumptions behind the way we were treating people were the same as the industrial revolution types. So we made some changes.

The first thing we did was to deliberately change our assumptions about people. We said that the assumptions need to be that people are thinking, creative, responsible individuals. And a whole panoply of things have followed from that. We've created an organization that has no more than two layers of supervision between my office and any entry-level position all around the world, just two layers. We have no shift superintendents or foreman in any of our plants. We have no major staff operations in our whole company. We have no general counsel's office. We have no finance department, and yet we've raised 2½ billion dollars over the past five years for our plants. Above all, we have no human resources or personnel department because we think this function is too important to be left to some specialist operation separate from our supervisors. We have no public relations department, no engineering department (although, of course, we have a huge amount of engineering going on), and no safety department, although we want to have the best safety record of any company in our industry.

We require every officer to work for one week every year in one of the plants, and our highest level meetings, the operating committee which meets once a month, are open to every person in the company who happens to be there. We sometimes go to the plants to hold these meetings so that people in the plants can attend as well. Every piece of financial information and every other information is delegated and given to every person in the company. There are no limits as to how much any one person can buy in the company with regard to capital investments, which are all delegated. There is no capital budgeting process as such. There are no salary grades. There are no job descriptions written, by design, and there are no employee handbooks to tell you that when your mother or dad or grandmother dies you can have four days off, but if they live in Stockholm you get five days off, and so on and so forth.

Notice that the element that has been left completely out of our company list of values is this business of profits, and on this point I agree completely with Max De Pree's view of profits. Profits are a likely and necessary result if in fact you are doing a good job of meeting a need in society. But the fact is that values ought to be separate from the issue of profits. Profits are not the goal, at least we're trying at AES not to make them *the* goal.

We articulated these goals about two years after we started the company, and there were a number of very skeptical folks among the leadership in the company. But we went ahead and articulated them and started trying to live by them, and I must say these values are much more a statement of who we would like to be, our aspirations, than a description of who we really are. We obviously are never going to fully reach where we'd like to be regarding these values; but we issued the statements anyway and started trying to apply them.

A couple of years later we had a group of leaders of the company together in a meeting. We were talking about how things had gone with regard to the values, and a couple of the vice presidents who had been really skeptical earlier said, "Don't worry about these, Roger, Dennis. These are fantastic. We love these values. They really work." There was dead silence, and both Roger and I turned somewhat white and thought to ourselves, we have, in fact, done something very wrong. We didn't choose these values because we thought they would work. We chose these values because they are right. We tried to explain that then, and we have continued to try to explain this every day of our lives. These values are an end in themselves and not a means to an end.

Bob Waterman, a good friend who is on our board and has had a great influence on our company, called about three weeks ago. He's writing a new book and AES is a major part of that book, and he said, "I finally realized after all these years what the difference is between the Hewlett Packards and the other great companies that I'm writing about in a values driven way and AES, and that is that the values of AES are not, in fact, part of your strategy. There's nothing that says if you do these values, that's going to lead to customers who like us better, or employees who are going to work better, or higher profits or whatever."

Some of you may have thought that the title of this talk, "Values Don't Work in Business," was a misprint, but I think that it is one of the major problems that exists in the country today with all the emphasis that now exists with regard to ethics and values. There are schools, fine old schools like Harvard and Kellogg, who were in fact thinking about setting up ethics programs and the like. I think that is extremely dangerous and something that Christians should not be fooled about.

Let me just tell you about another conversation I had with Bob Waterman last winter about this book he is writing. "Are there any companies out there that you know of who have the kind of values structure that we're talking about here, but are not doing very well economically, are doing lousy?" He thought for a moment and said, "Yes," and he named one. I said, "Why don't you write about them?" and he said, "It won't sell." It is simply the case that the hottest topic, the hottest technique for getting to the golden numbers today, is ethics and values. Another friend said in a recent little note, "There is money in green. There is money in being environmentally sensitive. Go for it!"

As I conclude, I'd like to point out several problems with that kind of mentality, the kind of thinking that asks, "What difference does it make when people start acting the right way?" I think there are three problems with this connection between values and profits or improved relations with customers and so forth. One, it's simply not true. Those of you who are believers know that the rain falls on the good and evil alike. In fact, there is an article that came out in the *Harvard Business Review* not too long ago that says something like, if honesty doesn't pay, why be honest? It's a whimsical article. I recommend it to all of you. It talks about this business, just exactly the problem that the good guys don't always win and the bad guys do win. I think that in fact God created the world to be a place where these kinds of values will probably produce better results, so it isn't surprising if good things happen. But we all know that we are in rebellion and that the world is not like that, and in fact often people who do not follow these values will do equally well or better.

The second problem with the "values equal profits" mentality is this. If in fact people start relying on this linkage and saying if I follow these values I'm going to get to the Holy Grail, then what happens when they don't? What happens to their behavior? That is the second problem. If, in fact, profits are the main objective and it doesn't happen, people are going to go back and change their values. They'll say, This technique is no good; let's throw it out. And that's very dangerous.

The third problem is that it's filled with hypocrisy. In effect we're doing something for someone else with an ulterior motive, in order to get something, and we're not being upfront about it. There can be no integrity in a company with that kind of hypocrisy built into its value system. It looks a great deal to me like the health and wealth gospel of some of our evangelists on television.

This kind of mentality is very prevalent in business circles and is being taught in business schools today. I want to encourage you to take your biblical values into business because they are right, not because they work, and to let the economic consequences fall where they may.

717

Section 3: Putting Faith to the Test

Challenges routinely arise for individuals whose Christian faith calls them to the business world. Personally acknowledging one's business career as a vocation is a first step. Securing a position of influence within a corporate culture may be the second. Yet persons who take on such challenges routinely can expect to face hard choices. Real people even in the best of corporate cultures will find ethical questions requiring decisions and action. These hard choices may occur when individuals are personally asked to participate in unethical business activity. They may also occur when Christians consider the broad social responsibilities of business. When faith is put to the test, how should Christians respond?

The first two articles focus on individual ethics, specifically, the challenge of unethical behavior. Larry McSwain laments the fact that the general American culture accepts the idea of an autonomous market system loyal first of all to its own values. In contrast, he believes that Christians are called to be disciples "living above the market." Thus for Christians the bases of choice arise from faith first and the market second, not vice versa. The result is that McSwain encourages Christians to work as change agents in business through innovation, example, and, if necessary, whistleblowing. While whistleblowers must examine their motivations carefully, in his eyes it may sometimes be the only reasonable moral choice available.

Richard Chewning focuses on specific strategies that may help Christians work through situations they believe to be unethical. His advice focuses specifically on subordinates torn between a desire to please their superiors and their sense of what is morally right. Chewning believes that putting faith to the test requires a careful analysis of the situation and a conscious plotting of ethical strategy. Even when whistleblowing becomes necessary, it should be done prudently as well as responsibly. Overcoming evil in the workplace should not require martyrdom, unless that is the only option.

The next two articles focus positively on the opportunities for corporate responsiveness in the social environment. Claudia McDonnell discusses the range of reasons businesses give for getting involved in community-based social programs. Her illustrations, along with other boxed examples, suggest strategies businesses use to respond to their social environments. McDonnell is honest about the mix of business self-interest, altruism, and religious concern that can motivate corporate responsiveness. Yet she still challenges business to have a heart.

Joseph Nolan and David Nolan describe the historical development of ideas about business social responsibility. They believe that during the twentieth century U.S. businesses have moved through several stages in developing their consciences about the broader social environment. Their article provides historical perspective on the evolution of business social responsibility and documents current public expectations. It suggests that, in the long run, the efforts of countless persons to exercise moral leadership in the corporations as well as in society has tended to lift our moral standards. The willingness to test one's faith in the workplace need not be seen as either fruitless or counterproductive.

Christian Ethics and the Business Ethos

Larry L. McSwain

. . . The business ethos of contemporary economic systems stands in stark contrast to the kingdom ethic of the Christian faith. Whether the system is a variant of capitalism, traditionalism, or socialism, it functions as a "principality and power" seeking autonomous loyalty to its values. The business ethos of free enterprise capitalism promises the material benefits of profit for those who will invest their life, time, and capital in its mechanics. Those mechanics are not inherently evil, for such a system has made possible the accumulation of resources for constructing an industrial machine which provides employment for millions, raises the standards of the world's economies, and creates whole new technical possibilities for exploring the frontiers of the universe.

But the business ethos also includes within it the demand for freedom. It is this systemic insistence upon autonomy that leads to idolatry. No system of the world can claim autonomy in relation to the kingdom of God. At this point all three major economic systems become idolatrous. Traditional economic systems claim the autonomy of religious organizational control as their primary right. Consequently the church, rather than the kingdom, becomes the means of economic salvation. Socialist systems claim the autonomy of state control as their primary right. Thus no individual has freedom in relation to the state dominations of one's means of livelihood. Capitalist systems claim the autonomy of the marketplace

as their primary right. As a result, freedom in the marketplace becomes the mechanism for exploitation of consumers and laborers.

All freedom for the Christian requires a certain kind of bondage. The truest form of freedom is to be found in being bound to the community of faith obedient to the will of God. For one to take seriously the claims of Christian discipleship requires living "above the market" of the capitalistic system. The result is a dialectic of both affirming and judging human systems, including economic ones. The ethos of the business community must be affirmed at the points of its just delivery of needed goods at competitive prices. When that same system becomes dishonest, exploitative, or unjust to create the market for its products, the Christian stands in judgment against it. . . .

The business employee has, to a considerable degree, no different ethical responsibilities than employees of any institution. Indeed, one of the least explored areas of ethical concern is the treatment of and responsibilities of employees of religious institutions.

Ethical concerns that will have impact must speak to both small and large business contexts. Novak reports there are some fifteen million small businesses employing forty-six million people and seven hundred thousand large corporations employing thirty-eight million in the United States alone. The largest single employment sector is governmental, employing or contracting for the services of twenty million people.

Given the importance of work in the total lives of persons, this is an area of training and concern to which the churches have given little attention. They can hardly decry the lack of ethical concern in the corporation if they do not exercise their own responsibilities in giving educational and spiritual leadership to developing sensitivity among laypersons to the moral values so important to the Christian faith. Indeed, any business person who would function as a change-agent in the corporate context must have groups of support for dealing with the pressures of work in ethically ambiguous settings.

The ethical ambiguity of the workplace is not so much knowing the right as knowing how to be influential in encouraging right behavior. What is the ethical responsibility of the female employee who is aware of sexual relationships between her

Larry L. McSwain, "Christian Ethics and the Business Ethos," *Review and Expositor* 82, no. 2 (1984): 197-207.

male supervisor and another female employee who receives special treatment for her favors? To report such behavior to company superiors jeopardizes relationships with the supervisor and may result in the loss of future advancement or employment. Not to report such behavior creates internal morale problems for the employee. To complicate the situation further, proving the indiscretion may be more difficult than knowing it exists.

A host of other kinds of behavior from petty stealing of company property to price fixing, producing unsafe products, and shoddy work are observed daily by persons of honesty who do not participate in them, but do not resist such actions by others either. What are the ethical responsibilities of the employee, whether of governmental, business, or church-related institutions?

The Change-Agent as Innovator

Creativity in response to the needs of any work setting is the most important quality of the Christian employee. There is hardly any job imaginable in which better service or products, improved processes of functioning, or new sets of policies for greater efficiency are not possible. The most significant resource of any capitalistic system is insight, as it is in any service or religious organization.

One of the ethical responsibilities of the Christian is to assist the business context to function profitably in a highly competitive atmosphere without resorting to unethical practices. The temptation to lower one's values can be met by more innovative ways of doing business. Such innovation becomes its own reward as the creative business delivers a finer product than its unethical competitor. The scriptural guide "Whatever a man sows, that he will also reap" (Gal. 6:7c) applies to the corporation which trades the short-term unethical profit for the long-term ethical value as much as it applies to individuals.

Facilitating change is therefore an ethical stance for the Christian. To resist the technology needed for a more qualitative life or to oppose processes of change which offer the potential for achieving ethical goals may be among the most unethical forms of human behavior the worker can commit.

One important role of the church must, therefore, be the encouragement of attitudes of flexibility, adjustment to change, and innovation in the minds of those it teaches and serves. If our God is the creative God who brought the world into being and charged humanity with the responsibility of developing its resources in a responsible manner, innovative leadership in developing new products and services and making them available to the peoples of the world is itself an ethical demand.

The Change-Agent as Example

A second primary opportunity of the Christian employee is to stand over against the prevailing amoral and immoral behaviors encountered in the work place. Given the extensive participation Americans report in the religious life of the United States, one cannot but wonder about the reporting of industrial theft, employee injustice, and discrimination. Either the reports are exaggerated or church members are responsible for many of the ethical problems in this area.

Surely the Christian has a responsibility to function within the framework of those Christian values of honesty, fairness in dealing with persons, giving work equal to one's compensation, and working with established procedures to promote those policies reflective of the highest human values. Regardless of the behavior of others, the light and salt qualities of Christian living dispel the darkness of iniquity and leaven the evil of our world. To such commitment every church must call its members. Every Christian must be encouraged to work with the conviction that right behavior is its own reward and is itself a form of judgment to the unethical who observe it.

The Change-Agent as "Whistle Blower"

In extreme cases of unethical business conduct, the Christian change-agent may need to risk employment itself to bring the ethical wrong to public awareness. Such a role is a sacrificial one. No corporation or government agency will reward the person who goes outside the channels of internal authority to correct a wrong. James M. Roche, former president of General Motors, shared a corporate perspective on this activity:

> Some critics are now busy eroding another support of free enterprise — the loyalty of a management team, with its unifying values of cooperative work. Some of the enemies of business now encourage an employee to be disloyal to the enterprise. They want to create suspicion and disharmony, and pry into the proprietary interest of the business. However this is labeled — industrial espionage, whistle blowing, or professional responsibility — it is another tactic for spreading disunity and creating conflict.

Yet some situations are critical to the point of danger if someone is not willing to make the sacrifice of risking employment for the public good. Certainly the nature of the Christian life would call for following the sacrificial example of Jesus Christ in doing the good. It was a welder going to the newspaper to report shoddy work at a nuclear power plant who may have saved the nation from a future tragedy. Yet he lost his job. Norman Bowie offers an excellent definition of the ethical whistle blower who is not acting to fulfill his or her own ego:

> A whistle blower is an employee or officer of any institution, profit or non-profit, private or public, who believes either that he/she has been ordered to perform some act or he/she has obtained knowledge that the institution is engaged in activities which a) are believed to cause unnecessary harm to third parties, b) are in violation of human rights, or c) run counter to the defined purpose of the institution and who inform the public of this fact.

There are dangers in encouraging Christians to engage in such behavior. It can lead to self-righteousness or incorrect or inadequate information being made public. To guard against such, Bowie offers several guidelines for the justification of this action:

1. It is done from the appropriate moral motive, namely, as provided in the definition of whistle blowing.
2. The whistle blower, except in special circumstances, has exhausted all internal channels for dissent before informing the public.
3. The whistle blower has made certain that his or her belief that inappropriate actions are ordered or have occurred is based on evidence that would persuade a reasonable person.
4. The whistle blower has acted after a careful analysis of the danger: (a) how serious is the moral violation, (b) how immediate is the moral violation, (c) is the moral violation one that can be specified?
5. The whistle blower's action is commensurate with one's responsibility for avoiding and exposing moral violations.
6. It has some chance of success.

Each of these change-agent roles requires a higher loyalty in terms of value than the ethos of the business community alone. The creation of that kingdom ethic of obedience to the One who must be served, whatever the consequences, is the task of every church and every minister. To apply such a value to the business community is a risky task. But to do less is to fail to serve the Christ who is the Lord of all life — including the life of work.

Whistleblowing may be defined as an effort to make others aware of some ongoing practices which seem to the whistleblower to be illegal; or harmful, or unjust. Further, the practices are only known to the whistleblower because he/she has some privileged access to information about the group engaging in the doubtful practice. Thus, it may be, the whistleblower learns of the practice because, as a fellow worker employed by the company in which the allegedly wrongful practices obtain, he or she is trusted with the information by those engaging in the practice. However, it is also possible that the whistleblower has never received any confidential disclosure but is merely unusually observant and thus discovers the practice on her own. Or the corporation may be flagrant in their disregard of employee awareness. Finally, it is possible that the privileged position may be held by an employee of some parallel bureaucracy, who because of that employment is given access to otherwise privileged information, and correlating this privileged information then reports the apparent misdeeds of a bureaucracy which does not directly employ him/her. . . .

For the most part, whistleblowers are vilified. They suffer a loss of reputation. Their motives, character, mental stability and trustworthiness become the subject of aspersions. They are often described as disgruntled troublemakers, people who make an issue out of nothing, self-serving publicity seekers, or troubled persons who have distorted and misinterpreted situations due to their own psychological imbalance/irrationality.

Yet, character assassination barely begins to describe the consequences that most often accrue to the whistleblower, even one who submits a well-founded and important alert. Beyond such disparagement, whistleblowers almost always experience retaliation. Those who work for private industry may be fired, or possibly blacklisted so that they cannot continue to work in their profession. Those who are not fired may be transferred with prejudice, demoted, given less interesting work (or sometimes no work at all). Staff may be transferred away so that the whistleblower can no longer continue to function efficiently, and this may become further ground for criticism. They may be denied salary increases. Letters of recommendation will subtly or overtly mention the trouble caused by this employee's actions. Where possible, their professional competence will be attacked. Certainly their professional judgement will be impugned.

— Natalie Dandekar, "Contrasting Consequences: Bringing Charges of Sexual Harassment Compared with Other Cases of Whistleblowing," *Journal of Business Ethics,* Feb. 1990, pp. 150, 152

When a Boss Asks for Something Unethical

Richard Chewning

Part I

We often hear that it is difficult to be a Christian in the marketplace. We hear of pressures being exerted on subordinates to do unethical things. We are even told that the words "business ethics" are a contradiction in terms. There are, however, some concrete ways of elevating Christian ethics in the marketplace.

How do Christians deal with a boss that asks them to do something unethical? I frequently hear of such pressure being felt by those who desire to be ethical, but who are also afraid of not "pleasing" their superior. The psychological pressure can be enormous. How are we to cope with it when it occurs?

First of all, we need to examine the *facts* of what is before us and not our *perception* of what is confronting us. The reason this is so important is that 98% of all boss-induced pressure to act unethically is *implied* in character and not an open request to be unethical.

The business environment is unusually competitive and "tight"; the sales manager may feel the pressure of those above him or her to keep the sales volume up so the year-end financial report will be favorable; and the sales manager is aware that you are approaching the end of four months of hard work to close a large and potentially profitable contract with a major customer. So the sales manager intones, "Bob, we are really looking to

you to close that contract next week with the Big Corporation. Your success will probably tip the balance for our profits this quarter. *You do whatever you have to do to get it.* It's that important to us."

What are the implications of the statement, "You do whatever you have to do to get it"? Even if the statement were stronger in its emphasis, we would not know the intentions behind it unless the boss gives us specific behavioral instructions ("If you have to, offer him a $5,000 bribe"). Anything short of a concrete directive leaves the listener only with the opportunity to reveal his or her own mental reaction to another's non-specific implication. (To be pure, everything is pure — Titus 1:15.)

Then how are we to act in the face of what we perceive to be an *implied* request to behave unethically? We are to act as if the implications were an innocent emphasis that asked us to "do whatever we have to do" within the confines of good company policy and high moral standards. It may mean, if working a 16-hour day will help, do it. It may mean, study our proposed bid carefully and see if there are other savings we can offer the customer.

Always turn an implied request for unethical behavior into a positive and ethical response. No one can fault someone *openly* for having worked hard in an ethical manner. Even if the boss's implied request did have bad intentions behind it, few people in business will actually suggest behavior that is unethical. Even the unethical do not want to be perceived as such in the open light. Besides, no one will publicly find fault with ethical conduct. Work hard as if the Lord is your employer. Don't fear people who imply that inappropriate conduct is acceptable.

The people who cave in to the psychological pressure to act unethically in order to please their boss have not thought clearly. Unethical conduct undermines our integrity. The superior will not respect unethical conduct even if he or she did imply it was "expected."

If a superior learns of any unethical conduct on the part of a subordinate, a discreet ostracism will take place. The boss will be very careful to keep from being "polluted" by association. If the unethical conduct should become public the superior will always deny any association with it.

Richard Chewning, "When a Boss Asks for Something Unethical," *Presbyterian Journal*, 24 Dec. 1986, 14 Jan. 1987, and 4 Feb. 1987.

Implied requests to violate moral standards will be reinterpreted by the originator of the implied statement with righteous indignation. The unethical party will be isolated quickly when an occurrence becomes public. The boss will appeal to his or her own historic record and ask when or where he or she has been involved in such a procedure. The "offender" will be dropped like a "hot potato."

Unrighteous conduct is foolish. It can only create negative consequences. To engage in what is wrong because another person implied it would be acceptable in the particular situation is analogous to believing that Satan has our best interests at heart when we are tempted. Only integrity can stand the test of time and the light of day.

What does one do if the boss goes beyond an *implied* request for unethical behavior and asks us to do a specific thing that we deem to be unethical? We will discuss this in the next article.

Part II

Rarely will superiors give a specific directive that is actually unethical. When they do, it is normally a request to do something that they would do themselves in their insensitivity. For them it may be a competitive norm. For example, a superior might ask Jack to see if he can get the customer's purchasing agent to tell him just how low other competitors are going in their bidding for a contract so that we can "do an even better job for the customer" by getting our bid lower — in order to secure the contract for ourselves.

A purchasing agent should not provide such "help" in a closed-bid situation. It is unethical (maybe illegal). Other firms making bids are treated unfairly. The purchasing company would not want their agent doing this, for it will eventually destroy the effectiveness of a bidding procedure. Our superior is probably not thinking about the integrity of the "other people." He probably sees nothing wrong with asking for such information. What happens is the other company's responsibility, not his.

On the other hand, an ethically sensitive Christian would feel it is not right to ask someone to do something that is fundamentally wrong in his or her judgment. Such a request would present us with an ethical problem. What should we do in the face of such requests?

First, never appear to be self-righteous, "holier-than-thou," or judgmental with a boss. No one (Christians included) likes a self-righteous person, and no boss will respond well to being told that he or she is unethical. Do not criticize a superior by revealing your opinion concerning his impropriety. A direct confrontation should be avoided if possible.

Respond kindly with a modicum of *self-exposure* regarding your personal sensitivity. "Mr. Big, I know that the suggestion to ask Bill Connors (the purchasing agent) for some 'bid' help is a common procedure in much of our industry. I also know that what he might do would be his own responsibility, but I have a personal sensitivity I need to share with you. I am a little uncomfortable exposing it, but I would ask that I not be given such an assignment. I know others do it, and I don't judge them for it, but my conscience would 'eat me alive' if I persuaded Bill to do what I wouldn't do. It would create a real 'downer' for me. I have a record of the last six winning bids, and I believe we can figure out what it will take to capture this one." (Note that elaborate details on "why it is wrong" are *not* necessary. The simple statement that "it" is something "I would not do" is sufficient. The boss would not really want any of his subordinates to do what he wanted another's employee to do — give out secret information.)

The subordinate has revealed his or her personal sensitivity to the ethical dimension of the initial request in a way that is not judgmental, but is considerate. Ninety-five percent of the time a superior will back away from the request and will respect such sensitivity, provided he or she does not feel chastened by a self-righteous attitude. A self-revealed sensitivity (provided we don't reveal such at every turn) will normally be *well* received as a mark of integrity. This generates respect and trust, desirable consequences.

When Christians will run the *very small risk* of exposing their ethical sensitivities in a manner that speaks of their personal *hurt* or of the *hurt* it inflicts upon others, few (very few) supervisors will challenge or react to override the exposed ethical nerve. To do so is almost like kicking someone who is wounded and lying on the ground. There are just not many people with so little sensitivity.

No, they will more than likely "read" the sensitivity as a real strength of character. They will likely interpret the courage to run the risk of self-exposure as a quality that will build confidence in the character of the subordinate. This must not be done manipulatively; but when it is genuine, it will normally result in a stronger bond between the supervisor and the subordinate.

Only rarely will someone actually "command" a subordinate to do something unethical. "I don't care about your personal sensitivity. Do what I told you. This is business and not a charity!" When this happens, an ethical confrontation is in full bloom. How do we ethically handle this kind of situation? The next article will address this.

Part III

This is the last of three articles dealing with the pressure a subordinate can feel from a superior to act unethically. The first essay pointed out that 98% of all such pressure is generated by statements implying that unethical conduct "is expected," but not by explicit instructions to act unethically.

The second article discussed the fact that when a boss does ask a subordinate to act unethically, the request is generally for an action that the superior would do himself without regarding it as unethical. In this case, we suggested that the subordinate expose his or her personal sensitivity in a non-judgmental, non-self-righteous manner. Ninety-five percent of the time this will be perceived as a mark of good character that will work to the benefit of the "self-exposed" subordinate.

A superior can, however, *command* a subordinate to do something that is unethical — "I don't care about your personal sensitivity. Pad the expenses another $2,000,000. That's only 3% of the total costs, and they won't know the difference. After all, we are only 'recovering' a little of our own tax dollars. Everybody twists the nose of the government occasionally."

Several things need to be foremost in our minds if a situation like the one just described should confront us. First, we need to understand that the real power rests with those who do what is *right* and not with the unethical superior. A request of this type puts the boss in an incredibly weak position. His command cannot stand up under open exposure. The subordinate is really in the stronger position in such circumstances, provided he or she continues to act ethically in both *what* is done and *how* the situation is handled.

In a corporate setting where a number of people are involved in working together, an unethical person is in an extremely weak position. A boss cannot fire an effective employee without a good reason. Questions *are* asked; others would become involved; so remain calm and confident. The next steps in handling such a situation are critical. Be super-sensitive to proceeding in a very professional, ethical, and non-threatening manner. The biggest danger a subordinate has in such a situation is one of being goaded into being insubordinate or unprofessional (unethical) in his or her reaction to the superior. The unethical superior will turn on the subordinate's unethical behavior, deny his or her verbal request, and act to remove the "embarrassing" subordinate — the subordinate now has damaging information from the superior's perspective.

The subordinate should politely decline the "request" and seek to change the subject. A statement such as, "John, the action you have just suggested is really not in the best interest of any of us individually or the corporation in the long run. I cannot do it, and I feel certain that upon further reflection you will agree. Let's just forget this and move on to other matters."

It would take a very weak — yes, desperate and weak — man to pursue a subordinate any further with a request for such unethical behavior. But should the demands continue, ask respectfully if he will accompany you to discuss the matter with his superior. He will in all probability refuse, for such a request will normally reflect the poor judgment of one individual. (If he will go, there is a *bigger* problem on a wider front within the company, and the subordinate should be prepared to continue on up the "chain of command," one rung at a time, in an ethical, factual, respectful way.)

When such an encounter has occurred, one should not be naive about what has transpired. The supervisor *will* experience a sense of embarrassment whenever he or she is in our presence unless the error of judgment is acknowledged and reconciliation is sought. More often than not, this will not be done. This means the superior will remain uncomfortable in our presence.

The subordinate should continue to be friendly and open to the normal direction of the superior and be certain to *do everything well and on time.* Any evident deficiencies exhibited by the subordinate will be picked up on and probably "blown all out of proportion." The righteous party may become the "hunted" one in circumstances of this type.

God may rescue us through a promotion and/or transfer. He may move the "boss." He may allow us to be the target of backbiting, gossip, and some persecution — overload in work assignments, assigned to all the unexciting work, etc. Whether we should stay or look for employment elsewhere is a personal matter. My belief is that one should always "go to" a genuine opportunity and not "run from" a bad situation. God has enormous lessons he can teach us at such times in our lives.

Above all, however, maintain a godly character in the midst of such experience. Make sure what is done and how it is done both reflect the Christlike attitudes and behavior revealed in the Scripture as Christ faced his temptation and enemies.

Does Big Business Have a Big Heart?

Claudia McDonnell

When a customer can't pay the electric bill, New York State Electric & Gas Corporation makes a house call to find out why. The privately owned utility sends Paula Ross, a social worker and consumer representative at NYSEG's Pittsburgh office, to the homes of customers with past-due accounts. Ross looks for ways to help poor, elderly, or ill people keep the power on.

A Medicaid worker alerted Ross to one woman's situation. The woman, 53, had been battling cancer for several years and was terminally ill with a brain tumor. She lived alone in a mobile home next to a church and rectory. She had an income of more than $1000 a month, but chemotherapy cost her $596 every three weeks. She hadn't known Medicaid would cover it. The Medicaid worker was making the necessary arrangements but told Ross it would take time. Meanwhile, the woman had "let every bill go," according to Ross, but did not tell any of her creditors why.

"I went to see her," Ross says. "She fell apart. It would have been easy for me to say, 'We aren't going to shut you off, don't worry, see you later.' " Instead, Ross sat down and made a list of agencies to call. When she realized the woman couldn't make the calls herself, Ross made them. She obtained grants from the Cancer Society, Catholic

Claudia McDonnell, "Does Big Business Have a Big Heart?" *Salt* (Claretian Press, Chicago, IL), Jan. 1988, pp. 6-11. The article has also appeared in the March/April 1988 issue of *The Marketplace,* Mennonite Economic Development Associates, P.O. Box M, Akron, PA 17501.

Charities, and two food projects that serve the needy.

The power stayed on. Ross adds, "We never took one penny from that woman."

Ross' work is one example of the various causes that attract corporate dollars. American businesses are investing both cash and employee time in programs for poor people, education, health care, small businesses (often minority-owned), neighborhood restoration, cultural institutions — just about every conceivable effort to improve society.

The results are visible and sometimes dramatic. The motivation is a little hard to track, and it can vary from one company to another. Humanitarian concern may play a greater or lesser role. One factor, however, holds constant: corporate giving makes good business sense. Corporations are in business to make money, and their profitability depends in large part on the health of the society in which they operate. Society's economic health, in turn, is tied into corporations' fortunes. In a phrase business executives and ethicists frequently use, corporate-giving reflects "enlightened self-interest."

"Society grants corporations the ability to do business," says David K. Cummings, second vice president for corporate relations at Northwestern National Life Insurance Company in Minneapolis. "Society says, 'Do business in an ethical manner, make good products, and you'll get an appropriate rate in return.'"

Businesses do not deny the benefits they receive from the dollars they give away, not only in economic terms but in public trust and a favorable image. Nor do they equate corporate contributions with donations made by nonprofit charitable organizations. Many executives avoid the term "corporate philanthropy" in favor of "corporate social involvement," "good corporate citizenship," and other ways of expressing the fact that business largess is a two-way street.

John E. Pearson, chairman and chief executive officer of Northwestern National Life Insurance Company, states in an employee publication, "The dollars and involvement we provide are not charity or philanthropy. They are an investment in our community and its future that will come back to us many times over in the form of a healthy economy and a deeper reservoir of goodwill." But "the bottom line of social responsibility," he adds,

is "helping the less fortunate and working in other ways to improve the quality of life in our community."

Many companies' corporate concern begins in the workplace. For example, Northwestern National Life's "employee wellness program" offers exercise classes as well as classes in nutrition and physical and mental health. Allstate Insurance Company offers its workers confidential counseling for any personal problem, including drug and alcohol abuse and marital tension. Employees can take seminars to learn how to cope with stress or to stop smoking.

Edward L. Morgan, Jr., assistant vice president of corporate relations at Allstate, points out that most corporations run similar programs. "It's good business," he explains. "If employees have problems, they're going to bring them to work. The faster and more completely we can help them solve problems in their personal lives, the happier they will be. And happy employees are more productive. Everybody wins."

Many companies apply similar standards outside their office doors. If a customer has a problem, they want to solve it. New York State Electric & Gas, the company that helps customers with overdue bills, is a case in point. "We've found that most people, once they receive help, have no recurring problems," says Paula Ross, NYSEG's consumer representative.

Irene Stillings, NYSEG's assistant vice president of consumer affairs, launched the consumer-representative program in 1978. The program doesn't aim to duplicate the work of social-service agencies, she points out, but to "catch people who are falling through the cracks," especially the working poor and the elderly who do not qualify for other forms of help.

"Older people will pay a bill and not eat or buy medicine," Stillings says. "We train our meter readers to recognize signs of confusion."

Both Stillings and Ross say that because NYSEG's service is essential to health and safety, it has a special obligation to its customers. But it also has an obligation to its shareholders, many of whom are elderly and depend on the utility as a safe investment.

"I'm willing to give anybody a chance to prove they need help," Ross says; but she is tough on able-bodied customers who lie or fail to follow her advice and help themselves. "The company respects the fact that I'm not going to give someone free electricity for months while they twiddle their thumbs."

While corporations benefit in obvious ways from social involvement — good publicity, tax write-offs, a better business climate — evidence suggests that genuine humanitarian concern also plays a role. Some corporations explicitly state their commitment to improve society, a commitment usually tied to the beliefs and principles of the founder or an influential executive officer.

Levi Strauss & Company, based in San Francisco, not only bears the name of its founder — a Bavarian merchant who called his product "overalls" — but also practices the tradition of philanthropy for which he became famous. With 38,000 employees and annual sales of more than $2 billion, Levi Strauss is the world's largest apparel manufacturer. Executives cite it frequently as a leader in corporate responsibility, and examples abound. It was the first employer in many communities in the South to open factories with an integrated work force. It encourages employees to join its "Community Involvement Teams" (CITs) to help communities around the world. Several years ago, for example, the CIT in Manila in the Philippines helped drill two water wells and install pumping equipment to provide drinking water for a fishing village.

The CIT at Levi Strauss' Cherry Street plant in Knoxville, Tennessee, hosts a monthly birthday party at a home for adults with cerebral palsy. At their own expense, CIT members presented a talent show as a fund-raiser for their activities at the home. Mary Ellen McLoughlin, manager of community affairs for the company's eastern region, says employees put in "a couple of hundred dollars and many hours" of their own, staging the show at a social center and rehearsing their songs and dances. Several years ago the Knoxville CIT sponsored a $15,000 grant for the home from the Levi Strauss Foundation.

When a corporation retains its founder's values, it is usually because the family is still running the store. Robert D. Haas, president and chief executive officer of Levi Strauss, is the founder's great-great-grandnephew.

Another leader in corporate social involvement, executives say, is Cummins Engine Company in Columbus, Indiana. J. Irwin Miller, former chairman of the board of Cummins and now chairman of its executive and finance committee, bases his business principles on deeply held religious values, says Adele Vincent.

"There is a strong moral tone in our management's dealings," according to Vincent, who is associate director of Cummins Engine Foundation, the corporation's philanthropic arm. She notes that Miller, a member of the Church of the Disciples of Christ, was the first lay president of the National Council of Churches and is still very active in the organization.

Cummins funds projects in five areas: education and youth; equity and justice; community development; arts and culture; and public policy. It supports numerous programs, including one in Jamestown, New York, that combines tutoring and track competition to motivate low-income and minority students to stay in school. Cummins also funds voter registration, small community-arts programs, homes for troubled youth, and a number of college and educational programs.

Cummins is the largest employer in Columbus and other industrial cities; and it takes seriously its responsibility to its "shareholders, employees, customers, and the people who live and work in the communities where it operates," Vincent says.

Corporate philanthropy clearly benefits both giver and receiver, but whether it is motivated by a concern for justice is hard to say. It also raises other questions: What is justice? What constitutes justice toward the individuals who are affected by business — employer, employee, shareholder, customer, citizen?

Sister Dianne Bergant, C.S.A., assistant professor of Old Testament Studies at Catholic Theological Union in Chicago, says that justice in the biblical sense means "all of us have a right to the goods of the earth."

"The land belongs to God; it is ours in trust," says Bergant. "The goods of the earth don't belong to any individual." Hence, sharing with others is a duty. "Philanthropy is justice, not charity."

According to Dick Westley, philosophy professor at Loyola University of Chicago, the American notion of justice deviates sharply from biblical justice. Americans define justice, says Westley, as "when I get what's coming to me." Biblical justice, on the other hand, calls for a right ordering of

Sam Williams, owner of a McDonald's franchise, is one of the many business people in Baton Rouge, La., participating in a program designed to show high-school students the critical link between their education and their job prospects.

One of the students who heard him was Lynda Stansell, a 15-year-old sophomore who was failing and about to drop out. But what she heard from Williams about employer expectations and the opportunities available to young people with the education and skills needed in today's marketplace changed her mind.

Today, she has a B average, will soon be working part time under the business program for the schools, and is getting ready to take college-entrance exams. "Business people come in to talk to us, and I'm learning a lot more because of it," Stansell says.

The Baton Rouge program's business participants represent a variety of industries. John Everett, a Holiday Inn manager, discusses careers in hotel management. Bobby Smith, owner of a building company, describes the construction industry and the skills needed to enter it. Michael Gramelspacher, manager of a Woolworth store, and Mickey Weaver, who owns a seafood restaurant, explain what they expect new employees to bring to their firms. Maxine Crump, a local television correspondent, conducts workshops to show the young women students how to improve their self-images.

That program represents just one of the many ways in which business people throughout the country are taking on one of the most serious problems facing the nation today — an educational system unable to produce students equipped for challenges ranging from entry-level to maintaining the U.S. position in an increasingly competitive world.

Meeting those challenges, the experts point out, must begin with the realization that an "educational system" consists of not only schools and teachers but also students, parents, and the entire community that depends on a well-educated population for its economic and social health.

The Business–Higher Education Forum, which brings together the chief executives of major U.S. corporations, colleges, and universities, says a key goal of education at all levels should be equipping "all of our young people to enter adult life with the basic education and skills essential in the modern world."

The organization, based in Washington, D.C., says that success in achieving that and other education goals "ultimately depends on the sustained individual and joint efforts of teachers, students, and parents, of managers and workers, of business executives and labor leaders, and on the encouragement of the private sector."

— Nancy Croft Baker, "Would You Hire Them?"
Nation's Business, April 1989, pp. 16-19

---

society, in the light of the Kingdom of God. Justice is done when "things turn out right."

With a touch of irony, Westley calls business philanthropy "part of the American heritage" and traces it back to the millionaire moguls of another era, who felt a sense of obligation toward the less fortunate.

"Philanthropy is almost a substitute for justice," he says. "It wouldn't be needed if things were right." To bring about a biblical vision of justice "would require a transformation of the American heart."

Westley is skeptical of the motives behind corporate philanthropy. "Corporations make inferior products, pollute the environment, and bury toxic wastes," he says. "Then with all the money they make, they're philanthropic. The question I'd raise is this: how much of what industry does is really a guilt trip?"

David Krueger, executive director of the Center for Ethics and Corporate Policy in Chicago, though less critical, also says philanthropy can be used for strictly self-serving motives. "I think it's probably beyond dispute that many corporations see their foundations and contributions as a way to offset public criticism of other corporate practices." He and Westley offer the same example. "The tobacco industry," Krueger notes, "has been very prominent in its corporate giving, especially in the arts and sports programs. It's a way to defuse public criticism of questionable practices or products."

Westley simply remarks that tobacco companies, if they were really philanthropic, would "voluntarily go out of business."

Despite his severe judgment, Westley does not condemn all corporate philanthropy, nor does he see any inherent contradiction in the "enlightened self-interest" philosophy. It's simply facing reality, he says, to acknowledge that "if you do good things, good things will come back to you." But if a company's only motivation is a good image, then its public giving is not philanthropy but "just another good business practice."

"From a Christian perspective, in order to find out whether a company is really concerned with human justice and righting wrongs, you would have to look at the business practices that generate the profits," Wesley says. "You can't make a moral judgment on philanthropy without looking at the way the corporation is run. If human values permeate the business enterprise — as much as they can, because it's a jungle — then at least the philanthropy is in keeping with the way it does business."

Corporate contributions have increased yearly for sixteen consecutive years, according to the Conference Board, a business research organization in New York City. The total for 1986 was $4.5 billion.

David L. Dodson, executive vice president of MDC, Inc., a private, nonprofit research firm in Chapel Hill, North Carolina, says most corporate giving "hovers around 1 percent of pre-tax profits." Dodson and other executives say an amount equal to 5 percent of pre-tax profits is a benchmark for a strong corporate-giving program. Consequently, "2 percent clubs" have sprung up in the corporate world to try to get businesses to come closer to the 5 percent figure.

"Many CEOs are spending their time looking for ways to fight off corporate raiders," says David Krueger. "They're devising strategies to maintain their corporate independence. The competitive marketplace has become so vicious that philanthropy has become an expendable item."

Dodson draws a distinction between philanthropy and the works of justice. Corporations are not obligated to be philanthropic, he says, but they do have a responsibility to work for justice. He explains the apparent contradiction. "A corporation can't be a philanthropy. In that sense, philanthropy would be at cross purposes with what business is all about, which is making a product and returning a profit to the shareholders." Corporate giving, he says, can only be justified if it benefits investors and the company as well as the community.

Asked whether the corporation can be a force for justice in the land, Dodson says, "I wish it did more of that." He isn't talking about gifts to worthy causes. "Philanthropy is one aspect of a corporation's corporate responsibility, and in one sense, a very minor aspect. The corporate activities that have the largest impact are the way a business hires, the way it manufactures, its labor relations practices, its marketing practices."

Dodson, who holds degrees in both divinity and management, says religion can influence the corporate world to work for a more just society. "One of the most important disciplines that comes out of a spiritual environment is reflection." He advocates "a systemic way to encourage corporate leadership to reflect on the impact that their actions have on society."

A good first step, he continues, is for religious leaders to approach corporate executives in their congregation and begin to talk with them "as people of faith." He also asks clergy to study the business world. "There is a lack of understanding on the part of the clergy about the economic system," Dodson says. "The tendency is to criticize what corporations are doing without understanding the system in which they work."

Efforts like those Dodson describes are already underway in many places. In Chicago, John Fontana is executive director of the Crossroads Center for Faith and Work at St. Patrick's Church. Fontana, a former corporate executive with a master's degree in management, says the center's purpose is "to develop a ministry and relationship with business people." Activities include programs for executives on values in management; discussion groups for members of various professions including law, finance, and medicine; and programs on poverty in the city.

"The response has been overwhelmingly positive," Fontana says. "A lot of people want to talk about the relationship between their work and their faith." He also says graduate schools of business are training managers to be aware of the social and ethical implications of their decisions.

"On the whole, corporations are a fairly positive force in our society," he says. "When they make profits and spread them out, it has an impact." Corporations provide jobs, and jobs mean dignity. But he warns against unrealistic expectations.

"If you work on a perfection model," he says, "you're going to be disappointed. All of us are saints and sinners."

While not a substitute for government services, the private sector, some executives say, has a responsibility to work with government and non-profit groups for the good of society. "If we refuse to join with those other two sectors in a partnership against our common problems, then the public has a right to hold us accountable," says Richard J. Haayen, Allstate's chairman of the board.

Haayen made the statement in Chicago last October during his address to corporate executives who participated in a two-day forum on coping with the AIDS crisis. Allstate, based in Northbrook, Illinois, sponsored the forum; speakers included Dr. C. Everett Koop, the U.S. Surgeon General, and experts in the fields of medicine, law, insurance, labor, and journalism.

Allstate says the forum aimed to "develop policy guidelines" for dealing with AIDS in the workplace. Allstate plans to present to the federal government ways for American businesses to cope with the crisis.

Allstate, like many other corporations, has a long tradition of public involvement, both long-term and short-term. One example is its volunteer program, Helping Hands. Allstate estimates that 75 percent of its more than 50,000 employees have participated in the program, which was launched in 1976. Helping Hands often puts employee volunteers in touch with community agencies that request help.

One Helping Hands bulletin carries "Want Ads" for volunteers to provide legal, financial, computer, and communications skills to various agencies. Other projects include visiting the elderly, tutoring, and sponsoring holiday parties at homes for children. Helping Hands has played a part in more than 10,000 community projects.

When floods devastated much of the Chicago area in 1986, forcing more than 400 families to evacuate their homes, Helping Hands was on the scene. More than 250 Allstate employee volunteers were given time off from work to join in relief and cleanup efforts. Volunteers were transported by company vans to the hardest hit neighborhoods. "We had over 400 volunteers in a three-day period," says Edward Morgan. "We couldn't place all of them."

Allstate worked closely with the American Red Cross during the emergency. The Allstate cafeteria prepared about 1800 meals a day for distribution; Red Cross trucks carried the food to victims, volunteers, and temporary kitchens set up in flood-stricken areas. Allstate also donated $5000 to the Red Cross for flood relief and gave a flat-bottom motorboat to the village of Gurnee.

Volunteers from Allstate and other corporations sandbagged and cleaned homes. Nancy Kluz, reporting for the *Park Ridge Advocate* in Wilmette, spoke with a woman named Rose whose house had been flooded. An assembly line of Allstate volunteers was emptying her basement. "I don't know where we would be right now without the help of these volunteers," says Rose. "Both my husband I are 75 years old. There's not much heavy lifting you can do at that age."

Another man said the volunteers "put a silver lining in the clouds."

Allstate invited employees and neighboring corporations to donate furniture, appliances, linens, and other necessities to flood victims. The items were collected in a large tent that Allstate set up on its grounds. Some volunteers logged in donations or drove trucks to pick up large items. Since many flood victims were Allstate employees themselves, the company enacted a temporary Disaster Relief Policy to compensate them for the loss of uninsured household goods destroyed by the flood.

Allstate received the President's Citation in 1987 for flood-assistance program. Morgan says the volunteer spirit that made the program successful is typical of Allstate workers. Volunteer work "is part of the culture here." Motivation comes in part from "top-management support." Nearly all senior management executives are involved in some form of volunteer work also.

David Krueger says the banking and insurance industries have "much stronger philanthropic arms" then many other businesses because of their investments in many communities. "The well-being of the community enhances their own well-being," he says.

Darwin N. Davis, a vice president at Equitable Life Assurance Company in New York, makes the same point. If a corporation takes no interest in society's condition, its own investments will be destroyed. He recalls the riots of 1968, when people "started burning down America."

"People felt disenfranchised," says Davis. "They had no opportunity. No one paid any attention to them. They felt no one cared about them. They weren't bad people; they were in bad situations."

Equitable is one of many corporations sponsoring or participating in educational programs. One is Join-a-School. Started by the New York City Board of Education in 1982, it encourages corporations to form an alliance with a high school and enhance students' educational opportunities. Equitable "joined" William Cullen Bryant High School in Queens. The student body is racially mixed, Davis says, with blacks, whites, Hispanics, and Asians represented.

Join-a-School links employees with students for personal and academic support, and provides a summer-job program and computer instruction for Bryant teachers. Executives and school faculty are now writing a curriculum for a course about corporations and finance, including the stock market, stocks and bonds, mortgages, interest rates, credit ("What does it mean to finance a car?"), and consumerism. Company executives will teach the course.

Last summer Equitable took Bryant's girls' softball team to Florida to compete with teams there. The kids raised the money for airfare through car washes, dances, and bake sales; Equitable picked up the tab for lodging and meals at a hotel owned by the corporation.

Equitable also helps higher education through its Minority College Liaison Program, which pairs a senior executive with a college founded to serve blacks, Hispanics, or Native Americans. Most of the executives become members of the college board of directors. Participating colleges, which will number 25 this month, include Morehouse College in Atlanta, Xavier University in New Orleans, and Bacone College near Muskogee, Oklahoma.

Each college receives a $10,000 grant at the outset. The executive partner can make subsequent cash grants out of his or her budget. The program, however, involves more than cash donations.

"We've helped with investment portfolios to give the colleges a financial base," says Davis. And Equitable showed one school how to turn 10,000 acres into income-producing property by building homes, apartments, and stores. The corporation also employs 60 summer interns, pays their airfare to New York, and arranges for housing at Columbia University.

Like David Cummings, Davis points out that society can take away a corporation's charter if the corporation doesn't benefit the public. The combination of a "sophisticated buying public" and a competitive market ensures that inferior products or poor standards will put a company out of business. He rejects the notion that corporate giving is token compensation for poor goods or services. "You can't give away money as a salve for your guilt," Davis says.

Until the 1970s, homelessness generally was regarded as a social disorder rather than an economic problem. Three decades ago, as the country released hundreds of thousands of institutionalized mental patients in what was intended as a beneficent reform, many of those people wound up on the streets. The totally disturbed still make up perhaps a third of the homeless and in some urban areas there has been an increased number of drug addicts who are homeless, but by far the largest share of the new homeless are those who simply cannot find shelter that they can pay for.

The problem runs far deeper than the homeless who monopolize the media spotlight. For every family with a home, there are thousands of others whose housing is more expensive than they can afford. These are near-homeless. . . .

Now, a remarkable coalition of state and local governments, charitable foundations, community organizations and major profit-making corporations has been developing across the country to tackle the job of rehabilitating low-income housing.

Take Chicago, for example. A drive through the city's west side with William W. Higginson, president of the Chicago Equity Fund, reveals block after block of sturdy five- and six-story brick apartment buildings, their windows shattered and their interiors largely destroyed by vandals or the effect of weather and neglect. All told, he says, there are an estimated 45,000 units of salvageable housing in vacant buildings in Chicago — many of them now seized for unpaid taxes. "Enough," says Higginson, "to accommodate all of the families on the waiting list for public housing if they could be rehabilitated." Three years ago, the Chicago Equity Fund set out to persuade local corporations to fund the rehabilitation of nonprofit housing and make a profit doing so by using the tax advantages that were written into the law specifically to encourage housing for low-income people. Says Higginson: "We showed companies that they could make $1.20 for every dollar they put in."

Initially, the tax advantage depended on accelerated depreciation — one of the tax shelters killed by the 1986 tax reform bill. But it has been replaced by a tax credit ranging from 4% of construction costs to 9% of rehabilitation costs for projects that set aside at least 20% of their apartments for families who earn no more than 60% of the local median income. While this provision has limited value as a tax shelter for individuals because it is phased out for personal incomes above $200,000 a year (although a number of limited partnerships for individuals have been sold successfully) the credit for corporations has no such restrictions.

So far, about two dozen major corporations have put a million into the Chicago Equity Fund, money that has resulted in the addition of $92 million worth of affordable housing for the city's poor. The list of corporate investors reads like a Who's Who of Chicago business: Amoco, Baxter Trade Laboratories, Commonwealth Edison, First National of Chicago, Harris Trust & Savings Bank, Illinois Bell, Quaker Oats, Sara Lee, Sears, Roebuck and United Airlines among others.

One successful Chicago Equity Fund project is the restoration of the historic Guyon Hotel. Once a luxury residential hotel, whose ornamental terra-cotta work won recognition on the National Register of Historic Places, the Guyon has gone steadily downhill as the neighborhood turned poor black. By 1985 it was a useless shell — occupied by drug dealing squatters.

Then Bethel New Life — a community organization associated with the neighborhood Bethel Lutheran Church — obtained title to the Guyon, which had been taken over by Cook County for nonpayment of taxes. The Chicago Equity Fund invested $1.3 million. Since the equity money was to be paid in over six years, the First National Bank make a brief loan to make the funds available immediately. Harris Trust accepted a first mortgage. The Chicago Department of Housing provided an interest-free second mortgage. The Illinois Development Finance Authority put up what amounted to a third mortgage at 3% interest with payments deferred for 30 years. The Chicago Department of Economic Development made a grant to restore the building's historic facade.

Today, the Guyon has been transformed into 66 spacious, modern, well-equipped one-bedroom apartments renting for $316 per month and 48 two-bedroom apartments that rent for $385. For a tenant earning around $14,000 a year (approximately 60% of the Chicago median income), those are affordable rents. For those below that level, government rent supplements are now available.

— Dan Cordtz, "On the Street," *Financial World*, 29 Nov. 1988, pp. 26-28

The Path to Social Responsibility

Joseph Nolan and David Nolan

When Johnson & Johnson, responding to a second wave of Tylenol poisonings in four years, recently discontinued the manufacture of all over-the-counter capsule medications, its prompt action was hailed by President Reagan as an example of "the highest ideals of corporate responsibility."

This Presidential commendation was notable for its sharp contrast with earlier chief executives' pronouncements on business behavior: Theodore Roosevelt's scathing denunciation of the "malefactors of great wealth"; his cousin Franklin's scornful broadsides at the "economic royalists"; and John F. Kennedy's derisive jab in the wake of a steel price increase, "My father always told me that all businessmen were sons of bitches." Even the usually controlled Woodrow Wilson blew his scholarly cool with the railroad operators when they fought him in the issue of an eight-hour workday — "which society is justified in insisting is in the interest of health, efficiency, contentment, and a general increase in economic vigor."

Business' route toward more responsible behavior over the past seven decades has been anything but smooth. Along the way there have been numerous backsliders whose misdeeds have been embarrassingly emblazoned in headlines. Still, there is today an acknowledgment among members of the business community of an obligation to protect and improve the welfare of society as a whole, along with their own interests. It is a view that is far from universal, but further still from the cavalier attitude summed up in William H. Vanderbilt's sneering remark "The public be damned!"

It is possible to discern at least four stages the development of a heightened corporate consciousness about the world beyond the plant and the executive suite. In order of appearance we can name these periods after the businessmen who epitomized them: the visionaries of the 1950s and before, the improvisers of the 1960s, the reluctant compliers of the 1970s, and the initiative-takers of today.

The Visionaries

In corporate responsibility as elsewhere there have always been people who projected something beyond the conventional wisdom of their day. They recognized well before their peers that management had develop a broader social role for the corporation — along with its traditional economic role — if business was to earn public confidence.

The founders of the Conference Board, in 1916, represented a quantum leap forward from the "public be damned" attitude in their candid admission of "the abuse of power by some employers" and the "disregard of rightful obligations to employees and society on the part of others." To combat these problems, they advocated an energetic self-reform effort. But despite its evident validity, self-reform has never proved an easy concept to sell, either to other business people or to an increasingly skeptical public.

One of the most farsighted of the visionaries was Theodore N. Vail, president of AT&T around the turn of the century, who reasoned that if households had no complaints about the telephone, there would be scant public support for a Government takeover. So he boldly proclaimed that "Our business is service" — a definition that served his company for two thirds of a century.

Other corporate "founding fathers" were similarly perceptive in charting their firms' missions. When James Cash Penney outlined the basic philosophy that has animated succeeding generations of management in the J.C. Penney Company, he put two commitments at the top of his list: "To serve the public as nearly as we can to its complete

Joseph Nolan and David Nolan, "The Path to Social Responsibility," *Across the Board* 23 (May 1986): 54-58.

satisfaction . . . [and] to test our every policy, method, and act in this wise: 'Does it square with what is right and just?' "

George Draper Dayton, founder of the Dayton-Hudson Corporation, challenged his business associates with the provocative question: "Shall we agree to start with the assumption that success is making ourselves useful in the world, valuable to society?"

General Robert Wood Johnson, in the 1940s, drafted Johnson & Johnson's now-famous credo, which began: "We believe our first responsibility is to the doctors, nurses, and patients, to mothers and all others who use our products and services."

A less philosophical example was the response to a disastrous 1947 freighter explosion that leveled a small Texas community in which Monsanto operated a chemical plant. The blast killed 145 Monsanto workers; the area was described as resembling "a flaming end of the world." Even though the explosion originated outside the plant and no Monsanto products were involved, chairman Edgar Queeny promptly reacted in a manner that has come to be seen as a classic assumption of responsibility above and beyond legal requirements. Cutting through corporate red tape, he ordered immediate payment of a wide variety of medical benefits and rebuilding assistance. Queeny directed his associates "to do all possible to alleviate hardship," and persuaded his board of directors to approve a half-million-dollar fund "to reward outstanding cases of heroism." Then he and Monsanto took the lead in rebuilding the plant and the community. Four decades later, those steps might have been considered normal procedure, but they set a new and higher standard in that time of tragedy.

But these visionaries were often voices crying in the wilderness of corporate indifference. In the first half of this century, the economic rationale was dominant. Most businessmen felt that they were behaving in exemplary fashion if they produced quality goods and services, sold them at fair prices, and appropriately rewarded the stockholders with dividends and the employees with wages.

It was fine for Andrew Carnegie — as an individual — to give away millions in the belief that "the man who dies rich dies disgraced." But it was quite another thing to engage in philanthropy with corporate funds at the expense of potential profits for the stockholders. Philanthropy was the first break from the economic rational for a long time, it was almost the only one.

The notion was widespread that social responsibility invariably came at the expense of profit. The fact that some corporations that embarked on creative programs in this area, such as Bob Cascade, wound up in financial difficulty serving to dampen the enthusiasm of others. By mid-century, the accepted concept of social responsibility was still primarily limited to goods, services, jobs, and philanthropy. But that definition was soon to be radically expanded.

The Improvisers

In the turbulent 1960s, public expectation of corporate behavior began changing with the emergence of three significant issues. The first was the urban issue, a witching brew blended of all the ills of those trouble times — racial discrimination, inadequate schools, hard-core unemployment, antiquat housing, poverty in the midst of plenty. The second was the environmental movement, which activists asserted that America was parting for a large part of its growth and affluence in mortgaging its environment, and that the business system effectively encouraged this. The third issue was consumerism, which surfaces when the buying public got fed up with products it felt were shoddily made and services perceived as being arrogantly offered and grudgingly performed.

These issues focused attention anew on the role and responsibilities of the corporation. Critics not only expected business to take material goods and produce something better, they wanted business to make employees better off. They expected business to be a better opportunity for investment, a better taxpayer and supporter of government, a better neighbor in the community, and a better contributor to social goals and human progress.

New York's Mayor John V. Lindsay epitomized the prevailing attitude in the 1960s with a frantic appeal to the business community to "adopt" the black ghetto neighborhoods. "Whatever government, social workers, or community action try," Lindsay said, "things seem only to get worse. Therefore, big business had better take responsibility."

In this volatile climate, fueled by race riots and burning cities, business people realized that they *had* to do more to improve conditions in the communities where their people lived and worked. So they began improvising.

One company tried rehabilitating run-down blocks of apartments in Harlem. Another financed bookmobiles. Insurance companies undertook extensive investments in slum reconstruction. IBM, Control Data, and Digital Equipment built inner-city manufacturing plants with work forces drawn largely from the adjacent neighborhoods. Banks, recognizing that minority entrepreneurs often needed more than just money, started assigning "business counselors" to help out with the thorny problems of accounting, marketing, and management.

There were false starts galore. Some companies, with more enthusiasm than common sense, got bogged down in projects far beyond their ability. Others, in their ebullient naïveté, intruded on the traditional terrain of government units and were summarily evicted. Still others made modest beginnings and were able to claim a measure of success. For example, business executives under the prodding of Henry Ford II formed the National Alliance of Businessmen, and made some headway in providing meaningful jobs for the hard-core unemployed.

For the most part, though, these first ventures into active social responsibility were seen by the public and their elected representatives as coming hesitantly, in insufficient doses, and only if they did not interfere with a firm's bottom-line results.

The Reluctant Compliers

In the 1970s, the public frustrations — vented in the civil-rights, environmental, and consumer movements, and given voice by activist-authors such as Rachel Carson (*Silent Spring*) and Ralph Nader (*Unsafe at Any Speed*) — boiled over into legislative and regulatory actions that told business precisely *how* it must behave responsibly.

In rapid succession there emerged the Occupational Safety and Health Act (1970), the Environmental Protections Agency (1971), the Consumer Product Safety Commission (1973), and a host of other regulatory agencies and measures.

From 1974 to 1978, Congress enacted no fewer than 25 far-reaching additions to the arsenal of regulatory power over business. *Time* magazine wrote that a "growing number of Federal rules and regulations . . . seem to float out of Washington as casually as children blow soap bubbles."

Just as in the 1930s the nation decided that acceptable labor-management behavior would include whatever accords emerged from collective bargaining, so in the 1960s and '70s it decided that acceptable behavior would include equitable participation of minorities, strict control of waste and pollution, and firm assurance that products were safe to use.

Many business people felt that the new laws and regulations were unwisely conceived, hastily enacted, and totally unnecessary. Most companies reluctantly complied, but a few, such as Sears, Roebuck & Company, fought back. The nation's largest retailer filed an unprecedented class-action suit against 10 Federal agencies in 1979 charging that they had imposed contradictory and unreasonable conditions on hiring and promotion policies. Last February, a Federal District Court in Chicago ruled in Sears' favor on the last remaining claims of a Government countersuit.

Most other companies confined their griping about "government by guideline" to the executive dining room, fearful that too much protesting would make a bad situation even worse. In moments of reflective candor, though, some managers conceded that business had brought on many of its own regulatory troubles. They noted that between 1965 and 1975, public confidence in business had plummeted from the high 70 percent area to the low 20s — buttressing the arguments of congressional critics for tougher laws and more rigorous enforcement.

The Initiative-Takers

With the election of a Republican Administration in 1980, the business community found itself being urged more insistently than ever to take heed of its responsibility "beyond the bottom line." President Reagan talked about the desirability of the private sector's making up the gap that resulted from Federal cutbacks in social programs.

While business executives were quick to point

out that "closing the gap" was an unrealistic expectation, they did take to heart the President's admonition that they explore what more could be done.

Forerunner companies, such as Johnson & Johnson, felt that taking public-spirited initiatives that went beyond the requirements of the law — often at great expense to themselves — made good sense because public confidence had to be maintained at all costs.

Procter & Gamble quickly removed its Rely tampons from store shelves after reports of a possible connection with toxic shock syndrome.

Johnson Wax withdrew all its fluorocarbon products in response to what it saw as a "genuine concern" about harm to the ozone layer.

General Motors managing director in South Africa publicly condemned that country's segregated beaches and offered legal aid to any GM employee prosecuted for swimming at a white beach — the first time a corporate executive had promised openly to support blacks engaging in acts of civil disobedience.

Executives from Exxon, Du Pont, and Monsanto worked with environmentalists and public officials to create a nonprofit corporation called Clean Sites Inc., to speed the cleanup of toxic-waste dumps through voluntary cooperation.

The Johnson & Johnson case has prodded serious students of corporate conduct to grapple with some difficult questions: What constitutes socially responsible behavior in the face of a major crisis, such as Bhopal, or Three Mile Island, or Love Canal? In view of information that has come to light since December 1984, could Union Carbide, for example, have foreseen and possibly prevented the gas leak in India that killed some 2,000 people? Should it have reacted differently than it did?

There are, of course, no simple answers. The enormity of Bhopal makes comparison difficult. But, in retrospect, at least a few elements are somewhat clearer now.

Warren Anderson's initial move of flying to India to express his condolences to families of the victims and to see what could be done to alleviate suffering was an instinctive gesture of human compassion that earned the Union Carbide chairman admiration in many quarters. In dealing with the news media, however, the company was per-

ceived to be following a reactive strategy rather than the proactive approach that worked so well for Johnson & Johnson. Anderson himself put his finger on a key conflict inherent in most crisis situations. "If you listen to your lawyers," he said, "you would lock yourself up in a room somewhere. If you listen to the public-relations people, they would have you answer everything. You would be on every TV program."

Indeed, for several days after the latest Tylenol episode, chairman James E. Burke of Johnson & Johnson seemed to be on almost every television program — a compassionate and reassuring figure voicing sympathy for the victims' family, explaining the decision to stop making Tylenol capsules, and urging consumers to give the caplets a chance.

By contrast, Carbide's more restrained approach made even its necessary cautionary details appear to some as sinister evasion, unquestionably damaged its reputation. But Bhopal, the company had ranked in the top of its industry group in the *Fortune* annual survey of executives, directors, and analysts in community and environmental responsibility. Afterward, it was rated near the bottom of the 292 companies evaluated.

Nevertheless, as Allied Chemical demonstrated in the aftermath of the Kepone pollution controversy, it is possible for a company to rebuild its reputation through socially responsible conduct. Fined $13 million for improper disposal of toxic wastes, the company overhauled its safety and environmental programs, cracked down on polluting plants, abandoned excessively risky products — and won commendation from the EPA and the news media as a model for other companies to emulate.

While effective communications in a crisis can help, companies must do something tangible to convince the public that they are, in fact, socially responsible. Actions still speak louder than words, and if they cost the company $13 million, which is what Johnson & Johnson estimates it will have to spend in the wake of the second Tylenol episode, they pack a lot of conviction. So the Crisis Management Task Forces that are springing up in many companies these days must examine action-oriented initiatives in their preparedness plans.

The idea of corporations taking initiative beyond the requirements of the law strikes a responsive chord with much of the public. Polls show that many Americans think that corporations operate too much for the benefit of managers and stockholders, and not enough for the benefit of customers, employees, and society.

The experience of the past 70 years strongly suggests that business must redefine its corporate interests with the broader framework of the public good, as some companies are beginning to do. The choice that companies face is clear-cut. Seize the initiative to take on new responsibilities voluntarily, or wait until that initiative has been preempted and new responsibilities are thrust upon them by law.

By all appearances the business closing issue is evolving much like many of the other social issues business has had to address during the last twenty years. The effect of the recession of the early 1980s has been to put the issue more dramatically on the front page. Though it is somewhat premature to assess where public opinion on the issue will eventually come to rest, a strong case could be made for a positive or proactive response given the magnitude of the problem, the level of legislative activity, and the activism of labor unions. In addition to the desire to circumvent more government regulation and continue hostile relationship with labor, responsive corporate action could be justified on the grounds of long-run, enlightened self interest, preserving business as a viable institution in society, preventing further social problems, and creating a favorable public image for the corporation.

Though the right to close a business down has long been regarded as a management prerogative, the business shutdowns since 1970 — especially their dramatic effects — call to attention the question of what rights and responsibilities business has vis-à-vis employees and communities.

The literature of business social responsibility and policy has documented corporate concern with the detrimental impact of its actions — indeed, businesses' social response patterns over the past 15 years have borne this out. No less a business advocate than Peter Drucker has suggested what business owes regarding the social impacts of management decisions:

Because one is responsible for one's impacts, one minimizes them. The fewer impacts an institution has outside of its own specific purpose and mission, the better does it conduct itself, the more responsibly does it act, and the more acceptable a citizen, neighbor and contributor it is.

The question is raised, therefore, whether businesses' responsibilities in the realm of plant closings and their impacts on employees and communities is any different than the host of responsibilities that have already been assumed in areas such as employment discrimination, employee privacy and safety, honesty in advertising, product safety, and concern for the environment. . . .

A number of executives have spoken to this issue and several have indicated that there is an obligation to employees and the community when a business opens up or decides to close. As D. Kenneth Patten, president of the Real Estate Board of New York, illustrates:

A corporation has a responsibility not only to its employees but to the community involved. It's a simple question of corporate citizenship. Just as an individual must conduct himself in a way relating to the community, so must a corporation. As a matter of fact, a corporation has an even larger responsibility since it has been afforded even greater advantages than the individual. Just as a golfer must replace divots, a corporation must be prepared at all times to deal with hardship it may create when it moves or closes down.

Others have also argued that there is a moral obligation at stake in the business closing issue. In a rather extensive consideration of plant closings, philosopher John Kavanagh has asserted that companies are not morally free to ignore the impact of a closing on employees and the community. His argument is similar to those that have been given on many other social issues: namely, that business should minimize the negative externalities (unintended side effects) of its actions. . . .

If this is so, why have we not seen more positive responses in business closings? There are a variety of answers. One would be that executives still regard as foremost their economic performance and survival. To the extent that this is the issue, of course, this is quite legitimate. Another answer might be that sufficient exposure and analysis as to what is really at stake in business closings has not taken place. Charles R. Dahl, past president and CEO of Crown Zellerbach, stated that

corporations do try to be aware of social trends and embryonic issues. But until there is sufficient evolution of the thought process among the various constituencies to clearly define the issues, the corporation is not in a position to make an appropriate response.

At this point we are just beginning to define the parties interested in the issue, the impacts that business closings are having on these interest groups, and the possible actions management can take to be more responsive. From past experience, one cannot avoid arguing that if further federal and state government regulation and social protests are to be avoided or minimized, positive and constructive steps must be taken by business to be responsive to the employee and community needs that arise when close-downs are imminent. What is needed is for business to engage in the same kinds of sensitive, thoughtful, and deliberate decision-making process when it is planning to leave a community as when it made the initial decision to enter the community.

— Archie B. Carroll, "When Business Closes Down: Social Responsibilities and Management Actions," *California Management Review*, Winter 1984, pp. 129-30, 138

Chapter Fourteen

The Global Economy

Massive changes in communication, transportation, and information networks have guaranteed that the future of economic life is global. Yet negotiating the path into that future is dependent on the real decisions of nations, businesses, authorities on economic development, and environmental activists. Each of these constituencies brings an economic perspective to the global negotiating network. That perspective is shaped by fundamental beliefs and religious values, some Christian and many non-Christian. Chapter 9 explored world religions and their influence on economic activity in the past. This chapter looks to the future and tries to determine the contribution that religion may make, among these other forces, in shaping a genuinely inclusive economic culture.

National governments have been among the most decisive factors in the global marketplace. They normally monitor national economic performance and comparative economic advantage based on geography, natural resources, infrastructure, developed labor force skills, educational capital, and financial clout. In consultation with world economic authorities, they try to shape policies that favor those economic sectors that promise global advantage. The global overview in Section 1 gives some inkling of the sweeping economic changes now occurring in one nation after another, the diverse religious and moral aspirations that are operative in them, and the challenge they pose to both the theory and practice of national economic policy.

Thousands of individuals drawn from virtually all the nations of the world spend their careers in multinational corporations. They often live in countries other than their own and traverse the globe in search of market opportunities and production locations. Their business decisions also shape the economic future and cannot be divorced from ethical concerns about appropriate treatment of global customers and worldwide resources. Section 2 examines the role and ethics of multinational corporations.

While the industrialized world struggles on one plane to build a truly global economy, there are many nations still operating in another dimension marked by the constraints of destitution and the imperatives of basic survival. Photos, stories, and experiences of less developed countries continue to haunt the global community. Section 3 considers Christian commitments to these so-called Third World nations and their impact on the prospects for economic development.

Finally, the natural and technological environment play a critical role in the global scenario. Concerns about ecology and technology press people of many cultures to ask fundamental questions about the future of this planet and our interactions with it. Section 4 addresses these issues.

As the global economy continues to grow, the emerging ethical questions are multiple and complex. The global economy is not merely the arena in which changing business corporations must compete, or the laboratory in which they must develop, test, and refine their capacities in various business specializations. The global economy provides the ultimate challenge to those who would exercise moral leadership in business. This chapter is meant to provide some insight into the range of forces transforming the world economic system and our responsibilities in relationship to them. The selections have been chosen particularly in the hope that they will suggest convergences between the Christian churches' agenda for social and economic justice on a global scale and the visions of moral business leaders seeking to establish a flourishing global economy.

Section 1: Challenges in Emerging Global Markets

The assumption that a market economy works only when wed to Western Judeo-Christian culture is dying rapidly. Yet it still appears that certain cultural patterns are more conducive to modern economic development than others. While many factors work together gradually to shape culture, religious belief is always one of them. As the world is rapidly adopting the decentralized market economy as its model, patterns of religious belief continue to affect the global marketplace. This section offers a brief survey of those points on the global economic map where the pathways of religious and economic change seem to intersect most prominently.

The key for interpreting this map is provided by Peter Berger's remarks on the idea of an economic culture. He contends that it is time to disabuse ourselves of any notion of an exclusive connection between Christian faith and modern economic development. However, using examples from around the world, he also suggests that certain economic cultures formed in conjunction with their social, familial, political, geographic, and religious circumstances have comparative advantage in the global economy. Thus certain values, such as education, self-denial, and frugality, derived from many cultural/religious systems, are important for the success of a market economy.

Several authors illustrate Berger's thesis about the connections between religious faith, cultural patterns, and economic development. George Lodge observes recent economic developments in China. He argues that defining China in terms of either capitalism or socialism is parochial and irrelevant for understanding that economy. By highlighting the influence of Confucianism and its distinctive support for extended family networks, he argues that China's economy should more aptly be called "communitarian." Lodge's piece therefore echoes Berger's skepticism about any exclusive connection between Christianity and modern economic development. Sang-Goog Cho, on the other hand, shows how economic progress and Christian conversion seem to have come hand in hand in South Korea. He believes that Christianity has played a significant role in South Korea's economic growth. In Cho's view, Christianity's influence may be even greater than that of the broadly Confucian morality that South Korea traditionally shares with the rest of East Asia.

But East Asia is not the only region where established economic structures and inherited cultural values are undergoing dramatic transformation. Arun Katiyar and Shefali Rekhi show how India's new openness to market capitalism can be sustained in a managerial ethic shaped by the shastras of traditional Hinduism. Leo Ryan adds a cautionary tale, however, that economic reformers and managerial visionaries should take to heart. In light of Poland's recent experience, transforming a command economy into a market economy is a painfully long-term process, dependent not only on structural changes but also on the residual ethical resources of the economic culture. Poland's recent bout of economic shock therapy suggests that the ethical and cultural disorientation provoked by radical change is not likely to be overcome, short of a massive spiritual regeneration of the nation as a whole.

Preston Williams's essay, penned in the waning days of South Africa's struggle against apartheid, outlines the scope of the challenge for spiritual renewal. A market economy, even one informed by religious faith, does not necessarily lead to justice, community, and the good life. Reconstituting civil society requires the construction of a moral, legal, and political framework in which economic activity takes place. The development of a global market economy will not insure that justice prevails, that inequality is ameliorated, or that human integrity is honored. A globally civil society, in Williams's view, must grapple with the problems of class, race, and sex. Williams encourages those of the Christian faith to aid the development of global justice in conjunction with the global marketplace.

The Gross National Product and the Gods: The Idea of Economic Culture

Peter L. Berger

Biblical scholars may disagree on just why Jesus drove the money-changers from the Temple, but at least in the Christian imagination this famous scene, often captured in works of art, expresses the intuition that economics and religion do not easily mix. What holds for religion holds also for other manifestations of culture — that is, the beliefs, values and lifestyles by which human beings organize their existence, find meaning and define who they are. Throughout history, and still today in most of the world, religion and culture are virtually synonymous. However, even in societies in which religion appears to have lost influence, culture determines the way people understand the world and themselves. At the same time, no society can exist without economic arrangements. Keeping these arrangements going requires actions and mind-sets that seem to be very different indeed from those that characterize religion — prosaic, pragmatic, calculating — far removed from the great passions and ecstasies of human experience. Human beings have always been prepared to sacrifice and even to die for their gods and their ideals. Nobody in his right mind, not even the most enthusiastic capitalist, is willing to die for business reasons. Is the case, then, that here there are two completely distinct areas of human reality, areas that have nothing to do with each other? Or, on

Peter L. Berger, "The Gross National Product and the Gods: The Idea of Economic Culture," *The McKinsey Quarterly*, 1994, no. 1.

the contrary, does one area finally determine and serve to explain the other? Or, more likely, do these two spheres interact in complicated ways without either one determining the other? In any case, what is the relationship between markets and sanctuaries, between economic rationality and morals, between the gross national product and the gods?

There are very few if any analysts of modern society who would argue that culture determines economic behavior. (There are, of course, such views regarding pre- or non-modern societies, especially by anthropologists. But this is a matter that cannot be pursued here.) In consequence, there are hardly any scholars in the humanities who would take it upon themselves to explain, say, the dynamics of Wall Street. By contrast, there is a sizable number of scholars, especially economists but with converts in other disciplines, who believe that the science of economics, or at least the reformulation of other human sciences in terms borrowed from economics, can explain all human behavior. The underlying assumption here is that human beings are essentially "rational actors" and that the rationality of the marketplace is the same rationality that governs all other areas of life as well. There are a number of reasons why economists, who have been so remarkably unsuccessful in clarifying let alone predicting the workings of the economy, should now be trusted with interpretations of politics or of interpersonal relations. Be this as it may, an explanation of Wall Street in terms of, say, theology is as unpersuasive as an explanation of the Iranian revolution in terms of economics. A different approach would seem to be called for.

The idea of "economic culture" is intended to open the way for such an approach, which would be a middle way between the deterministic perspectives of "culturalism" (where beliefs and values are supposed to explain everything) and "economism" (where politicians, lovers, spouses and Islamic revolutionaries are all assumed to act in accordance with the logic of capitalist investment bankers). By economic culture is meant, quite simply, the social and cultural context of economic behavior. Using this phrase does not assume causal determination in either direction — neither culture determining economics, nor the reverse. It only assumes that human beings

exist in society and that this context, with its baggage of cultural attitudes and habits, affects economic behavior and is in turn affected by the latter in ways that must be studied empirically, case by case, on the ground. For example, if American and Japanese business people negotiate a contract with each other, it may indeed be assumed that all of them are "rational actors" in that they intend to profit from the arrangement and that they are calculating the chances of making a profit as they haggle over the provisions of the contract. However, this does not mean that the participants in the negotiations check their respective cultures in the cloakroom before they go into the meeting. On the contrary, no matter how much the same capitalist rationality motivates both Americans and Japanese, the cultural differences will surface again and again, sometimes to the point where one side will completely misunderstand what the other side is saying. (Business people who have actually taken part in such negotiations will not need to be persuaded of this. Rather few economists have had the experience.)

In order to clarify the role of economic culture, it may be useful to introduce another term (borrowed, with due apologies, from economics) — that of "comparative cultural advantage." The Japanese, for reasons that are not mysterious but can be explained by the history of Japanese capitalism since the nineteenth century, have been very successful in building large organizations that command intense, sometimes passionate loyalty from its members. They have certainly been more successful in this than Americans. It can be said, therefore, that Japanese have a comparative cultural advantage in creating such organizations, in competing with large organizations (say, American ones) that cannot count on this degree of devotion, and in maintaining their organizations even through periods of economic difficulty. Now, this does not mean that Japanese are *always* successful in this way, nor that Americans can *never* be. It only means that, *comparatively,* the cultural baggage that Japanese bring with them into the economic arena is helpful in the task of organization-building. There is a further implication: What may be helpful at one time may not be at another time, may even be a handicap. Thus it is probably correct that Japanese culture was very advantageous throughout the period when Japanese corporations created the manufacturing achievements that have been scaring the wits out of Americans and Europeans for so many years. It is at least arguable that this cultural constellation of corporate loyalty and conformism (the Japanese call it "groupism") may be much less helpful, may indeed be a comparative *dis*advantage in a "post-industrial" period of high technology and information-driven services. Possibly, to their own surprise, Americans may yet discover that in this new situation their much-maligned individualism and irreverence toward institutions, including the ones that employ them, will turn out to offer a comparative cultural *advantage*.

The most astounding economic success story of the post-World-War II period has been the ascendancy of East Asia, led by Japan and now extending in a gigantic crescent of prosperity into the countries of Southeast Asia. The explanation of this economic miracle has preoccupied a good many people both inside and outside the social sciences, and among these there have been some who have stressed the role of East Asian culture. The most commonly cited cultural factor has been an allegedly common Confucian tradition, which inculcates discipline, hard work, frugality, no respect for authority and, last not least, a passion for education. A "post-Confucian ethic" would then serve as a functional equivalent of the so-called "Protestant ethic," which Max Weber saw as an important factor in the rise of modern capitalism in the West. But Confucianism is not the only "suspect" if one wants cultural explanations of this phenomenon. There are other religio-ethical traditions, notably Mahayana Buddhism and Shinto, folk religion, as well as distinctive features of kinship and household with the values attendant to them. Can the economic success of East Asia be explained, if only partially, by its culture? The practical implications of this question are immense. It is not just a question of satisfying one's intellectual curiosity as to why East Asia has succeeded where other developing regions have not. In recent years there has been much talk about an "East Asian development model." Supposing that there is such a thing, *is it exportable?* The answer to this strategically important question hinges in large part on the place one assigns to culture in the East Asian success stories. If culture is at most a minor factor, then it makes sense for, say, an African country to adopt various economic and social policies imitating Taiwan, or for management in America and Europe to adopt Japanese personnel practices. But if, on the other hand, such policies and practices depend wholly or even in large measure on Chinese and Japanese cultural traits, then an attempt to transplant them into a very different cultural milieu may turn out to be a big mistake. It may make sense for Nigeria to imitate Taiwan in its tax laws; it makes no sense to expect Nigerians to adopt the precepts of Confucian morality.

If one wants to assess the role of culture in contemporary East Asian economic behavior, one will not get very far *either* by reading ancient texts (few Taiwanese entrepreneurs are steeped in the Confucian classics or for that matter in any reading other than of the Asian edition of *The Wall Street Journal*) *or* by reading about comparative economic indicators (which will simply reiterate what is already known — namely, that Taiwan has been a monumental economic success, compared to almost anyone). Progress will only come from careful, ethnographically oriented study on the ground — of the sort that anthropologists engage in, when they endlessly interview and observe people in a culture they want to understand. It is this sort of study that has been undertaken for several years now by a team of researchers headed by Gordon Redding of the University of Hong Kong. This research has concentrated on the overseas Chinese, the approximately fifty million Chinese who live outside mainland China, though it has ongoingly compared them with their Japanese and Korean counterparts. The Overseas Chinese constitute an economic miracle in and of themselves. It is not only that the capitalist societies which they dominate (Taiwan, Hong Kong and Singapore) have been fabulously successful, but that Chinese minorities have played a vastly disproportional role in all the economies of Southeast Asia, and that Overseas Chinese capital and management are now playing a very important role in all the regions of the People's Republic where capitalist enterprise is allowed to unfold.

Redding's work has demonstrated in rich detail how distinctive Chinese cultural traits affect the business behavior of Overseas Chinese entrepreneurs and managers (significantly, the two functions usually coalesce in one individual in this population). Central in this is the Chinese family, its habits and its ethos. The great majority of Overseas Chinese firms are family firms. It is the ethos of the Chinese family which motivates the dedication, the self-denial and the sober pragmatism of the people who run and staff these firms. It gives them a high degree of cohesion and flexibility. In fact, superficially, the Chinese family firm bears some resemblance to the Japanese firm. There is, however, a very important difference, which Redding calls the size barrier: Chinese firms tend to be small and, if larger, capable of being run with a very simple organization that only requires a small managerial staff (shipping is a good example of this). This explanation lies in the cultural definition of trust. Human cultures differ greatly in the range of trust that an individual finds plausible. "Whom can I trust?" . . . The Chinese answer is very clear: *Close relatives.* Consequently, Chinese family firms are typically run by small circles of closely related individuals. The problem comes when the firm grows and one runs out of close relatives to fill the required management positions. Different scenarios may then ensue. Very often the firm will split; the more distantly related managers go off on their own. Or the close relatives are asked to take on more than they can efficiently do, with deleterious consequences for the firm. Or alternatively the firm may imitate non-Chinese businesses and hire managers outside the family. These individuals tend to be very unhappy in the situation: They know that they are not really trusted and that they will not be allowed to get to the top of the firm, and, good Chinese that they are, they will likely have one overriding ambition — to get out as soon as possible and start a family business of their own!

The family-orientation of Overseas Chinese businesses shows quite nicely what the idea of a comparative cultural advantage implies. Chinese do indeed have a culturally based advantage as they compete with many other ethnic groups, such as Malays in Southeast Asia. But this advantage may not outlive the particular circumstances of a particular moment in economic development. If at a further point in time it may be necessary to create and maintain large, complex organizations, the same Overseas Chinese will find themselves at a considerable *dis*advantage — as compared to Japanese or Westerners, and quite possibly as compared with Malays (who, for instance, might find sources of trans-familial loyalty in a modernized Islamic ethic).

Another interesting question arises from the study of the Overseas Chinese: Why did this particular "post-Confucian" ethic have such massive economic payoffs in all these places outside China, and not in China itself? The answer is easy, and uninteresting, if asked with regard to Communist China: Even the most dedicated capitalist is going to have a hard time making it in a socialist society (though, in China as in other socialist countries, there did develop a frequently dynamic underground capitalist economy). The answer is not so easy if one looks at pre-Communist China, and Chinese emigrants succeeded in many places in pre-Communist times, while the economy back home remained stagnant and unable to develop toward a modern capitalism. The answer becomes clearer if one looks at the social and political structures of China through most of its history, structures that were intrinsically antagonistic toward any form of modern economic development. The Confucian tradition itself, in its classical Chinese form, was deeply conservative and disdainful of mercantile values. The traditional Chinese state made modern economic development very difficult. Probably the Chinese family, in its native, pre-emigration form, did the same, being embedded in very wide networks of kinship obligations that made capital accumulation very difficult — too many relatives clamored for a piece of the action! The emigrants, the Overseas Chinese, escaped most of these obstacles to capitalist success. They did not have to cope with crippling state regulations or with disdainful Mandarins, and most of the clamorous relatives had been left behind in the ancestral village (they would get sent their remittances, but they could not stick their noses into the business).

These considerations allow the formulation of another helpful concept — one could call if "functional latency." Cultural traits, of whatever kind, do not lead to the same results at all times: In some cases, they may lie dormant, latent, for very long periods of time until the "right" moment when circumstances (economic, political, even ecological) are such that their hidden potential has an opportunity to become manifest. It is not the traits that change in such cases but the "external" circumstances (external, that is, to the culture). This appears to be so in the case of the Overseas Chinese. Here one finds one of the oldest cultures in human history. Some of its essential traits, such as its family ethos, have been transmitted successfully through many generations, with little change and with similar consequences. Then, all at once, as the people carrying this cultural heritage with them find themselves in radically different circumstances, the same traits take on very different social and economic functions. This is what has been happening throughout the Chinese diaspora (incidentally, not only in Asia but wherever Chinese emigrants have gone, including North America); it may happen once more if mainland China continues on its present economic course (which is, in effect, a capitalist revolution with a lot of waving of red flags).

There may be other such cases of functional latency. For example, it has been plausibly argued, given past history, that at least the Iberian version of Catholicism is dysfunctional in terms of modern capitalist development. Not only the societies of the Iberian peninsula itself but their overseas extensions, above all in Latin America, have been cited in support of this thesis. A piquant case in support of the same thesis may be the Philippines — the only Catholic society in Asia, culturally shaped by Iberian Catholicism — and the only economic disaster in capitalist Southeast Asia. But then there is the case of Spain itself, which since the demise of the Franco regime has transformed itself into a booming capitalist economy, recently having attained the highest growth rate in Europe. A strategic role in this transformation was played by the Catholic movement Opus Dei — fiercely conservative in its theology, but very much committed to capitalist economics. Opus Dei played an important role in the opening up of the Spanish economy to market forces in the last years of the Franco regime and just thereafter. Opus Dei runs two very influential management schools in Spain, with their graduates sprinkled through the top layers of the Spanish business community. Here, once more, it was not so much a matter of an ethic changing, but of change in the circumstances under which this ethic came to be practiced.

The importance of careful, case-by-case, em-pirical research in this area cannot be emphasized enough. Bold generalizations, such as are often made in the management literature, may be useful in stimulating such research and in being the source of hypotheses to be tested, but using them to avoid research is to invite grave misperceptions. Thus there has been talk about an alleged "Asian management style." It is not always clear just where the western boundaries of this "Asia" are supposed to be. The Urals? The Bosphorus? There is always the assumption that East Asia is part of this entity. Yet, as the above discussion indicates, lumping Japanese and Chinese management into the same category is gravely misleading. Both may indeed show influences from the same Confucian moral tradition, but the differences between them are massive. Both are the result of modernizations of old traditions, but very different traditions indeed — the latter a modernized family ethos (the village patriarch metamorphosed into a chief executive officer), the former an ingenuous translation of feudal, military values into a morality serving the modern corporation (samurais in business suits presiding over the most efficient industrial empires in history). It is accurate to say that Japanese and Chinese management styles differ from each other as much, possibly more, than either differs from an American management style.

If the relevance of the putative "Asian management style" is supposed to include India (let alone the Muslim world), the term loses all meaning. In all likelihood one cannot even speak of an *Indian* management style." Instead of one overarching economic culture, one finds many such cultures, differentiated by region, ethnicity, caste and religion. Thus Gujerat is a region that has produced a disproportionate number of successful entrepreneurs, as is the case with the Marwari caste, and strikingly so with the small religious minorities of the Jains and the Parsis. But there is one resemblance between the otherwise incredibly different cases of China and India: In both cases groups, who have not evinced much economic dynamism at home, have done remarkably well abroad. In the Indian case this is particularly so in eastern and southern Africa, where Indian business people have played and (where allowed) continue to play an important role in the economy (though, it must be added, not with the degree of success attained by the Overseas Chinese). To understand why and just how these different economic performances occur requires precisely the kind of on-the-ground ethnography by which Redding and his associates have shed light on the workings of Overseas Chinese business.

There is what might be called the ancient-curse theory of history — the notion that cultures somehow came into being in the remote past and that ever since people born into a culture are fated to repeat its ancient patterns over and over again. Both anthropologists and historians frequently adhere to such a view. Then Chinese individuals are destined to endlessly restage the ancient family dramas and Japanese individuals the theater of feudal fealty. While the circumstances may have changed, as they have for the Overseas Chinese and for the Japanese since the Meiji Restoration that initiated the country's modernization, the cultural patterns have continued in a seemingly unbroken continuity. There is, of course, a degree of validity to this view. Cultures do show a remarkable continuity, sometimes over long stretches of time, a fact to be explained by the basic dynamics of socialization by which each new generation absorbs the world of its progenitors. Now, even in the Overseas Chinese and Japanese cases, such a theory oversimplifies. A multi-million-dollar manufacturing company in Taiwan is not simply a peasant clan writ large and the chief executive officer of a Japanese corporation is not simply a samurai in a three-piece suit. In adapting to radically new circumstances, even very persistent cultural patterns undergo changes. The ancient-curse theory, however, breaks down completely in other cases. These are situations in which groups of people drastically change their beliefs and their behavior, creating drastically *new* cultural patterns, sometimes in an amazingly short time. This may occur when people are subjected to intense pressure due to economic and social transformations. Thus there is evidence to the effect that people who migrate from rural areas into the gigantic pressure-cookers that are the large cities of the Third World create genuinely new cultures with remarkable speed. But probably one of the most effective agents of cultural revolution is religious conversion.

Contrary to what many analysts of the contemporary world have said and to what is still the prevailing opinion among people who have gone through Western-type higher education, modernization has not led to a decline of religion in most of the world. With the exception of a few regions (Europe being the most important) and a rather thin cross-national stratum (the aforementioned graduates of Western-type universities), the world today is as intensively religious as it ever has been, and arguably more so. Passionate religious movements are pulsating all over the place, some in continuity with the great traditions, others innovating and often antagonistic to these traditions. The Iranian Revolution and its aftermath has made this fact evident to a broad public. And, indeed, the phenomenon of Islamic revival (rather misleadingly labelled "fundamentalism" by Western observers) is one of the most important religious movements in the world today. Throughout the vast area between the Atlantic Ocean and the China Sea it is inspiring masses of people to change their behavior, in the process shaking up governments and transforming entire societies. An equally important, possibly even more important movement is that of Evangelical Protestantism (most of it Pentecostal) which is rapidly spreading over huge areas of Asia, Africa and Latin America. Its geographical scope is actually wider than that of Islamic revival.

While the rise of militant Islam has been widely noted and commented upon, the rise of Pentecostalism and of Evangelical Protestantism generally still comes as a surprise to most people in the West when they first stumble on it. The origins of this movement are, of course, in the United States, where Evangelical Protestantism has experienced notable growth and at least since the mid-1970's has been noticed by the media and a broad public (Jimmy Carter's presidential campaign may have been a watershed event). It has been estimated that there are some forty million "born-again Christians" in the United States. The figure is unreliable, but there can be no question but that the Evangelical community, extending across many if not all Protestant denominations, is a formidable and a growing presence on the American religious scene. By the very nature of its creed, it is also a highly missionary-minded community, and eager young American Evangelicals have carried their religious message to every corner of the globe. Nevertheless, in most of the places where this message has taken root (including, significantly, Latin America), there are now strong indigenous churches, supporting themselves financially out of their own resources and led by indigenous pastors and evangelists. These churches are mostly fully independent of their sister institutions in the United States and would continue unimpeded even if all contacts with the latter were severed. The scope and dynamism of this movement are astounding. It is very strong in Asia — strongest in South Korea, but also vigorous in all the Overseas Chinese communities (anecdotal evidence suggests that it is spreading in a subterranean fashion in mainland China too), in the Philippines, and also throughout the Pacific archipelagos. It is very strong in sub-Saharan Africa where it has frequently entered into a syncretistic relationship with non-Christian indigenous African religions. But the most dramatic and unexpected growth has been in Latin America, where the number of Evangelical Protestants has by now almost certainly reached the number of their coreligionists in the United States. The movement has been strongest in Central America (thus it is estimated that between 25% and 30% of the population of Guatemala is now Protestant), but no country in the region has been untouched.

The most careful study of this phenomenon has been undertaken by the British sociologist David Martin and his associates, first in an overview of the entire Latin American situation, then in field studies in Brazil and Chile. What this study clearly shows is that conversion to Protestantism brings about what can only be called a cultural revolution. Individuals who join these Protestant churches abruptly, radically and in most cases permanently change their behavior. Defying all the stereotypes about Latin American culture, these people begin to act like, say, English Methodists in the eighteenth century. The break with traditional patterns of *machismo* is particularly startling. While most of the pastors are men, most of the evangelists and organizers of the new Latin American Protestantism are women. As Martin showed, these women "domesticate" their husbands — and, if the husbands refuse to be so resocialized, they find themselves out on their ears. The good Protestant husbands must stop drinking, gambling or having women on the side. Instead of celebrations with the godparents of one's children

(an important cause for consumption and income redistribution among Catholics), they now go to church services (often every night) and contribute a hefty portion of their income to the church (which redistributes by religious affiliation rather than kinship ties — a very important change). There is within these newly tightened families a strong interest in educating the children — which, as is well known from cross-national research, is a key factor in upward social mobility.

There has been a concomitant change in people's economic behavior. The people in these churches begin to practice in their lives the same virtues that Max Weber, in his classic work on the origins of capitalism, called the "Protestant ethic." (One commentator on Martin's work summed up its findings in the statement "Max Weber is alive and well and living in Guatemala.") This is an ethic of discipline and self-denial, of hard work, of favoring saving over consumption, and, last not least, an ethic associated with systematic planning for the future. A significant difference between the new Latin American Protestantism and its Anglo-Saxon antecedents is the mostly Pentecostal character of the former, bringing with it a highly emotional, even orgiastic style of worship. This emotionalism, though, does not seem to interfere with the new soberness in everyday life outside the sanctuary. It is even possible that it enhances the "Protestant ethic" in an original way, providing an emotional release in church which then makes it more possible for individuals to practice the new self-denying ethic in the outside world. Be this as it may, the economic consequences of the Protestant cultural revolution are beginning to come into view. In countries where the macroeconomic situation is depressed, this is not the case. If there are no objective opportunities for improving one's economic situation, it does not matter much *what* one's ethic is — one still stays in place. At best, then, one can once more speak here of "latent" cultural traits, which may come into their own if and when the overall circumstances change. Such is the case, for instance, in the Northeast of Brazil, a region of unrelieved economic depression. However, where the macroeconomic context is one of growth and mobility opportunities, it becomes clear that the Protestants have, precisely, a "comparative cultural advantage." Chile is a prime case of this. There we see the beginnings of a new

Protestant lower-middle class. If economic development continues successfully, there is every reason to think that this will become a full-blown *bourgeoisie,* including a well-educated upper-middle class. Not just the economic consequences but the social and political consequences of this for Latin America are staggering.

The comparison between this ethic and that of non-Protestant, non-Christian groups that have been economically successful is instructive. The Overseas Chinese are a good case for comparison. Despite the enormous religious and social differences, there are some obvious similarities — to wit, in the self-denying, gratification-delaying, frugal morality that Weber described as "inner-worldly asceticism" (living like a monk, but in the world, not in a monastery), in a pragmatic, activistic orientation in life, and, last not least, in a high regard for education. Chinese children may have literacy pounded in them so that they will grow up to be adults who can carry on a wide-ranging business correspondence, and Protestant children so that they can read the Bible. Either way, these children gain a "comparative cultural advantage" as against their illiterate non-Chinese or non-Protestant neighbors. Such a comparison suggests a general hypothesis: In an early stage of modern economic development, when there must occur an initial accumulation of capital and where much investment must be in the form of sweat, an ethic of self-denial, no matter how legitimated, is functionally necessary. Whether this behavior is motivated by fear of one's mother-in-law or fear of God, *economically speaking,* does not matter. An intriguing question, which will be raised below, is whether the same kind of ethic *remains* functional in a later state of economic development.

One more word here about the usefulness of looking at social change through the prism of economic culture: Some analysts of the contemporary religious scene have subsumed both the Islamic revival movements and the new Evangelical Protestantism under the category of "fundamentalisms." Let it be stipulated that there are some common features; after all, passionate movements of any sort, religious or secular, have some similar traits (it would be easy to list quite a number of purely secular "fundamentalisms" in the United States today). But the economic and socio-political consequences of the above two movements could not be more different. Both movements have been called "reactionary." This is correct up to a point, in that both movements react against certain aspects of modernity (notably its secularism and its alleged immorality) and that they look back to a supposedly better age. But *which* is the age they look back to? The Muslim "fundamentalists" look back to the golden age of Islam — say, some one thousand years ago; their putative Protestant soul-mates, if they look back at all (they do more so in the United States than in Latin America), look back to an earlier, simpler version of the bourgeois era — say, about a century ago. In other words, conservative Islam takes as its ideal an emphatically pre-modern society, while Evangelical Protestantism, insofar as it has any societal ideal at all, extols the virtues of Western culture at precisely the moment when it was in its most dynamic modernizing phase. One might venture a specific hypothesis: Protestant "fundamentalism" is itself a modernizing force; "Islamic fundamentalism" is counter-modernizing in its effects.

It has become a truism to say that in highly modern societies — that is, in the most economic and technologically advanced societies — all processes of change keep on accelerating. Like so many truisms, this one has a large kernel of truth. In contemporary North America and Europe, there have been many commentaries on economic changes and many on cultural changes, relatively few on how these two may relate to each other. Arguably the most dramatic cultural changes in recent Western history have been those that came about in the wake of what in the United States has been called "the late sixties." It is fairly clear that these changes did not come from nowhere, that they had roots in earlier developments. It was in the period roughly between 1965 and 1975, though, that in one country after another in the North Atlantic region there took place a series of events that, taken together, shook up the political, social and cultural scene. There emerged a constellation of beliefs, values and behavior patterns that defined itself as a "counter-culture." Counter to what? Well, counter to the political, social and cultural *status quo,* but significantly also counter to the economic *status quo* — that is, counter to capitalism. Broadly speaking, the new counter-culture was on the Left of the ideological spectrum, though there were great differences in political outlook (for example, in the degree of identification with Marxism). Culturally, the opposition was to a bourgeois society marked, precisely, by the "Protestant ethic." The counter-culture was hedonistic, self-affirming, consumption- rather than savings-oriented, averse to systematic discipline and planning, suspicious of education. In all of this, it seemed, the new cultural changes looked like bad news for capitalism, indeed for any sort of advanced industrial society. As Marxists used to say, "it was no accident" that these people liked to garb themselves in peasant costumes.

The perception of the counter-culture as inimical to capitalist modernity was shared by its critics and its proponents. In the United States there was a brief but interesting debate on the question of the so-called "New Class" — supposedly a new middle class based on the production and distribution of knowledge — knowledge of a special kind — non-material, symbolic, morally charged. The members of this new knowledge class — educators, therapists, "communicators," political activists, as well as segments of the bureaucracy and the legal profession — were taken to be the principal bearers of the counter-culture. At that time it was clear that these people were to the Left, not only of the population in general, but of members of the *old* middle class, which was seen to be broadly identical with the business community and most of the older professions. Commentators both from the Left and the Right concurred that there was indeed such a phenomenon. They disagreed, not on the putative facts, but on how to evaluate the facts: What one side understood to be the last, best hope for the longed-for revolution, the other side perceived as a decadent force subverting the economic, political and moral foundations of the society. As one looks back on the last twenty years or so, one can say with some confidence that both the hopes and the fears were exaggerated. "The system," as the counter-cultural revolutionaries called it, survived in its basic economic and political structures. What is more, the events that finally culminated in the collapse of the Soviet Union gave such a blow to Leftism in all its overtly political forms that it will probably take a considerable period of time, at the least, before this particular ideology becomes widely plausible again. Nevertheless, there *have* been sig-

nificant cultural changes in Western societies that have remained and that constitute a sort of institutionalization of "the late sixties." Some institutions, notably the universities and some of the major religious denominations, have been radically and apparently permanently changed. Politics has been strongly affected. In particular, views and behavior affecting relations between the sexes, interpersonal relations in general, sexuality in all its forms, child-rearing, attitudes toward racial and ethnic differences, and attitudes toward health and the physical environment — all these have undergone profound changes, probably most strongly in that part of the population categorized as the "New Class": in the earlier debate, but by now diffused through a much wider range of social strata. The sensibilities associated with feminism represent this cultural seachange very clearly; in that sense, one could say that North American culture, and to a slightly lesser degree the culture of western Europe, have become "feminized." How has this affected the economic culture of these societies? And, speaking economically only, has this enhanced or damaged the international competitiveness of the societies so changed?

The second question, at this point, must remain speculative. An attempt to begin to answer the first question was made by a team of social scientists headed by Hansfried Kellner of the University of Frankfurt. They studied "New Class" professionals in the United States and four countries in western Europe — business consultants in "soft" areas like personnel relations and corporate public relations, welfare-state bureaucrats, qualitative market researchers, and what the principal American researcher called "moral entrepreneurs" (such as anti-smoking and animal rights activists). These are all professional subcultures heavily affected by the values and lifestyles of what was once called the counter-culture, and many of these individuals had themselves been would-be revolutionaries in their younger years. What has happened to them in the meantime? Revolution in the literal sense of a radical restructuring of economic and political structures is no longer on the agenda. They have accepted "the system," with whatever inner reservations, and they are doing well working within it. On the other hand, however, they have retained much of their earlier outlook — on the egalitarian ideal, on "sensitive" interpersonal relations, on sexuality and gender, and they are still likely to be on the Left side of the political spectrum (liberal in American terms, social-democratic in European). Their own selves of twenty years ago, given the ability to peer into the future, would have said that they have sold out; their parents, if they are still around, are probably saying that they have settled down and become much more sensible.

More interesting, though, is another question: To what extent have they effected changes in the culture of business? The research by Kellner and his team cannot give a quantitative answer to this question; that is, their findings cannot indicate how large a sector within the business world has been changed by the arrival within it of these people. The findings do show, cross-nationally, that certain sectors have been affected to a considerable degree. Indeed, there has appeared a new market for products and services inspired by counter-cultural values. This is obviously the case with specific products, such as environment-friendly cosmetics, allegedly "natural" foods, equipment for an allegedly healthier lifestyle, and the veritable emporium of utensils (from meditation pillows to folk costumes) serving various "New Age" activities. The services offered in the same spirit are also manifold. Thus it has become possible to make careers and estimable incomes by advising corporations on how to develop executives who are "more sensitive" to various categories of employees or who have learned "to be in touch with their own bodies" (there is a whole category of "personal development programs" in both American and European corporations), on setting up affirmative action procedures, anti-smoking and weight-reduction clinics, on operating day-care facilities for employees' children, or on propagating a "socially responsible" corporate image in the wider public. What emerges here is a "kinder, gentler" capitalism, or at least the appearance of one — or, if one prefers, a more "feminized" capitalism.

Would such a new capitalism be internationally competitive? One can only speculate here. On the face of it, the answer would seem to be negative. East Asian capitalism, for one, is certainly made of harder stuff, and in a contest between hard and soft cultures it is the former that usually win. Put in more elegant scientific language, hard-nosed sons-of-bitches are likely to wipe the floor with sensitive types. But on the other hand, as anyone has learned who ever took an introductory sociology course (the famous "Thomas' dictum"), "if people define a situation as real, it is real in its consequences." If people really believe that they will produce better telecommunications equipment if they "get in touch with their bodies" or are more appreciative of alternative forms of sexual orientation, perhaps they will *really* produce better equipment — and beat out those uptight, insensitive Taiwanese in international competition. If this should actually turn out to be the case, it would support another hypothesis: Contrary to what is functional at an earlier stage of modern economic development, when something like the "Protestant ethic" is called for, a more mature economic stage ("post-industrial," "knowledge-driven") can accommodate and perhaps even requires a much more hedonistic ethos.

The problems of economic culture sketched here have great intellectual fascination. The social scientist requires no other motive than his own curiosity in exploring these problems. He can paraphrase for his own discipline the famous toast that used to be offered at the Royal Society of Mathematicians: "To pure mathematics, and may it never be of use to anyone!" People who must orient their activities by practical results, in business and at least some areas of government, cannot afford such luxury. They must ask what use there might be for their results-oriented projected from insights coming out of this particular intellectual inquiry. The answer would seem to be obvious. Insofar as cultural factors enter into economic and political life, no one who seeks results in these areas can ignore them. If he does, he is likely to be in for some unpleasant surprises.

A chemist trying to understand a particular chemical reaction will always carry out some sort of control experiment. The social scientist, of course, cannot carry on experiments of his own, but sometimes history provides him with the same experimental logic. Thus, anyone seeking to grasp modernity today may conjure up the image of a gigantic laboratory in which three test tubes are bubbling away, each containing a similar reaction ("modernization"), but with significantly different elements in each. There continues to be the case of advanced industrial capitalism in the West. There is also the . . . case of advanced industrial socialism, in the Soviet Union and in its European allies. The comparison between these two cases is very important, but it will not concern us here. But there is yet another case, that of advanced industrial capitalism in East Asia. It is my contention that this case is absolutely crucial for an understanding of modernity; it is, if you will, an essential "control experiment." In this logic, it is not just a question of understanding East Asia, but rather a question of understanding what happens elsewhere (including the West) in the light of this Asian experience.

The countries I have in mind here are, of course, the successful capitalist ones in the region: Japan, the so-called Four Little Dragons — South Korea, Taiwan, Hong Kong and Singapore — and, increasingly, at least some of the countries of ASEAN besides Singapore. Their economic successes have powerfully impressed themselves on the consciousness of people everywhere (not always pleasurably, i.e., the American automobile and steel industries). The same economic successes have induced both social scientists and politicians in other parts of the world to speak of an "East Asian development model." I recently met with a group of Senegalese intellectuals to discuss problems of African development; when they heard that I had just returned from East Asia, that was all they wanted to talk about. A few months ago I spent some time in Jamaica and, not really to my surprise, a question that kept coming up was what would have to happen to make Jamaica "another Taiwan."

It is my contention that these countries are sufficiently distinct, as compared with the West, that one is entitled to speak of them as a "second case" of capitalist modernity.

— Peter Berger, "An East Asian Development Model?" in *In Search of an East Asian Development Model,* by Peter Berger and Michael Hsiao (New Brunswick: Transaction Books, 1988), p. 4

The Asian Systems

George Lodge

The Asian Systems

. . . . Thus far in our examination of capitalism and socialism (including communism) we have seen that the words have carried many meanings. They embody certain theories about how economic and social systems *should* work. They contain analytical critiques of how these systems actually *have worked*. And inasmuch as they were mutually antagonistic, the meaning of one derived from one's conception of the meaning of the other; that is, in a real sense, they defined each other.

Socialism is deeply rooted in Europe, and capitalism in both Europe and the United States. They are inseparable from the religion, philosophy and economic theory peculiar to those regions. They were inspired and affected by Christianity, just as they in turn seem to have effected Christian thought. In spite of the Socialists' rejection of religion, it seems clear that their moral goals and thus their legitimacy was based in Christian thinking — Laski made this quite clear — as well as the philosophy of Kant and Hegel. And clearly Capitalism was legitimized by Protestantism, filtered through the thoughts of Locke and Adam Smith among others. As the 20th century drew to a close a synthesis of both had found favor with the Vatican.

Capitalism, even though not named until around 1800 — and then defined as much or more by its opponents as its adherents — dated from the middle of the 17th century. Socialism came later as a protest against capitalism's in-

justices. Ideologically speaking, capitalism conformed roughly to the tenets of individualism and socialism to one variation or another of communitarianism. By the end of the 20th century socialist concerns regarding egalitarian outcomes — i.e. affirmative action — and for guaranteed rights of membership to such things as income, health and shelter had become accepted principles throughout the industrial world. The dispersion of ownership and ecological imperatives had greatly diluted the importance of property rights.

It seems fair to conclude that events have passed the two words by, and whatever meaning the words may have had was peculiar to western civilization. It verges on the preposterous and certainly the parochial to call the economic systems of China, Japan, Taiwan, Korea, Singapore and other Asian countries by the words "capitalist" and "socialist" that are as irrelevant to their Confucian, Taoist, Buddhist and Shinto traditions as they are to their historic experience.

Although the literature of capitalism and socialism — Smith, Marx, Schumpeter, List, etc. — was certainly familiar to 19th and 20th century Asian intellectuals, one must suspect that the development of Asian economic systems had little to do with the western isms. While Schumpeter is known to have been popular in Japan in the 30s, it seems likely that it was because his views happened to coincide with and justify what Japan was in fact doing rather than because the Japanese had accepted the Harvard economist as a guide. Even the development of China since 1949 seems to have been far more Chinese in character than it was an outgrowth of Marx and European communism and socialism.

The Asian economic systems are clearly communitarian — not individualistic — and each represents a quite different form of communitarianism. In both China and Taiwan, for example, what might be called "familism" exists alongside "statism," the purpose of business invariably being the enrichment of the Chinese family. The purpose of business in Japan, on the other hand, is clearly to serve the greater glory of Japan as well as the welfare of all the corporate members. I recall once asking the president of Toyota who owned Toyota. The question was puzzling to him, but after a pause he said he thought Toyota was owned by "all its members."

George Lodge, "The Asian Systems," draft for a chapter in a forthcoming book by Pfeiffer and Co.

Asian systems such as Japan have familiar characteristics which have made them formidable competitors against their western rivals. These characteristics include:

Cooperative relationships between business and government and between managers and managed which produce a high level of consensus behind national goals. The consensus depends upon fairness in sharing both economic pain and gain: the Asian countries have the most equitable distribution of income in the world. (Ironically, Taiwan's is more equitable than the People's Republic.)

National goals give top priority to national competitiveness, that is to the acquisition of market share by the nation as a collection of producers in high value-added products. The distinction in this regard between public sector and private sector is insignificant.

Economic policies are designed to serve these goals. They are producer — not consumer — oriented. They encourage saving and investment, not consumption — but, let us quickly note, the motive for this is not individual salvation. It is community prosperity.

So we can say that the world's most competitive economies are neither socialist nor capitalist. They have elements of both but they are significantly, perhaps radically, different. Pretending otherwise leads to confusion and misunderstanding.

The Chinese System

S. Gordon Redding, dean of the Hong Kong University School of Business Administration, has interviewed hundreds of Chinese business managers. He has written that an understanding of Chinese business must begin with the Chinese people's religious and belief system. And this belief system, or what Redding calls "the prevailing ideology of China for most of its recorded history has been a set of ideas which go under the convenient label of Confucianism."

Confucianism constrains "the expression of individual desires" and encourages group sharing of limited resources. The family and loyalty to the family are of supreme importance. The family functions as "a rational collective" to insure individuals against disaster. This idea of the family carries over into the Chinese conception of the state which is quite different from the western idea. The Confucian state is

"seen by its members as an enormous, but nevertheless united group, while the western version is doctrinally at least an abstraction, a universal or absolute idea. Thus the Chinese state is in essence the super-family of Chinese people. Within this structure, the maintenance of order was founded on the morally enriched prescriptions for relationships. Thus the individual finds dignity and meaning in the maintenance of harmony in his own social context.

"The society is constructed of morally binding relationships connecting all. In this the self is not an enclosed world of private thoughts. The individual is instead a connection, and the totalness of society is passed down from one binding relationship to the next, rather than by the Western mode of uniting loosely coupled and free individuals by their separate espousal of coordinating ideas and principles. For the Chinese, fulfillment comes from the very structure and dynamics of the relationships and emphasis on belonging."

Inasmuch as the Chinese state tended toward despotism, the family was the protector of the individual against the state. "The family is the first and last resort, and for most the only resort." Welfare had traditionally been a family responsibility and schooling enforced the rigor of duty to family as a way of stabilizing the state.

"An inevitable consequence of this is the rivalry of families as they seek to control and accumulate scarce resources in competition with each other. Individual achievement becomes an aspect of family achievement and the spirit of family enrichment at the expense of other families becomes a primary force described as 'magnified selfishness,' and opposed to a wider sense of community and societal responsibility."

There are three important differences separating Confucianism from other religions: It contains no deity, only rules of conduct. It doesn't compete with other religions. And it has no large-scale institutional "church."

"Its dominance came about because it provided the philosophical basis for the filial piety which supported the family structures and in turn the state itself." It also provided the Chinese with their conception of the purpose of business: the long-term enrichment and preservation of the family.

"The son, pursuing a career in medicine in Canada, but called back by the father to Hong Kong in order to take over the responsibilities of the family business which has run into problems, must understand the duty imposed on him by the protocols of filial piety, must follow that duty without complaint, and must discipline himself to a new life-style."

Confucius lived between 551 and 479 B.C. Although his teachings have been packaged and re-packaged in a variety of ways over the years and although Mao tried to set them aside altogether, they have remained remarkably reliable and resil-ient. For most Chinese they are mixed with Taoism, a kind of nature religion, which is more sympathetic to individualistic concerns. Indeed, there is in Taoism a rather strong streak of what we in the West might call civil disobedience which combined with Confucianism produces a most non-Western approach to government. Govern-ment is to be respected but knowing how to cir-cumvent its strictures is admired. Putting it crudely perhaps: Respect government but its rules are made to be bent.

I recall a conversation with a senior minister of the Taiwan government who bemoaned the plethora of government regulations that hindered Taiwanese business people in world competition. But then the minister added cheerfully: "But you know our people are very good at getting around the laws."

The Chinese belief system produces family firms in which members and employees work ex-tremely hard, because their survival depends upon it. These firms often have far-flung connections through family members in the Pacific basin and the United States. But their growth is essentially limited by the extent of the family. It is a business system also, says Redding, that is anything but transparent and difficult to change.

He speaks of the "passivity induced by a system which places the individual in a powerfully main-tained family order, itself inside a powerfully maintained state order, itself seen as part of a natural cosmic order (Taoist and Buddhist tradi-tions), and all dedicated to the maintenance of the status quo. When the only true authority is tradition, and when deviant behavior meets heavy sanctions from an early age, when deference to elders is automatic, and when dependence on those same elders is non-negotiable, then all the ingredients are present for producing a social sys-tem characterized on the one hand by an impres-sive stability and on the other hand by a debili-tating incapacity to adapt, innovate, and change."

This brief look at traditional Chinese ideology helps us to understand why Chinese firms are quite different from the Japanese *keiretsu* and *kai-sha*, the Korean *chaebol*, and the western multi-national. We may also get an idea of some of the managerial challenges when the different organi-zational forms compete, cooperate, or collide.

The Future

Some paths to the future are already quite clear:

1. National systems — economic, social and political — are being forced to converge by two global forces: intensifying competition among the different systems and pressures to preserve eco-logical integrity. Those systems which respond most efficiently to those two forces will survive and prosper and tend to change those systems which are less responsive. This is not too surpris-ing. In fact, we have already seen the United States, which is perhaps as ideologically distant from Japan as any nation can be, changing its ways in a Japanese-like direction in order to become more competitive. And the pressures for ecological in-tegrity are causing all nations to bow to certain global constraints.

2. Even as competition among nations becomes more intense the nation-state itself is being forced to surrender sovereignty and power to a variety of international organizations and entities upon which it is increasingly dependent. These organi-zations include a melange of public and private entities ranging from multinational corporations, corporate alliances, business-government coali-tions, purely governmental regional associations,

trade blocs and the like, and the United Nations and its specialized agencies.

To seek to interpret such a future within the parameters of "capitalism" — or "socialism" — is fruitless. What is worse, it is virtually sure to lead to error. Those words carry blinders that restrict what we see and condition our interpretation of what we see.

Korean Economy: A Model Case of a Miraculous Growth?

Sang-Goog Cho

Introduction

By any measure, the performance of the Korean economy during the last three decades has been outstanding. From 1962 to 1991 the Korean economy grew at an average annual rate of nearly nine percent in real terms. In the span of roughly one generation, Korea has achieved the kind of economic development that today's advanced nations took almost a century to achieve from a similar stage of development. Many scholars call this the Korean miracle. Another story of miracle in Korea is, however, usually neglected.

Even though it was 1884 when the first resident Christian missionary, American medical doctor Horace N. Allen, entered Korea, Korea now has by far the highest proportion of Christians — nearly half of all professed religious believers — among the traditionally Confucian and Buddhist cultures of East Asia. The world's largest Methodist church (Kwang Lim Methodist Church, 50,000), Presbyterian church (Young Nak Presbyterian Church, 50,000), and Pentecostal church (Yoida Full Gospel Church, 500,000) are all to be found in Korea's capital city of Seoul. There are over 330,000 Protestant congregations in South Korea. Apart from the three mega-churches in Seoul, there are others numbering 10,000, and congregations of over 1,000 are common. Together these

Sang-Goog Cho, "Korean Economy: A Model Case of a Miraculous Growth?" unpublished paper, September 1993.

total around ten million Protestant believers and about two-and-a-half million Roman Catholics. The nation is effectively over 25 percent Christian. With spiritual new births taking place at around one million per year as against natural births at about 600,000 per year, the goal of being more than 30 percent Christian by the early 1990s and then going on to take the nation seems clearly attainable.

Many people, however, mention the Korean miracle only in terms of economy, not referring to it in terms of Christianity. What is the relationship between economic growth and Christianity in Korea? What are the problems in the Korean economy from a Christian perspective? I would like to discuss these. First, let's turn to the performance of the Korean economy.

A Brief Review of the Korean Economy

Korea is a small country in terms of area — about the size of Portugal or Hungary, or a quarter of California or Japan's size. It is a large country by population, however. With 42.8 million people in 1990, Korea is comparable in population to major Western industrial countries during their rise from developing to developed country status.

The history of Korea as an independent country goes as far back as A.D. 668, when the Silla Kingdom (57 B.C.–A.D. 935) completed the conquest of two other early Korean kingdoms — Koguryo and Paekche. With the unification of the country under the Silla, the Korean people came under the rule of a single monarch — marking the beginnings of a unified culture and history that were to persist, with only occasional interruptions, until this century. From the unification of the country by the Silla until the colonization of the country by Japan in 1910, Korea remained an independent nation for more than twelve centuries. Edwin Reishauer says that Korea and Japan have, after China, the longest histories as independent nations in the world.

Korea was one of the poorest countries in the world immediately after the Korean War. Even in 1960, after the damage inflicted during the war had been repaired, with a per capita GNP of US $80 in current prices, domestic savings were negligible. As a result, foreign aid financed well over 50 percent of the nation's investment. Unemployment and underemployment were widespread; urban unemployment in particular reached as high as 20 percent. Over 40 percent of the nation's population was suffering from absolute poverty. At the same time, as a resource-poor nation, Korea had no significant exports ($55 million in 1962), and the balance of payments had shown a chronic deficit since 1945.

Since 1963, however, Korea has entered a period of sustained high economic growth. As a result, it developed to the level of a "new industrializing economy" (NIE) by 1970. The economy entered a new phase in 1986 with the onset of the "three lows" — low oil prices, a lower dollar, and low interest rates. For the first time in the economic history of Korea, domestic savings began to exceed investment, and the international balance of payments turned from a chronic deficit position to a surplus. As a result, Korea was able to rapidly reduce her foreign debt, which had peaked at US $46.7 billion in 1985. It was no longer necessary for Korea to worry about foreign debt and rely on advanced countries for economic assistance. By 1986 Korea appeared to have achieved its earlier goal of realizing "economic independence" and reached the stage of self-sustaining growth. In that year the annual inflation rate as measured by the consumer price index stabilized at the 2-3 percent level, and the economic growth rate exceeded 12 percent in 1986, 1987, and 1988, the highest rates in the world.

Today, with a total trading volume of $153.4 billion in 1991, up from $477 million in 1962, Korea currently is the eleventh largest trading nation in the world. Korea's per capita income in 1990 surpassed the $5,000 mark ($6,498), a big leap from the meager $87 recorded in 1962. The nation's unemployment rate consistently remains below 3 percent, and absolute poverty has nearly disappeared. Indeed, Korea is on the threshold of joining the ranks of industrially advanced nations, and it may become the first nation from the developing world to achieve such status since World War II.

Korea's Strategy for Growth

There are many books and articles written on the Korean economy and on other Asian newly industrializing economies (NIEs). Since the Asian NIEs share a common heritage of Confucianism, this cultural factor is often emphasized in explanations of their successes. Their successes have sometimes been explained only in the context of pure neoclassical theories. Still others have emphasized institutional factors, such as political structures, while some have pointed to the government's ability to guide markets and thereby reduce risk for the private sector. It is also well known that Korea's economic success is due to a great extent to international factors: foreign markets, foreign capital, and important technology. All these factors must have played a role in producing the Korean success story.

As a Christian I am bold enough to argue that the Christianity in Korea has played one of the most important roles in Korean economic growth. We might find many evidences for this argument beyond the scope of this paper, but as an international economist I would like to take one example of government strategy as it intersects with Christianity.

Many economists agree that Korea's sustained growth since the early 1960s is due largely to the identification of and adherence to a growth strategy, namely, an outward-, industry-, and growth-oriented (or OIG-oriented) strategy. This OIG-oriented strategy is not unique in the Korean economy. Korean Christianity in general also is characterized by this strategy, perhaps due to the model of the government strategy or due to the positive faith or pentecostal fever in Korea. In other words, OIG-oriented strategy became a nationwide strategy both in the economy (the physical world) and in Christianity (the spiritual world).

Let's discuss three aspects of this parallel growth strategy in detail.

First, it is growth-oriented rather than equity-oriented. Driven by the urgent need to compete successfully with North Korea in the 1960s and to escape from the vicious circle of unemployment and poverty, Korea adopted a strongly growth-oriented strategy. This is also true of the Korean church. There has been a strong drive and enthusiasm for church growth in Korea. It seems that the criterion for church success was the number in the congregations, and bigness was the first priority in most churches. Yet while justification and blessings were loudly proclaimed to non-believers, sanctification in faith was not properly emphasized to the believers.

Second, Korea's strategy has been industry-oriented rather than resource- or service-oriented or agriculturally oriented. Lacking natural resources, Korea was not in a position to adopt a primary or resource-oriented development strategy. At the same time the Korean church also was industry-oriented. Lots of churches in the industrial cities were built and proliferated, but the number of churches in the rural areas diminished.

Third, Korea's approach has been outward-looking rather than inward-looking or neutral. The need to import food and other raw materials impels Korea to earn needed foreign exchange through the export of manufactured goods. The Korean church's approach also has been outward-looking for different reasons. The Korean church sent lots of missionaries to the third world and many students went to foreign countries — especially to the United States to study theology. The Korean church began to look around the world and feel some calling from God toward the world.

This is just one example of a strategy that has been commonly adopted by both the Korean government and the Korean church in general. Does this show a coincidence or a strong correlation? I think it is the latter. It is not always recommended that a developing country adopt an OIG-oriented strategy since it does not guarantee success. Yet the OIG-oriented strategy was very acceptable to the Korean people, of whom 25 percent are Christians. It seems this strategy brought about the economic miracle. It would be too much to argue that there is direct causality between the successes of Christianity and the economy of Korea. It would be safe, however, to say that Christian attitudes and values toward work, thrift, vocation, and positive thinking have been critically important for the success of Korean economy.

Challenges Ahead

Korea's phenomenal success brought its own problems. As Korea's export market grew quickly, its export share in the world naturally increased rapidly. Trade disputes and frictions with major trading partners were bound to arise. The United

States, traditionally the most important market for Korean exports, provided more than one-third of the market for Korea's exports in the 1980s. Furthermore, Korea began to record a trade surplus vis-à-vis the United States in 1982, when the U.S. was suffering from its twin deficit problem. Korea became one of the major targets for U.S. policies to restrict access to the U.S. market while increasing bilateral pressure for market opening and currency appreciation. The antidumping case of Korean album exports to the United States and U.S. pressure to open the Korean cigarette market are cases in point. Despite the relatively small amounts of money involved, these cases generated a high level of anti-American sentiment.

Korea is now caught between two competitive fronts. As it loses its competitive advantages in labor-intensive and middle-level, technology-intensive products, Korea now faces difficulties in establishing a competitive edge in capital-and technology-intensive differentiated products. Differentiated high-value-added products require constant product and process innovation and dynamic responses to market changes in addition to manufacturing excellence.

Despite the apparent trend toward favorable income distribution until very recent years, distributional issues have lately been drawing a great deal of attention in Korea. It could be that actual income distribution in recent years has, in fact, worsened. Another possibility is that published income distribution statistics do not accurately portray the actual distributional situation in Korea. Still another possibility is that a gap between actual and perceived income distribution may exist and has widened in recent years. Some believe that published statistics seriously underestimated income inequality in Korea, primarily due to problems of biased coverage in the data collection. The incomplete coverage of capital gains from real estate could be the most serious source of bias because Korea has experienced unprecedented and rapid real estate price increases in recent years. In addition to the possibility of actual worsening income distribution, it is also likely that the perceived income distribution gap has also widened in recent years. Recent rapid increases in housing prices may have left non-house-owners feeling further disadvantaged. The proportion of house-owning households in urban areas has dropped to less than 50 percent while housing prices have increased substantially in recent years.

Korea's most serious problem is the labor-management confrontation that began in 1987. Korean labor relations are still in their infancy and are reminiscent of those of the United States in the 1920s. Korean policymakers are particularly worried about the possibility of serious labor disputes that may impede growth. Korea has reached the stage where a competitive strategy based on quality differentiation rather than on price has to be pursued. Such a strategy can succeed only with appropriate human resource development and productive labor-management relations. In other words, economic environments are not as favorable now for growth in Korea.

How about spiritual environments in Korea? The most serious spiritual problem in Korea now seems to be "faith in progress." It is embedding itself in the majority of the Korean people. It is becoming a dangerous idol that will betray us soon; and furthermore there are not many strong Christians with world-formative views in Korea. It is well known that in recent years most big economic crimes involved some Christians. Since materialism is intertwined in Korea with economic success, there are also many Christians who associate material progress with spiritual values, looking upon riches as a proper reward for work combined with the proper virtues. Yet contrary to this view it is also said that the mainstream Korean Protestant church is pietistic, other-worldly oriented.

It is not rare to listen to the following criticisms of Korean Christians: Christians in Korea are mostly still passive and following government policy in practicing distributional justice; they are very sincere Christians in church but are not very distinctive in their public life; Christianity in Korea is being reduced to personal matters, not transforming the world; even though growth in the number of Christians is miraculous, influence of Christianity on society is not accompanying it but rather diminishing; Christians are familiar with the blessings from God but quite ignorant or negligent about his commands of justice and the doctrine of stewardship.

Recently Korean President Kim Youngsam has adopted a series of drastic changes in politics and the economy, eradicating corruption among public officials and establishing sound foundations for the economy. He opened up records of officials' wealth, and he requires using one's real name in financial accounting. Many representatives and high officials resigned due to their conspicuously suspicious accumulations of wealth. President Kim, who is an elder of the Presbyterian Church, asked that the Korean Christians repent and practice justice more vividly in their lives. Many Christian leaders agree with him. There is a growing awareness of the need for Christian reformation in every field of our lives, especially in the economy.

Do Koreans have pessimism about the future? Korean Christians don't, because they have hope. Many Christians believe that the economic miracle is grace from God and that there must be a reason for this grace from God. God's reason, related to the aspirations of Korean Christians, is described by the famous Dr. Han Kyung-Jik, the pastor emeritus of Young-Nak Presbyterian Church:

> We should pray earnestly, work harder, and be willing to give our lives to achieve true democracy in this land. We desire that freedom, equality, and a high respect of human rights will be practiced and enjoyed by all people and that our nation will prosper.... The reason God placed us in this land at this time is to evangelize our nation first, then North Korea, and then the whole world. We must recommit ourselves to the Lord with a new devotion, greater effort, and willing spirit of sacrifice to fulfill this great task.

Guiding Principles

Arun Katiyar and Shefali Rekhi

Kurukshetra. Arjun pauses, then declines to fight. Is there glory in a victory that kills fathers, sons, teachers and students? One of the most able warriors in the land is paralysed by emotion. Lord Krishna reminds him of the consequences to the state and society.

Modern day managers face the same situation every day — a conflict between tough decisions and the larger good. "Corporate playing fields are much like Kurukshetra," says Delhi-based management consultant M. B. Athreya. "They can be viewed as *Dharam Kshetra*, where the role of leadership is to re-establish *dharma* and resolve the conflicts that arise between customers and suppliers, pollution and the environment, manipulative politics in the organisation and unfair practices towards workmen."

Concepts like *Utthistha* (stand up and be counted), *Vishadha* (doubt), *Swadharma* (duty) and *Nishkama Karma* (work without attachment to results) have always existed in the *shastras*. Now, driven by the understanding that the Indian cultural tradition is rich in these leadership values, managements are beginning to examine the wisdom embodied in the scriptures. Many across the country who have tried to inculcate the values prescribed in the Gita are starting to show positive results. Says Dr. Subir Chowdhury, director, Indian Institute of Management (IIM), Calcutta: "It's back to basics. If traditional values are transplanted to modern times, a new management style can develop as opposed to the Japanese and the American style."

Companies like Crompton Greaves, Larsen &

Arun Katiyar and Shefali Rekhi, "Guiding Principles," *India Today*, 15 July 1994, pp. 42-43.

Toubro, Excel Industries and the Mafatlal Group are beginning to reinterpret business in the context of Indian heritage. Asea Brown Boveri Limited's (ABB) unit in Vadodara is one such place which has been experimenting with the Vedanta style as part of its total quality management programme for the past four years. Consultant Vanraj Jhala was called to hold workshops for workers. The results are visible and can be quantified.

At ABB, one group of workers reduced the time to make a circuit breaker from 120 days to 68 days, while customer delivery has improved 100 percent. "The foundation of the change programme lies in getting away from the hand-body syndrome and engaging the minds of people in a creative manner towards an overall vision," says ABB Vice-President K. K. Kaura.

The *shastras* have been used in more sophisticated management missions than improving shop floor objectives. Athreya, who earned his doctorate at Harvard and leads the new interest in the *shastras* today, has used his knowledge of the Gita to reorganise Indian family businesses like those of Harishankar Singhania, transform the political cultue of the L. M. Thapar group to that of a business culture and has helped workers at Shaw Wallace come to terms with the fight between brothers Manu and Kishore Chhabria.

At the Rs 240-crore Excel industries, says Managing Director K. C. Shroff, who bases his management methods on the *Upanishads*, the company hasn't wasted an hour on industrial disputes in its 53-year history. Shroff quotes the *Upanishads*: "Together we will work, together we will do great things. But never envy each other."

The rediscovery of ancient wisdom is quickly being recognised as turbo *vidya*. "The Bhagvad Gita works because it is about self-management," says Alok Chopra, an *acharya* at the Vedant Academy, a non-profit organisation which holds courses on vedic principles. "We tell people, if all you want is more money and power, go to a financial institution. If you want to know the rightful place of both, the Gita will help."

According to Bangalore-based economist, S. I. N. Simha, author of *Management with Dharma All the Way* and books on the Ramayan and the Mahabharat, values are critical to the performance of individuals and also to the outcome of corporate efforts. "The principles of manage-ment tell you how to acquire skills. But people don't have the courage or character to use those skills correctly," says Simha who was the founder-director of the Institute of Financial Management and Research, Madras, and currently lectures on the subject. Many are convinced that western management has outlived its relevance in the context of the Indian psyche.

Excessive emphasis on competition and not enough on integrative cooperation has begun to expose its imperfections. "In line with the integrative mode, companies like Thermax and Sundaram Fastners have been trying to evolve shared visions and core corporate values," says Jhala. "Once that is done, it has a powerful emotive appeal within the organisation."

Jhala says that he is amazed at the resonance with which Indian workmen take to concepts like Karma Yoga. His studies have shown that even three years after the training in *shastras*, the new set of values survive erosion. He thinks that when a management educator uses the *shastras*, he literally taps into what Carl Jung calls the collective unconscious or the *sanskaras*. Better work ethics, cooperation between departments and improved management-union relationships begin to emerge naturally.

Results appear to match the theory. And companies like Logic Control Private Limited, which manufactures voltage stabilisers, are beginning to experience them. "Most workers lack a purpose in life," says S. K. Bahl, managing director of the Rs 1.96-crore Logic Control. "Their lives are full of misgivings, doubts, and complexes." Within two months of lectures on the *Vedas*, the transformation at Logic Control became evident. Workers became aware of the contribution they make and began to appreciate their significance. "Things move so smoothly now that I'm sitting idle most of the time," says Bahl.

The changes caught the attention of a transporter who ships products between Logic Control and his company called Controls and Switchgear. "It seldom took the transporter more than 10 minutes to get material off loaded at Logic Control premises. But back at his own office, it took him hours. When the transporter decided to speak to the Logic Control people, he discovered that there was no bureaucracy or hierarchy. He was told that this was a result of the weekly Vedanta sittings. Soon, Controls and Switchgear's 2,000 employees, including the top management, were looking at the *Vedas* for corporate guidance. Says Controls and Switchgear Managing Director Ravindra Nath Khanna, "I too wanted to be in the same boat."

What Khanna discovered are key solutions which every management aims for. "The *Vedas* combine the dynamism of the West with the peace and serenity of the East," says Khanna. "Secondly, they tell you to be true to what you are doing." Khanna gives the example of standing for a *yagna*, throwing *ahuti* in the fire in the hope that the fire god will shower his blessings. A factory is like *havan kund;* your efforts are like *ahuti* — if they are pure and sincere, you will be rewarded. "We encourage workers to deliberate on their actions," says Khanna. "I've seen it transforming my people psychologically."

The transformation is inevitable, suggests Dr. Y. Jayadev, director of Bombay's 75-year-old Yoga Institute. His experience has shown that the *Vedas* as well as yoga help cultivate an otherworldly attitude. With industry and business showing an increasing interest in the value of the *shastras,* ITT Delhi is conducting an efficiency study at Logic Stat to quantify the gains. Whatever its findings, the need for a specifically Indian movement has become imperative to balance the western dynamics of progress. "A sobering effect to the mindless rat race is the need of the hour," says Chowdhury of IIM, Calcutta where Professor S. K. Chakraborty is setting up a Centre for Management of Human Values. Recognised as one of the first to use the *shastras* in management, Chakraborty has been holding workshops and lectures for managers for more than six years now.

Unfortunately, many consultants who use the *shastras* are sometimes viewed as cranks, or even religious fundamentalists. But they continue to look towards the great Indian epics for inspiration, helping resolve the conflicts between individual, corporate and social objectives. The attitude is in keeping with what Simha observes in his book: "Public interest must always take precedence over private interest. That is the path of *Dharma.*" A path that could help bring in improved work ethics and enhance productivity — a mission statement that any management would be proud of.

"Import substitution cannot be an end in itself. The very level of development we have reached is independent of the world economy in some respects, but more dependent on it in others. This is an important aspect of the complexity of modern development. There is hardly any country in the world, however developed, which insists on making everything it needs. Not that it does not possess the capacity to do so, but it finds it more economical, in its circumstances to buy a number of things from others who make them . . . the criterion of self-reliance today has to be not whether you can make whatever you need, but whether you can pay for whatever you need." These words of Prime Minister P. V. Narasimha Rao clearly defined the concept of self-reliance in the present-day world (1992).

So there is no reason why the economy of the country should remain insulated from the world economy in the name of an obsolete concept of self reliance. Any delay to overcome this will have disastrous consequences for a large country like India where it is unable to meet even the basic needs of the population with its own resources. There must be a two way traffic of capital, manpower, technology etc. . . .

Misplaced

The fears that the policy of welcoming foreign investment will hurt Indian industry and may jeopardize its economic sovereignty are totally misplaced. As the Union Finance Minister Dr. Manmoham Singh aptly said, "India as a nation is capable of dealing with foreign investors on its own terms. Indian industry has also come of age, and is now ready to enter a phase where it can both compete with foreign investment and also cooperate with it. This is the trend all over the world and we cannot afford to be left out. . . . We have enough policy instruments at our disposal to ensure that enterprises with foreign equity function in accordance with our national priorities." Stressing the country's confidence in this regard, the Prime Minister had this to say, "no foreign country or force could swallow India. No country is a big enough whale to swallow us."

The recent steps taken by the Government are not at the cost of self reliance. Self reliance does not mean cutting the country off from the world and reducing imports. It requires the creation of a competitive environment, in which enough is exported to pay for the imports without excessive dependence on aid or borrowing. Foreign investment is business. The era of dependence on international concessional assistance is virtually over with new claimants for it.

The Finance Minister has emphasized on more than one occasion that the bulk of the resources for India's development would continue to be mobilized domestically. A favorable macro economic environment for the growth of domestic savings and their deployment in productive channels has been provided. Foreign direct investment will enable the country to reduce its reliance on foreign commercial borrowings, thereby facilitating a more orderly management of the economy.

Phenomenal Increase

. . . Foreign investment and technology collaborations will help the country obtain higher technology, increase exports, expand the production base and generate new employment opportunities. Today, China and several South East Asian nations are able to attract much more foreign investment than India. As a nation, India stands to gain considerably by integrating into the global economic mainstream by harnessing our strengths and overcoming our weaknesses so that the country emerges as a vibrant and internationally competitive economy.

— Y. S. R. Murthy, "Indian Industry Comes of Age," *India News Magazine,* 16-30 April 1992, p. 6

The New Poland: Major Problems for Ethical Business

Leo V. Ryan

Throughout Eastern Europe, now preferably called again Central Europe, 1989 was a year of unprecedented political and economic change. Poland was the first Eastern European socialist country to initiate sweeping changes designed to transform the country from a centrally planned and controlled economy characteristic of "Real Socialism" to a system predicated on parliamentary democracy and a market economy based on a system of private property. However, early evidence indicates that Polish economic reform is not even primarily about new economic initiatives. The success of the programme of economic transformation depends heavily on the supportive attitudes of the public, on social consensus, on a willingness to sacrifice, on the acceptance of new responsibilities corresponding to newly acquired rights — all of which relate to values. Fundamentally, most of the issues facing the new Poland involve moral and ethical questions.

There is growing evidence to suggest that public attitudes are shifting, that the enthusiasm for change and the social consensus is weakening. Moreover, there is acknowledgement by a widespread cross-section of the population that Poland will require a much longer period of re-education than initially anticipated to recover from a forty-year period of passive aggression and the lack of

Leo V. Ryan, C.S.V., "The New Poland: Major Problems for Ethical Business," *Business Ethics: A European Review* (Blackwell's at Oxford, U.K.) 1, no. 1 (Jan. 1992): 9-15.

confidence in government, the erosion of the work ethic, the corruption of public and private morals, and a system rife with injustice.

The unprecedented changes of 1989 in Poland were the result of a decade of failures by the Communist Party system to meet the successive economic and political challenges facing the country. When General Wojciech Jaruzielski was eventually influenced (or forced) to initiate the "Round Table" talks in 1989, he invited several hundred representatives heavily reflective of the ruling Communist coalitions but also the opposition centred about the then still outlawed "Solidarity" movement. The so-called "Round Table" negotiations were to focus "on practically all significant spheres of social life, including economic matters." Partially free elections were authorized for June, trade unions were re-established on April 7, and this prepared the way to re-legalize Solidarity on April 17. A landslide victory of Solidarity supporters to the Parliament necessitated forming a new government under Tadeusz Mazowiecki as Prime Minister.

The Mazowiecki government faced a desperate situation which, in turn, demanded severe economic adjustments. Twenty-five new economic laws were prepared by the new government in December 1989 alone. The new laws paved the way for what has been called the Balcerowicz Plan after Leszek Balcerowicz, then, and still under Lech Walesa, Poland's Minister of Finance and Deputy Premier for Economic Affairs.

Economic Shock Therapy

The Balcerowicz Plan involves two strategic goals: stabilization of the economy (elimination of inflation) and transformation of the economic system to a market economy. In implementing this plan the government faced a choice between a gradual, step-by-step approach or a "shock" treatment. The government chose the latter, hence the plan was called "The Big Bang" or "The Shock Programme" or simply "Shock Therapy."

The transformation package aimed fundamentally to alter the economic system by introducing free market institutions and mechanisms within two years. It involves: (1) initiating widespread private ownership, privatization of state owned enterprises and the competitive sale of state assets; (2) demonopolization and fostering competition; (3) liberalizing foreign trade and establishing a foreign exchange market; (4) creating a land market; (5) modifying labour laws favourable to a free labour market; (6) establishing capital markets; (7) upgrading administrative and managerial skills; (8) introducing individual income and value-added taxes and reforming the tax system, and (9) adopting new joint venture laws to attract foreign investment.

The Balcerowicz "Shock Therapy" approach was an essential economic decision. But it proved to be more "shock" than "therapy" to the general population. The effects of the stabilization and transformation programmes challenged the public attitudes, work ethic, and the sociocultural characteristics which have prevailed in Polish society for the last forty (or more) years. Grey and Smeetzer define "The sociocultural environment" as "the prevailing values, attitudes, and the customs of the society or culture within which the organization operates." While "Shock Therapy" is an approach that can work in economic matters, it does not work as an instrument for changing attitudes, values or morality. Professor Stefan Kurowski of the Catholic University of Lublin observed: "It's possible to nationalize an economy by one decree but going in the opposite direction overnight inescapably becomes a long and difficult process which needs deliberation and careful handling." The Russian economist, Leonid Abalkin wrote, ". . . it is not easy to develop a stratum of talented people, with a good understanding of the market. For that it is necessary to put aside fixed patterns of thinking, inherited from the past, to consider afresh our morals, and our system of values in general."

In Poland people's ideas, patterns of thought and spirit of action or inaction have been shaped for forty years in the centrally planned, decreed and enforced mode. The shift to entrepreneurial, open, risk-taking, free market approaches to the economy and to social issues will come neither easily nor soon. There are no models to follow of transitions from "Real Socialism to market economics. A lack of experience in transition . . . and unpredictability of the behaviour of economic entities in the processes causes all the assumptions in the course of this process and of its outcome to lie in the sphere of conjecture" writes Professor Marian Paszynski.

Re-education, whether in economics or management or in attitudes, ethics or values, combined with positive reinforcing experiences, require time and usually long-suffering patience. Already "Better tomorrow was yesterday" graffiti are beginning to appear. To some the deprivations, hardships, unemployment, risks and uneasiness of the promised "New Order" are evoking a certain nostalgia for the "Old Order."

Unemployment, unknown in "socialist Poland," will probably reach 2 million by December 1991. Controlling hyperinflation remains a constant challenge. Productivity is on the decline. Privatization is moving very slowly; already corruption is widely rumoured about the process. The continuing presence in state firms of a great number of Nomenklatura who lack enthusiasm for the transformation process is influencing work attitudes and has had negative effects on production. Economic aid to Poland has not been as immediately forthcoming as anticipated, in part because of the Gulf War and German reunification, but also because of Parliamentary indecision and postponed elections. The Sejm (Parliament) to be elected October 28, 1991, will have only a short time in which to address these economic questions before the social acceptance of the effects of "Shock Therapy" erodes or completely evaporates.

Rebuilding Social Values

The success of Polish economic reform depends greatly on continued social acceptance. Calmness, discipline and sacrifice characterized the early months of reform. Initial acceptance of the demands of stabilization and transformation was widespread, even enthusiastic, and was certainly hopeful. But social consensus is tenuous. Already signs of a shift in social consensus are being observed.

A mid-year 1991 survey of "The Public Mood" reported by Andrzej Uznanski notes:

"The public mood is perhaps at its most critical point since Solidarity took power. . . . The respondents who feel that there has been a general improvement in the Polish situation have dramatically decreased since April while the number convinced that the situation is worse has increased. . . . Pessimists enjoyed a majority, namely 53%. . . . Social approval for the direction of change in Poland has decreased significantly."

"The May Poll . . . documents an increase . . . of negative opinions about all the most important state institutions, public personalities, and the economy. . . . The number supporting the Balcerowicz Plan has decreased (. . . to 21%) . . . the lowest rating . . . since its inception."

"An overwhelming majority, 90%, feel there is tension and unrest in Polish Society."

Uznanski concludes his analysis by noting that "The risks of the spreading of social conflict have dramatically increased" and he asks: "Is Poland threatened by an explosion of nationwide protest?" In Poland it appears that "the springtime of hope" is unfortunately deteriorating toward "a winter of discontent."

Reviewing the year 1989 in *Centesimus Annus*, the Polish Pope John Paul II observed:

"A great effort is needed to rebuild morally and economically the countries that have abandoned Communism. For a long time the most elementary economic relationships were distorted, and the basic virtues of economic life, such as truthfulness, trustworthiness, and hard work were denigrated. A patient material and moral reconstruction is needed, even as people, exhausted by long-standing privation, are asking their governments for tangible and immediate results. . . ."

What are some of the areas of "Moral Reconstruction" needed in Poland today? What are some of the moral and ethical reforms essential for social and economic progress?

To accomplish the political transformation to a democratically elected government involves restoring respect for laws, trust in government, confidence in public institutions and civic leaders and a belief in the value of one's voice and vote. For years the Polish public reacted to laws as "their laws, not ours" and so developed a pattern of ignoring, circumventing, or subverting the laws. Government promised, but consistently failed to deliver, thus eroding trust. Public agencies suffocated the spirit with enormous red tape, until all confidence in response was killed. And the socialist leadership cult left people skeptical of all politicians, including current Solidarity candidates. Respect, trust, confidence in government and self-worth need to be restored.

To achieve a market economy effectively involves accepting new responsibilities, renewing a commitment to elements of common morality and achieving a certain level of ethical behaviour. New freedoms demand acceptance of new responsibilities. Rights and obligations are handmaids. The socialist centralized system absorbed individual freedom into the collectivity. Initiative, creativity and self-assertion were discouraged and society languished from lack of personal responsibility and risk-taking.

Common Morality

The elements of "common morality" were systematically eroded. We think of "common morality" as those universal canons governing ordinary ethical behaviour — promise-keeping, non-maleficence, mutual aid, respect for persons and respect for property. Yet, official *promises* regularly made were regularly broken, denied or unfulfilled, and the same pattern often became common in society generally.

Non-maleficence requires that people avoid violence, and refrain from hurting others. But a police state, periods of martial law, known kidnappings, house arrests, imprisonment and disproportionate prison penalties inspire strikes, riots and violence as a means of achieving goals, the very opposite approach of democratic parliamentary governance. Rising tensions in Poland today could easily give way to public violence. Violent crimes are on the increase. Mutual aid fosters community and favours people helping one another, usually understood to be a moral duty "if the cost is not too great." Many people are even heroic in coming to the aid of others, even total strangers, without counting the cost. However, the fear of surveillance and intimidation, of spying and police questioning, often made the cost of mutual aid too great and caused people "to look the other way." Marxism exploited injustice and oppression causing in people a fear to act.

Again, *respect for persons* requires that persons are taken seriously, their aspirations and intentions are seen as legitimate and their desires and hopes are important. The opposite of respect for persons was the prevailing policy under Communism. People were chattels of the state. The state determined the needs and goals for the people. Injustices prevailed. People were dehumanized. Once self respect was lost, the virus spread, giving the state the upper hand.

Finally, *respect for property* is a corollary of respect for persons. But the confiscation and wanton destruction of property — public and private — also prevailed throughout much of the occupation and under Communism. The government constructed factories without respect to environmental damage. Rack, ruin, rubble and refuse give evidence of civic disrespect. Pollution abounds. (Poznan now has an active programme of civic cleanliness — gutter, streets, pedestrian underpasses, public parks — to restore respect for public areas and a programme of cleaning public statuary to restore respect for the historical beauty of the city.)

Four Levels of Ethical Analysis

Another framework of ethical analysis of the present situation in Poland can be drawn from the four levels of ethical analysis proposed by Stoner and Freeman: societal; stakeholder; "internal policy"; and personal morality.

That double standards in ethics exist in Poland should not come as a surprise. At the *level of society* many dualities existed. The occupiers and the occupied; the party and the proletariat; the army and civilians; active official communist efforts to discourage religion and increasing public displays of Roman Catholic religiosity. Moreover dual standards existed. The economy existed along with an active underground economy and a black market. Almost everybody knew someone who could get you what you might want if you could pay for it. Corruption was widespread. Sophisticated schemes to defraud government and avoid taxes existed. Disrespect and circumvention of the law was commonplace. Poland operated in an atmo-

sphere of public piety but also in an atmosphere of distrust, duplicity, deception and dishonesty. Moreover, the quality of family life deteriorated. Absence of housing for the newly-married, three-four generations living in congested quarters, lack of privacy, stress of intergenerational living, alcoholism, working mothers, government promotion of abortion — all weakened the fabric of family life. One of the first acts of the Russians in Poland was to build vodka factories as if somehow to anaesthetize people from their pending plight.

Democracy and free market behaviour reflects human values. To make a freely elected Parliament and a free market system work requires that many of the factors contributing to Poland's social disintegration must be overcome, old values restored, new values accepted and internalized. Church, education, family and government have a major challenge before them.

A second level of ethical evaluation relates to *stakeholders,* i.e. the rights of various groups who have a "stake" in the success of an enterprise. At present most large enterprises are still state-owned. Five large firms have been privatized; 400 firms are under consideration; and a total of 7000 may be privatized. After forty years of isolation from Western economic ideas and American management theory, "stakeholder analysis" will be somewhat new to Poland. Concepts of empowerment, self-directed management, teamwork and the emphasis on initiative, motivation and creativity will take some time to become common.

The idea that different groups have an interest in business success finds its most active voice in present unions and workers' councils at the factory level. Already debate exists about the proper future role for unions. Solidarity grew out of the Trade Union movement. Eventually it became recognized primarily as a cultural, political and social phenomenon, and after its success in the first partially-free elections Solidarity became an agency for economic reform. Workers already feel alienation from the new government. They fear that with privatization their union voice will be silenced, and that workers' councils may be dissolved or their representation greatly minimized. At present, the Nomenklatura, those who held jobs with party approval, have a great "stake" in retaining their present positions, despite their lack of enthusiasm for political change, and even less enthusiasm for a free market economy. Just how stakeholder rights will be recognized or honoured remains to be worked out.

"Internal Policy" as a third level of moral discourse about ethical business behaviour involves examining *issues internal to the business* which have ethical implications. These issues exist now within state-owned firms and will continue to manifest themselves further even as state firms are privatized. One problem which will be immediately evident is the failure of the socialist system to invest in human capital in a free market sense. All education and training was directed to serving government and state enterprise goals, and had a limited technical and skills orientation, rather than focusing on managerial, organizational behaviour, and human resource and organizational development.

The loss of the work ethic is a paramount problem, well expressed by the sentiment "They pretended to pay us, and we pretended to work." The loss of pride in workmanship, absence of standards and the acceptance of inferior production, diminished motivation, avoidance of responsibility, and minimal loyalty present a great challenge for re-education and re-training.

The attitude on the part of many people about businessmen is very negative. Referring to their wealthy compatriots other Poles say, "The first million is always gained dishonestly; probably the second million also. Only later do rich people become somewhat more honest." At a public lecture on business ethics in Poland last year one member of the audience remarked "Only a rich man can be just." Another person contended it was not possible to be a Catholic and a business person. A third person with a similar view strictly interpreted the biblical "eye of the needle" as condemning all business persons. Is this view isolated?

Economists Robert J. Shiller et al., in a recent survey of "Popular attitudes toward free markets: the Soviet Union and the United States compared" asked several questions among many to measure comparative attitudes towards business. One question is of special interest here:

"Do you think that those who try to make a lot of money will often turn out not to be very honest people?"

Response	USSR	USA
Yes	59%	39%
No	41%	62%

In the summer of 1991 the same 29 questions were put to a select group of 35 Polish University teaching staff in Economics, and their response was even more negative. 77% said Yes; 23% said No. While anxious for a free market system, many educated Poles also have reservations about capitalism and the consumerism of the west, and are alarmed at the values of the USA and Western Europe as conveyed in videos, on TV and in songs, and in pornographic publications now for the first time publicly available in Poland.

Unemployment was unknown in the Old Poland. Already the New Poland has experienced unemployment predicted to reach 2 million by the end of 1991. One Polish labour economist remarked that a possible positive aspect of the unemployment situation is that the remaining workers now realise that they must demonstrate a renewed work ethic if they also expect to avoid redundancy. Another economist suggested that a major ethical problem is that managers of public and private firms alike want to get as much work done as possible at the lowest wages, while the workers want to do as little work as possible for a much pay as possible. Until both sides change manager-worker relations productivity will remain problematic.

A fourth and final level of moral discourse in the area of business ethics is *personal morality*. We have already noted how the widespread problems of distrust and dishonesty cripple the social capacity to achieve a free market where commercial transactions clearly depend on honouring obligations, keeping promises, honesty and trust. Experience reveals that many Polish people are steadfast and consistent in adhering to their personal moral code and their respect for and treatment of other people "in season and out of season." Other persons less principled, and not only Poles, appear to adjust their ethics to the business cycle, with different codes depending on periods of survival, depression, recession or prosperity. We can observe the situation in Poland but we should not presume to judge individual motives.

However, several comments are appropriate. For many Poles the survival mentality pushed them to marginal ethical behaviour. Another explanation was the absence of ethically motivated role models in government, state enterprises and in the small private businesses that did function. Inexperience with proper business practice often leads to "cutting corners," especially in an environment where avoidance rather than acceptance of law prevails. The absence of larger, independent, professionally managed firms operating with codes of ethics and a sense of social responsibility left the system devoid of institutional role models. The absence of effective sanctions for unethical business behaviour permitted such practices to flourish. Moreover, it is not valid to compare the business ethics of mature mixed capitalistic countries with a centrally controlled socialist country, nor with a newly emerging national effort to achieve a free market economy. We have ample evidence that we in the West have not yet achieved the acknowledged ethical ideal in many of our business transactions.

In Spring 1991, the Catholic Intellectual Club of Poznan sponsored a public lecture on "Ethics in Business," an acknowledgment of the problem and of the need for discussion of the topic. Church leaders, clerical and lay, and educators alike are increasingly sensitive to societal, stakeholder, worker and personal ethical issues. Educators are making a concerted effort to understand Western business and management practices, including business and society relationships, moral, ethical and value issues in business. The challenge is enormous. Human behaviour often changes slowly, but education and positive reinforcement can accelerate the process. The Polish people are very adaptable. The vast majority still evidence a strong desire to build a new and more just society. Their determination to succeed despite so many obstacles and systemic problems augurs well for eventual progress in achieving higher standards of ethics in business.

Reconstituting Civic Societies: An Afro-American View

Preston N. Williams

This year I would urge that there is only one appropriate way to symbolize the opening of our academic year and that is by saying a word of thanks for the unexpected series of events which recently transformed the Soviet Union, Poland, Eastern and Central Europe, and South Africa. The significance of these events has not been fully appreciated. They will be celebrated more in the days to come than they have been by us, their stunned observers. These revolutions . . . are of peculiar importance to me because early in my ministerial and academic career I participated in church efforts to aid the victims of oppression in Eastern Germany, in student Christian movement efforts to supply scholarship assistance to the last class of black South African medical students admitted to Witwatersand University before South Africa transformed its policies of racial discrimination into apartheid, and in citizen-based efforts to ameliorate the cold war was confrontation characterized by McCarthyism. Contemporary history suggests that all these once dreaded evils have been greatly weakened and their demise seemingly assured. . . . command economies and racist market-oriented regimes fail.

Christians since the days of the Protestant Social Gospel and Roman Catholic *Rerum Novarum* have acted to inform governments and people of the perennial need to reconstruct civil society and that this need requires efforts to humanize capi-

Preston N. Williams, "Reconstituting Civic Societies: An Afro-American View," from a convocation address presented at Harvard University, Fall 1991.

talism. That task has not been wholly or everywhere successful even though it may have done much to mitigate the evils of capitalism and to make it the bearer of the expectations that many today have for the good life. Christians must continue to criticize the evils of capitalism even as they support its virtues in those tottering societies where newly liberated people seek to produce the goods that will help them live in charity and peace. For while it is important to acknowledge forthrightly the collapse of communism and the necessity of a market economy, it is also important to affirm the necessity of a constraining the market by mechanisms that make for a just economy and a communitarian society.

Adam Smith, the great advocate of capitalism, supports this view. He noted the failings of the market system and advised that governments act not only to defend their citizens "from the violence and invasion of other independent societies" but that they in addition protect "every member of society from the injustice or oppression of every other member of it" and provide "certain public works and certain public institutions which it can never be for the intent of any individual, to erect and maintain."

Certainly Adam Smith contemplated neither socialism, the welfare state nor affirmative action, but he did see that the so-called free market should operate in the context of a government that acts directly on behalf of justice among all its citizens as well as on behalf of business interests. Adam Smith knew, as I am sure the people of the Soviet Union, Poland, Eastern and Central Europe, and South Africa know, that a market economy is always linked to and shaped by a civil society and that the government ought to be fair enough to act directly on behalf of all its citizens as well as the interest of business. South Africa illustrates the injustices a market economy will accept. Its moral failure proves that government must "protect every member of society from the injustice or oppression of every other member of it."

South Africans have been oppressed for more than forty years because their market economy was put to the service of a regime which continued the racism of Hitler's Germany. The market economy provided neither freedom nor consumer goods for all South Africans. Rather it exploited blacks, Asians, and colored South Africans in order to pile up profits and privileges for white South Africans and their businesses. Moreover, the market economies of the West participated in and sanctioned this exploitation. Yes, Adam Smith was correct: market economies do fail and they fail not only in productivity but also in respect to justice. Market economies need therefore to be constrained by or regulated by government and, as John Rawls has stated, the primary concern of civil society ought to be the creation of just institutions. Multi-party systems are helpful but not sufficient; what is required are just social and economic institutions.

The activities undertaken by the Soviet Union, Poland, Eastern and Central Europe, and South Africa in restructuring their societies can provide us with larger and more certain understandings of social justice. Anxiety with respect to the redefinition of property rights, legal and social institutions, religious freedom, and the shock of economic reform — unemployment, high prices, loss of human service, the replacement of a party elite by a capitalist elite, as well as a fear of the collapse of the economy — point to a continuing need for an appropriate relationship among classes, to considerations of who bears the burdens of social existence and who reaps the rewards and benefits. If the necessities of a market economy entail inevitable economic inequality we must be more concerned than we are with the acceptable kinds and ranges of inequality. . . .

Reconstituting society in South Africa provides additional insight into the kind of inequality that a strong market economy may tolerate or support. There, society must be restructured because the market has been indifferent to the worth and dignity of non-white individuals and groups, stripping them of property, family life, and citizenship in order to ensure its own vitality and robustness. Justice requires constraints on this type of market operation, and mechanisms that would make the market sensitive to racial and other forms of injustice. In the light of America's own racial past and its increasing uneasiness about a future when the United States will have a non-white majority population, South Africa's pursuit of a non-racial democratic society and the keen attention that is paid to race should be instructive about how we as a society should define and move toward civil rights.

The experimentation in reordering social institutions now underway as a consequence of the revolutions of 1989-1990 has much to learn from the West and the history of protest by minorities in the West because we have experienced capitalism's successes and failures. We also can learn from them. At this juncture in our history the most important lesson may be the need for government to constrain the market and treat fairly the interest of every individual and group.

My references to Adam Smith should indicate that the constraints I would support would not be totalitarian and a guise for the reintroduction of centralized planning or a command economy. We must, however, provide incentives, both for individual initiative and productivity and for responsible participation in the common life. Our institutions must be strong enough to check the greed and ambition of the most powerful. The lessons of communism and of the South African type of capitalism will have to be learned, namely that no small group of individuals can be permitted to define the common good. The conflict of claims among the many units of society must not be settled by the imposition from above of an authoritarian conception of the good. Our understanding of freedom must arise from the joint participation of all in the quest for liberty. Freedom is not the property of political, business, religious, or intellectual authorities alone. Our new familiarity with the significance of particular traditions and values together with a framework of just law should guide us in the fabrication of constraints that will be light and flexible yet strong enough to provide safety nets for the disadvantaged. We welcome the revolutions of 1989-1990 because they provide new opportunity for us and the world to consider what constitutes basic needs and human rights in a society that urgently needs reforming. The universalism that is at the core of the Christian faith and the conviction that the person is end, not means, which is embedded in Western culture, should be the foundation for respecting all persons and cultures and reconstituting new social institutions.

How one deals specifically in respect to building social, legal, religious, and political institutions and relating them to the market are questions that can be dealt with only in the context of each society. John Rawls' suggestion that we think of justice as embodying two principles is helpful: One an absolute principle related to our integrity as a person that can never be broken and the other a less than absolute one embodying provisions for trade offs and a mechanism for limiting the inequalities that might exist, including those that result from differences in natural talents and abilities. In my opinion such a manner of procedure is more suitable for dealing with the conflict of aspirations possessed by the liberated people of Europe and Africa and the formation civil society than are Michael J. Sandel's notions about limiting justice and accommodating special relationships because some more or less enduring attachments and commitments when taken together partly define the person. Moreover, the efforts that must be made to recreate the Soviet Union, Eastern and Central Europe, and South Africa will indicate the fundamental error and injustice in our nation's policies of benign neglect, the cry to "get the government off my back." The quest for a positive though limited role for government and a less privileged role for business must be at the heart of the effort to reconstitute civil society. The fate of the poor, of human services, and of justice must not be left to the vagaries of the market, the charity of the rich, or the dividends of peace. They must become a part of the structure of society and a routine cost of productivity.

An aspect of social reconstruction greatly underdeveloped in the revolutions of 1989-1990 is that of gender relations. The inequalities and injustices are everywhere evident but there is little indication that this dimension of personal and institutional life needs specific attention. Here, if I am correct, the revolutions lacks imagination and is not helpful. It needs to reconsider its understanding of male-female roles and power relationships. It is difficult for me to provide precise insight about the needed changes because of the multicultural nature of the Soviet Union, Eastern and Central Europe, and South Africa. The communist conception of women in the states where its vision has collapsed is not consistent and varies over time. The new societies will require a variety of resolutions for these issues. In some instances there has been an enlargement of freedom and equality. Where this has occurred, the changes should be institutionalized and made more adequate. In other instances where there has been a diminution of liberty and greater intrusion of government into private life, attention must be called to the contradictions between the goals of the revolution and the consequences it has for the lives of women. In South Africa the radically different social location of white and black women under apartheid will require changes that address both issues of dignity and social welfare. In all these societies the market economy alone will not correct the evils of sexism. The ancient and complex nature of the problem will necessitate efforts to create institutions that are plural, inclusive, and fair and which constrain the indifference of market operation and the bias of governmental policies. Perhaps it is the responsibility of American women to take a more active role in working with their sisters in Europe and Africa to support them in their consideration of what they think is needful to forward their own liberation. The present moment when new social orders are being formed is an appropriate time to increase the pace of activity and to go beyond the concern for power sharing, family planning, domestic violence, and equal pay. Gender justice must be made an explicit dimension of concern in the reconstitution of societies in Europe, Africa, and the Americas. In this the American community might take a great leadership role in consciousness-raising and the design of social institutions.

In spite of the omission of a central emphasis upon sexism, the revolutions of 1989-1990 represent a most fruitful place for religiously and morally responsible individuals to work during the coming decades. The Soviet Union, Eastern and Central Europe, and South Africa have broken through the communist-capitalist encounter and made possible the unity of the first and second world and the engagement of their national states in institutional and social reconstruction. Although these states are fragile and face an uncertain future because of their economic weakness and internal conflicts, they nevertheless can contribute to a reconceptualization of what types of political order are needed in order to create a market economy that treats all its people fairly and abandons none to the flow of the tide. A reconstitution of the civil societies of the Soviet Union, Eastern and Central Europe can lead to a construction of a . . . European community that recognizes that markets are to a great extent directed by governments and can be made sensitive to justice. The market system in South Africa corrected by a Mandela-like leadership may become sufficiently strong and just that it provides equally for the well-being of all its citizens and serves as a model exerting transformative influence upon the other Southern African states as well as Nigeria, Kenya, and Liberia. Whether these revolutions of Europe and Africa become vehicles that provide us with societies that are more just in respect to class, race, and sex, or whether they are overtaken by greedy and unscrupulous market economy will not of course be determined by us. We may, however, influence the shaping of the new market economies and the governments that regulate them. As we celebrate the collapse of communism and the rebirth of Christianity in the Soviet Union, Eastern and Central Europe and its great growth in Africa, we might also ask how can we help this revived or newly acquired faith to aid in the construction of more just social institutions. . . .

Section 2: Multinational Corporations

Many business corporations have had international connections for decades. However, their international strategies have evolved over time to a much higher level of sophistication. The previous model of international business concentrated on import/export relationships and licensing arrangements. These international connections were interactions from a distance primarily controlled by citizens from the home countries. An international division in the company was viewed as a valuable complement to the home country's market.

In the past two decades many businesses have consciously left the previous model behind. Instead of viewing international divisions as extra arms of the company, many firms now believe a global strategy is at the heart of their enterprises. Corporations analyze customer markets, product concepts, resources for production, mechanisms for distribution, and competitive pricing on a global scale. It is no longer unusual for a product to have component parts designed in, say, Germany, produced in South Korea and Taiwan, assembled in Mexico, and sold in the United States. The company behind the product most likely makes each of those decisions based on a global analysis of the best opportunities available. Many business firms have now become truly multinational, interacting with many cultures and many governments simultaneously.

The global scope of such multinational companies raises a host of ethical questions unique to operating across national boundaries and beyond traditional cultural constraints. How should the Christian churches respond to the moral questions posed by such a change?

Michael Novak argues that multinational corporations provide an opportunity for great good: they can become for Christians signs of God's grace. He believes that such corporations offer opportunities for creativity, liberty, communal work, risk taking, and the development of wealth, all of which are measures of the ways in which God expects humans to live. Yet he cautions that such large-scale entities can also fall into the sin of autocracy, create alienation, and concentrate power inappropriately. Given that multinationals can operate for good or ill, he suggests that large corporations have broad responsibilities economically, politically, and morally.

Lee Tavis also issues a call for moral responsibility by multinational corporations, particularly because of their power to allocate resources. He recognizes that often such businesses operate in Third World economies with less than adequate accountability for resource use and market development. Tavis believes that multinationals should shoulder a special moral responsibility for the development of the poor. To do so, the planning and information systems of multinationals should be redesigned to integrate this commitment to the poor into their decision-making processes and systems for monitoring the effects of their activity.

Gene Laczniak and Jacob Naor flesh out the broad-based commentary of Novak and Tavis. They highlight specific ethical problems corporations confront when operating in global markets. Laczniak and Naor explain the difficulties companies face when operating in a world with pluralistic ethical standards, limited legal restraints, and shifting ethical criteria. Given the moral chaos that is too often encountered in international business operations, these authors recommend that corporate codes of ethics be formulated and that firms incorporate ethics into their strategic decisions.

Each of the authors above recognizes that berating multinational corporations for their failures or wishing they would simply disappear is not a useful way to usher in the twenty-first century. As global communication and transportation networks continue to develop, even more businesses will adopt global strategies. Indeed, these authors were selected precisely because they try to open up ways in which multinational corporations can institutionalize ethics in their strategic and operational systems. Global firms are moral agents. They cannot escape their responsibilities. If they come to terms with their moral responsibilities, they can serve all God's people more effectively.

Toward a Theology of the Corporation

Michael Novak

Our task is to set forth some steps toward a theology of the corporation. We need such a theology so that the ministers who serve businessmen and workers might be able to preach more illuminating and practical sermons and so that critics might have at their disposal a theologically sound standard of behavior for corporations.

For many years one of my favorite texts in scripture has been Isaiah 53:2-3: "He hath no form nor comeliness; and when we shall see him, there is no beauty that we should desire him. He is despised and rejected of men; a man of sorrows, and acquainted with grief; he was despised, and we esteemed him not." I would like to apply these words to the modern business corporation, a much despised incarnation of God's presence in this world.

When we speak of the body of Christ, we ordinarily mean the church, both invisible and visible, both sinless and marred by sin. God calls His followers to bring His presence to their work, to their daily milieu, to history. This is the doctrine of Christian vocation. A liturgy does not end without a word of mission: "Go out into the world of daily work to carry the peace and love of Jesus Christ." I do not mean by this to suggest that the Christian form is the only form of speech for this fundamental attitude. A sense of vocation infuses Jews, Muslims, and others of religious faith. Many who are not religious also regard their work as useful and ennobling. They feel called to the task of

From Michael Novak, *Toward a Theology of the Corporation*, rev. ed. (Washington, DC: American Enterprise Institute for Public Policy Research, 1981).

making life better for their fellow human beings. But I am a Catholic Christian, and it is better to speak in the idiom with most meaning for me than to pretend to an idiom that, by virtue of being no more than a common denominator, would appear superficial to all of us.

To work in a modern business corporation, no one need pass a test of faith or even reveal his or her religious convictions to others. But it would be a mistake to permit the business corporation's commendable acceptance of religious pluralism to mask the religious vocation that many see in it.

The Multinational Corporation

In speaking of the corporation, I will concentrate on those large business corporations that are found among the 300 or so multinational corporations, two-thirds of which are American.

The reason one must first consider these *big* corporations is that all but very strict socialists seem to be in favor of markets, ownership, cooperatives, and *small* business. Religious socialists like John C. Cort favor the private ownership of small businesses, ownership through cooperatives, and some free-market mechanisms.

What are multinational corporations? They are not those which merely sell their goods in other lands, buy goods from other lands, or trade with other lands. Multinationals are corporations that build manufacturing or other facilities in other lands in order to operate there. The building of a base of operations in other lands is an important condition for qualification as a multinational corporation in the strict sense. One should not think only of factories; banks and insurance firms — important for local investment — may also establish such operations.

The training of an indigenous labor and managerial force is not a strictly necessary condition for a corporation to be considered multinational, but is a common characteristic, particularly of American companies. Thus multinationals make four chief contributions to the host country. Of these the first two, (1) capital facilities and (2) technological transfers inherent in the training of personnel, remain forever in the host country, whatever the ultimate fate of the original company. In addition, products manufactured within

the nation no longer have to be imported; thus (3) the host nation's problems with balance of payments are eased. Finally, (4) wages paid to employees remain in the country, and local citizens begin to invest in the corporation, so that most of its future capital can be generated locally. These are important factors in any accounting of the relative wealth transferred to and from the host country and the country of the corporation's origin. Critics sometimes concentrate only on the flow of return on investment. They commonly neglect to add up the capital investment, training, balance-of-payments relief, salaries, and stimulation of local investment. . . .

Other contextual matters should be noted. In most nations of the world — notably the socialist nations — private corporations are not permitted to come into existence. Only a few nations of the world produce privately held corporations. Furthermore, some nations which do so (like the United States) were formerly colonies, and some others (Hong Kong) still are. Since economic development depends to a large extent upon home-based privately held corporations, differences in moral-cultural climate are significant. Some cultures seem to develop far higher proportions of skilled inventors, builders, and managers of industry than others do. In some cultures, the work force is more productive than in others.

Over time, education and training may provide new moral models and fairly swift cultural development. Simultaneously, of course such developments may provoke intense conflicts with guardians of the earlier cultural order. It cannot be stressed too often that corporations are not merely economic agencies. They are also moral-cultural agencies. They may come into existence, survive, and prosper only under certain moral-cultural conditions. . . .

Theological Beginnings

In thinking about the corporation in history and its theological significance, I began with a general theological principle. Georges Bernanos once said that grace is everywhere. Wherever we look in the world, there are signs of God's presence: in the mountains, in a grain of sand, in a human person, in the poor and the hungry. The earth is charged with the grandeur of God. So is human history.

If we look for signs of grace in the corporation, we may discern several of them — a suitably sacramental number.

Creativity

The Creator locked great riches in nature, riches to be discovered only gradually though human effort. John Locke observed that the yield of the most favored field in Britain could be increased a hundredfold if human ingenuity and human agricultural science were applied to its productivity. Nature alone is not as fecund as nature under intelligent cultivation. The world, then, is immeasurably rich as it comes from the Creator, but only potentially so. This potential was hidden for thousands of years until human discovery began to release portions of it for human benefit. Yet even today we have not yet begun to imagine all the possibilities of wealth in the world the Creator designed. The limits of our present intelligence restrict the human race to the relative poverty in which it still lives.

In 1979 Atlantic Richfield ran an advertisement based on a theme first enunciated, as far as I can tell, by Father Hesburgh of Notre Dame, namely, that 40 percent of the world's energy is used by 6 percent of the world's population residing in the United States. This way of putting the facts is an example of the cultivation of guilt that Professor Bauer has described. A moment's thought shows that it is a preposterous formulation.

What the entire human race meant by energy until the discovery of the United States and the inventions promoted by its political economy were the natural forces of sun, wind, moving water, animals, and human muscle. Thomas Aquinas traveled on foot or by burro from Rome to Paris and back seven times in his life. The first pope to be able to make that voyage by train did so six centuries later, in the mid-nineteenth century. Until then, people traveled exactly as they had done since the time of Christ and before — by horse and carriage, by donkey, or by foot. History for a very long time seemed relatively static. The social order did not promote inventions and new technologies, at least to the degree lately reached. The method of scientific discovery had not been invented.

In 1809 an American outside Philadelphia figured out how to ignite anthracite coal. The ability to use anthracite, which burned hotter and more steadily than bituminous coal, made practical the seagoing steamship and the locomotive.

In 1859 the first oil well was dug outside of Titusville, Pennsylvania. Oil was known in biblical times but used only for products like perfume and ink. Arabia would have been as rich then as now, if anybody had known what to do with the black stuff.

The invention of the piston engine and the discovery of how to drill for oil were also achieved in the United States. The first electric light bulb was illuminated in 1879 in Edison, New Jersey.

After World War II the U.S. government dragooned the utilities into experimenting with nuclear energy. They knew nothing about it. They did not need it. They did not want it. Oil and coal were cheap. The government, however, promoted the peaceful uses of the atom.

Thus 100 percent of what the modern world means by energy was invented by 6 percent of the world's population. More than 60 percent of that energy had been distributed to the rest of the world. Though the United States can, of course, do better than that, we need not feel guilty for inventing forms of energy as useful to the human race as the fire brought to earth by Prometheus.

The agency through which inventions and discoveries are made productive for the human race is the corporation. Its creativity makes available to mass markets the riches long hidden in Creation. Its creativity mirrors God's. That is the standard by which its deeds and misdeeds are properly judged.

Liberty

The corporation mirrors God's presence also in its liberty, by which I mean independence from the state. That independence was the greatest achievement of the much-despised but creative 6 percent of the world's population. Advancing the work of their forebears, they invented the concept and framed the laws that for the first time in history set boundaries on the state, ruling certain activities off-limits to its interference. Rights of person and home, free speech in public, a free press, and other liberties came to be protected both by constitutional law and by powerful interests actively empowered to defend themselves under that law. Legal autonomy was such that even the king could not forcibly enter the home of a peasant; a peasant's home was as protected as a duke's castle — rights which the colonists in America demanded for themselves. Private business corporations were permitted to become agents of experimentation, of trial and error, and for good reason: to unleash economic activism. The state retained rights and obligations of regulation, and undertook the indirect promotion of industry and commerce. The state alone was prohibited from becoming the sole economic agent. A sphere of economic liberty was created.

The purpose of this liberty was to unlock greater riches than the world had ever known. Liberty was to be an experiment, which Adam Smith and others advocated, that might (or might not) prove to be in accordance with nature and with the laws of human society. Pleading for room to experiment, their practical, empirical arguments flew in the face of entrenched ideological opposition. The case for liberty prevailed.

The foundational concept of democratic capitalism, then, is not, as Marx thought, private property. It is limited government. Private property, of course, is one limitation on government. What is interesting about private property is not that *I* own something, that *I* possess; its heart is not "possessive individualism," in C. B. MacPherson's phrase. Quite the opposite. The key is that the state is limited by being forbidden to control rights and goods. I cannot infringe on the privacy of one's home or on one's right to the fruit of one's labors and risks. Herbert Stein has a useful definition of capitalism: "The idea of a capitalist system has nothing to do with capital and has everything to do with freedom. I think of capitalism as a system in which ability to obtain and use income independently of other persons or organizations, including government, is widely distributed among the individuals of the population."

This is the distinctively American way of thinking about private property. In this framework, property is important less for its material reality than for the legal rights its ownership and use represent and for the limits it imposes on the power of the state. Such liberty was indispensable if private business corporations were to come into

existence. Such corporations give liberty economic substance over and against the state.

Birth and Mortality

In coming into being with a technological breakthrough, and then perishing when some new technology causes it to be replaced, a typical corporation mirrors the cycle of birth and mortality. Now corporations arise every day; dead ones litter history. Examining the *Fortune 500* at ten-year intervals shows that even large corporations are subject to the cycle: New ones keep appearing, and many that were once prominent disappear. Of the original *Fortune 500*, first listed in 1954, only 285 remained in 1974. Of the missing 215, 159 had merged, 50 had become too small or gone out of business, and 6 were reclassified or had unavailable data. Recently, Chrysler has been number 10. Will it by 1990 be gone from the list? Will Ford be gone from the list? It is entirely possible. As products of human liberty, corporations rise and fall, live and die. One does not have in them a lasting home — or even an immortal enemy.

Social Motive

Corporations, as the very word suggests, are not individualistic in their conception, in their operations, or in their purposes. Adam Smith entitled his book *An Inquiry into the Nature and Causes of the Wealth of Nations*. Its social scope went beyond individuals and beyond Great Britain to include all nations. The fundamental intention of the system from the beginning has been the wealth of all humanity.

The invention of democratic capitalism, the invention of the corporation, and the liberations of the corporations from total control by state bureaucracies (although some control always, and properly, remains) were intended to be multinational. Smith foresaw an interdependent world, for the first time able to overcome immemorial famine, poverty, and misery. He imagined people of every race, every culture, and every religion adopting the new knowledge about the causes of wealth. One does not need to be Christian or Jewish, or to share the Judeo-Christian world view, to understand the religious and economic potency of the free economy. Smith did not exactly foresee

Toyota and Sony. But he certainly would have been delighted to add a chapter to his immense study showing how the Japanese demonstrated the truth of his hypothesis.

Social Character

The corporation is inherently and in its essence corporate. The very word suggests communal, nonindividual, many acting together. Those who describe capitalism by stressing the individual entrepreneur miss the central point. Buying and selling by individual entrepreneurs occurred in biblical times. What is interesting and novel — at least what struck Max Weber as interesting and novel — is the communal focus of the new ethos: the rise of communal risk taking, the pooling of resources, the sense of communal religious vocation in economic activism. To be sure, certain developments in law and in techniques of accounting had to occur before corporations could be institutionalized in their modern form. In this sense, too, they are social creations.

Corporations depend on the emergence of an infrastructure in intellectual life that makes possible new forms of communal collaboration. They depend on ideas that are powerful and clear enough to organize thousands of person around common tasks. Moreover, these ideas must be strong enough to endure for years, so that individuals who commit themselves to them can expect to spend thirty to forty years working out their vocation. For many millions of religious persons the daily milieu in which they work out their salvation is the communal, corporate world of the workplace. For many, the workplace is a kind of second family. Even those who hate their work often like their co-workers. This is often true in factories; it is also true in offices. Comradeship is natural to humans. Labor unions properly build on it.

Insight

The primary capital of any corporation is insight, invention, finding a better way. Insight is of many kinds and plays many roles: it is central to invention; it lies at the heart of organization; it is the vital force in strategies for innovation, production, and marketing. Corporate management works hard at communal insight. Constantly, teams of persons meet to brainstorm and work out common strategies. Insight is the chief resource of any corporation, and there cannot be too much of it. Its scarcity is called stupidity.

Karl Marx erred in thinking that capital has to do primarily with machinery, money, and other tangible instruments of production. He overlooked the extent to which the primary form of capital is an idea. The right to patent industrial ideas is an extremely important constitutional liberty. It is indispensable to the life of corporations, as indispensable as the copyright is to writers. Money without ideas is not yet capital. Machinery is only as good as the idea it embodies. The very word "capital," from the Latin *caput,* "head," points to the human spirit as the primary form of wealth. The miser sitting on his gold is not a capitalist. The investor with an idea is a capitalist. Insight makes the difference.

A momentary digression. Money was more material before capitalism, when it was gold and silver coin, than it came to be afterward. Under capitalism, perhaps a majority of transactions are intellectualized "book" transactions. Moreover, paper money is necessary, as are stocks, bonds, constitutions, and legal contracts. Materialism is more and more left behind as money depends for its value less on material substance than on public confidence, the health of the social order, the stability of institutions. Let these be threatened and investments flee because deteriorating social health reduces the value of the amounts registered on paper. Materially, money is often "not worth the paper it's printed on." Its real value depends on sociality, trust, a sense of health and permanence. In this respect, a theological treatise on the symbolic nature of money is badly needed. Such a treatise would have to deal not only with the fact that most money exists only in the intellectual realm but also with the impersonality of money, which transcends discrimination based on race, religion, sex, or nationality, and with money's remarkable indeterminacy, according to which its moral value springs from how persons, in their liberty, use it. Money opens a vast range of freedom of choice. Accordingly, it is more closely related to insight and liberty than to matter. It no longer functions as it did in biblical times.

The Rise of Liberty and Election

A corporation risks liberty and election; it is part of its romance to do so. Tremendous mistakes in strategy can cripple even the largest companies. Easy Washing Machines of Syracuse once made an excellent washing machine, but Maytag's discovery of a new technology took away part of Easy's market. Easy had all its assets sunk in a plant that it could not redesign quickly enough to incorporate the new technology, and the company collapsed. Thus a sudden technological breakthrough, even a relatively minor one, can cripple a company or an industry. A simple strategic mistake by a team of corporate executives about where to apply the company's energies over a year or two can end up dimming the company's outlook for many years. A failure to modernize can bring about bankruptcy. The corporation operates in a world of no scientific certainty, in which corporate leaders must constantly make judgments about reality when not all the evidence about reality is in. Such leaders argue among themselves about strategic alternatives, each perhaps saying to himself, "We will see who is right about this," or "The next year or two will tell." But a judgment must be made and the investment committed before the telling is completed. Thus decision makers often experience the risks inherent in their decisions. At the very least they always face the risk of doing considerably less well than they think they are going to do.

In these seven ways, corporations offer metaphors for grace, a kind of insight into God's ways in history. Yet corporations are of this world. They sin. They are *semper reformanda* — always in need of reform.

Problems of Bigness and Other Accusations

Big corporations are despised and rejected even when the market system, small businesses, and private ownership are not. Some religious socialists do not absolutely reject certain elements in the democratic-capitalist idea. But they often bridle at the big corporations. Their accusations against such corporations — many of them as true as charges made against the universities or against any large institution — are many.

One accusation is that the corporations are autocratic, that internally they are not democratic. In trying to decide how true this charge is, one could undertake a survey of the management techniques of the *Fortune 500* corporations. How are they actually managed? How does their management differ in practice from the internal management of universities, churches, government agencies, or other institutions? Let us suppose that some autocrats still function in various spheres of authority today, including business. What sanctions are available to autocrats within a corporation? Leadership in all spheres today seems to depend upon large areas of consensus; leaders seem to "manager" more than they "command." I have roughly the same impression of the chief executive officers I have met as of the American Catholic bishops I have met; namely, that out of the office they would find it hard, as Schumpeter says, to say boo to a duck. Few, as I see them, are autocrats. Would that the world still saw the likes of Cardinals Spellman, Connell, Cushing, and Gibbons; or of industrial autocrats like Carnegie, Mellon, and others. Such types seem to have perished from the earth. In their place are men who, if you saw them in sport shirts at a Ramada Inn, would make you think you had dropped in on a convention of real-estate agents from Iowa. Very pleasant, nice men, they are nowhere near as assertive as journalists. They do not often have the occupational arrogance of academics. But empirical tests are in order to see how many autocrats are in corporations, in comparison with any other sphere of life.

A second frequent accusation against big corporations is the alienation their employees experience in the workplace. To what extent is such alienation caused by the conditions of modern work under any existing system or under any imaginable system? Do laborers in auto factories in Bratislava or Poznán work under conditions any different from those faced by laborers in the United States? One ought to compare hours of work, conditions of the workplace, salaries, working procedures, and levels of pollution. There is no evidence that any real or imagined socialism can take the modernity out of modern work. Nor is boring work unique to the modern factory; it surely dominated the ancient work of European peasants and continues to dominate the fourteen-hour day of the modern potato farmer. Farming is not, in my experience, inherently less alienating than working seven hours, with time off for lunch, on an assembly line.

Alienation is not a problem peculiar to capitalism or to corporations. Is work less alienating within a government bureaucracy? Instead of condemning political activists or politicians to jail for various crimes, suppose one simply condemned them to filing the correspondence of congressmen from state like Ohio and Arkansas for periods of up to three months.

A third accusation against corporations is that they represent too great a concentration of power. What is the alternative? There is indeed a circle within which small is beautiful, a relatively small and beautiful circle. But "small is beautiful" does not apply across the whole large world. When Jane Fonda and Tom Hayden made their pilgrimage to seventy-two cities carrying the word on economic democracy, they did not fly in airplanes made in mom and pop stores. Their travel arrangements were made not by small organizations working off a telephone in a back room, but by agencies with computers and Telex connections to operating stations in all airlines and in all airports, giving them the instantaneous information required to synchronize such a trip in a very short time.

Socialist economist Robert Lekachman has argued that the big corporations should be reduced in size to more manageable proportions. Maybe so. To my mind the question is a practical, experimental one. Consider the largest of all corporations, General Motors. It is already broken up into more than 200 units in more than 177 congressional districts in the United States. Its largest single facility, in Michigan, employs no more than 14,000 people. Many universities — the University of Michigan and Michigan State, to name two — comprise human communities two or three times that size. Corporations already follow the principle of subsidiary far more thoroughly than Lekachman seems to take into account. One might argue that they should be still smaller. Yet one must note that the smaller U.S. auto companies — American Motors, Chrysler, and Ford — are apparently in danger of perishing because of inadequate capital to meet the enormous expenses of retooling for new auto technologies. The foreign auto companies competing with General Motors (even in the United States) are also very large.

If small is beautiful, its beauty seems precarious indeed; big may be necessary.

In practice, I cannot imagine how human capacities and human choices of the sort needed by mass markets could still be made available except through large organizations. Small organizations may suit a small country, but it seems to me absurd to imagine that a continental nation with a population of 220 million can be well served in all respects only through small organizations in small industries. If somebody can invent a system of smallness, fine; I am not, in principle, against it. I just cannot imagine that it can work in practice.

Corporations are further accused of being inherently evil because they work for a profit. Without profit no new capital is made available for research, development, and new investment. Further, there is a difference between maximization of profit and optimization of profit. To aim at maximizing profit — that is, to obtain the greatest profit possible out of every opportunity — is to be greedy in the present at the expense of the future. The profit maximizer demands too much for products that can be produced more cheaply by somebody else and in the process narrows his market and destroys his reputation. Inevitably, he damages himself and, in time, destroys himself. Adam Smith made this point a long time ago, and history is replete with examples of it. By contrast, to optimize profit is to take many other factors besides profit into account, including long-term new investment, consumer loyalty, and the sense of a fair price.

The profit motive must necessarily operate in a socialist economy, too. Every economy that intends to progress must have as its motive the ability to get more out of the economic process than it puts in. Unless there is a return on investment, the economy simply spins its wheels in stagnation, neither accumulating nor growing. Capital accumulation is what profits are called in socialist enterprises. If the Soviets invest money in dams or in building locomotives, they must get back at least what they invest or they lose money. If they do lose money — and they often do — then they must draw on other resources. And if they do that throughout the system, economic stagnation and decline are inevitable. The same law binds both socialist and capitalist economies: Economic progress, growth, and forward motion cannot occur unless the return on investment is larger than the investment itself.

It is true that under socialism profits belong to the state and are allocated to individuals by the state for the state's own purposes. Such a procedure can be institutionalized, but the costs of enforcing it are great. It tremendously affects the possibilities of liberty, of choice. It deeply affects incentives and creativity. . . .

Three Systems — Three Fields of Responsibility

The most original social invention of democratic capitalism, in sum, is the private corporation founded for economic purposes. The motivation for this invention was also social: to increase "the wealth of nations," to generate (for the first time in human history) sustained economic development. This effect was, in fact, achieved. However, the corporation — as a type of voluntary association — is not merely an economic institution. It is also a moral institution and a political institution. It depends upon and generates certain moral-cultural virtues; it depends upon and generates new political forms. In two short centuries, it has brought about an immense social revolution. It has moved the center of economic activity from the land to industry and commerce. No revolution is without social costs and sufferings, which must be entered on the ledger against benefits won. Universally, however, the idea of economic development has now captured the imagination of the human race. This new possibility of development has awakened the world from its economic slumbers.

Beyond its economic effects, the corporation changes the ethos and the cultural forms of society. To some extent, it has undercut ancient ways in which humans relate to each other, with some good effects and some bad. After the emergence of corporations, religion had to work upon new psychological realities. The religion of peasants has given way to the religion of new forms of life: first that of an urban proletariat, then that of a predominantly service and white-collar society. The productivity of the new economics has freed much human time for questions other than those of mere subsistence and survival. The workday has shrunk, and "weekends" have been invented. After work, millions now take part in voluntary activities that fill, in effect, another forty-hour week (associations, sports, travel, politics, religion, and the like). Personal and social mobility has increased. Schooling has become not only common but mandatory. Teenagerhood has been invented. The "stages of human life" have drawn attention with the emergence of the private self.

But the corporation is not only an economic institution and a moral-cultural institution: it also provides a new base for politics. Only a free political system permits the voluntary formation of private corporations. Thus, those who value private economic corporations have a strong interest in resisting both statism and socialism. It would be naive and wrong to believe that persons involved in corporations are (or should be) utterly neutral about political systems. An economic system within which private corporations play a role, in turn, alters the political horizon. It lifts the poor, creates a broad middle class and undermines aristocracies of birth. Sources of power are created independent of the power of the state, in competition with the powers of the state, and sometimes in consort with the powers of the state. A corporation with plants and factories in, say, 120 congressional districts represents a great many employees and stockholders. On some matters, at least, they are likely to be well-organized to express their special political concerns. Political jurisdictions often compete to attract corporations; but their arrival also creates political problems.

Corporations err morally, then, in many ways. They may through their advertising appeal to hedonism and escape in ways that undercut the restraint and self-discipline required by a responsible democracy and that discourage the deferral of present satisfaction on which savings and investment for the future depend. They may incorporate methods of governance that injure dignity, cooperation, inventiveness, and personal development. They may seek their own immediate interests at the expense of the common good. They may become improperly involved in the exercise of political power. They may injure the conscience of their managers or workers. They are capable of the sins of individuals and of grave institutional sins as well. Thus, it is a perfectly proper task of all involved within corporations and in society at large to hold them to the highest moral standards, to accuse them when they fail, and to be vigilant about every form of abuse. Corporations are human institutions designed to stimulate economic activism and thus to provide the economic base for a democratic polity committed to high moral-cultural ideals. When they fall short of these purposes, their failure injures all.

Private corporations are social organisms. Neither the ideology of laissez faire nor the ideology of rugged individualism suits their actual practice of their inherent ideals. For corporations socialize risk, invention, investment, production, distribution, and services. They were conceived and designed to break the immemorial grip of mercantilist and clerical systems upon economic activity. On the other hand, they cannot come into existence, and certainly cannot function, except within political systems designed to establish and to promote the conditions of their flourishing. Among these are a sound currency, a system of laws, the regulation of competitive practices, the construction of infrastructures like roads, harbors, airports, certain welfare functions, and the like. The state, then, plays an indispensable role in democratic capitalism. The ideals of democratic capitalism are not those of laissez faire. The relations between a democratic state and a social market economy built around private corporations are profound, interdependent, and complex.

The ideals of democratic capitalism are not purely individualist, either, for the corporation draws upon and requires highly developed social skills like mutual trust, teamwork, compromise, cooperation, creativity, originality and inventiveness, and agreeable management and personnel relations. The rugged individualist of an earlier mythology may be an endangered species.

Great moral responsibility, then, is inherent in the existence of corporations. They may fail economically. They may fail morally and culturally. They may fail politically. Frequently enough, they err in one or all these areas. They are properly subjected to constant criticism and reform. But types of criticism may be distinguished. Some critics accept the ideals inherent in the system of private business corporations, and simply demand that corporations be faithful to these ideals. Some critics are opposed to the system qua system. Among these, some wish to restrain, regulate, and guide the business system through the power of the state and/or through moral and cultural forces like public opinion, shame, ridicule, boycotts, and moral suasion ("do not invest in South Africa," for example). In the theory of "mixed systems," the ideal of democratic capitalism shades off into the ideal of democratic socialism — one leaning more to the private sector, the other leaning more to the public sector. Still other critics wish to make the business system directly subject to the state. These last may be, according to their own ideals, corporate statists or socialists. They may be state socialists or local participatory politics socialists. Criticism from any of these quarters may be useful to the development and progress of democratic capitalism, even from those who would wish to destroy it.

There is plenty of room — and plenty of evidence — for citing specific deficiencies of corporations: economic, political, and moral-cultural. To be sure, there is a difference between accusations and demonstrated error. Like individuals, corporations are innocent until proved guilty. A passionate hostility toward bigness (or even toward economic liberty), like a passionate commitment to statism, may be socially useful by providing a searching critique from the viewpoint of hostile critics. But unless it gets down to cases and sticks to a reasoned presentation of evidence, it must be recognized for what it is: an argument less against specifics than against the radical ideal of democratic capitalism and the private corporation. It is useful to distinguish these two types of criticism, and it is helpful when critics are self-conscious and honest about which ideals actually move them. To criticize corporations in the light of their own ideals, the ideals of democratic capitalism, is quite different from criticizing them in the name of statist or socialist ideals incompatible with their existence. Clarity about ideals is as necessary as clarity about cases.

Theologians, in particular, are likely to inherit either a precapitalist or a frankly socialist set of ideals about political economy. They are especially likely to criticize corporations from a set of ideals foreign to those of democratic capitalism. To those who do accept democratic-capitalist ideals, then, their criticisms are likely to have a scent of unreality and inappropriateness. Wisdom would suggest joining argument at the appropriate level of discourse — whether the argument concerns general economic concepts, whether it concerns the rival ideals of democratic capitalism and socialism, or whether it concerns concrete cases and specific matters of fact. Each of these levels has its place. Wisdom's principal task is *distinguer*.

Managing a free society aimed at preserving the integrity of the trinitarian system — the economic system, the political system, and the moral-cultural system — is no easy task. An important standard set by Edmund Burke is cited as the epigraph of a masterly work by Wilhelm T. Röpke, *A Humane Economy:*

> To make a government requires no great prudence. Settle the seat of power; teach obedience: and the work is done. To give freedom is still more easy. It is not necessary to guide; it only requires to let go the rein. But to form a *free government;* that is, to temper together these opposite elements of liberty and restraint in one consistent work, requires much thought, deep reflection, a sagacious, powerful and combining mind.

To govern a free economy is yet more difficult than to form a free government. It is hard enough to govern a government. It is difficulty squared to govern a free economy — to establish the conditions for prosperity, to keep a sound currency, to promote competition, to establish general rules and standards binding upon all, to keep markets free, to provide education to all citizens in order to give them opportunity, to care for public needs, and to provide succor to the unfortunate. To have the virtue to do all these things wisely, persistently, judiciously, aptly is surely of some rather remarkable theological significance. It may even represent — given the inherent difficulties — a certain amazing grace. To fall short is to be liable to judgment.

Christians have not, historically, lived under only one economic system; nor are they bound in conscience to support only one. Any real or, indeed, any imaginable economic system is necessarily part of history, part of this world. None is the Kingdom of Heaven — not democratic socialism, not democratic capitalism. A theology of the corporation should not make the corporation seem to be an ultimate; it is only a means, an instrument, a worldly agency. Such a theology should attempt to show how corporations may be instruments of redemption, of humane purposes and values, of God's grace; it should also attempt to show their characteristic and occasional faults in every sphere. Like everything else in the world, corporations may be seen as both obstacles to salvation and bearers of God's grace. The waters of the sea are blessed, as are airplanes and plowshares and even troops making ready for just combat. A city in Texas may be named Corpus Christi, and a city in California, Sacramento. Christianity, like Judaism, attempts to sanctify the real world as it is, in all its ambiguity, so as to reject the evil in it and bring the good in it to its highest possible fruition.

Most Christians do not now work for major industrial corporations. Instead they work for the state (even in state universities), for smaller corporations, restaurants, barbershops, and other businesses. Still, a Christian social theology that lacks a theology of the large corporation will have no effective means of inspiring those Christians who do work within large corporations to meet the highest practicable Christian standards. It will also have no means of criticizing with realism and practicality those features of corporate life that deserve to be changed. Whether to treat big corporations as potential vessels of Christian vocation or to criticize them for their inevitable sins, Christian theology must advance much further than it has in understanding exactly and fairly every aspect of corporate life. The chief executive officer of General Electric needs such a theology. So do those critics of the corporation at the Interfaith Center for Corporate Responsibility. If we are to do better than clash like ignorant armies in the night, we must imitate Yahweh at Creation when he said, "Let there be light." We have not yet done all we should in casting such light.

Lenin wrote that foreign investment was a distinctive feature of the final stage of capitalism. It is a nice irony, therefore, that the world's greatest boom in corporate investment across borders took place in the dying years of Lenin's communism. From 1983 to 1990 such investment grew four times faster than world output and three times faster than world trade. Now, although the boom has faded in the recession-hit industrial countries, foreign investment is rushing enthusiastically to those countries that for decades were blighted by communism, by forms of state socialism and by authoritarian, isolationist government: to China, India, other parts of Asia, Latin America and even Eastern Europe. Not for the first time, Lenin's analysis missed the mark.

He is not alone, however, in having misunderstood and mispredicted the future of cross-border business. It is marching on, but not in the ways that were widely expected. A quarter of a century ago, when multinational firms suddenly loomed large on the radar screens of pundits and politicians, they aroused a mixture of awe and fear. The thought of the global enterprise, placing itself wherever costs and resources dictated, made business thinkers gasp with excitement. Such firms, fuelled by economies of scale and scope, would grow faster and bigger than whole countries and would soon dominate the world economy with their unbeatable effi-ciency. Echoing Marx and Lenin, many assumed this would entail the concentration of industries in fewer and fewer hands.

Similar ideas, also influenced by Marx and Lenin, led others to be terrified of multinationals: huge, ruthless and stateless, these firms would exploit the poor, manipulate governments and flout popular opinion. Raymond Vernon, a Harvard professor and one of the leading (and most sober) students of this phenomenon, observed in a 1977 book called "Storm over the Multinationals" that "the multinational enterprise has come to be seen as the embodiment of almost anything disconcerting about modern industrial society."

Yet now it is only a slight exaggeration to say that it is seen as the reverse, as the embodiment of modernity and the prospect of wealth: full of technology, rich in capital, replete with skilled jobs. Governments all around the world, especially the developing countries, are queuing up to attract multinationals. The United Nations, which spent decades tut-tutting about these firms and drawing up codes of conduct to control them, now spends much of its time advising countries on how best to seduce them.

— Bill Emmott, "A Survey of Multinationals —
Back in Fashion," *The Economist*,
27 March 1993, p. 5

Developmental Responsibility

Lee A. Tavis

This paper outlines the unique opportunity and responsibility associated with multinational corporate involvement in the economic and social development of Third World countries, and suggests ways that managers might begin to incorporate an awareness of this responsibility into the decision-making structure of their firms.

This developmental responsibility of multinationals derives from: (1) the leading role of these firms in allocating resources between the developed countries of the Northern Hemisphere and the less-developed ones in the Southern, as well as their position within Third World economies, (2) the desperate circumstances of the poor in the Third World, and (3) the lack of guidance to aid the multinational manager in deciding the "best" trade-off among the firm's various constituencies both within and among countries.

Multinationals are inextricably involved in the development process of the Third World. Not only do they affect the resource balance between countries through capital investments and profit repatriation, but they often dominate sectors within these economics. Thus, the results of multinational activities reach beyond the balance of resources between rich and poor countries, to the balance among groups of people within these countries. A wage decision in a rural area of the Philippines, for example, is a direct allocation between the Philippine laborer and the U.S. share-holder, with indirect connectors to other local constituencies such as the laborer's family, the community, and local and national governments.

More than economic resources are transmitted across national boundaries in the process. Social attitudes and values are also communicated. Take the example of a fruit packing facility. Modern equipment and production techniques introduced into a Third World location would bring increasing productivity to the operation. At the same time, cultural modernization takes place, with its social as well as its economic consequences. Not only are workers employed but, for many, this employment imposes a new regimentation of work hours and other requirements. When the multinational arrival is in a remote rural area, the overall social change is even greater, as structured, organized activities replace small, rural farming for the workers, and whole communities grow up around the multinational economic center. These social impacts are evidenced in the Dolefil case example.

In making decisions that necessarily affect the social as well as the economic position of their various constituents, multinational managers are not provided the kind of guidance available to a corporation operating in a single developed country. A firm in the United States faces product and financial markets where prices tend to be set by competitive pressures, and management faces strong unions where wages are negotiated. These market conditions exist in an environment where laws and governmental regulators are continually directing corporate activities to serve society, or to represent the needs of groups that are injured by the workings of unfettered markets.

Such is simply not the case for multinational firms with operations in the Third World. Too often, markets in these countries are inefficient, unions irresponsible, and government regulations, however well-intentioned, are not effective. Moreover, as resources are moved across national boundaries they are caught up in a host of conflicting political pressures and confusion with few institutions other than multinationals committed to long-term ties among countries.

This international environment can be viewed by managers in one of two ways. On the one hand, it provides an opportunity to pursue profit at the expense of local Third World constituencies, i.e.,

Lee A. Tavis, "Developmental Responsibility," in *Multinational Managers and Poverty in the Third World*, ed. Lee A. Tavis (Notre Dame: Notre Dame University Press, 1982), pp. 127-39.

push profit opportunities against less well-defined, and less well-organized limits on the freedom of corporate action. Alternatively, this environment can be viewed as one requiring management to establish its own constraints — to internally represent constituencies that cannot represent themselves.

The concept for developmental responsibility calls managers to the latter view. When a firm is in a position to contribute to the well-being of those in the Third World who are unable to change their own circumstances, the responsibility falls to the corporate management.

The internalization of economic and social guidelines adds a demanding new dimension to corporate decision structures. Managers are required to consider a full range of new social and economic parameters. Data on the local impacts must be collected and fed through the firm's information network. The nature of these data as well as the techniques for its transmission present new challenges.

The Productive-Social Role of Corporations

The allocation of corporate resources has a complex impact on any society. Factors are drawn from a number of constituencies — labor, management, suppliers, owners, lenders — and are combined synergistically into products that are sold to others — intermediate processors or consumers. The broader public is also included directly through unabsorbed externalities or indirectly through linkages with the firm's constituents. The managers charged with making these allocation decisions are responsible for the necessary trade-offs among the various groups and for the full range of direct or indirect impacts.

In classic Western social theory we have focused our attention on the corporate role of enhancing productivity, and have separated it from a responsibility to the constituents, save the owners. Management is assigned the task of enhancing productivity by optimizing shareholder wealth in efficient financial and product markets. Responsibility for the welfare of the other constituencies lies with the law, regulatory structures, or public opinion. These representatives of social consensus impose minimum performance re-

quirements, or constraints, that represent the interests of these other groups.

In most developed capitalistic countries, governmental regulation is based on the existence of relatively efficient markets. One part of regulation is directed to improving this efficiency. In the United States, the Federal Trade Commission and the Securities and Exchange Commission, for example, regulate the information flowing to consumers and investors, thereby enhancing their ability to make rational choices.

Paralleling this market focus, other legislation is designed to protect groups that may be injured by the workings of a free market. This regulation, based on broader social goals, is the role of the United States Consumer Product Safety Commission or the Occupational Safety and Health Administration.

This, in classical social theory, responsibility is separated — managers shoulder the productivity responsibility and represent the shareholders, while regulators and the courts bear the responsibility for the effect on other constituencies through the imposition of what might be termed social constraints.

The classic notion of corporate responsibility represents a conservative end of the spectrum. It is staunchly supported by a number of theoreticians and many managers. This position should not be seen as irresponsible. In this view, managers do not maximize short-run profits to the detriment of long-term wealth for shareholders; they do not violate their firms' enlightened self-interest; they would stay within the unenforceable limits of the law.

If this productivity-social separation of responsibilities is to work, however, the constraints on corporate activity must be clearly communicated to the decision-maker. This is the role of efficient markets and effective regulation.

Beginning in the 1960s, there has been a growing focus on non-owner constituents in the academic literature and in managerial attitudes. The notion of "trusteeship" is gaining support. In its statement *Social Responsibility of Business Corporations,* the Committee for Economic Development stated:

The modern professional manager also regards himself not as an owner disposing of personal property as he sees fit, but as a trustee balancing the interests of many diverse participants and constituents in the enterprise, whose interests sometimes conflict with those of others.

We should note that clear signals as to the societal limits on corporate actions are necessary conditions for managers who view their function as a trustee as well as those who hold to the classic view. The role of the law or regulation in establishing the boundaries beyond which one constituency cannot be traded off against another remains, regardless of a person's position on social responsibility.

Multinational Developmental Responsibility

The necessary clarity of signals from markets and regulators seldom exists for the multinational firm. Signals from inefficient markets carry little information about consumer preferences, and regulation that is confused, or itself socially irresponsible, can be destructive.

In Third World countries both regulators and managers must cope with inefficient markets. Governmental regulations tend to replace the free activities of efficient markets with sets of artificial market mechanisms such as price controls, quotas, and exchange requirements. The regulatory span becomes broader and regulations tend to overlap one another.

As the span is broader, the resources available for the regulatory process are narrower. In all of these countries there are well-trained and talented technocrats, but they are often too few relative to the task and have small staffs and inadequate information. The bureaucratic infrastructure can be seriously inadequate. In circumstances such as these, we find that the signals transmitted to the private sector are not very useful.

At the present time there are few clear signals emanating from the international sector. This is unfortunate since, as the world becomes more interdependent, fewer problems can be effectively treated in a national context. The development of codes of conduct by a number of international organizations such as the United Nations, the Organization for Economic Cooperation and Devel-

opment, and the International Chamber of Commerce, holds promise. Although these codes are general, and often contain conflicting requirements, they do indicate a direction and suggest a role that multinationals can play in our changing society.

With inadequate market and regulatory signals coming from national and international sources, the productivity-social separation principle does not hold. Managers cannot responsibly ignore the social impact of their firms' presence. They have no alternative other than to be developmentally responsive. Rather than the pursuit of wealth maximization to the limits of the marketplace, regulation, or enforceable laws, self-regulation through internal, managerially imposed constraints is in order.

As managers approach this new requirement for participation in Third World patterns of development they are morally called to a concern for the poor in those countries. When one person or group is in critical need, another individual or group in proximity to the situation must act to alleviate the need if they can. This is particularly true when other sources of assistance are not available in time to avoid a crisis. On this principle, a multinational manager who is in a position to aid the poor who cannot help themselves, incurs that responsibility. With the multinational direct and indirect links to the poor, managers would apply corporate resources where their firms could uniquely contribute to the relief of poverty, even though their firms were not involved in the cause.

Thus, the management of a multinational's activities in a Third World country is subject to a far different environment than is the case for a domestic American firm. The opportunities and the nature of the constraint set are derived from a fundamentally different context. While multinationals are powerful economic and social forces in Third World countries, managers seldom have the needed economic signals from efficient markets nor guidance as to social preferences necessary to allow the separation of the productive dimension of their decisions from their social impact. In exercising this involvement, managers are called to the responsibility of helping those who are in desperate need.

Executives who accept this expanded responsibility in the Third World will increasingly evaluate the social as well as the economic dimensions of their decisions. The action focus is transformed from externally imposed market and legal requirements to management-directed efforts. For example, a developmentally responsive multinational corporation would monitor the life style changes that it imposes upon its indigenous employees; it would be alert to the potentially damaging misuse of sophisticated products among technically backward peoples; it would measure its long-term impact on local suppliers and competitors; it might provide local housing, health, or transportation services; it would be concerned with the nutrition and health of employees and their families; it would anticipate the economic and social effects of a new production technology on the employees and the community. Whereas many or most managers would prefer to relinquish the social dimension of their decisions to other institutions, this is impossible in the multinational environment. Managerial social neutrality is simply not possible in much of the Third World.

Meeting Corporate Developmental Responsibility

If one recognizes the development cusp, particularly its poverty dimension, and accepts the argument that multinational managers need to address this concern, how do they get the job done? A firm cannot be developmentally responsive to the exclusion of its assigned productivity role. It must meet both responsibilities in an environment where the interests of the constituencies are generally quite diverse.

The local activities of a multinational operation are simultaneously an element of two systems — the multinational corporate system and the national economy — with close linkages to both. The key to multinational productivity lies in the multinational system, while developmental responsibility is a part of the national system.

Multinational managers must attempt to integrate their subsidiaries in order to achieve the efficiency associated with the international arbitration of factors of production if they are to meet their productivity responsibilities. Moreover, the advantages that multinationals gain through their ability to penetrate national boundaries is necessary to offset the disadvantages they incur as a result of absentee control. Thus, some degree of systematic optimization is an economic necessity.

To be developmentally responsible, however, the local operations must fit the needs of the national system. These needs can often be in conflict with multinational optimization. This kind of conflict is to be expected in any situation where systems with divergent goals overlap. Unfortunately, this conflict is too frequently played out between the multinational corporation and national institutions on the basis of power, with little room left for considering the needs of the poor. The rancor makes it difficult, indeed, for the manager to respond to the needs of the poor in the Third World.

The managerial entry point for a balanced developmental response is clearly the firm's planning and information system. This is true for the assurance of ethical performance by any institution. For multinational firms it is critical because of the complexity of their decision environment and the difficulty of the trade-offs that must be decided upon.

If an institution is to respond favorably to its environment, this impact is best anticipated and evaluated while the institution still has maximum flexibility — early in the planning process. Rigidity sets in at an alarming rate as managers proceed through the planning sequence to implementation. Once resources are committed to an alternative, the social as well as the economic die is cast. If, because of an early lack of concern, the social dimension is not properly anticipated, or if social impact information is filtered out of the system, unintentional and often unavoidable damage can result.

In order to effectively respond to the development needs of the Third World, multinational planning and information systems need to: (1) measure the full impact of the corporation's presence in host countries — both economic *and* social: (2) transmit the "soft" social impact data through the system to the decision-makers for both strategic and operations decisions, as well as those who are judging the performance of the decision-makers: and (3) establish a specific policy as to what information management will share with its various constituencies.

Environmental Monitoring

The goal of environmental monitoring is to identify the full range of corporate involvement in the host country. It includes the identification of the firm's linkages with the economic and social aspects of development. Monitoring must be undertaken on a country-by-country basis. The nature of the linkages with local poor can be very different among operating locations. Local environments are unique and what may be "best" for one multinational operating site may not fit the needs of others. Development patterns are incredibly diverse. And, social preferences in one location can be vastly different from those in others.

When monitoring is broadened to include the social dimension of developmental responsibility, the firm is extending its data collection into a much larger system with longer relevant planning horizons and more obscure linkages. The earlier developmental response examples of product use, employee life styles, family health, community development, and new technology reflect the firm's broader reach of information needs.

Even though we are suggesting an additional dimension to the firm's usual economic environmental measures, multinationals have access to the most sophisticated social monitoring techniques in history through market research methodology. Surely these skills could be applied to social measurement.

Internal Information Processing

Full environmental monitoring must be accompanied by an information system that transmits this expanded data to the relevant decision and performance measuring points. It must flow through very complex organizational structures. The general organizational pattern of multinationals has been one of decentralized decisions associated with increased reliance on financial reporting systems. In these structures more decisions are made locally with headquarters judging the decisions after the fact through the financial reporting network. This process can mask much of the developmental impact of resource allocation decisions. Local managers who are judged strictly on financial performance cannot be expected to be alert to the full impact of their activities. Moreover, top management, isolated from the local setting, cannot provide responsible guidelines to the operating executives. Thus, firms cannot simply feed locally monitored information to decentralized local decision-makers. It must be moved through the information system.

Information in multinational firms must span great geographic and cultural, as well as organizational, space. The tendency for "soft" social information to be filtered out in decentralized firms will be more prevalent in a multinational than in a firm operating in only one country.

Cultural differences must be faced at some point in an information network. Many firms employ nationals at local levels as a means of increasing their sensitivity to the local environment. For integrated planning, however, this sensitivity must become information and flow up through the organization. Without strong cultural sensitivity at the headquarter's level, the filter is simply moved from local monitoring to the division headquarters. For those situations where local secrecy and mistrust have developed, as is the case for many acquired firms, the filter is impervious, and most of the social as well as much of the economic data does not flow.

For performance evaluation, it is essential that data on developmental performance move through the firm, since managerial performance is always monitored at organizational levels above the manager who is being evaluated. The fact that the social dimension of developmental responsibility tends to be slow to develop exacerbates the problem of attempting to measure a long-term phenomenon in short, segmented, quarterly or annual time periods. We cannot expect the "soft" estimates of developmental impact that are slow to appear and hard to measure to readily pass through the geographic-organizational-cultural boundaries in typical information networks.

Sharing Information

Disclosure is an essential element of all planning and information systems. Through its disclosure policy, management decides the extent to which it will share its power. Clearly, multinationals must meet disclosure requirements imposed by both parent and host countries as well as those initiated through shareholder resolutions. Disclosure policy deals with the sharing of information in those all-too-frequent cases in which the requirements are not clear, or in sharing information which is beyond clearly stated minimums. Since information is power, disclosure becomes a particularly sensitive issue in conflict situations.

Multinationals that undertake expanded environmental monitoring will develop an in-depth understanding of the local environment. They have three options for the use of this information:

1. as a base for independent action,
2. to share with local governmental authorities,
3. for voluntary disclosure to the public.

The first two alternatives relate to our earlier conclusions concerning social neutrality. Where a firm must monitor and control its own social impact due to the lack of clear signals from legal structures or efficient markets, management can either use the information to plan a responsible economic and social program for the allocation of resources to and within the host country, or it can share this information with host country officials to jointly work through the productivity-social trade-offs.

A clear example of information sharing that could improve the living conditions of the poor in host countries is in the selection of technology. The capital intensity is in the selection of technology. The capital intensity of technology being transferred by multinational enterprises is currently a source of friction between multinationals and host countries. Whereas multinational technology from the developed countries is capital intensive, development planners in the Third World are calling for a more simple, labor-intensive, "intermediate" technology tailored to their labor skills and employment needs. The development planners have the power to control, but the multinational enterprise has the critical information. Managers know the technical limits of their production function — the limits on the substitutability of labor for capital and the related efficiency. Having worked with that technology, they understand how amenable it is to modification and are in a position to judge how it relates to the realities of production in that country. When confrontation can be minimized and information shared, development will be enhanced.

When managers opt for the first alternative (independent action), they incur the danger of paternalism and of imposing values from one national or managerial culture on host country peoples. Alternatively, only when governmental authorities represent the needs of the people and there is a basis of trust for meaningful multinational-host government interaction is information sharing in order.

To voluntarily disclose information to the general public beyond that which is required (alternative three) is a decision to be openly accountable for corporate actions. (This broad disclosure can, of course, occur as a result of sharing information with governmental officials in alternative two.) Disclosure relinquishes power to other groups in the community with no assurance that they will employ it effectively or responsibly.

In this paper, I have shared my world view and preferred role for multinationals — that poverty in the Third World is the most serious cancer in our global society and that effective action by multinational firms is an important ingredient for progress toward its relief. I have argued for a multinational form of corporate social responsibility designated as a "developmental responsibility."

Developmental responsibility is imposed on multinational corporations by conditions in Third World countries. Markets and regulatory regimes do not signal the requirements of a social consensus. In these conditions, multinationals must impose a form of self-regulation on their Third World activities. They are called to internalize a social responsibility. An extra dimension is added to corporate decision-making in what is already a complex and high-risk international environment.

The beginning point in implementing a policy of developmental responsibility is with the poor in Third World operating locations. This is the group universally in the greatest need, a need that should be recognized by all segments of society. Contributions to this group provide the most important measure of accomplishment for the developmentally responsive multinational corporation.

The managerial entry point for meeting developmental responsibility is with the firm's planning system. The extended planning horizons associated with this new dimension of the corporate role and the "soft" nature of its measured performance pose a real challenge to the multinational manager.

Global Ethics: Wrestling with the Corporate Conscience

Gene R. Laczniak and Jacob Naor

. . . . This article will try to define human welfare in international operations and the conduct necessary to promote it. We will advance six propositions dealing with issues involving ethical considerations that were judged to be of critical concern to international operations. As such, they are not all-inclusive or mutually exclusive. They should simply be regarded as first steps in the quest for a more rigorous outlook on multinational ethics. The propositions are intended *to reflect the ethical climate facing organizations operating in international markets, in a nonjudgmental fashion,* and are not presented in any particular priority. We will then outline the actions that might be taken by corporations concerned about the ethics of their worldwide behavior. Perhaps the issues raised here will help to better define the areas of agreement. Because U.S.-based multinationals now account for more than 10% of the world's GNP, the scrutiny of multinational activities, including their ethical postures, will no doubt increase in the future. One only has to look to the tragic events in Bhopal, India, to realize that a single unfortunate incident can focus worldwide attention on the operating procedures of a multinational corporation.

Gene R. Laczniak and Jacob Naor, "Global Ethics: Wrestling with the Corporate Conscience," *Business* 35 (July-Sept. 1985): 3-10.

The Propositions

Proposition 1: When operating in international markets, there is no single standard of ethical behavior applicable to all business decisions. In contrast to domestic operations, a wide spectrum of standards and modes of ethical behavior confronts decision makers involved in situations that transcend national boundaries. This makes the development of a corporate-wide ethical posture more difficult.

Discussion — Multinational corporations operate in markets that cut across cultures in which Christian, Moslem, Hindu, Buddhist, or socialist values may predominate. While production considerations often dictate an increasing globalization and homogeneity of products, the cultural value systems faced by these companies are strikingly diverse. Even when two countries share the same predominant religious denomination (the Philippines and the United States have Christianity in common, for example), economic and sociocultural values may greatly limit the similarity between the two nations.

In order to understand such cultural diversity, decision makers must consider a wide variety of ethical systems based on eastern and western cultures. Obviously, the more cultural boundaries that are transcended, the more philosophical perspectives confronting decision makers. The practical manifestation of this dilemma has been described as follows:

"This situation is not black and white. . . . It is clouded by the question of what is 'proper.' Practices illegal in one country may be accepted ways of doing business in another. A company that adheres strictly to a policy of restraint may find itself at a serious disadvantage in some countries. A company that goes along with the accepted practices in a country may find it has a different problem. A number of American companies have been criticized at home for engaging in practices [abroad] that are quite legal and aboveboard in those countries where they were used but are illegal in the United States."

Under such conditions, developing a "proper" corporate ethical posture is one of the most vexing challenges facing the multinational executive. Long-term success involves understanding the interaction of cultural and religious values on ethical perspectives.

Proposition 2: The laws of economically developed countries, such as those of the United States, generally define the lowest common denominator of acceptable behavior for operations in those domestic markets. In an underdeveloped country or a developing country, it would be the actual *degree of enforcement* of the law that would, in practice, determine the lower limit of permissible behavior.

Discussion — Many of the less developed countries (LDCs), as a result of their colonial past, have laws based on Western systems — often that of the former colonial regime. In many instances such laws are either not enforced or are ignored. For example, in Venezuela during the early 1970s customs officials exacted, as a matter of course, illegal (according to Venezuelan law) payments from foreign-owned organizations that imported raw materials into the country. Bribes were given in order to have those materials classified according to their appropriate import duty categories. Only as the result of concerted appeals to the Venezuelan government by several of the extorted firms were existing laws (which prohibited bribery of customs officials) finally enforced. Similarly, in Honduras, United Brands was forced to make payments into a Swiss bank account in order to receive a "more feasible" export tax treatment on their exports from that country.

In both of these situations the "official" law clearly did not define the lowest common denominator of behavior. "Business customers" were at variance with the law and took clear precedence over it. Thus a careful study of the de facto versus the *de jure* rules and regulations of the countries where an organization operates is a must for the international corporation concerned with defining benchmarks for "proper" ethical behavior. The organization must then decide if the "permissible" lower levels of behavior are the course of action that it will follow. The discrepancy between existing laws and the unlawful practices that are socially condoned is one of the dilemmas with which multinationals must grapple.

Proposition 3: The upper threshold of ethical behavior regarding either domestic or foreign operations is not clearly defined.

Discussion — In contrast to the lower limit of acceptable ethical behavior, no easily definable upper limit to such behavior exists as a guide to corporate decision makers. Companies can thus engage, for example, in "slightly more" or "much more" ethical behavior than their competitors. An example of a relatively higher ethical stance is provided by the IBM Corporation, which refused to pay even small "lubrication" payments permitted under the Foreign Corrupt Practices Act. The Dow Corning Corporation takes a similarly meritorious stand, due in part to their belief in the superiority of their products and technology. Thus, an elevated moral stance may in many instances depend on the motivation of top management itself, apart from environmental factors such as competitive behavior or accepted business customs. The cost of maintaining a high moral stance if the competition does not do the same may be considerable. In fact, the small firm in particular may not be able to afford the high price of morality. The reality of the situation may be that only the organization with superior technology or a lock on products badly needed by the host country can easily resist the temptation to behave unethically.

Proposition 4: Because of their visibility and their actual or potential impact on the economies of LDCs, multinational corporations have a heavier ethical responsibility than their domestic counterparts. Flagrant non-ethical behavior may attract substantial attention in host countries and may generate regulatory action aimed at the offender or at multinationals in general. This may result in adverse publicity affecting operations in other markets as well.

Discussion — Multinational corporations often provide major sources of employment and income either in LDCs or in underdeveloped regions of more developed countries. They often hold a pivotal position regarding the economic health of important market areas. The experience of the Singer Company is cited here, both for the host-country impact of particular overseas operations as well as for the apparent recognition and acceptance by the company of its ethical responsibility in the matter:

"In 1975, Singer decided to close a washing machine and refrigerator manufacturing plant in Leini, Italy. The closing would have put 2,000 workers out of jobs. And the timing could not have been worse. Other companies were closing plants in Italy and the government was alarmed. A committee of top executives from the United States and Italy, under the control of the European division president, worked out the step-by-step plan of action. A policy of frankness was followed for all public and private discussions. The result was government acceptance of the decision, an equitable settlement with labor, and much less publicity than accorded the closing of several plants by other multinationals at about the same time."

The acceptance of ethical responsibility by Singer and its explanation of the situation appear to have been major factors in motivating equitable behavior. Less enlightened behavior would have triggered host-country regulations aimed at averting major damage to the local economy. An example of less cautious behavior occurred when the Upjohn Corporation distributed a birth-control product called *DepoProvera* in Malaysia. This product had failed Food and Drug Administration license approval in the United States because of its link to menstrual difficulties as well as to heart cancer in laboratory rats. The resulting negative publicity caused embarrassment to Upjohn and generated considerable discussion about the obligations of multinationals to LDCs.

There have been other pressures on multinationals to reform their behavior. On the U.S. front, groups such as the Interfaith Center for Corporate Responsibility have emerged. This coalition of social-activist groups, representing 170 Catholic orders and 15 Protestant denominations (and influencing many large financial portfolios), has engaged in fact-finding trips abroad, research, testimony to the United Nations and the U.S. Congress, and stockholder resolutions in order to publicize and encourage ethically responsible behavior by corporations operating in international markets.

Also, social and religious doctrines including the 1981 encyclical by Pope John Paul II (*Laborem Exercens*), as well as the pastoral letter by American bishops on the U.S. economy (1984), have articulated the moral responsibility incumbent on those in corporations to provide economic opportunity and assure justice for all who live in less developed societies. These examples indicate that the acceptance of ethical responsibility is a fundamental prerequisite for development of managerial behavior that strives to be equitable to consumers and employees around the world.

Proposition 5: Because the top management of multinational organizations will tend to be less familiar with foreign markets than with domestic markets, and because of pervasive ethnocentric orientations, the likelihood of ethical misjudgments by top management regarding such markets will be greater.

Discussion — The well-known miscalculations of the Swiss-based Nestle Corporation in marketing infant formula in LDCs during the 1970s is an obvious illustration of this proposition. While there was indeed a need for improved infant nutrition in most of the markets Nestle sought to serve, Nestle failed to take into consideration basic social and economic conditions necessary for the proper and safe use of infant formula, namely proper sanitation, refrigeration, and the availability of clean water. Negligence and ethnocentrism appear to have combined in this instance to produce disastrous consequences that could have been avoided had adequate, unbiased research determined the conditions existing in the various foreign markets. Only in October of 1984, after an independent audit commission reported that Nestle was meeting all the nutrition safeguards proposed by the World Health Organization, was a worldwide boycott of Nestle products by numerous consumer groups ended.

The danger of an organization viewing foreign markets ethnocentrically — that is, only from the vantage point of one's own culture — is ever-present. One set of authors observed:

"In cross-cultural analysis, multinational organizations should be keenly aware of this one fact: we are all products of our own culture. We tend to interpret others from our own perspective. Other cultures do not necessarily hold the same values, use the same symbols, exhibit the same behaviors or use the same decision process. . . . Costly mistakes can be avoided by recognizing the differences that prevail between cultures. The differences seem to represent substantial obstacles for those who venture into international trade.

Nowhere is this more true than in the area of ethical conduct. 'The Ugly American' has become part of the world's vocabulary, due in part, to our ethnocentric views. Our views of right and wrong are not universally held."

Some social observers have suggested the use of periodic public opinion polls, culturally specific in their inception, to monitor whether the customers in a foreign market feel that a multinational firm is communicating clearly and honestly.

Proposition 6: Concern for ethics seems to rise proportionately with the degree of a country's overall development. The higher a country's economic, social, and technological development, the greater are the pressures in that country for higher standards of ethical business conduct. Conversely, the less advanced the level of economic development, the lower will be the concern within host countries with the ethics of business conduct.

Discussion — In many less developed or developing countries, pressures on a given organization to succeed may often be fierce, while effective environmental restrictions on business activities may often be lacking. Under such conditions, bribery, extortion, nepotism, and fraud may at times be considered necessary and essential modes of behavior in order to assure economic survival. Such behavior is consistent with psychologist Abraham Maslow's famous theory of needs, which suggests that the satisfaction of primary needs, such as economic safety, precedes the satisfaction of "higher order" needs. Some observers have noted that as certain Middle Eastern countries have increasingly clamped down on corruption and engaged in significant charitable activities. Under depressed economic conditions, multinationals may be tempted to apply lower standards of ethical behavior to LDCs, or may even be encouraged by host governments to operate in an environment that permits unethical behavior. The unfortunate result is that countries that are most vulnerable to the impact of the activities of multinationals will stand to lose the most under such a policy of "case-by-case" ethics.

Recommendations

The preceding discussion describes realistic ethical considerations for multinational decision makers. The following recommendations may provoke somewhat more dissent. The propositions relevant to particular recommendations have, in each case, been identified in parentheses in order to focus attention on areas requiring further clarification and thought. In the process, additional areas of concern may emerge. Perhaps the result will be gradual progress toward a more coherent analysis of multinational ethical issues.

Recommendation 1: Multinational corporations should develop clear codes of conduct that specify their objectives, duties, and obligations in the international markets in which they operate. To the greatest extent possible, such codes should be company-wide, regardless of the area of operation (Propositions 1, 4).

Discussion — Multinationals have incurred some of their harshest criticism by operating with divergent sets of rules in different countries, thereby giving the impression that the differences were motivated by the desire for exploitation. Thus, there should not be two or more sets of ethics, one for the United States and others for countries abroad. In addition, any code of ethics should take into account the legitimate interests of the host populations. The code developed can then perhaps serve as a policy guide to the propriety of a contemplated action. Several corporations, such as Caterpillar Tractor, Allis Chalmers, Johnson's Wax and Rexnord, have designed and used their own codes for ethics for worldwide operations. In the case of Caterpillar Tractor, the company published in 1974 a "Code of Worldwide Business Conduct." The code was distributed to its 1,300 managers around the world, and they are expected to adhere to it. A basic principle of this code (which has served as a model to other organizations) states that "we support laws of all countries which prohibit restraint of trade, unfair practices, or abuse of economic power. And we avoid such practices in areas of the world where laws do not prohibit them."

In addition to general principles, Caterpillar's code includes detailed guidelines dealing with payments of all kinds that may be "required" in various markets. Where unavoidable, they must be limited to customary amounts and made only to facilitate correct performance of officials' duties. In a sense, this portion of the code provides an explanation of the Foreign Corrupt Practices Act, which, according to law, the company must adhere to. Caterpillar even goes so far as to urge its dealers worldwide to adopt written codes similar to its own. The rationale for this strategy is that for both the dealers and for Caterpillar there is much more to lose than to gain by unethical practices.

Another way to minimize the temptation to engage in questionable strategies is for the multinational organization to provide high-quality, safe, and culturally appropriate products as standard worldwide operating procedure. This dictum applies equally well when dealing with developing or developed countries. Corporations should not assume that developing countries want and would be satisfied with "cheap" products (i.e., substandard by home country requirements). While a policy that strives to provide high-quality items may sometimes go unnoticed by the average citizen of the host country, it will go far in avoiding the negative attention received by a multinational corporation when the marketing of unsafe, substandard, or culturally inappropriate products becomes known. For example, Australian meat packers were subject to well-deserved censure as well as economic backlash when "beef" shipments to the Middle East were allegedly found to contain pork, and those destined for Japan to contain kangaroo meat. A major tobacco vendor suffered unfavorable publicity when it came to light that the company apparently sent inferior quality cigarettes to developing countries. Had these corporations adhered to clearly specified codes of ethical conduct, such behavior would not have occurred. Citicorp's International Code of Conduct captures these notions quite well. Their code states:

> "We must never lose sight of the fact that we are guests in foreign countries. We must conduct ourselves accordingly. We recognize the right of governments to pass local legislation and our obligation to conform. Under these circumstances, we also recognize that we can survive only if we are successful in demonstrating to the local authorities that our presence is beneficial. We believe that every country must find its own way politically and economically. Sometimes we feel

that local policies are wise; sometimes we do not. However, irrespective of our own views, we try to function as best we can under prevailing conditions. We have always felt free to discuss with local governments matters directly affecting our interests, but we recognize that they have final regulatory authority."

When multinational corporations point out the benefits of their presence in various reports and publications, they should strive to identify situations where they have been ethically sensitive to host governments and local consumers.

Recommendation 2: The ethical dimensions of multinational corporate activity should be treated as significant inputs into strategy formulation by top management of multinational corporations (Propositions 4, 5).

Discussion — Strides in this direction have already been made by some corporations. For example, the Norton Company has a corporate committee that tours the company's foreign operations on a regular basis and provides advice concerning troublesome areas, including those having ethical implications. Castle and Cooke Corporation has invited a panel of academics to study its Philippine plantations and to audit these operations for socially responsible behavior. Presumably the results of this evaluation would serve as feedback for future corporate behavior. Control Data has in recent years published a detailed report on its social performance in international markets. While many organizations make similar efforts, Control Data has subsequently attempted to generate some ethical guidelines, such as not selling computers to countries that are human rights violators.

An approach that might help corporate executives develop culturally appropriate responses would be the regular use of group discussions between headquarters management and management teams of nationals from the various international market areas. The goal of such meetings would be value clarification, value exchange, and consensus on problems confronting the corporations. Pillsbury Corporation reportedly has used a variation of this approach. At its core, this perspective implies that not only should a company study the characteristics of consumers in various markets but also should be familiar with the ethical norms of the cultures involved.

The inference one can draw from this approach is that top management should consciously and systematically determine and develop the ethical profile that it wishes to cultivate. In doing this, long-term consideration should predominate over short-run concerns. Corporate strategy will thus clearly be affected by the type of ethical profile the corporation chooses to project. The mere fact that the company states the principles to which it abides may earn it a measure of respect, if not approval. In any event, companies must increasingly consider the ethical impact of their strategies or face marketplace consequences that may be costly and damaging in both the short-term and long-term. The Nestle infant formula debacle, mentioned earlier, is a classic case in point.

Recommendation 3: When unbridgeable gaps appear between the ethical values of the host country and those of the multinational corporation, the multinational should voluntarily consider suspending activities (Propositions 1, 2, 3, 6).

Discussion — Examples of such situations would include the withdrawal of various corporations from operations in South Africa in response to apartheid policies, and the suspension of activities by IBM and Coca-Cola in India because of that country's policies concerning the extent of national ownership and control of organizations operating in the Indian subcontinent. Since many developing countries look to multinationals for leadership, due in no small part to the resources and expertise they command, a high moral posture may influence the competitive environment, even as that environment affects the strategies of the corporation. Thomas A. Murphy, former chairman and chief executive officer of General Motors Corporation, made the point this way:

"While we may not agree with the underlying philosophy of laws and institutions in certain countries where we conduct business, we nevertheless recognize that we have an opportunity, by our example and by our good business practice, to work within the existing framework and to act as a positive force for progressive change."

Recommendation 4: In order to encourage the consideration of ethical issues by multinational corporations, the regular development of "ethical impact statements" should be considered (Propositions 4, 5).

Discussion — Periodic reviews of ethical impact, which may be part of more broadly conceived social audits, should attempt to measure the influence of planned or ongoing corporate activities on the social and cultural welfare of the people concerned. This is the so-called "externalities effect," which means that organizations should make greater efforts to define, in addition to attempting to quantify, the impact of their activities on the financial health of the organization. The evolving thoughts on the techniques of social auditing apply directly to the analysis of issues of ethical concern. Thus while a social audit might examine, for example, the impact of a corporate decision on the employment and incomes of local workers, the ethical impact statement would examine the moral values involved in arriving at that corporate decision in the first place.

Some European multinationals are already engaged in social audits that attempt to identify the benefits (and costs) of particular operations for the local economy. Dunlop, Unilever, and ICI have in recent years prepared cost-benefit analyses of their subsidiaries in Malaysia, Nigeria, Zambia, and India. The inclusion of ethics-specific considerations, in the sense used here, is rare however. In other words, seldom do organizations attempt to quantify and report on the economic costs of decisions made on the basis of ethical concern.

The United Nations has called for formal agreements between multinationals and host countries that clearly define the public responsibilities of a corporation, specify sanctions against infringements, and require complete financial disclosure concerning operations. While most corporations would resist additional mandates for financial disclosure requirements, the social audit and its ethical impact might very well prepare a corporation to negotiate ethical guidelines, should these be necessary or advantageous in the future.

Conclusion

It is becoming increasingly clear that, acting in their own self-interest, multinational corporations should consider themselves as change-agents of economic and social development. Willingly or unwillingly, their impact in foreign countries is often crucial and long-lasting. Such influences on local cultures, institutions, religions, and ways of life therefore must be carefully ascertained. Companies should conduct periodic "ethical impact audits" to assess such effects. Ethical considerations must necessarily become a vital element in the multinational corporate planning process. Failing these, questions raised by multinational corporate behavior will result in regulations set by either the host government or larger regulatory bodies (such as the Organization for Economic Cooperation and Development or the United Nations) with regional or worldwide authority. This, it appears to be in the best interest of multinational organizations to set a single ethical posture for all worldwide operations, to set it at as high a level as possible, and to implement it consistently and conscientiously.

Section 3: Third World Development

While global networking among industrialized countries continues to grow, the world community also wrestles with the plight of the poor in less developed countries. Christianity affirms that they are, preeminently, God's own people. Concern for the Third World poor has been a consistent theme within the Christian churches for many decades.

Already in the 1960s, Catholic social teaching had focused on the wrenching lot of the less developed countries. Cardinal Maurice Roy in his 1967 speech encouraged American Christians to expand their vision of humanity: The new heaven and new earth envisioned in the Book of Relevation cannot fully unfold until the lives of the poor are dramatically improved.

Evangelical Christians have also implored believers to consider the Bible's message about the poor. Ron Sider provides a full range of evidence from the Old and New Testaments to support his thesis that God is not a neutral observer of history. Instead, God is actively working through history on behalf of the poor and expects believers to work for transformed economic relationships that empower the poor. Sider provides convincing evidence that in the Scriptures neglect of the poor is a sign of disobedience to God.

Yet even when there is a consensus that something must be done about global poverty, people of faith diverge in their thinking about appropriate strategies to address that problem. Cornel West argues that far too often the church has bought into the social logic of established powers. It has allied itself with existing governments and concentrations of economic wealth. The result has been "centralized economic power unaccountable to the majority of the populace," the building of an "iron cage" in which oppression is the norm for the majority. West argues instead for a church grounded in people's basic needs, which honors the diversity of human experience. He believes the end result might be some form of democratic socialism.

In contrast to West, Mark Amstutz critiques church support for development strategies that are heavily dependent on governmental intervention in the economy. He argues that such strategies are typically redistributional but do not create employment or generate wealth. Amstutz contrasts the structural and modernization theses about development, the former emphasizing the injustice of exploitative economic policies, the latter stressing the positive cultural values that contribute to economic progress. In his view the church has supported the structural thesis for change while support for a modernization thesis would be more helpful to the poor. On that basis he proposes that the church respond by recognizing that its primary competence is in moral analysis, not in development strategies. Yet he still exhorts churches to respond with humanitarian aid and private efforts that enhance the necessary preconditions for development.

Each of these authors is committed to answering the cry of the poor and is convinced that Christian faith requires collective action. Yet their analyses of the biblical basis for aiding the poor exhibit different emphases; and these emphases result in different strategies for assistance. Together they illustrate the broad range of discussion that occurs as people of faith grapple to connect faith and economic development.

The People of God and the Development of Peoples

Cardinal Maurice Roy

The unaided eye of man cannot see all of humanity in a single focus of vision. We can see successively only a few people — just a little portion of mankind. Now and then we can even see a crowd of a few hundreds at one time, such as here tonight. We can extend our horizon of mankind to 50 or 100,000 in a football or baseball stadium.

But until television our ability to see the whole human family was much restricted, very slight compared to that of God who sees us all at once. Today via television we can see much more of humanity on parade. Via satellite we can see our fellow man at work, at play, at war and at peace, on every continent with a sense of immediacy and shared experience. We witness the actual unfolding of the joys and hopes, the griefs and anxieties of the men of this age. To some degree we can even say: "Here is all of humanity. All men are present to me. I am present to all of them."

From this glimpse of all the human family, one frightful reality emerges in clear focus: All men are not yet equal; far from it. There are widespread inequalities and differences among men, physical or mental, social or political, economic or cultural, material or spiritual. But the most glaring inequalities are between the third that lives in luxury, and the two-thirds who live or verge on misery.

It is not my task here to draw for you in fine-line detail the awful portrait of the anguishing face

Cardinal Maurice Roy, "The People of God and the Development of Peoples," *Catholic Mind* 66 (Feb. 1968): 32-41.

of mankind today. The condition of the more than three billion persons who share this planet is common knowledge among all of you. You know the facts of hunger, misery, poverty and underdevelopment. You know, too, the dimension of affluence and the frightful drain of armaments that multiply misery.

Pope Paul VI has traveled widely throughout the world, and he has seen first hand the universal human condition. "We were able to see with our own eye," he says, "and virtually touch with our hands the acute problems pressing on continents full of hope and life." Viewing the world scene, the Pope in his Easter encyclical, On the Development of Peoples, diagnosed the human condition in one trenchant phrase: "The world is sick" (*Populorum Progressio*, § 66).

At the twilight of the second millennium after the birth of the Son of God, we stand looking at our Lord's good earth and we too must in candor affirm the Pontiff's evaluation: The world is sick! Paul's stated diagnosis of the global sickness is "the lack of brotherhood among individuals and peoples."

But how can this be? We might ask, how is it possible that the world lacks the healing balm of brotherhood when so many of us profess that the Messiah has already come, healing the aching, gaping wounds of humanity? We who profess the name of Jesus as our Lord and brother, we who dare address the Almighty Creator with the familiar term "Our Father," we stand in the midst of an infected world that aches from a lack of brotherhood.

We stand in the midst of a fantastic accumulation of scientific and technical apparatus. In this century we have been increasing our knowledge about ourselves and the universe at a geometric rate compared to all prior centuries. We have learned so much about the world, its energies and power, that we are perhaps at a point of breakthrough into a new era. We have solved mysteries of seed and fertilizer, insecticides and nutrients. We can now, in fact, destroy scourges that have enfeebled man since his beginning. We know how to produce enough food to feed all the men on this globe. We are approaching a new time when "we can liberate most of humanity from the misery of ignorance" (*The Church in the Modern World*, § 60).

On the other hand, we are standing on an atomic pile that can annihilate the globe and all mankind. So here we stand — modern man — sophisticated, yet frightened. For while we recently discovered the process of harmonizing vast forces of the universe, we are frightened because we have learned our planet is fractured and sick. The majority of our neighbors — of city and planet — are infected by diseases, and suffer from hunger, illiteracy, frustration, causing violence to explode erratically. And we are frightened; the epidemic might burst into a plague of global proportion and rage on out of control.

In the midst of this diseased globe, Pope Paul echoes the great note of human hope, when in his encyclical he says, despite occasions of individual sinfulness, and massive collective destructiveness, "Humanity is advancing along the path of history." This then that Paul calls "advancing humanity" places the Pope's thinking directly in line with his predecessor's vision of man's development. What Pope John XXIII called the "socialization" movement, Pope Paul sees as the development of man and the development of peoples.

When Paul addressed himself to this vast global view, he was not writing as an economist or a demographer, a statesman or an industrialist. Successor to the apostle Peter, he tries to state in modern language the meaning of his predecessor's epistle wherein the first Pope, Peter, wrote, "We are looking for the new heavens and new earth" (2 Pet. 3:13).

So the Pontiff writes as an enlightened visionary, one who has received from God's world the vision of a new world. Further, as Pope Paul told the United Nations on his visit here two years ago, he speaks as an "expert in humanity." This view of progressing man and "advancing humanity" is subject to the charge of being utopian.

However, Paul stands squarely in the context of the history of mankind — the history of salvation — as revealed by sacred Scripture, when he keynotes this realistic optimism. The first book of the Bible, Genesis, opens with a poetic account of God's victory over nothingness and chaos. Step by step God's creation progresses to reach man's beginnings in the virginal forest. In this primeval society, the Lord charges man with the task of populating the earth and conquering all its ener-gies and forces. Made in God's image, man is co-creator with God. Man's prime task on earth is to continue creation to refine the raw materials into higher levels of perfection, higher levels of being — thus aiding in the development of man himself.

The concluding book of the Bible gives the fantastic account of the terminus of God's initial creation. St. John tells again about "a new heaven and new earth." The metaphors used in the first book taken from the agrarian milieu — a tropical forest with man as its gardener — have dissolved. In Revelations St. John replaces fish and bird, and beast and seed-bearing plant of Genesis with the imagery of urban culture. St. John tells us of the formation of a giant megapolis so massive that the great city's proportions are incredible. The new creation is a city 1,500 miles in length, 1,500 miles in breadth, and 1,500 miles in height! (Apoc. 21:16-17).

Whatever the supernatural implications of St. John's prophecy, the fact is that the whole world is today become one, one huge city. Economically, technologically, scientifically, via communications, the human family is becoming an interdependent whole. The astronaut strolls around our globe in 90 minutes. A few hydrogen bombs could blow us all up in 90 seconds. But this small vulnerable planet that is, so far, the only habitation of the human race, still lacks moral, social and political institutions to match its physical unity: Our growing body lacks a soul.

Pope Paul VI in *Populorum Progressio* lays on Christians the important duty of confronting this crisis. He asks that we change the raw fact of the world's economic and material proximity into the moral fact of a fully human society. We must become the vanguard of a new kind of citizenship in the world's community, giving leadership toward a new planetary solidarity.

This task is, of course, not confined to any single group. All peoples, rich and poor, Christian, non-Christian, East and West, white and brown, yellow or black, all are called to the work of building a world society in which mankind as a whole can survive and prosper. But Christians, with their vision of humanity united in a single body under the headship of Christ, have a special responsibility to see that the essential, moral and political foundations of a true world order are securely laid.

A Biblical Perspective on Stewardship

Ronald J. Sider

God Is on the Side of the Poor

The Central Points of Revelation History

The Exodus

God displayed his power at the exodus in order to free oppressed slaves. When God called Moses at the burning bush, he informed Moses that his intention was to end suffering and injustice (Ex. 3:7-8; also 6:5ff). Each year at the harvest festival, the Israelites repeated a liturgical confession celebrating the way God had acted to free a poor, oppressed people.

> A wondering Aramean was my father; and he went down into Egypt and sojourned there. . . . And the Egyptians treated him harshly and afflicted us, and laid upon us hard bondage. Then we cried to the Lord, the God of our fathers, and the Lord heard our voice, and saw our affliction, our toil, and our oppression; and the Lord brought us out of Egypt with a mighty hand (Deut. 26:5ff).

The God of the Bible cares when people enslave and oppress others. At the exodus he acted to end economic oppression and bring freedom to slaves.

Before Yahweh gave the two tables of the Law, he identified himself: "I am the Lord your God who brought you out of the land of Egypt, out of

the house of bondage" (Deut. 5:6; Ex. 20:2). Yahweh is the one who frees from bondage. The God of the Bible wants to be known as the liberator of the oppressed.

The exodus was certainly the decisive event in the creation of the chosen people. We distort the biblical interpretation of this momentous occasion unless we see that, at this pivotal point, the Lord of the universe was at work correcting oppression and liberating the poor.

Destruction of the Nation and Captivity

When they settled in the promised land, the Israelites soon discovered that Yahweh's passion for justice was a two-edged sword. When they were oppressed, it led to their freedom. But when they became the oppressors, it led to their destruction.

When God called Israel out of Egypt and made his covenant with them, he gave them his Law so that they could live together in peace and justice. But Israel failed to obey the Law of the covenant. As a result, God destroyed Israel and sent his chosen people into captivity. Why? The explosive message of the prophets is that God destroyed Israel because of mistreatment of the poor.

The middle of the eighth century B.C. was a time of political success and economic prosperity unknown since the days of Solomon. But it was precisely at this moment that God sent his prophet Amos to announce the unwelcome news that the northern kingdom would be destroyed. Why? Penetrating beneath the facade of current prosperity and fantastic economic growth, Amos saw terrible oppression of the poor. He saw the rich "trample the head of the poor into the dust of the earth" (2:7). He saw that the affluent life-style of the rich was built on oppression of the poor (6:1-7). He denounced the rich women ("cows" was Amos' word) "who oppress the poor, who crush the needy, who say to their husbands, 'Bring that we may drink.'" Even in the courts the poor had no hope because the rich bribed the judges (5:10-15).

God's word through Amos was that the northern kingdom would be destroyed and the people taken into exile (7:11, 17).

> Woe to those who lie upon beds of ivory and stretch themselves upon their couches and eat

Ronald J. Sider, "A Biblical Perspective on Stewardship," *New Catholic World* 220 (Sept.-Oct. 1977): 212-21.

lambs from the flock and calves from the midst of the stall. . . . Therefore, they shall now be the first of those to go into exile, and the revelry of those who stretch themselves shall pass away (6:4-7).

Only a very few years after Amos spoke, it happened just as God had said. The Assyrians conquered the northern kingdom and took thousands into captivity. Because of their mistreatment of the poor, God destroyed the northern kingdom — forever.

God sent other prophets to announce the same fate for the southern kingdom of Judah (cf. Is. 10:1-4; Mi. 2:2; 3:12). But they continued to oppress the poor and helpless. As a result, Jeremiah declared that God would use the Babylonians to destroy Judah (Jer. 5:26-31; 7:5-6). In 587 B.C., Jerusalem fell and the Babylonian captivity began.

God destroyed Israel and Judah because of their mistreatment of the poor. The cataclysmic catastrophe of national destruction and captivity reveals the God of the exodus still at work correcting the oppression of the poor.

The Incarnation

Christians believe that God revealed himself most completely in Jesus of Nazareth. How did the Incarnate One define his mission?

His words in the synagogue at Nazareth, spoken near the beginning of his public ministry, still throb with hope for the poor. He read from the prophet Isaiah:

The Spirit of the Lord is upon me, because he has anointed me to preach good news to the poor. He has sent me to proclaim release to the captives and recovery of sight to the blind, to set at liberty those who are oppressed, to proclaim the acceptable year of the Lord (Lk. 4:18-19).

After reading these words, he informed the audience that this Scripture was now fulfilled in himself. The mission of the Incarnate One was to free the oppressed and heal the blind. The poor are the only group specifically singled out as recipients of Jesus' Gospel. Certainly the Gospel Jesus proclaimed was for all, but he was particu-

larly concerned that the poor realize that his Good News was for them.

Jesus' actual ministry corresponded to his words in Luke 4. He spent most of his time, not among the rich and powerful in Jerusalem, but rather among the poor in the cultural and economic backwater of Galilee. He healed the sick and blind. He fed the hungry. And he warned his followers in the strongest possible words that those who do not feed the hungry, clothe the naked and visit the prisoners will experience eternal damnation (Mt. 25:31ff). At the supreme moment of history when God himself took on human flesh, we see the God of Israel still at work liberating the poor and oppressed and summoning his people to do the same.

The foundation of Christian concern for the hungry and oppressed is simply that God cares especially for them. He demonstrated his concern when he freed oppressed slaves at the exodus. He underlined that concern in an awesome way when he obliterated the nation of Israel and Judah for their economic injustice. And he expressed that concern most vividly when he became flesh and walked among us to heal the broken and set at liberty those who are oppressed. At the pivotal points of God's self-disclosure in history, he revealed himself as the liberator of the poor.

God Identifies with the Poor

Not only does God act in history to liberate the poor. In a mysterious way that we can only half fathom, the powerful sovereign of the universe identifies in a special way with the poor and destitute.

Two powerful proverbs state this beautiful truth. Proverbs 14:31 puts it: "He who oppresses a poor man, insults his Maker." Even more moving is the positive formulation: "He who is kind to the poor lends to the Lord" (19:17). What a statement! Helping a poor person is like helping the Creator of all things with a loan.

Only in the incarnation can we begin dimly to perceive what God's identification with the weak, oppressed and poor really means. "Though he was rich," Paul says of our Lord Jesus, "yet for their sake he became poor" (2 Cor. 8:9). Born in a barn, raised a carpenter, he never owned a home, and died penniless. Yet he was God Incarnate.

Only as we feel the presence of the Incarnate God in the form of a poor person can we begin to understand these words:

> I was hungry and you gave me food. I was thirsty and you gave me drink. . . . I was naked and you clothed me. . . . Truly I say to you, as you did it to one of the least of these brethren, you did it to me (Mt. 25:35ff).

What does it mean to feed and clothe the Creator of all things? We cannot know. We can only look on the poor and oppressed with new eyes and resolve anew to heal their hurts and end their oppression.

If his first saying is awesome, the second is terrifying. "Truly I say to you, as you did it not to one of the least of these, you did it not to me" (v. 45). What does that saying mean in a world where millions die each year while rich Christians live in affluence? What does it mean to see the Lord of the universe lying by the roadside starving and walk on the other side? We cannot know. We can only pledge in fear and trembling not to kill him again.

Christian faith is a faith focused on the Incarnation. The Incarnate One tells us that God identifies in a special way with the poor.

God Casts Down the Rich and Exalts the Poor

Jesus's story of the rich man and Lazarus echoes a central, biblical teaching. The rich may prosper for a time, but eventually God will destroy them. The poor on the other hand, God will exalt. Mary's Magnificat puts it simply and bluntly:

> My soul magnifies the Lord. . . . He has put down the mighty from their thrones and exalted those of low degree; he has filled the hungry with good things, and the rich he has sent empty away (Lk. 1:46-53).

"Come now, you rich, weep and howl for the miseries that are coming upon you" (Jas. 5:1) is a constant theme of biblical revelation.

Why does Scripture declare that God regularly reverses the good fortunes of the rich? Is God engaged in class warfare? Actually our texts never say that God loves the poor more than the rich.

But they constantly assert that God lifts up the poor and disadvantaged, and they persistently assert that God casts down the wealthy and powerful — precisely because they became wealthy by oppressing the poor and because they failed to feed the hungry.

Why did James warn the rich to weep and howl because of impending misery? Because they had cheated their workers: "You have laid up treasure for the last days. Behold the wages of the laborers who mowed your fields, which you kept back by fraud, cry out; and the cries of the harvesters have reached the ears of the Lord of hosts. You have lived on earth in luxury and in pleasure; you have fattened your hearts in a day of slaughter" (5:3-5). God does not have class enemies, but he hates and punishes injustice and neglect of the poor. And the rich, if we accept the repeated warnings of Scripture, are frequently guilty of both.

Long before the days of James, the psalmist and the prophets knew that the rich were often rich because of oppression.

> Wicked men are found among my people: they lurk like fowlers lying in wait. They set a trap; they catch men. Like a basket full of birds, their houses are full of treachery; therefore they have become great and rich, they have grown fat and sleek. They know no bounds in deeds of wickedness; they judge not with justice the cause of the fatherless, to make it proper, and they do not defend the rights of the needy. Shall I not punish them for these things? says the Lord (Jer. 5:26-29).

Nor was the faith of Jeremiah and the psalmist mere wishful thinking. Through his prophets, God announced devastation and destruction for both rich individuals and rich nations who oppressed the poor. And it happened as they had prophesied. Because the rich oppress the poor and weak, the Lord of history is at work pulling down their houses and kingdoms.

Sometimes Scripture does not charge the rich with direct oppression of the poor. It simply accuses them of failure to share with the needy — but the result is the same. In the story of the rich man and Lazarus (Lk. 16), Jesus does not say that Dives exploited Lazarus. He merely shows that the affluent Dives had no concern for the sick beggar lying outside his gate.

The biblical explanation of Sodom's destruction provides another illustration of this terrible truth. Ezekiel says that one important reason God destroyed Sodom was because she stubbornly refused to share with the poor!

> Behold, this was the guilt of your sister Sodom; she and her daughters had pride, surfeit of food, and prosperous ease, but did not aid the poor and needy. They were haughty, and did abominable things before me; therefore, I removed them when I saw it (Ez. 16:49-50).

The text does not say that they oppressed the poor (although they probably did). It simply accuses them of failing to assist the needy.

The God of the Bible wreaks horrendous havoc on the rich, but it is not because he does not love the rich persons, it is because the rich regularly oppress the poor and neglect the needy.

God Commands His People To Have a Special Concern for the Poor

In every strand of biblical literature, we find God commanding believers to have special regard for the poor, and weak, and disadvantaged.

Equal justice for the poor in court is a constant theme of Scripture. The Torah commanded it (Ex. 23:6). The psalmist invoked divine assistance for the king so that he could provide it (Ps. 72:1-4). And the prophets announced devastating destruction because the rulers stubbornly subverted it (Am. 5:10-15).

Widows, orphans and strangers receive particularly frequent attention (e.g., Ex. 22:21-24). The Bible specifically commands believers to imitate God's special concern for the poor and oppressed (e.g., Ex. 22:21ff; Lk. 6:33ff; 2 Cor. 8:9; 1 Jn. 3:16ff). In fact, it underlines the command by teaching that when God's people care for the poor, they imitate God himself. But that is not all. God's word teaches that those who neglect the poor and oppressed are really not God's people at all — no matter how frequent their religious rituals or how orthodox their creeds and confessions.

Worship in the context of mistreatment of the poor and disadvantaged, God thundered again and again through the prophets, is an outrage. Isaiah denounced Israel (he called her Sodom and Gomorrah) because she tried to worship Yahweh and oppress the weak at the same time:

> Hear the word of the Lord, you rulers of Sodom! Give ear to the teaching of our God, you people of Gomorrah! What to me is the multitude of your sacrifices? . . . Bring no more vain offerings; incense is an abomination to me. New moon and Sabbath and the calling of assemblies — I cannot endure iniquity and solemn assembly. Your new moons and your appointed feasts my soul hates. . . . Even though you make many prayers, I will not listen; your hands are full of blood (Is. 1:10-15).

Nor has God changed. Jesus repeated the same theme. He warned the people about scribes who secretly oppress widows while making a public display of their piety. Their pious looking garments and frequent visits to the synagogue are a sham. Woe to religious hypocrites "who devour widows' houses and for a pretense make long prayers" (Mk. 12:38-40).

The biblical word against religious hypocrites raises an extremely difficult question. Are the people of God truly God's people if they oppress the poor? Is the Church really the Church if it does not work to free the oppressed?

We have seen how God decreed through the prophet Isaiah that the people of Israel were really Sodom and Gomorrah rather than the people of God (1:10). God simply could not tolerate their exploitation of the poor and disadvantaged any longer. Jesus was even more blunt and sharp. To those who do not feed the hungry, clothe the naked, and visit the prisoners, he will speak a terrifying word at the judgment: "Depart from me, ye cursed, into the eternal fire prepared for the devil and his angels" (Mt. 25:41). The meaning is clear and unambiguous. Jesus intends his disciples to imitate his own special concern for the poor and needy. Those who disobey will experience eternal damnation.

Lest we forget the warning, God repeats it in 1 John. "But if anyone has the world's goods and sees his brother in need, yet closes his heart against him, how does God's love abide in him? Dear children, let us not love in word or speech but in deed and truth" (3:17). Again, the words are plain. What do they mean for Western Christians who demand increasing affluence each year while fellow Christians in the third world suffer malnutrition, deformed bodies and brains, even starvation? The text clearly says that if we fail to aid the needy, we do not have God's love — no matter how punctilious our piety or how orthodox our doctrine. Regardless of what we do or say at 11:00 A.M. Sunday morning, affluent people who neglect the poor are not the people of God. But still the question persists. Are Church members no longer Christians because of continuing sin? Obviously not. We are members of the people of God not because of our own righteousness but solely because of Christ's death for us.

But that response is inadequate. Matthew 25 and 1 John 3 surely mean more than that the people of God are disobedient (but still justified all the same) when they neglect the poor. These verses pointedly assert that some people so disobey God that they are not his people at all in spite of their pious profession. Neglect of the poor is one of the oft-repeated biblical signs of such disobedience. Certainly none of us would claim that we fulfill Matthew 25 perfectly. And we cling to the hope of forgiveness. But there comes a point — and, thank God, he alone knows where! — when neglect of the poor is no longer forgiven. It is punished. Eternally.

Is it not possible — indeed very probable — that a vast majority of Western Christians have reached that point? Can we seriously claim that we are obeying the biblical command to have a special concern for the poor? Can we seriously claim that we are imitating God's concern for the poor and oppressed? Can we seriously hope to experience eternal love rather than eternal separation from the God of the poor?

God is on the side of the poor! The Bible clearly and repeatedly teaches that God is at work in history pulling down the rich and exalting the poor. At the central points of the history of revelation, God acted not only to reveal himself, but also to liberate poor, oppressed people.

God actively opposes the rich since they neglect or oppose justice because justice demands that they end their oppression and share with the poor. God longs for the salvation of the rich as much as the salvation of the poor. God desires fulfillment and joy for all his creatures. But that in no way contradicts the fact that God is on the side of the poor. Genuine biblical repentance and conversion lead people to turn from all sin — including economic oppression. Salvation for the rich will include liberation from their involvement in injustice. Thus God's desire for the salvation and fulfillment of the rich is in complete harmony with his special concern for the poor. The God revealed in Scripture is on the side of the poor and oppressed.

God's concern for the poor seems astonishing and boundless. At the pivotal points of revelation history, Yahweh was at work liberating the oppressed. We can only begin to fathom the depths of his identification with the poor disclosed in the incarnation. His passion for justice compels him to obliterate rich persons and societies that oppress the poor and neglect the needy. Consequently, God's people — if they are indeed his people — follow in the footsteps of the God of the poor.

"That There May be Equality": Economic Relationships among the People of God

The New Community of Jesus' Disciples

Jesus walked the roads and footpaths of Galilee announcing the startling news that the long expected kingdom of peace and righteousness was at hand. Economic relationships in the new community of his followers were a powerful sign confirming this awesome announcement.

The Hebrew prophets had inspired the hope of a future messianic kingdom of peace, righteousness and justice. The essence of the good news which Jesus proclaimed was that the expected messianic kingdom had come. Certainly the kingdom that Jesus announced disappointed popular Jewish expectations. He did not recruit any army to drive out the Romans. He did not attempt to establish a free Jewish state. But neither did he remain alone as an isolated, individualistic prophet. He called and trained disciples. He established a visible community of disciples joined together by their unconditional submission to him as Lord. His new community began to live the values of the promised kingdom which was already breaking into the present. As a result, all relationships, even economic ones, were transformed in the community of Jesus' followers.

Jesus and his disciples shared a common purse (Jn. 12:6 and 13:29). Judas administered the common fund buying provisions or giving to the poor at Jesus' direction (Jn. 13:29). Nor did this new community of sharing end with Jesus and the Twelve. It included a number of women whom Jesus had healed. The women traveled with Jesus and the disciples, sharing their financial resources with them (Lk. 8:1-3).

From this perspective, some of Jesus' words gain new meaning and power. Consider Jesus' advice to the rich young man in this context.

When Jesus asked the rich young man to sell his goods and give to the poor, he did not say, "Become destitute and friendless." Rather he said, "Come, follow me" (Mt. 19:21). In other words, he invited him to join a community of sharing and love, where his security would not be based on individual property holdings, but on openness to the Spirit and on the loving care of new-found brothers and sisters.

Jesus invited the rich young man to share the joyful common life of his new kingdom.

Jesus' words in Mark 10:29-30 have long puzzled me: "Truly, I say to you, there is no one who has left houses or brothers or sisters or mother or father or children or lands, for my sake and the Gospel, who will not receive a hundredfold *now in this time, houses and brothers and sisters and mothers and children and lands,* with persecutions and in the age to come eternal life."

Matthew 6 contains a similar saying. We are all very — indeed, embarrassingly — familiar with the way Jesus urged his followers to enjoy a carefree life unburdened by anxiety over food, clothing and possessions (vv. 25-33). But he ended his advice with a promise too good to be true: "But seek first his kingdom and his righteousness and all these things (i.e., food, clothing, etc.) shall be yours as well" (v. 33).

Jesus' promise used to seem at least a trifle naive. But his words suddenly come alive with fantastic meaning when I read them in the context of the new community of Jesus' followers. Jesus began a new social order, a new kingdom of faithful followers who were to be completely available to each other.

The common purse of Jesus' disciples symbolized that unlimited liability for each other. In that

kind of new community, there would truly be genuine economic security. One would indeed receive one hundred times more loving brothers and sisters than before. The economic resources available in difficult times would in fact be more compounded a hundredfold and more. All the resources of the entire community of obedient disciples would be available to anyone in need. To be sure, that kind of unselfish, sharing life-style would challenge surrounding society so pointedly that there would be persecutions. But even in the most desperate days, the promise would not be empty. Even if persecution led to death, children of martyred parents would receive new mothers and fathers in the community of believers. In the community of the redeemed, all relationships are being transformed. The common purse shared by Jesus and his first followers vividly demonstrates that Jesus repeated and deepened the old covenant's call for transformed economic relationships among the people of God.

The Jerusalem Church

However embarrassing it may be to some, the massive economic sharing of the earliest Christian Church is indisputable. "Now the company of those who believed were of one heart and soul, and no one said that any of the things which he possessed was his own, but they had everything in common" (Acts 4:32). Everywhere in the early chapters of Acts, the evidence is abundant and unambiguous (Acts 2:43-7; 4:32-7; 5:1-11; 6:1-7). The early Church continued the pattern of economic sharing practiced by Jesus.

Economic sharing in the Jerusalem church started in the earliest period. Immediately after reporting the 3,000 conversions at Pentecost, Acts notes that "all who believed were together and had all things in common" (2:44). Whenever anyone was in need, they shared. Giving surplus income to needy brothers and sisters was not enough. They regularly dipped into capital reserves, selling property to aid the needy. Barnabas sold a field he owned (4:36-37). Ananias and Sapphira sold property, although they lied about the price. God's promise to Israel (Deut. 15:4) that faithful obedience would eliminate poverty among his people came true! "*There was not a needy person among them,* for as many as were possessors of lands or houses sold them . . . and distribution was made to each as any had need" (4:34-35).

Two millennia later, the texts still throb with the first community's joy and excitement. They ate meals together "with glad and generous heart" (2:46). They experienced an exciting unity as all sensed they "were of one heart and soul" (4:32). They were not isolated individuals struggling alone to follow Jesus. A new community transforming all areas of life became a joyful reality. The new converts at Pentecost "devoted themselves to the apostles' teaching and fellowship, to the breaking of bread and the prayers" (2:42). The earliest Jerusalem Christians experienced such joyful oneness in Christ that they promptly engaged in sweeping economic sharing.

What was the precise nature of the Jerusalem church's costly *koinonia?* The earliest Church did not insist on absolute economic equality, nor did it abolish private property. Sharing was voluntary, not compulsory. But love for brothers and sisters was so overwhelming that many freely abandoned legal claims to private possessions. "No one said that any of the things that he possessed was his own" (4:32). That does not mean that everyone donated everything. Later in Acts, we see that John Mark's mother Mary still owned her house (12:12). Others also undoubtedly retained some private property.

The tense of the Greek verbs in Acts 2:45 and 4:34 confirms this interpretation. The verbs are in the imperfect tense. In Greek, the imperfect tense denotes continued, repeated action over an extended period of time. Thus the meaning is: "They often sold possessions." Or: "They were in the habit of regularly bringing the proceeds of what was being sold." The text does not suggest that the community decided to abolish all private property and everyone instantly sold everything. Rather it suggests that over a period of time, whenever there was need, believers regularly sold lands and houses to aid the needy.

What then was the essence of the transformed economic relationships in the Jerusalem church? I think the best way to describe their practice is to speak of unlimited liability and total availability. Their sharing was not superficial or occasional. Regularly and repeatedly, they sold possessions and goods and distributed them to all, "*as any had need.*" If the need was greater than current cash

reserves, they sold property. They simply gave until the needs were met. The needs of the sister and brother, not legal property rights or future financial security, were decisive. The brothers and sisters made their financial resources unconditionally available to each other. Oneness in Christ for the earliest Christian community meant unlimited economic liability for the total economic availability to the other members of the people of God.

The costly sharing of the first Church stands as a constant challenge to Christians of all ages. They dared to give concrete, visible expression to the oneness of believers. In the new messianic community of Jesus' first followers at Pentecost, God was redeeming all relationships.

Whatever the beauty and appeal of such an example, however, was it a vision which quickly faded? Many people believe that. But the actual practice of the early Church proves exactly the contrary.

The Pauline Collection

Paul broadens the vision of economic sharing among the people of God in a dramatic way. He devoted a great deal of time to raising money for Jewish Christians among Gentile congregations. In the process he broadened *intra*-church assistance within one local church into *inter*-church sharing among all the scattered congregations of believers. From the time of the exodus, God had taught the chosen people to exhibit transforming economic relations among themselves. With Peter and Paul, however, biblical religion moved beyond one ethnic group and became a universal, multiethnic faith. Paul's collection demonstrates that the oneness of that one multi-ethnic body of believers involved dramatic economic sharing across ethnic and geographic lines.

For several years, Paul devoted much time and energy to his great collection for the Jerusalem church. He discussed his concern in several letters (Col. 2:16; Rom. 15:22-28; 1 Cor. 16:1-4; 2 Cor. 9:7-9). Paul arranged for the collections for the churches of Macedonia, Asia, Corinth, Ephesus and probably elsewhere.

Paul knew he faced certain danger, possible death, but he still insisted on personally accompanying the offerings for the Jerusalem church. It was while delivering this financial assistance that Paul was arrested for the last time (Acts 24:17). His letter to the Romans showed that he was not blind to the danger (Rom. 15:31). Repeatedly, friends and prophets warned Paul as he and representatives of the contributing churches journeyed toward Jerusalem (Acts 21:4, 10-14). But Paul had a decided conviction that this financial symbolism of Christian unity mattered far more than even his own life. "What are you doing weeping and breaking my heart?" chided friends imploring him not to accompany the others to Jerusalem. "For I am ready not only to be imprisoned but even to die at Jerusalem for the name of the Lord Jesus" (Acts 21:13). And he continued the journey. His passion of commitment to economic sharing with his brothers and sisters led to his final arrest and martyrdom.

Why was Paul so concerned with the financial problems of the Jerusalem church? Because of his understanding of Christian fellowship (*koinonia*). *Koinonia* is an extremely important concept in Paul's theology. And it is central in his discussion of the collection.

The word *Koinonia* means fellowship with, or participation in, something or someone. Believers enjoy fellowship with the Lord Jesus (1 Cor. 1:9). Experiencing the *Koinonia* of Jesus means having his righteousness imputed to us. It also entails sharing in the self-sacrificing, cross-bearing life he lived (Phil. 3:8-10). Nowhere is the Christian's fellowship with Christ experienced more powerfully than in the Eucharist. Sharing in the Eucharist draws the believer into a participation (*koinonia*) in the mystery of the cross.

> The cup of blessing which we bless, is it not a participation (*koinonia*) in the blood of Christ? The bread which we break, is it not a participation (*koinonia*) in the body of Christ? (1 Cor. 10:16).

Paul's immediate inference — in the very next verse — is that *koinonia* with Christ inevitably involves *koinonia* with all the members of the body of Christ. "Because there is one bread, we who are many are one body, for we all partake of the one bread" (v. 17). As he taught in Ephesians 2, Christ's death for Jew and Gentile, male and female, has broken down all ethnic, sexual, and cultural dividing walls. In Christ, there is one new

person, one new body of believers. When the brothers and sisters share the one bread and the common cup in the Lord's supper, they symbolize and actualize their participation in the one body of Christ.

That is why the class divisions at Corinth so horrified Paul. Wealthy Christians, apparently, were feasting at the eucharistic celebration while poor believers went hungry. Paul angrily denied that they were eating the Lord's supper at all (1 Cor. 11:20-22). In fact they were profaning the Lord's body and blood because they did not discern his body (vv. 27-29) What did Paul mean by not discerning the Lord's body? He meant that they failed to realize that their membership in the one body of Christ was infinitely more important than the class or ethnic differences which divided them. One drinks judgment on oneself if one does not perceive that eucharistic fellowship with Christ is totally incompatible with living a practical denial of the unity and fellowship of all believers in the body of Christ. As long as one Christian anywhere in the world is hungry, the eucharistic celebration of all Christians everywhere is incomplete.

For Paul, this intimate fellowship in the body of Christ had concrete economic implications. Paul used precisely this same word, *koinonia,* to designate financial sharing among believers. Sometimes he employed the word *koinonia* as a virtual synonym for "collection." He spoke of the "liberality of the fellowship" (*koinonia*) that the Corinthians' generous offering would demonstrate (2 Cor. 9:13). He employed the same language to report the Macedonian Christians' offering for Jerusalem. It seemed good to the Macedonians, he said, "to make fellowship (*koinonia*) with the poor among the saints at Jerusalem" (Rom. 15:26). Indeed, this financial sharing was just one part of a total fellowship. The Gentile Christians had come to share in (he uses the verb form of *koinonia*) the spiritual blessings of the Jews. Therefore it was fitting for the Gentiles to share their material resources. Economic sharing was an obvious and crucial part of Christian fellowship for St. Paul.

Paul's guideline for sharing in the body of believers is startling. The norm he suggested is something like economic equality among the people of God. "I do not mean that others should be eased and you burdened, but that as a matter of equality your abundance at the present time should supply their want, so that their abundance may supply your want, that there may be equality" (2 Cor. 8:13-14). To support his principle, Paul quoted from the biblical story of the manna. "As it is written, he who gathered much had nothing over, and he who gathered little had no lack" (v. 15).

According to the Exodus account, when God started sending daily manna to the Israelites in the wilderness, Moses commanded the people to gather only as much as they needed for one day (Ex. 16:13-21). One omer (about four pints) per person would be enough, Moses said. Some greedy souls, however, apparently tried to gather more than they could use. But when they measured what they had gathered, they discovered that they all had just one omer per person. The account concludes: "He that gathered much had nothing over and he that gathered little had no lack" (Ex. 16:18).

Paul quoted from the biblical account of the manna to support his guideline for economic sharing. Just as God had insisted on equal portions of manna for all his people in the wilderness, so now the Corinthians should give "that there may be equality" in the body of Christ.

It may seem startling and disturbing to rich Christians in the northern hemisphere, but the biblical text clearly shows that Paul enunciated the principle of economic equality among the people of God to guide the Corinthians in their giving. "*It is a question of equality.* At the moment your surplus meets their need, but on one day your need may be met from their surplus. *The aim is equality*" (New English Bible).

However interesting it may be, what relevance does the economic sharing at Jerusalem and Corinth have for the contemporary Church?

Certainly the Church today need not slavishly imitate every detail of the life of the early Church depicted in Acts. But that does not mean that we can simply dismiss the economic sharing described in Acts and the Pauline letters.

Over and over again God specifically commanded his people to live together in community in such a way that they would avoid extremes of wealth and poverty. That is the point of the Old Testament legislation on the jubilee and the sabbatical year. That is the point of the legislation on tithing, gleaning and loans. Jesus, our only perfect model, shared a common purse with the new community of his disciples. The first Church in Jerusalem and St. Paul in his collection were implementing what the Old Testament and Jesus commanded.

The powerful evangelistic impact of the economic sharing at Jerusalem indicates that God approved and blessed the practice of the Jerusalem church. When Scripture commands transformed economic relationships among God's people in some places and describes God's blessing on his people as they implement these commands in other places, then we can be sure that we have discovered a normative pattern for the Church today.

What is striking in fact is the fundamental continuity of biblical teaching and practice at this point. The Bible repeatedly and pointedly reveals that God wills transformed economic relationships among his people. Paul's collection was simply an application of the basic principle of the jubilee. The mechanism, of course, was different because the people of God were not a multi-ethnic body living in different lands. But the principle was the same. Since the Greeks at Corinth were now part of the people of God, they were to share with the poor Jewish Christians at Jerusalem — that there might be equality!

Conclusion

By way of conclusion, I want to sketch a few implications of these biblical themes for contemporary Christian concern for world hunger.

In the Church

Central to any Christian strategy on world hunger must be a radical call for the Church to be the Church. One of the most glaring weaknesses of the churches' social action in the past few decades is that the Church concentrated too exclusively on political solutions. In effect, Church leaders tried to persuade government to legislate what they could not persuade their Church members to live. And politicians quickly sensed that the daring declarations and frequent Washington delegations represented generals without troops. Only if the body of Christ is already beginning to live a radically new model of economic sharing will our demand for political change have integrity and impact.

Tragically we must confess that present economic relationships in the worldwide body of Christ are unbiblical and sinful; indeed they are a desecration of the body and blood of our Lord. It is a sinful abomination for a small fraction of the world's Christians living in the northern hemisphere to grow richer year by year while our brothers and sisters in the third world ache and suffer for lack of minimal health care, minimal education and even just enough food to escape starvation.

We are like the rich Corinthian Christians who feasted without sharing their food with the poor members of the Church (1 Cor. 11:20-29). Like them we fail today to discern the reality of the one worldwide body of Christ. The tragic consequence is that we profane the body and blood of the Lord Jesus we worship. U.S. Christians spent 5.7 billion dollars on new church construction alone in the six years from 1967-1972. Would we go on building lavishly furnished expensive church plants if members of our own congregations were starving? Do we not flatly contradict St. Paul if we live as if African or Latin American members of the body of Christ are less a part of us than the members of our home congregations?

A radical call to repentance so that the Church becomes the Church must be central to a viable contemporary Christian strategy for reducing world hunger and restructuring international economic relationships. Unless the Church begins to live a new model of economic sharing in the local congregations in each geographic area, and in the one worldwide body of Christ, any political appeal for governmental action will be a tragic, irrelevant farce.

The Church is the most universal body in the world today. It has the opportunity to live a new corporate model of economic sharing at a desperate moment in world history. If even one-quarter of the Christians in the northern hemisphere had the courage to live the biblical vision of economic equality in the worldwide body of Christ, the governments of our dangerously divided global village might also be persuaded to legislate the sweeping changes needed to avoid disaster.

In Secular Society

The centrality of the Church as the new community for Christian social concern by no means entails the view that working to restructure secular political and economic systems is inappropriate or irrelevant.

From the preceding analysis, we can summarize a few of the fundamental biblical principles and norms we need to keep in mind as we think of structural change in society. The most basic theological presupposition is that the sovereign Lord of this universe is always at work liberating the poor and oppressed and destroying the rich and mighty because of their injustice.

Second, extremes of wealth and poverty are displeasing to the God of the Bible. Third, Yahweh wills institutionalized structures (rather than mere charity) which systematically and regularly reduce the gap between the rich and the poor. Fourth, although they do not suggest a wooden, legalistic egalitarianism, the biblical patterns for economic sharing (e.g., the jubilee, the Pauline collection) all push toward a closer approximation of economic equality. Fifth, persons are vastly more valuable than property. Private property is legitimate, but since God is the only absolute owner, our right to acquire and use property is definitely limited. The human right to the resources necessary to earn a just living overrides any notion of absolute private ownership.

The last principle is particularly significant for us. Some countries like the United States and the USSR have a bountiful supply of natural resources within their national boundaries. It by no means follows that they have an absolute right to use these resources as they please solely for the advantage of their own citizens. If we believe Paul's word, then we must conclude that the human right of all persons to earn a living clearly supersedes the United States' right to use its natural resources for itself. We are only stewards, not absolute owners. The absolute owner is the God of the poor and he insists that the earth's resources be shared.

The 1975 conference that marked the beginning of the United Nations Decade for Women stressed the huge economic cost of discriminatory practices — legal, financial, cultural, educational — that preclude women's active participation in the economic mainstream. Those attending closely examined women's economic role — their economic facts of life: women perform over 65% of the world's work, earn only 10% of the income, and own less than 1% of the world's property. Given this dramatic disparity, how could women achieve economic self-sufficiency?

WWB [Women's World Banking] was founded to advance and promote entrepreneurship by women, particularly those women who have not generally had access to the services of established financial institutions. Its objectives are:

- to help create an environment in which women have equal access to the benefits of the modern economy;
- to build within individual countries local support bases which can respond to the specific needs of its own entrepreneurs;
- to establish a global network of women leaders in banking, finance and business;
- to encourage women's confidence and trust in themselves as capable, professional businesswomen.

In meeting the needs of emprisers, WWB never seeks to control either the process or the beneficiaries of the process. It shows preference to no group — regional, ethnic, religious or political — nor is it beholden to any special interest group, agency, or nation in determining how best to meet its objectives.

WWB's approach as a financial intermediary is a sound one, charging going market rates of interest and expecting adequate return for those loans it guarantees or makes to local borrowers.

WWB is committed to keeping the authority and decisions at the community level where people understand the financial and economic realities faced by small business in the local area.

It relies on local leadership to establish relationships with the banking and business communities, and raise capital to fund most of its local programs. In addition, the local leadership group — the WWB affiliate — identifies women in that community as potential loan recipients, who must be willing to place as collateral some resources, small as they may be, in order to assume their share of the risk. The loans, made in local currency, may vary in size from less than one hundred dollars to thousands. . . .

But access to credit is not enough if women lack good business information, management skills, and marketing experience. WWB affiliates address these needs through a myriad of programs. Many have established training programs which provide basic business skills to their loan beneficiaries. Others provide free management consulting services to help women expand their enterprises. They link local women with the informational, technical, marketing and other production elements necessary to their business development.

The affiliates understand that their assistance should go beyond direct business needs. Some have established inexpensive health care programs for clients and their families. Others help women work through the conflicting demands of family and business. They hold local seminars and workshops, encouraging emprisers to share experiences and business problems to find workable solutions for each other.

The affiliate programs reflect the diversity of the social and economic contexts in which WWB affiliates operate. What they share in common is a deep commitment to help women gain the tools and confidence to realize their business potential.

But statistics cannot tell the full story. Even when the scale is small, the spirit is grand. Delegates to a WWB African Regional meeting visited one affiliate's loan beneficiaries and described their impressions:

"The kikapu is the ubiquitous shoulder bag that Kenyan women carry — and visitors purchase. The weavers whom we visited sit on a dirt island at the intersection of several traffic-congested streets. Here, they weave as well as market their bags. As we approached on foot, dodging cars with every step, the weavers jumped to their feet and welcomed us with hearty enthusiasm. We all shook hands and chatted about the success of their cooperative venture. By working together, they have been able to rent a nearby space for storage of their materials. Suddenly, they began to sing. Then, still singing, they wended their way into the street in a snake dance. The high spirits were contagious; we joined in, singing and dancing, as the cars whizzed by. As we drove back to the city, we discussed the initiative and reliance the women we visited had demonstrated. Along the way, we passed through over-crowded slum areas — strong reminders of the formidable task that many in the world face, just to survive. But the pockets of hope and purposeful energy that we had encountered that day gave strong meaning to the WWB mission."

— Michaela Walsh, "Women's World Banking," promotional booklet privately published in August 1987 by the Women's World Banking, 104 E. 40th, Suite 607-A, New York, NY 10016

The Political Task of the Christian Church

Cornel West

At the beginning of this century, we witnessed the Europeanization of the world. By 1918, a handful of states located between the Atlantic Ocean and the Ural mountains controlled over 87% of the land on the globe. By the middle of this century, European hegemony had been replaced by the Americanization and Sovietization of the world.

In this article, I shall attempt to discern the political task of the Christian church in view of prevailing institutional forms of injustice introduced first by the Europeans and later reinforced by the two superpowers. For Christian thinkers, political discernment rests upon systemic social analysis grounded in an interpretation of the Christian Gospel. Such analysis should take seriously the biblical injunction to look at the world through the eyes of its victims — to see through the lens of the cross. Therefore, I shall attempt to put forth a framework which highlights the global life-denying forces which victimize people.

Distinctions should be made between exploitation, repression, domination and subjugation. Each can be identified with a particular social logic promulgated first by Europeans and intensified later by the Americans and Soviets. Social logics are structured social practices which dehumanize people. I associate exploitation with the social logic of capital accumulation; repression with state augmentation; domination with bureaucratic administration; and subjugation with white, male, and heterosexual supremacy.

The development of capitalism is a basic fea-ture of the Europeanization of the world. Its operation is dictated by accumulation and powered by profit-maximization. Its aim is not simply to generate capital, but, more importantly, to reproduce the conditions for generating capital. As Marx noted, capital is neither mere revenue nor money, but rather a social relationship between persons which requires economic exploitation of those who work (e.g. sell their time, skills, energies). Since the ownership of the means of production (e.g. land, raw materials, instruments) is held by a small minority, the majority who must sell their labor are forced to live lives of material insecurity. *Exploitation* here is not so much a moral term as descriptive, denoting workers' lack of control over investment decisions, their work conditions, and how their products are used.

The capitalist mode of production, an international economic system, has undergone three stages: industrial capitalism, monopoly capitalism and multinational corporate capitalism. Its basic effect has been to privatize and centralize First World economies and to subordinate Third World economies to the First World. Capitalism's major competition has been the rise of the Soviet Union and its satellite countries. Yet their centrally-planned, hierarchical economies do not provide a feasible alternative.

The social logics of capital accumulation during the Europeanization, Americanization and Sovietization of the world have resulted in centralized economic power unaccountable to the majority of the populace and usually manipulative and abusive of the neo-colonial countries which depend upon them.

In the past decade, capital accumulation in the United States has undergone a deep crisis, principally due to increased competition with Japanese and European (and even some Third World) corporations; rising energy costs due to Third World oil cartels; the precarious structure of international debts owed American and European banks by Third World countries, and victorious anti-colonial struggles which sometimes limit lucrative capital investments. The U.S. response has been to curtail the public sphere by cutbacks of federal transfer payments to the needy; diminished public worker protection; erosion of unemployment compensation; diluted environmental protection; enlargement of low wage

Cornel West, "The Political Task of the Christian Church," *The Witness* 69, no. 1 (Jan. 1986): 6-8.

markets and incentives, and abatements to huge corporations. In short, this response promotes the dissolution of the public sector.

Repression and Augmentation

One of the ironies of the Europeanization, Americanization and Sovietization of the world is the increasing dissolution of the public sphere alongside the augmentation of the state. The state is understood more and more to be a channel through which public funds sustain centralized economic power (of multinational corporations in capitalist societies or bureaucratically-controlled economic firms in communist societies) as opposed to the public sphere which promotes the common good.

There has always been an intimate relationship between capital accumulation and the modern state, but the function of the state has changed radically. For example, industrial capitalism neither desired nor sought public regulation — yet it was buttressed by sympathetic courts, supportive military and police and financially helpful legislatures. Monopoly capitalism openly violated anti-trust laws enacted in response to peoples' movements, but is resiliency and resources — its capacity to insure economic growth — limited an expanding state to the roles of public regulation of monopolies, support for those outside the job market and protection of the marginal. And, of course, multinational corporate capitalism is saddled with a burdensome welfare state whose major recipients are not poor minority female heads of households (as is often believed) but rather corporations *qua* huge contract winners.

The salient feature of state augmentation since American and Soviet hegemony is the ever-expanding refinement of surveillance and control methods. The primary function of state apparatuses in U.S. and U.S.S.R. neo-colonial countries — from Chile to Cuba, South Korea to Poland — is to control and contain counter-insurgency movements with brutal techniques often learned from their hi-tech patrons.

The basic difference between the Americanization and the Sovietization of the world is that the United States was born with a precious rhetoric of rights. This tradition of liberalism, though circumscribed by racist, sexist and class constraints, provides crucial resources against the encroachment of repressive state apparatuses. Hence the scope of individual liberties remains broader in the United States — as well as in the U.S. neo-colonial countries — than in Soviet neo-colonial ones. This rich rhetoric of rights is politically ambiguous in that it can resist both state repression and state support for public life. By confusing state intervention in the economy with state interference in people's lives, healthy libertarian sentiments can lead toward a conservative ideology.

Domination and Bureaucratic Administration

The social logic of bureaucratic administration runs on impersonal rules and regulations that promote hierarchical patterns and steadfast submission. Its goals of institutional efficiency and self-preservation often enhance profit-maximization and disciplinary control. Capital accumulation, state augmentation and bureaucratic administration in both capitalist and communist countries constitute the major components of a growing "iron cage" in which labor is exploited and people are repressed and dominated.

The major responses to bureaucratic administration have been "therapeutic" releases such as alcoholism, narcotic subcultures, simulated sexuality, cults of sport and charismatic renewals of religion. These are earnest attempts to preserve some self-vitality and vigor and overcome the banality of modern societies. In the United States, such responses have often reduced religious rituals to packaged commodities, kerygmatic preaching to dramatic commercials, and protracted struggles of conversion to glib events of sentimental titillation. Rarely do these responses result in opposition to the status quo. Instead, they usually become escapist activities that reinforce it.

Capital accumulation, state augmentation and bureaucratic administration are shot through with white, male heterosexual supremacist discourses and practices. Such racist, sexist and heterosexist practices relegate black, brown, red, yellow, gay and lesbian people to marginal identities and cause them psychosexual anxieties.

Industrial capitalism boasted of overt racist

practices such as Jim Crowism, exclusionary immigration laws against Asians, and imperial conquest and geographical containment of indigenous peoples. Its cult of domesticity limited the role of heterosexual women, banished lesbians, and promoted a doctrine of masculinity which degraded "effeminate" heterosexual men and gay men. Monopoly capitalism tempered its racist practices and refined its ideologies against peoples of color, but nearly committed genocide against Jewish peoples in the midst of "civilized" Europe. It celebrated women who carried double work loads and castigated lesbians and gay men. Multinational corporate capitalism turns its racist ammunition on the black and brown working poor and under-class; focuses its right-wing movements on women's reproductive rights and often uses lesbians and gays as cultural scapegoats.

First World Church Resistance

Christians are deeply entrenched in the prevailing political situation, and our theologies are shot through with the social logics I have described. Are there any Christian resources left after one teases out the economic exploitation, state repression, bureaucratic domination, and racism, sexism, and homophobia?

Only if we can interpret dramatic biblical narratives and emphasize a morality which promotes the de-Europeanization, de-Americanization and de-Sovietization of the world. This should not result in a vulgar anti-European, and anti-American and anti-Soviet stance. Rather, it should build upon the best of the European, American and Soviet experiments. Further, it does not constitute a shift of the church to a "universal" faceless church, but rather from a church caught in European, American and Soviet captivity to a church more fully grounded in people's basic needs. In biblical language, I am promoting a church serious about rooting out its deep-seated idolatries.

Christian resources include the indispensable (yet never adequate) capacities of human beings to solve problems — hence the anti-dogmatic elements of Christianity which encourage critical consciousness and celebrate the good news of Jesus Christ which empowers and links human

capacities to the coming of the Kingdom. Thus too the warding off of disenabling despair, dread, cynicism, and death itself. Last, Christians view all human beings as having equal status, as warranting the same dignity, respect and love. Hence the Christian identification with the downtrodden and disinherited.

For those of us situated in the Christian tradition, there ought to be a deep bias against the prevailing forms of dogmatism and oppression. Yet this bias should be manifested without making criticism, hope and liberation a fetish or idol; for such reductions of the Christian Gospel result in impotent irony (as with some avant-garde postmodern theologians), shallow self-indulgence (as with many First World churches) or spiritless political struggle (as with some secularized political activists).

Another task of First World middle-class churches is to preserve the Christian ideals of individuality and democratic participation in the decision-making processes of the institutions which guide and regulate our lives.

This accents the Christian belief that all humans are made in the image of God, and are thereby endowed with a certain dignity and respect which include a chance to fulfill their potentialities. This interpretation acknowledges that the development of individuality occurs within groups and societies. Further, it recognizes the depravity of persons in the sense that institutional mechanisms must provide checks and balances for various forms of power, wealth, status and influence. These mechanisms seem to work best when regulated and enforced by democratic convictions. This condition of democracy not only calls for participation within a given set of structures, but also a share of power to change the structures themselves.

The Christian struggle for freedom is as much a struggle for moral norms and systemic social analysis as it is a struggle against the powers that be precisely because these powers must be adequately understood if they are to be effectively transformed. Battles within the Christian tradition are often fought over the kind of social analyses to be employed in understanding our lives, societies and world. Christian thinkers should employ elements of various social analyses of power, wealth, status and influence that look at the world from the situation of the "least of these."

Given the complexity and multiplicity of social logics of our world, an acceptable social and historical analysis must be both systemic and eclectic. My framework rests upon insights from the traditions of Marxism, anarchism, Weberianism, Garveyism, feminism, womanism, anti-homophobism, ecologism, liberalism and even elements of conservatism.

Affirming the Christian norms of individuality and democracy would more than likely lead to some form of democratic and libertarian socialism linked to anti-racist, anti-patriarchal and anti-homophobic ways of life: that is, a socio-economic arrangement with markets, price mechanisms, and induced (not directed) labor force, a free press, formal political rights and a constitutionally-based legal order with special protections for marginalized people. This social vision recognizes that centralization, hierarchy and market are inescapable realities for modern social existence; the crucial question is, how will they be regulated?

Finally, the preservation of individuality and democracy depends in large part, upon our understanding of and commitment to a deep sense of justice. And for Christians, justice has much to do with the depths of our faith.

The Churches and Third World Poverty

Mark R. Amstutz

The earth is a place of many sorrows. One of the sad aspects of our contemporary world is the extreme poverty found in many nations in Africa, Asia, and Latin America. Whereas living conditions in the Northern industrial states have allowed unprecedented comforts for its citizens, a large portion of the Third World's population lives in conditions of abject destitution. When he was president of the World Bank, Robert McNamara coined the term "absolute poverty" to describe the condition of life characterized by illiteracy, malnutrition, and disease as to be beneath any reasonable definition of decency. While there is much disagreement about the number of people living in such a state, it is possible that as many as 500 million persons (10 percent of the world's population) currently live in this subhuman condition.

How should the Christian church in the United States respond to this problem? What should it do directly and indirectly for the poor in foreign lands? Historically, North American missionaries have provided both physical and spiritual nurture to the poor, traveling to faraway lands to preach the gospel and to care for human needs. During the nineteenth and early twentieth centuries — the period of greatest North American missionary activity — countless Catholics and Protestants went to Africa, Asia, and Latin America to carry the good news of Christ while also providing material relief to those suffering from hunger, disease, and malnutrition. The tens of thousands of schools, agricultural communities, and hospitals

Mark R. Amstutz, "The Churches and Third World Poverty," *Missiology* 17, no. 4 (Oct. 1989): 453-64.

which have been built around the world and which continue to serve the needs of many bear witness to this generous outpouring of concern for the material and spiritual well-being of people.

Robert Bellah has written that North American churches have recently undergone a paradigm shift in the way they express public policy concerns. According to Bellah, for more than 150 years the missionary enterprise served as the major means by which the churches influenced foreign affairs. They did this by modeling Western social, political, and economic values, thereby contributing indirectly to the promotion of habits and institutions found in the United States. But more recently the churches have become directly involved in public policy debates through teaching documents and public pronouncements on important public policy issues, such as the nuclear dilemma and poverty. According to Bellah, this shift in paradigms is best symbolized by the issuing of the 1983 U.S. Catholic bishops' pastoral letter on nuclear weapons. Fundamentally, this shift in paradigms has involved a change in focus — from modeling to public policy analysis and advocacy, from micro concerns of the individual to the macro concerns of social and political structures. No longer are the churches concerned solely with preaching and teaching and the modeling of values. Rather, they have become major actors in dealing with domestic and international public policy concerns.

Consistent with this new paradigm, the Roman Catholic and mainline Protestant churches in the United States have endorsed numerous statements and resolutions and issued many teaching documents on national and international issues, including the economy. Some of the most important documents dealing with economic life include the U.S. Catholic bishops' 1986 pastoral letter titled *Economic Justice for All*, the Presbyterian Church (U.S.A.) 1984 study report, *Christian Faith and Economic Justice*, and the 1987 United Church of Christ report, *Christian Faith and Economic Life*. Although none of these reports are concerned alone with the plight of the poor in the developing nations, each of them provides general principals for assessing economic life and developing policy prescriptions.

The aim of this paper is to describe and assess briefly the churches' teaching documents on Third World poverty. While I applaud the concern expressed in these documents for justice and poverty, I question the adequacy of the social, political, and economic analysis of poverty and the resulting policy prescriptions. I do not take issue with these documents' moral and biblical analysis of poverty. Rather, I regard the theoretical and empirical judgments about Third World political and economic development as incomplete, if not misguided.

Common Themes

Church documents on national and economic life, such as the three listed above, are generally based on a number of shared moral and biblical principles. The following include some of the most significant of these:

1. The purpose of economic life is the affirmation of human dignity. The purpose of economic activity is not to acquire riches, but to enhance the quality of life.
2. Human dignity entails basic rights, including the right of participation in the economic life of a community. A priority of any economic system is to assure work for all its members.
3. The poor have a special claim on society. In fact, the 1986 Catholic bishops' pastoral letter suggests that the poor have the single most urgent economic claim on society.
4. A basic responsibility of a just economic system is the fulfillment of basic human needs.
5. Government has a major responsibility for promoting national and international economic justice, including the moderation of radical economic inequalities.

There can be little doubt that Christians and people of goodwill bear a moral responsibility to care for those in need. And for the Christian there is a special and compelling reason why the needs of the poor must have a priority — because that is what God expects of us. Christians must care for the weak, the poor, and the oppressed because God cares. This point, made repeatedly in the Scriptures, is most forcefully put by Jesus himself in his account of the Good Samaritan. According to Jesus, the Good Samaritan was the one who, unlike other more religious persons, responded directly to human needs. After suggesting that the person who demonstrated mercy and compassion was doing the will of the Father, Jesus said, "Go and do likewise" (Luke 10:37). In short, a manifestation of the Christian faith is the manner in which we personally and corporately respond to the poor.

Christians and people of goodwill can heartily agree with the churches' expressed concern for the poor. And since the people who have greatest physical and material needs are in the low-income countries in Africa, Asia, and Latin America, it is only appropriate that Third World needs should be at the forefront of the churches' international concerns. To the extent to which these documents increase awareness of, and interest in, the plight of the poor in the developing nations, they contribute to an important moral and biblical task.

One of the major emphases of these studies is the desire for increased government responsibility in providing jobs and a more equitable distribution of resources, both domestic and international. While the documents provide only general guidelines and principles for promoting economic justice, the general message is that an expanded government role is necessary for greater social justice and for meeting basic human needs. Although each of these reports makes an effort to affirm elements of free enterprise and socialism, the basic framework of analysis for each of the documents is a statist-interventionist-redistributional model of economic life. These reports assume that if justice is to be achieved and the needs of the poor are to be alleviated, greater governmental participation and regulation in economic life will be necessary.

Why do these documents emphasize resource transfers and structural reforms of the global economy? Why do they place so much emphasis on economic transfers, but neglect the topic of job creation? While there are several possible explanations for the statist orientation of these studies, the most persuasive explanation lies in the religious elites' underlying assumptions about political and economic change. Specifically, religious leaders prefer a political economy which places responsibility for social welfare and employment on the state and attributes poverty chiefly to exploitation and unfair economic structures.

Thomas Sowell has suggested that modern theories of political and economic change are rooted in fundamental assumptions about such issues as the nature of persons, the nature of community, the nature and role of government, and the perfectibility of the human condition. These basic presuppositions — which are generally clustered into a coherent set of beliefs or "vision" — provide the foundation for theories of political and social change. According to Sowell, since the seventeenth century two dominant visions or worldviews have dominated social and political thought. One of these he calls "constrained," and tends to be realistic and concerned with the development of institutions and rules for realizing the common good. The second vision is "unconstrained" and tends to be optimistic and idealistic and places great faith in the power of reason in promoting and improving community life.

To a significant degree, the religious elites' orientation tends to be "unconstrained," focusing on the prophetic call for social, political, and economic justice. While this approach is helpful in providing a standard by which to judge regimes and institutions, such a worldview also tends to overestimate the role of government and to underestimate the role of the individual in social and political change. Moreover, the unconstrained vision tends to underestimate the intractability of political and economic change.

Two Theses about Poverty

In order to assess the religious elites' political economy of Third World development, I shall compare two alternative models or theories of the poverty and wealth of nations. These approaches do not represent coherent social theories, but rather different perspectives about economic and political change. They represent, in effect, different ideals and analyses about the wealth, poverty, and unequal distribution of economic resources within the world.

The structural thesis is characterized by three distinctive features. First, it assumes that poverty is the result of unjust structures and exploitative economic policies. A feature of this approach is its assumption that the basic condition in life is sufficiency, not poverty. According to this model, the

The world is now at a historical juncture of great interest and importance because the processes of production and exchange have become so complex as to involve the whole of humankind in what is more and more a single exercise. Raw materials, intermediate goods, capital goods, methods of transport and communication, technology, capital, increasingly interact in a manner that has consequences for everyone on the other side of the globe though, obviously, not every economic act in a given place always affects every other place.

Thus, we now have a world that has become interdependent in the way in which this was true of the nation state in another age. But in today's world there are terrible disparities in power and wealth and hence in opportunity between the various national sections that make up this interdependent whole. However, equally, as with the nation state, the reality of interdependence places limitations upon the power of the strong and provides opportunities for the weak. We have contended that nations act most widely where they recognize that serious disparities within and between them in power, wealth and opportunity do not make for an acceptable and viable social organization. I believe the world community is just beginning to understand that this principle is equally true of this interdependent globe which we jointly occupy.

However in trying to do something about the disparities at the international level, we come up against difficulties a thousand times greater than those at the national level. Here we confront the divisive particularisms produced by differences of culture, language, history, location, area, population, ecology, resources and wealth that together define national interests. Add to that further differences of political ideology, economic organization, technological level and religion, and you can then form some preliminary idea of the enormous complexity and apparent intractability that confronts those who champion the politics of humankind as a whole in an arena of competing nation-states, multinational corporations, universal religions and radically opposed political and economic ideologies.

— Michael Manley, "Justice in a Developing Country's Perspective," *Ecumenical Review,* April 1979, p. 149

increase in absolute poverty is a direct byproduct of the expansion of capitalism. For example, Nicholas Wolterstorff in *Until Justice and Peace Embrace* writes that poverty in the Third World is a direct consequence of the expansion of Western capitalism. Wolterstorff argues:

It is now clear that the mass poverty is not the normal situation of mankind, nor is it the consequence of the actions of a few aberrant individuals. It is in good measure the effect of our world-wide economic system and of the political structures that support it.

Second, the structural thesis assumes that economic wealth is fixed. Since economics is a zero-sum game where the gain of one individual or nation must involve a corresponding loss to another, wealth creation is fundamentally exploitative. The gains of one person or community must of necessity involve a net economic loss to another person or community. Mutual economic expansion is not possible.

A third element of the structural thesis is that the international economic order is unjust, favoring the rich, powerful nations of the North. Ronald Sider explains this element as follows: "International trade patterns are unjust. . . . Every person in developed countries benefits from these structural injustices . . . which contribute directly to the hunger of a billion malnourished neighbors."

The alternative explanation for Third World poverty is the modernization thesis. This perspective provides a more adequate account of the

820

wealth and poverty of communities and is therefore more likely to aid in alleviating the Third World's problem of absolute poverty. According to this approach, the economic expansion of nations derives from a society's productive capacities, which are themselves based on different knowledge, technology, and skill, as well as access to primary and secondary commodities. To a significant degree, the features of this model can be expressed as direct opposites of the structural approach.

First, modernization assumes that the basic condition of life is scarcity and poverty. The major challenge, according to this approach, is the expansion of economic production, since it is the only means by which living standards can be improved long-term. While modernization has brought about much misery in the form of pollution, congestion, crime, and other related negative byproducts, economic expansion has improved the lot of citizens here and abroad. People are materially better off now than they were 50 or 100 years ago, this is true not only in the developed countries but also in the Third World as well.

Second, modernization assumes that economics is a positive-sum process where an increase in wealth in one state need not result in the decline in wealth of another. According to the modernization thesis, economic expansion can and will lead to significant disparities in income as it rewards groups, peoples, and nations that are most productive. But such rewards are not the consequence of exploitation, but of different productive capacities. International economic exploitation is not an automatic result of international economic relations.

Third, modernization assumes that the international economic order is a relatively neutral system, rewarding the firms and nations which are most efficient. The economic rise and fall of nations is explained not by the rules of international trade but by the ability of states to compete effectively in the world market of goods and services. The rapid economic rise of East Asian states is but the most dramatic illustration of this. There are no doubt injustices in the world economy, but there are too many poor countries which have prospered economically in the past two decades to assume that the existing framework impedes all economic progress.

To a large degree, the churches' approach to domestic and Third World poverty is based on a political economy based on the structural thesis. While the Presbyterian, United Church of Christ, and Catholic documents on economic life do not explicitly adopt such a paradigm, each of them leans heavily on this perspective. To the extent that Third World poverty is addressed, it is approached through the lens of structuralism. There is little or no discussion about the role of individuals and groups. The subject of culture is wholly missing from these studies. Virtually nothing is said about what the Third World nations themselves need to do to enhance human dignity. The prevailing assumption is that, since much of the poverty is the result of unjust structures, the major responsibility of the church is to help establish just public policies, both domestic and international. The way to achieve social justice is to establish just institutions and policies which assure just distribution of goods and services.

The major deficiency of the structuralist thesis is that it fails to provide an adequate explanation for the wealth and poverty of nations. Contrary to the dependency theorists and structuralist, the creation of wealth is a positive-sum process — a means whereby a net addition of economic value is possible. The wealth acquired by Japan and the Netherlands, for example, has not come from the exploitation of other states but from increased productivity. Nor is the poverty of Bolivia and Zaire a result of injury inflicted by multinational corporations or foreign governments. If this were the case, the Third World would have become increasingly impoverished as Western industrial states prospered economically in the postwar decades. But the results have been quite the opposite. As modern science and technology has spread throughout the world, improvements in living standards have occurred worldwide. To be sure, the largest increases in per capita income have taken place in the rich, developed states. But only a small portion of the world's nations have failed to take advantage of the expansion of modernization. Most First and Third World countries have improved their living standards in the past three decades.

These improvements in Third World living conditions are evident by the dramatic improvement in the living conditions of the average citizen. Comparative statistical data suggest that the average life expectancy and overall quality of life in the Third World has improved significantly since the 1960s. World Bank statistics reveal the following improvements between 1965 and 1985 in the 37 poorest countries in the world:

1. The annual crude death rate per thousand declined from 17 to 10.
2. Owing largely to a decline in the fertility rate, the annual crude birth rate per thousand people declined form 43 to 29.
3. Average life expectancy increased between from 47 to 60 years for men and from 50 to 61 years for women.
4. Infant mortality for children under one year declined from 127 per thousand to 72 per thousand.
5. The child death rate for children aged 1-4 declined from 19 per thousand to 9 per thousand.
6. Average daily caloric supply per capita also increased — from 2,046 to 2,339.
7. Finally, the average percentage of children in primary schools increased from 74 to 97 and in secondary schools from 21 to 32.

While the spread of modern medicine and technology has contributed greatly to increased living standards, it has also resulted in great misery. The cause of these contradictory outcomes lies in the different patterns of economic development. Whereas modernity evolved over several centuries in the North, most developing nations were thrust into the modern age in one brief period of time. This radical shift from an agrarian culture to an urban-oriented society has left profound consequences on the people of Africa, Asia, and Latin America.

One of the most fateful differences between the rich and the poor lands is that in the former modern medicine was introduced at the time that modern economic and political institutions were being established. But in the Third World modern medicine was introduced before social, political, and economic modernization had taken hold. The rapid spread of modernization has resulted in an imbalance in fertility and death rates, leading to a dramatic rise in the population.

The Third World's hunger and malnutrition are not new events in human history. What is new is the unprecedented scope of the needs created by a population explosion, whose great force is felt in the urban areas of the poorest countries. In light of the continuing population growth of more than 2.5 percent in many developing nations, the great challenge is how to expand the economic capacities of the poor societies by increasing employment opportunities. According to information published in the *The Christian Science Monitor* of August 30, 1985, the International Labor Organization has estimated that during the last 15 years of this century at least one billion new jobs will have to be created in the Third World in order to reduce current unemployment and provide jobs for those entering the work force.

Assessing the Churches' Political Economy

Is the churches' statist or structuralist political economy likely to help the poor in the developing nations? Is the socialist orientation of denominational studies and resolutions likely to assist those suffering from absolute poverty? Given the historical experience of capitalism and socialism in the Third World in the past three decades, there is reason to doubt the efficacy of a statist strategy of economic justice.

There are four reasons why churches should be wary of using a structuralist approach in caring for the Third World's poor. First, the statist approach to economic development has not worked well. Free enterprise strategies of economic growth have been more successful in creating wealth than socialist systems. The statist and socialist economic policies which many Third World countries have adopted have resulted in economic decay and the further impoverishment of the poor. By contrast, states which have encouraged private enterprise have experienced higher rates of economic growth and job creation. Peter Berger has suggested that if a nation wants to help the poor, it should become pro-capitalist. Ten years after he wrote his *Pyramids of Sacrifice*, Berger (1984) decided that he had been too even-handed in his earlier assessment of capitalism and socialism in the Third World. Because of the failure of socialist systems and the success of free enterprise regimes, Berger concluded that capitalism was a much more beneficial system for the poor. More recently, Robert Heilbroner has similarly written about the failure of socialism:

Less than seventy-five years after it officially began, the contest between capitalism and socialism is over: capitalism has won. The Soviet Union, China and Eastern Europe have given us the clearest possible proof that capitalism organizes the material affairs of humankind more satisfactorily than socialism: that however inequitably or irresponsibly the marketplace may distribute goods, it does so better than the queues of a planned economy; however mindless the culture of commercialism, it is more attractive than state moralism; and however deceptive the ideology of a business civilization, it is more believable than that of a socialist one. Indeed, it is difficult to observe the changes taking place in the world today and not conclude that the nose of the capitalist camel has been pushed so far under the socialist tent that the great question now seems how rapid will be the transformation of socialism into capitalism, and not the other way around, as things looked only a half century ago.

A second reason why churches should become less dependent on the structural thesis and more supportive of free enterprise is that the socialist systems appear to be no better at establishing social justice and economic equality than capitalist systems. Indeed, some social scientists have begun to challenge the widely held belief that socialist systems are better at creating equality. Thomas Dye and Harmon Zeigler have argued that the idea that socialism fosters equality rests on ideology and not on empirical observation. According to them, cross-national studies indicate that a) equality is primarily a result of economic development, not the consequence of a particular type of political system; b) capitalist systems are more successful at stimulating economic growth than socialist systems; and c) socialist and capitalist systems at the same level of economic development pursue essentially the same welfare and educational policies. In the light of these findings, the quest for greater social and economic equality will necessarily involve economic development. Despite its great mythic and moral appeal, a socialist strategy of development will not necessarily provide for the needs of the poor. Churches concerned with

devising a strategy based on a "preferential option of the poor" should, in effect, become more capitalistic and less socialistic.

A third reason for the inadequacy of the structural approach is its neglect of job creation. Since the low-income states have a population growth of 2.5 to 3 percent annually, economic expansion is essential in poor societies. What is desperately needed in countries like Bangladesh, Mali, and Zaire is the expansion of employment opportunities. A nation which seeks to maintain its standard of living must have an economy which expands at the same or higher rate than its population. Improvements in living conditions can occur only if the productive capacities of nations increase. Foreign assistance, as Tanzania discovered, can provide temporary relief for the poor, but will not alter their basic living conditions.

A fourth reason why the religious elites should not depend upon statist policies is that Third World governments are a major obstacle to the alleviation of poverty and the promotion of social justice. Because of the absence of accountability and the pervasiveness of corruption, there are greater temptations in the Third World to use political power chiefly to satisfy the economic and political wants of elites. Rather than serving the common good, governments have often become tools to oppress minorities and the poor. Government is essential in all community life, and good government is a blessing. But when greed and corruption infect government, the public good suffers and human needs remain unfilled.

Peruvian economist Hernando De Soto in his influential book, *The Other Path* (1989), writes that the major obstacle to Peruvian economic growth has been excessive government control. In his study, De Soto debunks the myth that the poverty of Latin America derives from too much capitalism. Indeed, he argues that Peru has never had a market economy. Its economy since colonial days has always been mercantilism — a system where economic and political power has been monopolized by a small elite. In his book De Soto describes graphically how the migrant poor, in order to overcome the discriminatory and unjust laws, have created a large black market of illegal economic activity in such sectors as transportation, housing, and trade. According to De Soto, this illegal or informal activity currently contributes nearly 40 percent of the gross domestic product, and involves 48 percent of the labor force.

Peruvian novelist Mario Vargas Llosa writes approvingly of the expansion of this illegal or "informal" activity. He notes that we should be glad that the poor have had the courage to demonstrate by their actions how poverty can be ameliorated. In his foreword to De Soto's book, Vargas Llosa notes:

> The path taken by the black-marketeers — the poor — is not the reinforcement and magnification of the state but a radical pruning and reduction of it. They do not want planned, regimented collectivization by monolithic governments; rather, they want the individual, private initiative and enterprise to be responsible for leading the battle against underdevelopment and poverty.... If we listen to what these poor slum dwellers are telling us with their deeds, we hear nothing about what so many Third World revolutionaries are advocating in their name — violent revolution, state control of the economy. All we hear is a desire for genuine democracy and authentic liberty.

Alleviating Absolute Poverty

The churches can, and must, contribute to the alleviation of Third World poverty. They can do this most effectively by modeling the habits and virtues which contribute to job creation and sharing. Given the unbelievable wealth in the United States, religious denominations can do more than they are now doing for the poor. American churches do not contribute a large enough proportion of their revenues to those suffering from absolute poverty. It is ironic that churches should seek to give public policy advice when they themselves could and should increase their financial transfers transnationally. The U.S. Catholic bishops' letter on the U.S. economy would have been more credible had the bishops indicated how Third World needs fit into the church's national and international priorities. The fact that the document neglects altogether its institutional responsibilities for the poor is most regrettable.

Churches can help alleviate Third World poverty in two distinct ways: first, they can respond in a humanitarian way to immediate human needs domestically and internationally; second, they can help establish the preconditions for long-term economic expansion. The first approach involves the transfer of financial and material resources to meet basic human needs, such as food, shelter, health care, and education. The second involves the sending of missionaries and volunteers to teach and to model practices and values essential to economic expansion. By seeking to model values such as organization, savings, planning, and rationality, Christian workers can contribute to the preconditions for job creation. Christian denominations have contributed much to the improvements in living conditions throughout the world, but more needs to be done.

To the extent that the churches become involved in public policy debates, such activity should not detract from their basic teaching, preaching, and modeling responsibilities. The churches can play an important role in illuminating relevant biblical and moral norms and can challenge individuals, groups, and governments to more just behavior. Participation in the public debate, however, should be undertaken with discrimination, competence, and caution. The church's competence, after all, is not the social sciences, but in moral and biblical analysis.

Governments in the West can of course help reduce Third World poverty. To the extent that churches seek to influence international economic policy towards the Third World, they should encourage foreign economic assistance which contributes to the enhancement of the private sector's job creation task. The following principles should govern the transfer of public funds from the United States to the poor lands:

First, the United States government should increase its material help to poor countries. The United States contributes one of the smallest proportions of aid of any of the Western developed states. Whereas most Western European nations contribute about .5 percent of their gross national product, the United States contributes about .25 percent of its GNP. The United States can and should do more for the poor.

Second, most aid should be given directly to Third World humanitarian and development organizations and to those American private development institutions concerned with job creation. Organizations such as Opportunity International — a small nonprofit development organization which makes available small-business loans in Third World countries — provide an effective method of transferring material aid. Economic transfers to Third World governments, however, will do little for the poor. Since most Third World countries are nonpluralistic, the transfer of resources is likely to increase the influence of ruling elites. Moreover, to the extent that governments invest foreign aid in infrastructure and other economic needs, the investment decisions are likely to be guided more by political considerations than by economic merit, especially by their impact on the poor and unemployed sectors of society. P. T. Bauer, who has devoted much of his professional life to the impact of foreign aid on Third World development, has observed that the poor are seldom the real beneficiaries of official aid. Bauer states:

> Official aid does not go to the poor people. . . . It goes instead to their rulers whose spending policies are determined by their personal and political interests, among which the position of the poorest has very low priority. Indeed, to support rulers on the basis of the poverty of their subjects is more likely to encourage policies of impoverishment than to deter them.

Third, official aid should emphasize nontangible resource transfers. The basic ingredients of wealth creation are intangible human qualities, not tangible resources, such as equipment, credits, raw materials, or new technology. United States aid programs have generally focused on tangible resources, partly because it is much easier to disburse financial assets than to promote human skills and attitudes. Organizations like the Peace Corps that emphasize education and human development can contribute greatly to the acquisition of skills, knowledge, and attitudes essential to economic growth.

In summary, the United States government can contribute to the improvement of living conditions in the Third World. It can do so by channeling increasing aid for famine relief and longer-term economic expansion. Since there can be no significant improvement in the living conditions of the poor apart from the expansion of employment opportunities, the chief aim of any official aid program must be the promotion of labor-intensive growth. This can be undertaken most effectively when the United States promotes those values, aspirations, and practices, as well as political and economic institutions, that have stimulated job creation in the West.

Section 4: The Economy and the Global Environment

Economic activity is dependent on the world's natural and technological environment. When national governments and business corporations have acted as if they were independent from the physical world, they only laid the foundations for long-term environmental problems. We now know what freon does to the ozone layer, what overuse does to topsoil, and what incessant technological change does to community life. The ensuing ecological disasters have made us all environmentalists of one sort or another.

Yet we need to think further about the balance between global economic development and global ecology. In Genesis 2:15 God instructed humans in the Garden of Eden to both "till it and keep it." Determining the appropriate balance of tilling and keeping is a reflection of our basic assumptions about nature and technology. Those assumptions necessarily involve parts of our theology, our basic beliefs about the nature of God in relationship to the world of nature. The readings in this section examine our understanding of theology in relationship to the environment and the implications for economic activity.

Wendell Berry begins by suggesting that our implicit model for an industrial economy has led us down the wrong path. When the industrial economy is the only economy acknowledged, assumptions about control, domination, and use of resources can be destructive. Berry's understanding of industrial economy as the lesser economy inside the greater economy of God provides a useful starting point for challenging conventional assumptions about economic development and the environment.

Robert Nelson also considers how theology and environmentalism can be related. Not only does he argue that contemporary environmentalism has an implicit theological foundation, but he also believes that Christian theology in its many forms has influenced Western culture's foundation for environmental concern. One's stand on environmentalism is in part dependent on one's theology of sin and salvation.

James Nash's contribution supports the broad theological assumptions shared by Berry and Nelson. While he acknowledges that ecological concern has not been a dominant feature of Christian theology or practice, he argues that Christian faith does offer an ultimate grounding for a strong environmental ethic. Nash demonstrates the practical consequences of this hypothesis by calling our attention to the public policy implications of a Christian approach to the environment.

While developing the connection between theology and environmental perspective is critical, so is the global concern for integrating ecology and economic development. Andrew Steer argues that developing strategies that serve both ecology and economy are critical for the future of the Third World poor. As an economist and policy maker, he suggests not only an appropriate Christian theology for balancing the two but also practical approaches that can make the balance work in favor of, rather than at the expense of, the poor.

Environmental concern related to economic development is no longer a silent stream. It is a turbulent river gaining force from multiple tributaries. Continuing debate about the balance between the economy and the environment needs adequate theological and ethical underpinnings. In the writings selected we have tried to highlight some of the most promising and provocative attempts to provide these.

Two Economies

Wendell Berry

Some time ago, in a conversation with Wes Jackson, the Kansas plant breeder and agriculturist, in which we were laboring to define the causes of the modern ruination of farmland, we finally got around to the money economy. I said that an economy based on energy would be more benign because it would be more comprehensive.

Wes would not agree. "An energy economy still wouldn't be comprehensive enough."

"Well," I said, "then what kind of economy *would* be comprehensive enough?"

He hesitated a moment and then, grinning, said, "The kingdom of God."

I assume that Wes used the term because he found it, at the point in our conversation, indispensable. I assume so because, in my pondering over its occurrence at that point, I have found it indispensable myself. For the thing that so troubles us about the industrial economy is exactly that it is not comprehensive enough, that, moreover, it tends to destroy what it does not comprehend, and that it is *dependent* upon much that it does not comprehend. In attempting to criticize such an economy, it is probably natural to pose against it an economy that does not leave anything out. And we can say without presuming too much, that the first principle of the kingdom of God is that it includes everything; in it the fall of every sparrow is a significant event. We are in it, we may say, whether we know it or not, and whether we wish to be or not. Another principle, both ecological and traditional, is that everything in the kingdom of God is joined both to it and to everything else that is in it. That is to say that the kingdom of God is orderly.

A third principle, which may be sufficiently demonstrable, is that humans do not, and can never, know either all the creatures that the kingdom of God contains or the whole pattern or order by which it contains them.

The suitability of the kingdom of God as, so to speak, a place name is somewhat owing to the fact that it still means pretty much what it always meant. Because, I think, of the embarrassment that it has increasingly caused among the educated, the phrase has not been much tainted or tampered with by the disinterested processes of academic thought. It is a phrase that comes to us with its cultural strings still attached. To speak of the kingdom of God, if we know something of the origins of our minds, is both to suggest the difficulty of our condition and to imply a fairly complete set of culture-born instructions for living in it. These instructions are not always explicitly ecological, but it can be argued that they are always implicitly so.

The instructions are always implicitly ecological because all of them rest ultimately on the assumptions that I gave as the second and third "principles" of the kingdom of God: that we live within order, and that this order is both greater and more intricate than we can know. The difficulty of our predicament is made clear if we add a fourth principle: though we cannot produce a complete or even an adequate description of this order, severe penalties are in store for us if we presume upon it or violate it.

I am not, of course, talking about a perception that is only biblical. The ancient Greeks, according to Aubrey de Selincourt, saw "a continuing moral pattern in the vicissitudes of human fortune" — a pattern "formed from the belief that men, as men, are subject to certain limitations by a Power — call it Fate or God — which they cannot fully comprehend, and that any attempt to transcend those limitations is met by inevitable punishment." The Greek name for the pride that attempts to transcend human limitations was *hubris*, and *hubris* was the cause of what the Greeks understood as tragedy.

Nearly the same sense of *necessary* human limitation is implied in the Old Testament's repeated remonstrances against too great a human confi-

Wendell Berry, "Two Economies," *Review and Expositor* 81, no. 2 (1984): 209-23.

dence in the power of "mine own hand." Gideon's army against the Midianites was reduced from 32,000 to 300 expressly to prevent the Israelites from saying, "Mine own hand hath saved me" (Judg. 7:2-21). A similar purpose was served by the institution of the Sabbath, when, by not working, the Israelites were meant to see the limited efficacy of their work and so to understand their true dependence.

Though I hope that my insistence on the usefulness of the term *the kingdom of God* will be understood, I must acknowledge that the term is local, in the sense that it is fully available only to those whose languages are involved in Western or biblical tradition. A person of Eastern heritage might, for example, make a similar use of *the Tao* to refer to the totality of all creation, visible and invisible. I am well aware also that many people would not willingly use either term or any such term. Because, for those reasons, I do not want to make a statement that is specially or exclusively biblical, I would like now to use a more culturally neutral term for the economy that I have been calling the kingdom of God. Sometimes I have called it the Great Economy, which is the name I am going to make do with — though I will remain under the personal necessity of biblical reference. And that must be one of my points: We can name it whatever we wish, but we cannot define it except by way of a religious tradition. The Great Economy, like the Tao or the kingdom of God, is both known and unknown, visible and invisible, comprehensible and mysterious. It is, thus, the ultimate condition of our experience and of the practical questions rising from our experience, imposing on our consideration of those questions an extremity of seriousness and an extremity of humility. (In such shiftings of terms, we should be mindful of the probability that, for Westerners, Western culture is inescapable. If we try to behave mechanically, we may think that we have escaped it. But if we try to behave courteously or respectfully or reverently we can do so only by remembering. And so if we speak of a Great Economy, meaning that it is greater than ourselves and greater than our comprehension, and if we capitalize the name, we become inevitably the neighbors and debtors of our forebears who spoke of the kingdom of God.)

I am assuming that the Great Economy, whatever we may name it, is indeed, and in ways that are to some extent practical, an economy: it includes principles and patterns by which values or powers or necessities are parceled out and exchanged. But that the Great Economy comprehends humans, and so cannot be fully comprehended by them, suggests that it is not an economy that humans can participate in directly. What this suggests, in fact, is that humans can live in the Great Economy only with great uneasiness, subject to powers and laws that they can understand only in part. There is no human accounting for the Great Economy. This obviously is a description of the circumstance of religion, the circumstance that *causes* religion. De Selincourt again states the problem succinctly: "Religion in every age is concerned with the vast and fluctuant regions of experience which knowledge cannot penetrate, the regions which a man knows, or feels, to stretch away beyond the narrow, closed circle of what he can *manage* by the use of his wits."

If there is no denying our dependence on the Great Economy, there is also no denying our need for a little economy — a narrow circle within which things are manageable by the use of our wits. I don't think that Wes Jackson was denying this need when he invoked the kingdom of God as the complete economy. He was, I think, insisting upon a priority which is both proper and practical. If he had a text in mind it must have been the sixth chapter of Matthew, in which, after speaking of God's care for nature, the fowls of the air and the lilies of the field, Jesus says: "Therefore take no thought, saying, What shall we eat? or, What shall we drink? or, Wherewithal shall we be clothed: . . . But seek ye first the kingdom of God, and his righteousness; and all these things shall be added unto you" (vv. 31, 33).

There is an attitude that sees in that text a purely spiritual denial of the value of *any* economy of this world — which makes the text useless and meaningless to humans who must live in this world. These verses make usable sense only if we need them as a statement, of considerable practical import, about the real nature of worldly economy. If this passage meant for us to seek *only* the kingdom of God, it would have the odd result of making good people not only feckless in this world but dependent upon bad people busy with quite other seekings. But it says, instead, to seek the kingdom of God *first;* that is, it gives an obviously necessary priority to the Great Economy over any little economy made within it. The passage also clearly includes nature within the Great Economy, and it affirms the goodness, indeed the sanctity, of natural creatures.

The fowls of the air and the lilies of the field live directly within the Great Economy; whereas humans, though entirely dependent upon it, may live in it only indirectly, by choice and by artifice. The birds can live in the Great Economy only as birds, the flowers only as flowers, the humans only as humans. The humans, unlike the wild creatures, may choose not to live in it — or, rather, since no creature can escape it, they may choose to *act* as if they do not, or they may choose to try to live in it on their own terms. If humans choose to live in it on *its* terms, then they must live in harmony with it, learning to live in it by considering the lives of the wild creatures, and in trust of it.

Certain economic restrictions are clearly implied, and these restrictions have mainly to do with the economics of futurity. We know from other passages in the gospels that a certain preparedness of provisioning for the future is required of us. It may be that such preparedness is part of our obligation to today, and for that reason we need take no thought for the morrow. But such preparations can be carried too far; we can provide too much for the future. The sin of "a certain rich man" in the twelfth chapter of Luke is that he has "much goods laid up for many years," and so believes that he can "eat, drink, and be merry." The offense seems to be that he has stored up too much and in the process has belittled the future; he has reduced it to the size of his hopes and expectations. He is prepared for a future in which he will be prosperous, not for one in which he will be dead (vv. 16-20). And we know from our own experience that it is impossible to live in the present in such a way as to diminish the future practically as well as spiritually. By laying up "much goods" in the present — and in the process using up such goods as topsoil, fossil fuel, and fossil water — we incur a debt to the future that we cannot repay. That is, we diminish the future by deeds that we call "use" but which the future will call "theft." We may say, then, that we seek the kingdom of God, in part, by our economic behavior, and we fail to find it if that behavior is wrong.

If we read Matthew 6:24-34 as a teaching that is both practical and spiritual, as I think we must, then we must see it as prescribing the terms of a kind of little economy or human economy. Since I am deriving it here from a Christian text, we could call it a Christian economy — and there is certainly an urgent importance for Westerners in the recognition that an economy may be Christian or unchristian. But we need not call it that. A Buddhist might look at the working principles of the economy I am talking about and call it a Buddhist economy. (E. F. Schumacher, in fact, says that the aim of "Buddhist economics" is "to obtain the maximum of well-being with the minimum of consumptions," which I think is partly the sense of Matthew 6:24-31.) Or we could call this economy (from Matthew 6:28) a considerate economy, or simply a good economy. The human economy, then, if it is to be a good economy, as prescribed by Matthew 6:24-34, would fit harmoniously within, and would correspond to, the Great Economy. In certain important ways, it would be an analogue of the Great Economy.

A fifth principle of the Great Economy, that must now be added to the previous four, is that we cannot foresee an end to it: the same basic stuff is going to be shifting from one form to another, so far as we know, forever. But from a human point of view that is a rather heartless endurance. As cynics sometimes point out, conservation is always working, for what is lost or wasted in one place always turns up someplace else. Thus soil erosion in Iowa involves no loss because the soil is conserved in the Gulf of Mexico. Such people like to point out that soil erosion is as "natural" as birdsong. And so it is, though these people neglect to observe that soil conservation is also natural and that, before the advent of farming, nature alone worked effectively to keep Iowa topsoil in Iowa. But to say that soil erosion is natural is only a way of saying that there are some things that the Great Economy cannot do for humans. Only a little economy, only a good human economy, can define for us the value — and not only the quantitative value — of keeping the topsoil where it is.

A good human economy, that is, defines and values human good, and, like the Great Economy, it conserves and protects its goods. It proposes to endure. Like the Great Economy, a good human economy does not propose for itself a term to be set by humans. That termlessness, with all its implied human limits and restraints, is a human good.

From a human point of view, the difference between the Great Economy and any human economy is pretty much the difference between the goose that laid the golden egg and the golden egg. For the goose to have value as a layer of golden eggs she must be a *live* goose, and therefore joined to the life cycle, and therefore joined to all manner of things, patterns, and processes that sooner or later surpass human comprehension. The golden egg, on the other hand, can be fully valued by humans according to kind, weight, and measure — but it will not hatch and cannot be eaten. To make an egg fully accountable by humans, then, we must make it "golden," must remove it from life. If in our valuation of it we should wish to consider its relation to the goose, we will have to undertake a different kind of accounting, more exacting if less exact. If we wish to value the egg in such a way as to preserve the goose that laid it, we find that we have to define ourselves as humans as fully as our traditional knowledge of ourselves permits. We participate in our little human economy to a considerable extent, that is, by factual knowledge, calculation, and manipulation. But we participate in the Great Economy also by cultural knowledge and by humility, forebearance, charity, generosity, and imagination.

Another critical difference, implicit in the foregoing, is that though a human economy can evaluate, distribute, use, and preserve things of value, it cannot make value. Value can originate only in the Great Economy. It is true enough that humans can add value to natural things. We may transform topsoil into walnut trees, and transform the trees into boards, and transform the boards into chairs, adding value at each transformation. In a good human economy these transformations would be made by good work, and a good human economy would place a proper value upon good work and properly reward the workers. But a good human economy would recognize at the same time that it was dealing all along with materials and powers that it did not make. It did not make soil fertility, or walnut trees, or walnut wood, and it did not make the intelligence and talents of the human workers. What the humans have added at every step is artificial, made by art, and though the value of art is critical to human life, it is a secondary value. Without the things of primary value, the things of secondary value would not exist.

When humans presume to originate value, they make value that is first abstract and then false, tyrannical, and destructive of real value. Money value, for instance, can be said to be true only when it truly and stably represents the value of necessary goods, such as clothing, food, and shelter, which originate in the Great Economy. Humans can originate money value in the abstract, but only by inflation and usury, which falsify the value of necessary things and damage their natural and human sources. Inflation and usury, and the damages that follow, can be understood, perhaps, as retributions for the resumption that humans can make value.

We may say then that a human economy originates, manages, and distributes secondary or added values but that if it is to last long it must also manage in such a way as to make continuously available those values that are primary or given, the secondary values here having mainly to do with husbandry and trusteeship. These primary values all originate in the Great Economy. The best a little economy can do with them is to receive them gratefully and use them in such a way as not to diminish them. We might make a long list of things that we would have to describe as primary values, that come directly into the little economy from the Great, but the one I want to talk about, because it is one with which we have the most intimate working relationship, is the topsoil.

We cannot speak of topsoil, indeed we cannot know what it is, without acknowledging at the outset that we cannot make it. We can care for it (or not), we can even, as we say, "build" it, but we can do so only by assenting to, preserving, and perhaps collaborating in its own processes. To those processes themselves we have nothing to contribute. We cannot make topsoil, and we cannot make any substitute for it; we cannot do what it does. It is apparently impossible to make an adequate description of topsoil in the sort of language that we have come to call "scientific." For though any soil sample can be reduced to its inert quantities, a handful of the real thing has life in it; it is full of living creatures. And if we try to describe the behavior of that life we will see that it is doing something that, if we are not careful, we will call "unearthly": it is making life out of death. Not so very long ago, had we known about it what we know now, we would probably have called it "miraculous." But in a time when death is looked upon with almost universal enmity, it is hard to believe that the land we live on and the lives we live are the gifts of death. Yet that is so, and it is the topsoil that makes it so. A fact we had better learn to deal with is that in talking about topsoil it is hard to avoid the language of religion. When in "This Compost," Whitman says, "The resurrection of the wheat appears with pale visage out of its grave," he is talking directly out of Christian tradition, and yet he is describing what happens with language that is entirely accurate and appropriate. And when at last he says of the earth that "It gives such divine materials to men," we feel that the propriety of the words comes not from convention but from the actuality of the uncanny transformation that his poem has required us to imagine, as if in obedience to the summons to "consider the lilies of the field."

Even in its functions that may seem, to mechanists, to be mechanical, the topsoil behaves complexly and wonderfully. A healthy topsoil, for instance, has at once the ability to hold water and to drain well. When we speak of the health of a watershed, this is what we are talking about, and the word *health*, which we do use in speaking of watersheds, warns us that we are not speaking merely of mechanics. A healthy soil is made by the life dying into it and living in it; and to its double ability to drain and retain water we are complexly indebted, for it not only gives us good crops but also erosion control and both flood control and a constant water supply.

Obviously, topsoil, not energy or money, is the critical quantity in agriculture. And topsoil *is* a quantity; we need it in quantities. We now need more of it than we have; we need to help it to make more of itself. But it is a most peculiar quantity, for it is inseparable from quality. Topsoil is by definition *good* soil, and it can be preserved in human use only by *good* care. When humans see it as a mere quantity, they tend to make it that; they destroy the life in it and they begin to measure in inches and feet and tons how much of it they have "lost."

When we see the topsoil as the foundation of that household of living creatures and their non-living supports that we now call an ecosystem, but which Westerners would understand better as a neighborhood, we find ourselves in debt for other benefits that baffle our mechanical logic and defy our measures. For example, one of the principles of an ecosystem is that diversity increases capacity. Or, to put it another way, complications of form or pattern can increase greatly within quantitative limits. I suppose that this may be true only up to a point, but I suppose also that point is far beyond the human capacity to understand or diagram the pattern.

On a farm put together on a sound ecological pattern the same principle holds. Henry Besuden, the great farmer and shepherd of Clark County, Kentucky, compares the small sheep flock to the two spoons of sugar that can be added to a brimful cup of coffee, which then becomes "more palatable, and doesn't run over. You can stock your farm to the limit with other livestock and still add a small flock of sheep." He says this, characteristically, after rejecting the efforts of sheep specialists to get beyond "the natural physical limits of the ewe" by out-of-season breeding to get three lamb crops in two years, or by striving for "litters" of lambs rather than nature's optimum of twins. Rather than chafe at "natural physical limits," he would turn to nature's elegant way of enriching herself *within* her physical limits by diversification, by complication of pattern. Rather than strain the productive capacity of the ewe, he would, without strain, enlarge the productive capacity of the farm — a healthier, safer, and cheaper procedure. Like many of the better traditional farmers, Henry Besuden is suspicious of "the measure of land in length and width," for he would be mindful as well of "the depth and quality."

A small flock of ewes, fitted properly into a farm's pattern, virtually disappears into the farm and does it good, just as it virtually disappears into the time and energy economy of a farm family and does it good. Or one might say that, properly fitted into the farm's pattern, the small flock virtually disappears from the debit side of the farm's accounts but shows up plainly on the credit side. And this "disappearance" is possible, not insofar as the farm is a human artifact, a belonging of the human economy, but insofar as it remains, by its obedience to natural principle, a belonging of the Great Economy.

A little economy may be said to be good insofar as it perceives the excellence of these benefits and husbands and preserves them. And it is by holding up this standard of goodness that we can best see what is wrong with the industrial economy. For the industrial economy does not see itself as a little economy; it sees itself as the *only* economy. It makes itself thus exclusive by the simple expedient of valuing only what it can use, that is, only what it can regard as "raw material" to be transformed mechanically into something else. What it cannot use it characteristically describes as "useless," "worthless," "random," or "wild," and gives it some such names as "chaos," "disorder," or "waste" — and thus ruins it, or cheapens it in preparation for eventual use. That western deserts or eastern mountains were once perceived as "useless" made it easy to dignify them by the "use" of strip mining. Once we acknowledge the existence of the Great Economy, however, we are astonished and frightened to see how much modern enterprise is the work of *hubris,* occurring outside the human boundary established by ancient tradition. The industrial economy is based on invasion and pillage of the Great Economy.

The weakness of the industrial economy is clearly revealed when it imposes its terms upon agriculture, for its terms cannot define those natural principles that are most vital to the life and longevity of farms. Even if they could *afford* to do so, the industrial economists cannot describe the dependence of agriculture upon nature. If asked to consider the lilies of the field, or told that the wheat is resurrected out of its graves, the agricultural industrialist would reply that "my engineer's mind inclines less toward the poetic and philosophical, and more toward the practical and impossible" — unable even to suspect that such a division of mind induces blindness to possibilities of the utmost practical concern.

That good topsoil both drains and retains water and that diversity increases capacity are facts similarly alien to industrial logic. Industrialists see retention and drainage as different and opposite functions, and would promote one at the expense of the other, just as — diversity being inimical

to industrial procedure — they would commit themselves to the forlorn expedient of enlarging capacity by increasing area. They are thus encumbered by dependence on mechanical solutions that can work only by isolating and oversimplifying problems. Industrialists are condemned to proceed by devices. To facilitate water retention they must resort to a specialized waterholding device such as a terrace or a dam; to facilitate drainage they must use drain tile or a ditch or a "subsoiler." It is possible, I know, to argue that this analysis is too general and to produce exceptions, but I do not think it deniable that the discipline of soil conservation is now principally that of the engineer, not that of the farmer or soil-husband — a matter of digging in the earth, not of enriching it.

I do not mean to say that the devices of engineering are always inappropriate; they have their place, especially in the restoration of land abused by the devices of engineering. My point is that to facilitate both water retention and drainage in the same place it is necessary to improve the soil, which is not a mechanical device but, among other things, a graveyard, a place of resurrection, and a community of living creatures. Devices may sometimes help, but only up to a point, for soil is improved by what humans do not do as well as by what they do. The proprieties of soil husbandry require acts that are much more complex than industrial acts, for these are acts conditioned by the ability *not* to act, by forbearance or self-restraint or sympathy or generosity. The industrial act, that is, is simply prescribed by thought, but the act of soil-building is also *limited* by thought. One builds soil by knowing what to do, but also by knowing what not to do and by knowing when to stop. Both kinds of knowledge are necessary because invariably, at some point, the reach of human comprehension becomes too short. At that point the work of the human economy must end in absolute deference to the working of the Great Economy. This, I take it, is the practical significance of the idea of Sabbath.

To push our work beyond that point, invading the Great Economy, is to become guilty of *hubris* or pride, the sin of presuming to be greater than we are. We cannot do what the topsoil does any more than we can do what God does nor what a swallow does. We can fly, but only as humans, very crudely, noisily, and clumsily. We can dispose of corpses and garbage, but we cannot, by our devices, turn them into fertility and new life. And we are discovering, to our great uneasiness, that some of our so-called wastes — those that are toxic or radioactive — we cannot dispose of. We can appropriate and in some fashion use godly powers, but we cannot use them safely and we cannot control the results. That is to say that the human condition remains for us what it was for Homer and the authors of the Bible. Now that we have brought such enormous powers, as we hope, to our aid, it seems more necessary than ever to observe how inexorably that condition still contains us. We only do what humans can do, and our machines, however they may appear to enlarge our possibilities, narrow our limitations and leave us more powerful but less content, less safe, and less free. The mechanical means by which we propose to escape the human condition only extend it. Thinking to transcend our definition as fallen creatures, we have only colonized more and more territory eastward of Eden.

Like the rich man of the parable, the industrialist thinks to escape the persistent obligations of the human condition by means of "much goods laid up for many years" — by means, in other words, of quantities: resources, supplies, stockpiles, funds, reserves. But this is a grossly oversimplifying dream, and thus a dangerous one. All the great natural goods that empower agriculture, some of which I have discussed, have to do with quantities, but they have to do also with qualities. They involve principles that are not static but active; they have to do with formal processes. The topsoil exists as such because it is ceaselessly transforming death into life, ceaselessly supplying food and water to all that lives in it and from it. Otherwise, "All flesh shall perish together, and man shall turn again unto dust." If we are to live well on and from our land, we must live by faith in the ceaselessness of these processes, and by faith in our own willingness and ability to collaborate with them. Christ's prayer for "daily bread" is an affirmation of such faith, just as it is a repudiation of faith in "much goods laid up." Our life and livelihood are the gift of the topsoil and of the human willingness and ability to care for the soil, to grow good wheat, to make good bread — not of stockpiles of raw materials or accumulations of purchasing power.

But the industrial economy can define potentiality, even the potentiality of the living topsoil, only as a *fund,* and thus must accept impoverishment as the inescapable condition of abundance. The invariable mode of its relation both to nature and to human culture is that of mining: withdrawal from a limited fund until that fund is exhausted. It removes natural fertility and human workmanship from bread. Thus the land is reduced to abstract marketable quantities of length and width, and bread to merchandise, high in money value, low in food value. "Our bread," Guy Davenport once said, "is more obscene than our movies."

But the industrial use of any "resources" implies its exhaustion. It is for this reason that the industrial economy has been accompanied by an ever-increasing hurry of research and exploration, the motive of which is not "free enterprise" or "the spirit of free inquiry," as industrial scientists and apologists would have us believe, but the desperation that naturally and logically accompanies gluttony.

One of the favorite words of the industrial economy is "control." We want "to keep things under control." We wish (we say) to "control" inflation and erosion. We have a discipline known as "crowd control." We believe in "controlled growth" and "controlled development," in "traffic control" and "self-control." But we are always setting out to control something that we refuse to limit, and so we make control a permanent and a doomed enterprise. If we will not limit causes there can be no controlling of effects. What is to be the fate of self-control in an economy that encourages and rewards unlimited selfishness?

More than anything else, we would like to "control the forces of nature," refusing at the same time to impose any limit on human nature. We assume that such control and such freedom are our rights," and that assumption seems to assure that our means of control of nature, and of all else that we see as alien, will be violent. It is startling to recognize the extent to which the industrial economy depends upon controlled explosions — in mines, in weapons, in the cylinders of engines, in the economic pattern known as "boom and bust." This dependence is the result of a progress that can be argued for. But those who argue for it are obliged, it seems to me, to recognize that in all these means good ends are served by a destructive principle, an association difficult to control if not limited. They must recognize too the inevitability that our failure to limit it has raised the specter of uncontrollable explosion. Nuclear holocaust, if it comes, will be the final detonation of an explosive economy.

An explosive economy, I take it, is not only an economy that is dependent upon explosions but one that will set no limits on itself. Any little economy that sees itself as unlimited is obviously self-blinded. It will not see its real relation of dependence and obligation to the Great Economy. It will not see that there *is* a Great Economy. It will call the Great Economy "raw material" or "natural resources" or "nature" and proceed with the business of putting it "under control."

But *control* is a word more than ordinarily revealing here, for its root meaning is to roll against, in the sense of a little wheel turning in opposition. The principle of control, then, involves necessarily the principle of division: one thing may turn against another thing only by being divided from it. This mechanical division and turning in opposition William Blake understood as evil, and he spoke of "Satanic wheels" and "Satanic mills": "wheel without wheel, with cogs tyrannic/Moving by compulsion each other." By "wheel without wheel" Blake meant wheel outside of wheel, one wheel communicating motion to the other, in the manner of two cogwheels, the point being that one wheel can turn another wheel outside itself only in a direction opposite to its own. This, I suppose, is acceptable enough as a mechanism. It becomes "Satanic" when it becomes a ruling metaphor and is used to describe and to organize fundamental relationships. Against the Satanic "wheel without wheel," Blake set the wheels of Eden, which "Wheel within wheel in freedom revolve, in harmony and peace." This is the "wheel in the middle of a wheel" of Ezekiel's vision (Ezek. 1:16) — an image, though not of course a description, of harmony. That the relation of these wheels is not mechanical we know from Ezekiel 1:12: "the spirit of the living creature was in the wheels." The wheels of opposition oppose the spirit of the living creature.

What had happened, as Blake saw accurately and feared justly, was a fundamental shift in the relation of humankind to the rest of creation. Sometime between say, Alexander Pope's verses on the Chain of Being in *An Essay on Man* and Blake's "London" the dominant minds had begun to see the human race not as a part or a member of Creation but as outside it and opposed to it. The industrial revolution was only a part of this change, but it is true that when the wheels of the industrial revolution began to revolve they turned against nature, which became the name for all of Creation thought to be below humanity, as well as, incidentally, against all once thought to be above humanity. And this would perhaps have been safe enough if nature, if all the rest of Creation, had been, as proposed, passively subject to human purpose.

Of course, it never has been. As Blake foresaw, as we now know, what we turn against must turn against us. Blake's image of the cogwheels turning in relentless opposition is terrifyingly apt, for in our vaunted war against nature, nature fights back. The earth may answer our pinches and pokes "only with spring," as E. E. Cummings said, but if we pinch and poke too much she can answer also with flood or drought, with catastrophic soil erosion, with plague and famine. Many of the occurrences that we call "acts of God" or "accidents of nature" are simply forthright natural responses to human provocations. Not always; I am not implying that by living in harmony with nature we can be free of floods and storms and droughts and earthquakes and volcanic eruptions. I am only pointing out, as many others have done, that by living in opposition to nature we can cause natural calamities that we would otherwise be free of.

The problem seems to be that a human economy cannot prescribe the terms of its own success. In a time when we wish to believe that humans are the sole authors of the truth or that truth is relative or that value judgments are all subjective, it is hard to say that a human economy can be wrong; yet we have good, sound, practical reasons for saying so. It is possible for human economy to be wrong; not relatively wrong, in the sense of being "out of adjustment," or unfair according to some human definition of fairness, or weak according to its own definition of its own purposes, but wrong absolutely and according to practical measures. Of course, if we see the human economy as the *only* economy, we will see its errors as political failures and will continue to talk about "recovery." But to think about only one thing is not to think at all. To think, we have to think about two things and the differences between them. It is only when we think of the little human economy in relation to the Great Economy that we begin to understand our errors for what they are and to see the qualitative meanings of our quantitative measures. If we see the industrial economy in terms of the Great Economy, then we begin to see industrial wastes and losses not as "tradeoffs" or "necessary risks" but as costs which, like all costs, are chargeable to somebody, sometime.

That we can prescribe the terms of our own success and that we can live outside or in ignorance of the Great Economy are the greatest errors. They condemn us to a life without a standard, wavering in inescapable bewilderment from paltry self-satisfaction to paltry self-dissatisfaction. But since we have no place to live but in the Great Economy, whether or not we know that and act accordingly is the critical question, not about economy merely but about human life itself.

It is possible to make a little economy, such as our present one, which is so short-sighted, in which accounting is of so short a term, as to give the impression that vices are necessary and practically justifiable. When we make our economy a little wheel turning in opposition to what we call "nature," which is in reality the Great Economy, then we set up competitiveness as the ruling principle in our explanation of reality and in our understanding of economy; we make of it, willy-nilly, a virtue. But competitiveness, as a ruling principle and a virtue, imposes a logic that is extremely difficult, perhaps impossible, to control. Competitiveness asks for the maximum of profit or power with the minimum of responsibility. That logic explains why our cars and our cloths are shoddily made, why our "wastes" are toxic, and why our "defensive" weapons are suicidal. And it explains also why it is so difficult for us to draw a line between free enterprise and crime. If our economic ideal is maximum profit with minimum responsibility, why should we be surprised to find our corporations so frequently in court and robbery on the increase? Why should we be surprised to find that medicine has become an exploitive industry, profitable in direct proportion to its hurry and its mechanical indifference. People who pay for shoddy products or careless

services and people who are robbed outright are equally victims of theft, the only difference being that the robbers outright are not guilty of fraud.

If, on the other hand, we see ourselves as living within the Great Economy, under the necessity of making our little human economy within it, according to its terms, the smaller wheel turning in sympathy with the greater, receiving its being and its motion from it, then we see that the virtues are necessary and are practically justifiable. Then, because in the Great Economy *all* transactions count and the account is never "closed," the ideal changes. We see that we cannot *afford* maximum profit or power with minimum responsibility, because in the Great Economy the loser's losses finally afflict the winner. Now the ideal must be "the maximum of well-being with the minimum of consumption," which both defines and requires neighborly love. Competitiveness cannot be the ruling principle, for the Great Economy is not a "side" that we can join, nor are there such "sides" within it. It is not the sum of its parts but their membership, the parts inextricably joined to each other, indebted to each other, receiving significance and worth from each other and from the whole. One is obliged to "consider the lilies of the field" neither because they are lilies nor because they are exemplary but because they are fellow members and because, as fellow members, we and the lilies are in certain critical ways alike.

To say that within the Great Economy the virtues are necessary and practically justifiable is at once to remove them from that specialized, sanctimonious, condescending practice or virtuousness that is humorless, pointless, and intolerable to its beneficiaries. For a human, the good choice in the Great Economy is to see its membership as a neighborhood and oneself as a neighbor within it. I am sure that virtues count in a neighborhood — to "love thy neighbor as thyself" requires the help of all seven of them — but I am equally sure that in a neighborhood the virtues cannot be practiced as such. Temperance has no appearance or action of its own, nor does justice or prudence or fortitude, faith or hope or charity. They can only be employed on occasions. "He who would do good to another," William Blake said, "must do it in Minute Particulars. . . ." To help each other, that is, we must go beyond the cold-hearted charity of the "General Good" and get down to work where we are:

Labour well the Minute Particulars, attend to
   the Little-ones,
And those who are in misery cannot remain so
   long
If we do but our duty: labour well the teeming
   Earth.

It is the Great Economy, not any little economy, that invests minute particulars with high and final importance. In the Great Economy each part stands for the whole and is joined to it; the whole is present in the part and is its health. The industrial economy, by contrast, is always striving and failing to make fragments (pieces that *it* has broken) *add up* to an ever-fugitive wholeness.

Work that is authentically placed and understood within the Great Economy moves virtue toward virtuosity: skill and technical competence. There is no use in helping our neighbors with their work if we do not know how to work. When they are rightly practiced within the Great Economy, we do not call the virtues virtues; we call them good farming, good forestry, good carpentry, good husbandry, good weaving and sewing, good housewifery, good parenthood, good neighborhood, and so on. The general principles are submerged in the particularities of their engagement with the world. Lao Tzu saw the appearance of the virtues as such, in the abstract, as indicative of their loss:

When people lost sight of the way to live
Came codes of love and honesty . . .
When differences weakened family ties
Came benevolent fathers and dutiful sons;
And when lands were disrupted and
   misgoverned
Came ministers commended as loyal.

Those lines might be read as an elaboration of the warning against the appearance of goodness at the beginning of the sixth chapter of Matthew.

The work of the small economy, when it is understandingly placed within the Great Economy, minutely particularizes the virtues, carries principle into practice, and to the extent that it does so it escapes specialization. The industrial economy requires the extreme specialization of work, the separation of work from its results, because it subsists upon divisions of interest and must deny the fundamental kinships of producer and consumer, seller and buyer, owner and worker, and work and product, parent material and product, nature and artifice, thoughts and words and deeds. Divided from those kinships, specialized artists and scientists identify themselves as "observers" or "objective observers," that is, as outsiders without responsibility for consequences or involvement in results. But the industrialized arts and sciences are false, their division is a lie, for there is no specialization of results.

There is no outside to the Great Economy. There is no escape into either specialization or generality. There is no "time off." Even insignificance is no escape, for in the membership of the Great Economy everything signifies; whatever we do counts. If we do not serve what coheres and endures, we serve what disintegrates and destroys. We *presume* that we are outside the membership that includes us, but that is only to damage the membership, and ourselves, of course, along with it.

In the industrial economy, the arts and the sciences are specialized "professions," each having its own language, speaking to none of the others. But the Great Economy proposes arts and sciences of membership: ways of doing and ways of knowing which cannot be divided from each other or within themselves, speaking the common language of the communities where they are practiced.

Unoriginal Sin: The Judeo-Christian Roots of Ecotheology

Robert H. Nelson

Many participants in environmental decision-making have assumed that the goal of environmental policy is to reduce pollution, improve air and water quality, and achieve other environmental objectives in an efficient way. Yet, experience has shown that magnitudes of benefits, levels of costs, and other factors affecting efficiency often play little part in environmental policy-making. Decisions are instead frequently made as an act of symbolic affirmation, to make a statement for or against a particular set of values. Indeed, on close inspection, environmental policy-making often turns out to be a battlefield for religious conflict. Rather than rational policy analysis, the making of natural resource and environmental policy in the United States has become an exercise in theological controversy.

Many environmentalists today have no objection to the characterization of their outlook as a religion. They readily acknowledge a goal to change the values of society and that the values they seek to promote rest on what is fundamentally a religious underpinning. The leading historian — an energetic advocate as well — of American environmentalism, Roderick Nash, recently described environmental views as deriving from a set of "eco-theologians" who propound a new "gospel of ecology." There is in the "recent concern for nature" what Nash describes as a

Robert H. Nelson, "Unoriginal Sin: The Judeo-Christian Roots of Ecotheology," *Policy Review,* no. 53 (Summer 1990): 59-94.

"quasi-religious fervor." Joseph Sax, in making the case for reducing the human presence in the national parks, states candidly that he and other preservationists are in truth "secular prophets, preaching a message of secular salvation."

Environmentalism is, to be sure, a diverse movement. Many people support environmental improvements for practical reasons that have nothing to do with environmental theology. They simply want clean air and water, parks for recreation, and protection of wildlife. Nor are all environmentalists skeptical of science or opposed to economic argument. For many environmentalists, taking care of the environment is simply a matter of doing economics better — factoring in all the benefits (including nonmarket benefits) and taking proper account of private actions that have impacts not accurately reflected in market profits and losses.

Yet, the growing importance of the theological element means that those who would engage environmentalists in constructive dialogue may find that they have no choice but to enter the realm of theological discussion. Increasingly, the environmental policy analyst must address matters not only of physical science, economics, and other conventional policy subjects, but of theology as well.

Greener Pastors

Modern discussions of environmental theology have been strongly influenced by a 1967 article in *Science* in which the historian Lynn White Jr. asserted that contemporary environmentalism required a sharp break from the Judeo-Christian heritage. Because the Bible teaches that the earth and its creatures are created to serve the purposes of mankind, according to White, "Christianity made it possible to exploit nature in a mood of indifference to the feelings of natural objects." White believed the environmental crisis of the current age required "a new religion," perhaps inspired by the faiths of "ancient paganism and Asia's religions," in which humanity must be understood as part of and not distinct from nature. White also drew inspiration from some Christian teachers, particularly St. Francis of Assisi.

The messages of contemporary environmentalism are widely seen — by environmentalist supporters and critics alike — as a major step toward the fulfillment of White's prescription of the pantheistic veneration of nature. Yet, despite its wide influence, White's argument has served more to confuse than to illuminate the actual tenets of environmental theology. The laws of nature frequently are not the laws of an idyllic or pastoral world; they are the Darwinian laws of the jungle — "Nature, red in tooth and claw," as Tennyson put it. Indeed, rather than becoming a part of nature as White asserted, the actual goal of environmentalism is the opposite: to inculcate a new morality with respect to the natural world that is found nowhere else in nature. No other creature is obligated to protect other species — as the Bible says that Noah was once commanded to do, and as the Endangered Species Act of 1973 again seeks to accomplish.

Environmental theology typically says little or nothing about God: it offers no answers concerning the hereafter; it is vague about the route of personal salvation; and in other respects it departs from basic tenets of the Judeo-Christian heritage. Yet, perhaps more remarkable is the extent to which environmentalism actually incorporates elements from the western religious heritage. Indeed, the real source of the appeal of environmentalism may be that it offers traditional religious messages of the West in a new secular form — a form that, in an age of rampant secularism, lends these traditional messages great authority for large numbers of people.

Devil's Design

One source of modern environmental theology is the long, powerful tradition within Christianity that regards wealth and riches, sophisticated reasoning, the structures of the law — all the formal institutions of society and of the good life — as dangerous and corrupting influences. These instruments all too often serve, not the will of God, but the devious designs of the devil. Since the fall of man from the Garden of Eden, human weakness has rendered the products of human reason unreliable, often deluding man to false optimism and excessive confidence in his powers. The leading American Catholic theologian of the 20th century, John Courtney Murray, once labeled this tradition within Christianity as one of "contempt of the world" and found that it has seen "sin as a permanent human fact that casts a shadow over all human achievements." This tradition encourages asceticism (and had an important influence on a number of monastic orders), spurns the attempt to perfect an earthly existence, and suggests that man "should by right neglect what is called the cultural enterprise — the cultivation of science and the arts, the pursuit of human values by human energies, the work of civilization." This outlook often asserts that the world is about to be overcome by the forces of evil — but there can still be hope that "in the moment [of collapse] the light disperses the darkness."

Contemporary environmentalism shares a closely related outlook: a sense that modern civilization tempts man to evil and represents retrogression rather than progress; an apocalyptic foreboding concerning ecological catastrophe and the near-term future of the earth: an attitude that human reason, as today embodied in science, offers false promises and alienates man from his true self; a view that a widespread sinfulness has infected the world (now seen in the "assaults" on and the "raping" of nature that meet popular indifference); a condemnation of the pervasive greed that motivates current evils (found especially in corporate "profiteers" who abuse nature); a view that urban and industrial civilization cuts men off from deeper and truer natural instincts; and a desire for a return to an earlier and more natural existence — the existence of the earth long ago — in which the products of modern science and economics would be banished. The deliverers of such environmental messages today issue a new call for men to renounce their evil ways and to live in simple harmony with their true natures and with the divine order that governs the universe — much as Christianity has preached repentance and deliverance from sin, and obedience to God.

Unheavenly City

This belief in the alienation of man from his true nature existed in the western tradition even before the advent of Christianity. For Plato, the undermining and corrupting power of greed and other economic influences — destroying the virtues of the citizenry — explained the decline of man. In the latter part of the ancient Roman empire, Augustine brought together the Platonic tradition and Christian theology. For Augustine, life on earth offered an existence of sin and depravity, characterized by "the love of self" and the pursuit of self-interest, as exemplified by the corruption and debauchery of ancient Rome.

In the history of western religion, Martin Luther and the Protestant Reformation represent the next great statement of such a theology. Owing to the fall of man, reason is subverted; government, the law, and other institutional products of man's rational faculty will reflect the corrupted nature of man, exemplified for Luther by the Catholic Church. Reunion with man's true nature is not to be achieved in this world, but is possible only in a heavenly future. Luther also continued the Platonic and Augustinian tradition of seeing economic competition and the pursuit of self-interest as forces of darkness. . . .

Is Man Part of Nature?

Despite drawing heavily on the Judeo-Christian tradition, environmental theology also contains major new theological elements. In the western religious tradition, to return to an original state of nature has been to return to the sinless condition of mankind in the Garden of Eden — or, for many secular theologies of the modern age, to some primitive tribal existence. Current environmental theologians, however, now have available to them the fairly recent scientific knowledge that for all but a very limited recent span, nature did not include human beings. To return to the original nature of creation thus might now be interpreted to mean a return to a state of nature that preceded human influence.

This theological logic is today exhibited in the formal criteria for designation of wilderness areas, where it is precisely the absence of signs and human presence that must be documented. Following a similar logic, the National Park Service maintains a policy to avoid interfering with nature and to seek to return to original natural conditions preceding human influence (thus, manmade fires are fought but "natural" fires are allowed to burn).

The government goes to great lengths to regulate very small quantities of manmade pesticides, but sees little problem in the widespread presence of dangerous pesticides that are created naturally by plants and vegetables. Global warming due to natural causes would be a cause for concern, but would no doubt stimulate much less public alarm than warming due to a buildup of gases caused by human activities. In each case the violation of nature is the basic concern, not the risk or other impact on human well-being.

"The AIDS of the Earth"

Environmental theology faces a dilemma that could prove insuperable: How can mankind find harmony with and return to an original state of nature when the very presence of man may now be seen as foreign to original nature? One theoretical answer would be the disappearance of mankind. Many environmental proponents seeking to limit the violation of nature support a sharply reduced human population on earth. A former leader of Greenpeace, Paul Watson, recently commented that "our species [is] the AIDS of the Earth: we are rapidly eroding the immune system of the Earth . . . destroying [her] ability to cleanse herself." If so, perhaps the proper fate of humanity might even be the same that medical research today seeks for AIDS.

Such theological logic was actually carried to this extreme by the author of a proposal — hopefully offered somewhat tongue-in-cheek — that appeared a while ago in a radical environmental publication: "Only a very few of human pathogens are shared by other partners on our planet. Biological warfare will have no impact on other creatures, big or small, if we design it carefully." Although few if any environmentalists would so advocate, in some fringe groups serious proposals are being made to exclude signs of human presence from as much as one-third of the land area of the earth.

Some environmentalists have avoided this theological difficulty by arguing that man should be seen not as foreign to but as an inherent part of nature — no different in any fundamental way from the plants, animals, and perhaps even inanimate objects of the natural world. A faith of an animistic or pantheistic character would result: worshipping nature and seeking a unification of man with the divine element to be found directly and literally in the natural world.

However, these environmentalists face a theological problem of equal severity. If the lion is not to be condemned morally for wanton acts of cruelty against other creatures, why, then, should mankind be judged harshly for making practical use of the natural world? This brand of environmental theology ends up in a virtual self-contradiction: men are to look to the current natural world for their values and spiritual sustenance, yet are instructed to behave and are to be judged by a standard found nowhere else in nature.

Law of Nature and of Nature's God

Lynn White's influential argument that only a new and nonwestern religion could protect the environment has diverted attention from a more promising theological direction for the environmental movement. Few would dispute that there are new threats to the world ecology; that there are growing numbers of people, creating increased demands on natural resources; and that quality of life becomes a greater concern as other basic human needs are met. These factors and others suggest the necessity of taking active steps to maintain and improve environmental quality. Yet, it does not follow that a brand-new theology is needed to justify such efforts. Indeed, perhaps reinterpreted a bit to take account of improved ecological knowledge and other changing circumstances, the messages of the Judeo-Christian tradition not only offer ample scope for environmentalism but firmer grounds for the development of an environmental ethic and a theology of environmental protection.

While deep ecology and other branches of environmental theology have borrowed from the ascetic tradition of Christianity, there are other theological outlooks of equal importance. Besides the tradition of "contempt of the world," John Courtney Murray labeled a second and much different central tradition of Christianity as one of "affirmation of the worldly." There is no need to reject the current social order and its values, but man should set about "building himself a world"

through the historical processes already at work. Although this theological tradition recognizes man's sinful nature, it sees history as not the story of a fall into every greater sin and evil, but potentially of the progressive realization of "the life of reason" with the help of God.

Such a worldly and rationalist outlook reached a high point in Christianity in the theology of Thomas Aquinas. If Martin Luther saw rational argument as often subversive of strong faith, for Aquinas a life of reason brought man closer to God. Much of Christian theology over the centuries has been grounded in a natural law tradition that finds in reason the means to discover the divine intent for this world.

Worldly Environmentalism

Murray argues that the natural law outlook could also be found at the core of "the American proposition," which was embedded in the Constitution and had been closely reflected in American institutions ever since. Americans saw the world in optimistic terms, believed in progress here on earth, saw reason as the means to progress, and regarded a life lived according to reason as a correct life. To the extent that American environmentalism seeks to deliver an opposing ascetic and antirational message, its probable fate will be rejection in America — much as the Marxist message of ever-deepening alienation was earlier rejected.

The worldly and rational tradition in western theology, moreover, offers a more promising route for actually achieving practical improvements in man's relationship to the environment. A deep concern for the environment is a logical part of the advancement of man's worldly condition. Rather than representing an alienating and subversive influence, science and other rational inquiry may be required to find a superior means of protecting the environment. Indeed, it is an other-worldly theology that is more likely to end up neglecting the environment, because results in this world count for so little. In short, those who see the realization of God's design taking place at least partly here on earth are most likely to regard environmental protection and improvement as an indispensable part of the divine plan for the world.

The role of man as steward of the earth is an important biblical theme. Although environmentalists have often found fault with the dominion themes of the first chapter of Genesis, the second chapter asserts that God has placed man in the Garden of Eden "to till it and care for it." While men are directed to use the earth for their own purposes they are not to do so in irresponsible or uncaring ways. As eloquently expressed in Psalms 8 and 24, man's dominion is clearly a delegated dominion, leaving him accountable to God, who maintains actual ownership of the earth. While God has created man "a little lower than the angels and . . . has made him to have dominion over the works of [His] hands" (Psalm 8:5, 6), still, "The earth is the Lord's, and the fulness thereof: the world and they that dwell therein" (Psalm 24:1).

However, a return to the biblical mode of stewardship may deprive environmentalism of some of the spiritual force that it currently derives from the conviction of having discovered new religious truths and a new faith. Yet, by often failing to acknowledge its original inspiration, environmentalism today is guilty of historical ignorance and is unable to draw upon theological lessons learned over many centuries — sometimes at great cost in human lives and effort. For example, history shows that to seek to guide technological and economic advances more successfully may be possible, but to seek to reverse them and to return to a state of nature of the distant past is another matter altogether. More and more, however, environmental theology today is preaching the latter — a goal of renouncing modern ways of living and seeking in actual practice to organize society on the basis of achieving a "natural" existence in which "artificial" signs of human presence would be minimized. . . .

Those who seek an impossible and utopian goal tend to forfeit the opportunity to shape the future constructively. While winning many symbolic victories, contemporary environmentalism has often failed to win the larger wars. The impractical and unworldly side of environmentalism shows up, for example, in the strong resistance shown by many environmentalists to use of market methods and incentives to bring about environmental improvements. If environmental theology preaches a return to original nature and an elimination of signs of human presence, some policy successes may be achieved, such as creating wilderness areas, but there is likely to be little impact over broad areas of political and economic concern. If environmental moralists ultimately have much practical impact, it might be to sow economic and political disorganization. Well-intended but misconceived environmental policies could impose large costs on society without much corresponding real gain to the environment.

The Christian ascetic tradition has often been in conflict with the Christian concern for uplifting the poor. So, too, many of the actions supported by environmentalists would be detrimental to the less advantaged people of the world. One prominent environmentalist, Paul Ehrlich, has suggested that the poor in some nations may have to starve if world population is to be effectively controlled. At a local level, the effect of rigorous environmental controls on growth is frequently to drive up the cost of living, restricting the housing opportunities of the less advantaged. Policies that restrict pollution without attention to costs and benefits can needlessly take away job opportunities. In preaching that material possessions and the good life are unnatural and to this extent evil, environmental theology suggests that the poor should be content with their condition and are perhaps even better off for it — an outlook that could eventually shape government policies.

In the future, environmental theology will have to recognize that man and physical nature are distinct. According to the very framework of environmental thought, man has obligations in the world that no other animal, plant, or inanimate object in nature possesses. Such a message is not found in science, which regards man as another mere object subject to the same laws as found elsewhere in nature. It is instead a biblical message. The responsibility to be good stewards of the earth follows from the essence of the biblical creation message — that man alone among creatures was created in the image of God and that man therefore has unique responsibilities for the rest of the earth. Environmentalism and the Judeo-Christian heritage are not necessarily in conflict; indeed, modern environmentalism is in some respects another theological variation of this heritage, one that could benefit from a greater recognition of the original inspiration.

Ecological Integrity and Christian Political Responsibility

James A. Nash

The Bishop of Bamberg in 1338 and his successor in 1398 were required to take an intriguing environmental pledge. In an age of dangerous deforestation in parts of Europe, when the food, fuel, and building materials of the woodland were vital to the economy, the bishops vowed to take the forests, not only the people, under their faithful protection!

This historical tidbit suggests a model for the churches in our ecologically distorted times — so long as we make due allowance for the fact that all Christians, not only the overseers, are entrusted with the gift and task of ministry. In an age when even *Time* magazine has become an environmental prophet, dramatizing humanity's profligate mismanagement by selecting the Endangered Earth as Planet of the Year, rather than its Usual Man or Woman of the Year, the circumstances indicate that all Christians and their communions should take the pledge to become faithful protectors of the ecosphere.

The ecological crisis can no longer be dismissed with caricatures, like the charge that environmentalism is the idle luxury of elites who prefer the preservation of puffins and peccaries to poor people. A wealth of empirical data confirms that the crisis is severe, systemic, and multi-dimensional. The problem is local, having its own forms in each place, and global, expressing itself in

James A. Nash, "Ecological Integrity and Christian Political Responsibility," *Theology and Public Policy* 1 (Fall 1989): 32-48.

forms, carried by the wind and water, which affect every place. It is a hydra-headed monster.

The major dimensions of the crisis include: 1) *Pollution.* A multitude of chemical and radioactive toxics, from pesticides to plutonium, are dumped into the world's waters, air, soils, and stratosphere, poisoning and genetically distorting humans and other creatures. A recent EPA survey documented the disposal of 10.4 *billion* pounds of toxics by major industries in the United States alone in 1987 alone — and the survey was significantly incomplete! 2) *Resource Exhaustion.* Non-renewable resources, like fossil fuels and major minerals, are being exhausted at an accelerating pace without regard for the future. Renewable resources, like water and soil, fish and trees, are being overconsumed through unsustainable practices in agriculture, forestry, fisheries, and industrialization. 3) *Gobal Warming.* The world's temperature is rising, perhaps 3-8 degrees F in the next 50 years, as a consequence of a "greenhouse effect" caused by levels of carbon dioxide in the atmosphere (induced largely by the burning of fossil fuels) which exceed the capacities of the oceans and depleted forests to absorb. The likely results include weather changes and sea-level rises, destroying wetlands, armlands, forests, and cities, and forcing mass migrations. 4) *Ozone Depletion.* The stratospheric ozone layer, which absorbs dangerous ultraviolet radiation, is itself endangered primarily by manufactured chlorofluorocarbons which destroy ozone molecules. The probable results are increased cancers, genetic aberrations, and shifts in ecological balances. 5) *Over-Population.* The world's human population of roughly 5.2 billion probably will increase to 10 billion by 2025 and 14 billion before 2100 unless the use of birth control increases substantially. The grim consequences will likely be further destruction of species and their habitats, increased pollution and consumption of scarce resources, and extensions of poverty and starvation. 6) *Maldistribution.* Less than one-fourth of the human population consumes more than three-fourths of the world's goods, and this minority is responsible for the bulk of the world's environmental degradation. The poor, moreover, are often forced to destroy their environments — causing deforestation and desertification — in order to avoid starvation and pay their debts. 7) *Radical Reductions and Extinc-*

tions of Species. Within the upcoming decades, at least hundreds of thousands, perhaps millions, of the earth's 5 to 30 million unique, irreplaceable plant and animal species, with their genetic secrets and evolutionary potential, could be irreversibly exterminated, largely as a consequence of the fragmentation and destruction of specialized habitats.

The nations are committing ecocide and, in the process, homicide. The ecological crisis, therefore, warrants a prime place on the churches' political agenda, ranking with the quest for economic justice and the banning of nuclear weapons (the ultimate environmental threat). The problems are too radical to be resolved by modest means. Changing our personal life-styles — for instance, by turning down thermostats and driving fuel-efficient vehicles — are necessary and valuable, but insufficient. Solutions must be proportionate to the problem. Serious governmental action and international collaboration are essential — and so is Christian advocacy to urge effective and equitable responses by public policy-makers.

For the churches, however, the ecological crisis is more than a political challenge. It is initially a theological-ethical challenge. The crisis is partially rooted in theological-ethical convictions about the rights and powers of humankind in relation to the rest of the biophysical world. According to one prominent conception, humankind is a distinctive creation — a species segregated from nature and possessing ultimate sanctions to dominate and exploit nature's bountiful supply of the "raw materials" provided for human benefit, without regard for physical limitations, biological connections, or moral obligations. This viewpoint reflects the fundamental failures which are at the bottom of the ecological crisis: the failure to adapt to the limiting conditions (the carrying and recuperative capacities) of our earthly habitat, the failure to recognize the intricate and interdependent relationships between humankind and the rest of the ecosphere, and the failure to respond benevolently to the fact of human kinship with all creation.

The Christian traditions bear at least some responsibility for propagating these failed perspectives. But the Christian faith is not confined by these environmental distortions. It embodies theological affirmations which provide solid groundings for environmental ethics and political action.

Two questions, then, must occupy our atten-tion: What are the implications of the central affirmations of the Christian faith for an environmental ethic? What directions are suggested by such an ethic for public policy in the 90s?

Theological Foundations

Ecological concern has rarely been a prominent, let alone a dominant, feature in Christian theory or practice. In fact, the mainstream traditions in the West generally have perceived the ecosphere as theologically trivial, if even relevant. The biophysical world has been treated either as the scenery or stage for the divine-human drama (which alone has redemptive significance) or as a composite of "things" which have no meaning or value beyond their utility for human production and consumption. The theological mainstreams, though by no means every tributary or every element in the mainstreams, have displayed, as Donald Worster charges, "a calculated indifference, if not antagonism, toward nature." Anthropocentrism has been and remains a norm in the dominant strains of Christian theology and piety, and it has served as both a stimulus and a rationalization for environmental destruction in Christian-influenced cultures.

Nonetheless, minority voices for ecological sensitivity have been present in Christian history. The Orthodox churches, for example, in their theology and piety, have retained the expectation of redemption for all creation and sanctification of matter through the incarnation. The popular stories of St. Francis and the Celtic saints, filled with embellished accounts of mutual affection and service between saints and animals, have been influential as ecological models throughout Christendom. Some prominent theologians in all traditions have expounded what Paul Santmire calls "the ecological motif." But even in these contexts, environmental consciousness generally is not only marginal, but also ambiguous. This fact is hardly surprising, since the untamed ecosphere is itself, from a human perspective, ambiguous, containing both beneficial and harmful elements, and generating mixed attitudes of antipathy and appreciation.

Despite the apparent ecological weaknesses in Christian traditions, the Christian faith is certainly not ecologically moribund. During the last three decades, a growing number of scholars, from "progressive evangelicals" like a team of scholars from Calvin College to process theologians like John Cobb, have been discovering or rediscovering the ecological potential in Christian convictions. In its central affirmations, not simply in its peripheral elements, the Christian faith offers a solid, ultimate grounding for a strong environmental ethic. In a sense, the churches do need "new" theological and ethical bases for sustaining environmental integrity. But this need does not entail the abandonment or replacement of Christianity's main themes. Rather, it requires extensions and reinterpretations of these themes in ways which preserve their historic identity and which are consistent with ecological data. To illustrate the promising dimensions of the Christian faith, I will outline some of the implications of several key Christian doctrines for environmental ethics and action.

1. Creation

The church confesses its faith in God as Maker of heaven and earth. God is the Pantocrator, the sovereign source and sustainer of all being and becoming, the ultimate provider and universal proprietor. All inhabitants of this planet or any planet, from humans to single-cell organisms, are creatures — creations of God and totally dependent on God's providential preservation and parental care. The whole of nature — the biophysical universe — is not the antithesis of grace, but rather an expression of grace, God's lovingkindness, which characterizes God's nature and acts. God *is* love. Therefore, the creative process is an act of love, and its creatures are products of love and the ongoing recipients of love.

Since God is the source of all, all creatures share in a common relationship. Thus, St. Francis called other creatures, from worms to wolves, brothers and sisters, "because he knew they had the same source as himself." This kinship of all creatures is symbolized in Genesis 2:7, 19 where both human and other animals are formed by God from the same element, the earth. It is enhanced, incidentally, by the theory of evolution, which describes humans as related to every other form of life through our common beginnings in one or more living cells and through our subsequent adaptive

interactions. The doctrine of creation implies that nature is not alien to humans; we are inter-related parts and products of a world which is continually being made and nurtured by God.

The creation is also "good" — indeed, as a whole, "very good" (Gen. 1:31). God takes delight in the results of the creative process (Ps. 104:31), because they correspond with God's intentions and expectations. Thus, the ecosphere is valued by the Source of Value even in all its moral ambiguity — including the predation, parasitism, and prodigality which are inherent parts of the dynamics of evolution and ecology. The creation and its creatures are declared to be "good," according to Genesis 1, *before* the emergence of *homo sapiens*. In other words, they have value independent of human interests, and this value exists even in a wild, virginal state, prior to the taming, technological transformations of human managers. Divine valuations, therefore, appear to be cosmocentric and biocentric, not simply homocentric. The world was created as a habitat not only for humanity but also for all created beings. Since fidelity to God implies respect for the divine purposes, we are called to love what God loves, and that includes the whole good creation.

For the Christian faith, however, the affirmation of the goodness of creation is also an expression of ultimate confidence in the goodness of God. The world now has an interim goodness; it overflows with marvels and sustains diverse forms of life, for a time. But it is also a world of systemic alienation, in which all life is temporary and destructive of other life. The creation needs liberation and reconciliation. Thus, the Christian church has always linked creation and redemption. Christ is the mediator of creation (John 1:1-3; 1 Cor. 8:6; Col. 1:15-17; Heb. 1:2-3). To say with the Nicene Creed that "all things were made" through Christ is to affirm that creation has a redemptive purpose from the beginning. The creation is very good because it is in the process of being brought to fulfillment by a good God — an expectation which, as we shall see, enhances Christian responsibility for environmental protection.

2. Covenant

The Noahic or Rainbow Covenant (Gen. 8:9-17) is a powerful Biblical symbol for ecological responsibility. God is portrayed in this story of the Flood as making an unconditional pledge in perpetuity to all humanity, to all other creatures, and to the earth itself, to preserve all species and their environments, so that *all* can "increase and multiply." This "ecological covenant," along with the story of the Ark itself, implicitly recognizes the interdependent relationships of all creatures in their ecosystems, and suggests that the Creator's purpose is to provide living space for all organisms. It is a symbol of the unbreakable bonds among all creatures and with their Creator.

This story provides a symbolic mandate for responsive loyalty to God's ecological fidelity. Environmental contempt, manifested, for example, in pollution, dehabitation, and extinctions, is a violation of the Rainbow Covenant and, therefore, an attack on the created order. It is disloyalty to God, other creatures, other humans, and ourselves, for we are all bound together with common interests in saving the integrity of our home, the Earth.

3. Incarnation

The Word became flesh (John 1:14). In the life and ministry, humiliation and glorification, of the fully human Jesus of Nazareth, the Christian church experienced its definitive encounter with the saving Christ. The fullness of divine grace entered the human condition, becoming immanent in the material, identifying with the finite, in this Representative Human. In doing so, however, God united with the whole biophysical universe which humans embody and on which their existence depends. The Representative Human, therefore, is also the Representative of the Biosphere, indeed, the Ecosphere. Humans are *imago mundi*, a reflection of the world of nature. We are the microcosm which represents the macrocosm, past and present. The atoms in human bodies were once part of other creatures, including the original organisms. The chemical structure of the cells in our bodies is remarkably similar to that of the cells in all other creatures. We have evolved through adaptive interactions, along with all other creatures, from common ancestors. We are products of photosynthesis and every other earthly process. Through the flora, fauna, minerals, chemicals, and radiation we imbibe by eating, drinking, breath-

ing, and simply being, humans embody a representative sampling of all the elements of the ecosphere. Humans are of the earth, interdependent parts of nature — and this totality is what God associated with in the incarnation.

The ecological implications of the incarnation are significant. The doctrine confers dignity not only on humanity, but on biophysical materiality, everything earthly and heavenly. It sanctifies creation, making all things meaningful and worthy in the divine scheme. It sanctions human humility, reminding us of our common rootage and connections with other kinds. It justifies "biophilia," the affiliation with and affection for the diversity of life forms. When we destroy life, as predatorial creatures must to survive in this unredeemed world, we should do so sparingly and reverently, in recognition of the incarnation and in respect for our co-evolving kin. Wanton pollution, profligate consumption, and extinctions are sins from the perspective of the incarnation.

4. Sacramental Presence

We live in a "sacramental universe," as William Temple eloquently argued, in which the whole of material existence can be an effective vehicle of communion with God, a means of grace. Creation is a sacramental expression of the Creator. Since the transcendent God is also immanent, dwelling in the creation and not in deistic isolation, the world is the bearer of the holy, the temple of the Spirit. For the spiritually receptive, the cosmos is a complex of sacramental signs which convey the hidden but real presence of the Spirit "in, with, and under" the natural elements.

This intuition of the Spirit's presence in power and love has been a potent force in the development of a human affection for nature, with both spiritual and ethical consequences. The raw, natural world has been a prime place for encounters with the grandeur and glory of God. This world, however, cannot be romanticized. It remains an ambiguous reality — hostile yet hospitable, a threat to survival yet the means to survival, a source of joy and fear. Nonetheless, the natural world is omnimiraculous, filled with the extraordinary in the midst of the ordinary. As such, it arouses in many of us an awareness and appreciation of its Source. Whether stalking an elegant trogon in an Arizona canyon, or microscopically examining the marvelously intricate and dynamic interactions within a single, organic cell, or gazing into infinite space at an uncountable multitude of blazing stars, or exulting with that pious naturalist John Muir over the "wild beauty-making business" of "a noble earthquake" as an "expression of God's love," men and women have been filled with awe and wonder, moved to humility and contemplation, perplexed by the paradox of holistic order through brutal predation, overpowered by a sense of mystery, and yet strangely grasped by the consciousness of God's loving presence. This sensate spirituality experiences God in and through the "distractions" of the biophysical world, not by blocking the senses and transcending them.

As the habitation of the Spirit and the context of sacramental presence, the cosmos is a sacred place. Its integrity, therefore, demands respect. Its diversity and stability must be protected and nurtured, not only for its own sake but also for the sake of our physical *and* spiritual well-being.

5. Dominion and Sin

Humans are created — through the evolutionary process, we now know — to be the *image* of God and to exercise *dominion* (Genesis 1:26). The two concepts are closely related. Too frequently, and falsely, both have been interpreted as the divine grant of a special status making humanity the sole bearer of intrinsic value in creation, or of a special mandate to pollute, plunder, and prey on creation to the point of exhausting its potential. Biblically, however, the image is basically the God-given assignment to exercise dominion *in accord with God's values*. The image is not so much a unique status or sanction, but rather a special role or function — a vocation or calling, in recognition of humanity's peculiar creative powers and moral capacities. This interpretation does not diminish human dignity, but, instead, accentuates it. Humans act in the image of God when they are *responsible representatives*, reflecting, like governors or ambassadors of antiquity, the interests of their Sovereign. They exercise dominion properly when they are faithful stewards, who care for God's good creation in accord with the will of the ultimate owner. In fact, when interpreted in the context of Christ (the fulfillment of the image), the realiza-

tion of the image and the expression of dominion are representations of nurturing and serving love.

None of this denies, however, that humans must "subdue" — yes, trample, conquer — the earth's resistance in order to survive and maintain civilizations. The much-maligned but realistic writer of Genesis 1:28 chose the right word! The ecosphere is potentially hospitable to human interests, but that hospitality must be coerced by overcoming the earth's manifestations of seeming hostility or neutrality — predators and parasites, floods and flames, for example. From the beginning, the survival of the human species has been a struggle for food, shelter, fuel, health, and other basics. And human ingenuity — manifested in plows, shovels, axes, weapons, medicines, and their modern, sophisticated equivalents — has been a necessity for both primitive and civilized survival. The ecological crisis, however, is a result of imperialistic over-extension — the abuse of what was divinely intended for use, subduing far beyond the point of necessity, failing to nurture benevolently nature's potential hospitality. It is sin.

Sin is a declaration of autonomy from the sovereign source of our being. It is the refusal to act in the image of God as responsible representatives. It is the distortion of dominion into despotic domination. Ecologically, sin is expressed as the arrogant denial of the creaturely limitations on human ingenuity and technology, a defiant disrespect for the interdependent relationships of all creatures and their environments established in the covenant of creation, and an anthropocentric abuse of what God has made and values. Seeing the ecological crisis in the context of sin alerts us to the powers behind the plunderings and the intimidating obstacles to reform.

6. Consummation

John Muir berated Christianity for its "stingy heaven," since it allegedly had no room in the realm of redemption for a Yosemite bear. This charge is only partially justified. The hope for cosmic redemption is rooted in scripture (Isaiah 11:6-10; 65:17, 24-25; Col. 1:15-20; 1 Cor. 15:28; Eph. 1:10; Rom. 8:19-22). It has been preserved in the theological traditions of the Orthodox churches and, although generally not prominently, in a variety of Western theologians, including Luther, Calvin, and Wesley. This hope, however, has become fairly common among theologians in the last couple decades, perhaps spurred by ecological consciousness. Nevertheless, the predominant characteristic of Western traditions has been the absence of the hope for the consummation of creation. Heaven is exclusively for humans, or some of them, who alone have "rational, immortal souls." This belief has served as a major justification for depreciating the value of creation and destroying its allegedly valueless components.

The expectation of universal redemption is a necessarily vague vision of the consummation of shalom — reconciliation among all creatures (Isaiah 11:6-10) and liberation from the bondage to transience (Romans 8:21). Fundamentally, it is a statement of hope in the goodness and trustworthiness of God. The value-conserving God, who embraced all creation in the incarnation, and who inhabits all creation through the Spirit, will fulfill the creation, making it perfectly good.

Ecologically, this vision gives ultimate meaning and worth to the cosmic ecosphere. Nothing is any longer valueless or irrelevant; everything counts for itself and others ultimately. This perspective stands in judgment on anthropocentrism. If the natural world as a whole will participate in God's redemption, then all things must be treated as ends in themselves, and not simply as means to human ends. Moreover, this vision suggests a style for our relationships with the rest of nature. In the midst of the moral ambiguities of creation, we cannot yet experience the full harmony of the New Creation. The vision itself prevents such romantic illusions. Nonetheless, the vision represents the ultimate goal to which God is beckoning us. Our responsibility, then, is to approximate the harmony of the New Creation to the fullest extent possible under natural conditions.

7. Church

Prominent contemporary ecclesiologies virtually compel the role of the church as an advocate of ecological integrity. In theologies of hope, liberation, and even the classical Social Gospel, the church, ideally, is "the avant garde of the new creation." This conception reflects a widespread theological consensus that the originating tradition of the church — the apostolic witness in scripture — is thoroughly eschatological in orientation. The essence of the Gospel is the good news of the coming commonwealth of God, of which the resurrected Christ is the promise of our destiny and the life-giving Spirit is the power prodding us toward that destiny. From this perspective, the church is in the apostolic succession when it is a sign of this coming Commonwealth, proclaiming and participating in the divine mission to consummate communion with the whole creation. The church, then, is called to make its vision visible, in maximum conformity with the new creation. God's future goal is not simply our final destiny; it is also our moral responsibility. It is a summons to action, to shape the historical present, as the Lord's Prayer suggests, on the model of God's new heaven and earth. The church's ethical orientation is "eschatopraxis," doing the final future now in anticipation. Since God's ultimate goal is the perfection of harmonious relationships (shalom), the church's present task includes the pursuit of justice, peace, and ecological integrity.

The church's classical definition of itself as "catholic" or universal corresponds with this perspective. The term historically has connoted wholeness and fullness — including a comprehensiveness of concern to re-present the all-encompassing love of God. If ultimate catholicity is the consummation of liberation and reconciliation for all creation in the Reign of God, then the church is truly catholic — and truly reformed — when it anticipates and contributes to this Reign by embodying the whole Gospel for the full needs of all persons and other creatures in all places and times. Ecological responsibility, then, is a vital part of being the church catholic.

Love: The Ground of a Christian Ecological Ethic

What kind of ethic is consistent with the ecological implications of Christian doctrine, and also adequate to address the ecological crisis? From a Christian perspective, the answer must be an ethic of love — the humble, self-giving, other-regarding, compassionate, and passionate service embodied in Christ. Love is the integrating center of the whole of Christian faith and ethics — including, therefore, an ecological ethic.

Christianity affirms that love is the ground and goal of all being. As Christians, we trust in a God whose character is love. We experience that love in the mysteries of creation, in the cause of Jesus, in the grace evident on the cross and confirmed in the resurrection, and in the empowering and reconciling presence of the Holy Spirit. We hope for God's liberation of creation through love, and eternal life in a new order whose constitution is love. In imitation of Christ and in anticipation of the coming Commonwealth of God, the church is called to produce the fruits of justice and generosity, peace and unity, compassion and community, liberation and reconciliation — all of which are expressions of love. We seek to love as a grateful response to the grace-filled fact that God first loves us (1 John 4:19, Eph. 5:1) — and we are empowered to love by God's love working through us. In essence, therefore, the Christian faith is the confidence that the comprehensive ministries of God to the creatures of God are a mission of love, and our ministry in Christian ethics and action is to be a mirror image of that love.

Consequently, an ecological ethic which is grounded in the Christian faith is simply a reasonable extension of love to the whole creation, in order to represent the all-encompassing affection and care of God. Albert Schweitzer enlarged the meaning of love to cover every organism: "The ethic of Reverence for Life is the ethic of Love widened into universality. It is the ethic of Jesus, now recognized as a logical consequence of thought." Aldo Leopold, knowing the ecological connections between life and its habitats, broadened the boundaries of love to the whole ecosphere, "the land": "That land is a community is the basic concept of ecology, but that land is to be loved and respected is an extension of ethics." Christian love, similarly, is inclusive, because God's love is unbounded. The "love of nature" is simply the "love of neighbor" universalized, in recognition of our common origins, mutual dependencies, and shared destiny with God's whole creation.

Interpreting the meaning of Christian love for an ecological ethic, however, is a mental quagmire. Debates abound in Christian ethics about the definitions, types, characteristics, possibilities, demands, and dilemmas of love. And nearly all of these complicated controversies have focused exclusively on divine-human and interhuman relationships. In all situations pertaining to the demands of love, moral dilemmas and other conflicts of values are inevitable; purity and perfection are impossible. In ecological situations, however, these complexities are compounded. The tragedy of the human condition is that we must destroy other forms of life and their habitats in order to satisfy basic human needs and maintain the essentials of civilization. We cannot live without disrupting and killing. How is it possible, then, to express environmental love in this context? An adequate answer is hardly possible here, but it is important to suggest a rough outline of an answer.

Ecologically, Christian love is caring and careful service to retain and restore the integrity of the ecosphere, out of respect for the intrinsic worth of this community and its biotic components, human and otherkind. This love is beneficent, doing good by maintaining the health of the air, water, soil, and stratosphere, and by preserving the stability and diversity of species and their necessary habitats. This love is also just, protecting the earth and its species (collectively and individually) from wanton consumption, destruction, and pollution, and insuring the necessary conditions for ecological integrity and sustainability. (Indeed, the language of moral rights seems appropriate in this context, despite the objections of some ethicists who want to reserve this vocabulary exclusively for interhuman relationships.) Under the conditions imposed by universal love, human values remain primary. Yet, humans are bound by certain obligations and the nonhuman world is entitled to certain protections of its needs. The claims — or "rights" — of nature are not absolute. They can be overridden, but only with just cause, such as: satisfying basic human needs or valuable human benefits; exercising self-defense against, for example, crop pests, viruses, urban rats, and, yes, mosquitoes; or preventing the population of a species from exceeding the carrying capacities of its environment.

Christian environmentalists have a difficult time ahead in developing the meaning of love in an ecological context. The task, however, is essential and should be beneficial for understanding both the meaning of love and ecological responsibility.

Directions for Public Policy

Legislative and regulatory proposals for environmental protection are abundant, reflecting the breadth and dangers of the crisis. For example, *Blueprint for the Environment,* a comprehensive product of twenty major environmental organizations, contains 511 proposals for Federal action — and nearly all of these are important and reasonable. Political action by the churches requires involvement in such specifics, but the process does entail some risks. No straight line can be drawn between theology-ethics and public policy; too many factual disputes, judgment calls, value conflicts, and moral dilemmas block the way. The translation of Christian faith into moral norms and then into prudential laws and regulations is a complex and ambiguous process, and that translation becomes more tenuous with each step toward specificity. Yet, the risk of specificity must be taken to avoid ineffectiveness and innocuousness. The intention here, however, is not to add to the multitude of valuable policy proposals, but rather to suggest a few directions to guide churches in formulating and assessing political specifics. These directions seem to be compatible with the moral demands of Christian theology and especially important in light of the character of the ecological crisis.

First, the ecological crisis must be treated with the utmost seriousness. The counsel seems obvious, but it is also imperative. The churches too often have succumbed to faddism, focusing on a concern for a time, perhaps a biennium or even a quadrennium, and then neglecting it when a new and more glamorous issue seduces our attention. Environmentalism suffered that fate from the hands of the churches in the early 70s. The crisis, however, has intensified — partly because of neglect in the interim — and now demands tenacious attention. The planet and its diverse populations are in peril, poisoned and impoverished on a score of fronts simultaneously. The problems are serious and persistent, and the responses of the churches must be equally so. Environmental responsibility entails a stalwart and sustained commitment.

Second, the churches have a duty to insist that the interests of future generations be protected in current legislation and regulations. The tragedy of the ecological crisis is not only the damage done to the present generation, but also the harm caused to future generations — if, indeed, they will have the opportunity to exist. The vital interests of coming generations in a healthy and whole habitat are being sacrificed for the comforts and gratifications of the affluent in the present generation. Some in the present are receiving dubious benefits from resource depletions, extinctions, and toxic wastes, while future generations, if any, must bear the risks and costs. This mortgaging of the future is morbidly captured in a recent cartoon, "Washingtoon" by Mark Alan Samaty. It portrays a self-indulgent, anti-environmentalist emerging from a theater which is showing the movie "Global Warming Holocaust." He says: "Yeh! It was great! It was really scary, because you know it could really happen, but at the same time you feel sort of safe, because it might not happen until five minutes after our lifetime!" Contrary to those who deny obligations to future generations primarily because they do not yet exist, and despite the major difficulties and dilemmas in balancing allocations between present and future, the Christian faith assumes the legitimacy of intergenerational justice. Just as we have duties of hospitality to strangers in remote lands, so we have similar duties to future strangers in remote times. God's covenant is with "you and your descendants forever" (Gen. 13:15). Moral responsibilities apply not only to our children and grandchildren, but to the children and grandchildren of every generation in perpetuity, until the end of the age.

In light of the churches' role in anticipating the Reign of God, responsibility to future generations means not only that each generation should leave the ecosphere to its successors in as healthy a condition as it was received, but also that each generation should seek to enhance that condition by cleaning up the messes that its forebears left behind. No generation, moreover, should use more than its "fair share" of non-renewable resources like fossil fuels and minerals. If, however, this standard can be given some precision and if it is violated, excessive depletions should be "counterbalanced by the devising of new techniques so that succeeding generations have opportunities matching those of their predecessors." The compulsive overuse of fossil fuels in our generation, then, would seem to require the compensatory development of ecologically friendly energy technologies, like photovoltaics. Equally, just as the present generation cannot be sacrificed for a better future, so future generations should not be endangered irreversibly for the sake of the benefits of the present generation. If so, this criterion provides a compelling argument against nuclear energy. Plutonium wastes, stored in containers that will endure for only a few decades or even centuries, retain their potentially lethal effects through the lives of ten thousand generations!

In assessing public policy, therefore, the churches must be a voice for the unrepresented — future generations of both humans and otherkind, to insure that they have an opportunity to be and that their environment is sustained in a sound state.

Third, the churches must respond to the ecological crisis holistically and relationally. The crisis is not a single, discrete problem, like pollution. It is, instead, a massive mosaic of problems, which affects humans and "every creeping thing." The crisis is local and global, multidimensional and interrelated. Environmental problems cover everything from resource depletion to overpopulation. And each of the many specialities includes an array of subspecialties, so that our minds are overwhelmed by the volume and complexity of that monumental understatement: "the environmental problem."

Strategically, therefore, it is impossible — and even if it were possible, imprudent — to focus on all facets of the environmental crisis simultaneously. We must pick priorities rationally and concentrate resources efficiently to be politically effective. Obviously, then, the counsel to respond holistically and relationally does not mean to act imprudently. Instead, this counsel means to be aware of the multiple dimensions of the ecological crisis and their linkages, and to act in a way that the solution to one environmental problem does not cause or aggravate another environmental — or social — problem. It is a way to avoid the "tall stacks syndrome": the high smokestacks at coal-burning utilities in the Ohio River Valley prevent local pollution, but kill lakes and forests through acid rain in New England! Holistic and relational perspectives provide protection against the multiple forms of this syndrome.

Fourth, the churches must struggle to resolve the dilemma between environmental integrity and economic development. Increasingly, it appears that the nations cannot sustain both. Growthmania is a prime tenet of the American economic faith, and, in fact, an obsession which unites capitalism, socialism, and mixed economic ideologies. Allegedly, the perpetual expansion of production and consumption is necessary for progress and prosperity (measured quantitatively in GNP) — to satisfy the insatiable wants of consumers and to provide employment values — profits, capital for investments and improvements, employment, tax revenues for governmental programs, technological innovations, and philanthropic benefits. But economic growth is also a major factor in destroying the ecosystems on which the well-being of social and economic systems ultimately depends. Promiscuous production and consumption — industrial, agricultural, and land development, for instance — are key causes of resource depletion, pollution of various sorts, global warming, extravagant waste, species' reductions and extinctions, deforestation, erosion, and economic maldistribution in which multiple millions are starving or malnourished. The ideology of economic growth assumes the indestructibility and inexhaustibility of the products and capacities of nature — and this assumption makes this ideology a *utopian illusion!* It ignores the ecological reality of limits — the limits of renewable goods and non-renewable resources on a finite planet, the limits on the atmosphere to absorb toxic wastes, the limits on delicate ecosystems to survive the stresses of human interventions. Unbridled economic development is eventually destructive of the conditions for economic health. Economic systems — indeed, all social systems — cannot be sustained unless environmental systems are sustained, because human welfare depends on the productivity and integrity of the natural world.

Economic conversion to ecological sustainability, then, appears to be a social, economic, and ecological necessity. Some forms of economic development, of course, are environmentally neutral or friendly — various services and "soft" technologies, for example — but we can neither tolerate nor survive the indiscriminate material development which has characterized the "American way of life." We need alternatives — and they must include simpler lifestyles, stringent conser-

850

vation, rigorous regulations, pollution taxes, international cooperation, and equitable sharing of resources. One option that needs to be explored seriously is economist Herman Daly's model of a steady-state economy, with its emphases on population control, qualitative rather than quantitative development, production and consumption within the bounds of ecological sustainability, and the elimination of poverty through an equitable re-distribution of wealth. This model has been rejected by most conservative and liberal economists, but it is certainly compatible with traditional Christian norms for economic life. And some version of this model may be the only realistic means of resolving the economics-ecology dilemma. A major challenge to the churches of the 90s and beyond, therefore, will be to propose an alternative to our present brand of economic growth — one which enables the *sustainability* of a sound economy, one which preserves the *integrity* of the environment, and one which provides *sufficiency* for the basic needs of all humanity.

Fifth, the churches should be protectors of non-human species, insuring the conditions necessary for their perpetuation and ongoing evolution. This role of guardian of biodiversity does not mean the displacement or diminution of human values, but rather the enhancement of these values by embracing the human need for inclusive relationships. It is an expression of genuine dominion, in respect for our kinship and interdependence with other creatures, in acknowledgement of their intrinsic value, and in fidelity to the biocentric valuations of God. This role entails habitat protection in wildlife refuges and a variety of other sanctuaries integrated with human habitats, to insure that all species have sufficient space and other basic necessities to thrive. It means clean air, clean water, and clean soil. Generally, it means a *laissez faire* strategy — leaving the non-human world alone to work out its own adaptations and interactions without benefit of human managers, except insofar as interventions are necessary to correct for the disruptive influences of humankind (like the threat of extinctions). Defending biodiversity also requires controlling anthropocentric imperialism — for instance, by halting human population growth, so that all species can have a place in the sun.

Sixth, the churches' quest for ecological integrity must be pursued in alliance with the struggles for peace and justice. These concerns are interdependent and inseparable. That is the message implied by the World Council of Churches' slogan, "Justice, Peace, and the Integrity of Creation," by Christian environmentalists' stress on "ecojustice," and, indeed, by the Biblical concept of "shalom." Environmental problems cannot be fully resolved unless economic maldistribution, for example, is remedied. Otherwise, the people of poor nations are forced to exploit their natural resources beyond the limit — for example, by deforestation, overgrazing, overhunting, and unsustainable agriculture — in order to stay alive. The precipitous decline of roseate terns along the beaches of the northeastern United States is a simple illustration of this problem and its global consequences. These long-range migrants are being killed for food by hungry people in the southern hemisphere, prompting one naturalist to note, "The situation of the roseate terns is a microcosm of all our environmental problems: these problems can be alleviated by traditional conservation measures but cannot be solved without fundamental changes in the social and economic systems from which they derive." For the sake of environmental integrity and social justice, therefore, massive doses of economic assistance to impoverished nations — including debt relief and "debt for nature swaps" — will be helpful, and authentic economic equity among nations will be far better.

Equally, peace and justice are not achievable apart from environmental integrity. A stable and diverse ecosphere is a necessary condition of peaceful and just relationships within and among nations, for humans depend upon environmental health to make life possible and productive. Indeed, it is alarming to contemplate the social consequences of an environmental apocalypse: mass poisonings, leaps in cancer rates, increased poverty, more starvation, massive migrations, wars for scarce land and other resources, economic collapses, political dislocations, and spiritual lamentations. Environmental and social concerns, therefore, are not alternatives or competitors; they are inseparable partners.

These political directions for ecological integrity, of course, will be dismissed by many critics as unrealistic, idealistic, and/or utopian. Frankly, these criticisms have considerable merit. Knowing what we do about human resistance to fairness and attraction to self-gratification (sin!), achieving these goals seem at least uncommonly difficult, if even possible. But the church is not motivated merely by the calculation of possibilities or projections from the past! Rather, we are propelled by the consciousness of screaming needs and the vision of God's intended future. All we can do is work with faithful perseverance to achieve whatever is possible now, and hope that with each step forward, Providence will create new possibilities for the future.

This brings us to a . . . crucial point: markets and prices are not necessary conditions for economic value. Rather, markets and prices emerge from collective economic behavior when people can be excluded from the use and benefits of things unless they pay for them. Property rights protect owners' claims to things while prices facilitate an allocation of their claims. Without exclusivity, there is little reason for people other than a philanthropist to supply a commodity or an environmental resource, since without it they would not be compensated. Without exclusivity on the supply side and a sufficient interest or demand on the part of others to pay for something, markets and prices would not emerge.

Contrast things that are exchanged in markets with scenic vistas, clean ground water, national forests, and blue whales. Although the latter usually are not priced in traditional single-commodity markets, economic man still gets personal satisfaction from their existence. In fact, it seems difficult to argue that marketlike mechanisms, albeit nontraditional, do not allocate resources to protect environmental quality, wilderness, wildlife, and the likely interests of future generations when we pay taxes (and in many cases vote to raise taxes) for pollution control, ecosystem preservation, endangered species programs, and so on. In addition, conservation organizations are in effect voluntary, market-like systems for providing nonconsumptive recreation, species preservation, and environmental protection. Traditional markets and prices provide only one mechanism whereby these values are revealed. Limiting economics to the analysis of traditional markets is arbitrary.

— Steven Edwards, "In Defense of Environmental Economics," *Environmental Ethics* 9, no. 1 (1987): 77

How Green Is Our Gospel?

Andrew Steer

Seven months ago in June 1992, 178 nations gathered together in Rio de Janeiro for the earth summit. This was the largest international conference in the history of the world. The outcome was not spectacular, but nonetheless that conference, I believe, marked an agreement on a consensus concerning what sustainable development is and what kinds of policies are required for its implementation.

At the end of the conference, 116 heads of state and government sat around one table to discuss the conclusions. What was it that they agreed to? They agreed that the environment and development are not enemies as is commonly believed, as in the past, but are partners. They agreed that the old regime whereby economists promote growth at any costs and environmentalists try to stop economic growth has been bad for economic development and has been bad for the environment. They agreed that economists have seriously failed by underestimating the cost of environmental damage, and they agreed that the environmentalists have failed by failing to note the benefits of economic growth. They agreed that the environmental agenda has been excessively dominated by the environmentalists in rich countries and has failed to adequately reflect the more urgent needs and the environmental priorities of the poor. They noted above all that poverty is strongly related to the environment, poverty is exacerbated by environmental damage, and in turn, causes further environmental damage. Thus they concluded that if we claim to be interested in the environment we must be interested in reducing poverty. They concluded that some greed-driven, environmentally damaging, excessive consumption needs to be stopped; but they also agreed that accelerated development and accelerated economic growth in many developing countries is absolutely essential if we are to have any hope of a sustainable future. The conference produced an 800-page document called *Agenda Twenty-One* which was crammed-packed full of suggestions and policies in a number of key environmentally relevant areas. They also reached agreement and opened for signature a biodiversity convention and a framework convention on climate change.

A striking feature of the conference was its spiritual tone and its openness to spiritual concerns. Representatives from every faith on earth were evident all over the place. Symposiums and seminars on the link between nature and faith were given every day. Buddhists, Hindus, Muslims, indigenous people were seeing each other in small conclaves all over Rio. The New Agers were there in great forces, as you could imagine. Shirley MacLaine organized a prayer meeting with the Dalai Lama. Striking also, however, . . . was the lack of a distinctively Christian voice. Some church groups were there in some force but their message was not distinctive. It seemed to stem from the same broad mystical pantheism that seemed to drive many of the other spiritual groups there. The evangelicals and . . . the reformed faith adherents, were conspicuous by their absence of a distinctive voice. It got me to wondering why is it that those people that seem to take the Bible very seriously don't seem to take the environment terribly seriously? And the more serious churches are about Bible study, in many instances, although one shouldn't generalize too much, the less interested they are in environment.

I think there are three broad sets of reasons for this lack of interest historically. First, I think Christians would argue that restoring the human soul is more important than restoring ecosystems. People, they would argue, are more important than trees. Second would be the Christian eschatology. The Bible seems to say that things will get worse before the endtime. Creation, we believe, groans as it awaits the final culmination of history, and, so some Christians would argue, who are we to relieve its pain? A third reason for a lack of

Andrew Steer, "How Green Is Our Gospel?" edited from a speech delivered at Calvin College, Grand Rapids, Michigan, 18 January 1993.

interest historically has been, I believe, a sort of fear of guilt by association and a dread of idolatry with regard to nature. Environmentalism has been dominated by a group of people who have very faulty theology, and so some Christian churches don't want to have much to do with them. And the worship of nature has been a dreaded heresy in the church since early times.

Thus, those Christians who seem to take the Bible very seriously have often left the environmental field to those who don't. Now this is a great pity, of course, and is now being remedied by a number of good books that have come out over recent months giving a biblical environmental perspective. Why, incidently, should the church be interested in the environment? Why should they take it seriously? Well of course most obviously because we're told we should in the Scriptures. The first great commission of Genesis chapter 1 commands men and women to be good stewards. Subdue the earth, have dominion. Now this of course has been interpreted wrongly for so much of church history. It's been used, the concept of dominion and submission and subduing, as an excuse to squeeze the earth for as much short-term gain as possible. The word "subdued" has been mistranslated in many people's minds. In fact it doesn't have an aggressive meaning of wrestling the earth into subduing it. Rather, it has a gentler meaning, a meaning that you might use when you're breaking in a horse, for example. One scholar likened this word "subdue" to the activities of love-making where husbands and wives subdue each other in gentleness in the act of making love.

Now in addition to the general command to take creation seriously, there are two specific reasons why in the Scriptures we are told to take the environment seriously. First, the environment, we are told, is God's messenger. It's the first great evangelist. The heavens, we're told in the Psalms, declare the glory of God, the skies proclaim the work of his hand. Day after day they pour forth speech. The second reason is that the creation, we're told, was made to serve mankind. Destroying nature destroys the livelihood of mankind. In the Psalms, God's creation is likened to God's open palm, from which he makes available all of the things that we need. If we destroy nature, we destroy that wonderful provision. The title of this talk asks the question "How Green Is Our Gospel?"

Well, the answer is that our gospel is a green one; but we must remember as we approach our environmentalism that people really are more important than trees; and we really must eschew any form of idolatry.

President Bill Clinton has proposed a "people-first" presidency, and we, I believe, need to propose a people-first environmentalism. I would like to show some slides to illustrate what seem to me to be the most important environmental problems that we are facing today. And I make no apology for the fact that they almost all relate to developing countries, and we are not in a developing country today. But if, as we like to think, we are global citizens, and as environmentalists we take global welfare seriously, we have to be primarily interested in those environmental problems that threaten the largest number of people today, and those happen to be in developing countries. Later on, I'm going to say what it is we might do about it. But most of the problems I'll be looking at are from the standpoint of developing countries.

Now, I'm not going to talk about global warming. . . . Nor am I going to speak about ozone depletion. I would be happy to address that in the questions afterwards, because I do believe those two problems are extremely serious, and we do need to address them urgently. Nor am I going to address issues such as the oceans, and pollution in the deep oceans. . . . I'm not going to address this kind of environmental problem. Nor am I going to address the problems that some people think are the most important — climatic changes brought about by major geological shocks. Rather, I'm going to talk about three sets of problems that today affect the largest number of people. I believe if one did a poll throughout the world one would find that these are considered to be the most important environmental problems today.

Number one on the list must be water and sanitation. One billion people today have no access to clean water. 1.7 billion people in the world today don't have access to sanitation. Rivers and streams are polluted by human waste and industry. As a result, between two and three million children die every year unnecessarily. Now for this one-third of humanity who don't have sanitation or clean water, this is the most important issue of all. It's the most important environmental problem. It's also the most important health and development problem. Surely we, as Christians, in particular, would want to take water very seriously indeed. Listen to this from Psalm 104, "Praise the Lord, O my soul. You are very great. You make springs to gush forth into the valleys. They flow between the hills, they give water to all creatures." Isn't it clear that the pollution- and disease-ridden water that a billion people will have to drink today hardly fits in with what the psalmist had in mind?

A second set of issues concern damage to the land and the undermining of productivity. I want to make it clear that not everything is going wrong as one reads sometimes in environmental literature. There has been huge progress over the last quarter century in agriculture. In the last twenty-five years, food production in the world has doubled. That has never happened before in such a short space of time. Food prices are now lower than they have been at any stage during the last century in real terms. As we have doubled food production, ninety percent of that has come from yield increases, and only ten percent has come from area expansion, a remarkable achievement in a brief space of time. So what's the problem? The problem is that over the next forty years food production will need to double all over again. And while the rate of growth of food production required, which will only be about 1.6 percent a year, is smaller than the growth that has been achieved over the last twenty-five years, which is about 2.5 percent a year, nonetheless, almost all of the agronomists believe that the future will be much more difficult than the past. Irrigation water is becoming scarcer. The sources of growth that came from double and triple cropping will not be there anymore; and there are problems associated with excessive fertilizer and pesticide use. There are already signs that fertility of soils in some areas is declining. The misuse of livestock such as goats has caused overgrazing, which causes excessive run-off and soil erosion. Similarly, the passion and craving for fuel and energy has led to the cutting down of trees that have held the soil in place, and so watersheds are being destroyed. Similarly, the craving for forest products has led to the destruction of significant areas of forest. In the Amazon, for example, one percent of the forest has been lost each year in the 1980's. This has been due mainly not to rapacious commercial logging operations but rather to small holders who simply haven't had the wherewithal to make a living elsewhere and so they have encroached into the forest. The other cause has been livestockers who have been heavily subsidized by the government. So the second problem is degradation of the land.

The third problem is degradation of the air. Now listening to the media or reading environmental literature one would get the impression that the most serious problems here relate to hazardous emissions, to CFCs or carbon dioxide. These are important, but I believe they're not the most important today. The most important are simpler and more deadly than those. The most serious problem is what we call particulates, soot and smoke. This slide shows Jakarta in Indonesia. This could be one of a hundred cities in the developing world and indeed in parts of the industrialized world. Today there are 1.3 billion people in the world who are inhaling soot and smoke at dangerous levels. As a result, something like 700,000 people every year are dying prematurely and unnecessarily. Possibly even more serious than that outdoor form of pollution is this indoor form of pollution from cooking stoves. Today 700,000,000 women and children will be cooking on open stoves with health effects that are very serious. The health effects are equivalent for those women and children to smoking something like three to five packs of cigarettes a day; and yet this issue very rarely finds its way onto the environmental agenda. A third serious problem is lead in the air. This is Bangkok, as you know a very busy city, but the same is true of Mexico City and many other large cities. The average child of seven in Bangkok today has had his or her IQ lowered by four points because of lead in the air. These are some of the problems that are affecting poor people around the world. They deserve our urgent attention.

Now, if that seems bad, wait to see what happens next. If pressures upon the earth's productive and sustaining ecosystems are severe today, they clearly are bound to intensify. Why is that? Well, first, population growth. The next four decades will see growth like never before. Each year, one hundred million people are being added to the world's population. In the four decades that were the focus of our work over the last year, 1990 to the year 2030, 3.7 billion people will be added to the earth's population. Today, there are over one billion people in the world in acute poverty, living on less than a dollar a day in terms of their consumption. Most of the increased population will be born into poor families. Now if one joins population growth with the required income growth, we have a dramatic growth in the world economy and in pressures on the ecosystems. Energy consumption in the next forty years will triple worldwide. In developing countries it will increase sixfold. Industrial production in developing countries will also increase sixfold.

Some environmentalists think this is bad news. I believe it is not at all. I believe it is very good news and essential news. Without increased energy consumption, without industrial production to fuel income growth, there will be no hope, it seems, for sustainable development. The bad news would be, of course, if environmental damage were to grow at the same rate as the economic growth. What would happen over the next forty years if environmental damage rose commensurately with population and economic growth? By the year 2030, twenty million people would be dying every year simply because of particulate emissions. Under present trends, the number of people without access to clean water and sanitation would grow, and brain damage from lead would increase dramatically. Another one-third of all tropical moist forests would be lost. Aquifers would be irreparably depleted. Soils in many parts of the world would be irreparably lost. That's the bad news. The good news is that these bad things need not happen and will not happen if sensible policies and behaviors are adopted in both rich and poor countries. This might sound easy. It's not. It is extremely difficult.

What needs to be done then? Let me suggest that there are two sets of policies that need to be followed. They stem from a recognition that there are really two primary causes of environmental damage: first, causes related to inadequate development, such as soil erosion, the lack of clean water and sanitation, and indoor air pollution, which are related to a lack of income growth; and second, causes related to too much of the wrong kind of development. Let me first of all address what we call the win-win policies, policies that are good for development, good for poverty alleviation, good for economic efficiency, and good for the environment. What are they? Let me just give

you some examples. Investing in sanitation and water has some of the highest economic rates of return in the world. It's good for health. It's good for the environment. It's good for poverty reduction. It's good for GDP growth. Slum upgrading is another area that is good for economic growth. It's good for the environment, reducing unsanitary conditions. . . . Agricultural research on ecologically benign agricultural forms has been shown to have extremely high rates of return in terms of production. It also has high environmental rates of return. Agriculture research in Brazil on possibilities for inter-cropping to protect those fragile tropical soils in Brazil has very high economic rates of return, very high environmental rates of return. Involving local beneficiaries in projects has extremely high ecological and environmental rates of return. Empowering local people is something that clearly is dramatically good for development and for the environment. This slide shows a slum in Indonesia. When the squatters, who are illegal here, were given the legal rights to the land, they quadrupled their investment in sanitation. When these herders in Burkina Faso were given the legal right to their tribal traditional land, overgrazing fell dramatically; they managed it well because they had an incentive. When these fisherman in Sri Lanka were encouraged to get together to jointly manage their fishing, overfishing fell sharply. Empowering people is good for social and economic development. It's also powerfully good for the environment.

Perhaps the most powerful environmental policy of all is education. Education empowers people to make better decisions about their own futures. It's good for the environment, and it is very good for the people. Research in Thailand that we did recently showed that the single most important policy that would prevent deforestation in Northern Thailand was education of the rural squatters who were slashing and burning. The reason is simple. Once one can read and write, one can find better things to do with one's life than slashing and burning.

Educating girls is perhaps the single most important long-term environmental policy in the world. This is a major message of the report that we wrote. The reasons are very clear. They are twofold. First of all, the effect on fertility is astonishing. If you take a thousand girls in Africa today, and give them one more year, just one more year of primary education, five hundred fewer children will be born as a result. We have learned that it is impossible to reduce population growth without educating girls. The second reason to give girls and women an education is a more direct one. Women are the primary resource managers in many parts of the world. Half of all natural resources in Africa are managed by women. Seventy percent of all the farms in Congo are managed by women. Yet these women often lack access to education. They often have no legal rights. They are bypassed by the extension and credit services, and they can't even read the labels on their fertilizer packages. Is it surprising, then, that there is environmental damage? If there is a single win-win policy in the world it must be educating women. To remove discrimination against girls throughout the world simply by putting into schools the same number of girls as there are boys would require that twenty-five million girls today enter primary schools that are not there now, and twenty-five million enter secondary schools. That would cost only 2.4 billion dollars a year. There is no better use of such money anywhere. It is an environmental investment, but much more important, it is also a developmental and a human investment. We should stop arguing with each other and get to work on it and support countries that are willing to take this seriously.

Education empowerment of women is perhaps the most powerful way of reducing fertility rates, but it's not the only one. In addition to that, it's necessary to have a rising income standard for families and improved health of children. Fertility declines, then, depend strongly also on child health and nutrition. One of the things we have learned in the last ten years is that couples make decisions about how many children they will have based in part on the likely health of the children they have. We can now demonstrate that investment in child inoculation, for example this slide in Bolivia, or investment in pre-natal and post-natal care, such as this in Bangladesh, have extremely powerful impacts upon fertility decisions. A final element in bringing down fertility growth, which is clearly so essential to the long-term sustainability of the way that we interact here on earth, is of course family planning. It's a great shame that family planning has been assumed to

be in the driver's seat of the population debate and even more of a shame that abortion has been there. In fact family planning is necessary, but it follows the demand side of the equation which comes from education and increased income levels. It must be put in place.

Let me move on to some other win-win policies, some that don't cost any money at all for example. Some actually make money and help finance other forms of development. Most countries actively encourage the wasteful use of resources. Energy subsidies around the world amount to 230 billion dollars a year. That's five times the total amount of foreign aid in the entire world. As a result energy is wasted in places like eastern Europe and the former Soviet Union. Half of all air pollution would disappear if energy subsidies were removed. If energy subsidies, that is, actively paying and subsidizing prices so that people consume more energy than is efficient, were removed, that would reduce carbon emissions worldwide by over 10%. Doing that would be good for development. It would be very good for the environment.

There are many other commodities and inputs around the world, in this country and in developing countries, that are subsidized. Pesticide subsidies, for example, amounted to something like 200 million dollars a year in Indonesia. When they removed those subsidies, the quality of the rural environment improved, and because they introduced what we call integrated pest management, supported by foreign aid from the United States, the productivity of their agriculture did not decline. They could not have done this obviously good thing for the environment and development, however, had they not had the resources and inputs to introduce a new, more environmentally benign form of development supported by the United States.

Water is perhaps the most subsidized commodity on earth. When China reduced the subsidies of water and stopped giving it away for free, over-depletion of aquifers in the North China plain declined sharply. It's very difficult to do, but it's important that we recognize the value of these natural, God-given commodities. When Bangkok started charging for the use of water in the city, the city stopped declining. Up until that stage, because of overpumping of the aquifer under the ground, the entire city was falling by several inches a year, leading to acute flooding at certain times of the year. That would have just gone on happening. Removing subsidies stopped it because water was used more prudently. A place like Mexico City spends one billion dollars a year in cash subsidies to water users. As a result, the aquifer underlying Mexico City has fallen by 90%. Some people worry about removing subsidies on water because they think it will hurt the poor, and one does have to be careful. But the real poor, of course, don't benefit from subsidies because they don't have access to the piped water. They are part of the one billion people in the world that have to travel long distances for water or drink dirty water. The average poor person in the world spends ten times as much as the average rich person on a liter of drinking water through having to go long distances or through buying from vendors or through disease.

The final win-win policy relates to technology transfer. The best policy here is to promote open trade and investment. Some environmentalists argue that free trade and free investment hurts the environment, and we certainly need protection and the right policies in place. However, I would argue that without free trade there will be no technology transfer. We can demonstrate that countries with more open trading systems have newer and cleaner technologies. They have more efficient production processes.

Well, so far this all sounds very easy. It's good for poverty. It's good for the environment. Everything I've said has been sort of win-win. Why don't we get on with it and do it? Surely we should agree on all of these things. Well, we don't. There are political vested interests stopping these things happening, but in addition resources will be required and those resources have not been forthcoming. I should also discuss the second set of policies I mentioned earlier. We need to break the negative links between economic growth and the environment. For example, we need more technology development in fuel-efficient stoves. We need more innovative experiments in solar and alternative energies such as this wind-powered electricity generating site in Kenya. We need better regulations. For instance, in Hong Kong, which along with many countries in Asia now is putting in place lead free gasoline, they are charging people for taking cars downtown to reduce congestion. There are over 100 developing countries at the moment who are requesting us and other agencies to help them strengthen their environmental capacity. They are building environmental protection agencies. They desperately need help from countries such as the United States.

Another thing we need to do to break the adverse links of economic growth is to do better environmental assessments. The institution I work for, the World Bank, has financed a large number of large projects. Some of these in the past have been damaging to the environment. We have looked at just one side of the equation. We have looked to the benefits without looking at the environmental costs. We need to do a much better job than we have done. The United States has a tremendous background and experience in that. Roads into the forests may still on occasion be required, but we now have learned a great deal about their damaging impacts. We need to break that link. We need to do careful environmental assessments, and in some situations we need to ban such investments altogether. We need to recognize above all people who benefit from the natural environment. Here is a slide of some Amer-Indians in Rendonia, or in Brazil, where I spent a week last year. We need to recognize that these people have rights to remain undisturbed.

Well, so far this all seems very well, but surely it is all the responsibility of the poor countries, and shouldn't we tackle the problems at home first? Yes, we should. I haven't addressed those because one can read so much about those in so many newspapers and articles. I do believe we should tackle our problems at home. But in addition, we need to support developing countries. . . . I believe the Christian church and the nation of the United States need to renew their vision of supporting those who are most needy. Environmentally sustainable development requires investment. It requires knowledge. It requires technology. How should we help in funding? The most direct thing we can do is to engage in free trade. One of the sad things has been the failure to reach agreement on the Uruguay round. Every year, if we halved our barriers to trade to developing countries, that would put seventy billion dollars in the hands of developing countries who could then make the required investments for sustainable development. It would also facilitate environmentally benign technologies.

Foreign aid also needs to be increased. How sad it is that we in this country — and indeed, I am from England, so I will include my own country in it too — both America and the United Kingdom have lowered the share of their income that goes to foreign aid very dramatically over the last decade or so. Some of this is predicated on the assumption that foreign aid has failed. Not at all. The average dollar of foreign aid has had a very dramatic and positive impact. A country like India has received on average $1.50 per head of population in foreign aid over the last thirty years. That is not very much. One should not expect radical results. And yet food production and poverty reduction has been dramatically positive. We need to redirect our foreign aid toward those investments that benefit the poor and the environment: sanitation, health, female education, and the like. We need to regain our vision for our role in the world. We need to expand our technology transfer. We need technical assistance. We need agriculture research, which we have done too little of over the last decade.

Finally, we do need to address the global environmental problems. I haven't discussed global warming or the depletion of the ozone layer. I would be happy to in the discussion time, but I wanted to focus on those other issues.

Now, what about the personal level? Let me address a couple of constituencies here. I presume that some of you students here are about to enter into the work force. We desperately need people to commit their careers to environmentally sustainable development. We need agronomists, foresters, water engineers, ecologists, biologists, teachers, scientists, and so on. And when I say *we* need them, I don't mean we at the World Bank need them. I mean the world as a whole needs them. There are huge opportunities for serving in developing countries.

Let me suggest that there's another important element of our own personal responsibility. It relates to life-style, of course. We in this country have the lowest savings rate in the world. That explains why we are not able to afford so much of the foreign aid that we wish we could afford. Why do we have such a low savings rate? It is because we just love consuming things. And you and I are probably as guilty as any of the rest of them. Let

me leave you with a passage from Ezekiel, chapter 34. "Is it not enough for you, says the Lord, to feed on the good pastures? Must you also trample the rest with your feet? Is it not enough for you to drink clear water, must you also muddy the rest with your feet?" Don't you feel that somehow, sometimes, this is the way that we live — not satisfied with sufficiency, rather demanding more?

The next forty years pose extraordinary opportunities and challenges. For those of you who are about to enter the work force, an interesting question to ask is, what will the world look like the day after you retire when you wake up and you look out of your window? What will the children of the world have to look forward to in that period? Will things have gotten worse? Will there be great malnutrition? Will more people be dying of pollution? Or by that stage will clean water have been brought to every man, woman, and child on the earth? Will the soils have been stabilized? Will deforestation have been reduced? I believe we can achieve those things. I believe we know the policies and the programs. I believe they have been documented. Now they need commitment from rich and poor countries.

Today is Martin Luther King Day. He had a dream. It seems to me we need to rekindle a dream for our role in the world in promoting the dignity of every person — man, woman, and child, but especially children. When George Marshall, the Secretary of State, visited Harvard in 1948 to inaugurate what became the Marshall Plan, he said, "We will support countries in Europe, those that have suffered from the war. We will rebuild them at any cost." When we were at war in the Cold War with the Soviet Union, and we had an enemy, we defended ourselves at any cost. What greater challenge is there for us in the remaining decade of this century and the first three decades of the next century?

The challenges are so enormous to raise living standards, to promote human dignity, and to protect the planet through environmentally sustainable development. It is a huge task. It is a long task. I'll close with a story you may have heard, the story of the man who wanted to plant a tree, and he asked the expert, "If I plant it today how long will it take to grow?" The man said, "Well, it will take forty years." The other man said, "Well, we'd better get on with it right away. We have no time to lose."

Chapter Fifteen

The Ongoing Discussion

Economic life and business systems continue to change. The 1990s, so far, have generated more than their share of new words to describe these evolving patterns. *Downsizing, shamrock organizations, core competencies, multicultural management, virtual corporations, leadership jazz, economic shock therapy, NAFTA, GATT, multigenerational unemployment, information superhighway* — all of these words mark shifting scenes in the global economic drama. We thus cannot presume that the discussion relating the life of Christian faith to economic choices is finished or ever will be finished. Before the dust settles on old issues, new challenges emerge for the churches, the business community, and those who develop Christian paradigms for global economic life.

In many ways the public conversation relating Christian faith to economic life has only begun. The church documents excerpted in Chapter 10 opened a new era for discussion in the public square. Christian churches once again recognized that faith has profound implications for views of economic reality and norms for economic life. Churches worked closely to form a chorus of prophetic witnesses. Yet there is still work to be done. Churches must continually reexamine their theologies in light of further — and especially, unexpected — developments in the global economy. They must listen to new voices as new groups emerge to claim their rightful place in society. They must encourage new forms of ministry that actually help laypersons make their working lives integral to their understanding of Christian faith. The challenges ahead are major ones.

Businesses as well face new challenges in this public conversation. As individuals and as organizational representatives, business professionals must learn to practice the social responsibility so ardently preached in the past few years. Public expectations of business are rising. We expect businesses to operate ethically, to embrace employee diversity, and to resist the chronic and pervasive evils of exploitation, racism, and sexism.

For the churches and economic actors to find their ways and to find each other, the dialogue about broad Christian paradigms for economic life must continue. How should Christians find their economic souls among diverse global religions tied to multiple variations on economic systems? How should a Christian understanding of reality inform economic theorizing and policy? What principles should people of faith employ to balance the multiple economic mandates of the Scriptures in their own decisions and practices?

An ongoing public conversation can provide perspective and guidance for the years ahead. You are invited into that discussion to participate, learn, and make your own contribution.

Section 1: Challenges for the Church Community

While admiring church contributions to date, the authors represented in this section are convinced that churches should not rest content with yesterday's achievements. We begin, then, with an assessment of one of the churches' most successful efforts to transform corporate cultures, the past generation's movement to use the churches' investment portfolios and their unparalleled access to consumers to increase business's accountability to its stakeholders. We then highlight examples of new forms of Christian social action, as the churches experiment with new ministries in light of the experiences of blue-collar workers, black entrepreneurs, and Christian executives. These reports from the field hardly exhaust the rich diversity of contemporary church initiatives, but they are meant to stimulate your own thinking about what is possible in your own community, and who your potential collaborators might be.

The paired essays from Prakash Sethi and Philip Wogaman are offered as a reflection on what has been learned within both business and church circles from historic encounters like the Nestlé boycott and the movement for divestment in apartheid South Africa. Both authors urge the churches to think carefully about the premises and strategies for Christian social action, but from different perspectives. Sethi welcomes the church as an instrument for social change, yet warns against the resistance that overzealous and uninformed activists can provoke among business leaders. Once mobilized for action in the public square, the church is subject to the same scrutiny of its policies and performance as any other organization would be. Wogaman, based on his experience with the Nestlé boycott, responds to Sethi's warn-

ings by suggesting specific public strategies that churches can use to generate more effective results in their economic activism.

Steve Boint offers a different challenge to the Christian churches, a growing responsibility to hear the voices of those not coping well with economic change. He ponders the support, or lack thereof, that churches provide for those traditionally classed as blue-collar workers. Boint's concern is for those silently left behind by economic restructuring. What should the church do for those whose life patterns are shredded by economic change? Boint is convinced that basic Christian theology is the foundation for comfort, empowerment, resistance, and community for those who never expected to be economically marginalized. His observations suggest that churches have more options than pointless resistance to the inevitabilities of economic restructuring.

African-Americans coping with economic change are the focus of Lloyd Gite's contribution. This author gives examples of how black Christian churches offer one of the primary sources of hope in both urban and rural areas. Gite suggests that the black church is a critical source of economic vision and development for the future. It has demonstrated the capacities that all Christian churches can acquire for stimulating entrepreneurship and joint ventures in the local community.

David Krueger is also aware of the economic significance of innovative forms of Christian ministry. He challenges the clergy to engage in an ongoing dialogue with Christian business executives. Convinced from his experience in organizing such dialogues that the church has much to learn from listening more carefully to economic practitioners, he urges it to reexamine its theological language to build better connections between faith and business and to expand its repertoire of models for economic systems.

Each of these authors believes that the church's witness to and interaction with powerful economic forces in the public square is important. However, they encourage the church to be sure that its own house is in order, that it improve the economic understanding and practice of its own members, and that it choose its public concerns and strategies judiciously.

The Righteous and the Powerful: Differing Paths to Social Goals

S. Prakash Sethi

An ever-increasing number of church-related institutions that influence the behavior and performance of economic organizations, notably large corporations in the united States and, indeed, in the entire world, are an undeniable fact of life. The following examples would serve to point out both the enormity and the complexity of the many ways in which organized religious bodies intervene in the decision-making processes of our economic institutions.

On May 20, 1985, the Interfaith Center on Corporate Responsibility (ICCR) and its associated religious organizations announced that they have targeted twelve U.S. corporations as "key supporters of apartheid" for special action to induce them to disengage from the South African operations. This was the latest, but certainly not the last, step in a movement started in 1971 when the Episcopal Church launched the first church-sponsored shareholder resolution challenging General Motors management in regard to its South African operations.

In November 1984, a committee of Catholic bishops issued a draft letter on "Catholic Social Teaching and the U.S. Economy," setting forth a national agenda and a set of priorities on what the Catholic Church considered to be the desirable course of action that this country's political and economic institutions should follow.

S. Prakash Sethi, "The Righteous and the Powerful: Differing Paths to Social Goals," *Business and Society Review* 54 (Summer 1985): 37-44.

The pastor of a small Lutheran church in Clairton, Pennsylvania (a suburb of Pittsburgh), has been waging a relentless battle against U.S. Steel and Mellon Bank for their actions in "causing" the unemployment and misery of thousands of steel workers. The tactics included, among other things, picketing executives' homes, confronting them in their churches, disrupting prayer, visiting schools of their children and using a host of other tactics designed to intimidate people. Backed by a militant professional organizer he has defied his own church leaders' orders to refrain from such disruptive and abusive behavior. Furthermore, he and his supporters ordered those church members who disagreed with their actions to leave the church or face unmentioned consequences.

In many ways, this was a replay of some of the more violent business-church confrontations of the late 1960s and early 1970s, involving such professional activists as Saul Alinksy, who sought to build power among the poor people through strong organizational effort and confrontational tactics. The most notable of these conflicts was the drive in 1966 against Eastman Kodak in Rochester under the aegis of a local minority group FIGHT (Freedom, Integration, God, Honor — Today). A large number of the tactics used by many activist groups today were honed during this heyday period of activist struggles against large corporations.

In 1984, Nestlé Corporation jointly agreed with a church-supported activist group whereby the latter consented to terminate its worldwide boycott against Nestlé, recognizing the efforts the company had made in the Third World countries to comply with the WHO Code on the marketing of infant formula foods. The announcement culminated a seven-year struggle which was probably unprecedented in the annals of business-society conflicts for the intensity and extensiveness of church involvement.

These examples illustrate the many facets of church involvement in this nation's economic life and range all the way from active confrontation, to conciliatory engagement and constructive rapprochement. That business and church must interact in the economic arena is inevitable. That the two will often conflict is also understandable given the overlapping nature of their societal concerns and a divergence in their goals and strategies to achieve them. The challenge in an open society, therefore, is not to avoid conflict, because that would be impossible. Instead, our efforts should be focused at understanding the nature of this conflict and in harnessing it for the common good. . . .

Role of the Church

Normally the church has been associated in the popular mind with prayer, charity, and service, having little interest in economic pressures and confrontational policies. However, the church has always related itself to its social and political context. The leadership of the Catholic Church has always maintained that its responsibility extends into all arenas of human endeavor, personal and social, including the economic enterprises that occupy such a large part of most people's lives.

One of the reasons Jesus of Nazareth was crucified was because he was viewed as a threat to Caesar in Rome. With the "conversion" of Constantine, the church was plunged into affairs of state. From the Holy Roman Empire through the Huguenot-Wallon Wars to the role of colonial clergy in setting the stage for the American Revolution; from the churches' role in the abolition and temperance movements to the civil rights and peace activism of the 1950s and 1960s, convinced persons have used the institution of religion to further their social and political views. In so doing, they have seen themselves as obedient servants of the prophetic traditions of the Judeo-Christian faith. . . .

And yet the church also recognizes the tension that exists between the prophetic teaching of Jesus, in blessing the poor and warning against the spiritual perils of attachments to material wealth, and the compelling needs and desires of imperfect men and women to pursue their own material self-interest. Christian teachings and capitalistic values have not always been considered inseparable. Even Adam Smith assumed that people pursuing self-interest could also serve the public good by increasing a society's ability to produce greater wealth. Smith, himself a clergyman, believed that an acquisitive society would also make possible a more humane society. The problem arises when we divorce the moral and ethical underpinnings of the rationale for acquisition and retention of wealth, and when it appears unrelated, and even contrary, to our notions of social welfare and a sense of fair play and justice.

The rise of social activism has had a salutary influence in the United States since the early 1960s and has been instrumental in raising public consciousness and social change in such areas as race, age, and sex discrimination, conservation, and environmental protection. The 1970s brought a partial resolution of these problems. Large-scale, overt inequalities were outlawed. The resolutions of past inequalities have largely been institutionalized and the probability of their significant resurgence in the United States in the foreseeable future is highly unlikely.

The churches and their affiliated institutions and agencies provide us with a distinct form of social activism. The institution of church has an ideological core and a value-set. Its concern for the poor and the downtrodden is rooted in both its values and traditions, and yet as a well-established institution with strong historical roots, it also has a long-term perspective in dealing with issues and other institutions of society.

The examples of church intervention in economic affairs cited in the early part of this article provide an illustration of the dual set of strategies and tactics pursued by the activistic church-related organizations. We see certain church-related groups resorting to direct pressure and confrontation tactics — and often disregarding the niceties of means — to achieve their desired goals. At the same time, we see church groups and agencies insisting on a quite different posture — one that examines all relevant aspects of an issue and questions the strengths and deficiencies of various positions, including their own, and puts more emphasis on rapprochement and alleviation of the problem. Business-church conflicts may appear to be isolated incidents when viewed through the eyes of the parties immediately involved. However, when strung together temporally and contextually, their implications must be analyzed for the long-run consequences for both the institutions involved and the entire social system.

Because religion is used as a tool for social change, it subjects itself to societal evaluations. When it moves against prevailing attitudes and practices, when it seems to challenge public opinion, when it utilizes confrontational tactics, employs power plays, and uses forms of economic and political leverage, it offends many of its constituents, creating a body of skepticism within its own ranks, and undermines belief in and popular support for its programs and leadership. Some social analysts argue that the declining influence and membership of "mainline churches" is attributable to the aggressive activism of some Protestant leaders and Roman Catholic hierarchies. . . .

Activist Mentality

To an extent, some of the alleged excesses of activist groups are inherent in the nature of the movement itself and are common to most emerging groups that seek a greater share of power from the established sociopolitical order. While the power imposes its discipline, those who lack power are not so restrained. The activist mentality — a feeling of being under constant siege — creates an approach to problems that is born of reaction to the exercise of power rather than the wielding of it. Confrontation becomes their lifeblood and they are energized by defeats and rebuffs. Issues are simplified because to allow for complexity is to concede that the issues might be multisided. Solutions become all pervasive. They feel compelled to design comprehensive solutions to every problem, ignoring the ones that are difficult and messy. Imbued with the righteousness of their cause and the correctness of their advocated solution, they ignore those aspects of the problem that don't fit the mold. Skilled in the art of confrontation and opposition, they are untutored in the defensive compromises of power.

And herein lies one of the major dilemmas of our times. As activists become more influential in the process of social intervention, they become an important element in the process of social change. However, their value-set and self-perception may cause them to adopt attitudes and means for achieving their objectives that may have the potential of causing great social harm through severe rupture in the established order with no better or effective alternative in sight.

Problem Areas

The moral force of church involvement in social and economic issues makes it imperative that religious institutions take the utmost care in selecting issues that reflect the will of its body politic, meet with its core values, and conform to the highest standards of fairness and truth in dealing with those whose behavior it seeks to influence and change. An analysis of church activism over the last fifteen years leads to the suggestion that certain problem areas need careful attention from church leadership.

A significant part of current church-supported activism in the economic arena is accompanied by exaggerated, and often strident, rhetoric-making demands that are usually difficult to meet without imposing serious costs on other groups. As a matter of fact, rhetoric and its attendant news media attention are considered an integral part of the tactics used by the activist groups — church-related groups included — to bring pressure on the recalcitrant corporations to change their behavior. And yet, rhetoric has a way of becoming rigidified into nonnegotiable demands and unfinished agenda, thereby creating a divisiveness in society with potentially harmful effects for all concerned.

There is a growing recognition among the church leaders that the "movement" is dominated and controlled by a committed minority that could lead the church into issues and engage it in confrontations in a manner that might not take into account the sensibilities of the body politic; it might even diverge from the core values it purports to espouse. However, there is as yet little open dialog within the church and with other societal groups with a view to developing a code of conduct by which the constituent groups would behave and to creating new measures of external accountability to ensure that the church lives up to the highest standards of ethical behavior in the marketplace.

And finally, one of the more critical areas for the church is developing defensible criteria and an order of priorities by which it selects issues for intervention, and how it might measure success in achieving its goals of sociopolitical intervention. Too often we confuse achievement of process-related targets with accomplishment of verifiable goals. To an extent, this is in the nature of social conflict. When opposing groups confront each other, there is a need to define objectives in tactical terms. For the activists, it is necessary to score victories in order to maintain momentum, increase their stature with their followers, and also gain credibility with the general public for their successes in achieving results. However, success so defined has the danger of short-changing the ultimate objectives on the one hand, and, on the other, inflicting unbearable costs on individuals and groups which may not have had much to do with the activists' assumption of the role as their chosen leaders, and which certainly had very little to do with the choice of strategies and goals pursued by the activists on their behalf. . . .

The ethical problems of the 1980s pertaining to social conflict between business and society are not between right and wrong, between guilty and innocent, but between one type of inequity and another, between giving one group more while taking from another group, between the virtue of frugality and the sin of accumulation, and between morality of principle and morality of situations. In an unjust world, the distinctions between the guilty and innocent have become ambiguous. What we are confronted with is the realization that we live in an increasingly interdependent society where individual good is not possible outside the context of common good. It makes no sense to separate moral principles from institutional behavior, political power from economic influence, and environmental values from material rewards. To do so is to divorce the social system from its basic element, the human being, who does not behave in a fragmented manner.

The Ethical Premise for Social Activism

J. Philip Wogaman

The deepening involvement of American churches in corporate responsibility issues has given rise to intensified conflict and misunderstanding. Conflict is not necessarily bad, but it often breeds the kinds of bitter feelings and misunderstandings that make constructive solutions more difficult to achieve. Truth itself can be the first victim, since people who are deeply involved in conflict absolutize their own goodness and caricature their adversaries. For the sake of churches and corporations alike, it is imperative that both seek to understand each other better and that both recognize the ethical perspectives out of which church groups properly engage corporations on corporate responsibility issues. It is important for corporations to know where church groups are "coming from," and it is important for churches to have a clear sense of the basis of their actions and the kinds of restraints they need to observe.

My own general involvement with such issues spans a career of teaching and writing Christian social ethics. But the issues came more sharply into focus for me during the four years (1980-1984) I served as chairperson of a Task Force on Infant Formula for the United Methodist Church. We were charged by our denomination with responsibility to engage the giants of the infant formula industry: Nestlé, Abbott-Ross, Bristol Myers (Mead Johnson), and American Home Products (Wyeth). Taking note of widespread publicity during the 1970s about exploitative practices

J. Philip Wogaman, "The Ethical Premise for Social Activism," *Business and Society Review* 54 (Summer 1985): 30-36.

in the marketing of breastmilk substitutes, particularly to Third World women, the denomination asked us to engage these corporations in dialog seeking to bring an end to the objectionable forms of marketing. The church's action in setting up our Task Force was an alternative to direct involvement in the Nestlé boycott, then actively supported by dozens of church groups and other kinds of organizations. But the church also made it clear that if our dialogs should fail, we ought to recommend United Methodist endorsement of the boycott of any or all of the corporations. Our dialog proceeded vigorously and (usually) cooperatively, but we also found ourselves caught in the wider crossfire of church groups and corporations. From the start, we had to deal with very basic questions as we struggled to be effective while keeping faith with our identity as representatives of a Christian denomination. . . .

Is Involvement Legitimate?

The foundational question is whether churches really have any business getting involved in seeking changes in corporate behavior. Occasionally one hears it said that churches should stick to "spiritual" matters and leave "secular" matters to the people who know something about them.

Of course, nobody seriously believes that church involvement is illegal in any way. Church groups have the same rights as any others to become involved in economic problems. It would be difficult, indeed, for churches as institutions to escape serious involvement with the economy. Individual churches and national denominations handle business transactions involving billions of dollars each year. Through pension funds and institutional endowments, churches must make investment decisions with important ramifications for themselves and for banks and corporations. Church groups are major purchasers, and the individual economic decisions of individual Christians constitute, no doubt, a majority of the business transactions of the American economy each year. Aside from such obvious facts, there is something to be said — on a purely secular plane — for constructive participation in economic controversy by groups whose primary motivation is the public interest and the general well-being of the world's people. The good intentions of church groups do not guarantee the wisdom of their proposals or even the decency of their behavior. But such participation at least helps to lift social controversy about pure self-interest. That is to view the matter from the secular plane. People who take the public good and corporate responsibility seriously have good reason to welcome church participation in public dialog on economic problems.

The church's own self-understanding of these matters cuts more deeply. Viewed in theological perspective, there is no aspect of worldly life that does not affect God's purposes one way or another. The world was created by God with loving intention. In the Genesis narratives of creation, it is said that God, after creating the world and its contents, "saw that it was good." But the Bible also makes clear that the world and its contents can be misused. Economic life can be an expression of sin; it can be destructive of God's life-giving purposes for humanity. The great prophets of Israel heaped their scorn on those who exploited the vulnerable, making clear that the oppression of others is an offense against God. Hebrew law arranged economic matters in such a way that the poor, the orphans and widows, the "sojourners," would be given special protection. Dishonest business practices were condemned. Parts of the New Testament express similar concern for the poor and judgment on the abuses of wealth. . . .

In response to its faith in the love of God, church people are committed to the service of humanity. All human beings are perceived as sisters and brothers — no matter whether they are rich or poor, no matter where they live, no matter how old they are, no matter whether they attend church or even belong. The well-being of other people is God's business, and therefore it is perceived by church people as their business as well. . . .

Clearheaded

As an ethical rule of thumb, it seems clear to me that the more negative or coercive the actions taken by churches (or contemplated by churches), the more carefully disciplined and accountable they must be. In general, the burden of proof ought to be against church use of pressure tactics. Use of raw institutional power, while sometimes necessary, often risks distortion of moral issues. The church needs to be clearheaded about the conditions under which it believes such tactics justified. For example, such a serious measure as an economic boycott should not be undertaken unless (1) it is on a relatively grave issue, (2) it is a last resort after serious dialog has been tried and proven ineffective, (3) there has been "due process" consideration of the issue by church membership, (4) the reasons for the boycott, and their ethical/theological rationale, can be made clear to the church constituency and to the target of the coercive action, (5) the leaders of the offending corporate body know what they must do to bring the action to an end, (6) the action is likely to be reasonably effective, without unacceptable side effects, and (7) the church body would be capable of ending the action when there was no longer reason to continue it. The fact that actions like boycotts are often undertaken by broader coalitions of organizations makes it important to emphasize that church bodies should never simply delegate decision-making authority to others. The theological/ethical integrity of the church requires that it remain accountable for its own actions even when, as may frequently be the case, it is necessary for it to act in concert with others.

Such guidelines, by themselves, will not guarantee wisdom in church actions. Churches, like individuals (and like corporations), can make real mistakes. That lamentable fact should not inhibit churches from acting in the world. But it should lead them to be careful, open and creative, if it is possible to be all of those at the same time.

Respect for People

The endlessly fascinating thing about the interaction of churches and corporations is that both are represented by real people, and who those people are and the way they relate to one another can make a real difference. The fact that Helmut Maucher and Carl Angst assumed leadership of Nestlé in 1981-1982 was very important in resolving the Nestlé controversy. Both of them deserve high marks for openness, creativity, and integrity in dialog and decision-making. Sensitive church representatives can observe that different corporations do indeed have different personalities, and the peculiar mix of leadership in corporations can make a substantial difference. On many corporate social responsibility issues it is possible to identify some within a company's leadership who seem much more responsible than others — and an important task for the church representatives, then, is to try to strengthen the hand of those who seem to have a more sensitive social conscience. It is also important to try to recognize the limiting parameters within which these more sensitive leaders must operate. In particular, those who wish to improve corporate social responsibility will be aware of market constraints and not act so as to weaken the market position of those who are most responsible. That means focusing on whole industries and markets, not simply on particular companies. And it means working for acceptable guidelines and regulations to discipline the marketing behavior of all involved.

Since not all corporate leaders are equally sensitive to moral problems, church representatives must sometimes confront corporate representatives as adversaries in conflict. That is inevitable. Corporate leaders also confront church representatives whose integrity they cannot bring themselves to respect. But it is well to remember, from both sides, that the people we confront as adversaries are still people and they do not need to be treated as enemies. Part of the genius of the civil rights movement of Dr. Martin Luther King, Jr. and others is that they could conduct very hard-headed campaigns while at the same time honoring the personhood of the adversary. Church people are committed to a life of love, and that means loving the adversary even in the midst of struggle. It also means not judging the sinfulness of others. None of us is quite good enough to be the judge of another's humanity — that is God's responsibility, not ours. We are indeed called on to judge actions and policies — to identify injustice and oppression and all that dehumanizes people — as best we can. But the adversary we meet is a brother or sister, and when treated as such it is surprising what a difference it can make even at the practical level. Undertaken in that spirit, churches have a major contribution to make to the cause of corporate social responsibility.

The Blue-Collar Worker and the Church

Steve Boint

Blue-collar workers are found in a wide spectrum of economic, racial, political, and geographic situations. They are defined by the type of work they do — physical labor. Some are at the top of the economic spectrum with relatively satisfying jobs; others have tedious jobs which pay no better than minimum wage. But while there will always be a need for plumbers and other highly skilled and paid workers, the total job market for high skill/high pay blue-collar jobs is shrinking drastically.

This shrinking is due in large part to four trends in American society. First the de-industrialization of the United States is eliminating jobs traditionally held by blue-collar workers and replacing them with jobs in the service sector which pay much less, require little skill, and have no security. Second, the growth of a global economy has given birth to multi-national corporations which relocate their production facilities in foreign countries where labor is cheaper. [Third,] automation is also eliminating some traditional blue-collar jobs. Fourthly, the remaining blue-collar jobs are becoming more production line–oriented, requiring less skill. This leaves workers vulnerable to easy replacement and therefore with little power.

Because highly skilled, highly paid blue-collar jobs are already so few and are shrinking in number, this article will focus predominantly upon those people living slightly below middle-class income levels. As I have indicated, many blue-collar

Steve Boint, "The Blue-Collar Worker and the Church," *Urban Mission* 6 (March 1989): 6-17.

individuals are finding jobs in the service sector, a market not traditionally considered blue-collar. Because the same class of people who were once blue-collar are now being forced into the service sector, we will consider people in this occupational line part of the low income blue-collar group.

Blue-collar workers are found all across the United States, but the heaviest concentration is found in the large urban areas with more industrial jobs. This is changing, though, as more and more companies move to the rural South and Midwest to escape high city taxes and labor unions. Company towns built around the steel, coal, and auto industries are heavily blue-collar areas. Farmers are not considered blue-collar in this article because their extreme rural isolation adds enough unique characteristics to their social situation for them to be viewed separately.

The American Dream

I will focus first on the unique influences upon blue-collar people. But in the U.S. it is impossible to live without being influenced by major societal beliefs. As Tex Sample explains in his book, *Blue-Collar Ministry,* much of the working class lifestyle can best be understood as a reaction to the American religion of achievement. This religion has its most compelling form in what is usually called the American dream: to own your own home, to slowly accumulate wealth, and to use this as a springboard from which your children can have just a little more of the pie of wealth, power, and status.

This is the dominant value orientation of the American people. It is built upon two major presuppositions: that there is individual freedom with social problems the sum of individual actions, and that everyone has equality of opportunity. Buying into the religion of achievement is common in blue-collar society, as it is throughout the U.S., and yet this is particularly destructive for working-class people. This dream forces people to prove their dignity and worth, something the Bible says can't be done, and something society's structures deny working-class people. Belief in individual freedom and the attainability of the American dream change social criticism into self-criticism, so that failure to succeed is blamed solely upon

one's self. Therefore the religion of achievement justifies the structured inequality of society by convincing everyone that it is right and good for society to be this way. This causes severe tensions within the life of the working class as they try to square their belief in achievement with the reality of their failure — reality which confronts them every time they look around or watch T.V.

Buying into the American dream is largely an unconscious act; it's just the way life is, and is only questioned after a worker loses his or her job or is unable to gain meaningful employment. In other words, it is only questioned once the person is forced to face his or her failure and powerlessness. Once this is faced, it leads to a strong feeling of being betrayed by society. And this often leads to alienation from friends who are still "making it" and believing in the American dream, as well as from one's spouse, though the latter response is more a need to blame someone than an actual anger.

Blue-Collar Values

Probably the definitive characteristic of life peculiar to the low pay/low skill, blue-collar person is work. The work experience of blue-collar people involves taking orders, paying respect to superiors, and experiencing failure. Failure especially confronts those in service sector jobs which provide them with little financial remuneration and almost no job security. The increasing deindustrialization of America also threatens those in traditional high paying and/or secure jobs with failure through loss of work. Work influences all of their lives, even down to their preferences for strict, conventional morality. In most of their jobs, there is only one way to do it, the right way. Pipes only fit together in one specific way, or they have to do it the way the boss says. There is no room for decision-making. The lack of gray area and decision-making during their working lives provides no background for situational ethics. To blue-collar workers, there is only the disciplined keeping of the rules. This and only this is rewarded.

Work also influences the leisure time activities of the poor working-class. Work, especially on the production line, is so boring and so discouraging to creativity that its mold can't be broken during leisure time. Workers come home and watch T.V. They have to have their entertainment fed to them, just as they are required to have their working decisions fed to them. All creativity is sapped from them. They get no relief from the monotony of their work.

Failure is a haunting reality for the poor. The structures of society seldom allow any of the working class to rise economically to the middle-income level or higher. And even if their income level does rise, their class status does not. To compensate, the blue-collar people tend to emphasize the importance of being respectable. Respect is sacred because it fills up the gap left by a lack of class status, and is therefore vehemently upheld. Of course, the poorer the blue-collar individual, the less he or she is concerned with respectability. If it appears that even respectability is forever beyond your economic grasp, the time spent trying to uphold it even in lip service seems a waste. So preoccupation with respectability depends upon how economically close one is to the upper classes of American society. . . .

Failure and Self-Blame

This brings us to a discussion of the particular effects of failure upon blue-collar people. As has already been suggested, failure results in self-blame, instead of a measured understanding of the structural evils of American society. Since the existence of structural evil is not admitted with the religion of achievement, those still operating within this religion must find someone to blame for their failure, and this can only be themselves. Often, if they have jobs that are high-paying, they also shift the blame to liberals, who take from those who have and give to the poor. Blame-shifting also leads to racism — it's not that they believe blacks are inferior, it's just that they feel the need to hang onto every penny they get, and it hurts to see money taken from their pockets and given to those who have nothing.

A recent example of this took place in Philadelphia when 500 whites demonstrated in front of the home of a black couple who had moved into their neighborhood. The whites in this blue-collar neighborhood did not understand why all the out-siders were calling them racist. For them it was simply an economic decision. Blacks lower the property value and the stability of the neighborhood, they said. The whites were just working together to insure that the sanctity of their neighborhood and their own respectability were maintained. It wasn't a racial decision from their perspective.

But always in back of this victim-blaming is the belief that the failure they live in is their own fault. This is especially true for the poorest blue-collar workers. Often this leads to the blue-collar tendency to put on an air of toughness. It also leads to the more destructive loss of personal dignity, which often gets drowned in alcohol. For most poor working-class individuals, alcohol is a regular part of life and a regular part of family problems.

Dependence on alcohol often brings about alienation from family and friends. But alienation is even more severely increased by the insecure job situation most blue-collar individuals survive in. As jobs end, they move to another area looking for more work. This rootlessness keeps them from being involved in community organizations like churches. They are then locked into a severe individualism that keeps them from ever developing a power base that would enable them to confront the practices of the upper classes. So politics is a dirty word to them. It merely stands for the way the rich take the poor person's money. Most blue-collar individuals don't bother to vote.

There is also alienation toward those of the upper classes, often expressed in derogatory remarks about "college boys" doing blue-collar work to get through school, desk jobs, etc. because they sense that they are being exploited by those who have so much more than they do.

Failed Men, Fractured Families

Lack of personal dignity, alcohol dependence, or alienation from family and society can each on its own ruin a marriage; but in cases combining all three, there is little hope. Marital instability is common among the poorer blue-collar individuals. In the working class community surrounding Emmanuel Chapel in Philadelphia, there is a high ratio of families headed by women. There is also an exceptionally high ratio of alcoholism among the men. These two seem to go together. But there is no direct and necessary link between the two.

When I worked as a security guard in North Philadelphia, I worked with several women who were the heads of their families. Betty Leonard was married and provided the sole income for her family. Crystal James was a single mother who was trying to provide for her child. She had never been married. As we talked, they both painted the same picture of men. Once the men were faced with their powerlessness and forced to admit failure, especially at an early age, they lost their sense of dignity.

Because male dignity is culturally tied to providing for one's family, a man who has difficulty doing so often gives up and assumes that he is worthless. The man sees himself as financially dependent upon the wife and guilty of only spending her money. Paradoxically, this often drives him into the bars to spend money drinking with his friends. Infidelity often results because the man longs for a sexual relationship where he does not need to face his dependence. In an affair, it is much easier for him to pretend. Few marriages survive these problems.

This situation is one of the reasons for the growing number of female-headed, single parent families. Crystal often stated that she had no intention of ever marrying because she couldn't afford to have a husband. A child, on the other hand, was seen as providing more emotional support than a husband. And children provide a form of retirement security in old age. Husbands are often viewed in poor communities as drains on an already bad financial situation. . . .

The Church and the Blue-Collar Worker

This is the world of the blue-collar American, at least in a small part. But where does the church fit into this world? First the reality. The church for the most part ignores blue-collar people. They, for their part, ignore the church. They feel alienated from the class of people usually found in the church and since they move often, they do not have time to put down roots and get involved in community organizations. I am not so sure that this is not a trait found among churchgoers of

every class in the U.S., since evangelicalism has tended to focus on the spiritual in a sense that excludes all social dimensions of life.

The most effective method of curing this alienation and segmentation of the church is to attack the religion of achievement head on by providing an alternative to it. The doctrine of grace provides the most radical means for doing this. It teaches that human dignity is not earned or deserved in any way, but is a free gift of God. Human dignity can only be found in a correct relationship with God. Being a human of worth means living to fulfill God's purposes in reaching and changing society. The ability and inclination to do this come from God, and this provides a new and constructive direction for changed lives to take, one which is dignity-affirming. In other words, if the church is to reach the blue-collar person, it must emphasize that Christianity is not for the powerful of this present evil age, but for the victims, the losers. Jesus sides with the poor. And in the Christian life, cross-carrying, the refusal to play the world's game, must be emphasized over developing theological sophistication.

It may even be that the emphasis of our Christology should change. Could it be that we have emphasized Christ as a victor and powerful because we white, male, American Christians are the powerful and victorious in society? Maybe it would be more beneficial to focus on a Christ who was fully human, powerless, and picked on.

A Christ who maintains his fidelity to the kingdom when he has no power to control history from the outside, who immerses himself in it in self-surrender, can speak to those who have no earthly reason to hope for liberation. He can help them to keep on keeping on or to "hang in there."

What is needed is a recognition that the gospel is for the people labeled failures by society, couched in hope and grace so that they find their dignity renewed in the fountain of life. On the practical level of preaching, this means that they don't hear sermons lambasting them for, say, drinking too much, and just calling upon them to quit drinking. When they fail to quit, as usually happens, this just adds another failure to their list, and attending church, their last hope for dignity, becomes a guilt trip. Rather, in calling upon them to quit drinking we must follow Paul's outline: Look what Christ has already done in saving you, just imagine your worth; now, you need to change in this area, so do it before you bind yourself again under sin; I'm confident that you'll change because God is in you, just look at all he's accomplished so far. They need to hear the ethical imperatives of the gospel couched in the indicative of the hope they have in Christ Jesus. It is only from a base in dignity-affirming hope that they will ever find the strength to change.

Addressing Structural Evil

In order to speak relevantly to the world of the working classes, the U.S. church must force itself to recognize the existence of structural evil. The Fall not only placed mankind in the situation of original sin, it also made them masters of a twisted world. The structures we totally depraved individuals have made are anything but just or neutral. It must be recognized that not all sinful or destructive situations in people's lives result from personal sin. Many result from structural evil alone. Many others stem from structural evil causing personal sin in the believer's life.

For example, I do a little work with street people. In Pennsylvania, if you are between the ages of eighteen and forty and are an unmarried, able-bodied individual (as the welfare agency defines this when your application comes in), you can collect welfare three months a year, $170 a month. Even during these three months, you aren't given enough money to rent an apartment. To get enough money, you need a job. But to get a job, you need to dress neat, look neat, and smell clean. To do this, you need an apartment, both for the opportunities it provides for cleanliness and the security it affords in hindering people from taking your presentable clothes. The structures of society force you not to be able to work. You become "lazy" because no other choice is open to you.

Perhaps the largest group of street people are those over sixty-five who never made enough money to receive large Social Security payments. This group constitutes about ten percent of the homeless in the U.S. Many of them worked at low-paying, service sector jobs all their lives, and at forced retirement didn't have enough money to live in an apartment. Some of these people drink heavily. In order to help them quit drinking, we must recognize the structural factors pushing them toward alcoholism and deal with these as well as the personal sin in their lives.

Often, when we come from the suburbs and are on the victorious side of society's structures, we are too quick to accuse the counselee of blame-shifting when he claims he is a victim of the system. We have to open our eyes and recognize the truth often present in this statement. It would be wrong to leave it here, saying, "It's really too bad that you are a powerless victim." Rather, we need to show them how, through Christ and their Christian friends, they can conquer the structures and change the resultant sin in their lives. Counseling is not a simple situation of merely dealing with individual sin.

This willingness to recognize structural evil will also determine the style of our evangelism. Explaining to people that they are sinners is necessary, but it is only one side of their lives. People are also the sinned against. This is especially true in the case of working-class individuals, because of their low position on the power ladder. They know that their bosses take advantage of them and abuse customers through false advertising and packaging. Traditionally, the church focuses on individual sins like laziness, anger, addictions, and infidelity. But when the blue-collar fellow hears this, he feels even more like a failure. What he does is evil, but his boss's actions don't seem to be viewed as nearly so bad. If it doesn't lead to despair, this recognition leads the worker to reject Christianity as just one more tool for keeping him inferior, echoing the message of American culture.

We must first recognize the violation of the blue-collar worker by society and other people. Only then will they listen to the message of the gospel delivered to them as willful violators of God. Only then will they come to a God who can free them both from being violated and from being violators. This is the path evangelism must take. In my year and a half as a security guard, I witnessed to nearly a dozen different guards. The path I have just outlined was the only one which led — and almost every time it did lead to this — to their coming to me the next day and asking to hear more about God. They often told me that they never heard a Christianity like this: this was a relevant Christianity.

If the church is to successfully combat the alienation and compartmentalization it tends to produce in the minds of the working-class, it must change its attitude toward work. It must hold that Christianity determines how you do your work and which jobs you may hold in a far more radical degree than just promoting witnessing to co-workers. It must maintain that God is relevant to all of life. In doing this, the church must cease siding with the upper-class in seeing that the most common sins involved with the work place are worker laziness and cheating the boss by taking a few too many minutes at break. These shouldn't be ignored. But underpaying workers, withholding holiday pay, unsafe work areas, lack of adequate insurance, harassment of employees, cheating employees out of benefits, and demanding that employees participate in unethical business transactions are all extremely common practices of corporate leaders, but practices seldom addressed by churches. We must recognize the need to fight for justice in the work place.

But while fighting for work place justice, we must remember to do so within the outlines provided by working-class culture. Overstepping these bounds, though done with the best intentions, will turn the very people we are trying to help against us.

An example of this is the story of Douglas Roth and the other pastors of the Denominational Ministry Strategy (DMS) of the Mon Valley in western Pennsylvania in 1984-85. As unemployment began to grip the steel industry, and the banking practices of Mellon and other smaller Pittsburgh banks exacerbated the problem, the ministers of DMS decided to fight for the lives of their congregations. They were seeking to provide employment and financial relief for the unemployed, but only succeeded in alienating most of them. They used leftist rhetoric, calling the banks and steel industry evil monoliths, and used terrorist, though non-fatal, tactics.

For the working class, this was just too radical a break with the American dream and life as they've been taught to understand it. They abandoned the ministers of DMS. Instead of instilling a concern within the middle-class for the less for-tunate, they alienated them. And those blue-collar individuals who had "made it" were too wrapped up in respectability to be associated with DMS.

In order not to fail as DMS did, we must be sensitive to the people as we work for justice *with* them. The best way is to let them lead, and listen to their plans to change things, and use these when possible.

The Church as Relational Community

The most successful model for the church in working-class areas is that of a community. When blue-collar individuals are active in the church, it is because they see the church as a community, a place where they can meet and do things with their relatives and friends. The church needs to provide for them what society cannot: friendship, mutual dignity, a sense that they are needed and irreplaceable. This involves including single parent families as real families.

This has implications for involving the laity in the ministry of the church. They need to be given responsibility in ministry and allowed to make decisions concerning the fate of the church, though it takes time to develop these qualities and interests in people who have been trained all their lives to obey others' decisions. This would also reinforce the servant model for all Christians, the model which says grace is the basis of dignity, and caring for others provides meaning for life. It helps them repudiate society and its evaluation of them.

In doing evangelism, door-to-door methods don't work in the city. If you are working with urban, blue-collar individuals, and often even in smaller communities, the best method of evangelism is friendship. At Emmanuel Chapel, most of the evangelism is done by friends talking to other friends and inviting them to Bible studies, church, etc. This method has begun to produce good results.

The amount of relational work that must go into providing a community for the congregation will eventually exhaust a minister. At Emmanual Chapel, our pastor has carried most of the relational work of the church, having for the most part only the elders to help in this. Recently he has experienced chest pains and has been forced by the doctor to slow down. The sheer amount of work demands that the laity be mobilized. The problems of the people, given their personal and structural make-up, aren't just solved at conversion, but take many years of counseling and fighting the structures of society. No one man can do this. The whole congregation must be active in helping each other.

This also works itself out in a lack of structure in church life. Programs and structures only alienate the working class. Most things must be done in informal, relational ways. In talking with Wilson Cummings, pastor of Emmanual Chapel, he mentioned that they could get no Bible study system of core groups going until, on their own, different people of the congregation began meeting together. After these groups were started, they could be tied into a network. All attempts to organize home Bible studies in the different areas where members live had failed; but the Bible studies have recently been starting as people informally banded together to study the Bible. He also mentioned that in training one of the deacons recently, the man was unable to complete the program designed to prepare him for ordination. But when the pastor met with the candidate and just asked him to read the books because the pastor thought they were good, the man did read them and fulfilled all other requirements for the diaconate.

The religion that is attractive to the working class tends to be less rational and sophisticated, and more relational and dogmatic. Their faith is believed without qualification, emotionally; and they express themselves through a strong creedalism and dogmatism. Their work and life experience teach them that there is only one right way to obey the rules, so they value dogmatic conviction over intellectual broadmindedness. In preaching and teaching, it is important to remember that spontaneity and emotion are valued over the formal and rational. They respond better to repeated eternal truth which they can feel in their bones than to theological insight and argumentation.

To sum up, the best way for the church to go to the blue-collar world is not to enter as a saviour claiming, "Here we are to save your souls and get your lives on the right track." Nor must we go in and merely import our categories and forms into their world. We must take the years to listen to them and learn their concerns. And where possible, we must let them take the active leadership.

Both as ideal and as reality, the family-wage norm has waned. Is it a norm worth retrieving? I am convinced it is. The great numbers of households in which adults are unable to support their families with the wages they are able to attain for their work is just as morally intolerable today as it was in [Monsignor John A.] Ryan's time. Such families, so many of them headed by women, testify to the continued relevance of framing wage questions in terms of basic human rights and social morality. The injustice these families suffer is still usefully expressed as the denial of sufficient remuneration to ensure a decent livelihood for self and family — that is, as the denial of a family living wage.

If the family living wage is to recapture public attention as a compelling agenda, however, both its rationale and its description require revision.

It plainly will not do to frame the moral agenda for a family living wage *in the form or with the justification* familiar to Ryan and much modern Catholic social teaching. That form and justification were bound to patriarchal presuppositions that have bred an overly individualistic construal of men's public economic rights, while socially and economically devaluing women and children, homemaking and parenting. Economic justice today will require a new, more equitable, marriage of home and workplace. . . .

If we can agree that childrearing and homework should be regarded a full-time occupation, *for which just remuneration in some form is due,* we then face difficult policy questions: how much remuneration? delivered in what form? from whom? under what system of accountability? Given that change starts from where we presently stand, what is the most promising path toward realizing the family living wage agenda sketched here? Let me propose for debate a two-staged approach.

A first step, one that may already be gaining some implied consent in contemporary U.S. practice, is to press for full employment and for a "family living wage" (an amount sufficient to reasonably support self, spouse, and children) for every adult wage worker, male or female, regardless of marital or family status. This goal has the advantage of being simple and clear, and it avoids applying different wage scales to people in different life situations — an option that was rejected by Ryan for prudential reasons (though he accepted wage differentials for single women and single men). Today the female employee is at least as likely as her male counterpart to be head or sole breadwinner of her household. Since at present, white women employed full time make, on the average, only two-thirds of the salary of white men — black and Hispanic women only about one half of white male salaries — the struggle to achieve comparable worth for female-concentrated occupations is of critical importance. Such an approach can draw on many of the arguments advanced by Ryan, extending the designation of individual familial rights and duties to adult women as well as men. Choice and monetary freedom would be maximized for individual adults in this "liberal" expansion of Ryan's proposal.

If this level of remuneration were accorded all adult workers, dual-earner households could in theory afford for either worker to forego earnings during periods of high familial intensity, or to pay a fair rate to competent assistance in upholding domestic duties while both parents work outside the home. Single household heads could afford full-time domestic and child care help and could, at least theoretically, choose to work part time at different points in the family and child-rearing cycle. Lacking some family allowance system, single parents would not, however, have the option of caring for their own home and children full time. Nor, given present workplace practices, could dual-earner families expect to periodically switch to part-time status without paying penalties in salary scales, advancement, and job security.

These limitations return us to a central point. Short of qualitatively upgrading the social and economic value placed on the domestic activities of citizens, and adjusting the mutual expectations of employers and employees accordingly, simply upping or equalizing wage scales will not change much. To truly accomplish the sense of "family living wage" introduced here, "living wage" must come increasingly to mean not just cash amounts, but hours and conditions of work, career tracks, benefits and leave policies, pension and insurance plans that conduce to the fulfillment of one's domestic, along with one's public vocation.

— Christine Firer Hinze, "Bridge Discourse on Wage Justice: Roman Catholic and Feminist Perspectives on the Family Living Wage," *Annual of the Society of Christian Ethics* (1991): 119-20, 124-26

The New Agenda of the Black Church: Economic Development for Black America

Lloyd Gite

Hartford Memorial Baptist Church leaders laid out a plan in 1985 to reclaim their northwest Detroit community. It involved no small endeavor. All the telltale signs of a neighborhood beyond hope were there: doors of once prosperous businesses were shuttered; abandoned buildings sat crumbling for blocks; rats and vermin had overtaken vacant lots and the streets had become a public dumping ground.

Even longtime residents thought only a miracle could restore their neighborhood and provide much needed jobs for its people. Well, if a sound business plan and the means to carry it out qualifies as a miracle, they were right.

Today, that once vacant land is leased to African-American entrepreneurs operating McDonald's and KFC franchises. Several social service agencies and a school also use the land. In August, the church broke ground on a reported $17-million, 80,000-sq. ft. shopping center that will include a supermarket, drug store and restaurant.

"Hartford Memorial also has plans to construct a 40,000-sq. ft. auto-care and commercial center and a multimillion-dollar housing project. Initially, church members paid $500,000 for the vacant properties now under development. Today, the land is believed to be worth more than $5 million.

Lloyd Gite, "The New Agenda of the Black Church: Economic Development for Black America," *Black Enterprise*, December 1993, pp. 54-59.

Hartford Memorial Baptist Church has established a grand model for other churches to follow," declares Arthur L. Johnson, vice president for university relations at Detroit's Wayne State University. "This is a city where economic resources have been sharply curtailed and white flight has occurred on a massive scale. White business interests have withdrawn and in large measure they have failed to be active partners in the rebuilding of Detroit. Hartford is now a partner."

Rev. Charles Adams, Hartford Memorial's pastor, sees the church's mission and impact from a personal and practical vantage point. "The church needs to concentrate on the business of creating economic institutions," declares Adams. "The issue is jobs. People being laid off through all this corporate downsizing is affecting every black community in this country. The church finds itself in a situation where it is the best continuing, organized entity in the black community for the acquisition and redevelopment of land, the building of business enterprises and the employment of people."

Adams' view of the church as a vehicle for economic empowerment in African-American communities is not novel. Dating back to slavery, the black church has been an epicenter for spurring social, political and economic self-help among its congregations and extending out into the community. Then as now, bad times breed activism. But driving this new movement is a population of pastors and parishioners who are better educated, more sophisticated, and have far more political and economic clout than their predecessors. This generation of church leaders fully recognizes the power of ownership and entrepreneurship. And they realize that, given their collective money and expertise, they are in a unique position to jump-start their communities. "Given our tremendous economic resources, it is possible for the church to create projects that will revitalize our communities, empower our people and revive their spirits," says Rev. W. Franklyn Richardson, General Secretary of the National Baptist Convention, USA. Furthermore, says Richardson, who is also pastor of Grace Baptist Church in Mt. Vernon, N.Y., "Our churches have millions of dollars invested in banks. We must ensure that banks reinvest in our communities."

Nonbelivers need only check the black churches'

collective spreadsheet. A 1981 study by Martin Larson and Stanley Lowell estimated that African-Americans contributed about $1.7 billion to their churches annually. C. Eric Lincoln, author of *The Black Church in the African-American Experience* and professor of religion and culture at Duke University, places the amount today at roughly $2 billion. Emmett D. Carson, author of *A Hand Up: Black Philanthropy and Self Help in America*, notes that "90% of all black giving is channeled through the church," making it the one enduring institution in low-income black communities with the ability to secure major credit.

Nor is there any question about the commitment of these churches. "The black church recognizes it has to be in the forefront of economic development," says Lincoln. "It has become evident that black people are simply going to have to stand on their own feet and the black church, with all of its economic power, can help facilitate that by creating businesses."

The churches profiled below are among a growing number doing exactly that. They are multidenominational, stand in distinctive parts of the country, and haven't all been blessed with massive congregations and overflowing coffers. What they do share is a belief that the salvation of their communities depends on basic business and economic development. Behind them are pastors and church leaders who view the church's role as not just social or spiritual, but entrepreneurial as well, and can rely on congregants who are willing to pool their resources to create a strong business arm for the church.

Rebuilding Blighted Areas in New York

In 1978, Allen African Methodist Episcopal Church, inspired by its ambitious pastor, Rev. Floyd H. Flake, took the first giant step in what would become a major community redevelopment campaign. Using a $10.7 million HUD grant, it built a 300-unit senior citizens housing project. Over the next 15 years, Allen Church established numerous service institutions, including a school and a multiservice center housing a prenatal and postnatal clinic. But it also became a builder of businesses, buying and rehabilitating more than 15 boarded-up storefronts in its Queens, N.Y., community. Today, these storefronts house a travel agency, medical and legal professional offices, a barber shop, a restaurant, a home-care agency and a preschool.

The initial financing of these projects began with money from the collection plate. But as its holdings grew, Allen Church was able to secure several hefty loans to keep up the momentum for these projects. Today, Allen Church continues to set aside one-third of the $3 million it collects annually from its 6,500 members for development projects. The church is currently negotiating to buy a Burger King and a Ben & Jerry's ice cream franchise. Also in the works is a $9-million new home for the church itself. "If our churches ever learn the power that they have, we can turn the urban communities of America around and have control of them," says Flake, who is also a U.S. congressman.

Nearby, in the Bedford-Stuyvesant section of Brooklyn, Bridge Street African Methodist Episcopal Church is also transforming one of the most blighted areas of the city. The church owns and operates the Bridge Street Preparatory School, a credit union, apartment buildings and a soon-to-be-built 86-unit, $7.2-million senior citizens housing complex.

Bridge Street has also joined forces with 10 other local churches to revitalize the 40-block area surrounding the church. The massive project is spearheaded by the Consortium for Community Development, a nonprofit corporation. With financial assistance from several city, state and federal housing agencies, hundreds of vacant apartments and storefronts have been purchased and are currently being renovated. Several multimillion-dollar grants are enabling Bridge Street to renovate 40 housing units and erect 22 duplexes with the Enterprise Foundation and the New York Housing Partnership. Of the more than $1.3 million in tithes and offerings the church collected last year, over $600,000 was spent on renovation and construction projects. Among them is the ongoing renovation of a former drug den, which will eventually house Bridge Street's Head Start Program.

"The black church is the one place in our community where people come together and pool their resources to better minister to the church and the community," says Rev. Barbara Lucas,

Bridge Street's assistant pastor. "But it's big business, and we must run it like a business."

L.A. Church Provides Lifeline

Shortly after the 1992 riots in Los Angeles, the mammoth 9,500-member First African Methodist Episcopal (FAME) Church of Los Angeles swung into action. As an economic lifeline for the devastated community, the church created the FAME Renaissance Program to fund community services, business and economic development programs through private and public funding sources. FAME Corp. is a nonprofit organization established by the church.

Shortly after the Renaissance Program was formed, church officials competed for and received a $1-million grant from the Walt Disney Co., leading to the creation of the Micro Loan Program, which supplies low-interest rate loans of $2,000 to $20,000 to minority entrepreneurs in the area. So far, the program has approved about 34 loans totaling more than $500,000. Among the beneficiaries are day-care centers, transportation companies, restaurants, a medical billings business, cosmetics companies and a manufacturing firm. "We deal with people who won't qualify for a bank loan," explains Mark Whitlock, executive director of the Renaissance Program. "We don't mind if you have a couple of bad nicks on your credit. We don't mind if you're a brand new business that has never received a business loan before."

But FAME does mind delinquent repayment. It requires applicants to present their business plans to a panel of experienced entrepreneurs and bankers. Loan recipients whose businesses have been in operation less than two years must also go through the church's 10-week entrepreneurial training program.

Once completed, the church's moral and technical support network kicks in. "Our membership base has some 300 attorneys, 200 CPAs and 700 business owners," explains FAME's Whitlock. "For every loan we make, the recipient also gets a mentor to help support that business." Finally, there's that crucial bottomline edge: "We suggest to the congregation that they do business with the company owner we just made a loan to."

The Micro Loan Program recently received a $500,000 grant from Atlantic Richfield Corp. Ultimately, the church hopes to raise $10 million from corporations to fund as many as one thousand businesses.

Atlanta Church Spreads the Wealth

While a number of African-American churches have just begun to launch the economic redevelopment projects for their communities, Atlanta's Wheat Street Baptist Church began changing the face of its historically black neighborhood in the early '60s. Today, it boasts more than $33 million in real estate holdings, making it one of the wealthiest African-American churches in the nation.

The church's nonprofit corporation, the Wheat Street Charitable Foundation, owns and manages two housing developments, several single-family dwellings and an office building. The foundation also owns Wheat Street Plaza North and South, two shopping centers located in the heart of the Martin Luther King Jr. historic district. They were built in 1969 on land purchased with church monies and bank loans, and are currently getting a $120,000 face-lift thanks to an interest-free loan from the City of Atlanta.

Says Rev. Michael Harris, the church's pastor: "Before we can think in terms of heaven by and by, we've got to live here on earth. And Wheat Street, through its economic development projects, wants to make sure life on earth is as good as it can be."

Rural Churches Build Businesses

Not all African-American churches involved in economic redevelopment are located in major cities. A growing number of rural churches are launching businesses providing job opportunities for their members, many of whom are poor people with few skills.

When the nondenominational Mendenhall Bible Church was formed in the early 1970s in Mendenhall, Miss., church leaders knew that if they didn't provide jobs for their members, nobody would. So, they created Mendenhall Ministries, a nonprofit corporation, and built a business complex that today includes a health clinic, law office, elementary school, thrift store and recreation center. The projects were funded by private and public grants and a few bank loans.

In building its school, Genesis I, Mendenhall Ministries bought a long-abandoned school building for $20,000 — it took church members one week to solicit this money from residents and corporations. But the building was in such poor condition they soon realized that renovation would easily run into the tens of thousands of dollars. That's when the church network stepped in.

"A church group from Aurora, Ill., brought 162 people down here to completely remodel and refurbish the building," recalls Rev. Dolphus Weary, associate pastor and president of Mendenhall Ministries. "They also brought about $75,000 worth of materials to do the job." Flooding the community with skilled and unskilled volunteers, the Aurora group spent one week reinforcing the two-story building's foundation, making it possible for the rest of the Mendenhall community to finish the restoration in about four months.

Mendenhall Bible Church, with only 125 members, is now trying to lure a manufacturing plant to the community to provide even more jobs for its people. It stands as proof that a church doesn't have to be large or rich to bring about tangible, positive change.

Another church making a difference in its rural community is Greater Christ Temple Church in Meridian, Miss. Bishop Luke Edwards, the church's pastor, believes in the power of pooled resources. When he founded the Pentecostal church in 1974, it had only 35 members, 96% of whom were on welfare. Edwards, now 67, got them to pool their food stamps and buy wholesale. Four months later, church members were selling food to community members out of a makeshift grocery store set up in the church auditorium.

In 1978, they parlayed proceeds from that grassroots enterprise into the $18,000 purchase of a small supermarket, which they ran for several years before selling it. Today, under its REACH Inc. (Research Education and Community Hope) nonprofit corporation, Greater Christ Temple owns three restaurants, a bakery, an auto repair shop and a 4,000 acre farm with 700 head of cattle and two meat processing plants.

Greater Christ Temple has 200 members who have "delivered themselves from welfare by pooling their resources," says Edwards. "Being black, it's very difficult to get loans. We realized we had to turn to one another. We just had to work together."

Should Your Church Get Involved?

Though increasingly essential to the redevelopment of their communities, church-related business ventures can be risky. It's crucial that such endeavors be set up and run like businesses.

One of the most common problems with church-related businesses is tax problems and the commingling of funds. Under no circumstances are church funds to be mixed with foundation or community development corporation monies. In 1991, the Department of Justice subpoenaed all the records of Allen Church in Jamaica, N.Y.

After a four-week trial and $2 million worth of defense work paid for by the church, the Justice Department dropped their case, prompting Flake to chalk up the entire episode to political harassment. Still, the minister says he learned a valuable lesson about running church-related businesses. "When we began developing these organizations, we did not have CPAs and lawyers on base all the time," Flake says. "We did more by heart and instinct. Of course we did everything by the book to the best of our knowledge, but one has to be very careful."

Increasingly major corporations, cities, foundations and private individuals are offering grants to churches to help fund redevelopment projects. But not all churches are comfortable with such financial arrangements, which frequently have strings attached.

Hartford Memorial Baptist Church learned a painful lesson when it received a grant in the hundreds of thousands of dollars from a conservative foundation based in Washington, D.C. Hartford's credit union complied with the grant's requirement to make loans to high-risk business ventures. Unfortunately, "the economy turned and many of the persons who were borrowing this money had good ideas, but that was it," explains Adams, Hartford's pastor. "They didn't have a good business plan; they didn't have a good handle on cash flow. Their ideas went down the drain and so did our credit union."

Bridge Street pastor, Rev. Fred Lucas, also advises caution when seeking such funds: "We actually received a grant for $15,000, but we felt the stipulations were too stringent and were taking us in a programmatic direction that we felt uncomfortable with. So we sent the money back. You always have that option. Just have your attorneys and program managers read the fine print," he advises.

Churches must also realize that not every business venture is going to succeed. In 1980, Mendenhall Ministries first got into farming by purchasing a 120-acre farm for $90,000. At its peak, the farm had 45 head of cattle and crops of peaches, watermelons, peanuts, cucumbers and peas. The crops were sold to help raise money, but it wasn't enough. The farm was closed in 1991. The church paid off the loan, but lost about $60,000 on the venture. "The same kinds of risks that are associated with economic development normally will be associated with church-related efforts," warns Emmett Carson.

Despite the risks, most ministers say they wouldn't have it any other way. Without such involvement, they say, black communities across this country would face extinction. "The risk of not doing it is greater than the risk of doing it," declares Adams of Hartford Memorial. "If we take the risk, we can provide employment opportunities, and our children can begin to acquire the skills that will take them up the ladder of economic independence."

Clearly white America has never been a friendly environment for blacks. White America has always hindered black Americans from flourishing either as individuals or as a group. In the past blacks have not despaired to the extent that many do today. The reasons are largely economic. Blacks are dispensable today in ways that they were not even one generation ago. The principal causes of this recent discovery are twofold: first, the postindustrial structural changes in our economy caused by the technological revolution in communications; and second, the rapid growth of a new immigrant class eagerly absorbing domestic and other unskilled jobs previously held by blacks.

Ironically, though a stereotype of blacks is that they are lazy, they were imported for centuries as slave laborers to build much of this country's infrastructure. There was no unemployment in slavery, and the only lazy people were the slave owners. And though there was malnutrition, there was no starvation. This does not mean that things were better then than now. It does suggest that even the most perilous suffering did not prevent people from creating a culture of hopefulness that inspired constructive strategies of survival and resistance. . . .

The face of contemporary racism is mirrored in the fact that white America can flourish without blacks. This is the first time in the nation's history when such a claim has been plausible. Hence the nation feels no sense of moral outrage about the plight of the black poor; the delayed maintenance on urban infrastructures; the low educational performance of poor black children; the cutbacks in domestic assistance programs and the removal of job accessibility; the warehousing of blacks in prisons; the billion-dollar drug industry that flourishes at the expense of black lives; or the astounding levels of toxic waste stored in poor black neighborhoods.

Significant advance out of this crisis can occur only with the emergence of creative, effective black leadership. Is it platitudinous to say that we who remain among the shrinking class of hopeful citizens must support all endeavors that "keep hope alive"?

— Peter J. Paris, "In the Face of Despair," *Christian Century*, 27 April 1994, pp. 438-39

Connecting Ministry with the Corporate World

David A. Krueger

For some people religious life and business practice are integrally related in a creative tension. For others — both clergy and business professionals — the worlds of church and corporate life are galaxies apart, separated by ignorance, hostility, apathy, language, interests, values. But to profess Christ and participate in the Christian community requires us to affirm a connection between faith and economic life. The faith of the Hebrew and Christian Scriptures is that God is ruler of all creation and all realms of human life — economic, political, cultural and personal. To assert otherwise is to suggest that the God of the Scriptures is but a god among gods with competing spheres of sovereignty.

To profess Christ as Lord of all is to suggest that God's kingdom penetrates all of life and that the moral demands of discipleship — love, justice, faithfulness — reach into every system and institutional arrangement. To affirm such a universalism of faith requires us to denounce dichotomies like "sacred and secular," which can provide conceptual crutches for the artificial compartmentalization of faith and various spheres of life. Whatever our occupation, each of us is called to a vocation of service to neighbor and community, be we priest or hangman, as Luther said. The U.S. Catholic bishops affirm the connection eloquently in *Economic Justice for All* when they write, "To worship and pray to the God of the universe is to acknowledge that the healing love of God extends to all persons and to every part of existence, including work, leisure, money, economic, and political power and their use, and to all those practical policies that either lead to justice or impede it."

Neither church nor business is monolithic. The pluralism of theologies and ecclesiologies makes it difficult to generalize about ministry. The multifaceted texture of American corporate life and practice and the enormous diversity of people's experiences within business make it difficult also to generalize about ministry to the business world. Our different foundational notions of God and church as well as our various empirical impressions of the corporate world inform our models of ministry to business.

When the primary posture of the church's ministry to the corporate world is a critical, prophetic one of denouncing corporations for their alleged ills and failings, business can seem utterly godless. The other extreme is an uncritical accommodation to corporate culture, assuming its practices are fully consistent with God's intentions for the world. Business becomes a god.

Both attitudes are theologically and descriptively unsatisfactory. As we are both saints and sinners, so our social institutions embody both good and evil — at the same time. Somewhere in between these two extreme approaches lies a proper connection between the church and the world of business, a relationship of critical, healthy, lively tension that is both prophetic and supportive, critical and constructive, challenging and affirming. Such ministry embraces both the radical transformative demands of love and the prudent recognition of the permanence of sin in the human heart and in the structures of society.

At the Center for Ethics and Corporate Policy we have sponsored an annual clergy education project that attempts to enhance clergy sensitivity to economic and workplace realities. For part of the program, clergy spend a day in the workplaces of one or two congregants. This permits clergy to see how faith might connect to work in practical ways and also to gain insight into the ethical dilemmas inherent in corporate life. In all cases, the executives claim that this is the first time their clergy have visited them at work. In most cases, clergy say this is the first time they have set foot in their congregants' workplaces. In all cases,

David A. Krueger, "Connecting Ministry with the Corporate World," *Christian Century*, 30 May–6 June 1990, pp. 572-74.

clergy say the experience heightens their own understanding of the realities laity face as they attempt to be Christians in the corporate world.

We try to operate with certain principles about the nature of ministry to the corporate world. First, one should engage in such ministry with humility and openmindedness. While Scripture and the Christian tradition have much to say about discipleship, they provide neither a blueprint for the rapidly changing, increasingly global economic order nor easy answers to the myriad of ethical issues in modern corporate practice: work force reductions, plant closings and corporate restructuring, corporate governance, the role of women and minorities within organizations, concern for sustainable ecosystems, relationships with local communities, business-government relations and the reality of multinational businesses. Scriptural norms, principles and visions of life are often articulated in highly poetic, paradigmatic, allegorical, even cryptic language that does not lend itself to easy application. Scripture articulates general norms of love, justice and community, often conveyed in concrete narrative illustrations, but rarely provides the systemic and institutional strategies and tactics to accomplish those ends in a complicated technological age.

Second, one should engage in ministry with businesspeople as a listener and mutual learner. Church professionals have much to learn from laity in the corporate world who profess allegiance to both the church and the corporation. Countless people in the private sector struggle every day to relate faith to work and to embody within their occupations a larger sense of religious vocation and calling. Often, though, they feel that their concerns and experiences are not primary to the agendas of their congregations. Likewise, the laity have much to learn from church professionals — both clergy and educators. Clergy can increase effective lay ministry in the workplace by nurturing members of congregations in the basic fundamentals of the faith — literacy in Scripture and Christian traditions and participation in liturgy and the rhythms of the church year. Seminaries can function as creative centers for the continuing education of the laity in the workplace.

Listening and mutual learning are essential given the partial nature of knowledge and experience. We know less than the full truth; we see less than the whole of reality. When people generalize from their own partial experience and vision of the world, they run the risk of falsely characterizing the whole — an easy pitfall when reflecting on the religious and moral character of business. It is easy, for instance, to generalize from a particular corporate takeover and conclude that all mergers and acquisitions are bad. Anecdotal evidence is usually insufficient for moral conclusions.

Rarely are there sustained opportunities within communities of faith to reflect upon the ethical dimensions of work in light of faith. Congregations must become, to use James Gustafson's expression, "communities of moral discourse" where congregants debate in a spirit of civility and openness social issues of the day in light of their faith. Faith communities and religious traditions, by themselves, cannot provide answers to all moral questions of modern corporate life. But they can become seedbeds of creative thought and action for church members who desire to embody the vision and norms of faith in the policies and practices of their corporations.

Third, the church must seek links between its language and values and those of the corporate world. The language of faith — prophetic, narrative, symbolic, allegorical, unconditional — often stands in contrast to the language of business — strategic, operational, quantitative, measurable, conditional. Churches must work to find common words and values that permit more explicit connections between faith and work, thereby giving clarity and substance to the ministry of participants and shapers within business organizations. The corporate trend toward articulating mission, corporate values and ethics statements, as well as attending to corporate culture and external constituencies, points to areas laden with notions of purpose, value, obligation and community — notions inherent in faith communities. Similarities and distinctions can be probed between the economic value of efficiency and the religious value of stewardship. The corporate push for quality, excellence and customer satisfaction can have religious dimensions — analogues to service and servanthood. Demographic trends are forcing employers to take greater account of growing numbers of women and minorities in the workplace in such areas as recruitment, career development, employee benefits and family policy.

Fourth, faith communities must be discerning and strategic about the use of prophetic, pastoral and other expressions of ministry. Ideally, a prophetic ministry allows people to recognize sin and calls them to the ideals of the kingdom — justice in the workplace, the diminishing of racism and sexism, and the support and building up of people. But clergy must engage in more tenuous and ambiguous constructive task as well. Critical denunciations of systemic and institutional practices can prompt recognition of social and personal sin and unmet human needs. But they can also function narcissistically and irresponsibly, unnecessarily alienating others and avoiding the more difficult, messy task of reform and transformation. Prophetic denunciation is often of little moral assistance to the manager seeking to discern what is morally possible within the bounds of circumstances, resources and competing claims. It is not helpful, for instance, for the manager to hear the preacher offer wholesale denunciation of workforce reductions and plant closing as a symptom of corporate greed and the triumph of profits over people. Causal factors are rarely so simplistic.

It is more helpful, and more difficult, to ask how biblically informed norms might be sustained and embodied in a rapidly changing global economy. Decisions within the corporate world are shaped not merely by ethical ideals but also by economic social, political and legal constraints. Christian ethics, for most people, becomes the art of discerning the morally "more or less," the less than perfect "better or worse," in the myriad of trade-offs among competing values and interests. As the reform movements sweeping through Eastern Europe are learning, denunciation of evil and corruption is a necessary first step toward social change, but constructing new institutional arrangements is by far the more arduous task.

Fifth, the church's efforts at ministry with the corporate world must begin with self-reflection and evaluation. Churches are themselves corporations. As the U.S. Catholic bishops acknowledge, churches must judge themselves by moral standards that are at least as rigorous as those to which they would hold other corporations accountable. As churches model their own convictions and norms in their institutional policies and practices, their capacity to influence the corporate world will strengthen. Does it matter that the Evangelical Lutheran Church in America asks its Board of Pensions to divest itself of all securities of companies doing business in South Africa but at the same time signs a multimillion-dollar contract to purchase IBM computers for its entire headquarters? How rigorous and pure must the church be?

Finally, churches must let the very categories and frameworks by which they construct ministry to the corporate world adapt to the larger political and economic trends that are revolutionizing the globe. In past decades, larger debates about the merits of capitalist and socialist systems colored visions of ministry. As the ills of capitalism became apparent in the late 19th century and as various forms of socialism — Soviet, democratic, Chinese — developed in the 20th century, notable Christian theologians — Tillich, the early Reinhold Niebuhr, the early Brunner and more recently, liberation theologians — have advocated the wedding of Christian ethics with socialist economic practice. With such an intellectual heritage within the church, it is no wonder that helping to formulate business ethics policies and ministry to the corporate world has been low on the agendas of many churches and church professionals. But if recent events in the Soviet Union and Eastern Europe are any indication, single-party politics joined with centrally controlled economies are no longer viable experiments in political economy. Capitalism, consisting of heavy doses of free markets and private capital, coupled with a pluralistic democratic political order, may be the only game in town for creating wealth in the ways that satisfy the masses. If this trend is indeed the case, the need for the church's ministry to the corporate world is only magnified.

Theologians throughout Christian history have envisioned the church as a community of believers not separate from the ambiguities of a sinful yet graced world but fully immersed in that world. That vision is also one for Christians in a corporate world that will be called upon to make even greater contributions to the well-being of peoples across the globe. The church must be a critical and constructive partner.

It is in this triangle of people's work, family and people's basic values that a convergence of concerns is now occurring. It is in this nexus that people live out some of their most important values and aspirations. Yet, ironically, it is these very matters which we are least able to discuss. We are freer to discuss sex and corruption than faith and family in the typical business or academic setting. They are too important to talk about. Family and religion have been off limits for business concern. Churches and synagogues have seen their main mission in terms of families and consider economic organization foreign to their task. Family services have tended to focus exclusively on the psychological dynamics of family systems and bracketed off people's religious roots or their economic context. This is the constricted pot that is stunting the flowering of business ethics as well as management theory.

The kind of broadened perspective we need is not a deepening of the rutted paths of our usual conversation but an awareness of the depth energies and structures that integrate people's actual lives. It is in the profound interplay of workplace, family, and faith that we have enormous difficulty coping with the profound changes that are upon us. . . .

Now it is quite clear that we cannot recover the same pattern of integration as that in ancient Greece or in traditional agrarian culture. However, the concept of the *oikos* gives us an orientation toward the process of integration. It symbolizes the human desire to relate these crucial dimensions of existence. *Oikos* is a heuristic concept for analyzing a set of relationships that shapes the way people relate to work, family, and faith. It can be applied to individuals as well as to organizations. It is both psychological and structural.

A person's *oikos* is the way he or she relates these three dimensions to each other. Each of us has an *oikos* of some kind. Some are more explicit than others. Some are more internally congruent and coherent than others. Recognition of our own *oikos* and the way we are struggling toward congruence and integration is a funda-

mental life task. The vision of an ideal *oikos* shapes our judgment about personal relationships as well as institutions, whether they be businesses, families, or churches.

Likewise, each organization has its *oikos* — its model of the way it wants its members to organize their various *oikoi*, the plural of *oikos*. Moreover, each organization, no matter how "rationally" it has been separated from religion and family, tends to develop its own *oikos* to embrace these perennial human dynamics. Firms in the past have given considerable attention to the role and character of the employee's wife (to say spouse in this context would be disingenuous indeed). Her role in the corporate *oikos* was to provide a safe haven and launching pad for her husband. Faith and values were construed in individual terms of personal morals and conformity to the ethos of marketplace dynamics — honesty, promise-keeping, obedience, and rational even-handedness. The function of religion was to keep home life stable so that men could be raised and supported in their economic pursuits.

The religious concept of vocation was transformed into the commitment to a life-long career — at least for professionals. For the entrepreneurs and managers it was a vehicle for expressing their vocation or peculiar talents. For workers, the workplace was to be a source of money to support their family. From a religious standpoint it was a discipline for selfish and sexual inclinations. This pattern dominated the industrial *oikos*. Both the firm and the family were to be run by a lofty patriarch guiding and disciplining weaker and more unruly subordinates. Both poles were united by a religious vision of a divine Father, obedient Son, and dutiful, devoted inspiring mother — the social vision of the traditional Christian Trinity.

Now, however, there has been a shift in the official *oikos*. Religion is no longer content with supporting the family alone. Or, more precisely, many religious groups are no longer committed to the patriarchalism and male individualism that permeated the industrial *oikos*. Not only do they seek to make direct impact on the marketplace or on corporations. They also lift up other models for human relationships — of collegiality, friendship, equality, or nurture.

Correlatively, wives are no longer so content to hitch their wagons to their husband's corporate star. And women don't have to be wives at all to get a piece of the managerial cake. Moreover, sharing of parental tasks has meant that people want flexible hours, job and career patterns, allowances for child-care, home health emergencies, and even paternity leave. Many men are no longer solely committed to their occupational career but see their life's vocation in broader terms that encompass occupational changes, community service, family life, and ongoing personal reassessment.

In short, corporations cannot assume the existence of a single type of *oikos* among their members. Moreover, the *oikos* pattern the corporation projects, whether explicitly or implicitly, greatly affects how employees will relate to it, if they choose to at all. We are therefore confronted not only by a change in our dominant *oikos,* but the presence of a variety of *oikoi.* Families, corporations, and religious bodies all want a say in how this is to develop, because each has a primordial claim on the integrated reality they all participate in.

— William Johnson Everett, "Oikos: Convergence in Business Ethics," *Journal of Business Ethics* 5 (1986): 318-20

Section 2: Challenges for the Business Community

Not only must the churches be open to changes in the way they approach economic questions, but the business community must also work to improve its capacities for addressing moral issues. A decade or more of focus on business ethics has witnessed some change in the business community, but hardly enough. The readings in this section have been organized to reflect a trajectory, beginning with the previous status quo in which business managers seemed to operate in a moral vacuum, and going on to encouraging signs that talk of moral business can no longer be dismissed as a pious oxymoron. The moral voice of business must be cultivated in the voices of its managers and in the structures and opportunities it creates for all those who must work for a living.

Frederick Bird and James Waters reflect conventional worries that professional business managers have not yet acquired a moral voice. Managers expect to use moral standards in their conduct but do not understand either their own sources of moral insight or the moral reasoning justifying their policies and actions. Bird and Waters see serious consequences if businesses are allowed to remain morally mute. Managers may submerge their moral sentiments or experience moral stress. The only answer is cultivating the habit of ethical reflection within the decision-making processes of their organizations. Bird and Waters's brief in behalf of explicitly ethical discourse is still a useful token of the starting point for contemporary business ethics.

One important factor in improving businesses' ethical performance during the recent past has been the movement for corporate social responsibility. This movement has pioneered a shift in corporate accountability structures in favor external stakeholders. Business analyst J. Richard Finlay describes this shift from a shareholder to the stakeholder paradigm. He interprets the converging interests of individual minority shareholders, ethical investment funds, and institutional investors, all looking for recognition of a wider set of corporate values. Finlay sees these trends as supportive of improved ethical performance. He challenges companies to respond to their many stakeholders, believing that more open and constant communication with many external parties will be imperative in future business practice.

The selection from Michael Novak's writings chosen for inclusion here dramatizes the kind of lay theological reflection that such business practice is likely to stimulate. The practice of entrepreneurship raises questions about the theological paradigm of a finished creation, still held by some Christians. He argues that God's creation is not finished. Humans in God's image are gifted with the task of co-creation: they collaborate with God in rendering the earth more amenable to God's purposes. On this foundation Novak argues that there is virtue in economic creativity, entrepreneurial activity, and the wealth such activities generate. He sees business as a community of workers, managers, and entrepreneurs operating together as God's co-creators, and he endorses market economies as decentralized systems that honor human creativity.

Novak's lofty theological vision, while widely shared among Christian business leaders, does not directly specify how business activity ought to be structured and evaluated. Shirley Roels's piece scrutinizes business goals and processes from a

Christian perspective. She examines the three questions central to any effective business plan: Why do businesses exist? What are they to produce and sell? How are they to arrive at the desired results? Roels is concerned to show, concretely, how businesses can be seen as institutions that do fulfill some of God's purposes. Her reflections on the practice of entrepreneurship and management demonstrate that a theological vision of business, articulated from a business perspective, can have significant impact on how businesses are organized.

The Moral Muteness of Managers

Frederick B. Bird and
James A. Waters

Many managers exhibit a reluctance to describe their actions in moral terms even when they are acting for moral reasons. They talk as if their actions were guided exclusively by organizational interests, practicality, and economic good sense even when in practice they honor morally defined standards codified in law, professional conventions, and social mores. They characteristically defend morally defined objectives such as service to customers, effective cooperation among personnel, and utilization of their own skills and resources in terms of the long-run economic objectives of their organizations. Ostensibly moral standards regarding colleagues, customers, and suppliers are passed off as "street smarts" and "ways to succeed."

Many observers have called attention to this reluctance of managers to use moral expressions publicly to identify and guide their decision making even when they are acting morally. A century and a half ago, de Tocqueville noted the disinclination of American business people to admit they acted altruistically even when they did. More recently, McCoy has observed that managers are constantly making value choices, privately invoking moral standards, which they in turn defend in terms of business interests. Silk and Vogel note that many managers simply take for granted that business and ethics have little relation except negatively with respect to obvious cases of illegal activities,

Frederick B. Bird and James A. Waters, "The Moral Muteness of Managers," *California Management Review* 32, no. 1 (Fall 1989): 73-88.

like bribery or price-fixing. Solomon and Hanson observe that, although managers are often aware of moral issues, the public discussion of these issues in ethical terms is ordinarily neglected.

Current research based on interviews with managers about how they experience ethical questions in their work reveals that managers seldom discuss with their colleagues the ethical problems they routinely encounter. In a very real sense, "Morality is a live topic for individual managers but it is close to a non-topic among groups of managers."

This article explores this phenomenon of moral muteness and suggests ways that managers and organizations can deal openly with moral questions.

Actions, Speech, and Normative Expectations

To frame the exploration of moral muteness, it is useful to consider in general terms the relationships among managers' actions, their communicative exchanges, and relevant normative expectations. Normative expectations are standards for behavior that are sufficiently compelling and authoritative that people feel they must either comply with them, make a show of complying with them, or offer good reasons why not.

While normative expectations influence conduct in many areas of life from styles of dress to standards of fair treatment, in most societies certain types of activities are considered to be morally neutral. Choices of how to act with respect to morally neutral activities are considered to be matters of personal preference, practical feasibility, or strategic interest.

Although managers often disagree regarding the extent to which business activities are morally neutral, their interactions in contemporary industrial societies are influenced by a number of normative expectations. These expectations are communicated by legal rulings, regulatory agencies' decrees, professional codes, organizational policies, and social mores. Considerable consensus exists with respect to a number of general ethical principles bearing upon management regarding honest communication, fair treatment, fair competition, social responsibility, and provi-

sion of safe and worthwhile services and products.

Through verbal exchanges people identify, evoke, and establish normative expectations as compelling cultural realities. Moral expressions are articulated to persuade others, to reinforce personal convictions, to criticize, and to justify decisions. Moral expressions are also invoked to praise and to blame, to evaluate and to rationalize. Moral discourse plays a lively role communicating normative expectations, seeking cooperation of others, and rendering judgments.

For those decisions and actions for which moral expectations are clearly relevant, it is possible to conceive of four different kinds of relationship between managers' actions and their verbal exchanges. These are depicted in Figure 1 (p. 888).

One pattern (Quadrant I) identifies those situations in which speaking and acting correspond with each other in keeping with moral expectations. A second congruent pattern (Quadrant III) is the mirror image of the first: no discrepancy exists between speech and action, but neither is guided by moral expectations.

The other two patterns represent incongruence between speech and action. In Quadrant II, actual conduct falls short of what is expected. Verbal exchanges indicate a deference for moral standards that is not evident in actual conduct. Discrepancy here represents hypocrisy, when people intentionally act contrary to their verbalized commitments. Discrepancy may also assume the form of moral backsliding or moral weakness. In this case, the failure to comply with verbalized commitments occurs because of moral fatigue, the inability to honor conflicting standards, or excusable exceptions. Because they are intuitively understandable, none of these three patterns are our concern in this article.

Rather, our focus is on the more perplexing fourth pattern (Quadrant IV) which corresponds with situations of moral muteness: managers avoid moral expressions in their communicative exchanges but would be expected to use them either because their actual conduct reveals deference to moral standards, because they expect others to honor such standards, or because they privately acknowledge that those standards influence their decisions and actions. In other words, with respect to those instances where the mana-

Figure 1. Relations between Moral Action and Speech

	Actions Follow Normative Expectations	Actions Do Not Follow Normative Expectations
Moral Terms Used in Speech	I Congruent Moral Conduct	II Hypocrisy, Moral Weakness
Moral Terms Not Used in Speech	IV Moral Muteness	III Congruent Immoral or Amoral Conduct

gers involved feel that how they and others act ought to be and is guided by moral expectations, why do they avoid moral references in their work-related communications?

For example, a given manager may argue that the only ethic of business is making money, but then describe at length the non-remunerative ways she fosters organizational commitment from her co-workers by seeking their identification with the organization as a community characterized by common human objectives and styles of operation. In another example, managers may enter into formal and informal agreements among themselves. In the process they necessarily make promises and undertake obligations. Implicitly, they must use moral terms to enter and confirm such understandings even though explicitly no such expressions are voiced. This discrepancy occurs most pervasively in relation to countless existing normative standards regarding business practices that are passed off as common sense or good management — e.g., taking care of regular customers in times of shortage even though there is opportunity to capture new customers, respecting the bidding process in purchasing even though lower prices could be forced on dependent suppliers, and ensuring equitable pricing among customers even though higher prices could be charged to less-knowledgeable or less-aggressive customers.

Causes of Moral Muteness

Interviews with managers about the ethical questions they face in their work indicate that they avoid moral talk for diverse reasons. In the particular pattern of moral muteness, we observe that in general they experience moral talk as dysfunctional. More specifically, managers are concerned that moral talk will threaten organizational harmony, organizational efficiency, and their own reputation for power and effectiveness.

Threat to Harmony

Moral talk may, on occasion, require some degree of interpersonal confrontation. In extreme cases, this may take the form of blowing the whistle on powerful persons in the organization who are involved in illegal or unethical practices and may involve significant personal risk for the whistleblower. Even in less-extreme cases, moral talk may involve raising questions about or disagreeing with practices or decisions of superiors, colleagues, or subordinates. Managers typically avoid any such confrontation, experiencing it as difficult and costly — as witnessed, for example, by the frequent avoidance of candid performance appraisals. Faced with a situation where a subordinate or colleague is involved in an unethical practice, managers may "finesse" a public discussion or confrontation by publishing a general policy statement or drawing general attention to an existing policy.

In the case of moral questions, managers find confrontations particularly difficult because they experience them as judgmental and likely to initiate cycles of mutual finger-pointing and recrimination. They are aware of the small and not-so-small deceits which are pervasive in organizations, e.g., juggling budget lines to cover expenditures, minor abuses of organizational perks, favoritism, nepotism, and fear that if they "cast the first stone" an avalanche may ensue.

Many managers conclude that it is disruptive to bring up moral issues at work because their organizations do not want public discussion of such issues. We interviewed or examined the interviews of sixty managers who in turn talked about nearly 300 cases in which they had faced moral issues in their work. In only twelve percent of these cases had public discussion of moral issues taken place and more than half of these special cases were cited by a single executive. Give-and-take discussions of moral issues typically took place in private conversations or not at all.

Threat to Efficiency

Many managers avoid or make little use of moral expressions because moral talk is associated with several kinds of exchanges that obstruct or distract from responsible problem-solving. In these instances, moral talk is viewed as being self-serving and obfuscating. Thus, for example, while moral talk may be legitimately used to praise and blame people for their conduct, praising and blaming do not facilitate the identification, analysis, and resolution of difficult moral conundrums. Similarly, while moral talk in the form of ideological exhortations may function to defend structures of authority and to rally support for political goals, it does not facilitate problem solving among people with varied ideological commitments.

Because of the prevalence of such usages, many managers are loathe to use moral talk in their work. Blaming, praising, and ideological posturing do not help to clarify issues. Moreover, such moral talk frequently seems to be narrowly self-serving. Those who praise, blame, or express ideological convictions usually do so in order to protect and advance their own interests.

In addition, managers shun moral talk because such talk often seems to result in burdening business decisions with considerations that are not only extraneous, but at times antagonistic to responsible management. Moral talk may distract by seeking simplistic solutions to complicated problems. For example, discussions of justice in business often divert attention to theoretical formulas for distributing rewards and responsibilities without first considering how resources as a whole might be expanded and how existing contractual relations might already have built-in standards of fair transactions and allocations.

Moral talk may also be experienced as a threat to managerial flexibility. In order to perform effectively, managers must be able to adapt to changes in their organizations and environments. They are correspondingly wary of contractual relations that seem to be too binding, that too narrowly circumscribe discretionary responses. They therefore seek out working agreements, when they legally can, that are informal, flexible, and can be amended easily. They assume that if the stipulations are formally articulated in terms of explicit promises, obligations, and rights, then flexibility is likely to be reduced. In order to preserve flexibility in all their relations, managers frequently seek verbal, handshake agreements that make minimal use of explicit moral stipulations.

Many managers also associate moral talk with rigid rules and intrusive regulations. Too often, public talk about moral issues in business is felt to precede the imposition of new government regulations that are experienced as arbitrary, inefficient, and meddlesome. Complaints about particular immoral practices too often seem to lead to government harassment through procedures and rules that make little economic sense. Managers may therefore avoid using moral expressions in their exchanges so that they do not invite moralistic criticisms and rigid restrictions.

Threat to Image of Power and Effectiveness

Ambitious managers seek to present themselves as powerful and effective. They avoid moral talk at times because moral arguments appear to be too idealistic and utopian. Without effective power,

Figure 2. Causes of Moral Muteness

Moral talk is viewed as creating these negative effects . . .	. . . because of these assumed attributes of moral talk.
• Threat to Harmony	• Moral talk is intrusive and confrontational and invites cycles of mutual recrimination.
• Threat to Efficiency	• Moral talk assumes distracting moralistic forms (praising, blaming, ideological) and is simplistic, inflexible, soft and inexact.
• Threat to Image of Power and Effectiveness	• Moral talk is too esoteric and idealistic, and lacks rigor and force.

the uses of moral expressions are like empty gestures. Many managers experience futility after they attempt unsuccessfully to change corporate policies which they feel are morally questionable. They privately voice their objections but feel neither able to mount organized protests within their organization nor willing to quit in public outcry. Defacto they express a loyalty they do not wholeheartedly feel.

This sense of futility may even be occasioned by management seminars on ethics. Within these workshops managers are encouraged to discuss hypothetical cases and to explore potential action alternatives. Many find these workshops instructive and stimulating. However, when managers begin to consider problems that they actually face in their organizations, then the character of these discussions often changes. Moral expressions recede and are replaced by discussions of organizational politics, technical qualifications, competitive advantages, as well as costs and benefits measured solely in economic terms. In the midst of these kinds of practical considerations, moral terms are abandoned because they seem to lack robustness. They suggest ideals and special pleadings without too much organizational weight.

Managers also shun moral talk in order to not expose their own ethical illiteracy. Most managers neither know nor feel comfortable with the language and logic of moral philosophy. At best they received instruction in juvenile versions of ethics as children and young adults in schools and religious associations. They have little or no experience using ethical concepts to analyze issues. They may more readily and less self-consciously use some ethical terms to identify and condemn obvious wrongdoings, but do not know how to use ethical terms and theories with intellectual rigor and sophistication to identify and resolve moral issues.

Finally, the "value of autonomy places great weight on lower managers' ability to solve creatively all their own problems they regularly face." They observe how this valuing of autonomy actually decreases the likelihood that managers will discuss with their superiors the ethical questions they experience. . . .

Consequences of Moral Muteness

The short-term benefits of moral muteness as perceived by managers (i.e., preservation of harmony, efficiency, and image of self-sufficiency) produce significant long-term costs for organizations. These costly consequences include:

- creation of moral amnesia;
- inappropriate narrowness in conceptions of morality;

- moral stress for individual managers;
- neglect of moral abuses; and
- decreased authority of moral standards.

Moral Amnesia

The avoidance of moral talk creates and reinforces a caricature of management as an amoral activity, a condition we describe as moral amnesia. Many business people and critics of business seem to be unable to recognize the degree to which business activities are in fact regulated by moral expectations. Critics and defenders of current business practices often debate about the legitimacy of bringing moral considerations to bear as if most business decisions were determined exclusively by considerations of profit and personal and organizational self-interest. In the process they ignore the degree to which actual business interactions are already guided by moral expectations communicated by law, professional codes, organizational conventions, and social mores.

When particular business practices seem not to honor particular standards, then it may be wrongly assumed that such actions are guided by no normative expectations whatsoever. Actually, specific business practices which are not, for example, guided primarily by particular standards such as social welfare and justice may in fact be determined in a large part by other moral expectations such as respect for fair contractual relations, the efficient and not wasteful use of human and natural resources, and responsiveness to consumer choices and satisfactions. Often, when businesses act in ways that are judged to be immoral, such as the unannounced closure of a local plant, they may well be acting in keeping with other normative standards, regarding, for example, organizational responsibility. To assume that conduct judged to be unethical because it is counter to particular standards necessarily springs solely from amoral consideration is to fail to grasp the extent to which such conduct may well be guided and legitimated by other, conflicting norms.

The moral amnesia regarding business practices is illustrated by the debate occasioned by an article by Friedman entitled "The Social Responsibility of Business Is to Increase its Profit." To many, Friedman seemed to conclude that business people had no moral responsibility other than to use any legal means to increase the returns on the investments of stockholders. He did argue that business people were ill-equipped to become social reformers and that such moral crusading might well lead them to do harm both to those they sought to help and to their own organizations. Both defenders and critics assumed that Friedman was defending an amoral position. However, although cloaked in the language of economic self-interest, Friedman's article alluded in passing to eight different normative standards relevant for business practices: namely, businesses should operate without fraud, without deception in interpersonal communications, in keeping with conventions regarding fair competition, in line with existing laws, with respect to existing contractual agreements, recognizing the given rights of employees and investors, seeking to maximize consumer satisfactions, and always in ways that allow for the free choices of the individual involved. It can be argued that Friedman invited misunderstanding by polarizing issues of profit and social responsibility. It cannot be argued that according to his position profits can be pursued without any other moral criteria than legality.

It is characteristic of this moral amnesia that business people often feel themselves moved by moral obligations and ideals and find no way to refer explicitly to these pushes and pulls except indirectly by invoking personal preferences, common sense, and long-term benefits. They remain inarticulate and unself-conscious of their convictions.

Narrowed Conception of Morality

In order to avoid betting bogged down in moral talk which threatens efficiency, managers who are convinced they are acting morally may argue that their actions are a morally neutral matter. They "stonewall" moral questions by arguing that the issues involved are ones of feasibility, practicality, and the impersonal balancing of costs and benefits, and that decisions on these matters are appropriately made by relevant managers and directors without public discussion.

We interviewed a number of managers who made these kinds of claims with respect to issues that others might consider contentious. A utilities executive argued, for example, that studies had exaggerated the impact of steam plants on water supplies. He also contended that no moral issues were relevant to the decisions regarding the domestic use of nuclear power. A pharmaceutical company manager criticized those who attempted to make a moral issue out of a leak in a rinse water pipe. An accountant criticized a colleague for arguing that the procedure recently used with a customer involved moral improprieties. These managers attempted to treat issues that had been questions as if they were not publicly debatable.

Insofar as it is thought that moral issues are posed only by deviance from acceptable standards of behavior, then managers have a legitimate case to shun moral discussions of their actions which are neither illegal nor deviant. However, while appropriately claiming that their actions are not morally improper, managers stonewall whenever they insist, in addition, that their actions are constituted not only by deviance, but also by dilemmas (when two or more normative standards conflict) and by shortfalls (from the pursuit of high ideals). In the examples cited above, the managers were correct in asserting that no illegal nor blatantly deviant actions were involved. However, they were incorrect to argue that these actions were morally neutral.

Moral muteness in the form of stonewalling thus perpetuates a narrow conception of morality, i.e., as only concerned with blatant deviance from moral standards. Most importantly, moral muteness in this case prevents creative exploration of action alternatives that might enable the organization to balance better conflicting demands or to approximate better the highest ideals.

Moral Stress

Managers experience moral stress as a result of role conflict and role ambiguity in connection with moral expectations. They treat their responsibility to their organizations as a moral standard and, when confronted with an ethical question, they frequently have difficulty deciding what kinds of costs will be acceptable in dealing with the question (e.g., it costs money to upgrade toilet facilities and improve working conditions). Moreover, moral expectations (for example, honesty in communications) are often very general and the manager is frequently faced with a decision on what is morally appropriate behavior in a specific instance. He or she may have to decide, for example, when legitimate entertainment becomes bribery or when legitimate bluffing or concealment of basic positions in negotiations with a customer or supplier becomes dishonesty in communication.

A certain degree of such moral stress is unavoidable in management life. However, it can be exacerbated beyond reasonable levels by the absence of moral talk. If managers are unable to discuss with others their problems and questions, they absorb the uncertainty and stress that would more appropriately be shared by colleagues and superiors. In the absence of moral talk, managers may cope with intolerable levels of moral stress by denying the relevance or importance of particular normative expectations. This may take the form of inappropriate idealism in which the legitimacy of the organization's economic objectives is given inadequate attention. Conversely, and perhaps more frequently, managers may cope with excessive moral stress by treating decisions as morally neutral, responding only to economic concerns and organizational systems of reward and censure. In either case, moral muteness eliminates any opportunity that might exist for creative, collaborative problem solving that would be best for the manager, as well as for the organization and its stakeholders.

Neglect of Abuses

The avoidance of moral talk by managers also means that many moral issues are simply not organizationally recognized and addressed. Consequently, many moral abuses are ignored, many moral ideals are not pursued, and many moral dilemmas remain unresolved. Managers we interviewed readily cited moral lapses of colleagues and competitors. The popular press continually cites examples of immoral managerial conduct, often failing in the process to credit the extent to which managers actually adhere to moral standards.

Just as norms of confrontation contribute to moral muteness, in circular fashion that muteness reinforces those norms and leads to a culture of neglect. Organizational silence on moral issues makes it more difficult for members to raise questions and debate issues. What could and should be ordinary practice — i.e., questioning of the propriety of specific decisions and actions — tends to require an act of heroism and thus is less likely to occur.

Decreased Authority of Moral Standards

Moral arguments possess compelling authority only if the discourse in which these arguments are stated is socially rooted. It is an idealistic misconception to suppose that moral reasons by virtue of their logic alone inspire the feelings of obligation and desire that make people willingly adhere to moral standards. Blake and Davis refer to this assumption as the "fallacy of normative determinism." The pushes and pulls which lead people to honor normative standards arise as much, if not more, from social relationships as from verbal communication of moral ideas. The articulations of moral ideas gain compelling authority to the degree that these expressions call to mind existing feelings of social attachments and obligations, build upon tacit as well as explicit agreements and promises, seem to be related to realistic rewards and punishments, and connect feeling of self-worth to moral compliance. That is, moral expressions become authoritative, and therefore genuinely normative, to the degree that they both arouse such feelings and reveal such agreements, and also connect these feelings and recollections with moral action.

Moral ideas communicated without being socially rooted simply lack compelling authority. Such expressions are like inflated currency: because they possess little real authority, there is a tendency to use more and more of them in order to create hoped-for effects. Such language, unless it has become socially rooted, is experienced as disruptive, distracting, inflexible, and overblown. Simply attempting to talk more about moral issues in business is not likely to make these conversations more weighty and authoritative. What is needed is to find ways of realistically connecting this language with the experiences and expectations of people involved in business.

Indeed, in an even more general effect, the resolution of organizational problems through cooperation becomes more difficult to the extent that managers shun moral talk. Cooperation may be gained in several ways. For example, it may be inspired by charismatic leadership or achieved by forceful commands. Charisma and command are, however, limited temporary devices for gaining cooperation. Many managers do not have the gift for charismatic leadership. In any case, such leadership is best exercised in relation to crises and not ordinary operations. Commands may achieve compliance, but a compliance that is half-hearted, foot-dragging, and resentful. Cooperation is realized more enduringly and more fully by fostering commitments to shared moral values. Shared values provide a common vocabulary for identifying and resolving problems. Shared values constitute common cultures which provide the guidelines for action and the justifications for decisions.

It is impossible to foster a sense of ongoing community without invoking moral images and normative expectations. Moral terms provide the symbols of attachment and guidelines for interactions within communities. In the absence of such images and norms, individuals are prone to defend their own interests more aggressively and with fewer compromises. Longer range and wider conceptions of self-interest are likely to be abandoned. Without moral appeals to industry, organizational well-being, team work, craftsmanship, and service, it is much more difficult to cultivate voluntary rather than regimented cooperation.

The Nature of Change Interventions

Several factors must be taken into account by those who wish to reduce this avoidance of moral talk by managers. Those who wish to "institutionalize ethics" in business, "manage values in organizations," or gain "the ethical edge" must take into account the factors which give rise to this avoidance. It is impossible to foster greater moral responsibility by business people and organizations without also facilitating more open and direct conversations about these issues by managers.

First, business people will continue to shun open discussions of actual moral issues unless means are provided to allow for legitimate dissent by managers who will not be personally blamed, criticized, ostracized, or punished for their views. From the perspective of the managers we interviewed, their organizations seemed to expect from them unquestioning loyalty and deference. Although many had privately spoken of their moral objections to the practices of other managers and their own firms, few had publicly voiced these concerns within their own organizations. Full discussions of moral issues are not likely to take place unless managers and workers feel they can openly voice arguments regarding policies and practices that will not be held against them when alternatives are adopted.

Business organizations often do not tolerate full, open debate of moral issues because they perceive dissent as assuming the form either of carping assaults or of factional divisiveness. Carping is a way of airing personal grievances and frustrations, often using moral expressions in order to find fault. Ideally, managers ought to be able openly to voice dissent and then, once decisions have been made contrary to their views, either respectfully support such choices or formally protest. However, business organizations that stifle open discussions of moral concerns invite the carping they seek to avoid by limiting debate in the firs place. Managers are most likely to complain, to express resentment, and to find personal fault in others if they feel they have no real opportunities to voice justifiable dissents.

Legitimate expressions of dissent may be articulated in ways that do not aggravate and reinforce factional divisiveness. Before considering recommendations for organizational change (about which various managers and workers are likely to have vested interests), it is useful to set aside time for all those involved to recognize the degree to which they both hold similar long-run objectives and value common ethical principles. These exercises are valuable because they help to make shared commitments seem basic and the factional differences temporary and relative. In addition, factional differences are less likely to become contentious if these factions are accorded partial legitimacy as recognized functional subgroups within larger organizations. Finally, legitimate dissent is less likely to aggravate factional diviseness if ground rules for debate and dissent include mutual consultations with all those immediately involved. These rules can help reduce the chances of discussions turning into empty posturing and/or irresolute harangues.

Second, if business people are going to overcome the avoidance of moral talk, then they must learn how to incorporate moral expressions and arguments into their exchanges. Learning how to talk ethics is neither as simple nor as difficult as it seems to be to many managers. Initially, managers must learn to avoid as much as possible the ordinary abuses of moral talk. In particular, efforts must be made to limit the degree to which moral talk is used for publicly extolling the virtues or excoriating the vices of other managers. Evaluations of personal moral worth ought to remain as private as possible. Furthermore, the use of moral expressions to rationalize and to express personal frustrations ought to be censored. In addition, the use of moral expression to take ideological postures ought to be minimized. Moral talk ought to be used primarily to identify problems, to consider issues, to advocate and criticize policies, and to justify and explain decisions.

Managers should recognize and learn to use several of the typical forms in which moral arguments are stated. An elementary knowledge of moral logics as applied to business matters is a useful skill not only for defending one's own argument, but also for identifying the weaknesses and strengths in the arguments of others. It is important, however, to recognize that verbal skill at talking ethics is primarily a rhetorical and discursive skill and not a matter of philosophical knowledge. Like the skill of elocution, learning how to talk ethics involves learning how to state and criticize moral arguments persuasively. What is critical is that managers are able to use moral reasoning to deal with issues they actually face in their lives and to influence others to consider carefully their positions.

Managers must regularly and routinely engage with each other in reflection and dialogue about their own experiences with moral issues. The attempt to overcome the avoidance of moral talk by managers by introducing them to formal philosophical languages and logics not rooted in their social experiences is likely to fail. Philosophical ethics is indeed an instructive and critical tool that can be used to analyze moral arguments of business people and to propose creative solutions to perceived dilemmas. It is improbable, however, that many managers are likely to adopt philosophical discourse on a day-to-day basis to talk about moral issues. At best, this language might serve as a technical instrument, much like the specialized languages of corporate law and advanced accounting used by specialized experts in consultation with executives. Such technical use does not overcome the moral amnesia that infects ordinary communications among managers. To be compelling, moral discourse must be connected with, express, foster, and strengthen managers' feelings of attachment, obligation, promises, and agreements.

Moral ideas rarely possess compelling authority unless some group or groups of people so closely identify with these ideas as to become their articulate champions. Moral ideas are likely to gain widespread following by business people as smaller groups of managers and workers so closely identify with these ideas — which in turn express their own attachments, obligations, and desires — that they champion them. This identification is most likely to occur where business people with existing feelings of community, due to professional, craft, or organizational loyalties, begin to articulate their moral convictions and to discuss moral issues. It is precisely in these sorts of subgroups of people who have to work with each other as colleagues that managers will be willing to risk speaking candidly and see the benefits of such candor in fuller cooperation.

The role of senior managers in fostering such "good conversation" among managers in an organization cannot be overemphasized. If they seek to provide moral leadership to an organization, senior managers must not only signal the importance they place on such conversations, but also demand that they take place. They need also to build such conversations into the fabric of organizational life through management mechanisms such as requiring that managers include in their annual plans a statement of the steps they will take to ensure that questionable practices are reviewed, or that new business proposals include an assessment of the ethical climate of any new business area into which entry is proposed.

Finally, interventions require patience. Open conversations of the kind we have been describing will, in the short-run, be slow and time-consuming and thus reduce organizational efficiency. They will, in the short-run, be awkward and fumbling and appear futile, and thus they will be quite uncomfortable for managers used to smooth control of managerial discussions. Patience will be required to persevere until these short-run prob-

lems are overcome, until new norms emerge which encourage debate without carping and acrimony, until managers develop the skills necessary for efficient and reflective problem solving with respect to moral issues, until moral voices and commitments are heard clearly and strongly throughout their organizations.

Ethics and Accountability: The Rising Power of Stakeholder Capitalism

J. Richard Finlay

There is a revolution of a kind which is beginning to confront the major corporations of North America. Its driving force is a combination of minority shareholders seeking recognition of their rights and a new breed of ethical investor striving for greater social justice. Together, these groups are united in their determination to extract a higher level of accountability and responsibility from today's major corporations. This is the rise of stakeholder capitalism, and if it is successful it could fundamentally alter accepted standards of corporate responsibility and performance.

The principle underlying the concept of stakeholder capitalism is both straightforward and far-reaching. It is based on the belief that society's most pressing concerns — including the health of customers and workers, the livelihoods of employees and whole communities, women's equality, the fare of causes like South Africa, environmental safety, the integrity of the financial and capital market system and indeed, much of the world's future — are heavily influenced by what its corporations do or do not do. Accordingly, it is felt that these same constituencies have a stake in the kind of decisions corporations make and how they make them.

J. Richard Finlay, "Ethics and Accountability: The Rising Power of Stakeholder Capitalism," *Business Quarterly* 51, no. 1 (Spring 1986): 56-63.

The Pressures From Within

Ironic as it may seem, the impetus behind the current drive to strengthen corporate ethics accountability comes not from the ideological enemies of business, but from those who have chosen to operate within its ranks. These include enlightened financial institutions and pension funds, minority shareholders and ethical investors. Their tactics are not taken from the time-worn twilight of socialist theory, but from the foundations of the corporate system itself — the stock market, consumer marketplace and the arena of public opinion.

The evolution of this phenomenon should come as no surprise. The modern private sector is itself a child of the struggles against concentration of power in 18th century Britain. There, a new class of mercantilist and business professional began to emerge and press for an opening-up of power and a widening of benefits beyond the Crown. Today, as a major concentration of power, the corporation is itself the centre of efforts to have its power controlled and its benefits broadened by a similarly determined new class of activist.

Another aspect of this phenomenon is its battle ground upon which it is being fought. For years business has toiled mightily to create a most sophisticated consumer marketplace. It is one in which price and economics are but one part of the decision-making process — and frequently downplayed in the face of other more heavily promoted factors such as taste, image, convenience or even patriotism. So it is that business should not be surprised that the same marketplace has begun to evaluate corporate contributions not just in terms of the bottom line but also on the basis of much larger human, social and emotional considerations. As more and more individuals begin to see the stake they have in corporate decisions and actions, they will seek to influence the marketplace in such a way as to reflect their interests. The good news for business is the fact that these stakeholder groups have decided to meet corporations on their own "turf" — in the marketplace instead of at the barricades.

So it is that social responsibility advocates and minority investors have found themselves occupying the common ground of similar needs and complementary abilities. Social responsibility activists have begun to use the financial marketplace and techniques of corporate share ownership as means of advancing their causes and influencing positive corporate behavior — while at the same time putting financial assets to good use. For their part, minority shareholders have increasingly sought to make management more accountable for its actions and conscious of a larger commitment beyond its own short-term self-interest. As well, individual investors have become more sensitive over the years to the potential damage associated with corporate activities that are unethical, illegal or just badly conceived. And they have begun to look with more curiosity on the role that social responsibility advocates — and now ethical investors — have played in reading the danger signals arising from such corporate action. Together, these two groups share a growing disdain for corporations and management styles that are unresponsive to the needs of society's various public and financial constituencies, and a growing desire to change those conditions.

Primum Non Nocere: The Legitimacy and Ethics of Power

The notion of social responsibility is deeply rooted in North America's attitudes toward large corporations. Almost three decades ago, A. A. Berle offered the following explanation for the reasons behind such concern:

> Whenever there is a question of power there is a question of legitimacy. As things stand now, these (corporations) have the slenderest claim of legitimacy, which also means finding a field of responsibility and a field of accountability. Legitimacy, responsibility and accountability are essential to any power system if it is to endure.

Long before these issues were raised in North America, however, the German industrialist Walter Rathenau (1867-1922) was posing the questions: "What is the place of the large enterprise in modern society and in the modern nation? What impact does it have on both? And what are its fundamental contributions and its fundamental responsibilities?" But it was the sudden burst of major concerns over environmental quality and pollution, consumer health and safety, and corporate ethical abuses of price-fixing and political pay-offs in the early '70s that took the issue of corporate power out of the realm of philosophy and forced it onto the agenda of public action.

Such concerns continue to dominate the public's view of its major corporations. They are given all the more weight by what has become a growing litany of egregious activities on the part of some of North America's largest corporations. A. H. Robbins, for example, faces years of costly litigation and lost consumer confidence for its handling of problems arising from the dalkon shield contraceptive device. Johns Manville sought voluntary bankruptcy in an effort to save all legal action due to health damages resulting from its manufacturing of asbestos. The deaths of thousands in Bhopal remains a permanent legacy for horror for Union Carbide. The giant brokerage house of E. F. Hutton pleaded guilty last year to an elaborate scheme to defraud millions of dollars from U.S. banks. Major defence contractors General Electric and General Dynamics were the subject of public repudiation and Congressional censure regarding over-billing and padded invoices. . . .

The message would seem clear enough. Matters of poor ethics, unresponsive behavior or lack of concern for the health and safety of consumers, workers, and the public can carry with it enormous costs — not the least of which are financial. And they serve to emphasize that the first responsibility of any business is to not knowingly do harm — and to make certain that it knows no harm is being done.

The Prescience of Social Responsibility

The fact that many examples of corporate disaster and disgrace were first spotted or predicted by social responsibility advocates has not gone unnoticed by many minority shareholders and institutions. Indeed, there seems to be an increasing awareness that the insights and sensitivities offered by social responsibility activists can provide an important window into the future of certain corporations. Long before North American auto makers began to lose out to Japanese imports, Ralph Nader and others had warned that the domestic car industry would pay a heavy price for its smugness and failure to change. The same kind of corporate thinking that was reluctant to build in added safety features in North American cars was also slow to adapt to the growing demands of customers for greater reliability and fuel-efficiency. Domestic auto makers lost billions as a result. Such examples vividly demonstrate that a weak sense of corporate responsibility will almost invariably lead to a condition of financial loss of some kind, whether in the form of foregone business, unrealized opportunity, erosion of share values or civil and criminal penalties. Almost always, it is the shareholder who winds up footing the bill for such financial fiascos. . . .

The Coming Coalition for Corporate Change

Major change is clearly at the doorstep of the corporate sector. On the one hand, there is a growing segment of socially concerned institutions and individuals who have discovered that by becoming a part of the capitalist system they are better able to give life and heft to their convictions. The expansion of ethical investment funds and the determination of various individuals and organizations to invest in those corporations they believe socially responsible represent the vanguard of a trend of potentially enormous impact. Its power will be greater if it is able to attract the increasingly affluent children of the activist sixties into its ranks — enabling the socially conscious so-called "Big Chill" generation to leave its special mark on this aspect of society as it has done with so many others.

On the other hand, this is a change that comes equally from a more traditional source of business participation. It is spurred by an ever increasing population of individual minority and institutional investors who have begun to consider themselves no longer the passive coupon clippers and dividend takers they once were and more as active stakeholders in the decision-making process of their corporations. One of the more important aspects of this new role is that shareholders no longer see themselves as the simple captives of management's convenience but more as surrogates for the integrity and perceived fairness which

a healthy capital market requires and an increasingly skeptical public demands.

Where these two new trends converge — social responsibility advocates in search of better ways to influence the advancement of corporate values and traditional shareholders seeking more recognition for their wider interests — the prospect of a formidable fusion of forces exists. Add to this the many pension funds, levels of government, churches and universities which are active in the equity markets and are under increasing pressure to have their investment decisions reflect and support their social values, and what emerges is a powerful coalition for corporate change.

The power of these two groups is all the stronger because of their symbiotic relationship. To be effective, social responsibility advocates and ethical investors require the greater market clout and investment sophistication that traditional shareholders and institutions can offer. And to ensure better the integrity of their own investment and financial marketplace, these same shareholders need the business and political prescience enjoyed by the new breed of social-investment activist.

Together, these two groups have a common need in pressing corporations to be more open and accountable for their actions, in transforming what is frequently seen as the narrow self-interest of management into a wider commitment to the interest of all stakeholders, and in making sure that corporate resources are used fairly and in ways that avoid posing danger to consumers, employees, the environment, the public interest or the political "capital" of the corporation. . . .

Choices and Tactics

Apart from investing in existing ethical funds, shareholders and social responsibility advocates have a number of other ways by which to advance their common interests. The fact is existing ethical investment funds may not offer all investors the kind or size of choices they require. In some cases, investors are committed to their holdings in particular corporations. In other cases, social advocates may have a genuine desire to attempt to change the direction of certain corporations which affect them or their society in undesirable ways.

What is paramount in social responsibility or ethical investment decisions is that they be based on intelligent and deliberate analysis. Given the complexity of the capital market today and all the financial and social ramification it entails, all investors should reflect more frequently on what they are trying to accomplish, what is important to them and how consistent their investments are with those values.

How should such shareholders go about advancing their concerns? The creation of more independent forums for discussion and consultation would seem part of the answer. Information sharing among institutions, pension funds, church, university, ethical and minority investors could provide added perspective and lay the groundwork for shared action.

Investors wishing to improve the level of accountability and ethical performance of their corporations would do well to find ways of improving communications with management. There is probably no better way of achieving better understanding of complex matters than through face-to-face discussions. Certainly, shareholders and management would have to concede that such methods for gaining information or influencing action are far preferable to the various other remedies which are at the disposal of and are being increasingly employed by aggrieved shareholders.

A Stakeholder Strategy for Smart Business

Increasing trends toward corporate accountability and social responsibility bring with them profound consequences for the world of business. How should it respond? The first step is for top corporate decision-makers to understand the dynamics of the challenge that faces them. Persistent assertions on their part, for instance, that corporate and capital decision-making is "value free" and based solely on economics and not social or moral concerns will continue to do more harm than good. The public and its investing community alike know from painful and costly experiences — many of which have been discussed throughout this article — that social and moral impacts or omissions by the corporate sector can and do have far-reaching costs — financial and otherwise.

Moreover, for their part, major corporations are increasingly seen as major players in the social and political arenas: contributing to charitable causes and political campaigns, as well as lobbying for and against all kinds of legislation. Whether the issue is day care or tax reform, business seems more and more to have an opinion and is often highly active in influencing political acceptance of its views. Clearly, if business is concerned about things that lie beyond its formal functions of, say, building cars or finding oil, it should not be surprised that others are interested in its own impact on social concerns too.

How corporations organize themselves to deal with these new pressures is another indicator of their enlightened thinking — or its absence. Gone are the days when the full spectrum of investor and other stakeholder concerns can be met once a year at the annual meeting. One-way communication, such as quarterly and annual statements, is also not sufficient. Suggestions as to the advisability of holding more frequent meetings with shareholder and other interested groups have already been expressed. Management can be assured that if it fails to hold such meetings, shareholder groups will find ways of meeting among themselves to combine forces and chart strategy.

A New Lease on Corporate Governance

It now seems that the rising tide of shareholder and ethical investor activism is really part of a much larger wave of public concern that has been sweeping across the boardrooms of the business world for several years. It is, therefore, not likely to make a fast retreat. Wise corporate strategy would recognize both its importance and its potential value, and accord such concerns the highest level of attention in the organization.

At a time when a good deal of criticism — in business, regulatory agencies and political circles — has been focusing on matters of corporate governance in general and the role of the board of directors in particular, issues of ethics and accountability seem timely and tailor-made for board review. Part of that process should take the form of a special committee established by boards of major corporations to examine all aspects of investor relations and social responsibility. Matters such as management codes of conduct, share-holder communications and grievance procedures and relations with socially concerned organizations are obvious topics for such review. Furthermore, directors more than any group in the corporation need to be concerned about where future risks lie, about potential disaster areas and about the consequences of courses of action — or lack of them — which are unforeseen. Directors often have the ability to bring a greater level of objectivity to such concerns. And while many would say that directors have the moral obligation to undertake such examinations of their corporations and their impacts, they clearly have an even more powerful motivation. More and more, individual directors are being held legally culpable for major oversights and misdeeds on the part of the corporations they govern. And they would likely gain considerable respect in many quarters if directors began to assume more responsibility as the ultimate guardians of corporate integrity within their organizations.

Turning Expectations into Assets

Success in business is often the difference between corporations that find ways of turning challenges and difficulties into their advantage and those that do not. There can be little question that major corporations are being challenged by a whole flock of new constituencies — and some of them among its own ranks.

There is also little question that the many mergers and acquisitions that have occurred of late will have an impact upon how such concentrations of power and capital are viewed. At the very least, it appears that the public will demand a level of perceived and demonstrated responsibility and accountability on the part of these larger corporations that is more commensurate with the scale of their influence.

At the same time, it seems apparent that minority shareholders, pension funds, social responsibility advocates and other groups will also look for ways of expanding their power and influence over the organizations in which they have a stake. If they are unable to achieve their objectives in the marketplace and in the corporate sector, history suggests that they will seek their objectives in the

political arena. For a business community that has only recently been freed from the heavy shackles of government over-regulation, this is a prospect that ought not to be ignored.

To the extent that society may well evaluate its major concentrations of private power in terms of how responsibly and accountably they operate, a considerable opportunity exists for individual corporations to make a strategic difference. Those who choose to be known for the standards of their integrity, ethics and responsibility to society may also find a good deal of added support in their traditional business market. Such genuinely held convictions would obviously appeal to this new breed of shareholders, ethical investors and accountability-conscious pension funds. Indeed, improved relations among corporate stakeholders would seem to hold the greatest hope for continued success in the future.

Finally, it would seem logical that wise corporations acquaint themselves with the skills of those who have a proven record in anticipating the futurity of corporate impacts. The same skills, for instance, that allow social responsibility analysts to discern emerging issues of corporate folly can also be used to determine new and untapped opportunities down the road. As such, an important strategic tool is available to the innovative corporations.

Clearly, it is one that sensible investors will find more and more difficult to ignore. The counsel of one astute social observer stands the test of time:

> . . . for knowing afar off (which is only given a prudent man to do) the evils that are brewing, they are easily cured. But when, for want of such knowledge, they are allowed to grow until everyone can recognize them, there is no longer any remedy to be found.

Those words were written by Niccolo Machiavelli more than three hundred years ago. For corporations and investors looking for the most successful path to the future, no more timely advice could be offered.

The Lay Task of Co-Creation

Michael Novak

Capitalism and Creation

"Man," writes Pope John Paul II in *Laborem Exerens,* "is the image of God partly through the mandate received from his Creator to subdue, to dominate, the earth. In carrying out this mandate, man, every human being, reflects the very action of the creator of the universe." In America, the image of God as Creator compelled admiration through the beauty of the mountains, the prairies, and the oceans and — as an exemplar in the immense task of creating a new civilization in the wilderness.

Nature was not always kind. Many perished from impure water, in blizzards, in desolate climates, in swamplands, in places of rocky and barren soil. It may be easy enough today, in a civilization of air-conditioners, to imagine that "the environment" is naturally hospitable to humans, and that humans add nothing to nature but to pollute it. In the early days of this country, the very beauties of the natural environment of this continent were juxtaposed to the relentless power of nature to destroy human life. Wind, flood, desert, and erosion needed to be tamed; resources hidden in nature needed to be brought to human usefulness. The expression "subdue the earth," according to John Paul II, has an immense range:

Michael Novak, "The Lay Task of Co-Creation," in *Toward the Future: Catholic Social Thought and the U.S. Economy, A Lay Letter,* Lay Commission on Catholic Social Teaching and the U.S. Economy, North Tarrytown, N.Y., 1984, pp. 25-45.

It means all the resources that the earth (and indirectly the visible world) contains and which, through the conscious activity of man, can be discovered and used for his ends. And so these words, placed at the beginning of the Bible, never cease to be relevant. They embrace equally the past ages of civilization and economy, as also the whole of modern reality and future phases of development, which are perhaps already to some extent beginning to take shape, though for the most part they are still almost unknown to man and hidden from him.

Creation is not finished. Much of use to humans remains hidden within it. Humans become co-creators through discovery and invention, following the clues left by God. Yet human beings are creators not only in changing the world, but also in realizing their own inner possibilities. Every human being who works must be respected as a person. None is merely "an instrument of production," mere "merchandise," whose labor is merely purchased. Since the early nineteenth century, John Paul II writes, expressions of this sort "have given way to more human ways of thinking about work and evaluating it." Free labor is neither slave labor nor a mere instrument; freedom flows from personality, autonomy, and choice. Yet a materialistic civilization may reverse the priority of looking at humans as true makers and creators, in the image of God, and instead treat man solely "as an instrument of production." "Precisely this reversal of order, whatever the program or name under which it occurs, should rightly be called 'capitalism,'" the pope adds.

While Pope John Paul II clearly defines the term "capitalism" in this way, and while abuses of that sort do occur here, this is not the meaning of the term in the United States. Abraham Lincoln described the system of "free labor" as "the just, the prosperous system," precisely because of the dignity it afforded every free economic agent. Only a market system allows economic agents regular, reliable, ordinary liberties. Only a market system respects the free creativity of every human person, and *for this reason* respects private property, incentives (rather than coercion), freedom of choice, and the other institutions of a free economy. A market system obliges its participants to be other-regarding, that is, to observe the freely expressed needs and desires of others, in order to serve them. A market system is not morally validated because it is productive; command economies, after all, achieve capital accumulation and other material goods through coercion. A market system is validated because it is the only system built upon the liberty of its participants. That it also works better to promote invention and to yield an incredible bounty is a secondary (although not insignificant) advantage. A market system values new ideas, the inventor, the entrepreneur, the creator, and it values the free, individual choices of every worker and participant. It values the free individual, skilled in cooperating in association with others. In no other economy does the worker command more social respect.

Pope John Paul II is clearly in favor of a "reformed" capitalism. Yet Catholic social thought needs to examine more carefully the institutional causes of economic creativity. Creativity does not just happen; in world economies, it is relatively rare.

The Innate Virtue of Enterprise

Experience around the world since 1945 teaches us that the innate virtue of enterprise is universal. It is distributed among the poor as widely as, perhaps more widely than, among the children of the affluent. Like all talents, it is no regarder of birth or station. What is most required for its appearance and its flourishing, however, is a *system* which encourages it. The importance of system — as we said near the beginning — can hardly be exaggerated. In many parts of the world, alas, the natural talents distributed by the Creator are left to wither on barren or rocky ground, and the dynamism of whole peoples is unnaturally repressed.

Catholic social thought itself grew up in an agrarian age. It was shaped through long centuries in which static societies, rather than dynamic developing societies, were the norm. It remains relatively underdeveloped in its conceptions of how new wealth is produced, and how co-creation is accomplished. To create new wealth, specific institutions are required. Specific virtues are required. A specific ethos is required. The gate to creativity is narrow, and the way is strait.

The term "enterprise" is sometimes used to designate the business firm, in a static way, rather than to designate the dynamism impelling a free economy: the *virtue* of inventiveness, risk-taking, and creativity. This virtue, more than any other factor, makes an economy dynamic and leads to economic development. Enterprise is a virtue relatively neglected by theologians, although perhaps included by them as the economic aspect of creativity. In most cultures during most of history, neither the wealthy nor the poor have been enterprising. The miser sat counting up his money, not investing it. The poor saw little prospect of bettering their condition in a sustained and progressive way. Among those with savings, enterprise requires the opposite of possessiveness; it consists in a willingness to lose gains already acquired by placing them at risk. Among the poor, it inspires imagination and adventure, rather than resignation. The incentives for enterprise are more than material. They include the excitement, the beauty, and the satisfaction of making to exist what did not exist before.

Like Abraham Lincoln, Pope John Paul II, as we have seen, speaks of "the priority of labor over capital." Considered as a final cause, the human person is indeed prior to inanimate capital. Yet capital is not only inanimate; knowledge and skills, habits and attitudes are also forms of capital. The fact of widespread unemployment shows beyond a doubt that, as an efficient cause, labor is not prior to capital but, on the contrary, requires new investment as its own prior cause. The creation of new enterprises depends upon the cooperation of others, investors, for example. Capital and labor are both human, and both are present in every economic activity.

The father of Pius XI was a businessman, and so with uncommon insight Pius XI stressed three things: creative intellect, the enterprise, and its work. A business enterprise is not simply assets and liabilities listed on a balance sheet. It "consists in the first place of the human beings who work in it; it essentially consists of them, in association." The business enterprise is "an association of persons who co-operate in production by contributions of different kinds, especially by employing their person ("labour") or property ("capital"); the result (yield or return) of this production is intended to serve the various interests of those involved." Without question, *intellectus* comes first, that is, the initiative and enterprise of management, in personal terms therefore the directors, the top management, whose function is to combine the productive factors, labour and capital, and to get them to co-operate effectively." In short, the relation is triadic: not only labor and capital but also creative intellect. The entrepreneur, who supplied the intellectual vision putting labor and capital together, is a co-creator. In our experience, this role can scarcely be stressed enough. Along with workers and managers — and millions of others in every social role — entrepreneurs are co-creators.

The Entrepreneur

In this respect, the distinguished German Jesuit Oswald von Nell-Breuning, one of the authors of Pius XI's *Quadragesimo Anno,* has criticized the economic teaching of Vatican II precisely because, while praising the dynamism of modern economics, it fails even to mention its chief instrumentality: the entrepreneur. Since Vatican II praised the economic miracles of the reformed capitalist West "in glowing terms," von Nell-Breuning notes, "it is therefore all the more odd that the key-figure in this economy, *the entrepreneur* is not mentioned in any way." Catholic social thought has not yet put sufficient emphasis upon the creative instrument through which new ideas and inventions are brought into service to human beings: the practical insight of the entrepreneur. By themselves brilliant ideas do not serve humankind; to be brought into service to man, they must be transformed through complex processes of design and production. The talent to perform this transformation is as rare and as humanly precious as talent in any other field. Indeed, the promotion of entrepreneurial talent is indispensable if the "cry of the poor" is to be heard. If not the man or woman of enterprise, who else will create new wealth? Who else will invent new opportunities for employment?

Pope John Paul II seems to have come to this same point in his address to businessmen and economic managers in Milan (22 May 1983):

The degree of well-being which society enjoys today would be unthinkable without the dynamic figure of the business man, whose function consists of organizing human labour and the means of production so as to give rise to the goods and services necessary for the prosperity and progress of the community.

In Barcelona (7 November 1982), the pope was more emphatic:

Allow me now, dear men and women workers of Spain, to address my words to another class of workers in Spain: businessmen, industrialists, top administrators, qualified experts in socio-economic life and backers of industrial complexes.

I greet and pay honor to you, the creators of jobs, employment, services and job training, all of you in this dear Spain who provide work and support for a great number of men and women workers. The pope expresses his esteem and gratitude to you for the high function which you perform in service to man and society. To you, too, I proclaim the gospel of work. . . . do not waver, do not doubt your mission. Do not fall into the temptation to give up business, to shut down, to devote yourselves egoistically to calmer and less demanding professional activities. Overcome such temptations to escape, and keep on bravely at your posts, trying to give a more humane face every day to your enterprise and keeping in mind the great contribution you make to the common good when you open up fresh work possibilities.

Major errors were committed by entrepreneurs during the development of the industrial revolution in the past. But that is no reason for failing, dear industrialists, to give public recognition and praise to your dynamism, your spirit of initiative, your iron wills, your creative capacities and your ability to take risks. These qualities have made you key figures in economic history and in confronting the future.

Willingly, we embrace this teaching, confirming it from our own experience. The task of lay persons in the economic order, whether investors, workers, managers, or entrepreneurs, is to build cooperative associations respectful of each other's full humanity. Such enterprises should be so far as is feasible participative and creative, in order to bring out from creation the productive possibilities and the human resources that the Creator, in his bounty, has hidden within it. Economic activism is a direct participation in the work of the Creator Himself.

Economic Talents

Under the leadership of Pope John Paul II, the Church has been placing more emphasis upon creativity — and, particularly, upon the creative task of the entrepreneur and the inventor and all other workers — than ever before. This emphasis is timely. Furthermore, it is important to see that a business depends for its creativity not only upon inventors and entrepreneurs, but also upon an adventurous and skillful work force. Creativity is necessary at every level. Thus, many have come to see that economic activism is as much a vocation for lay Catholics as is political activism — indeed, much more so, given Catholic teachings on the limited state, on the principle of subsidiarity, on liberty, on property and creative action, and on the need for economic development. Naturally, as in the American scheme, the political system, including the state, plays a major role both in empowering and in regulating the economic system. Catholic social teaching has never accepted the strictly libertarian view of "the night watchman state," on the one hand, nor the socialist view of "the managerial state," on the other hand.

The concern for government activities to promote commerce and industry is present on virtually every page of *The Federalist*. The new nation was hardly born when Alexander Hamilton wrote his *Report on Manufactures*. A sound banking policy, it was speedily seen, is an essential contribution of government to economic dynamisms, since government policy disproportionately affects the soundness of money. The U.S. Congress decided through the Homestead Act to settle the West through multiplying the number of owners and economic activists — rather than according to the plantation system of the South (and of Latin America). The government saw its role as that of taking on tasks that would lead to greater productivity: from helping build canals, railroads, ports, and interstate highways to sponsoring rural electrification, farm credit, great dams, and countless other initiatives. Not all of these were wise, or

conducted without corruption. But all vindicated the principle that government, too, has a role in the economy, as the phrase "political economy" explicitly suggests. As distinct from socialism, a democratic capitalist regime seeks to empower others, not to manage all things.

We who are laypersons have learned through our own experience, however, how precious are the liberties which encourage economic creativity, and how easy it is to stifle those liberties through neglect, indifference, excessive state entanglement, imprudent regulation, a decline in capital formation, and the unwise monetary, fiscal, and credit policies of governments. Persons of superb talents in economic creativity are found in every nation, in every ethnic group, in every social class, at every level of formal education. Economic talents, as we learn in the Parable of the Talents (Matt. 25:14-30), are not intended to be buried — but to be employed in wise and creative stewardship, reaping the return for which creative efforts are intended:

[A] man who was going on a journey . . . called in his servants and handed his funds over to them according to each man's abilities. To one he disbursed five thousand silver pieces, to a second two thousand, and to a third a thousand. Then he went away. Immediately the man who received the five thousand went to invest it and made another five. In the same way, the man who received the two thousand doubled his figure. The man who received the thousand went off instead and dug a hole in the ground, where he buried his master's money. After a long absence, the master of those servants came home and settled accounts with them. The man who had received the five thousand came forward bringing the additional five. "My lord," he said, "you let me have five thousand. See, I have made five thousand more." His master said to him, "Well done! You are an industrious and reliable servant. Since you were dependable in a small matter I will put you in charge of larger affairs. Come, share your master's joy!" The man who had received the two thousand then stepped forward. "My lord," he said, "you entrusted me with two thousand and I have made two thousand more." His master said to him, "Cleverly done! You too are an industrious and reliable servant. Since you were dependable in a small matter I will put you in charge of larger affairs. Come, share your master's joy!"

Finally the man who had received the thousand stepped forward. "My lord," he said, "I knew you were a hard man. You reap where you did not sow and gather where you did not scatter, so out of fear I went off and buried your thousand silver pieces in the ground. Here is your money back." His master exclaimed: "You worthless, lazy lout! You know I reap where I did not sow and gather where I did not scatter. All the more reason to deposit my money with the bankers, so that on my return I could have had it back with interest. You, there! Take the thousand away from him and give it to the man with the ten thousand. Those who have will get more until they grow rich, while those who have not will lose even the little they have. Throw this worthless servant into the darkness outside, where he can wail and grind his teeth."

This parable, in fact, stresses not only stewardship but creativity: preserving capital is not enough — it must be made to grow.

In the Catholic tradition, von Nell-Breuning observes, there was for too long a "skeptical, critical attitude to economic life, so frequently found in ascetical writings and in official ecclesiastical pronouncements, which asserts that it diverts men's minds from higher things and attaches them to lower things." Yet in a world in which early mortality is being swept away by advances in medicine and hygiene, a world, therefore, of growing populations, this negative attitude toward economic activism is blessedly being set aside. The task of feeding the hungry, clothing the naked, educating the unlearned, and assisting the millions of all nations to attain their own economic well-being is now a matter of vast social necessity. Economic activism is no longer an avocation of comparatively few; it is indispensable for the entire human family.

Cross-Cultural Clarifications

To make our own position clear, we wish to distinguish it sharply from three common misperceptions. Some hold that anyone who supports a capitalist economy: (a) places all responsibility upon individuals, without reference to social institutions or the social system as a whole; (b) holds to a purely "free market" approach to society, is libertarian, or even "Darwinian"; and (c) excludes the political system, especially the state, from public policy reforms. These claims are false. Our own views are as follows.

The United States differs from the individual nations of Western Europe in its continental size, in its diversity of cultures drawn from the entire planet, in its vast range of regional climates, economic strengths and needs, and in the churning mobility of its population. Thus, it is no wonder that individual U.S. citizens often find themselves far from their neighborhoods of origin, their families, and other familiar social networks, and, through no fault of their own, become vulnerable to chance events. Thus, too, there is great flux into and out of poverty. For such reasons, we strongly support the social welfare systems which help the truly needy until they regain their self-reliance. And we recognize that because of age or disability or other necessity, some cannot be self-reliant.

Second, the very concept of political economy implies that the economic system of democratic capitalism does not stand by itself. The American system is not a free-market system alone, or a free enterprise system alone. The political system has many wholly legitimate and important economic roles, including care for the truly needy. To the one side, we reject statist views which would swallow all of life under state control. To the other, we reject libertarian visions of an "unfettered" economic system, which would measure all matters merely in their economic aspects.

No economic system can pretend to do everything sufficient for a good society. Many human requirements must be met outside and beyond it. The young, the elderly, the disabled, those visited by sudden misfortune, and many others are permanently or for a time unable to work. In a good society, the moral system and the political system must come to the assistance of such persons in ways the economic system alone cannot. In fact, one of the moral obligations of the economic system is to produce the wealth necessary so that the political and moral systems can accomplish these and other tasks.

Third, it is clear from the foregoing that we are

not opposed to the state. We are watchful, as all free citizens must be, lest it abuse its enormous powers, overstep its proper competence and limits, and through unwise actions not only fail to achieve its proper purposes but make matters worse for all. Criticism of errors by the state is no more a failure to respect the legitimate roles of the state than criticism of the economic system is a failure to respect its legitimate roles. Particularly in its welfare functions, as a last resort, the state is an indispensable institution of the good society.

In this context, several major terminological difficulties seem to arise from the differences between Continental and Anglo-American cultures. "Liberalism" on the Continent seems to have connoted a strongly anti-religious animus. This connotation is not typical of Anglo-American liberalism. Further, the Anglo-American concept of liberty, as Archbishop Hughes tried to explain to Rome, means liberty under law, "liberty and justice for all," a liberty constrained both by moral and by political safeguards. On the Continent, by contrast, "liberty" is sometimes defined in opposition to law and to moral constraint, in an alleged contrast between "unfettered" liberty and social good. In Anglo-American culture, the fetters of law, virtue, and custom are normally thought of as indispensable to the constitution of liberty.

Yet again, the term "capitalism" has negative connotations on the Continent which, except among those who approach these matters as socialists do, it does not have in America. Capitalism on the Continent is associated with Darwinism, the survival of the fittest, and contempt for the weak. Yet Darwin's work became popular nearly a century after Adam Smith, whose concern for the poor and moral sense are quite prominent. More to the point, the record of capitalist societies in providing personal liberties, a creative economy, high wages, and unprecedented standards of living for the formerly poor is beyond dispute. The aim of capitalism has been to overcome the tyranny of poverty not solely for the few (who did not need such liberation), but for all, and not solely in one nation, but in all nations.

Finally, on the Continent and in Anglo-American culture, there appear to be quite different concepts of the self. On the Continent, the self is sometimes regarded as if in opposition to society, public order, and the common good. By contrast, in Anglo-American culture, the self is often viewed as having internalized such crucial social values as self is often viewed as having internalized such crucial social values as sympathy, fellow-feeling, benevolence, a sense of fair play, and a due regard for the way the self would be regarded by an objective observer. From among a multitude of texts, we cite but one:

When the happiness or misery of others depends in any respect upon our conduct, we dare not, as self-love might suggest to us, prefer the interest of one to that of many. The man within immediately calls to us, that we value ourselves too much and other people too little, and that, by doing so, we render ourselves the proper object of the contempt and indignation of our brethren.

The judgment of a contemporary social critic is worth including here by way of summary:

A close reading of the *Wealth of Nations* itself suggests that political economy as Smith understood it was part of a larger moral philosophy, a new kind of moral economy. Schumpeter complained that Smith was so steeped in the tradition of moral philosophy derived from scholasticism and natural law that he could not conceive of economics per se, an economics divorced from ethics and politics.

The nature of poverty has changed in two key respects, and this has changed politics. First, the poor are less often self-reliant than they were before 1960. Above all, many fewer are employed. Using the government's definition of poverty, in 1959, 68 percent of the heads of poor families worked at some time in the year, and 31 percent did so full-year and full-time. By 1990, these figures had fallen to 51 and 15 percent. While there still are working poor, they are considerably outnumbered by the nonworking. As fewer of the needy held jobs, more became dependent on welfare. The numbers living on Aid to Families with Dependent Children (AFDC), the main federal welfare program, grew from 3 million in 1960 to over 13 million in 1992.

Of course, many people fall on hard times briefly, and these needy are not distinct from the general population. More significant politically are the 6 to 7 percent of the population, about half of the poor in a given year, who are needy or dependent for more than two years at a stretch. These poor comprise the long-term welfare families, jobless youth, homeless, and panhandlers who have become conspicuous in urban areas. As these groups suggest, poverty today connotes more than low income. It has become associated with a number of other social disorders that are distressing to poor and nonpoor alike — crime, drug addiction, and troubled schools.

The second great fact about recent poverty is that it is much less attributable to outside forces than the destitution of the past. Today's poverty, unlike that of the Depression, is seldom imposed on people by impersonal adversities such as depression, racial exclusion, or starvation wages. Decades of economic growth and equal opportunity policies have abolished the hard-and-fast impediments to self-support by the nonwhite and unskilled that were commonplace before 1960. Most often, today's poverty arises in the first instance from the behavior of the poor themselves, such as crime, drugs, and unwed parenthood. Above all, it results from the fact that poor fathers today often do not support their children, while the mothers usually go on welfare, which pays less than poverty, rather than work themselves.

Many politicians and researchers have supposed that today's poverty, like yesteryear's, must be traceable to outside "barriers" that depress incomes, but the evidence for these is weak and disputable. It has been argued that low wages keep the unskilled poor even if they work, jobs are no longer accessible to the poor of the inner city, racial discrimination keeps the poor out of jobs, welfare mothers cannot work for lack of child care, and welfare receipt discourages work, since recipients with earnings have their grants cut. But research suggests that none of these factors is more than a minor cause of nonwork. The chance to work at wages sufficient to escape poverty and welfare, if not to enter the middle class, appears to be widely available. While barriers to equal opportunity remain, they mainly explain inequality among workers rather than failure to work at all.

It appears that contemporary poverty is due mainly to cultural factors. While most poor adults want to work, some refuse to take the menial jobs that are most available to them. A larger number are simply too defeated by past failures and personal disorganization to work consistently. The poor seem prone to these responses because most of them come from groups — blacks and Hispanics — that have been denied equal opportunity in the past. The reactions have also been exacerbated by the isolation of the inner city from mainstream society.

Without clear-cut barriers to attack, the usual prescriptions of either liberals or conversatives no longer achieve much. The period of larger government of the 1960s and 1970s, known as the Great Society, aimed to overcome poverty by providing a range of new benefits to the poor. But poverty dropped sharply only during the 1960s and early 1970s when there were still enough working poor to benefit from a growing economy. After that, progress was halted, partly by a troubled economy, but mainly because the great majority of poor now were outside the labor force. Voluntary programs such as improved work incentives for welfare recipients and education and training programs for the disadvantaged achieved little, mainly because they could not motivate sustained work effort by their clients. The Reagan era placed new reliance on the private sector, but the boom of the 1980s reduced poverty hardly at all, again because of the work problem. Mere opportunity is apparently no longer sufficient to cause many poor to "get ahead."

— Lawrence Mead, "Dependency and Liberal Political Theory," unpublished paper delivered at the 1992 Annual Meeting of the American Political Science Association, pp. 6-8

Business Goals and Processes

Shirley J. Roels

The call to be God's trustees, to develop image-bearers, and to serve the unfolding kingdom is not limited to our personal economic decisions. It extends as well to the businesses that we create. Without our Reformed theology, businesses are not necessary evils in society. To treat them as such denies that Christ's redemption opens the way to restore economic organizations. Granted, our businesses have falling victim to sin, as has all of culture. But in New Testament times, businesses now can be transformed into instruments of kingdom service. In redeemed times we can view a career in business as a major part of our call from God. Abraham Kuyper argued long ago that we must extend God's kingdom to every square inch of this world. Business occupies millions of kingdom square inches that we must monitor with care. If we assume that our business has a valuable role to play in God's kingdom, our key concern is to determine how we can best fill our roles as God's agents in business.

Three Questions and Answers to Help Us

1. Why are we in business?

Think about commonly assumed business goals. Whether a business is large or small, one commonly hears profit-making suggested as a goal. After all, profit — making money — is what keeps

the economic system working. Upon digging a little deeper, however, we discover that *Christian* business people think beyond that one-word answer.

A small-business owner may suggest that he or she wants to provide a healthy family income. Furthermore, accumulated wealth provides opportunities to tithe to the church and to charities.

Managers in larger companies may suggest other goals. Profit means long-term profitability as measured by return on investment or earnings per share. As such, it provides for the survival and growth of the business. Some of these companies argue that their economic activity helps to raise the American standard of living by providing stable jobs and producing income. They believe that both of these in turn raise the poorer classes of society. Other companies may suggest that providing interesting, creative, and satisfying work is a goal in itself. They pride themselves on developing their human resources. Publicly owned companies may perceive their role as providing a return on the investment of their stockholders. They feel strong obligations to their investors. Finally, some companies may simply state that their goal is to provide economic values to customers — a quality product at a fair price.

Is anything wrong with these goals for business? Most people, Christian and non-Christian alike, would not reject them. There are communal obligations — responsibilities to family, employees, stockholders, and customers. In addition, these goals have created vast benefits for many American households.

The Christian should note, however, that there are also certain pitfalls that should be avoided. Most Christians recognize that profit merely for family income purposes can become an obsession which the Bible condemns. Small-business owners must be very careful in balancing family desires with the needs of employees and customers. We cannot, in good conscience, underpay our help or overcharge our clients to support excessive personal consumption.

For larger businesses, Christians would not quarrel that providing good jobs is a noble goal, especially if it is done by selling quality products at fair prices. Certainly for publicly owned companies, obligations to stockholders are important aspects of good stewardship. For Christians in

---

Shirley J. Roels, "Christians and Economic Life," *Occasional Papers from Calvin College* 8, no. 1 (March 1990): 27-37.

such businesses, the issue is not often whether one should accept certain economic obligations. Rather, the difficult issue is determining by what standards a firm decides on the balance between prices, wages, product costs, dividends, charitable contributions, and retained capital for growth. What framework provides the criteria for distributing accumulated wealth?

The goal statements above, though not bad, are still too narrow. They do not ask: income for what purpose? An increased standard of living for what purpose? What is the best way to distribute a firm's profits? Overall, these goals are not linked to a broader Christian perspective. These goals in no way distinguish Christians' motives from those of decent secular humanists.

These goals, further, do not question the nature of products and services provided and to whom they are distributed. Any product or service which is not illegal is acceptable, presumably, since it provides income, jobs, consumer satisfaction, and investor returns. Little attempt is made to look beyond the current short-term demands of our culture to consider God's intentions.

It is time that we began to evaluate business goals by stricter criteria. Short-term goals defined only by the immediate demands of society should not be ultimate goals for Christians. Instead, we should perceive business goals as the implementation of God's goals for creation.

Let me suggest that we should not cite profit for survival, growth, wealth production, family income, job creation, or even charitable contributions as ultimate goals. Rather, our over-arching business goal is economic service unfolding God's kingdom on earth. Such a suggestion does not deny our more specific objectives. It simply enables us to see them as strategies to achieve our ultimate goal.

If our goal is economic service in the kingdom, our work in business will be characterized by a much broader set of concerns than those cited thus far. First, we will see ourselves as God's trustees both working and caring for the world. Power over resources implies first of all responsibility, not status or private economic gain. Second, our businesses will be characterized by a strong emphasis on service to God's people, image-bearers who come to us as customers and employees. We will serve them with honesty and re-spect. Third, we will work to achieve the common good in our enterprises. Such a commitment will help us develop a basis on which to balance shareholder gains with the needs of employee, customer, and supplier. Fourth, since a vision of kingdom service is global, our business goals must operate within a world-wide perspective. We are interested in doing more than simply raising the North American standard of living, whether our businesses are large or small.

What, then, do we do with the concept of profit? Profit is still crucial to business growth, survival, and all other healthy benefits of production; but now profit becomes a means to an end instead of an end in itself. It is a means by which service to God's kingdom can survive and grow. Max DePree, the former Chairman of the Board of Herman Miller, Inc., and author of the book *Leadership Is an Art*, explains that profit is like breathing. You don't live to breathe, but without breathing you cannot live. Profit allows our businesses to live, but it is not the reason they should live.

Profit remains an important *tool* which permits a business to continue. It can provide for wage increases, finance capital improvements, give returns to owners and investors, and support charitable contributions the company chooses to make. If we have analyzed a business (as owners, stockholders, managers, or other employees) and concluded that the business does provide a kingdom economic service, there is nothing wrong with generating the profit that lets our good activity continue. We must, however, constantly be on guard to see profit as a tool of kingdom service, not an end in itself.

Profits are also a *measure* of the effectiveness and efficiency of our kingdom service. A lack of long-run profitability should cause us to ask important questions about our kingdom service. Are we being efficient in our use of resources? Inefficiency, the poor stewardship of natural, human, and productive resources, results in higher costs and thus lower profits. A lack of profit might signal such inefficiency. Are we being effective in meeting human needs? A lack of profit may indicate that we have missed our target in providing for humankind. This may signal a need to re-evaluate the nature of what we are providing to consumers.

The answer is not quite this simple, however. Many other forces may contribute to profit or a lack of it. Changing consumer tastes and new product innovations affect the results as do economic conditions around the globe. It also is possible that a product or service is needed, but not possible for a profit-making institution to render it. A non-profit structure may be better in some cases. Profitability, or lack of it, cannot, therefore, be completely equated with the quality of one's kingdom service. However, lack of profits at least sends up a warning flag, prompting us to ask questions about what we're doing.

In measuring whether we have met our goals, we also must consider our effects on the *broader* society. Service in God's kingdom is not characterized by narrow boundaries on our responsibilities for the world and its people. We have obligations beyond those to our customers and employees. Although these responsibilities are important, we are still accountable for all the facets of creation which our businesses touch. We should develop a broader mental-performance index, one which considers a stewardship of natural resources, concern for the disadvantaged locally and globally, and sensitivity to the common good — in addition to profit.

Even in a successful business, profit, or lack of it, does not tell us everything we need to know about a business's goals and whether they have been met. Contemporary businesses readily admit that a business has multiple responsibilities and must have multiple measures of success. Peter Drucker notes that since the 1950s General Electric has had eight criteria by which it measures its overall success as a company, including market standing, new-product innovation, community service, and employee well-being. So it should not seem strange to suggest that a kingdom perspective will require additional measuring devices besides profit in any evaluation of the company's performance.

2. What should we produce and sell?

If we agree that our business goal is to provide economic service which unfolds God's kingdom, we must be discriminating in what we choose to produce and market. Traditionally, Christians in business have shunned certain product lines. We agree that Christians shouldn't produce pornogra-phy or market crack cocaine. The avoidance of such obviously harmful products is important. However, for Reformed Christians such an approach is too limited. We need to evaluate more carefully the types of products and services which should be created and distributed as part of God's kingdom.

Many products and services are good and helpful ones in a society. I am grateful for companies that produce the steel used in washers, dryers, and microwave ovens. We should not underestimate the contributions electricity, plumbing, and insulation have made in our lives. Travel agencies provide useful information and helpful tips for vacations and business trips. Health-care providers have improved the well-being of our children and the elderly.

Not all products and services, however, have primarily good effects on us and our earth. Non-degradable plastics and throw-away cans pollute the land. Adding to the range of small appliances on our household shelves may lead to frustration over too many choices, instead of the real satisfaction over a useful purchase. An illconceived condominium development can drain wetlands critical to wildlife. Marketing soda pop in less-developed nations can harm children's nutrition. Manufacturing and selling cigarettes contributes significantly to cancer-related deaths. Offering TVs with 40-inch screens in a disadvantaged area encourages misuse of limited resources. Providing Rambo toys or violent videotapes does not encourage Christian approaches to resolving conflict.

We should carefully evaluate whether the products and services in which we involve ourselves are good ones by asking:

a. Will it likely harm the physical environment?
b. Will it likely have an unhealthy effect on consumer habits, values, or attitudes?
c. Will it exacerbate obvious imbalances in the types of purchases made by consumers?

Of course, no product is perfect. Even good products can have ill effects that we don't intend; and we all would agree that consumers must each evaluate their own situations. A good purchase for one buyer might be a poor choice for another.

As Christians, however, we should not suppose that proclaiming consumer sovereignty will resolve all the issues. Granted, consumers must be responsible for what they buy; but that does not absolve us as producers and marketers of our responsibility. God expects both buyers and sellers to develop the kingdom's character. As manufacturers and distributors, we should bear our share of responsibility for what we offer to consumers.

Finally, Reformed Christians should not simply focus on avoiding unhealthy products. Of equal importance is searching for new opportunities to serve. We should constantly ask ourselves, "What new products and services could aid God's developing kingdom?" As new-product developers and marketers, we are key people affecting future society. In every product idea we generate, in every design we shape, every raw material we use, and every buyer we target, we can aid or thwart the restoration of God's creation.

Perhaps an example will help. Several years ago I worked with students on a new-product development case. The issue was whether a food manufacturer, highly skilled in working with grain products, should launch a new line of toaster ovens, electric knives, corn poppers, and fry pans. We analyzed all the prices and costs. We dissected market demand and distribution strategies. As a group we debated whether the company should go ahead with this investment. Finally one student said, "You know, I don't think they should do this even if it is profitable. This company has resources to produce better food in a world with lots of hungry people. Why are they considering the small-appliance market?" We didn't have the details to answer the student's question, but he focused on a critical issue.

Businesses are always involved in setting priorities. Every choice in product research, development, and marketing involves claims on the resources of God's world and the responses of image-bearers. As God's stewards in business, we should choose our business priorities carefully. We should always ask whether, given the situation of our business and the resources at our disposal, we are doing our best to provide products or services matching important, healthy customer desires.

3. How should we produce and sell?

Finally, Christians also must apply the Bible's perspective to the business processes we use. We must be concerned with our stewardship of financial and production resources. Our superiors and subordinates must be treated as God's creatures. We must uphold honesty, fairness, and healthy motivation in our marketing.

As God's trustees, we must realize the importance of the materials we use and the processes we choose. We must use resources which avoid unnecessary scrap and waste. We should also carefully evaluate the effects of our production materials and processes on the environment. This means we must recycle materials and scrap where possible. Such production decisions matter! Imagine the difference it made when Amway Corporation, a large consumer-products company, decided to use biodegradable plastic for the containers it filled with liquid soaps, cosmetics, and cleaning fluids. Millions of plastic bottles would no longer add to litter and landfill problems.

Our human-resource decisions are equally important. Whom we hire should reflect our business needs; but it also should reflect our concern for the disadvantaged in society. That concern may push us to hire some employees who are not as perfect or as polished as we desire. One group of Christian business owners in the Milwaukee area is currently working to employ minorities from the inner city, some of whom have never held a regular job. These employees require special training, communication, encouragement, and even boundaries. This is no easy undertaking; but these Christian business owners believe it is part of God's call to them to provide jobs to those who most need jobs.

In addition, the way we design jobs, develop an employee's talents, dialogue regularly, and distribute rewards should reflect our Christian perspectives on individuals at work. We must treat each employee as God's image-bearer, respecting each employee's work-related talents and performance as well as the need to balance work with rest and worship.

Marketing strategies also should reflect our Christian faith. Our prices, arrangements with wholesalers and retailers, behavior toward competitors, and promotion strategies all must be fair and honest. Certainly there is a range of options. In establishing prices, one must consider costs, competitors' strategies, research and development needs, and responsibilities to employees and shareholders. Sales promotions could appeal to a variety of health desires while giving accurate information about the product's value. Yet in all our marketing efforts we should remember that our primary goal is economic service in God's kingdom. We should not be concerned first of all with meeting sales quotas, winning prizes, or getting job promotions. Our objective is to match the customer's need as best we can with the products we have available.

Financing strategies must be stewardly ones. Managing the cash flow well can be good kingdom work. We also can build our businesses through retained earnings, stock offerings, partnership arrangements, or debt. Each option has its advantages and disadvantages. Whatever one's financial-management strategy, however, we must carefully balance the desire to expand our business with existing commitments to employees and customers. We should take risks for the kingdom, but these risks must always be weighed against our current responsibilities.

Finally, good management systems can build a sense of human community among employees. We all are God's trustees together, cooperatively engaged in economic service to God's world. We can build a sense of community in our workplaces through good supervisory strategies, adequate opportunities for communication, sound strategies for profit-sharing, responsive organizational structures, and rational planning practices.

No matter how good the products or services we offer, the methods we use to create and distribute them should be pleasing to God. Our products must be kingdom ones; but our *processes* must build God's world as well.

Being Realistic about Our Business Situations

All of us recognize that our reasons for being in business, as well as our production and marketing choices, are affected by the Fall. We should not be grandiose in our vision. Relationships with employees, customers, and suppliers are imperfect. We cannot ignore the actions of our business competitors and must regularly respond to them. All of us have limited business resourses. Most uses of them involve trade-offs. What we give to em-

ployees as salary increases we cannot give to investors as dividends or customers as discounts. A kingdom perspective does not easily resolve all the daily dilemmas we face.

Several suggestions may help us handle these limitations. First, we should not be discouraged when our contribution to God's work seems small. Whether we run a print or a bike shop, sell computers, design tools, produce auto parts, build houses, or market condominiums, we can be God's servants. If God has called us to serve our neighbors in business, that call is not "be powerful," but "be faithful." God wants us to be faithful in being effective trustees, serving as image-bearers, and working for the common good. God will examine our *faithfulness* in business, not its size or relative profitability.

Second, as we make decisions we should regularly seek the help of other Christians in business. William Diehl, a Christian sales representative and manager at Bethlehem Steel for 30 years, created a business breakfast club. Each Monday morning he and about a dozen other Christian business managers discussed business problems and pending decisions. They debated as Christians what they should do with difficult decisions about employees, product lines, and sales approaches. We should form similar groups to help us consider Christian approaches to the complex business issues with which we struggle.

Despite our limitations, we must, as heirs to the kingdom, take risks for the Master. The risk of running a business based on Christian principles is a small price of gratitude compared to the risk Christ took for us. God does not ask that we complete the economic tasks in this world, only that we add to the kingdom. What we cannot accomplish, God will do. Because the kingdom will come, the future of all business goals is held in God's hands. All our Creator asks is that we follow in faith.

Section 3: The Call for New Christian Paradigms

A fruitful public conversation among people of faith and economic decision makers would be enhanced by general agreement on the appropriate frameworks for ethical and economic analysis. New theological, economic, and public policy paradigms are needed, as many Christians already know, to address changing global structures and emerging human aspirations. Such paradigms will surely advance the discussion. This section samples some of the voices involved in the search for new paradigms and seeks to provide some insight into where the search may be heading.

Robert Benne opens the discussion by describing his own struggle to overcome what he considers the inherited paradigm in Christian social ethics, namely, an implicit or explicit commitment to the ideology of democratic socialism. Benne attributes the persistence of the inherited paradigm, not to a basic lack of familiarity with economic theory, but to the academic influence of the New Class knowledge elite as well as underlying societal problems with modernization. On the surface the transparent values of democratic socialism are more attractive than the more complex value dynamics of democratic capitalism. They appear to fit more comfortably with the ideas of those in the postindustrial knowledge sector and also with the prevailing religious eschatology of American society. Yet Benne warns other Christian theologians to break with what he takes to be the reigning orthodoxy so that a fairer and more perceptively critical assessment of democratic capitalism can be developed.

Amy Sherman shares Benne's point of view, but she makes her case for a paradigm shift specifically in light of the lessons learned in the struggle for global economic development. She, too, is convinced that "oldline" Protestant thinking focused heavily on distributional issues instead of issues related to the generation of wealth in Third World economies. In her critique she agrees that God demands that we care for the poor and recognize economic injustice as a crucial challenge to Christian faithfulness. On that basis she affirms the work of evangelical groups doing relief and development work who consider spiritual and economic development together. She outlines a revisionist theology of development that, honoring individual dignity and freedom, encourages democracy and private ownership. Sherman contends that government assistance channeled through private, often religious, organizations will offer the most effective strategy for overcoming global poverty in the long run.

Daniel Rush Finn pursues the need for new paradigms at the level of basic economic theory. His goal is a broader, and hence more useful, concept of self-interest. He agrees with Sherman that wealth generation is important but believes that human motivation in the economy has often been misunderstood. Finn argues that the conventional understanding of self-interest is too narrow a concept on which to base an adequate paradigm for public policy analysis. Instead he suggests a broad social paradigm that focuses on four economic problems, those of resource allocation, benefit distribution, the proper scale for an economy, and the quality of human relationships in community. He suggests that the more effective frameworks for the future will be those which balance and integrate concern for all four economic and social problems.

The move to a global economy that Finn describes has also seen the need for new economic paradigms reflected in contemporary Christian debates about specific policy issues. The words of John Cobb and Robin Klay illustrate opposing Christian frameworks for considering free trade on a global scale. Cobb is concerned about the implications of free trade for those less well served by structural shifts. Klay suggests that Cobb underestimates the range of beneficiaries and the depth of benefit as trade opens up.

Finally, Max Stackhouse and Dennis McCann conclude this section by presenting in manifesto form the case for a new paradigm relating theology to the economic and political order. The old debate by Christians over the relative merits of communism, socialism, and capitalism — the previously reigning paradigm for public discussion among both Protestants and Catholics — is dead. With its demise a new public theology is needed, one that goes beyond confessional particularities, exclusive church histories, and privileged realms of discourse. They believe this new theology must highlight stewardship, covenant, and vocation for a global society.

The call for new Christian thinking in theology, economic life, and public policy goes out to all who can enrich the conversation. Theological ethics must convince by persuasion, and that involves feedback, criticism, and refinement. Many voices must be heard, including those of theologians and laity, academicians and practitioners, the powerful and the oppressed, the pragmatists as well as the pious. For only when all Christian voices are represented can new concepts and practices in economic life emerge to shape a world reflecting the reality of God.

The Great Refusal and My Discontent

Robert Benne

It is often the case that creative reflection emerges from anguishing situations. I can point confidently to many anguishing situations in recent years related to the ethical assessment of capitalism at home and in the world. Although much reflection has been generated out of these situations, I can with less confidence call the situations themselves creative. One such situation occurred recently in Dublin, Ireland, where I was attending an international consultation on human rights. I chose to attend a working group on human rights and the economic order because I thought there might be an enlightening discussion on the complexities of national and international economic problems.

I had — perhaps naively — little expectation of what was in store. The group was made up of Catholic missionary teachers from Third World countries and Protestant and Catholic officials of various international church agencies. Rounding things out were a highly articulate Hungarian Marxist and myself, the lone American. The full-blown theory of dependent capitalism came out quickly and unanimously — the Western industrial-capitalist nations were wealthy primarily because of exploitation of the Third World; the United States through its CIA kept all oppressive governments in power; the world was neatly divided into oppressors and oppressed; democratic governments were simply the tools of the ruling capitalist classes and therefore shams (the

From Robert Benne, *The Ethic of Democratic Capitalism: A Moral Reassessment* (Minneapolis: Fortress Press, 1981), chapter 1.

917

choices offered in democratic elections were between Tweedledum and Tweedledee); arms sales by capitalist countries were the primary source of war and the threat of war; and so on. Every last bit of cant and hypocrisy on the part of the West was sniffed out and "unmasked." Participatory socialism was the answer, and on the other side of the revolution workers and peasants would manage their destinies with productivity, peace, and justice.

I put up some resistance at first. I knew enough of development studies to believe that poor countries faced tough economic problems common to them whether they were socialist or capitalist, and I knew there were competing, credible theories of what was happening in the emerging international economic order. But my arguments got nowhere. I decided to sit back and take my lumps as an American and see if I could learn any new twists in the theory of dependent capitalism. I didn't learn any and endured that part of the consultation under conditions of acute distress.

It would not always have been that way. Earlier in my teaching career, when I was more susceptible to "liberal guilt," I would have eagerly and gratefully assimilated this "prophetic" perspective into my teaching agenda. It would have fit neatly with the clear and coherent synthesis I have constructed out of the theology of Reinhold Niebuhr and the economic interpretations of John Kenneth Galbraith. The two thinkers made a nice fit; I knew as a trained theologian that Niebuhr wrote theology and ethics credibly, and I assumed that Galbraith's theories were all I needed to know about economic analysis. Wasn't he the economic beacon for the liberal intelligentsia? Such a Niebuhr-Galbraith synthesis gave me a persuasive position from which to criticize a decadent and dying capitalism — oligopoly, private affluence and public squalor, stagnation, consumerism — and to pursue the expected coming of democratic socialism. The Dublin conference would have simply given me macrocosmic data for an interpretation that had been worked out on the domestic level.

But, alas, the tidy, coherent, "prophetic" synthesis was shattered. I began eating from the tree of economic knowledge, and the unified world I had constructed came down in shambles. I had gotten acquainted with faculty members of the University of Chicago Business School and Economics Department, and each one of my pet Galbraithian notions was cut to shreds by sharp, and empirically documented, rejoinders to the conventional wisdom I floated out. At the root of their perspective was a radically different assessment of the realities and values of democratic capitalism. And they could make intellectually respectable what I had always viewed as the barely concealed ideology of the business world. This newfound challenge was hard to assimilate, so I began reading economic texts and delving into the mountains of economic literature dealing with the American economy. As the interpretations of mainstream American economists began to be taken more seriously, I began to doubt both the Galbraithian analysis of the American economic world and the assessment of democratic capitalism as a socio-political system. Perhaps our economy was workably competitive; perhaps profits had a useful economic function; perhaps free markets were the most efficient way of allocating economic resources; perhaps there was a connection between economic freedom and civil and political liberties; perhaps capitalism fostered a separation of economic and political power and enhanced social pluralism; perhaps the private sector, if used imaginatively, could handle more of our social problems better than an ever-enlarging public sector; and perhaps the poor were faring better under capitalism than under socialism. Indeed, I began to believe that the particular combination of democratic polity and capitalist economy found in many Western lands was defensible not only on economic grounds but also on technical grounds. Not — heaven knows! — that these systems are perfect or even near perfect, but they have enough going for them to legitimate them and to warrant pressing for reforms to make them more just. Now this was really too much — a Christian ethicist seeing enough reformable virtue in democratic capitalism to assess it as "ambiguously positive." A voice was crying in the wilderness, and it was not a voice announcing the Messiah but a voice that was willing to say some good things about capitalism.

Further, it was not as if the world of theological ethics had stood still while I had moved out of my synthesis to a new appreciation of democratic capitalism. Indeed, the Galbraithian view now seems to constitute the right wing of most theological ethicists who write about political and economic matters. The center has moved decidedly leftwards. Those who carry forward the legacy of Niebuhr and Tillich — the Shaulls, Bennetts, and Browns — carry forward a vision of democratic socialism supplanting a decadent capitalism. Even so mild and balanced a commentator as Philip Wogaman in his *The Great Economic Debate* opts for socialism as the embodiment of Christian ethical hope.

To the left, the field is dominated by the various strands of liberation theology. Bonino, Segundo, Assmann, Gutiérrez, and others take as their prime target the capitalism represented by American multinational corporations. They have swallowed the Marxist analysis of dependent capitalism and hope for a revisionist socialism in Latin America. Indeed, as Dom Helder Camara has succinctly put it: "The Church must now do with Marx today what Thomas did with Aristotle in medieval times." The social ethics of both the World Council and the National Council of Churches are hostile toward Western capitalism and partisan toward the socialist movements of the developing world. Marxist thought has become the major tool of economic analysis and prescription for Christian liberation theology and ethics.

This completes the description of the polarities of my schizophrenic world. The mainstream of American economic thought leads toward an appreciation of market economies on both economic and ethical grounds. The mainstream of Christian social ethics leads toward outright condemnation of democratic capitalism and a passionate hope for an ideal democratic socialism. It is difficult to get these two streams to flow together. One either has to choose minority economists to fit with majority ethicists or minority ethicists to fit with majority economists. (The minority of ethicists who are willing to dissent publicly are gathered under the umbrella of *Worldview* magazine. They are quickly written off by the majority as the religious part of the "neoconservative reaction" led in the secular world by figures such as Irving Kristol, Daniel Bell, and Edward Banfield. Other prominent figures in theological ethics — Ramsey and Gustafson, inter alios — are involved on other fronts and write little on political economy.)

This unhappy situation creates a good deal of pain in my life. I share enough basic theological and ethical convictions with the Christian ethics fellowship to want to be critical of all systems but especially our own democratic capitalism. But I share enough of the viewpoint of the mainstream of the American economics establishment to arrive at quite a different interpretation of the American economy than that of the ethics establishment. I find that many of the judgments of the ethics establishment are imposed simplistically upon ambiguous and complex economic phenomena and their "prophetic insights" are often misguided.

All this might possibly be interesting as an example of a painful personal odyssey or as a colorful internecine fight among a small group of Christian ethicists — possibly, but not probably. But this little story takes on added gravity, I believe, when one views it as a small reflection of a much broader public rift.

The bias against democratic capitalism is not simply the province of a small fellowship of Christian social ethicists at war with American society. It rests in a much broader spectrum of society that has increasing power to delegitimate the social order that I have been calling democratic capitalism. It attacks at both a theoretical and a practical level the shared values and assumptions that have undergirded our social system. It has enough power and influence to provoke in time a crisis of legitimation.

This sector of society has emerged from broad changes in the social structure of postindustrial society. Daniel Bell has provided the most important profile of this new society. As industrial societies mature into postindustrial societies, there is a shift from manufacturing to services, an attendant emphasis on the "knowledge" component within those services, and an elevation of a new elite that deals with the codification of theoretical knowledge for directing innovation and the formulation of policy. This "New Class" embraces a large number of occupations, ranging from intellectuals to technicians.

Like previous classes, the New Class is stratified within itself; in this hierarchy, no doubt, those deemed to be the cultural elite occupy a high position. Institutionally, prestige universities and other centers of knowledge production (such as think tanks) are centers of New Class Power, while publishing houses, periodicals, and foundations serve as distributing agencies. . . . Below these elite institutions, however, there is a much larger complex of New Class population in the lower reaches of the educational system. . . . Then, of course, there is the powerful center of national communications media which is allied with the cultural elite through a network of interlocking occupations that provide services through the administration of symbols, most though not all in the public sector of employment — people who staff the welfare and regulatory agencies on all levels of government, the planning and propaganda arms of these agencies, and the miscellaneous therapeutic, guidance, and counselling institutions.

The phenomenon of the New Class is characteristic not only of American society, since Raymond Aron and Helmut Schelsky have sketched portraits of it in Western Europe, but it is more advanced and numerous in the United States because the transition to postindustrial society is further along here. The minions of the New Class are in competition with the old business elite, which is losing the battle for the legitimation of democratic capitalism. The business elite has few intellectuals within it or supporters within academe in general who make a credible case for the present order. A good share of intellectuals — particularly those of a humanist bent — are aligned with the left-liberal or socialist propensities of the New Class. And although they are less important to the broader society than they believe, they do occupy positions in which they define reality for a large number of people.

What holds the New Class together ideologically is so well stated by Peter Berger that it is worthwhile to quote him at some length:

The New Class is marked by a strong hostility to the capitalist system and to the business community. This animus ranges from the left-liberal orientation of the majority to more pronounced socialist view of a vocal minority. . . . The greater part of the New Class derives its livelihood from public-sector employment; it has the most tangible interest in expanding this type of employ-

ment. Thus the vested interest in this group in replacing market forces with government intervention is, at the very least, as important in explaining the statist inclinations of the New Class as more idealistic aspirations. . . . Because government interventions have to be legitimated in terms of social ills, the New Class has a vested interest in portraying American society as a whole, and specific aspects of that society, in negative terms. Bad news about America is *ipso facto* good news for New Class aspirations. This ideological function serves to explain the consistently "critical" orientation of New Class interpretations (such as the facts of income distribution, poverty, the state of civil rights, or the changes in the racial situation). The same ideological function helps to account for the consistent sympathy of New Class individuals for foreign movements and regimes, provided these can plausibly be pictured as some sort of antithesis to American society.

This broadly sketched picture is no doubt too simplistic, but it does have persuasive commonsense appeal. We shall later have occasion to look more closely at the characteristics of and reasons for the alienation of the New Class from the social system of democratic capitalism. Be that as it may, the New Class is in considerable tension with the older business elite, the "heartland" population of farmers and small-town people, middle-class suburbanites, and a considerable portion of blue-collar workers. These segments have very few articulate spokespersons who can provide a more positive rationale for the evolving democratic capitalism of our time.

This very large public rift is duplicated in many of the institutional structures of our society, among them the church. The laity and local clergy — especially after they have been socialized for some years in parish life — tend to side with the "unenlightened," old "producer" segments of the population, whereas the thinkers of the church — particularly those who are the most distant from the currents of local life — tend to side with the New Class. This is not to say that these "cosmopolites" have no useful prophetic function, but their bread is buttered by coming up with enough critical interpretations to keep them in the business of being "change agents" in the church and society. They also have an "interest." They tend not to understand or be sympathetic with the struggles of the producer elements of society but rather are concerned with the distribution of what is produced. This makes them indifferent or hostile to the productive possibilities of democratic capitalism and friendly toward the interventionist tendencies of left-liberalism or democratic socialism. Meanwhile, the patient but somewhat befuddled producer elements continue to pay the bill for the delegitimating activities of their own intellectual elite. Great patience have they who are willing to finance the destruction of their own cherished beliefs and practices. . . .

It is important to offer some brief reflections on why such a large majority of the American intelligentsia, at least that section of the intelligentsia that deals publicly with economic and political matters, harbor such antipathy toward democratic capitalism.

The first possibility is that they may be right. And this possibility accounts for some of the anguish in my own reflective life. Certainly the socialist passion for social justice is admirable. Perhaps the sociopolitical system we have known as democratic capitalism is in principle inefficient, unjust, and destructive of higher human values. It is obsolete, so we should move on to the next stage of social evolution — democratic socialism. Hasn't this been the consensus of the great Christian theologians of the twentieth century? Certainly Barth, Tillich, and the early Reinhold Niebuhr were socialists of a sort. There seems to be a religious consensus on the prima facie appeal of socialism. Indeed, Tillich's *Religious Socialism* has just been translated and will find a good deal of renewed attention among Christian social ethicists. How can one fight such a consensus? One reality that keeps disturbing my faith in such a consensus is the fact that socialism is no longer simply a vision. It has been incarnated in many nations, both developed and underdeveloped; socialism now has a historical track record. And that record is certainly not obviously superior to that of Western democratic capitalism in key categories — liberty, democracy, equality, quality of life, productivity, peaceful intentions and actions, cultural creativity, and others. The most dramatic symbol that sums up the limitations of the vast majority of mature socialist lands is that of the fence. Generally, the citizens of these lands are forcibly

kept within their boundaries. If free emigration were allowed, the population would decline drastically as people made their way to better opportunities. But few seem to be fleeing the horrors of democratic capitalism. Even those who "know" how bad it is remain. The harshest critics seem to have little aversion to reaping the benefits from sales of their books. And, irony of ironies, some of those who are cast out of socialist lands spend most of their efforts attacking the systems that harbor them.

Why are there so few measured defenses of democratic capitalism and so many attacks on it in the wider intellectual world? Joseph Schumpeter, whose classic *Capitalism, Socialism and Democracy* remains a continuing source of penetrating insight, gives a compelling answer to this very question. "Unlike any other type of society capitalism inevitably and by virtue of the very logic of its civilization creates, educates and subsidizes a vested interest in social unrest." Then follows what he calls an "excursion into the Sociology of the Intellectual." This is a much earlier interpretation of the New Class phenomenon proposed later by Bell and Berger.

First, Schumpeter notes that two of the characteristics that distinguish intellectuals from other people who wield the power of the spoken and written word are the absence of direct responsibility for practical affairs and of the firsthand knowledge of them that only actual experience can give. "The critical attitude, arising no less from the intellectual's situation as an onlooker — in most cases also as an outsider — than from the fact that his main chance of asserting himself lies in his actual or potential nuisance value, should add a third touch." . . .

As capitalist society develops, there is a vigorous expansion of the education apparatus. This provides more ground upon which intellectuals may operate. The expanded educational apparatus produces a growing number of trainees who increasingly occupy the administrative and bureaucratic niches of the society. There they have a vested interest not only in expanding the competency of the state but also in denigrating the capacity of the private sector to handle the social challenges that emerge. Thus, Schumpeter asserts, hostility toward the capitalist order increases instead of diminishes with every achievement of capitalist evolution.

Although Schumpeter accounts for a good number of the reasons why the New Class, and particularly its intellectuals, are aligned as adversaries of "bourgeois society," he does not delve very deeply into the reason why those intellectuals have, and historically have had, an affinity for socialism as the alternative to democratic capitalism. One obvious reason is that the rhetoric of socialism contains many close parallels to deeply embedded values in Judeo-Christian tradition. Moral rhetoric is very close to the surface in the theory of socialism whereas the moral values of democratic capitalism are much less visible, at least in its theoretical foundations. The convergence of value systems in the traditions of socialism and Judeo-Christian humanism is readily grasped; the case for democratic capitalism is much more subtle and complex. Indeed, the fact that the concrete embodiment of values in its practice is more convincing than its present theoretical justifications dictates that its case can never be made simple.

But the appeal of democratic socialism is simple and coherent. Justice, cooperation, democracy, peace, community, equality, and ecological sanity are all a part of the promise. What is more convincing, the very poor shall be lifted up, the rich sent away empty-handed, and the oppressed set free. Further, we will live according to ennobling values and be liberated from repression. This vision is in direct continuity with the eschatological hope of the great religious traditions of the West; Marxism and socialism are clearly secular offshoots of Western religion.

It is easy to see why economists who keep these values visibly active in their analyses and prescriptions are appealing to humanist intellectual readers. From the Galbraith-Lekachman pole leftwards toward the more Marxist-oriented Union of Radical Economists, such value visibility is evident. This approach is very appealing to sociologists, political scientists, historians, philosophers, and theologians who read these authors. Moreover, most of these liberally trained readers are not known for their economic sophistication. Many have avoided the "dismal science" for much of their academic careers and are therefore unable and unwilling to go after their economic analysis firsthand. They gravitate toward writers on economic affairs who write for lay audiences and whose value orientations are close to their own and readily visible. Thus, they tend to accept too quickly the economic analyses that go with the value orientations they admire. By a neat methodological leap, highly dubious economic analysis is accepted primarily because writers exhibit persuasive and coherent value systems. Humanist readers swallow Marxist and socialist economic interpretations for their moral appeal, not for their empirical validity. And then, as is the case with the theory of dependent capitalism, morality tales with all their righteous indignation and revolutionary flourish are substituted for the hard intellectual grappling that gets at a highly variegated and complex reality.

Another variation of this interpretation of intellectuals' affinity for socialism is put forward by Peter Berger. He believes that the crucial reason for this affinity lies in the specific characteristics of what he calls the "socialist myth." By "myth," of course, he means not something false or imaginary but rather a paradigmatic drama which interprets and organizes experience, judges the present, and provides a prescriptive model for the future.

The socialist myth derives much of its power from its unique capacity to synthesize modernizing and countermodernizing themes. Modernization — its ideas, values, aspirations — continues to be the dominant theme of our time, and it is fully integrated into all the various versions of socialism. The socialist program is based on all the standard cognitive assumptions of modernity — history as progress (an idea which must be understood as a secularization of biblical eschatology), the perfectibility of man, scientific reason as the great liberator from illusion, and man's ability to overcome all or nearly all of his afflictions by taking rational control of his destiny.

Socialism thus takes up the trends of modernity within its myth, as does its cousin of the Enlightenment, liberalism. But socialism has also incorporated into its myth some of the powerful protests against modernity, that is, themes dealing with a renewed community. Liberalism, in contrast, has not been able to bring off such an incorporation.

Berger believes that modernity has been brought

about only at great cost. The forces of industrialization — with attendant urbanization and secularization — have eroded the small social settings marked by intense solidarity and moral consensus that have constituted normative human habitation for most of human history. With these organic social settings went the comforts of shared, stable systems of meaning and identity. These settings were often stifling, stagnant, and oppressive, but they never suffered from *anomie*. The community was real and all-embracing, for better or worse.

Modernity, on the other hand, means the movement away from *Gemeinschaft* — organic, "given" community — to *Gesellschaft* — voluntary association built upon individual choice. The individual participates in many associations of limited ends. Market economies eat away at traditional ways of doing things. Technical rationalism erodes the metaphysical verities. We live in an increasingly "disenchanted" world. Shared meanings are replaced by a great marketplace of competing worldviews. It is not surprising in this situation of modernity that countermovements arise. Indeed, we see such a countermovement in the present resurgence of conservative Islam. It longs for restoration of community, for overcoming the fragmentation of modernity.

. . . Socialism, in other words, promises all the blessings of modernity and the liquidation of its costs, including, most importantly, the cost of alienation. To grasp this essentially simple fact about the socialist myth and to recall at the same time that modern secularism has greatly weakened the plausibility of competing religious eschatologies is to remove the mystery of the magnetic appeal of socialism. Indeed, if any mystery remains, it is that socialism has not yet triumphed completely.

In our society those most alienated from traditional "competing religious eschatologies" are the intellectuals. Religious commitment tends to be part of the "bourgeois" background that is sloughed off as persons make their way toward intellectual respectability. But a vacuum of religious and moral meanings can be tolerated by only a very few; the socialist myth provides a persuasive alternative for the many.

Even religious intellectuals are prey to the synthesizing qualities of the socialist myth. Protestants flee from the otherworldly tendencies of pietism and evangelicalism by historicizing their own Christian eschatologies. Christian theological ethics becomes "relevant" again by clothing its social ethics in the socialist myth. The heavenly hope is brought down to earth. Particularly for those Protestants who accept historical guilt for unleashing unguided technical rationalism on the world through a secularized Protestant ethic, the appeal of renewed human and ecological community inherent in the socialist myth is persuasive. Protestantism tends to patch up its social-ethical deficiencies by appropriating the relevant aspects of the socialist myth.

Roman Catholics do not need to participate in such strategies of compensation. Their traditional social theories have often been unitive. The Christian revelation, with its hierarchy of values, is to be synthesized with one political and social philosophy. Medieval civilization at its apex was such a synthesis: one God, one pope, one king, one realm, and one system of shared values and meanings that order politics, economics, and culture. Catholicism fought a long rearguard action against the forces of modernity that were intruding themselves into the synthesis. The old synthesis holds sway in very few places, although the legacy of the old synthesis continues in the travail of many "Catholic" lands — a legacy of semifeudalism, authoritarian government, and a conservative church. Curiously, the anguish of these lands is all too simply blamed on the dominating economic power of the democratic capitalist world.

Now the assumptions of modernity are making their way into the post–Vatican II church. The old synthesis is being jettisoned. Modernity is being embraced. But the old dreams of synthesis do not disappear. They only search for new partners in the wedding. And what will pull together the assumptions of modernity with a hope of Christian community in society? Why, socialism, of course. The socialist myth combines modernity with the yearning for "Catholic substance." It is a potent combination.

Meanwhile, mainstream economists bury the moral appeal of democratic capitalism under the baffling equations of welfare economics. They pursue their specialities without addressing directly either the values they hold or the direction in which they think society should move. Their concern for the poor is covered over by technical argument, which is rarely appealing to social idealism. Is there any doubt why the socialist myth holds such appeal for intellectuals — religious and secular alike? Socialism, as Michael Novak quips, has become the thinking person's economics. More than that, it has become the thinking person's religious myth.

Christians and Economic Development

Amy L. Sherman

The 1980s may well be looked back upon as a decade of intellectual reformation in the so-called North-South debate. A burst of revisionist thinking has affected recent discussions of Third World economic development and may offer a harbinger of better policies vis-à-vis the world's poor. There are signs of an emerging consensus that the development approach followed until very recently — one that emphasized large wealth transfers from the developed to the underdeveloped world, worried about the "population explosion" draining natural resources, and questioned capitalism's ability to "trickle down" prosperity to the masses — has not brought sustained and stable growth to the Third World. Revisionists have questioned Club of Rome pessimism about the prospects for world development and recaptured the enthusiasm for market development strategies that characterized post-World War II U.S. foreign aid policy.

One example of renewed appreciation for market oriented approaches is Pope John Paul II's recent encyclical *Sollicitudo Rei Socialis*. *Sollicitudo,* written on the twentieth anniversary of Pope Paul VI's *Populorum Progressio,* rejects that document's predominantly statist model for development and endorses both the democracy-development connection and the crucial role of individual initiative in economic advancement. A more surprising example is prominent liberation theologian Gustavo Gutiérrez's tentative rethinking about democracy, development, and socialism.

Amy L. Sherman, "Christians and Economic Development," *First Things,* March 1990, pp. 43-50.

Peter Steinfels of the *New York Times* reported not long ago that Gutiérrez is willing — even if only "very theoretically" — to entertain the idea that "if evidence showed capitalism effectively relieving poverty, there could be a capitalist liberation theology."

Mikhail Gorbachev's *perestroika* tacitly admits serious doubts about the efficacy of centralized economic planning, which, as Nicholas Eberstadt's latest work *The Poverty of Communism* (1988) demonstrates, has failed to provide freedom (which few expected) or bread (which many hoped for). Economic performance in terms of health and nutrition has been so shoddy that in some communist-bloc countries, life expectancy is actually declining.

Perhaps the most significant rethinking in the development community has been done by sociologist Peter Berger. In an article in *Commentary* ("Under-development Revisited," July 1984), Berger reconsidered the conclusions of his remarkable *Pyramids of Sacrifice,* published ten years earlier. *Pyramids* had evaluated the prevailing models of economic development, examining Brazil as a test-case of capitalism, and Mao's China as an experiment in socialism. Throughout the book, Berger struck an evenhanded posture, arguing that both systems had "generated myths that had to be debunked," and advocating an "open, non-doctrinaire approach" to development. "What came through," he reflected in 1984, "was some vague notion of a 'third way.' . . . I had no clear conception of what this might look like. . . ." With ten years of hindsight, Berger articulated his new position on development: "Not to put too fine a point on it, I am much less evenhanded today in my assessment of capitalist and socialist development models: I have become much more emphatically procapitalist." His *The Capitalist Revolution: Fifty Propositions About Prosperity, Equality & Liberty* sets forth the reason why.

The most important reason is that not one case of successful socialist development can be found in the Third World. Socialism has proved unable to produce material prosperity and has failed even to live up to its pledge to distribute resources equitably. Rather, as Berger puts it, what has occurred with "disturbing regularity" in new socialist regimes is the establishment of an inefficient Soviet-style *nomenklatura.* At the same time, the "success stories" of Japan, Hong Kong, Singapore, and South Korea have demonstrated the economic superiority of market-oriented models of development. The experience of these so-called "Four Little Dragons" indicates that an exuberant embrace of capitalism doesn't have to mean brutish consequences for the poor — indeed, the benefits of economic growth have "lifted the poor from grinding poverty and wiped out Third World misery."

The Capitalist Revolution's evaluation of capitalism follows the criteria of success Berger proposed in *Pyramids of Sacrifice;* namely, that the benefits of development must reach the poorest members of society and that development ought not to require the abrogation of human rights or the demeaning of cherished cultural values. For Berger, the evidence suggests that if one truly wants to adopt a "preferential option for the poor," one should exercise a preferential option for capitalist models of development.

Christian participation in debates over development policy follows from the concern for the poor that is central to the Gospel message. That concern, if it is to be effective, needs to be informed, and it is unfortunate that key sectors of the Christian community have failed to keep up with empirical developments in the field. Protestant oldline (a term empirically more accurate than the former "mainline") churches in particular have remained unaware of or stubbornly resistant to the wealth of new data on development that has emerged in recent years.

The oldline, in deliberations on economic development, is at best stuck in a nebulous "third way"; between capitalism and socialism; at worst, it advocates discredited statist (socialist) models of development. That it has failed to "catch up" with the economic realities of the eighties is readily apparent from analysis of four recent church pronouncements on economic development: the United Church of Christ's (UCC) 1987 study paper, *Christian Faith and Economic Life;* the United Methodists' 1988 "Resolution on Economic Justice"; the Episcopal Urban Bishops Coalition's 1987 study guide, *Economic Justice and Christian Conscience;* and the 1984 Presbyterian Church (USA) statement, *Christian Faith and Economic Justice.*

Oldline church activists base their conclusions

about development economics to a considerable degree on their understanding of biblical theology regarding poverty. They seek to identify themes and biblical principles that, coupled with prudential judgments about the world economy, provide a conception of "economic justice." All four documents argue that any "just" economic system will reflect, at minimum, the following biblical principles.

1. Special concern for the basic human needs of the poor. According to the oldline, God wills that all people have access to the basic necessities of life. The Methodists' 1988 "Resolution on Economic Justice" notes that "law codes in Exodus, Leviticus, and Deuteronomy show a special concern for the resources necessary to meet human needs and guarantee basic rights such as food, clothing, just business dealings, and access to the juridical process." God's love for the poor is also expressed, the oldline claims, in Old Testament regulations promulgated to prevent gross economic disparities among the Israelites. The New Testament continues these themes. The 1987 UCC study paper reminds readers that Jesus came to "preach good news to the poor" and to "set at liberty those who are oppressed." It argues that the Parable for the Great Judgment (Matt. 25:31-46), in which the righteous are defined as those who have fed the hungry, clothed the naked, and ministered to the poor, "discloses God's fundamental relationship with and intentions for humanity."

2. Stewardship. This theme has two implications for oldline economics. First, it teaches that "the earth is the Lord's and all that is in it." For the Presbyterians, this implies that "human domination over material things is limited." For the United Church of Christ, it means that private property rights are similarly limited: "as the stewards of God's creation, humanity's access to resources, including ownership of private property is conditional. . . . [A] recognition of the right of private property does not mean that anyone has the right to unlimited accumulation of wealth." The Episcopal Bishops concur: "private ownership of property, in the biblical view, is never ultimate."

Second, stewardship means taking care of God's earth. Environmentally insensitive economic practices are immoral. The UCC argues that humans have already wreaked havoc on God's earth; we have "violated our role as stewards" by failing to "live in harmony with nature." Faithful stewards would follow development strategies that protect the earth, even if by doing so they sustained economic losses. The UCC contends that "as stewards of the earth, we must recognize the fragility of the ecosystems which sustain all of creation. This will require us to identify and enforce limits on economic growth."

3. Recognition and avoidance of structural sin. Drawing on the Old Testament prophets, oldline analysts insist that sin must be recognized as both individual and corporate. The prophetic message, they argue, should be understood primarily as an economic one, condemning *structural injustice* in Israel. The economic, social, and legal arrangements of the society were "sinful" because they were based on greed, exploitation, and indifference to the poor. They produced gross disparities in wealth, and economic systems that do the same today also stand under prophetic judgment.

These principles taken together lead the oldline to define a just economic system primarily in terms of its ability to ensure an equitable distribution of resources that guarantees the fulfillment of basic needs. At that level of generalization, few would disagree. Problems develop, however, as the discussion gets more specific.

Having defined the kind of economic system it wishes to attain, the oldline analyzes the present global economic order to identify obstacles to the achievement of a just world economy and to offer guidelines for its establishment. Four key themes emerge from their deliberations: a "limits to growth" mentality, agreement with dependency theory, sympathy toward the "basic human needs" strategy for development, and confidence in government-led programs of redistribution.

Essentially, *limits to growth* philosophy holds that the world is in the grips of a severe economic crisis; that reckless use of resources has led to critical ecological damage; that the world is rapidly running out of resources and radically new ways must be found to reverse the ominous trend; and that traditional emphasis on economic *growth* (as opposed to more equitable distribution) is no longer appropriate or feasible. This philosophy was publicly advanced in the Club of Rome reports during the 1970s that have since been brought into serious question by the new thinkers in development. Reflecting the old view, the Presbyterians suggest ominously that "warnings of a severe and multidimensional crisis abound." The economic pie is no longer growing: resources are being depleted and growth cannot be pursued in the reckless, environmentally insensitive way it has been in the past. "The world's present resources are dwindling . . . and at some point they will all be gone. Oil, water, valuable minerals and even arable land itself, are all limited." The UCC argues for an "ecologically sustainable" system in which the rate of population growth and pollution are "within the capacity of the earth to support." The upshot of all this is a renewed emphasis on redistribution. If there is only so much to go around, and the present distributional patterns are leaving so many without basic material resources, then radical new ways of distributing wealth must be adopted.

The fundamental assertion of *dependency theory* is that the international economic system is structured in a "core-periphery" relationship; the "core" being the rich, industrialized "North," and the "periphery" being the poor, underdeveloped "South." The periphery is said to be "dependent" upon or dominated by the "neo-colonialist" economies of the core states. This arrangement has presumably had various adverse consequences for the South, most notably the "immiseration" of the population. In dependency theorist André Gunder Frank's words, the relationship leads, necessarily, to the "development of the underdevelopment"; in other words, the poverty of the periphery is brought about by its relationship with the core. As the relationship continues, the gap separating rich and poor grows. In short, poor nations entering the international system are made worse off by so doing.

Oldline statements reveal a deep indebtedness to dependency analysis. All four agree the "gap" between the rich and the poor is widening. All four believe that the international order is characterized by gross and unjustified disparities in income. All four worry about the negative influence of

multinational corporations on the Third World's poor. The UCC notes that "in its extreme form dependency theory asserts that in order for the rich to remain rich, the poor countries must stay poor." It goes on to state both that "many thoughtful Third World Christians subscribe to dependency theory" and that "some of the claims of dependency theorists can be substantiated."

The oldline looks favorably upon dependency theory's call for a "new international economic order" (NIEO) in which resources will be distributed more evenly among nations — even if this requires involuntary resource transfers executed by powerful new international economic institutions. The UCC's enthusiasm for NIEO spills over into a suggestion that a "progressive global tax of between one and five percent of GNP be levied on all countries with per capita incomes of over $2,000 per year." The tax revenues would then be redistributed to "the two-thirds of the human family who live in the low-income and middle-income economies" — presumably by national and multinational agencies.

The oldline favors the so-called "*basic human needs*" approach to development that focuses on providing health services, schools, housing, and food to the poor. In this model, development aid is judged by its ability to relieve the material suffering of the poor, as against the "cold" standards by which the other prominent development strategy, industrialization, is measured: real GNP per capita growth, increases in investments, balance of trade, etc. The UCC statement is forthright in its preference for models of development which "focus more on meeting key national or basic human needs and which promote a more equitable income distribution within Third World countries."

The Methodist statement holds that "covenant people are committed to equitable distribution of resources to meet basic human needs and to social systems that provide ongoing access to those resources." For the Presbyterians, income disparities between the North and the South mean that "the world is characterized by grave economic injustice" and needs to be brought into line with biblical teaching, i.e., *redistribution*. The oldline insists that redistribution is the only practical and "biblical" solution to poverty. Its intense attachment to redistribution leads it to favor an expansion of government's sphere of authority. The Episcopalians submit that "government at all levels must be challenged once again to play a responsible role in correcting the inequities in the economic crisis." In a section entitled "The Limits of Friendly Persuasion," the Episcopal Bishops wonder whether "we are willing to mobilize ourselves" for the radical reform measures necessary to carry out redistribution. And if such will cannot be summoned, the bishops confess that they "do not know" whether alternatives to "revolution" can be found.

The oldline's program of theological economics yields its conception of itself as being in "solidarity with the poor." But slogans should not substitute for analysis, and careful examination of the oldline philosophy reveals that it relies on insufficient biblical analysis and clings stubbornly to dubious economic propositions. That being the case, one wonders about the actual value to the poor of the oldline's "solidarity" with it.

The oldline's theology of economic development would be much improved, to begin with, by more serious reflection on the doctrine of creation. One obvious lesson of creation is that man is created in God's image, meaning, man is a creator. Since He creates, we should as well, and this includes the *creation of wealth.* God's commandment to "be fruitful and multiply" may well have significant implications beyond procreation; it may be interpreted as a general encouragement to productive labor. The oldlines' discomfiture at economic inequalities leads it to suggest a moral necessity for an equality of outcomes, and thus to emphasize not production but distribution. The Presbyterians, for example, accept John Rawls' formula for distributional justice: distribution of all social resources should be equal, unless an unequal distribution benefits the disadvantaged of society. But as Michael Novak has commented, "the Jewish and Christian view shows that God is not committed to equality of results. One steward differs from another in his performance; some virgins are foolish, some wise."

The oldline statements also fail to draw important distinctions as to *who* is responsible for carrying out God's commandments with regard to the poor. Doug Bandow's recent book, *Beyond Good Intentions* (1988), helps demarcate the lines of responsibility, noting biblical instruction on the proper roles of individuals, family, and church. The responsibilities of civil government in executing charitable duties are less certain. But the oldline statements indiscriminately apply biblical injunctions to care for the needy to believers and nonbelievers, to the Church and the civil government. In addition, they seriously alter the biblical message when they pass from admonitions to give *voluntarily* to policies which *compel* redistribution. The Episcopal and Presbyterian statements, for example, call for more government taxation, redistribution, and expanded provision for material needs. This indiscriminate application of biblical injunctions clouds the Church's understanding of the right role of government, and tends to increase government's sphere of influence. In effect, these churches encourage the state to enforce upon nonbelievers the standards of charitable conduct to which believers aspire. Moreover, they encourage economic policies whose actual results in helping the poor are ambiguous at best.

In addition, the oldline's conception of solidarity with the poor suffers from excessively economic interpretations of certain biblical passages. For example, the oldlines' interpretation of stewardship emphasizes only the *distributional* aspects of the doctrine (i.e., personal accumulation of wealth at the expense of others is bad stewardship) and disregards equally important productivity issues encompassed in the notion. As the Parable of the Talents suggests, good stewards are also good investors, creatively using God-given resources to produce new wealth. Moreover, the oldline's economic interpretation of the prophetic message misses the larger point: the prophets' *primary* lament is that Israel has departed from its God. Economic injustice is but one result of this disobedience. The prophets' call is not for an overhaul of "sinful structures" as much as it is for spiritual repentance and the conversion to God-centered attitudes that will allow needed socioeconomic reforms to take place. The prophets' agenda starts with transformation of individuals and leads to transformation of society, not the reverse.

While the oldline's theology reminds Christians of the importance of being involved in ministry to the poor, it does not provide sufficient guidelines for relating faith to economic questions. Although the oldline statements appear to begin with the biblical text and end with policy pronouncements, the economic philosophy advanced seems to have been predetermined.

, In any case, that economic philosophy does not bode well for the poor. In recent years, writers such as Julian Simon, P. T. Bauer, Michael Novak, and Ronald Nash have effectively debunked both the "limits to growth" mentality and dependency theory. As with ideas, so with practice: three decades of underdeveloped countries following the types of economic policies advocated by the oldline have resulted in anything but a liberation of the poor. The 1987 "Index of Human Suffering" report of the Population Crisis Committee rated nations on a scale of human misery using various data including GNP per capita, inflation rate, infant mortality, access to clean water, literacy and general personal freedoms. The eleven countries with the *worst* ratings have followed internal economic policies that closely resemble the measures advocated by the oldline.

The oldline's conception of solidarity with the poor, fortunately, is not the only Christian development philosophy available. Five evangelical relief and development agencies — Food for the Hungry, Transformation International, World Concern, World Relief, and World Vision — are already performing relief and development tasks. These evangelicals can lead the way to a reformation in Third World development strategy because they have for the most part avoided the errors of their oldline co-activists and have shown more sensitivity to the forceful empirical analysis of the 1980s.

These five organizations do not represent the full spectrum of evangelical engagement with questions of poverty and development. Rather they reflect only a small part of "evangelicaldom," that complex social movement that includes hundreds of denominations and independent churches; publications such as *Christianity Today, Soujourners, Moody Monthly,* and *World;* evangelical colleges and seminaries; evangelistic and discipleship groups such as InterVarsity Christian Fellowship and Navigators; Christian television and radio networks, stations, and programs; the National Association of Evangelicals and a host of other Wheaton-based Christian ministries; and activist groups such as Evangelicals for Social Action.

Many evangelical scholars, publicists, and activists participate in the development debate. At times their involvement largely echoes the perspectives of their new-class peers in the oldline church, and to the extent that evangelicals buy into the oldline's conception of solidarity with the poor, their contribution to the reformation of development policy will be limited. (One sees signs of this on the evangelical left.) But there is reason to hope that they can resist that temptation.

The five agencies considered here carry out similar programs. All except Transformation International are involved in emergency relief efforts and in traditional community development projects: digging wells, building health clinics, constructing irrigation systems. All are involved as well in vocational training, technical assistance programs, and micro-economic development. Some are active in "development education," seeking to inform American Christians about the problems of hunger and underdevelopment; proportionally, though, only a small share of their budget is earmarked for this. The agencies also employ similar development methods. Wherever and whenever possible, they work through local churches — believing this provides greater financial accountability and more opportunity for spiritual witness-and invite the active participation of local people in development projects.

One notable feature of evangelical involvement in economic development is its relative lack of visibility. Due in part to the oldline's liberationist rhetoric and in part to the relatively unpublicized activities of evangelical relief and development agencies, many people believe that oldline churches are far more active in efforts to alleviate poverty than are evangelicals. Evangelicals, so it is thought, are much more interested in the "vertical" side of ministry, bringing people to faith in God, than in the "horizontal" aspect, caring for the neighbor. In fact, in terms of financial commitment to development, it appears that evangelicals are doing more on the ground to help the poor than their oldline counterparts. Although differences in methods of financial reporting among church agencies make the comparisons difficult, the available evidence indicates that the evangelicals are spending more than twice as much as oldline agencies in Third World relief and development ministries.

The evangelicals' theology of development coincides with the oldline's in its concern for the poorest of the poor. Each agency is committed to helping the most vulnerable members of poor societies: widows, children, orphans, and the disabled. But several significant differences distinguish the evangelicals' development theology from the oldline's.

First, while the evangelicals accept the oldline's twofold understanding of Christian ministry, they place greater emphasis on spiritual outreach. Each of these agencies has struggled with the delicate balancing act between food for the body and food for the soul. Staff are confronted with overwhelming and desperate physical deprivation; response to the simple physical needs of people can become all-consuming. Bryant Myers, vice president for corporate services at World Vision, notes that while the agency has always linked spiritual and material sides of its ministry "in word," it has sometimes struggled with the problem of how to combine them "in deed." Following a three-year consultation on "philosophy of mission," World Vision issued a policy paper strongly affirming the significance of spiritual ministry. As Myers puts it, World Vision came to the recognition that "there are two destinations for mankind, heaven or hell." "We had to realize," he reflects, "that we might be improving the standard of living for people, but they were still on the wrong path." As with the other evangelical agencies, World Vision stresses both the need for redemption in Christ and the need for renewed communities to reflect "Kingdom-like values." In this view concern for salvation includes the desire to help those who have been saved better reflect the transforming experience of Christ in their behavior, attitudes, and relationships.

The agencies also relate spiritual ministry to tangible results in economic affairs. Jerry Ballard, executive director of World Relief, notes that "unless people have a good concept of God's love for them, they may find it hard to be motivated to change their situation." Fred Gregory, executive director of World Concern, believes that acceptance of the Gospel can bring hope to the poor and liberation from fatalistic attitudes that are barriers to development.

Second, and more significant, while the oldline's theology is rooted in concern for distributive justice, the evangelicals' is centered in their understanding of human nature. "Man made in the image of God" has several specific implications for these agencies. First, it means that *all* people have inherent worth and are due the Christian's attentive concern. Relief and development assistance will be offered not only to fellow believers, but to people of other faiths as well. Second, all people have God-bestowed dignity. Abject poverty and the slow death of starvation are affronts to this dignity; the Christian's response is to help meet the basic physical needs of the poor. Evangelicals recognize that man's dignity requires much more than basic material provision: the ultimate goal in development is to help people "be all God intended them to be." At the core of man's dignity is his *freedom,* and the evangelicals seek to recognize that God-given freedom in implementing their development policies. "Unless people participate in the decision making," says Fred Gregory, development "is not going to be a very liberating experience." Ballard believes that charitable activity must be designed in such a way as to avoid negatively affecting the self-esteem of the recipient.

Recognizing that man is but "a little lower than the angels," these groups also stress that man is sinful. For evangelicals, the effects of the Fall are pervasive, affecting individuals, communities — even nature itself. In this view, all sufferings and evils, including poverty, can be traced to sin. This is particularly stressed by Transformation International and World Relief. For example, Robert Hancock of Transformation International argues that greed, dishonesty, and moral compromise are more a reflection of individual character than they are of economic and political systems. "The problem is not in the economic system, but in moral degeneration."

Some evangelical development leaders follow their oldline counterparts — at least part way — in speaking of "structural" sin. Bryant Myers believes that "institutions are fallen," and that "evangelical theology is badly underdeveloped on the concept of the principalities and powers. Both individuals and structures need transformation." Dr. Manfred Grellert, regional vice president for Latin America at World Vision and a Brazilian theologian heavily influenced by liberation theology, goes even further. For him, the international economic order embodies structural injustice; it is "anti-Kingdom." Grellert concedes that "evil resides in the human heart," but he sees its presence also "in socio-economic and political structures. These structures are at the service of a privileged few . . . and they generate misery and poverty for many."

Because their theology of development rests on their understanding of who man is and what he is meant for, it is not surprising that the evangelicals define development as more than the alleviation of poverty. World Concern believes that there are choices people can make in determining their futures. The agency speaks of liberating people from the bondage of contemplating only "what is" and helping them to see "what can be." Its intention is to increase people's freedom over their entire lives — not just their economic life. Similarly, World Vision defines development as "a process by which people in a community work together to remove those individual and corporate barriers which prevent them from moving toward a better future." It recognizes that some of those barriers are internal — individual feelings of worthlessness and powerlessness — while others are external — oppressive political, economic, and social structures. Tetsunao Yamamori, president of Food for the Hungry, defines development as "a process of positive change by a community or an individual in values, behavior, attitude, and the quality of life."

The evangelical agencies differ within and between themselves in their attitudes toward dependency theory. Dr. Grellert of World Vision wholly accepts it; he believes that "underdevelopment and development are two different sides of the same coin." But his does not appear to be the dominant view among World Vision executives. His colleague Bryant Myers agrees with Grellert that the "results of the international economic system are unambiguously unjust" and that the gap between rich and poor is increasing; unlike Grellert, however, Myers sees shortcomings in dependency theory. It is too simplistic, he says, and tends to search for an economic answer to a problem that is "fundamentally spiritual." However, Myers estimates that many World Vision field workers in Latin America would tend to agree more with Grellert's position than with his own: "many field staff personnel buy the North-South paradigm of a rich core that oppresses the periphery."

Leaders of World Concern and World Relief have adopted two components of the dependency theory: that the "gap" between the rich and the poor countries is widening, and that the international economic system consistently favors the "haves" at the expense of the "have-nots." For example, Gregory of World Concern argues that "economic power is becoming more and more concentrated in fewer and fewer hands" and that "the gap between those who have and those who don't is becoming greater." Ballard believes that it is the function of the international economic order that has produced the Third World's crushing debt, and he suggests that debt forgiveness may be in order.

Yamamori of Food for the Hungry and Hancock of Transformation International are the most skeptical of dependency theory. For example, Hancock calls dependency theory "simplistic" and argues that "win-win" relationships are possible in our global economic system, as the experiences of several East Asian countries attest. Yamamori is also impressed with the Four Little Dragons and believes that their commitment to economic growth, encouragement of private enterprise, and willingness to compete vigorously in the international export market have been the keys to their success.

Even those within the evangelical agencies who see some truth in dependency theory join their more skeptical colleagues in rejecting outright its call for a global redistribution of resources as the key to alleviating Third World poverty. Evangelicals, because of their appreciation of individual freedom and their sober assessment of personal evil, are naturally suspicious of government-led redistribution schemes. Rather than redistribution, evangelicals place emphasis on the importance of wealth creation. Mike Still, an economist for World Vision, sees wealth creation as the best strategy to combat Third World poverty. Yamamori states simply that "new wealth can and should be created. . . . There is no limit to value added." Hancock believes that wealth creation is the only enduring solution to poverty. World Relief emphasizes microeconomic development and operates programs aimed at improving farmers' productivity. Fred Gregory argues that "wealth is dynamic . . . not static," and adds that "for someone to get ahead, someone else does not have to be diminished."

Taken all in all, the views of the five evangelical agencies seem more attuned to the realities of economic development than do those of oldline groups. The evangelicals show more awareness of and willingness to learn from the revisionist studies of recent years. For that reason, they would seem better suited than the oldline to establish a "solidarity with the poor" that would in fact go beyond rhetoric and offer genuine hope for long-range alleviation of Third World poverty.

There have been signs in recent years that U.S. foreign aid policy is beginning to take into account the emerging scholarly consensus on development. Though a combination of bureaucratic inertia and reluctance to forsake old orthodoxies has hindered those developments, the policies of the Reagan and Bush administrations indicate receptiveness to new thinking. An opening therefore exists for Christians to participate in the defining of a new foreign aid policy consensus. Evangelical relief and development agencies like those described above could help in a variety of ways to further this reformation.

First, evangelicals can expand their "theology of development," building on foundations they have already laid. An "evangelical statement of development" along the lines of the impressive NAE Peace, Freedom, and Security Studies *Guidelines* would provide a valuable resource for foreign aid policy makers. As it happens, a number of far-sighted activists have already taken steps toward development of such a document.

Forty evangelicals, concerned over the emergence of liberationist currents within evangelicalism, met in 1987 in Villars, Switzerland, to consider the proper role of evangelicals in "opting for the poor." The Villars participants noted a number of disturbing tendencies in development thought within the churches:

> . . . the tendency [of development ministries] to focus on meeting material needs without sufficient emphasis on spiritual needs . . . the attempt to synthesize Marxist categories and Christian concepts, to equate economic liberation with salvation . . . the emphasis on redistribution of wealth as the answer to poverty and deprivation without recognizing the value of incentive, opportunity, creativity, and economic and political freedom . . . and the attraction to centrally con-

trolled economics and coercive solutions despite the failures of such economies and their consistent violation of the rights of the poor.

The conference's resulting "Villars Statement on Relief and Development" represents a first step toward a comprehensive evangelical vision for development. The statement notes that the "causes of hunger and deprivation . . . are spiritual as well as material and can only be dealt with adequately insofar as the spiritual dimension is taken into account." Its policy recommendations include support for private property and for the "the family as the basic social and economic unit."

Second, evangelicals can press their broad definition of human development in the public debate over foreign aid. If development is understood as something including but transcending the alleviation of material poverty, internal economic and human rights policies of recipient countries may be scrutinized far more carefully than has been the case in the past. If development is conceived of as both the alleviation of poverty and an increased scope of human freedom, recipient countries' records on religious tolerance, democratization, and human rights may take their place alongside traditional strategic considerations in decisions on foreign aid.

Third, evangelicals can improve the quality of "development education." Thus far, efforts to inform the public by (mainly oldline) Christian development agencies have been limited to relating the gruesome facts of human deprivation and hunger. Rarely are explanations for poverty given other than the standard dependency arguments. Internal causes of poverty, such as corrupt or oppressive political systems, are neglected — unless the nation under consideration is a right-wing military dictatorship. If the subject is poverty in Ethiopia, Vietnam, or Kampuchea, seldom are the disastrous political and economic policies of their totalitarian Marxist-Leninist governments raised as possible explanations.

Fourth, based on their conception of development, evangelicals can press the argument for three critical "pro-poor" institutions: private property rights, the rule of law, and democracy. The religious left views private property rights with suspicion, believing that they lead to the massive and unjust accumulation of wealth by the wealthy. Nicholas Eberstadt notes that in societies where private property rights are disregarded, the state can, in the "interests of the poor," expropriate at will the property of the wealthy. But surely, he argues, a state with sufficient power to steal from the rich and powerful may with even greater ease steal from the poor and vulnerable. Private property rights, in other words, ought to be understood as potentially critical for the poor as well as the rich.

Evangelicals can also press the rule of law — with its attendant virtues of order, fairness, and impartiality — as precondition to sustainable development. The absence of the rule of law may stymie development in that it may adversely affect the investment climate, individual savings rates, and productivity. Furthermore, the rule of law, as Eberstadt contends, "affords to society's most vulnerable members the protection that can only be brought by wealthy people in a 'state-of-nature' situation."

Moreover, evangelicals can publicize the democracy development connection. They already recognize the critical role of local participation by citizens in development projects. Local citizens ought to be involved both because they best know their own needs and because their freedom and dignity are demeaned if they are not included. Evangelicals should press the analogy to the national level, arguing that democratic and participatory forms of government best "fit" with man's freedom and capacity to decide what is best for his own welfare. Evangelicals need to carry the argument for expansion of civil and political freedoms in the underdeveloped world because too many other Christians have succumbed to the Marxist siren song of bread before freedom. Evangelicals must remind those who argue that the poor lack interest in "bourgeois" civil rights and political freedoms that none of us lives by bread alone. They can also publicize the strong empirical evidence linking freedom to material prosperity and authoritarian and totalitarian control to poverty.

Finally, evangelical private organizations can encourage vigorous consideration of government assistance programs to the private sector. Government-to-government transfers have often failed to improve the lot of the poor, either because they were diverted by corrupt leaders into Swiss bank accounts or because they enabled ruling elites to persist in following repressive political policies and/or destructive economic agendas. As Eberstadt has eloquently commented: "Transfers of wealth enlarge the capacity of recipient governments to pursue their intentions; they do not change those intentions. If the intentions have consequences that are economically destructive, the government will be empowered to act more destructively." In contrast, government-to-private-sector projects bring funding close to local problems, and they use resources in ways that villagers themselves, and not distant government bureaucrats, determine are most efficacious in addressing local needs.

Evangelicals are poised at the cutting edge of a reformation in development policy. Their contribution to that reformation can be significant if they forthrightly reject conceptions of solidarity with the poor that in fact lead to greater suffering for the poor. The task is theirs, in solidarity with oldline and Catholic co-activists willing to share an empirical temper, a comprehensive conception of development, and an appreciation for market-oriented economic models. For the sake of the poor, one hopes that the opportunity will not be missed.

The Four Problems
of Economic Life

Daniel Rush Finn

Any attempt to simplify the complexities of life to improve our understanding entails the imposition of a structure. Thus, the schema of four problems of economic life to be presented here cannot hope to outline the issues in any universally valid manner. The critical moral issues approached here clearly transcend economic activity; to approach them from the perspective of the economy alone will mean representing them in a way that is less than fully adequate. It is also the case that gathering a multitude of moral issues into a general category like "the quality of relations" clearly leaves racism, sexism, and many other particular issues unarticulated. This typology also exhibits the deficiencies inherent in focusing on the national economy rather than the international, and on the industrialized countries rather than the Third World, although the basic interdependencies among the four problems can be witnessed in those settings as well. Nonetheless, I hope the perspective outlined here will be helpful in advancing the dialogue between defenders and critics of the economic system currently prevailing in most of the Western world.

I have adopted the broader usage of the term "economic" in identifying "economic problems." From one point of view, it might be preferable to limit the term more narrowly in an attempt to rein in the over-confidence which many economists have shown in applying economic analysis to all sorts of areas of human life. Nonetheless,

From Daniel Rush Finn, "Self-Interest, Markets and the Four Problems of Economic Life," *Annual of the Society of Christian Ethics* (1989): 23-53.

"economic issues," broadly construed, already have center stage in public discourse in the nation, and it seems more likely that additional concerns may be added to these ongoing discussions under the umbrella of "economic" issues than it does that economic concerns might give way to other "non-economic" values and goals.

Looking at these four basic problems of economic life will, I hope, cast economic issues in a way that will press Christian ethicists, their students, and perhaps even persons in economics, business, and elsewhere to look more carefully at the tradeoffs and interdependencies that exist between and among several of the most basic goals we pursue in our common economic life.

Allocation

The first of the four problems to be faced in any economy is that of allocation. The problem itself is an old one in economics though calling it "allocation" is a twentieth-century phenomenon. The general goal implicit here is the production of goods and services or, in Adam Smith's terms (though not exactly his meaning), the production of wealth. Economists today understand the problem as one of the allocation of *resources* principally because of a shift in the self-understanding of the discipline. Mainstream economics now understands itself as the study of the allocation of scarce (i.e., costly) resources to alternative uses. The primary value understood to be at stake in this problem of allocation is still that of wealth-creation, the production of those goods and services which people find beneficial.

The primary evil confronting efforts at production is waste. Waste can occur in the production process if more resources than necessary are used to produce a certain amount of a particular good. Waste might also occur at the point of the marketing of products when the overproduction of a particular good means that we have more of it than we need or want at current prices and that we should have instead used some of those resources to produce goods in short supply. This understanding of the importance of waste in the process is exactly the point at which the notion of efficiency enters the discussion. No one is in favor of inefficiency. Everyone from profit-maximizing entrepreneurs to environmentally-conscious Christian stewards wants resources to stretch as far as possible.

The primary locus of decision-making in the process of allocation is clearly the market. That is, since individuals and institutions control resources, it is they who ultimately decide what to do with them, even though these individual decisions are always limited by the technological possibilities of the era and are often severely constrained by cultural, moral, and/or governmental standards. This is true, of course, in more or less capitalist economies, but it is even true to a surprising extent in centrally planned socialist economies. While a government might subsidize the production of rice to make it more easily available, the amount which farmers produce will still be sensitive to the incomes which farmers receive for producing it.

Because the primary method of governmental influence of persons making market decisions is to offer incentives (whether tax relief or Pentagon weapons contracts) or impose disincentives (whether taxes or prison sentences), there is the constant danger that government interference will lead individuals or institutions to react to these new "signals" in ways not foreseen by the legislators who created them. For example, the standard economic argument against rent controls or gasoline price ceilings is that although those people will gain who *can find* apartments to rent or gasoline to buy, builders of apartments and refiners of gasoline will slow or even cease production of these products, and fewer people will be *able to find* them for sale. Similarly, without competition in the market, monopoly (one seller), cartels (collusion among sellers), or organizations with such "market power" will employ that power to their own advantage and to the detriment of others. Anti-trust laws exist to prevent such abuses.

Thus, the problem of allocation features the self-interest of economic actors prominently. Advocates of free markets, of course, also combine this feature with an advocacy of personal freedom as a value in itself, something which in this schema is better considered in connection with the problem of the quality of human relations. This is not an insignificant issue in a world where the people of some nations might lead healthier, better educated lives if more economic decisions were left to the local level. Still, compared to the other three problems, allocation is preeminently dependent on active, free persons and institutions making decisions largely out of their own self-interest. The primary goal of those most concerned with the problem of allocation in our current context is to increase efficiency.

Distribution

The second of the four problems is that of distribution, the distribution to individuals and institutions of the products and services available each year. When we ask *to whom* the benefits of the economy should go, we ask a question of equity, and, by and large, economists recognize this. If we were to look at distribution as a problem in isolation from the other three, values such as these come to mind: meeting human needs; rewarding productivity, effort, sacrifice, and risk; obtaining security; and even achieving fair relative incomes. The primary perceived evils in distribution are poverty, the existence of great concentrations of wealth, faulty incentive structures, and the self-interest of persons who "have something to lose" in redistribution. Among institutionalized disincentives are welfare policies that discourage the seeking of employment, legal structures that foster costly litigiousness, and policies on legislative lobbying where a million dollars spent trying to change the rules of the game in one's own favor can at times improve a firm's profitability more than spending that million productively in renovating the plant or increasing efficiency.

While local considerations are important and international discrepancies are morally distressing, the primary locus of decisions in matters of distribution is the national community, principally the national government. Charitable, voluntary efforts are important at all levels, but the most basic need for a structure of justly distributed wealth is that embedded in the national economy. In a radically egalitarian commune, the primary goal related to distribution might be to increase income differentials to compensate individuals more fairly. In our context, the primary goal of those most concerned with this problem is clearly to reduce inequality.

Describing distribution as a separable problem

has certain disadvantages, primarily because it might be argued to be a subset of the fourth problem, the quality of relations in the economy. Separating it out would seem to give it a greater importance than other issues related to the quality of relations which are in fact equally crucial. Still, economists (and the wider public) have traditionally acknowledged that distribution is a problem separate from allocation and one which the market is not well suited to solve. Thus, treating distribution as one of the four basic problems builds on an existing understanding that allocation, for all its importance, is but a part of the question.

Scale

The third problem is that of achieving the proper scale for the economy. This is a relatively new problem. There have been examples of pre-modern problems of scale, but these have been localized phenomena. The cliff-dwelling Anasazi of what is now southwestern Colorado flourished for several hundred years and then disappeared in a matter of decades in the early thirteenth century, probably because they over-taxed the environment in a period of drought. Similarly, citizens of the large industrial cities of England in the nineteenth century repeatedly experienced winters during which the smoke from coal-stoked heaters all too often filled the air and their lungs. Still it has been only in the last few decades that a general sense of the limits of our biosphere as a storehouse for resources and a sink for wastes has become acute.

Fundamentally, of course, problems of world-wide scale are completely beyond the reach and ken of unconstrained individual economic activity. Economists have long known that common pool depletion of, say, oil or water resources will occur at beyond-optimal rates unless coordination is imposed either by outside powers like government or possibly by the group of all owners of rights to deplete the pool. Economists have similarly noted the existence of "externalities" or "neighborhood effects." These are either negative effects of economic actors felt by others where the costs are not paid by those causing them, or, in some cases, positive effects caused for others where those causing them cannot reap the benefits.

Still, such acknowledgments have been added to the structure of mainstream economics as minor corrections, as Ptolemaic epicycles, without causing any major revision of the paradigm whose validity is weakened the more seriously externalities are taken. Clearly, today the problem of scale is not only real but immensely important. The greenhouse effect and depletion of the ozone layer are perhaps the two most pressing issues, but the list of real concerns is far longer: waste treatment and storage, resource depletion, etc. While some of these may be made more tractable by technological breakthrough, the point here is that treating the problem of allocation as if it were far and away prior to the problem of scale is shortsighted and foolhardy. As Herman Daly and John Cobb put it in the language familiar to economists, determining the appropriate scale for the economy is a distinct optimization problem, one that cannot be subsumed under the effort to achieve an allocative optimum.

The general goal guiding responses to the problem of scale is sustainability. The time frame for this sustainability is not easy to specify. While a thousand years is tempting, nearly everyone admits that technological change over that time will likely be unthinkably immense and that presumptions of zero or small technological change are ludicrous. A time frame of a century may be more appropriate, but any line drawn here is clearly arbitrary.

The primary perceived evil when talking of scale is mindless, unsustainable growth. If world industrial production continues apace, serious climactic temperature shifts of even a few degrees Celsius could quite easily impose economic (not to mention human) costs that are both staggering and irreversible. If the production of energy continues to require more and more energy inputs to produce the same amount of energy to be sold (and this is likely as the more accessible sources of energy are consumed first in good economically rational fashion), petroleum may in the next five or six decades vanish altogether as a significant world energy source.

Historians of the next century may shake their heads at what look like reasonable market decisions today, for these may appear as short-sighted choices based on a naive extrapolation of a two-hundred-year era of good fortune which in reality was built on the exhaustion of a resource base that took ten thousand times that long to create. Technological innovations may indeed come to the rescue for a time, as could happen if effective and cheap smokestack "scrubbers" made the world's coal resources less threatening, but that possibility only brings us round again to the limits established by the greenhouse effect. Fusion remains a hope, but a very uncertain one. Fundamentally, the problem of scale is an immense and intractable one for any modern economy.

The Quality of Human Relations

The fourth problem is that of the quality of human relations. This is without doubt the most complex of the four in that it is perhaps more accurately described as a complex of related problems. Still, as our purpose here is the development of a framework for thinking about the economy, many of the subtleties must be neglected; the general governing goal related to the quality of relations is to develop and sustain strong persons in active communities. This problem needs to be seen as integral to economic life (and not a peripheral concern attended to by the moral or cultural realms) because economic life generally, as well as economic life considered narrowly as allocation, is only possible to the extent that the individuals and communities involved are well constituted.

The primary values to be achieved under the heading of the quality of relations are individuality, creativity, community, and participation. The meaning of any one of these is widely debated and heavily influenced by a nation's culture and informal traditions, but clearly in the United States these include democracy, freedom, and accountability. The primary perceived evils are polar opposites: the loss of the individual in the group and the loss of community as a result of individualism. The locus for decisions affecting the vitality of persons and communities is more diffused than in the other three cases: individuals' decisions and those taken at any level of group interaction.

Any specification of the major goal to be accomplished in our current context will also be subject to controversy. Nonetheless, two possibilities are particularly compelling: strengthening communal economic control at each level and limiting the psychic distance that threatens human relations in bureaucratic government. These two, of course, are themselves in tension, but together they mark the importance of responsive and robust channeling of economic activity. Note here that there are other and more chronic objections to tendencies within bureaucracy, most notably that it can obstruct good allocation (the first problem), but it qualifies here as well because the rigidities and unresponsiveness that attend bureaucracy in any environment are detrimental to individuals and community.

Negative Interactions among Efforts to Address the Four Problems

This framework of four problems is designed simply to distinguish, organize, and relate the basic problems facing any modern economy. It cannot of itself resolve the truly critical questions about the relative importance of the four problems or the relative importance of the various values and goals implicit within each one. To take just one example, Robert Nozick and Michael Walzer have widely divergent views on the relation of individual and community, and the schematic framework I am developing here provides little, if any, help in adjudicating their differences. However, it is clear that if any serious attempt at adjudication is to be made, it will have to begin with a clear differentiation among the problems, and it will require that all four sets of issues be laid on the table. In current practice we find that some parties to the economic policy debate conveniently forget about three of the problems in their enthusiasm for solutions to one of them.

This forgetfulness is not difficult to understand. It is much harder to develop simple and satisfying solutions when all four problems are considered together. Compromises have to be made and costs have to be accepted.

Let us begin by considering ways in which solutions to other problems can have an adverse impact on successful allocation. Actions oriented to improving distribution can impair production through a loss of incentive on the part of those receiving government transfer payments (whether the unemployed, farmers, or big business) or through a drop of savings and investment if taxes on these were raised dramatically to pay for redistribution. The sort of controls needed for solving the problem of scale can easily lead to special interest distortions and bureaucratic blunders harmful to allocation. Worthwhile efforts to improve the quality of relations in economic life often have significant costs (e.g., the cost of court systems to enforce contracts, the cost of education on the dangers of drugs or smoking, the cost of due process requirements within firms); and special interest distortions are always possible as individuals and groups seek gains for themselves under the banner of improving the quality of relations generally.

In the case of distribution, it is clear that actions oriented to improving allocation often and even generally have some effects that work against the goals of distribution. Some bases for desert — need, for example — are entirely ineffective within the market. Other bases for desert — like effort or risk — are indeed rewarded by the market, but only the most doctrinaire marketeers or libertarians would assert that this is the morally optimal scheme for rewarding effort and risk. Goals related to the problem of scale can likewise threaten the general goal of equity in distribution, as when special interest effects (always oriented to the powerful not the poor) or environmentally necessary economic retrenchment leave fewer resources available for redistributive efforts. Similarly, efforts to improve the quality of relations would impair distributive efforts if higher costs of achieving some other goals diminished wealth, making redistribution harder, either economically or politically.

Efforts to solve the problem of scale are threatened by actions in service to allocation in that individuals and institutions have economic incentives to ignore the social costs they cause. Because improvements in both distribution and the quality of relations are generally costly, and thus easier to accomplish under conditions of robust economic growth, efforts to solve these problems will often conflict with simultaneous efforts to solve the problem of scale.

Similarly, efforts to improve the quality of relations are threatened by pursuit of the goals related to the other problems. The tendency for the market to undercut communal ties and traditional values has been well documented and critiqued. Some, such as Joseph Schumpeter and Thorstein Veblen, have even argued that this tendency in capitalism erodes the moral foundations on which capitalism stands, thereby leading toward the demise of capitalism itself. Similarly, some attempts to improve distribution (e.g., welfare rules that refuse benefits to two-parent families) may erode family ties, individuality, customs, etc. The strong national or international authorities that may be needed to address the problem of scale could entail the sort of restrictions on democratic freedoms feared by Robert Heilbroner in *An Inquiry into the Human Prospect*.

Positive Interactions among Efforts to Address the Four Problems

At the same time, of course, solutions to these four problems are not simply mutually exclusive.

The most important of these positive interactions are those between allocation and the latter three problems. I say "most important" because so much of recent neoconservative writing on ethics and economics has been directed against those trying to address one of the other three problems; the neoconservative argument rests on the claim that other approaches threaten the production of goods and services. As we have just seen, there are tradeoffs between and among these four basic goals, but the simplistic form of the argument heard so often takes an ahistorical view of production as somehow prior to the others and views those other goals as unidirectionally dependent on production. This argument goes on to endorse (more or less) the current state of social legislation but offers no justification of its implicit demand that we stop the development of social legislation at its current position and go no farther.

This argument is shortsighted. Efforts to improve distribution can indeed conduce to better productivity. Without a broadly accepted conception of equity in a society, both workplace predictability and political stability are at risk. Efforts to improve distribution affect workplace loyalty and motivation and enable lower-income citizens to become better educated and thereby better able to advance economically through productive contributions in the economy.

Steps to address scale are also crucial for allocation. Unless a sustainable economic process is established, impressive gains today may well look shortsighted and even foolhardy fifty years from now. When intergenerational equity is taken into consideration (and there are few morally weighty arguments for discounting the welfare of future generations in the way self-interest in the market discounts it), sustainability moves from a prudent reasonableness to a moral obligation.

As important as the goals of equity and sustainability are for allocation, the goal of developing strong individuals and communities is even more critical. Neoconservative defenders of the market system often praise the productive, wealth-producing capacity of capitalism as the engine providing the means for accomplishing other goals in life like equity or environmental improvements. However, it is certainly more accurate to say that it is the presence of strong, creative, and public-spirited individuals in strong, creative and caring communities and institutions that have made possible the dramatic advances in productivity within the market system. The arguments of Schumpeter and Veblen and others are telling when they point out that the rationality of the market (a means/end rationality) tends to undercut the values and communal ties without which the freedom and individuality that fuel the market will burn too hot and consume the very network of relationships that supports the interrelated productive centers we call the economy.

For the same reasons the quality of relations has been essential to our current prosperity, improvements in this quality can have still further positive effects on the allocative process. Political economists engage in strenuous debates on this issue, of course, and I do not take my asserting such positive effects to be adequate argumentation for them. Nonetheless, I am convinced that stricter workplace safety standards, more aid to education (particularly for low-income groups), security for medical catastrophe, and many other particular goals would contribute to our national welfare and would have beneficial effects in production by creating the context — increased motivation, better education, stronger personal and familial security — from which market-oriented ingenuity and risk-taking arise.

Some neoconservatives do explicitly praise the many historic steps taken through government action (social legislation) to humanize capitalism, but nearly all of them oppose further steps in this direction. Peculiarly, however, there is almost always an asymmetry in their rationale. While they usually oppose further social legislation on the grounds that it would interfere with allocative efficiency, that could also be said (and was!) about the social legislation that they now take for granted. When an issue is one of tradeoffs between say, allocation and the quality of relations, it is insufficient to consider only the benefits and costs within allocation. A responsible argument requires that benefits and costs within the quality of relations be carefully attended to as well.

While the positive interaction among the other permutations of these four problems are important, they are both less intricate and less controverted. Improving distribution is easier, other things being equal, with growth and is more difficult without it. While many efforts to improve sustainability compete for resources with efforts to improve distribution, it is clear that long-run improvements in distribution require sustainable long-term economic prosperity. With the improvement of the vitality of individuals and communities comes a greater appreciation of the value of equity within the nation. The very possibility, mentioned earlier, of subsuming the goals of distribution under those of quality of relations speaks to the positive interaction of efforts to address these two problems.

The goals related to the problem of scale clearly conflict with the unencumbered operation of the market, but it is also true that environmentally necessary changes in production will be easier to make with rising per capita GNP, particularly if that growth is an environmentally benign sort. Advances in equity will probably bring about a greater willingness to sacrifice for sustainability, as will advances in the quality of individuals and communities.

While some of the goals related to the quality of relations are in critical ways threatened by the market, others, like creativity and individuality, are rewarded and encouraged. Improvements in productivity make it easier to afford expenditures to improve the quality of relations. Improvement in equity might be seen as a subset of improvements in the quality of relations, and a greater sense of equity can increase one's sense of self and of the importance of appropriate communal ties. Enhancements in sustainability benefit the quality of relations in that they serve to prevent the social dislocations which would surely follow upon environmentally induced economic crises.

Conclusion

The strength of the capitalist form of economic organization has been its unprecedented success in the allocation of resources in the market. Relying upon and rewarding self-interested activity of individuals and organizations has led to the greatest outburst of economic productivity in the history of humankind. As Bernard Mandeville put it nearly three centuries ago, the system is one where "the very Poor Lived better than the Rich before." From the point of view of ethics, this favorable consequence is significant and weighs heavily in favor of a generally free market. Still, there are negative effects of the system and these weigh heavily on the other side of the balance. The productive process, here referred to as allocation, is but one of the basic problems to be addressed in setting the rules of the game for economic life. Although self-interested activity deserves to be endorsed *within* the process of allocation, the extrapolation of the legitimacy of self-interested behavior outside the allocation process cannot rely on arguments that it simply helps allocative efficiency. That is not the issue.

Neoconservatives are owed a debt of gratitude for disclosing the moral foundations of capitalism and for reminding business practitioners and others of the importance of such foundations. Recognizing the many benefits of self-interest within markets may be difficult for some critics of the system. Recognizing the restricted nature of the legitimacy of self-interest may be difficult for some defenders of the system. Attempting to adjudicate the differences in opinion about the relative weights of the various goals in economic life will not be easy, but since we face multiple problems, it is critical to recognize vividly the tradeoffs that will have to be made.

Ethics, Economics, and Free Trade

John B. Cobb, Jr.

Issues of profound ethical importance are sometimes put before us as technical economic policies. The Uruguay Round proposals for revision of the General Agreement on Tariffs and Trade, for instance, are presented as an extension of "free trade," a principle we have been taught to honor from our childhood. If fully implemented, these proposals will profoundly affect hundreds of millions of lives.

What we read about these discussions suggests these proposals involve ethical issues. The obstacles they face are depicted as the expression of narrow vision and corrupt self-interest on the part of small groups willing to risk the well-being of the whole for the sake of retaining the unjust advantages they now enjoy. It is assumed in almost all the published reports that the well-being of the whole will be advanced by extending the scope of free trade. Since this is what the Uruguay Round proposals do, they are evidently good. Hence it is the moral responsibility of governments to accept these proposals rather than to heed the protests of those special interests who will be harmed by their implementation.

Even if the issue really was as depicted — that is, the well-being of the many versus that of the few — ethicists would have reason to examine matters with some care. The suffering of a few million people is not to be taken lightly. For example, the wiping out of the European family farmers, the only people who have thus far protested effectively against the proposed agreement,

John B. Cobb, Jr., "Ethics, Economics, and Free Trade," *Perspectives* 6, no. 2 (Feb. 1991): 12-15.

is surely a social change of such scope that it should not be treated as a minor loss. Still, if the issue is as depicted, ethicists will be inclined to support the proposals if ways are found to ease the adjustment of family farmers into urban life.

Before such a decision is made, ethicists should look further into what is proposed and into its probable effects. For example, the Uruguay Round proposals include the removal of restrictions on investment and services in the Third World. Currently, many countries try to ensure that foreign investment works with local capital in ways that help build up the indigenous economy. Many have regulations that help the enterprises of their own citizens, especially in the service sector (banks and insurance companies, for example), to compete with multinational corporations. The new proposals forbid all of these practices, thus insuring that the service sector of Third-World economies, like the industrial sector, will be owned and managed by foreigners whose only professional interest is corporate profit. Similarly, a Third-World country will not be able to protect its natural resources from international market forces. Any country that fails to abide by these agreements will find markets closed to its exports.

The negative effects of these proposals extend to the areas of health and environment. For example, the United States now prohibits the use of certain poisons in the production of food. It can also refuse to import food produced with those poisons. Under the new rules, it could refuse to import such foods only if a small committee in Rome, noted for its very low standards in such matters, declares the food a health hazard.

Examples such as these give us a clearer picture of what "free trade" means. It means that governments can no longer steer economic development within their boundaries. Such development is to be determined by the global market. Capital will flow around the world to those places where it can be most profitably invested. Goods will be sold to the highest bidder. All other considerations will be drastically subordinated. Free trade also means that governments cannot set standards for health and the environment above those of the rest of the world. Otherwise, local producers must compete with others who are not regulated in these ways.

As the negative consequences of free trade be-come more evident, ethicists can begin to ask some critical questions. What does "free trade" really mean? What are its positive values? Are these so important as to justify support despite the losses they entail?

"Free trade" is trade between firms that is free from regulation or interference by governments. Generally, the term applies to trade that crosses national boundaries. "Free trade" means that goods, services, and capital can flow across national boundaries as easily as they flow within a single country. Today, concretely, it means that transnational corporations can invest freely where and for what purposes they will and that governments give up the right to regulate them. "Free trade" is the means whereby the most important decisions about human welfare are shifted from the political sector to the market, and that means to the major players within the market.

The first step in the argument for free trade is, therefore, the argument for the market economy. History has frequently demonstrated that efforts to guide the economy by bureaucratic decisions break down in inefficiency and delay even if they do not become blatantly corrupt. The collapse of the Eastern European economies has confirmed this lesson in a decisive and unforgettable way. It seems that only the market can make the requisite decisions for the efficient use of resources that will lead to an adequate supply of the desired goods.

The second step in the argument — that the larger the market is the better — is based on the evidence that a larger market allows for greater specialization, and specialization makes greater efficiency in production possible. This means that the larger the market, the more efficiently capital will be invested and the greater will be the resultant gross product. The global market toward which the Uruguay Round proposals move us will assure the most rapid possible growth in gross world product.

This argument is valid as far as it goes. If the proper goal of policy is to increase total production, then the extension of markets free from governmental interference should be consistently supported. But ethicists must ask whether this goal of increasing the gross product should override all other goals. Among the goals overridden — as illustrated above — are those of the social ideal of the family farm, the desire of Third-World peoples to participate in the control of their own destiny, and the right of people to set standards for their own health and environment. Should all of these goals be subordinated to that of increasing gross product?

The ethical argument for a positive answer is that, speaking globally, there is still a woeful shortage of goods, even of necessities. Hundreds of millions of people are living in abject poverty. The global population continues to grow rapidly. Unless gross product grows more rapidly than population, there will not be enough product to meet human needs in the future. Those of us whose basic needs — and more — are comfortably met have no right to place secondary considerations above these primary ones.

But there is a strong counterargument as well. When market forces are not directed by political concern for the poor, they increase the gap between the rich and the poor. Indeed, the poor often become poorer and more numerous. In a global market without political control, the rich nations grow richer and the poor poorer. The same is true within nations. What is advocated as free trade involves the removal of political influence from the market. It will not improve the lot of the poor.

Defenders of free trade or of the expansion of market size may acknowledge that the market tends to increase the gap between rich and poor. But, they argue, the poor do not become poorer in absolute terms, Instead, even if they benefit less from the increased production than do the rich, the poor still benefit. As the pie enlarges, even if their share is smaller as a percentage of the whole, it is still larger in absolute terms.

An example will help clarify the relative strengths of these arguments for and against free trade. Consider what is happening in the United States and Mexico. As trade becomes freer between the two nations, more and more U.S. companies relocate across the border where wages are much lower and governmental regulations in the interest of health and environment are fewer. They then sell their products in the U.S. market, pricing them lower than domestic producers.

This movement of capital out of the United States has a negative effect on wages here. On the other hand, the wages paid to Mexican workers, while very low by our standards are fairly good by

theirs, and U.S. capital does employ persons who might otherwise have no job at all. In the long run, free trade between the United States and Mexico will tend to equalize wages in the two countries. It can be argued that this is a movement toward global justice.

How is this dynamic to be evaluated ethically? Obviously, it involves enormous hardship for U.S. workers. But is this suffering compensated by the gains of Mexican labor? If Mexican labor could be expected to rise toward First-World standards, then ethicists might decide they should support this development and seek to ameliorate the hardship of the labor force in this country.

Let us assume that increasing U.S. investment in Mexico will benefit Mexican labor. The question is, how much? The answer is discouraging. Mexican labor is so abundant that the movement of more factories south of the border is unlikely to raise Mexican wages above subsistence, especially in a time when technology is continuously reducing the amount of labor required in production. If, in spite of these factors, Mexican wages did begin to rise significantly, the market forces that moved capital to Mexico would move it elsewhere. Thus, the rapid decline in the standard of living of U.S. workers will not be compensated by a significant rise in the standard of living of Mexican workers.

The situation for investors, of course, is different. As they are free to seek more profitable investments elsewhere, and as labor costs and governmental restrictions decline at home, their income will rise. In this way the gap between the rich and the poor will widen.

Is the increase of gross world product the ethical end of policy even though it is accompanied by widening gaps between the rich and the poor? Will it in the end allow for the employment of more people and thus the reduction of utter destitution? Since bureaucratic management of the economy has demonstrated its incapacity, is there really any alternative to pressing forward to a free global market?

This last question is the most poignant and the most urgent for ethically sensitive persons. If there is no defensible alternative to a single global market, then ethicists must support this goal while seeking to ameliorate the harmful consequences. Since such amelioration can scarcely occur unless there is a political body that has authority over the market, the ethically concerned will devote their energies to generating stronger international institutions. Since the ethical reason for wanting such governmental authorities is that they may ameliorate the suffering of the market's victims, these institutions must be responsive to those who suffer and to those concerned for them. Some way must be devised for the expression of these human interests in the selection of the leaders of global organizations. Overall, the move must be toward world government.

If we accept the globalization of the economy, then we must work for globalization of political authority as well. Otherwise we abandon all possibility of ethical influence on those decisions that will most determine human well-being. But if we develop a world government for the sake of those who suffer from market forces, would there be any way of preventing such authority from coming under the control of precisely those economic interests it was instituted to monitor? This control of political decisions by economic interests is already a serious problem at the national level. The global level is so remote from ordinary citizens that competition for influence with multinational corporations is unlikely to succeed.

If it is ethically unacceptable to have the world controlled by transnational corporations alone, and if we cannot trust global political authority to represent the interests of ordinary citizens, ethicists are under pressure to devise alternative images of a desirable future. The second of the two steps given above as the argument for free trade — that the larger the market is the better — is based on the assumption that the greater the increase of gross product the better; that has already been shown to be a weak argument. The increase of gross product is not commonly associated with improvement in the welfare of the poor. And it is not clear that the increase of the wealth of the rich justifies the many negative consequences already noted as accompanying the extension of the market.

Another important objection against working primarily for the increase of total production is the close connection between growth of this kind and resource exhaustion on the one side, and pollution on the other. In general, the more rapid the growth, the faster the exhaustion of resources and the greater the pollution. (The qualification "in general" is needed, since there can be carefully directed growth that does not have these effects.) But it is just this kind of careful directing of growth by governmental regulations that is excluded by the extension of the free market. The growth engendered by global free-trade will be the kind that exhausts resources and pollutes the environment.

The implication of what has been said is that growth of gross product is not necessarily improvement of human welfare. To state it even more strongly, per capita gross product is not even a measure of economic welfare. Even the most orthodox economists agree on this, although both they and government officials often neglect this point in their public communications. Recognizing the difference between gross product and economic welfare, some have developed measures of economic welfare and applied them to the economy of the United States. The results have shown, with some consistency, that welfare has not grown proportionately to per capita GNP in recent decades. Indeed, it seems apparent that growth of GNP can be accompanied by declining economic welfare, especially when the welfare considered is sustainable welfare. (See the appendix to *For the Common Good,* by Herman Daly and myself.) Ethicists should work for policies that enhance human welfare in general and for an economy that enhances economic welfare.

If increase in gross product is not the ethical goal, then there is not ethical reason to increase the size of markets. It is clear that some groups, especially those who live from the investment of capital, will gain by increasing the size of markets and that labor now living above the global subsistence level will lose. All will suffer through the decline in health and environmental protection, the exhaustion of resources, and the pollution of the environment. The ability of people to participate in making the decisions that shape their lives will decline. Ethical considerations, far from supporting free trade, as is still generally supposed, count strongly against it.

The alternative to free trade is a system of relatively self-sufficient markets in relatively small regions. In each of these regions the community can organize to express its concern for all its members through political and social institutions. There would be a market economy instead of central planning, but the community would establish rules, applied equally to all the layers in the market, designed to support the public good in health, environmental well-being, and the conditions of labor. Those who played by these rules would not be forced to compete with other producers who played by less demanding rules in other markets. Of course, the market would need to be large enough to insure competition in as many types of business as possible. Where that is not possible, business would be closely regulated or even owned by the community. The ability of ordinary people to participate in important decisions at this level is incomparably greater than their ability to participate in global government.

In a world like this there could be trade that is in fact much freer than what is now called "free trade." Today free trade means the freedom of multinationals from governmental interference. The effect on people everywhere is to make them dependent for their very existence on a trade whose terms are set by others. They are not free not to trade and hence must trade on whatever terms are imposed on them. In the scenario proposed here, each community would be free to trade or not to trade as it chose. It could survive without trade, and therefore each community would trade only when the terms of trade were advantageous to it.

Since many issues cannot be dealt with at the local level, these relatively self-sufficient communities would organize themselves into communities of communities, and these into communities of communities of communities, up to the global level. No local community should be free to export its pollution to others or to exclude minority groups from participation in its own life. Communities of communities would require considerable power in order to enforce such rules. More power is needed at the global level, for example, to enforce decisions of the World Court and of the United Nations. The goal is not a return to political isolationism. But the ideal is free people participating in shaping the conditions within which free markets operate, freely determining when trade is advantageous to them. Political institutions should retain power over economic ones even if they choose to give free reign to market forces within the community. In such a world, communities could measure their eco-

nomic well-being by whether the basic needs of all citizens are met, not but by the growth of their product, a far more ethical approach.

Liberating Thoughts about the Ethics of Exchange and Trade

Robin Klay

When will theologians and ethicists learn the most heartening and demonstrable truth of economics, namely that free exchange and trade result in mutual ties and benefits?

If an Indian entrepreneur, Feler Bose, invents, produces, and markets a more fuel-efficient, wood-burning stove, should he not rejoice in the service he renders to his peasant customers, who are converting much of the time and energy they previously spent gathering scarce cooking fuel into more intense farming on higher-yield crops? Should he not take pride in the difference this will make to this region, where erosion, caused by rapid deforestation, can now be reversed? Should he not also enjoy the profits he makes, both for the increased opportunities they give him and his extended family (partners in this enterprise) and for the part those profits play in funding an expansion of their business? Or, should he instead confess his guilt for having put several older stove-makers out of business because his stoves attracted so many new buyers — due to their great savings in time and energy?

Suppose my name is Alice Bos and I own some Xerox stock, which I bought when I heard the company was setting up production facilities across the border in Mexico. Should I feel glad about the dividends and grateful for what they will mean to my daughter's college education? Per-haps, instead, I should feel some collective guilt for having improved my lot "on the backs" of Mexican workers hired in the new Xerox plant. And what should U.S. consumers think of their part in the global economy? Should we carry a sense of guilt for buying less expensive imported cars, TVs, and clothing? After all, their cheaper prices may result from foreign labor being less expensive, per unit of output, than American labor with the same skills — which translates into fewer such jobs in Michigan and North Carolina at the same time that jobs are expanding in Mexico, Korea, and the Philippines. Or, instead, should U.S. consumers delight that their imported purchases not only enhance their own lives but also mean higher standards of living for Mexican and Philippine workers — as well as greater sales of U.S. exports to increasingly better-off consumers in those countries?

Such mixed messages about the morality of our roles in the marketplace as workers, entrepreneurs, stockholders, and consumers can seem confusing and frustrating. But it is possible to enjoy reasonably clear consciences as participants in a market economy. Economists have attempted to answer the above questions for generations by affirming the social value of exchange (and trade) in markets open to competition; but there always seems to be a need to repeat the analysis and to reconfirm the answer.

The gist of their argument is this: when any two parties freely make an exchange, both enjoy some benefits from the trade. The worker who takes a job at the Xerox plant in Nogales gains a job and income better than his or her alternatives (lower-paying jobs elsewhere or unemployment). At the same time, the stockholders of Xerox gain more in dividends if the employment of Mexican workers allows Xerox to remain competitive and profitable in the world market. And U.S. consumers of products manufactured by Xerox in Mexico gain from the exchange, because their alternative is to buy higher-priced or lower-quality products made elsewhere.

None of this is to say that the market does not produce losers as well as gainers. It does so all the time. For instance, the U.S. worker who was working in a Xerox factory making typing ribbons lost a job when the plant moved to Mexico. Yet, in the many situations where competition is able to har-

Robin Klay, "Liberating Thoughts about the Ethics of Exchange and Trade," *Perspectives* 7, no. 10 (Oct. 1992): 10-13.

ness productive efforts to produce goods and services efficiently, consumers, workers, and producers gain collectively through free exchange.

This is the case for Xerox production in Mexico. By moving lesser-skilled jobs to Mexico, Xerox is better able to protect the more skilled jobs in its U.S. plants from foreign import competition. Why? Because Xerox products can remain competitive with Asian producers due to the reduced cost of ribbons installed in them. Furthermore, the money U.S. consumers save on their purchases of the now-cheaper Xerox products will go toward purchases of other goods and services, most of which entail American jobs. Finally, Mexican workers with new jobs and higher incomes stimulate growth of the Mexican economy resulting in greater imports from the United States — again, a source of new America jobs.

The general argument for free markets, both domestically and across international borders, is that when people freely produce and sell products or services in a competitive market, both they and their customers gain from the exchange. Competition among sellers for customers forces costs as low as possible. In some industries, the products of developing countries can successfully compete with similar products from advanced economies, on the basis of low wages. In many other industries, products of high-wage workers in advanced economies successfully compete with Third World exports, due to the greater education and skills of these workers and due to the large amounts of sophisticated capital with which they work. In both cases, international competition makes for efficiency in the use of scarce world resources (land, labor, and capital), thereby insuring the greatest possible output and highest possible living standards.

Unfortunately, the truth of this argument for free trade frequently gets lost in a morass of nationalism, romantic notions of self-sufficiency, and narrow producer interests. The great period of ascendancy of protectionist logic and policy, known as mercantilism, covered the years between 1500 and 1776. During that period, a nation's interest was thought best pursued by governments promoting exports and limiting imports, thus bringing gold into the national treasury. Such ideas encouraged colonialism, whereby cheap sources of materials could be mo-

nopolized and new, captive markets for manufacturers created.

It was Adam Smith's revolutionary *Wealth of Nations,* published in 1776, that first powerfully made the case for free trade. It makes no more sense for a nation to produce for itself one item that it could obtain more cheaply from another country than it would for an individual person to grow her own rice, when she could instead teach music and buy the rice more cheaply (with fewer hours of labor) from a farmer. As Smith said: "What is prudence in the conduct of every private family, can scarce be folly in that of a great kingdom."

When Americans bow to Detroit's pressure to raise tariffs 25 percent against Japanese minivans, we are making precisely the mistake that Adam Smith warned against — insisting that American consumers pay more in order to buy domestically-produced minivans. And when the relatively small numbers of farmers prevail in Japanese political circles, they persuade the Diet to maintain bans against foreign rice imports at the expense of Japanese consumers, who must then pay a price several times higher than the world price for their most important staple. In both cases, Adam Smith's lesson has been lost to the benefit of narrow economic and political interests.

When some politicians in Third World countries argue that tariffs and quotas against foreign imports are necessary to promote greater economic self-sufficiency, again Adam Smith's lesson is being lost. The history of economic development of nations confirms Adam Smith's expectation that expanding trade within domestic markets, and among nations, would prove to be a veritable engine of growth, raising the average standards of living everywhere. It was his observation that larger markets make specialization in production easier, thereby increasing productivity, output, and incomes. Countries that, instead, attempt to be self-sufficient end up severely compromising their chances for economic growth and higher standards of living.

Adam Smith's lesson gets lost not only in political debates, responding to narrow commercial interests, but also in explorations of the ethical nature of trade by some Christians. John Cobb, Jr., for instance, in "Ethics, Economics, and Free Trade" reasoned that free trade endangers the world's health and environment, equitable income distribution between rich and poor countries, and the ability of people to control their own destinies.

Cobb's evaluation of the freeing of trade between Mexico and the United States (whose completion in the form of a North American Free Trade Area was negotiated in 1991 and 1992) is an example of the ethical issues as he sees them. He pits the losses of American jobs in industries that have opened plants in Mexico against the hoped-for gains in Mexican jobs and wages. As an ethicist, his evaluation seems to hinge on whether any benefits to Mexican workers outweigh the losses to certain American workers (those who lost their jobs).

Cobb's assumption appears to be that if the economic gains to Mexican workers (who are very poorly paid compared to U.S. workers) could be shown to exceed the losses to U.S. workers, then the movement of manufacturing plants to Mexico could be judged ethically good. However, he argues that, due to a large Mexican labor supply, the added demand for labor in "maquiladora" industries (set up by U.S. firms on the Mexican side of the border) will do little to raise Mexican wage rates. Thus, he reasons that the gains do not outweigh the losses — with the implication that the plant moves are therefore ethically bad (even if they may raise world output).

Unfortunately, Cobb's analysis is seriously flawed at various points. Wage rates in maquiladora plants have, in fact, been higher than elsewhere in Mexico, exerting an upward pull on Mexican wage rates generally. Furthermore, as long as workers willingly take jobs in the maquiladoras (many people having moved long distances to border towns from the interior of the country), we know that *they* perceive themselves to be better off. Either they currently have jobs, after being counted among the large numbers of Mexico's unemployed, or their earnings are higher than in previous work. In either case, their lives have been improved by moving to a place where new jobs have opened. Over time, the lives of those left behind also improve, as employers there must pay higher wages as an incentive to keep their employees from moving toward new opportunities.

However, the most serious flaw in Cobb's analysis is his assumption that the potential gainers from the plant moves to Mexico are only two:

Mexican workers (whose expected gain he judges to be small) and U.S. investors, whose profits increase with the new investment in Mexico. Furthermore, he assumes that U.S. workers, as a group, lose from the transaction. This is not likely the case. As we noted earlier, expanded Mexican employment and incomes make Mexico — the third most important buyer of U.S. exports — an even better customer. Thus, as the economic pie expands output and opportunities in Mexico, flows of trade and finance across borders make it likely that the U.S. economy and total jobs in the United States will also expand.

Although Cobb concentrated on maquiladora plants, there is much more than border assembly operations in the offing. The North American Free Trade Agreement (NAFTA), which the legislatures in Canada, the United States, and Mexico must ratify before taking effect in January 1994, is designed to free trade among these three nations over a fifteen-year period. If approved, NAFTA will comprise a market of 364 million people, whose total trade volume now exceeds $200 billion annually. Rapid economic reform in Mexico and the anticipation of NAFTA have already boosted expansion of the Mexican economy (and the U.S. economy along the Mexican border). U.S. exports to Mexico over the last five years have nearly tripled, with expectations that Mexico will soon surpass Japan as America's second-largest trading partner (after Canada). Consumers throughout North America stand to gain greatly from prices lowered by the elimination of tariffs and the vigorous competition. Furthermore, economists estimate that net job creation in the United States alone will be at least seventy-five thousand by 1995, steadily growing along with continued economic expansion throughout the continent. The prospects for important mutual gains to the people of Mexico, Canada, and the United States should prompt vigorous support by Christians for NAFTA's ratification.

That Cobb's ethical reservations about trade are widespread in the general public and very ancient in origin does not make them valid. Since early times, religious thinkers have tended to suspect that often in buying and selling there is a gainer exploiting a loser and have, therefore, urged the authorities to regulate prices and other terms of exchange. In both the medieval world and the mercantilistic period that followed, regulations of price, permission to produce, wage rates, and product quality were pervasive and largely pernicious to output and material well-being.

Yet, this is precisely how Cobb also reasons. First, he considers the possibility of creating a global political authority to ensure that trade takes place in ways beneficial to all parties. This he quickly backs away from, out of fear that political forces at the global level would be no more just in their handling of trade than those at the national level. Alternatively, Cobb suggests that the world be divided into many small economic regions with relatively self-sufficient markets. This he recommends because he believes that the large size of current markets has benefited the owners of capital but hurt labor.

Cobb would have us more in the opposite direction from that in which world economies have been moving since the Middle Ages — and even more so during the twentieth century. Developments in multinational trade negotiations through GATT (as in the current Uruguay Round aimed at reducing trade barriers among most trading countries) and bilateral negotiations (as in the North American Free Trade Area) aim to go even further in opening markets. Why the persistent move to greater *interdependence* (less self-sufficiency)? Precisely because self-sufficiency means a lower standard of living than is possible with trade along the lines of comparative advantage (i.e., exporting products in which a nation has a cost advantage and importing those in which it has a cost disadvantage).

Cobb wants to deny the economic importance of large market size and to contrast it with what he supposes to be the moral advantage of small market size — namely, that people can have a greater say in the direction of their economy for purposes of justice when it is small. But enormous increases in the standard of living in the developed world since the early nineteenth century and rapid economic progress in East Asian economies over the past two decades stand as monuments to the benefits of large and growing free markets! In contrast, poor economic outcomes for India's masses and corruption in high places testify to the barrenness of a policy of regulated self-sufficiency — even in that relatively big economy. Largely for this reason, since 1991 India has embarked on radical

economic reform aimed at freeing her market to international trade and greater domestic competition. Eastern Europe's even more dramatic rediscovery of the benefits of markets and trade testifies to the evident power of free domestic and international trade to improve the material lot of millions.

Instead of engaging in ethical handwringing about trade, Christian ethicists would do well to join most economists (Christian and otherwise) in supporting further measures for lower barriers to trade and financial flows and in celebrating the moves from self-sufficiency to interdependency. If the current major round of trade negotiations, known as the Uruguay Round, is unsuccessful in lowering certain quantitative barriers to trade (like quotas), ethicists and economists both will have something big to worry about. They should worry about the injustices and inefficiencies that would flow from a failure of the Uruguay Round — thereby setting the stage for a continuation of two decades of increased governmental resort to quotas on imports. Not only has this trend impeded trade expansion in general, but it has especially hurt Third World countries, whose chances for development are directly linked to export success. Unfortunately, setbacks in Uruguay Round negotiations have been promoted by "pockets of privilege" in industrialized countries, like French farmers, who prefer to remain insulated from world competition by protective farm and trade policies. Christian concerns for justice should motivate strong support for the Uruguay Round negotiations, which would open markets to the world's *underprivileged* competitors.

The world stands to gain greatly from freer trade because resources are thereby redirected into more productive channels, expanding the economic pie and raising living standards. Protectionists in high-wage countries complain about "unfair competition" from exports produced at low wages in the Third World. Protectionists in the Third World complain about unfair competition in exports produced with cheap capital in the industrial world. But free traders understand that when products effectively compete in world markets — whether due to less expensive labor, or cheap capital, or better technology — there is nothing "unfair" about it. It is the market's way of signaling more effective ways for world support of land, labor, and capital to be used for the greater benefit of the whole.

It would be especially helpful to Christian economists if they could count on Christian ethicists and theologians to explore the possibilities for freer trade and financial flows to help break down barriers between peoples. After all, inherent in exchange is the possibility of converting foreigners into partners and strangers into neighbors.

We need a better understanding of ethics in market economies that are increasingly open to the world. Armed with such understanding, ministers could more effectively engage parishioners from the business world with some very important ethical issues of our own day — issues that differ from those addressed by medieval ethicists who wrote in economically stagnant, highly stratified societies. Ours is a world of economic growth and change, whose challenges can engage our very best creativity and most productive efforts while advancing our concern for justice.

A Postcommunist Manifesto: Public Theology after the Collapse of Socialism

Max L. Stackhouse and Dennis P. McCann

The specter that haunted the modern world has vanished. That specter is communism. Nobody who has been paying attention takes it seriously anymore, although a few will echo its slogans for generations. To be more specific: no one thinks anymore that the route to social justice and prosperity necessarily lies in the political control of the marketplace and the means of production. Along with Soviet communism, forms of Marxism, even the gentler forms of European socialism, are under pressure.

We can neither ignore this fact nor deny its implications for Christian social ethics. The Protestant Social Gospel, early Christian realism, much neo-orthodoxy, many forms of Catholic modernism, the modern ecumenical drive for racial and social inclusiveness, and contemporary liberation theories all held that democracy, human rights and socialism were the marks of the coming kingdom. For all their prophetic witness in many areas, they were wrong about socialism. The future will not bring what contemporary theology said it would and should.

This is not like other recent crises. The current crisis in the Middle East makes American complacency impossible. The upheavals in Central Amer-

Max L. Stackhouse and Dennis P. McCann, "A Postcommunist Manifesto: Public Theology after the Collapse of Socialism," *Christian Century*, 16 Jan. 1991, pp. 1, 44-47.

ica have chastened American paternalism. Vietnam struck at national arrogance. The civil rights era demanded the repudiation of racism. The defeat of fascism vindicated democracy. And the crash of 1929 demanded the reform of the industrial order. All these altered the social landscape. But they did not require repentance of modern Christianity. Indeed, they clarified before the world deep though obscured social principles held by the ecumenical church.

The failure of the socialist vision, where it does not bring a crisis of faith, demands repentance. All too many religious leaders still cling to the belief that capitalism is greedy, individualistic, exploitative and failing; that socialism is generous, community-affirming, equitable and coming; and that the transition from the one to the other is what God is doing in the world.

The truth is: no system has a monopoly on greed; modern capitalism engenders greater cooperation; socialism is more exploitative; and no one who has experienced "really existing socialism" now believes that it was God's design. What we now face is more than a delay in the socialist *parousia*. It is the recognition that this presumptive dogma is wrong.

If we can no longer affirm the socialist decision, must we now become libertarian neoconservative? The answer is No, for questions of social justice are a necessary part of modern economics, not an intrusion into it. The economics of the future cannot be based on 18th-century theories or a return to 19th-century practices. Is it possible that, in face of the new evidence, everyone who holds to a "preferential option for the poor" must now embrace capitalism, since socialism itself impoverishes? In some measure, the answer is Yes. But it must be a reformed capitalism — one that uses law, politics, education and especially theology and ethics to constrain the temptations to exploitation and greed everywhere.

Whenever capitalism rapes the earth or becomes a pillar of racism, sexism, classism or nationalism, it must be resisted. But if the age of individualist greed is past, so is the age of collectivist protest against it. Aggregates of possessive egos, each making bottom-line decisions by the utilitarian calculation of cost and benefit, are as false as command economies where political and military leaders control the whole society.

Of course, socialism and Christianity are in theoretical accord on one key point: society is and must be prior to both government and business. But on the issue of what constitutes the core of society the differences appear immediately: more important than class conflict is theology and communities of faith. These transcend political economy both locally and historically and provide the model for the common life.

All politics and all economics must be conducted under the context-transcending principles of truth, justice and love. Concretely understood, these protect the moral and spiritual rights of persons and groups and disclose purposes for living that are not of this world. Such principles and purposes are, and must be, the formative force in all public life, as well as in personal piety. They must enhance the salvation of both souls and civilizations.

At once more personal and more cosmopolitan than any political ideology or economic interest can be, a genuinely theological vision must constitute the ethics of our postsocialist economic order. Every authority and every policy that is deemed legitimate must recognize the integrity of both material and spiritual matters, of both historical consciousness and the awareness of eternity, of both humanistic interests and metaphysical-moral visions.

Theology is indispensable to the analysis of the human condition and the historical ethos. Interests not guided by theology and channeled by covenanted communities of faith march through the world like armies in the night; but they do not build civilizations and cultures that endure. Communities of intimacy and ultimacy, not class consciousness; institutions of affection and excellence, not revolutionary cadres; organizations of creativity and cooperation, not bureaucritized control mechanisms; and associations dedicated to what is true and just and loving before God, not quasi-scientific dialectics, are what shape social destiny in the long run.

Any account, including a Marxist one, of why things are the way they are that does not speak of theology and ecclesiology errs. It is doomed to fail. But where the political economy honors these, society can become open to a redemptive spirit. Modern theology and ethics have not said this clearly enough.

Yet it is one of the providential aspects of this moment in human history that the failure of communism, and consequently the doubt now thrown on all forms of socialism, cannot justify triumphalism in the West generally or among Christians particularly. The fact that "they" are sick does not prove that "we" are well. The new situation merely means that we can and must examine the relations of theology to political economy with a new openness that does not simply sprinkle holy water on materialist theories, outdated ideologies and special interests.

The ensemble of problems which we confront is formidable. A full repertoire of solutions is not at hand. Optimism is soured by the nation's growing addiction to debt, a dependence on oil, recurrent hunger in far too many parts of the world, the peril of ecological disaster, the probability of a recession, the high visibility of ethical rot (as in recent junk-bond trading and the savings-and-loan crisis), a lack of commitment to educational excellence, the growing disparity between conspicuous consumption for some and conspicuous poverty for others, and the loss of hope and talent due to discrimination and drugs among far too many.

Even more, many contemporary forms of theology — fideist, fundamentalist and liberationist — are so alienated from modern science, technology, culture and especially business that they cannot discern where, in the midst of these sectors of our contemporary life, God is accomplishing something new. And now that the socialist forms of analysis have proven empty, even modern ecumenical thought will have to struggle to prove the framework of meaning, the principles and purposes necessary to face the new situation.

Any theology able to address the future must reach beyond confessional particularities, exclusive histories and privileged realms of discourse. In constructing a cosmopolitan social ethics, certain dimensions of theology are more important than others. If theology is only the proclamation of personal sin and redemption, of course, let some continue to preach to their choirs. This message has partial validity, and the old songs replenish the soul. If theology is essentially narrative or metaphor, let others take time to write a novel or a poem. The world needs good ones. If theology is essentially a tradition's confession of faith, still

others will want to study their catechisms. People ought to know what their communities believe. And if theology is primarily the reflected experience of some particular gender or race or support group, let them serve the needs of their sectarian enclaves. This, too, is a valid ministry.

But theology adequate to the cosmopolitan challenges that await us must have another dimension as well: it must develop a social ethic of the emerging world in which democracy, human rights and a mixed economy are acknowledged as universal necessities. It must address a world linked by technology, trade and a host of new interdependencies.

This agenda for Christian thought requires a "public theology," a way of speaking about the reality of God and God's will for the world that is intellectually valid in the marketplace of ideas and morally effective in the marketplace of goods and services.

Of course, there are some aspects of Christianity that stand as perennial constraints on every effort of this kind. On the one hand, the Bible knows no economic blueprint. Further, it tells us that to take economic matters too seriously is to miss the point of the lilies of the field, to decline the invitation to the banquet, to turn away sadly, indeed, to worship mammon. This prevents all Christians from identifying any economic system with the Kingdom of God.

On the other hand, the Bible also calls us to be responsible stewards — not only of our talents and personal possessions but of all that is the Lord's until he returns. We are to labor in the vineyards of the world — even when the vineyards reach around the globe in new patterns of corporate capitalism.

We dare not shrink from this task. We cannot say that the new economy now taking shape globally is without theological roots. Nor can we say that it needs no theological help. We must not give the impression that Christianity has nothing to offer it other than condemnation. Islam, and for that matter Hinduism, Buddhism and the host of secular humanisms and neopagan spiritualities that seek to capture the soul of our times, should not be allowed to shape the future by default. They need a Christian theological perspective to fulfill them and, where necessary, to correct them.

If we refuse the challenge to which providence

951

has called this generation, we betray the gospel. Any pastor who does not preach on these matters, any congregation that does not study them, any seminary that does not teach about them, or any baptized Christian who does not pray about them with a depth that can overcome old ideologies and alter common practices denies that God is lord over all of creation and history.

What issues, then, are central to this challenge?

1. *The Stewardship of Capital.* Vast amounts of capital are necessary for the 21st century. We must invest in research and development, in new equipment for robotic production, in the development of nonfossil fuels and biotechnology, and in the training of a highly skilled work force. Failure to capitalize means not only economic stagnation but environmental destruction, unemployment, wider hunger and further homelessness. The undercapitalization that results from policies directed against economic growth inevitably compounds social injustice. The challenge is to capitalize in ways that reflect our responsibilities as faithful stewards. How ought we do it?

Precisely because capitalization by state fiat under socialism has failed to promote economic development and has worsened most of the evils it intended to correct, contemporary Christians must think more deeply about the morality of profits in a world oriented toward markets, corporations and global competition. Creating wealth is the whole point of economic activity, as known to folk wisdom: "If your output is less than your intake, your upkeep is your downfall." What is true of the body's energy level and the family budget is true of every economic effort.

If profits are made by honorable means, we must recognize that working to serve people's needs in the marketplace may be a holy vocation in and for the salvation of the world. We are bound therefore to help businesspeople discover how to exercise this vocation with due respect for employees, customers and suppliers. Further, public theology must insist upon a regard for the larger social and natural environment. In these ways, the disciplined pursuit of profits within a responsible strategy of capitalization can be a modern form of stewardship — one finding much precedent in the biblical record.

Indeed, a new form of Christian mission today emerges precisely at this point. Converting hearts to God through the grace of Christ is paramount, of course. But outward and material signs of this grace are required. If we care for people's material conditions, the churches should send out to the poorer regions people who can teach others how to develop their own resources — how to form corporations and manage them, how to find markets, how to develop technology, how to work with employees, and how to make profits for the common good.

Enhancing the capacity for capitalization in responsible corporations is as much the new name for mission as development is the new name for peace.

2. *The Covenant for Corporations.* The corporation has already become the social form distinctive of every cooperative human activity outside the family, the government and personal friendships. It is historically based on the patterns of association worked out by the church beyond tribe, patriarchy and nation. The modern business corporation could become a worldly ecclesia no less than hospitals, unions, parties, schools, voluntary organizations and cultural institutions, virtually all of which are incorporated.

Further, the business corporation has, as much as any other institution, leaped cultural and social boundaries and broken down the walls that divide people. It has found a home in societies far from its roots. Where the opportunities to form corporations are constricted or the skills to sustain them are absent, people remain in an underdeveloped condition. Societies stagnate and people die for want of the ability to form corporations.

Businesses need all the spiritual and moral guidance they can get. The financial environment is in constant flux. Accountability to investors requires a devotion to efficiency that may threaten other principles and goals of covenantal association. Moreover, businesses increasingly operate in a context of global competition. Comparative advantages can make selling out, closing down or moving to other lands imperative. The failure to move is in some cases a manifestation of a misplaced patriotism, and may fail to aid underdeveloped regions.

Further, such pressures put corporations in a moral bind. On the one hand, the corporations that focus most directly on short-term, bottom-line considerations are those least able to sustain the loyalty of their employees and the trust of the communities they serve. On the other hand, those that spend the most resources on benefits to promote community service and encourage the personal and social development of their employees are often least equipped to defend themselves against hostile corporate takeovers. For them, liquidation can bring a greater immediate return than quarterly performance. For businesspeople to resign themselves to either alternative, and for the church not to address such questions, is to fall short of the covenantal implications of public theology in corporate life.

If the modern business corporation is to fulfill its calling as a secular form of covenantal community, Christian leaders must assist businesspeople to understand the fateful choice between building an association of interdependent persons seeking to produce goods and services that benefit the commonwealth, and being reduced to an instrument with interchangeable parts, seeking maximum immediate advantage.

If public theology can help us overcome our contempt for corporations as mere money machines, then Christians can begin to articulate what we expect of these institutions. We can even learn to love them as we have learned to love our churches, neighborhoods, nations, schools and hospitals — although we must not be tempted to seek from them the loves that are proper to other relationships.

We can demand moral responses from them, put a decent measure of loyalty and trust in them, be alert to the strong possibility of sin within them, judge them, forgive them and convert them when we find them snared in corrigible error. Further, we can encourage churchpeople to work in them and find their callings there, precisely because they may discover valid moral principles already operative there.

While rejecting as both false and unjust the view of the corporation as an inhuman piece of organizational machinery, public theology also must be aware of the limits of this form of covenantal community. Corporations become idols when we become married to firms, when our loyalty is to them only, when we bend all politics to their service, when their distinctive modes of operation get confused with the ideals that must govern health care, education and culture. Corporations become idols, in short, when we think that they can bring salvation to human life.

The question of limits, however, is not simply one of public ecclesiology. The modern business corporation is not only a voluntary association but an economic institution designed to achieve a degree of control over markets. To the extent that corporations are successful, markets cannot be relied upon exclusively to control corporations. The voice of labor, the demands of government, the rule of law must also be developed.

Furthermore, dramatic increases in corporate mastery of the latest advances in technology enormously enhance any industry's capacity to have a decisive impact on its environment, both culturally and ecologically. While affirming the corporation as a covenantal community, a public theology fully resonant with our emerging world will have to collaborate in developing new systems of public accountability to ensure that corporations respect God's gift of creation.

3. *The Vocation of Management.* Business managers have not yet become members of a genuine profession in the ways that clergy, teachers, doctors, lawyers and architects have. There were many reasons for this in the past. They are less valid now, and will become increasingly less so. Managers, no doubt, are already professionals in the way that baseball players, rock stars, and talk-show hosts are: they are experts at what they do, they work at it full time, and they make big bucks. And many do what they do with personal standards of integrity at least as high as those of the clergy. But management itself has not yet developed the rich texture of public responsibility that emerged from the sense of "high" calling historically characteristic of the traditional professions.

In the emerging world of global economic interdependence, management can and should be professionalized. Christians should come to regard it as an honorable and specialized ministry of the laity. If we can no longer dismiss corporations as inhuman machines, we must also confess that it is false and unjust to categorize managers only as bosses. A public theology that is open to the experiences of those who exercise responsibility in modern business corporations will soon discover that managers have more in common with community organizers, pastors and teachers than they do with impersonal systems of mechanical control. Granted, they must measure performance, both personal and corporate, by standards that aspire to objectivity; but ultimately so must all those who genuinely empower others. There is no longer any reason to deny the holiness of a vocation to business management.

4. *A Public Theology for a Global Civilization.* Capitalization and profits, the corporation as a covenanting community and worldly ecclesia, the professionalization of management technology? As theological topics? Yes. These are key examples of a public theology that respects the ordering principles of trinitarian thought, with its fundamental commitment to the inclusive community of persons and its dynamic reconception of the biblical message in nonbiblical social and intellectual environments. In a postsocialist world, these are among the decisive areas where the righteous sovereignty of God, the sacrificial presence of Jesus Christ and the dynamic novelty of the Holy Spirit must become concrete.

Such topics are at least as important for the human future as today's theologies of sexuality, literary criticism and biomedical ethics. The biblical and doctrinal, the ethical and interpretive resources of the ecumenically open traditions have more to offer this new world than we have yet seen. To rediscover these resources is the first requirement for those Protestant and Catholic communities of faith that hope to speak socially and ethically to the momentous changes of our times.

Christians of the world, awake! Now that the specter of communism has vanished, cast off the spell of economic dogmatism! There is nothing to lose but ideology and irrelevance.

Where Do We Go from Here?
Some Thoughts on Geoeconomics

Dennis P. McCann

This anthology has aimed to identify classical and contemporary resources in Western Christian thought for interpreting the religious and ethical significance of business and economics. It also stands as an invitation to present and future leaders in the churches, in businesses, and in the professions to bring these resources to bear on the geoeconomic reality that will shape the twenty-first century. Christian social ethics in the twenty-first century, to a great extent, developed within the framework of the great economic debate over capitalism versus socialism. The ways in which theologians evaluated the traditions of Western Christian thought were heavily influenced by where they stood in that debate, just as where they stood in the debate was influenced by how they interpreted these traditions. There is nothing dishonorable or surprising about this, for it is a reflection of the normal operations of what critical theorists call the hermeneutic circle.

The twentieth century's great economic debate over capitalism versus socialism, however, seems to have been rendered moot by the revolutions of 1989. The ensuing collapse of the hermeneutic circle predicated upon that debate signals neither the end of history nor an end to ideology, as if the future contained only technical questions for bureaucrats to decide. We believe instead that a new geoeconomic reality is emerging beyond the stalemated polarizations of the past. It is a morally ambiguous reality, to be sure, but one that ought to challenge Christian social ethics as deeply as the clash of twentieth-century ideologies, and the world's apparently successful resistance against totalitarianism, ever did. Christian theologians and ethicists, we believe, will find themselves constructing a new hermeneutic for the twenty-first century, a rethinking of our ethical responsibilities in light of a fresh reading of the Western Christian tradition.

This epilogue is meant to illustrate how that rethinking might proceed. Though it highlights some of the themes that are implicit in the overall design of this anthology, the questions raised here are merely my own. The other editors, as well as any of you, our readers, might formulate an entirely different set of questions. Mine, I hope, may help to stimulate your own efforts. Let me first establish the context for our reflections by reviewing some of the defining characteristics of the geoeconomic challenge. Then I will try to formulate the theological questions that the new reality raises for me. To those familiar with the history of Christian theological reflection, these questions will be unmistakably perennial. They are new only in the sense that they seem to have been forgotten over the decades when Christian social ethics responded to the call for a fateful and faithful decision for or against capitalism and socialism.

Geoeconomics is characterized by several converging trends, the most salient of which is the declining economic significance of the public sector and any national government's ability to shape its own economic policy autonomously. Various studies issued by the Office of Economic Cooperation and Development (OECD) show that this trend is pervasive and long-term. It is not simply a reflection of the collapse of "really existing socialism" in Russia and Eastern Europe, nor is it to be identified exclusively with the political agendas of Margaret Thatcher and Ronald Reagan. All regimes of whatever ideological orientation have had to face the combination of significant new constraints upon their ability to generate revenue and the accumulated momentum of previously mandated expenditures, not all of which are for social welfare programs. The result has been chronic budgetary crises that have eroded the power of national governments to affect national economic policy.

This practical problem of governance is matched by a theoretical problem: it has become increasingly difficult to conceptualize, let alone monitor the performance of, a national economy. What once many of us fervently hoped for, the dawning of a new era of global economic interdependence, has in fact arrived with unexpected challenges to the conventional assumptions of neoclassical economics, both of the Friedmanesque and of the Keynesian variety. National policies that stimulate economic growth through deficit spending have consequences in global financial markets that may undermine the nation's existing comparative advantages in world trade. Recent technical innovations in these same markets, particularly the proliferation of new financial instruments, make conventional measures of the nation's money supply increasingly unreliable as a guide to national monetary policy. The theoretical implications of these problems are leading some economists to question whether it makes sense to conceptualize governmental policy in terms of an increasingly fictive national economy.

The unexpected consequences of global economic interdependence have also challenged conventional assumptions governing debates over free trade and protectionism. The new reality of geoeconomics seems to have bypassed neoclassical arguments in favor of the one and opposed to the other. The recent political struggles in the U.S. over NAFTA and GATT, seen in geoeconomic terms, were wrongly posed as a forced choice between the two. The issue, instead, is how trade is to be managed, by whom, and according to which rules. The need for some brokered international regime of managed trade signals not the triumph of neoclassical economics but its increasing irrelevancy. Managed trade becomes necessary when no consensus can be assumed among the nations on either the significance of economic activity or the goals and methods of national economic policy.

As various readings presented in this anthology have suggested, the forms of capitalism emerging in East Asia and elsewhere diverge significantly from the conventional Anglo-American model. As a theoretical paradigm, geoeconomics is challenged to account for these differences so that appropriate trade relationships can be negotiated. The differences can no longer be ignored or explained away as the result of some sort of cultural lag.

For the churches and other institutions committed to global economic justice, these trends call for a reexamination of our customary patterns of thought regarding economic development. They challenge us to recognize that the globalization of market economics that has already been achieved entails a recognition of new agents for change, the development of new institutional alliances, and experiments testing new strategies for economic justice. Precisely for justice's sake, the churches can no longer remain fixated on questions of distributive justice conventionally played out in debates over what the U.S. can or cannot do for the poor of the Third World. If the health of the U.S. economy is increasingly tied to the complex interdependencies emerging in the global economy, the churches must seek an appropriately global understanding of that economy and the ways in which it can be influenced for the good of all nations.

The shape of this global understanding, the editors all agree, raises theological questions. Based on the readings that we have selected for this anthology, I intend to pursue three of these. The first, which concerns corporate culture and Christian vocation, presupposes that business corporations — characteristically, multinational corporations, only some of which are based in the U.S. — will be among the primary moral agents shaping the global economy. Ethical reflection on the nature of multinational corporations has been going on for some time now; but geoeconomics may suggest that a shift in focus is in order — from concern over how, in the absence of world government, to make U.S. multinational corporations socially responsible to a question of what the limits may be on the influence that business ethics should have on the moral and spiritual development of the people who work for the firm. We all assume that working for a corporation can be a form of Christian vocation, but in the new geo-economic reality I am struck by the extent to which corporate cultures are often shaped by religious values that may be alien to the traditions of Western Christianity. On the horizon of inter-religious dialogue, this leads me to speculate on how far corporations are likely to go in becoming communities of faith, either in alliance with the Christian churches or as alternatives to them. This question will seem strange only to those who lack familiarity with the ways in which spirituality, often based on non-Western religious assumptions, is fast becoming part of the standard repertoire of consultants specializing in the management of corporate cultures.

My second theological question, which concerns economic policy and the rediscovery of sacrifice, stems from an awareness of the declining significance of the public sector, which the new geoeconomic reality brings in its wake. The erosion of national economic policy, among other things, may be the coup de grace for the ideology of interest-group liberalism. If any given nation's economy is beyond its own government's span of effective control, not even the government of a political superpower can guarantee an ever-expanding pool of material benefits with which to ease social conflicts. One sign of the demise of interest-group liberalism is the recent vogue for the rhetoric of sacrifice among U.S. politicians and pundits. Sacrifice, of course, is a term loaded with crosscultural religious significance. How are we to understand, and theologically evaluate, its use in the public domain — both here and abroad — in light of the new geoeconomic reality?

My third theological question, which concerns God and geoeconomics, is as global as it is traditional. If Western modernity's utopian aspirations for a perfectly just society have been indefinitely postponed by the constraints and opportunities of the global economy, how are we to apportion responsibility for the inequalities in life chances that, despite global economic development, are likely to endure as far into the future as anyone can reasonably anticipate? If national governments — primarily, the victorious superpower and its allies — are not in a position unilaterally to transform the structures of economic opportunity worldwide, to what extent do the persisting inequalities we suffer raise basic questions of

theodicy? How is it possible to confess the will of God in the obstacles to global economic development that we continue to face, without undermining the churches' theological commitment to economic justice and social progress?

I have no easy answers to any of these questions; and, obviously, they hardly exhaust the theological challenges that geoeconomics represents. Nevertheless, let me expand upon each of these, if only to stimulate your own thinking.

(1) *Corporate Cultures and Christian Vocation.* The readings we've selected consistently propose a view of business ethics in which matters requiring theological interpretation are prominent. Our surveys suggest that the myth of amoral business no longer reigns unchallenged in management circles. The issue is no longer whether a concern for business ethics will be internalized within the firm but rather whose religious and ethical perspectives will be implemented and with what consequences for the spiritual and moral development of the firm's employees. While it may have been possible to ignore theological questions when business ethics consisted mainly of identifying moral dilemmas and applying secularized paradigms of deontological and teleological moral reasoning, such questions have been given new vitality by the competitive pressures that today's managers experience in diverse organizational cultures that no longer are modeled exclusively on the Protestant work ethic. If spirituality is increasingly seen by management consultants as the key to organizational innovation and increased productivity, how can employees be empowered to participate without some critical perspective on the ultimately religious sources of the firm's corporate values?

In the future, this question is likely to concern whether and how a Christian can work for a corporation shaped by, say, neo-Confucian values; but even today, the question surfaces whenever a concern for spirituality is identified with business leadership. Christians familiar with leadership studies ought to recognize this as a secular variant on the traditional question of vocation. The Protestant affirmation that all persons have a calling in this world has become part of the lingua franca that consultants use to convey the meaningfulness of work in business and the professions. One striking example of this secularized theology is the little book *Leaders: The Strategies for Taking Charge* (1985) by Warren Bennis and Burt Nanus. The role of vision in defining the corporate mission and the challenge of motivating personal commitment to it are presented by Bennis and Nanus in terms strikingly similar to those familiar from Christian practical theology.

The churches ought to be challenged, both positively and negatively, by such secularized adaptations of the norms of religious community. The recovery of the strategic role of corporate culture in business enterprises may echo the churches' traditional wisdom in asserting the priority of questions of meaning and value over narrow measures of economic self-interest in motivating people for a common goal. But the promise of value-based management may also carry a threat, not just to the churches but also to business enterprises as such. Given the eroding bonds of social solidarity, should corporations seek to become functional substitutes for the specific kind of covenantal community that churches ought to be? Or are traditional forms of explicitly religious community, which provide space for exploring the ultimate sources of meaning and value, still an essential basis from which to pursue the common good?

Despite welcome progress in improving ethical standards in business, should the churches actively resist the tendency in some corporations to co-opt at least the symbols, if not the substance, of the primary institutions in which persons are socialized — namely, families, schools, churches, and the various forms of private voluntary associations? Conversely, can businesses retain their capacities for flexible response to the challenges of global competitiveness if they have encumbered themselves with the covenantal responsibilities specific to these other institutions? How far, for example, can other businesses realistically be expected to go in emulating the covenantal ideals that Max DePree, for example, helped institutionalize at Herman Miller, Inc.? Even if new forms of organizational learning require some focus on the spiritual and moral development of a firm's employees, should the churches resist such developments as a usurpation of their role or cooperate with them so that any dissonance between corporate and ecclesial values can be minimized?

These are not merely organizational questions,

to be resolved on a business-as-usual basis. Pursuing them theologically may set the pattern for future interactions between the churches and business corporations. In light of the new geo-economics, we can foresee that these questions increasingly will focus our attention on inter-religious dialogue at the global level. Exercising one's Christian vocation in a multinational corporation will require not just a general awareness of the role of spirituality in business but a growing realization of the specific religious traditions animating the firm's distinctive history and corporate culture. A working knowledge of the history of the world's religions, as well as an understanding of comparative religious ethics, will become indispensable resources for managing cultural diversity. The recovery of the role of spirituality in business, while certainly a welcome development, provides an unprecedented challenge to the Christian churches, especially for the laity. If and when this challenge is taken up, we hope that it will be seen as an opportunity for critical theological reflection and not simply as confirming the wisdom of a deceptively secular approach to business ethics.

(2) *Public Policy and the Rediscovery of Sacrifice.* Though any number of observers have documented the morally destructive consequences of the late twentieth century's absolute faith in self-realization, it has taken firsthand experience of the social dislocations caused by economic globalization to awaken the public generally to the failure of interest-group liberalism. The M.I.T. economist Lester Thurow, for example, pointed out more than a decade ago that public policy discussion was fast becoming a zero-sum game. He demonstrated that, left to its own devices, the politics of interest-group liberalism could only end in gridlock. In a democracy where the costs attached to various proposals, and who would bear them, were generally known, each special interest group would seek to minimize those costs to itself either by exercising a veto over new policies whenever possible or by devising a variety of cost-shifting strategies.

In his proposals for breaking the anticipated political gridlock, Thurow did not explicitly refer to community or sacrifice. But *The Zero-Sum Society* did identify a structural weakness — a growing deficit in "civic disinterestedness," that is, the willingness to sacrifice personal gain for the common good — something that, alas, has continued to distort public debate over economic policy ever since. Indeed, Thurow's analysis may be even more pertinent today than it was a dozen years ago, for it reminds us that this structural impediment to U.S. economic development was in place long before the impact of the new geoeconomic realities had been fully absorbed. In retrospect, the politics of cost-shifting that Thurow denounced is just one symptom of the U.S.'s declining hegemony in the global economy. Overcoming that decline — as Thurow makes clear in his recent work *Head to Head: The Coming Economic Battle among Japan, Europe, and America* (1992) — means defining economic development in terms of production rather than consumption. The development of U.S. productive capacity, however, depends to a great extent upon our capacity to generate capital, which in turn means reversing the long-term weakness in the U.S. savings rate. Overcoming economic decline, in a word, requires sacrifice.

But who can demand sacrifice or impose it for the sake of the common good in a nation whose public morality has been shaped by a debauched form of interest-group liberalism? Ironically enough, before he signed on with the Clinton administration, Robert B. Reich made the geoeconomic context for raising this question explicit in his seminal essay *The Work of Nations: Preparing Ourselves for 21st Century Capitalism* (1990). Like Thurow, Reich offered a penetrating analysis of declining U.S. competitiveness in the global economy, and also like Thurow, he suggested that this trend could not be overcome through any conventional package of national economic policies. Proposals for rebuilding the U.S. economic base — that is, the educational system, communications networks, and transportation systems — as well as effective strategies for managing trade and technology were important as means. But none of them could either be enacted into law or implemented effectively unless we learned to overcome "the politics of secession," his term for our liberal resistance to sacrifice for the common good.

The stunning difficulties that the Clinton administration has had in Congress seem not only to confirm the analyses of both Reich and Thurow

but also to require us to press their diagnoses further. Though both strike me as essentially correct, neither of them seems to have a clue as to how, precisely, either to overcome the nation's accumulating deficit in moral disinterestedness or to renew a sense of national community powerful enough to create a new politics. Early in the campaign of 1992, Clinton's supporters did distribute literature that spoke of a new national "covenant" that they hoped to evoke as the moral basis for an equitable distribution of the sacrifices required. But this idea seems to have been abandoned even before the primaries had run their course, and Clinton has generally presented his policies in strictly secular terms.

Pious talk of national community and allusions to the need for sacrifice, however nebulous, ought to alert us that public discourse once again has crossed the threshold of theological inquiry. I want to underscore the significance of this threshold. What is the relationship between sacrifice and the self-interest ostensibly pursued as a matter of principle in a market economy? Do sacrifice and self-interest stand in contradiction to one another, or do they mutually reinforce one another as moral imperatives, rendered all the more indispensable by the challenge of geoeconomics? Learning and teaching the social logic of sacrifice, of course, has always been a function of organized religion. In the history of Western Christianity sacrifice has served as the root metaphor most often invoked to interpret the theological significance of the death and resurrection of Jesus. Even in this century inquiries into the ethical significance of sacrificial love have played a major role in the development of Christian social ethics, as generations of students have sharpened their dialectical skills on the Niebuhrian realism that places self-sacrifice at the pinnacle of the struggle for social justice.

This theme, so prominent in the history of Christian ethics, remains relevant to public policy questions that others treat as purely technical and value neutral. Not only Christian believers but all concerned citizens ought to be challenged by the way in which the logic of geoeconomics forces us to reconsider the theological implications of public policy debate. It is not just a matter of taking a position on the merits of specific policy proposals. We must return to these sources in order

to rediscover the religious meanings of covenanted community and sacrifice and their moral
relevance for economic life, in order to form some
reasonable expectations about what we still owe
to one another as we all seek to cope with the
realities of geoeconomics. Do we still believe in
the deepest truths of our own heritage? Is the
connection between self-realization and self-sacrifice, once central to authentically Christian communities, still cultivated as a way of seeing the
demands of the common good in a certain way
and acting upon them magnanimously? If the
analyses offered by economists like Thurow and
Reich are at all on target, a renewed, though
chastened awareness of traditional Christian models of community may hold the key to any national
recovery of civic virtue and the bonds of social
solidarity. And lacking such a recovery, we will
render ourselves less and less capable of either
participating effectively in the global economy or
understanding the ultimately religious challenge
of geoeconomic development.

(3) *God and Geoeconomics.* This final theological question concerns God's own hand in the dramatic events that are shaping our geoeconomic
future. If there is reason to think that a robustly
Christian interpretation of contemporary history
forms the core of any viable public theology,
Christians must take the risk of asking where, concretely, God is leading us as we try to determine
where we go from here. The world now emerging
from the wake of the Cold War abounds with
ironies that force us to think again about God's
own vulnerabilities within history. During the
Cold War, which many people understood in
apocalyptic terms, it was common to attribute an
uncaring omnipotence to whichever superpower
we distrusted the most and to hold them solely
responsible for virtually all the sufferings that
humanity continues to endure. Now that the Cold
War is over, we may be forced to look elsewhere
for an explanation of human suffering.

If during the Cold War each of the superpowers
could plausibly identify the other as the Great
Satan, the theodicy issue — the perennial question of God's own justice — could easily be ignored. For demonizing one's adversary as the
Great Satan is useful, to be sure, for resolving any
ambiguities about good and evil. But the Soviet
Union no longer exists, and Russia, in all likeli-

hood, is not about to audition for the part of
Goliath, opposite our less than convincing attempts to go on playing David. By finally bringing
down the curtain on the Cold War, God has acted
mercifully to dispel our apocalyptic fantasies. But
the nature of God's mercy, in this instance, forces
me, at least, to consider once again the moral ambiguities of history — above all, the meaning of
human suffering and God's own complicity in it.

Pope John Paul II's *Centesimus annus* (1992),
for example, obliquely raises the theodicy question by making a useful distinction between the
marginalization and exploitation of the Third
World's poor. The major obstacle to geoeconomic
development, the pope accurately observes, is not
that the poor are being exploited by rich oppressors but that for one reason or another the poor
are not yet capable of taking advantage of the new
geoeconomic opportunities. Their sufferings, in
other words, result not from capitalist exploitation
but from the fact that they lack basic access to
capitalist development, especially in their own
homelands.

When I am struggling with the question why
such a baseline of economic marginalization exists, I am comforted by Job and the other biblical
voices who contested the justice of God the Creator and Lord of history. The unequal patterns of
natural resource distribution and human settlement, as well as the varying adaptive capacities of
specific human cultures that have existed from
before the dawn of recorded history, cry out for
theological response. As with other forms of the
classical question of theodicy, reflection upon
these patterns ought to instill in us a certain sense
of humility, as it did in Job, particularly as we
come to recognize the extent to which the inequalities that divide us are beyond human devising. Without deflecting the Christian impetus for
social change, we must enhance our capacity for
a truly demythologized social praxis in which it
becomes increasingly difficult to demonize those
who differ with us economically, culturally, and
politically. Covenantal partnership with the Creator and Lord of history may also become more
plausible when we recognize that God, too, shares
our burden of responsibility to the extent that
God's will is served by geoeconomic development.

The world's rapid movement toward genuine
interdependence, an interdependence that is cul-

tural and political as well as economic, is bound to raise theological questions about the grand design of the divine order. Contemporary theologians are rightly suspicious of a neoclassical theism that canonizes the metaphysical prejudices of Plato and Aristotle, but this does not relieve us from the need to develop an adequate theological understanding of the emerging realities of geoeconomics. Given the role of relatively unfettered market activity in creating unprecedented levels of global interdependence — particularly in effecting a massive flow of capital and technology from North to South — perhaps theologians were wrong to assume that God abhors the social dislocations caused by market forces. Perhaps the cycle of "creative destruction" marking the advent of geoeconomics is, after all, an inevitable consequence of the search for full covenantal partnership with the Creator and Lord of history.

In this area, as in each of the others, I am, of course, speaking only for myself. These questions are meant to illustrate, in a personal way, how the resources Max, Shirley, and I have assembled in this anthology might stimulate fresh theological thinking on where God seems to be taking us, as each of us seeks to formulate his or her own considered response to the new geoeconomic reality.

Acknowledgments

The editors and publisher gratefully acknowledge permission to include material from the following sources:

Introduction

Paul Tillich, *The Shaking of the Foundations* (London: SCM Press, 1949). Reprinted by permission of the publisher.

Chapter 1

George N. Monsma, Jr., *Through the Eye of the Needle*, 3rd ed. Copyright © 1989 Department of Economics and Business, Calvin College, Grand Rapids, Michigan. Reprinted by permission.

Barry Gordon, *The Economic Problem in Biblical and Patristic Thought.* Reprinted by permission of E. J. Brill Publishing Co.

Paul D. Hanson, *The People Called.* Copyright © 1986 by Paul D. Hanson. Reprinted by permission of HarperCollins Publishers Inc.

The New Revised Standard Version Apocryphal/ Deuterocanonical Books, copyright 1989 by the Division of Christian Education of the National Council of the Churches of Christ in the USA. Used by permission. All rights reserved.

Martin Hengel, *Property and Riches,* copyright © 1974 Fortress Press and SCM. Used by permission of Augsburg Fortress.

Chapter 2

Stephen Charles Mott, "The Use of the New Testament in Social Ethics," *Transformation* 1, no. (April/June 1984): 21-26. Reprinted with permission.

Lisa Sowle Cahill, "The Ethical Implications of the Sermon on the Mount," *Interpretation* 41 (April 1987): 144-56. Reprinted with permission.

Work and Leisure in Christian Perspective by Leland Ryken. Copyright © 1987 Multnomah Press. Reprinted by permission of Questar Publishers.

Bruce J. Malina, "Wealth and Poverty in the New Testament and Its World," *Interpretation* 41 (October 1987): 354-66. Reprinted with permission.

Faith and Wealth: A History of Early Christian Ideas on the Origin, Significance, and Use of Money by Justo L. Gonzalez. Copyright © 1990 by Justo L. Gonzalez. Reprinted by permission of HarperCollins Publishers Inc.

In Memory of Her: A Feminist Theological Reconstruction of Christian Origins. Copyright © 1983 by Elisabeth Schüssler Fiorenza. Reprinted by permission of The CROSSROAD Publishing Co., New York, and SCM Press Ltd., London.

Max L. Stackhouse, "What Then Shall We Do? On Using Scripture in Economic Ethics," *Interpretation* 41 (October 1987): 382-96. Reprinted by permission.

Chapter 3

Works and Days by Hesiod, translated by Dorothy Wender (Penguin Classics, 1973), copyright © Dorothy Wender, 1973. Reprinted by permission.

The Politics of Aristotle, edited and translated by Ernest Barker (1946). Reprinted by permission of Oxford University Press.

Cicero, *The Laws,* translated by Francis Barham, in *Introduction to Contemporary Civilization in the West*, 3rd edition, volume 1, pp. 61-73. Copyright 1960 © Columbia University Press,

New York. Reprinted with the permission of the publisher.

Chapter 4

Augustine, *The City of God*, trans. D. B. Zema and G. G. Walsh, in *Fathers of the Church*, vol. 8. Reprinted by permission of Catholic University Press.

The Rule of St. Benedict, abridged edition in English and Latin, with notes and commentary by T. Fry, O.S.B. (1981). Copyright © 1981 by The Order of St. Benedict, Inc. Published by The Liturgical Press, Collegeville, Minnesota. Used with permission.

St. Thomas of Aquinas, *Summa Theologiae*, translated by T. Gilby, O.P., Blackfriars edition, vol. 37 (New York: McGraw-Hill, 1975). Reprinted by permission of Cambridge University Press.

Thomas of Aquinas, *Summa Theologica*, trans. D. Biogniari (New York: Hafner Publishing Co., 1957). Reprinted by permission of MacMillan Publishing Company.

"The Myth of Self-Interest: Hobbes Had It Wrong" by Michael J. Himes and Kenneth R. Himes, *Commonweal*, Sept. 23, 1988. Copyright © Commonweal Foundation, 1988. Reprinted with permission of the Commonweal Foundation.

Chapter 5

Luther's Works, volume 45, edited by Walter I. Brandt, pp. 245-72, copyright © 1962 Muhlenberg Press. Used by permission of Augsburg Fortress.

Aristotle, *The Politics of Aristotle*, edited and translated by Ernest Barker (1946). Reprinted by permission of Oxford University Press.

John Tiemstra, "Stories Economists Tell," *Reformed Journal* 38 (February 1988): 15-16. Reprinted with permission of *Perspectives*.

Ulrich Stadler, "Cherished Instructions," in *Spiritual and Anabaptist Writers*, edited by George Hunston Williams and Angel M. Mergal (The Library of Christian Classics). First published MCMLVII by SCM Press and The Westminster Press. Used by permission of Westminster John Knox Press and SCM Press.

Gerrard Winstanley et al., "The True Levellers' Standard Advanced," in *Puritanism and Liberty*, edited by A. S. P. Woodhouse (London: Dent, 1938). Reprinted by permission of Everyman's Library, David Campbell Publishers Ltd.

John Wesley, "The Use of Money," in *Standard Sermons*, edited by E. H. Sugden. Used by kind permission of the Epworth Press.

Chapter 6

Immanuel Kant, *The Philosophy of Law*, trans. W. Hastie (Edinburgh: T&T Clark, 1887). Reprinted by permission of T&T Clark Ltd.

Excerpts reprinted by permission of the publishers from *A Theory of Justice* by John Rawls, Cambridge, Mass.: The Belknap Press of Harvard University Press, copyright © 1971 by the President and Fellows of Harvard College.

Chapter 7

Material reprinted with the permission of Simon & Schuster from the Macmillan College text *The Protestant Ethic and the Spirit of Capitalism* by Max Weber, translated by Talcott Parsons. Copyright © 1958 Charles Scribner's Sons.

Revolution in Time by David Landes, Cambridge, Mass.: The Belknap Press of Harvard University Press, copyright © 1983 by the President and Fellows of Harvard College. Reprinted with permission.

Law and Revolution: The Formation of the Western Legal Tradition by Harold J. Berman, Cambridge, Mass.: Harvard University Press, copyright © 1983 by the President and Fellows of Harvard College. Reprinted with permission.

Material reprinted with the permission of The Free Press, a division of Simon & Schuster from *Social Theory and Social Structure* by Robert K. Merton. Copyright © 1957 by The Free Press; copyright renewed 1985 by Robert K. Merton.

Material reprinted with the permission of The Free Press, a division of Simon & Schuster from *Sociological Theory and Modern Society* by Talcott Parsons. Copyright © 1967 by The Free Press.

Chapter 8

"Marxism" by Charles C. West. Excerpted with permission of Simon & Schuster Macmillan from *Encyclopedia of Religion,* Mircea Eliade, Editor in Chief. Vol. 9, pp. 240-48. Copyright © 1987 by Macmillan Publishing Company.

John A. Ryan, "The Church and the Workingman," *Catholic World* 89 (April-September 1909): 776-82. Copyright 1909 The Catholic World. Reprinted with permission.

Reinhold Niebuhr, "Marx, Barth, and Israel's Prophets." Copyright 1935 Christian Century Foundation. Reprinted by permission from the January 30, 1935 issue of *The Christian Century.*

James W. Skillen, "Human Freedom, Social Justice, and Marxism: A Biblical Response," reprinted with permission of the author.

Excerpts from "The Business of Slavery" and "The Lives of the Slaves" in *Slavery: History and Historians* by Peter J. Parish. Copyright © 1989 by Peter J. Parish. Reprinted by permission of HarperCollins Publishers.

Janet Thomas, "Women and Capitalism: Oppression or Emancipation?" *Comparative Studies in Society and History* 30 (July 1988): 534-49. Copyright © 1988 Cambridge University Press. Reprinted with the permission of Cambridge University Press and the author.

Gustavo Gutiérrez, *A Theology of Liberation,* 15th Anniversary Edition, Maryknoll, NY: Orbis Books, 1988. Reprinted with permission of Orbis Books and SCM Press.

Excerpts from David Martin, *Tongues of Fire* (London: Basil Blackwell, 1990). Reprinted with permission.

Peter Berger, "Social Ethics in a Post-Socialist World," *First Things* 30 (February 1993): 9-14. Reprinted with permission.

Chapter 9

Excerpts from *The Koran,* translated by N. J. Dawood (Penguin Classics 1956, fifth edition 1990), copyright N. J. Dawood 1956, 1959, 1966, 1968, 1974, 1990. Reprinted by permission.

Excerpts from Mahmud Shaltout, "Islamic Beliefs and Code of Laws," in *Strait Path Islam Interpreted by Muslims,* edited by Kenneth W. Morgan. Copyright © 1958 by John Wiley & Sons, Inc. Reprinted by permission of John Wiley & Sons, Inc.

Robert Hefner, "Islam and the Spirit of Capitalism." Used by permission of the author.

Ken Brown, "Islamic Banking: Faith and Creativity." Copyright © 1994 by the New York Times Company. Reprinted by permission.

Kautiliya, "Artha Shastra," in *Sources of Indian Tradition,* edited by William T. DeBary, copyright 1957 © Columbia University Press, New York. Reprinted with the permission of the publisher.

Max L. Stackhouse, "The Hindu Ethic and the Ethos of Development: Some Western Views," *Religion and Society* 20, no. 4 (1973): 5-33. Reprinted by permission of the Christian Institute for the Study of Religion and Society.

Phra Rajavaramuni, "Foundations of Buddhist Social Ethics," in *Ethics, Wealth, and Salvation: A Study in Buddhist Social Ethics,* edited by Russell F. Sizemore and Donald K. Swearer. Columbia: University of South Carolina Press, 1990. Reprinted by permission of the Center for the Study of World Religions, Harvard University.

"Buddhist Economics" from *Small Is Beautiful* by E. F. Schumacher. Copyright © 1973 by E. F. Schumacher. Reprinted by permission of HarperCollins Publishers, Hutchinson of Random House UK Ltd., and the estate of the author.

Confucius, "Selections from the Analects," Ch'eng Hao, "Ten Matters Calling for Reform," and Mao Tse-Tuung, "On Contradiction," in *Sources of Chinese Tradition,* vol. 1, compiled by William T. DeBary et al. Copyright 1960 © Columbia University Press, New York. Reprinted with the permission of the publisher.

Wei-ming Tu, "Is Confucianism Part of the Capitalist Ethic?" Used by permission of the author.

"How to Get Rich Quickly" in Ibn Khaldun, *The Muqaddimah: An Introduction to History,* translated by Franz Rosenthal. Copyright © 1967 by Princeton University Press. Reprinted by permission of Princeton University Press.

"Zulu Wisdom," from *Zulu Proverbs,* rev. ed., by C. L. S. Nyembezi (Johannesburg, South Africa: Witwatersrand University Press, 1963). Reprinted by permission of the author.

Bill Keller, "A Surprising Silent Majority in South Africa." Copyright © 1994 by The New York Times Company. Reprinted by permission.

Richard E. Sincere, Jr., "The Churches and Investment in South Africa." Reprinted with the permission of Richard E. Sincere, Jr., and America Press, Inc. Originally published by America Press, Inc., 106 West 56th Street, New York, NY 10019, in *America*'s March 3, 1984, issue. © 1984. All Rights Reserved.

Chapter 10

Material condensed from *Economic Justice for All: Catholic Social Teaching and the U.S. Economy.* Copyright © 1986 by the United States Catholic Conference, Inc., Washington, D.C. Used with permission. All rights reserved.

Larry Rasmussen, "Economic Policy: Creation, Covenant, and Community." Reprinted with the permission of Larry Rasmussen and America Press, Inc. Originally published by America Press, Inc., 106 West 56th Street, New York, NY 10019, in *America*'s May 4, 1985, issue. © 1985. All Rights Reserved.

Paul F. Camenisch, "Recent Mainline Protestant Statements on Economic Justice," *Annual of the Society of Christian Ethics* (1987): 71-73. Reprinted with permission.

"The Villars Statement on Relief and Development," *Stewardship Journal* 1, no. 1 (Winter 1991): 3-5. Reprinted by permission.

"The Oxford Declaration," *Transformation* 7, no. 2 (April-June 1990). Reprinted with the permission from *Transformation*.

Pope John Paul II, *Centesimus Annus*, copyright 1991 Libreria Editrice Vaticana. Reprinted with permission.

Chapter 11

Dennis P. McCann and M. L. Brownsberger, "Management as a Social Practice: Rethinking Business Ethics after MacIntyre," *Annual of the Society of Christian Ethics* (1990): 223-45. Reprinted with permission.

Stewart W. Herman, "The Potential for Building Covenants in Business Corporations," *Annual of the Society of Christian Ethics* (1992): 201-23. Reprinted with permission.

Douglas Sturm, "Corporate Culture and the Common Good," *Thought* 60, no. 237 (June 1985). Reprinted by permission of the publisher from *Thought* (New York: Fordham University Press, 1994). Copyright 1985.

Donald W. Shriver, Jr., "Three Images of Corporate Leadership and Their Implications for Social Justice," used by permission of the author.

"Ethics and Management in the Corporate Arena," prepared for Angelo State University Symposium, 1985, by Michael Rion, Resources for Ethics and Management, West Hartford, Connecticut. Used by permission of the author.

"Creating Ethical Corporate Structures" by Patrick E. Murphy, *Sloan Management Review* 81 (Winter 1989): 81-87, by permission of publisher. Copyright 1989 by the Sloan Management Review Association. All rights reserved.

Harold M. Williams, "Corporate Accountability: The Board of Directors," *Vital Speeches of the Day,* vol. 44, no. 15, pp. 468-72. Reprinted with permission.

John C. Cort, "Is Mondragon the Way?" *New Catholic World* 226, no. 1354 (July/August 1983): 153-54. Reprinted with permission.

Excerpts from *Leadership Is an Art* by Max De Pree. Copyright © 1987 by Max De Pree. Used by permission of Doubleday, a division of Bantam Doubleday Dell Publishing Group, Inc.

Robert Kinloch Massie, "Corporate Democracy and the Legacy of the South African Divestment Movement," *The Christian Century,* 24 June 1991, pp. 716-20. Reprinted with permission of the author.

"Position Paper on South Africa," Trinity Center for Ethics and Corporate Policy, March 1986. Used by permission.

Barnaby J. Feder, "Seven Companies May Back a South African Code." Copyright © 1994 by The New York Times Company. Reprinted by permission.

Chapter 12

Paul F. Camenisch, "Business and Ethics: On Getting to the Heart of the Matter," *Business and*

ACKNOWLEDGMENTS

Professional Ethics Journal 1, no. 1 (Fall 1981): 59-68. Reprinted with permission of the author.

"Challenging a Commodity Culture" by John Kavanaugh, *Commonweal,* Nov. 2-16, 1984. Copyright © Commonweal Foundation, 1984. Reprinted with permission of the Commonweal Foundation.

Jon P. Gunnemann, "Capitalism and Commutative Justice," *Annual of the Society of Christian Ethics* (1985): 101-23. Reprinted with permission.

William J. Kehoe, "Ethics, Price Fixing, and the Management of Price Strategy," adapted with the permission of Lexington Books, an imprint of Macmillan Publishing Company, from *Marketing Ethics: Guidelines for Managers* by Gene R. Laczniak and Patrick E. Murphy, editors. Copyright © 1985 by Lexington Books.

Robert S. Bachelder, "Have Ethics Disappeared from Wall Street?" Copyright 1987 Christian Century Foundation. Reprinted with permission from the July 15-22, 1987, issue of *The Christian Century.*

Dennis P. McCann, "The Church and Wall Street," *America* 158, no. 4 (30 January 1988): 85-94. Reprinted with the permission of Dennis McCann and America Press, Inc., 106 West 56th Street, New York, NY 10019, 1988. All Rights Reserved.

Paul Hessert, "Theology and Money," *Explor* 4, no. 2 (1978): 21-32. Reprinted with permission of *Explor,* Garrett-Evangelical Theological Seminary.

Ian C. Stewart, "Accounting and Accountability: Double Entry, Double Nature, Double Identity," *Crux* 26, no. 2 (June 1990): 13-20. Reprinted with permission of the author.

Philip M. Piaker, "Accounting and Sentiment." Reprinted with permission from *The C.P.A. Journal,* November 1984, copyright 1984.

"Meeting the Financial Reporting Needs of the Future: A Public Commitment from the Public Accounting Profession." Reprinted with permission by the American Institute of Certified Public Accountants, Inc.

Elmer W. Johnson, "Shaping Our Economic Future: Dignity in the Workplace," *Vital Speeches of the Day,* vol. 52, no. 11, pp. 332-35. Reprinted with permission.

Lennie Copeland, "Learning to Manage a Multicultural Work Force." Reprinted with permission from the May 1988 issue of *Training* Magazine. Copyright 1988. Lakewood Publications, Minneapolis, MN. All rights reserved. Not for resale.

Barbara Hilkert Andolsen, "The Social Self at the VDT: Exploring the Advantages and Limitations of the Relational Model of Agency," *Annual of the Society of Christian Ethics* (1988): 205-20. Reprinted with permission.

Chapter 13

M. L. Brownsberger, "Christian Faith and Business: A Story," Chicago Theological Seminary *Register,* Fall 1989, pp. 56-63. Reprinted with permission.

Joseph P. Sullivan, "The Christian Vocation of a Business Leader," *Origins* 16 (16 October 1986): 325-28. Reprinted by permission of the author.

Penelope Washbourn, "Women in the Workplace," *Word and World* 4, no. 2 (1984): 159-64. Reprinted with the permission of *Word and World.*

Sir Fred Catherwood, "The Protestant Work Ethic: Attitude and Application Give It Meaning," *Fundamentalist Journal,* September 1983, pp. 22-24, 48. Reprinted with permission.

John C. Haughey, "Affections and Business," from the Proceedings of the Second National Consultation on Corporate Ethics, Center for Ethics and Corporate Policy, May 13-15, 1987. Used by permission of the author.

Robert A. Sirico, "A Worthy Calling," *FORBES,* 22 November 1993. Reprinted by permission of FORBES magazine. © Forbes, Inc., 1993.

William F. May, "The Virtues of the Business Leader," from the Proceedings of the Second National Consultation on Corporate Ethics, 13-15 May 1987, Center for Ethics and Corporate Policy, Chicago, Illinois, edited by David Krueger. Reprinted with permission.

William L. Weiss, "Minerva's Owl: Building a Corporate Value System," presented to the Workshop on Business Ethics, DePaul University, Chicago, Illinois, 26 July 1984. Reprinted with permission.

J. Irwin Miller, "How Religious Commitments

Shape Corporate Decisions," *Harvard Divinity Bulletin,* February-March 1984, pp. 4-6. Reprinted with permission.

Dennis W. Bakke, "Values Don't Work in Business," speech given at Calvin College, Grand Rapids, Michigan, 16 April 1991. Used by permission of the author.

Larry L. McSwain, "Christian Ethics and the Business Ethos," *Review and Expositor* 81, no. 2 (1984): 197-207. Reprinted with permission.

Richard Chewning, "When a Boss Asks for Something Unethical," *Presbyterian Journal,* 24 December 1986, 14 January 1987, and 4 February 1987. Reprinted with the permission of Richard C. Chewning, the Chauvanne Professor of Christian Ethics in Business at Baylor University.

Natalie Dandekar, "Contrasting Consequences: Bringing Charges of Sexual Harassment Compared with Other Cases of Whistleblowing," *Journal of Business Ethics,* February 1990, pp. 150, 152. Reprinted by permission of Kluwer Academic Publishers.

Claudia McDonnell, "Does Big Business Have a Big Heart?" Reprinted with permission from *Salt* magazine (now *Salt of the Earth*). Published by Claretian Publications (1-800-328-6515).

Nancy Croft Baker, "Would You Hire Them?" Excerpted by permission. *Nation's Business,* April 1989. Copyright 1989. U.S. Chamber of Commerce.

Joseph Nolan and David Nolan, "The Path to Social Responsibility," *Across the Board* 23 (May 1986): 54-58. Reprinted with permission of the authors.

Archie B. Carroll, "When Business Closes Down: Social Responsibilities and Management Actions." Copyright © 1984 by The Regents of the University of California. Reprinted from the *California Management Review,* vol. 26, no. 2. By permission of The Regents.

Chapter 14

Peter L. Berger, "The Gross National Product and the Gods: The Idea of Economic Culture," *The McKinsey Quarterly,* 1994, no. 1. Reprinted with permission.

"An East Asian Development Model?" by Peter L. Berger, in *In Search of an East Asian Development Model,* by Peter Berger and Michael Hsaio. Copyright © 1988 by Transaction Publishers. Reprinted by permission of Transaction Publishers. All rights reserved.

George Lodge, "The Asian Systems." Used by permission of the author.

Sang-Goog Cho, "Korean Economy: A Model Case of Miraculous Growth?" Used by permission of the author.

Arun Katiyar and Shefali Rekhi, "Guiding Principles," *India Today,* 15 July 1994, pp. 42-43. Reprinted with the permission of the publisher.

Y. S. R. Murthy, "Indian Industry Comes of Age," *India News Magazine,* 16-30 April 1992, p. 6. Reprinted with permission of the author.

Leo V. Ryan, "The New Poland: Major Problems for Ethical Business," *Business Ethics* 1, no. 1 (1992): 9-15. Reprinted with permission of the publisher.

Michael Novak, *Toward a Theology of the Corporation,* revised edition, 1981. Reprinted with the permission of The American Enterprise Institute for Public Policy Research, Washington, D.C.

Bill Emmott, "A Survey of Multinationals — Back in Fashion," *The Economist,* 27 March 1993, p. 5. © 1993 The Economist Newspaper Group, Inc. Reprinted with permission.

Lee A. Tavis, "Developmental Responsibility," selection taken from *Multinational Managers and Poverty in the Third World,* edited by Lee A. Tavis. © 1984 by the University of Notre Dame Press. Reprinted by permission.

Gene R. Laczniak and Jacob Naor, "Global Ethics: Wrestling with the Corporate Conscience," *Business* 35 (July-September 1985): 3-10. Reprinted with the permission of the publisher and authors.

Ronald J. Sider, "A Biblical Perspective on Stewardship," *New Catholic World* 220 (September-October 1977): 212-21. Reprinted with permission.

Michaela Walsh, "Women's World Banking," promotional booklet privately published in August 1987 by the Women's World Banking, 104 E. 40th, Suite 607-A, New York, NY 10016. Reprinted by permission.

Cornel West, "The Political Task of the Christian Church," *The Witness* 69, no. 1 (January 1986):

6-8. Reprinted with permission of *The Witness,* 1249 Washington Blvd., Suite 3115, Detroit, MI 48226-1822.

Mark R. Amstutz, "The Churches and Third World Poverty," *Missiology* 17, no. 4 (October 1989): 453-64. Reprinted with permission.

Michael Manley, "Justice in a Developing Country's Perspective," *Ecumenical Review,* April 1979, p. 428. Reprinted with permission.

Wendell Berry, "Two Economies," *Review and Expositor* 81, no. 2 (1984): 209-23. Reprinted with permission.

Robert H. Nelson, "Adam and Eve Meet the Sierra Club," *Policy Review* 53 (Summer 1990): 59-94. Reprinted with permission of the publisher.

James A. Nash, "Ecological Integrity and Christian Political Responsibility," *Theology and Public Policy* 1 (Fall 1989): 32-48. Reprinted with the permission of the publisher and author.

Chapter 15

S. Prakash Sethi, "The Righteous and the Powerful: Differing Paths to Social Goals," *Business and Society Review* 54 (Summer 1985): 37-44. Reprinted by permission of the author.

J. Philip Wogaman, "The Ethical Premise for Social Activism," *Business and Society Review* 54 (Summer 1985): 30-36. Reprinted by permission of the author.

Christine Firer Hinze, "Bridge Discourse on Wage Justice: Roman Catholic and Feminist Perspectives on the Family Living Wage," *Annual of the Society of Christian Ethics* (1991): 119-20, 124-46. Reprinted with permission.

David A. Krueger, "Connecting Ministry with the Corporate World." Copyright 1990 Christian Century Foundation. Reprinted with permission from the May 30–June 6, 1990 issue of *The Christian Century.*

William Johnson Everett, "Oikos: Convergence in Business Ethics," *Journal of Business Ethics* 5 (1986): 313-25. Reprinted by permission of Kluwer Academic Publishers.

Frederick B. Bird and James A. Waters, "The Moral Muteness of Managers." Copyright © 1989 by The Regents of the University of California. Reprinted from the *California Management Review,* Vol. 32, No. 1, by permission of The Regents.

J. Richard Finlay, "Ethics and Accountability: The Rising Power of Stakeholder Capitalism," *Business Quarterly* 51, no. 1 (Spring 1986): 56-66. Reprinted with permission.

Michael Novak, "The Lay Task of Co-Creation," in *Toward the Future: Catholic Social Thought and the U.S. Economy, A Lay Letter,* Lay Commission on Catholic Social Teaching and the U.S. Economy, North Tarrytown, New York, 1984, pp. 25-45. Used by permission of the author.

Lawrence Mead, "Dependency and Liberal Political Theory." Used by permission of the author.

Shirley J. Roels, "Christians and Economic Life," *Occasional Papers from Calvin College* 8, no. 1 (March 1990). Reprinted by permission.

Robert Benne, "The Great Refusal and My Discontent." Reprinted from *The Ethic of Democratic Capitalism: A Moral Reassessment* by Robert Benne, copyright © 1981 Fortress Press. Used by permission of Augsburg Fortress.

Amy L. Sherman, "Christians and Economic Development," *First Things,* March 1990. Reprinted with permission.

Daniel Rush Finn, "Self-Interest, Markets and Four Problems of Economic Life," *Annual of the Society of Christian Ethics* (1989): 23-53. Reprinted with permission.

John B. Cobb, Jr., "Ethics, Economics, and Free Trade," *Perspectives* 6, no. 2 (February 1991): 12-15. Reprinted with permission of *Perspectives.*

Robin Klay, "Liberating Thoughts about the Ethics of Exchange and Trade," *Perspectives* 7, no. 10 (October 1992): 10-13. Reprinted with permission of *Perspectives.*

Max L. Stackhouse and Dennis P. McCann, "A Post-Communist Manifesto: Public Theology after the Collapse of Socialism," *The Christian Century,* 16 January 1991. Reprinted with permission.

Index of Names

Index of Subjects